THE NEW PRESS GUIDE
TO MULTICULTURAL RESOURCES
FOR YOUNG READERS

THE NEW PRESS
GUIDE TO
MULTICULTURAL
RESOURCES
FOR
YOUNG READERS

EDITED BY DAPHNE MUSE

The New Press New York

Published in the United States by The New Press, New York
Distributed by W.W. Norton & Company, Inc., New York

*The New Press was established in 1990 as a not-for-profit alternative
to the large, commercial publishing houses currently dominating
the book publishing industry. The New Press operates in the public interest
rather than for private gain, and is committed to publishing,
in innovative ways, works of educational, cultural, and community value
that might not normally be commercially viable. The New Press's editorial
offices are located at the City University of New York.*

Book design by BAD
Production management by Kim Waymer
Printed in the United States of America

9 8 7 6 5 4 3 2 1

THIS BOOK IS DEDICATED

TO SOME OF THE EARLY VISIONARIES

~~~~~~~~~~~~~~~~~~~~~~~~

Augusta Baker

Charlemae Rollins

WEB DuBois, Jessie Redmond
Fauset, and the Staff and writers for
The Brownies' Book

A.E Johnson, Editor of *The Joy*

Arna Bontemps, author, librarian,
and one of my best teachers

Effie Lee Morris

Arthur Schomburg

Ellen Tarry

Shirley Graham

Lorenza Graham

Yoshiko Uchida

For Tatiana, Mookie, Trinh, Talia,
Jamal, Mae Mae, Ling, Manuel,
Jeffrey, Crystal, Lequita,
and the millions of children
across the country who still languish
in the love of the bedtime story,
find both adventure and peace
in books, and search through
the words and pictures to find
their own stories and learn from
those of others.

To all the writers who labor
and toil creatively to give our
children powerful stories
that can serve as a foundation
for developing vital lives
and building viable futures
for themselves.

And especially for John Steptoe,
a brilliant man who left a precious
legacy that will nurture
generations yet to be born.

CONTENTS

〜〜〜〜〜〜〜〜〜〜〜〜

ACKNOWLEDGMENTS

In 1967, a search for black children's books to use in my first grade classroom in Washington, D.C., put me on a course that would result in my devoting much of my life to the field that has come to be known as multicultural children's literature. That search also resulted in my joining Judy Richardson in developing a "Third World" children's literature section for Washington's Drum and Spear Bookstore.

Based on a sense of how stories had shaped and fueled my own black, working class community in Washington, I worked with Richardson to assemble a substantial collection of books by Arna Bontemps, Walter Dean Myers, John Steptoe, Muriel Feelings, Arnold Adoff, Virginia Hamilton, Tom Feelings, Yoshiko Uchida, Dorothy Sterling, Ellen Tarry, Shirley Graham, and others, and to get those works into classrooms, libraries, community centers, and homes across the United States. During my two years at Drum and Spear, I met thousands of teachers, librarians, parents, wonderful children, and a then-small but emerging cadre of African, African American, West Indian, Asian, and Native American children's authors. The "University of Drum and Spear" and its "faculty," including Ralph Featherstone, Joe Gross, Charlie Cobb, Jeniffer K. Lawson, Tony Gittens, Willard Taylor, Juadine Henderson, Anne Forrestor, Marvin Holloway, Cortland Cox, and Judy Richardson, opened me up to a world of learning and opportunities for which I will always remain deeply grateful.

A phone call in 1993 from Diantha Schull, on behalf of The New Press, combined with encouragement from author and friend Herb Kohl, and funding from The Hitachi Foundation, The W. K. Kellogg Foundation, The Lilly Endowment, and The Aaron Diamond Foundation, helped to "grow" the idea of *The New Press Multicultural Resource Guide for Young Children* into a reality.

Literally hundreds of people were involved in assembling this catalogue, and many of them endured through major personal and professional transitions, including floods, deaths of loved ones, surgeries, job searches, and other life-altering experiences. I thank them all for their perseverance.

My heartfelt gratitude goes out to the scores of dedicated and resourceful librarians from San Leandro, California, and Seattle, Washington, to Milwaukee, Wisconsin, and Montgomery, Alabama, who answered my queries and researched obscure data.

Angela Morton, Joanna Johnson, and Dr. Jeniffer Johnson provided administrative support in the early stages of this project. Editorial Intern Angela Watrous worked conscientiously to provide essential research-related data. Kudos to Joi Rhone, the ever-ready, on-the-case computer consultant, who rescued us from "techno hell."

The critical and theoretical works of Violet Harris, Jack Zipes, Donna Rae MacCann, Rudine Sims Bishop, Sonia Nieto, Masha Rudman, and all of those who poured their hearts and minds into the Council on Interracial Books for Children, continue to serve as both an inspiration and an intellectual barometer of the vigorous discourse that continues to take place in this field. I would also like to thank the reviewers, essayists, and contributors whose voices and views make *The Guide* a significant contribution to the field. Thanks especially to Binnie Tate Wilkin and Barbara Smith Palmer for their early contributions.

I am indebted to Rima, Sule, and Ayo, who nurtured their mom and my California editorial coordinator, Rosa Warder, through a maze of details. Rosa, one of my most outstanding students, was a gem, and working with her was one of the most gratifying experiences I've had in many years.

Nancy Pearl brought a critical eye and a breadth of knowledge to reading the manuscript in various stages of development. Special thanks also goes out to David Gancher who listened to my ideas early on and provided guidance and solid suggestions. Jessica Lewandoski input and fact-checked miles and miles of copy efficiently. I also thank Laurie Regelbrugge of The Hitachi Foundation; Emily Bittner, director of the Kids Project on Disability Awareness and Education; author Tonya Bolden; Susan Hinkle of The Diversity Resources Collaborative at The Packer Collegiate School; Hazel Rochman of The American Library Association; Mel Leventhal of Leventhal, Slade; author Jacqueline Woodson; Jean Poderos for his unmatched computer expertise and patience; Randy Carter of NAIS; Max Rodriguez of *The Quarterly Review of Black Books*; Ann Sandhorst; and New Press interns Carrie Schoen, Carlie Berwick, and Denise Clegg.

Organizations including the American Library Association, Bank Street Bookstore and Bank Street College, Poets and Writers, The Children's Book Council, Children of the Sun Books, Childlore Inc., The Chinese American Library Association, Multicultural Publishers Exchange, Oyate, and TEC Computer Consultants provided technical and informational support that helped to move the project forward.

A very special thanks goes out to Jodie Patterson, the New York Editorial Coordinator, who for three years managed the project from the New York office, hung in there for the long haul, and persevered as we blazed new trails through mountains of details and mazes of technical challenges beyond our wildest imaginations. Many thanks also to Molly Gould who spent the last six months of the project attending to the constant and often demanding administrative tasks. I remain grateful for every hour of toil and precious labor both Jodie and Molly contributed to this effort. Marie Brown, my patient and reassuring agent, was always there when I needed her counsel, laughter, and New York wisdom.

I also thank The New Press Education Advisory Comittee, who helped shape the idea for *The Guide* and confirmed the very real need for a collected gathering of resources:

Naomi Barber, *Director, New Visions for Public Education*

Gladys Hardy Brazil, *Education Consultant*

Randolph Carter, *Director of Diversity & Multicultural Services, NAIS*

Milly Daniel, *The Girl Scouts of America*

Julie Diamond, *Pre-school Teacher, Westside Community PS 166*

Mary Frosch, *English Department Head, The Spence School*

Linda Gold, *English Teacher, Packer Collegiate Institute,*

Ellen Goldberg, *Teachers College (Columbia) Writing Project*

Susan Hinkle, *Director, Diversity Resource Collaborative*

Michael Holzman, *former Director, Elementary and Secondary Schools Programs, ACLS*

Robert Mitchell, *Chelsea High School, author of The Multicultural Students' Guide to Colleges*

Pedro Pedraza, *The Center for Puerto Rican Studies, Hunter College*

Thomas Roderick, *Director, NY Educators for Social Responsibility*

Diantha Schull, *Director, Libraries for the Future*

Nancy Shapiro, *Director, Teachers and Writers Collaborative*

Michele Sola, *Manhattan Country School*

Eileen Wasow, *Associate Dean, Bank Street College of Education*

Mark Weiss, *Director, The School for the Physical City, New York*

I especially want to thank my partner, companion, and fellow traveler David Landes. He patiently and lovingly put up with hundreds of papers, thousands of books, and three computers spread out on the kitchen table, in the studies, and on our living room floor. His love, compassion, and sense of humor always helped me see through to the commitment and vision that brought me to the project. I also want to thank Jackie Nash, my three-day-a week, four-miles-at-a-stretch walking partner, who held my hand through many of the tough challenges and "moments of growth" that arose during this project. My internet colleagues responded to my queries, and delivered great information, identified excellent resources, and provided solid reviews.

This acknowledgment would not be complete without thanking the now hundreds of writers who, for well over a century, have had the courage, imagination, wit, passion, and creative acumen to tell the often untold stories of women, people of color, gay men, lesbians, and other oppressed and disenfranchised people who continue to be an integral part of the foundation of this country. Your stories have taught me how to honor my power and stand in my truth, and they allow me to continue my relationship with the child I know I will always be.

The New Press Guide to Multicultural Resources for Young Readers Staff:

Daphne Muse, *Editor-in-Chief*

Diantha Schull, *Consulting Editor*
Dr. Sonia Nieto, *Contributing Editor*

Dr. Elaine Aoki, *Associate Editor*
Dr. Nola Hadley, *Associate Editor*
Dr. Violet Harris, *Associate Editor*
Masha Rudman, *Associate Editor*
Dr. Debbie Wei, *Associate Editor*
Dr. Naomi Caldwell Wood, *Associate Editor*

Susan Hinkle, *Curriculum Editor*
Nehru Kehlev, *Curriculum Editor*

Rosa Warder, *Editorial Coordinator*
Nancy Pearl, *Editorial Consultant*
Molly Gould, *Editorial and Administrative Assistant*

The New Press Staff:

Jodie Patterson, *Project Manager*
Jerome Chou, *Project Manager*
André Schiffrin, *Director*
Diane Wachtell, *Associate Director*
Dorothy Regan, *Business Manager*
Grace Farrell, *Managing Editor*
Hall Smyth, *Art Director*
Ellen Reeves, *Editor*
Matthew Weiland, *Associate Editor*
Deborah Bernstein, *Editorial Assistant*
Jessica Blatt, *Editorial Assistant*
Greg Carter, *Editorial Assistant*
Jim Lavendos, *Copy Editor*
Christine Johansen, *Office Manager*
Davia Smith, *Designer*
Jenna Laslocky, *Writer/Researcher*
Sue de Lara, *Researcher*
Carlie Berwick, *Intern*
Joanne Chen, *Intern*
Denise Clegg, *Intern*
Marisa Miller, *Intern*
Carrie Schoen, *Intern*
Angela Watrous, *Intern*

Permissions

INTRODUCTION

~~~~~~~~~~~~~~~~~~~~~~

DAPHNE MUSE

Children's books are cultural products whose existence straddles various realms, including the worlds of education, entertainment, illustrations, and literature. Further, this kind of literature appeals to our basic human needs for storytelling and story hearing and the often accompanying illustration appeals to our eyes. We utilize children's books as agents of socialization, politicization, and of formal education. Parents and school systems make careful as well as ill-informed decisions about reading materials; materials which have the power to influence the attitudes of youth as they attain literacy and grow into various cultures.

—DIANNE JOHNSON PH.D
Telling Tales: The Pedagogy and Promise of African American Literature for Youth (New York: Greenwood Press, 1990)

 nyone who has ever raised, taught, or cared for a child who is exploring the world of books knows that world may be a distorted, discouraging one. Only forty years ago, with rare exception, children's books were replete with images of girls who fussed endlessly with their hair; people of color described and illustrated as alien, frightening, one-dimensional creatures; disabled people portrayed as pitiful, helpless beings; and white boys and men who reached insurmountable heights, brought great innovations to civilization, and lived exemplary, memorialized lives. The idea of a biracial character, a gay man, or a smart, sassy African American girl was simply inconceivable for most of the book industry.

 t is equally apparent to even the casual observer that children's literature today—much more than in the past — reflects the actual lives, emotions, and concerns of young readers and their families and friends. Aekyung and Rashawn have joined Dick and Jane in books that chronicle, acknowledge, and examine the values, perspectives, and experiences of groups that have been marginalized because of race, gender, ethnicity, language, ability, age, social class, religion/spirituality, and/or sexual orientation. Multicultural children's literature includes works written for, by, and about people of all cultures and backgrounds. It draws upon long traditions of storytelling: legends, folktales, and myths passed down over hundreds of years. As is still true in cultures around the world, storytelling is a way of passing on traditions, preserving history, and providing information vital to the future. Centuries before the arrival of European explorers, Native Americans had developed a strong storytelling tradition. Africans brought the tradition of the griot with them on board the slave ships. Across sometimes treacherous seas, through wars, rebellions, and famines, Europeans, Latinos, Asians, Middle Easterners, and Pacific Islanders immigrating to this country brought their stories with them as well. In folktales, slave narratives, and family stories passed from generation to generation, marginalized people preserved their humanity in the face of prejudice, unjust laws, and violence.

2

 n many ways the history of multicultural children's literature in this country mirrors the history of this country's tremendously diverse cultural, ethnic, and spiritual populations. Historically, most American children's literature has addressed only European American and European themes, cultures, and pedagogy. Despite many changes in the past half-century, demeaning characterizations, stereotyping, and exclusion of people of color, women, people with disabilities, gay men, and lesbians are still common in children's literature. Yet, even as we come to understand the full legacy of an often racist, discriminatory body of children's literature, we need to acknowledge the resistance, from very early on, to that legacy. *The New Press Guide to Multicultural Resources for Young Readers* honors and builds on a multicultural tradition forged by countless librarians, teachers, parents, activists, and many young readers themselves from all cultural and ethnic backgrounds.

 lthough stereotypical and demeaning images remain an issue in children's literature, just as they do in the larger society, some significant progress has been made primarily as a result of stories being told through authentic voices, and a greater level of knowledge and sensitivity toward other cultures. With broad and imaginative strokes, children's authors and illustrators are providing a much more inclusive picture of U.S. history and culture, and capturing the diverse, complex range of ideas, practices, and values that exist within a given community.

 ulticultural children's literature does not exist to fill a quota, or simply to provide a quantitative "representation" of quickly changing demographics. Rather, just as European American and European children's literature imparts information and supports general educational goals, many multicultural children's books provide greater access to literacy, encourage critical thinking and philosophical discourse, and teach valuable skills, as well as promoting cultural understanding. Multicultural literature also includes stories that excite imagination, give credence to creativity, and expand overall literary appreciation.

 aving grown both in stature and scope, this literature has earned the right to lay claim to its classics. And like most classics they will stand boldly and gain a readership that will span the generations and cultural chasms. Within the past thirty years, multicultural/multiethnic children's literature has gained wider institutional recognition and pedagogical permanency through inclusion in the curricula, reference bibliographies, and teaching methodologies. This literature is certain to play a significant and reflective role in the intellectual, artistic, and pedagogical enlightenment of the twenty-first century, especially with communities increasingly responding to immigration, the development of bilingual and multicultural education, and a growing number of cross-cultural alliances.

THE HISTORY OF MULTICULTURAL CHILDREN'S LITERATURE

efore 1960, only a handful of children's books included strong and affirming images of Native American, Latino, African American, or Asian American people. Shirley Graham, Jade Snow Wong, Lorenz Graham, Langston Hughes, Arna Bontemps, and Yoshiko Uchida were among a very small and visionary group of authors who wrote powerfully affirming and historically compelling stories that focused on people of color and women. But as early as 1887 Mary V. Cook presented a paper to the National Press Convention in Louisville, Kentucky, asking rhetorically, "Is Juvenile Literature Demanded on the Part of Colored Children?" According to African American scholar and children's literature historian Dianne Johnson, in 1896 the National Baptist Publishing Board began to publish Sunday School materials for African American youth as a result of Cook's work.

 uring the 1940s, a series of articles were published on the African American and intercultural books. Among them were Augusta Baker's "The Negro in Literature," published in *Child Study* (Winter 1944–45); Eva Knox Evans's "The Negro in Children's Fiction," which appeared in *Publishers Weekly* (August 1941); and Helen Trager's "Intercultural Books for Children," published in *Childhood Education* (November 1945). The articles documented an early, serious interest in the development of literature that included African American values, characters, and themes for young readers.

 ut it was Nancy Larrick's 1965 landmark study "The All-White World of Children's Books," first published in the *Saturday Review* (and reprinted as part of this guide), that created a major uproar that would have a long-range impact in the world of children's literature. That study reported the results of analyzing children's trade books published between 1962–64. Not surprisingly, the analysis showed that African Americans were consistently portrayed as slaves, sharecroppers, and in other menial roles in contrast to their more "successful and respectable" white counterparts. Combined with the groundbreaking work of librarians, such as Augusta Baker and Charlemae Rollins, Larrick's work remains a turning

point in the field. Although the article focused on images of African Americans in children's books, profound questions were raised among librarians, educators, and parents regarding demeaning images of all people of color in children's books. The reverberations from the Larrick piece would be felt for decades to come.

 ith the coming of the civil rights movement of the 1960s and the cross-cultural relationships built with other political and social movements, books began to appear about other traditionally underrepresented groups and topics, including, for example, the internment of Japanese Americans during World War II, and the Latino and Native American experiences. That initially small group of visionaries began to expand, and writers including Virginia Hamilton, Cruz Martel, Virginia Driving Hawk Sneve, Lucille Clifton, and Walter Dean Myers began to write stories that reflected and mined the wealth of their respective cultures.

 uring the seventies, a number of explicit efforts were made to diversify children's books. The Council on Interracial Books for Children essay "Chicano Culture in Children's Literature: Stereotypes, Distortions and Omissions," published in *Cultural Conformity in Books for Children* (edited by Donnarae MacCann and Gloria Woodard, Scarecrow Press, 1977) was critical of depictions of Mexican Americans in children's literature. After analyzing two hundred books, the Council concluded that little in the stories would enable children to recognize a culture, history, or set of life circumstances. The essay also criticized the recurrent theme of poverty as a natural element in Chicano life. Later in this decade, the Council took on the challenge of analyzing class issues in children's books as well.

4

eviews, critical essays, and books by educators and critics including Bettye Latimer, Donnarae MacCann, Gloria Woodard, and Donna E. Norton began to appear. For example, Laura Herbst's essay "That's One Good Indian: Unacceptable Images in Children's Novels," also published in *Cultural Conformity in Books for Children*, brought attention to the prevalence of the wooden Indian and other stereotypical images of Native Americans.

ttempts were also made to address the lack of diversity in the publishing industry itself. In 1969, the American Book Publishers Council hired a special minority recruiter who was able to place six people of color in industry jobs within three months and also developed a plan to capitalize minority publishing firms by acting as a liaison between potential publishers and backers.

ut, while the social movements of the '60s and '70s had a tremendous impact on the historical and political consciousness of the country, major trade publishers were still slow to take risks, saying that multicultural books did not enhance their bottom line. Financial backers for ethnic presses also proved hard to find. Many of the titles from what we now think of as a fertile period in multicultural publishing actually came from small presses with non-existent budgets, who took leaps of faith and published on a shoestring small editions of manuscripts the major trade publishers would not consider. (A notable exception has been Scholastic. As one of the largest publishers of elementary and secondary school books, they have maintained a huge paperback distribution program and proven that fiscal success and social responsibility can coexist.)

t is important to recognize that some multicultural authors fought the commercialization of their books in the hands of trade publishers whom these writers did not trust to maintain the vision or cultural integrity of their stories. These authors chose to publish with small houses including Just Us Books, Lollipop Power, Drum and Spear, and Third World Press, relying on word-of-mouth marketing and the intergenerational appeal of many of these books to sustain their work. During this period, Lollipop Power forged a mission dedicated to addressing sexism in children's books. As a result of their efforts and the "Free to Be Series" that appeared in *Ms.* magazine, girls began to have real voices, their own dreams, and a powerful identity in a growing number of children's books. Drum and Spear broke new ground by publishing a children's book in English and Kiswahili.

y the early '80s, the social issues landscape had broadened significantly in children's books. Rape, homelessness, incest, drugs, and racism were addressed, and multiple controversies ensued. But the sense of wonder, the powerful use of imagination and creativity also continued to expand in the works of authors such as Candy Dawson Boyd, Arnold Adoff, Laurence Yep, and Francis Lea Block. Along with works featuring non-nuclear families, stories about gay men and lesbians, and bilingual books began to appear in stores, classrooms, and home libraries.

s movements to dismantle affirmative action gained ground over the course of the '80s, and the social movements of the previous two decades receded in a political backlash, many inroads made by people of color in mainstream children's book publishing were lost. There was a tendency to cast multiculturalism as a passing trend at some of the major publishing houses, ignoring its integral role in American life. Encouraged and supported by organizations including the Cooperative Children's Book Center and the Multicultural Publishers Exchange, a number of new independent and ethnic presses appeared as a result.

 number of small houses that had perservered through the decades also experienced a revitalization. Wade and Cheryl Hudson of Just Us Books and Harriet Rohmer of Children's Book Press repositioned themselves strategically, becoming '90s economic, educational, and cultural success stories. The Hudsons get calls from major publishers asking them to suggest ideas, concepts, and even marketing strategies. Children's Book Press has done a wonderfully popular series of bilingual/bicultural books, and Just Us Books has made a number of smart editorial decisions including publishing anthologies and an affirmation book for children.

 long with a growing number of young adult novels and brilliantly illustrated picture books including Candy Dawson Boyd's (Floyd Cooper, illustrator) *Daddy, Daddy Be There*, the '90s have brought us multicultural joke books including Barbara K. Walker's *Laughing Together: Giggles and Grins from Around the Globe*, and holiday books that celebrate Kwanza, Diwali, Hanukkah and 'Id al-Fitr. While story lines focusing on social realism have diminished in picture books during the '90s, many more folktales were published from a range of cultures whose literary tongues had not been heard in this country before.

ut despite these changes, few writers of color have experienced the major print runs and mass marketing approaches—including movie deals, t-shirts, buttons, and lunch box tie-ins—afforded the work of many children's book authors. And even those multicultural authors whose books have brought in millions of dollars to large, mainstream publishers have often had to fight to maintain the literary integrity of their powerful words.

THE CURRENT SITUATION

oday, readers are more likely than ever before to find titles such as Laura Rankin's *The Handmade Alphabet*, Alma Flor Ada's *Gathering the Sun: An Alphabet in Spanish and English* and Simon Ortiz's *The People Shall Continue*, anthologies such as Diane Bauer's *Am I Blue*, and comprehensive bibliographies including Frances Ann Day's *Latina and Latino Voices in Literature* in their local libraries or bookstores.

hough improved, however, the current situation is far from ideal. The *New York Times* recently reported that a number of ethnic and multicultural presses including Lee and Low, Just Us Books, and Winston-Derek Publishers sold over $1 million worth of books in 1995, and that over 350 books stores across the country are owned by African Americans. But while part of the picture is bright, some truly disconcerting facts remain. According to the Cooperative Children's Book Center, of the 4,500 children's books published in 1995, 100 titles were created by black authors and illustrators, and 70 titles were from Hispanic authors. Books with Native American themes have generated perhaps the most controversy; eighty-three titles were published, but not all were by Native Americans. Contemporary Asian American themes were the rarest; most of the ninety-one Asian American titles published were folk tales.

oday people of color write and illustrate fewer than 7 percent of the books published for children and young adults. This low level of editorial input has serious consequences for young readers, the education system, and society as a whole. The recent publication of three new versions of *Little Black Sambo*, for instance, reflects ongoing instances of what children's literature scholar Violet Harris refers to as "nostalgic racism." And who knows how many wonderful book projects have been killed by the lack of a broader vision of cultural inclusion.

inally, censorship and attempts to ban books plague children's literature, as they do works for adults. In 1995, a Spokane, Washington, elementary school librarian challenged Faith Ringhold's award-winning *Tar Beach* based on the author's memoirs of family rooftop picnics in 1930's Harlem, "because it stereotypes African Americans eating fried chicken and watermelon, and drinking beer at family picnics." *Heather Has Two Mommies* has caused entire school districts to issue culturally restrictive and intellectually repressive guidelines.

THE FUTURE OF MULTICULTURAL CHILDREN'S LITERATURE

lthough the preponderance of cultural misrepresentation, incorrect use of dialect, and ethnically, racially, or sexually offensive stereotypes has decreased in children's literature, a dire need remains for more multicultural books. Especially needed are books that reveal untold stories including those about refugee communities such as the Hmong, about biracial or working class characters, or children who do not conform to gender stereotypes; books that reflect the rich diversity within various cultures that have been portrayed as monolithic communities or have been thought of in only a few limiting ways; and books that offer new possibilities for cross cultural understanding.

ulticultural children's literature must also continue to expand its scope. While folktales abound, there are still far too few interestingly conceived and well-written biographies, poetry anthologies, and bold young adult novels. Accounts of Native Americans in contemporary cities still lag far behind people's lived experiences.

n addition, while the various transformative social movements of the last three decades have led white ethnics to rediscover and affirm their own cultural spiritual heritage, there has not yet been a significant body of work that portrays or examines the efforts of Americans of European descent to deal with their own racism. Today, white characters who study themselves in the same ways that people of color are studied, are rare. As the movement examining what it means to be white expands, it is important to ensure that this topic appears in young adult literature of the twenty-first century.

rom the look of things now, a handful of small, multicultural presses will move into the twenty-first century with solid fiscal and editorial reputations behind them. Ideally these publishes will supplement ongoing efforts by major commercial houses to publish books that include and appeal to all Americans. But it remains to be seen whether these small presses will be able to sustain themselves at a time when big conglomerates consume smaller businesses on an almost daily basis. Judging from the past decades, the existence of these independent publishers will be crucial to intellectual freedom, pedagogical diversity, and the development of twenty-first-century visionaries.

ifteen years ago, a teacher asked me who was really going to read these books and how on earth would they impact the curriculum. I think the answer has become clear to publishers and certainly to generations of children

who have been culturally and intellectually nurtured by an Allen Say picture book, Muriel Feelings and Tom Feelings counting book, a Nicholas Mohr young adult novel, or Joseph Bruchac story. It is my hope that *The New Press Guide to Multicultural Resources for Young Readers* will become a standard reference and resource guide for your classroom, library, home, or office. But it is my dream that many of these books, and hundreds of others not included here, will become an important part of the literary, cultural, and intellectual lives of children across the country.

7

About This Book

WHY A MULTICULTURAL GUIDE?

As a result of major curriculum, pedagogical, and social reforms that have taken place in the past thirty years, the twenty-first-century classroom will include educational materials that more than ever reflect this country's ethnic and cultural diversity. In many cases, the mandate to reform the school curriculum involves both the introduction of literature that more adequately represents the varied cultural perspectives of students and the use of innovative supplementary materials including films, posters, music, and CD-ROMs. This growing body of multicultural works now constitutes an important resource for educators, librarians, parents, and the general public.

While the existence of materials is no longer a major issue, the selection of appropriate materials remains a critical challenge. In the absence of a major clearinghouse of information about alternative print and audio-visual materials, the most creative models for teaching and learning are usually known only within limited markets. In a letter of complaint to the *New York Times*, a librarian with many Puerto Rican students wrote that she lacks materials about the history and literature of Puerto Rico. She also emphasized

how important it is for these books to be written in English.

If a professional librarian, trained to use bibliographies and databases, has trouble locating appropriate materials — materials which in many cases exist in abundance — this search is even more difficult for less-skilled users. Most multicultural and intercultural materials are aimed at a single audience and are not included routinely in the reference and finding aids regimens used by other audiences. Few of these reference volumes — most of which emphasize printed materials exclusively — cross-list the wide range of related materials, so that teachers and librarians can identify films, CD-ROMs, and audio tapes to use in conjunction with books. And many existing guides are merely bibliographic, lacking annotations or evaluations of the materials listed.

National and regional educational and library organizations publicly recognize the need for better dissemination of critical information. The American Council of Learned Societies (ACLS) has gone so far as to suggest that an annotated bibliography for primary school teachers might be more useful than a project that actually produced material for classroom use.

The New Press, a not-for-profit, public interest book publisher founded in 1990, was established to serve audiences traditionally neglected by mainstream publishing houses. Five years ago, at the first meeting of The New Press's Education Advisory Committee, committee members including teachers, librarians, administrators, policy makers, and others, were asked to prioritize among education projects The New Press might undertake in its first five years. The committee unanimously rated a critical guide to existing multicultural educational resources as the single most important project the Press could publish. No other project the committee could envision had the potential to affect more people — children, parents, teachers, librarians — or to have a greater impact on curriculum across the country.

The resulting reference guide — five years in the making and funded in part by major grants from The Hitachi Foundation, The W.K. Kellogg Foundation, The Lilly Endowment, and The Aaron Diamond Foundation — is by no means exhaustive, but it does provide an enormous amount of thoughtful information about materials that have not been listed or reviewed together in a mainstream publication before. We hope it is offered in a way that will be useful to a wide range of audiences, from the librarian in Queens seeking to serve a Puerto Rican audience meaningfully to the classroom teacher in Oakland looking for ways to help her diverse students find common ground, to parents everywhere in America looking for books that will help their children see and understand themselves and others.

WHAT THIS BOOK CONTAINS

THE REVIEWS

The Guide's primary feature is over a thousand critical reviews of multicultural children's books for young readers in grades K-8, written specifically for this volume by more than a hundred writers and educators who are actively using these works in their daily interaction with children. While no one guide can comprehensively catalog such a wide-ranging and constantly changing field, *The New Press Guide* — in its scope, diversity of opinion, pooling of expertise and resources, and innovative organi-

zation — in every way breaks new ground in surveying and assessing multicultural children's materials.

Review Components
Each review lists the name of the author, editors, illustrator, and translator as appropriate; the publisher and year of publication; and the overall ethnicity or distinguishing feature of the characters in the work. Any special editions (foreign language, Braille, audio cassette, etc.) are also noted as are other related titles that are not reviewed in this guide but that may prove helpful in combination with the book being reviewed (related works that *are* included in this guide may be located using the indexes at the end of the book).

A synopsis with a brief assessment is provided in large type, and a more comprehensive review of 250 to 500 words follows. In many cases, specific teaching suggestions are included at the end of reviews.

Assessment Criteria
In consultation with teachers, librarians, and others who work with children, *The Guide's* writers and editors evaluated books using the following criteria:

* the overall quality of writing and illustration
* accuracy and nuance of treatment of different cultural groups
* the extent to which the item provides a critical or fresh perspective on traditional concepts of race, ethnicity, and gender
* the item's effectiveness in generating or complementing thematic and intercultural approaches to teaching
* accessibility of the text or narrative to the intended audience
* sensitivity and appropriateness of illustrations or artwork
* attractiveness and/or effectiveness of design

Treatment of Classics
As the central problem in this field concerns quality, not quantity, we did not set out merely to create a list of laudable titles. Although it is essential that progressive, well-written books are recognized for their merits, an important

part of our mission is also to challenge existing curricula and criticize flawed books that long have been deemed classics. Thus enormously popular books such as *Charlie and the Chocolate Factory*, *The Indian in the Cupboard*, and *The Cay* are taken to task for the often hurtful ideas and stereotypes they promote.

THEMATIC ORGANIZATION

Perhaps the most unconventional (and we think helpful) feature of *The Guide* is its organization by themes or topics intended to assist teachers and others in using culturally diverse materials across the curriculum. Themes including Community, Family, Social Justice, and Building Cross-Cultural Bridges should stimulate ideas for integrating materials from different ethnic and cultural groups, and should encourage a reconsideration and reform of traditional approaches to history, language arts, science, and the arts. Within each themed chapter reviews are listed by grade level: K-3, 4-6, and 7-8; within each grade level reviews are listed alphabetically by author.

Using *The Guide*'s thematic and grade-level organization, teachers can adapt entire sections into units and develop comprehensive, often interdisciplinary lesson plans, including books and ancillary materials. For example, in Chapter Three, "Community/Friendship," a sidebar of "Recommended Titles on Homelessness" appears along with a review of Eve Bunting's *Fly Away Home*. This review and sidebar are easily adapted into a unit on understanding and sensitizing children to homelessness, using books with different cultural orientations that support children's language and reading development skills.

While one of *The Guide*'s many indexes does list titles by broad cultural/geographical groups that include all the major groups comprising American society today (for example, items that deal primarily with Native Americans are categorized as such), we hope organizing materials by theme will help teachers and programmers who seek to revise strict disciplinary approaches to phase in cross-cultural materials. We hope this format will benefit both teachers without the personal experience and background to enhance the diversity of classroom materials on

their own, as well as those accustomed to working with diversity-oriented materials who would like exposure to new perspectives.

The Guide contains a number of helpful features for teachers who want practical ways of integrating these materials into classrooms and curricula. Wherever relevant, a review includes specific teaching suggestions, including classroom activities and related materials that can accompany a given title in a teaching unit or in a discussion.

OTHER FEATURES

* *An extensive appendix of resources* includes listings of book awards and notable bookstores, library collections, multicultural organizations, relevant magazines and newsletters.

* *Indexes cross-reference books by author, title, and ethnicity* make the search for any given title a quick one.

* *Essays by leading writers and educators on a wide variety of central issues in multicultural education* provide historical context and a pedagogical framework for facilitating classroom use. The essays include:

"Ethnic and Gender Stereotyping in Recent Disney Animation"

"Let Me Tell You A Story: Storytelling in Multicultural Literature"

"I See Myself In There: Experiencing Self and Others in Multiethnic Children's Literature"

"Illustrating the Point: A Commentary on Multicultural and Stereotypic Picture Books"

"Why You Always Giving Us That Black, Latino, Gay, Asian (Fill in the Blank) Stuff?"

"Images of Arabs in American Children's Literature"

"Ebony Visions and Cowrie Shell Dreams: Black American Classics in Fiction and Poetry for Young Readers"

"Behind the Golden Door: The Latino Immigrant Child in Literature and Films for Children"

9

"CD-ROM Technology in the Multicultural Classroom"

"Building Trust and Community in the Classroom"

"Addressing Concerns about Teaching Culturally Diverse Students"

*   *Two classic essays,* "The All-White World of Children's Books" by Nancy Larrick and "10 Quick Ways to Analyze Children's Books for Racism and Sexism" from The Council on Interracial Books for Children, have also been included for their timeless insights into the key issues surrounding multicultural children's literature.

*   *Information on multimedia resources* including movies and videos, CD-ROMS, audio cassettes, and teacher's guides, offer additional ways to broaden the curriculum.

*   *Sidebars, vignettes, illustrations, and other special features* interspersed throughout the book introduce more voices—from students, concerned readers, activists, parents—and show, on the most practical levels, how to incorporate multicultural books into curricula and everyday life.

*   *A timeline of milestones in children's literature* traces the history of publishing for diverse audiences in this country.

*   *Reviews of bilingual books from many cultures* offer a wonderful resource for English As a Second Language students.

Obviously, there is no one way to use *The Guide*. Hopefully readers will find both general "directions" to a complex and compelling landscape of new resources, as well as some specific examples that will help them teach and work with children differently. Ideally, the scope and variety of *The Guide* will provoke creative, new approaches not included in this volume.

10

KEY TO THE REVIEWS

※ SPECIAL AVAILABILITY
including part of series,
audio, video, Braille, foreign
language, etc.

GRADE LEVELS
K-3 (triangle), 4-6 (circle), 7-8 (square)
are identified at top and in margins
of review pages

11

✎ ILLUSTRATOR(S)

TITLE AND SUBTITLE

▣ RELATED TITLES

▣ AUTHOR(S)

ETHNICITY
special features
of the characters

All titles indexed by author,
ethnicity, and title at the
end of The Guide

MOST RECENT
PUBLICATION DATE
(date of first publication
if different), publisher

SYNOPSIS

CRITICAL REVIEW

TEACHING
SUGGESTIONS

REVIEWER
reviewer biographies
appear at end of
The Guide

GRADE FOUR TO GRADE SIX

The Invisible Thread: An Autobiography

▣ Yoshiko Uchida ※ Various sources
Asian American, Japanese American
1991, Julian Messner, ※ Series, ▣ Day, Frances Ann,
Desert Exile; Uchida, Yoshiko, *Journey Home*;
Uchida, Yoshiko, *Journey to Topaz*.

In this moving autobiography, Uchida writes about her beloved family, the Japanese American community, the social and political climate of the time, and her early experiences as a writer. She reflects on her school experiences, including unhappy days as an outsider in junior and senior high school, when she longed to be accepted as an American. Her pain was further compounded by a trip to Japan with her family during the 1930s. There she was perceived as a foreigner; the language and customs were new to her and she came away even more confused about where she belonged.

A moving book about growing up as a second-generation Japanese American in California.

Prejudice against Asian Americans, which had heretofore been barely held in check, was unleashed during World War II. When Japan bombed Pearl Harbor, 120,000 West Coast Japanese Americans were uprooted and incarcerated in concentration camps. Uchida's father, who was born in Japan, was abruptly seized and held incommunicado; Uchida, her mother, and her sister were interned in a horse stall at a nearby racetrack. Later, they were sent to Topaz, a bleak prison camp in the Utah desert where her father eventually joined them.

With insight and clarity, Uchida describes what it was like to be sent by her own government to live behind barbed wire. Her firsthand account of the deprivations of the desolate, dusty prison camp is a revelation, especially for readers who are unfamiliar with that shameful chapter in United States history. Uchida writes, "The ultimate tragedy of that mistake, I believe, was that our government betrayed not only the Japanese people but all Americans, for in its flagrant violation of our Constitution. It damaged the essence of the democratic beliefs on which this country was founded." It was not until 1987 that the Supreme Court reversed its wartime stance on the incarceration of American citizens of Japanese descent and acknowledged that the event was one the worst violations of civil liber-

ties in American history. The United States government belatedly issued a formal apology, concluding that the causes of the uprooting were racial prejudice, war hysteria, and a failure of political leadership. In 1988, Congress passed a redress bill to mitigate some of the massive losses suffered by Japanese Americans, but it came too late for many of those who, like Uchida's parents, were deceased.

After the war, Uchida graduated with honors from the University of California. She later earned her master's degree at Smith College. She taught elementary school in Topaz, Utah, while incarcerated, and later in Philadelphia. The last chapter in this autobiography ends with Uchida happily standing in front of her first class ready to start her new career.

In the epilogue, Uchida describes how a second trip to Japan on a Ford Foundation fellowship in 1952 began to turn things around for her. She perceived Japan in a new light and found a wholeness of spirit that spoke to something deep inside herself, making her aware of the invisible thread that linked her with her Japanese heritage for the first time. She describes her growth and her development in her youth, when she was imbued with the melting pot mentality and wanted to be like everyone else, to later in her life when she became more self-conscious, and proud to be a Japanese American. Having transcended her pain and confusion, she can serve as an inspiration for others who are suffering the rejection and anguish of being an outsider.

It was Uchida's quiet strength that enabled her to infuse this poignant memoir with power and warmth. *Illustrated with family photographs, this autobiography from the In My Own Words Series is fascinating reading for writers, history students, Japanese Americans, lovers of children's literature, and people committed to cultural sensitivity.*

Uchida's experiences during World War II provide the basis for two of her novels: Journey to Topaz *and its sequel,* Journey Home. *Reading both novels along with this autobiography will help students gain insight into how life experiences provide inspiration for writing fiction. The Invisible Thread might also be used with a unit on World War II, an author unit or a unit on prejudice.* FRANCES A. DAY

101

Milestones in Children's Literature

ROSA E. WARDER

hile the voices of new immigrants, descendants of slaves, women, gay men and lesbians, and the indigenous people of the nation can be found in all manner of young adult novels, biographies, and picture books today, far too many people remain unaware of this growing body of literature. Tongues and feet are unbound and stereotypes are overturned in books written to honor, celebrate, and illuminate the lives and struggles of disenfranchised people in this country.

his timeline continues to be a work in progress. It provides some sense of the breadth of this body of literature and the range of people who have cultivated and nurtured it for over a century. As more writers, illustrators, and independent booksellers bring powerful and innovative stories to young readers, this timeline is bound to expand and reflect an even broader collection of voices and visions from America's multicultural landscape.

1817 The first African American firm to issue children's books, A.M.E. Book Concern, is founded in Philadelphia by the African Methodist Episcopal Church.

1855 J.W. Leonard and Co. of New York becomes the first commercial African American publisher.

1887 Amelia E. Johnson, wife of a Baltimore minister, founds *The Joy*, an eight-page monthly periodical for African American children.

1889 Amelia E. Johnson writes *Clarence and Corrine or God's Way*. The book was published by the American Baptist Publication Society, a white-administered organization.

1896 The African American-administered National Baptist Publishing Board begins publishing Sunday School material for African American youths in response to a paper entitled, "Juvenile Literature Demanded on the Part of Colored Children?"

1920 African American author, scholar, and philosopher W.E.B. DuBois founds the *Brownies' Books*, a monthly magazine that includes fiction, poetry, and a column called, "The Crow Flies," providing a African American perspective on world events. Harlem Renaissance author Jessie Redmond Fauset serves as editor during its two years of publication.

1933 African American author Charles C. Dawson, founder of the Association for the Study of Negro Life and History (1916), writes *ABC's of Great Negroes* (Dawson Publishers), one of the earliest books to treat the subject of African American history in an alphabet format for young readers.

1934 African American author Arna Wendell Bontemps offers a realistic depiction of black life and history through a series of books he writes for his children, beginning with *You Can't Pet a Possum*.

1937 Dr. Carter G. Woodson, an African American, Harvard-trained historian, produces the first curriculum material for African Americans, through *The Negro History Bulletin*. In 1938, Dr. Woodson writes *African Heroes and Heroines* (Associated Publishers); and in 1945 Dr. Woodson writes *African Makers of History* (Associated Publishers).

1938 The James Weldon Johnson Memorial Collection is started at the County Cullen Regional Branch Library in New York with a gift of $77 from the James Weldon Johnson Literary Guild. The goal is to establish a collection of children's books accurately and sensitively reflecting black history and culture. Under the direction of librarian Augusta Baker, books are selected based on the appropriateness of language, theme, and illustration. At its height, the collection contains over 1,600 books.

1940s Julian Messner publishes African American Shirley Graham's biographies of George Washington Carver (1944), Paul Robeson (1946), Frederick Douglass (1947), Phillis Wheatley (1949), Jean Baptiste de Sable (1953), and Booker T. Washington (1955). This is the earliest known collection of biographies focusing on the accomplishments of African Americans published for young readers.

1946 African American writer Ellen Tarry writes *My Dog Rinty* (The Viking Press), a photo essay featuring contemporary African American children living in Harlem. This book is the first to portray urban African American life.

1946 Lorenz B. Graham's publisher first accepts and then rejects his manuscript for *South Town*, saying that the characters did not seem like real Negroes; they were too much like other people. During the next ten years, *South Town* is rejected by nearly every publisher for the same reason. Graham refuses to give in and is dismissed as an uncooperative writer. The book is finally published by Follett Publishing Co. in 1958.

1946 Just one year after the internment of 110,000 Japanese Americans ended, Mine Okubo, an established artist, publishes the first book of line drawings and narrative, depicting life in the internment camps with satirical humor. (Columbia University Press in New York). This book is such a standard that it is still in print from the University of Washington Press. Okubo still lives in New York.

1950 Kenneth Clark's study of the psychological impact of racial segregation on children is released. The results of the study influence the landmark school desegregation decision in 1954.

1951 Japanese American author Yoshiko Uchida writes *New Friends for Susan* (Scribner), about a girl's experience after she and her family are released from a West Coast internment camp following World War II. This is the first book for children published after WWII that authentically portrays the effects of the war on Japanese Americans. Uchida continues to create an impressive body of books on the Japanese American experience until her death in 1994.

1954 The Supreme Court hands down its school desegregation ruling in *Brown v. Board of Education*. As a result, mainstream publishing houses are forced to confront their abuse of ethnic stereotypes in children's literature and begin to recruit African Americans into the field as authors, illustrators, and editors.

1956 Arna W. Bontemps wins the Jane Addams Children's Book Award for *Story of the Negro* (Knopf), becoming the first person of color to receive the award.

1957 The New York Public Library publishes its first annual annotated bibliography, *Books About Negro Life for Children*. In 1963, the title is changed to *The African American Experience in Children's Books*. The bibliography continues to be published sporadically, the last edition in 1994. This publication helps to legitimize the need for multiethnic voices in children's literature.

1958 Although many publishers are reluctant to take on white author Dorothy Sterling's book *Captain of the Planter: the Story of Robert Smalls*, claiming that southern markets would be closed to the book because of its sympathetic portrayal of blacks, Doubleday takes the risk. Ironically, shortly after its publication, the book is included on a list of approved books for schools by the South Carolina State Department of Education.

1958 Lorenz B. Graham's *South Town* is published. Considered a courageous book for its time, the story tells of the hardship, violence, and prejudice to which a black family in the South is subjected. The book has been criticized for the stereotypical benevolent white savior roles of the European American characters in the story.

1965 Doubleday-Zenith releases its Black Heritage Series, with publications including *Great Rulers of the African Past*, by Lavina G. Dobler and William A. Brown, originated by Charles Harris. This is the earliest known series of its type released by a major publishing house that focuses on positive images of Africa and African life before slavery.

1965 European American educator Nancy Larrick's landmark study, "The All-White World of Children's Books," appears in the *Saturday Review*. It outlines her study of more than 5,000 children's trade books published between 1962 and 1964. Of these, only forty include illustrations or text depicting contemporary African Americans. The article influences publishers and the public, and is responsible for increased sensitivity to ethnicity in children's books.

1966 The Association for the Study of Negro Life and History publishes a series of Negro History Kits in response to the increasing demand for multicultural teaching materials, marking the beginnings of multicultural education and curriculum materials in the U.S. school systems.

1966 *The Council on Interracial Books for Children Bulletin*, edited by Bradford Chamber, begins publication in order to provide support for authors of color. By introducing them to publishing houses, the *Bulletin* plays a key role in shaping multicultural children's literature.

1967 *The Council on Interracial Books for Children* (CIBC) is founded by writers, librarians, teachers, and parents to promote anti-racist and anti-sexist children's literature and teaching materials, and to provide a forum for socially conscious analysis of children's books. CIBC's Contest for Third World Writers, started in 1967, provides a starting point for multicultural writers and illustrators.

1968 African American author Walter Dean Myers wins CIBC's contest and publishes his first children's book, *Where Does the Day Go* (Parents Magazine Press). It is one of the earliest books published in which the protagonist is both disabled and positively portrayed.

1969 At age nineteen, John Steptoe publishes his first book *Stevie* (Harper & Row).

1969 *The Black Panther* coloring book is published by party members. Unauthorized by party leadership, the book is suppressed by the organization upon publication. The story line follows an African from a past time of dignity in Africa through slavery, exploitation, and persecution in the United States, culminating in a violent resurgence of self-esteem.

1969 The annual Coretta Scott King Award for African American illustrators is established. The award's purpose is to encourage creative writers and/or illustrators to promote the cause of brotherhood and peace through their work.

1970 Arnold Adoff's *Malcolm X* is published. During the early 1970s, children's books begin to look at African American characters in relation to one another, rather than simply in relation to white society. Several other biographies of civil rights activists are published, including Eloise Greenfield's *Rosa Parks*.

1970 Lollypop Power Press is founded. Run by a women's collective, it merges with sister press Carolina Wren in 1986 and is devoted to publishing non-sexist multicultural picture books and bilingual titles. *In Christina's Toolbox* and *I Like You to Make Jokes with Me, But I Don't Want You to Touch Me* exemplify their approach.

1970 The American Indian Historical Society puts out *Textbooks and the American Indian*, an analysis by Native American scholars of over 300 books used in schools. Not one of the books examined (many of which remain in use today) was deemed a good source of information about the culture and history of Native Americans. The analysis charged: "Everybody has a right to his own opinion. A person also has a right to be wrong. But a textbook has no right to be wrong, or to lie, or to invade the truth, falsify history, or insult and malign a whole race of people. That is what many textbooks do."

1971 Kazue Mizumura, author and illustrator, becomes the first Asian woman to win a Boston Globe-Horn Book Award for illustration for her book *If I Built A Village* (Crowell).

1971 The Japanese American Curriculum Project, Inc., (now Asian American CP) of San Mateo, California, becomes the first Asian American organization nationally to promote the awareness of Asian American children's books. A non-profit, voluntary organization, it still promotes selected good Asian American children's books. JACP writes the first supplementary text on Japanese Americans written by Japanese Americans. Titled *Japanese Americans: An Untold Story* the text contains history, biographies, and three short stories (Holt, Rinehart & Winston). This is the first text to realistically describe the internment for children from the point of view of the former internees. It is revised in 1985 as *The Japanese American Journey*, published by JACP .

1972 Native American author Virginia Driving Hawk Sneve's *Jimmy Yellow Hawk* (Holiday House) is one of the earliest books by a Native American author about the Native American experience.

1972 Tom Feelings is the first African American artist to win a Caldecott Honor Award for his illustrations of *Moja Means One: A Swahili Counting Book* written by Muriel Feelings (Dial). He goes on to win the Boston Globe-Horn Book

Award and the Caldecott Honor again in 1975 for *Jambo Means Hello: A Swahili Alphabet Book* by Muriel Feelings (Dial).

1973 Arnold Adoff's *Black Is Brown Is Tan* (Harper & Row) is the first children's book to feature an interracial family. Previous to this book, the theme of interracial relationships in children's literature was portrayed only through animal characters and imaginary creatures, as in *Rabbit's Wedding* (Harper 1959) by Garth Williams and *Little Blue and Little Yellow* (Aster-Honor 1959) by Leo Lionni.

1973 *Ebony Jr!*, a monthly magazine focusing on the African American experience and designed for young readers, begins publication. The last issue is published in October 1985.

1974 African American author Virginia Hamilton's *M.C. Higgins, the Great* (Macmillan) wins the National Book Award and Boston Globe-Horn Book Award.

1974 The first annual Carter G. Woodson Award from the National Council for Social Studies is presented. The annual award is given to encourage the writing, publishing, and dissemination of outstanding social studies books for young readers that treat topics related to ethnic minorities and race relations sensitively and accurately. The first author honored with this award is African American author Eloise Greenfield for her book *Rosa Parks* (Crowell).

1974 Nicholasa Mohr wins the Jane Addams Children's Book Award for *Nilda* (Harper 1973). She is the earliest known Puerto Rican author to be honored with this award.

Mid 1970s The Council on Interracial Books for Children (CIBC) expands its goals to include fighting sexism, homophobia, and discrimination on the basis of handicap, age, and class.

1975 Virginia Hamilton is the first author of color to be recognized with the Newbery Medal for her book, *M.C. Higgins the Great* (Macmillan). First awarded in 1922, the Newbery Medal, named after the famous eighteenth-century publisher and seller of children's books John Newbery, is offered by Fredric G. Melcher as an incentive for better quality children's books.

1975 Chinese American author Laurence Yep's *Dragonwings* (Harper & Row), a true story of an early-twentieth-century Chinese boy and his father who built and flew an airplane, is published. In 1976, Yep receives a Newbery Honor Book Medal, the first Chinese American author to receive this award.

1975 *Why Mosquitoes Buzz in People's Ears* (Dial), as retold by Verna Aardema and illustrated by Leo and Diane Dillon, is published. In 1976 it receives the Caldecott Award. Named after Randolph J. Caldecott, the famous English illustrator of children's books, the Caldecott is awarded to the artist of the most distinguished picture book for children in the United States. In 1976, Leo and Diane Dillon are the first illustrators of color to win the award.

1977 Children's Book Press publishes *The People Shall Continue* by Simon Ortiz, the first children's history of the western hemisphere written from a Native American perspective.

1977 Mildred D. Taylor's *Roll of Thunder, Hear My Cry* (Dial) wins the Newbery Medal, becoming the second work by an African American author to receive this award.

1977 The Council on Interracial Books for Children publishes Robert Moore and Arlene Hirschfelder's *Feathers, Tomahawks and Tepees: A Study of Stereotyped "Indian" Imagery in Children's Picture Books*. This groundbreaking book shows that most "Indian" imagery in children's books consists of illustrations of Caucasian children playing Indian by putting on a feather and argues that to suggest that other people can become Indian simply by donning a feather is to trivialize Native people's diversity and to assault their humanity.

1978 Children's Book Press publishes the first bilingual Korean-English book for children, Min Paek's *Aekyung's Dream*. Children's Book Press goes on to publish folktales from around the world using side-by-side country of origin and English texts.

1978 The Right-On Rainbow festival is established at Mills College in Oakland, California, to celebrate and honor cultural diversity in children's literature and film. One of the first festivals of this type, the Right-On Rainbow festival results in materials that are used as building blocks for multicultural literature and media festivals nationwide.

1979 "Guidelines for selecting bias-free text-books and storybooks" are published by CIBC. These guidelines are distributed through libraries and professional teaching associations nationwide and are still used by parents, educators, and librarians.

1982 African American scholar Rudine Sims writes *Shadow and Substance: Afro-American Experience in Contemporary Children's Fiction* (American Library Association), the first substantial examination of literature written by African American authors for African American children.

1982 Arlene B. Hirschfelder's *American Indian Stereotypes in the World of Children: a Reader and Bibliography* (Scarecrow Press) is published. With a foreword by scholar and author Michael Dorris, the book clearly documents the continuing stereotyping of Native Americans.

1983 "Reading Rainbow," a public television show hosted by African American actor LeVar Burton, featuring a read-aloud of multicultural children's literature and reviews by children, premiers. In 1995, Reading Rainbow publishes and distributes a handbook, *The Reading Rainbow Guide to Children's Books: The 101 Best Titles.*

1985 The Cooperative Children's Book Center at the University of Wisconsin-Madison begins to document the number of books written or illustrated by African Americans. Eighteen of the 2,500 children's books published in the United States in this year were written and/or illustrated by African Americans.

1986 African American author Jeannette F. Caine's *Chilly Stomach* (Harper & Row) relates the tale of a girl who, after being sexually abused by her uncle, decides to reveal what happened and get help. This groundbreaking book paves the way for children's literature aimed at informing and supporting children dealing with trauma.

1986 The earliest books on AIDS for young adults appear: *AIDS* by Allan E. Norse, M.D., highly recognizable because of the *Scarlet Letter* type *A* printed on the book jacket; and *AIDS: Deadly Threat* by Alvin and Virginia Silverstein.

1987 *Publishers Weekly* publishes its first announcement of the Cuffies Awards: Favorites and Not-So-Favorites of Children's Booksellers, including off-the-cuff categories such as Worst Celebrity Book, Most Annoying Hype, and Most Garbled Title Request.

1989 Rosmarie Hausherr's *Children and The AIDS Virus* (Clarion), the first children's book on AIDS, is published.

1989 The Center for the Study of Books in Spanish for Children and Adolescents/Centro para el Estudio de Libros Infantiles y Juveniles en Español, at California State University, San Marcos. The Center is the only one in the world, and now includes more than 60,000 books and a World Wide Web site with recommended books.

1990 Author Ed Young's *Lon Po Po: A Red-Riding Hood Story from China* (Philomel) receives the Caldecott Award, becoming the first book by a Chinese American to win the award. This book also receives the Boston Globe-Horn Book Award for illustrations.

1990 Giuseppe Verdi's opera *Aida* is published as a children's book, told by Leontyne Price and illustrated by Leo and Diane Dillon. In 1991, it receives the Coretta Scott King award for illustrations. This book is renowned for destroying stereotypes about African Americans and classical opera.

1990 Of the 5,000 children's books published in this year in the United States, fifty-one were written and/or illustrated by African Americans. The number of books published by Native Americans, Latinos, and Asians is far lower, according to the Cooperative Children's Book Center.

1991 *Judge Rabbit and the Tree Spirit: a Folk tale from Cambodia* (Children's Book Press), told by Lina Mao Wall, adapted by Cathy Spagnoli, and illustrated by Nancy Hom, is the first Cambodian-English book published for children.

1993 *Who Belongs Here? An American Story* (Tilbury House), written by Margery Burns Knight and illustrated by Anne O'Brien, tackles racism and political activism through the experience of Nary, a young Cambodian immigrant.

1993 The Skipping Stones Book Awards are established for children's book authors and illustrators whose work addresses multicultural issues.

1994 Tom Feelings receives the Caldecott Award for *Soul Looks Back in Wonder* (Dial). This is the first children's anthology of poetry by African American authors to receive this recognition.

16

1995 Virginia Hamilton is the first author of color to receive the Laura Ingalls Wilder Award, established in 1954 to honor an author's collected works and contributions to childrens literature.

1995 Hispanic author Evelyn Cisneros and African American author Virginia Hamilton are awarded MacArthur Foundation Fellowships Genius Awards for their contributions to literature.

Rosa Emilia Warder is an artist and writer living in Oakland, California. Her work centers on issues of importance to women, children, and bicultural peoples. She is the writer and illustrator of three children's picture books, and is at work on a youth novel.

Rosy Elliott, an intern with Children's Advocate Newspaper, *and Angela Watrous, a student at Mills College in Oakland, California, contributed to the research of this timeline.*

10 Quick Ways to Analyze Children's Books for Racism and Sexism

Since their publication in 1979, these guidelines from The Council on Interracial Books for Children have been widely recognized as a milestone in multicultural children's literature and have become an invaluable resource in teaching concerned children and adults how to select children's books free of stereotypes.

Both in school and out, young children are exposed to racist and sexist attitudes — expressed over and over in books and in other media — gradually distorting their perceptions until stereotypes and myths about minorities and women are accepted as reality. It is difficult for a librarian or teacher to convince children to question society's attitudes, but if a child can be shown how to detect racism and sexism in a book, the child can proceed to transfer the perception to wider areas. The following ten guidelines are offered as a starting point in evaluating children's books from this perspective.

1. CHECK THE ILLUSTRATIONS
Look for Stereotypes. A stereotype is an oversimplified generalization about a particular group, race, or sex, which usually carries derogatory implications. In addition to blatant stereotypes, look for variations that in any way demean or ridicule characters because of their race or sex.

Look for Tokenism. If there are non-white characters in the illustrations, do they look just like whites except for being tinted or colored in? Do all minority faces look stereotypically alike, or are they depicted as genuine individuals with distinctive features?

Who's Doing What? Do the illustrations depict minorities in subservient and passive roles or in leadership and action roles? Are males the active "doers" and females the inactive observers?

2. CHECK THE STORY LINE
The civil rights movement led publishers to weed out many insulting passages, particularly from stories with black themes, but the attitudes still find expression in less obvious ways. The following checklist suggests some of the subtle (covert) forms of bias to watch for.

Standard for Success. Does it take "white" behavior for a person of color to "get ahead?" Is "making it" in the dominant white society projected as the only ideal? To gain acceptance and approval, do people of color have to exhibit extraordinary qualities — excel in sports, get A's, etc.? In friendships between white children and children of color, is it the child of color who does most of the understanding and forgiving?

Resolution of Problems. How are problems presented, conceived, and resolved in the story? Are people of color considered to be "the problem?" Are the oppressions faced by people of color and women represented as causally related to an unjust society? Are the reasons for poverty and oppression explained, or are they just accepted as inevitable? Does the story line encourage passive acceptance or active resistance? Is a particular problem that is faced by a person of color resolved through the benevolent intervention of a white person?

Role of Women. Are the achievements of girls and women based on their own initiative and intelligence, or are they due to their good looks or to their relationship with boys? Are sex roles incidental or critical to characterization and plot? Could the same story be told if the sex roles were reversed?

3. LOOK AT THE LIFESTYLES

Are people of color and their setting depicted in such a way that they contrast unfavorably with the unstated norm of white middle-class suburbia? If the non-white group is depicted as "different," are negative value judgments implied? Are people of color depicted exclusively in ghettos, barrios, or migrant camps? If the illustrations and text attempt to depict another culture, do they go beyond oversimplifications and offer genuine insights into another lifestyle? Look for inaccuracy and inappropriateness in the depiction of other cultures. Watch for instances of the "quaint-natives-in-costumes" syndrome (most noticeable in areas like costume and custom, but extending to behavior and personality traits as well).

4. WEIGH THE RELATIONSHIPS BETWEEN PEOPLE

Do the whites in the story possess the power, take the leadership, and make the important decisions? Do people of color and females function in essentially supporting roles?

How are family relationships depicted? In African-American families, is the mother always dominant? In Latino families, are there always lots of children? If the family is separated, are societal conditions — unemployment, poverty — cited among the reasons for the separation?

5. NOTE THE HEROES

For many years, books showed only "safe" non-white heroes — those who avoided serious conflict with the white establishment of their time. People of color are insisting on the right to define their own heroes (of both sexes) based on their own concepts and struggles for justice.

When minority heroes do appear, are they admired for the same qualities that have made white heroes famous or because what they have done has benefited white people? Ask this question: "Whose interest is the particular figure really serving?"

6. CONSIDER THE EFFECTS ON A CHILD'S SELF-IMAGE

Are norms established which limit the child's aspirations and self-concepts? What effect can it have on African American children to be continuously bombarded with images of the color white as the ultimate in beauty, cleanliness, virtue, etc., and the color black as evil, dirty, menacing, etc.? Does the book counteract or reinforce this positive association with the color white and negative association with black?

What happens to a girl's self-esteem when she reads that boys perform all the brave and important deeds? What about a girl's self-esteem if she is not "fair" of skin and slim of body?

In a particular story, is there one or more person with whom a child of color can readily identify to a positive and constructive end?

7. CONSIDER THE AUTHOR'S OR ILLUSTRATOR'S BACKGROUND

Analyze the biographical material on the jacket flap or the back of the book. If the story deals with a multicultural theme, what qualifies the author or illustrator to deal with the subject? If the author and illustrator are not members of the group being written about, is there anything in their background that would specifically recommend them as the creators of this book? The same criteria apply to a book that deals with the feelings and insights of women or girls.

8. CHECK OUT THE AUTHOR'S PERSPECTIVE

No author can be wholly objective. All authors write out of a cultural as well as personal context. Children's books in the past have traditionally come from white, middle-class authors, with one result being that a single ethnocentric perspective has dominated American children's literature. With the book in question, look carefully to determine whether the direction of the author's perspective substantially weakens or strengthens the value of his/her written work. Are omissions and distortions central to the overall character or "message" of the book?

9. WATCH FOR LOADED WORDS

A word is loaded when it has insulting overtones. Examples of loaded adjectives (usually racist) are "savage," "primitive," "conniving," "lazy," "superstitious," "treacherous," " wily," "crafty," "inscrutable," "docile," and "backward."

Look for sexist language and adjectives that exclude or ridicule women. Look for use of the male pronoun to refer to both males and females. The following examples show how sexist language can be avoided: "ancestors" instead of forefathers; "firefighters" instead of "fireman;" "manufactured" instead of "manmade;" the "human family" instead of the "family of man."

10. LOOK AT THE COPYRIGHT DATE

Books on "minority" themes — usually hastily conceived — suddenly began appearing in the mid-1960s. There followed a growing number of "minority experience" books to meet the new market demand, but most of these were still written by white authors, edited by white editors, and published by white publishers. They, there-fore, reflected a white point of view. Only recently has the children's book world begun to even remotely reflect the realities of a multiracial society or the concerns of feminists.

The copyright dates, therefore, can be a clue as to how likely the book is to be overtly racist or sexist, although recent copyright is no guarantee of a book's relevance or sensitivity. The copyright date only means the year the book was published. It usually takes a minimum of a year — and often much more than that — from the time a manuscript is submitted to the publisher to the time it is actually printed and put on the market. This time-lag meant very little in the past, but in a time of rapid change and changing consciousness, when children's book publishing is attempting to be "relevant," it is increasingly significant.

Information collected by the Council on Interracial Books for Children, and first developed in 1979.

The All-White World of Children's Books

Nancy Larrick

"Why are they always white children?"

The question came from a five-year-old Negro girl who was looking at a picturebook at the Manhattanville Nursery School in New York. With a child's uncanny wisdom, she singled out one of the most critical issues in American education today: the almost complete omission of Negroes from books for children. Integration may be the law of the land, but most of the books children see are all white.

Yet in Cleveland, 53 percent of the children in kindergarten through high school are Negro. In St. Louis, the figure is 56.9 percent. In the District of Columbia, 70 percent are Negro. Across the country, 6,340,000 non-white children are learning to read and to understand the American way of life in books which either omit them entirely or scarcely mention them. There is no need to elaborate upon the damage —much of it irreparable to the Negro child's personality.

But the impact of all-white books upon 39,600,000 white children is probably even worse. Although his light skin makes him one of the world's minorities, the white child learns from his books that he is the kingfish. There seems little chance of developing the humility so urgently needed for world cooperation, instead of world conflict, as long as our children are brought up on gentle doses of racism through their books.

For the past ten years, critics have deplored the blatant racial bias of the textbooks. Last August, Whitney Young, Jr., executive director of the National Urban League, attacked the trade books as well. In a nationally syndicated column, he berated American trade book publishers for omitting Negroes from their books for children. As an example, he singled out a

Little Golden Book, entitled *A Visit to the Zoo*, which pictures New York's Central Park Zoo in realistic detail except that no dark face is shown. "The entire book-publishing industry is guilty of this kind of omission," charged Mr. Young.

Are the publishers guilty as charged? To find the answer, I undertook a survey of more than 5,000 trade books published for children in 1962, 1963, and 1964. Surely the effect of Little Rock, Montgomery, and Birmingham could be seen by this time, I reasoned.

As a start, I turned to the seventy members of the Children's Book Council who published trade books for children in each of these three years. Sixty-three of them (90 percent) completed my questionnaire; many gave anecdotal information as well.

Analysis of the replies and examination of several hundred books led to the discouraging conclusion that the vast majority of recent books are as white as the segregated zoo of Golden Press. Of the 5,206 children's trade books launched by the sixty-three publishers in the three-year period, only 349 include one or more Negroes (an average of 6.7 percent). Among the four publishers with the largest list of children's books, the percentage of books with Negroes is one-third lower than this average. These four firms (Doubleday, Franklin Watts, Macmillan, and Harper & Row) published 866 books in the three-year period, and only 4.2 per cent have a Negro in text or illustration. Eight publishers produced only all-white books.

Of the books which publishers report as "including one or more Negroes," many show only one or two dark faces in a crowd. In others, the litho-pencil sketches leave the reader wondering whether a delicate shadow indicates a racial difference or a case of sunburn. It would be easy for some of these books to pass as all-white if publishers had not listed them otherwise.

The scarcity of children's books portaying American Negroes is much greater than the figure of 6.7 percent would indicate, for almost 60 percent of the books with Negroes are placed outside of continental United States or before World War II, an event as remote to a child as the Boston Tea Party. There are books of African folktales, reports of the emerging nations of Africa, stories laid in the islands of the Caribbean, biographies of Abraham Lincoln and Jefferson Davis and historical studies about the Underground Railroad. Most of them show a way of life that is far away from that of the contemporary Negro and may be highly distasteful to him. To the child who has been involved in civil rights demonstrations of Harlem or Detroit, it is small comfort to read of the Negro slave who smilingly served his white master.

Over the three-year period, only four-fifths of 1 percent of the children's trade books from the sixty-three publishers tell a story about American Negroes today. Twelve of these forty-four books are the simplest picture books, showing Negroes in the illustrations but omitting the word from the text. Examples are *Benjie* by Joan M. Lexau (Dial Press); *Tony's Birds* by Millicent Selsam (Harper&Row) *The Snowy Day* and *Whistle for Willie* by Ezra Jack Keats (Viking).

Those for readers of twelve and up mention the word Negro, and in several the characters tackle critical issues stemming from school integration, and nonviolent demonstrations. But these books are usually so gentle as to be unreal. There are no cattle prods, no bombing, no reprisals. The white heroine who befriends a Negro in high school enjoys the support of at least one sympathetic parent and an admiring boyfriend.

Several books do have outstanding literary merit. Among them are *Roosevelt Grady*, by Louise Shotwell (World), the story of a Negro boy whose parents are migratory workers; *I Marched with Hannibal*, by Hans Baumann (Henry Z. Walck), a boy's report of the brilliant Carthaginian general; *Forever Free: The Story of the Emancipation Proclamation*, by Dorothy Sterling (Doubleday); *The Peoples in Africa*, by Colin M. Turnbull (World); and *The Peaceable Revolution*, by Betty Schechter (Houghton Mifflin), a beautifully written report of three phases of the nonviolent revolution as seen in the work of Thoreau, Gandhi, and the American Negro today.

But these notable titles are the exceptions. "Really fine books are still scarce," says Augusta Baker, coordinator of Children's Services in the

New York Public Library. Most of the books depicting Negroes are mediocre or worse. More than one-third have received unfavorable reviews or been ignored by the three major reviewing media in the juvenile book field; *The Horn Book, School Library Journal*, and *Bulletin of the Children's Book Center of the University of Chicago.*

How well do recent children's books depict the Negro? To answer this question I enlisted the help of four Negro librarians who work with children in New York, Chicago, and Baltimore. They rated 149 of the books "excellent" and thirteen "objectionable" in their portrayal of Negroes either through illustration or text.

Among those listed as "objectionable" are three editions of *Little Black Sambo*. Another is *The Lazy Little Zulu*, which a reviewer in *School Library Journal* rated as "Not recommended because it abounds in stereotypes."

The identification of Negro stereotypes in adult fiction is vividly spelled out in the unpublished doctoral dissertation (1963) of Catherine Juanita Starke at Teacher's College, Columbia University. By analyzing the work of popular American novelists of the past hundred years—from James Fenimore Cooper to James Baldwin and Ralph Ellison—Dr. Starke shows how the Negro in fiction has changed from the ridiculous stock character to the emerging individual who is first a human being and second a Negro.

Early novelists called the Negro "gorilla-like," gave him a name that ridiculed his servile status (Emperor, Caesar, or Brutus, for example), and made his dark skin and thick lips the epitome of the ludicrous. The Negro mother was described as uncomely and ungraceful, clothing her stout body in gaudy calico.

Concurrently there were protest novels which showed the "counter stereotype," the Negro of unsurpassed grace and beauty, poetic language, great wisdom, and unfaltering judgment.

In the 1920s, the *Saturday Evening Post* was building circulation on the Irvin S.Cobb stories of Jeff, the comic Negro menial. Twenty years later, the *Post* was still doing the same with stories by Octavius Roy Cohen and Glenn Allan, who wrote of Negroes who ridiculed themselves and their race.

Perhaps the public opinion that applauded this kind of adult fiction was responsible also for the 1946 Caldecott Medal award to *The Rooster Crows: A Book of American Rhymes and Jingles,* illustrated by Maud and Miska Petersham and published by Macmillan. Apparently the librarians who selected this book as "the most distinguished American Picture Book for Children published in the United States" in 1945 were not bothered by four pages showing Negro children with great buniony feet, coal black skin, and bulging eyes (in the distance, a dilapidated cabin with a black, gun-toting, barefoot adult). White children in this book are nothing less than cherubic, with dainty little bare feet or well-made shoes. After eighteen years enough complaints had been received to convince the publisher that the book would be improved by deleting the illustrations of Negro children. In the new edition of *The Rooster Crows* (1964) only white children appear.

The 1964 Caldecott Award went to *The Snowy Day*, written and illustrated by Ezra Jack Keats and published by Viking. The book gives a sympathetic picture of just one child, a small Negro boy. The Negro mother, however, is a huge figure in a gaudy yellow plaid dress, albeit without a red bandanna.

Many children's books that include a Negro show him as a servant or slave, a sharecropper, a migrant worker, or a menial.

On the other hand, a number of books have overtones of the "counter stereotype" observed by Dr. Starke, the Negro who is always good, generous, and smiling in the face of difficulties. The nine-year-old hero of *Roosevelt Grady* is one of these. Cheerfully and efficiently he looks out for the younger children or works alongside his parents in the fields, does well at school when there is a school to go to, never loses his temper, and in the end finds a permanent home for the family. The book won the Nancy Bloch Award for the Best Intercultural Children's Book for 1963, although it includes no whites except the teacher, the social worker, and the owner of the trailer camp. Only the pictures indicate that the Gradys and their friends are Negroes.

When the Cleveland Board of Education recommended *Roosevelt Grady* for children's reading, a Negro newspaper deplored this choice because one picture shows a work-gang leader grappling with a fat knife-toting Negro who has threatened a young boy. "This is a gross stereotype," was the objection. "But the main story shows beautiful family life among Negroes," was the reply, and *Roosevelt Grady* remains on the Cleveland list.

It is not unusual for critics to disagree as to the effectiveness of the pictures of the Negro in a book for children. For example, one of the librarians who helped me gave *Tolliver*, by Florence Means (Houghton Mifflin), a rating of "excellent" for its pictures of the Negro. Another criticized it as a modern story set in Fisk University as it was twenty-five years ago. "There has been a revolution down there since then," she wrote. "As a result the book seems somewhat condescending."

Whispering Willows, by Elizabeth Hamilton Friermood (Doubleday), also brought mixed response. It tells of the friendship of a white girl who is a high school senior in the class of 1911 and a Negro girl who works as a domestic in a white home. One librarian gave the book top rating. Another objected to the stereotype of the gentle Negro serving-girl who "knows her place."

These divergent opinions point up the dilemma faced by publishers of children's books. As Albert R. Levinthal, president of Golden Press, explains it, "Golden Press has been criticized from both sides... Almost every time we reissue *Little Black Sambo* we receive mail deploring it. When it is not available in our Little Golden Book Series, we have had letters asking why we do not keep this classic in print!"

One irate Mississippi mother (white) denounced a Little Golden Book of Mother Goose rhymes in a long letter to the *Jackson Clarion-Ledger*. She was aroused by the old rhyme, "Three babes in a basket/And hardly room for two/And one was yellow and one was black/And one had eyes of blue."

"I bought one of the Little Golden Books entitled *Counting Rhymes*," she wrote. "I was horrified when I was reading to my innocent young child, and behold, on page fifteen there was actually the picture of three small children in a basket together... and one was a little Negro! I put my child and the book down and immediately called the owner of the drugstore and told him he would not have anymore of my business (and I buy a lot of drugs, for I am sick a lot) if he didn't take all the rest of his copies of that book off his shelves."

The illustration shows the Negro baby looking down at a mouse. Determined to get the whole truth about basket integration, the Mississippi mother said she got in touch with the author, presumably Mrs. Goose herself. She said the author gave this explanation of the black child: "He was aware he didn't belong there, and he was looking down in shame because somebody (a symbol for the outside meddling Yankees) has placed him in the same basket with the white child, where he didn't really want to be. Also he was looking down at the mouse as if he recognized some kinship to animals."

It's an amusing story. But the sad fact is that many publishing houses are catering to such mothers of the South and of the North. As one sales manager said, "Why jeopardize sales by putting one or two Negro faces in an illustration?"

Caroline Rubin, editor at Albert Whitman, tells of three books brought out in the 1950s: *Denny's Story*, by Eunice Smith, which shows Negro children in illustrations of classroom activity; *Fun for Chris*, by Blossom Randall, with Negro and white children playing together; and *Nemo Meets the Emperor*, by Laura Bannon, a true story of Ethiopia. "The books won favorable comment," writes Mrs. Rubin, "but the effect on sales was negative. Customers returned not only these titles but all stock from our company. This meant an appreciable loss and tempered attitude toward further use of Negro children in illustrations and text."

Jean Pointdexter Colby, editor of Hastings House, faced similar opposition in 1959 when she told her salesmen about plans for *A Summer to Share*, by Helen Kay, the story of a Negro child from the city who visits a white family in the country on a Fresh-Air-Fund vacation. "Galleys on the book had been set and art work was in preparation," Mrs. Colby wrote in the April 1965 issue of *Top of the News*, published by the American Library Association. "I told the salesmen present about the book and immediately encountered such opposition that I felt we either had to cancel the book entirely or change the book to an all-white cast. I wrote apologetically to the author and artist, explaining the situation. They were both cooperative and the racial switch was made." *A Summer to Share* came out in 1960 with the Negro child turned into another white one.

Mrs. Colby's experience with *New Boy in School*, by May Justus (1963), was quite different. This is a simple story for second and third graders about a Negro boy who enters an all-white class. "We had a great deal of trouble selling *New Boy in School* in the South," she writes. "Ed Jervis, our southern salesman, reported that one big jobber would neither stock nor sell it. Another would only fill special orders." But then favorable reviews began to come in from *School Library Journal*, the *New York Times*, the *Chattanooga Times*, the *Savannah News*, the *Raleigh Observer*, and the *Tulsa World*, among others. "Now it is a real bestseller!" she reports.

Mrs. Colby is also feeling pressure from those who deplore a story that shows the Negro as a slave, a servant, a railroad porter. "Slavery has been practically taboo for many years now as a subject for children's literature," she writes, "and depicting the Negro as anything but perfect is not welcome either. White children and adults can be bad, but Negroes cannot. So my job has been to tone down or to eliminate such people and situations... But when can we lift the shroud from the truth?"

Not all editors speak as frankly as Mrs. Colby. One, who asks to remain anonymous, says it took her two years to get permission to bring out a book about children in a minority group. Another reports a leading children's book club rejected a 1961 book "especially because Southern subscribers would not like the way this heroine tackled the problem of prejudice." Although no other publisher commented on book club selection, this is undoubtedly an important influence in editorial decisions.

When the directors of eight children's book clubs were questioned about the books they have distributed since September 1962, they listed only a tiny fraction that listed Negroes. Four hardcover book clubs offered 230 of which only six mention Negroes. Four paperback book clubs distributed 1,345 titles with Negroes included in fifty-three.

Not one of the fourteen Negro books on the ALA list of Notable Children's Books in 1962, 1963, and 1964 won the more lucrative award of book-club selection.

In the two Negro books distributed by the Weekly Reader Children's Book Club, *Long Lonesome Train*, by Virginia Ormsby (Lippincott), and *Skinny*, by Robert Burch (Viking); the Negro characters are Aunt Susan, her son Matt, a fireman, and the handyman, Roman. Richard R. Repass, director of this hardcover book club, says, "These I would consider neither germane to the plot, nor particularly flattering to our Negro citizens. The main reason why there are not more books with Negro characters among our book club selections is the general dearth of good candidates."

It should be explained that the hardcover book clubs send the same book to every child while the paperback book clubs ask each member to choose one title from a list of ten to a dozen. Perhaps for this reason the paperback clubs have distributed certain titles which the hardcover book clubs would not take a chance on. One of these is *Mary Jane* by Dorothy Sterling, published by Doubleday in hardcover and given a two-star rating by *School Library Journal*. It also received the Nancy Bloch Award for 1959. This is the realistic story of a Negro girl who is the first to enter an all-white junior high school that bristles with prejudice.

Mary Jane has not been selected for hardcover book club distribution. But after several years of deliberation, the Arrow Book Club, one of the paperback clubs, offered *Mary Jane* to its fifth and sixth-grade members. By December 1964, 159,895 copies had been sold. "Only six letters of complaint were received," reports Lilian Moore, Arrow Book Club editor, "all from adults in the South. And many warm comments have come from the children who read *Mary Jane*."

By March 1965, *Mary Jane* had been published in Swedish, Dutch, Czech, German, and Russian editions. According to *Publishers Weekly*, the Children's Literature House of Moscow reports 100,000 copies of *Mary Jane* have been printed there and are stirring up "lively interest." But, consciously or unconsciously, most writers

23

and artists have long been following the formula for pure white books. Some of the distortions caused by this formula are ludicrous. For example, *We Live in the City*, a simple picture book by Bert Ray (Children's Press, 1963), tells of Laurie and Gregg looking over the city of Chicago, a city that apparently has no Negroes.

Only white people appear in *Your Brain*, by Margaret O. Hyde (McGrawHill, 1964). In books of science experiments, it is usually a white hand that holds the thermometer, a white arm reaching for a test tube, white children feeding the guinea pig. In books of poetry, it is a white face smiling over the first stanza.

While making a survey of G. P. Putnam's list, juvenile editor Tom MacPherson came upon an illustrated novel about professional football with not a single Negro playing among the professionals. "That embarrassed us considerably," he wrote.

Several juvenile editors expressed similar concern. "I was surprised," wrote Virginie Fowler, editor of Knopf's Borzoi Books for Young People, "to realize how few books we have on our list that accept an integrated society... as I look at my titles and think of the books [I realize] in many instances they could easily have been books about Negro child or could have been shared books of child and friend."

Executives at Golden Press analyzed the Little Golden Books of 1962, 1963, and 1964 and decided that thirteen of their all-white books could have included Negroes in a perfectly natural way. One of these is *A Visit to the Zoo*, cited by Whitney Young, Jr. ("He is certainly right," said the Golden Press editor. "A missed opportunity for a natural handling of the situation.")

In the meantime, the Negro market has expanded to at least $25 billion in consumer purchasing power, according to John H. Johnson, publisher of *Ebony*. The Negro school population and the number of Negro teachers are growing rapidly, particularly in the large urban centers. With vastly increased funds available through government sources, a huge economic force is building up for integrated schools and integrated reading materials.

Lacking good children's book about Negro history, many school libraries are purchasing the $5.95 adult book, *A Pictorial History of the Negro in America* by Langston Hughes and Milton Meltzer (Crown). Boards of education in both New York and Detroit have written and published their own paperback Negro histories for young readers.

The integrated readers produced by the Detroit Board of Education and published in 1964 by Follett for in-school use are now being sold in paperback in the bookstores, where parents are reported to be buying eagerly.

The market that most publishers are avoiding is being cultivated by, of all corporations, the Pepsi-Cola Company, which has produced an excellent LP recording *Adventures in Negro History*. This has been made available to schools through local soft-drinks distributors. The first pressing of 10,000 copies was grabbled up almost immediately, according to Russell Harvey, director of special market services. After a year, 100,000 copies had been distributed and a second record is being made.

What about children's books coming out in 1965? According to reports from editors, about 9 percent of their 1965 books will include one or more Negroes. This is 1.5 percent above the average for 1964.

In addition, there will be a continuing trend to up-date or reissue earlier books that include Negroes. Among those reissued in the past three years: *My Dog Rinty*, by Ellen Tarry and Marie Hall Ets (Viking); *Black Fire: A Story of Henri Christophe*, by C. Newcomb (McKay); *Famous Women Singers*, by Ulrich (Dodd, Mead); *The Story of The Negro*, by Arna Bontemps (Knopf); and *The Barred Road*, by Adele DeLeeuw (Macmillan). *Ladder to the Sky*, by Ruth Forbes Chandler (Abelard), which went out of print for several years, has returned in 1965.

This year Doubleday is launching its new Zenith Books, "to explain America's minorities." These books are planned for supplementary reading in high school English and social studies classes. The accompanying teacher's manual puts them more definitely with textbooks than with trade books.

Many juvenile editors who state determination to present a completely fair picture of Negroes in our multicultural society add the reservation: "where it seems natural and not forced."

"We don't set about deliberately to do these things," writes Margaret McElderry, editor of children's books at Harcourt, Brace & World, "but take them as they seem natural and right."

"We plan to continue to introduce Negroes where it can be handled in context and illustrations in a normal way," says Margaret E. Braxton, vice president of Garrard Publishing Company. "Artificial books forcing the racial issue are not a part of our future plans."

"Most publishers are eagerly looking for manuscripts that deal with integration and the problems faced by Negroes in our country," writes Mrs. Esther K. Meeks, children's books editor of Follett Publishing Company. "If we found twice a many publishable books that included Negroes in a natural and sympathetic manner, we should be happy to publish them." *South Town*, by Lorenz Graham, winner of the Follett Award of 1958, is one of the few books for young people that tells a realistic story of the violence resulting from racial prejudice.

Fabio Coen, editor of Pantheon Books for children, makes this comment: "A book even remotely discussing racial problems has to deal with the subject with the same spontaneity and honesty that is basically required of any book. To my mind, it is therefore impossible to commission one."

The newly formed Council for Interracial Books for Children operates on the principle that, given encouragement, authors and artists will create good children's books that include non-whites, and that, given the manuscripts, publishers will produce and market them. The Council, sponsored by a group including Benjamin Spock, Ben Shahn, Langston Hughes, Mary Gaver, Alex Rosen, Harold Taylor, Harry Golden, and Sidonie M.Gruenberg, will offer prizes for outstanding manuscripts and will negotiate with editors for their publication.

The crisis that brought the Council into being is described by one of its organizing members, Elinor Sinnette, district school librarian for the Central and East Harlem Area of New York: "Publishers have participated in a cultural lobotomy. It is no accident that Negro history and Negro identification have been forgotten. Our society has contrived to make the American Negro a rootless person. The Council for Interracial Books for Children has been formed to relieve this situation."

Whether the Council gets many books into print or not, it can accomplish a great deal simply by reminding editors and publishers that what is good for the Ku Klux Klan is not necessarily good for America — or for the book business. White supremacy in children's literature will be abolished when authors, editors, publishers, and booksellers decide that they need not submit to bigots.

Nancy Larrick is the former president of the International Reading Association and a well-known writer about children and their education.

This article first appeared in a 1965 edition of the Saturday Review. *Reprinted with permission of* Saturday Review *(380 Madison Ave., N.Y., N.Y.10017).*

CHAPTER I

WHO AM I? WHO ARE WE?

 friend of mine is an Eastern European Jew married to an Irish Catholic. I recall her trying to explain to their three-year-old son Peter his ethnic heritage. He looked at his elbow and asked if that was the Jewish or Catholic part. Another child I know asked if the pink of her palms was the European part of her ancestry, while the darker brown of her skin was the African part.

 nyone who has been around children very long understands that these are not simply cute episodes, but very often a child's first attempts to make sense of our notions of race, nationality, religion, class, and gender, and to say "This is me."

n the most basic sense, multicultural literature helps children answer questions of identity and understand how others are answering these questions as well. It supports the development of a positive sense of self and allows children of very different backgrounds to empathize with others' life experiences. In books covering a range of cultures and peoples that could not be found in print only a few decades ago, a child can find authentic images, languages, and experiences.

 his section of the guide addresses issues of identity and diversity in multicultural children's literature. Donnarae MacCann gives a comprehensive and incisive overview of multicultural picture books in "Illustrating the Point." Two pieces deal with how young readers come to form images of self through books: Candy Dawson Boyd's "I See Myself in There" and "Are Mexican American Females Portrayed Realistically in Fiction for Grades K-3?" by Osbelia Juárez Rocha and Frances Smardo Dowd.

NOLA M. HADLEY, PH.D.

Nola Hadley Ph.D. is an Appalachian Cherokee woman who teaches American history and culture at Vista Community College in Berkeley, California, and has been a board member of the Indian Historian Press in San Francisco, California, and of Oyate, an American Indian educational resources project in Berkeley, California. She leads faculty and campus trainings on diversity, and workshops and classes in peer counseling and leadership training for young people of color and their families.

Kindergarten to Grade Three

Borreguita and the Coyote: A Tale from Ayutala, Mexico

📖 Verna Aardema 🖊 Petra Mathers
Hispanic, Mexican
1991, Alfred A. Knopf, ✳ Series, Spanish
📖 Carle, Eric, *Twelve Tales from Aesop*; Kherdian, David, *Feathers and Tails: Animal Fables from around the World*; Lionni, Leo, *Frederick's Fables: A Leo Lionni Treasury of Favorite Stories.*

Borreguita is an English translation of "La Zorra y el Coyote," a witty and provocative tale, originally published in *Tales from Jalisco, Mexico*. Using her cunning and wits, Borreguita—

A little lamb outwits a hungry coyote in this engaging traditional Mexican tale.

which literally means little lamb— produces one clever excuse after another to avoid becoming the coyote's next meal. Each tactic that Borreguita uses to survive is better than the one before. At the story's end, an older, plumper Borreguita frolics on the farm while the Coyote slinks away in disgust and humiliation.

The spare, yet colorful drawings by Petra Mathers support the story line well. This starkness in the illustrations makes the story more engaging. It's also a story that invites the use of the imagination.

Borreguita *would work well in thematic units on Mexico, on folklore, or on fables from around the world. It also works as a great allegory for women or girls who refuse to become victims.* ANDREA L. WILLIAMS

Black Is Brown Is Tan

📖 Arnold Adoff 🖊 Emily McCully
African American
1992 (1973), HarperCollins

Black Is Brown Is Tan, is a story-poem about family life in an interracial African American/European American family. The delightful language brings to life the everyday events of a family with young children—from playtime to bedtime—in a celebration of love. The author, Arnold Adoff, is married to African American author Virginia Hamilton, and he draws upon his personal experience as the father of two biracial children as he honors the differences in his family.

Describing herself, the mother says, "i am brown sugar gown, a tasty tan and coffee pumpkin pie," while the father is named as white, but not the color of snow or milk: "i am white, i am light, with pink and tiny tans." The child says he is brown: "i am black, i am brown, the milk is chocolate brown, i am the color of the milk, chocolate cheeks and hands that darken in the summer sun, a nose that peels brown skin in august."

A story-poem that celebrates differences and similarities among members of an interracial family.

The lyrical prose is enhanced by Emily McCully's vibrant illustrations of the family at work and play. Her simple yet colorful paintings bring the similarities and differences of the family's many ethnicities to life. The extended family is included in this portrait of multiracial life, "daddy's sister florence with the gold gold hair and mama's tan man brother who plays the frying pan; granny white and grandma black kissing both your cheeks and hugging back."

The simple and important message in this story-poem embraces love and acceptance and the joy of a happy home. The text is spare, original, and full of joy. Certainly, this is a much-needed message that extends beyond the preschool years for which this book is written. ROSA E. WARDER

I'm Deaf, and It's OK

📖 Lorraine Aseltine 🖊 Evelyn Mueller, Nancy Taid, and Helen Cogancherry
Physical Disability
1986, Albert Whitman Concept Books

For those of us without disabilities or physical challenges, there are so many things we never even think about: the shape of a curb, the act of holding a fork, physical access to a theater, school, or a friend's home. But the seven-year-old deaf boy in Lorraine Aseltine's story describes the fear of going to bed without his hearing aid, or getting lost in a department store because no one can understand him. His fear turns to anger when he finds out that he will remain deaf. That anger changes when he befriends a seventeen-year-old boy who comes to visit his classroom. His admiration for Brian provides proof that he too can grow up and be a whole person.

While the prose and illustrations convey an awareness of, and sensitivity to, the feelings of a deaf boy, some of the negative behavior exhibited by the non-disabled is also portrayed. A waitress treats him inappropriately when she almost yells and overemphasizes her words. When his sister talks on the phone, she always keeps her back turned to him. His grandmother reads to his sister, but not to him. The preferential treatment hurts and annoys him. The boy makes it clear that he just wants people to treat him the way they treat his sister and others. He is portrayed as competent, curious, and eager to learn.

A sensitive portrayal of the everyday life of a deaf boy.

With the exception of the fact that all his classmates wear hearing aids and his teachers use sign language, his classroom is like any other. On the last page of the book, we see the young boy using sign language to communicate. Although this book helps children to identify with some of the feelings of a deaf child, it also makes them aware of the similarities and differences that exist between them.

The book is an excellent vehicle for developing discussions with young children about deafness and other disabilities. This book might be used as a catalyst for other activities, such as encouraging children to learn to "sign" their names and the words in the back of the book, and inviting a teacher of the deaf and deaf students into come to classroom to teach sign language.
BARBARA A. KANE

Cleversticks

📖 Bernard Ashley ✎ Derek Brazell

Asian American, Chinese American

1992, Crown Publishers

Ling Sung has just started school, and he hates it. It seems that all the other kids are good at something: tying shoes, printing their names, buttoning jackets. Ling Sung wants to be good at something too, but he hasn't discovered what that is yet.

Because Ling Sung is fiddling with a pair of paintbrushes when cookies are passed around during snack time, he drops his plate and breaks a cookie. He then uses the paintbrushes as chopsticks and puts the bits of cookie into his mouth—the way he eats at home. His classmates and teachers see this

and suddenly everyone wants to learn how to use chopsticks. Ling Sung shows them and everyone tries, laughing as they drop cookies all over the place.

Only Ling Sung knows how to use chopsticks! Finally, he has found something he is good at. This realization gives him confidence to feel part of the group. He no longer feels isolated. Now he loves school.

What's wonderful about this book is that it focuses on Ling Sung's feelings. It emphasizes his struggle to be able to do something and how badly he feels at first about not being able to do "something clever." The book does not fall back on the cliché that "children can be cruel" when one of their peers cannot do what they can do. It also keeps the adult characters—teachers and parents—incidental to the story line. They praise the children who are able to complete certain tasks, but are not shown coaching or comforting Ling Sung. A weakness, perhaps, but the story takes place in the first days of school and their lack of intervention might be forgiven.

Wishing he had a special talent, an Asian American boy discovers that his classmates admire his prowess with chopsticks.

The illustrator carefully depicts the 1990s school experience. There's a computer in the classroom. One teacher is dressed in a sari. One of the fathers wears jogging pants and a sweatshirt when he picks up his daughter. The book truly reflects the changing face of American schools by showing the multicultural nature of the classroom. Many readers will identify with Ling Sung and his situation.
LESLIE ANDERSON MORALES

The Wall

📖 Eve Bunting ✎ Ronald Himler

Hispanic, Multicultural

1990, Clarion Books

A father and his young son travel to see the Vietnam Veterans Memorial in Washington, D.C., a wall listing the names of more than 58,000 people who died or were missing in action during the Vietnam War. In this touching story, the father and son browse through the list of names, searching for the father's father, the boy's grandfather.

Bunting skillfully presents readers with an emotionally charged story seen through the eyes of the boy. The idea that the father never knew his father

29

makes the father and son's trip together all the more important. When they finally find the boy's grandfather's name, George Munoz, the father and son together rub the name on paper. (It is interesting that he is Hispanic. Perhaps Bunting is making a statement on minorities who fought in the war.) Although they are sad, the father and son feel pride. The father bows his head in front of the name, and the boy notices other visitors. He sees a grandfather walking with his grandson, and at that moment he understands what the loss means to him. He leaves a picture of himself in front of the memorial, hoping his grandfather will recognize him.

A Latino boy and his father visit the Vietnam Veterans Memorial.

Ms. Bunting is a prolific author of high-quality picture books that deal with difficult issues. With so few picture books on the Vietnam War, it is especially fortunate that this one is well written. Himler's soft watercolor paintings capture the quiet honor of the story, reaffirming the stirring nature of Bunting's words. LISA FAIN

Abuela's Weave

Omar S. Castaneda / Enrique O. Sanchez

Guatemalan, Hispanic, Mayan

1995 (1993), Lee & Low Books, Inc., ✳ Spanish

In *Abuela's Weave*, Omar Castaneda tells an intergenerational story about a grandmother and her granddaughter, Esperanza, who are both weavers in Guatemala. Esperanza knows that Abuela's skill with a loom is renowned, but she is just learning about selling their weavings at the marketplace. Abuela has a birthmark that scares people, and Esperanza is afraid that she will not be able to sell the goods by herself.

A Mayan family journeys to market in Guatemala in a charming story that unfortunately ignores recent political developments.

The marketplace reveals to readers the variety of modern Guatemalan life: the mission structure in the background, crowds of Indians and Latinos, cars rushing past horse-drawn carriages, handmade pottery, homemade pastries, and tourists with cameras.

Since people seem to be afraid of her grandmother's birthmark, Esperanza travels to the market and sets up her wares, seemingly alone. Abuela stays in the background, her face hidden in a dark robe. The *huipils* and the weavings immediately gain a lot of attention in the market.

The largest tapestry "blossomed with images of Guatemala....There were heroes and heroines inspired by the glorious Popul Vuh, the sacred book of the Maya. In one corner a *quetzal* seemed to watch over it from within a white cage." They all sell quickly. On the way home the two ride together holding hands. Their pride is visible.

There is much to enjoy in this story, including brightly colored illustrations by Enrique Sanchez. The main characters look Mayan, and there are several visual and textual references to Mayan history and culture. Author and artist refer to the *huipils*, the *quetzals*, and the Mayan glyphs and designs. There is a tapestry design on the bottom of every page with text.

Unfortunately there is no indication of the specific place and people Esperanza comes from and the book does not address the political situation of contemporary Guatemala or the long history of human rights abuses against people of Indian descent. Any contemporary Mayan in Guatemala would be far more terrified of the government's death squads than of birthmarks. A more complete account of Mayan characters also would include Mayan names and would address issues of spirituality. NOLA HADLEY

Hairs: Pelitos: A Story in English and Spanish from the House on Mango Street

Sandra Cisneros (translated by Liliana Valenzuela) / Terry Ybanez

Latino

1994, Alfred A. Knopf, 📖 Deveaux, Alexis, *An Enchanted Hair Tale*; Kroll, Virginia, *Hats Off to Hair!*

First published in *The House on Mango Street*, *Hairs: Pelitos* is an endearing vignette about a family whose members each have different type of hair. All too often, long blonde hair has been used as a symbol for beauty in children's books. The reissuing of this vignette from Cisneros's celebrated collection of stories as a children's book is an especially welcome development.

The overarching theme of this warm family portrait is the acceptance of physical differences and the celebration by people of color of those physical traits that distinguish them from the others. The father's hair is like a broom; and the mother's hair is soft, arranged in little rosettes, and sweet smelling. The daughter's hair is lazy; "it never obeys barrettes or bands." Childlike, dreamy illustrations invite young readers into the story, as does the clarity and ease of Cisneros's writing. This story can help to unravel some common prejudices about "good hair and bad hair."

An endearing vignette dealing with hair as cultural tradition.

Other books dealing with this theme include Alexis Deveaux's *An Enchanted Hair Tale*, the first children's book to celebrate the wearing of dreadlocks, and Virginia Kroll's *Hats Off to Hair!*, From curls worn by Hasidic Jews to cornrows worn by African American girls, from the shaved head of a Masai girl, to the cascading ringlets of a teenage white girl, Kroll explores hair as a cultural tradition around the world. DAPHNE MUSE

213 Valentines

Barbara Cohen ✎ Wil Clay

African American

1993 (1968), Redfeather Books for Young Readers

✳ Series

Transferred to a school for the gifted and talented, fourth-grader Wade Thompson resents leaving his neighborhood friends and facing new challenges at Kennedy School. The schoolwork is easy for him; his difficulties lie in making friends with his new classmates, most of whom come from a more affluent background. This becomes clear with their first assignment, the perennial "What I Did Over Summer Vacation" essay. While his new classmates write about going to hockey camp or trips to Greece and Hawaii, Wade writes about his trip to the municipal pool. Dink Worth, a girl

An African American boy tries to fit in with his new classmates at a school for the gifted.

who attended Wade's old school, also feels left out and lonely at Kennedy. Part of the problem is that both children are African American in a predominantly white school, but there are differences in economic background and class as well. Wade labels most of his new classmates as snobs.

Fearful that he will be left out of his class's Valentine swap, and eager to show up his new classmates, Wade buys hundreds of cards which he addresses to himself, signing the names Oprah Winfrey, Ronald Reagan, Michael Jordan, and dozens of luminaries, living and dead. Wade had always regarded Dink as a "lady nerd," but as she assists him with his holiday plan, he begins to see her as a friend. A classroom incident in which some students tease Dink helps Wade realize that some of  his new classmates are genuinely nice. Ultimately, he passes out cards to most of his class, including more than fifty to Dink, proving that he is on his way to reaching out to others and fitting in.

This easy going story contains interesting characters and good humor and is perscient in describing the concerns of elementary school students. Although Wade cites race as one reason he doesn't fit in, the book is not an examination of racism in the classroom. Instead, it's a story about the difficulty that many children have adjusting to a new school situation. Although race may play a role in Wade and Dink's situation, they learn to adjust by befriending each other as well as accepting the tentative gestures of friendship they receive from some of their new classmates. *The book is well-suited for reading on Valentine's Day*, but has year-round appeal with its focus on friendship and loneliness. PETER D. SIERUTA

Coming Home: From the Life of Langston Hughes

Floyd Cooper

African American

1994, The Putnam Publishing Group

Floyd Cooper is well known for his children's book illustrations in burnished oils. In the first book that he has written and illustrated, his evocative prose brings to life the story of poet Langston Hughes.

Hughes had a lonely childhood in Lawrence, Kansas, with his Grandma Mary Langston. His father worked as a lawyer in Mexico "after they wouldn't let him be a lawyer in Oklahoma because he was a black man." His mother was pursuing an acting career in Kansas City. Only rarely were the three of them together as a family, times that Hughes cherished and longed for.

The text emphasizes the importance of home to Hughes. At first "he dreamed of the three of them together, of having a home with his ma and pa. A home he would never have to leave." As he grew older he understood that home could be many things: "For him home was a blues song sung in the pale evening... Home was the theater where his ma performed... Home was the church, alive with music...."

We also learn about Hughes's childhood heroes. It was his grandmother who took him to hear Booker T. Washington speak in Topeka. She regaled him with stories of his grandfather, who died helping John Brown free slaves; of his uncle, John Mercer Langston, the first black American to hold office; and of her own exploits while working on the Underground Railroad. She told him "stories of heroes. Heroes who were black, just like Hughes."

A wonderful tribute depicting the early years of poet Langston Hughes.

These role models inspired Langston and made him proud of his relatives and his race. They peopled the stories that he would tell to friends, and later, infused his poetry.

This book is a wonderful tribute to Langston Hughes and gives a fine sense of his early years. Cooper's illustrations capture young Hughes's hopes and dreams. It is a pity, however, that Cooper did not include more of Hughes's poetry. Only one poem, "Hope," appears in the book. A reference to further reading would also have been useful.
LINDSEY TATE

Palm Trees

🎨 ✏️ Nancy Cote
African American
1993, Four Winds Press 📖 Gouch, Patricia L., *Christina Katorina and the Time She Quit the Family*; Hoffman, Mary, *Amazing Grace*; Kasza, Keiko, *The Pig's Picnic*.

Now that her mom has returned to work, Millie must take responsibilty for fixing her own hair. At first she thinks her bushy hair won't stay put and behave like her mom's wavier locks. Finally, she plunges ahead and puts her hair in two self-styled pony tails. They look a lot like palm trees, but Millie is excited to have styled her hair herself. These feelings change when her best friend Renee laughs at her new "do," calling Millie "Palm Trees." Later, Millie is about to clip her hair when Renée shows up —her hair styled in palm tree fashion! Renée's imitation and flattery make Millie feel good. By the story's end Millie and Renée are full of laughter. Millie now realizes that she need not look like anyone else.

Humor and a unique hair style help two African American friends gain new respect for each other.

The illustrations sell the book. *They are clear and defined enough for a small group read-aloud session.* The characters act like real children. While the story might appear to be minor slice of life, it is about an incident that matters a lot to children. Do I look OK or do I seem weirder than my friends? The use of humor and the lack of heavy-handedness are pluses along with attractive gouache drawings. *A teacher who wanted to read a series of stories throughout the school year emphasizing self-determination would find this story a good one.*
ANDREA L. WILLIAMS

Katie's Alligator Goes to Day Care

📘 Ann Decter ✏️ Bo-Kim Louie
Multicultural
1988 (1987), Women's Press

This story takes place in a setting many children will find familiar: day care. When Katie's mom gets a new job, she enrolls her daughter in a day care program. Katie is worried about spending all day without her mother so she takes her toy Alligator with her. Katie joins the other children but leaves her toy in some water, which causes it to expand and dissolve slightly. The story ends happliy when Katie's playmates make a home for Alligator in a big glass bowl full of water and pebbles on the bottom. They plan to watch the toy grow everyday.

A multicultural daycare story.

This book addresses fears any child may have entering a new situation with new people. This story depicts a caring, friendly, multicultural group. There are children of color and an Asian teacher, for instance. The illustrations are somewhat inconsistent; Katie's face changes from page to page and she doesn't appear to be the same child throughout the book. Nevertheless, the black-and-white drawings have an unexpected depth, and both the illustrations and the story are attractive. LESLIE ANDERSON MORALES

Oliver Button Is a Sissy

Tomie dePaola
European American
1979, Harcourt Brace and Company

A charming picture book that traces the difficulties of gender nonconformity.

Endearing illustrations show a young boy who doesn't "do things boys are supposed to do." Instead of playing football, Oliver likes walks in the woods, reading, drawing, and even playing with paper dolls. His father disapproves, angrily telling him to go play ball. But the other kids don't want him on their team, complaining, "now we'll lose for sure." When his mother worries he isn't getting enough exercise, Oliver explains that he does—from dancing. So his parents send him to dance school— "especially for the exercise," according to his father. Bullies, noticing Oliver's tap-dancing shoes, write "Oliver Button Is a Sissy" on the school wall. When Oliver enters a talent contest, his abilities surprise his classmates. Though he doesn't win, he returns to school the next day to find "Oliver Button Is a Star" on the school wall.

This charming picture book traces the difficulties of gender nonconformity without losing sight of the gift that difference can give. Oliver's parents appear by no means united on the issue of Oliver's hobby, but his father's anger is transformed into pride by this creative attempt to assuage his anxieties. While the story does not downplay the difficulties of not fitting in, it does show that there is hope for people who don't. CHRIS MAYO

An Enchanted Hair Tale

Alexis Deveaux Cheryl Hanna
African American, Caribbean American
1991 (1987), Harper & Row

Focusing on a sensitive and imaginative young boy named Sudan, this story demonstrates how lack of acceptance can shape people's lives and shows the transformative effects of supportive communities. Although he looks like his father, Sudan has his mother's thick and coarsely textured hair which he wears in dreadlocks. He refers to his dreadlocked hair as enchanted because of the way it moves. But adults don't like his hair. They whisper behind his back that it is ugly and unkempt. Children consider him strange and different, teasing him wherever he goes. When people talk about him, Sudan becomes upset, often getting into fights.

Criticized for his hairstyle, an African American boy soon finds acceptance and friendship.

One day when he is being mercilessly teased, he leaves and walks a long way from home. He comes upon a circus in the street with animals and acrobats. He notices that the performers have hair like his. There he is not ridiculed, but admired. Sudan discovers that one of the circus performers is a friend of his mother's. The performer takes him back to his neighborhood and talks with him about the ways in which people can be unkind when they see people with "enchanted hair." Once at home, Sudan looks in the mirror and admires his own enchanted hair.

The story supports children who are different, or may simply feel different, and encourages them to address

what their difference means to them. The circus performers have given him the validation he needs to realize that he and his hair are okay. An interesting twist in this story is the fact that adults are also guilty of teasing and whispering behind Sudan's back. In other words, adults are as capable as children of being rude and mean. The way in which the story addresses difference, and a child's ability to accept his own difference, is provocative. The author's rhythmic prose and the exciting illustrations are complemented by beautiful black-and-white illustrations creating a fairy tale-like aura. MICHELLE GARFIELD

The Twins Strike Back

Valerie Flournoy ✏ Melodye Rosales
African American
1994 (1980), Just Us Books

Natalie and Nicole are twins. Their cousin Nate and big sister Bernardine are always teasing them that they think exactly alike. Their mother expects them to have identical accomplishments. Everyone seems to ignores their given names, referring to them simply as the twins.

Twin African American sisters come up with a plan to show everyone how different they are really are.

Natalie and Nicole decide to show everyone that they really are two different people. *The Twins Strike Back* is a story that will resonate with any two siblings who are seeking independent identities, and anyone who has ever said "I just want to be myself."

Humorously illustrated, *The Twins Strike Back* is a lighthearted story about dealing with other people's expectations. YOLANDA ROBINSON-COLES

How My Parents Learned to Eat

Ina R. Friedman ✏ Allen Say
Asian American, Japanese American
1987 (1984), Houghton Mifflin, ✴Cassette, Cole, Ann, *Children Are Children Are Children*; Downer, Leslie, *Japanese Food and Drink*; Gray, Nigel, *Country Far Away*.

The narrator of *How My Parents Learned to Eat* is the young daughter of an American man and a Japanese woman. The book begins as she explains that "In our house, some days we eat with chopsticks and some days we eat with knives and forks. For me, it's natural."

A Japanese American girl describes her interracial family and their eating habits in this gentle, amusing story.

We learn that her parents met when her father, John, was a sailor stationed in Yokohama, Japan, and her mother, Aiko, was a schoolgirl. Quickly growing fond of one another, the two secretly dread eating a meal together. Aiko thinks John will find she looks silly trying to use a knife and fork, and John is sure his inexperience with chopsticks will leave him hungry and frustrated. When he receives orders to return home, John finally musters the courage to ask Aiko to dinner, then promptly rushes off to a Japanese restaurant for lessons in using chopsticks. Aiko goes to her well-travelled great uncle to learn to eat with western utensils. The story is amusing, thought-provoking, and thoroughly satisfying in its resolution.

This is a particularly nonthreatening introduction to the idea of "different, not better or worse." There is also a subtle message that even within similar traditions there are differences: Aiko's great uncle shows Aiko how to eat mashed potatoes and peas like an Englishman; she is surprised to learn that Americans use a knife and fork differently than the British.

The soft watercolor pictures by Japanese American illustrator Allen Say realistically depict differences in the faces of the Japanese and Caucasian characters without stereotypes or caricatures. The biracial narrator is featured with physical characteristics from both her parents. LYNN EISENHUT

Death of the Iron Horse

✏ Paul Goble
Cheyenne, Native American
1987, Simon & Schuster

When scouts report the approach of the Iron Horse, the Cheyenne wonder if the words of their prophet, Sweet Medicine, are finally coming to pass. In a dream, Sweet Medicine has seen strange people coming from the East to kill his people and the buffalo, binding Mother Earth with iron bands. Surely this roaring, smoking monster moving along the wooden and iron trail will bring destruction.

A group of young Cheyenne men ride out to meet the Iron Horse and inspect its strange trail. The men

A valuable story of young Cheyenne men resisting white settlers' encroachment upon their lands.

chop the ties and pull the spikes. The freight train derails, killing the white people inside the cab. The Cheyenne find pans, kettles, ribbons, hats, blankets, food, and bolts of beautiful cloth inside the cars.

The illustrations burst with color as paper money is scattered to the winds in a game, and bolts of cloth become banners held by the Cheyenne as they gallop their horses around the train. In the distance, another Iron Horse approaches. The men gather as much as they can and set the boxcars on fire. They return to their people with joy, bringing gifts and thinking that the Iron Horse is an enemy easily defeated.

Paul Goble's singular illustrations capture the poignancy of the young Cheyennes' exuberance in taking on this new iron enemy, confident that they can defeat it.

Although there are disturbing aspects to this story, it is especially valuable in the way it counteracts stereotypical train raids depicted in movies and on television. Most never even hint at the Cheyenne view of the railroad's arrival. Goble reminds us that for the Cheyenne, the arrival of trains signaled the start of a fight for survival. JANIS O'DRISCOLL

Nathaniel Talking

📖 Eloise Greenfield ✒ Jan Spivey Gilchrist
African American
1988, Black Butterfly Children's Books

This is a unique book of rap and poetry, told from the perspective of a nine-year-old boy. The book begins with "Nathaniel's Rap," introducing the reader to Nathaniel B. Free, who says that he's got something on his mind and has a lot to say.

The poem "Nine" has Nathaniel thinking that "nine is fine" because it is an important time for a young boy to learn about becoming more independent. In "Missing Mama," he talks about dealing with grief and anxiety when his mother dies. Nathaniel admits that he sometimes still cries but tries to remember the good times. "Missing Mama" and "I Remember" are two poems that refer specifically to memories.

An African American boy expresses himself in rhythm, rhyme, and rap in this engaging book.

Nathaniel also reflects on the consequences of misbehaving in school and the uselessness of fighting.

Several other poems talk about important family members. Nathaniel praises his father in "My Daddy," who, even when playing the blues on his guitar, sings about loving Nathaniel. In "Grandma's Bones," Nathaniel is awed by his fun-loving grandmother who shares her musical talent with the family.

The longing to be useful is a powerful theme in the companion pieces titled "A Mighty Fine Fella" and "I See My Future." The first poem is a look at the pitfalls of materialism and the realization that character is more important. Imagining his adult life, Nathaniel sees himself "moving through the world doing good and unusual things." He speaks of great optimism while recognizing the difficulties that are pervasive in the world.

The book explores the mature and complex concerns of young children today. Young readers will enjoy Nathaniel's engaging and candid character. The subtle, silhouetted cityscapes and dynamic faces drawn by illustrator Jan Spivey Gilchrist are a good complement to this story of a young boy's serious inquiry into life. SHIRLEY R. CRENSHAW

Something on My Mind

📖 Nikki Grimes ✒ Tom Feelings
African American
1990 (1978), Dial Books for Young Readers

Life in the city is portrayed sensitively in the prose poetry of Nikki Grimes and the haunting illustrations of Tom Feelings. Both author and illustrator capture the complex lives of youth who are growing up in multiple-family residences in a crowded city setting.

Grimes's text allows readers to experience the thoughts, anxieties, and hopes of individual young people.

A sensitive collection that reflects the feelings of black children living in an urban setting.

Several themes are interwoven: the need to belong; the desire to escape; difficulty in trusting adults; questions about education; and the hope for a meaningful future.

Tom Feelings uses both bold strokes and sparse outlines in his black ink-and-charcoal drawings. All of the faces are serious, thoughtful, or wondering, and some are etched with sorrow or disappointment. There is little eye contact—most eyes are downcast or looking away. Most of the illustrations include fences; some iron with sharp points and others chainlink. One wonders if the fences are there to keep the youth in or to keep other influences out. Many children are shown sitting on steps or stoops at entries to the apartment buildings, close enough to doorways to escape outside dangers or inside pressures.

The opening poem sets the tone. Three children are talking about going somewhere else. One longs to go down South, another thinks Africa would offer the most promise. The third child expresses the desire to go someplace that has no name where she can be herself, and "not have to feel worse or better than white people—just a place where she can feel at home." This sense of longing pervades the book. There is a longing for friends, for family solidarity, for understanding, for material needs, for something to do, and ultimately for a future.

One poignant illustration captures a young girl questioning the education she receives. She wonders what "good English" has to do with having better clothes, enough food, and blankets.

This beautifully written, powerfully illustrated book is a valuable resource for teachers, students, parents, and should be required reading for politicians. SHIRLEY R. CRENSHAW

"Mush-hole": Memories of a Residential School

📖 Maddie Harper ✏ Carlos Firere
Native American
1994, Sister Vision, Black Women and Women of Color Press, ✳ Video

"Mush-hole": Memories of a Residential School by Maddie Harper is one of the few books for early readers about the hardships of the Indian boarding school experience. Harper speaks to the struggles of several generations of Native Americans in overcoming the difficulties of low self-esteem developed during boarding school years.

The year is 1914. Harper describes her experience as she and 200 other girls are taken away from their tribe to an Indian boarding school. The children are told when to get up, when to eat, and when to go the bathroom. They are not allowed to speak their own languages. Whipping is a common form of discipline. The students call the school the "Mush-hole" because of their diet of mush.

A rare book, set early in this century, about the harsh Native American boarding schools.

Harper recounts how she feels confused about her identity after she leaves the school and returns home. She no longer really fit in to life on the reservation. She has few friends and, like many on the reservation, eventually turns to alcohol. Finally Harper receives guidance from some elders who teach her about traditional ways and ceremonies. Through the reclaiming process, Harper heals herself, regains her identity, and shares this traditional way with other indigenous peoples in Central and South America.

Although the author is never specific about her tribal affiliation, this story manages to capture both the pain and healing that has occurred in many tribes provoked by the assimilationist policies of the boarding schools and the Christian religion. Although Harper is very direct about calling the schools assimilationist, she never fully analyzes her experience with Christianity, which has also been an assimilating force in indigenous communities. She does, however, cover a lot of territory in this twenty-four page book.

The illustrations are not as strong as the text. Firere's four-color pictures are bright and active, but the depictions of the faces of Indian people are distorted. The elder in this book look's remarkably like a stereotypical witch.

I would recommend this book to accompany discussion of Native American history. Young readers will be interested in the social justice issues, but it also might be helpful to remind young ones who are trying to adjust to their own school experience that Indian schools have been struggling and are beginning to succeed in establishing a healthy, culturally relevant educational experience for Indian students. The video White Man's Way, *about the boarding school experience, provides useful background information for teachers.*
NOLA HADLEY

Amazing Grace

📖 Mary Hoffman ✏ Caroline Binch
African American
1995 (1991), Dial Books for Young Readers

An imaginative and confident young black girl, Grace loves to act out all kinds of stories. When she performs them, she always gives herself the most exciting part. In fact, if there is no one else to play with her, Grace plays all the parts. At times, she even convinces Ma and Nana to join in playing the parts.

An African American girl stars in Peter Pan *in a story that will engage readers.*

When Grace's teacher asks for volunteers for various parts in the play *Peter Pan*, everyone wants to be Peter, including Grace. One classmate tells Grace that she can't be Peter because she is a girl; and another tells her she can't be Peter because she is black. But Grace decides to audition for the part anyway, and she takes the lines home to learn. When she tells Ma and Nana what the other kids have said, they encourage her to audition for the part, reminding

Grace she can be anything that she wants.

On Saturday, Nana takes Grace to a ballet performance of *Romeo and Juliet*. Juliet is played by a young black woman whose grandmother grew up with Nana in Trinidad. Seeing the young black woman in the role of Juliet strengthens Grace's resolve.

When she auditions for *Peter Pan*, she receives the unanimous support of her classmates to play the part. The play itself is a huge success and Grace does an excellent job. While Grace is convinced that she can do anything she puts her mind to, the story is also a reminder of how much harder women and people of color often have to work in order to gain acceptance.

This children's story is a creative affirmation of a child's imagination and determination. Although the story takes place in Britain, the issues that confront Grace are common to children on both sides of the Atlantic. The story highlights the role that adult support and encouragement can play in the life of young children. The text of the story is straightforward and easily understood. The colorful illustrations vividly support the story line. MICHELLE GARFIELD

Joshua's Masai Mask

Dakari Hru Anna Rich

African American

1993, Lee & Low Books

Joshua's Masai Mask is a contemporary fable of a young boy who wishes he were anybody but himself. Fearing ridicule from his classmates at the school talent show, Joshua hides his inclination to play African rhythms on the kalimba and wishes he were the popular Kareem who amazes the other children with his dancing and rapping. Much to Joshua's surprise and ultimately his horror, with the aid of a Masai mask given to him by his Uncle Zambezi for the kalimba performance, his wish comes true. He becomes Kareem. Through the course of the story, Joshua transforms himself into a rap star and the mayor, but finds that he would rather be himself than

A boy longing to play African drums faces peer pressure at school.

someone else. In the end, it is Joshua's own performance in the talent show that invigorates the audience, pleases his parents, and reassures him that his own identity is valuable.

Rich's brightly colored illustrations add to the ebullience of this celebration of self. CHRISTINE PALMER

Jamal's Busy Day

Wade Hudson George Ford

African American

1991, Just Us Books, ✳ Series

Jamal's Busy Day is the delightful tale of an African American boy and his family as they go through their workdays. Jamal's workday takes place at school, his mother's at her job as an accountant, and his father's as an architect. The story is told through Jamal, who appears to be approximately ten years old. We see the family as they groom themselves, dress, and eat breakfast to be ready for their "busy day." The father goes off to his day as an architect who "makes drawings to guide the people who build houses." We see him at a building site, going over his drawings with the construction workers. Jamal says, "He works very hard." The mother goes off to her job at an office surrounded by the tools of her trade—computers, adding machines, and fax machines—where she is always busy with numbers. Jamal says, "Mommy works very hard." It is clear that he is proud of the work they do.

An African American boy compares his "work day" at school to his parents' work.

The story moves on to Jamal, who says, "I work hard, too." We go with him to school where his day is described in occupational terms. As opposed to math, science, and art classes, Jamal describes his morning as working with numbers, trying experiments, and making drawings. When he selects a book from the library he says, " I do research," and when he attends an assembly program of African drummers, he says, "Then there are meetings to attend." Jamal refers to his classmates as his co-workers, and his teacher as his supervisor. What comes across so well in this book is Jamal's confidence that he is doing something important in his life by going to school—and that he knows this is his job as a member of his family.

The story also balances the workday with the rest of the family's life. We see them relaxing, playing games, and helping prepare their evening meal together. At the dinner table, they all discuss their busy days. George Ford's illustrations are detailed and realistic as he takes the family through their day. His drawings include fine points that add cultural and social perspective to the book. The parents are dressed professionally, with Afrocentric touches; the construction site includes a woman and a primarily black crew, and the classmates are shown in every ethnicity, working and playing together. Ford also depicts the parents with happy and loving expressions as they speak with each other and Jamal.

This is a lovely story that brings cultural sensitivity, pride, and accomplishment to the daily life of Jamal and his family. With the help of the excellent illustrations, readers relate to his "work terminology" as he describes his day. There is also a message implicit in the story that work can be fulfilling and enjoyable when you are doing things that you feel good about, a message we can use at any age.
ROSA E. WARDER

When I Am Old With You

📖 Angela Johnson 🖌 David Soman
African American
1993 (1990), Orchard Books

Following a child's sense of time and logic, the book begins with "When I am old with you Grandaddy, I will sit in a big rocking chair beside you and talk about everything," the child naturally assumes that the grandfather will remain ageless, while the child grows older. The familiar concept is both tender and sad, for the child sees both her grandfather and herself as being immortal. As the child recites all the things she and her grandfather will do together "when I'm old with you," the use of imagination is reassuring in this warm and endearing story. The most important thing they will do is spend time enjoying each other's company as they already do. "We can look at the old pictures and try to imagine the people in them. It might make us cry. But that's O.K. In

An African American child imagines growing old with her grandfather.

the morning, Grandaddy, we will cook bacon for breakfast and that's all. We can eat on the porch, too."

The warm expressions and tender thoughts of both the child and the grandfather are lovingly captured in vibrant watercolor illustrations by David Soman. The illustrations are rendered in such a way that the gender of the child is not clear. It is difficult to find books that are written without gender specificity and nearly impossible to find any with illustrations that reflect the universality of childhood beyond gender boundaries.

The book features an African American grandparent and grandchild, yet the theme is universal. This is a book in which the relationship between grandchild and grandparent is celebrated. At a time when ageism is especially pronounced in our culture, *When I Am Old with You* provides a reassuring sense of bonding across the boundaries of age.
DEBBIE WEI

The Girl Who Wore Snakes

📖 Angela Johnson 🖌 James Ransome
African American
1993, Orchard Books

Ali is fascinated by the snakes the man from the zoo brings to her classroom. The other children are surprised when Ali parades around with the snakes on her shoulders, arms, and ankles. Ali saves up her money to buy snakes from the local pet store. But her newly found passion is not embraced by her family and friends who are appalled, and Ali must listen to disparaging remarks about her new pets. Only one of her aunts understands and Ali is pleased that someone close to her supports her interests in snakes.

Environmental issues figure in this book about an African American girl interested in snakes.

Snakes remind Ali "of the sun and the earth and everything in between." She sees them as an integral part of nature and demonstrates a strong compassion for them and their right to be on the planet. As we distance ourselves from our natural surroundings, there remains a growing need for books that address the relationship between man and nature.

Author Angela Johnson emphasizes that all creatures have a role in the ecosystem. She also encourages both an aesthetic appreciation for and understanding of the role other species play in our lives. With books often portraying girls as fearful and hysterical when it comes to bugs, snakes, and many other animals, it's refreshing to read a story with a bold and adventurous girl. While Ali is African American, she could be a girl from any culture.

This book will help children understand that animals, even reptiles, are not ugly—that all creatures have their role in the ecosystem essential to human existence. It could also help children overcome phobias of snakes and all other animals. Children should be encouraged to read and learn about whatever they find interesting. This book may encourage them to be like Ali and do just that. MARTHA L. MARTINEZ

The Four Gallant Sisters

📖 Eric A. Kimmel (editor) adapted from the Brothers Grimm ✒ Tatyana Yuditskaya

Feminist

1992 (1991), Henry Holt and Company

This folktale depicts four young sisters who set out to seek their fortune after the death of their mother. They agree to dress as young men and cut their hair, for they believe this will increase their chance of success. They also agree to meet at their mother's grave in seven years. Each sister becomes apprenticed and receives a magical object in payment for her good work. The first sister becomes a tailor and is given a magic needle that will sew anything. The second sister becomes a hunter and is given a magic gun that will never miss its mark. The third sister becomes a magician and is given a magic belt that enables her to become invisible. The fourth sister becomes a skilled stargazer and is given a telescope from which nothing is hidden. Having learned their trades, they return home and seek employment with the King. After proving their skills, they are hired to rescue the King's promised bride and her brothers from a dragon. With the help of their magical equipment, they are successful in the rescue mission. The four sisters' true identity as females is revealed, and they marry the four res-

A sexist adaptation of a Brothers Grimm story.

cued princes. The King marries the rescued princess, and they all live happily ever after.

While the four sisters are portrayed as gallant, brave, and intelligent, they unfortunately must dress as males to prove it. *Readers might discuss whether or not they could be respected as females.* The "happy ending," in which the sisters marry the princes, should also be challenged. This is a traditional notion that women's happiness depends on marriage. *Children may be invited to invent alternative paths to happiness and fulfillment.* Would four such gallant and capable women give up their exciting lives and be content as sedentary and docile princesses? It is interesting to note, also, that the King's mother is suspicious of the four sisters from the beginning. Convinced that they are actually females disguised as males, she sets out to trap them into revealing themselves. Not only is the King's mother portrayed in a negative and stereotypical light (suspicious, vengeful, jealous) but she uses highly stereotypical measures to trap the sisters into revealing their gender. For example, she sets out food for the sisters and then watches to see whether they feed themselves first, or feed their friends first. She decides that if they think of themselves first, they are men, but if they put their friends' needs first, they are women. One could argue that the Queen celebrates femaleness and nurturing by using these types of tests, but given the sexist overtones of the book, the tests also appear to be highly sexist in nature.

BARBARA SMITH REDDISH

Wood-Hoopoe Willie

📖 Virginia Kroll ✒ Katherine Roundtree

African American

1995 (1992), Charlesbridge Publishing

Wherever he goes, seven-year-old Willie is constantly rapping out "the beat" with his knuckles. But when his aunt tells him that he will ruin his joints, he stops rapping and begins tapping out a tune on his drinking glass with his fork. When his mother disapproves, he begins tapping out the beat with knives on the tabletop. Everywhere Willie goes, his hands are in constant motion, eager to keep the beat going, shaking jars of dried pepper flakes together, drumming chopsticks on a glass, tapping pencils on his desk.

Whenever adults tell Willie to stop, his grandfather, who has spent time in Africa, remembers the drumming sounds that he has heard there. Finally his grandfather says that perhaps Willie has a wood-hoopoe trapped inside. He says that a wood-hoopoe is an African bird that is always pecking or crackling out some type of rhythm. When Willie does not hear music he makes his own.

It is on the fifth night of the Kwanza Nia (the Kidevahili word for "purpose") that a real disappointment turns into a great opportunity for Willie to show off his talent—-and what he has learned from his grandfather. Upon arriving at the Kwanza celebration, they discover that the drummer has been hurt in an accident. Everyone is upset except Grandpa, who tells Willie that it is time to set his wood-hoopoe free. As Willie begins to play the drums, the other musicians also run to their instruments and the celebration begins. Willie smiles at Grandpa and they both look up as he is sure that he sees something flapping and flying across the ceiling.

An African American boy shares his musical talent and energy in a Kwanza celebration.

This story is a provocative look at one child's special talent and the way in which he is allowed to effectively channel that energy. While most of his family see him as simply an active and precocious child, his grandfather recognizes and encourages his true talent. His grandfather's description of the wood-hoopoe bird provides Willie with the language to describe his constant drumming. Throughout the text, the grandfather offers both encouragement and information about the African roots of various musical instruments. The illustrations contribute to the festive and celebratory mood of the story. The pictures are colorful and there are African musicians performing in the background. Included in the text is a chart that outlines the seven days of Kwanza and what each means. The author does an excellent job of linking Willie's talent and energy to a collective history of music and celebration. MICHELLE GARFIELD

Africa Brothers and Sisters

📖 Virginia Kroll   ✏ Vanessa French

African

1993, Simon & Schuster Children's Books

With subtle eloquence, Kroll teaches her readers about the continent of Africa and the many people who reside there. With the use of the characters Jesse and his Daddy, who through an imaginative game verbally and pictorially travel around Africa, Kroll offers insight into the traditions and talents of twenty-one African tribes. Through Jesse and his Daddy, we learn about the beautiful woven cloth of the Ashanti (Ghana), the wondrous carved masks of the Guere (Ivory Coast), and the stunningly masterful gold and silver jewelry of the Djerma (Niger Valley). We see tribal and metropolitan Africans, ranging from warriors to engineers.

A complex portrait of the people and culture of Africa emerges as an African American boy and his father discuss their heritage.

Furthermore, Kroll instructs her readers about the diversity of African peoples in terms of language, customs, and dwelling places. *The author takes readers far beyond the monolithic view of this very complex continent, making this an excellent resource for a teacher preparing a unit on African studies.*

Kroll includes the pronunciation of the names of each of the twenty-one peoples that she includes in the text, as well as a page-long note on other African peoples and their specialties. The Turkana, Karqmojong, Ituri, Sotho, and Malinke are among the others to whom she refers. And for those teachers interested in helping their students develop a more realistic image of Africa as a continent rather than as a country, Kroll includes an ethnogeographic map of the continent. *With French's bright watercolor and colored-pencil illustrations, African Brothers and Sisters serves as an excellent tool with which to introduce young minds to the global perspective of multiculturalism.*

CHRISTINE PALMER

Starting Home: The Story of Horace Pippin, Painter

📖 Mary E. Lyons ✏ Horace Pippin and other sources
African American
1993 (1992), Charles Scribner's Sons, ✳ Series

Horace Pippin was born in Westchester, Pennsylvania, in 1888. He later moved to Goshen, New York, with his mother and his siblings. He soon began to sketch in pencil and crayon, but as soon as he was old enough, he had to go to work. In 1917, he joined the army and was sent to France to fight in World War I. While there, he kept notebooks in which he made notes and drawings. He had to leave most of them behind, however, to prevent the Germans from coming into possession of them.

An introduction to Horace Pippin, one of the foremost African American painters.

The war left Pippin with frightful memories. His right shoulder was shattered and his upper arm had to be reattached to his body with a steel plate. These experiences colored the rest of his life, and his demons gave him no peace. He was often in pain.

Pippin married when he returned home and found he could use his strong left arm to support his weaker right arm. Soon, he was making etchings on wood with a hot fireplace poker. Later, he transferred this technique to painting in oil on canvas.

Mary Lyon's book is richly illustrated with Pippin's art. His work was often dark and terrifying, filled with blacks and grays. He gave his paintings grace with splashes of red and white. The story of his life is told in such works as *Cabin in the Cotton III, Self Portrait*, and *The End of the War: Starting Home*.

Pippin died in 1946. His *The Milkman of Goshen* sold in 1988 for $100,000.

This is a wonderful introduction to Pippin's work. He said, "I take my time and examine every coat of paint carefully. When I'm through with a picture, I've put everything in it I've got to give." BETTYE STROUD

You Be Me, I'll Be You

📖 ✏ Pili Mandelbaum
African American, Biracial
1990, Kane/Miller

Anna wants to look more like her white father than her African American mother. Her father tries to provide her with a lesson in self-acceptance. They "trade places." He rubs coffee grounds on his face and braids his hair; Anna puts on a hat and rubs powder on her face. Each tries to feel what it's like to be a different race.

While Anna's concerns are dealt with gently, many questions remain unanswered. Because Anna's mother isn't a main character, the reader never knows

A story of a biracial girl that fails to address key issues.

Anna's inability to come to terms with her biracial identity. Why is Anna dissatisfied with her skin color? Why is it that she prefers to look like her white father, rather than her black mother?

We also see a disproportionate number of white images in this story, such as Anna's dolls and the ladies in the beauty parlor. The neighborhood, however, appears to be urban, and the people on the streets are depicted as coming from a variety of cultures.

Of special note is the way in which Anna and her father are depicted by the illustrator. While the father is portrayed with somewhat chiseled features and a lined face, Anna appears more cartoon-like. She has a round smooth face and a pink circle for a nose, making her look like a little doll. BARBARA SMITH REDDISH

The Girl Who Loved Caterpillars: A Twelfth-Century Tale from Japan

📖 Jean Merrill ✏ Floyd Cooper
Asian, Japanese
1992, Philomel Books · Putnam & Grosset Group

Jean Merrill captures the wonder of an ancient Japanese folktale in *The Girl Who Loved Caterpillars*. The story chronicles the attraction of a young woman, Izumi, to the beauty of nature. The daughter of an inspector in the emperor's court, Izumi is known throughout the province as "the girl who loved caterpillars." Despite her parents' wishes that she model her behavior after that of her neighbor, "the lady who loved butterflies," Izumi refuses

A Japanese folktale about a strong-minded young woman who refuses to conform.

to conform to the dictates of society. She collects insects instead of flowers, leaves her teeth their natural sparkling white instead of blackening them according to fashion, and does not pluck and shape her eyebrows into thin lines as other women do,

41

preferring to leave them in their unadorned caterpillarlike form. Though the servants and other courtesans gossip about Izumi's behavior, she contents herself in the knowledge that she is yet another of nature's miraculous and beauteous creations, and befriends several village boys who bring her the insects she wishes to observe.

When a young nobleman hears of Izumi's behavior, he decides to send her a surprise (a mechanical snake), to determine the extent of Izumi's adherence to her beliefs. Delighting in the gift, Izumi responds to the young man with a poetic letter. A friend of the young man, the Captain of the Stables, is intrigued by her response, and travels to the garden of Izumi's home to watch her. He is struck by her unconventional beauty and sends his compliments to her. In the end, the Captain leaves, and Izumi is left to enjoy her caterpillars.

According to an endnote by the author, the abrupt ending is due to the content of the older versions of the tale in which the suggestion is made that there is a second part to the tale, a part which has not yet been discovered. In any event, the tale that Merrill presents, along with Cooper's rich oilwash illustrations, is an amazing exploration of individuality and pride. CHRISTINE PALMER

Zora Hurston and the Chinaberry Tree

William Miller Ying-Hwa Hu
African American
1994, Lee and Low Books

This picture book biography focuses on the childhood of Zora Neale Hurston, an important American writer. As viewed from the chinaberry tree in her backyard, Hurston's world comes alive in lyrical prose and richly hued watercolors. The focus here is on Hurston's relationship with her mother, who taught her "that everything had a voice.... and that the world belonged to her." Curious and adventuresome, Zora immerses herself in the life of the all-black town of Eatonville, Florida, asking questions of the men playing checkers and listening to folktales told around the campfire. When her mother gets sick, Zora sits by her bedside every day, telling her sto-

An inspiring account of Zora Neale Hurston's childhood, focusing on her relationship with her mother.

ries. Her mother reminds her always to remember the stories, because "stories...kept their people alive. As long as they were told, Africa would live in their hearts."

When her mother dies, "Zora felt as if she had died too." She runs to climb the chinaberry tree, to see the world her mother had given her, and to renew her promise that she would never stop climbing but always "jump at the morning sun."

Hurston went on to become a controversial Harlem Renaissance writer, anthropologist, and folklorist. Though her works and life remained obscure for many years after her death, Hurston's voice has once again become an integral part of the American literary landscape through the efforts of Alice Walker. William Miller's text and Ying-Hwa Hu's watercolor paintings are a visual treat, with emotionally expressive characters and lush landscapes. *This inspiring story about a remarkable woman could be used with older elementary and possibly middle school students.* LAURI JOHNSON

Hue Boy

Rita Phillips Mitchell Caroline Binch
Caribbean
1993, Dial Books for Young Readers

Although this story's title is somewhat misleading (since the focus is on size, not color), this is an interesting novel, a kind of parable of self-acceptance. Hue Boy is constantly teased by his classmates because of his small size. His mother thinks that if he eats fruits and vegetables he will grow.

At the harbor, Hue Boy notices a tall man getting off a ship and then realizes that the man is his father. As they walk into the village, Hue Boy stands tall, walking proudly along with his father. He comes to the realization that while he is small now, he may grow as tall as his father in time.

Hue Boy comes to realize that there are other things more important than physical appearance, such as his father returning to his family after being away at work. He also learns that what others perceive is not what really counts; it's what one feels on the inside that truly matters.

Touching on the themes of self-acceptance and

A story of self-acceptance about a Caribbean boy who yearns to grow taller (not more colorful, as the title suggests).

pride in the face of mockery, this story reminds us how important it is to know who we truly are and not yearn to be what others think we should be.
MARTHA L. MARTINEZ

Angela's Wings

Eric Jon Nones

Hispanic

1995, Farrar, Straus and Giroux, Dorros, Arthur, *Abuela*; James, J. Alison, *Eucalyptus Wings*; Mills, Lauren, *Fairy Wings*; Small, David, *Imogene's Antlers*.

Angela wakes up one morning to find that she has sprouted wings. "Oh, terrific, what am I supposed to do with these things?" she asks. Her Mama, Papa, and brother are all aghast. "They noticed." Her parents launch into an argument about which side of the family the wings might have come from. "Think they'll attract attention?" Angela asks. She walks past the local grocery where everyone is staring and pointing.

A Hispanic girl wakes up one morning with wings in a book that celebrates difference.

The janitor tells Angela that he knew a man in Toledo with a beautiful set of wings. "He didn't do much with 'em though—a real pity." Her grandmother says, "Everyone's got something special, child. Just depends on what you do with it, that's all." So Angela starts to use her wings. She dunks a basketball, plays an angel in St. Bartholomew's Christmas pageant, and soars among kites over the city. She's still "different," but she's discovered she likes that. In the last picture, she stands exuberantly in front of a glorious fireworks display.

Nones's artwork shows real people from a number of ethnic groups. He captures Angela, a preadolescent Latino girl, perfectly: she slouches the right way, rolls her eyes, hunches like a gargoyle on the school building, hovers demurely over the manger. The fact that she looks and acts like a real girl, wings and all, underscores the subtle message that whatever makes us different can be something to celebrate. *The book may be used to illustrate the importance of accepting others—and ourselves—as unique individuals, encouraging discussions about how things that appear to be disabilities can become useful.*

Nones's short text, including some pages with very few words and some pages with illustrations only, makes this book accessible to readers as young as kindergarten age. With Angela as a realistic, looking nine- or ten-year-old, however, it will not seem "baby-ish" for children up to fifth grade.

A number of other books can be used with this one. Students can look for plot differences in Imogene's Antlers *by David Small (Crown, 1985), the story of another girl who wakes up shockingly different.* Fairy Wings *by Lauren Mills (Little Brown, 1995), in which Fia—a fairy born without wings—saves her people from the Troll, delivers a similar, less subtle message. In* Eucalyptus Wings *by Alison James (Atheneum, 1995), two girls find a magic cocoon and go flying through the night on a warm ribbon of air. Students can compare Demi's illustration of Mica and Kiria floating over a Southwest city with Spanish-style houses on nearby hills to the illustration of Angela swooping over New York City.* Abuela *by Arthur Dorros (Dutton, 1991), with pictures of a grandmother and granddaughter flying over New York City, provides another useful comparison.* JANE KURTZ

Somebody Called Me a Retard Today...and My Heart Felt Sad

Ellen O'Shaughnessy   David Garner

Mentally Disabled

1992, Walker Publishing Company

Ellen O'Shaughnessy shares her professional expertise in educating developmentally disabled children in this useful book. With simple language and delicate watercolors, young people are encouraged to empathize with those who are "different," especially important now that more and more mentally retarded children are being mainstreamed in schools.

An excellent treatment in a story of a girl ostracized for her disability.

The book's main character does well in school, plays with the other children, and takes on real responsibilities at home. She feeds the cat, helps care for her baby brother, and spends time with her dad, just like many other children.

This is an excellent book for teachers or parents to use when dealing with teasing and name-calling.
DAPHNE MUSE

Handicapism Checklist: What Do We Mean by "Handicapism"?

ELOISE GREENFIELD

In the late sixties and early seventies, as part of the overall battle for civil rights that was taking place all over the country, people with disabilities were becoming vocal and visible: stopping buses during rush hour to protest the lack of wheelchair access on public transportation; demonstrating for curb cuts; and sitting in city hall to demand equal, integrated education.

As a result of these struggles, section 504, the Rehabilitation Act of 1973, was passed; and in 1975, public law 94-142, the Education for All Handicapped Children Act mandated that all children with disabilities are entitled to a free education "in the least restrictive environment."

Also in the late sixties—and continuing to the present—a plethora of children's books were published featuring children with disabilities or issues concerning disability. The need for more complex, sympathetic, and challenging works about disability becomes evident if we consider some of the most popular disabled storybook characters we know from childhood. Tiny Tim in A Christmas Carol and Rumplestilskin, and Long John Silver, and the nearsighted Mr. Magoo, and Porky Pig, just to name a few.

Now let's ask ourselves this question: When we were growing up, did we see disabled people as grotesque, evil, ugly, pitiable, laughable, weird, outsiders? Or if we had disabilities, did we see ourselves this way?

There are many more stereotypes that inundate childrens literature—both "classics" and contemporary stories. When choosing books (or reviewing TV shows, movies, videos, plays, etc.), here are some questions you might ask about disabled characters or stories featuring them. This is not a checklist to be applied to each and every story involving disability; these are simply questions we can have in mind as we read, questions that will help us understand the ways in which disabled people for so long were depicted in childrens literature.

1. Are the disabled/different characters one-dimensional (clumsy or foolish, evil or malicious)? Are they depicted as childlike even if they are adults?

2. Are they always sad, receiving pity or preoccupied with the hope of recovery? Are they more sensitive, angry, or bitter than the average person? Is the disability synonymous with their being somehow incomplete? Are they capable of a full range of emotions?

3. Are they passive and dependent, or are they active, independent people?

4. Are they described as beautiful or handsome, except for their disabilities? Are their clothing, activities, or aspirations described only in terms of the limitations of the disability?

5. Are they attractive people who could have a sweetheart or sexual partner? Do they see themselves as capable, loving, or sexual? Do they have homes or children? Are they part of a community?

6. Do they have special powers because of their disability? Is there a relationship between their attractiveness and goodness and physical improvement?

7. In the course of a story, are they cured solely because of a positive attitude? Is a bad attitude the only thing standing in the way of success? Are societal barriers explored in discussing attitudes?

8. Do they have a miraculous recovery because of the intervention of the main characters? Can they find their own strengths and answers without having to be rescued?

9. Are the nondisabled characters always helping them? Are they depicted as helpers or good friends?

10. Are they just like you? Is each person seen as an individual with similarities to and differences from you?

11. Is there anything in the story line that would embarrass or humiliate a disabled child?

From *Writing for Children—A Joy and a Responsibility*.
© 1978 by Eloise Greenfield.

Dinner at Aunt Connie's House

Faith Ringgold
African American
1993, Hyperion

Melody loves to visit the beautiful beach home of her Uncle Bates and Aunt Connie. This summer she finds two surprises: a newly adopted son that her aunt and uncle have brought into the family, and an attic full of Aunt Connie's paintings. But these paintings can speak! Altogether, there are twelve paintings, each a portrait of a courageous African American woman, who tells a short history of herself. "I am Fannie Lou Hamer, born in 1917 in Mississippi," says one painting. "I was a civil rights activist and public speaker. I worked with Martin Luther King for voters' rights in the South.

African American women's history comes alive when twelve "talking paintings are found in an attic.

I helped thousands of people register to vote." From Sojourner Truth (born in 1797) to Dorothy Dandridge (born in 1922), the stories told by these paintings give children great pride in being African American and also inspire them to accomplish great things as adults.

Ringgold's illustrations are bold and vibrant. At the end of the story she tells the true account of her "Dinner at Aunt Connie's House" story quilt, which combines painting, sewing, and storytelling. A small illustration of the quilt is shown. *The "Dinner at Aunt Connie's" quilt is a great motivator to use with any subject taught for any age, including adult. You can draw a table setting, with the food, plates, and silverware to depict any theme. Lastly, the people would be drawn to add to the dinner table. For instance, it could be one's own family, showing relatives, food, and settings. Or it could show important people from a certain period, such as the Civil War, and also depict the food of that time. It has been used for study of Native Americans, the farm, etc.* On the last page, there is a biography of Faith Ringgold and an accompanying photo. She said, "After I decided to be an artist, the first thing that I had to believe was that I, a Black woman, could be on the art scene without sacrificing one iota of my Blackness or my femaleness or my humanity."
DORIS COSLEY

Ahyoka and the Talking Leaves

Peter Roop / Yoshi Miyake
Cherokee, Native American
1994, 1992, Beech Tree Press, Klausner, Janet, *Sequoya's Gift.*

This short, readable book for elementary grades provides some insight into the formidable task of creating a written language. By 1821, Sequoyah, a Cherokee, with help from his daughter Ahyoka, accomplished something no one person had ever done before: he had created a written language from a spoken language.

With clear and simple language, the authors have crafted an interesting book, fleshing out the character of young Ahyoka. They

A short, readable account of the origins of the Cherokee language.

explain how she and her father used pieces of charcoal and sycamore tree bark to draw hundreds of pictures representing words in their Tsalagi language. Their tribal community considered these activities evil and drove the father and daughter from the camp. However, the two continued their search and

spent eighteen years exploring the English alphabet and words, devising a syllabary of eighty-six signs to represent the sounds in their own language. The book makes the reader aware of the genius of Sequoyah and the Cherokees, not savages as stereotypically portrayed, but an intelligent people who were able to produce and read their own newspapers as early as the mid-1800s. The story is a blend of details about Indian life, coming-of-age rituals, and exciting quests.

The black-and-white illustrations have interesting depth through shadings and fine, nonstereotypical features in the characters' faces. There is a five-page epilogue in which the authors document their research. The resource bibliography lists thirteen books and articles written between 1870 and 1987.

The young-adult biography Sequoyah's Gift *by Janet Klausner (HarperCollins, 1993) can serve as a teacher resource and read-aloud text.*
GLORIA D. JACKSON

45

El Chino

Allen Say
Asian American, Chinese American
1990, Houghton Mifflin

Bong Way "Billy" Wong was a Chinese American man who knew the importance of dreams. Billy's parents immigrated from Canton, China, at the turn of the twentieth century. The family settled in Nogales, Arizona, and later in California. His dream was to become a famous basketball player, much to the amusement of his five successful siblings. But Billy followed his dream, remembering his father's promise that in America "you can become anything you want to be." He became Berkeley high school's star player but was not tall enough to be accepted at college level. He received an engineering degree and traveled throughout Europe. In Spain, he discovered bull-

A charming portrayal of a legendary Chinese American bullfighter in Spain.

fighting. He reveled in the excitement of the crowd as it encouraged the matador and decided this was the sport for him. But the Spanish matadors laughed at him. He was not Spanish. How could he possibly become a bullfighter? Defiantly, Billy donned a Chinese costume and successfully escaped from the bullring, attracting the attention and admiration of the matador school and eventually becoming the first famous Chinese bullfighter: El Chino!

Allen Say learned of this legendary Chinese bullfighter at the school his daughter Yuriko attended with one of Bill Wong's relatives. This charming story is a distinctive contribution to biography for children. Say's evocative watercolors perfectly complement the crisp, concise storytelling for which the author-illustrator is so well known. His skillful account captures Bill Wong's determination and courage in pursuing his dream. Say's use of shadow and black-and-white shading effectively evoke the past, in photograph-like images. *His frank and honest portrayal is a tribute to this Chinese American man and is a useful addition to any multiethnic list of biographies, especially for crosscultural themes or assignments.* PATRICIA WONG

Ragtime Tumpie

Alan Schroeder   Bernie Fuchs
African American
1993 (1989), Little, Brown and Company

This is a fictional account of the real-life story of the world-renowned dancer and entertainer Josephine Baker. It is an exciting tale of the humble beginnings and determination of a famous African American entertainer. Growing up in the poorest area of St. Louis, Missouri, "Tumpie," as Baker was called, regularly walked two miles to a large market to pick up the vegetables and fruits that fell on the ground beneath the

An exciting fictional account of Josephine Baker's girlhood.

stalls. As she walked to the market, she passed a café where she heard ragtime music. She always stopped and tapped her foot to the beat. The music made Tumpie think of her father, a honky-tonk drummer. Now that he was gone, she lived with her mama and stepfather.

On her way home from the market, she would stop at the train station to pick up the coal that fell from the hopper cars. Her family used this coal to keep warm at night. As she walked, she dreamed of boarding the train, going far away, and becoming a famous ragtime honky-tonker. During the winter when their apartment was very cold, she and her mama would dance just to keep warm. During the spring she danced in all the vaudeville shows that the neighborhood kids put on.

One morning a medicine man arrived in town. At the end of the day he held a dance contest for which the prize was a silver dollar. Tumpie entered at the last minute and stole the show. The crowd loved her. As she carried her silver prize home, Tumpie promised her mother that she would never stop dancing.

Although the story ends while Tumpie is still a small girl, there is an author's note that outlines some of the highlights of her future career as Josephine Baker. The author attempts to describe the music through Tumpie's dreams and observations outside the cafe. Yet this text would be more effective if it were accompanied by audio examples of ragtime music. The illustrations are both excellent portrayals of what is occurring in the story, as well as beautiful examples of African American art. The movement and energy of the illustrations convey a sense of rhythm and excitement. MICHELLE GARFIELD

The Gifts of Wali Dad: A Tale of India & Pakistan

📖 Aaron Shepard ✒ Daniel San Souci

Asian, East Indian, Pakistani

1995, Atheneum

This retelling of a folktale attributed to northwestern India and Pakistan rings in the ear like a lesson once learned, now long forgotten. *The Gifts of Wali Dad* is a story of the joys of simple living. Set in rural India, it reflects a culture grounded in reciprocity; gifts cannot simply be given, but must be generously exchanged. The tale revolves around an old grass-cutter who lives in a little hut far from town. Each day he cuts and bundles wild grasses to sell in the market as fodder. He earns thirty pias a day—the smallest Indian coin—ten of which he spends for food, ten for other necessities. Each evening, he adds the remaining ten coins to the clay pot he keeps beneath his bed.

A rich East Indian tale about a poor grass-cutter who is transformed into a wealthy man.

Wali Dad lives contentedly until he decides to drag the pot from under the bed. A fortune in coins has accumulated over the years, but he has no need for wealth. He gathers the money into a sack, exchanges the coins for a gold bracelet and visits a traveling merchant in hopes of ridding himself of this excess by giving it away to "the noblest lady" in all the world. When the queen of Khaistan returns Wali Dad's gift by sending back a camel laden with the fine silks, he begs the traveling man to tell him who the "noblest man" on earth is, so that he can pack off the queen's gift to someone in need of such finery. The series of gift exchanges which follow land the grass-cutter in the middle of a wackily humorous game of one-upmanship as the queen and king try to out-give the mysterious Wali Dad. From silks to horses to a caravan of elephants with gold tusks, gifts flow from east to west as Wali Dad tries to rid himself of these unwanted riches.

Daniel San Souci's muted watercolors are a perfect match for a story that eloquently mixes simplicity and grandeur. Wali Dad is almost a caricature: with exaggerated nose and spindly legs, he leaps off the page with exuberance. Other characters are portrayed more realistically. San Souci chooses telling detail throughout: a line of mules loaded with chests of silver trot toward the reader. Three sketches of Wali Dad at the top of a page portray the changes in his expression from surprise to dismay. The artist uses this split-page technique effectively throughout the book to give the reader multiple images. Close-ups of stately monarchs, grand panoramas of rural India, and comical views of Wali Dad complement Shepard's straightforward text.

The tale reaches its climax when the queen and the king journey to Wali Dad's hut, laden with riches and determined to meet the man whose generosity seems to know no bounds. Two angelic peris have turned Wali Dad's rags to finery and replaced his hut with a sparkling palace so that he can greet his guests without shame. Predictably, the king of Nedabad and the queen of Khaistan meet at Wali Dad's palace, fall in love and marry. Not so predictably, Wali Dad still longs for the simple life. This twist lifts *The Gifts of Wali Dad* above the abundance of folktales of the deserving man who rises from poverty. Few tales offer the richness of the conclusion of this retelling. As the story ends, the peris grant Wali Dad's heart's desire: he becomes a grass-cutter once again and joyfully lives out his days in his simple hut far from town.

The final act of Wali Dad may seem foreign to children living in a country where material wealth is the ultimate indicator of success. *Classroom discussions might range from enjoying one's own "gifts" to the value of living simply, depending on students' ages. The idea of reciprocity leads to discussions of the meaning of gift-giving in a variety of cultures.* KIM GRISWELL

Blue Jay in the Desert

📖 Marlene Shigekawa ✒ Isao Kikuchi

Asian American, Japanese American

1993, Polychrome Publishing Corporation

Junior and his family once lived in California. But now they find themselves at a desert outpost in Poston, Arizona, along with thousands of other Japanese Americans brought to internment camps "for safe keeping." Junior's grandfather is a wood carver known throughout the camp for his talent. One day, Junior finds out that his grandfather is working on a special carving just for him. He imagines it to be a lion,

A Japanese American in WWII internment camp learns the value of freedom from a blue jay in this beautiful, thoughtful tale.

47

stallion, or a great bear. Much to Junior's dismay, he finds out it is a blue jay, not the wild beast he has set his sights on.

Junior decides to find out more about blue jays so he can better understand why his grandfather has chosen to carve one for him. He learns that blue jays fly quickly, they are not afraid to express anger, and they help farmers by eating insects. But it is still not clear to him why he should have a blue jay.

One night, Junior dreams that he rides the bird's wings over the barbed wire and back to his home in California. When he wakes up, Junior understands his grandfather's choice. He thinks, "This blue jay is like us. We all want to go home where we belong. This blue jay doesn't belong here either. Blue jays belong in the woods…not in the desert…" He finds that his grandfather has finished his carving. The blue jay becomes a symbol to Junior of his need for freedom and his need to be brave in order to survive.

Beautifully written and thoughtfully told, this story demonstrates how an older, wiser man passes on the value of freedom to his grandson. The whimsical, stylized illustrations are colorful and work well with the text. There is a certain sadness in the ending. Though the book ends with Junior's family receiving word that they are to be released from camp and the last illustration shows the family standing in front of a rainbow, they are off to a bittersweet new beginning. DEBBIE WEI

The Pool Party

🎴 Gary Soto ✒ Robert Casilla
Hispanic, Mexican American
1993, Delacorte

When ten-year-old Mexican American Rudy Herrara is invited to a pool party on the rich side of town, his entire family prepares him for the event. His father tries to tells him: "Rudy, we're just ordinary gentle people. We get by. We're honest. She's gonna see that you're real." Their advice and support make this a loving story about a boy who is uncomfortable with the idea of leaving his neighborhood for the day and unsure how to behave.

An effective story featuring a Mexican American boy learning about class and family.

The book raises issues about family relationships, pride in one's work, and class conflict. It fits perfectly into a unit on community or family, addressing such universal concerns as security and the desire for social acceptance.

Readers learn about the workings of a loving family in a Mexican American neighborhood in a small California town. Soto's story effectively undermines Mexican stereotypes. His easy and engaging style in this novel will appeal to readers young and old. DORIS COSLEY

Three Strong Women: A Tall Tale from Japan

🎴 Claus Stamm ✒ Jean and Mousien Tseng
Asian, Japanese
1993 (1962), Viking Children's Books

One of the strongest, most powerful wrestlers in Japan is on his way to the capital to demonstrate his prowess before the emperor and bask in the admiration of the court. So enamored is he of himself and his might, that he decides to have a some fun with a jolly little girl he comes across on the roadside. He tickles her. Ha Ha, laughs the jolly girl. But the joke is on Mr. Big, for she clamps her arm down over his and he can't get away.

An updated version of a delightful Japanese tale about one family's strong women.

At first he is bemused, then startled, then downright bewildered. How can such a small girl be so much stronger than he, and sassy besides? She

takes him home to show her mother, who is bringing home the cow on her shoulders, and her grandmother, who picks up a tree out of the ground, roots and all. The mother hurls it across the valley and far up the mountain. "Oh, bother, I missed," she exclaims. "I meant to throw it over the mountain."

"Let's teach him how to be really strong," they chuckle to themselves. Forced to submit to the whims and wiles of the three women, the big, strong man lives with them for three months, doing chores, working out, learning about living happily with a family whose real strength lies in appreciation for one another and delight in a simple lifestyle. Finally, having come to love his life with them and having forgotten all about showing himself off to the emperor, he sets out again for the capital, this time with a measure of humility but with even greater strength than before. He amazes the court with his feats, but casts aside their adulation and returns to his sassy girl and her family.

The original edition, which came out in 1962, is the same delightful story, but in the 1993 edition, the clever and personable illustrations of Jean and Mousien Tseng enhance the tale considerably. GINNY LEE

Maria, A Christmas Story

📖 Theodore Taylor

Hispanic, Mexican American

1993 (1992), Avon

This short book tells a story based on the traditional Christmas parade held in the town of San Lazaro, California. It is the story of the Gonzaga family's Christmas float, conceived of envy, nurtured with pride, produced in desperation, and remembered for a generation. The Gonzaga's Mexican American nativity float wins the prize against all odds and is reenacted each year in remembrance.

An excellent Christmas story about a girl who changes an annual parade that traditionally excludes the Mexican American community.

Maria Gonzaga and her family live on a meager ranch surrounded by the large ranches and homes of wealthy Americans. In school Maria hears about the expensive floats that these families are planning for the Christmas parade; they spend up to sixteen thousand dollars. One day, in a fit of envy and desperation, Maria says that her family will also be entering a float, and to back up her determination, she signs the entry form. How Maria overcomes the reluctance of her family, appeals to their sense of heritage, gets her teenage brother to be part of the float, and eventually mobilizes the whole Mexican American community is a gentle story brimming with good humor, healthy conflict, quiet suspense, and a moving climax. *This is an excellent Christmas read-aloud for children ages ten and up.* GLORIA D. JACKSON

Brown Honey in Broomwheat Tea: Poems

📖 Joyce Carol Thomas   ✒ Floyd Cooper

African American

1996 (1993), HarperCollins Chidren's Books

African Americans range in color from very fair to very dark. They range from short to tall, from thin to wide and from young to old. How can a family be so diverse yet have sprung from the same seeds?

Brown Honey in Broomwheat Tea draws its explanations of physical characteristics from the environment. What starts as an examination of color and physical features culminates in a strong sense of self and family love.

The poems affirm an inner strength ("I am the pot that boils the potion.") but expresses a need for love. "Hide me in the cradle/ Of your love."

Halfway through the collection is a poem entitled "Family Tree." It describes the experience of being torn from the shores of Africa, being brought to America, and then having to build new family bases.

Warm-hearted poems that deal with African American identity and self-esteem.

The painting accompanying this poem captures all the written words and many of those unspoken. It is a painting that would clarify for anyone, young or old, exactly what a family tree is.

A poem entitled "Bitter" captures hard times when parents cannot adequately provide for their children. Yet the family unit remains intact. Here, Cooper captures the sense of failure in the faces of the parents and still manages to reinforce the bond of family.

Perhaps the best painting and poem are at the end. The last painting shows a family on a porch with the family tree within reach. It's the kind of scene of which childhood memories are made, the kind that makes an adult share these memories with a child. Therefore, it is quite fitting that the final verse should remind the reader of the lessons and the warmth that has been shared:

A spoonful of thought and time
helps keep a brood growing
A cup of loving kindness
helps keep a family going.

When added to the backdrop of Floyd Cooper's paintings, a sense of peace and security envelops the reader. Mr. Cooper's paintings are done in soft colors with an extensive use of browns. The colors reflect the soft warm tones of a people born of Mother Earth, nourished by the Sun, and nurtured by Father Time. YOLANDA ROBINSON COLES

The Day They Put a Tax on Rainbows

Johnny Valentine Lynette Schmidt
Gay, Lesbian, Bisexual
1992, Alyson Wonderland Publications, Inc.

This collection of three fairy tales emphasizes the importance of being generous, honest, and clever. In the first story, a father gives his daughter a magic ring that gives the wearer a wish. He tells her that he once had been lonely and wished to fall in love. Soon after, he fell in love with Brendan, a man, and was very happy. The daughter ends up using her wish to save herself from drowning by turning into a mermaid. She falls in love and marries a "mer-prince" under the sea.

A collection of three original fairy tales involving gay/ lesbian parents.

The second tale relates the adventures of three brothers as they look for a chest of gemstones. The talent of each brother is needed to complete the journey, and all three are rewarded in the end by finding the chest.

In the last story, a king puts a tax on everything, including rainbows, in an attempt to raise money to build a castle for himself. A clever boy, with two mothers, hatches a plot to convince the king that he doesn't want a new castle, and the king repeals the rainbow tax.

These stories are typical fairy tales where goodness, cleverness, and righteousness prevail against all odds. The only element that makes these different from *Cinderella* or *Snow White and the Seven Dwarves* is the inclusion of same-sex parents. This is not an integral part of the stories, but rather just one piece of information among others. While this is a welcome change from traditional fairy tales, too many other pieces remain the same to recommend these tales over the traditional ones: the rich and power-

ful remain rich and powerful; the beautiful girl marries a gorgeous prince; people are portrayed as all good and therefore win the prize. No challenges to any of these attitudes are raised. SUE FLICKINGER

Nene and the Horrible Math Monster

Marie Villanueva Ria Unson
Asian American, Filipino American
1993, Polychrome Publishing Corporation

Nene, a young Filipino American girl, faces double pressure to conform to expectations. Not only does she face the familiar problem of following in her older siblings' footsteps, but she also faces the model minority myth: that all Asian Americans do well in math.

Nene's older brother and sister are good at math, but Nene must study constantly to maintain her good grades. When her teacher, Mrs. MacKenzie, announces that because of her high scores, Nene will represent her school in an annual academic competition in the math category, Nene panics.

Villanueva does a fine job of helping children understand the complex topic of stereotyping. Nene confides to her sister: "I've heard other kids at school say that all Asians are supposed to be good at math. You're good and Bobby's good. There must be something wrong with me because I'm not." When her sister Tessie tells

A Filipino American girl confronts the myth that all Asians excel in mathematics.

Nene that this is a stereotype, she explains, "When you were younger, you probably believed that all birds could fly. Then as you got older, you found out that there are birds that don't fly, like chickens and ostriches . . . Saying that all birds fly is what stereotypes are all about. A stereotype is an idea people have about a group's identity that may not be true for everyone in the group. Sometimes it hurts people."

Villanueva goes on to explain to Nene that even seemingly "good" stereotypes can hurt people. She explains that the model minority myth may hurt Asian American students who really are struggling academically, but who don't receive help because everyone assumes they are doing fine. This important concept is developed in the story in a way that helps children understand stereotypes and their role in limiting people's aspirations.

Nene, who really enjoys writing, finds the strength to ask her teacher if she can enter the writing contest instead of the math contest. Her teacher is surprised at Nene's request. As though seeing Nene for the first time, Mrs. MacKenzie says, "I had no idea you liked writing so much." Nene, in her attempt to make herself less invisible, also finds her voice to ask Mrs. MacKenzie to call her by the name she prefers, Elizabeth, instead of the "Maria Elizabeth" Mrs. MacKenzie always uses.

Nene enters both the math and writing contests. She is determined to work hard to prove herself. Children will be amused by the Math Monster of Nene's nightmares who has numbers for teeth and spits flash cards at her. In her nightmare, when Nene complains that the cards are coming too fast, the monster replies, "Too fast! My dear child, these are flash cards. They are supposed to be fast, otherwise they would have named them drip cards!"

This is a delightful book with some important lessons embedded in the text. It is rare to find children's literature with a Filipino American protagonist and, this is a most welcome addition to the field of Asian Pacific American literature. DEBBIE WEI

Diego

📖 Jonah Winter (translated by Amy Prince)
✏ Jeanette Winter

Hispanic, Mexican

1991, Alfred A. Knopf Books, ✳ Spanish

Diego offers autobiographical sketches of the life of Diego Rivera, the renowned Mexican muralist of the 1930s and '40s. This beautiful book should make even the youngest child appreciate art and artists. Each page is adorned with colorful illustrations reminiscent of Diego Rivera's murals. A colorful band adorns each page, surrounding each of the illustrations. Through this account, readers are not only informed of an important figure in art but are also encouraged to note and develop their own talents.

Diego Rivera's childhood is recreated in a colorful and informative text.

Diego grows up a sickly child and is sent to live with a Native healer. He spends the first few years of his life in the mountains, surrounded by nature, and returns to his family once he is healthier. He receives chalk as a welcome-home present and begins to draw everywhere, including the living room walls.

His parents note their young son's talent, and encourage him greatly. His father goes as far as to build him his own studio. Diego's parents enroll him in a prestigious art school, despite his young age. Here, Diego learns the techniques to further his natural talent. Diego never loses sight of *"la raza,"* the people, and his favorite subject to paint is, in fact, real life. Once the young Diego paints a scene of the bloody Mexican Revolution.

So talented is this young man that he studies in Paris on a scholarship. Traveling to Italy, he is introduced to religious murals, and it is here that he develops the idea to paint murals of and for the Mexican people. So dedicated is this artist that he spends hours on the scaffold, even eating meals there. The narrator includes an interesting example: once, he falls asleep on the scaffold and falls off!

The illustrations do justice to the magnificent Rivera murals. Diego was not only famous in his own country, but also abroad. He was asked to paint in New York City, Detroit, and San Francisco. This amazing man painted close to two and a half miles of surface.

In this delightful picture book, the essential information about Rivera's life is presented in a manner that never trivializes Rivera's contributions to the art world, but makes it accessible so that young readers can grasp the importance of Rivera's talent and dedication. MARTHA L. MARTINEZ

Journey to the Bright Kingdom

📖 Elizabeth Winthrop ✏ Charles Mikolaycak

Japanese, Physically Disabled

1979, Holiday House

Kiyo's mother used to go to the fields to sketch. The villagers would say, "She has shown us things we never noticed before." But one day she goes blind due to a mysterious malady, and when Kiyo is born her mother cannot even see her face.

At one point, Kiyo's mother says, "No doctor will cure me of this disease (her depression) unless he can give me back my eyes." Her blindness makes her angry at the world. She tells the doctor she does not want to go on living if she cannot see again.

Kiyo used to stop in the fields to feed her rice cakes to the mice. When it seems

A girl seeks help for her blind mother from magical mice in this tender Japanese tale.

her mother might die of unhappiness at being blind, Kiyo pours out her feelings to the mice as they gratefully nibble at her cakes.

The mice invite Kiyo and her mother to spend an afternoon in Kakuresato, where "we have the riches

of the earth." On one level she refers to the grains, the trees, the birds, the produce of the earth. But there is also the deeper level of richness of spirit, which is part of the gift of the mice. Kakuresato is the kingdom of mice, a magically perfect place where "no one is ever unhappy, tired, hurt, or lonely or blind." Everyone in Japan knows about Kakuresato. Mothers tell their children about this wonderful paradise; everyone would like to go there, but only a very few are ever chosen. The mice decide who may enter.

One mouse says to Kiyo's mother during the visit, "But you are a different person from the woman we used to watch painting in the fields. Back then you saw only with your eyes. Today you saw Kakuresato with your ears and your fingers and your nose."

Her deprivation of sight has enhanced her other senses without her realizing it. On returning to her world of darkness above, she would retain those extra powers, and they will allow her to cope and even be happy and independent in the rest of her life.

Oliver Wendell Holmes once said, "Once you've had your mind stretched to accommodate a new idea, it never goes back to its original dimensions." The sight of her daughter's face, the wisdom of the mice, and the image of their bright kingdom stay with Kiyo's mother. She plants her own garden and takes long walks in the fields. "It's almost as if she can see," says Kiyo's father. "I can smell my way home," she says with a laugh. But it is the change in her own attitude that makes her life bright again.

The message of this story is that all of us have handicaps. Sometimes they can be advantages; sometimes they make us angry. We may be too tall, too short, too fat, too easily angered, "not college material," "lacking gymnastic aptitude," blind, deaf, or quadriplegic. Some things can be worked on and improved; other things must be accepted. But there is always something positive we can do in spite of what we might think of as our "handicap." That is

the message of this delicate story whose culture is part Japanese, part the world of the blind.

Elizabeth Winthrop has taken the magic of Kakuresato to create a glimmer of hope for the courage to face one's life, complete with all its advantages and disadvantages. This is not a hope for a cure for blindness, but hope for the courage to count one's blessings in the face of great adversity.

Though elegantly illustrated, this slim volume is not a picture book. The illustrations are drawings done in black and white in Japanese wood-block fashion with flowing lines and Japanese perspective, balancing large sections of black with large sections of white. They greatly enhance the story, adding character, charm, and delicacy to the already tender tale. GINNY LEE

Sundiata: Lion King of Mali

David Wisniewski
African, Mali
1992, Clarion, Houghton Mifflin Company

The story of Sundiata, king of medieval Mali, is a dramatic and exciting tale that has been passed down through the centuries by the griots (greeohs), oral historians of West Africa.

Sundiata's story is inspiring. Before becoming the undisputed ruler of Mali, he has to overcome physical hardships and court intrigue. His early years are marked by the scorn of his relatives and the derision of members of his father's court, who mock him for being unable to walk or talk. Sundiata eventually conquers his physical ailments and perseveres, only to have to flee his country when threatened by his stepmother and her allies, who have placed Sundiata's half-brother on the throne after the boys' father dies.

A centuries-old tale of medieval Africa, with excellent cut-paper illustrations.

Under the tutelage of his wise mother, Sogolon, and the king of the city-state of Mema (who later makes Sundiata his heir), Sundiata bides his time and learns how to rule a kingdom. When the evil sorcerer-king Sumanguru invades Mali, messengers from his late father's kingdom come to Sundiata begging him to return home and save his country. In dramatic fashion, Sundiata meets and defeats Sumanguru on the battlefield, then assumes his father's throne and the loyalty and love of his people.

This retelling by David Wisniewski is particularly memorable for its attractive cut-paper illustrations, which make the book a visual treat for young readers or listeners.

The lion Wisniewski has put on this banner symbolizes Sundiata, the king. Sundiata's father is also compared to the lion and his mother to a strong and courageous buffalo. *Students can imagine which animal they would compare themselves to and why and they can make cut-paper illustrations of their chosen animals. If the students do their work on nine-inch squares of construction paper, the squares can later be joined together to form a quilt to display proudly at school. Students' descriptions of their squares can be bound together to form a museum catalog to hang next to the quilt.* SANDRA KELLY

Ashok by Any Other Name

Sandra W. Yamate   Janice Tohinaka
Asian American, East Indian
1994 (1992), Carolrhoda Books

Ashok is a winsome young boy of East Indian descent who wants to belong but whose name sets him apart in an American classroom. He decides to change it. He tries Tom, but there are four other Toms in class. He tries Walter, but forgets to answer to it. He settles on Frances, only to find a girl in class with that name.

One day he talks with the African American librarian in his school who tells of his own "ever-so-great-grandfather" who came here as a slave and was not allowed to keep his own name. They discuss the implications of this name-stealing and Ashok decides to keep his own name. There is an endpaper note on the life of the great Indian king, Ashoka, who believed in nonviolence and ruled wisely for thirty-seven years during the third century B.C.

An East Indian immigrant tries to change his name, but then learns to take pride in it.

The subject matter is relevant to the many diverse students whose names seem "different" to Anglo Americans. The pastel illustrations are simple enough to have been drawn by any artistic young student, and they show flesh shades of tans and browns. *The book is an excellent model to encourage children to write and illustrate picture books reflecting their own experiences.*

Though the author is not East Indian, the acknowledgments in the preface name several East Indian American people as sources of information. GLORIA D. JACKSON

Are Mexican American Females Portrayed Realistically in Fiction for Grades K-3?: A Content Analysis

Osbelia Juárez Rocha and Frances Smardo Dowd

RESEARCH CONFIRMS THAT MULTICULTURAL materials do affect children's attitudes, achievements, and concepts.[1,2] The value of utilizing books to foster cultural awareness and appreciation, therefore, is particularly effective. Contrary to the "color blind" ideology, children develop an awareness of cultural and physical characteristics among people at a very early age, and they do so more by exposure to prevailing community attitudes about other racial groups than by immediate contact with their members.[3,4]

Forming a positive cultural/racial identity can be especially difficult for young Mexican American girls. As "minorities," Mexican American girls may learn not to expect to see themselves reflected in the world around them, so they may assume that the dominant culture is "best." In addition, studies have shown that sex-role concepts and gender stereotyping, influenced by societal standards and the familial environment, are evident in children as young as two.[5,7] It is not surprising, then, that inaccurate stereotypic and caricatured portrayals of cultural/racial groups are particularly harmful during the developmental stage when children are forming clear concepts of themselves and others.[8] To avoid this potential harm, "we must foster a children's literature that turns the diverse raw material of life into artistic products which…celebrate the dignity…of other people and their cultures."[9] Yet few realistic books for young children depict female characters of Mexican descent. Moreover, a thorough search of professional literature in the fields of both education and library science revealed only one study, now almost twenty-five years old, that investigated the extent of authenticity or stereotyping of Mexican American characters in children's books.[10] D. K. Gast concluded that inaccurate, oversimplified views of this group existed, citing Mexican Americans portrayed in the titles analyzed as living in barrios, as shopkeepers, and dressed in ethnic garb. Because of the lack of recent research regarding the image of females of Mexican descent in children's literature, a content analysis was warranted.

METHODOLOGY

The major purpose of this study was to investigate the portrayal of Mexican American females in fiction appropriate for children in kindergarten through third grade. Secondary purposes were to determine (1) whether a difference exists in the portrayal of Mexican American girls and women in fiction published from 1950 to 1969 and that published from 1970 to 1990; (2) characteristics of Mexican Americans revealed in these books; and (3) what, if any, stereotypes of the Mexican American culture these books convey.

SAMPLE

The following five procedures identified sixty titles containing Latino/a characters. First, retrospective and recent catalogs from eighteen of the leading children's book publishers (Atheneum; Bantam; Collier, Greenwillow; Harcourt Brace; HarperCollins; Houghton Mifflin; Lothrop, Lee & Shephard; Morrow; and Random House, among them) and seven small/ethnic presses (Children's Book Press, Fielding Publications, Lectorium Publications,

Multnomah, and Santillana, for example) were examined for potential titles. Second, reference works were checked (such as *A to Zoo, A Guide to Children's Picture Books, Best Books for Children: Preschool through Middle Grades, The Best in Children's Books; The University of Chicago Guide to Children's Literature 1966-1972, Bookfinder; A Guide to Children's Literature About the Needs and Problems of Youth Aged 2-15, Guide to Non-Sexist Children's Books, Latino Materials: A Multimedia Guide for Children and Young Adults, Picture Books for Children, The Southwest: Reading for Young People,* and *Subject Guide to Children's Books in Print*).[11-19]

Next, periodical articles were examined (such as "Ethnic Groups in Children's Books: Hispanics," "Recent Children's Books About Hispanics," "Recent Outstanding and Ordinary Books about Mexico, Mexicans, and Mexican Americans," "Using Books to Help Teachers and Children Develop Multicultural Awareness").[20-23] Fourth, titles were requested through interlibrary loans from Electric Paso Public Library, a facility serving primarily Mexican Americans due to its location near the U.S./Mexican border. Last, holdings were checked to communities with large Mexican American populations: Martin Luther King Center, a federally funded library program operated through the Emily Fowler Public Library in Denton, Texas; Diamond Hill-Jarvis Branch Library in Diamond Hill, a suburb of Fort Worth, Texas; George and Helen Mahon Public Library in Lubbock, Texas; Ector County Public Library in Odessa, Texas; and Abilene Public Library in Abilene, Texas) as well as the School of Library and Information Studies libraries at both the University of North Texas and Texas Woman's University. The library at Texas Woman's University includes the 25,000 volume Hispanic Heritage Collection titled Proyecto LEER, an acronym for Libros Elementales Educativos Recreativos (Essential, Educational, Entertaining Books). Proyecto LEER represents the first evaluation and research center in library education focusing on the information needs of American Latinos/as and includes children's materials in both English and Spanish published in Latin America, Spain, and the United States.[24]

Since the study undertaken pertained only to stories set in the United States with female characters of Mexican descent, twenty-nine of the sixty titles identified by the procedures described above were eliminated either because all the characters were males; all the female characters were of Cuban, Puerto Rican, or Spanish descent; the settings were in countries other than the United States; or the books were not written solely in English, but rather were bilingual. Two of the thirty-one remaining titles were utilized to test the evaluative instrument.

The final sample of twenty-nine titles, which contained only one book written by a Mexican American (De León's *I Will Catch the Sun*), consisted of the following: one title from the 1950s, eight from the 1960s, twelve from the 1970s, and eight from the 1980s. Three multiracial titles by V. B. Williams from the latter time period include Latina characters whose ethnic group is not specifically described, but who, for the purpose of this study, were assumed to be Mexican Americans. Implementation of these procedures for the sample selection revealed that few books about Mexican Americans have been published by the major presses. No titles with a 1990 copyright date were identified.

EVALUATIVE INSTRUMENT

The primary sources used to develop the evaluative instrument, in addition to personal experience, were *Analyzing Children's Books From a Chicago Perspective* (Uribe and Martinez) and *Resource Materials for the Creative Curriculum* (with Special Articles on Evaluating the Black and Hispanic Image in Children's Books) (Frisby).[25,26] Evaluation included elements from seven categories—plot, setting, theme, point of view, style of writing, characterization, and special features—and was designed to analyze both text and illustrations. The instrument was revised according to recommendations from three validators knowledgeable in children's literature and familiar with the Mexican American culture. The final evaluative instrument was coded, when applicable, to differentiate between components used to analyze characteristics (C) and those that examine potential stereotypes (S). For example, with regard to plot, the term dealing with stereotypes (S) was

fiestas, while the following were specific phrases pertaining to characteristics (C): religious faith, superstition, preoccupation with contemporary concerns, and involvement in politics.

DESCRIPTION OF MEXICAN AMERICAN CULTURE AND EXPLANATION FOR CODING EVALUATIVE INSTRUMENT

Some Mexican Americans who have lived away from the *barrio* have been embarrassed about the prevailing Mexican stereotypes in their predominantly white neighborhoods, and they have suppressed their language and culture in order to gain acceptance. These Americans are now realizing that "assimilation doesn't have to mean homogenization." As a result, they are making a conscious effort to rediscover various aspects of their culture. For some this may mean celebrating *quinceañeras* (parties for a girl's coming of age on her fifteenth birthday), *dia de los muertos* (November 2; commemoration of the dead that combines pre-Columbian and Spanish customs with contemporary U.S. Halloween celebrations), *diez y seis de septiembre* (September 16; commemoration of Mexico's independence from Spain in 1821); or *Cinco de Mayo* (May 5; commemoration of the Mexican army's victory over the French in Puebla, Mexico, in 1862); for others it may entail sharing cultural experiences with Anglo friends.[27]

If children's books are to represent authentically the Mexican American lifestyle, they should reflect contemporary life in the United States; which means that characters from other racial/ethnic groups are also depicted. Realistic titles should also portray variety in Mexican American families in terms of number of children and income (rather than depicting solely large, impoverished Mexican American families with two parents).[28] Books for children set in the United States, where females are often assertive and are achieving parity with their male counterparts, should include Mexican American female characters from all age groups in diversified roles, such as members of team sports or the school's Mariachi band. Women from the same ethnic group could be presented not only in traditional roles (cooking or keeping house) but also in nontraditional roles (such as a school P.T.A. official, police officer, mail carrier, or

55

56

lawyer), since many females of Mexican descent do indeed hold such positions.

COMPARATIVE FINDINGS AND DISCUSSION

This section describes the findings from the content analysis of the nine books for grades K-3 published from 1950–1969 as compared to the findings from the twenty titles published from 1970–1990. After each general statement, specific examples from sample books are provided to illustrate and substantiate the conclusions. In addition, available findings from research about culture are discussed to provide a factual basis for the designation of "stereotypes" for this group.

CHARACTERIZATION

Comparatively speaking, the image of the female of Mexican descent presented in fiction for grades K-3 published since 1970 is considerably more authentic than previously published work. Almost all of the components designated by a (C) code show a positive percentage of net change, while almost every component designated by an (S) has a negative percentage of net change. For example, from 1950–1969 to 1970–1990 the portrayal of females of Mexican descent as strong and enduring increased by 16 percent, while the weak/docile image decreased by 5 percent. Similarly, authors in the latter time frame more frequently depict these females as employed (although none were found to be working in professional positions), respecting elders, attending school/receiving an education, and serving as leaders in school or the community, while they less frequently portray girls and women of Mexican descent as emotional, present-oriented, wearing a traditional Mexican hairstyle or dress, and submitting to gender subordination.

Research confirms the fact that at least some of the stereotypical (S) Mexican American traits above have no factual basis. For example, Trambley found evidence to disprove the misconception that this group is by nature/culture present-oriented and incapable of delaying gratification.[29] Furthermore, Mirande concluded that a significant trait of women of Mexican descent was their strength and endurance, in contrast to their stereotypical depictions as weak

and submissive.[30] The absence of portrayals of Mexican American women in professional positions also belies census data which indicate that as many as 29 percent of Mexican Americans (and surely women account for a portion of this percentage!) hold professional positions. Adams's *Fidelia* (1970) illustrates several of the above-mentioned comparative changes in the portrayal of Mexican American females in fiction for young children. The title character, Fidelia, is depicted as a leader because she asks for admittance to the school orchestra, even though second graders had not been allowed to join in the past. Fidelia shows strength/endurance by making her own violin from a cigar box and practicing in preparation for the all-city tryouts. After crashing into the instruments in the orchestra room, she faces Miss Toomey with downcast eyes (respect for elders). Although Fidelia wears Mexican braids, she does not wear traditional Mexican clothing. Her ability to delay the gratification of being in the special orchestra illustrates that she is not present-oriented.

In *A Chair for My Mother* (Williams, 1982), Mama is employed as a waitress; she also exhibits tremendous strength/endurance in managing to cope with the devastation of losing every possession in an apartment fire. The Mexican American mothers in *Victor* (Galbraith, 1971) and *I Speak English for My Mom* (Stanek, 1989) enroll in night classes to learn English to end dependence upon family members to interpret what doctors or others say.

The one exception to the generalization that stereotypes (S) have decreased in the past twenty years pertains to involvement in music/dancing, which occurs more frequently now. This increase may be due to the fact that Mexican Americans are rediscovering cultural traditions (such as Mexican holiday celebrations) lost in the process of assimilation.[31] The many guests of José and María in Bolognese's *A New Day* (1970) love music and dancing so much that they celebrate the birth of a child by creating their own song and dancing in the street.

The sole exception to the generalization that characteristics (C) have decreased in titles since 1970 regards the female serving as a leader in the home. This trait is seen less often now, but it is evident in *I Speak English for My Mom*.

Lupe Gomez takes on a leadership role at home by helping her mother make payments on payday, interpreting when necessary, and encouraging her mom to seek a better-paying job to make ends meet.

PLOT

Several specific findings indicate that the contemporary portrayal of females of Mexican descent is still somewhat stereotypical. Not only are fiestas/celebrations (S) more often a part of plots now than in the 1950–1969 time period, but there is also a 17 percent decrease in the presentation of information about contemporary concerns/activities of Mexican Americans (C).

Taylor's *The Corn Festival* (1971) incorporates information about realistic Mexican American issues (unfavorable living conditions and ethnic discrimination) as well as a fiesta (the Annual Street Corn Festival). When Grandmother King says that Felipe and his people are "just some of the migrants from the canning company" and blocks their view by placing her stool in front of them, she is rejecting members of this cultural group.

Neither *Where Is María?* (Gunther, 1979) nor *A New Day* (Bolognese, 1970), however, touches upon any contemporary activities or concerns of Mexican Americans. The only concern of the characters in the former title is finding a lost Mexican American girl at a street fair; the latter book deals primarily with the celebration following the birth of a child.

Since the content analysis also revealed that no sample books from any decade included politics (C), the image of females of Mexican descent in the plots of these books did not change. Becerra found Mexican Americans to be markedly involved in the political process, so this topic should be mentioned in at least one recent title so that this group's presentation in literature would be more realistic.[32] Perhaps the topic of politics was omitted for developmental reasons; the target age group for the books analyzed would be too young to understand the abstract concept of political affiliations.

Inclusion of expressions of religious faith (C) in the sample books decreased by 8 percent in the more recent time period, in comparison to the titles published in the 1950–1969 era, thus making the overall portrait of females of Mexican heritage less genuine. One example of a current title that does deal with religion, however, is *María's Grandma Gets Mixed Up* (Sanford, 1989). María prays to God daily to help her understand what is happening to her grandmother who has Alzheimer's disease.

THEME

The portrayal of Mexican American girls and women in relation to themes has become more realistic in the past twenty years. Later-era authors have written books with themes related to Mexican history (brief stories, including lessons in Mexican culture and Mexico's past), helping/sharing (promoting the concept of assisting others, especially family members), goals or dreams (having aspirations of achieving success in some form), noncultural differences (conflict resulting from something other than intolerance of another person's culture), the need for privacy (living conditions that allow individuals some personal space), satisfaction with life/self (contentment with lifestyle, achievements, financial situation, and so on), and acculturation (assimilating or adapting to the dominant cultural group's way of life). Previously these themes were not addressed at all.

This last theme is depicted in *Mexican Soup* (Hitte and Hayes, 1970). Mama, proud of her heritage, finds assimilation difficult when her family leaves "the mountains of the West for the city where people live differently." The family pleads with Mama to cook like other Americans instead of using spicy ingredients.

The focus of Politi's *Three Stalks of Corn* (1976) is a grandmother's concern for inculcating Mexican history and cultural traditions in her grandchild, Angélica. Helping/sharing takes place twice in *A Gift for Tía Rosa* (Taha, 1986). The Mexican American protagonist shares her time and talent to teach Carmelita to knit; but when Tía Rosa dies, Carmelita, feeling that a person's kindness should be passed on instead of returned, decides to finish the quilt Tía Rosa was knitting for her grandchild. McInnes' *How Pedro Got His Name* (1974) centers upon a Mexican American boy who works at a shoe repair shop to fulfill his dream of purchasing a particular puppy from a pet shop.

57

Satisfaction with life is identifiable in *Music, Music for Everyone* (Williams, 1984). When Rosa plays her accordion with her friends in the Oak Street Band to earn money to help her mother with expenses for her sick grandmother, she realizes that sharing brings satisfaction and happiness for all. Themes unrelated to and independent of Mexican American culture (that is, noncultural differences) are recognizable in both *Where Is María?* (Gunther, 1979) and *María and Mr. Feathers* (Kimball, 1982). In the former title, children find their lost friend at the street fair and learn that helping others can be fun. In the latter title, María wishes she were a pirate so that no one would tell her what to do; the theme is that merely wishing for the impossible will not change anything. The actions/messages of neither book are limited to Mexican American culture.

Other terms or phrases used in themes of books include: English (referring to problems arising from a character's inability to speak English), familism (alluding to the great importance of the family to its members or to members of the extended family), life's prerequisites (describing requirements that must be fulfilled in order to reach a goal, such as the minimum age requirement for obtaining a driver's license), material goods (suggesting that the character is concerned with obtaining tangible possessions), nature (relating to a preoccupation with the outdoors and with elements of nature), and personality (referring to the importance of having a pleasant attitude/outlook).

POINT OF VIEW

More recent sample books analyzed indicate a departure from gender stereotyping, and this change adds to the stories' realism and gives due credit to the female characters. One-fourth of the authors from the 1970–1990 time frame relate their stories from a Mexican American female's perspective, in contrast to the period from 1950–1969, in which none of the titles is narrated by a girl or woman of Mexican heritage. In *Something Special for Me* (Williams, 1983), Rosa relates how she selected an accordion as a birthday present. In *María's Grandma Gets Mixed Up* (Sanford, 1989), the protagonist tells about family life when a relative has a disease that causes strange behavior.

SETTING

Initially, the presentation of females of Mexican descent seems less realistic and less believable because there appears to be an inaccurate imbalance between the percentage of Mexican American characters residing in barrios or lower-class neighborhoods (60 percent) and the percentage living in middle-class neighborhoods (25 percent). Both categories show a net gain: 16 percent and 3 percent, respectively. Moreover, stories analyzed from both time periods are totally void of characters of Mexican descent residing in upper-class neighborhoods. While the above-described fictional situation may appear to convey incorrectly the socioeconomic status of this group, it should be noted that the National Council of La Raza, after examining census data and national studies, found the following distressing trends among Latino/a families: (1) this was the only ethnic group showing no improvement in socioeconomic status between 1980 and 1990; (2) compared with Anglos of similar educational levels, Latinos/a with four years of high school were 2.3 times as likely to be poor in 1988; and (3) Latino/a children represent 11 percent of U.S. children but 21 percent of U.S. children living in poverty.[33]

In *Just for Manuel* (Hampton, 1971), a large family lives in a lower-class neighborhood in an apartment so crowded that Manuel wishes for a place to call his own where he can play by himself. Sonneborn's *Friday Night Is Papá Night* (1970) is also set in a lower-class area; Pedro sleeps in the kitchen of his family's small apartment. Josefina and her mother live in an urban, racially mixed, middle-class environment with contemporary apartment buildings in Bunting's *Josefina Finds the Prince* (1976).

Comparatively speaking, there has been a substantial net increase in percentage (21 percent) in the past twenty years of stories portraying Mexican American characters living in contemporary dwellings, accompanied by a decrease in the depiction of typical lower-class homes (that is, subsidized housing, -6 percent; mobile homes/trailers, -11 percent; crowded quarters, -11 percent; and, in some cases, old-fashioned dwellings, -18 percent).

STYLE OF WRITING

The components of writing style considered in this study include use of "standard" English (conventional English-language usage); use of stilted-sounding language (unnatural or awkward-sounding language, such as sentences with repetitive phrases that sound like beginning readers); use of Mexican American language style (direct translations that result in incorrect adjective and noun order, such as "the red dress" translated to *el rojo vestido* instead of *el vestido rojo*; language that includes a Spanish/English mixture, such as "Es que I don't like that type of dress"); use of language that demeans the user (stilted Mexican American language style); explanation in the text for Spanish terms (inclusion in the same sentence or paragraph of the definitions of Spanish terms used); and use of symbolism.

The style of writing has improved somewhat during the past twenty years. But in a more recent book, *Roland's Grandfather's Stories from México* (1986), the dialogue is awkward and the language sounds stilted, condescending, and childish: "They dress just like you and they play games just like you…[and they] go to school just like you do."

SPECIAL FEATURES

Although of minimal significance in fiction and representative of only a nominal number of books, special features were also considered in this study, and there is a slight improvement in quality in this category. The inclusion of a glossary of Spanish terms (in *Victor*), a note acknowledging the author's relevant experiences (in *Three Stalks of Corn*), and/or recipes for Mexican foods (also in the latter title), is seen in the sample books published since 1970. These features are assets because they provide cross-cultural access points for teachers and librarians, and they may be of particular interest and value for children unfamiliar with Mexican American language or culture.

CONCLUSIONS AND IMPLICATIONS FOR PRACTITIONERS

The primary conclusion from the study findings is that the portrayal of women and girls of Mexican descent in fiction for children in kindergarten through third grade has improved since 1970. Female images are now less stereotypical and more accurately reflect contemporary demographic and research data. For a more authentic representation of females of this cultural group, however, additional improvement is needed. In particular, women and girls of Mexican heritage need to be depicted more often as leaders in homes and professional positions and less often as emotional, present-oriented, and "frivolous" (partying with music/dancing). Plots should contain fewer fiestas and more information regarding the religious faith, politics, and contemporary activities/concerns of this cultural group. At least some percentage of Mexican Americans should be portrayed in upper-class neighborhoods.

The major implication from these findings is that school library media practitioners and teachers still need to be critical in selecting even recent fiction depicting females of Mexican descent, so as not to condone the remaining stereotypes and inaccuracies these books contain. Another implication, based upon the process of sample selection for this research rather than from the content analysis, is that there is a pressing need to recruit authors of Mexican descent to write fiction for young children portraying their heritage. No titles published from 1990 or 1991 that met the criteria specified for inclusion in this study could be identified.

RECOMMENDATIONS FOR FURTHER RESEARCH

This content analysis could serve as a springboard for other studies about children's literature depicting Mexican Americans, especially in light of the scarcity of research on the topic. A representative sample of Mexican Americans and of Anglo females could be surveyed or interviewed to determine their perceptions about the extent to which female characters in these same books are accurately or stereotypically portrayed. Results could be analyzed separately by ethnicity to learn if the groups have significantly different perceptions.

This study could be replicated by using the same evaluative instrument but selecting a sample of books for older children. Researchers also could adapt the evaluative instrument as needed to investigate another ethnic/cultural group infrequently represented in realistic fiction for children, such as Native Americans or Vietnamese.

Others could design and conduct experimental studies by sharing the books in this sample with young Mexican American and Anglo children to determine whether such exposure/immersion contributes to a change in attitude about this cultural group, and, if so, whether the modification is positive or negative.

REFERENCES

1. P. Campbell and J. Wittenberg. "How Books Influence Children: What the Research Shows," *Interracial Books for Children Bulletin* 11:6 (1980): 3-6.

2. D. Milner, "Are Multicultural Classroom Materials Effective?" *Interracial Books for Children Bulletin* 12:4 (1981): 9-10.

3. "Racism in Children's Books: A Report on the Arnoldshain Conference." *Interracial Books for Children Bulletin* 10: 1&2 (1979): 4-8.

4. Mary Ellen Goodman. *Race Awareness in Young Children* (New York, N.Y.: Collier, 1952).

5. B. I. Fagot and M. D. Leinbach. "The Young Children's Gender Schema: Environmental Input, Internal Organization. *Child Development* 60 (June 1989): 663-73.

6. G. Cowan and C. Hoffman. "Gender Stereotyping in Young Children: Evidence to Support a Concept Learning Approach." *Sex Roles* 14 (February 1986): 211-24.

7. I. Collins, B. Ingoldsby, and M. Dellman. "Sex-Role Stereotyping in Children's Literature: A Change from the Past." *Childhood Education* 60 (March/April), 1984): 278-85.

8. Louise Derman-Sparks, Carol Tanaka Higa, and Bill Sparks. "Children, Race and Racism: How Race Awareness Develops," *Interracial Books for Children Bulletin* 11: 3&4 (1980): 3-9.

9. J. St. Clair. "Recreating Black Life in Children's Literature," *Interracial Books for Children Bulletin* 19:3&4 (1989): 7-11.

10. D. K. Gast. "Minority Americans in Children's Literature. *Elementary English* 44 (January 1967):12-23.

11. C. W. Lima and J. A. Lima, eds. *A to Zoo: Subject Access to Children's Picture Books*, 3rd ed. (New York N.Y.: R. R. Bowker, 1989).

12. J. T. Gillespie and C. B. Gilbert, eds. *Best Books for Children: Preschool through Middle Grades*. (New York, N.Y.: R. R. Bowker, 1985).

13. Z. Sutherland, ed. *The Best in Children's Books: The University of Chicago Guide to Children's Literature 1966-1972* (Chicago: University of Chicago Press, 1973).

14. S. S. Dreyer. *The Bookfinder: A Guide to Children's Literature About the Needs and Problems of Youth Aged 2-15* (Circle Pines, MN: American Guidance Service, 1977).

15. J. Adel and H. D. Klein, comps. *A Guide to Non-Sexist Children's Books* (Chicago, Ill.: Academy Press Limited, 1976).

16. D. F. Duran. *Latino Materials: A Multimedia Guide for Children and Young Adults* (New York, N.Y.: Neal Schuman Publishers, 1979).

17. P. J. Cianciolo, ed. *Picture Books for Children* (Chicago, Ill.: American Library Association, 1973).

18. E. A. Harmon and A. L. Milligan. *The Southwest: Reading for Young People* (Chicago, Ill.: American Library Association, 1982).

19. L. N. Gerhardt, ed. *Subject Guide to Children's Books in Print: A Subject Index to Children's Books* (1984 to 1989 eds.), (New York, N.Y.: R. R. Bowker, 1984-1990).

20. L. Y. Zwick and M. M. Salinas. "Ethnic Groups in Children's Books: Hispanics," *Booklist* 83 (June 1987): 1611-1612.

21. I. Schon. "Recent Children's Books about Hispanics." *Journal of Youth Services in Libraries* 2 (Winter 1989): 157-161.

22. I. Schon. "Recent Outstanding and Ordinary Books about Mexico, Mexicans, and Mexican-Americans," *Top of the News* 41 (Fall 1984): 61-64.

23. F. Smardo and V. Schmidt. "Using Books to Help Teachers and Children Develop Multicultural Awareness," *The Southeastern Librarian* 34 (Summer 1984): 47-51.

24. "Proyecto LEER" flyer. (Denton, Tex: Texas Woman's University, no date).

25. Oscar Uribe and Joseph S. Martinez. *Analyzing Children's Books from a Chicano Perspective*, (Washington, DC: National Institute of Education, ERIC Document Reproduction Service No. ED 129 458, 1975).

26. Deborah Frisby. *Resource Materials for the Creative Curriculum* (with Special Articles on Evaluating the Black and Hispanic Image in Children's Books), (Washington, DC: Creative Associates, Inc., ERIC Document Reproduction Service No. ED 194 219, 1979).

27. Gayle Reaves. "Renewing Cultural Ties: Many Hispanics are Rediscovering Mexican Heritage," *Dallas Morning News* (October 13, 1991): 35A.

28. L. Derman-Sparks and the A.B.C. Task Force, "Anti-Bias Curriculum: Tools for Empowering Young Children," (Washington, DC: National Association for the Education of Young Children, 1989).

29. J. P. Trambley. "Time Orientation and Delay of Gratification as a Function of Social Class in Mexican American and Anglo Adolescents," *Dissertation Abstracts International* DA 8916111, 50:4 (1989): 1639B.

30. A. Mirande. *The Chicano Experience: An Alternative Perspective* (Notre Dame, IN: University of Notre Dame Press, 1985).

31. *United States Bureau of the Census, Persons of Spanish Origin in the United States, March 1985*, Current Population Reports, Series P-20, No. 203 (Washington, DC: United States Government Printing Office, 1985).

32. R. M. Becerra. "The Mexican-American Family," *Ethnic Families in America: Patterns and Variations*, C. H. Mindel, R. W. Haberstein, and R. Wright, eds. (New York, N.Y.: Elsevier, 1988): 141-157.

33. Mercedes Olivera. "Hispanic Children at Risk: Poverty Statistics Indicate Dismal Future for Many," *Dallas Times Herald* (July 14, 1991): 34A.

APPENDIX A
Sample Titles Analyzed

1950 - 1959

FELT, S. *Rosa-Too-Little*. (Garden City, N.Y.: Doubleday and Co., 1950).

1960-1969

CLARK, A. N. *Tia Maria's Garden*. (New York: Viking Press, 1963).

ETS, M. H. *Bad Boy, Good Boy*. (New York: Thomas Y. Crowell, 1967).

FREEMAN, D. R. *A Home for Memo*. (Chicago: Elk Grove, Press, 1968).

GREENE, C. *Manuel: Young Mexican-American*. (New York: Lantern Press, 1969).

KRAMON, F. *Hipólito and Eugene G.* (Chicago: Follett, 1967).

LEXAU, J. M. *Maria*. (New York: Dial Press, 1964).

SCHWEITZER, B. B. *Amigo*. (Toronto, Ontario, Canada: Collier-Macmillan, 1963).

SONNEBORN, R. A. *Seven in a Bed*. (New York: Viking Press, 1968).

1970-1979

ADAMS, R. *Fidelia*. (New York: Lothrop, Lee & Shepard, 1970).

BOLOGNESE, D. A. *A New Day*. (New York: Delacorte Press, 1970).

BUNTING, E. *Josefina Finds the Prince*. (Champaign, Ill.: Garrard, 1976).

DE LEÓN, N. *I Will Catch the Sun*. (Lubbock, Tex.: Trucha Publications, 1973).

GALBRAITH, C. K. *Victor*. Boston: Little, Brown and Co., 1971.

GUNTHER, L. *Where Is Maria?* (Champaign, Ill.: Garrard, 1979).

HAMPTON, D. *Just for Manuel*. (Austin, Tex.: Steck-Vaughn, 1971).

HITTE, K., AND HAYES, W. D. *Mexicali Soup*. (New York: Parents Magazine Press, 1970).

MCINNES, J. *How Pedro Got His Name*. (Champaign, Ill.: Garrard, 1974).

POLITI, L. *Three Stalks of Corn*. (New York: Charles Scribner's Sons, 1976).

SONNEBORN, R. *Friday Night Is Papá Night*. (New York: Viking Press, 1970).

TAYLOR, F. W. *The Corn Festival*. (Minneapolis: Lerner Publications, 1971).

1980-1990

KIMBALL, H. *Maria and Mr. Feathers*. (Cleveland: Modern Curriculum Press, 1982).

ROLAND, D. *Grandfather Stories from Mexico*. (El Cajon, Cal.: Open My World Publishing, 1986).

SANFORD, D. *Maria's Grandma Gets Mixed Up*. (Portland: Multnomah, 1989).

STANEK, M. *I Speak English for My Mom*. (Niles, Ill.: Albert Whitman and Co., 1989).

TAHA, K. T. *A Gift for My Mother*. (New York: Dillon Press, 1986).

WILLIAMS, V. B. *A Chair for My Mother*. (New York: Mulberry Books, 1982).

———— *Something Special for Me*. (New York: Greenwillow Books, 1983).

———— *Music, Music for Everyone*. (New York: Greenwillow Books, 1984).

Osbelia Juárez Rocha, M.L.S., is a librarian at the Bowie Junior High School, Ector County Independent School District, in Odessa, TX. A frequent contributor to Multicultural Review, *she is listed in* Who's Who in American Education 1994-1995, 4th ed. *(Marquis, 1994).*

Frances Smardo Dowd, PH.D., is an associate professor at Texas Woman's University in the School of Library and Information Studies who teaches children's literature. Her article titled "An Annotated Bibliography: Recent Realistic Fiction and Information Books for Young Children Portraying Asian-American and Native American Cultures" appeared in the April 1992 issue of MultiCultural Review *(vol. 1, no. 2).*

61

Illustrating the Point: A Commentary on Multicultural and Stereotypic Picture Books

Donnarae MacCann

THE PICTURE BOOK IS BY DEFINITION A merger of two distinctive kinds of expression, the literary and the visual, requiring a harmonious relationship between picture and text.

While no general guideline for an artist is possible, there are features we should learn to look for in multicultural illustrations. For example, are the characters placed in subordinate roles? Are European features used for all ethnic groups?

Two-time Caldecott award-winner Leo Dillon notes that the challenges in picture books have gradually changed for him, moving him from a single-minded concern with the "slick and beautiful" to an interest in getting the "feeling across." With few exceptions, children's picture books about African Americans published prior to the civil rights movement are perhaps best characterized in Carole Parks's incisive comment, "Black youngsters who sought reflections of themselves or projections of what they could be were subjected to insignificant pickaninnies languishing contentedly on plantations, their past frozen in slavery." For example, in the 1940s, Little Brown Koko "wasn't studying a lick, for he was so sleepy he could hardly hold his big round eyes open." Only when his "big, ole, good, fat black Mammy" came to school did the protagonist begin to study "for dear life." Images of Asians, Hispanics, and Native Americans were likewise stereotypically skewed in books such as Claire Bishop's *The Five Chinese Brothers*; Marie Ets's, *Bad Boy, Good Boy*; and Walter D. Edmonds's *The Matchlock Gun*.

In the early 1960s, through the creative and political insight of individual writers and illustrators, sometimes working with mimeographs and publishing with small independent presses (such as Lollipop Power Press, Third World Press, and Drum and Spear Press), new images of African Americans and Puerto Ricans began to appear in literature from the new Freedom Schools. The Freedom Schools had been organized by young civil rights workers as a way to stop the miseducation of children of color. The literature written to support the teaching in these schools retold old stories and offered new ones that communicated some of the most important goals of the civil rights movement—the ability of people of color to see, embrace, and own their history, beauty, and power. Such tests include *Puerto Rico: Our People's History* by Orlando Ortiz, and *Our Folktales*, a privately printed book compiled by Julius Lester, edited by Mary Varela, and illustrated by Jennifer K. Lawson, whose work inspired later groundbreaking illustrators such as John Steptoe, Leo and Diane Dillon, and Tom Feelings.

Steptoe went on to become a bold experimenter, exploring highly innovative uses of materials and techniques in such books as *Mother Crocodile* and *Story of Jumping Mouse*. The Dillons gained early recognition as designer/decorators noted for their unique blends of realistic portraiture and original, jewel-like abstractions. Their embellishments are particularly effective in *Who's in Rabbit's House*, where the story is formulated as a staged event with animals in decorative masks, and in the stunning black-and-white patterns for the African tale, "The Song of the Boat." Feelings distinguished himself as a sensitive portrait painter. In *Soul Looks Back in Wonder*, for instance, he creates monumental, three-dimensional portraits and draws upon the African experience in his abstract textile patterns and vast African landscapes.

These artists tend to emphasize emotion over technique. Feelings treats as a maxim the comment by early twentieth-century African American artist Aaron Douglas that "the artist's technique, no matter how brilliant it is, should never obscure his vision."

Artists who followed this group in the 1970s and beyond maintained high standards in both areas: technical expertise and aesthetic sensitivity or vision. The physicality of black people, was, for instance, redefined by these standard bearers; Feelings's portraits depicted broad noses, night-dark skin, and coarse-curly hair with a beauty heretofore unseen. The deep skin tones ridiculed in books like *Little Brown Koko*, *Little Black Sambo*, and *Jake and Honeybunch Go to Heaven* are a positive trait in Steptoe and Dillon books.

By the time the New York Public Library issued its 1984 and 1989 editions of *The Black Experience in Children's Literature*, the list included works by about two dozen black illustrators, and the number has increased noticeably in the 1990s. Some world-famous artists are accessible to the young through the picture book: Jacob Lawrence, whose work has most recently been made available to children in *John Brown: One Man Against Slavery*; Romare Bearden, whose collages and paintings have been compiled in *I Live in Music* in conjunction with a poem by Ntozake Shange; Faith Ringgold, whose *Tar Beach* includes reproductions of some of her well-known pieces of quilt art; and Elizabeth Catlett, whose bold linocuts enhance *Lift Every Voice and Sing* (the African American national anthem with words from a poem by James Weldon Johnson). Black artists who are known to picture book specialists include Carole Byard, Jerry and Brian Pinkney, Will Clay, Floyd Cooper, Moneta Barnett, Pat Cummings, Jan Spivey Gilchrist, James Ransome, Amos Ferguson, Kathleen Atkins Wilson, Ashley Bryan, and Jonathan Green.

With the coming together of statistical research, political pressure, newly available federal dollars, and the "Black Is Beautiful" movement in the late 1960s, the stage was set for groundbreaking works including Steptoe's *Stevie* in 1969, writer and poet Lucille Clifton's *Some of the Days of Everett Anderson*, illustrated by Evaline Ness, in 1970, and Eloise Greenfield's *Bubbles*, illustrated by Eric Marlow,

in 1972. All were pioneering books in ethnic and racial inclusiveness. *Bubbles* was the first picture book done by Drum and Spear Press, and sold between 4,000 and 5,000 copies during the first two years of its release. (It was subsequently reissued under the title *Good News* with illustrations by Pat Cumings and Coward McCann in 1977.)

After *Bubbles*, Greenfield would take her commitment a step further with the inclusion of an affable disabled girl pictured in a wheelchair in her 1980 picture book *Darlene*. One of the earliest picture books to include a child with a physical disability, *Darlene* shows a young girl who is not greatly impeded by her use of a wheelchair, and who is notably lacking in self-pity and self-rejection.

In examining cultural inclusiveness in the field of picture books since the civil rights movement, it is important to look at how certain organizations and mindsets have either sustained multiculturalism or proven counterproductive. Even as educators, sociologists, and librarians have worked to promote understanding and tolerance, old racial and cultural biases have reemerged.

At the forefront of multiculturalism, Interracial Books for Children (CIBC) made one of the earliest efforts to introduce African American graphic artists to the publishing world. Under the heading "Art Directors, Take Note," the work of Leo and Diane Dillon (an interracial couple) and Donald Crews was featured in the spring 1970 issue. The artwork on display in this feature revealed a rich source of new talent, but all too few of the featured artists made their way into the children's book field.

In 1969, four years after the founding of the Council, the Coretta Scott King Award was established through the initiative of publisher John Carroll and librarians Mable McKissick and Glyndon Greer. Named after the widow of civil rights leader and philosopher Dr. Martin Luther King, Jr., this prize originally was bestowed on a black author whose work was an "outstandingly inspirational contribution." In 1979, the award committee began to honor black illustrators. There was little hope that African American artists would receive the

63

recognition they deserved unless such a prize was established. Blacks, and other people of color, had essentially been locked out of the children's book world until civil rights pressure was applied to the publishing industry. With the creation of CIBC and the Coretta Scott King Award, two important changes came into play: organized political and educational opposition to the white supremacy myth in all its guises, and needed support and visibility for African American authors and artists. However, just as new flack and ethnic studies departments were causing near panic in academia with their demands for unbiased scholarship, so antiracist activism stirred a backlash in the well-established children's book institutions. The King Award was barely able to survive until it found a home in the Social Responsibility Roundtable of the American Library Association (ALA) in 1979. The award had been denied official status as an "ALA Award and had been refused listing as an ALA activity until the early 1980s. CIBC was under constant attack from the mainstream children's book press, the Children's Book Council, and various sections of ALA."

Organizations that began as part of the African American civil rights struggle often increased their scope to include the other traditionally oppressed "minorities": Asian, Hispanic, and Native American groups. CIBC opened its contest for unpublished minority writers to include all these ethnic populations. It established the Asian American Children's Book Project and similar task forces on Puerto Rican and Chicano books to evaluate current publishing practices. In 1978, The National Council of Teachers of English (NCTE) passed a resolution in support of authentic Native American literature at all grade levels. As part of NCTE's current "bibliographic series," a multicultural committee created a booklist covering material related to Hispanic Americans/Latinos, Native Americans, Asian Americans and African Americans. (See *Kaleidoscope*, edited by Rudine Sims Bishop.) The American Indian Library Association staged important conferences on children's books at conventions, including the now groundbreaking "'I' is not for Indian" confer-

ence in Atlanta in 1991. As a result of these concerned efforts, stereotyping came to be understood as an injustice to be opposed unconditionally.

Webster's Third International Dictionary defines a stereotype as "something repeated or reproduced without variation; something conforming to a fixed or general pattern and lacking individual distinguishing qualities, especially a standardized mental picture held in common by members of a group and representing an over-simplified opinion, affective attitude or critical judgment." The "mental picture" referred to here is transformed into a literal visual image in children's literature. And since stereotypes are created by groups of people, a stereotype has a political connotation; it serves perceived group interests. Well-worn images of lazy, dishonest, lustful, or exotic people of color depicted with exaggerated costumes or features served to reassure whites of their alleged superiority; the stereotype worked as an implicit rationalization for oppression.

The misrepresentation and misidentification of various cultures remain a problem in children's books even today. In the lavishly illustrated *Brother Eagle, Sister Sky: A Message from Chief Seattle*, the "message from the chief" actually was contrived by Euro-American writer Ted Perry. Illustrator Susan Jeffers clothes the Suquamish people in Lakota garments, and implies in her images that whites can ravish the land with impunity as long as they replant. Native peoples, who strive to maintain the natural balance, are not depicted as participants in the restoration work.

These are some of the flaws referred to in an interview with Naomi Caldwell-Wood, president of the American Indian Library Association. She also notes the way stereotypes still abound in the typical "Thanksgiving" book and the "playing Indian" book. Even sacred costumes are among the "play" clothes suggested in books about holidays (e.g., in Mary Anne Pilger's *Multicultural Projects Index: Things to Make and Do to Celebrate Festivals, Cultures, and Holidays Around the World*). The double standard here is obvious; European cultures are not the target of sacrilegious treatment. Children are not encouraged to play the part or dress up as nuns. And "playing" Jesus is relegated to Christian pageants.

Yet gains have been made. During the past decade, authors and illustrators from the various Native American nations have been increasingly participating in picture book making. Navaho artist Shonto Begay brings magical tonal qualities to *The Boy Who Dreamed of an Acorn* by Euro-American author Leigh Caster. Sometimes the text is from a Native American source and the artist is a non-Native. For example, Joseph Bruchac collaborated with Euro-American Susan L. Roth in *The Great Ball Game: A Muskogee Story*, Craig Kee Strete collaborated with Craig Brown in *Big Thunder Magic*, and Virginia Driving Hawk Sneve's *Dancing Tepees* is illustrated by Stephen Gammell. As noted above, such cross-cultural collaborations are becoming more commonplace.

Whether illustrators are members of a Native American nation or not, their visual stylistic features are sometimes borrowed from indigenous cultures, as when Graciela Carrillo draws upon Aztec motifs in *How We Came to the Fifth World/Como Vinimos al Quinto Mundo*. Similarly, Murv Jacob utilizes Southeastern Indian traditions in *How Turtle's Back Was Cracked*, Virginia A. Stroud demonstrates her Cherokee and Kiowa influences in *A Walk to the Great Mystery,* and Paul Goble's many books suggest decorative Plains Indian styles (e.g., *Iktomi and the Berries*). Arthur Dorros's *Tonight Is Carnival* uses reproductions of the actual *arpilleras* (a South American quilted art form) produced by an art cooperative: the *Club de Madres Virgen del Carmen* of Lima, Peru.

Giving Thanks (Lee and Low, 1995), a new picture book written by Tekaronianeken Jake Swamp of the Mohawk nation and illustrated by Erwin Printup, Jr., a Cayuga/Tuscarora painter, will do a great deal to redefine the meaning of Thanksgiving as rooted in the ancient Haudenosaunee Thanksgiving Address, which is recited at all gatherings of the six nations: Mohawk, Oneida, Onondaga, Cayuga, Seneca, and Tuscarora. Also of great benefit to multiculturalists is *Through Indian Eyes: The Native Experience in Books for Children* edited by Beverly Slapin and Doris Seale. This work, writes Caldwell-Wood, helps book specialists

"re-examine, understand, and identify stereotypes." It is a vital tool for evaluating both fiction and nonfiction.

Spanish-speaking American children have access to a greater number of picture books published in Spanish than in earlier decades, but, given the fact that two million children fit the "limited proficiency in English" category and 73 percent of these children have a competency in Spanish, more Spanish texts are needed. Hispanic children rarely see themselves in contemporary settings, or postindustrial worlds. What continues to dominate the market are stories about handicraft-makers (*Abuela's Weave*), shrewd barterers (*Saturday Sancocho*), or children who rescue an otherwise botched Christmas ceremony (*Carlos, Light the Farolito*).

A laudable exception is the Children's Book Press, a nonprofit educational press whose materials about Latino life have broken new ground. The founder, Harriet Rohmer, draws upon talents within a collective of women muralists in the San Francisco area, and also keeps alive the great tradition of Mexican mural art by recruiting important Mexican painters as illustrators. Bay area muralist Consuelo Mendez is the illustrator of the Puerto Rican legend, *Atariba and Niguayona*. Mendez is a striking colorist and bold designer in this tale of selfless love in a holistic universe. For a modern text, Rohmer adapted a production from Nicaraguan National Television: *Uncle Nacho's Hat*. In this comedy about well-meaning neighbors versus a wise child, illustrator Veg Reisberg uses a blend of naturalistic and flat poster styles. The Indian tradition undoubtedly inspired Enrique Flores, illustrator of a satisfying story about a triumphant farmer: *The Harvest Birds/Los Pajaros de la Cosecha*. And *The Woman Who Outshone the Sun* is the work of a well-known painter from Oaxaco, Fernanco Olivera.

While the Children's Book Press has been providing leadership in this field for more than a decade, other publishers also have started recruiting skilled Hispanic illustrators. Bridgewater Books commissioned Maria Antonia Ordonez for the boldly illustrated story, *The Red Comb*. Using vividly contrasting colors, Ordonez interprets pictorially a nineteenth-century Puerto Rican community that outwits a band of slave catchers. Francisco X. Mora gives Juan Tuza a convincing comic personality in *Juan Tuza and the Magic Pouch*, a book published by Highsmith Press.

The near absence of the modern Asian world in children's literature is a puzzling phenomenon. The emergence in the 1950s and 1960s of Japanese artist Taro Yashima, whose works, *Umbrella* and *Momo's Kitten*, received critical praise, is an exception. Such artists as Suekichi Akeka and Mitsumasa, Chihiro Iwasaki (illustrator of *The Fisherman Under the Sea*) and Yasuo Segawa (*The Witch's Magic Cloth*) are well-known in the West. Examples of books with a modern setting include Taro Gomi's *Coco Can't Wait*, Kiyonori Kaizuki's *A Calf Is Born* and Allen Say's *Grandfather's Journey* (a 1993 Caldecott winner).

An increasing number of books about World War II are now being issued with impressive, emotionally charged graphics: Norituki Ando illustrates the horror of the day the atomic bomb exploded in Hiroshima in *Shin's Tricycle*; and Ken Mochizuki depicts life in a Japanese internment camp in *Baseball Saved Us*, illustrated by Dom Lee. The all-Japanese American combat unit is featured in Mochizuki's *Heros*, also illustrated by Lee.

Among the Chinese artists, Ed Young is well-known for his 1990 Caldecott winner, *Lon Po Po: A Red-Riding Hood Story from China*, and for a long and distinguished career. Young often works on cross-cultural projects, one of the most distinguished being his artwork for Isaac Olaleye's *Bitter Bananas*, an original Nigerian story.

We cannot discount the impact the women's movement has had on picture books, especially during the 1970s and 1980s. The emergence of picture book biographies on Rosa Parks, Maria Tallchief, Fannie Lou Hamer, and Mother Jones, as well as feminist fairy tales and gay and lesbian stories, have become part of the genre. Picture books focusing on gender roles have also provided new images of boys, and John Steptoe's *My Special Best Words* addresses sexist stereotypes about girls and boys.

A continuing obstacle to intelligent, challenging multicultural work are the official standards for children's literary prizes, whose impact on sales are tremendous. The most well-known prize for illustration, the Caldecott Awards, often accounts for as many as 100,000 new copies being printed of a winning title. Additionally, a "best book" designation by the *New York Times* carries great weight. Clearly, books that receive this kind of promotion warrant serious analysis; their harmful social impact is undeniable if they stereotype a group or distort history. Several books featuring distorted portraits of African Americans are cases in point.

Rachel Isadora's *Ben's Trumpet*, a 1980 Caldecott Honor book, depicts a stereotypically dysfunctional black family. Critic Opal Moore sums up the book's symbolic message when she writes that "the entire family seems stratified and isolated from each other.... Even baby brother seems overwhelmed by the lethal lethargy...as he sits nude and unattended on a blanket."

Margot Zemach's *Jake and Honeybunch Go to Heaven*, A *New York Times* best book for 1982, is described by critic Nancy Arnez in *Crisis Magazine* as a work with "more of the demeaning derogatory, negative references and illustrations of black life than any children's story that I have ever read." The picture book author claimed that her intention was to give children aspects of black experience, but her images are actually carryovers from the minstrel stage and such white supremacist tracts as Roark Bradford's 1928 publication, *Ol' Man Adam an' His Chillun* (later reincarnated as *Green Pastures*, a play and film by Marc Connelly.)

In a similar misguided decision by the 1995 Caldecott jury, Eve Bunting's *Smoky Night* received the top award in 1995. The book reduces the 1992 Los Angeles rebellion to the work of "hooligans" in a disturbingly reactionary analysis. When such misrepresentations are given the stamp of approval by professionals, the miseducation of children and the decline of race relation continues.

The picture book lends itself to countless expressions of beauty, humor, ingenuity, and poignancy. For such a rich art form to be turned into a weapon against traditionally oppressed groups is untenable, but not unexpected. Institutional structures still provide support for racist practices, as when staffers at the ALA Office for Intellectual Freedom argue that the rejection of racist books denies children their rights or when the *Newsletter on Intellectuals Freedom* states: "Whether or not [a book] is guilty of racial stereotyping... is not for the librarian to judge." Such statements validate prejudice that begin in early childhood unless texts and illustrations receive our careful scrutiny and the benefit of our best thought. Anything less than this vigilance is an open invitation to those fear-driven adults who would pass racism along to upcoming generations.

Critics of multiculturalism sometimes charge that it is a subtle means of politicizing art. But we are naive if we have not noticed the connections among economic, political, and cultural institutions. African American author Eloise Greenfield echoes George Orwell in writing "it is true that politics is not art, but is political. Whether in its interpretation of the political realities, or in its attempts to ignore these reali-

ties...all art is political." Similarly, critic Addison Gayle sees no conflict between art and politics. He notes that "the true beauty of art is...in the potential of [a] particular work to make more meaningful and more beautiful the lives of people. This, of course, is the function of politics at its best." Moreover, "freedom for the writer is linked to freedom for [people]... Racial, social, and economic freedom...are prerequisites for human and artistic freedom." The opposite condition—liberty for some and denial of liberty for others—would hardly warrant the name "multiculturalism."

Donnarae MacCann earned a doctorate in American studies at the University of Iowa, where she is now a visiting assistant professor in the African America World Studies Program. She has been a children's librarian and has taught children's literature at UCLA, Virginia Tech, and the University of Kansas.

67

Grade Four to Grade Six

All the Colors of the Race: Poems

Arnold Adoff ✏John Steptoe

African American

1992 (1982), Beech Tree Books

All the Colors of the Race is a new collection from award-winning poet Arnold Adoff. The poems are about the many different ways people look—skin color, hair texture, facial features—and celebrates those differences as part of the beauty of our world. Mr. Adoff brings a particular perspective to this

An inviting book of poems that celebrates the beauty of people of all colors.

work. His personal life, as the husband of the African American author Virginia Hamilton, and the father of two biracial children, clearly serve as a catalyst for this work. (Mr. Adoff previously explored this subject in his book, *Black Is*

Brown Is Tan, which won the 1988 National Council of Teachers of English Award for Excellence in Poetry for Children.)

The illustrations by the late John Steptoe, an award-winning author and illustrator, are intense portraits of a young brown girl and her family. Mr. Steptoe uses only shades of brown, black, and white in his drawings, visually reinforcing each "piece" of the girl's world. (Steptoe was the recipient of two Caldecott Honor Awards, an ALA Notable Book Award, and a gold medal from the Society of Illustrators.)

All the Colors of the Race is an inviting collection of short poems delivered through the persona of a young biracial girl. The language honors the emotions and sensations that biracial, bicultural children experience when they begin to examine their family histories. Many of the poems are about discovery and acceptance, and they range from serious to highly amusing. In "Trilingual" the idea of

68

having to compartmentalize your ethnicity to fit others' expectations is perceptible in its simplicity. "I can talk black, and I can talk white, and I can talk so no one understands." Mr. Adoff uses clear, understandable language that doesn't force the young reader to wade through obscure symbolism.

Arnold Adoff also includes directions: "This book is a presentation of power and love. Celebrate the meaning and music of your lives. Stand free and take control." The book is dedicated to his children and every combination of races. Mr. Adoff's work will help deepen the understanding children and adults have about growing up biracial.
ROSA E. WARDER

My Black Me: A Beginning Book of Black Poetry

Arnold Adoff
African American
1995, Puffin, Sanchez, Sonia, *It's A New Day: Poems for Young Brothas and Sistuhs.*

Through poems like Langston Hughes's "My People," Bob O'Meally's "It Ain't No," Barbara Mahone's "What Color Is Black," and the spirited voices of twenty-three other African American poets, this rich treasury of words explores the black experience in America. First published in 1974, the book also contains Vanessa Howard's "Monument in Black," whose message of exploding black communities still resonates clearly twenty years later:

*Put my Black father on the penny
let him smile at me on the silver dime
put my mother on the dollar
for they've suffered for more than
three eternities of time
and all money can't repay.*

*Make a monument of my grandfather
let him stand in Washington
for he's suffered more than
three light years
standing idle in the dark
hero of wars that weren't begun.*

*Name a holiday for my brother
on a sunny day peaceful and warm
for he's fighting for freedom he
won't be granted
all my Black brothers in Vietnam
resting idle in unkept graves.*

Though many of the references are to times long gone, young readers will find real connections between the deferred dreams about which Langston Hughes wrote and the dreams that racism still puts on hold for so many children and young adults. *Many of these poems are also excellent points of departure for tracing important milestones in black American history; others will touch chords in all of us. Poetry remains a tool for engaging even the most reluctant reader, and many of the poems in this volume lend themselves to the same kind of rhythmic adaptation so popular in today's rap lyrics.*

The black experience is eloquently documented through poems by distinguished African American poets.

In this new edition of the book, Adoff has updated the biographical information on each poet and provided an index to authors and first lines of poems. As a recipient of the National Council of Teachers of English Award for Excellence in Poetry for Children, Adoff here sustains his reputation as one of the leading anthologizers in the country. DAPHNE MUSE

My Painted House, My Friendly Chicken, and Me

Maya Angelou Margaret Courtney-Clarke
African, Ndebele
1994, Clarkson Potter Publishers

In *My Painted House, My Friendly Chicken, and Me,* Maya Angelou skillfully introduces us to the Ndebele culture of South Africa through the eyes and words of Thandi, an eight-year-old Ndebele girl.

Thandi invites us into her village and takes us on a delightful tour, where she introduces us to her family and friends, including her best friend, a chicken. Thandi's conversational, interactive narration makes for a very engaging story. Greeting the reader at the beginning of the book with "Hello Stranger-friend" is a clever way for inviting even some of the more reluctant readers into the story. When talking about her little brother, Thandi asks us if "the little brothers in your village (are) as mischievous as

A wonderful stroll through a Ndebele village with a young girl who describes her culture.

my little brother?" She jumps naturally from topic to topic. After explaining the rationale behind names for Ndebele girls, she turns immediately to bragging about the signature painting of Ndebele homes. She tells us about the games Ndebele children enjoy, and complains about the dull uniforms she and her friends must wear to school. Margaret Courtney-Clarke's photographs illustrate the incredible scenery. She captures the life and color of the village in great detail. The photographs are divided between close-ups of expressive faces and wider shots of the beautifully painted homes. The artistry of the layout of *My Painted House, My Friendly Chicken, and Me* is also worthy of mention. The background color behind the text and photographs is bold and vibrant. The font and type size change throughout the book and become an extension of the feelings that Thandi's words and the photographs evoke. When Thandi talks about her brother, "mischievous" and "shouting" are the dominant words on the page. When she's telling a secret or making an aside, the type size is reduced.

Thandi is very proud of her village and her people and seems to enjoy telling us all she can about her world. "All Nbedele women paint their houses, and I want you to know, stranger friend, that no one's house is as good as my mother's," Thandi boasts. She tells us why she feels sorry for the city women who stare at her and her relatives when they go to town.

Besides being a wonderful story for children, *My Painted House* also provides rare insight into a contemporary African female character who is active, strong, and willful. She takes what seem like small details of her world and presents them to us in engaging ways. When children read this story, they will be drawn into Thandi's world, which may lead to more reflection about their own. MAGNA M. DIAZ

Voices from the Fields: Children of Migrant Farm Workers Tell Their Stories

📖 ✒ Beth S. Atkin
Hispanic, Mexican
1993, Little, Brown

The dreams and day-to-day lives of nine children of migrant workers are presented in their own words and a combination of documentary-style, black-and-white photographs and bilingual (Spanish and English) poems.

In often moving personal narratives these children tell their stories of struggle. Each chapter opens with a poem. For many of us strawberries are fruit whose aroma and taste we savor. But "The Strawberry" describes the often backbreaking work of picking this difficult-to-harvest fruit.

Third-grader Jose Luis Rios tells how his parents, nine brothers and sisters, and other family members labor together in the fields. When not working, Jose helps care for his younger brothers and sisters. If he had the money, he says he would buy milk and food for his family. The mother of twelve-year-old Julie Verlarde works in the fields and must move from town to town searching for work. Julie and her sister long for the day when their mom will hold one job in one place.

A memorable picture/photograph book of Mexican migrant workers and their children.

These children will not soon be forgotten by any reader. Those inspired to learn more about the conditions of migrant workers can draw on the list of suggested readings included. KATHY COLLINS

Bastoor

📖 Mehrdad Bahar ✒ Nikazad Nojoomi
Ancient Persian, Arab American, Middle Eastern
1983, Mazda

In the old days, when Persians and Turans were enemies, they fought many battles. Their most famous battle was won by a young Persian boy named Bastoor.

When this battle begins, no one in the Turan army is able to fight Zarir, the mightiest warrior of Persia. But when Jasseb, the Turan king, announces that whoever defeats Zarir can marry his beautiful daughter, the wicked wizard, Bederaf, changes himself into an old man and slyly kills Zarir by plunging a poisoned dagger into his back. Bastoor, the seven-year-old son of Zarir, decides to avenge his father's death, and with the help of Zarir's horse, defeats the Turan army.

A retelling of an epic legend by Ferdowsi, a great Iranian poet of the tenth century.

69

This captivating story reflects the extraordinary courage of a determined little boy. Through color illustrations that capture the excitement of this ancient legend, the young reader can take a trip to tenth-century Persia. The illustrations depict the ancient Persians and their style of dress. *Teachers can use this book as an accompaniment to a history lesson on ancient Persia.* SHAHLA SOHAIL

The Mishomis Book: The Voice of the Ojibwa

📖 Edward Benton-Benai ✏ Joe Liles

Native American, Ojibway

1988, Red School House

Edward Benton-Banai grew up in a family and community where the history and traditions of the Ojibwa, were valued, and this book represents what he learned. Several aspects set the book apart as a distinctly Indian approach to history. First, Benton-Banai does not omit the spiritual aspects of daily life. For example, Benton-Banai states, "I hope you take what I seek to put down and use them in a good way. Use them to teach your children about the way life has developed for the native people of this country. Use them to redirect your life to the principles of living in harmony with the natural world." Second, the value of women is clear. "The earth is said to be a woman. In this way it is understood that woman preceded man on earth. She is called Mother Earth because from her come all living things."

A clearly written history of the Ojibway nation.

In the final chapter, entitled "Stepping into Modern History," Benton-Banai discusses the impact of colonization upon tribal history and culture. He takes us through missionaries and government policy to the present period.

It is the author's belief that learning about these Ojibway teachings can help restore the strength and continuity of indigenous communities.

The lessons develop in complexity as the book goes on, and rarely have I seen a children's book explain topics as clearly as this book does. Every page of this text is illustrated with clear line drawings printed in brown ink on textured tan paper. Maps are included. Ojibway language is used throughout along with pronunciation guides, so that it is easy to understand and learn the words presented. NOLA HADLEY

Blubber

📖 Judy Blume

European American

1982 (1976), Simon & Schuster, The Bradbury Press

Using fear as the basis for leadership, Wendy organizes Jill and other fifth graders in heaping cruel and abusive treatment onto a slightly overweight classmate. When the classmate, Linda, presents a school report on whales, Wendy nicknames her "Blubber." Linda is taunted by both friends and classmates throughout the novel. Linda's lack of assertiveness and self-confidence are her real obstacles to dealing with the taunting, teasing, and abuse.

A girl teased about her weight overcomes peer pressure in this well-known adolescent novel.

On Halloween, Jill and a friend are caught playing a trick on a neighbor whom they dislike. They have to make restitution by doing yard work and are convinced that "Blubber" informed on them. During a lunch period, Wendy stages a mock trial in the classroom, but fails to provide Linda with a defense lawyer. Surprisingly, Jill protests the unjust treatment of Linda and the trial is canceled. Jill becomes the target of Wendy's vengance and is mocked and ridiculed like Linda. The story becomes more intense and somewhat more complicated when Wendy befriends Linda who in turn treats Jill in the same cruel manner she once treated Linda.

At no point in the book do any of the adults intervene or question the bullying. It is unclear why Jill, who was a follower, suddenly asserts her independence and sees through Wendy's inappropriate behavior. Physical appearance, group acceptance, and peer pressure become focal points in Blume's some-

times confusing novel. The sudden shift in Jill's behavior, and Wendy's manipulation of Linda needed to be dealt with more directly. But the constant focus on physical appearance affords the reader an opportunity to examine the cruelty and injustice of ridiculing people based on their physicality.

The story clearly details the difference between leaders and followers. In this case, the leadership is built on fear, disrespect, and put-downs. The inherent strength of self-confidence, fairness, and independence come through when Jill stands up for Linda's right to have a lawyer. Blume's work consistently reflects independent strong-minded girls who struggle with the challenges of adolescence, sexism, and peer pressure. BARBARA A. KANE

Among the Volcanoes

📖 Omar S. Castañeda

Guatemalan, Hispanic, Mayan, Native American

1991 Dutton Children's Books

Isabel, a Mayan girl of about fifteen, lives in the mountains of Guatemala with her parents and siblings. She has been attending the rural school, but as the oldest daughter, she is needed at home to care for her very ill and dying mother, her father, and the other children. She under-

A moving story of a Mayan girl living in the mountains of Central America.

stands her responsibilities and does what is expected of her, but dreams of becoming a teacher.

Isabel discovers that dreaming is the least of her problems. She is caught between the modern world and the customs of her village. For example, her people believe in the powers of herbs and *curanderos* (a spiritual healer). When a visiting American doctor doing research in her village tells her that he believes her mother might be cured with modern medicine and new technology, the villagers turn against her. Isabel feels torn between her desire to be a teacher and to learn about the world outside. Her cultural traditions require that she settle down at fifteen or sixteen with a husband and take

care of him and her family. To discover the answer, Isabel must look within herself and express her feelings to those she loves. She can only hope that her loved ones also want what is right for her and will allow her to pursue her dream.

This is an exceptional story of a Mayan teenager who is trying to pursue a dream and search for her identity in a world fraught with upheaval and change. MAGNA M. DIAZ

The Christmas Revolution

📖 Barbara Cohen 🖋 Diane De Groat

Jewish

1993 (1987), Dell Publishing Group, Inc.

Emily and Sally Berg are fraternal twins who are very much different, but who generally enjoy each other's company. According to Emily, Sally is "perfect." She is bright, talented, academically adept, tolerant, polite, and pretty. The twins are Jewish, but their family is not strictly observant. Their teacher enjoys making a big fuss about holidays (all holidays). When Christmas comes Emily is always uncomfortable, but Sally enjoys the celebration.

The picture changes when Simeon Goldfarb joins the class. Although this is a public school, there are very few non-Christians in attendance. Simeon's family are observant Jews, and Simeon speaks out firmly against being included in the Christmas preparations. He refus-

A thoughtful story of two Jewish children in a predominantly Christian community who oppose the celebration of Christmas in their school.

es to sing carols and opts out of making Christmas wishes with the rest of the class. Emily decides to join him in his nonparticipation. This results in a number of children who used to be Emily's friends now ostracizing her.

Things come to a head when the school's decorated Christmas tree is knocked down. Emily and Simeon are suspected of the vandalism, and they and Sally decide to become detectives and discover who really knocked down the tree. They do find out who the culprits are, and they are reconciled with their former friends, who now are very apologetic. In addition, Emily directs a Hanukkah play and invites some of her friends to a Hanukkah party at her grandmother's house.

The author accurately describes Hanukkah's status as a minor Jewish holiday that commemorates a significant historical event but is not accompanied by religious traditions and ritual. There are no special feasts or fasts associated with the holiday, but there are customs that are practiced, such as the lighting of candles and eating special foods. Adults do not stay home from work and children attend school during Hanukkah.

In the end, Emily is content with the way things worked out, but she understands that next year she will again have to grapple with the problem of the universal celebration of Christmas in her community.

The issues of minorities being expected to conform to the majority's customs is an important one for children to consider. Sometimes the "norm" as set by the immediate community is so widely assumed that others' views and customs are not at all acknowledged. The teacher in this story is not an evil person, nor is she unkind. But she is ignorant of the implications of her behavior. She is also not adept at handling the interactions among her students.

This book helps to point out some of the complicated issues involved in the celebration of a Christian holiday that many people simply view as an American holiday. No really clear stand is taken by anyone except Simeon, and he is seen as a "slightly weird" character. No permanent resolution is in effect at the end of the story. The open-endedness is realistic, but one wishes that the parents and other adults had taken more of a position on the separation between church and state. There is also no indication that the child who was Emily's worst tormentor (although she was a "good friend") understands the lesson she should have learned. MASHA RUDMAN

Chingis Khan

📖 ✎ Demi
Asian, Chinese, Mongolian
1991, Henry Holt and Company, Inc., ✳ Chinese

Chingis Khan, the famous Mongol leader and military strategist in world history, conquered many places from East Persia and China, to the Western part of Russia in his time. Born the son of a clan chieftain, Chingis Khan learned how to survive on the Mongolian steppe, how to unite the feuding tribes, and how to train his military and defeat his enemies. At last he established the greatest contiguous land empire in history and became the first emperor of the Yuan Dynasty in China.

An account of Chingis Khan, a famous Mongol leader, conquerer, and military strategist.

Based on both history and legend, Demi mainly describes Chingis Khan's military career through his iron strategies, but does not give much detail to show his humanity. It gives a strong impression that Chingis Khan is a cruel, stern, fierce, and powerful leader with strong ambitions to conquer the world, and that he is great but not kind. The text and pictures show that Chingis Khan shot his half brother in the heart because his half brother broke discipline. He killed his last enemy who had been a boyhood friend on the steppe, because only one of them could be the leader of all the Mongols. He killed innocent people with his "fire that flies" from one country to another.

Chingis Khan is a historical figure. From what the book shows, young readers may ponder whether he was a good or a bad man. Do his achievements outweigh his cruelty? This kind of picture book can not provide many details or different aspects for readers because of its space limitations. Readers cannot appraise his achievements and errors only as represented in this book; they have to read more books about this mystical historical figure. Demi's wonderful pictures exactly convey the main details and plot of the story, and this wonderful book may stimulate young readers to read more books about historical figures. LI LIU

Arctic Memories

📖 ✎ Normee Ekoomiak
Eskimo/Aleut/Inuit, Native American
1982 (1988), Henry Holt and Company, ✳ Bilingual English/Inuktitutther, 📖 Arvaarluk, Michael, *Baseball Bats for Christmas*; Steltzer, Ulli, *Building an Igloo*.

There are approximately one hundred thousand Inuit living in Denmark, areas of Siberia, and Alaska. In Canada there are twenty to twenty-five thousand who mostly live in the Arctic, an area of snow, ice, and rock, with no trees. Most Inuit were hunters and trappers who traditionally built housing from the snow packs around them during the winter months and tents of animal hides during the summer. Today most Inuits no longer live through the winter months of the year in igloos and many travel by snowmobiles as well as dog sleds.

But Normee Ekoomiak has captured aspects of his childhood in the arctic. Fort George, the area where the author grew up with his grandfather, is now flooded

Through the author's childhood memories and traditional legends, this picture book depicts Inuit life in the Arctic.

from the Hydro-Quebec James Bay project, but the book is a testament to its memory. Ekoomiak has designed a picture book using traditional Inuit needlework with felt applique, embroidery, and prints and acrylic paints that clearly depicts Inuit

ARCTIC MEMORIES
Normee Ekoomiak

life in the Arctic. Memories of Ekoomiak's childhood are vivid in his art work: hunting, fishing, children playing in the snow at the string game and the blanket toss. Pictures also depict traditional legends and local animals: dog sleds, huskies, polar bears, snowy owls, igloos, frozen woolly mammoths, and narwhals. Ekoomiak even presents a nativity scene. The text next to the illustration tells a story or explains the picture.

In one striking photo the picture Ekoomiak shows the High Kick game and several other recreational games the Inuit's played when they were not hunting or busy with other tasks. One of the games was to keep do a push up while trying to pick up a stick with one's mouth!

The Inuit did not have written language until the nineteenth century, when they devised a system based on one used by the Cree. This is one of the first children's books to be printed bilingually in Inuktitut.

Other good materials about the Inuits are Michael Arvaarluk's *Baseball Bats for Christmas* and Ulli Steltzer's *Building an Igloo*. NOLA HADLEY

History Of Women in Science for Young People

Vivian Sheldon Epstein
Feminist
1994, VSE Publishers, Day, Frances Ann, *Teacher's Guide in Multicultural Voices in Contemporary Literature*; Lowe, Rebecca, Thompson, Warren, and Thompson, Mary H., *The Scientist Within You: Experiments & Biographies of Distinguished Women in Science*; McKissack, Patricia and Frederick, *Taking a Stand Against Racism and Racial Discrimination*; *"You Can Be a Scientist, Too"* (video).

Vivian Sheldon Epstein traces the history of women scientists from pre-civilization to the present, describing their exclusion and gradual acceptance in a field dominated by men.

The exciting and challenging lives of twenty-nine women scientists in diverse scientific areas will inspire young women to become involved in science and consider it as a part of their life's work. Some of the women scientists highlighted in this much-needed book include Hypatia, a fourth-century Greek astronomer, inventor, and mathematician; Chien Shiung Wu, a Chinese American experimental physicist; and Myra Adele Logan, an African American surgeon; as well as Maria Mitchell, Elizabeth Blackwell, Antonia Coella Novello, Margaret Sanger, Marie Curie, Rachel Carson, Jane Goodall, and Sally Ride.

Responding to a dearth of books on female scientists, this volume provides brief biographies of twenty-nine women scientists from diverse backgrounds and a wealth of related information.

Epstein introduces this excellent book with a quote from Rosalyn Yalow, the 1977 Nobel Prize winner in medicine: "The world cannot afford the loss of talents of half of its people if we are to solve the many problems which beset us." Accompanied by color and black-and-white illustrations, the succinct biographies feature the specific contributions of each woman, often tracing her development as a scientist to her childhood interests. The author expands the reader's awareness of the many options available in science by including women from a wide variety of fields such as marine biology, archaeology, anthropology, industrial medicine, aeronautics, chemistry, physics, environmental science, medical science, computer sciences, psychology, and genetics.

HISTORY OF WOMEN IN
SCIENCE
FOR
YOUNG PEOPLE

As a result of long-standing prejudices and widely-accepted stereotypes, women have had to struggle for acceptance in the science world even more than they have in other fields. Educators have become increasingly alarmed at the results of studies like the one recently conducted by the American Association of University Women which conclude that most girls begin to avoid science when they reach middle-school age. Similar research indicates that the culture of the classroom discourages girls from pursuing their interests in science. Unfortunately, few materials are available to counteract the notion that girls cannot be scientists.

Epstein responded to the need for books that provide a positive image of women in science. Her growing reputation for creating books that enhance the awareness of the contributions of women is greatly augmented by this title. To dispel the myth that there were no women scientists until recently, the author uses the last six pages of her book to list, by century, hundreds of women scientists and their contributions. This extensive list, plus a bibliography, provides both the student and the educator with a wealth of information for further research. Epstein writes, illustrates, publishes, promotes, and markets her books. In taking complex subjects and skillfully simplifying them for the young reader, she is making a significant contribution to the field of children's literature.

Students might be interested in the following related activities: Examine the biography section of your library. Make a list of the biographies available about women scientists. Compare your list with the scientists featured in History of Women in Science for Young People. *How many are missing? Request that these books be added to your library collection.*

Read the other books written by Vivian Sheldon Epstein. Discuss gender bias. What can we each do to insure that all people have equal opportunities? Why is this important?

Read Taking a Stand Against Racism and Racial Discrimination *by Patricia and Fredrick McKissack. In what ways are racism and gender bias similar? How might we use some of the recommendations in Taking a Stand to combat sexism?* FRANCES A. DAY

The Great Brain

📖 John D. Fitzgerald ✏️ Mercer Mayer

Jewish

1985 (1967), Dell, Dial Press

Ten-year-old Tom Fitzgerald is a very intelligent boy who likes to brag about his "great brain," which he often uses to cheat his friends or shirk his reponsibilities, and sometimes uses for good. Tom lives with his prominent, well-respected family in a predominantly Mormon town in Utah at the turn of the nineteenth century. The book is narrated by Tom's younger brother, who reports that he and Tom taught the Mor-

A well-known book that harbors undercurrents of cultural intolerance.

mons tolerance by beating them up. "After all, there is nothing as tolerant and understanding as a kid you can whip."

The book follows various events that illuminate the townspeople's cultural intolerance. A Jewish peddler, Abie Glassman, who has regularly come through town for many years, is invited to open a store, despite his doubts about competing against Mormon-run stores. Abie's store fails and he eventually dies of starvation. Tom's father comments that Abie died because he was a Jew, and no one in town paid attention to the fact that a Jew was in dire straits. The townspeople give Abie a Christian burial, at which the Mormon bishop says, "I am sure both God and Abie will understand." A wreath is placed on the grave. It is never mentioned, however, that this is a symbol of oppression, and that either of the ministers probably could have given Abie a Jewish burial, or at least a non-denominational burial.

When a family from Greece moves to town, bullies torment the family's young boy, Basil. Tom derides Basil for being a "cry-baby" and a "mother's boy" and says he will not be Basil's friend until he learns to fight. Tom earns the Greek father's undying appreciation when he promises, "I'll make a hundred per cent American kid out of him." Then Tom teaches Basil how to fight, after first goading Basil into getting beaten up very badly by one of the bullies.

Although Tom's father explains that it is wrong to harbor prejudices, and although Tom is well-meaning, the undercurrent of bigotry still surfaces. *Although the book's main characters are portrayed as essentially just, honest people, the prejudice and lack of cultural understanding evident throughout the book should be discussed.* MASHA RUDMAN

The Adventures of Connie and Diego

📖 Maria Garcia ✏️ Malaquias Montoya

Hispanic

1994 (1987), Children's Book Press,
✶ Audio Cassette, Bilingual English/Spanish

In the Land of Plenty, twins Connie and Diego are different from other children: they have varied colors all over their bodies, and their brothers and

Feeling like outcasts, Hispanic twins, Connie and Diego, run away in a tale about mixed-race heritage.

sisters always laugh at them. Convinced that they will never fit in, they decide to run away to find a place where they will belong. Though they travel to many places, they cannot find a place that is congenial.

Finally, they find themselves in a jungle no friendlier than any other place. Confronted with an angry tiger, they ask him if they can all live together.

"No, we cannot! Tigers and humans do not get along together."

Connie and Diego bemoan their many colors, but the Tiger admonishes them: "Bah! That's not important! You're human! Can't you see?"

"We're human," echoes Connie, "just like our brothers and sisters. Let's go home."

Connie and Diego return to the Land of Plenty and to their sisters and brothers, and discover that in accepting themselves, they are also accepted by others.

This story gives support to children of mixed heritage who are confused about their identity. Author Maria Garcia writes about herself: "I am Chicana. I am Black. I am Native American. I am Asian. I am White. What does this mean? To children it can be very confusing."

The text is in English and Spanish, set on colored paper, and illustrated expressively in bright poster-like scenes. The boldness of the art affirms the message to children to be bold and proud in their lives. Maria Garcia has given children a valuable lesson in a beautiful book. JANIS O'DRISCOLL

We Adopted You, Benjamin Koo

📖 Linda Walvoord Girard, Edited by Abbey Levine
✒ Linda Shute

Asian American, Korean American

1989, Albert Whitman & Company, 📕 Boyd, Brian, *When You Were Born in Korea*

Benjamin Koo was born in Korea and adopted as an infant by an American couple. The book's first illustration shows him, age nine, sitting at his desk, speaking into a tape recorder. This "biography" gives a straightforward account of his initial six months in Korea, his adoption, and his life in America. The story will be familiar to any adopted Korean child or that child's parents. Abandoned at an orphanage, Benjamin, or Koo Hyun Soo as he is initially named, is well taken care of until his adoption can be arranged with the Andrews, a nice middle-class couple. Coming to the United States on one of the famous international baby flights, he is picked up at the airport by his new parents and made much of by his new extended family. Benjamin's parents make no effort to hide from him the fact that he is adopted, but the concept doesn't mean much to him until age eight when he begins to

A helpful but uneven book about a Korean boy adopted by a white American family.

take serious note of the physical differences between himself and his friends and family. As is typical, Benjamin goes through a period of anger and rebellion, worries about why his birth parents abandoned him, and even denies that his American parents have the right to tell him what to do.

Although *We Adopted You, Benjamin Koo* is labled as a biography, Benjamin's story is so typical that the book can serve, and undoubtedly is intended to, as a manual for dealing with the issues that adopted Korean children frequently have to come to terms with. Benjamin's parents, for example, behave appropriately when he's angry, staying calm and emphasizing both their love for him and their parental rights. Later he visits his school counselor who gives him the standard good advice on why his adoptive parents are his real parents in every important sense. Eventually Benjamin gets past his anger, things settle down, and the Andrews decide to adopted a second child, a little girl from Brazil.

Girard deals briefly but effectively with some of the other problems faced by adopted children who are racially different from their parents, specifically nosy adults who ask, "Are they yours?" and other kids who use racial slurs. She also emphasizes some of the unique benefits of living in a multicultural family.

We Adopted You, Benjamin Koo is a good book on Korean adoption, and is entirely appropriate for either adopted children or other young people who might want to find out more about the subject. It has a couple of weaknesses, however. The illustrations by Linda Shute are not particularly engaging. Further, many of the difficulties involved in overseas adoption are underplayed. One final note: Although the book is entirely appropriate for the children who are its intended audience, it does not speak adequately (and should not be expected to do so) to the emotional needs of prospective adoptive parents. MIKE LEVY

75

Alesia

📖 Eloise Greenfield and Alesia Revis
🖌 George Ford and Sandra Turner Bond
African American, Physically Disabled
1981, Philomel Books

Using a diary format, Greenfield and Revis discuss the everyday challenges for a teenage girl who uses braces and a wheelchair for her mobility. Engagingly and realistically written in very simple prose, the story provides an insightful look into the life of fifteen-year-old Alesia Revis. As a result of an accident in which a car hits Alesia while she's riding her bike, the young girl is seriously injured and unable to walk. Longing to walk, dance, and acquire the ease of mobility again Alesia reflects:

Told in diary format, an insightful story of a physically-handicapped girl who discusses her crippling accident.

"Walking, real walking, is gliding. Just gliding along and not thinking about it. Not having to hold on to anything or worry about stepping on a rock and losing your balance.... You just glide."

Along with discussing a range of support services from camps to occupational training programs, the book documents the long, demanding process of rehabilitation including the physical pain of therapy. While providing a look into the world of a disabled teenager, it does not go along the pity path. The authors also examine the frustration of adjusting to a disability and convey the determination it takes to "step" boldly into the world and continue being a whole person. One profound example comes when Alesia decides that her prom is very important and she plans to be there.

Disguising her crutches becomes an issue, but only briefly.

With confidence, spirits and a desire to have just as much fun as her peers, Alesia attends the dance. Her creative approach to doing the latest dance also results in her having a great time. The upbeat tone of the book serves to dispel many of the stereotypes about young people with disabilities. Shopping, being active in her church, and doing well in school remain a part of Alesia's life and she does not allow the disability to prevent her from finding and embracing joy in her life. Strong parental encouragement, peer acceptance, and being part of an understanding community provide her with the support needed to make her way in the world. Through her parents, friends, and her own sense of self-determination, Alesia also learns to deal with situations that make her uncomfortable.

Illustrated with both black-and-white photographs and line drawings, we see her evolution from a careless nine-year-old on a bicycle who runs into an oncoming car to a poised young woman ready to graduate from high school. Young readers will find the story interesting and engaging. *The story line and focus provide a launching point for teachers to discuss disability and what it means personally and in the larger world.* MEREDITH ELIASSEN

Plain City

📖 Virginia Hamilton
African American
1995 (1993), Scholastic, Inc.

Buhlaire, an almost-thirteen-year-old free spirit, has always considered herself an outsider. Because of her independence, love of solitude, and different look, she doesn't fit in with her classmates, her family, even, she thinks, her own body. Her family runs and owns a group of secluded rental properties on long stilts by the river in Plain City, and Buhlaire is essentially alone. Her mother, a singer and fan dancer, is often travelling, so Buhlaire is raised by her strict Aunt Digna and blind Aunt Babe.

Buhlaire believes her father is dead and knows little about him until she is told he is alive and back in Plain City. Thus begins Buhlaire's quest for her identity, her memories and history, and the truth about her family and her father. Along the way, she makes a friend in Grady, a classmate who alternately torments and protects Buhlaire, and ultimately learns her family's secrets. Buhlaire discovers her father homeless and sees her family's collective cover-up of his stealing and drifting. She also learns of her father's feelings of alienation, particularly because he comes from an interracial family.

Buhlaire's father is mentally ill, but she chooses not to avoid him as her family has done. Buhlaire

An African American girl sets out to find her homeless father in this intelligent story.

forces the rest of her family to address her confusion and feelings of betrayal while she tries to understand why they kept information from her. She finds a large piece of herself when she finds her father, and she works to integrate him into the puzzle that is her life.

Hamilton crafts a tale about identity, family, homelessness, self-assurance, and acceptance with an adept sense of a reader's intelligence. As always, she challenges readers with language, sentence rhythms, and sensitive issues while allowing them to listen in on Buhlaire's thoughts. ALISON WASHINGTON

Cousins

Virginia Hamilton

African American

1993 (1990), Philomel Books

Eleven-year-old Cammy loves her grandmother, Gram Tut, for her wisdom, generous spirit, and concern for Cammy's family. Cammy visits Gram Tut at the nursing home and is mortified to see that the woman is nearing life's end. The precious minutes she shares with Gram Tut temporarily help Cammy forget how she feels around the rest of her family. Her mother Maylene is always working, and her often kind, protective brother Andrew can be mean to Cammy with little warning. Cammy endures the remarks of crabby, sniping Aunt Effie; Effie's cold, spoiled, and perfect daughter Patty Ann; Effie's troubled, directionless son Richie; and their poor relation, Elodie. Cammy is often overwhelmed and not sure how to react to them.

A complex, realistic story about a family conflict and losing loved ones, featuring an African American girl.

Although she wishes to be like Patty Ann, Cammy dislikes her cousin's stuck-up attitude and disregard for others' feelings. Cammy also knows Patty Ann's secret: she is constantly making herself throw up after meals. So when Patty Ann cruelly remarks that Gram Tut is a "smelly old bag of bones that's dying," Cammy wishes that Patty Ann would disappear. But when Patty Ann drowns at day camp, Cammy is forced to rethink her feelings about her cousin, family, and dying. Cammy realizes that her cousin could be caring despite her spoiled nature, and that enjoying those we love while they live can help ease the pain when the loved one dies.

Hamilton's knack for writing dialogue and her empathy for her characters are evident in *Cousins*. Her portrayal of the cousins and their intertwined lives is complex and realistic. ALISON WASHINGTON

Calling the Doves

Juan Felipe Herrera / Elly Simmons

Hispanic, Mexican

1995, Children's Book Press, ✳ Bilingual English/Spanish

This is a beautiful bilingual memoir of Juan Felipe Herrera's childhood as a migrant farmworker. Juan Felipe Herrera grew up the son of migrant farmworkers. In *Calling the Doves*, he has created a beautiful, evocative memoir of his childhood. The language is precise, and the book's imagery is mirrored in Elly Simmons' richly painted illustrations.

Both Spanish and English text are presented together, mostly on the same page and occasionally side by side. The resulting layout is effective and inviting. Full of sounds, smells, and flavors, Herrera's memories engage the senses. Herrera is especially good at depicting his family members: his mother is an artistic woman who often sings to him; his father is a lively and poetic storyteller.

A portrait of migrant farmworkers vividly evoking the authors' childhood memories.

Farmworkers are often a forgotten segment of American society, and this book, focusing on the author's generally warm childhood memories, does not address the hardships farmworkers face. While children should understand that farmworkers are exploited, some books, however, make the mistake of portraying farmworkers simply as victims.

This book is extremely valuable for its multidimensional human portrait. It is appropriate both for children living the farmworker life and for those learning to appreciate it. JANIS O'DRISCOLL

Letters from Rifka

Karen Hesse

Jewish

1993 (1992), Puffin Books

Twelve-year-old Rifka tells her story through letters she writes to her cousin Tovah, who remains behind in Russia. Rifka hopes to actually mail the letters one day, but for now she keeps them safely stashed in a book Tovah gave to her as a gift.

A compelling tale of a Jewish girl's escape from czarist Russia and her nearly disastrous attempts to come to America.

Rifka and her immediate family have escaped from Russia as illegal emigrants. Rifka is instrumental in their successful escape because with her blonde hair and blue eyes, and her flawless, unaccented Russian speech, she can distract the guards while the rest of her family sneaks onto a train.

The trip to Poland is difficult, and Rifka and other family members fall ill. After more than two months, the family sets off for America. Rifka, however, contracts another illness and must stay behind. After a long year of convalescence, Rifka finally journeys to America. Even after her arrival at Ellis Island, she is detained for nearly a month and leaves only after persuading officials of her cleverness.

The epistolary format is very engaging, though the series of disasters that befalls Rifka may disturb some readers. Moreover, the book successfully evokes the climate for Jews in Russia and America at the turn of the century and skillfully develops Rifka's determined, mature, and resilient character.
MASHA KABAKOW RUDMAN

The Ballad of Belle Dorcas

📖 William H. Hooks 🖌 Brian Pinkney
African American
1995 (1990), Alfred A. Knopf, 🎞 Parks, Van Dyke, *Jump! and Jump Again! Adventures of Brer Rabbit* .

Belle Dorcas is free issue—her mother is a slave and her father is her white owner. Her mother hopes her daugher will marry a free-issue man, but Belle has her heart set on a slave named Joshua. She will not be swayed in her decision, and the two are set to wed. But when the master is killed in an accident, his replacement tries to sell Joshua.

Belle Dorcas summons up her courage and visits the local conjure woman, Granny Lizard, who gives her a special magic bag. When Belle uses it, wishing that Joshua will never leave, he is transformed into a tree. The master cannot find him and soon gives up the search. The lovers' secret is that Belle can turn Joshua back into a man by rubbing the conjure bag on him.

Belle's hopes, however, are dashed again when the Joshua tree is chopped down and used to build a smokehouse. Unable to bear the loss, Belle visits the smokehouse everyday for years. On the day of her death, the smokehouse disappears and in its place are two cedar trees growing side by side.

Hooks based this powerful love story on a tale he heard during his childhood. In his author's note he tells of conjure men and women who can still be found in the South today. The colorful etchings against a black background reflect the element of magic swirling through the story. Readers will find Belle's depth of emotion compelling. Sometimes words are not needed, as in the double-page spread showing Joshua's transformation into a tree. PAM CARLSON

A free African American woman uses magic to keep her fiancé from being sold to another slave owner in this powerful story.

Cherokee Summer: Cwy ay

📷🖊 Diane Hoyt-Goldsmith and Lawrence Migdale
Cherokee, Native American
1993, Holiday House, ✳ Braille,
📖 Hoyt-Goldsmith, Diane, *Artic Hunter*; *Totem Pole*; *Apache Rodeo*.

The team of Diane Hoyt-Goldsmith and Lawrence Migdale have developed a fine series of photo essays of Native American children. Each title introduces the reader to the family and life of a Native American child from ten to twelve years old with the child serving as the boy or girl narrator. In *Cherokee Summer*, our guide is ten-year-old Bridget Russell, a member of the Cherokee Nation of Oklahoma.

This book contains an impressive variety of information in its thirty-two pages. Bridget explains how her people got to Oklahoma from their southern Appalachian homeland and describes how the Cherokee Nation governs its citizens today from the Cherokee Nation's capital of Tahlequah, Oklahoma. Bridget then introduces the reader to her family and

An informative photo essay tracing Cherokee history.

to Cherokee traditions such as basket making, blow-gun making, and crawdad hunting. Each of these brief sections is enhanced by superb photographs of Bridget and her family, and the captions present additional information not found in the text. A very informative section explores the Cherokee language and syllabary (an alphabet of syllables rather than letters), presenting the entire alphabet and several words in Cherokee. Bridget tells us about the Cherokee stomp dance, a spiritual tradition shared by other tribes in northeastern Oklahoma, and includes a recipe for the traditional "hog fry" that is always served to everyone at the stomp dance.

Besides an excellent glossary and useful index, the authors offer a page of portraits of people who attended the stomp dance that they photographed for this book. Earlier, Bridget had talked briefly about "full-bloods" and "mixed-bloods," and this portrait gallery simply illustrates the variety of physical features that make up Indian country today. This, and the other, Hoyt-Goldsmith/Migsdale volumes are highly recommended for all public, school, and tribal libraries. LISA A. MITTEN

Helen Keller

📕 Nigel Hunter 🖉 Various sources

Physically Disabled

1986 (1985), Wayland, The Bookwright Press, ✳ Series

This biography highlights Helen Keller's most important breakthroughs. It also focuses on Anne Sullivan, Helen's teacher and companion, who helped Helen to communicate with and understand the world around her. Anne taught her the manual alphabet and gave her the key to language. Helen also learned to read braille and to hear through her fingers by placing them on the speaker's lips and throat. Further, she learned to speak and could lip-read by feeling the speaker's lips.

When she was sixteen years old, Helen entered Cambridge School for Young Ladies in Massachusetts and, with Anne beside her, she studied and went on to Radcliffe College. In 1903, she wrote *The Story of My Life*. She was politically active, joining the Socialist Party, and wrote about her beliefs.

As Anne Sullivan's health declined in the early 1930s, Polly Thompson replaced Anne as Helen's colleague and companion. Helen and Polly toured the globe, and Helen's life became the subject of films and books. Helen died in 1968, leaving her legacy as an inspiration to us all.

This excellent biography is written in simple language, easy for young children to comprehend. The word "handicap" is used in this book, but does not imply that Helen's disabilities ever restricted her opportunities. The book contains both illustrations and photographs that depict Helen from the age of seven up until her late sixties and covers important events and people in her life. The back of the book contains a chronology of important dates, a glossary, and a list of related books.

Activities:
1. Blindfold one student and have another guide him or her through a maze without speaking so that he or she can sense what it feels like to be totally dependent on others and learn to trust them.
2. Work with a partner and try the manual alphabet.
BARBARA A. KANE

An excellent, accessible biography of Helen Keller.

Revisiting the Life of Helen Keller

MICHELLE ELWOOD

From the age of one and a half, Helen Keller could not hear, see, or speak. She lived in a dark and isolated world until Anne Sullivan came to teach her. As an adult, Helen Keller traveled all over the world and raised money to start schools for the deaf and blind children. Her courage and determination earned her admiration and respect as she set out to help others conquer the odds against them.

Dear Helen Keller,
Your book, The Story of My Life, has changed my whole outlook on life. I now feel that anyone can accomplish just about any goal they choose to. You have shown the whole world that being disabled does not mean you are stupid or untalented. Your story gives hope to many. I used to think that disabled people just could not do very many things.

I am totally deaf in my left ear. I do not know if I was born this way, or if my loss was caused by an infection or a high fever. My parents did not realize I had a problem until I was about two and a half years old. I have a twin sister, and her hearing is fine.

Before my parents realized that I had a problem, they thought I just did not listen to them. When someone spoke on my left side, I simply did not hear everything. I was very frustrated, as were my parents. Sometimes I threw tantrums. People began to think I was a brat. Finally, my hearing loss was discovered, and as long as everyone talked to me on my right side, and made sure I heard them, I listened to what I was told. My parents decided that I was not such a brat after all.

When I started school, I wore a hearing aid that crossed the sound over to my good ear. It helped me some, but it was also a pain. Kids were always making fun of me, always asking questions. My hearing aids made me different. They always fell out if I tried to play on the playground equipment also. I felt sorry for myself.

At age eleven, I decided I was not going to wear them anymore. I learned to make do with one ear.

I always turn my head toward my good ear when someone is talking to me. I manage fine.

Until I read your book, I think I felt a little sorry for myself. I resented not having normal hearing like my sister and brother. Now, I know just how lucky I am. You accomplished so much with your disabilities, it almost made me ashamed for feeling so sorry for myself. There are so many people with problems worse than mine. Your story gives hope to people with any type of disability.

I will never forget this book and how much courage you had.

MICHELLE ELWOOD, 14
Eagle Point High School, Eagle Point, OR
Teacher: Mrs. Elaine Ledbetter

Michelle Elwood wrote this letter when she was a fourteen-year-old student at Eagle Point High School in Eagle Point, Oregon.

Excerpt from "Dear Author" collected by Weekly Readers Magazine. © 1995 by *Weekly Readers Corporation. Reprinted by permission of Conari Press, Berkeley, California.*

Class President

📖 Johanna Hurwitz ✒ Sheila Hamanaka
Latino, Puerto Rican
1991 (1990), Morrow Junior Books, ✱ Spanish

Class President's star is fifth grader Julio Sanchez. He is a Puerto Rican who ends up as class leader, although he doubts his intelligence and popularity.

A Puerto Rican teacher helps a student become class president and learn about true leadership.

Over the year, however, Julio begins to view himself differently due to the influence of the new teacher, Mr. Flores. Mr. Flores is also Hispanic, and wows the class with interesting assignments and novel activities, including the class election. Mr. Flores emphasizes the correct pronunciation of Julio's name and forces students to reconsider their prejudices.

This is an engaging, believable chapter book that will especially appeal to children who enjoy positive, upbeat endings. ANDREA L. WILLIAMS

Believers in America: Poems about Americans of Asian & Pacific Island Descent

📖 Steven Izuki ✒ Bill Fukuda McCoy
Asian Pacific American
1994, Children's Press, ✱ Series

As part of the "Many Voices, One Song" series developed by Children's Press, this book features poetry about Asian Pacific American history and individual Asian Pacific Americans. It is refreshing to see a different approach taken to the presentation of history and the experiences of Americans of Asian and Pacific Islander descent. Following in the tradition of epic poetry, the book seeks to provide historical perspective in manageable portions for young readers. As a historical text, the book

A set of poems that recounts Asian American history with mixed success.

does an admirable job. It deals both with groups of people and with individuals. Some of those groups are distinguished by ethnicity (Hawaiians, Korean

Americans, Vietnamese, refugees and Southeast Asians in the United States. Here are the "Manila-men," the first Asian immigrants to America. They came from the Philippines to the Louisiana delta region in the 1500s. Here, too, are the Angel Island detainees, the 1442nd Regiment, and the Chinese railroad workers. There are also notable historical events such as the Chinese Exclusion Acts and the internment of Japanese Americans. Telling history in poems is a challenging task, and as poetry, this collection only works sometimes. Many of the poems seem to be paragraphs which have been cut up to mimic poetic form.

Much of the text lacks the emotional pull that characterizes poetry or lyrical prose. This becomes most pronounced when the author attempts rhyming verse. "Sammy Lee served as a member of the President's Council on Physical Fitness/ Then coached another Olympic diver Samoan American gold medalist Greg Louganis." While I really like the concept of this book, the poetry is strained. Perhaps the book would have worked better as a mixture of prose and poetry. Nonetheless, for what it seeks to do, the book has some value. The history chronicled is often neglected in accounts of U.S. history for children. The groups and people honored are important for children to know about. Like the text of this book, the illustrations have strengths and weaknesses. The illustrations are best when portraying groups or significant events. The work is less compelling when portraying specific individuals. DEBBIE WEI

All About You: An Adventure of Self-Discovery

📖 Aylette Jenness   ✏ Illustrated and designed by Laura DeSantis; Photographs by Max Belcher; Video frames by D'Arcy Marsh
Multicultural
1993, The New Press, ✳ Series

Another book in the Kids Bridge Series, *All About You: An Adventure of Self-Discovery*, is executed with the same youthful enthusiasm as *Come Home with Me: A Multicultural Treasure Hunt* (also available in translation, *Ven a Mi Casa: Una Busqueda de Tesoros Multicultural*).

Drawn from the work of a curriculum research project in multicultural studies at The Children's Museum in Boston, this books encourage

A multicultural workbook that enables kids to learn about themselves and each other.

the reader to embark on an adventure of self-discovery and self-knowledge, and through this inquiry, to develop a positive self-image. Its primary purpose is to help kids value themselves and others.

As readers journey through this book, they are led to reflect upon themselves and their lives, and to discover themselves, their families, their friends, and their world. *Through the exercises in the autobiographical activity book, children are encouraged to view themselves in relation to family, friends, and the world in a nonthreatening way. Progressive activities begin with a sequence of readings, pictures, drawings, and questions to answer about where one lives; the reader is asked to write his or her life's story, to interview family members, and to examine his/her culture. The book culminates with an exploratory activity comparing individuals of diverse ethnic backgrounds. The readers write stories about their own cultures. The books in the Kids Bridge Series are a thoughtful collection of* each reader's sense of identity, family, ethnic heritage, and culture, and a cherished keepsake of a journey into adulthood. As with the other books in this series, the photographs are splendid, the glossary useful, and it will prove adaptable to readers of all ages and all areas of the curriculum.
MELVINA AZAR DAME

Bird Talk

📖 Lenore Keeshig-Tobias   ✏ Polly Keeshig-Tobias
Native American, Ojibway
1991, Sister Vision, Black Women and Women of Color Press, ✳ Bilingual Anishinabe/English

In *Bird Talk*, a mother and her children come to terms with racism and misperceptions of who they really are.

Based on a true story, the book tells how a "seemingly" innocent game turns into a lesson in racial understanding. At recess one day, the children decide to play Cowboys and Indians. Polly tells them that it really isn't a nice game and she goes on to explain that she is Indian. They tell her she can't be because she's not wearing feathers. One girl asks her why she doesn't come from India if she's an Indian. Another says that if she's Indian, her skin should be red.

The family photo album and some stories her

A girl draws on family history to handle slurs against Native Americans in one of the few bilingual books on Native Americans.

82

grand-parents used to tell help reassure Polly. Her mother promises to come to the school to tell Polly's class about Columbus, cowboys, and Indians. Polly takes a walk in the park to let off some steam. While in the park, she hears all the voices and different languages, and she is reminded of the many languages that birds use in speaking to their young. The reader, as well, is reminded of the intense variety of living things in our universe. "I thought it was like waking up early in the morning before rush hour. You can hear all the different birds singing their different bird songs in their own bird language. Sparrow, robin, wren, chickadee, and gull."

Simple black-and-white line drawings by Polly Keeshig-Tobias convey the deep emotions recounted in this painful, yet uplifting story. With cowboys and Indians remaining a prevalent theme in children's books and movies, there remains a critical need for more books that address the issues Keeshig-Tobias raises.

Written in Anishinabe and English, this book is important because it is also one of the few bilingual Native American books. It will be particularly helpful for indigenous youth living or going to school outside of the Native American community who might be facing similar confrontations and stereotypes about their identity.

NOLA HADLEY

Shannon: An Ojibway Dancer

📖 Sandra King ✎ Catherine Whipple

Native American, Ojibway

1993 (1993), Lerner Publications, ✳ Series,
📼 Braine, Susan, *Heartbeat: A Collection of the Powwow, Into the Circle* (video).

Shannon: An Ojibway Dancer is one of the rare books focusing on contemporary urban Native American communities. Seen through the eyes of

An Ojibway girl prepares for a powwow, in a rare look at contemporary Native American life.

an adolescent girl living in Minneapolis, the book takes the reader through the entire process of her creating dance regalia for the Mille Lacs Reservation Powwow. En route, the reader learns about contemporary urban Ojibway life, ties to the reservation, Indian schools in Minneapolis, the Minneapolis' Urban Indian Center, and powwows. Color photographs by Lakota photographer Catherine Whipple highlight home life,

school, friendships, Indian stores, and the Indian center, as well as the music and dancing at a powwow and the process of beading and making dancing costumes.

Sandra King explains: "Powwows are traditional Indian social events that feature drumming and dancing. They take place all over the United States and Canada throughout the year. They are held in cities and on reservations, indoors and outdoors, in winter and summer. Summer, though, is consid-

ered powwow season. Some reservations have held powwows for more than 100 years."

For weeks before the powwow, Shannon, the book's protagonist, works diligently making the beading for her moccasins, leggings, belt, cape, and braided hair ties. The rest of the family helps, too. Shannon's grandmother taught her to bead when Shannon was about seven years old. She also helps make her shawl and takes Shannon to buy beads. Shannon's sister, Nicole, who is fifteen, helps Shannon practice her dances. A cousin, Chantelle, also beads, and is a dancer as well.

In this book as well as in many of the others in this series, indigenous peoples living in urban areas still have strong bonds with their reservations. Young people are shown growing up with a strong sense of identity—knowing where they are from and knowing many members of their extended families. Although Shannon lives in the city, she is emersed in Indian culture in a vital Indian community. She is even able to attend a school, the Four Winds School, where she can participate in an American Indian language immersion program.

This book is a welcome addition to the Native Americans Today: We Are Still Here Series.

It is highly recommended for teenage and preteen girls of all cultures who are interested in learning more about powwows and other aspects of various Native American cultures. The book is also helpful to Native American girls who are interested in learning more about their roles in indigenous societies.

Photographs are excellent throughout. Included in this book are a foreword by Michael Dorris, a map of Minnesota locating seven Ojibway reservations, and a short glossary and bibliography.

NOLA HADLEY

Ordinary Splendors

📖 Toni Knapp ✏ Kevin Sohl

Multicultural

1994, Roberts Rinehart

Author Toni Knapp retells eighteen animal stories from around the world which illustrate universal human values such as friendship, loyalty, persistence, acceptance, love, and integrity. The stories are divided into three separate sections that tell of creatures who live in the water, on land, and in the sky. Some are familiar, such as Aesop's fable about the tortoise and the hare. Other stories, equally delightful but less well known, include a Mayan tale of a buzzard who learns that everyone has an important place in the world; a story from India's *Jataka Tales*, which shows how a rhinoceros teaches a prince about friendship; and a Chinese tale in which a little rat proves that you don't have to be big to be clever or important.

Proceeds from sales of this book of animal tales from around the world go to a substance abuse treatment program.

Knapp has definitely done her homework researching world folklore. Her book's bibliography lists over fifty resources dating from the early years of this century to the present. This bibliography is in itself a valuable resource for anyone interested in folklore and is a good supplement for a unit on folklore.

Ordinary Splendors is illustrated with Kevin Sohl's artwork, created as presents for his mother between his eighth and fourteenth birthdays. Designer Jody Chapel has incorporated Sohl's artwork into a unique and pleasing picturebook look. The young artist's unusual illustrations of animals are set against backgrounds of bold color. Simple geometric shapes in contrasting colors highlight an introduction to each tale. A copy of the main illustration of each story appears at the bottom of the pages in silhouette.

Sohl died prematurely of a heroin overdose when he was twenty-eight-years old. The proceeds of this book, illustrated with his artwork, benefits The Scott Newman Center, an organization devoted to the prevention of substance abuse through education. Paul Newman and Joanne Woodward, who also lost a child to substance abuse, wrote the book's foreword. Roberts Rinehart, the publisher of this book, has a history of supporting nonprofit organizations by giving a portion of the proceeds from various books to good causes, and this book continues that tradition. SANDRA KELLY

The Great Migration: An American Story

📖 Walter Dean Myers ✏ Jacob Lawrence

African American

1992 (1993), HarperCollins

Near the time of the first World War, large numbers of African Americans migrated from their homes in the rural South, seeking employment and prosperity in the North's burgeoning industrial cities. Internationally acclaimed artist Jacob Lawrence has chronicled this journey in his series of paintings called "The Migration of the Negro," which are reproduced in this volume. Part of this migration himself, Lawrence uses tempera and gesso to create poignant representations of the hopefulness of migration, as well as the desperation and violence that are involved in this struggle for a better life. The actual paintings can be found in the Museum of Modern Art, New York, and in the Phillips Collection. Washington, D.C. *Not a storybook in the traditional sense, Lawrence's piece could easily serve as the introductory text for a lesson on art history, African American history, or migration studies.*

A masterful collection of paintings addressing the migration of African Americans to the North during WWI.

Walter Dean Myers contributes to this effort with the inclusion of his poem, "Migration." A piece that is equally compelling as Lawrence's paintings, Myers's "Migration" lends a literary component to this folio that is otherwise lacking.

CHRISTINE PALMER

Stella, On the Edge of Popularity

📖 Lauren Lee

Asian American, Korean American

1994, Polychrome Publishing Corporation

Seeking to capture a young Korean American's experience, this somewhat contrived novel only partially succeeds. Stella Kim's story is familiar to many young Korean American immigrants. Her

83

father, a former engineer, and her mother, a former nurse, have given up their former professions to open a dry cleaning store in America. Stella's grandmother usually runs the household, allowing the parents to work the long hours necessary to keep the business afloat. As the oldest child and only daughter, Stella feels intense familial pressure. She must help her two younger brothers do well in school, and obey three elder figures. Outside the family, faced with the peer pressure and demands of seventh grade, Stella wants desperately to fit into her school. Stella's nemesis (formerly her best friend) is Eileen Englehart, the most popular girl in school and the one Stella most wants to emulate.

A predictable book in which a Korean American girl gains a better sense of her identity.

Unfortunately, Stella and the other characters in the book are not simply familiar, but are actually little more than stock figures. Stella is the oppressed Asian American girl struggling for acceptance while trying to bridge the expectations of her family and her peers. The book reinforces the myth of Asian Americans as "model minorities." Stella is described as being very good in math "like all Asians are." Stella's grandmother, father and mother are wise stoics; her brothers are smart-alecky pests. Eileen is the prototypical WASP snob.

The book takes an "oh, by the way" detour to address racism. Stella's father and his friends are kicked off of a soccer field, and they sue the owner for discrimination. Elieen's father turns out to be the lawyer who represents the racist owner of the field.

Although the book is well-intentioned, ultimately it is simply a series of clichés grounded in superficial understanding of a young girl's experience. It is difficult to feel sympathy or attachment to any of the characters. The bad guys are very bad; the good guys are very good. In the end, of course, Stella becomes popular. There are a few moments of insight when Stella learns not to be ashamed of her class background and begins to understand her parents' motivations better. Perhaps part of the problem here is that Lee is struggling to convey something which she does not seem to have experienced firsthand. In the author's notes, she thanks a number of young people for informing her "about being twelve years old, being a person of color, or being Korean American." While not an insurmountable task, I think dramatizing experiences outside of one's own experience requires insight and a deft control of writing that Lee has yet to develop.

While this book is not highly recommended, it does raise some good issues for discussion and in a field with few books on the Korean American experience, it does have some value. DEBBIE WEI

The Rose-Colored Glasses: Melanie Adjusts to Poor Vision

📖 Linda Leggett ✒ Linda Andrews and Laura Hartman
Physically Disabled
1979, Human Sciences Press

As a result of an accident, Melanie becomes visually impaired. Using a class project to reach out to her classmate, her friend Deborah makes it possible for Melanie to develop a real friendship with someone who understands her disability. While the book's language may seem somewhat dated, the issues addressed are relevant.

Deborah reaches out to Melanie, a classmate who is visually impaired, and helps her overcome her handicap in a slightly dated book.

Deborah emerges as a very strong character in the story, often resolving conflicts in the classroom that the teacher can't seem to handle. The friendship helps Melanie gain confidence in herself both as a person and as a student.

With black-and-white illustrations portraying a classroom filled with children from various cultures, this book could prove useful in helping a teacher or counselor share greater understanding about how young children meet the challenges that come with being disabled. The upbeat tone of the story and the absence of a "woe is me" theme makes this an effective book to use in the classroom. MEREDITH ELIASSEN

From Anna

📖 Jean Little ✒ Joan Sandin
Physically Disabled
1972, Harper & Row, 📚 Gormley, Beatrice, *The Ghastly Glasses.*

This story is set in 1933 in Germany. Anna's parents are uncomfortable with the atmosphere in Germany and have decided to emigrate to Canada.

But this story is not really about the adjustment to Canada as much as it is about the change in Anna when her health is attended to.

Anna has always been considered clumsy and slow by her family, but once in Canada, it is discovered that Anna has very poor eyesight. With glasses and a special school to help her catch up with her schoolwork, the true Anna is revealed to be funny and artistic.

An unrealistic treatment of a physical disability.

The story does not seem realistic. Eyesight as bad as Anna's would have to be accompanied by eyestrain, and it borders on child neglect that her parents would simply write her off as clumsy. Throughout the story, it seems as though Anna's job is to prove her worth to her parents, rather than her parents' job to help Anna find her talents. Everyone (including Anna's) complete acceptance of this situation is maddening.

Contemporary children who have a similar vision experience will be unbelieving that Anna was not teased about her glasses, and therefore was never torn between wanting to see and hating her glasses. This book is not recommended.

JANIS O'DRISCOLL

Stitching Stars: The Story Quilts of Harriet Powers

Mary E. Lyons

African American

1993, Scribner's Sons, ✳ Series, 🏛 Coerr, Elanor Josephina, *Story Quilt*; Johnston, Tony, *Quilt Story*.

In Mary Lyons's adept hands, this introduction to nineteenth-century folk artist Harriet Powers and her two story quilts becomes a celebration of creativity and an invitation to the rich cultural traditions of West African textile art, African American religion and spirituals, and Southern folklore—all of which, Lyons suggests, contributed to Powers's work.

A fine illustrated biography of Harriet Powers, a nineteenth-century African American folk artist.

Little is known of the first years of Harriet Powers' life. She was born into slavery in Clarke County, Georgia, on October 29, 1837. By the time she was eighteen, she was married and had had the first of her seven children. With her growing family, she watched the progress of the Civil War, celebrated emancipation, and began a new life as a free woman. Lyons fills out this skeletal story with well-selected quotations from other former slaves who lived in Georgia during these years and several period photographs. By 1886, Powers had completed the first of her story quilts. That year she exhibited the quilt at a cotton fair and received an offer to buy it, which she reluctantly accepted.

The quilt Powers exhibited that year (now in the Smithsonian) and a second she undertook as a commission for Atlanta University (now in the Museum of Fine Arts, Boston) were, according to Lyons, diaries of Powers's spiritual life, histories written with needle, thread, and cloth. As she guides us panel by panel through each quilt, Lyons quotes generously from Powers's own description of the quilts' narrative elements. In addition, Lyons offers her own observations on the quilts' subject matter, filling in details about the dramatic weather incidents like the "Dark Day of 1780," which Powers records, and drawing intriguing connections between Powers's use of biblical figures like Moses, Jacob, Jonah, or Satan and their appearance in spirituals or African American folktales. The design of the quilts, Lyons suggests, may well owe a direct debt to the appliqué work of West African banners and flags and the rhythm echoes of the call-and-response pattern of an African American preacher and his congregation.

It is unlikely that Harriet Powers ever left Georgia, but as Mary Lyons writes, "when she sat down each evening to work on a story quilt, she traveled to a different world." *Stitching Stars* is a wonderful guidebook to that world. Includes both an index and a list of sources. ANNE DAVIES

Skin Deep and Other Teenage Reflections: Poems

Angela Shelf Medearis ✏ Michael Bryant

Multicultural

1995, Macmillan Books for Young Readers, 🏛 Wong, Janet, *Good Luck Gold*.

Medearis is a prolific author whose body of work includes a cookbook, picture books, and now poetry. The poems are reflections of the doubts, angst, joys, frustrations, and uncertainties faced by teenagers. The book addresses such concerns as peer pressure and teenaged pregnancy. The poems are not complex in terms of structure or content and their messages are easily discernible though somewhat didactic. For example, "Black Barbie Doll" explores how cliques form around how one talks or performs in

A didactic collection of contemporary poetry expressing the pleasures and dilemmas faced by adolescents.

school. Medearis ends the poem in this manner: "Nobody is going to squeeze me into a box labeled black or white. Okay?" Undoubtedly, many young people, especially young people of color, will understand and identify with these feelings.

The simple illustrations are in pencil, charcoal, and ink. Several of the faces are distinctive, but many of the illustrations are somewhat mundane. The full-color jacket is inviting. VIOLET HARRIS

Winnie Mandela: The Soul of South Africa

📖 Milton Meltzer ✒ Stephen Marchesi
African, South African
1987 (1986), Viking, ✳ Series, 📖 Evans, Michael, *South Africa*; Green, Carol, *Desmond Tutu: Bishop of Peace*; Haskin, Jim, *Winnie Mandela: Life of Struggle*; Naidoo, Beverley, *Journey to Jo'burg*; Vennema, Stanley and Peter, *Shaka: King of the Zulus*.

With deft research and outstanding writing skills, Meltzer has created an insightful biography of one of the world's most well-known women. Although the controversy surrounding her later years is not detailed in this biography, and little is done to place her life in the context of the fierce and complicated history of South Africa, Meltzer sensitively draws a detailed personal portrait focusing on the earlier parts of Winnie Mandela's life. (He does, however, describe her efforts to gain her husband's 1990 release from prison.)

An insightful but incomplete look at a controversial woman.

Winnie Mandela's work with the African National Congress is highlighted, and much detail is provided about the black and white women who worked with her to fight apartheid. Mandela was only twenty-seven years old, with two small children, when her husband was arrested, tried, and sentenced to life in a Pretoria prison, and Meltzer effectively depicts her life at the time. But the lack of historical context or a time line of events and a bibliography weaken the biography.

While the writing is fluid and clear, I think this book would work best in conjunction with some others, including Carol Green's *Desmond Tutu:*

Bishop of Peace, Beverley Naidoo's *Journey to Jo'burg* and Michael Evans's *South Africa*. Jim Haskin's *Winnie Mandela: Life of Struggle*, which is more suited to grades 7 and up, provides a richer overview of Winnie Mandela's journey from medical social work to a major freedom fighter and antiapartheid spokesperson. Although Diane Stanley and Peter Vennema's *Shaka: King of the Zulus* traces Shaka Zulu's rise from an obscure place in his nation to the position of King of the Zulus, the Eurocentric misrepresentations in the illustrations are troubling. For example, in the time of Shaka, Zulu boys and young soldiers did not wear sandals. Nor does Vennema capture the stature and dignity of this military genius. But Stanley does provide readers with a look into the strategically focused mind of this warrior and empire builder often compared to Napoleon, Alexander the Great, and Julius Caesar. DAPHNE MUSE

Elliott and Win

📖 Carolyn Meyer
Gay/Lesbian/Bisexual
1986, McElderry

Fourteen-year-old Winston has a mother who thinks he needs a male role model, so she enrolls him in Los Amigos, where he meets Elliott. Elliott, a middle-aged confirmed bachelor, is intent on fixing the grammar of American youth and introducing Winston to the finer things in life, like gazpacho and opera. Winston's hypermasculine friend Paul concludes that Elliott is a "faggot" and tries to get Winston to stop seeing him. But Winston begins to change his life—cooking better, reading more, taking an interest in classical music—despite Paul's chiding.

Though Elliott's sexuality is never defined, his nontraditional gender roles wear off on Winston. As it turns out, Paul's father, whom Paul has not seen for years, is gay. Paul recounts to

A sometimes lighthearted book about a teen challenging traditional gender roles.

Winston his angry reaction toward his father, and his father's caring and understanding response. Although Paul is not entirely comfortable with his father's gayness, Elliott's new girlfriend Heather is perfectly at ease and doesn't understand why people are upset about homosexuality. Indeed, this seems to be one of the central points in *Elliott and Win*: though sexuality or gender-role conformity may initially seem to be an important facet of a person, the more one gets to know the person, the less central these become, until the issue is moot.

When Win witnesses the gang rape of Heather, unable to stop it, his feelings of guilt and powerlessness overwhelm him. The book deals with the gang rape and its aftermath with great sensitivity and complexity. Elliott understands Win's pain and teaches him ways to regain a sense of control over his life. In the end, Paul's warnings about gay men rectify themselves in heterosexual men—the only sinister behavior in the book is heterosexual, while two of the more supportive relationships in the book are between boys and nonconforming men. While sometimes lighthearted and amusing, the book also addresses serious and painful issues with insight and hope. CHRIS MAYO

All It Takes Is Practice

Betty Miles
African American, Biracial
1976, Alfred A. Knopf

This book explores the world of a ten-year-old boy named Stuart, who lives a simple existence as an only child in an affluent Kansas family. His days consist of school, dreaming of being a basketball star, and his friendship with Allison, a neighborhood friend whom he has known all his life. Stuart's world is challenged and enriched when he is chosen by his fifth-grade teacher to help the new boy in town get acquainted with school. Stuart is seen as a loner who craves a best friend, and he finds that he really likes Peter, the new boy. The two become friends and discover a great deal about each other and themselves in the process.

A wonderful still-fresh story of the friendship between a Caucasian and biracial boy.

Peter is a biracial child whose mother is African American and whose father is European American. Peter's is the first "black family" to move into the small town, and they have chosen the "fanciest street in Clayton," a street known for its large homes with swimming pools.

The story line follows the townspeople's various and sometimes dangerous reactions to Peter's family as seen through Stuart's and Peter's eyes. Peter is described as a very light-skinned boy who "doesn't look black." His older brother is pictured as darker skinned with an Afro hairstyle like his mother, and his little sister is light brown. What is important in the text is that Peter's identification as a black person is clearly stated in his dialogue with Stuart. When Peter tells Stuart about an experience he had with a family who didn't want him to come over to their house because he was black, Stuart says, "You aren't black!" Peter responds by saying, "Yes, I am. You better get that." He goes on to say, "It's not just looks. It's how you feel, and who your ancestors are." Through this dialogue and other moments throughout the book, although Peter is described as "looking white," he is depicted as a young boy who is very clear about and proud of his identity.

Although the book deals with racism, it focuses on Stuart's coming-of-age. It is through Stuart that we see both the impact racism has on white and black people and the prejudices people draw upon to judge each other. Betty Miles skillfully weaves the events in the town, from Stuart and Peter being chased and beaten by a gang of rednecks to Allison's father's constant running commentary of racist and sexist remarks. The reader also gets to observe Stuart's personal reactions, his need to question people, and his desire to be friends with both Peter and Allison. It is through this process that we see the good and bad of of their hometown as we watch Stuart's own growth into a young man.

The magic of *All it Takes Is Practice* is that these complex issues are presented in very simple, descriptive language while maintaining the emotionally charged and exciting story line. Stuart's desire for a "best friend" and Peter's need to be accepted by his peers are universal preadolescent themes. Young readers of all ethnicities will identify with the characters and the issues. ROSA E. WARDER

Reflections of a Black Cowboy

Robert Miller ✎ Richard Leonard
African American
1992 (1991), Silver Burdett Press, ✶ Series

Four larger-than-life African American heroes people the pages of this, the fourth book in Miller's Reflections Series. Their lives offer a glimpse of the role African Americans played in the development of the United States. African Americans have made significant contributions to American history in every era. In his preface, the author states this series was written to introduce the reader to people who helped settle the West.

87

88

Continuing the format of his previous works, Miller has the Old Cowboy relate tales to his constant companion, his loping old yellow dog, Sundown. In "Esteban and the Seven Seas of Gold," Sundown hears about a black slave born in the African nation of Morocco around 1500, who spent many years seeking treasures in Mexico.

This fascinating book in the Reflections Series retells the lives of four African Americans in the American West.

The adventures continue with the exploits of Jean Baptiste Pointe Du Sable. He set up a trading post on the banks of Lake Michigan in a place called Eschikagou, which endured to become the modern city of Chicago. The retelling of the life of Jim Beckwourth includes his adventures as a mountain man, but more importantly as a Crow Indian Chief. George McJunkin, cowboy and scholar, discovered Folsom Site, where bones and relics have been discovered that suggest man roamed the plains of New Mexico as long as 10,000 years ago.

These adventuresome tales make for a fascinating read, while a bibliography provides sources for further study. Richard Leonard's dramatic woodcuts add the perfect touch needed to personify these larger-than-life heroes.

This book may also be used in lessons along with the other three books in the series. They all offer examples of perseverance, steadfastness, and the pursuit of dreams. BETTYE STROUD

Brown Angels: An Album of Pictures and Verse

Walter Dean Myers
African American
1993, HarperCollins

Myers has spent years browsing through flea markets and antique shops to amass the collection of photographs of African American children from which this book finds its inspiration. The poetry, most often imbued by the spirit of the images of children, offers a starting point from which readers may begin to muse upon and analyze the photographs. Jubilant, bright-eyed, tenacious, smiling faces greet the reader with the turn of each page; though the reader is met

A collection of photographs of African American children enhanced by poetic verse.

only with images, it is difficult to remain passive with this book in hand.

Brown Angels is the perfect medium through which an active imagination can frolic, amusing and entertaining itself. A compelling piece, Myers's effort is more than worth the expense, if only to admire the bright young faces. *However, teachers could easily employ this book in a history unit, or even a creative writing exercise in which children imagine who these faces are and what their lives must be like.* Strongly suggested for any shelf, *Brown Angels* is sure to delight readers of all ages.
CHRISTINE PALMER

Zia

Scott O'Dell
Native American
1995 (1976), Dell Publishing Company, Inc.,
O'Dell, Scott, *Island of the Blue Dolphins*.

Zia is the sequel to *Island of the Blue Dolphins*. In *Island*, an Indian woman named Karana remains alone on an island off the coast of California for eighteen years. Her niece, Zia, who lives on the mainland near the Santa Barbara Mission finally manages to contact her. Zia is the story of Karana's life after leaving the island, and the effect of her life on her niece.

A one-dimensional sequel to Island of the Blue Dolphins.

Although these books have been popular in schools for many years, the characters are one-dimensional and *Zia* is mostly plot—unrealistic plot. The depiction of mission life is hazy at best and misleading at worst.

Mission life for California's Indians was harsh and demeaning. Their cultures were diminished and devalued by priests, but one would never guess this from reading *Zia*.

The characters are so flat that one cannot get a sense of Karana or Zia's cultures, much less their feelings about their plight. Too much is left out here and what remains makes mission life seem "not so bad."

Unfortunately, both of these books remain in California's fourth-grade literature curriculum. *It is crit-*

ical, then, that students who are asked to read these books also be made aware of the real conditions that comprised California mission life. JANIS O'DRISCOLL

Thunder Rolling in the Mountains

Scott O'Dell Elizabeth Hall

Native American

1992, Houghton Mifflin

Many people are acquainted with the removal of the Nez Perce from the Wallowa Valley in Oregon. Chief Joseph and his people resisted the initial attempts to remove them. Finally, they had no choice and were told that

A historical account of the struggle the Nez Perce people encountered before surrendering their land in the late 1800s.

they must leave or be forced to move. With little time to prepare and numerous physical obstacles along the way, many of the Nez Perce perished during the trip. This well-researched account follows the precise trail taken by Chief Joseph in 1887.

O'Dell has written several historical children's novels, one of which, *Island of the Blue Dolphins*, won the Newbery medal.

O'Dell's engaging writing and adept storytelling engage the reader. The image-filled language captures the courage, fear, and despair of these people as they flee their tormentors. This fine novel provides young readers with a rarely voiced view of American history. JUDITH CASTIANO

Standing Tall: The Stories of Ten Hispanic Americans

Argentina Palacios

Hispanic

1994, Scholastic, Inc.

According to the 1990 U.S. Census, there are roughly 22.4 million "Hispanic" people in the United States. Throughout many grammar schools and high schools, topics related to Latinos and Hispanics are largely ignored and thousands of children grow up without any heroes or figures that they can directly link to their heritage. The author has selected ten individuals from different fields including science, sports, and music to provide inspiring examples of what youth can achieve. This book provides readers

with profiles of people from Puerto Rico, Mexico, Bolivia, and Cuba.

Each story reflects the enormous challenges these people faced. The profile of baseball star Roberto Clemente illustrates how some have chosen to meet these challenges. Clemente, from a humble background, had a talent for baseball as well as a true passion for the

Ten upbeat autobiographical sketches of people of Latin descent.

sport. Unfortunately, ignorance and racism forced Clemente to play in racially segregated baseball leagues until Jackie Robinson broke the color line in 1947. Despite this, he obtained numerous batting titles, Most Valuable Player awards, and a total of 3,000 hits during his career. Clemente was inaugurated into the baseball Hall of Fame in 1973.

After struggling to gain his success, Clemente never lost sight of people who were less fortunate. He died on his way to Nicaragua to deliver food and supplies after the 1972 earthquake.

Clemente's story and those of the others included in this book will encourage readers to remain hopeful in their own struggles.
MARTHA L. MARTINEZ

Red Dancing Shoes

Denise Lewis Patrick James E. Ransome

African American

1993, Tambourine Books

This collection of brief biographies of fourteen important African American men and women is interesting enough to hold the attention of young readers. The subjects are selected from a variety of fields, including politics, medicine, sports, and theater. Some, such as Frederick Douglass, Martin Luther King Jr., and Rosa Parks, are well known; others, such as organizer and school founder Mary

Fourteen brief biographies of important African American men and women.

McCleod Bethune or Dr. Charles Drew, who helped perfect blood transfusion techniques, are less known but deserving of greater recognition. Ironically, the book notes that Charles Drew died as a result of blood loss because he was refused admittance to an all-white hospital. This controversial point has been disputed, however, by his daughter, Charlene Drew Harris. According to

89

90

Charlene, her father was treated in the emergency room and never formally admitted to the hospital. Because of the extent of his injuries, he was transferred to another hospital because it had a better trauma unit.

The text is well written and a black-and-white portrait of each subject is included. *The most unique feature of this book is the inclusion of simple skits about key events in each subject's life.* For example, the skit about Charles Drew has a group of children attending a school named after him. They are curious as to why their school is named after him. With the help of a former student of the doctor, they (and presumably the audience and actors) learn about Dr. Drew's accomplishments. Due to the subject matter and brevity of the skits, they tend to be didactic. *Nevertheless, it can be fun and educational for children to act them out.* JODIE LEVINE

The Sunita Experiment

Mitali Perkins
Asian American, East Indian American
1994 (1993), Hyperion Book for Children

Sunita Sen is a first-generation Indian American trying to figure out her identity in this mild and not especially poignant book. Most of her friends in her unnamed San Fransisco suburban town are WASP-like, with the exception of one other Asian and one African American. Herein lies this book's first problem: Because San Francisco is extremely culturally diverse, the ethnic makeup of Sunita's world does not ring true. Another problem with *The Sunita Experiment* is its shallow treatment of too many topics. Between a budding romance, culture clash, environmentalism, and racism, this book does not focus on any topic long enough to satisfy.

An exploration of East Indian culture that unfortunately features a protagonist whose sole wish is to assimilate into mainstream culture.

In the book's basic plot, Sunita's Indian grandparents are spending a year with her family, and Sunita's mother disregards Sunita's fourteen years of American cultural assimilation to appease Sunita's traditional grandparents. One of her concessions is not allowing boys in the house, thus putting Sunita's romance with Michael in peril. However, it soon becomes apparent to everyone but the characters in the book that Sunita's Indian grandparents are receptive to American ways, as when the grandmother wins a soap opera-writing contest and goes to New York instead of attending the annual Bengali festival. While this blindness on behalf of the mother and others advances the plot, it makes for a very ineffectual reading experience.

Perkins also introduces racism into the story. Someone whispers, "Check it out—the colored girls stick together" when Sunita and her African American friend walk together down the hall. Sunita subsequently decides not to hang out with her friend for fear of attracting too much attention. From time to time she ponders the insult, but no substantial resolution ever comes from the incident. This makes Sunita appear extremely cold hearted.

Woven throughout the story are dreams where Sunita dons designer duds and lounges around acting glamorous. These passages only make readers feel that since Sunita feels this way, perhaps being Indian is not as grand as being white. In the end, her friends are impressed with her Indian culture, yet the reader may still sense Sunita is not. Her feelings of wanting to fit in are natural for junior-high students, but it is troubling to see her abandon her cultural heritage to reach her goal. There are so few children's books on the Indian American experience that it is a shame to see a book whose main character spends so much time regretting being Indian. However, this book does a fine job of explaining Indian culture. *A good point of discussion after reading this book is what exactly is an American, and what occurs in American society to make immigrants feel they have to renounce their native culture.* LISA FAIN

Clambake: A Wampanoag Tradition

Russell M. Peters and John Madama
Mashpee Wampanoag, Native American
1992, Lerner Publications, ✱ Series, 📖 Braine, Susan, *Drumbeat Heartbeat: A Collection of the Powwow*; Ortiz, Simon, *The People Shall Continue*.

Steven Peters, or Red Mink as his tribe call him, is a twelve-year-old Wampanoag who lives with his mother, stepfather, and younger sister. Steven's tribe is in Plymouth, on a Massachusetts peninsula that reaches into the Atlantic Ocean between Cape Cod and Martha's Vineyard. An avid fan of sports and Nintendo, Steven also enjoys spending time with his relatives, who live in Mashpee on tribal lands. Steven especially likes his grandfather, Fast Turtle, who is interested in passing on the traditional ways of his tribe to his own children and grandchildren.

While visiting relatives, a Wampanoag Indian learns the importance of honoring elders.

During one of Steven's visits the tribe honors an elder at an appanaug, a traditional clambake. Fast Turtle explains that this important event requires special preparations and cooking techniques. The photographs in the book take the reader through the entire process of preparing for and enjoying the appanaug.

First, Fast Turtle chooses the site for the appanaug, and he and Steven pick out rocks for the fire and collect firewood. Steven digs a shallow oval fire pit. The next day Steven and two friends, Nebosett and Mishanagqus, collect clams, and Steven and his grandfather collect rockweed. The rockweed has

bubbles filled with saltwater that will help give the foods a naturally salty taste while they are cooking.

The guests begin to arrive and the fire is started. After burning for several hours, the hot ashes are raked down around the stones, a bed of rockweed is placed on the stones, food is placed on the top, covered with another layer of rockweed and a layer of plastic, which holds in the steam.

While the food cooks, the guests pray together and thank Hazel Oakley for all her work on the tribe's behalf. The celebration includes teaching tribal history, drumming, dancing, and thanking Fast Turtle and Red Mink for their labors in preparing for the appanaug. Then, at last, the food is ready. After a fabulous feast, Steven thanks his grandfather for teaching him how to hold an appanaug, "Thanks, PaPa, I'll never forget this."

This book is a vital addition to the Native Americans Today: We Are Still Here Series. It teaches about respect between generations and passing on tribal customs and spiritual traditions.

This book is highly recommended for use in classrooms that are teaching about Squanto and the Pilgrims. It is a nice replacement for the oversaturation of Thanksgiving stories during the month of November and is a good resource for younger children, along with

The People Shall Continue by Simon Ortiz. It also would be good for units on the ecology of tidal zones.
NOLA HADLEY

The Almost Year

Florence Engel Randall
African American
1971, Atheneum

The unnamed narrator of this book is a fifteen-year-old African American girl sent to live with an upper-class white family on Long island for the school year. As the angry visitor arrives at her new home, a shower of stones begins to fall from the sky. Are racist neighbors protesting her arrival? Are the children in the family playing a trick on her? From the first moment, *An African American girl is sent to live with an upper-class white family for the school year.* the protagonist feels isolated from the Mallory family, which consists of the unaccepting and unfriendly fourteen-year-old Jolly, the bespectacled and frightened twelve-year-old Gary, their little sister Laurie, their businessman father, and stay-at-home mother. The children make tentative gestures toward their visitor, but she remains aloof, smoldering in anger over living in a world where she feels she does not belong.

The family home seethes with unspoken emotions, and soon unexplained phenomena begin to occur. The doorbell rings for no apparent reason; food flies off dinner plates; the grandfather clock chimes thirteen times. The poltergeist activity reaches its zenith one night when the family is snowbound. Footsteps and pounding resound from the attic bedroom where the young visitor sleeps. The narrator believes that she is responsible for the turmoil, though she has no idea how to control it.

Ultimately, the story is less about psychic phenomena than it is self-discovery, individual growth, and the need for reaching out. By the end of the year, the young narrator has matured as a human being, and is able to accept the well-meaning yet flawed members of the Mallory family because she has learned to understand herself.

Young readers gobble up paperback horror stories, but this one is the real thing—a literary novel that deals with horror but also has a psychological component. The elliptical prose style may be challenging for readers nourished on a steady diet of

91

commercial horror fiction, but would be satisfying for the somewhat better-than-average upper elementary or middle school student. Because it was originally published in 1971, there is a bit of dated slang ("dig," "groovy") and talk about the generation gap, but the emotional life of the characters remains right on the mark. Some readers may be offended that the African American protagonist is never named, but this literary device is quite effective in showcasing the isolation and alienation of the character. PETER D. SIERUTA

Cut from the Same Cloth: American Women of Myth, Legend and Tall Tale

Robert D. San Souci ✦ Brian Pinkney

Multicultural

1993, Philomel Books

Most of these tales are the author's retellings of little-known but authentic folktales recorded in a number of sources. The fifteen stories are presented geographically, three from each region, and represent a range of cultures including American Indian (Chippewa, Seneca, Pueblo, Tewa, Miwok, Sugpiaq), African American, Anglo American, Mexican American, and Hawaiian. A stylized map shows the area of each story's origin. The author introduces the culture or circumstances that may have led to the creation of each heroine, and includes a section of source notes that will help those interested to further their own research.

Occasionally, he adds his own research to the tales, as he does in "Pale-faced Lightning." In this story, he "intermingled details of Pueblo life from a variety of sources." In the story of "Sweet Betsy from Pike," from the song of the same name, San Souci creates a prose tale from the experiences mentioned in the lyrics and research he conducted on his own journey to the west. Source notes are helpful in indicating how much of each story is actually San Souci's work, and purists can choose not to use the stories that cannot be authenticated.

Imaginative stories of little-known heroines of American folklore.

In his preface, Robert D. San Souci suggests why American folktales featuring women are not as well known as those relating the exploits of men. Again, not all of this material is supported with scholarly evidence, but rather presents a common-sense argument.

Overall, this is a successful, imaginatve volume. The inclusion of tales from a number of indigenous nations provides a broader view into native cultures. An extensive bibliography of folktales, with an emphasis on those featuring strong female characters, is included. LYNN EISENHUT

The Ink-Keeper's Apprentice

Allen Say

Asian American, Japanese Japanese

1994, Houghton Mifflin

This semi-autobiographical account of the author's own boyhood touches on the universal elements of what it means to be a teenager and having a determined mission in life, and suggests to us in the West the elements that make life in Japan unique.

A boy in post-war Tokyo wants more than anything to become a cartoonist.

This coming-of-age story follows Koichi as he pursues a life's longing to become a cartoonist and inadvertently grows up in the process. He knocks on the door of the well-known artist Noro Shinpei, intent on lessons, an unlikely move either in Japan or in the West. After an eccentric interview, the boy is accepted and set to grinding ink and other beginning tasks along with Tokida, another apprentice, slightly older and slightly more experienced both in life and in cartooning.

The decidedly eccentric sensei misreads the characters of Koichi's family name, Seii, and calls him Kiyoi for the rest of his life. The boy, in an eccentricity of his own, decides to let it stick.

The lessons the sensei (master) offers the boys on cartooning teach personal integrity as well as the craft of drawing: "...when I ask you to draw a Shinto temple, I don't mean just any old temple, but a Shinto temple. Most of the time, no one will know the difference, but I want YOU to know it. If you're not sure, look it up..."

Together the boys roam the streets of Tokyo, armed with their sketchbooks, practicing their drawing on the things of the real world, and trying out their own new urges in the flow of city life, frequenting coffee shops, experimenting with cheap wine, and attending life drawing classes, to both the excitement and embarrassment of Kiyoi. There are even current politics to be dealt with, including student riots in the streets.

The influence of both the elder apprentice and the Sensei have profound effect on the future of the young boy, who became the author and illustrator of the wonderfully sensitive picture books we know as *The Bicycle Man, The Tree of Cranes, The River of Dreams, The Boy of the Three-Year Nap,* and *Grandfather's Journey.*

The novel is, by admission of the author, a tribute to his sensei, who taught him that "to draw is to discover...and to be astonished." His master also told him to take control of his own education, to learn as much as he could from each teacher, and then move on. "Be ruthless...Be true to your art. One day you'll see that it's harder for the master to let go of a disciple." But the teacher (and the parent) remembers: "Let your beloved child journey."

The jacket illustration is done by Allen Say, but there are no illustrations in the body of the book.
GINNY LEE

The Whispering Cloth: A Refugee's Story

📗 Pegi Deitz Shea ✒ Anita Riggio

Asian American, Laotian American

1995, Boyds Mills Press

A refugee from Laos makes a traditional story cloth of her life.

Longing to understand the killing and devastation of the Vietnam War, young Mai sorts through her feelings related to the death of her parents during the war. Although their Hmong village was in Laos, the war encompassed all of what was then known as Indochina. Mai and her grandmother, Ban Vinai, make it to a refugee camp in Thailand, where she spends her days learning to make the embroidered Hmong story cloths.

Being pushed out of their settlement is nothing new to the Hmong. Prior to migrating from northern to southern China, North Vietnam and Laos became their points of settlement before thousands of them immigrated to the United States after the war in Vietnam. Many sought refuge at Ban Vinai, a noted refugee camp just across the river from Laos in Thailand.

Mai's search for a story worthy of stitching onto her cloth takes her memory back to her mother and father, her flight to Thailand, details of her life in

the camp at Ban Vinai, and her dreams of a new life in "the Big Country."

With her subtly discerning grandmother as a catalyst, Mai pours her being into the story cloth. The sale of the cloth is intended to bring enough money for airfare to a new land and a new life. However, she has stitched the spirits of her mother and father into her cloth, and those spirits are not for sale at any price.

Like any good piece of writing, the story to be stitched into a story cloth must come from inside. The process of introspection and contemplation described here so simply is what most writers go through. *This book would make a good springboard for a creative writing class or for any creative activity involving putting oneself on the line wearing one's heart on one's sleeve.*

The poignancy of the story is enhanced by Anita Riggio's simple, sweet watercolors of Mai's life in Ban Vinai. Mai's story cloth was stitched by You Yang and is presented in two double spreads. Full of clear detail it is an excellent example of what a Hmong story cloth is all about and is especially intriguing for those who have never seen one.

A glossary, placed advantageously at the beginning of the book, defines and pronounces a few Thai and Hmong words and gives us an idea of the significance of the Mekong River for the people of Indochina. GINNY LEE

Extraordinary Asian Pacific Americans

📗 Susan Sinnott ✒ Lindaanne Yee-Donohoe

Asian Pacific American

1993 (1992), Children's Press, ✳ Series

Books about "extraordinary people," often ignore the collective work and actions of groups of people. Greatness seems to be reserved for selected individuals. The "famous people and contributions" approach to multiculturalism presents children with a lopsided view of history. The Extraordinary Asian/Pacific Americans Series is a welcome exception and a useful addition to the non-fiction biographical genre.

The book pays tribute to masses of unnamed heroes—the working people of various Asian coun-

94

tries who have made significant contributions to United States history. There are chapters devoted to "Travelers to Gold Mountain," "Chinese Railroad Workers," "The Chinese Laundry Business," "Raising Sugar Cane in Hawaii," and "Inmates in America's Detention Camps." The book proceeds in chronological order, and, as such, presents a panorama of Asian Pacific American experience in the past 150 years. The book includes many people who may have been neglected previously. The contributions of labor leaders Pablo Manlapit and Philip Vera Cruz are addressed. There are also sections of such distinguished individuals as Lydia Liliuokalani, "Queen of Hawaii," who resisted American colonialism. When discussing renowned sculptor Isamu Noguchi, the author points out how, during World War II, despite the fact that Noguchi lived in New York and was considered to be "safe," he voluntarily went with other Japanese Americans to an internment camp in Poston, Arizona, with the intention of helping other inmates construct playgrounds and parks. When discussing famed Asian American actress Anna May Wong, the author notes her life long struggle to find roles which defied stereotypes, only to be pigeonholed by the U.S. film industry. So frustrated was Ms. Wong with her inability to find decent roles as an Asian American actress that she went to Europe where she became an international film star.

A tribute to Asian Pacific Americans who have made significant contributions to U.S. history.

Well-chosen photographs on almost every page provide a sense of atmosphere for these well-written biographies. The book also includes a bibliography of recommended readings and a comprehensive index. *This is an excellent book for use with anyone interested in developing children's knowledge of Asian Pacific American heroes.* DEBBIE WEI

Louise's Gift or What Did She Give Me That For?

📖 Irene Smalls ✏ Colin Bootman

African American

1996, Little Brown

Louise is disappointed when her grandmother pulls precious gifts from a magic shopping bag for Louise's sisters and brothers, but for Louise, just a crumpled, blank piece of paper and a prediction for her future. The grandmother tells Louise, "I give you the gift of a blank page on which you can put whatever you wish." She responds, "Is this all I get?"

An African American girl is disappointed by Nana's gift, but comes to realize how special her gift truly is.

Hurt, Louise retreats to the kitchen to sulk. When her grandmother joins her with the reassurance that "your gift is the sum of all those others but greater," Louise reluctantly joins her siblings in play and saves the day by using her clever wits to rescue a ring her sister was not supposed to be wearing in the first place.

As the children march home, they come upon a truck stuck under a bridge. The whole neighborhood turns out to watch fancy machines try to retrieve the truck. Louise suggests that they let the air out of the tires, once again saving the day.

Louise's grandmother tells her she now has the right word to put on that piece of paper — creativity. From this, Louise realizes that she has a very special gift.

For the most part, the illustrator captures the great expressions in the brown faces of the characters. The story line emphasizes the value of creative action as opposed to material things and reinforces the importance of cooperation and respect, especially for one's elders. It is also heartening to see a young black girl solving problems with creativity and logic. DAPHNE MUSE

Canto Familiar

📖 Gary Soto ✏ Annika Nelson

Hispanic, Mexican American

1995, Harcourt Brace

Just as he does in his richly written stories like *Neighborhood Odes* and *Baseball in April and Other Stories*, Gary Soto tells great stories even in his poetry. Writ-

Twenty-five beautiful poems about growing up Mexican American.

ing about the extraordinary and the ordinary, Soto captures the daily life of growing up Mexican American and what that means spiritually and culturally. In "Doing Dishes," he writes with an eloquent wit often found in the voices of teenagers to the tedious task of washing dishes :

We have a stack
Of plates
The color of chickens,
White and red.
That's what we
Had tonight— chicken mole,
A messy meal
That leaves stains
On your mouth
And greedy fingers.

Poems like "Eating While Reading" and "Eyeglasses" take young readers into very personal experiences. Sometimes personal and cultural experiences combine to reflect an emerging being. "Ballet Folklorico" speaks to how a cultural experience shapes the core of a young girl.

"Spanish" adeptly describes the power of a language to paint the most colorful pictures using tantalizing words:

Spanish is a matter
Of rolling rrrrs,
Clicking the tongue,
And placing
Your hands
On your hips
When your little brother
Pours cereal
Into your fishbowl.

At times playful and painful, these poems take young readers around the barrio, around the world and through the hearts and minds of young Mexican Americans. Annika Nelson's colorful illustrations are perfectly companioned with Soto's poems. They form a wonderful chorus that invite young people to return to these poems for numerous visits.

DAPHNE MUSE

Let the Balloon Go

📖 ✎ Ivan Southall

Physically Disabled

1990 (1968), Reed Books (Mammoth)

Reminiscent of Thurber's *The Secret Life of Walter Mitty*, this story explores the fantasies, dreams, and reality of a child with a physical disabililty. "Ordinary boys had arms and legs that did the right thing; John's arms and legs only sometimes did the right things; and when his mum got upset about it, John usually got worse. He would start stumbling and dropping things and stammering, and sometimes

On the first day at home alone, a boy with cerebral palsey climbs a tree.

had to beat his thigh with his fist over and over again very hard, to get his words out. His heart would pound like a hammer and sometimes (to his horror) he would cry."

John lives with his overly protective parents in Australia. He has a physical disability that makes his body move in jerks, fits, and starts, but John wants to be like the other boys and girls and even dreams of getting the same kind of knocks, kicks, and bruises other children get from playing ball, running, or climbing a tree. John seizes an opportunity to assert himself when his mother leaves him home alone for the first time; he climbs a tree. This monumental victory signals a major step in his life. The time comes when everyone must cut the string and let the balloon go. John's newfound sense of independence shores him up against the challenges of his disability.

The illustrations are interesting and effective. They are fluid and contain logical movement and scale; the tree is tall, the ladder is heavy, and in one illustration you cannot tell if John is holding the tree or if the tree is holding John. They do not convey how monumental John's adventure is; he looks like a normal child doing something average; in fact, you cannot tell who has the disability.

Southall's accuracy in describing John's psychological need to do something that he thought he could not accomplish (even if he did it to excess), and to press his physical limits in order to reverse the derogatory comments of others, is impressive and noteworthy. The author's skill is also apparent in his ability to engage the reader's sympathy with John's point of view. Even though John's disorder is never named, the reader is put into his body in order to experience things that most of us take for granted.

This story would be ideal for use in the classroom. Most children have thought that their parents are overprotective, but the deceptive simplicity of this story will make them think about family relationships. While the reader is sympathetic to John's plight, there are reasons for the parents to be concerned, which come out in the story. At the end of the story his father makes the statement that sums up what John's odyssey has been for: "Ordinary boys and girls get knocks and bruises you've never dreamt of. Ordinary people have to live with ordinary treatment, and that's not what you are used to. You've been given special treatment; I doubt if you'll ever know how special it has been. But I gather you've had your fill of it. You'd prefer the knocks and bruises."

"A balloon is not a balloon until you cut the string and let it go." Although this story describes the emotions and experiences of a child with disabilities, the theme is universal. There is a time when everyone must "let the balloon go" and see what he or she can do. MEREDITH ELIASSEN

Call It Courage

📕 🖋 Armstrong Sperry

Pacific Island, Polynesian

1990 (1940), Simon & Schuster

✳ Braille

On an impulse Mafatu, son of the Great Chief, decides to paddle to a distant island, accompanied by his only friend, a little dog. Unhappy because he is known as a coward, Mafatu plans to gain his place among strangers, and then return home a real warrior.

Sperry's straightforward, unsentimental storytelling will appeal to those who like uncomplicated plots, lots of action, and little dialogue. Although Sperry's drawings are a bit stylized—they remind one of wood cut drawings—they are beautiful. From them, the reader gets a sense of the vastness of the ocean which Mafatu bravely confronts, as well as his terrible isolation.

Thoroughly entertaining, *Call It Courage* is an excellent read for youngsters. *Further, its simple story can be helpful to any teacher looking for material illustrating the universal themes of courage and self-reliance.*

Aside from the issue of values, *Call It Courage* is impressive for at least one other reason: it takes place on the sea under open skies and in "the forgiving jungle." From Mafatu's experience children may learn that the natural world can be of service to man, and not just an awful threat.

Winner of the Newbery Medal, *Call It Courage* is indeed a gem. ADRIENNE MARSHALL

Shaka: King of the Zulus

📕 Diane Stanley 🖋 Peter Vennema and Diane Stanley

African

1988, Morrow

This picture book biography chronicles the life of a Zulu king from birth to death. The author draws on European accounts of Shaka's life as well as Zulu perspectives. In the late eighteenth and nineteenth centuries, profound changes occurred in southern Africa. Many village and town communities were subsumed into nations, consensus decision making sometimes gave way to autocratic rule, and inequalities in wealth became more pronounced. Warfare shifted from stylized combat with little loss of life to total war and massive deaths. These changes were the result of population pressure, drought, and competition for trade. Groups vied with each other to meet European demand for goods. The new societies of southern Africa demanded new leaders. In this context Shaka, an outstanding soldier who had proven himself on the battlefield, assumed leadership of the Zulu people.

Much of the book focuses on Shaka's military technology and strategies. His innovations are correctly described and impressively illustrated. Balanced in its approach, the book records Shaka's excesses but places him in a global perspective: "Throughout Shaka's life he ruled through force and fear—that is how he made his soldiers obey him, and that is how his army won battles. It is not an approach that is admired today, as we dream of a world at peace. But Shaka lived in a different age, when nations all over the world went to war to build great empires, believing it was honorable."

Much of the book focuses on Shaka's contacts

A Pacific Islander frightened of the sea tries to prove his bravery in a Newbery Award-winning book.

A picture book biography of Zulu leader Shaka and his powerful military genius.

with British visitors to Zululand. As the authors correctly note, the British were able to obtain an agreement from Shaka that gave them limited use of land. They comment, however, that "Shaka always considered the English his good friends." This is highly questionable. Shaka, the politician, viewed the British primarily as a means to increase trade and gain access to guns. He wanted to establish friendly relations, but it is doubtful that he saw the British as friends. When he provided the British with coastal land for a settlement, he also appointed a Zulu governor to study their activities and authorized the creation of a special regiment to watch them. The regiment was called "The watchers over the monster" (*u Khangela amankengane*).

Stanley's illustrations complement the text well. The depiction of Zulu life is authentic and often breathtaking. A minor inaccuracy appears in the illustration of Zulu sandals. According to anthropologist Bernard Magubane: "The typical Zulu sandals have straps that run across the foot rather than straps between the toes." More important, however, is Professor Magubane's overall assessment of the work: "This beautifully illustrated book for children is a welcome departure from the calumny Shaka's childhood has been subjected to in the past. Shaka's difficult childhood, his achievements as youth and adult are not only placed in proper historical context but are done with a great deal of empathy and understanding. Reading the book and looking at the illustrations made me nostalgic about my country."

The pronunciation guide that appears in the front of the text will help teachers and students master Zulu names and places. The best audience for this book will be upper-elementary grades. The text is longer than the typical read-aloud and touches on subjects such as politics and war that older students are better equipped to understand. Picture book biographies of Africans are virtually nonexistent. Recommended titles on southern Africa for younger people are also rare. This book fills an important void.

Teachers who wish to read more about Shaka should consult The Illustrated History of South Africa: The Real Story *(Reader's Digest, 1989), Neil Parsons'* A New History of Southern Africa *(Holmes and Meier, 1993) and Mazisi Kunene's* Emperor Shaka the Great: A Zulu Epic *(Heinemann, 1979).*

BRENDA RANDOLPH

Zekmet, The Stone Carver: A Tale of Ancient Egypt

📖 Mary Stolz   ✏ Deborah Nourse Lattimore

African, Egyptian

1988, Harcourt Brace and Company

The greed of the pharaohs surpasses understanding, thinks Ho tep, the pharaoh's vizier. After nearly completing the pyramids, Pharaoh Khafre wants yet another monument to himself to ensure that his name will last through all eternity. Ho tep enlists Zekmet, a lowly stonecarver, to do the work and plans to claim the credit for himself.

A common Egyptian stone carver creates a monument to immortalize the king.

Dorothy Lattimore has studied extensively the art of ancient Egypt and has brought her erudition to her illustrations. The text is retold in hieroglyphs that line the borders of each page that also tell the story. The book's endpapers repeat the story line by line — a line of hieroglyphs and a line of English — attractively and accurately laid out as though it were taken directly from an ancient papyrus text. The hieroglyph story, however, conveys none of the pharaoh's vainglory, but rather emphasizes great respect for both gods and pharaohs. This tone doesn't match the cynicism that characterizes the main text.

There is a popular packet called Fun with Hieroglyphics, *which includes a number of hieroglyph stamps and a book describing their history and meanings. An older group of children could write (and illustrate) their own stories using the abbreviated, terse hieroglyphs in the same way.*

Khafre, son of Khufu who began the project of building the pyramids, was indeed known as a tyrant. Whether or not this story reflects historical fact is not known, but in any case it does provide a compelling glimpse of ancient Egypt and makes accessible the ancient hieroglyphs. GINNY LEE

97

Children of Clay: A Family of Pueblo Potters

📖 Rina Swentzell and Bill Steen
Native American, Santa Clara Pueblo
1993 (1992), Lerner Publications, ✳ Series,
📖 Ortiz, Simon, *The People Shall Continue.*

Part of the Native Americans Today: We Are Still Here Series, this book teaches about respect between generations and passing on tribal skills and spiritual traditions. The story focuses on one family that works together in the process of making pottery.

Working with clay provides a window on intergenerational relationships in Pueblo society.

Readers learn from the book that working with clay is a long process that takes patience and craftsmanship, and that it is best shared among several people. Together the family collects, cleans, presses, shapes, and fires the clay. The children in the story learn far more than technique, however. Throughout the long process, Rosie tells her two daughters, Judy and Tessie, stories connected with the various stages of their work. One story is about Clay-Old-Woman:

"Clay-Old-Woman lies within the earth and the clay. If people talk to her with respect, she will help them to make beautiful things. Gia Rose says that the pots and figures they make will be alive because Clay-Old-Woman will continue to live and breathe inside them. In order to know that Clay-Old-Woman is breathing within their pieces, they must be quiet and listen."

From these stories, and Rosie's instruction, the children learn to treat the clay with spiritual reverence.

Of the ancient practice of clay working, the author writes, "Although many things are changing at Santa Clara Pueblo, pottery-making is still much the same as in the past. Making pottery helps children…remember the place, the mountains, and the sky as they work and play in clay with their mothers, aunts, grandmothers, and great-grandmothers."

This book is highly recommended for use in classes on cultural traditions or in conjunction with The People Shall Continue *by Simon Ortiz. It is a good resource for students examining indigenous history and cultures of the Southwest.* NOLA HADLEY

It's Crazy to Stay Chinese in Minnesota

📖 Eleanor Wong Telemaque   ✒ Various sources
Asian American, Chinese American
1978, Thomas Nelson

This collective biography is a testament to Chinese Americans who have fought the odds and have endured. McCunn has compiled seventeen profiles of men and women from all walks of life and has organized these profiles into three sections: pioneers, generations, and contemporaries. Written in a lively narrative style, these profiles include people like China Mary, an Alaskan frontierswoman; Harry Lee, a "cowboy" who became Louisiana's first Chinese American sheriff;

Profiles of seventeen interesting Chinese American men and women who have fought incredible odds.

Li Khai Fai and Kong Tai Heong, a husband and wife doctor team who diagnosed and fought the bubonic plague in Honolulu at the turn of the century; Lue Gim Gong, developer of frost-resistant strains of oranges; and Arlee Hen, a black Chinese woman from Mississippi. The chronicling of these biographies also provides young readers with an opportunity to ask questions related to the presence of a black Chinese woman in Mississippi, a Chinese cowboy in Louisiana, and a highly educated Chinese wife and husband doctor team who fought a life-threatening disease at the turn of the century.

Relevant historical information is interwoven throughout the stories and there is an extensive bibliography provided at the back of the book to place individual lives in a historical context. Each profile is liberally illustrated with rare archival photographs and detailed captions that tell the compelling stories of the struggles and triumphs of ordinary and extraordinary Chinese Americans. By chronicling the diversity of interracial backgrounds, geographical locations, and the depth of discrimination in the Chinese experience, some stereotypes are dispelled and the record is set straight. *An enlightening work of scholarship, this book is accessible to an upper-middle school audience.* LAURI JOHNSON

98

When the Nightingale Sings

📖 Joyce Carol Thomas

African American

1992, HarperCollins

In this updated Cinderella story, gentle, hardworking Marigold is an orphan living by a swamp with Ruby and her twin, tone-deaf daughters Arlita and Carlita. Marigold is the cook, housekeeper, seamstress, teacher, and the golden-throated voice instructor for the snippy girls who abuse her every chance they get. Far across the swamp, the Rose of Sharon Baptist Church is searching for a sincere, magically voiced singer to replace the Queen Mother Rhythm lead voice in the choir.

A Great Gospel Convention brings together an African American singer and her dead sister's long-lost daughter.

The Minister of Music and Queen Mother decide to host the Great Gospel Convention, where the sweet strains of Marigold's song enchant the crowd. Marigold's vocal talents are revealed; furthermore, she discovers that she is the niece of Queen Mother Rhythm. The Minister of Music gallantly divulges his love for Marigold and her voice, and Marigold's song harmoniously reunites her torn family.

In this version of the classic tale, Marigold is not loved for her looks but for her caring personality, intelligence, and talent. The melding of gospel, dreams, and nature only enhance this distinctive and down-to-earth story. At the end, Marigold embraces her once abusive relatives, reinforcing forgiveness. ALISON WASHINGTON

Naya Nuki, Shoshoni Girl Who Ran

📖 Kenneth Thomasma ✏ Eunice Hundley

Native American

1992 (1983), Baker Book House, ✳ Series

Based on a true story, *Naya Nuki, Shoshoni Girl Who Ran* is the story of an eleven-year-old Shoshoni girl who is captured by an enemy tribe and forced to march one thousand miles away from her home to become a slave. Throughout her ordeal, the protagonist, Naya Nuki, refuses to give up hope of returning to her village. She plots an escape and travels alone through the wilderness back to her own tribe. Thomasma takes us step by step through Naya Nuki's courageous journey.

The story begins in 1801 as Naya Nuki's tribe moved closer to the prairie to hunt buffalo. A summer drought left the tribe weakened, hungry, and vulnerable to attacks from other tribes. Nevertheless, Naya Nuki and her best friend, Sacajawea, remained optimistic and playful as they imagined the nights ahead when they would fall asleep with full stomachs. They fantasized about new buffalo skin robes. They listened closely each night around the fire as their elders regaled the group with inspirational stories and tribal lore.

In an uneven book based on a true story, a Native American girl in the nineteenth century escapes her captors.

Then one morning, as the girls chatted and gathered water at a stream, a scout from their tribe blazed by on horseback shouting, "The enemy is coming. Prepare for attack!" Confusion ensued, shots were fired, and Naya Nuki, Sacajawea, and others were taken prisoner by the attacking Minnetares.

The Shoshoni captives were taken clear across the prairie, about one thousand miles from their home, to become slaves. Naya Nuki, given to a crabby old woman, immediately set about plotting to escape. She tried to persuade Sacajawea to go along, but her best friend was too frightened to join her. Days later, Sacajawea was sold to a white man.

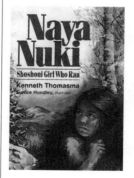

One night, all the conditions were right, and Naya Nuki decided to flee by herself. She ran for hours through the night, and rested by day. Throughout her escape, Naya Nuki faced many predictable obstacles, such as dangerous animals, other tribes, hunger, and sickness. She maintained composure at all times and often drew upon the inspiration and survival knowledge she had acquired from her elders. She eventually reached her village and the arms of her mother.

Unfortunately, at times the story becomes repetitive and predictable: Naya Nuki travels by night, rations her food, rests during the day, and faces a suspenseful event every few days. Interest is revived when Naya Nuki reminisces about her village life, thinks back with tenderness to her family, and expresses her fears.

Thomasma doesn't present Native Americans as a monolithic population. He shows them as belonging to separate groups, each with a unique language, style of dress, and culture. At times this differentiation is simplistic. Thomasma portrays the Shoshoni tribe sympathetically and as a peaceful group simply looking for food. Other tribes—the Crow, Blackfoot, and Minnetares—are depicted as fierce and aggressive. Thomasma writes, "These warlike tribes came to steal Shoshoni horses, to kill Shoshoni warriors, and to take their women and children prisoner." It is the usual good vs. evil dichotomy applied to Native Americans.

Similarly, in the end Sacajawea, married to Charbonneau, the French guide to Lewis and Clark, is reunited with her tribe. This happily-ever-after ending feels too neatly sewn up.

Naya Nuki, Shoshoni Girl Who Ran will appeal to middle-grade readers and will be easy for them to read. The history and survival lessons the story provides are more entertaining than informative. The book also provides a valuable text for critique, especially about contact between whites and Native Americans.
KATHY COLLINS

The Real McCoy: The Life of an African American Inventor

📖 Wendy Towle ✒ Wil Clay
African American
1993, Scholastic, Inc.

Elijah McCoy's parents escaped slavery in the South by moving to Ontario, Canada, where McCoy was born. Educating slaves was illegal in the United States, but in Canada McCoy was able to attend school. He took an interest in the ways in which mechanical devices worked. At sixteen, he was sent to Scotland and became a master mechanic and engineer. When the American Civil War ended, he returned to Michigan as a free man.

An appealing picture-book biography of the prolific African American inventor Elijah McCoy.

McCoy initially was unable to utilize fully his talents, as discrimination forced him to become a railroad worker. In 1872, however, he patented his first automatic lubricating cup, which oiled the locomotive while the train was in motion, thus eliminating the need for frequent stops for oiling. Others tried to copy his invention, but were not successful. People wanted not the imitations but the "the real McCoy"—hence the expression. McCoy patented over fifty inventions in his lifetime, including the lawn sprinkler and the ironing board, but died an impoverished, forgotten man. In 1975, he finally gained recognition in the form of a historic marker at the site of his home and a street named in his honor.

The picture-book format makes the story appealing not only for elementary students but also for middle and high school students with reading difficulties. The full-page illustrations are very colorful and rich in authentic detail. DORIS COSLEY

Faith Ringgold

📖 Robyn Turner ✒ Various sources
African American
1993, Little, Brown

Faith Ringgold's art heralded a new trend in children's book illustrations. In this biography, Turner discusses many of the influences that shaped Ringgold's work, including the social and political milieu in which Ringgold lived. Most importantly, Turner demonstrates how Ringgold's family defied and overcame many of the strictures that might have prevented her from reaching her full potential.

A biography of the famous African American artist Faith Ringgold.

The story begins with life among the Ringgolds prior to Faith's birth. Turner goes on to major events in Faith's life such as childhood illnesses that prevented regular attendance in primary school, the encouragement of artistic talent she received from family members, the loving familial environment, the divorce of Ringgold's parents, her education, teaching career, marriages, children, and art. *Ringgold lived a relatively privileged life, and careful discussion can elicit this observation among children. One can share information about Sugar Hill, the privileged African Americans who resided there, and the influence of African-American artists on U.S. culture through discussion about Ringgold's life.*

The highlights of the book are discussions about Ringgold's art as well as photographs of her major works. Some of her best-known works are included. However, more discussion about her three children's books would have added substantially to the work. VIOLET HARRIS

The Invisible Thread: An Autobiography

📖 Yoshiko Uchida   🏷 Various sources
Asian American, Japanese American
1991, Julian Messner, ✳ Series, 📖 Day, Frances Ann, *Desert Exile*; Uchida, Yoshiko, *Journey Home*; Uchida, Yoshiko, *Journey to Topaz*.

In this moving autobiography, Uchida writes about her beloved family, the Japanese American community, the social and political climate of the time, and her early experiences as a writer. She reflects on her school experiences, including unhappy days as an outsider in junior and senior high school, when she longed to be accepted as an American. Her pain was further compounded by a trip to Japan with her family during the 1930s. There she was perceived as a foreigner; the language and customs were new to her and she came away even more confused about where she belonged.

A moving book about growing up as a second-generation Japanese American in California.

Prejudice against Asian Americans, which had heretofore been barely held in check, was unleashed during World War II. When Japan bombed Pearl Harbor, 120,000 West Coast Japanese Americans were uprooted and incarcerated in concentration camps. Uchida's father, who was born in Japan, was abruptly seized and held incommunicado; Uchida, her mother, and her sister were interned in a horse stall at a nearby racetrack. Later, they were sent to Topaz, a bleak prison camp in the Utah desert where her father eventually joined them.

With insight and clarity, Uchida describes what it was like to be sent by her own government to live behind barbed wire. Her firsthand account of the deprivations of the desolate, dusty prison camp is a revelation, especially for readers who are unfamiliar with that shameful chapter in United States history. Uchida writes, "The ultimate tragedy of that mistake, I believe, was that our government betrayed not only the Japanese people but all Americans, for in its flagrant violation of our Constitution. It damaged the essence of the democratic beliefs on which this country was founded." It was not until 1987 that the Supreme Court reversed its wartime stance on the incarceration of American citizens of Japanese descent and acknowledged that the event was one the worst violations of civil liber-

ties in American history. The United States government belatedly issued a formal apology, concluding that the causes of the uprooting were racial prejudice, war hysteria, and a failure of political leadership. In 1988, Congress passed a redress bill to mitigate some of the massive losses suffered by Japanese Americans, but it came too late for many of those who, like Uchida's parents, were deceased.

After the war, Uchida graduated with honors from the University of California. She later earned her master's degree at Smith College. She taught elementary school in Topaz, Utah, while incarcerated, and later in Philadelphia. The last chapter in this autobiography ends with Uchida happily standing in front of her first class ready to start her new career.

In the epilogue, Uchida describes how a second trip to Japan on a Ford Foundation fellowship in 1952 began to turn things around for her. She perceived Japan in a new light and found a wholeness of spirit that spoke to something deep inside herself, making her aware of the invisible thread that linked her with her Japanese heritage for the first time. She describes her growth and her development in her youth, when she was imbued with the melting pot mentality and wanted to be like everyone else, to later in her life when she became more self-conscious, and proud to be a Japanese American. Having transcended her pain and confusion, she can

serve as an inspiration for others who are suffering the rejection and anguish of being an outsider.

It was Uchida's quiet strength that enabled her to infuse this poignant memoir with power and warmth. *Illustrated with family photographs, this autobiography from the In My Own Words Series is fascinating reading for writers, history students, Japanese Americans, lovers of children's literature, and people committed to cultural sensitivity.*

Uchida's experiences during World War II provide the basis for two of her novels: Journey to Topaz *and its sequel,* Journey Home. *Reading both novels along with this autobiography will help students gain insight into how life experiences provide inspiration for writing fiction. The Invisible Thread might also be used with a unit on World War II, an author unit or a unit on prejudice.* FRANCES A. DAY

Juanita Fights the School Board

📖 Gloria Velasquez

Hispanic, Mexican American

1994, Arte Publico Press

Juanita (sometimes called Johnny) Chavez, a student at Roosevelt High School, has been expelled from her school and the whole district. Her fight with a racist Anglo girl at the school dashes her hopes of becoming the first person in her hard-working, low-income Mexican American family to graduate from high school.

A coming-of-age story about a remarkable Mexican American girl who is expelled from high school.

Told in chapters that alternate between being narrated by Jaunita and Sharon Martinez, a child psychologist, and an attorney who helps Juanita fight the school board, the creative structuring of the narrative provides a depth and complexity that enriches the story line.

Juanita emerges as a real person—no angel—capable of losing self-control in a conflict, and of lying to her family to get out at night. Juanita also has a strong sense of fairness and appreciation of goodness in others. Her fairly typical teenage sense of humor adds a wonderfully realistic dimension to the story as well. Without turning into a goody-goody, Juanita comes to recognize her mistakes and bad habits and begins to change.

The story falters in that much more emphasis is placed on the lawyer and other adults in the story than on the teenagers. The warmth of Sharon, who gives herself totally to Juanita's struggle, and the financial generosity and legal brilliance of the attorney, who charges no fee to the Chavez family, tend to dominate the reader's attention. Yet, while at times the plot feels paternalistic, the problems in the book are overcome by Juanita's solid presence.

A pattern of racial bias emerges which exposes a broad range of school board practices, including the failure to give the Chavez family case-related documents in proper order, and the failure to investigate the other girl's actions, including her history of racist remarks.

With a well-deserved reputation for publishing new poetry and prose by Latino/a authors, often bilingually, the publisher Arte Publico's entry into this arena is significant. Hopefully, author Velasquez will offer young readers more as well. ELIZABETH MARTINEZ

Mariah Keeps Cool

📖 Mildred Pitts Walter ✏ Pat Cummings

African American

1990, Bradbury Press

In a sequel to her *Mariah Loves Rock*, Walter explores the reaction of a family to the arrival of a child from the father's first marriage.

Mariah is looking forward to summer. She plans to host a surprise party for her sister Lynn and to train hard for diving competitions with her swim team. As it turns out, the summer is filled with activities and involvements Mariah did not expect. She is shocked that Lynn is volunteering at a homeless shelter, and finds that her half-sister, Denise, is having difficulty fitting into her new home.

However, by summer's end all is well. Mariah and her friends have helped celebrate Lynne's birthday

Realistic characters populate this family drama focusing on an African American girl's coming-of-age.

by collecting food and clothing for the people at the shelter. Mariah has helped Denise settle into a loving family. And she goes to the swim meet determined and confident that she can prevail against even the stiffest competition.

This book portrays a wonderful sense of family through realistic characters with whom readers can identify. Problems arise and are dealt with or solved. Support is given to family members, and love and caring abound. *Mariah Keeps Cool* is an uplifting portrayal of an eleven-year-old's resolve to do her very best for herself, her family, and her team. This book is recommended. BETTYE STROUD

Definitely Cool

📖 Brenda Wilkinson

African American

1995 (1993), Scholastic, Inc.

Roxanne begins her school year with a whole list of "news": new outfit, new style, new school, new school year, and new friends. She is sure entering the seventh grade at the upscale Riverdale Junior High will make her a new, cool person. But when her first day is harried, confusing, and lonely, Roxanne fears becoming an outcast.

Roxanne misses her old neighborhood elementary school when she sees the many divisions at

An African American girl must deal with peer pressure and fitting in at a new school.

Riverside; people there group themselves by social status, race, age, and "coolness." Roxanne confronts peer pressure, and has to decide if popularity is worth risking friendships, her reputation, and her academic life. Roxanne learns about true friendship, how to face bullies and pressure, how to treat others, and how to have confidence in her ability to choose the correct course despite what all the "cool" kids do.

Students identify with Roxanne because Wilkinson seems to tap into all the fears and anticipations they face on entering junior high. Roxanne makes choices that are not easy; she sometimes gives in to pressure and sometimes avoids it, but she knows that either way she must deal with the consequences. Wilkinson is dead-on with the language, attitudes, feelings, and reactions of this age group and treats the kids with respect. The adults are not merely didactic, moral guides but also imperfect beings, thus allowing Roxanne to make her own decisions with some adult input. ALISON WASHINGTON

The Shimmershine Queens

📗 Camille Yarbrough

African American

1989, Putnam

This novel for middle-school audiences addresses hierarchies of skin color among African Americans. Teased by the other students because of her full features and dark skin, Angie confides in her visiting "Cousin" Seatta (who is ninety years old), "Sometimes people say mean things — Say I'm too black, my hair is bad. Call me names." Cousin Seatta reassures Angie that her classmates are confused because they don't know their history.

Yarbrough emphasizes the importance of community elders in this coming-of-age story set in a predominately African

An African American girl learns about self esteem and achievement from an older relative.

American neighborhood in New York City. Cousin Seatta carries on the tradition of African griots by passing on history and wisdom through story. She encourages Angie to be proud of her past and to "glory in knowledge." Determined to excel in school, Angie faces opposition from a group of tough-talking girls. Only her friend Michelle stands by her.

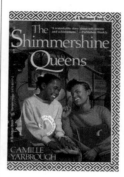

They are the "shimmershine queens." As Angie explains about the shimmershine feeling, "You get it when you do the best you can....You feel like you be shining all over."

Despite peer pressure and family problems (her parents have recently separated), Angie enrolls in an African dance and drama class taught by a visiting performing artist, finds her voice, and lets her talents and intelligence shine through. The black English dialogue and classroom scenarios ring true. This is an important book about identity and the need to know one's history. LAURI JOHNSON

The Lost Garden

📗 Laurence Yep ✐ Various sources

Asian American, Chinese

1991, Julian Messner, Simon & Schuster, ✶ Chinese, Series, 📖 Yep, Laurence, *Serpent's Children*; *Sweetwater*; *Dragon of the Lost Sea*; *Dragon Steel*; *Dragon Cauldron*; *Dragon War*; *The Mark Train Murders*.

Chinese American author Laurence Yep provides us with a moving account of his search for identity. Yep values his heritage, questions some of its traditions, and writes meaningfully to engage the minds of young people. His reflections on growing up as a Chinese American are often candid and humorous.

Yep recounts the pain he felt when people were surprised by his ability to speak English clearly. But there were also times that he forgot who he was. He recalls watching a television program in which the bad guys were Chinese. Imitating the villains, Yep ran around the

A humorous autobiography of a Chinese American writer's adolescence in San Francisco.

room pinching his eyes trying to "look Chinese," until his mother stopped and made him look in the mirror.

Yep, who grew up Catholic, also writes about serving as an altar boy. At one particular service, his job involved carrying the cross. The pole was twice his size and difficult to balance. He lost control of the pole, which almost took on a life of it's own:

"I lurched, almost taking out some of the other servers who managed to get out of the way in time. Like a drunken lancer, I struck one side of the door-way. Thrown off balance, I staggered back as every-

one ducked. Even more determined, I took aim and tried to charge through the sacristy door but missed and hit the other side of the doorway. By the time I actually made it through the door, even the nuns were laughing."

The rich and visually powerful writing for which Yep has become known engages even those readers who might not have an interest in the story of a young Chinese American boy growing up in the fifties and sixties. The field of children's literature is far richer for including Yep's vision, voice, and humor in its canon. MAGNA M. DIAZ

Between the Lines:
Literature As a Tool for Tolerance

Sheri Bauman

SCHOOL STORIES

Young people are drawn to stories written in the first person. Hearing the subjective voice, they see the world through another person's eyes.

As a teacher committed to tolerance, I often use novels and short stories to help students explore the lives of people whose cultures are very different from theirs. In one unit, I use stories that enable my students to enter other cultures through the familiar environment of school. Because their own lives are centered in school, students often have strong personal reactions to stories that explore the hazards of that environment.

In the following stories, students will find youthful first-person narrators whose interests and dreams are familiar to them but whose cultural background may be quite different. By experiencing discrimination and hardship with the characters, students become aware of the intolerance around them and are able to identify with the victims of intolerance.

"A BUNCH OF LOSERS"

In *American History*, by Judith Ortiz-Coffer, the narrator is a teenager of Puerto Rican descent named Elena who has repeatedly felt the pain of being an outsider. She is disqualified from taking honors classes (although she is a straight-A student) because English is not her

native language. She and her black and Puerto Rican classmates are called a "bunch of losers" by their teacher.

Elena begins the day excited at the prospect of going to the home of her only friend, Eugene, to study for a test in American history. Elena is a resident of "El Building," a tenement inhabited primarily by Puerto Ricans, and had gazed with longing at the only house remaining on the block where Eugene lives. When she arrives, however, she is turned away at the door by Eugene's mother.

Students can appreciate the irony of the book's title. "Where in American history do we learn about people like Elena?" I ask them. We discuss the kinds of people who are absent from the pages of our history textbooks, and we speculate about how their absence might affect the self-esteem of someone like Elena. Such discussions heighten my students' sensitivity to their peers' experiences and deepen their understanding of how history is written.

A HAWAIIAN QUEEN

Another piece that highlights the problems of minorities in school is *Fourth Grade Ukus* (1952), by the Hawaiian author Marie Hara. The character Lei attends Kaahaumanu Elementary School, which served the Native Hawaiian and Asian population prior to statehood. She encounters daily contempt for her language and culture, including degrading head inspections for *ukus* (headlice).

One day Lei is introduced to the story of Queen Kaahumanu by the sensitive school principal. Although Lei's teacher continues to treat her students with disdain, Lei is comforted by the portrait of the Queen (the school's namesake) that hangs on the wall. She says, "Every day the Queen's round face gave me a signal that I was okay; a small thing, but necessary for someone so hungry for *signs.*"

Lest my students believe that such situations occur only in fiction, I invited the grandfather of one of my students to talk to the class about his experiences in school as a Mexican American growing up in Colorado. Students were shocked to hear that he was punished for using Spanish in school and were saddened to learn that he refused to use Spanish with his own children, in an attempt to spare them the humiliation that he had experienced.

SINGLED OUT

In Sherman Alexie's lean and powerful work, *Indian Education,* Victor reflects on his experiences as a student and an Indian. A series of vignettes, one for each grade of school, depicts with irony and humor recurring incidents of humiliation that Victor endures. A unique feature of this story is the series of "proverbs" or "lessons" that end many of the sections.

One vignette focuses on Betty Towle, a missionary teacher who regards her pupils with undisguised scorn. At one point, Victor tells us, the teacher mutters, "indians, indians, indians". "She said it without capitalization," Victor says. "She called me 'indian, indian, indian'." This single sentence offers many possibilities for lessons. How does one speak without capitalization? Why does Alexie use language in this way to show us how Victor feels?

ONLY ONE WAY OUT?

The story *Training,* by Susan Straight, captures the sadness of a ten-year-old black child in a class for learning disabled students at a mostly white school. Demone's well-meaning teacher tries to engage him but Demone is preoccupied with fears for his older brother. Max has given up on life and has told Demone that he is

going to "kiss the trains. Ain't no other way."

As they recognize the school's inability to offer Demone any security or hope, students can use this story to discuss the subtle ways in which schools can discount the personal needs of minority students. The story can also be used to spur an inquiry into the number of minorities in special-education programs.

Students may know of someone like Demone, whose "learning problems" stem from poverty, discrimination, or even poor nutrition, rather than from limited natural ability. Since all students can identify with the intrusion of personal stresses on their performance at school, they can also be led to see how those stresses increase with the hardships of poverty or discrimination.

NO PLACE TO CALL HOME

Writer Francisco Jimenez sheds light on the education challenges of children in migrant families. In *The Circuit,* Panchito struggles to adjust to another new school and welcomes the help and mentorship of an understanding teacher, Mr. Lema. On the day that Panchito hurries home to share his excitement about learning to play the trumpet, he finds out that his family will be moving again.

These stories typically will generate discussion about acts of prejudice or discrimination that students themselves have experienced in schools. I have noticed that white students are often surprised to learn that incidents of intolerance are happening here and now to their own peers. That awareness is an important step toward understanding and examining their own values and behavior.

As I watch the power of literature at work in my classroom, I share the hopes of Abraham Rodriguez, a young writer from the South Bronx, who said, "I wish stories could change people.... Maybe stories can break down walls."

ACTIVITIES

1. To encourage the development of empathy, ask students to rewrite a story, or crucial episodes, from the point of view of another character in the story.
2. Several of these stories capture the idiom or vernacular of the characters especially well. Ask the students to write a dialogue from

their own experience in school, focusing on an incident or situation that made a deep impression on them.

3. The question of labels and their relationship to stereotypes generates a lively discussion. How do the terms we use to identify various racial and ethnic groups affect our identity? How can the answers to this question improve relations between these groups?

4. Assign students to write an epilogue to each story, telling what became of each character later on in life. This exercise requires the students to think deeply about the traits or qualities of each character.

5. Because these stories all deal with education, and perhaps reflect the weaknesses rather than strengths of the system, students could be asked to try their hand at persuasive writing, using these stories as a springboard. Composing letters to the editor, to the school board, to an organization that could be enlisted for help, etc., would allow students to practice another style of writing while teaching them one response to the frustrations these stories may provoke.

6. If you work with high-school students, an excellent follow-up project would be to pair an interested student with an elementary child who would benefit from extra attention.

Sheri Bauman is a teacher and counselor at Centennial High School in Ft. Collins, Colorado.
Reprinted with permission from Teaching Tolerance, *Southern Poverty Law Center, Montgomery, Alabama.*

I See Myself In There: Experiencing Self and Others in Multiethnic Children's Literature

Candy Dawson Boyd, Ph.D.

A good book is a garden carried in the pocket. —*African adage.*

What one reads becomes part of what one sees and feels.
—*Ralph Ellison, "Remembering Richard Wright,"* Going to the Territory, *1986*

THE CHILDREN OF AMERICA
The children of America represent a remarkable range of racial, ethnic, and linguistic diversity. Immigrant growth is evident in the doubling of the Latino population since the 1970s. Seventy percent of the Asian American population are immigrants from the 1970s and 1980s. Every day in America monolingual, monocultural teachers face as many as seventeen different languages in their classrooms.

At a time when the political system too often seems to ignore the needs of families and children, education that is rigorous, relevant, and resolute in its commitment to equity, offers a potentially life-affirming opportunity for youngsters. Certainly, multiethnic literature cannot be relied on alone to reduce racial prejudices, build self-determination, and portray accurately people of color. Yet these stories do have the power to provide solace, escape, nurture, and insight.

THE VALUE OF MULTIETHNIC CHILDREN'S LITERATURE
In a profound sense, children look to story for self. Stories are a critical source for discovering where they stand in the world. Adopting a new language of empathy, caring, compassion, and courage through reading multiethnic books enables children to experience issues of identity and beliefs in all their wonderful complexity. The following excerpt from a letter written to me by a young white reader in South Carolina reveals the power of this new language:

Dear Ms. Boyd,

Every aspect of your book, Fall Secret, *touched my heart. Even though I don't share Jessie's race, we are much the same. I feel as if it could be me at O.P.A. [Oakland Performing Arts School]. I hope there is, or will be a sequel to Fall Secrets. Is it fun to live in California? Have you ever experienced an earthquake? Please write back.*

From Cathy Hanson.

Recognition of oneself in others can be an exhilarating discovery. Jessie, the main character in *Fall Secrets* is an African American sixth-grader who yearns to be a famous actress. Her life is fraught with the uncertainties of early adolescence and complicated by issues of race. For this reader, Jessie's difficulties seemed accessible and familiar.

It is the work of the young to make sense of the world and to live what they understand. Children seek emotional truth, about themselves and those they love. Adults involved with multiethnic children's books thus bear an inevitable ethical responsibility. A crib found to harm children receives more attention than a book that demeans them but the emotional damage of being rendered invisible or worthless in the language of literature deserves equal consideration.

MULTIETHNIC CHILDREN'S AUTHORS

As an African American female child, I never saw my face or the lives of my family, friends, and neighbors in the books I read. Every Saturday I would eagerly trek to the small storefront public library on the Southside of Chicago, under the El station. I read horse books, mysteries, science fiction, girl series, and whatever else was available. The characters were always white, nice, safe, and perfect, in their own distant way. I realized that I was invisible, excluded, disaffirmed, spurned, discarded, scorned, and rejected in the white world of children's literature.

Without the steady, strong teachings of my parents and relatives, my ethnic identity would have suffered immensely. But they told me that I came from a proud, brilliant people—Africans; that I was surrounded by ancestral heroes and heroines named David Walker,

Marcus Garvey, Harriet Tubman, Denmark Vesey, W.E.B DuBois, Mary McLeod Bethune, Hannibal, Aesop, Alexander Dumas, and hundreds more. They also made it clear that I had inherited a rich history upon which to build my own dreams and life.

Daddy lectured, Mama talked and read to us. I listened to my adult relatives share personal stories of racism and pain. I learned their lessons—the lessons needed to walk the world and hold my head high as an African American woman. In the world of my family and community, I was treasured.

The search for self is particularly complex for the multiethnic author, who is always both "something different" and in some way "American." The writer Laurence Yep shares his own difficulties:

I was the Chinese American raised in a black neighborhood, a child who had been too American to fit into Chinatown and too Chinese to fit in elsewhere. I was the clumsy son of an athletic family, the grandson of a Chinese grandmother who spoke more of West Virginia than of China.

When I wrote, I went from being a puzzle to a puzzle solver. I could reach into the bag of rags that was my soul and begin stitching them together. Moreover, I could try out different combinations to see which one pleased me the most. I could take these different elements, each of which belonged to something else, and dip them into my imagination where they were melted down and cast into new shapes so that they became uniquely mine.

Nicholasa Mohr, the Puerto Rican author of *El Bronx Remembered*, a young-adult novella and stories, elucidates the worlds that constitute the inner life of a writer who is a Puerto Rican, an American, and a human being:

I just write about what I know and care very deeply about. I think that the more specific you are in your work, the more universal you become. If I can appreciate a story by Sholem Aleichem about someone in an eastern European village, someone else can certainly appreciate a story about a Puerto Rican child. So I just write about the human drama, the human struggle of an ongoing life to the best of my knowledge. I write about Puerto Ricans because that's what I am.

108

Many multiethnic stories are the first of their kind to swim in the sea of mainstream children's literature. The books contradict widely institutionalized ethnic group stereotypes: the exotic Asian; the savage, drunk Indian; the lazy black; and the ignorant, rural Mexican. A stereotype is an in-group's oversimplified conception of members of an out-group. The conception is devoid of traits valued by the in-group and is loaded with traits devalued by the in-group. Plains Cree Nation author/illustrator George Littlechild offers needed perceptions in his bold picture book, *This Land Is My Land*:

> I paint at night. I'm inspired to paint at night. I stand outside staring at the night sky and I begin to dream. The sky is like a doorway into the other world, the Spirit World.

> I am inspired by the ancestors. When I look back on our history and see all the difficulties our ancestors had to face, I can only honor them. Through the wisdom of our Elders and the courage of all our people we have survived the past 500 hundred years. I thank the Creator for Wahkomkanak, our ancestors.

In another selection from the same text, Littlechild describes his painting of the costume of a young Plains Cree woman who has won the Miss Hobbema Indian Princess Pageant:

> The feathers are from the air. The shells are from the water. The fire is her spirit. During the pageant she will thank everyone in the community, especially the grandmothers, for all that they have given her.

> My intention in this painting is to break down stereotypes and help restore a sense of dignity, pride, and elegance to the women of the Plains Cree.

A sound, accurate knowledge of and personal experiences with the values of the white Anglo Saxon in-group provides crucial perspectives for the multiethnic author. Christine Bennett presents one of the clearest topologies of American values categorized by worldview, self, and relations with others. A multiethnic child adrift in the sea of in-group values soon learns that individual achievement, personal initiative, independence, self-sufficiency, pragmatism, technological superiority, and short-term perspectives are prized by the culture of authority.

The task of the multiethnic author is enormous: challenging and transcending past and present ignorance and positing a hopeful future. Each must constantly combat a language embedded in racism and marginality. Nobel Laureate Toni Morrison, author of *The Bluest Eye*, which is widely read as an adolescent novel, explains:

> I am a black writer struggling with and through a language that can powerfully evoke and enforce hidden signs of racial superiority, cultural hegemony, and dismissive "othering" of people and language which are by no means marginal or already known and knowable in my work.... The kind of work I have always wanted to do requires me to learn how to maneuver ways to free up language from its sinister, frequently lazy, almost always predictable employment of racially informed and determined chains.

The intimate knowledge that a multiethnic author brings to her reader is not always conscious. An author may not realize that in millions of black households, there are "nine family structures." This was outlined by Billingsley, whose work was based on 1983 and 1986 United States Bureau of the Census statistics and includes the following:

Single-Person Households	26 percent
Cohabitation	3.2 percent
Children, No Marriage	33 percent
Marriage, No Children	19 percent
Marriage and Children	20 percent
Children and Relatives	7 percent
Blended Family	no statistics
Dual-Earner Family	no statistics
Commuter-Couple Family	no statistics

The work of multiethnic children's writers certainly incorporates this information. Prior to reading Dr. Billingsley, I couldn't list the nine familial structures, but, as a black female living in black communities, I had experienced each one personally or vicariously. Using Billingsley's categories, I reviewed some of my own books:

Circle of Gold
A young girl, Mattie, believes that her mother loves her twin brother, Matt, most of all. She tries to win her mother's love by struggling to buy her a gold pin. Single-person household (widowed). (Scholastic, 1984)

Breadsticks and Blessing Places
Toni, Mattie's best friend, also has another best friend, Susan. Mattie and Susan are quite different. When Susan is killed by a drunk driver, Toni is trapped by her grief. With Mattie's help, she create a unique way to go on. Single-person household. (Macmillan, 1985)

Charlie Pippin
Bold, brash Chartreuse "Charlie" Pippin discovers that her stern father was a Vietnam hero. In uncovering the truth of what happened to him in Vietnam, Charlie's world is turned upside down. Marriage and children with dual earners. (Macmillan, 1986)

Chevrolet Saturdays
Stricken by the remarriage of his mother, a difficult fifth-grade teacher, class bully, and a new stepfather, fifth-grader Joey Davis searches for a way to recreate his "old" family. When Joey makes a serious, heartrending mistake, he has to grow up. Blended families with dual earners. (Macmillan, 1993)

Fall Secrets
Sixth-grader Jessie Williams yearns to be a famous actress. In her first year at Oakland Performing Arts Middle School, she makes unexpected new friends at school and at home. Marriage and children with dual earners. (Puffin, 1994)

Daddy, Daddy, Be There
In a series of verses, and the emotionally driven art of Floyd Cooper, important relationships between children and their fathers are revealed. All except for cohabitation. (Philomel, 1995)

The representation and inclusion of all household types is so important and cannot be overemphasized. While family composition and number of wage earners often determines a child's access to resources, it does not always determine that child's destiny. Being mired in poverty as a child does not mean you can't become a caring and compassionate person who also provides significant leadership in your community as an educator, chief executive officer, artist, or scientist. Children who read this body of work encounter a balanced portrayal of black family life. This was deliberate on

my part. Supplanting hundreds of years of racist propaganda with truths demands informed vigilance. But most of all, I want my writing diligently to capture the voices, hearts, spirits, and minds of children. While the data are real and often disturbing, they do not provide us with the substance of who we are: our dreams, our complex dimensions, and our often unrecognized power.

Ethnic stereotypes thrive on exaggerated and demeaning depictions of the physical self— hair, skin color, noses, hips, sizes, shapes, eyes, ears, and every other aspect of the human body. For African Americans, the dark, oversexed, violent male savage; fat, big-breasted mammy; thick-lipped, nappy-haired girl; or fair-skinned, straight-haired mulatto are the images inherited from American culture. Sadly, some of these distortions have been integrated into the taxonomy of African American beauty. Even within various ethnic and cultural groups many members have yet to comprehend and celebrate differences.

These are matters of serious import. In *Circle of Gold*, I took care to create a contrasting physical picture of Mattie and Toni, long-standing best friends:

…[Mattie's] thin brown face would have been unremarkable except for her eyes. Intelligence and caution existed together in those huge brown orbs. Mattie was all dark brown eyes and copper-colored angles. Not Toni Douglas. She was a chocolate bubble floating through life. (p. 5)

Mattie muses about the impact of another black classmate, Angel Higgley, who is a manipulative bully:

There was no telling what Angel would do to her for this, but Mattie didn't care. Not too many kids dared to cross Miss Queen Bee. Mattie was angry with the bunch of dopes who always hung around Angel. Girls who dreamed their eyes were gray instead of black. Girls who dreamed of having long wavy hair like the white girls on television. Girls who didn't realize that they, too, were lovely and special.

Ten years later, in *Fall Secrets*, this tragic, debilitating legacy perseveres. Issues of skin color, hair texture, eyes, and body shapes threaten to

109

separate Jessie from her older sister, Cassandra, and damage Jessie's self-image. Mamatoo, Jessie's grandmother, attempts to counsel her in this excerpt:

And she [Cassandra] loves you very much, and she did not ask to be born light-skinned like her father and me with hazel eyes and straight hair. I've told you time and time again that we are a rainbow people. African-Americans come in all shades of black and browns and creams—just like our family. When you celebrate your beauty, I'll rejoice. I wish I knew what makes you feel this way about yourself. You weren't always like this.

The book probes problems associated with physical differences. When Cassandra finally forces Jessie to listen to her side, their relationship changes for the better:

I'm light skinned. You're brown skinned. My eyes are lighter than yours and my hair is straighter. That just means that the white in our family came out more in me. What's so great about knowing that I'm light not because there was intermarriage in our family history, but because there was slavery and the abuse of our women! Think about what that means for me, Jess!

Later Cass says to Jessie: "I don't feel ashamed. But looking like this is nothing to flaunt."

Struggling with the English language to describe shades of skin color like organic peanut butter or brown-sugar taffy; nose shapes that are small, thin, flared, pointed; curly, tangled, straightened, permed, thick, crisp, short, tightly curled, shoulder length, plaited, beaded hair; all manner of arms, legs, breasts, chests, chins, ears, cheekbones, hands, feet, legs, behinds, sizes, and hips is an eternal war. Sometimes I use photographs from magazines, family albums, newspapers, and books. Black children of all ages face the lasting legacy of slavery—the way they look. But they are not alone. The African American author/illustrator stands right there with them, books in hand.

THE WORK OF MULTIETHNIC LITERATURE

In very recent history, the world of children's literature has seen a small but potent surge in stories by ethnically diverse authors and illustrators who are more a part of the American stew than the American melting pot. Such literature recreates the lore of the world. But books need time and attention to mature. The rewards of a sustainable readership and popular acceptance are great. What is written, accepted, distributed, and read becomes the lore, way, and wealth of the world.

Over time, selected stories are shared and read generation after generation. But increasingly, for stories to reach a wide audience, they first must be accepted by the billion-dollar industry of children's literature. A multiethnic book travels a daunting, perilous journey to reach the hands of a child reader. The manuscript must make its way through agents, editors, marketing departments, powerful organizations, librarians, booksellers, teachers, parent committees, reviewers, censors, and more before it is available for a child to choose to read. All too often, these people do not read biased books critically or multiethnic works sympathetically.

Research studies conducted since the 1940s reveal the positive effect of multiethnic teaching materials on children's racial attitudes toward ethnic groups and themselves. Crago and Litt assert that the power of story in literary form can "alter the course of lives."

With an increasing multiethnic population of school children, the urgency to teach them resounds in journal after journal. The implications for multiethnic literature are obvious. Reading educators are clamoring for literary experiences that will be part of every child's school curriculum for at least thirty minutes per day. But there is recent evidence that reading and writing activity occupy less than 10 percent of the child's school day. An emphasis on meaning explored through literate talk and conversations dominates suggested pedagogical practices. One researcher has said, "I suggest that the essence of reading is getting lost in a story—literally entering the text world."

Still, the body of multiethnic children's literature is comparatively small in size, constituting 1/2 percent of the three-to-five thousand children's books published each year. Despite its size, the collective impact of this body of literature has charged a passive philosophy of education with robust, vital vision; redefined the role of child and adolescent literature; dramatically altered educational pedagogy in the areas of reading, language arts, and content areas like social studies and history. It has also recreated ethnic white groups, anchoring a healthier sense of ethnic identity for white children, which is something that certainly cannot be overlooked. This is laudable given the reluctance of many major mainstream publishing, library, and educational institutions to affirm multiethnic authors. In writing about the paucity of multiethnic books, one critic notes: "Providing information about European and white American cultures is not difficult. The majority of the books listed on the Newbery, Caldecott, Carnegie, Greenaway, and Touchstone lists reflect these two cultural backgrounds. [T]here is still a disproportionately small number that deals in any way with minorities."

In 1994, using two categorization systems—one related to ethnic groups and one related to the substance of ethnic characters in the stories—a survey of the seventy-three Newbery Medal books from 1922 to 1994 was conducted. The study found that sixty-six (90 percent) of the books had white Anglo Saxons as main, minor, or mentioned characters, with the vast majority as main characters. By creating a separate category called "non Anglo-Saxon," which included Polish, Tartars, Bulgarians, Hungarians, Dutch, Moroccan, French, Scottish, Danish, and Middle Easterners, the authors managed to reduce the total dominance of white authors and characters. Only two subgroups would be challenged as "nonwhite" —Moroccan and Middle Eastern. They constituted two of the seventy-three books.

Two authors of color are Newbery Medal winners: Virginia Hamilton for *M. C. Higgins, the Great* and Mildred Taylor for *Roll of Thunder, Hear My Cry.* We have yet to see a Latino, Asian American, or Native American author be recognized at that level by the Newbery Committee. There is also the matter of books with gay and lesbian themes as well as books focusing on disability being honored. Of the nineteen books with some appearance of black characters, seventeen were written by white authors. At the very least, the lack of recognition of works by multiethnic authors and the continued rewards for white authors writing about Asians, blacks, Latinos, and Indians is questionable.

Issues of authenticity are not about philosophy or morality. They are issues of power and authority. If only books written by those privileged by virtue of race, gender, education, and/or money are available, these works become the accepted and cherished lore of the world. When writers privileged by race decide to write stories about people who are not so privileged, their stories take on the mantle of "reality." It is rare to read such a work and not find serious flaws and distortions. Such flaws or distortions can rob children of an authentic story. The lore of the world is depleted, and that strongly needed sense of self is diminished further.

Multiethnic books and the language of this literature create a vital element in transformative curriculum. According to educator and scholar James Banks, transformative curricula designed to impact the values and beliefs of students "challenge the basic assumptions and implicit values of the Eurocentric, male-dominated curricula institutionalized in U.S. schools, colleges, and universities. It helps students to view concepts, events, and situations from diverse racial, ethnic, gender, and social-class perspectives. The transformative curriculum also helps students to construct their own interpretations of the past, present, and future."

It is now possible for an African American, Latino American, Asian American, Native American, gay, lesbian, or special needs child to find his or her real face, feelings, thoughts, family, or community in children's literature. And European American children can recreate themselves and engage others as equals. Some of the most imaginative, authentic, and engaging stories that affirm that sense of self, self-acceptance, and self-determination, include:

AFRICAN AMERICAN

Nikki Giovanni, *Knoxville, Tennessee.* Very simple picture book with one-line pages of black girl telling about her summer activities.

Jeanne Moutoussamy-Ashe, *Daddy and Me: A Photo Story of Arthur Ashe and His Daughter Camera*. Beautiful black-and-white photos of daily father and daughter activities, told by Camera in "I" language; for example, "But sometimes Daddy gets sick because he has AIDS. Do you know what having AIDS means? I do."

Walter Dean Myers, *Brown Angels: An Album of Pictures and Verse*. Collection of photographs of African American children of all ages culled from the author's treasure searches in antique shops, flea markets, and auction houses. The photographs are of children from the 1800s and early 1900s.

NATIVE AMERICAN
Shonto Begay, *Navajo: Visions and Voices Across the Mesa*. Twenty of Begay's powerful paintings of his people and their lives are coupled with chants, stories, and poems explaining and sharing the world of the Navajo people.

Joseph Bruchac, *Fox Song*. Breathtaking picture book story of Jamie and her beloved grandmother, Grama Bowman, who teaches her about nature and animals. She dies and Jamie still feels her presence and her songs. Jamie sings to the fox and learns she will never be alone.

ASIAN AMERICAN
Marie G. Lee, *If It Hadn't Been for Yoon Jun*. For seventh-grader Alice Larsen, being Korean in a white school is no problem until Yoon Jun, a Korean immigrant, arrives. Adopted, Alice believes that she belongs until Yoon's obvious cultural differences make it impossible for her to ignore her heritage.

Allen Say, *Grandfather's Journey*. Using his own life, Japanese American author/illustrator Allen Say traces his family's journeys across the ocean carrying their conflicting emotions, hopes, and dreams.

LATINO AMERICAN
Gloria Anzaldua, *Friends from the Other Side, Amigos Del Otro Lado*. Prietita, a young Mexican American girl, befriends an illegal alien boy named Joaquin. In the course of a few days, her values are tested and Prietita honors her loyalty to Joaquin in important ways.

Carmen Garza, *Family Pictures*. Short stories about Mexican American life accompany illustra-

tions created from the author's family album.

Gary Soto, *Too Many Tamales*. Picture book with realistic illustrations. Christmas Eve tale about a girl named Maria making tamales with her mother. Maria wants to wear her mother's ring. She puts it on and loses the ring in the tamales.

CULTURAL WHITE
Sonia Levitin, *Journey to America*. The compelling story of one Jewish family's struggle to stay together and alive. Winner of the National Jewish Book Award.

Joanne Ryder, *My Father's Hands*. A father takes his young daughter on a nature treasure hunt.

Marilyn Sachs, *The Bears' House*. Ten-year-old Fran Ellen has more problems than most adults. Her father has left and her mother cannot function. With her brother, she tries to keep the family together and loses herself in a pretend world inside a doll house. (Sachs' *Almost Fifteen* and *Class Pictures* are noteworthy.)

Susan Terris, *Nell's Quilt*. It is 1899 and Nell wants to go to college, but her parents tell her she must marry. Unable to have the life she wants, Nell creates a beautiful quilt and starves herself.

Ann Turner, *Nettie's Trip South*. The illustrated, true story of the author's great-grandmother's trip to the South in 1859. There, Nettie witnessed a slave auction, plantation life for the slaves, and siblings separated and sold. She returned home a committed abolitionist.

MULTIETHNIC
Marion Dane Bauer, *Am I Blue? Coming Out from the Silence*. Collection of sixteen short stories by noted authors such as Lois Lowry, Jane Yolen, Jacqueline Woodson, and Bruce Coville. The book explores aspects of growing up gay or lesbian, or with gay or lesbian friends or parents.

Joyce Carol Thomas, *A Gathering of Flowers: Stories About Being Young in America*. Eleven new short stories written by authors from different cultural backgrounds: rural Oklahoma, Chicago Latino barrio, Chippewa Indian Reservation, and urban San Francisco.

When a white child writes to me and says, "I just finished *Circle of Gold*. I didn't know that black people have feelings. But now I do. Are you going to write any more books about Mattie and Toni?," the lore of that child's world shifts. One multiethnic book has elicited honesty, reflection, and the recognition of shared humanity from a child within the secure context of literature. The reader can lay the book down, think, reread, discuss, and write. Her understanding of the world has been transformed. Little by little the accretion of experiences with others within the pages of multi-ethnic books enlarges and fashions the mirror in which children envision and define themselves, their community, country, and world. Gradually, the multicolored, multihued new American child discovers that she is not alone in her living. Her ethnicity, gender, spirituality, special challenges, family structure, and socioeconomic class invigorates the lore of the world. And the lore of the world is richer because through multiethnic story, she searches, stumbles, and soars in all of her wondrous splendor.

Candy Dawson Boyd is the first tenured African American professor at Saint Mary's College of California in Moraga and recipient of the school's first Professor the Year award. She is the distinguished author of several children's books, including Charlie Pippen *and* Breadsticks

REFERENCES

1. Allington, R. L. "The Schools We Have. The Schools We Need." *The Reading Teacher* 48 (1993): 14-29.
2. Banks, J. A. *Multiethnic Education: Theory and Practice.* Boston: Allyn and Bacon, 1994.
3. ———. *An Introduction to Multicultural Education.* Boston: Allyn and Bacon, 1994.
4. Bennett, C. I. *Comprehensive Multicultural Literature: Theory and Practice.* Allyn and Bacon, 1995.
5. Billingsley, A. "Understanding African-American Family Diversity." *The State of Black America 1990,* edited by Jo Dewart, New York: National Urban League, Inc. 1990.
6. Crago, H. and M. Litt. "The Place of Story in Affective Development: Implications for Educators and Clinicians." *Journal of Children in Contemporary Society,* 17 (1985): 129-42.
7. Day, F. A. *Multicultural Voices in Contemporary Literature.* Portsmouth, N.H.: Heinemann, 1994.
8. Ellison, R. *Going to the Territory.* New York: Random House, 1986.
9. Fisher, F. "The Influence of Reading and Discussion on the Attitudes of Fourth Graders Toward American-Indians." Ph.D. diss., University of California-Berkeley, 1965.
10. Garcia, R. L. *Teaching in a Pluralistic Society.* 2d ed. New York: HarperCollins, 1991.
11. Gillespie, C. S., J. L. Powell, N. E. Clements, and R. A. Swearingen. "A Look at the Newbery Medal Books From a Multicultural Perspective." *The Reading Teacher* 48 (1994): 40-50.
12. Harris, V. J. ed. *Teaching Multicultural Literature in Grades K-8.* Norwood, Mass.: Christopher-Gordon Publisher Inc., 1992.
13. Johnson, C. *Being & Race.* Bloomington and Indianapolis, Ind.: University of Indiana Press, 1988.
14. Litcher, J. and D. Johnson. "Changes in the Attitudes Toward Negroes of White Elementary School Students After Use of Multiethnic Readers." *Journal of Educational Psychology* 60, (1969): 148-52.
15. Mohr, N. "Why Do I Write About Puerto Ricans?" *The Lion and the Unicorn: A Critical Journal of Childrens' Literature* 11, (1987): 1.
16. Norton, D. E. *The Impact of Literature-Based Reading.* New York: Merrill, 1992.
17. Morrison, T. *Playing in the Dark: Whiteness and the Literature Imagination.* Cambridge, Mass.: Harvard University Press, 1992.
18. Olsen, L., proj. dir. *The Unfinished Journey-Restructuring Schools in a Diverse Society.* San Francisco: California Tomorrow, 1994.
19. Piper, D. "Language Growth in the Multiethnic Classroom." *Language Arts* 63, (1986): 23-36.
20. Rudman, M. K. *Children's Literature: An Issues Approach.* 3d ed. New York: Longman, 1995.
21. Sleeter, C. and C. Grant. *Making Choices for Multicultural Education: Five Approaches to Race, Class, and Gender.* 3d ed. New York: Merrill, 1994.
22. Stephan, W. G. "Intergroup Relations." In *The Handbook of Social Psychology.* 3d ed. edited by G. Lindzey and E. Aronson, 599-658. Hillsdale, N.J.: Lawrence Erlbaum Associates, 1985.
23. Tidwell, B. J. *The State of Black America 1992.* New York: National Urban League, Inc., 1992.
24. Trager, H. G. and M. R. Yarrow. *They Learn What They Live.* New York: Harper, 1952.
25. West, C. *Race Matters.* Boston: Beacon Press, 1993.

CHILDREN'S BOOKS CITED

ANZALDUA, G. *Friends from the Other Side. Amigos del Oro Lado.* San Francisco & Emeryville: Children's Book Press, 1993.

BAUER, M.D. *Am I Blue? Coming Out from the Silence.* New York: HarperCollins, 1994.

BEGAY, S. *Navajo: Visions and Voices across the Mesa.* New York: Scholastic, 1995.

BOYD, S. *Circle of Gold.* New York: Scholastic, Inc., 1984.

———. *Breadsticks and Blessing Places.* New York: Macmillan, 1985.

———. *Charlie Pippin.* New York: Macmillan, 1987.

———. *Chevrolet Saturdays.* New York: Macmillan, 1993.

———. *Fall Secrets.* New York: Puffin, 1994.

———. *Daddy, Daddy, Be There.* New York: Philomel, 1995.

———. *A Different Beat.* New York: Puffin, 1996.

BRUCHAC, J. *Fox Song.* New York: Philomel, 1993.

GARZA, C. *Family Pictures.* San Francisco: Children's Book Press, 1990.

GIOVANNI, N. *Knoxville, Tennessee.* New York: Scholastic, 1968.

HAMILTON, V. *M.C. Higgins, The Great.* New York: Macmillan, .1974.

KRAMON, F. *Hipólito and Eugene G.* Chicago: Follett, 1967.

LEE, M. G. *If It Hadn't Been for Yoon Jun.* Boston: Houghton Mifflin, 1993.

LEVITIN, S. *Journey to America.* New York: Macmillan, 1970.

LEXAU, J. M. MARIA. New York: Dial Press, 1964.

LITTLECHILD, G. *This Land Is My Land.* Emeryville, Cal.: Childrens' Book Press, 1993.

MOUTOUSSAMY-ASHE, J. *Daddy and Me: A Photo Story of Arthur Ashe and His Daughter Camera.* New York: Knopf, 1993.

MYERS, W. D. *Brown Angels: An Album of Pictures and Verse.* New York: HarperCollins, 1993.

RYDER, J. *My Father's Hands.* New York: Morrow, 1994.

SACHS, M. *The Bears' House.* New York: Avon, 1971.

SAY, A. *Grandfather's Journey.* Boston: Houghton Mifflin, 1993.

SCHWEITZER, B. B. *Amigo.* Toronto, Ontario, Canada: Collier-Macmillan, 1963.

SONNEBORN, R. A. *Seven in a Bed.* New York: Viking Press, 1968.

SOTO, G. *Too Many Tamales.* New York: G. P. Putnam Sons, 1993.

TAYLOR, M. D. *Roll of Thunder, Hear My Cry.* New York: Dial, 1976.

TERRIS, S. *Nell's Quilt.* New York: Scholastic, 1987.

THOMAS, J. C., ED. *A Gathering of Flowers: Stories About Being Young in America.* New York: Harper & Row, 1990.

TURNER, A. *Nettie's Trip South.* New York: Macmillan, 1987.

YEP, L. *The Lost Garden.* New York: Julian Messner, 1991.

114

Grade Seven to Grade Eight

Slow Dance Heart Break Blues

👤 Arnold Adoff 🖊 William Cotton

Multicultural

1995, Lothrop, Lee & Shepard Books

In this collection of poems, award-winning poet Arnold Adoff addresses the tumultuous adolescent years—sweaty palms, pimple cream, and first dates. Interspersed with artwork by William Cotton and a compilation of photographic images and collage depicting the "stuff" of teens, Adoff's poems deftly

A light, eclectic collection of poems about adolescence.

capture the tone and terror of teen angst. His style is quick, precise, and rhythmic with echoes of rap and hip-hop. Although Adoff deals with both the ups and downs of adolescence, the work is fun and full of energy.

In the poem "Now," the prepubescent female protagonist is summed up in a few phrases: "This time —from trolls to tampax—says it all." For all of us who have been caught in an embarrassing moment, we have "Freeze Frame": "My / right / pinkie/ is / in / my / left / nostril / digging / for / gold / when / you / walk / by."

This volume contains many such familiar moments. Readers should expect mostly light fare with a good comic touch. ROSA E. WARDER

Life Doesn't Frighten Me

📖 Maya Angelou, Edited by Sara J. Boyers

✒ Jean-Michel Basquiat

African American

1993, Stewart, Tabori and Chang, Inc.

In *Life Doesn't Frighten Me*, editor Sara Jane Boyers successfully matches the Maya Angelou poem by the same name with Jean-Michel Basquiat's childlike paintings to create a picture book that adults and children of all ages will enjoy.

Maya Angelou's poem and artist Jean Michel Basquiat's paintings celebrates our ability to conquer fear.

First published in 1978, the poem "Life Doesn't Frighten Me" celebrates our ability to face and conquer our fears. In almost every refrain, the scary images conjured up by Angelou's words ("Shadows on the wall/noises down the hall,") are followed by the reassuring line, "Life doesn't frighten me at all." Most of the images—fear of a new classroom, dragons breathing fire, ghosts in clouds—seem particular to childhood. Angelou's direct, singsong language and easy rhymes evoke childhood, as well: "I go boo/make them shoo/I make fun/the way they run/I won't cry/so they fly."

Basquiat's paintings illustrate Angelou's poem so well that they seem to have been commissioned specifically for the text. Basquiat's body of work has been characterized as childlike and humorous, but there's also a very unsettling quality to it that suits Angelou's poem perfectly. He often uses stick figures or crudely depicted human forms for his characters who seem both innocent and menacing.

In Life Doesn't Frighten Me, Boyers includes biographies of both Angelou and Basquiat, as well as recommendations for further explorations of their work. The biographies are brief but very insightful in that they not only detail the accomplishments of the writer and illustrator, but they also discuss some of the struggles and demons these two have faced. Through the biographies, the reader gets a behind-the-scenes look at what may have been the seeds for Angelou's poem and Basquiat's art.

In addition to its literary value, the book would be a wonderful resource for poetry and picture book genre studies, as it provides a powerful example of how the exploration of one's own life experiences provides fertile ground for writing.

Important discussions inevitably will arise as children relate personally to Angelou's poem and talk about their fears. Although some of the pictures could be frightening to very young children, there are many familiar objects among the abstract images.
KATHY COLLINS

Herstory: Women Who Changed the World

📖 Ruth Ashby (editor) ✒ Deborah Gore Ohrn, Introduction by Gloria Steinem

Multicultural

1995, Viking Penguin

This well-written, thoughtfully compiled reference book will be helpful to readers from twelve through the early years of college.

An inclusive volume of 120 biographical sketches of famous and unsung women.

Introduced by Gloria Steinem, the volume includes brief biographies of such well-known women from history as Catherine the Great, Sojourner Truth, Eleanor Roosevelt, Eva Perón, and Jacqueline Kennedy Onassis. Also included are women who may be less well-known to American youngsters who have also made incredible contributions to science, art, literature, history, and social justice movements. I was pleased to see women such as Hypatia, Sor Juana Ines de la Cruz, Qiu Jin, and Wilma Mankiller included in this impressive volume.

Although some of the women profiled were revolutionaries and athletes, others made names for themselves in the kitchen and in the corridors of political power. In sum, their lives provide a broad range of the female experience. Sidebars, quotes, and archival photographs place their lives in context and the inclusion of geographical, alphabetical, and occupational indexes encourages further research. Herstory *is a useful educational tool that raises intriguing questions about the relative absence of women's history from school curricula in the United States and other countries around the world.*
DAPHNE MUSE

Growing Up Latino: Memoirs and Stories

📖 Harold Augenbraum (editor) ✒ Ilan Stavans

Hispanic, Mexican

1993, Houghton Mifflin

Growing Up Latino is a comprehensive collection of short stories by twenty-five Latino authors. This collection is a particularly useful for someone who wants to get a sense of the breadth of Latino literature, as well as an introduction to the books from which most of these stories were selected.

The editors organized the short stories into three sections. In "Imagining the Family," there are eight stories that recount memories of home and domestic relationships both in the United States and abroad. In "Gringolandia," eight stories describe marginalization and racism experienced by Latinos living within the United States. "Songs of Self-Discovery," a title inspired by nineteenth century American poet Walt Whitman (1819-1892), contains nine stories that describe the mediation and conflict in trying to balance two cultures. Of special note is the inclusion of a story "The Autobiography of a Brown Buffalo" by Oscar "Zeta" Martinez, a politically active Chicano writer who has been missing since 1974.

A comprehensive collection of short stories by twenty-five Latino authors.

Although the use of "Latino" in the title suggests a more diverse selection, in fact the majority of the works (sixteen) describe the Mexican American experience. There are seven stories by Puerto Rican authors, one by a writer of Cuban descendent, Oscar Hijuelos, and one by Julia Alvarez, who is from the Dominican Republic. Alverez is one of nine Latina authors included. Each author has an established place in the Latino/Chicano literary canon. Suggestions for further reading include titles of major and lesser-known works. Also, there is a short biographical sketch describing each author at the end of the book. Overall, this is an excellent collection and an engaging introduction to Latino literature for secondary-level reading.

HERIBERTO GODINA

Am I Blue?: Coming Out from the Silence

📖 Marion Dane Bauer

Gay/Lesbian/Bisexual, Multicultural

1994, HarperCollins

Sixteen well-written, original short stories that explore growing up gay, lesbian, or bisexual.

Supported by consistently fine writing and imaginatively crafted storylines, this groundbreaking collection of original short stories focuses on growing up bisexual, gay, or lesbian. The book is a dream come true for accomplished writer and editor, Marion Dane Bauer. Bauer, a lesbian, conceived and developed the idea for the book and gathered talented writers whom she believed could write responsibly and have the courage to speak out on the subject of homosexuality.

The contributors include Bauer, Francesca Lia Block, Bruce Coville, Nancy Garden, James Cross Giblin, Ellen Howard, M.E. Kerr, Jonathan London, Lois Lowry, Gregory Maguire, Leslea Newman, Christina Salat, William Sleator, Jacqueline Woodson, and Jane Yolen. The resulting collection reads more like a collaboration than an edited anthology. The authors that contributed to the collection are diverse in age and experience, and each shares a personal vignette detailing why he or she became involved in the project. The emotional range of the stories is vast, some of them are funny, serious, irreverent, or heartbreaking, with several managing to be all of the above and more.

As the reader moves from story to story, the experiences portrayed and the ideas discussed create a gratifying mosaic. The title story by Bruce Coville, takes the reader on a fanciful journey, where a fairy godfather named Melvin grants a teenage boy, who is questioning his own sexuality, the chance to have three wishes; one wish being the ability to see those around him in a new light:

"'We used to imagine what it would be like if every gay person in the country turned blue for a day.'

"My eyes went wide. 'Why?' 'So all the straights would have to stop imagining that they didn't know any gay people. They would find out that they had been surrounded by gays all the time, and survived the experience just fine, thank you. They'd have to face the fact that there are gay cops and gay farmers, gay teachers and gay soldiers, gay parents and gay kids. The hiding would finally have to stop.'"

A valuable addition to young adult literature, *Am I Blue?* will serve to enhance a greater understanding of the challenges facing young gays and lesbians. In addition, the royalties from this book are being shared with Parents, Families and Friends of Lesbians and Gays (P-FLAG) for their Respect All Youth Project, which aims to disseminate information about healthy sexuality to all youth. ROSA E. WARDER

The Tale of the Little Black Fish: Mahi Siah Kuchulu

📖 Samad Behrangi (translated by Eric Hooglund and Mary Hegland) ✒ Yousef J. Javan

Iranian, Middle Eastern, Persian

1992 (1969), Three Continents Press

This is a collection of five stories, which were published in Persian as individual books. Samad Behrangi (1939-1968), a teacher and author of many remarkable books, was born in Tabriz, in the Azarbayjan Province of Iran. He believed that Iranian children should read literature that focused on the lives of all Iranians, including the poor people in the villages.

Five Persian short stories that focus on social problems in Iran.

This collection, *The Little Black Fish*, first published in 1967, won the gold medal at the 1969 Bologna International Book Exhibition. It is a story about a little black fish who decides to leave his small stream and explore the world. His mother tries to discourage him, but her efforts are useless. The curious little fish, has made up his mind to go and find the ocean. Through the Little Black Fish's journey, the young readers learn about self-determination and courage.

"24 Restless Hours," "The Little Sugar Beet Vendor," and "One Peach, a Thousand Peach" deal with children who live in impoverished families and struggle hard to survive. These stories highlight the gap between the rich and the poor in Iranian society. "The Bald Pigeon Keeper" is inspired by the folktales of Azarbayjan, the author's homeland. The bald pigeon keeper is a poor young man who lives with his mother and begins to resist the king's cruelties.

These are engaging stories that also focus on the causes of social problems such as hunger and poverty and what can be done to eradicate them. SHAHLA SOHAIL GHADRBOLAND

Weetzie Bat

📖 Francesca Lia Block

Gay/Lesbian/Bisexual, Multicultural

1991 (1989), Harper & Row

In an unusually candid story filled with a barrage of fabulously colorful images and characters, we meet blonde flat-topped Weetzie and her gay mohawked friend, Dirk. The two friends are on the lookout for their ideal partners: a secret agent for Weetzie and a surfer for Dirk. To help them, Dirk's grandmother gives Weetzie a genie in a bottle. After several unsuccessful wishes, Weetzie settles on wishing for the above-mentioned men and a house where they can all live happily ever after.

In due course, Dirk meets a surfer named Duck and Weetzie meets a man named My Secret Agent Lover Man, who moves in with the trio.

Weetzie and her gay friend Dirk search for their respective ideal men in this quirky, funny book.

Weetzie decides she wants a baby, but My Secret Agent Lover Man refuses because he thinks the world is not a good place. Dirk and Duck volunteer, having seen a a talk show in which "two gay guys and their best friend all slept together so no one would know for sure whose baby it was." When the child, Cherokee, is born, she has Dirk's cheekbones, Duck's hair and nose, and My Secret Agent Lover Man's eyes.

Things go along fairly smoothly, but when Duck finds out that one of his best friends is dying of AIDS, he becomes scared of a world "where love can become death," and he runs away. Dirk tracks him down, brings him home, and they decide to "become more politically active." Weetzie thinks "love and disease are both like electricity...they are always there...[but] we can choose to plug into the love current instead."

This unconventional family applies a creative approach to building an unusual, yet loving, home. CHRIS MAYO

Andy

📖 Mary Christner Borntrager ✒ Paula Johnson

Amish

1993, Herald Press, ✳ Series

In this sixth book in a series about the Amish, Andy Maust, the younger brother of Ellie (*Ellie*, the first book in the series), is a curious sixteen-year-old boy who becomes fascinated with the stories of a drifter his father hires. The drifter describes sunsets and blue skies, wheat fields with golden grain, and green fields of Iowa corn.

An Amish boy wrestles with peer acceptance, an eating disorder, and his temper.

Andy is fascinated with the drifter because he himself feels very much an outsider. Andy wrestles with an eating disorder—"Food is a comfort to Andy...he eats because he is unhappy. He is unhappy because he is too heavy." The boys in the community tease him about his weight and bully him.

Drawn by the drifter's lifestyle, Andy runs away, only to discover that home is the best place to be. Any young adult who has found it difficult to be part of the crowd will identify with Andy's struggle.

Although life seems somewhat less complex for the Amish than for other communities, the stories clearly convey the fact that young Amish people face difficult challenges as well. But in these stories they have the unwavering support of a community steeped in spirituality that has buoyed them over the years. NANCY PAQUIN

Midget

📖 Tim Bowler

Physically Disabled

1995 (1994), Simon & Schuster

With all the trappings of a psychological thriller, Midget is a spellbinding young adult novel spilling over with rage. Fifteen-year-old Midget lives at the mercy of his abusive seventeen-year-old brother, Seb. Midget, named because of his small stature, also has some physical disabilities. His mother died when he was born and his father is not a strong figure in his life. Constantly taunted, abused, and put down by Seb, Midget seeks comfort in his dreams about sailing.

When an older boat builder named Joseph, who has befriended Midget, dies, he leaves Midget his partially built dingy. In sailing the boat, Midget builds strength and character. Ultimately, he learns to "sacrifice the part of you that hates until you love what you once hated. Whatever its faults."

Although the novel is set in Essex, England, the pain, suffering, and torture inflicted by Seb and felt by Midget are universal. The novel focuses on an intense hatred that threatens to annihilate and finally defeat the spirit. But Midget finds something at the very core of his being that keeps him from being destroyed.

In a highly engaging work, Midget, an abused child, takes control of his life when he gets his own sailboat.

Well written in engaging and very visual language, Midget will help young people learn that abuse may look like power, but it is really a mask for weakness. Tim Bowler clearly demonstrates how dreams have the power to take us beyond life's horrors and into a place of self-discovery. DAPHNE MUSE

Grandfather Stories of the Navaho People

📖 Sydney Callaway ✒ Gary Witherspoon, Hoke Denetsosie, and Clifford Beck

Native American, Navajo

1968, Board of Education, Rough Rock Demonstration School

Developed as a tool for young people in the reservation schools, *Grandfather Stories of the Navaho People* instructs readers about Navajo life and culture. The book covers creation stories, Navajo history and tribal relations, family life, religion, and health and healing. Stories include "The Navajo Ceremony for Rain," "The Lake That Got Angry," and "The Holy People and the First Dog." The chapters emphasize the value of traditional Navajo life. Illustrations include fine black-and-white traditional drawings and contemporary art, and black-and-white photographs of the Navajo reservation and of the herbs that grow there.

Developed for use in Native American reservation schools, this valuable book, now out of print, explores Navajo life and culture.

One chapter tells the story of a young Navajo boy who falls ill and is sent to a hospital, where he must adjust to non-Indian society. Eventual-

118

ly the doctor sends for his parents, who take him home and successfully treat him with a traditional ceremony. "[The boy] had seen the ceremony succeed for others, and he knew it would work for him. He knew this because the Holy People had done it that way from the beginning. The doctors and the nurses at the hospital had been good to him. They had done everything to make him comfortable. He was happy there, in a way. But, with his people, he found true happiness and a feeling of belonging."

The book discusses the spiritual dimensions of everyday life in many things, such as housing and tools. One chapter explains the uses of hogans: "The Navajo hogan is not just a place to sleep and eat; it is…also a temple. It is a 'being' which must be fed and kept strong and good."

Few other sources mention this spiritual aspect of Navajo housing.

Unfortunately, this valuable book has gone out of print. Hopefully students, teachers, and librarians will be able to find copies. NOLA HADLEY

Imagining Isabel

Omar S. Castaneda

Guatemalan, Hispanic

1994, Lodestar Books, Casteneda, Omar S., *Among the Volcanoes.*

Isabel leaves her village in Guatemala to become a teacher in this sequel to Among the Volcanoes.

A sequel to *Among the Volcanoes, Imagining Isabel* allows readers to come into an even greater understanding of Isabel's life and the cultural framework around which it is structured. Having decided to marry Lucas, she also continues to pursue her commitment to teach. Her mother passes on a sacred bundle to her. What Isabel finds inside is not quite what she thought it would be.

A letter from the Commission of Education in Guatemala City notifying her that she has been selected for the teacher training program puts her another mile further along the path to her dream. The reality of the opportunity jars her and for a moment she considers not going; but Lucas clearly

understands what this means to Isabel and their village. At the training school, a life-threatening experience teaches Isabel that politics is very much a part of her education.

While the first few chapters are very slow, the pace of the writing quickens once Isabel goes to school. The strong sense of danger and intrigue enhance the story. The result is a political education for Isabel and for readers as well. MAGNA M. DIAZ

The Last of the Menu Girls

Denise Chavez

Hispanic, Mexican American

1991 (1986), Arte Publico Press

Denise Chavez presents an integrated collection of seven stories featuring Rocio Esquibel, a seventeen-year-old Mexican American girl who reflects upon her life in New Mexico. Roco asks the difficult questions probably every teenage girl at some time or another asks:

"What did it mean to be a woman? To be beautiful, complete? Was beauty a physical or spiritual thing, was it strength of emotion, resolve, a willingness to love?"

The personal narratives examine many such questions and topics as Rocio takes stock of her family, community, and self. Interspersed throughout the book are a few Spanish words that can be easily defined through context; however, no glossary is provided to assist monolinguals.

Insightfully describing the human condition through personal narratives, Chavez writes in a colloquial style that is easily understood by most high-school and middle-school students, yet does not compromise intellectual quality. Also, the stories do not dwell on the negative aspects of social and personal identity, but infuse important implications related to gender and ethnicity through reflective insight. *It is* The Last of the Menu Girls'

A collection of stories featuring a Mexican American girl who asks difficult questions.

accessibility as an intellectual inquiry into the identity of an individual that makes it an excellent text for adolescent readers. Its value in a multicultural classroom setting is also punctuated by the seldom heard Mexican American female perspective. HERIBERTO GODINA

A Hero Ain't Nothin' but a Sandwich

📖 Alice Childress

African American

1989 (1977), Bantam Doubleday Dell, ✳ Braille

Thirteen-year-old Benjie Johnson of Harlem has an anxious mother with a well-meaning live-in boyfriend, a deeply religious grandmother, and a nascent heroin habit. This demanding, uncompromising book asks, what can save Benjie? Benjie and his world emerge from the first-person narratives of the protagonist and his mother, grandmother, would-be stepfather, and best friend, as well as a well-meaning white teacher, an angry black nationalist teacher, a school principal, a drug dealer, and a manipulative neighbor.

The characters reveal themselves with varying degrees of integrity, bravado, intelligence, and self-deception. For example, Benjie is brutally honest about the hypocrisy, platitudes, and incompetence he confronts in school, in his neighborhood, and in the larger society; but he rationalizes his own drug use, steals from his grandmother's purse, and avoids taking responsibility for his choices. With the cruelty of youth, he belittles the pride and past achievements of his mother's boyfriend, who was involved in the civil rights movement of the 1960s. The white teacher is dedicated and concerned about his students, but while he is ready to acknowledge past injustices, he is unwilling to deal with present racial injustices. It is the black teacher, however, who ultimately cares enough about Benjie to report his drug use to the authorities.

An African American child deals with his slide into addiction in this provocative classic.

The fact that this book was first published almost twenty years ago suggests that it may be dated. To an unsettling degree, this is not the case. To be sure, in the 1990s Benjie would face many different problems. On the whole, however, the characters' struggles, hopes, and challenges remain relevant to this country's current social, educational, and moral crises. *With its textured and honest exploration of loneliness, peer pressure, pride, self-delusion, and self-respect, this provocative book offers tremendous possibilities for discussion.* ROBIN BERSON

An Island Like You: Stories From El Barrio

📖 Judith Ortiz Cofer

Hispanic, Puerto Rican

1995 (1978), Orchard Books

Teenagers of Puerto Rican heritage growing up in Paterson, New Jersey, people this excellent book. Most of the stories are set in the barrio, an area of the city where the largely Hispanic population forms a cultural community.

Twelve revealing stories about teenagers of Puerto Rican descent growing up in New Jersey.

Family ties, peer interaction, competing and nurturing customs are presented in a lively and personal set of accounts. The protagonists are all teenagers, most of whom are experiencing difficulties either at home or at school. They have uneasy relationships with their peers, and they are struggling for identity. Each of

the twelve stories enriches the readers' knowledge of the barrio as well as its teenage inhabitants. A community and its varied perspectives emerges.

Most of the stories have a bittersweet flavor, such as "An Hour With Abuelo," in which a young man is forced by his mother to visit his grandfather in a nursing home. To his surprise, his visit is an interesting one, largely consisting of his grandfather's reading aloud from a notebook in which the grandfather has set down his memories. The grandfather is an intelligent, literate man who loves words and knowledge. He has been thwarted by external circumstances and people who have cruelly used him, but he retains his dignity. His grandson promises he will never permit others to stop him from doing whatever he wants to with his life.

Some of the stories deal with intergenerational respect, or lack of it; most convey issues of growing up and making decisions. Spanish words and phrases are interlaced appropriately. The writing flows well and captures each character as well as the setting. The flavor is unmistakably Latino and the Puerto Rican heritage comes through as an element greatly to be valued. MASHA RUDMAN

People of the Short Blue Corn: Tales and Legends of the Hopi Indians

📖 Harold Courlander ✒ Enrico Arno

Hopi, Native American

1996 (1970), Henry Holt & Company, Inc,

📚 Courlander, Harold, *The Cow-Tail Switch and Other West African Stories*; Courlander, Harold, *The Fire on the Mountain and Other Stories from Ethiopia*; Courlander, Harold, *Eritrea*.

A collection of seventeen traditional tales from the Hopi people.

Folklorist Harold Courlander has devoted his life to collecting the myths and stories of African, Native American and Asian people. He has preserved their stories and traditions in such outstanding books as *The Cow-Tail Switch and Other West African Stories, The Fire on the Mountain and Other Stories from Ethiopia* and *Eritrea*, and this fine collection of Hopi myths and folktales. Courlander spent two summers with the Hopis to collect these stories, which were first published in 1970. Clever and intriguing, these stories reveal many aspects of Hopi culture , including traditions of sorcery and mysticism. These stories also depict the interdependence of nature, humans, and spirit. Older, more sophisticated readers will find these stories especially engaging.

Most of the stories are written in such a way that reading them will not be nearly as exciting as listening to them being told by masterful tellers. "The Beetles's Hairpiece," "The Sun Callers," and "Coyote's Needle" in particular require the voice of superb storytellers to convey the message.

The black-and-white pen-and-ink illustrations are filled with symbolism. Courlander also provides a "Pronunciation Guide and Glossary," which explains

that numerous Hopi words vary in their pronunciation from village to village. The glossary also reflects the influence of Spanish on the Hopi language. The notes include information about the origin of names, and some discussion on the inability of English to convey fully the meaning of some Hopi words.

DAPHNE MUSE

Coyote Sun

📖 Carlos Cumpian ✒ Carlos Cortez

Hispanic, Mexican

1990, March/Abrazo Press

Chicano poet Carlos Cumpian presents thirty-four short poems in *Coyote Sun*. His poetry will satisfy many students' counterculture tendencies. This collection offers a refreshing departure from traditional representations of poetry. This poetry makes no compromises between the mainstream culture's distorted images of Chicanos and the social realities affecting many Mexican Americans today.

The poems invoke topics often ignored in the school curriculum, such

Thirty-four off-beat poems that focus on social realities affecting many Mexican Americans today.

as the concept of Aztlan, illegal immigration, gangs, homelessness, racism, and violence. Throughout the poetry, Cumpian conveys an acknowledgment of resilience, and even defiance, in the face of institutionalized racism. Chicano Calo, the Mexican dialect of Spanish, is interspersed throughout the selection, and Cumpian provides a short glossary at the end of each poem to assist non-Calo speakers. *These poems were very popular with the Mexican American high school students that I shared them with, even though like many other high school students, they were initially reluctant to engage in classroom poetry reading.*

HERIBERTO GODINA

I'll Get There, It Better Be Worth the Trip

📖 John Donovan

Gay/Lesbian/Bisexual

1969, Harper & Row, ✷ Spanish

Davy Ross is living with his grandmother and his dachshund, Fred, in a coastal New England town when his grandmother dies. As she was his primary care giver and confidante, he is devastated by this loss. At thirteen, he is compelled to move to New York City to live with his alcoholic mother, whom he hardly knows. He spends Saturdays with his father and stepmother. He discovers that his parents don't know much about

An intimate but dated look at a teen's sexuality that discourages homosexuality.

121

him, and in fact don't seem interested in learning about him. In his loneliness, he spends considerable time observing the behavior and needs of his best friend, Fred, his dog.

At school Davy becomes acquainted with another boy named Altschuler, and they develop a friendship. One day while on the floor playing with Fred, Davy tries to describe the feelings inside himself when he finds himself in close proximity to Altschuler, with Fred licking both their faces; they end up kissing. Both he and Altschuler avoid each other intermittently for the next several weeks, and finally come to blows. However, they renew their friendship and do talk about their intimacies; each reassures the other he is not ashamed. Davy assures himself this does not mean he is gay.

John Donovan succeeds at capturing the authentic voice of a lonely thirteen-year-old boy in journal form. Davy ponders the subtleties of friendship, adult respect and appreciation, animal behavior, popularity, and budding sexual expression. However, the reaction of all the adults to the potential sexual relationship is alarm. Davy tells his father he is not "queer" and his father is relieved. By the end of the novel, Davy is saying the important thing is "not to do it again," and his friend agrees.

The novel is certainly linked to the late 1960s and early 1970s stereotypical norms. The mother's character seems especially dated. It attempts to explore the possibilities of same-sex sexual expression in early teens in a nonjudgmental light, but succeeds in implying this is acceptable only if nobody is really gay. SUE FLICKINGER

Morning Girl

📕 Michael Dorris

Caribbean, Native American

1992, Hyperion Books for Children

This is an intriguing fictional account of Columbus's fateful "discovery" told from the perspective of two youngsters living in an idyllic world. It's provocative reversal of the traditional story should encourage fruitful discussion. Morning Girl and her brother, Star Boy, are Taino Indians living on a Bahamian island in the late fifteenth century. They have little experience with strangers, and greet every day with vigor and eagerness. Life for the Taino is quite full; they depend on the gifts from

An intriguing fictional account of Taino life before Columbus.

the sea and their island for survival. It always seems to Morning Girl that "if the day starts before you do, you never catch up. You spend all your time running after what you should have already done, and no matter how much you hurry, you never finish the race in a tie. The day wins." The family is full of life and humor and love for one another and the world in which they live. They are the first to encounter a group of men, in a fat canoe, that fateful day in 1492 when Columbus "discovered" the New World. They embrace these strangers as they would any other people. Author Michael Dorris, an anthropologist and member of the Modoc tribe, ends the story with a haunting excerpt from Columbus's log. *Morning Girl* is an enlightening addition to any study of American history. PATRICIA WONG

Coming of Age in America: A Multicultural Anthology

📕 Mary Frosch (editor)

Multicultural

1994, The New Press

As Gary Soto points out in his thoughtful foreword, we can all recognize similar feelings of greed, fear, and love, even in the very different experiences of others. We might not have experienced the pain of wearing an ugly "guacamole-colored jacket," as Soto describes in his own story, but we can all recognize the peculiar adolescent shame of standing out in a crowd.

Writers from fifteen different ethnic groups explore adolescence.

The collection of short stories and fiction excerpts in this anthology portrays varied experiences of childhood. A young black girl in rural Maryland rages against her poverty by destroying a neighbor's marigolds. A young white girl on Long Island recalls

a quiet sense of betrayal, both external and internal when she overhears her immigrant neighbors denigrated as "shanty Irish," and she makes no protest. Frosch identifies these intense adolescent emotions as "awakening moments." Lizabeth, the marigold-stomper, recalls that "that violent, crazy act was the last act of childhood."

These and other stories eloquently capture incidents where perspective changes, and possibilities open or close forever. The twenty-one stories are organized into four categories: "Fitting in," "Family matters," "Affairs of the heart," and "Crisis." Frosch explains in her preface that these categories follow the process of coming-of-age. Our first step in self-identification is to try to fit in, then we tackle our relationships with our families, then we approach the critical moments of our lives, where we meet face-to-face something ugly or frightening. *Carla's story in particular contains some explicit sexual content that may be disturbing to a young reader. This passage is essential to the story, which is itself disturbing. However, teachers may wish to review the story before making it available in the classroom.*
RENEÉ HAYES

Annie on My Mind

Nancy Garden

Gay/Lesbian/Bisexual

1992 (1982), Farrar, Straus & Giroux, ✻ Spanish, ▥ Bauer, Marion Dane, editor, *Am I Blue? Coming Out From the Silence*; Brett, Katherine, *S. P. Likes A. D.*; Day, Frances Ann, *Teacher's Guide to Multicultural Voices in Contemporary Literature*; Garden, Nancy, *Good Moon Rising*; Garden, Nancy, *Lark in the Morning*; Heron, Ann, editor, *Two Teenagers in Twenty: Writings by Gay and Lesbian Youth*; Rench, Janice E., *Understanding Sexual Identity: A Book for Gay Teens and Their Friends*; Scoppettone, Sandra, *Trying Hard to Hear You*; Scoppettone, Sandra, *Happy Endings Are All Alike*.

This classic story is told from the point of view of a young first-year student at M.I.T. looking back on her relationship with another young woman during their senior year in high school. Although Liza Winthrop was student council president in her private high school, she never felt like she belonged. Annie, from an Italian American working class family, attended a public high school where she was a gifted musician.

Shortly after the two girls meet for the first time, they develop a strong relationship. Liza struggles to accept her feelings for Annie and to come to terms with her lesbianism. "It was like a war inside me; I couldn't even recognize all the sides," she says. One day she and Annie are caught making love in the house of two of Liza's vacationing teachers, who are also lesbians. The ensuing fallout leads to the teachers' dismissal. Confusion and guilt prevent Liza from

contacting Annie for several miserable months during which they both leave for college. At the book's end, however, Liza telephones Annie and they reaffirm their love for each other.

Nancy Garden's bittersweet, tender love story is a classic in the field. Beautifully written, the book also skillfully tackles tough topics such as lesbianism and the complex and often overlooked issue of class differences in relationships. An excellent book about two real and likeable young women, *Annie on My Mind* provides much needed information about lesbianism as well as the prevalent homophobia that, unfortunately, is typical of our society.

A classic, groundbreaking story of love between two young women and the bigotry that threatens it.

This award-winning, groundbreaking book is especially important because, unfortunately there are still very few books for young people about homosexuality. It is crucial that books such as *Annie on My Mind* be available to all young students—whether they are homosexual or not—who are searching for

information about sexuality. Nancy Garden responded to this need for a well written, realistic book about young lesbians when she wrote *Annie on My Mind* in 1982; the second edition in 1992 finds the body of adolescent literature still suffering from a paucity of quality books about homosexuality. Garden's 1991 book, *Lark in the Morning*, presents us with another likeable, admirable lesbian protagonist who is an important role model for young lesbians searching for positive images in books. Garden skillfully weaves information and insight into her compelling books. Readers will also want to watch for ways to counteract the homophobia that is injuring and killing many of our most creative young people.

In areas where books such as Annie on My Mind *might be considered controversial, educators should first become familiar with their district's policy on the use of controversial materials. They should always notify their principals in advance about their plans to use these materials. Advice and additional resources for students and teachers are available in books such as* Two

Teenagers in Twenty: Writings by Gay and Lesbian Youth *edited by Ann Heron,* Understanding Sexual Identity: A Book for Gay Teens and Their Friends *by Janice E. Rench and* Am I Blue? Coming Out From the Silence *edited by Marion Dane Bauer.*
FRANCES ANN DAY

Sister

📖 Eloise Greenfield ✎ Moneta Barnett

African American

1987 (1974), Thomas Y. Crowell, ✳ Series

Shortly after breaking her leg, thirteen-year-old Dorthea, or Sister as her family calls her, begins a memory book—to pass the time, recount her dreams, and describe her parents' happy marriage. She continues her journal over the next four difficult years in her life as her family goes through a series of changes. The entries tell about her father's death, her older sister Alberta's pulling away from the family, and her mother's loneliness and financial struggles, as well as Sister's new feeling about boys, her difficulties in school, and her fears about all that happens.

Dorthea idolizes Alberta, and, in fact, everyone says the two girls are exactly

In her journal, an African American girl wrestles with turning points in her life including the death of her father.

Annie on My Mind

FRANCES ANN DAY

Despite gains made by the gay rights movement, there are still very few books for young people about homosexuality. As an author and educational consultant, I know how crucial it is for books such as Annie on My Mind to be available to all young students who are searching for information about sexuality. Our society is still appallingly misinformed about homosexuality; books such as Annie on My Mind are desperately needed to support lesbian and gay youth in the process of coming to terms with their sexuality to support heterosexual youth in the process of coming to terms with their sexuality and to help heterosexual students support their lesbian and gay friends.

Many adult lesbians and gay men report having searched in vain for information when they were younger. Omission is one of the most insidious and painful forms of bias; the implicit message is that homosexuality does not exist or is deviant. Invisibility is extremely destructive to young lesbians and gay men as well as to the larger society. Growing up in a society that teaches these young people to hide their sexual orientation and to hate themselves has resulted in a national tragedy: lesbian and gay youth who take their own lives account for 30 percent or more of all suicides in the United States.

As educators, we are responsible for reaching out to gay and lesbian teenagers. In places where books such as Annie on My Mind might be considered controversial, educators first should become familiar with their district's policy on the use of controversial materials, and should always notify their principals in advance about their plans to use these materials .

Advice and additional resources for students and teachers are available in books such as Two Teenagers in Twenty: Writings by Gay and Lesbian Youth, edited by Ann Heron, Understanding Sexual Identity: A Book for Gay Teens and Their Friends, by Janice E. Rench, and Am I Blue? Coming Out From the Silence, edited by Marion Dane Bauer. These books recommend that teachers make clear that bigotry of any kind will not be tolerated and that we must stop students who are harassing other students. Even one positive comment from a teacher can mean a great deal to an isolated teenager who faces prejudice and hostility from the larger society.

Frances Ann Day is the author of a reference book and teaching guide of the works and lives of multicultural authors and illustrators.

alike. But when Alberta begins to worry her mother by staying out late, getting into fights, and being sullen at home, Sister is angry and wants to be anything but Alberta's carbon copy. Through her memories, Sister discovers that she is not a replica of Alberta but a changing, distinct, and empathetic individual.

Sister is a short, easy-to-read book at a growing girl's changing viewpoint and world. When her familiar security is taken from her, Dorthea copes by writing about the situations, her feelings, and reactions. What emerges is a distinct portrait of a child maturing that articulately voices Dorthea's fears about death and her changing family.
ALISON WASHINGTON

A White Romance

📖 Virginia Hamilton

African American

1989 (1987), Philomel Books

Talley Barbour is slowly adjusting to her formerly all-black high school's integration. The changes come quickly, and there seems to be a tentative truce between students. Talley releases her energy by running and meets a soulmate in Didi, a white girl who shares Talley's love for running. Didi is deeply in love with Roady Dean, a drugged-out, heavy metal music lover who depends on her for stability. Talley can't understand what keeps Didi and Roady together but is fascinated by their "White Romance," as she calls it. Talley and Didi have a close friendship, but that is strained when David, a Svengali-like charmer, focuses his attention on Talley. Didi's warning that "David Emory would be a joke if he wasn't an absolute zero to begin with," falls on Talley's deaf ears. Talley is hesitant to return any affection because she can't understand why David is interested in her; he's white, well-known in school, and has a shady reputation. Still, Talley is drawn in by David's sudden, intense devotion to her and is swept into his life despite her reservations.

Troubled teenaged love, complicated by race, motivates this story of an African American girl's relationship with a white boy.

David introduces Talley into a world of heavy metal music, sex, self-doubt, and his business as a drug dealer. Later, Talley must face the truth: David is using her and will eventually cut off all his attention to her. Talley is broken-hearted by the break up even though she knows it is the only way for her to regain her sense of balance and control. In the end, Talley can clearly see what real friendship and devotion is, through people like Didi, who really care for her.

A White Romance describes the turmoil of teens in love, or in at least what they think is love. It discusses drug use, race relations, sex, and gives a chilling description of what goes on at a heavy metal rock concert. The story falters when showing the consequences of Talley's choices, especially in an age when what she does can have life-altering results. Parents are almost nonexistent in this world and exert no influence in their children's lives. Without moralizing or becoming preachy, Hamilton could show more of what might have happened to Talley as she makes risky choices in her life. ALISON WASHINGTON

Against the Storm

📖 Gaye Hicyilmaz

Middle Eastern, Turkish

1992 (1990), Little Brown & Company

A Turkish proverb says that against a storm, the upright tree may finally break, but the one that bends survives. In this story of a Turkish boy's thirteenth year, young Mehmet finds that with both steadfastness and resilience, he too can survive.

Mehmet's family have left their village for Ankara, hoping for a better life with the help of a rich uncle, who already has a thriving business in the capital city. All too soon they are disillusioned; Mehmet is forced to leave school and get a job collecting bus fares. Thrown on his own, he makes one good friend in a young boy, Muhlis, who is living on the street. Fortunately, a wealthy old woman takes an interest in the boys and hires them to do gardening.

A Turkish boy and his family move to the capital city in hopes of a better life.

During this time Mehmet grows in self-reliance and confidence; he has learned to take care of himself, make careful judgments, and stand up for what he wants. He also has grown angry at poverty and the general mess he sees surrounding him. With financial help from the elderly woman, he returns to his village.

125

This is a story full of adventure for its protagonist. There is a Dickensian quality in the black villainy of the rich uncle, and his obnoxious family, and in the convenient appearance of a few good-hearted persons who help the boys in their times of need. One could question the story's realism. What is certain, however, is that this is an unusually gripping and well-written book. The portrait on the striking book jacket supports the image of an "ordinary" child quickly becoming what may be an extraordinary man.

The splintering of families is a theme in the book that bears further discussion. Mehmet comes to reject his parents for their toadying to the rich uncle and their abandonment of him.

Against the Storm is convincingly grounded in present-day urban Turkey, though not lavish with colorful detail of setting or culture. Rather, *it has a universal quality; Mehmet's story could be that of a poor boy in Mexico or Morocco. This quality brings the story closer to home and could lend itself to discussion of "real life," ethics, and "what I would do in Mehmet's sandals."* ELSA MARSTON

I Be Somebody

❧ Hadley Irwin
African American, Creek Indian, Native American
1988 (1984), Atheneum

Ten-year-old Rap finds his everyday life in Clearview colored with mystery words such as Athabasca, overheard in conversations between adults—his aunt, with whom he lives; a Creek Indian, who is like a grandfather to him; and others who figure in his life. As the story unfolds, Rap discovers more about the mystery words, about his father, and about his aunt's wish to travel to Athabasca. The town of Athabasca, located in far-away Alberta, Canada, has been settled by blacks seeking a better life. In the year of 1910, Rap and his aunt travel by train to the Canadian town.

A boy's search for identity touches upon African American history in Canada.

Based on a little-known historical fact, this is a worthwhile story of a boy's search for identity, but as a narrative, it lacks drama and ultimately fails to involve the reader fully. There are fuzzy areas in the progression of the plot. Even so, *the story is good enough to use as a catalyst for the discussion of this period in black history.*

The images of Rap and his family are mostly positive. BENNIE TATE WILKIN

A Rock and a Hard Place: One Boy's Triumphant Story

❧ Anthony Godby Johnson, Foreword by Paul Monette, Afterword by Fred Rogers
Gay/Lesbian/Bisexual
1994 (1993), Dutton

Fourteen-year-old Tony Johnson finds his solace in school and on the streets of New York, not with family or with a long-standing community of friends. Though not his biological family, the people who love him show a compassion and demonstrate real concern for Tony, his tenacity, and his future.

A former victim of abuse, now diagnosed with AIDS, Tony remains optimistic. While the disease afflicts him physically, he refuses to allow it to destroy his spirit. The author provides the reader with a real person, not a sociological statistic. Tony's sense of determination and self-reliance will encourage young readers to face those "hard places" in their own lives whether those adversities are abuse, peer pressure, or a terminal disease. *A Rock and a Hard Place* also clearly demonstrates how important community is to the lives of young people and how critical it is for us to hear their pleas for something beyond this often terrifying world in which they are growing up. While the book's gripping social realism can be disturbing, it can also help readers grow in understanding about how adversity shapes our lives.
FRIEDA K. TAKAMURA

A fourteen-year-old victim of abuse and AIDS refuses to let adversity destroy his spirit.

The Arizona Kid

❧ Ron Koertge
Gay/Lesbian/Bisexual
1989 (1988), Joy Street Books

In this coming-of-age novel, sixteen-year-old Billy spends the summer with his gay uncle in Tucson, Arizona. Ostensibly, he is there to work with the horses at a racetrack. (He plans to become a veterinarian.) But his personal goals for the summer are to find a girlfriend and lose his virginity. He arrives in Arizona from Missouri, a complete greenhorn: he is unfamiliar with the desert heat, the single gay lifestyle of his uncle Wes, and how to pick up girls. He knows absolutely nothing about horses. He is, however, endearingly self-deprecatory and has a lively sense of humor. He finds his romance with a feisty horse rider named Cara Mae, learns a lot about horse racing, and also becomes friends with his uncle Wes. From Wes he learns about AIDS activism, about the sorrow of friends dying from AIDS, about safe sex, and about having a better understanding of others. Billy's learning process also includes how to be a supportive romantic partner for Cara Mae, who experiences some disappointments during the summer.

Living with his gay uncle, Billy learns much about himself and one single gay man's lifestyle.

Billy is an amiable, believable character whose wry comments on his surroundings make the reader laugh out loud. Wes is also a complex character who reveals generosity, fears, faults, and a dry sense of humor. What gay men do on dates is discussed explicitly, along with a strong bid for safer sex for both gay and heterosexual couples. This discussion between Billy and Wes is touched with sadness, humor, and anger at having to worry about it all; in short, realistic without being preachy. The book is well written, with intelligent, fast-paced dialogue and characters so likable that one is sorry to see the book end. SUE FLICKINGER

Wilma Unlimited: How Wilma Rudolph Became the World's Fastest Woman

Kathleen Krull David Diaz and Cecelia Zieba-Diaz

African American, Physically Disabled

1996, Harcourt Brace & Company

No one expected Wilma Rudolph to make it to her first birthday. Born in Clarksville, Tennessee, in 1940, she suffered more from childhood diseases than did her nineteen brothers and sisters. With severely limited resources, living in an area where only one doctor would treat black people, Wilma and her family faced daunting days. When she turned five, Wilma was diagnosed with polio. At that time, most people who contracted the disease were permanently crippled or died. Wilma learned to manage life by hopping on one foot. But twice a week she took the bus fifty miles to Nashville to the nearest hospital that would treat black people. There, doctors and nurses helped her to strengthen her paralyzed leg.

Once her leg was fitted with a brace, she was able to move around more easily. Although her classmates teased her, she refused to let their taunts or the pains in her leg discourage her. Her perseverance paid off; one day, Wilma boxed her brace and sent it back to the hospital. She went on to win a full athletic scholarship to Tennessee State University. During the summer of 1960, she represented the United States as a runner at the Olympics in Rome. She won the 100-meter and 200-meter dash, bringing home two gold medals. In the 400-meter relay, Rudolph almost dropped the baton, but went on to earn a third gold medal.

Her return home from Rome was the first time in the history of Clarksville, Tennessee, that blacks and whites sat together to celebrate anything.

A biography of an African American woman who overcame childhood polio to win three gold medals in a single Olympics.

Rudolph went on to become a second-grade teacher and high school coach. She also founded a nonprofit foundation to support young athletes and to teach them to overcome adversity. Although she died in 1994, she left a legacy that is sure to endure.

David Diaz, a 1995 Caldecott Medal-winner, collaborated with his wife Cecelia Zieba-Diaz, to create the book's illustrations and paintings. Created with acrylics, watercolor, and gouache on Arches watercolor paper, the paintings bring a rich dimension to the book. I especially like the way in which the Diazes capture the runner's motion. Some young people may question the portrayal of several of the members of the media with darker skin tones. During the early sixties, it was extremely rare to see any people of color in front of the camera.

While capturing a real sense of the times in which Rudolph grew up, Krull truly honors the dignity and power of Rudolph in this well-written biography. It is sure to inspire generations of young women and men. DAPHNE MUSE

127

128

Asian American Oral Histories of First to Fourth Generations Americans from China, the Philippines, Japan, India, the Pacific Islands, Vietnam, and Cambodia

Joan Faung Jean Lee (editor)

Asian American

1991, The New Press

Lee offers the reader a collection of first-person accounts of life in the United States. Based on her interviews with people from many walks of life, fifty-two short passages in this book paint a vivid impression of what it means to be Asian American. This book's subtitle, "Oral Histories of First to Fourth Generation Americans from China, the Philippines, Japan, India, the Pacific Islands, Vietnam, and Cambodia," only hints at the diversity of life experience revealed within these pages. The author's personal testimonies range from an eleven-year-old U.S.-born Indian girl's account of racial hatred to a seventy-four-year-old Chinese woman's description of her carefree retirement in the United States.

Each personal narrative is brief, between one and ten pages long. They are grouped thematically into three sections: "Living in America," "Aspects of Americanization," and "Reflections on Interracial Marriage." The narrator is introduced by a brief biographical vignette, no more than a few lines. In fact, except for her short introduction and these brief biographies, there is no authorial voice here at all. Yet the theme of self-identity emerges strongly from these disparate voices, creating a unity of focus unexpected in such a collection.

A diverse set of short, personal reflections by first-to-fourth-generation Asian Americans.

Perhaps the most compelling aspect of this collection is that not everyone defines themselves as Asian American. The author addresses this in her introduction, explaining that some dismiss the concept of Asian as inaccurate. She points out that people living in various Asian countries have very different cultures, and do not identify themselves as "Asians." However, she argues, the different Asian groups in the United States have a lot in common through a shared history and experience.

These Asian American narrators all address this question of ethnic identity differently. A man from Korea who immigrated to the United States as a teenager laments that he will never speak English without an accent, and yet has lost fluency in his first language. A son of Chinese immigrants considers taking Chinese language classes, although he does not feel Chinese. An Indian father resigns himself to the fact that his daughter can best be defined as an American, while his daughter insists that she prefers being Indian.

My only regret about this book is that the author did not add her own voice to the chorus. She identifies herself at the end of the introduction as the daughter of a Chinese immigrant, and very briefly wonders what her life might have been like if her father had chosen to stay in China. It might be interesting to hear the personal narrative of someone inspired to gather such a moving collection of other people's stories.

This book can easily be read cover to cover, or can be used as a resource book. The simplicity of language and brief narrative form make it accessible to middle-grade readers, yet the fascinating accounts and strong theme of identity make the book rich enough to satisfy more sophisticated readers as well. MARTHA L. MARTINEZ

Three Friends

Myron Levoy

Gay/Lesbian/Bisexual

1984, HarperCollins

Joshua is a chess champion. At fourteen, most of his time outside of school is spent reading books on chess and going over previous chess matches. Then one day at the mall, he meets Karen and Lori, two girls from school, and the three of them begin to spend time together, both in and out of school. Karen has an even temperament and a good sense of humor. Lori has mood swings and often daydreams in a fantasy world. Karen and Josh soon begin dating and Lori finds herself on the outside. She fantasizes about both Karen and Josh, finding herself attracted to them both. She spends more and more time by herself, fantasizing about how she wants life to be.

One Saturday while home alone, Lori takes an overdose of her mother's sleeping pills. Her parents find her that evening and barely get her to the hospital in time to save her. Josh and Karen race to the hospital when they get the news and make it very clear to Lori that even though they're a couple, she is very important to them. The three of them discuss their relationship. Lori tells Karen and Josh that she's attracted to both of them. Josh makes clear it doesn't matter to him that she's "half gay," he likes her as she is and wants to remain good friends. He also makes clear that he doesn't think attempting suicide is a good way to deal with her unhappiness.

Very few young adult books address the topic of bisexuality. It is a relevant issue for some teenagers and books are needed that present a variety of bisexual characters. In this book, Lori is portrayed as confused and unstable, somewhat disconnected from reality. The extent to which her bisexuality is a part of the problems she's having is not made clear. The response of both Karen and Josh to the news that she's attracted to both of them is sensitive, but they don't talk much about it, focusing instead on her mood swings and depression. The author leaves the reader with the impression that while being bisexual is not necessarily a bad thing, it does add problems and causes confusion. The story line is weakened by the fact that her bisexuality seems not to be connected to the other problems she's having. SUE FLICKINGER

Three friends broach the subject of bisexuality, which in this book seems to bring confusion and problems.

A Piece of My Heart/Pedacito de mi corazón: The Art of Carmen Lomas Garza

Carmen Lomas Garza

Hispanic, Mexican American

1991, The New Press

This book was not originally intended as a children's book, but, rather, as a portfolio of paintings, drawings, etchings, and works in mixed-media. However, the naive style of this artist relates well to people of all ages. This is an engaging and insightful aesthetic tale that is well suited for the multicultural classroom.

Garza's art is rich in metaphorical symbolism related to Mexican American culture, and her paintings have been featured in exhibits across the country. (An impressive exhibition history is appendixed in her book.) Garza's themes, revealed through a simplistic painting style that pays careful attention to detail, makes her art very accessible and a strong vehicle for classroom and family discussions. Prevalent themes include a strong sense of community and family that is both warm and mysterious. Many scenes include the preparation of meals, which are treated by Garza as celebratory events that are joyful and inviting. They include the family eating watermelon on a porch and the preparation of tamales. The accompanying text, more suited for secondary-school students, describes some of the cultural elements found in the pictures. These include some

An artist's representation of Latino culture and life through thirty-seven works of art.

mystical aspects of Mexican culture such as *curanderismo* or faith-healing.

Since faith healing and spiritual practices from other cultures are often looked upon suspiciously or without a real understanding of the cultural context, further readings in the literature would provide teachers with detailed information on curanderismo. Many elements of culture portrayed in the book, such as curanderismo or making tamales may be discussed with supplementary texts. HERIBERTO GODINA

Twelve Days in August

Liza Ketchum Murrow

Gay/Lesbian/Bisexual

1993, Holiday House

Sixteen-year-old Todd is about to begin his junior year in high school. Tryouts for the varsity soccer team have started during August, and Todd has high hopes of making the team this year. On the first day of practice a new player shows up. Alex has just moved from Los Angles and is a very talented soccer player. His skill is very threatening to Randy, the star player from the previous year. Randy begins taunting Alex at every opportunity, calling him "fag" and convincing many of the other players to ostracize him. Todd feels caught in the middle. He is impressed with Alex's skill and doesn't want to hurt him, but at the same time he is intimidated by Randy and doesn't want to cross him. He discusses the situation with his uncle, who tells him that he himself is gay. That changes Todd's perspective on what is happening on the soccer team and he stands up to both Randy and the coach, insisting that the name-calling has to stop. In the end, the whole team, including Randy, works together to win a soccer game.

Liza Ketchum Murrow has created believable characters in this story. The reactions from many of them regarding the suspicion that Alex is gay— from overt rejection to avoidance of both the topic and Alex—are typical. Todd's rethinking of his perspective, once he finds out his uncle is gay, is not surprising; many people respond differently when they find out a family member or someone very close to them is gay or lesbian. The reader is never told whether or not Alex is really gay. The focus is on heterosexual people's reactions to the issue, the effects those reactions may have on others, and how reactions may change over time.

Todd faces difficult choices when the new kid on the soccer team is ostracized because his teammates think he's gay.

The ending is the only unbelievable part of the story. The players and coach briefly confronted the issue at halftime and then all the players pull together to win the game. Randy's sudden willingness to work with Alex rather simply for the sake of the game felt a little too contrived. Though the author doesn't pretend that Randy's attitude had changed completely, she didn't provide a solid enough base for why it would change even the little that it did.

The book could facilitate some good discussions about attitudes toward and treatment of gay and lesbian people. It could also raise some good questions about assuming someone is gay and whether or not it matters. SUE FLICKINGER

Hoops

Walter Dean Myers
African American
1983 (1981), Delacorte

Lonnie Jackson has only one constant in his life— his game. His father has left home, he can't seem to get along with his mother, his dreams of the future are evaporating, but he is a phenomenal basketball player. Lonnie feels trapped until he becomes part of a winning city league basketball team coached by a former NBA player, Cal Jones. Cal was released from professional ball because of a point-shaving scheme years ago, and has stopped drinking long enough to coach the talented teens to the city's special, televised, championship game. Lonnie begins to see Cal as the encouraging but tough father figure he never had and really begins to care for the fallen idol.

Problems arise when college scouts promise players the moon, bookies and gamblers want to run the games, and pressure is put on Cal to step down as coach. When heavy bettors force Cal to keep Lonnie on the bench so the team will lose the tournament, Cal risks everything to redeem himself and allow Lonnie to play. Lonnie has closed himself off to anyone who tried to get close to him, but as he begins to put his faith in his teammates and Cal, Lonnie opens himself to relationships with others. He expresses love and confusion about Mary-Ann, sister of his friend Paul. Lonnie helps Paul get out of the clutches of a loan shark/thief while understanding Paul's desire to have money and be like some well-off blacks. Still, the idea of becoming basketball stars allows them to dream. Lonnie soon sees how seeking happiness in his present reality is better than placing all his hope for love, admiration, and success on a tenuous fantasy.

An outstanding African American basketball player learns about trust and setting goals.

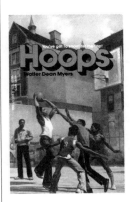

Hoops is replete with exciting, detailed basketball sequences, action-filled episodes, and humor, but the levity is balanced by corrupt and greedy individuals, fragmented families, and those affected by alcoholism. What redeems the story is its honest look at Lonnie's fears, frustrations, trials, and successes as he struggles. Lonnie is no model character, but his intensity for the sport and people he loves as well as his innate yearning for something better makes him admirable. *The basketball theme might draw in readers who typically wouldn't choose a story about a boy making decisions about growing up.* ALISON WASHINGTON

Talent Night

📖 Jean Davies Okimoto

Asian American, Biracial, Japanese American

1995, Scholastic Inc.

High school student Rodney Suyama, half Caucasian and half Asian, wants to become the first Japanese American rap star. He has the requisite earring and ponytail, drum machine, and perhaps even the talent, but he never had the nerve to perform before an audience. With his school's annual Talent Night approaching, Rodney decides to sign up for the event. In the meantime, he is having romantic problems. He's interested in classmate Ivy Ramos, who is also biracial — Filipino American and African American — but Ivy is dating the school football star. Their off again-on again relationship is an appealing element in a novel that also touches on racial pride, family heritage, and prejudice.

Rodney plans to start a career as an Asian American rap star by preparing for a school talent show.

Although Rodney and his sister Suzanne are quite comfortable with their biracial background, the imminent arrival of Uncle Hideki makes them question just how much they know about their Japanese ancestry. Uncle Hideki, a Japanese American interned during World War II, is considering bequeathing part of his reparations money to the younger generation if he feels they are honoring their heritage. Eager for the inheritance, Rodney and Suzanne begin studying Japanese phrases, cooking ethnic foods, and attempting to perform traditional arts and crafts.

Uncle Hideki's short visit is a disaster. The fussy elderly man clearly finds Rodney and his sister lacking in character. When Ivy drops in for a visit, Uncle Hideki is perturbed and utters an ethnic slur in Japanese. The furious family is happy when the uncle cuts his visit short. This incident, plus an episode in which a stranger bashes Rodney's ethnicity, inspire him to write a rap song about prejudice and brotherhood. With Ivy's onstage assistance, Rodney performs a rap number that brings down the house on Talent Night.

Likeable characters and a fast-moving plot make the novel an enjoyable reading experience. Although Rodney is seventeen-years-old, the book seems to be directed at a much younger audience. There are a few mild vulgarities, but otherwise the story is unpretentious and the romance is awkward and mild, with Rodney and Ivy behaving more like twelve- or thirteen-year-old kids than high school seniors. Therefore, the book seems most appropriate for upper-elementary or middle-school readers. One of the most interesting features of the story is the depiction of prejudice from an ethnic minority. Since so many books depict Caucasian prejudice, it is interesting — and unfortunately honest — to see bias displayed by other races as well. *Another intriguing aspect of the novel is that excerpts from many other works of literature are incorporated into the story as Rodney and Ivy study for their language arts class, making* Talent Night *a special interest for English classes. Music fans will be intrigued by the focus on rap, although some may find Rodney's rap number to be rather lame; students might enjoy writing their own rap lyrics for Rodney's big number.*

PETER D. SIERUTA

Rap to Live By

📖 Don Roberts   ✒ Sherman Edwards

African American, Multicultural

1993, Hampton Roads Publishing Company Inc.

Although its popularity was heightened by hip-hop, rap is not new. Today's style and delivery give rap a new face in a world often oblivious to teen or young adult concerns. *Rap to Live By* looks candidly at those worries and discusses the consequences of inappropriate choices.

The author, Don Roberts, is a television news anchor who has covered many stories dealing with violence, addiction, and abuse. He knows firsthand that these conditions often provide him with the lead story for his newscasts. Tired of this reoccurring trend, he wrote *Rap to Live By* to open a line of communication between young people and adults. He hopes that his book of verse can serve as a means of stopping the extreme violence perpetrated by today's youth.

Positive rap for children and young adults.

Using the rhythm of the streets of the world, *Rap to Live By* captures the emotions and concerns of

131

today's young adults. Further, it deals with the fears experienced by youth, while encouraging each person to find the answer best for him or her. On topics such as love, sex, drugs, and friendship, this book discusses both sides of each issue. *Rap to Live By* deals with these issues and explores some of their negative aspects, but offers a positive path. The message is delivered in a vernacular that would appeal to young people. The offer of adult assistance is clear but not overpowering.

This book has a positive message. It gives hope to all that there is an end to violence and restores the ability to dream of a future.

YOLANDA ROBINSON-COLES

The Drowning Boy

Frank Rodgers
Emotionally Disabled
1992 (1972), Doubleday and Company

This sensitive, well-written, and complex story shows how a confused teenager successfully copes with feelings of inadequacy. Surrounded by a domineering father and a passive mother and grandmother, Jason tries to find his way in the world. The father's fierce domination results in the mother's withdrawing from her satisfying career into a world that supports the father's image. Jason's grandmother lives with the physiological ravages that sometimes come with aging, and she cannot care for herself. Jason struggles to evolve beyond this dismal morass.

A sensitive book in which a boy exposed to children with disabilities for the first time develops new respect for life and relationships.

In forming a friendship with his teacher's autistic nephew, Buddy, Jason learns about the challenges that come with a tough and unyielding physical disability that also impairs one's intellectual and reasoning skills. His character develops dramatically as he is taken outside his own problems. But the motives of the domineering father are never explained, and the mother is too submissive. In a young adult novel where emotions are so articulately defined, it would be valuable for the reader to have a better understanding of why the adults escape into dysfunction in much the same way as the autistic child retreats into his own private world.

MEREDITH ELIASSEN

Always Running: La Vida Loca, Gang Days in L.A.

Luis J. Rodriguez   Julie Scott
Hispanic, Mexican American
1994 (1993), Curbstone Press

In *Always Running*, Rodriguez relates an autobiographical account of his teenage days as a gang member in East Los Angeles. Written in a style that often integrates Chicano Calo, the Mexican dialect of Spanish, non-Calo speakers will need the glossary provided. However, even with the aid of a glossary, this may be a difficult text to read because many of the cryptographic phrases are used mostly among Mexican American gang members.

In the preface, Rodriguez describes some of his rationale for writing this dark account of his gang life. He intended his son, Ramiro, to read it as a way of understanding what was happening out in the streets. Rodriguez writes from a personal perspective that authentically captures the experience of what it means to be a Mexican American gang member.

A vivid autobiographical account of the author's teenage years as a Mexican American gang member in East L.A.

Teachers whose students entertain or are sympathetic to such affiliations may find this text instructive as its characters are consumed by tragedy. As Rodriguez relates, the prominence of gang membership and the victimization of youth in urban areas is a serious problem. This story also calls attention to violence and drug abuse. There is a negative, hopeless tone throughout the book that makes it difficult to salvage something redeemable from this account of pariah youth. However, students who are more closely oriented toward this life-style should find the story dramatically engaging. Unfortunately, there still remains a dearth of non-gang-centered autobiographical selections for young readers and especially autobiography that is not gang-focused.

HERIBERTO GODINA

Happy Endings Are All Alike

📖 Sandra Scoppettone

Gay/Lesbian/Bisexual

1991 (1990), HarperCollins

Happy Endings Are All Alike, focuses on two high school seniors who are engaged in a lesbian relationship, a first for both. Even as they try to define their own relationship, they struggle with family condemnation and societal pressure to conform. The book also reveals the inner thoughts of certain family members and acquaintances, all struggling with their reactions to the idea of a lesbian relationship. Included in the thoughts of acquaintances are the diary entries of a young man who plans a rape and assault on one of the main characters. After the rape, the victim plans, with her family's encouragement, to press charges and consequently to pursue a very public trial. As the rape, and subsequently the relationship of the main characters, becomes public knowledge in their small town, the girls' relationship falls apart. In the end, however, the two girls reconcile, and the reader is left with the impression that there might be some chance of their staying together.

A somewhat one-dimensional look at two high school girls' love.

This is one of the few but slowly growing number of young adult books to deal with a romantic involvement between two girls. The author's style is realistic; nothing is glossed over. The plot is engaging. Although the characters are unique, with thoughts and reactions that vary widely, they generally lack depth. The rape victim's recovery seems simplified; she bounces back too easily from this traumatic event. Because everything in the book focuses on the lesbian relationship (even the rape is seen by most characters in that context), the book has a "flat," single-issue feel to it. SUE FLICKINGER

Unlived Affection

📖 George Shannon

Gay/Lesbian/Bisexual

1995, Harper & Row, ✳ Braille

Eighteen-year-old Willie Ramsey is getting ready to go to college. His grandmother, who raised him, has just recently died and he is now alone. His mother died when he was very young and he never knew his father. The only thing his grandmother would say was that his father was "unfit to be a father. He's better off dead." Willie is left to clean out the house, sell everything off at auction, and leave for school.

As he's cleaning out his mother's old room, he comes across a shoe box full of letters from his father to his mother. He sits down to read the letters, full of anticipation that he will finally get to know something about his father. As he reads through them, he begins to understand why his grandmother never talked about his father. His father was gay and left Willie's mother for another man. From the letters it's clear that Willie's mother and father maintained a good friendship and regular communication, though Willie's mother never told his father that he had a son. Willie is reading his father's talks about men, wishing that he had written about his boss or his work making chairs. By the end of the letters, Willie realizes that his father may not be dead— which was just what his grandmother had led him to believe.

A teenage boy discovers some letters revealing his father's homosexuality in this imaginative, perceptive book.

Even though the majority of the book is made up of letters from only one person, the reader gets a clear picture of the events that occurred before Willie was born and of the people who were important to his father and mother. The author convincingly uses the letters to portray the father's love of the mother, the gradual drawing away from her as he gets to know a man with whom he falls in love, and the difficult time he has explaining his feelings to his own mother and eventually his family. The fear of rejection and ostracism that many gay people feel is clearly depicted as is the eventual turning toward not wanting to hide or lie anymore.

Nothing is resolved by the end of the book; indeed, very little has changed except that Willie now knows why his father was "out of the picture." Whether or not the father is still alive is unknown. Willie's plans for the future do not seem to have changed. The author does not make Willie automatically accept that his father is gay; Willie's discomfort with the whole issue remains obvious. This is a good book to get one gay man's story of both the difficulties and satisfaction of becoming more open about who he is; in the end, the father struggles to accept his identity. Willie is just beginning to understand what all of this means. SUE FLICKINGER

133

134

Growing Up Gay: A Literary Anthology

Bennett Singer (editor)

Gay/Lesbian/Bisexual, Multicultural

1993, The New Press

As Martina Navratilova writes in the foreword, magazine articles and movies may provide positive gay role models, but they are impersonal. Only through personal contact with real people who share with us their homosexuality can we begin to realize that sexual orientation is only a small part of who we are, that being gay should be no more an issue than being heterosexual.

The first literary anthology geared specifically to gay and lesbian youth.

This bold literary anthology includes fifty-six separate and very different stories with one common theme: self-acceptance. Singer writes in his introduction that nobody decides to become gay. Gay people can't choose their sexual orientation, but they can choose to accept and even celebrate this essential aspect of their identity.

"Invisibility can be deadly" reads the book's inscription. Singer relates in his introduction that his own tremendous sense of isolation in high school was first challenged when he read a novel about a love affair between two gay men. This anthology offers similar insights to today's gay and lesbian youth. The stories are very personal, sometimes painful and sometimes joyful, but together they make homosexuality a visible possibility for anyone who, like Singer, might feel like the only gay student in the entire school.

Most of the passages are autobiographical, first-person narratives, although some are identified as fiction, including the lyrics of a rap song, one of Walt Whitman's poems, and an excerpt from M.E. Kerr's novel *Night Kites*. A brief biographical sketch before each story provides an even more personal touch.

The stories themselves provide some surprising insights into gay adolescence. Kevin Jennings reveals his decidedly unaccepting upbringing during the sixties, recalling that he was taught to believe in a Communist government plot and a Jewish media conspiracy. His uncles joined the Ku Klux Klan. He recalls trying to stifle his "perversion" by telling "fag jokes" and making sexual advances toward women. After his first sexual experience with a boy in high school, he tried to kill himself. These revelations support Singer's argument that people don't choose their sexual orientation. Jennings's story of personal acceptance reads more like a battle against the inevitable which is finally lost and, only in the losing, won.

A gay Chinese American relates the double dose of stereotyping he has endured, an immigrant writes that homosexuals were hospitalized in her native country, and a Cuban American writes that boys of "uncertain" sexuality were given hormone shots in Little Havana, Miami. These different voices all speak to the tremendous psychological, and sometimes physical, stress endured by young homosexuals everywhere. These stories, therefore, can be read as something more than encouraging therapy for gay

youth. Many are heroic tales of struggle and success that can serve as inspiration for anyone.

The book can be used as a resource. Appendix 1 lists selected books, magazines, newspapers, and videos. Appendix 2 provides information on hotlines, support groups, and pen pal programs. One caution about this anthology: some of the stories include some explicit sexual content. These few scenes are not gratuitous, but clearly belong in stories about emerging sexuality. I would recommend that teachers using this anthology first screen the book before providing access to students in schools and communities where sexual content is censored. RENEÉ HAYES

Hispanic, Female and Young: An Anthology

Phyllis Tashlik (editor)

Hispanic

1993, Piñata Books Arte Publico

It began in a circle at a public school on East 99th Street in Spanish Harlem (el barrio). For a year, twelve eighth-grade girls in an elective class called *Las Mujeres Hispanas* (Hispanic women) began to share their life stories, rites of passage and cultural traditions, journeys beyond their homelands, and struggles to overcome racism and sexism. The group represented a veritable mosaic of cultures, backgrounds, and histories ranging from Dominican and Puerto Rican to Mexican and Cuban. Although their school system is one-third Hispanic, these young women had been denied the rich legacy of their own literary tradition. They had never read a single novel written by an Hispanic author. Their teacher provided them with the opportunity to create something that would honor the pioneering work of writers like Nicholasa Mohr, Roberta Fernandez, and Judith Ortiz Cofer.

An intergenerational dialogue of stories on growing up bilingual and bicultural written by a diverse group of Hispanic women.

Hispanic, Female and Young is the result of their literary and cultural odyssey. But this anthology is more than a collection of stories, poems, and essays. Under the guidance of a rather visionary teacher — Phyllis Tashlik — *Las Mujeres* searched for novels, read back issues of journals such as *Revista Chicano-Riquena*, and found the power in their own voices to express rage, love, despair, and new possibilities.

Containing examples of *Las Mujeres'* own creative efforts and the works of well-established writers who inspired them, this intergenerational dialogue contains short stories, poems, interviews, and essays that reflect the diversity of the Latina teenagers at Manhattan East, a public school in New York City.

In Sara Rodriguez's piece "Interviewing My Mom, Dolores Rodriguez," a young girl is transported in her mind to Chihuahua, the small village in Mexico where her mother was born. Her mother talks of working in a Chinese restaurant. There were times when she was called upon to cook when the chef was out, and those opportunities resulted in some interesting cross-cultural dishes that combined pescado al vapor with chop suey.

Cofer's bold and poignant poem "Lost Relatives" speaks volumes about the strong sense of alienation that often comes with leaving one's homeland and living under the guidelines of another culture:

In the great diaspora
of our chromosomes,
we've lost track of one another.
Living our separate lives,
unaware of the alliance of our flesh,
we have at times recognized
our kinship through the printed word:
Classifieds, where we trade our lives

in two inch columns;
Personals, straining our bloodlines
without lonely hearts; and
Obituaries announcing a vacancy
in our family history
through names that call us home
with their familiar syllables.
DAPHNE MUSE

Tommy Stands Alone

Gloria Velasquez

Gay/Lesbian/Bisexual, Hispanic, Mexican American
1995, Piñata Books, ✶ Series

Gloria Velasquez continues her enjoyable Roosevelt High Series with this sensitive book about coming of age and sexual identity. Tommy Montoya, a young Chicano boy, believes he is gay. The novel centers on the pain he endures while he tries to hide his sexuality from his friends and family. The Mexican American/Chicano culture he belongs to is emphasized through the inclusion of Spanish in the text (with a glossary for non-Spanish-speaking readers) and the references made to the machismo role of men in Tommy's household. Tommy's anguish and inability to talk with anyone about what he is feeling results in alcohol abuse and a suicide attempt. With the help of his friend Maya and a Chicana therapist, Ms. Martinez, Tommy learns to communicate and deal with his life, his sexuality, and his family.

A Chicano boy accepts his sexuality and finds acceptance from family and friends.

What is particularly special about this work is Ms. Velasquez's willingness to tackle obstacles and not give in to easy solutions. Tommy is not portrayed as a wimpy victim, but rather as a smart but troubled youth. The school friends and family are not depicted as simple bigots or as freely accepting of his sexual orientation, instead they range the gamut from name-calling school kids to compassionate friends. Tommy's parents are shown as very traditional Catholics that have two very different reactions to his declaration of homosexuality. The father, who loves wrestling and boxing and the status of his role as a man in his home, finds it impossible to accept Tommy initially and throws him out of the house. His mother reacts with horror that she is to blame and seeks the help of a priest to "cure him." Thankfully, Maya brings Ms.

135

Martinez into the situation to act as both a bridge between Tommy and his tumultuous feelings, and between his parents beliefs and their child's reality. Ms. Martinez is also shown as a person outside of her role as a therapist, and the reader witnesses her struggles regarding homosexuality and AIDS within her own family dynamics.

This is an excellent novel for young teens and anyone who works with or lives with children of this age group. The text is concise and easy to read, with the point of view changing back and forth between Tommy and Ms. Martinez. Once again, Ms. Velasquez manages to tell a difficult story with sensitivity and grace. ROSA E. WARDER

Peter

🔖 Kate Walker

Gay/Lesbian/Bisexual

1993, Houghton Mifflin Company, 📖 Lynn Hall, *Sticks and Stones.*

Peter is fifteen years old when he meets his older brother's friend, David. Peter is drawn to David from the first, unusual in Peter's aggressively mas-

An Australian boy questions his sexual identity after meeting his older brother's friend, David.

culine Australian world. David is a sensitive, caring male and is only slightly taken aback when Vince, who is heterosexual, warns him away with the news that David is gay. Partly to annoy his brother and partly out of curiosity, Peter pursues his acquaintance with David. It's easy enough: David is interested in Peter's hobby as a photographer, and is a skilled small-engine mechanic who helps Peter tune his dirt bike.

Much of the value of this book lies in the fact that the author doesn't find it necessary to irrevocably label Peter's feelings. Peter finally comes to terms with the fact that, at fifteen, he doesn't have to make any binding decisions about his sexuality. He leaves it open, accepting David as a friend: "And maybe someday, in a couple of years' time, if I still felt the same about him, I'd turn up on his doorstep again."

The Australian setting does not create too many problems for American readers; a few slang expressions may defy literal translation, but their intent is clear. LYNN EISENHUT

Just Be Gorgeous

🔖 Barbara Warsba

Gay/Lesbian/Bisexual

1989 (1988), Harper & Row

Heidi Rosenbloom is a challenge to her glamorous mother—she wears a long men's overcoat, wool watch cap, and orders the barber to cut her hair very short. Though she feels like she isn't accepted anywhere, she meets up with a young, gay, homeless, street tap dancer who takes immediate notice of her fabulous coat and hair. Jeffrey even manages to temporarily win over Mrs. Rosenbloom with his "beautiful manners," despite his short fur jacket and blue eye shadow. He teaches Heidi about the gay world, contending that it is "only a mirror image of the straight world," that not all gay people are like him. Helping her define her aspirations, his courage and drive are an inspiration to her and he supports her gender nonconformity. Jeffrey also explains the dangers of forging a different path in the world. He is, after all, living in an abandoned building with no heat and water. He has also been the victim of constant harassment and bashing in his native Chicago. When he and Heidi are attacked on the street, Heidi's anger and attempts to fight back encourage Jeffrey to do the same. For the first time in his life, he resists and the bashers run off. Though he and Heidi mutually support one another, Heidi knows that she is not part of the gay "club," which will

A lovely story of two outcasts who help each other to develop self-confidence.

mean her eventual exclusion from his life. When he moves in with a gay couple, she is happy for him, but increasingly removed from his life. *Just Be Gorgeous* is a lovely story of two outcasts who help each other to develop more confidence in themselves, even knowing they will grow apart. CHRIS MAYO

Like Sisters on the Homefront

🔖 Rita Williams-Garcia

African American, Multicultural

1995, Lodestar Books

Teenage pregnancy has become a major social issue and contributed significantly to the increased dropout rate and lowering of the median family income. Some believe it has also had a real impact on the rise in child abuse. *Like Sisters on the Homefront* deals with the drastic changes in one family brought about as a result of a fourteen-year-old girl's second pregnancy.

Gayle has discovered that she is pregnant, again. In her mind, it's no big deal because she has "homegirls" who help her care for her son. Gayle's mother feels differently. As soon as she realizes Gayle is pregnant, she whisks her off to a woman's clinic to confirm the pregnancy. At the clinic, she signs papers for an abortion, but Gayle is upset because she can't see her boyfriend to tell him.

A troubled four-teen-year-old African American girl is sent to Georgia to live with her aunt and uncle.

Drama and attention are what Gayle is interested in most, not what's best for herself and her son, Jose. When the summer began, she was hanging with her homegirls on a regular basis. But each girl's parents find something for the girls to do that keep them from hanging with Gayle. After the abortion, Gayle's mother sends her to Columbus, Georgia, to live with her uncle who is a preacher.

Down South, Gayle is like a fish out of water. She's living in a big house in the country with many chores to do. During all this, she must watch her son continually. Her cousin Cookie is the polar opposite to Gayle's street-tough exterior. Cookie doesn't drink, doesn't smoke, doesn't have a boyfriend, and she listens to church music all the time. Gayle hatches a plan to humiliate her.

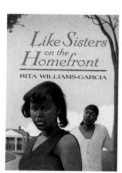

Then Gayle meets her great-grandmother Abigail Coston Gates. Great, as everyone calls her, is just waiting to die, waiting for someone to give the responsibility of "The Telling," an oral version of the family's history. At first, Gayle is overwhelmed by Great's "Telling" and feels that it's a burden. Indeed, it will be years before she fully understands "The Telling." But slowly, Gayle begins to come into her own as a person. She learns that pain is different for each of us and the survival of our families depend on how we use our experiences.

Like Sisters is a coming-of-age story for the '90s, addressing contemporary attitudes and behaviors against a backdrop of how things used to be. Gayle's pregnancies do much to bring about difficult changes in her immediate family; by the same token, it must be Gayle who brings her family together again. As Gayle painfully discovers, no person is an island, and her actions impact on all of her family. The book also shows strong and loving families can support young people through the harshest changes in their lives. YOLANDA ROBINSON-COLES

Maizon at Blue Hill

Jacqueline Woodson

African American

1994 (1992), Delacorte, Woodson, Jacqueline *Last Summer With Maizon.*

Maizon at Blue Hill tells the story of Maizon Singh, a bright and precocious black pre-adolescent who wins a scholarship to a prestigious boarding school, but fears that she will lose her racial and cultural identity.

Raised by her paternal grandmother in a working-class neighborhood in Brooklyn, Maizon shares a special friendship with Margaret, a black peer who also is bright and talented. Margaret plans to attend a local public high school. Maizon is the only girl in Brooklyn to pass the admissions test for Blue Hill, an all-girl institution in Connecticut that offers her a generous scholarship.

Maizon is not impressed when Mr. Parsons, a recruiter from Blue Hill, comes to visit the Singh home. "You're going to love it, Maizon," Parson says, while Maizon's grandmother looks through the school's colorful brochures. "You don't even know me," Maizon thinks. "How do you know what I'm going to like?" When Maizon asks why there aren't any pictures of black girls in the school's brochure, Parsons explains that Blue Hill is working on recruiting more minorities. Maizon's temper flares. "I hate the word minority," she moans under her breath. "I mean, who decides who becomes a minority?"

Accepted at a prestigious prep school, an African American girl from a working-class family worries about fitting in.

Maizon is filled with fear. If she goes to Blue Hill, she might lose Margaret's friendship. Nothing will be the same. She will be different and all alone. Grandmother Singh listens to Maizon's reservations, but she encourages her granddaughter to move beyond the boundaries of Brooklyn. "There is more to this, Maizon. You need to see that," Grandmother Singh says. "You and Margaret will always be together. Right here in your heart."

When Maizon arrives at Blue Hill, she meets a diverse group of peers who open her eyes to the complexities of race and class. Is Maizon "hip, cool, and sophisticated" like the five black "sisters" she meets on campus? Is she "smart, well-bred, and rich" like her liberal white peers? Or is she an independent thinker, like Pauli, a black student who risks being called a "traitor" to make friends with girls of other races?

Woodson's storytelling is insightful and real. The young women we meet at Blue Hill are true adolescents, struggling to find their own identity and a measure of acceptance in a world that can be unkind to people of color and women. Maizon is courageous, honest, and vulnerable. Young people will empathize with her fear of rejection and her determination to define her own world. LISA RHODES

From the Notebooks of Melanin Sun

Jacqueline Woodson
African American, Gay/Lesbian/Bisexual
1995, Scholastic, Inc.

Melanin Sun is a thirteen-year-old African American boy living in Brooklyn with his mother. Mel and Mama have always been a solid team, but lately the connection does not seem as strong and clearly Mama's keeping secrets. To work out these changes, Melanin Sun writes in his notebooks about Mama, his friends, and the feelings that he does not always understand: "I am tired now, of being thirteen. Tired of having to figure stuff out by myself. What matters is the people in your life, I think. Who they are and how they treat you. Mama matters. The Mama I used to know. Now everybody in my life is unfamiliar."

Melanin Sun struggles with the knowledge that his mother is a lesbian.

When Mama reveals her secret to Mel, it is more jolting than he could ever have imagined. Mama is a lesbian and is in love with a white woman. He feels humiliated, angry, and scared, and his confrontations with his own prejudices and intolerance fill his notebooks.

Mama's new life is the subject of discussion in the neighborhood and is the reason for his friend Sean's rejection of Mel. As Mel becomes more accepting, he finds that Mama, and his true friends Ralphael and Angie, have not abandoned him, though the break from Sean is permanent.

This is a sensitive, complex portrayal of a boy sorting out his feelings on sexuality, tolerance, and peer pressure. Mel's evolving beliefs are played out not in melodramatic shouting matches but in his quiet and intense journal entries. His reactions, ranging from hatred and disgust to acceptance, are entirely realistic. Readers in seventh and eighth grades will understand the pain of Melanin Sun's changing life, and will have a good model of mature introspection. JANIS O'DRISCOLL

Woodson's "Girl" Stories
DIANE PAYLOR

When it comes to choosing the subject matter for her books, Jacqueline Woodson is fearless. Her five novels for and about young people have addressed alcoholism, lesbianism, racism, class tensions, and other issues that affect us every day. "People say you can't put all that material into a book for young people because it'll distress them or they won't be able to absorb it all," she says. "But I believe children's minds compartmentalize— they will put stuff away until they're ready to deal with it."

Woodson's understanding of young readers has established her as one of the foremost African American women writers of young-adult books. "Girl Stories" has always been Woodson's mission, beginning with a trilogy exploring the complexities and strength of the friendship between pre-teens Maizon and Margaret. In Dear One (Dell), a pregnant fifteen-year-old girl from Harlem moves in with an upper-middle-class black family where the mother is a recovering alcoholic whose best friend is a lesbian. I Hadn't Meant to Tell You This (Delacorte) depicts the unlikely friendship between a poor white girl from a racist family and an upper-middle-class black girl.

Woodson says she learned at a very young age that the world is not a girl-friendly place. "Girls are desperate for identity and love," she says. "Society says if you go out and do A, B, and C, this is how you can get it."

Having spent her adolescence being shuttled between South Carolina and New York City, Woodson never quite felt a part of either place—a feeling intensified by being raised as a Jehovah's Witness. Although no longer a Witness, Woodson has retained the religion's "be in the world but not of the world" ideology. "I've been in the children's publishing world long enough to know I'm on the outside of it," she admits. "I'm never going to write best-sellers." She says people often judge her work by who she is. "I have these qualifiers: Jacqueline Woodson, African American lesbian writer. No one ever says 'Hemingway, a misogynist, anti-Semitic, white, male writer.' How come I can't just be a writer?"

"I'm always happy when someone comes up to me and says, 'I read your book and I really loved it; it changed my life.' It's like, wow, I really touched this person. Which is what I want to do as a writer."

Diane Paylor, a contributor to Ms. *magazine, clearly captures the spirit, tenacity, and willingness to take on hard issues Woodson achieves in her boldly written young-adult novels.*

Reprinted by permission from Ms. Magazine *1994 Nov./Dec. issue p.77.*

A Brown Bird Singing

📖 Frances Wosmek 🖋 Ted Lewin

Chippewa, Native American

1993 (1985), Lothrop, Lee and Shepard

In Frances Wosmek's lightly illustrated book, *A Brown Bird Singing*, Anego, a young Chippewa girl is raised by a white family, the Veselkas, in the Minnesota countryside. Her father, Hamigeesek, left her under their guardianship and will return one day to take her to be with her own people. *A Brown Bird Singing* tells the story of Anego's final year with the Veselkas, her anxiety concerning her father's return and her alienation in the all-white Minnesota town.

The book's greatest success is the exploration of Anego's mixed feelings, which revolve around not wanting to leave the Veselkas. They have raised her with as much love and care as their own daughter. Besides food, shelter and clothing, they also provide equal education, involve her in family activities and encourage her to pursue her talents and undertake responsibility. When Pa finds an orphaned fawn in the woods, he allows Anego to nurse it to health. This animal's recovery and membership in the family's group of domesticated animals, including a dog, horses and cows, stands as a metaphor for Anego's adoption. Having been a member of this happy family as far as she can remember, it is no wonder Anego fears her father's return and the uncertain future with the Chippewa people, with whom she has never interacted.

A Chippewa girl is raised by a white family in the Minnesota countryside.

A Brown Bird Singing is a well-written story that balances the internal and external forces of Anego's world in a very compelling way. All of the characters are three-dimensional and well-developed. Besides Anego's conflict, Wosmek has created duality within each character that increases through the year the book depicts. Mama Veselka treats Anego as her own child, but like any temporary guardian, grows distant to her over time. Sheila, the Veselka's daughter is reaching adolescence, and becomes more interested in clothes and city life than playing on the farm. Pa Veselka bestows responsibility and duties upon Anego, but then patronizes her with the gift of a rubber doll.

Young readers, especially those figuring out their identity and place, will be able to identify with Anego and her feelings of alienation and uncertainty. In her family and in the town, there are also many faces readers will recognize, from the schoolmates who maintain negative stereotypes of Native Americans, to the schoolhouse teacher who encourages Anego to be less shy.

All readers, regardless of race or gender, will benefit from the message in *A Brown Bird Singing*. With acceptance that she is an Indian and that the Veselkas are not like her, she starts to understand her place and see that those around her are not faultless: her one friend at school is a compulsive liar; Pa wishes he had a boy; and mocassins are more comfortable than Sears Roebuck cowboy boots. Only when Anego remains true to herself is she able to hear the voice inside her, the brown bird singing.

Briar Rose

📖 Jane Yolen, Edited By Terri Windling

Jewish

1994 (1992), TOR, ✳ Series

Briar Rose is a wonderfully imaginative and moving book that blends the fairy tale of Sleeping Beauty with the grimness of those who lived during the time of the Holocaust. Becca is a young journalist in her twenties who has been her grandmother's favorite. She remembers her grandma's obsessive retelling of her version of Briar Rose. Her grandma's last words before dying had to do with this story. After the funeral Becca's family finds a box of her grandmother's with photographs, a ring, and other objects. Becca feels obliged, due to respect and general curiosity, to piece together who her grandmother really was. The resulting story is *Briar Rose*.

Yolen manages to blend superbly alternating chapters of grandma's weird retellings of Briar Rose with Becca's journey to Poland to find out the truth. The book ends with an author's note that says the real life Chelmno, the site of an extermination camp, was the site of no known female survivors and was the killing field of over 30,000 people viewed as expendable. Knowing this makes the fairy tale ending of Becca's discovery in Poland even more poignant. There is also a recommended reading list of fairy tales and nonfiction titles relevant towards the study of folklore.

In a wonderfully imaginative book, a Jewish girl finds a box filled with things that help her recover her grandmother's past during the Holocaust.

I would suggest anyone planning to use Briar Rose or other Holocaust centered literature consult the U.S. Holocaust Memorial Museum for curriculum ideas and lesson plans. Another step in the right direction is to read Social Education's October 1995 issue that is devoted to teaching about the Holocaust. It makes the point throughout the articles that failure to plan teaching activities suitable for students is as bad a practice as the desire to not mention the Holocaust out of a fear it will be "upsetting." Appropriateness means not "destroying the subject matter though dilettantism," says Henry Friedlander, a scholar and a Holocaust survivor. Frequently, teachers resort to too graphic a presentation in order to create student interest. They may assume simulations, crossword puzzles, etc., are useful when the net result is to trivialize the subject matter.

Book Links *(March 1993) provides an annotated listing of books for children grades 1-8. It is divided into categories such as information books, fiction/picture books, first-person accounts, and biographies. There are also discussion ideas and suggested activities. Another source of books are two lists in* Youth Services in Libraries, *Winter 1994 and Summer 1995. Both lists are divided between nonfiction, information books, autobiographical and biographical accounts plus fiction. The topic of the Holocaust is too important an issue and cuts across so many areas of the curriculum to result in literature or classroom activities chosen helter-skelter without any sense of thought. The result is not only an insult to Holocaust survivors, but simply bad educational practice.* ANDREA L. WILLIAMS

CHAPTER 2

FAMILY

In recent years, blaming the decline of the family for a host of societal problems has become fashionable. While the foundations of family are indeed under attack—from factors such as divorce rates, lack of child care, economic pressures—the very notion of family also has undergone remarkable and long overdue transformations. Immigrant families from across the globe establish every day a fluid mix of language and cultures; gays and lesbians are at the center of a national debate over marriage rights and adoption; single mothers, interracial couples, and children of divorce all expand the narrow definition of family that for so long dominated societal expectations and children's literature.

This chapter deals with marriage, siblings, divorce, single parents, blended families, foster care, adoption, and aging. Of special note in this chapter is Janus Adams's incisive essay "Children's Books: Buyer Beware."

Adams takes a hard look at the children's book industry and finds that, despite much progress, there is still much to critique from the shrinking number of choices offered by publishers to the sales strategies of some large bookstores. Also included is Peggy Gillespie's "Other," an essay on the growing numbers of interracial families and the unique pressures, challenges, and joys they encounter. Along with the reviews are activities—from reading aloud to creating a photo album—designed to bring family members together.

VIOLET J. HARRIS

Violet Harris is an associate professor in the department of Curriculum and Instruction at the University of Illinois, and teaches undergraduate and graduate courses in children's literature. She is an active member of the International Reading Association and the National Council of Teachers of English where she presents regularly on issues in children's literature.

Kindergarten to Grade Three

Sleepy River

📕 Hanna Bandes   ✒ Jeanette Winter
Native American
1993, Philomel

This peaceful story unfolds as a mother and child take in the star-filled night and embrace the comforting sounds that accompany a river. While men and boys bonding at the river are not rare portrayals in children's books, a mother and son enjoying and appreciating nature has not been frequently depicted in literature.

A Native American mother and child experience nature as they canoe down a river.

The simplicity of life and its beauty are very much a part of this poetically alliterative story. Lulled to sleep by the reassuring sounds of nature and the confident voice of his mother, the child begins to build a relationship with nature. Written in a soothing tone, the story is also accompanied by rather unusual illustrations that include blue trees and purple water. These rather subtle, end-of-the-day colors add to the magical quality of the setting. MARTHA L. MARTINEZ

Saturday at the New You

📕 E. Barbara Barber   ✒ Anna Rich
African American
1994, Lee & Low Books, 📖 Tamar, Erika, *Garden of Happiness.*

Every Saturday, Shauna helps her mother at the family beauty parlor, The New You. Momma trusts Shauna with many important tasks. She is already an experienced coffee server, and could probably organize rollers in her sleep. What she really wants, however, is a chance to try her hand at hairstyling. So far, her expertise is limited to her dolls. Her opportunity comes on the day that bratty Tiffany Peters refuses to cooperate in the styling chair. Shauna's talents are put to use on her very first customer.

An African American girl helps her mother in the family-run beauty parlor.

This is a realistic story with believable characters. Shauna's interaction with her mother as they work together during a busy day is sometimes tense but always close. Children will identify with Shauna's desire not only to be included in the action but also engaged in useful tasks.

The behind-the-scenes look at the adult world of the beauty shop will fascinate children. The text evokes the fragrant shampoos, sugary sweets that the customers bring, the music Momma plays in the background, and more.

SATURDAY AT The New You
Barbara E. Barber • Anna Rich

Anna Rich's palette lives up to her name. She uses a full range of bold colors throughout the book and depicts distinctive characteristics: a double chin, for instance, or a star-studded sweatsuit. She also has the ability to maintain the focal point of each illustration amidst loads of clutter and topical detail. HEATHER ELDRIDGE

Daddy, Daddy Be There

📕 Candy Dawson Boyd   ✒ Floyd Cooper
Multicultural
1995, Philomel

Like a jazz musician who has found a universal riff, Candy Dawson Boyd has created a compelling refrain in this tenderly written plea to fathers to be present for their children. Through a wide range of voices, from children to adults, Boyd captures the emotions

In tender, honest words, children of all races ask their fathers to be there with them.

and bonds that children seek in relationships with their fathers. Refusing to be bound by any stereotype, Boyd issues this plea to fathers from all cultures and socioeconomic backgrounds:

Daddy, Daddy,
Be there,
During the Hard times when the money go,
During the saxophone-blowing-blues nights,
During the in-between, weary working months,
During the string of long years,
Daddy, Daddy,
Be there.

Daddy, daddy,
Be there,
When I dye my hair green or cut it off
Or pierce my ears and nose,
When my music rocks the house.
But grab me when I wander too far from home,
Too close to a danger I cannot see.
Daddy, Daddy
Be there.

Even though his illustration style is softly stated by gentle brush strokes, Floyd Cooper captures the anger, sadness, love, and joys shared between these children and their fathers.

Illustrations of fathers lovingly and patiently listening to their sons or hugging and holding their hands demonstrate a strong, all-too-often unseen nurturing side of men. With only a few exceptions, Cooper succeeds in creating facial expressions and gestures that compliment the passion and presence in Boyd's words. The honest and powerful father-child relationships demonstrated in this story will encourage young listeners and readers to ask for this story time and time again. DAPHNE MUSE

The First Strawberries: A Cherokee Story

📕 Joseph Bruchac ✒ Anna Vojtech

Cherokee, Native American

1993, Dial Books for Young Readers

In *The First Strawberries*, Joseph Bruchac retells a traditional Cherokee story about the creation of the first strawberries. The story is still a model for managing and resolving family disputes.

As the story goes, a man and his wife have been living together in harmony for some time, until one day they argue. The man resents the fact that his wife has been picking flowers rather than preparing his dinner. He is disrespectful and says some hurtful things to her. She turns to the west and leaves him. In time, the husband regrets his harsh words, but he cannot catch up with her to apologize.

A traditional Cherokee tale that traces the origin of strawberries.

The sun takes pity on a man trying to make up with his wife and attempts to stop the woman. He creates raspberries, blueberries, and blackberries in the hope that as she pauses to eat the fruit, her husband might catch up with her. She is not interested and passes them by. She stops to eat only when the sun creates the first strawberries. The moral of the story is clearly stated near the end of the book: "To this day when the Cherokee people eat strawberries, they are always reminded to be kind to each other; to remember that friendship and respect are as sweet as the taste of ripe, red berries."

There are also some powerful unstated morals: men need to respect women; husbands need to respect their wives; and abuse is not to be tolerated.

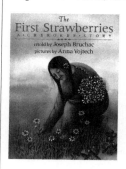

On the other hand, women need to show compassion for the stress their husbands experience through hunting or working. The story ends on a compassionate, loving note, with the strong feelings of anger, resentment, remorse, and regret having been exposed and resolved. The husband has had to take the initiative to correct his behavior and heal the impact of his harsh words. When he does so, he is rewarded; even the sun itself supports his efforts.

Although I enjoy Anna Vojtech's watercolor illustrations, I believe an Indian artist could have given the book, and therefore the story, a less dreamy quality. The book is, after all, a morality tale meant to instruct and set boundaries for proper human behavior. Although the facial features of the characters are Native American, there is nothing in the design that makes it clear that the people are Cherokee. It is rather generic Indian.

This book is a good tale for young girls needing strong female adult models and young boys who are working on feelings of anger and aggression. It would be a good impetus to discussions about resolving disagreements, anger and other emotions, family bonds, and responsibility, as well as discussions about the seasons, and walking in the woods. Of course, this reading could be followed by a bowl full of fresh strawberries.
NOLA HADLEY

The Wednesday Surprise

📕 Eve Bunting ✒ Donald Carrick

European American

1989, Clarion Books, ✳ Audio Cassette

This is a heartwarming story about Anna and her family, with an exciting and endearing ending. Anna's grandmother provides childcare for the family every Wednesday night because Anna's mother works outside of the home and her father is away from the house for long periods of time driving his truck. Every Wednesday Anna and her grandmother read together. For weeks they plan a surprise birthday party for Anna's dad, who is due to return home soon. The day finally arrives, but Anna and her grandmother are so excited they can barely eat the special birthday dinner they've prepared. They have an extra special birthday surprise planned.

A European American girl teaches her grandmother to read and surprises the whole family when the secret is revealed.

After the meal the family gathers in the living room and Anna's grandmother reads a book to them. Anna's parents are astounded because Anna's grandmother was unable to read until Anna taught her—every Wednesday night!

This intergenerational story depicts Anna and her family as honest, hard-working, intelligent people who love and respect each other. They rejoice when Anna's grandmother learns to read: "'Are you going to read everything in that bag, Mama?' Dad asks her. He's grinning, but his eyes are brimming over with tears and he and mom are holding hands across the table."

This is not only a poignant story about family bonds, but a powerful statement in support of literacy, and against ageism. Anna believes her grandmother is not too old to learn. Anna's grandmother is portrayed as a capable, intelligent person who undertakes a difficult task and, through her tireless efforts, succeeds in reaching her goal.

BARBARA SMITH REDDISH

Daddy

📖 Jeanette Caines ✒ Ronald Himler
African American
1995 (1977), HarperCollins

In *Daddy*, a little girl, Windy, looks forward to Saturdays, when she spends the weekend with her father and his new wife, Paula. Windy is always

A child of separated parents describes the activities she shares with her father on Saturdays.

afraid that Daddy might not come for her, but he always does.

Using very simple language, Jeannette Caines captures Windy's feelings, as do Ronald Himler's black-and-white il-

lustrations. Neither the author nor the illustrator understate Windy's feelings. They focus on the father's relationship with his daughter and not the conflict, if one exists, among the adults.

Windy's parents try to make her life as normal as possible. They want her to know that she is loved by both of them. The author does not deal with the reason the parents split up, nor does she focus on any bad experiences by either side. Instead she shows that family can still be family even when they live apart. YOLANDA ROBINSON-COLES

Just Us Women

📖 Jeanette Caines ✒ Pat Cummings
African American, Hispanic
1982, HarperCollins, 📖 Hamanaka, Sheila,
Be Bop A Do Walk.

"Saturday morning is jump-off time," and the reader is invited to join Aunt Martha and the narrator in Martha's brand-new convertible as they streak down the highway on their long-awaited adventure. The reader is privy to the narrator's anticipation of the time spent in transit when she is beyond the reach of restrictive adult supervision. There are no curfews or deadlines on the high-

Aunt Martha and her niece — just the two of them — plan a long-awaited road trip.

way. She and Aunt Martha dictate their own schedule, eating when they like, stopping whenever they choose, and splurging at roadside yard sales.

A mission such as this requires the type of preparation that would be impossible for a child to manage on her own. However, Aunt Martha occasionally "forgets things" and the child's input becomes essential, allowing her a role in the adult world. The adult relies on the child and the shared responsibility makes this trip truly their own.

Simplicity is this book's strength. The narrator's voice is clear and the text is succinct, allowing the pictures to provide added detail. The artist's depiction of the characters as individuals lends credibility to the account, which would have been lost had the figures been more generalized.

Some of the most interesting details emerge even before the trip begins, as the narrator imagines the adventures that await her: for instance, eating breakfast at night or getting out of the car to walk every time it rains. Since the journey has not yet begun, the narrator only describes the events as she predicts them, but the illustrations portray the events as if they are occurring in the present. Both travelers are pictured in different outfits and hairstyles every couple of pages. This technique provides a gentle pacing and a subtle suggestion of the passage of time. Effectively, the child's expectations are being realized as she speaks.

The narrator's exuberance is the driving force throughout the journey. Her fascination with every aspect of her special trip makes this book as relevant today as it was more than a decade ago. Keen observers may note the outdated fashions, but there is nothing to keep today's children from imagining themselves on the joyride. HEATHER ELDRIDGE

Julian, Dream Doctor

📖 Ann Cameron
African American
1993 (1990), Random House, ✳ Series

African American siblings work together to find their father a birthday present.

This novel is part of the Julian series also including *Julian, Secret Agent,* and *Julian's Glorious Summer,* which feature an imaginative, smart, and resourceful ten-year-old boy. In this story, Julian presents his father with a most unusual birthday gift. Julian discovers that his father's deepest secret wish is to have two snakes for his birthday. But the father is actually deathly afraid of snakes.

The story makes for a wonderful comedy, focusing on fears and how to deal with them. Although the father confronts his fear of snakes, the story does not end with him embracing or developing a

passion for them. He does develop a respect for them and even manages to hold one of the snakes.

Sibling camaraderie and cooperation are stressed, and Julian's sister is portrayed as just as involved and brave as the boys in searching for a snake. Materialism is downplayed throughout, and the ability of the characters to use things at hand is emphasized. Although this and the other books in the series are labeled "easy-to-read," the storylines are well developed so even advanced readers will enjoy them. DAPHNE MUSE

Everett Anderson's Goodbye

📖 Lucille Clifton   ✏ Ann Grifalconi
African American
1983, Holt, Reinhart & Winston, ✳ Series

In this quiet yet poetic picture book, Clifton effectively explains and illustrates the five stages of grief. She then sets out to show her popular young urban African American character, Everett Anderson, working through each of the five stages.

In stage one, he continually dreams of his father who has died. She writes, "Daddy always laughing or never just Daddy, Daddy, forever and ever." His words ring true and Grifalconi's pencil illustration is heartfelt; Everett's mother is holding him, looking strong and compassionate as she looks down on his tormented face.

In stage two, Everett decides to stop loving, even candy and his mother. His mother's resigned response is "Well, Everett...who do you love?" Grifalconi makes excellent use of body language in this illustration, showing Everett with his back to his mother, his arms wrapped around his shoulders, blocking out the world.

An African American boy works through the five stages of grief in an inspiring blend of text and illustration.

In stage three, Everett claims he will learn his multiplication tables, never sleep late, and eat all his bread in order to see his father again. In stage four, he cannot sleep, and he cannot eat. Grifalconi depicts him looking sorrowfully out the window.

The next couple of pages are wordless, with poignant illustrations of his mother reaching out to him and Everett walking alone in the park, until he reaches stage five. He then says that he knew his daddy loved him, but when people die, love does not stop. Everett is shown looking lovingly at a picture of his father, while his mother is sitting behind him with her hands on his shoulders.

The marriage of these two elegant artists' creativity makes this book cohesive and inspiring. Clifton's use of rhyme is smooth without being choppy and redundant. Also, Grifalconi's use of touch in most pictures lends warmth and love to each stage. This book presents a beautiful portrait of an urban African American family, which is not only an effective book on the subject of death, but also a heartfelt portrait of healthy family life. LISA FAIN

Don't You Remember

📖 Lucille Clifton ✒ Evaline Ness

African American

1973, E. P. Dutton

In an enduring work from the 1970s, an African American girl remembers everything everyone has promised her.

Four-year-old Desire Mary Tate remembers everything, but her father remembers nothing. Tate, as her family calls her, gets angry because no one remembers promising her the things they do, and they always tell her "next time" when she asks for something. From the first thing in the morning, until it is time for bed at night, she constantly reminds her parents and her brothers of their promises. But everyone surprises Tate on her birthday by showing up with a beautiful big black cake, with "Tate" written on it in pink letters. While the family gently teases Tate about forgetting her own birthday, they also demonstrate a strong sense of love for her and she for them. She also dreams of going to work at the same plant as her daddy, and on her birthday he remembers his promise to take her to work with him.

Tate is sassy, self-assured, and assertive. These characteristics reflect the impact of both the black power and the women's movement on children's literature in the early 1970s. Clifton, who has written several other children's books including *The Boy Who Didn't Believe in Spring* and *The Black ABC's*, has consistently incorporated strong-willed children in her books.

Ness captures the spirit and presence of Tate from her skinny braids to her spindly legs. The colors and shades of black, pink, and brown work especially well in the illustrations.

The storyline endures and Clifton continues to gain a wide readership for her wonderful stories about the day-to-day lives of children and their families. DAPHNE MUSE

See the Ocean

📖 Estella Condra ✒ Linda Crockett-Blassingame

Physically Disabled

1994, Ideals

Estella Condra's *See the Ocean* tells the story of Nellie, who has loved the ocean for as long as she can remember. Nellie is a self-contained child who seems quiet compared to her two rowdy older brothers who jostle and compete constantly. One of their yearly competitions comes while driving to a beach vacation —who will be the first to spy the ocean?

One year, as usual, Nellie sits quietly between them until, under a thick veil of fog, she claims she sees it. Her brothers accuse her of cheating and only then does she softly, lyrically, begin, "The ocean is an old, old man born at the beginning of time." And there follows one of the most poetic descriptions of the ocean you'll ever read, one that will stun you as much as it stuns Nellie's family. Silent for a long time, they acknowledge the truth of what she says, and another truth… that she can't see.

A young blind girl "sees" the ocean on a family trip.

This is a book you'll want to reread immediately. Suddenly you notice how the author has filled her story with smells, sights, and feelings of ocean and beach, and how right it is when Nellie's mother tells her sons, "Though your sister's eyes are blind, she can see with her mind."

Happily this book is not one bit sentimental, though it relates a sensitive story with tenderness of feeling. There is so much to treasure: the family's very individual way of caring for each other, the gifted main character, the incredible portrait of an ocean. Linda Crockett-Blassingame chooses soft oil colors, and her evocative images make this book equally satisfying to look at. SUSIE WILDE

Will There Be a Lap for Me?

📖 Dorothy Corey ✒ Nancy Poydar

African American

1992, Albert Whitman and Company, ✷ Braille

Mom is pregnant and the bigger she gets the less lap she has for Kyle. Kyle's sense of physical and emotional displacement results in finding other laps to substitute for his mother's until she gets hers back. But those other laps simply are not the same.

With baby brother on the way and changes about to come, Kyle is even more surprised when the baby arrives. Thinking the arrival of the baby will make things better, he quickly learns that his mom has even less time for him. He resents being displaced by the new baby. But with his mother's guidance and his own lessons in

An African American toddler must cope with a new addition to the family.

patience, he learns how to be around the baby.

Realizing the importance of habits that keep us connected to one another, she continues the daily ritual of having Kyle join her in feeding the birds —something they both really cherish doing together. On one occasion while watching the birds eat, she places Kyle on her lap and reads him a story. He has regained his favorite place with his mother, while hoping that he has also regained a favorite place in her heart.

Temporarily displaced, but not put out, we see Kyle and his mother lovingly struggle with the changes in their lives. While this story could have taken place in almost any family, having African Americans as the characters brings about another kind of understanding of the commonalities we all share. MARTHA L. MARTINEZ

Mama Zooms

Jane Cowen-Fletcher

Physically Disabled

1993, Scholastic, ✳ CD-ROM

A little boy explores the world with his mama in her wheelchair.

Filled with energetic illustrations and the simplest of language, *Mama Zooms* tells the story of a wonderful relationship between a little boy and his mother. The boy's life becomes a series of wonderful adventures as his mother puts him on her "zoom machine" to explore the world around them. The mother's disability is never explicitly explained, but the joy and love they share for one another is clearly portrayed in highly spirited, bold illustrations and the text:

Mama zooms me down a smooth sidewalk and she's my race car.
Mama zooms me fast down ramps.
We love ramps!

Mama's zooming machine takes the little boy on train rides, into outer space, and across open fields on a buckboard wagon. Young readers and listeners will enjoy the tantalizing sense of adventure and use of imagination very much apparent in this wonderfully told and powerfully optimistic story.

The mother is attractive, active, and very much engaged in the day-to-day parenting and nurturing of her son. Cowen-Fletcher includes an illustration of the father and son helping the mother up a steep hill. There is no prose about the mother's disability in the book; the child sees her as having special abilities as opposed to a disability.

This story allows young children to gain an understanding of people who use wheelchairs and to set aside some of their fears and prejudices about the disabled. While I have seen few children's books work well on CD-ROM, I think this one does because of its focus on motion and mobility. DAPHNE MUSE

Bigmama's

Donald Crews

African American

1991, Greenwillow, ✳ Audio Cassette, Series

Bigmama's, written and illustrated by Donald Crews, is a story about summer traditions. Each summer, Crews travels by train with his sisters, brother, and mother to visit his grandmother (known as Bigmama not because she is a large woman but because she is "Mama's Mama"). The first thing the children do when they arrive is check to be sure that everything is the same as they left it last summer. They find the kerosene lamps, wind-up record player, the washstand on the porch (with

Every summer, the family returns to Grandma's farm, a place that never seems to change.

the yearly reminder not to fall in), and the outhouse. Although Bigmama's house has no indoor plumbing or electricity, these are not drawbacks but an integral part of the experience.

This book is a joyous celebration of family getting together to share summer days. It offers a positive model of an African American family enjoying each other's company and maintaining their extended family. The author dedicates the book to the people of Bigmama's town and ends it by wishing that he could return for another summer. The book evokes an earlier time and lifestyle. *Children might enjoy looking*

through the book to find aspects that are similar to or different from experiences with their own grandparents. They might also be encouraged to talk with adults in their families about their memories of family traditions or vacations.

The watercolor and gouache paintings that illustrate the story are filled with movement and color. Each of the items or activities noted in the text is

clearly represented in the illustrations. These illustrations are important, as many of the items mentioned may be unfamiliar to young readers.
DEBORAH PATTERSON

Carousel

📖 🖊 Pat Cummings

African American

1994, Bradbury Press

Today is Alex's birthday. As her mother struggles to get her dressed, Alex searches for her father. She doesn't want to celebrate anything until Daddy gets there. The house is decorated, her aunts arrive, and a birthday dinner is served, but still Alex looks for Daddy.

An African American girl's father misses her birthday party and everything is spoiled until his gift comes to life.

Her mother and her aunts try to get Alex to enjoy her day. Alex is angry that her father, who had promised to come, is not there. She takes the carousel that Daddy left as a gift for her up to her room.

Sometime during the night she is awakened by the escape of the animals from the carousel. She chases after them, and when she finds them, they give her the ride of her life. Then one by one, the animals make their way back to Alex's bedroom. Alex is too tired to remember that she is angry at her Daddy.

Carousel is a story that explores a child's feeling when a favorite person is missing from an important event in his or her life. In this case, Alex feels as if her father has lied and never intended to be there. The author downplays Alex's anger, focusing instead on her strange night ride.

Carousel is bright and colorful. Most children will recall instantly their own birthdays and the gifts that they thought so special. But most of all they will remember the people that made them so happy. YOLANDA ROBINSON-COLES

Asha's Mums

📖 Rosamund Elwin and Michele Paulse

🖊 Dawn Lee

Gay/Lesbian/Bisexual

1990, Women's Press

This short picture book tackles opposition to lesbian-headed families in terms a preschooler can understand. Asha's preschool class is taking a field trip to the science museum, and the teacher, Ms. Samuels, questions her about why there are two women's names on her permission slip. When Asha responds that both of the women are her mothers, Ms. Samuels insists that she take the form home and have it filled out correctly. That night, as Asha worries about not being able to go on the field trip, Mum Alice reassures her that the form was filled out correctly and she'll talk to the teacher.

Asha explains to her preschool class that she has two mothers.

The next day during show and tell, Asha shares a drawing of her family on the way to the science museum which includes two mothers. When one of her classmates questions the appropriateness of having two mothers, saying, "my dad says it's bad," Asha replies, "It's not bad.... My mummies said we're a family because we live together and love each other."

The teacher is saved by the bell when one of the children begins to ask her if it's wrong to have two mommies and her hesitant reply is interrupted. In the final pages, Asha's moms come to school to straighten things out. Asha has a successful field trip, and her classmates seem satisfied that she really does have two mothers.

This is a gentle story, somewhat didactic in tone, but one of the few books for young children on a much needed topic. The Canadian spellings in the story (mummies, centre) are not overly distracting for a U.S. reader. The focus is on the familial roles of lesbian parents, which seems appropriate for the developmental level of a preschool audience.

Dawn Lee's pencil drawings are most effective when they are accented with soft watercolors on alternate pages. LAURI JOHNSON

Li'l Sis and Uncle Willie: A Story Based on the Life and Paintings of William H. Johnson

Gwen Everett William H. Johnson

African American

1994 (1991), Hyperion Books for Children

Good, sensitive biographies for young children are difficult to find, and when one attempts to include the life stories of African Americans, the task becomes even more difficult. While *Li'l Sis and Uncle Willie* is a fictionalized account of the life of African American artist William H. Johnson, it is based on actual events and is enhanced through its illustration with his paintings.

Told through the voice of his niece, Li'l Sis, this story weaves African American culture and history of the period together with the life of an important artist. Li'l Sis first meets Uncle Willie when she is five years old after he returns to South Carolina for a visit. Having traveled extensively around the world to study and paint, Uncle Willie expands the horizons of one child through his stories of living and working in Harlem and picking cotton in the South. When he leaves to return to his home in Denmark, Li'l Sis has difficulty understanding why her uncle does not stay. Her aunt explains to her that "Uncle Willie first went to Europe to study art, but he liked living there because people were friendlier to black people." Uncle Willie returns to New York at the beginning of World War II, and he continues to correspond with Li'l Sis, sending her photographs of his paintings of famous African Americans and telling her their stories. When the letters finally stop, Li'l Sis learns that her uncle became depressed after his wife's death and was hospitalized. According to the story, he remained there until his death.

The life of African American artist William Johnson told through the voice of his niece.

Taken from the collection of one thousand of Johnson's paintings that are housed at the National Museum of American Art, those chosen to illustrate this book give the reader a tantalizing introduction to Johnson's art. They not only depict scenes from his life, but also important events and people from African American history. Johnson's story is told without romanticizing it, and it is clear that he did not have an easy life. However, his story is related in a way that presents difficult issues to children appropriately and in a manner that will provoke discussion about important events and ideas. So important are these events and ideas that, although this may seem at first glance to be a picture book designed for younger children, it is equally valuable as an introduction to this artist for those who are older. DONNA GAGNON

Feast for Ten

Cathryn Falwell

African American

1996 (1987), Houghton Mifflin Company

Numbers from one to ten are used to tell how many members of a family shop and work together to prepare a meal. Not only are children able to develop counting skills with the rhyming text, they are also able to learn the names of several foods. More importantly, they can see that everyone helps with the shopping, cooking, and setting the table.

Observant readers will notice that family members who were dressed casually during the meal's preparation change clothes before sitting down to dinner with a pair of older adults—presumably grandparents—and another grown-up relative or friend. The reason for this feast is never stated. It's either a holiday or a family gathering, but this means that the story has more versatility than other books that are tied specifically to a Thanksgiving or Christmas dinner.

Readers count from one to ten as they follow an African American family shopping and preparing for a feast.

Careful attention has been given to an accurate presentation of contemporary life in this large family of three girls and two boys. Family members are shown recycling cans, and Mom drives a mini van. She also wears short, natural hairstyle, and dangling earrings popular in the African American community. The female children also wear hairstyles and barrettes that will be familiar to the African American reader.

The artwork features a collage of paper and fabric in the tradition of *The Snowy Day*. Although their faces seem a little stiff, the characters are happy, and it's great to see the entire family joined in a cooperative effort. LESLIE ANDERSON MORALES

End of the Game

📖 Lila Colman ✏ Melton Charles

African American

1971, Collins Worlel, 📖 Neufeld, John, *Edgar Allan*

Feeling it is their obligation to help society's oppressed, the Stevenses, a well-intentioned white family, invite an African American boy from a Brooklyn ghetto to share their Connecticut home for three weeks during the summer. Timmy Stevens is unsure how he'll feel about this newcomer, but when Donny Brown arrives by train, the two boys

A wealthy white family takes in a disadvantaged African American boy in a some- what dated book.

begin to develop a close friendship—talking, playing catch, and swimming in the lake. Timmy and his older twin sister observe that their mother is lenient with the young visitor, allowing him extra treats, second helpings at meals,
and not becoming angry when he accidentally breaks a favorite antique lamp. Because Mrs. Stevens is so intent on doing a good deed for this disadvantaged youth, she doesn't realize that she is going overboard in treating him well. Her own children soon take advantage of this, asking Donny to accept the blame when they lose the family dog and later cause the maid to quit. In each instance, Mrs. Stevens forgives Donny for things he has not done. However, out of Donny's hearing, she delivers a sharply racist condemnation of African Americans, all the while proclaiming that she herself is not prejudiced.

When the twins start a kitchen fire, Donny realizes he will be blamed for this too, so he and Timmy run away, spending the night in the woods. Just as Donny predicted, Mr. and Mrs. Stevens again blame him for the fire, expressing some shocking convictions about African Americans until the older girls break down and tell the truth that—except for the incident with the lamp—they were responsible for all the household problems over the summer, though Donny took the blame. Donny's mother arrives while the boys are missing, but when they are found and returned home, she expresses great anger and sadness upon learning that Donny has been playing "the white man's fool" and accepting blame for things he has not done. She angrily takes her son back to Brooklyn, refusing to accept even a ride to the train station from the Stevens family.

This hard-hitting, but perhaps overly purposeful novel examines hidden prejudices, as the deep-seat-ed racism of the do-gooder Stevens family comes to light during moments of crisis. The book is illustrated with black-and-white photographs which give the volume a documentary feeling. Although dated, the book still presents a meaningful message in depicting the awkward attempts at making the world a better place demonstrated by Mrs. Stevens, contrasted with the real friendship that develops between the two young boys. Some readers may be offended by Mrs. Stevens's indictment of blacks, as well as comments by Donny's older brother about being a "white nigger" if he goes to live with a white family for the summer.

Nevertheless, the book provides an interesting, early look at how race relations were tackled in the children's book field during the early 1970s, and can still provoke spirited classroom discussion. An interesting comparison may be made between this novel and John Neufeld's *Edgar Allan* (also illustrated by Feelings), which also concerns an ill-fated effort to integrate a white family. PETER D. SIERUTA

Tanya's Reunion

📖 Valerie Flourney ✏ Jerry Pinkney

African American

1995, Penguin/Dial Books

In this joyful sequel to *The Patchwork Quilt*, Tanya, a young African American girl, travels with her grandmother to a family reunion. It is a special treat for Tanya, as this is her first trip to the South, and she is allowed to travel across the country with her grandmother alone, with the rest of her family following a few days later. Tanya has listened to tales about the family farm all of her life and has imag- ined what it will look like. However, she finds the farm to be rundown, full of old people and old things, and not at all what she had pictured.

An African American visits her grandmother's farm and learns about her family's history and traditions.

With the help of her grandmother and other relatives, Tanya learns to
appreciate the farm for what it is now and what it has meant to their family. Tanya is caught up in the constant work needed to maintain the farm: feeding chickens, harvesting food, and preparing the meals for the big family reunion. But it is the special time she spends with her grandmother that transforms the visit into a treasured memory for

Tanya's old age. On a rainy day, Tanya sits with her grandmother and listens as her grandmother speaks of her memories of the people who lived there in the past. As her grandmother's story unfolds, Tanya discovers the true beauty of the farm and sees her history in it, too.

Tanya's Reunion is brought to life for the reader by Caldecott Honor Book artist Jerry Pinkney, whose watercolor and pencil illustrations lovingly portray the family and the old farm. *Tanya's Reunion is a wonderful book for reading aloud to children from preschool age on, and an excellent reader for elementary children.* ROSA E. WARDER

Billy and Belle

▨ ✎ Sarah Garland
African
1992, Viking Children's Books, ✳ Series

As *Billy and Belle* opens, Dad, who is black, has to drive Mom, who is white, to the hospital for the birth of their third child. The setting is an unnamed city in Great Britain, presumably London. Their daughter, Belle, who seems to be four or five, is going to spend the day at school with her older brother, Billy. It happens to be pet day, and Billy has brought his hamster. Other children in the multiracial classroom have brought frogs, mice, guinea pigs, and tortoises, so Belle catches a spider and declares it to be her pet. The teacher puts the animals out on the playground in their various containers and asks the children to draw them from memory. Because she cannot remember how many legs a spider has, Belle goes looking for her pet and accidentally releases all the other animals. Needless to say, chaos ensues until the pets are all recovered. When the school day is done, Billy and Belle go home to meet their new baby brother.

The story of British children from a multi-cultural family at school in a book that is unfortunately out of print.

Billy and Belle is one of the best non-didactic picture books to be published in the last few years on the topic of multiracial families. Such stories are in relatively short supply—ask anyone who lives in a mixed-race family—so it's a shame that the book has been allowed to go out of print. Garland depicts a warm and loving if somewhat chaotic home with two highly competent, slightly disheveled parents.

Dad routinely cooks and performs chores around the house, and Mom, though in labor, thinks nothing of rooting Billy's socks out from under the bed or forcing a very necessary comb through Belle's snarled and tangled hair. All of the characters seem very real and believable. Garland has illustrated the book deftly, sometimes placing multiple panels on each page and combining a standard printed narration with cartoon style, hand-lettered dialogue balloons. Her often humorous watercolor/pen-and-ink drawings are at once delicate and cluttered in a rather pleasing fashion. She is adept at portraying urban scenes. Of particular note is the two-page spread illustration in which Billy and his classmates search for their pets on the playground. It's one of those complex pictures that children love, where all of the pets are visible and it's up to the reader to find them.

There is absolutely nothing in the text of *Billy and Belle* that takes note of the fact that this is a mixed-race family. It's simply a normal part of the children's environment, which is, of course, as it should be. MICHAEL LEVY

Something from Nothing: Adapted from a Jewish Folktale

▨ ✎ Phoebe Gilman
Eastern European, Jewish
1993 (1992), Scholastic, Inc.

In Phoebe Gilman's *Something from Nothing*, adapted from a Jewish folktale, a little boy named Joseph and his grandfather, a tailor, find a clever way to help Joseph give up his beloved blanket. When his mother chides Joseph, telling him that his blanket is too old and dirty and must be thrown away, Joseph turns to his grandfather. Snipping and sewing, the grandfather transforms the blanket first into a jacket, then a vest, and then into progressively smaller articles of clothing until it is nothing more than a button. When this button is lost, Joseph realizes he has enough "material" to make something of his own: he writes a story, which tells the tale of his ever-evolving blanket. Set in an Eastern European shtetl around the turn of the century, this entrancing book helps children understand a time and place in the past. At the same time, it helps them deal with a

A grandfather finds a clever way to help his grandson give up his security blanket in this Jewish folktale.

problem that is always contemporary: giving up one's beloved transitional object.

While the visual element is important to any picture book, Gilman's beautiful oil-and-egg tempera illustrations are especially significant. Every picture is detailed and informative, conveying what life in the shtetl was like. Readers can see how Joseph's family, like so many other shtetl dwellers, lived and worked in the same place; his father's boot shop, his grandfather's tailor shop, and the living quarters for all six members of his family are squeezed into two rooms. Mother does her laundry in the river, people shop in open-air markets, and a gaggle of geese walk down the cobblestoned street. Joseph's Jewishness is similarly conveyed. His grandfather's tallis peeks out from under his vest, his grandmother lights Sabbath candles, and Joseph does his schoolwork in Hebrew-lettered Yiddish. These historical and religious details are perfect starting places for discussions about ancestors, traditions, and identity.

As all this life bustles on floor level, Gilman delightfully supplies a true sub "text." Under the floorboards of Joseph's home lives a charming and growing mouse family, whose presence is intrinsic to the story. Whenever the grandfather snips Joseph's blanket, coat, or whatever its current transformation, the discarded pieces fall through the floor, and the mouse family makes good use of the treasure raining down on them. As the lovely blue-starred material shrinks for Joseph, it fills the mouse house, providing blankets, tablecloths, and clothing for the mice and reassuring readers that Joseph's blanket still lives on in some way.

The only sour note is the portrayal of Joseph's mother, who comes across as a nag unable to understand her son's need for his blanket. Gilman risks succumbing to the stereotype of the Jewish mother as a clean-obsessed pleasure-denying harridan. Otherwise, the book will provide hours of delight as parents and children alike are enchanted with this ingenious reworking of a traditional story and the absorbing illustrations that so well complement and enhance it. JUNE CUMMINS

My Working Mom

📕 Peter Glassman ✏ Ted Arnold

Feminist

1994, Morrow

This is the story of a working mom, narrated by her young daughter. The narrator begins, "It isn't easy having a working mom. Especially when she enjoys her work." She continues to explain why it isn't easy. Her mother is always flying off somewhere, or yelling at her for playing with something that her mother is working on. She does say, however, that her mom gives the greatest birthday parties, cheers for her soccer team, and always goes to the school plays.

A girl discusses her mom's profession as a witch in a book that unfortunately reinforces some stereotypes.

The mom's occupation, apparently, is "witch." She is dressed in a long black robe and pointed hat, flies around on a broomstick, and conjures up magic potions in a big black kettle. The other characters are dressed in typical Western dress, including the father and the daughter. The author's intent is whimsical, portraying the mother as having a highly unusual profession, and a family that loves her just the way she is. Unfortunately, our society tends to portray women in stereotypic roles, and "witch" is one of them. While this could have been cleverly done, it is poorly handled. The author states that it is particularly difficult to have a working mom who enjoys her work, the implication being that women's work is usually tedious, boring, and nonpaid. When it is interesting, or takes her away from the home, it is undesirable. The story also implies that moms who work outside of the home are crankier: "always yelling at me for something ..." This book perpetrates undesirable gender stereotypes.

A productive way of teaching My Working Mom *is to discuss ones own family using questions such as, "Do the adults stick to traditional gender roles?" "What are the pros and cons?" "Do children help with the household chores?" and "What type of chores do individual members do?" Another series of questions such as, "What do you want to be when you grow up?" "Why?" "How will you achieve this goal?" and "What, if anything, will prevent you from achieving it?" can allow for discussion of the drawbacks of gender stereotypes.*
BARBARA SMITH REDDISH

First Pink Light

📖 Eloise Greenfield ✒ Floyd Cooper

African American

1991 (1976), Writers and Readers Publishing, Inc.,
📖 Greenfield, Eloise, *My Daddy and I.*

Young Tyree has a plan for how he is going to stay up, hide, and then surprise his father who is returning after a month away taking care of grandma. But his mother knows that daddy will not be home until dawn, and that Tyree must go to sleep. They work out a deal: he may sit in the big chair in his pajamas and watch through the window for the first pink light when his father is due.

Tyree, with the pillow and blanket suggested by his mother, cuddles up and soon falls into a pleasant sleep, knowing that his mother has won but not caring. Even when his father returns and gently awakens him to carry him to bed, he does not mind that he has not carried out his plan. Tyree feels only love for his father and wishes that he never has to go away again.

The strength of this story lies in the portrayal of a loving, unified family. Even the father's absence from home is for family reasons. The mother allows Tyree to interrupt her, so that they can communicate and compromise. She is gentle and understanding.

An African American boy insists on staying up until his dad, who has been away taking care of grandma, comes home.

The illustrations are in soft-toned gouache and pastels, which suit the sleepy tone of the story. There is little action, so there is little change of scene depicted. The greatest action is in the changing emotions, which are described in the text and shown clearly on the faces and in the posture of the characters. We see playful joking, anger, concern, support, peacefulness, love, and pleasure.

The characters are African Americans in the illustrations. Yet, there is only one reference in the text, when the father is referred to as "the man with the strong brown face." This is a positive aspect of this book as the family's experiences ring true for any loving, caring, cooperating family, and all children should feel satisfaction identifying with Tyree.

JACKIE LYNCH

Grandpa's Face

📖 Eloise Greenfield ✒ Floyd Cooper

African American

1993 (1988), Philomel, ✳ Series

In *Grandpa's Face*, Eloise Greenfield has written an intergenerational story of a loving African American extended family. Tamika loves to spend time with her grandfather, especially to see him perform as an actor or on "talk-walks" in the park.

But one day when Tamika comes into her grandfather's room to ask him to tell her a story, she sees her grandfather rehearsing for one of his plays. He looks very angry. The expression surprises and frightens her, leaving Tamika feeling like she wants to cry. "She had not known that Grandpa could look like that, and now that she did know, she couldn't be sure that he might not someday look at her with that face that could not love."

At first Tamika can't speak about her feelings. She just wants to do "all the things that Grandpa didn't like." Over dinner she plays with her food until her father asks her to leave the table and go to her room. She starts to cry and accidentally spills her water all over her grandfather's shirt. When she looks at her grandfather's face, Tamika realizes that he is angry but that he still loves her. Realizing that she is upset, Tamika's parents ask her what is going on when her grandfather goes to change his shirt. Rather than wanting to punish Tamika, her parents clearly express a deep concern for her well-being.

An African American and her grandfather find a meaningful way to express their love for one another.

Tamika's grandfather invites her for another "talk-walk" in the park. With a little prodding, Tamika tells how her grandfather's expression had frightened her. When her grandfather reminds her that acting is just pretend, Tamika still isn't sure. Her grandfather responds, "I love you....I could never, ever look at you like that. No matter what you do, do you hear?"

The image of a stable, multigenerational African American family and tender, clear-headed, and powerful African American

153

men refutes some of the stereotypes about black men and how they function in relationships with their families. Overcoming fears and building trust are very much a part of this story. In her usual manner, Greenfield has given us dignified characters who look for realistic and meaningful ways to handle fears and resolve conflicts in their lives. The strong and dignified images she creates with her words are reflected in Floyd Cooper's illustrations. Through the warm pastel colors, Cooper gives us a spirited grandpa with a truly loving face. NOLA HADLEY

Luka's Quilt

Georgia Guback
Hawaiian, Pacific Islander
1994, Greenwillow

When grandmother makes Luka a Hawaiian quilt, the young girl is displeased that it has only two colors. Luka and her grandmother, Tutu (Hawaiian for grandmother), are best friends. One day Tutu awakens from a dream about a lovely garden and decides she will make a quilt for her granddaughter. Luka is delighted and brimming with unanswered questions. Tutu keeps her guessing especially as to why Tutu asked her to pick only one color for her quilt.

Luka watches the cutting, pinning, and basting, as Tutu tells her, "you'll see." But when the quilt is com-

pleted, Luka looks for her garden of lovely flowers and sees only the green and white quilt. Her grandmother points out the many flowers stitched into the quilt and explains that she has made this quilt in two colors, in keeping with island tradition. Tears come to Luka's eyes, and relations between the two become strained and sad.

Tutu eventually calls a truce when they go to a Lei Day celebration. Again, disagreement arises when Tutu urges Luka to pick only one or two colors. Luka insists on having her way and makes a beautiful multicolored lei, and this gives her grandmother an idea. Gathering scraps of many different colors, Tutu makes a cloth lei to crown the traditional green and white quilt on Luka's bed. Luka is pleased with her quilt in both forms and, best of all, she is happy that she and her grandmother are close once more.

The author-illustrator incorporates important details that bring this Hawaiian story to life. The book is filled with bright, flowery illustrations that convey colors of tropical life and the playful relationship between grandmother and grandchild. SUSIE WILDE

I Remember "121"

Francine Haskins
African American
1991, Children's Book Press

Extended families have been a hallmark of African American life for generations. The movement of family members from the deep South to the upper South, Midwest, North, and West remains a central theme in African American literature. *I Remember "121,"* a memoir, *An African American adult reminisces about the fun times shared in her family's childhood home in Washington, D.C.* continues this literary tradition. Haskins does not focus on social or political issues such as segregation or discrimination. Rather, she presents the comforting world of an extended family that is part of a vibrant African American community.

Francine's grandparents migrated from South Carolina to Baltimore, Maryland. There, they purchased a three-story home that enabled other members of the family to migrate to the mid-Atlantic area. Francine's memoir begins at age three when she announces the birth of her baby brother to the neighborhood. Other memories include her jealousy of the new sibling, family meals prepared and served by women of the family, a proud papa creating a song for his beloved daughter, playing with neighborhood friends, misbehaving and receiving punishment, and the bittersweet moving day to a single-family home.

Haskins tells her story in a matter-of-fact tone. Each episode is introduced with the phrase "I remember." This becomes redundant after several sequences. Interest is retained by flashes of humor such as: "Hey everybody, I've got a brand new television set and a new baby brother named Michael Mouse!" The illustrations add levity and lessen the didacticism that creeps in periodically. Bold colors, flowing lines, oversized body parts, shifting perspectives, and juxtapositions of shapes and colors all create a lively tone. VIOLET HARRIS

The Day of Ahmed's Secret

Florence Parry Heide, Edited by Amy Cohen and Ted Lewin ✏ Judith Heide Gilliland

African, Arab, Egyptian

1995 (1990), Lothrop, Lee and Shepard

This popular book, set in Egypt, can be a starting point for a discussion about many aspects of Arab culture. Ahmed's secret, divulged at the end of the story, is that he has learned to write his name. He writes it in Arabic, a language spoken by more than 250 million people from the Arabian peninsula to Morocco to Detroit, Michigan, and the source for many familiar English words (e.g., admiral, alfalfa, algebra, almanac, cotton, guitar, and safari). Arabic is also the language of the *Koran,* Islam's holy book, and it is therefore an important language for Muslims the world over.

An Egyptian boy keeps a secret, eventually revealing to his family that he can write his name!

Children may wonder why Ahmed is working and not in school; although Egyptian children can begin formal schooling at age six, many do not begin until they are older because of overcrowding in the schools. In addition, many Egyptian families are very poor, and even small children work to help make ends meet. Ahmed takes great pride in assuming work responsibility—an example of commitment and loyalty to the family that is an integral part of Arab culture. Philosophical for one so young, Ahmed is conscious of his place not only in the family, but also in the city and in the continuum of time.

The watercolor illustrations in combination with the text convey the sights and sounds of traditional Cairo, including the foods people eat, their modes of transportation, and their dress. The latter might prompt a discussion about why so many people cover their heads (e.g., protection from the hot sun; Islamic traditions related to modesty), and why men and women alike wear long, loose clothing (a comparison can be made between the comfort of this attire with that of a suit and tie in a hot, dry climate). It is also worth noting that Ahmed is not wearing pajamas; rather, his clothing is one of the traditional forms of dress for Egyptian boys, popular because of low cost, light weight, and comfort.

Like so many other examples of children's literature about the Arab world, *The Day of Ahmed's Secret* depicts an almost exclusively traditional lifestyle. Ahmed's clothing and daily activities are certainly characteristic of millions of Egyptians, but millions more who live less traditional lives are just as authentically Egyptian. It should also be noted that the scene on pages twelve and thirteen is set not in Egypt, but in Morocco, where the traditional dress and typical architectural features are distinctly different from those in Egypt. Pointing this out can help to avoid perpetuating the stereotype of all Arabs (or Arab countries) as alike.

Even with the above points in mind, The Day of Ahmed's Secret *can be a creative means of introducing traditional Egyptian life and culture to children in the lower elementary grades. They might even remember the excitement and pride they felt when they first learned to write their own names, feelings obviously shared by children elsewhere in the world.*
LESLIE NUCHO

155

Boundless Grace

Mary Hoffman ✏ Caroline Binch

African, African American, Gambian

1995, Dial, ✳ Series

The picture book *Amazing Grace* introduced children to a spunky African American girl named Grace. In this sequel, she travels to Gambia, West Africa, to visit her father and his new family. This is a simply told but multilayered story. The obvious message is that "families are what you make them." More subtly, the tale suggests that parents should maintain family bonds despite divorce.

In this well-crafted sequel to Amazing Grace, *Grace visits her father and his new family in West Africa.*

The pivotal issue for Grace is her father's absence. Grace lives in a warm extended family with her mother, grandmother, and a cat named Paw-Paw. Yet she feels that, "Our family's not right. We need a father and a brother and a dog." At times, Grace even denies that she has a father. A trip to Banjul, Gambia, helps Grace come to terms with her father and understand that there are many types of families. Grace does a lot of growing in this story. She overcomes jealousy, homesickness, and the fragmented feeling children in separated families often experience. Caroline Binch's expressive illustrations perfectly mirror Grace's emotions.

The Gambian setting is not essential to the events in the story. It is gratifying, however, to see a beautifully illustrated book that depicts an African country in a nonstereotypical and authentic manner. Binch traveled to Gambia twice to collect images for the illustrations. Howard University professor Sulayman Nyang, a former resident of Banjul, found the illustrations accurate in almost every detail.

This is a carefully crafted book. Succinct text, wonderful illustrations, and a solid message make *Boundless Grace* a winner.

Grace is the central character of the book, and children will naturally focus on her actions and feelings. Teachers will have to help students see the role the adults play in the story. After reading the story, the teacher might ask the children to study the adults and explain how each acted in Grace's best interest. The book may also spark a discussion about various types of families. Grace is disturbed by books that show only one type: a mother, a father, a boy, and a girl. At the conclusion of her trip to Gambia, she resolves to find books about families like hers and write her own story. Students can follow Grace's example by identifying books that showcase alternative families, or by writing their own stories.

Teachers will also have to help students see commonalities between Gambia and the United States. Grace focuses on activities and objects that are different from those at home. Teachers should encourage students to study the illustrations for similarities (e.g., there are trucks, sodas, telephones, an airport).
BRENDA RANDOLPH

How Many Stars in the Sky?

📖 Lenny Hort   ✏ James Ransome
African American
1991, Tambourine Books

This story of an African American father and son exploring an age-old question begins late one night when the boy wonders how many stars there are in the sky. His mother, who "knows all about the sun and stars," is away so he tries to find an answer for himself. His dad finds him outside in the middle of the night and joins in finding an answer. They drive to other places to view the stars: into town, into a nearby city, past mama's office, and

An African American father and son travel to various countries and cities counting the stars in the sky.

finally out into the country where there are no streetlights. The boy realizes that it's nearly impossible to count all the stars but wants to know if they can try again sometime. His father says "Anytime," and that next time mama will come too.

The oil painting illustrations by James Ransome use many shades of deep blue, creating a feeling of darkness. Reading this book is like holding a small piece of the night in your lap. The father and son are softly painted and dressed in warm colors. This warmth is a lovely, visual metaphor for the love shared between father and son in the story.

Although she is away, the mother's presence is felt throughout the story. Both father and son look forward to her return and mention how she would contribute if she were home. The book offers a strong sense of love and support and a positive model of an African American family. *This book also could be used in a mathematical context to explore the concept of infinity.* DEBORAH PATTERSON

Aunt Flossie's Hats (and Crabcakes Later)

📖 Elizabeth Fitzgerald Howard   ✏ James Ransome
African American
1995 (1991), Clarion Books, ✱ Audio Cassette

Spirited Susan and sassy Sarah always look forward to regular visits with their great-aunt Flossie. Afternoons spent in her home, where books and joy abound, are always filled with memories, surprises, and imaginatively told stories rich with history. Great-aunt Flossie

Two African American sisters visit their great-aunt, who has a collection of hats and a story to go with each hat.

also has one of the most wonderful collections of hats, and with each comes an intriguing story. One such story is of a huge fire that took place in Baltimore and another is of a big parade that was held after the soldiers returned home from World War II. The parade clearly includes the presence of African American soldiers who had gone off to war to fight for their country.

Through this creative approach, centered around a family and their joys, the reader also gets a rich series of lessons in history without the usual didactic, did-you-know tone.

One of their great-aunt's favorite stories is also the girls' favorite. It centers on a big pink and yellow

Easter hat that flies off great-aunt Flossie's head and into the river. The girls especially like this story because they too are a part of it. As the story continues to be told and shared with other family members, they know that their names will go down in family lore. Howard's storyline also demonstrates how essential children are to family stories.

The wonderful afternoon culminates with great-aunt Flossie inviting the girls and their parents to join her for some of Baltimore's finest crabcakes at a very elegant restaurant. Through the thoughtfully and imaginatively written text, the love, tender feelings, and respect they have for one another is apparent. Howard's beautiful written images are accompanied by the heartwarming illustrations of James Ransome.

Ransome's movie-set-like illustrations portray a middle-class family that dines in fine restaurants, wears tastefully elegant clothing, and are clearly comfortable without being pretentious. With her art on display throughout and bookshelves lining her walls, great-aunt Flossie provides readers a peek into a kind of home rarely seen in African American children's books.

MARTHA L. MARTINEZ

Papa Tells Chita a Story

Elizabeth Fitzgerald Howard Floyd Cooper
African American
1995, Simon & Schuster Books for Young Readers,
Howard, Elizabeth Fitzgerald, *Chita's Christmas Tree.*

In a nightly ritual after the dinner dishes are done, Papa tells Chita stories. Chita has heard many of them before and chimes in with comments. One of her favorite stories relates Papa's involvement in the Spanish-American War.

Chita's father shares a story about his involvement as an African American soldier in the Spanish-American War.

Howard renders the story as a "tall tale." Some of the elements are true, others are exaggerations. Papa receives a medal for his service in Cuba. He "battled" giant snakes, alligators, eagles, and slimy swamps in order to convey a message to the comman-

der. Chita delights in each act of bravery recounted by her father.

This book follows another Elizabeth Howard/ Floyd Cooper collaboration, *Chita's Christmas Tree*, also involving the author's real-life cousin Chita. Once again, author and illustrator combine to create a wonderful story. Howard's writing is lively and Cooper's oil washes and mixed media help create the soft and warm feelings conveyed in Howard's prose. Helpful additions include the author's note about African American military involvement, a brief bibliography, and a photograph of Chita and Papa. This portrait of an upper-middle-class family helps expand the images of African American cultures.
VIOLET HARRIS

I Love My Family

Wade Hudson Cal Massey
African American
1995 (1993), Scholastic, Inc., ✱ Series

Through the charming narration of this story, a young boy invites readers to journey along with him to his family reunion in North Carolina. Relatives come from all over the country to pick peaches, dance, play basketball, and eat huge, memorable meals prepared by women and men with a history of turning meager vittles into sumptuous feasts. Scary stories by Uncle Lawrence and Great Aunt Nell, who is almost one-hundred years old, also highlight the festivities.

Written with an easy hand and a loving heart, this story captures the bonding and memorable moments that often surface when families reunite to celebrate their history

An African American boy has a wonderful time during a big family reunion.

and themselves. Family unity is important to this little boy, and he is neither ashamed nor embarrassed to say that he loves his family. This family even has a poster that outlines the family tree, and the young narrator explains that on the very last day, photos of everyone are taken, including a family portrait. He is saddened when he realizes that it is time to leave, but his mother reminds him that they will be back for Thanksgiving.

This is a wonderful book to share with a child who has been asked to research his or her family. The young boy's enthusiasm for his growing clan will encourage children to find out about their own families. The narrator has an encompassing acceptance for all his family mem-

bers, despite the differences they may have. He notes, "Uncle David, my father's brother isn't married. He brings a different girlfriend to every reunion." Children are exposed to the concept of loving family members simply because they are family.
MARTHA L. MARTINEZ

Do Like Kyla

📖 Angela Johnson ✒ James Ransome
African American
1990, Orchard Books

In this portrayal of a tender sibling relationship, an adoring younger sister incessantly imitates a patient older sister. Throughout a day of routine activities such as getting dressed, having breakfast, or running errands, Kyla's little sister mimics her every move. Each time, she repeats the phrase, "I do like Kyla." But by bedtime, the younger sister has occasion to say, "Kyla does just like me."

Through the day, African American Kyla's younger sister imitates her, but at day's end, Kyla follows her sister's lead.

Kyla respects her sister, and lovingly tends to her needs or desires, helping her put on her coat and read a book. The parents appear in one illustration and are mentioned in the accompanying text, showing the part they play in the children's lives. But this is a story of the girls' relationship. It shows there is no better way to learn than by following the behavior of an older sister, but that the tables can be turned as well.

The language used is simple and repetitive, like that of a young child. Bright, warm illustrations provide the only indication that this is an African American family. DAPHNE MUSE

Joshua by the Sea

📖 Angela Johnson ✒ Rhonda Mitchell
African American
1994, Orchard Books

Angela Johnson's board book series—featuring Joshua, his sister, father, and mother—is a welcome addition to a genre of multicultural children's literature.

Joshua by the Sea is a simple text that comes to life through an interactive read aloud. The family spends a day frolicking at the beach. Johnson uses verses to convey the family's close ties as well as the joy they find while playing in the sand and sea. The illustrator uses a subdued color palette with periodic splashes of intense colors to depict the shells, sea, sky, and other objects. The cover illustration shows a smiling Joshua holding a starfish near the sea. Of special note is the illustrator's decision to portray the variation in skin color found among African American families. Father is light skinned, Mother is dark skinned, and Joshua and his sister fall along this spectrum of skin-color.
VIOLET HARRIS

In one of a very few multicultural board books, two African American children and their parents enjoy a day at the beach.

Joshua's Night Whispers

📖 Angela Johnson ✒ Rhonda Mitchell
African American
1994, Orchard Books, ✻ Series

Literary depictions of African American fathers and their children are somewhat limited, although Lucille Clifton and Eloise Greenfield have bucked this trend for more than two decades with memorable picture books featuring fathers, stepfathers, and grandfathers. Angela Johnson and Rhonda Mitchell's *Joshua's Night Whispers*, part of a series of books by this team, offers a gentle portrayal of a father comforting his son, and is a delightful addition to any collection.

Like countless other children, adolescents, and adults, Joshua sometimes fears night noises. Johnson's characterization of the noises as "night whispers" is poetic and lessens some of the fears. The illustrations depict Joshua's fears via his somber looks rather than imagined monsters. The gently swaying curtains, soft pastels, and relaxed, comfortable furnishings also create a mood of safety and love, as does the boy's father. The cover illustration of Joshua snuggled in bed with a stuffed pink bunny helps lessen anxieties about nighttime. An adult sharing this book with a young child who fears the dark and night whispers can help children understand that their response is normal and that parents can provide comfort in the night.

An African American boy is afraid of the "night whispers" and seeks comfort from his father.

Typical of this genre, the text is sparse and written in simple phrases. Johnson manages to create some tension with descriptions such as, "In the nighttime the wind brings night whispers, so I follow them... past my toybox...." *The simple format encourages interactive reading and opportunities for children to imagine themselves in Joshua's situation and their responses to nighttime fears.* VIOLET HARRIS

Mama Bird, Baby Birds

📖 Angela Johnson ✏ Rhonda Mitchell
African American
1994, Orchard Books

Joshua and his sister discover a nest of birds near the stairs to their house. They observe that the mother bird flies overhead and, later, flies in to feed her babies. Joshua and his sister decide that the mother bird cares for her family in the same way that their mother cares for them.

Illustrator Rhonda Mitchell uses a subdued palette highlighted with more intense colors. The illustrations are realistic with soft, flowing lines.

Two African American children observe a bird family.

Several images convey the idea of a mother caring for her children: mother and baby birds on the cover; Joshua and his sister held by their mother as she shares fruit with them, contrasted with the mother bird feeding a worm to her babies. These peaceful images reinforce one of the book's themes — mothers care for their children by providing for their basic needs and showering them with love and affection.

The language is short, poetic, and simple. A loving mood is apparent despite the brevity of text. *The simple structure allows for extended discussion and exploration in a shared read aloud.* VIOLET HARRIS

Tell Me a Story, Mama

📖 Angela Johnson ✏ David Soman
African American
1992 (1989), Orchard Books

After asking her mother to tell her a bedtime story, an African American girl proceeds to retell her mother's often-shared stories of her childhood. The tales of the mean neighbor, the lost puppy, the trip to St. Louis, and finally the mother's moving away from home are familiar and treasured. They contain memories of her grandmother, grandfather, sister, and aunt, with the major family roles held by females.

An African American girl retells the familiar stories of her mother's childhood.

The mother responds to questions with comfort, love, support, and honesty. When the child asks whether Grandmama will stay forever, the mother replies, "She won't be here forever, baby, but long enough for you never to forget how much she loves you." When the child asks, "Would you cry if I moved away, Mama?" the mother answers, "Yes, I will...."

The language is simple and direct, very much the way a young child would speak, with the mother making appropriate interjections. Words such as "kissing," "love," "squeeze," "baby," and "miss" abound, and it is made clear that it is okay to cry.

There is an ease and love within this family.

The watercolor illustrations are sketchy and cheerful. This is a universal story, about an African American family in the illustrations only. It portrays a caring, loving family where traditions, including family stories, are valued. Ending with the mother and child hugging and laughing, the child says, "I like it when you tell me stories, Mama. Tell me more tomorrow." JACKIE LYNCH

159

The Aunt in Our House

📖 Angela Johnson ✏ David Soman

Biracial

1996, Orchard Books

160

Angela Johnson had already proven that she has vision and a real future in children's literature. In her most recent book, *The Aunt in Our House*, Johnson seemingly effortlessly writes with a kind of simple compassion that looks at the complex issue of biracial families. The story "breathes" easily, as though it is fueled by the purest of air.

An interracial relationship between an "aunt" and a special family.

The children call their weekly visitor Aunt, and she, like their daddy, is white. Her visits become weekly sojourns into fun, special times, and thoughtful gifts. She brings a fishbowl, a great joy-filled smile, and her somewhat mysterious self. She also helps Mama, who is black, weave rugs and blankets, and her portrait, painted by the daddy, hangs where the children can see her when they wake up. Their home is filled with the spirit of artistic vision and power, as well as a strong sense of acceptance.

Without moralizing, the author provides a real tribute to people's ability to see, find, and rejoice in harmony. The story is also richly organic with none of the formulaic feel of many contemporary books for young children.

David Soman, who also illustrated *Grandpa's Hotel* and *When I'm Old With You*, fully captures every joyous and mysterious moment about this fine book with endearing, almost photo-like art. His full-color illustrations reveal the same kind of creative compassion demonstrated in Johnson's writing. DAPHNE MUSE

A Writer on Reading to Her Children

DEBORAH FRAISER

My work revolves around stories. I collect picture books, study them, and write and illustrate on occasion. Yet I used to be too tired to read goodnight stories to my daughter.

Then one late October day, my two-and-a-half-year-old daughter stepped outside and, looking up at the sky with her hands stuffed in her coat pockets, said, "Winter day, cold and gray."

I stopped in my tracks. Those are the opening words to Doug Florian's book, A Winter Day, one of my favorite picture books for very young children. Suddenly my work seemed very immediate. My daughter's perception of the world had been shaped by the words she heard from a book.

I now read to my daughter much more readily. I've learned to enjoy the physicality of sitting together with a book, even using it as a rest period for myself. I think my daughter likes the closeness of reading together as much as the words or pictures. Right now she loves a book called Sesame Street Visits the Hospital. I have come to dread this book, but we have cut a bargain. I read one she likes, then we read one of my choice.

Over the last year her vocabulary has bubbled over, and the books we read are now here with us: "Milk in the batter, Milk in the batter" (In the Night Kitchen), she sings when we're in the kitchen; "The night bus arriving" (The Night Ones), she says when the city bus pulls in front of us at dusk; and today, in the yard, "a monarch butterfly, Mama, like the eve of my birth." And I stopped in my tracks, again. Those were my words given to her from my own books. Maybe I am not just reading words. Maybe in the shapes of those shared words reflected in the world I am also sending up flags, reminding her of the love that holds us together.

Deborah Fraiser is the author of The Day You Were Born *(Harcourt 1991).*

The Leaving Morning

📖 Angela Johnson ✒ David Simon

African American

1992, Orchard Books

Early on a gray day, a young girl waits for movers to come and take her family's belongings to their new home. While trying to reassure her younger brother that everything will be just fine, she begins to feel how hard it will be to say good-bye: leaving friends and neighbors is difficult, but leaving family is even more painful. The young girl is sad and scared of

An African American girl tells about her family's moving day.

leaving what is familiar for what is unknown. "We woke up early and had hot cocoa from the deli across the street. I made more lips on the deli window and watched for the movers on the leaving morning. Got a moving hat and a kiss on the head from Miss Mattie upstairs." Trusting her mother's word that the movers will take good care of their belongings and that they really will love their new home, the girl begins to understand that change can be good.

Young readers sometimes have difficulty relating to stories like *The Leaving Morning*, in which the characters are not named. While the illustrations help bring the reader closer to the girl and her brother, naming them would have strengthened the story line. MARTHA L. MARTINEZ

Your Dad Was Just Like You

📖 ✒ Dolores Johnson

African American

1993, Macmillan Publishing Company

Following a confrontation with his father, Peter goes to see his grandfather to explain what happened: "I was just playing around, you know, and that ole' stupid purple thing on dad's dresser just seemed to jump on the floor and break…He was so mad, he just walked away."

In the minds of many young children, things do seem to just "jump on the floor and break." But Peter is often comforted by the fact that his grandfather is more understanding and patient than his father. After taking a walk with his grandfather, he learns that his dad was very much like him as a child.

His grandfather tells him that his father loved to run and wanted to compete in a race. Peter's father

had prepared in earnest for the race. But the day of the event, it rained. Despite the rain, he persevered and ran to the finish line. No one was there to congratulate him. Peter's grandfather went to the finish line to pick up his exhausted son and take him home. The grandfather goes on to tell Peter how he made his dad a trophy, and when Peter asks of its whereabouts, Grandfather replies, "It was…. " Peter realizes that it was the purple thing he broke that morning.

Peter runs home and tries to repair his father's trophy. An apologetic Peter approaches his father with the "fixed" trophy behind his back. Attached is a note saying, "Dad, I love you!"

While Peter and his father may have trouble communicating, the grandfather is there for Peter. The grandfather shares a truly tender story with Peter that results in the boy's fixing the trophy. Punitive demands can often bring about punitive results. As this story demonstrates, when dealt with thoughtfully, children can often respond in kind.

Books with boys telling their fathers they love them are still too rare,

An African American boy learns about his father through stories told by his grandfather.

and this particular story says it in a most wonderful, yet simple way. Peter's efforts to repair the trophy speak volumes about that love. This story provides a clear example of the importance of listening, and having someone to listen to. MARTHA L. MARTINEZ

Ravi's Diwali Surprise

📖 Anisha Kacker ✒ Kusum Ohri, Anisha Kacker, and the Air India Library

Asian, East Indian

1994, Modern Curriculum Press, ✳ Series

Festivals and special holidays are one way that teachers often bring multiculturalism into the classroom. But there are many pitfalls inherent in such an approach. For one, the concentration on

A South Asian boy and his family prepare for a traditional Diwali celebration.

ethnic celebrations often highlights the foreign and exotic nature of peoples. The unstated message children sometimes get is that these festivals are so different they need to be explained, as opposed to American celebrations such as the Fourth of July,

St. Valentine's Day, and Christmas, which need no explanation. There are also the problems of seeing cultures solely through festivals and of missing deeply spiritual, personal, and cultural connotations of many celebrations.

Few children's books focus on the Southeast Asian experience in America, and in that respect, *Ravi's Diwali Surprise* is a welcome addition. This book focuses on Diwali, a Hindu festival of lights, and covers food, clothes, and some ritual. The surprise arrival of Ravi's brother, Shankar, from college provides the subtext. An element of family ritual is introduced when Ravi thinks about how, until this year, he and Shankar always hung the lights together for the Diwali celebration. When Ravi reluctantly begins to hang the lights without Shankar, his brother returns just in time to ensure that the family ritual continues. While there is no in-depth discussion of the ritual's history or Hindu focus, some understanding of the Southeast Asian presence in the United States is provided.

The book is nicely illustrated, with actual photographs interspersed in the text. With careful attention to the above mentioned pitfalls this is a valuable book, one that adds a Southeast Asian American voice to children's literature. DEBBIE WEI

Songs of Papa's Island

Barbara Kerley Katherine Tillotson

Pacific Islander, Guam

1995, Houghton Mifflin Company

From the damp, dark places of the bush, to the gooey, gluey mud, Barbara Kerley draws the reader into a sultry reminiscence of life on a tropical island in *Songs of Papa's Island*. Written as a dialogue between mother and child, the narrative invites sharing aloud; a gentle refrain begins each chapter: "Before you were born, you lived on an island in the middle of the ocean." This lullaby sets the tone for the conversational, yet luxuriously descriptive stories the mother tells her child. Frogs rumble and grumble and croak, vines wrap like serpents around tree trunks, and geckos cling to the ceilings with Velcro-like toes. Each chapter is a separate tale which coincides with a stage in the gestation and birth of the child listening to the stories. Mother and father

A mother's tales of life on a tropical island give her daughter a sense of her birthplace.

snorkel, race hermit crabs, and bicycle after wild boars—adventures the listening child wishes she had experienced. Giant blob frogs and raccoon pufferfish speed the pace toward adventure while the gentle progression of embryo to baby slows the tempo for reflection. Kerley's combination of humor and humanity appeals to both genders. In the final adventure, the listener, a baby at the time the tale takes place, helps her parents rescue forty frogs from certain death at the bottom of an empty swimming pool.

Kerley offers a refreshingly realistic view of island life, which Katherine Tillotson captures in stylized black-and-white illustrations reminiscent of wood cuts. Butterflies flutter above a lone palm, a one-eyed cat pounces from the bush, geckos emerge from whirls in the ceiling, and frogs nearly spring from the page. *Text and illustrations combine to make this book an excellent choice to set the scene for a classroom discussion of tropical island cultures. The clear picture of place Kerley paints will make islands come alive for students who may have limited, travel-poster views of islands. Other suggestions for classroom use include comparing Papa's Island to other islands: Baffin Island, Easter Island, Greenland, or Sri Lanka; inviting students to bring in stories of the places they were born; and locating the tropics on a map.*

Songs of Papa's Island was chosen by the New York Public Library as one of the 100 best children's books of 1995. KIM GRISWELL

Don't Forget

Patricia Lakin Ted Rand

Jewish

1994, Tambourine Books

Sarah wants to surprise her mother by baking her a birthday cake. She walks along Blue Hill Avenue in Roxbury, Massachusetts, a Jewish neighborhood in the post–World War II days, collecting the necessary ingredients and taking advice from each grocer: "For perfect sponge cake, whip the egg yolks. Don't forget," advises Mrs. Koretsky. Each grocer offers his or her own secret for perfect sponge cake and adds, "Don't forget."

For the eggs, Sarah must go to "Singer's." She is uncomfortable about shopping there because Mr. and Mrs. Singer have blue numbers tattooed on their left arms, which Sarah thinks she is not sup-

A Jewish girl talks about the Holocaust with a neighbor.

posed to look at, or even talk about. While paying for the eggs, Sarah's eyes move to the numbers on Mr. Singer's left arm. She cannot help but stare, and feels ill at ease. Mrs. Singer senses her embarrassment and asks her to come out back, into the kitchen. Together they prepare Sarah's surprise cake, and chat while it bakes. Sarah apologizes for staring at the numbers, and Mrs. Singer replies, "Why?... The numbers should NEVER be a secret, my little Sarah. If no one knows about bad things, they can happen all over again. Don't forget."

Perhaps Sarah's confusion over keeping secrets stems from her neighbors, who all offer their "secret" advice. It bears mentioning that there are different types of secrets; some harmful or serious, such as the secret of abuse, and others trivial or playful, like secret birthday surprises. The differences between them make good discussion topics for children and adults.

Children deserve to have an accurate account of world history, for perhaps our greatest fear is that of the unknown. We need not graphically depict the heinous atrocities of the Holocaust to teach children about war crimes, but should include in the curriculum an accurate portrayal of historical events. *Don't Forget* approaches this sensitive subject in an age-appropriate yet genuine and forthright manner. It is a deeply moving story, ending on an affirming note, with the actual recipe for Sarah's sponge cake. BARBARA SMITH REDDISH

Our Home Is the Sea

Riki Levinson   Dennis Luzak

Asian, Chinese

1992 (1988), Puffin Books

The small boy we follow through the streets of Hong Kong from school to home remains nameless, as do all the other people we meet in this picture book that introduces Hong Kong life in as many aspects as can be contained in the boy's route home.

A Chinese boy introduces the daily life of a fishing family in Hong Kong on his way home from school.

We see the high-rise offices packed together on the Hong Kong hillside overlooking the harbor; the towering apartments with their "laundry" (international flags) flying on poles from every window; the double-decker bus, also packed full, with a dolphin drawn larger than life on its side; the markets with the fish spread out in baskets; old men serenely practicing the slow dance of martial arts in a park, and others who have taken their birds in their bamboo cages to the park for an outing.

Finally it turns out that "home" is a boat in the harbor which lies packed in with other boats. The boy's father is a fisherman. The family spends its whole daily life aboard the small boat, as thousands of families live in Hong Kong.

The mother wants the boy to become a schoolteacher, but he doesn't really want to go to school. He wants to be out on the sea with his father. The author makes no apology for the boy's desire to become a fisherman, for which a formal schooling will not be necessary.

The illustrations are paintings that could well be modeled after actual photographs taken in Hong Kong, they are so specifically vivid and detailed. GINNY LEE

Tucking Mommy In

Morag Loh   Donna Rawlins

Asian American

1991 (1988), Orchard Books

At bedtime, two sisters, Jenny and Sue, find that their extremely tired mother is falling asleep. Consequently, they switch roles with their mother for the evening, taking her to her bedroom, helping her to undress, getting her into bed, and telling her a good-night story. Later, their father returns from work and provides closure to the evening and the book by tucking in his daughters, restoring their customary family roles.

Two Asian American sisters help their exhausted mother into bed and tell her a bedtime story.

This calm book, beautifully illustrated with clear, naturalistic pictures in the warm colors of muted sunshine, is perfect bedtime reading for two- to six-year-old children. Without being heavy-handed, the book provides realistic, honest portrayals of believable people in a common situation. Mommy really is "so tired that [she] can't think straight," the house is comfortably messy, and the sisters squabble just a little bit.

Because much of the information is conveyed through the illustrations rather than the words, a subtle effect is maintained. The characters' dark hair and almond-shaped eyes, for example, suggest an

Asian heritage, but their ethnicity is not mentioned in the text itself. Similarly, the father is clearly a blue-collar worker (he comes home from work late in the evening, wearing overalls and carrying a thermos), but the author, Morag Loh, lets the pictures make this point without bringing it up in the narrative.

The book's strength lies in the role reversal undergone by the sisters and their mother. By creating a mother who, for one evening, has to be taken care of by her children, Loh shows both kids and parents that sometimes parents can be like children and children can be like parents. Jenny and Sue sweetly take up the responsibility of getting Mommy into bed, using her words ("You'd better go to bed right now!") and physically leading her into her bedroom. Some readers may be taken aback by the picture of the sisters undressing their mother—her brassiere is plainly in sight—but this illustration provides important counterbalance to earlier ones that show the mother bathing the girls and helping them dry off. By caring for their mom, the girls show resourcefulness, self-sufficiency, and capability.

Lest parents or teachers worry that too much is expected of the sisters, Loh thoughtfully includes the last section of the book, where Daddy returns home and tucks in the girls, allowing them to be kids again. Some anxious readers may still worry about the greatly fatigued mother, and indeed, the book provides no explanation for her exhaustion. Most adults, however, can identify with her plight. The silence here offers adults and children an opportunity to discuss these issues, perhaps investing parents with some individuality that children had not previously realized. A further strength of the story is that it shows two girls as active and intelligent without being addressed only to female readers. Both boys and girls will be intrigued and comforted by this lovely picture book. JUNE CUMMINS

The Hundred Penny Box

Sharon Bell Mathis Leo & Diane Dillon

African American

1986 (1975), Viking, ✱ Video

This is the story of an African American family who's Aunt Dew, short for Dewbet Thomas, is one hundred years old and has recently been brought to live with Michael's family. Michael is excited to have Aunt Dew, his great-great aunt, join their home and is particularly interested in the hundred penny box she always keeps with her, which contains a penny for each year she's been alive.

Michael loves to take the pennies out one by one and hear the stories Aunt Dew has to tell for each year. He learns about his heritage and family history through her stories. Aunt Dew's presence is a delight to Michael but a challenge for his mother, who views Aunt Dew as a disruption in her family life and treats her as if she were another child requiring constant care.

Michael hides some of Aunt Dew's things so his mother can't throw them away. When she focuses on the hundred penny box, Michael talks with his mother about how important the box is to Aunt Dew and determines not to let her substitute it with a newer version, or burn the old one.

An African American woman has one penny for every year she's been alive, and an equal number of stories to tell her great-great nephew, in a still-fresh book from the '70s.

The illustrations, by Leo and Diane Dillon are soft and dreamy. They use only shades of black and white echoing colors of old photographs. They give a sense of a past time and provide a visual representation for Aunt Dew's remembering the past and haziness about the present. The issue of aging stands out clearly as a topic for examination. Michael's interest in Aunt Dew's life and curiosity about what it is like to be old is in strong contrast to his mother's view that Aunt Dew is an added responsibility. *Children might relate their own experience with older members of their families and try to understand where the different perspectives come from.*

The hundred penny box itself is a project children could start for themselves or with other family members. Finding out something that happened for each year of their lives, children may discover some interesting family stories or historical information. In a classroom, math stories using the years could provide some fun computation practice and the pennies themselves could be used for developing money and time concepts.

DEBORAH PATTERSON

A Million Fish...More or Less

📖 Patricia McKissack ✒ Dena Schetzer

African American

1992, Alfred A. Knopf, 📖 McKissack, Patricia, *Flossie and the Fox.*

Strange things happen around the fishing waters in Louisiana bayou country. Papa-Daddy and Elder Abbajon elevate exaggeration to a fine art when they spin incredible tales to pique a young boy's curiosity. Hugh Thomas, interested in fishing, learns quickly from the older men about hyperbolic storytelling.

An African American boy in Louisiana bayou country learns the art of hyperbole.

Papa-Daddy's story about catching a 500-pound turkey and finding a 350-year-old lantern that was still burning develops into an account of being chased by a huge, multi-legged snake and a swarm of giant mosquitoes. When Hugh Thomas asks if the story is true, the men simply respond "more or less."

Soon after Hugh finds himself in a tall tale of his own. He catches so many fish that he quickly attracts the attention of the bayou's residents. Atoo, the dreaded, old alligator, blocks his way and demands some fish. An army of raccoons with their bandit leader, Mosley, stop Hugh as well and force him to relinquish half of his remaining fish. When he finally gets home to show his fine catch, the neighbor's cat is also extremely interested.

Hugh finds he has only three fish left to show Pappa-Daddy and Elder Abbajon. They congratulate him on having such a fine catch for his dinner. Hugh insists that he really caught a million fish — more or less — and starts telling the story of his adventures.

The brilliant paintings by Dena Schetzer bring this story to life. The multicolored fish are depicted in a lush green setting of trees, bushes, and grasses that are indigenous to swamp-land habitat.

A Million Fish...More Or Less was a notable Children's Trade Book in the field of Social Studies in 1992, and would be a great introduction to a unit on storytelling. SHIRLEY R. CRENSHAW

A Visit To Amy-Claire

📖 Claudia Mills ✒ Sheila Hamanaka

Asian American, Biracial

1992, Macmillan Publishing Company

Excited about seeing her seven-year-old cousin again, five-year-old Rachel is disappointed to discover that all Amy-Claire wants to do is play with Jessie, Rachel's two-year-old sister. Jealous, Rachel refuses to play house with the other girls until she realizes that if Amy-Claire is the mother, and Jessie is the baby, she can be the big sister. And that isn't such a bad thing to be after all.

Although no mention is made of ethnicity, Rachel's mother and Amy-Claire's family are depicted as Asian American, while Rachel's father is portrayed with reddish-brown hair and European American features. Thus, Rachel and Jesse are biracial Asian European Americans. The illustrations, however, make *A Visit to Amy-Claire* one of a growing number of children's books to recognize the multiracial makeup

A book dealing with sibling rivalry in the context of a biracial family.

of America and incorporate families of varied ethnic backgrounds into stories with themes of universal interest. Children need to see themselves in the books they read, in the characters they meet and admire. The matter-of-fact representation of characters with non-European backgrounds, in stories that do not make an issue of race, helps all children feel included in, rather than excluded from, American society.

LYNN EISENHUT

Uncle Jed's Barbershop

📖 Margaree King Mitchell ✒ James Ransome

African American

1993, Simon & Schuster, ✶ Audio Cassette, Braille, CD-ROM

This touching book will pull at the heartstrings with its story of one man's commitment and sacrifices to make his dreams come true. Told from the perspective of a woman looking back, this is the story of her beloved Uncle Jed and his desire to own his own barber shop.

An African American works his whole life to open his own barbershop.

The setting is the Deep South during the early part of the century. Uncle Jed is the only black barber for thirty miles, so he is always guaranteed hair to cut, but he dreams of having his own shop. He speaks to his niece of the shiny sinks it will have, the four barber chairs, and the floors glistening like mirrors. Since most of his clients are poor, and pay him with only eggs or a hot meal, the money is slow coming, and a couple of incidents set him way back. First, his niece needs an operation, and Uncle Jed is the only person with money. Then the Great Depression closes a bank, taking Uncle Jed's life savings with it. In both cases, Uncle Jed exhibits a quiet calm, saying he will just have to save a bit longer. Not until he's seventy-nine does he finally open his shop, and he is so excited that he cuts hair for three days straight.

Woven throughout the appealing plot are snippets of African American history. Mitchell writes about how poor many African Americans were and defines sharecropping. She also describes segregation and its injustice, even in a hospital emergency room. The plot itself makes clear that no one else would cut African Americans' hair. Details like these are what lend poignancy to this story of one man's triumph over racism and adversity with nobility and grace. LISA FAIN

A Birthday Basket for Tia

Pat Mora Cecily Lang
Hispanic
1993 (1992), Macmillan Publishing Company,
✳ Audio Cassette, Series, Hammond, Anna, *This Home We Have Made*.

Cecilia and her great-aunt Tia have a relationship that transcends all others in their family. Cecilia wanders around the house collecting items that remind her of special things she and her great aunt do together; she has a surprise in store for great-aunt Tia.

When her mother becomes suspicious, Cecilia asks her to keep the secret as well. In no way is the elderly aunt portrayed as a burden; rather her presence in the household gives Cecilia greater self-esteem and is presented in a positive light. The importance of the inter-generational bond and the cultural ties to that bond are very much apparent in this story. The warmth and love of an extended family in this Latino household are captured in Cecily Lang's brightly colored illustrations.

A Hispanic girl hopes to give her aunt a wonderful basket for her ninetieth birthday.

The repetition of the poetic prose and rhythmic sound of words such as Tia Bizcochos, *hierbabuena*, and *piñata* add to the festive atmosphere of the story. Pat Mora, who is also a poet and novelist, provides a glossary with translations of the Spanish terms. MARTHA L. MARTINEZ

Daddy and Me: A Photo Story of Arthur Ashe and His Daughter, Camera

 Jeanne Moutoussamy-Ashe
African American
1993, Alfred A. Knopf, Levinson, Riki, *Dinnieabbiesister-r-r!*.

Although the young narrator, the "me" of the title, tells us early on that Daddy is sick with AIDS, *Daddy and Me* is really about a warm father/daughter relationship of which Daddy's illness is simply one part. Large black-and-white photographs illustrate the minimal text, that nonetheless manages to explain in terms a child can understand how AIDS makes one feel: "...sometimes Daddy runs a fever and feels very tired. Like when you have a stomach ache. You just don't feel very good." And how Daddy got the illness from a blood transfusion ("when you transfer blood from one person to another") during a heart operation. The matter-of-fact photographs show Camera and her father at home, on the tennis court, and at the doctor's for tests. Shots of Camera helping her daddy use a machine that assists his breathing are given no more weight than those of

Text and photographs show young children how families deal with AIDS.

Daddy combing her hair, primarily because the text and pictures are all focused on the child; she is in every photo except one. The camera also captures the endearing compassion with which this family deals with AIDS and eventually death.

An author's note, directed toward adult readers, explains that Jeanne Moutoussamy-Ashe and her husband, tennis star Arthur Ashe, conceived this book to give other parents a way to discuss AIDS with their young children, and notes Ashe's death from AIDS in 1993. The text, however, ends with "I love my daddy and my daddy loves me. That is the best medicine and we both agree!" LYNN EISENHUT

The Sea and I

Harutaka Nakawatari

Asian, Japanese

1992 (1990), Farrar, Straus & Giroux, ✳ Japanese

As a storm approaches, a Japanese child watches for his father, a fisherman, to return home safely from sea.

The beauty of *The Sea and I* lies not only in its impressive artwork, but also in its potential appeal to readers around the world. The translation of Nakawatari's story presents, simply and eloquently, a day in the life of a young child living on an island near the sea.

The book's text and illustrations allow us to experience and appreciate the unpredictable moods of the ocean as well as the love between a parent and child. Although one might presume that the characters depicted are Japanese and that the story is autobiographical, the faces of the child and father are never clearly revealed, contributing to the universal themes and quality of the book. From sunrise to sunset, the reader is captivated by Nakawatari's presentation of respect for family and nature.

This story contains excellent examples of common experiences shared among people, regardless of cultural background. *In the classroom, children might be asked to share their own experiences and feelings associated with the ocean, beaches, storms, boats, or separation from a loved one. Certainly, the rich vocabulary used in the book's translation would make* The Sea and I *a wonderful addition to a study of the ocean or coastal regions, placing terminology in a meaningful and illustrated context.* Nakawatari's work is a fine example of children's literature that can be appreciated at a variety of levels—personal, informational, artistic, and universal. KARLEEN H. TANIMURA MANCHANDA

Is That Josie?

Keiko Narahashi

Asian American

1994, McElderry Books

In this book, the text and illustrations work together to recreate a child's imaginative game with her mother. The book first presents a picture of Josie followed by the mother's question, "Is that Josie peeking out of bed?" Josie's answer, "No, it's a sly fox hiding in her den," is supported by a picture showing both her and the animal she is pretending to be. This pattern is repeated through a day's activities, with Josie, for example, imagining herself to be an eagle soaring when she is on a swing, or a smiling crocodile when she is brushing her teeth. The book ends with "And is this Josie all ready for bed?" Finally, she answers with a "Yes!"

An Asian American girl and her mother play an imaginative game.

The text is clear and simple, identifying insects, reptiles, and animals, from ant to turtle. The author uses interesting action verbs such as thumping, dangling, and soaring, and supplies basic adjectives such as high, big, fast, and deep. Children will be drawn into the book's rhythm and repetition. Even the youngest child will quickly catch on to "Is that Josie?" and be ready to answer with a resounding "No!"

The illustrations are pastel-toned watercolors, which have a pleasing fluidity, and capture the action of the text and extend it. Josie, sleekly stretched out, dives like a dolphin or stands tiptoed to brush her teeth. Depicting her hiding behind open fingers or crouched down with turtleneck pulled over her nose to be a turtle, the illustrations also add to the gentle humor of the book.

This book works on many levels. It can be a bedtime story, reflecting the kind of ruses that children use to avoid the inevitable. It can be an action game, with children acting out Josie's imaginary animals. Or it can be a language game with children making up their own responses to satisfy their own imaginations. Josie is loosely pictured as Asian, but she could be any child, and her inventiveness and good nature will be appreciated by all. JACKIE LYNCH

Saturday Is Pattyday

Leslea Newman ✎ Annette Hegel
Gay/Lesbian/Bisexual
1993, New Victoria Press

Frankie is upset because his lesbian parents, unable to stop their fighting, have gotten divorced. He tries to make himself feel better by placing his stuffed dinosaur, Doris Delores the Brontosaurus, in Patty's chair, but it doesn't help. Allie takes him to Patty's apartment on Saturday so he can visit all day. Patty has a shelf set up in her closet with his name on it and shows him his special place to sleep when he stays over.

Frankie is forced to deal with the divorce of his lesbian parents.

He has a tantrum in the park that sparks a conversation in which he voices his concern that if he and Patty fight like Allie and Patty did, they'll also get a divorce. Patty reassures him that only grown-ups divorce and that he'll always be her son. When it is decided they will see each other every Saturday, Frankie declares it "Pattyday." When the time comes for Allie to take him home, Frankie decides to leave Doris Delores behind to stay with Patty.

While this is clearly a story about a lesbian couple, the central issue is how a child begins to reestablish feelings of security after a divorce. This works well to shift the focus from the relationship itself to the universal problems encountered in a wide spectrum of relationships and how understanding and honesty can help children through a crisis. CHRIS MAYO

Too Far Away to Touch

Lesleá Newman ✎ Catherine Stock
Gay/Lesbian/Bisexual
1995, Clarion Books

This moving picture book is a rarity: a fictional treatment by a mainstream publisher of the affection between a young girl and her implicitly gay uncle who is living with AIDS. Uncle Leonard is Zoe's favorite relative, the one who takes her on special outings and makes her laugh. During a trip to the planetarium, Zoe asks Uncle Leonard, "How far away are the stars?" His response, "Too far away to touch but close enough to see" foreshadows their later discussion of his own possible death.

Zoe notices that Uncle Leonard is tired, has lost much of his hair, and must take frequent medication. But he still tells silly jokes and finds ways to surprise her. Uncle Leonard's partner, Nathan, accompanies them on an outing to a seafood restaurant and the beach, and is shown tenderly but unobtrusively assisting him. The book ends on a reassuring but realistic note. As Zoe and Uncle Leonard gaze up at the stars on the beach and Zoe realizes that her beloved Uncle might die, he tells her that his presence will always be with her, "too far away to touch but close enough to see" in her mind's eye.

Zoe's uncle has AIDS and explains that if he dies he will be like the stars, "too far away to touch but close enough to see."

The realities associated with living with a chronic illness are dealt with throughout the book. Catherine Stock's soft watercolors in mauves and blues set a gentle, contemplative mood that is perfectly matched to the story. Infused with both warmth and sadness, this picture book can serve as a supportive launching point for developing some understanding of and compassion for those suffering with AIDS and other life-threatening illnesses. LAURI JOHNSON

Abuelita's Paradise

Carmen Santiago Nodar, Edited by Judith Mathews ✎ Diane Paterson
Hispanic, Puerto Rican
1993 (1992), Varsity Reading Services, ✱ Audio Cassette, Series

An inviting book, *Abuelita's Paradise*, is the story of a little girl, Martita, who, while sitting in the rocking chair which belonged to her grandmother, reminisces about her *abuelita's* fond memories of Puerto Rico.

Nestled in her grandmother's arms and wrapped in the old blanket with paradiso written on it, Martita asks her grandmother countless questions about what life was like growing up in Puerto Rico. "Tell me more," Martita would ask, and images of life in Puerto Rico come alive through *abuelita's* vivid descriptions. In several passages the imagery is especially beautiful:

Marissa recalls the stories her abuelita (grandmother) told her about growing up in Puerto Rico.

"When the trade winds blew, the plumes of the flowering sugarcane bowed and curtsied. They reached up like feathery angels, dancing and floating toward heaven."

"I lived on a farm in Puerto Rico...Where night creeps over the mountains and down again. Where sunlight sparkles the day, and sugarcane reaches the sky."

The soft watercolor illustrations acccompany the text perfectly. Drawings of the countryside in Puerto Rico are both lush with deep green palm trees and mountains and rich with exquisite flowers and pastel sunsets.

Although it is quite clear to an adult from the beginning, the author chooses to wait until the last few pages to declare to its young audience that Abuelita has died. At the end of the book, curled in the paradise blanket on her grandmother's rocker, Martita falls asleep in her mother's arms as she is comforted also by Abuelita's imagined embrace. The author's approach to revealing the grandmother's death, together with her writing style, work successfully to evoke a soothing tone throughout the book. The subject of death is dealt with in a very relaxed and comforting fashion.

A well written and beautifully illustrated children's book, *Abuelita's Paradise* would make a fine addition to any home or classroom library. *As a teacher, I have used it in many ways: as a part of my Spanish and social studies curricula, as a resource for addressing the subject of dying with young children, and as an example of a story with strong female characters.* The author dedicated the book to four generations of grandmothers. MARY TROWBRIDGE

Grandpa's Town

Takaaki Nomura (translated by Amanda M. Stinchecum)

Asian, Japanese

1995 (1989), Kane Miller Book Publishers, ✳ Japanese

When Yuuta visits his newly widowed grandfather, they go to the public bathhouse together. On their way to the bathhouse, Yuuta greets many of Grandpa's friends and realizes that Grandpa is not as lonely as he thinks.

The public bath is a place where Japanese people come to socialize, in addition to having a soothing hot bath. In many Japanese small towns, it is difficult and expensive to heat up a big tub of water for a daily bath at home. Therefore, it is more convenient for people to go to public baths to soak and relax in hot-water pools. Children learn that the bathhouse has a male and a female section. People use small basins to clean themselves before soaking in the hot bath. Going to the public bath is not just for cleaning oneself, but also for visiting with friends.

A Japanese boy spends the day with his newly widowed Grandpa, and gains a better understanding of him.

This book can also be used for learning about the loss of loved ones. How can children comfort one grandparent when the other one passes away? Yuuta goes with Grandpa to visit his friends and shows his loving concern.

The authentic illustrations of a Japanese town are filled with details about places and people's actions. Almost one-third of the illustrations are about the public bathhouse. Teachers can use this opportunity to explain this important Japanese practice. BELINDA YUN-YING LOUIE

Fireflies for Nathan

Shulamith Levey Oppenheim   John Ward

African American

1994, Tambourine Books

While visiting his grandparents, Nathan learns, just as his father had many years before, that he must be patient in order to capture fireflies.

Like his grandfather, Nathan loves to catch and then release fireflies during the intense heat of summer. On his "bugs in a jar" expeditions, Nathan gets some fundamental lessons in nature. He also learns a lot about family traditions.

African American Nathan spends time with his grandparents and catches fireflies.

Peacefully capturing the family's relationship with nature, the illustrations reflect the warmth and simplicity of Nathan's family. The soft, gently rendered illustrations are peaceful representations of family time with nature. The story and the illustrations underscore the importance of elders in the learning process. MARTHA L. MARTINEZ

I Have a Sister—My Sister Is Deaf

📖 Jeanne Whitehouse Peterson 🖊 Deborah Ray
Physically Disabled
1984 (1977), Harper & Row, ✳ Series

We are all challenged by our inabilities to communicate with one another. But for a deaf child, that challenge is intensified. In this wonderful poem, a sister describes how she builds a real friendship with her younger, deaf sister. In the poem, she describes the many ways in which they communicate without words, by expressions and touch: "Last night I asked, 'Where are my pajamas?' She went into the kitchen and brought out a bunch of bananas."

In an enduring rhyming story from the '70s, a girl describes her loving relationship with her deaf sister.

The fact that the sisters can laugh at one another without putting each other down, will endear many young readers to this story. The book also deals well with the reality of the deaf sister's world without making her weak or pitiful.

The tender and loving relationship between the two sisters is well portrayed, and their different reactions to the same things are portrayed realistically. This is a book that will also help very young children allay some of their fears about being around a disability. MEREDITH ELIASSEN

My Mama Sings

📖 Jeanne Whitehouse Peterson 🖊 Sandra Speidel
African American
1994, HarperCollins

A young boy and his mother have a close, loving relationship cemented by the songs she shares from earlier years. Mother has special songs for changes in the seasons, household chores, leisure activities, and company. Their happiness is disrupted when Mother is dismissed from work because of lateness.

Songs keep the loving relationship between an African American boy and his mother alive.

The mother is momentarily depressed, and her somber behavior puzzles her son, who wants to help her make things better. He does so with a song about summer activities. Mother regains her equilibrium, apologizes, explains what happened, and life returns to normal.

The chalk, crayon, and paint illustrations make use of soft, gentle tones, lines, movement, and color. Although touching, the story presents some difficulties. For example, the mother and son remain nameless, even as the cat and neighbors are named. This may present a problem for young readers or listeners. Additionally, the mother's dismissal from her job is abruptly introduced and not explained in a satisfactory manner. The poetic text, however, will appeal to some readers and listeners. VIOLET HARRIS

Eagle Feather, An Honour

📖 🖊 Ferguson Plain
Native American, Ojibway
1992, Pemmican Publications, Inc.

Nooshen, a young Ojibway boy, grows up under his grandfather Mishoomis's guidance. He learns to love Mishoomis as he learns about songs, stories, tribal history, values, and Mother Earth from him. As Nooshen prepares to dance in a powwow, his grandfather becomes ill and knows that he will die soon. Despite his illness, Mishoomis makes arrangements for his grandson to receive an eagle feather at the powwow, a high honor. The eagle is considered to be the all-seeing messenger of the Creator, the Great Spirit. Once you are honored with an eagle feather you must do good deeds for the tribe or the clan.

An Ojibway boy learns about his history, culture, and Mother Earth from his dying grandfather.

When Nooshen is surprised upon receiving such an honor, Mishoomis explains to him that he is a blessing—his birth was a good deed. After Mishoomis dies, Nooshen grows up with the knowledge of his grandfather's love.

The intergenerational male relationships pictured in this book are full of love and tenderness. The elder is valued as a transmitter of culture and wisdom. The youngster develops pride as he is treated with full respect and complete appreciation when his grandfather states, "You are my Nooshen and I could not have asked for anything more."

More remarkable than the text of this story are the monochromatic illustrations. The main characters have clear, almost cartoonlike, qualities and are depicted against a background of faded, spiritual images of animals, hoops, and feathers upon a surface that looks like tanned hide. The pictures graphically display the many dimensions of our daily reality, with the spirit world, represented by the background images, being far more detailed and developed than the material world, represented by the clear line drawings.

Because these illustrations are rather delicate and in subtle gray tones, they would not be readily visible for large group readings. However, each page offers a lot to discuss with a single listener or a small group sitting very close. This is a good book for discussing family relationships, specific tribal customs, spirituality, aging, death, grief, and responsibility. If you are going to specifically discuss the Ojibway culture in conjunction with this book, you should read The Mishoomis Book *to understand and explain the meaning of specific images and customs described in this story. The book also contains a small glossary.* NOLA HADLEY

The Outside Dog

📖 Charlotte Pomerantz   ✏ Jennifer Plecas
Hispanic, Puerto Rican

1995 (1993), HarperCollins, ✳ Series, 📚 Ellis, Anne Leo, *Dabble Duck*; Graham, Amanda, *Who Wants Arthur?*; Phillips, Joan, *My New Boy.*

Marisol, a little girl who lives in a Puerto Rican hillside village with her grandfather, has always wanted a dog. Although there are many strays living on the hill, Grandfather has never allowed Marisol to have a pet, stating "they have fleas and ticks and who knows what." Yet when a small brown dog wanders near their home, Marisol wants to keep him. This book from the I Can Read Series is written in the limited,

Against her grandfather's wishes, Marisol, a young Puerto-Rican girl, decides to keep a stray dog.

simple prose which is the series' hallmark. The four episodes include Marisol's first meeting with the dog and Grandfather's grudging acceptance of the animal; a trip to the local *colmado* (grocery store), where Marisol and grandfather buy a flea collar for the animal that Marisol names Pancho; Pancho's two-day disappearance, during which Marisol searches for her pet; and Pancho's barking when rice begins burning on the stove.

The book serves as an easy introduction to multicultural literature for beginning readers. A number of Spanish words and phrases, including *abuelito* (grandpa), *vete* (scram) and *que cosa* (my goodness),

are seamlessly woven into the text. Neither the text nor the simple color illustrations overemphasize the Puerto Rican setting. At the forefront are a child's desire for a pet, the warm relationship between grandfather and grandchild, and the drama of Pancho's disappearance and return. By focusing on these universal experiences, the multicultural components of *The Outside Dog* are smoothly and naturally presented as background for the engaging story.
PETER D. SIERUTA

The New King: A Madagascan Legend

📖 Doreen Rappaport   ✏ E. B. Lewis
African, Madagascar

1995, Dial

Prince Rakota runs the show in Doreen Rappaport's *The New King*. He is a determined young African boy who gives everyone around him orders. However, no one can fulfill his command to bring his father back to life.

African Prince Rakoto grieves for and replaces his father, who is killed on a hunt.

By the end of the story, he finally accepts his father's death, when a wise woman tells him how children continue the life of someone who dies. Prince Rakota grows up to be a kind king who passes on the important lessons his father taught him.

The illustrations in *The New King* use a lot of dark colors to represent the death in the story. Their realism really made us feel like we were part of the book.

We had mixed opinions about this book. Some of us thought there were too many repetitive questions. We wished there was more action, more detail, and a faster pace. Others liked the theme of acceptance, the strong feelings, and the small boy's struggle to understand death.
MRS. CHAPIN'S 5TH GRADE CLASS

Aunt Harriet's Underground Railroad in the Sky

Faith Ringgold

African American

1992, Crown Publishers, Inc.

Cassie and her younger brother are flying among the clouds when they discover an old railroad train in the sky. When a woman appears wearing a conductor's uniform, hundreds of people come and board the old train. Cassie's brother Be Be also boards because he wants to ride. Before Cassie can get him off the train, it disappears through the clouds, leaving the message, "Go free North or die!" As Cassie screams for her brother, the female conductor introduces herself as Harriet Tubman, the woman who carried hundreds of slaves to freedom on the Underground Railroad. Aunt Harriet, as she was called, explains some aspects of slavery to Cassie. She also says that the old train will follow the same route that she had traveled one hundred years ago so that the cost of freedom won't be forgotten. In order for Cassie to find Be Be, she has to follow the Underground Railroad as the slaves did.

Cassie's adventure begins with her escape from the plantation. Along her route, Cassie finds notes of encouragement from Be Be and receives directions from Aunt Harriet. She hides in farmhouses, graveyards, wagons, and coffins. Finally when Cassie reaches Niagara Falls, she can fly once again and she is free. She sees Be Be and the other passengers from the train flying around also free. Be Be tells Cassie that although he loves her dearly, freedom is what is most important. The story ends with a giant celebration of the one hundredth anniversary of Aunt Harriet's first flight to freedom.

Written as a type of historical fantasy tale, this children's story is actually a spin on a dream that Harriet Tubman had when she was ill and dying. The story describes and explains the role that the Underground Railroad played in the escape of runaway slaves. The story also demonstrates the importance of remembering and celebrating what the railroad and Harriet Tubman meant for hundreds of fleeing slaves. At the end of the book the author provides an historical sketch of Harriet Tubman. There is also a map outlining some of the many routes taken by escaped slaves.

The illustrations in this book are among its greatest strengths. The descriptive portrayals enable the reader to follow the storyline easily. The main weakness of the text is that the focus is on slave escape rather than the institution of slavery itself. Escape is seen as the only real option for slaves. Although the Underground Railroad, and thus slave escapes, forms the central theme of the book, it is important to note that the decision to stay was often just as dangerous and difficult. Therefore *this book would be most effective if it were accompanied by other historical material on slavery and freedom.*

MICHELLE GARFIELD

> *A historical fantasy tale that celebrates the triumphs of Harriet Tubman and her Underground Railroad.*

Carry, Go, Bring, Come

Vyanne Samuels Jennifer Northway

African American

1989 (1988), Macmillan Publishing Co., Four Winds Press

On the day of his sister's wedding, Leon's whole extended family is busy in preparation—all except Leon, who sleeps through the commotion. At last, his grandmother wakes him with a whisper and sends him on an errand to deliver a silk flower to his mother. He never completes the errand, though, because on his way, his sister tells him to "wait a little," then hands him a veil to carry back to his grandmother. One by one, family members stop him and add to his burdens until finally, with the veil on his head, the flower in his teeth, the bride's shoes on his feet and gloves on his hands, balancing a bottle of perfume, he can go no farther. The family laughs at the sight of him, but poor Leon is appalled. At last, relieved of his burdens, he asks when he should get dressed for the wedding. He is again told to "wait a little," and becomes so exasperated that he jumps back into bed.

> *In preparation for African American Leon's sister's wedding, his family runs him ragged.*

The theme presented here is a universal one. It's frustrating not to be noticed. It's hard to be laughed at, too, as all young children know, and though they will laugh at the humorous illustrations, they will also empathize with Leon's plight. Readers may wish to discuss how Leon must feel and if they have ever felt like this themselves.

The family portrayed is a happy, loving one, and children from any culture can relate to it. Although the illustrations portray the wedding accouterments to be Western, the family is from the Caribbean, as is the author. Children may also wish to discuss their own families' traditions involving large gatherings such as weddings to see how their experiences resemble and differ from the one portrayed here. JODI LEVINE

Two Pairs of Shoes

📖 Esther Sanderson   ✎ David Beyer

Cree, Native American

1990, Pemmican Publications, Inc.

For eight-year-old Maggie, learning which pair of shoes to wear goes beyond proper etiquette. She receives for her birthday a pair of shiny patent leather shoes from her mother. In her excitement, she runs to show Kokom, her grandmother, the present from her mom. Despite the fact that she is almost blind, her grandmother has made Maggie a pair of beautifully beaded moccasins. Maggie is astounded. Maggie wonders, how could her grandmother see well enough to do such intricate and beautiful beadwork? As Maggie hugs her grandmother in appreciation, Kokom advises her that she now has to learn when and how to wear each pair.

A Cree child receives a pair of patent leather shoes and a pair of moccasins.

Emphasizing the value of women and family, this story also provides a wonderful example of how children can learn to balance the traditions that come with being bicultural. The author does not place a greater value on the patent leather shoes than she does on the handmade moccasins. In Maggie's heart, both are precious. With a few Cree words interspersed throughout the story, readers have an opportunity to see another language in print.

Bright, bold illustrations by David Beyer capture the warmth and energy of this picture book. *This book would be a wonderful choice for reading out loud to a group of children, starting a discussion about fam-*

ilies, *traditions, and making choices.* Although it emphasizes Indian life and values, children and adults of many backgrounds will enjoy and benefit from reading it. NOLA HADLEY

Down the Road

📖 Alice Schertle   ✎ E.B. Leiws

African American

1995, Harcourt Brace & Company, 📖 Brown, Don Brown, *Ruth Law Thrills a Nation*; Naylor, Phyllis, *The Fear Place.*

In this Junior Library Guild Selection, Alice Schertle has written a gentle story depicting a loving and understanding family.

Up to now, Hetty has never been allowed to go to the store alone. But one day when both Mama and Papa are too busy to go themselves, they send Hetty. With egg money in her pocket and a wicker basket over her arm, Hetty sets off for Mr. Birdie's store. She buys the eggs, thanks Mr. Birdie, and heads home feeling very grown up.

A beautifully illustrated tale of the trouble faced by an African American girl.

Hetty carries her eggs carefully. However, there are obstacles: a stream to cross, bumps in the road, and an apple tree laden with sweet, juicy, crackly-crisp apples. When Hetty stops to pick some, disaster strikes. She breaks the eggs—all twelve of them.

When Hetty does not return home, Papa and Mama go looking for her. They find their daughter, sad and ashamed, sitting in the top of the apple tree. Her parents are supportive, loving, and understanding. Pretty soon, Papa, Mama, and Hetty are all sitting in the tree.

E.B. Lewis's glorious, translucent watercolors are large and colorful, sweeping across whole double-page spreads, depicting a splendid summer day in wonderful detail. Hetty and her parents are black, but race does not figure prominently in the story. This book is especially appropriate for younger children as they take on more and more responsibility. It teaches that one does not always have to be perfect; one is permitted mistakes. *Students can use this story in an exercise to write their own stories of mistakes and forgiveness.*

BETTYE STROUD

On Mother's Lap

📖 Ann Herbert Scott ✏️ Glo Coalson

Eskimo, Native American

1992 (1972), Clarion Books/Houghton Mifflin Co.

A recurrent theme in children's literature is the relationship between children and members of their families. *On Mother's Lap*, depicts the warm, loving relationship between an indigenous Alaskan mother and her children.

The story begins with Michael climbing onto his mother's lap to be rocked while his baby sister sleeps on a nearby bed. Michael then decides he needs his doll, his boat, his reindeer blanket, and his puppy to be comfortable as his mother continues to rock and cuddle with him. When his sister awakens and his mother suggests that she would like to join them, Michael is not pleased by the proposal and protests that there is not enough room. However, his mother manages to find room for both children and all of Michael's belongings under the reindeer blanket, and Michael decides that his mother's lap is still a comfortable place to be.

A reissue of a '70s story of a warm, loving relationship between an Eskimo mother and her children.

Although this story could have taken place almost anywhere, its treatment of a mother's love and sharing with a sibling is enriched by its setting in an indigenous Alaskan household. These themes are universal and are readily recognized by most children. The objects depicted in the story are appropriate to that setting. Hence, the doll is dressed in indigenous Alaskan attire, the boat resembles a rough canoe, and the blanket is made of fur. These are surely different from items found in the homes of many American children. However, they are merely different and not unknown, since many children are familiar with dolls, boats, and blankets, and they might be as attached to these objects as is Michael. This story helps children understand that families from other cultures share feelings and experiences much like their own. Thus, the differences between families become superficial, while the common features are much more meaningful. DONNA GAGNON

The Skirt

📖 Gary Soto ✏️ Eric Valasquez

Hispanic

1995 (1992), Dell

In this novel portraying a warm, loving Mexican American family, fourth grader Miata Ramirez has a reputation for losing things. So she is understandably reluctant to admit to her mother that she has left her folklórico skirt on the school bus the Friday before she is scheduled to dance on Sunday. In desperation, she hatches a plan with her best friend to retrieve the skirt before her parents discover it missing. Miata's anxiety over losing her skirt is due less to a fear of punishment than of disappointing her parents, who she knows are looking forward to watching her dance.

Miata speaks English at home and with friends, but easily switches to Spanish when speaking with a friend's grandmother. The illustrations continue this theme: characters are drawn as individuals with Latino features, and Miata's home has Mexican art on the wall.

A young Latina leaves her folklórico skirt on the school bus just when she needs it for a performance.

The Skirt is an excellent self-acceptance builder for young Mexican Americans searching for stories about "kids like me." But the matter-of-fact treatment of the protagonist's cultural heritage, coupled with a realistic problem, create an early chapter book to which any child can relate. A native of Fresno in California's San Joaquin Valley, Gary Soto was a respected poet before being recognized as an author of notable books for young people featuring Mexican Americans. His stories reflect his own background, with naturally bilingual characters. LYNN EISENHUT

Daddy Is a Monster... Sometimes

📖✏️ John Steptoe

African American

1980, J.B. Lippincott Co., ✶ Series

Daddy Is a Monster...Sometimes, written and illustrated by John Steptoe, has been a favorite book among young children for over a decade, both as a read-aloud story and as an easy reader for early elementary school students. Steptoe tells a semiautobiographical tale of a single parent of two curious and rambunctious children, a daughter, Bweela, and a son, Javaka, narrated in truly authentic preschool/first-grade dialect, complete with sound effects that delight young readers.

The children recount the many times when they behaved inappropriately and "Daddy gets like the monster in the scary movies, with teeth comin' out his mouth and hair all over his face," and says, "Grrraaw, go to bed! Grrraaw!" The mischief that provokes their father's transformation is illustrated with imaginative, dreamlike clarity by Steptoe, the recipient of a gold medal from the Society of Illustrators and an ALA Notable Book Award for his book *Stevie*.

An African American brother and sister recount situations when their loving father, a single parent, turns into a "monster."

Daddy Is a Monster... Sometimes is an entertaining look at a kind of African American family rarely depicted in the media, with a single black man as the head of household. The special relationships between "Daddy" and his children come alive as we see them go through the daily tasks that make up family life everywhere, bedtime rituals and delays, rough play and household accidents, and shopping trips. In one scene the family is at a restaurant and the children are playing with their food and teasing each other. Bweela describes how the public monster comes out, "When we go out to a restaurant Daddy sometimes turns into a monster, but only just a little bit so nobody sees him doin' it."

When the children ask their father why he turns into "an ugly old monster sometimes," he says, "What? Me—a monster? I'm never a monster." "Yes, you are," they say. "Sometimes you a scary monster and you say, 'Go out and play. Grrraaaw.' And sometimes you say, 'Javaka, pick up all your toys. Grrraaw!'" The father responds with, "Oh, yeah. Well, I'm probably a monster daddy when I got monster kids." *This book is a fun read for all "monster kids" and a gentle springboard for discussions about behavior.* ROSA E. WARDER

Baby Says

John Steptoe, Edited by ALC Staff
African American
1988, Lothrop, Lee and Shepard

Initially, Kevin is not impressed with his white-haired baby-sitter, Lovey Pritchard. His tantrums and attempt to leave with his mother get no response from Ms. Pritchard. But he becomes intrigued and pleasantly surprised to find out she reads books, loves baseball, and roots wildly for her team. Shocked, surprised, and lured by curiosity, Kevin takes a liking to her.

He finds himself so engrossed with her that he does not even hear his mother when she comes in the door from work.

An African American boy of five learns to get along with his baby brother.

Instead of the soap opera-watching, nail-polishing, romance-novel-reading baby-sitter he expected, Kevin gets a wonderfully energetic and enthusiastic friend.

This almost wordless picture book relies on the illustrations to capture the feelings and moments shared by Kevin, his baby brother, and the baby-sitter. Especially nice are the illustrations clearly depicting his curiosity about the baby-sitter and the love he has for his baby brother. While the characters depicted are African Americans, this story provides all parents struggling with issues around childcare, insight into children's responses to being left with people they don't know. *It's a great story to share with young children when you're preparing them to adjust to someone other than Mom or Dad taking care of them.* MARTHA L. MARTINEZ

My Special Best Words

John Steptoe
African American
1974, Viking Children's Books

Illustrated in gorgeous, brightly colored cutout photographs, this storybook is told from the perspective of three-year-old Bweela. Describing her interactions with her little brother, cat, baby-sitter, and father, she points out the "special best words" of each. Her brother Javaka's standard response at her attempts to correct his hygiene is "takeabreak". Among Gunkie, her babysitter's, special best words are "ssshtheladydownstairsissleeping." Bweela's own special best word is "prettyful." Her father's is "Iloveyou."

175

Because this book does not represent a heterosexual nuclear family, it provides an encouraging model for children of gay parents or single parent household. It also shows children interacting with one another with and without adult support. Bweela takes initiative in helping her brother toilet-train, for example. Her father is a playful and supportive parent shown in all kinds of domestic interactions, not just as the man who tosses the ball around with his son on Saturday, which shows children that fathers and siblings can also play roles that children's books usually assign only to mothers. CHRIS MAYO

African American Bweela describes her interactions with her brother, cat, baby-sitter, and father in a classic from the '70s.

Stevie

📖 ✒ John Steptoe
African American
1995 (1969), HarperCollins, ✳ Audio Cassette

Before Stevie came, Robert played with his friends and spent time with his mother. But one day Stevie shows up and everything seems to change. One day, Stevie comes to live with Robert and his family temporarily. Stevie, by Robert's account, is spoiled. He is used to having his way, he gets Robert into trouble with his mother, and he tags along everywhere Robert goes. To top it all off, he seems to be getting all of Robert's mother's hugs and kisses. What Robert wants more than anything is for Stevie to go home.

African American Robert is put out by having to share his things with Stevie, until Stevie moves away.

Then one Saturday, Stevie's parents pick him up and announce that they are moving so Stevie won't be back. Robert should be happy, so why is he moping?

Stevie was written and illustrated by John Steptoe. It was published when he was just sixteen. Although it is his first published work, the story and illustrations are timeless.

Most children can sympathize with Robert's plight. They understand his feelings of jealousy and abandonment. Children can understand Robert's feelings of loneliness when Stevie leaves. Even though Stevie seemed to be a pest, he was still a companion and playmate.

Stevie explores many topics: extended families, mother-son relationships, sibling rivalry, and the loss of a friend. YOLANDA ROBINSON-COLES

The Tangerine Tree

📖 Harvey Stevenson
Caribbean, West Indian
1995, Clarion Books, 📕 Wyeth, Sharon Dennis *Always My Dad*.

The Tangerine Tree offers an honest, if difficult, portrayal of the separation of a close-knit family forced to split for survival. The events are described in frank terms, and the characters are believable, including young people with whom children will be able to identify. Because of this book's subject, it is not recommended for standard storytime reading but is best used to assist children in similar circumstances to talk about their experiences.

Ida's father is leaving her family's home in Jamaica in order to try to secure a better life for his family elsewhere. The entire family rallies around Ida to ease the blow, but despite this support, Ida is incredulous, then enraged. She retreats to her favorite hideout, the tangerine tree of the title, in a cascade of tears. Finally, however, Ida forgives her father and hope is restored to the whole family.

Stevenson's illustrations manage to capture rural Jamaican homelife with color. His combination of searing brights with cool, muted pastels evokes both the intensity of the Caribbean landscape and the somber mood of the characters. HEATHER ELDRIDGE

Ida is distraught that her father must leave their Jamaican home to find work in the United States.

The Dove

📖 Diane Stewart ✒ Jude Daly
African, Natal
1993, Greenwillow Books

Set in Natal in the eastern part of South Africa, this novel centers on the lives of Lindi and her grandmother, Maloko, who struggle to survive the elements and other harsh realities of their daily lives. A recent flood

An African girl saves herself and her grandmother through her creative efforts.

has ruined their chances for living off their crops or animals, so Lindi journeys into town with her grandmother to sell beadwork. The shop owner turns them down, suggesting they try near the beach. With scores of other women selling there, the odds for selling their work are slim.

Inspired by a beautiful dove, the grandmother places the bird's image on the beadwork. Seeing more than a beautiful dove, Lindi encourages her grandmother to show it to the shopkeeper they had spoken with the day before. The shopkeeper finds the dove fascinating and buys it, asking them if they can produce more. Their creativity, hard work, and persistence pay off. The grandmother's work sells well at the shop. Their hopes are also restored when spring comes and renews the barren earth.

Diane Stewart has created two very endearing characters in this tenderly written story. How people who are often faced with adversity can create something both inspiring and utilitarian is something that needs to be understood by more of us.
MARTHA L. MARTINEZ

On the Riverbank

📖 Charles Temple 🖌 Melanie Hall
African American
1992, Houghton Milton Company

A young boy eagerly awaits the end of the school year so that he can go night fishing with his parents. The story is written in a rhythmically soothing prose that conveys the often peaceful and serene atmosphere of the country.

We witness family togetherness as they all partake in the ritual of fishing. At the end, they work together to tug at the heavy line, weighed down by the many catfish they have caught. The story shows that even a small child can participate in such "grown-up" activities and is useful in helping. At the end, all have put in their share of work, and are pleased to know that shortly they will be enjoying a catfish fry.

An African American boy learns to fish with his mother and father by the riverbank at night.

Although the natural surroundings are represented as a comforting and giving environment, the child has some initial fears of his surroundings. But the fear is assuaged by his comforting parents and a sense of familiarity and security that they bring to the surroundings. Harmony, unity, and peace become underlying themes for this simple and endearing little story. The softly colored illustrations beautifully capture the mood and feeling of a country sunset. MARTHA L. MARTINEZ

Maria's Secret

📖 June Toretta-Fuentes 🖌 Mikki Machlin
Hispanic
1992, Paulist Press, 🎁 Palacios, Argentina, *Christmas for Chabelita*.

Going from store to store and place to place in her village, Maria sings of a secret that no one can bribe out of her. Even when Juan the fisherman attempts to pry the secret from Maria by offering her "a nice big fish" for dinner, Maria manages to guard her precious secret until the day of her great-great-grandmother's 100th birthday celebration.

In accordance with tradition, everyone in the village has prepared something to give to Mamacita, Maria's great-great-grandmother. On the appointed day, all the villagers walk to Mamacita's celebration to give her the presents. When it comes to Maria's turn, she does not have one. Instead, Maria tells the villagers that Mamacita knew they were going to celebrate her birthday and that she and Maria have, in turn, prepared presents for the villagers. With that, Maria helps Mamacita distribute the packages. The villagers are pleased at the gesture of kindness and reciprocity and also thank Maria for not spoiling Mamacita's surprise.

A young Latina has a big secret that she won't reveal until her great-great-grandmother's one-hundredth birthday celebration.

MARIA'S SECRET
by June Toretta-Fuentes
Illustrated by
Mikki Machlin

Although not everybody lives in such a tightly knit community, such gestures of kindness can still be encouraged and instilled in young children. Stories such as *Maria's Secret* provide creative venues for teaching young children the value of kindness and reciprocity. The simple pen and ink illustrations provide soft and tender renderings of Mamacita and Maria.
MARTHA L. MARTINEZ

Five Things to Find: A Story from Tunisia

Verna Wilkins   Barry Wilkinson

African, Tunisian

1993 (1991), Tamarind Books

North Africa is often neglected in the context of the Middle East as well as Africa, so it is particularly pleasing to find a children's story set in Tunisia. *Five Things to Find: A Story from Tunisia* is the tale of a wise man with three children, each of whom is gift-ed in a different way; Hassan is strong, Yasmin can run as fast as the wind, and little Fatima is clever. Everyone feels sorry for Fatima because she is little and shy. The children's father chal-lenges them to find five cleverly defined items, and he urges them to work together in this task. Hassan and Yasmin, eager to please their father and bring favor to themselves, each rush off alone; however, both fail. In contrast, Fatima spends most of the allotted time thinking about the puzzle that her father has posed, and she alone succeeds in solving it.

A wise man from Tunisia teaches his children that by working together, they can accomplish difficult tasks.

The message that the father—and the story—seeks to convey is obvious but important: each child has a special but different skill or talent, and by working together, they complement each other and can accomplish difficult tasks more easily. This may be a particularly appropriate moral for young children in the intended age range who will proba-bly already have become conscious of the differ-ences between themselves and their friends and classmates. Through discussion, this point can be extended from the realm of individual skills and talents to that of peoples and cultures.

Five Things to Find illustrates one of Arab society's basic values: respect for one's elders, and one's father in particular. Like most Arab children even today, Hassan, Yasmin, and Fatima would be unlike-ly to consider arguing with their father, and each wants above all to please him. The extended family remains the predominant social unit in Arab society, and although the story includes neither a mother figure nor an extended family, the action takes place within a family context. As in other families through-out the Arab world, Hassan, Yasmin, and Fatima are expected to depend on each other.

The watercolor illustrations in *Five Things to Find* depict a traditional lifestyle, justified by the story's "once upon a time" setting. However, as American children's exposure to North African society is like-ly to be minimal, this would be a good opportunity to point out that the lifestyles of most Tunisians today bear little resemblance to that depicted in the story; this is particularly true in urban areas.

A two-page discussion guide at the end of the book provides a basic framework for discussing the story's emphasis on problem solving. Other suggested activities and discussion questions focus on agricultural resources and the environment, and would be more relevant to a general discussion of Tunisia than to the story itself. A final series of questions about the story are posed in the present tense (e.g., "What do people wear?") and are potentially misleading if care is not taken to distinguish between the past (in which the story is set) and the pre-sent. LESLIE NUCHO

Daddy's Roommate

Michael Willhoite

Gay/Lesbian/Bisexual

1990, Alyson Wonderland Publications, Inc.

A young boy describes spending weekends with his father and his father's partner and lover, Frank. The story depicts typi-cal family activities, rang-ing from making dinner to going to the beach to working around the house. The boy seems happy and the pictures imply that his mother is very accepting as well.

A young boy talks about the time he spends with his father and his father's "signifi-cant other."

This simple picture book emphasizes the fact that gay relationships look very much like heterosexual relationships. Working, playing, fighting, and lov-ing are all present. This can be a reassuring book for young children who have gay parents or who have

friends whose parents are gay. The use of the term "roommate" is unfortu-nate, however, that word implies a less serious or permanent relationship than is portrayed.

This book would be a good addition to a collec-tion of books on families, though it should be recognized that it portrays a white, middle-class couple. More books are needed that include gay couples who are African American, Asian American, Native American, and working class. SUE FLICKINGER

Working Cotton

Sherley Anne Williams, Edited by Carole Byard
Carole Byard
African American
1992, Harcourt Brace and Company

Written in the Southern black dialect unique to that time period, this picture book is narrated by a girl who describes the process of working the cotton fields with her family. The entire family works in the field. Even

A young African American girl relates what it is like to work in the fields with her family.

the mother who must tend to her infant does so on the field next to those picking cotton.

The girl wishes she were bigger in order to help out her family by taking on a greater share of work. She knows that because of her size there are limits to the amount of work she can contribute. "If I was old as Ruise or Jemarie, I could pick fifty, even a hundred pounds of cotton a day," she says. She

looks at her older sisters with envy.

The narrator observes that the only constant in her life is her family. All the others on the field she may never see again because, after

the season is over, they all go their separate ways. This makes it notably difficult for her to maintain friends. She notes that picking cotton is an all-day event and her family is weary at the end of each day.

This book makes the life of cotton workers and struggles of slavery easy to understand at a very basic level. The author makes it obvious that the children working in the fields do not have a true childhood because of the labor that they must perform. They are not allowed the freedom that other children may have. Readers are given an idea of what it is like to be a migrant child, and what the daily routine is like. The illustrations are done in soft colors and capture the essence of nature.
MARTHA L. MARTINEZ

A Chair for My Mother

Vera B. Williams (translated by Aida Marcuse)
African American
1994 (1982), Greenwillow Books, William Morrow, ✳ Series, Spanish

179

A Chair for My Mother, written and illustrated by Vera B. Williams, tells the story of a girl, her mother, and her grandmother saving money in a large jar to buy a comfortable chair when all of their possessions are destroyed in a fire. After a move to a new apartment and a party to which their neighbors and family each bring something for their new home, they have the basics. But they have nothing soft to really get comfortable in. The

three of them have their heart set on a chair that is fat, soft, and covered in velvet with roses all over it.

Each contributes what she can to the jar. The girl sometimes helps out at the diner where her mom works and puts in her pay. Her mom puts in tips from the diner, and grand-

An African American family lose all of their belongings in a fire and save their money to purchase a new chair.

ma puts in change from grocery shopping. Gradually, after about a year, the jar is filled, and they shop for their dream chair. After trying out chairs in four stores, they find what they are looking for. The story ends with a picture of the three of them snuggled in the chair.

The illustrations in this book are rich with color and detail. The chair, painted in a deep magenta with large pink roses and small green leaves, looks like you could sink right in. Williams uses a lot of yellows throughout the book to give a sense of warmth and light on all the pages except those describing the fire. These are gray and smoky looking, giving the sensation that your hands will get dirty when turning the page.

This book has three strong female characters who provide a positive model for getting things done. They function well as a family working together toward a common goal. They are also clearly part of a larger community, helping to break down an urban stereotype of people not caring about or willing to help others in a city. *Along with the strong people elements, this story could be used to explore math concepts of money, time, and interest.*
DEBORAH PATTERSON

Three Days on a River in a Red Canoe

Vera B. Williams

Gay/Lesbian/Bisexual

1986 (1981), William Morrow & Company

Illustrated with maps, detailed pictures of flora and fauna, recipes, and instructions, this picture book tells the story of a canoe trip taken by a family composed of two women and their children. Armed with dried apricots, freeze-dried chicken, and loads of gear, and a detailed map with routes marked out from trips taken by the two women before the children were born, the four set out. Besides detailing events along the way, like catching crayfish and observing a swallow's apartment building, the book contains instructions for simple knot tying, fire building, simple camp recipes, and how to put up a tent. CHRIS MAYO

An early picture book that tells the story of two women and their children's canoe trip.

Jalapeño Bagels

Natasha Wing   Robert Casilla

Jewish, Hispanic, Mexican

1995, Simon & Schuster

The scent of baking bread rises off the pages of this realistic celebration of the cultural diversity of the American family. Few books reflect the richness of families with roots in more than one culture as well as Natasha Wing's *Jalepeño Bagels*. Pablo's Mexican mother and Jewish father own a bakery, a *panderia* as his mother calls it. When Pablo tells his parents that he must select something that reflects his culture to share with other students on International Day, his mother suggests that he choose a baked good to share. Pablo agrees to help his parents in the bakery on Sunday to help make his decision.

Pablo assists his mother first, making traditional Mexican treats: *pan dulce* (Mexican sweet bread), *empanadas de calabaza* (pumpkin turnovers), and *chango* (bars filled with nuts and chocolate chips). As he pours, stirs, and kneads, Pablo considers each treat for sharing at school the next day. When Pablo's father calls from the back room for help making bagels, the boy shapes dough into circles, then tries his hand at braiding a traditional Jewish challah (a bread leavened with yeast and glazed with egg before baking).

Wing's succinct style is as easy to follow as a recipe. Casilla's realistic artwork not only illustrates the story, but provides visual cues to the book's underlying theme: the richness of multiple cultures. Mexican *ristras* hang heavy in the front window of the bakery framing baskets overflowing with Jewish bagels and stacks of braided challah. Toasted browns peppered with bright red and green bits of jala-peño evoke the mother's Mexican roots, while a framed prayer recalls the father's heritage.

Pablo selects a mixture of both his parents' cultures to represent his family's heritage for International Day.

When all three family members come together to make their own specialty—jalapeño bagels—Casilla's double-page spread readies the reader for Pablo's choice. The heart of the book lies in Pablo's reason for choosing to share his family's jalapeño bagels on International Day. "They are a mixture of both of you," he tells his parents. "Just like me!"

This book pleases the eye, the ear, and the palate. Recipes are included at the end of the story, along with a glossary of Spanish and Yiddish words used in the text. Beyond the value of the story itself, Jalapeño Bagels *offers teachers a number of options for classroom usage. Teachers may wish to use this book to introduce the idea of sharing the cultures of their students by having their own International Day.* KIM GRISWELL

Children's Books: Buyer Beware

Janus Adams

ONCE UPON SOME NOT TOO FUTURE TIME, IN *a land with neither snow nor particular sun, a community lives a strange existence. Devoid of memory, the people are without feeling. Devoid of a past, they know no sadness, fear, or repercussion—except for the Giver, who bears Memory, with its pain and life-sustaining lessons for all. As the time comes for this mysterious elder to pass on his burden of history and truths of this strange life, Jonas, a boy coming of age, is chosen. As the Receiver, he will know hunger, feeling the fulfillment of life, and eventually the choices he must make will affect everyone.*

So goes the plot of Lois Lowry's *The Giver* (Houghton Mifflin), winner of the 1994 John Newbery Medal—the American Library Association's highest honor for a children's book. Dedicated to "all the children to whom we entrust the future," *The Giver* has been widely praised as one of the most sensitive, powerful, compelling books to be published in years. Not only is *The Giver* a best-selling gift book for teens, it is a read-aloud favorite of parents eager to share this allegory with younger children.

On the surface, its warning against the devastating effects of forgetting our past is laudable. Then we learn that the Giver has actually rejected the opportunity to impart knowledge to his only child—a daughter—whom we never meet and who, it is implied, will take care of him in his declining days.

While one book does not a trend make, this book has received some of the publishing industry's highest accolades—not only in the United States but also internationally. Yet it is a book in which life-giving roles of male and female are reversed. The choice of who will bear future life-giving responsibilities deliberately rejects females in favor of males. The figure of the African oral historian, the griot as holder of memory-in-mind and relayer of divine wisdom and guidance is supplanted by a white man. What's going on here? We are now twenty-five years into the crusade to provide children with gender-neutral, nonracist materials. While truly excellent works

are being written and published, children's literature is far from being free of sexism and racism. Often, these and other forms of bias are merely more implicit and more subtle than in the past. To complicate matters, independent and specialty bookstores, which are more likely to stock a range of non-mainstream, progressive titles, are being squeezed out by huge chain stores in many areas.

In the now ten-year-old Eyewitness Series from the highly respected publisher Dorling Kindersley, elegant and realistic books use design elements to carry the theme or story. In the book focusing on botany, the flowers look as though you can pick them right off the page; the musical instruments are just waiting to be played in the book on music. In *I Can* and *Me Too*, author and illustrator Susan Winter brings us a pair of books for two-to-five year olds. The same children are pictured throughout—a young boy and his younger sister. Every other page proclaims what he can do; the facing page shows what she cannot do. And so it goes through both books—exalting his skills and laughing at her weaknesses. While the books are meant to show a younger sibling emulating an older sibling, it is notable that the younger, less competent one is a girl. This subtle gender patterning is not uncommon in today's children's books.

Caron Chapman, executive director of the Association of Booksellers for Children, says: "A parent may think in the dead of night, 'I've got to find a book for my child to read that shows a positive female role model.' But by noon the next day, they're totally burned out and the act of getting to a bookstore—especially a specialty bookstore—may be beyond their reality. The values are there, but the time isn't." Chapman closed her own feminist children's bookstore five years ago when customers started passing her by for the convenient locations and longer hours of the chains.

While chains will special order books, most customers choose from the limited number of books that are displayed in the racks. And what can be found there? At a mid-Manhattan Barnes & Noble, the racks upon rows of Sweet Valley High and the New Nancy Drew Series are disturbing. For those of us who grew up with neither the idea nor the reality of "nonstereotyping books," Nancy Drew was a true oasis. But readers who grew up as fans of that Nancy may not know that the series has been revised; the capable, independent, self-motivated problem solver has been rewritten to be more passive and appearance obsessed. Now, face out on bookshelves nationwide, our Nancy is barely recognizable on her girl-as-seductress covers — although, when placed next to the mindless, terminal cuteness of Sweet Valley High, Nancy seems like the pick of the litter.

A search for images of people of color at the same Barnes & Noble yielded two revealing titles: *The Indian in the Cupboard* and *Return of the Indian*. Published by Avon as recently as 1986, they cannot be explained away as so-called classics of a past time. In both stories, a plastic toy comes to life: "The Indian's eyes are black and fierce" as he jumps upright, knife in hand. Within two pages, he is "taking scalps."

In the children's section of Waldenbooks, younger children are treated to heavy doses of Disney movie tie-in books and the charming but limited Dr. Seuss. For older children, Roald Dahl and the slasher mysteries of R.L. Stine dominate. But there are some positive surprises — a wholesome (though scant) array of faces and stories more reflective of the real world.

At Borders — arguably the best of the chains, with 30,000 children's titles — many of the salespeople are former librarians and teachers. Yet, on the three tables and on all the racks in Stamford, Connecticut, the only female images on books featured face-out were a nebulous watercolor woman and the cover art of *Sea Witches*, with its stereotypical witch-as-scraggy-granny images.

Florence Howe, founding publisher of the Feminist Press and a scholar who helped lead the charge to improve images of women and girls in books, offers this perspective:

The reason the Feminist Press started to publish children's books was that there was a woman in Baltimore in 1970 whose seven-year-old daughter wanted to be a doctor. They went around to all the libraries and all the bookstores, and they could not find a book. And so we published The Dragon and the Doctor. *But just a year ago, I was at a conference where a lot of publishers of children's books were exhibiting. I decided that it was the right time to look for a book for my African American grandchild, who had always wanted to be a doctor. I started out by saying, "Do you have any books about African American women doctors or about an African American girl who wants to be a doctor?" I got the most offensive responses like "Why would anybody want such a book!" "Are you kidding?" "Don't be silly." So I just asked for books about girls who want to be doctors. I got exactly the same responses.*

The strange life of Charlotte Pomerantz's *The Princess and the Admiral* is especially enlightening. This fable, about a thirteenth-century Vietnamese princess whose knowledge of tides foils an attempted invasion by Kubla Khan, was originally published in 1974 and received the Jane Addams Children's Book Award (for outstanding children's books that nurture peace). Despite the prize, critical acclaim, and strong sales, paperback rights to the book were rejected by twelve different publishers, and the book went out of print. Even though the fable was based on a true story, prospective publishers insisted that the princess be made into a prince. Thankfully, the Feminist Press has reprinted *The Princess and the Admiral*, but the book's history points to an infuriating manipulation of images.

The facts of life on the business end of publishing also influence our choices. The biggest consumers of children's books are libraries and schools. The library market alone yields 60 to 80 percent of children's books sales. And because more children are now learning to write in school from commercially available books instead of textbook "readers," schools are an increasingly important market. But due to government-funding cutbacks, the library market (both school and public libraries) has shrunk dramatically, and schools do not have the money to present a solid variety for students in the classroom. The drop-off in library and school funding therefore puts more of a burden on concerned parents.

The declining demand from libraries and schools also puts pressure on the publishing companies. The trend toward corporate mergers and downsizing affects the availability of a range of quality children's books. For example, three literary houses (Bantam, Doubleday, and Dell) have been combined and acquired by a larger media conglomerate. Last year, there were layoffs at Little, Brown. Do shrinking staffs produce a commensurate shrinking point of view? Craig Virden, publisher of Bantam Doubleday Dell Books for Young Readers, admits: "I want to say no, and the answer probably is no. But anytime there's downsizing you run the risk of changing the size of the pool of opinion." If the opinion pool is shrinking, so are the number and variety of new books we can expect each year. Three years ago Little, Brown was producing more than 199 new children's books per year; it is now down to about 80.

Parents and other concerned adults can often find greater variety by looking to small, unique companies like Glenn Thompson's Black Butterfly Children's Books (with its African American themes), Mark Sottnick's Rabbit Ears Productions (with its audiobooks featuring celebrities retelling classic tales) and Sasha Alyson's Alyson Wonderland (with its emphasis on lesbian and gay families). It is also worthwhile to seek out local independent children's bookstores for quality and variety.

For me, this article began writing itself a year ago, when my daughter purchased an innocent-looking book, *The Courage of Sarah Noble*, at her school's book fair — an event intended to provide children with an opportunity to choose their own "affordable" books. Settling in at home with her treasure, she was quickly disappointed. The story of a Puritan child in seventeenth-century New England was sprinkled with sketches of Sarah and her "Indian friend." Sarah was dressed in every piece of clothing she could find; her "Indian friend" was one loincloth from naked. Having learned early lessons of hatred only an African American child can know, my daughter took the slander of Native Americans personally when they referred to the "Indians" as "little brown mice running across the

field." I was incensed that this ignorance was being revived for my child even after my mother had fought so hard against it for me.

We both learned a lesson that day about the way long-out-of-print negative images could worm their way into our lives. Out-of-print "backlist" titles can return at any time. Reprinting backlist books can be immensely profitable, since the publisher already owns the property, and up-front costs such as editorial, layout, and design are already paid. Over the years, experiences such as my daughter's have also been a lesson about the continuing lack of people of color as decision makers in the publishing industry. So even when titles are published with "multicultural" content, few people of color are in places to determine what that content is to be.

Clearly, the adults who are the consumers of children's books must heed many lessons as we navigate this landscape. We must learn to be discerning readers of works that may be sending subtle messages of race or sex stereotyping. Even more of a challenge is making sure we go out of our way to find those books that dare to envision a truly new world, one that celebrates our diversity. These will be our children's classics.

Janus Adams is founder and publisher of Back Pax, a multimedia company that is devoted to producing multicultural, non-sex stereotyped books and cassettes for young people. The company received a Parents' Choice Award in 1990.

Grade Four to Grade Six

Where the Flame Trees Bloom

Alma Flor Ada ✦ Antonio Martorell

Caribbean American, Cuban, Hispanic

1994, Atheneum, Ada, Alma Flor, *My Name Is Maria Isabel*; Ada, Alma Flor, *Serafina's Birthday*.

184

Alma Flor Ada, author of *The Gold Coin*—a 1991 Christopher Award winner—shares eleven family stories from her childhood in Cuba. From her blind, uneducated great-grandmother to her grandfather Modesto, a stowaway from Spain who settled in Cuba, to her parents, aunts, uncles, and cousins. Ada's family members have helped her revisit some truly memorable moments in their lives.

Alma Flor Ada shares eleven family stories— memories of her childhood in Cuba.

The Cuba Ada recalls was one that was still young and filled with Spanish settlers. In the family stories, Modesto is helped by the captain of the ship he arrived on. Once on the island, he settles in Camaguay, Cuba, where eventually Alma Flor Ada was born. In another story, Modesto makes a fortune selling an RCA gramophone, but then the family falls on hard times. With the economy failing and his wife ill, Modesto has to decide between staying with his wife or saving his money.

In "Samone," the family houses a homeless man in exchange for his doing household chores and gardening. Although they have no "need" for another person on the grounds, the family takes him in. He works diligently and brings pleasure to the family by playing his accordion. But one day Samone has a terrible accident and loses the use of his hand. The music stops.

Through "Samone" and stories like "Rag Dolls," "Mathematics," and "The Surveyor," the flavor of this island and its rich history are vividly portrayed. Ada continues the family tradition of passing on these stories: several of them were translated by her daughter, Rosa Zubizarreta.

Antonio Martorell's creative illustrations bring the family history and lore alive. A close examination of the cover illustration will reveal the many faces of Ada's family in the tree. MAGNA M. DIAZ

Youn Hee and Me

C. S. Adler

Asian American, Korean

1995 (1968), Harcourt Brace

Eleven-year-old Caitlin Lacey lives comfortably in the suburbs with her divorced mother and younger brother, Simon. Although she isn't the best student in the world, she has several good friends, likes her school, and does well in sports, especially basketball. But life changes when Mrs. Lacey announces the family is adopting another child.

A European American family adopts an eleven-year-old girl from Korea in an enduring work from the '60s.

As the story opens, it has been three years since Simon was adopted, as a two-year-old, from Korea. His name has been changed from Si Won to Simon, he has learned English with ease, and he has grown into a typical American child, quickly establishing himself as a well-loved member of the Lacey family. However, it has now been discovered that Simon has an eleven-year-old sister still living in Korea. Youn Hee needs a home, and the Laceys believe that it's only right for Simon's blood sister to join their family.

Caitlin, who narrates the story in a likable, unpretentious voice, has mixed feelings about a third child joining the family. It may be nice to have a sister who is the same age, but what if they have nothing in common? Caitlan's fears prove to be well-founded when Youn Hee arrives. The undersized girl appears years younger than eleven. She speaks almost no English. She instructs Simon to address her as "Noona" but becomes angry when Caitlin calls her by that name. (Caitlin doesn't learn for months that the term means "older sister.") One of the most interesting aspects of the story is the tug-of-war between Caitlin and Youn Hee for the affections of Simon.

As his natural sister, Youn Hee expects obedience from the younger boy and is frustrated that he has become so Americanized that he no longer retains much of his Korean heritage. Caitlin feels her own responsibility as Simon's older sister slipping away and regards Youn Hee's attempts to "mother" Simon with jealousy and anger. She also feels frustration that Youn Hee continually rebuffs her attempts at friendship, and constantly talks about returning to her orphanage in Korea.

Strong characterization is the key to the novel's success. Caitlin, Simon, and Youn Hee are three-dimensional characters who speak, think, and behave as real children. Youn Hee is a particularly interesting character. She is fiercely independent and determined to follow many of her ethnic traditions. Although her understanding of the English language occurs almost too quickly to be believed, it's a necessary device because the reader then has the opportunity to understand Youn Hee's behavior through her own dialogue, rather than through Caitlin's observations. As Youn Hee slowly lets down her defenses and comes to accept the Laceys and their American lifestyle, the Laceys, in turn, become more accepting of Youn Hee and her background. The happy ending is well-earned in this satisfying story that realistically examines important issues of cross-cultural adoption. PETER SIERUTA

The Future-Telling Lady and Other Stories

James Berry
Caribbean, West Indian
1993 (1991), Harper Collins, Joseph, Lynn, *The Mermaid's Twin Sister*.

These stories are rooted in the folk traditions of Jamaica. Only two, "Cotton-Tree Ghosts" and "Mr. Mongoose and Mrs. Hen,"

A collection of West Indian children's stories that range from pourquoi tales to magic tales.

contain the elements that are standard in folktales. In "Cotton-Tree Ghosts," a girl sneaks off to pick almonds on a Sunday rather than attend church or complete her lessons. As a result, she is transported back in time to a plantation of old, complete with slaves and white plantation owners. There, she is greeted by a ghost who tells her a story about her family. "Mr. Mongoose and Mrs. Hen" inverts the tale whereby the weaker animal defeats the stronger through its intelligence.

The moral of the story seems to be that the weak should not let down their guard or seek justice from the predatory. The remaining stories feature children who attempt to render a bothersome brother invisible, struggle with homesickness, learn to control an ornery mule, and discover the course of their future.

Berry's writing is exuberant. He renders various Jamaican dialects that are easily read and understood. His signature repetition of words or phrases is in full effect in these selections. For example, in "Magic to Make You Invisible," Yunni believes she has made her brother permanently invisible. She cries out: "Oh God, my brother's bodyless! Dear God, Dear God, give him back a body to go with his voice. Do, give him back his body to go with his voice. Do..." Berry describes his settings with details that evoke vivid images. For instance, Boy-Don's loneliness is palpable in "Banana-Day Trip" as he searches for activities to fill the time with his elderly aunt and grandmother. Boy-Don's romp in the sea as well as his tearful interlude on the uncomfortable sofa in the quiet living room conjure up vivid images of homesickness. The characters are fully realized and embody many moods and attitudes of children everywhere. VIOLET HARRIS

A Day's Work

Eve Bunting ✏ Ronald Himler
Latino
1994, Houghton Mifflin

Francisco's *abuelo* (grandfather) has come to help his family now that Francisco's father has died. Because the grandfather speaks only Spanish, Francisco goes with him to the parking lot where many men wait for work. It is Francisco who lands the jobs by saying that that his grandfather is a fine gardener. But when the employer returns to find that they have pulled out all the flowers and not the weeds, Francisco

Francisco learns about integrity when he is caught lying for his grandfather, who speaks only Spanish.

must admit that he lied about his skill. It is his Grandfather who puts things right by offering to return to undo the damage and by refusing any pay until the work is complete. He tells his grandson that missing church and the Lakers on TV "is the price of the lie." The employer values integrity and allows them to return, offering further work because "The important things your grandfather knows already. And I can teach him gardening." The text and the watercolor-and-gouache illustrations are the fine collaboration of the team who has collaborated on previous titles. VICKI MERRILL

The Pinballs

📘 Betsy C. Byars

Multicultural

1987 (1977), Harper Collins, ✳ Audio Cassette, Series

Carlie, Harvey, and Thomas J. are three children who for very different reasons end up in a foster home. Sexually and physically abused by her stepfather, Carlie is rude and distant. Abandoned by his mother and left with his alcoholic father, Harvey suffers from two broken legs and the trauma of having been run over by his father. When he was only two, Thomas J. was abandoned by his mother on the doorstep of the elderly Benson twins.

The three meet when they are placed in the loving foster home of Mr. and Mrs. Mason. The Mason's have raised and shared their love with seventeen other foster children. Each child comes with his or her own unique set of emotional baggage. Carlie is afraid to love because it hurts too much. Harvey feels ashamed of his father's alcoholism and, denied his mother's lack of responsibility, Thomas J. needs desperately to find out where he came from. Each confronts, discusses, and struggles to accept their problems. Carlie compares herself and the other children to pinballs because they were continually bounced around, with little control over their lives.

In an early work of social realism, three children of different races are sent to live in the same foster home.

Never maudlin or misguided, the story revolves around the compelling emotional evolution of each child. Although they rage and hate, they also learn to love and find compassion for themselves and one another. Through their friendship, they come to realize that they can play a role in shaping their futures.

While the subject is tough and the discussions painful, Byars has also invoked humor to give the story a sense of a fuller reality. No predictable storybook ending exists to tie up loose ends neatly, but there is lots of insightful dialogue that helps young readers examine their own lives and where they stand in relationship to their families. Byars has also done a solid job of portraying how some of those who have been abused and abandoned can find themselves and the love and support of others.

Activities:
1. *Pick one of the three main characters and for a week write a daily journal as that character.*
2. *Show the movie* Pinballs, *an Afterschool Special Presentation.*
3. *Write about one of the main characters fifteen years into the future.*

BARBARA A. KANE

Our Brother Has Down's Syndrome: An Introduction for Children

📘 Shelley Cairo, Jasmine Cairo, Tara Cairo, and Irene McNeil

Mentally Disabled

1991 (1985), Annick Press, Ltd.

"Everyone is special" is the opening line of this beautiful children's book and it is also a ground rule for Jai's family. Written by members of his family—Jai's sisters, Jasmine and Tara—the book tells what it is like to have a brother with Down's Syndrome. Jasmine and Tara explain the ways that they help him and how he helps them. Though it may take Jai longer to learn how to do things, they emphasize that in many ways he is like other children.

Throughout the story, Jai's family speaks directly to the reader in a forthright, yet loving and sensitive manner. The girls explain Down's Syndrome though illustrations of a cell and a chromosome.

Written by the siblings of a child with Down's Syndrome, this book depicts their love and admiration for their special brother.

They explain that most people have forty-six chromosomes in each of their cells, but Jai, like other people with his disability, have forty-seven. They inform the reader that a person with Down's Syndrome takes longer to do things and that they look different from most other people. It saddens the girls when their brother is referred to as retarded. They recognize he has talents and ways of doing things that are different but effective. Jai's sisters feel that disabled individuals are just as special as everyone else.

The beautiful photographs invite the reader into Jai's home and into the family's lives. The reader also gets to see Jai interacting with his teacher, parents, and sisters in much the same way other children would. His family's love for each other is openly displayed with hugs, kisses, and companionship.

In the end, the sisters let us know, "Jai may be a little different (we all have different things about us), but mostly he's just like the rest of us." Powerful language and just as powerful love help these children build a strong and wonderful relationship with their brother. Pity and sympathy play no role in their relationship with their sibling. With so much written about sibling rivalry, it's refreshing to see a story in which siblings share love and respect for one another. BARBARA A. KANE

Walk Two Moons

Sharon Creech
Native American
1994, HarperCollins

This is the poignant story of a thirteen-year-old Native American girl's journey to find her mother, to know her grandparents, to accept her father, and to discover herself.

Salamanca Tree Hiddle wants to visit her mother on her mother's birthday, so her grandparents agree to drive her. During the trip from Ohio to Idaho, Salamanca entertains her grandparents with the life story of her friend, Phoebe. Phoebe's life is more outlandish than Sal's, but occasionally there are parallels. During the long trip, much is revealed about Phoebe, Sal's grandparents, and Sal's star-crossed mother and father. The trip is nearly complete before Sal sees how much has been revealed about herself. This coming-of-age journey, however, ends with a tragic death.

A Native American girl learns her family's history as she and her grandparents set out to find her missing mother.

This is a wonderful story, told with humor and tenderness, and is fully deserving of its 1995 Newbery Medal. Although the book's publisher positions it as a "Native American book," *Walk Two Moons* in fact does not focus on cultural or racial heritage, and references to Sal's Native American heritage are fleeting and undeveloped. For example, the mother is presented as exotic and mysterious. Further, the reader never finds out which tribe Sal's family belongs to, and none of her grandparents' stories delves into issues of Native American heritage. JANIS O'DRISCOLL

The Watsons Go to Birmingham — 1963

Christopher Paul Curtis
African American
1995, Delacorte Press

Kenny Watson is in the fourth grade. He can read books upside down and has an impressive dinosaur collection. But life is not without problems: At school he has to be careful of Larry Dunn, the king of kindergarten to fourth grade, who is prone to giving unsuspecting kids the Maytag treatment with fistfuls of snow. And at home there is Kenny's older brother, Byron. Byron is thirteen and an "official juvenile delinquent." Kenny likes to watch Byron's series of "Fantastic Adventures" at a safe distance, but sometimes there are penalties to pay. Kenny's parents try their best with Byron; but when Kenny gets conked, his mother becomes angered. This time, however, the consequences are worse than Kenny could imagine: The family is going to drive to Birmingham in their 1948 Plymouth, the "Brown Bomber," and there Byron is going to be turned over to the legendary disciplinarian, Grandma Sands, for the summer, possibly the whole year.

Told with humor and affection, this is a wonderful story about two brothers growing up. When the family reaches Birmingham, fiction is interwoven with fact and the mood shifts from comic to tragic. Throughout, author Christopher Paul Curtis masterfully maintains the perspective of his young narrator. In an epilogue, Curtis gives a concise, moving introduction to the civil rights movement of the 1950s and 1960s and the background of heroism and violence against which the story concludes. There are no easy answers here, but there is a family strong enough to pull through.

An alternately comic, tragic, and touching story of two African American brothers.

Since its publication, this novel has won numerous honors and awards. It has been named a Newbery Honor Book, a Coretta Scott King Honor Book, an American Library Association Best Book for Young Adults, and a *New York Times* Book Review Best Book, among others. Each honor is well deserved. This is a book that has much to offer any child. ANNE DAVIES

187

Abuela

📖 Arthur Dorros ✏ Elisa Kleven

Hispanic

1995 (1991), Dutton Children's Books

A young Hispanic girl in New York City goes on an outing with her abuela (grandmother). In the park, she imagines that she is able to fly, and invites her grandmother to join her in an imaginary flight. They soar over the Statue of Liberty and New York skyline, and visit the city's many neighborhoods. Once back in the park, Abuela suggests a boat ride. The young girl comments, "That's just one of the things I love about Abuela. She likes adventures."

A Latina Hispanic girl invites her grandmother on a fantasy flight around New York.

The grandmother is shown in a refreshingly non-stereotypical way. Although white haired, she is trim and attractive in her bright clothes. She is portrayed as youthful, spirited, and active, and the reader senses that this duo always enjoys doing things together. The gentle humor of this book underscores the affection between these charming characters. The story is told in simple and clear language. The Spanish words and phrases the characters use are skillfully integrated, and a glossary is provided at the end.

The real magic of this book, however, is provided by the vibrant, joyous illustrations. Everything, from the clothing to the windows to the kites in the sky, is beautifully detailed and filled with cheer. This book is highly recommended for younger readers. DAPHNE MUSE

Radio Man: A Story in English and Spanish

📖 ✏ Arthur Dorros (translated by Sandra Dorros)

Hispanic, Mexican

1993, HarperCollins, ✷ Spanish

Diego has a fascination with his radio and takes it everywhere that he and his migrant family travel. On their lengthy trips throughout the expansive Southwest harvesting the nation's crops, the radio becomes a source of news and information as well as a way to keep track of friends and other families through call-in shows. But it also serves as a way for older family members to share stories with the younger generation. The songs on the radio, for example, permit grandparents to share their lives with the younger generations.

Traveling with his family of migrant farmworkers, Diego relies on his radio to keep him company.

While the story is a great way for children in urban enclaves to learn more about those who bring our food to the table — especially migrant workers — the storyline does not provide a detailed view of how this lifestyle affects school, social lives, and the basic family structure. But the reader does get to see a Mexican American family, strong at the core and sharing some memorable times in the midst of grueling work and circumstances. MARTHA L. MARTINEZ

The Ear, the Eye, and the Arm

📖 Nancy Farmer

African

1995 (1989), Orchard, Puffin Books, 📖 Lowry, Lois, *The Giver.*

Only an author who has lived in Africa could have written *The Ear, the Eye, and the Arm.* Although this novel is set in the future — Zimbabwe, 2194 — strong elements of Zimbabwean culture permeate each page. Farmer did indeed live in Africa for a period of approximately twelve years, and her intimate knowledge of the country allows her to ground this highly imaginative work firmly in reality. First published in Harare, Zimbabwe, in 1989, this fast-paced thriller offers a richness lacking in many science-fiction novels for children. The strangeness of a foreign culture combined with the wonder of a future time excite the imagination and pull the reader into the intrigue of this futuristic world.

A science-fiction book set in Zimbabwe in the year 2194.

A robot doberman guards the house of General Matsika, Chief of Security for the land of Zimbabwe, and a genetically engineered blue monkey plays a role in the kidnapping of three important characters: Tendai, Rita, and Kuda — the general's children. When he discovers that his trusted Mellower has tricked him into allowing his children to journey into the city where they have been kidnapped, Matsika hires Africa's most unusual detectives to track the missing children. Known as the Ear, the Eye, and the Arm for their unique abilities to see, hear, and feel, the trio stays a step behind as they track the children from the underworld of Dead Man's Vlei (an early twenty-first century toxic dump populated by people so deformed they can hardly be called human anymore) to the soaring opulence of the swaying Mile-High MacIlwaine Hotel.

Tendai, Rita, and Kuda first fall into the clutches of the She elephant, a woman the size of an armchair who rules the vlei. A series of twists and turns winds the plot like a watchspring toward the climax, which finds Tendai in the hands of the Gondwannan Ambassador. His greatest desire is to sacrifice the lion-spirited son of his enemy, General Matsika, to the Big-Head Mask, the most ancient and powerful fetish of the Gondwannan people. Will the Ear, the Eye, and the Arm save the children, or will the mhondoro, the spirit of Zimbabwe which now resides in Tendai, rescue them from the clutches of death?

While exploring the realm of a possible future, Farmer's book shows a deep respect for Zimbabwe's past. The character Farmer calls the "Mellower" is reminiscent of the traditional Praise Singer common to many African cultures. Tendai, General Matsika's eldest son, wears the ndoro, an important symbol of rank once worn into battle by the ancient kings of Zimbabwe. The spirit world which flows in and out of Farmer's book provides a glimpse into a system of beliefs that guides this strongly religious culture. And the political turmoil that moves the plot recalls the ongoing strife between Africa's peoples.

A 1995 Newbery Honor book, Farmer's work is also the perfect book to pair with Lois Lowry's *The Giver. The book's appendix offers a number of ideas for further classroom study of Zimbabwe and its culture. The various tribes of Zimbabwe are discussed, as well as the importance of the Praise Singer in many African cultures. The book could also be used to encourage discussion of the issue of slavery, both in Africa and in the United States.* KIM GRISWELL

The Patchwork Quilt

📕 Valerie Flournoy   ✒ Jerry Pinkney

African American

1995 (1985), Puffin Books, ✳ Series

To Tanya, a year seems too long too wait for the patchwork quilt that her Grandma has promised

to make for her. Grandmother and Granddaughter have an understanding which grows as the quilt they share takes shape. Tanya's mother, distracted by her work and caring for the family, can't enter the quilting bee and the spirit of the project. She walks around the living room complaining about the mess that the scraps of materials are making on the rug. She suggests that she can buy a quilt at the department store. Grandma patiently understands her daughter and the many frustrations that she is encountering. Grandma says, "sometimes the old ways are forgotten." A quilt is a good way to bring back some of these ways.

This story portrays a strong middle-class African American family, a family structure not often seen in other children's books. The family is loving and caring to each other and to their Grandmother when she becomes ill. The family is dressed well, lives in a very nice home, where the father is a constant support to the mother and the children, especially when the grandmother becomes

An African American family captures their history in a patchwork quilt.

very ill. However, as Flournoy attempts to build a strong family image, she sacri-fices the characters, who accept stereotypical roles in the family. Father and sons are seen outside building in the yard, while Mother and Tanya are inside baking biscuits.

The scraps of material are all important to the quilt; each one traces and captures a piece of family history. There is a scrap of gold from Mother's Christmas dress, a scrap of blue from her brother Jim's favorite pants, a bright red square from her own Halloween costume. Jerry Pinkney's paintings and beautiful colors help children see how a family's history can be told by reading a patchwork quilt.

The reader can also explore the notion of how delicate one's health becomes with age. All ends happily in the story as Grandma recovers from her illness and completes the colorful quilt by adding a special dedication which she stitches into the corner of the quilt. The dedication reads, "For Tanya From Your Mama and Grandma." Grandma includes the three generations of women in the family and inscribes them into the quilt forever.

This book is well received by readers of all ages. The family reading this together may even feel like making their own "masterpiece" quilting project with their own family members.
MARILYN S. ANTONUCCI

Family Pictures/Cuadros De Familia

Carmen Lomas Garza

Hispanic

1990, Children's Book Press

Carmen Lomas's autobiographical story focuses on a girl in a traditional Hispanic community as she celebrates major rites of passage, including celebrating birthdays, picking nopal cactus, finding a hammerhead shark on the beach, and making tamales.

Family pictures and celebrations in the daily life of an Hispanic family.

The story focuses on Carmen's dreams of becoming an artist. Carmen shares her dream with her sister, and seeks her mother's support early in life, demonstrating her own commitment to her own life and earning her mother's respect. Carmen chooses to function in a role that is not usually looked upon favorably, especially for girls, but through hard work and her mother's love, Carmen achieved her dream.

This strong and compassionate story portrays the strength of this cohesive, functional, and loving family. The various pictures in the home speak volumes about their lives and the love and support they provide for one another.

Supported by good writing and a readable text, the magical colors and the spirited illustrations make for a solid book that may spark courage in readers to pursue their dreams.

DAPHNE MUSE

Talk About a Family

Eloise Greenfield   James Calvin

African American

1993 (1978), J. B. Lippincott Co., ✳ Series

Genny, her brother Mac, and sister Kim anticipate their brother Larry's return from the army because he can make things right again. Their father has not been working steadily, and he and their mother always seem to be angry at each other. Everyone in the house tries to hide behind smiles, but anger hangs in the air. Genny believes the welcome-home party planned may bring happy feelings back into the house.

Before the party, Genny hears her parents fighting, and the raised voices make Genny feel as if she's being hit. All the kids are affected and express their frustrations differently. Little Kim locks herself in her room, Mac stays out of the house, and Genny wants to wish the tension away.

Larry's return is joyous and Genny begins to believe her family is coming together again. Unfortunately Larry cannot fix what has fallen apart; Genny's father moves out, and none of the children can change the situation. Genny is confused, not sure where to direct her fear, anger, and hurt. All she knows is that she needs to be with her siblings. Genny begins to realize that although families may change, they still can be full of love. She simply has to get used to the new shape of her family.

An African American girl copes with her parents' separation in a book first published in the '70s.

This story focuses on children's perceptions and reactions to a family's break-up. The family's conflict is not resolved, so students may enjoy predicting what lies ahead for Genny and her siblings. *Talk About a Family* allows young people to discuss and identify with Genny's feelings. The illustrations lock the story into a specific era, the early 1970s, but the emotions Genny's family experience are timeless.

ALISON WASHINGTON

Not Home: Somewhere, There Must Be Love: A Novel

Ann Grifalconi

African American

1995, Little, Brown and Company

Not Home is a poignant novel about a family forced to separate by their economic and social circumstances. The novel is set in New York City, and the "home" which is "not home" is a church shelter for temporary and permanent wards of the court. Here two young brothers, Tommy and Dicky, are sent to live for several months while their mother undergoes treatment for a serious illness. Tommy, who is ten, is forced to live and sleep in the older boys' dormitory away from Dicky who is five. Through his narrative, Tommy explores the most frightening of scenarios for a child: loss of parents and loss of home.

Ann Grifalconi, a writer and artist, was inspired to write this book by her experience as a counselor at a children's home. She successfully transfers her memories into a detailed account of the emotional and physical world of the residents and staff there.

The reader learns in the first chapter that the brothers' father was hit by a stray bullet and killed five years earlier, and that Tommy has been the "man of the house" ever since. Tommy's warm memories of the love and support in his "real home" give him the strength to endure his own troubles and look after Dicky.

Jacob and Cara are the two primary staff characters, and their impact on the lives of stricken families is portrayed sympathetically. The characteriza-

During their mother's hospitalization, two African American brothers are sent to live in a church home.

tions of Tommy's roommates show the myriad ways they each learn to cope: Pinky is a prankster and bully; Sam is a tiny comedian with the manners of an old country gentleman; Joe is a big-muscled boy, and his equally big but none-too-bright sidekick Don, and the cool and silent Jimmy, have spent many years in the "home."

The relationship between Tommy and Jimmy best evokes the fear and isolation all the boys feel, as well as their sense that they need to protect themselves and each other from the "outsiders." Jimmy takes

the risk of breaking his cool silence to respond to Tommy and Dicky while Tommy finds a way to help Jimmy through the hardest challenge of his life.

Not Home is a unique novel full of themes to discuss with children in a school or home setting. The tone throughout the novel is sad, yet hopeful. The author portrays with sensitivity and compassion the vicious cycle of poverty and its effect on families. At the same time, she brings to light the judgmental attitudes many people direct toward the disadvantaged or homeless.

ROSA E. WARDER

The Ups and Downs of Carl Davis III

Rosa Guy
African American
1994 (1989), Delacorte Press, ✳ Series

Carl Davis III, a self-described teenage genius, is completely befuddled by his parents' decision to send him to South Carolina to live with his grandmother. A savvy and wise New Yorker, Carl finds the people of Spoonsboro dull, simple-minded, and oblivious to the challenges that affect blacks. In a series of letters to his parents and friends, Carl describes his loneliness, his exasperation with the seemingly backward black students, and the racist attitudes he faces in school, as well as his inability to connect with the grandmother he loves.

Slowly Carl begins to like the country, finds peace fishing, and befriends a dog. The dog's owners are Inge and Johan, two kindred spirits and Swedish outsiders to the Spoonsboro community.

An African American boy from New York learns to enjoy life with his grandmother in the South.

In school, Carl battles a teacher who doubts his intelligence and belittles him publicly. He faces scorn from the white students and mistrust from the blacks in class. Along the way, Carl sees his grandmother's quiet intelligence and deep love for him and finds out about his parents' personal struggles as they fought an unjust social system in the 1960s and 1970s. He also must deal with the death of his best friend from home and the almost fatal drug overdose of Johan in Spoonsboro. Carl sees that despite his intelligence, he has much to learn about social interactions and making friends. In the end, he doesn't want to leave his grandmother and decides "to devote my entire life to her—to live down here, with her, in the great outdoors." Although he must return to New York, Carl feels he has connected with others, affected attitudes, and understood some of the tenuous interactions of the people of Spoonsboro.

Carl's sensitive letters allow him to work out his mixed feelings about his family, come to terms with his grief and confusion over his changing world and friends, and rejoice in his family's solidity and his own well-developed self-esteem. The letters also serve as succinct history lessons for the reader. The reader may sometimes wonder if the words come from a child (even an intelligent one), but the letters do convince us that the voice heard is one of someone coming of age. ALISON WASHINGTON

191

A Girl Called Boy

📘 Belinda Hurmence
African American
1990 (1982), Ticknor & Fields

Blanche Overtha Yancey appreciates neither her name—passed down from generation to generation—nor the hardships that her ancestors were forced to endure. Then she is transported back in time to 1853 and witnesses slavery. A blend of history and fantasy, Hurmence's story provides the reader with vivid details related to the day-to-day lives of slaves: What they wore, what they ate, where they slept, how they acknowledged and celebrated various rites of passage are all beautifully woven into the story.

In this captivating and informative book, an African American girl transported back to 1853 becomes a witness to slavery.

With the exception of the traitorous Gump, "Boy" meets slaves who are generous as well as clever. Her experiences during her transformation back in time help her to understand rather than ridicule the plight of slaves.

A Girl Called Boy is wonderfully written, filled with suspense and finely drawn characters and the sheer sense of adventure in the story may appeal to some young readers who would not otherwise be interested in a story about slavery. Many youngsters rebel at the thought of reading stories about any kind of holocaust. But good writing with an overlay of drama and adventure can engage their minds and teach them about history at the same time.

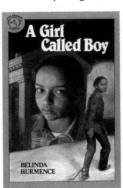

While some younger children can be introduced to basic information about slavery, children over twelve can engage in the discussion of the political and economic forces that drove this institution. ADRIENNE MARSHALL

When I Was Little

📘 Toyomi Igus   ✒ Higgins Bond
African American
1992, Just Us Books

When his young city-bred grandson Noel visits, Grandfather Will shares stories with him about what it was like to grow up in the early part of the twentieth century. The conveniences that exist in Noel's life were unknown to his grandfather, who had to hand wash and hang the laundry and carry blocks of ice from the store.

An African American grandfather takes his grandson fishing and shares stories of when he was a young boy.

While the story can be used to discuss how far we have come technologically, it can also serve to point up the fact that many people throughout this country and around the world do not have many of the conveniences young children often assume everyone has. Another important aspect of this story lies in the fact that Noel and his grandfather are African American men who have a refreshingly warm relationship.

Higgins Bond's black-and-white, photolike illustrations give a feeling for the early period of Grandfather Will's life and capture the essence of the stories he shares with Noel. MARTHA L. MARTINEZ

Losing Uncle Tim

📘 MaryKate Jordan, Edited by Abby Levine
✒ Ron Wennekes
Gay/Lesbian/Bisexual
1989, Albert Whitman & Company

Losing Uncle Tim shows, in a non-judgmental manner, a family confronting AIDS. In a somberly illustrated book, Daniel recollects the fun and conversations he had with his uncle Tim before Tim's death from AIDS. He recounts their closeness and his own fears of getting AIDS from his uncle. Reassured by his father that AIDS cannot be transmitted from visiting or hugging, Daniel continues to visit and talk to Tim even when he is in a coma. After Tim's death, Daniel finds that his favorite uncle had paid careful attention

Daniel recollects the fun and conversations he had with his uncle Tim before Tim's death from AIDS.

to what Daniel had admired in his antique store; Uncle Tim has left those things to Daniel.

Though not the main theme of the book, the parents' ease at having their son visit a presumably gay uncle and to continue to be close with him until his death shows what a nonhomophobic, non-AIDS-phobic family can do to help an ill relative and to help a child understand illness and death. In contrast to other representations of people with AIDS, Tim continues to be supported by his friends and family. But despite the author's subtly coding Uncle Tim as gay by making him owner of an antique store, Tim does not appear to have a partner, or even male friends. While this is a potentially positive move to dissociate gayness from AIDS and to make the book accessible to a variety of children whose relatives with AIDS may reflect a range of identities, Tim appears isolated from a gay community that has provided much care and support for people with AIDS. Still, this is an important book in its clear message of care and support for family members with AIDS. CHRIS MAYO

How My Family Lives in America

📦 ✒ Susan Kuklin

Multicultural

1992, Bradbury Press

Susan Kuklin, whose books have been hailed as "models of photojournalism for young readers," could be called the Bill Moyers of children's documentary books. She is the Listening Ear, the Asker of Good Questions. *How My Family Lives in America* takes us into the daily lives of three children: an African American, a Puerto Rican American, and a Chinese American. Each child introduces us to his or her family, and we learn about their customs and activities. Richly eloquent and lively photographs bring it all to life.

Three ethnically diverse children describe their families' cultures and traditions in this model of good multicultural literature.

Foreign words scattered liberally throughout the text are natural and unintimidating in the context of the stories. Also included in this book are tasty recipes from each home and culture.

How My Family Lives in America will leave children with a sense of the fabulous texture of voices and tra-

ditions woven into our land. Some fastidious critics, however, may blanch over her use of "America" instead of "United States" in the title and text, "Hispanic" for "Latino/a." *The book may also be used as a model for an activity in which students document ethnic traditions alive in their own homes.* NAOMI SHIHAB NYE

The Magic Moth

📖 Virginia Lee ✒ Richard Cufari

Physically Disabled

1972, Seabury Press

Chronicling a family's efforts to come to terms with the death of a child, *The Magic Moth* strives to demonstrate how children can develop a thoughtful attitude towards people with life-threatening illnesses. Told from the siblings' point of view, the book is an admirable, if sentimental, attempt to deal with this difficult subject in an honest way.

A somewhat misguided story about a young girl who is dying from a heart defect.

The story describes serious cardiac dysfunction, the process of dying and its aftermath. However, the dying girl, Maryanne, is never made a full-fledged character, and while the dialogue is well meaning and sensitive, it is sometimes misleading. When one of the characters asks why Maryanne died, for example, the mother's response is weak and ineffective: "That is something I don't know for sure, Mark-O, but some people do not seem to be meant to live very long." Moreover, the plot often feels contrived, and too many things go unexplained. There is also a real lack of interaction between Maryanne and her siblings. More thoughtful writing and a more multidimensional portrayal of the family would have enhanced both the plot and power of this story.

With death from illness occuring at alarming rates among young children, there is a need for more books that comfort souls and answer questions. While this one poses more questions than it answers and is not as comforting as it ought to be, it does provide some insights into the struggles that families encounter when dealing with a terminally ill child. MEREDITH ELIASSEN

Full Worm Moon

📖 Margo Lemieux ✒ Robert Andrew Parker
Algonquin, Native American
1995 (1994), William Morrow & Co,
📚 Quiri, Patrici Ryan, *The Alonquins*; Severson, Leigh, *Native American Primary Thematic Unit.*

A portrait of family togetherness that encorporates Algonquin history and folklore, *Full Worm Moon* is a warm, beautifully illustrated picture book. The afterword explains that this is Lemieux's attempt to imagine what life might have been like for the Algonquins

A warmly illustrated story of an Algonquin family on the night of the Full Worm Moon.

before the Pilgrims came, but the book will seem relevant to contemporary families as well.

The book is set on the night of the Full Worm Moon. Algonquins measured the calender year by the cycles of the moon, and named each full moon after significant natural occurrences. The Full Worm Moon takes its name from the worms that rise to the surface of the ground to fertilize the soil.

Atuck and Mequin, the children of the family, beg their mother to tell them the story about the coming moon. Their father suggests that they stay up to view the event. After dinner the four of them go out to the field to wait. Once outside, the mother begins telling the story, which explains why there are seasons and why worms rise in the spring. The story emphasizes the relationship between humans and nature.

The illustration is particularly effective in these scenes, in images of the family cuddled together under a blanket, and in depictions of the mother's story. A gradual transformation occurs, and the reader can see, as the children do, that the worms are rising in the morning light.

Full Worm Moon ably introduces and explains a little-known folktale and tradition of the Algonquins. Presented in clear, accessible language that is also sometimes poetic, the book offers children enjoyable characters who will seem very familiar.

LISA MOORE

Imani and the Flying Africans

📖 Janice Liddell ✒ Linda Nickens
African American
1994, Africa World Press

One perennial motif in African American folklore and literature is the idea of Africans who fly away from slavery. Several versions of the tale are available, notably those of Julius Lester and Virginia Hamilton. Liddell presents the tale in a different format. She maintains some folkloric elements such as passing down important cultural information via storytelling and also includes the literary device of transporting a contemporary character to another time in order to convey an essential history.

A scary contemporary retelling of the African American folktale in which slaves "fly away" from slavery.

Imani and his mother are driving from Detroit to Savannah, Georgia, to meet his grandparents, and great-grandmother. Imani is bored and tired by the long drive. His mother tells him a story in order to help the time pass quickly. She tells him about Savannah, some of the historic sights, and the tale about "flying Africans" who dance in a circle while singing. They lift into the sky one-by-one and fly back to Africa.

Imani falls asleep dreaming of flying Africans when his mother stops for gas, and Liddell begins her fantasy. Imani is kidnapped and taken deep into the woods by a fearsome stranger. He escapes when he runs into an elderly African American woman, who tells him to remember the powers and spirits of his ancestors. He does and flies away to his grandparents' home. When he discovers that the elderly woman who aided his escape is his great-grandmother, Imani gladly meets his family members.

This book is frightening. The surrealistic illustrations add to the terror of Imani's kidnapping. Harsh lines that emphasize a wild scraggly body with facial hair, jagged, rotten teeth, and fiery red skin combine to create a horrific kidnapper. Liddell's story grabs the reader, and tension is not eased until Imani flies away and the reader becomes aware of the fantasy.

Imani is the most complex character in the story. His mother, grandparents, and great-grandmother remain nameless except for terms of endearment such as Bigmama, Bigdaddy, and Granny. Some readers may want to know why Imani's mother has not informed her family of their grandchild and great-grandchild's existence until now, given her strong belief in family. Adults should prepare to discuss these and other aspects of the text.

VIOLET HARRIS

My Mother and I Are Growing Strong

📖 Inez Maury ✏ Sandy Speidel

Hispanic

1979, New Seed Press, ✳ Spanish

When Emilita's father is sent to prison, her family and world change forever. She and her mother, Lupe, take over his job, gardening in Ms. Stubbeline's flower garden. Emilita and her mother learn new skills and discover inner strengths that sustain them financially and ultimately protect them from a thief who tries to threaten them.

In a 1970s book with new relevance, a Latina girl is determined to help her mother during her father's incarceration.

These are not weepy women overcome by their circumstances. Lupe's determination serves as real support for Emilita. Their relationship is honest and inspiring. Emilita's mother is forthright in telling her young daughter how her father ended up in prison. She is also very reassuring in her efforts to instill a sense of the importance of fairness and justice. Maury provides a realistic yet tender portrayal of the fears that arise when Emilita goes to visit her father.

My Mother and I Are Growing Strong was put out in 1979 by New Seed Press, as part of its innovative program of children's books dealing with difficult social issues. Unfortunately, as the prison population soars, it is now more timely than ever.

DAPHNE MUSE

Somewhere in the Darkness

📖 Walter Dean Myers

African American

1994 (1992), Scholastic, Inc.

Fourteen-year-old Jimmy Little is not unhappy with his life; school may be hard, but Mama Jean, the aunt who raised him after his mother died, loves and understands him. So when a man called Crab appears and tells Jimmy that he is his father, Jimmy is stunned. Crab says he's been released from prison, is on his way to a job in Chicago, and wants Jimmy to come along so they can get to know each other.

A sensitive story of a teenaged, African American boy who meets his estranged father.

Jimmy hasn't seen or thought about his father in the nine years since his father was involved in a botched robbery that resulted in the killing of a guard. Torn between the security of Mama Jean's New York home and the possibility of having a relationship with his father, Jimmy warily decides to take a chance and sets out on a trip of revelations.

Crab has lied to Jimmy on most accounts: Crab actually escaped prison when he was being treated at an outside hospital, and Chicago is a pit stop on the way to Crab's hometown in Arkansas. Crab wants his son to know that he was not responsible for the guard's death and hopes Rydell, an accomplice in the robbery, will verify that. Crab is very ill and needs Jimmy to believe that his father made mistakes but was not a killer. After the lies, the apparent coldness, and the distance between them, however, Jimmy decides, "he didn't really like Crab .... He almost had to know about him, but he really didn't like him. But he thought that one day, if things worked out, he could." An ailing Crab wants to begin again in California with Jimmy, but knows a life on the run is not possible for them. Although Jimmy believes Crab is not a murderer and even begins to like the man a little, he decides to go home to Mama Jean.

Myers writes sensitively of two people linked by family but separated by painful circumstances and time. Jimmy is not lambasted for his decision to go with Crab but applauded for his sense in the topsy-turvy situation. A fast read, the story deftly tackles the strained father-son relationship and two people's attempts at forging a connection.

ALISON WASHINGTON

Turning Pictures into Words

ANYA MUSE

*Having grown up on a healthy diet of multicultural
children's literature, including books by Eloise
Greenfield, Virginia Hamilton, Candy Dawson Boyd,
and Laurence Yep, I realize how much the illustrations in those books meant to me. When I saw
Walter Dean Myers' Brown Angels, it looked so
much like my own family photo album. As a mother
of a three-year-old child, I want my own daughter to
use the family photo album as a way of knowing and
accepting who she is.*

*As Walter Dean Myers does so well in his books
Brown Angels: An Album of Pictures and Verse
and Glorious Angels: A Celebration of Children,
you can find many stories in your family photo
albums. I grew up in a house where the walls were
covered with photographs of generations of family
history. When I was a young girl, I would study those
photographs and those in my family photo album,
making up stories about the people in them. Here is
a recipe for a family album storybook:*

- ✷ Select a series of three to five photographs.
- ✷ Write what you know about the people in
  the photographs or make up stories to go
  with the pictures.
- ✷ Take the photos to a copy center and have them
  reproduced, along with your stories.
- ✷ Put the stories and photographs together
  and have them bound at the copy center.

*Now you and your family have a book that you
have created about people you know. You can also
make multiple copies to give as gifts to other family
members.*

*Anya Muse lives in Oakland, California and is
preparing her four-year-old daughter for the 21st century
by filling her literary and technological diets with
great multicultural books, CD-ROMS and expansive
experiences.*

Edgar Allen

🔖 John Neufeld

African American

1969 (1968), Dutton, 📕 Randall, Florence Engel,
The Almost Year.

Narrated by Michael Fickett, the twelve-year-old son
of a white minister, *Edgar Allen* describes what
happens to Michael's family—which includes his
fourteen-year-old sister Mary Nell and their two
much younger siblings—when Reverend and Mrs.
Fickett adopt a two-year-old African American boy
named Edgar Allen. Michael and his parents are
charmed by the bright-eyed,
intelligent child, and the two
younger children immedi-
ately accept him as a playmate, but Mary Nell, swayed
at least in part by her school
peer group, is resistant to
the idea of a black child
joining a white family.

The adoption is also challenged by the community.
A cross is burned on the
Ficketts' front lawn. Children are withdrawn from
the pre-school that Edgar Allen attends. The family is
ostracized in stores, school hallways, and church
itself. Ultimately, Michael's parents decide that the
situation is not working out and return Edgar Allen to
the orphanage.

The last chapters of the book reveal the detrimental consequence of this action. Mary Nell
finally agrees that Edgar Allen should not have
been removed from the family and Michael loses
faith in his father, a man who has suddenly
betrayed his own conscience. Even the community,
which has shown its disapproval of the cross-cultural adoption, now rejects the Ficketts. Michael's
father is asked to find another church because the
congregation cannot respect a man who did not
defend his convictions.

Although the family gains some insight into
their own prejudice, this is not a story with a happy
ending. Reverend Fickett loses his job; his family
loses respect for each other and slowly tries to
rebuild their faith in one another; and Edgar Allen,
who had grown to love this family, is taken away,
too young to understand why any of this occurred.

The slim volume, divided into many small chapters, makes fast reading, although the emphasis is
on philosophy rather than plot. *There is lots to think
about in discussing the motivations of these well-rounded characters. Are the Ficketts well-intentioned or self-
serving in their adoption? In sending Edgar Allen back
to the orphanage, who suffers most—the Ficketts, the
community, or Edgar Allen himself? Are Edgar Allen's
feelings considered at all? Why do those who resent the
adoption, such as Mary Nell and the parishioners,
resent it even more when Edgar Allen is sent away?
And though the book was published in the late sixties,*

*A provocative
story of inter-
racial adoption
first published
in the 1960s
that is still
popular and
relevant today.*

would the same situations occur today in this country? These questions can stimulate some very constructive classroom discussion for a book that may require some adult guidance in its depiction of racism and occasional racial epithets.

While this title presents interracial adoption from the perspective of the white adopting family, a book for somewhat older readers, *The Almost Year* by Florence Engel Randall, shows an interracial family situation from the point of view of the African American child trying to fit into a white family. PETER D. SIERUTA

Forbidden Talent

Redwing T. Nez, as told to Kathryn Wilder
Native American, Navajo
1995, Northland

A young Navajo boy's grandfather warns him that he must use his artistic talent respectfully.

Ashkii, a young Navajo boy, is a talented painter. But he uses his skills mischievously: he paints spots on his dog and turns a horse into a zebra. He also drinks from the forbidden Owl Springs and climbs cliffs to look at secret designs made by the Ancient Ones. Ashkii's grandfather warns him that his talent is a gift from the Creator that must be used purposefully. Unable to understand or accept what his grandfather says, Ashkii sets out on a path of defiance and rebellion. Though some of his acts are humorous for the reader, they are nonetheless disturbing to the grandfather, who ultimately shares his wisdom and brings about a greater sense of respect and understanding in his grandson.

For many younger readers, *Forbidden Talent* may have to be read more than once for a full understanding of the grandfather's teaching, but the oil-on-canvas illustrations nicely capture Ashkii's mischievousness as well as the loving and tender wisdom of his grandfather. DAPHNE MUSE

Sitti's Secrets

Naomi Nye   Nancy Carpenter
Arab American, Middle Eastern, Palestinian
1994, Simon & Schuster Children's Books

"People are far apart," says Mona, an American child of Palestinian parentage, "but connected." She is thinking especially of her grandmother Sitti in a Palestinian village on the other side of the world. With her father, she goes there to visit and quickly forms an attachment to Sitti.

Though neither speaks the other's language, Mona and Sitti work out their own ways of communicating and spend many hours together. Mona helps her grandmother and observes life in the village and the little delights that the old woman finds in life, such as the fragrance of fresh mint. When the sad day of her departure comes, Mona takes with her many memories of her grandmother and the bond between them. Sitti also gives Mona a little handmade purse with a picture of Sitti's lemon tree stitched on it, a symbol of simple daily pleasures and continuity.

The author clearly writes with knowledge of the details of Palestinian village life, and the illustrator conveys the idyllic, almost mystical quality of Mona's visit. Text and pictures are well matched in the child's poetic, subjective description of her experiences. The reader will enjoy the images, learn something about another culture, and gain a positive impression of the traditional lifeways of Palestinian Arabs, an impression sorely needed to counteract the all-too-prevalent negative notions about Palestinians that Americans tend to acquire from the inadequate and biased way that information reaches us.

An Arab American girl visits her grandmother in Palestine in a warm story that tries too hard to be positive.

In this sense, the book represents a significant break-through in American publishing for young people, and many readers and their children will

find this lyrical story totally satisfying. For me, however, something seems to be missing. The author seems to avoid any suggestion of a harsher reality. Not that the political situation of the West Bank has to intrude and not that we need any grim social problems pointed out, or reminders of the hardships of a traditional woman's life, but too much sweetness leaves one with little food for the emotions.

Moreover, a jarring note comes toward the end. Upon her return, Mona writes a letter to the American president, telling about her grandmother, "worrying" about the news on TV, and "voting" for peace. The "peace message" strikes me as an intrusion, as if added on to make the story fully acceptable. A more natural way to handle it might have been for Mona to tell her friends about Sitti.

Because Sitti's Secrets *does not address the many issues surrounding Palestinian life in the West Bank, the book probably would not in itself inspire much discussion in the classroom. What it does offer is reaffirmation of connectedness, along with a charming glimpse of traditional Arab home life. It could supplement further reading or presentations on Palestinian culture (such as food, crafts, and the exquisite embroidery on women's dresses, attractively hinted at in the illustrations)—and Palestinian history.* ELSA MARSTON

Shaina's Garden

📖 Denise Lewis Patrick ✏ Stacey Schuett

African American

1996, Aladdin Paperbacks/Simon & Schuster, ✳ Series

Another title in the Gullah, Gullah Island series, *Shaina's Garden* combines magic realism with a tranquil portrait of family life, as Shaina explores her new garden. Her father takes her to pick out the prettiest tomatoes in the world and she wonders if her vegetable beds will have patchwork quilts tucked under them. But her older brother James laughs and explains that a "vegetable bed is the place in the ground where plants can grow." The entire family joins her in raking the soil and sowing the seeds. And the magical Binyah Binyah Pollywog helps her keep the plants from being thirsty. After weeks of anticipation, her father brings her bounty from the harvest and Shaina realizes her dream as a real gardener.

An African American girl and her family discover the magic of a garden in this book of the Gullah, Gullah Island series.

The book is cleverly written and also beautifully illustrated. *The story is especially useful for providing teachers with some creative strategies for building their student's vocabulary.* The skin tones and physical features of the characters vary, and Shaina displays a wide range of expressions on her face during the course of the story.

Through this series, young readers come to know this family and their lives on their island.

There are coloring books, board books, sticker books, toys, videos, and software that are part of the Nick Jr. Series as well. DAPHNE MUSE

Amy and Laura

📖 Marilyn Sachs ✏ Tracy Sugarman

Jewish, Physically Disabled

1966, Doubleday and Company

Amy and Laura's lives have been permanently changed by their mother's serious injury in a car accident. Returning as a stranger to her own home, the mother feels alienated and the family tries to understand how the accident has affected their lives.

A useful but flawed story of two Jewish American sisters whose mother has a car accident.

Sachs's portrayal of the girls' reaction to their mother's accident is realistic. Amy and Laura are depicted as neither heartless nor callous, simply unable to understand what all this means, due in part to their father's "protective" shielding and in part to their own fears about their mother's injury and her future.

The story also follows the two girls outside of the home, as they attend school, make friends, and fuel their sibling rivalry. Unfortunately, the storyline stumbles. Amy and Laura's relationship is well developed, but the father's remote relationship to the daughters is not fully addressed. The language is also somewhat dated, and the sophomoric dialogue sometimes slows the pace of the story. Even with these flaws, more and more young people find themselves helping their parents through major illnesses, stories that demonstrate how some young people meet that challenge are very useful.
MEREDITH ELIASSEN

Marilyn Sachs
Amy and Laura
Illustrated by Tracy Sugarman

The Bears' House

📖 Marilyn Sachs ✒ Louis Glanzman

Emotionally Disabled

1989 (1971), Doubleday and Company, ✳ Series

In this beautifully written account of a family under tremendous emotional and financial duress, a young girl takes the leadership role and tries to keep her mother and siblings from being institutionalized. Fran Ellen and her brothers and sisters love their emotionally disturbed mother deeply. They are keenly aware of the fact that their mother can't really care for them, and their new baby sibling. Their father is both emotionally and physically absent.

A beautiful story of five siblings trying to cope with an absent father and an emotionally dysfunctional mother.

Sachs delicately explores the world of children who are forced to take on responsibility too soon — children who have to abandon childhood in order to survive. Caring for the baby, her mother, and her siblings disrupts Fran Ellen's life. She ignores her hygiene and becomes passive and friendless. At school, she immerses herself in fantasy play with a toy dollhouse that belongs to the teacher. In it is a miniature orderly world where life is manageable and people love her.

The Bears' House
by Marilyn Sachs
illustrated by Louis Glanzman

A home visit results in Fran's teacher being shocked by the conditions she finds. But she is also impressed by Fran Ellen's efforts to deal with her problems. Sachs's story clearly demonstrates how the fragmentation of families and the lack of societal support often place an undue burden on children. While Sachs does no real finger pointing in the novel, the harsh burden of what Fran Ellen must deal with is conveyed forthrightly.

The powerful illustrations, sometimes used in double-page spreads, underscore the dismal reality of Fran Ellen's life.

MEREDITH ELIASSEN

Living in Secret

📖 Cristina Salat

Gay/Lesbian/Bisexual

1994 (1993), Bantam

Many children of all ages are familiar with the problems of divorce and custody, either by firsthand experience or through their schoolmates. In this novel, the principal character, Amelia, who is eleven, has been ordered by the court to live with her father. Her mother, who is a lesbian, has only limited visitation rights. Amelia and her mother decide to run away and live together with her mother's girlfriend in San Francisco. Because they are breaking the law, they must change their names and identities, and they must live with many secrets, as the title implies.

An engaging novel about a young girl who runs away from her father to live with her mother and her mother's girlfriend.

Living in Secret is an engaging novel written in clear descriptive language, centering on Amelia as she works to integrate herself into the new roles she must play to protect her newly formed family. Salat manages to weave many sensitive issues into the story — homophobia, emerging teen sexuality, racism, financial worry, and the complexity of human relationships — while keeping Amelia's voice genuinely youthful and full of emotion. Amelia learns to examine her own tumultuous feelings about her parents' divorce and the differences in their beliefs and lifestyles. Salat skillfully moves between Amelia's internal conflicts about her own integrity and her struggle to protect herself and her family from detection by the police. The reader experiences Amelia's difficulties keeping secrets as she works to create a new life, develop friendships of her own, and keep up with her schoolwork. Since the story is set in San Francisco, the depiction of a community of nontraditional family groups is more convincing. Amelia takes comfort in the company of other children with lesbian or gay parents.

Living in Secret is a realistic account of the issues and dangers of living in secret, and living as a lesbian. Amelia's mother and girlfriend are nicely developed as loving and concerned and as painfully imperfect as any other parents. Amelia does not simply live happily ever after in San Francisco. Her father's hired detective finds her new home, threatens her mother with legal action, and drags her back to her old life with her father. Again, Amelia is thrown into conflict by her desire to live with her mother and the relief of living without secrets in her father's home. As the story ends, Amelia has many decisions to make. The reader is left with the lesson that everyone makes choices and that each choice has its consequences.

Living in Secret creates an opportunity for parents and teachers to discuss the many difficult social issues children face on a daily basis. This novel would work nicely in conjunction with a school course in social studies or health and sexuality. ROSA E. WARDER

When Megan Went Away

📓 Jane Severance 🖊 Tea Schook
Gay/Lesbian/Bisexual
1979, Lollipop Power

Shannon is very sad that her mother's partner, Megan, has moved out. She wants to ask her mother about it, but her mother doesn't seem to want to talk. Shannon remembers the good times the three of them had together and also some of the times she made Megan angry. She begins to worry that it is her fault Megan left. Shannon finally gets angry with her mother and tells her that she doesn't like it when her mother is so quiet. The two of them begin to talk about Megan and how sad they are that she is gone. The mother assures Shannon that though they will be sad for a while, they will not always feel this way.

A sensitive but somewhat dated look at a girl's sadness after her mother's lesbian partner moves out.

This book, like many others, addresses the feelings children often have when one of their parents leaves. Children worry that they were the cause of the breakup and also don't know how to react to the parent who has been left. These issues are dealt with realistically and sensitively. This book highlights the fact that the ending of a relationship is difficult for all involved, regardless of the gender of the people involved.

The loosely rendered pen-and-ink illustrations are obviously dated, depicting the characters in the clothes and hairstyles of the late 1970s. While the inclusion of women who do not fit the stereotypical notion of beauty is admirable, the drawings present an almost stereotypical view of the dress and activities of lesbian women and their daughters. The timelessness of the story is not matched by the illustrations. SUE FLICKINGER

Welcome Home, Jellybean

📓 Marlene Fanta Shyer
Developmentally Disabled
1988 (1978), MacMillan, ✳ Series

Family life with a severely developmentally disabled sibling is portrayed in this fast-paced novel told from the perspective of Neil, a likable and sensitive twelve-year-old. His older sister Geraldine, who has unspecified developmental disabilities, has been placed in a series of hospitals and residential schools her entire life. Her latest placement, the Green Valley Regional Training Center, is depicted as particularly custodial in nature, with the residents spoon-fed baby food and receiving little attention from the staff. Mrs. Oxley has decided to bring Geraldine home to live and to devote herself full time to her care. It is apparent from the beginning of the story, however, that Mr. Oxley is not supportive of this decision.

A story about life with a developmentally disabled sibling, told from the point of view of her nondisabled brother.

A series of mishaps — Geraldine pushes the emergency button on the elevator, ruins Neil's homework, and throws the groceries down the incinerator (imitating Neil throwing away the garbage) — are shown as largely the result of Geraldine's institutionalization and lack of training. Under her mother's and Neil's tutelage, Geraldine slowly makes progress, learning to feed herself and speak in one-word utterances. Mr. Oxley, an aspiring musician, has been unable to adjust to Geraldine's need for constant attention, and decides to move into his own apartment to write music, suggesting that Neil might want to join him.

Neil is portrayed as a realistic middle schooler, alternately embarrassed by and supportive of his sister. When Geraldine disrupts his performance at the talent show in front of the entire school, however, Neil decides he's had enough and will move out with his dad. Neil's generous and wise nature wins out in the end in a poignant scene in which he reaffirms his loyalty to his sister.

This book emphasizes the family stresses of caring for a severely disabled child without including any of the community support services available; one wonders why Mrs. Oxley decides to go it alone without help. *Told from the perspective of the nondis-*

abled sibling, Welcome Home, Jellybean *can serve as a good discussion starter about family decision making and solidarity, but would need to be supplemented with other titles that show the disabled child's perspective.*
LAURI JOHNSON

The Boy of the Three-Year Nap

📖 Dianne Snyder   ✒ Allen Say
Asian, Japanese
1988, Houghton Mifflin

Laziness is dealt with in a most creative way in this picture book. In Japan, when a boy living alone with his mother grows up, he is expected to support her. Thus, the mother has a serious interest in encouraging her son to be a productive person.

A Japanese fable in which a lazy boy plots to marry a beautiful rich girl so he won't have to work.

Taro is healthy and clever, but he is "as lazy as a rich man's cat…if no one woke him, he would sleep three years at a stretch. And so he was called 'The Boy of the Three-Year Nap.'"

A wealthy merchant with a beautiful daughter moves in next door. Taro, the clever boy, comes up with a scheme to fool the merchant into offering him the daughter's hand in marriage, thinking that with a wealthy father-in-law, he would be set for life.

Dressed as a local god, he startles the merchant into an agreement. But Taro's mother has plans of

her own. She plants in the merchant's head the notion that Taro will not be much good without a job. As a result, the merchant arranges to put Taro to work as the family storehouse manager. This causes Taro to exclaim: "That was not part of my plan!" His mother replies "Do you think you are the only one who makes plans?"

Both the dialogue and the author's commentary elicit chuckles. Allen Say's masterful illustrations reflect the country of his own childhood. Full-page illustrations face each page of text. The details of Japanese life in an earlier time are especially intriguing, and the humor in the pictures matches the humor in the text. GINNY LEE

The World in Grandfather's Hands

📖 Craig Kee Strete
Native American
1995, Clarion Books/Houghton Mifflin,
📚 Copage, Eric, *A Kwanzaa Fable.*

Surrounded by huge concrete buildings, unfriendly people, and noisy neighbors, eleven-year-old Jimmy is angry and homesick since he and his mother moved from the pueblo to the city after his father's death. They now live with Grandfather Whitefeather in a place with "No trees, no tall corn, no vegetable gardens. Just concrete everywhere." Jimmy feels imprisoned by the tall buildings and, in this environment, struggles to heal from the loss of his father and his "home."

A Native American boy is upset when he and his mother must move from the pueblo to the city.

Grandfather Whitefeather advises Jimmy to carry the pueblo with him wherever he goes. With this advice in mind, Jimmy manages to find reassurance in ice cream, freshly mowed lawns, and pueblo memories. Through his mother's courage and his grandfather's patience, Jimmy learns to trust and open his eyes to new, but still scary possibilities.

Author Craig Kee Strete writes with an eloquence and ease that conveys vividly Jimmy's struggle to live in both worlds. Too few novels focus on Native Americans who reside in urban areas: this is an exceptionally good one. *Teachers might find it interesting to use Strete's book with Eric Copage's* A Kwanzaa Fable *in the same unit.* Both deal with young boys who lose their fathers and must adapt to big changes in their families and their lives.
DAPHNE MUSE

A Blessing in Disguise

📖 Eleanora Tate
African American
1995, Delacorte, ✳ Series

This modern cautionary tale shows how drugs destroy African American families and communities. The narrator, twelve-year-old Zambia Brown, lives with her aunt and uncle because her mother is hospitalized (ravaged by prostitution, drugs, alcohol, and AIDS), and her drug-dealing father, Snake La Range, has another family and refuses to take responsibility for Zambia. Nevertheless, Zambia is so dazzled by her father's glamorous lifestyle—fine clothes, fancy cars, and successful nightclubs—that she cannot appreciate her adopted family's love and moral values, taking a walk on the wild side, ignoring her aunt's warning about associating with the wrong crowd. Then a drug deal goes bad, leaving one child dead and one wounded in a drive-by shooting. These tragic events make Zambia finally understand her aunt's wisdom.

In a shocking, sometimes sensationalist, realistic portrait of an African American adolescent, Zambia is tempted by her father's glamorous drug-filled lifestyle.

Tate writes about multi-generational black family relationships; she targets adolescent readers who are at a pivotal point in the formation of their values. This is the third work in a trilogy (along with *The Secret of Gumbo Grove* and *Thank You, Dr. Martin Luther King, Jr.!*), focusing on youngsters searching for a sense of self-identity, peer approval, and parental love.

The novel's strengths include an authentic setting, credible plot, believable characters, consistent viewpoint, and engaging dialogue; it would appeal to readers all too familiar with the media's glorification of drugs and violence. While it seems unlikely that so many calamities could happen at once, this family represents much of what has gone wrong with the African American community. Zambia's narrative voice rings true: "Check this out...I had nothing to do again but sit on my bike in the middle of dull, dusty Silver Dollar Road. Worse, I was still in itsy-bitsy, countrified, do-nothing Deacons Neck, South Carolina." The author manipulates her audience with the stereotype of the "bad guy," sleazy Snake, but her portrait of a community trashed by drugs is convincing.

A Blessing in Disguise may not be wholly realistic, but the use of violence helps dramatize the situation effectively for an adolescent audience. Tate startles her readers, but more importantly, she affirms hope. With the strong positive influences of a loving family and other caring adults who believe in religion, hard work, and responsibility, Tate shows that communities can bond together to eradicate drugs and violence. If airing "dirty laundry" (and the laundry list here includes deadbeat fathers, incompetent mothers, violence, abused children, drug and alcohol addiction, and AIDS) can benefit children, then it is a blessing in disguise. LAURA ZAIDMAN

Grab Hands and Run

Frances Temple
Hispanic, El Salvadoran
1995 (1993), Orchard Books, Garlan, Sherry, *Shadow of The Dragon*; Temple, Frances, *Tonight by the Sea*.

Twelve-year-old Felipe must run with his mother and younger sister from El Salvador to escape the death squads. Felipe's father has already disappeared, and the family has agreed that if they must ever flee, they will go to Canada.

Having made the decision to escape, the family finds that there is help for people who are running away, but the journey is still very dangerous. Those who do not die are often left wounded, alone, or with a lifetime of nightmares. Everyone pays somehow—little children and old people, too.

After their father disappears, a family escapes from El Salvador to Canada, in a realistic story of refugee life.

The greatest fear the family has is for Felipe's missing father, Jacinto. While the family is in a U.S. detention camp waiting for admission to Canada, news of Jacinto's death arrives. They have no choice but to push on to Canada. At last, Felipe and his family do arrive in Canada to live every refugee's dream: "... to lead an ordinary life."

The frightening and challenging journey is told clearly and realistically from Felipe's perspective. He learns quickly that "Growing up is something you decide to do. It takes courage." The whole book reflects this matter-of-fact approach; there is no yielding to sensationalism. The story does not linger on the work of the death squads, but focuses on the family's frantic escape, a description of flight and the exhausting search for refuge that will ring true for too many young people. JANIS O'DRISCOLL

Gingerbread Days

📖 Joyce Carol Thomas ✏ Floyd Cooper
African American
1995, HarperCollins/ Joana Cotler Books

A series of poems celebrating family, one for each month of the year.

These poems and paintings celebrate the seasons of a family's love, from a January filled with the reassuring smells of fresh-baked gingerbread, to the gift-giving days of December. Along with an excellent selection of Floyd Cooper's paintings, Thomas's poetry stirs memories, celebrates the love of family, and affirms African American identity.

> *Daddy hands me a shirt of many blues*
> *And I've polished my sturdy shoes*
> *And Mama's pressed my overalls*
> *For the very first day of school falls*
> *in September*
> *I reach for new book*
> *And read about old heroes*
> *I compute numbers*
> *I calculate zeros*
> *Then pages of poems I memorize*
> *And paint the pictures*
> *Behind my eyes*

Floyd Cooper's illustration shows a young African American boy sitting on logs and reading a book, a

sight seen all too rarely in children's books — African American boys.

In "April Medicine," a mother's healing touch steadies a child. "December Song" acknowledges a father's love as the best present of all. These and other memorable, healing, and celebratory poems insure that Thomas's book will be read time after time and shared with brothers, sisters, aunts, uncles, and friends, in the true spirit of family love.

Teachers will find Gingerbread Days *to be a wonderful companion to the author's* Broomwheat Tea, *another fine collection of tenderly written and inspiring poetry.* DAPHNE MUSE

Waira's First Journey

📖 ✏ Eusebio Topooco
Aymaran/Bolivian, Native American
1993 (1987), Lothrop, Lee and Shepard

In this semi-autobiographical tale, Topooco introduces the reader to the Aymara — a people native to the South American country of Bolivia. First published in Sweden in 1987, *Waira's First Journey* recounts how the Spanish destroyed a relatively intact society and how that destruction has carried over into the present. Along with stories passed on by his parents, he tells of the current struggles to preserve ancient traditions.

Waira's First Journey allows younger readers to gain a limited knowledge of indigenous societies and civilizations. It also helps them to understand that the term Native American goes beyond the original

An introduction to the life of an Aymara Indian family before their people were colonized by the Spanish.

inhabitants of the United States. The accomplishments, contributions, and struggles of those societies require more in-depth presentation than Topooco has made in this book, but at least young people will come to know that the Aymara existed and can raise questions regarding this society's dwindling numbers. The illustrations provide a very detailed look at the ancient Aymara ruins in the city of Tiwanaku. MARTHA L. MARTINEZ

A Jar of Dreams

📖 Yoshiko Uchida
Asian American, Japanese American
1981, Aladdin Books, ✳ Series

Set in California during the Depression, this novel about the Tsujimura family depicts the struggles of early Japanese American immigrants in America. Aunt Waka, who is visiting from Japan, helps the family maintain its dreams, and struggle to survive in a hostile environment.

Uchida raises hard issues in a thoughtful way, staying true to the voice and perspective of eleven-year-old Rinko. After Rinko and her brother are taunted on the street, for example, she writes, "It made me really mad, but it also made me feel as though I was no good. I felt ashamed of who I was and wished I could shrink right down and disappear into the sidewalk. There are a few white girls in my class at school who make me feel that way too. They never call me "Ching Chong Chinaman" or "Jap" the way some of the boys do, but they have other ways of being mean. They talk to each other, but they talk over and around and right through me like I was a pane of glass. More than anything, I wish I could be like everybody else."

A girl grows up in a tightly knit Japanese American family during the Depression.

Everyone in Rinko's family has dreams: Rinko wants to become a teacher. Her older brother Cal has plans to study to be an engineer, but of that he says, "That doesn't mean anybody's going to hire me. I'll probably end up selling cabbages and potatoes at some produce market just like the other Japanese guys I know." Rinko finds out that her mother had dreams of becoming a teacher as well when she was in Japan, but, instead, she came to America to marry Rinko's father. Rinko's father has a dream of opening his own garage, but is afraid to make the investment during the Depression.

The characters are clearly drawn and have distinct personalities. While everyone's dreams are threatened or deferred, this book is ultimately about hope, struggle, and survival. Rinko raises questions in a way immediately identifiable to young readers.

One day, at Aunt Waka's urging, Rinko's father decides to confront the racist bully, Wilbur Starr, who is attempting to sabotage his family's business. When this happens, Rinko begins to feel less invisible. Rinko's family begins a collective struggle for pride and courage and this struggle gives us an insight into the hearts of thousands of Asian immigrants who faced and continue to face similar conditions. DEBBIE WEI

Justin and the Best Biscuits in the World

Mildred Pitts Walter ✎ Catherine Stock

African American

1990 (1986), Alfred A. Knopf Books for Young Readers

A novel for children that focuses on the maturation of a ten-year-old African American boy, *Justin and the Best Biscuits in the World* serves as an excellent prelude to a conversation about gender roles. Surrounded by women—his mother and two older sisters—since his father's death, Justin longs for the company of other males. Belittled by his sisters' constant nagging about chores that escape him and by his inability to complete tasks correctly, Justin considers cooking, cleaning, making his bed, and general housework to be "women's work." He would rather spend his time in the park playing basketball with his friend Anthony.

Elated by the visit of his grandfather and the chance to associate with another man, Justin jumps at the offer to go with his grandfather to the family ranch to take care of the animals and attend the local rodeo festival. During his brief sojourn in the wilds of Missouri, Justin learns how to make his bed, wash the dishes without splashing water, fold his clothes, and make the best biscuits in the world. He learns all of this from his grandfather, who assures Justin that these things are not women's work. When Justin returns from his visit to the ranch, he eagerly demonstrates to the surprised women he loves all that he has learned.

An entertaining story that addresses gender stereotypes and teaches about the history of African Americans in the American West.

Walter's effort not only addresses the issue of gender roles, but it also paves the way for a discussion of African American contributions to the westward movement, as Justin learns about Bill Pickett, Nate Love, and other legendary African American men of the West. Central to this lesson in African American history is the history Justin learns of his own family and their migration story, which he reads in a book written by one of his ancestors. An amusing tale, *Justin and the Best Biscuits in the World* also offers food for thought. CHRISTINE PALMER

Poor Girl, Rich Girl

Johnniece Marshall Wilson

African American

1992, Scholastic, Inc.

Miranda Moses is the only child of middle-class African American parents in a middle-class neighborhood. Her major concern is purchasing contact lenses to replace her thick glasses. Her parents, who also wear thick eyeglasses, resist buying the contact lenses because Mr. Moses has opened a new business and the family must depend on Mrs. Moses's dietitian's salary. Undeterred,

Miranda concocts a scheme to purchase the contact lenses herself.

The novel focuses on her setbacks and triumphs in a series of jobs (baby-sitter, grocery store stock clerk, summer camp counselor, and dog walker) as well as in her household duties such as cooking—which she dislikes but improves upon as she does it more and more.

Miranda and her family are believable characters. Other characters are primarily used as foils and are not well developed, such as Miranda's best friend Teena and her erstwhile "enemy" Catriona. Fuller development of these characters is missed; Wilson drops tantalizing hints about them but does not follow through. For example, Teena is afraid of the dark and seems timid because her family's home was burgarlized. Catriona is the spoiled princess but the reader discovers that her family depends upon her summer earnings. Despite these distractions, the novel is breezy and easy to read and presents a vision of healthy, "normal" African American life. VIOLET HARRIS

A precocious African American pre-teen wants contact lenses and is willing to work in order to pay for them.

205

"Other"

Peggy Gillespie

IN A WORLD OF RACIAL AND ETHNIC CHAUVINISM, multiracial families provide convincing evidence that races can coexist not only in the same neighborhood but also in the same home. Whether formed through marriage or adoption, these families have become a common sight in America. In the past twenty years, the number of interracial marriages in the United States has risen sharply, from 310,000 to more than 1.1 million, and the incidence of births of mixed-race babies has multiplied twenty-six times as fast as that of any other group. According to the National Council on Adoption, more than 8,000 foreign and transracial American adoptions occurred in 1992 alone. Despite these large numbers, standard demographics do not yet acknowledge multiracial categories. Instead, this expanding population of families must check the category marked "other" on official documents to indicate their race.

"The demographer's practice of fitting people into the available categories is part of the lingering legacy of slavery and results in imprecise information about the breadth of diversity in our communities and in our country," says Jacqueline Bearce, assistant to the superintendent for affirmative action in the Amherst-Pelham regional schools. "Consequently, there are people in our communities who are essentially invisible in terms of their racial and cultural identities." University of North Carolina freshman Ifeoma Nwokoye is the daughter of a Nigerian man and a white American woman. After her parents divorced, she and her two sisters left their home in Africa and came with their mother to live in the United States. Nwokoye's keen intellect and self-confident manner would seem to make her stand out wherever she goes. However, in her college application essay, titled "Mixed Blessings," she described the inner turmoil caused by her struggle with this enforced racial invisibility.

"All humans are confronted with an 'identity crises.' Biracial children too, must go through it and for them it is a greater challenge because it is doubly hard," she wrote. "In America, the idea of a biracial person is something that people are unwilling to accept as a 'legitimate' claim. In our daily lives, we are constantly confronted with times when we must define who we are. We check the boxes marked 'White,' 'Black,' or 'Other' on our college forms, but there is no space marked 'Biracial.' There is no place for me."

State Senator William R. Keating of Massachusetts has recently introduced Senate Bill 275 to mandate a "multiracial" category on forms requiring racial data. "Those of multiracial and multicultural heritage can feel very negative about themselves when they can only check 'other' — the last choice," Keating says. "Also, those of only one heritage may well be adopted and raised in families of a different background, and a child may wish to acknowledge this, too." Many states are now considering this type of change, and Massachusetts could be among the first to do so.

My husband and I are Caucasian, and our six-year-old daughter's heritage is African American, Native American, and Caucasian. If Bill 275 passes, Julianna will be able to check the new "multiracial" category by the time she is old enough to fill out her own school forms. Having a multiracial daughter has permanently changed my identity, too.

When I became a mother, at thirty-nine, I was deeply struck by the powerful rush of love I felt the moment my four-week-old daughter was placed in my arms at an American Airlines gate. Apart from her inherited beauty — lustrous dark eyes and a full head of black hair — my baby's racial composition was an irrelevant fact as we became a family. My concerns then were simple: learning how to change diapers and getting enough sleep. Six years later, my concerns are still fairly straightforward: making play dates, learning about Egyptian mummies, getting to soccer practice on time, and setting limits with an increasingly clever negotiator. However, my husband, Gregory, and I also take our daughter to almost every multicultural event within a reasonable distance and provide her with a multitude of books featuring children of color. We have begun talking with her about discrimination and prejudice, as well as racial pride — Julianna often dresses in her favorite kente cloth sneakers and matching raincoat, and she knows that her Native American ancestors were here long before Columbus. She does not appear to be perturbed by issues of racial identity yet; however, I am aware that our family will certainly confront complex and controversial issues related to race as Julianna grows older. As a way of investigating many of the unique challenges and concerns of multiracial families, I interviewed more than thirty families for a traveling photographic and text exhibition, titled "Other: Portraits of Multiracial Families." When the exhibit first opened in Northampton, a reviewer wrote, "Most obvious and important is something we suddenly realize we almost never

see: relaxed, intimate, tangible affection among people of different colors."

"As a family, we drive people nuts," says Eileen Madison of Amherst, an exuberant bilingual teacher with a Spanish accent. "Nobody can figure us out. I'm Puerto Rican, and I was married to a Cuban man who is the father of my first three kids — Luis, Patricia, and José. Six years ago, I married Rodney, who is African American, and I gave birth to little Reggie four years ago. Last year, Reggie kept asking me when he would start looking like his half-brother José, who has very pale white skin. Now, Reggie realizes that he's always going to have beautiful brown skin like his daddy's."

Although Madison's family may sound confusing to outsiders, twelve-year-old José is quite clear about the benefits of being part of a multiracial family. "People shouldn't judge others by what their skin color is but by their personality — just like my mom did when she married my stepdad," he says. "Kids don't *decide* to be racist. They are *taught* to be racist. So, I'm very lucky. I love my Puerto Rican culture, and now I have relatives on Rodney's side who tell me about their lives as African Americans, so I'm learning a lot about another race besides my own. In fact, I think there should be a lot more families like ours."

José's mother shares his enthusiasm. "Being in a family like ours, you grow so much to a point where you feel pity for the people who are not capable of seeing and getting something from all cultures. Before I fell in love with Rodney, I couldn't see beauty in black people. I didn't even look for their beauty," she admits. "But when you are in a multiracial situation, you start seeing beauty in *all* races. I feel like somebody took a blindfold from my eyes and I started appreciating people for who they are, not because of what color they are. And here's the confession of the day: the first time Rodney kissed me, all I could see was my parents' faces. I was imagining what awful things they would say if they caught me kissing a black man!"

Upon hearing this, her husband slaps his head in mock amazement and shouts, "I always wondered why that kiss was so limp!" The three older children laugh uproariously at this image of their parents' first kiss.

Interracial marriage was prohibited in most states for many years. It wasn't until the height of the civil rights movement in 1967 that the United States Supreme Court declared the last of the laws against miscegenation unconstitutional.

Maki Hubbard grew up in postwar Japan at the same time her future husband, Jamie, was being raised in a Milwaukee neighborhood composed entirely of white middle-class Catholics. "When I first went to study in Japan," Jamie recalls, "my grandmother told me, 'You better not bring a Jap home — they're sneaky.' And the level of prejudice wasn't much different in Japan. When I first started to date Maki, her mother thought that all foreigners were barbarians and didn't want me to visit her house." Maki's mother mellowed over time. "When my mother met Jamie formally, and he was speaking Japanese and he knew more about Buddhism than she did," Maki says, "she was overwhelmed and impressed. These days she listens to him more than she does to me!"

The Hubbards are respected professors at Smith College, in Northampton; Maki teaches Japanese linguistics, and Jamie is in the department of religion. When the Hubbards travel to Japan with their two school-age children to visit Maki's family, strangers clamor to get a closer look at them — especially at seven-year-old Alicia, who has light brown Shirley Temple curls, big dimples, and a disarming grin. "Because of Alicia's looks and light skin, people often ask if I'm her baby-sitter," Maki says. "In Japan, the word for biracial is *haafu,* or half, but we are careful to tell both our children that they are *not* half anything. After all, they've got twice as much as most people — two countries, two cultures, two languages."

There are extreme cases as well. A white woman from the Boston area was officially disowned and declared "dead" by her Jewish family when she married a non-Jewish black man. Her parents will never meet their two granddaughters; to them, these children do not exist.

Penny Rhodes, a Jewish Bostonian with a no-nonsense Yankee manner, is married to Irv, a fifty-year-old African American business consultant. She views black women's criticisms of their marriage as just one of the many "side effects" of any multiracial relationship. "When you make a commitment through marriage or by adoption to love a person of color," she says, "you cease to be the regular white person you were before. Automatically, you're agreeing to take on the impact of racism."

Penny and Irv Rhodes see their marriage as having a broad impact on people in their families, on friends of their kids, and especially on white friends whose children date people of other races. "In a way, Penny and I are like guideposts," Irv says. "If a friend's child goes out with a black person, they know that lightning is not going to strike when they walk out the door."

Their daughter, Lauren, a witty sixteen-year-old, agrees with her parents' views — at least on this topic. "Nobody's pure, anyway, so why make a big deal about it?" she says. "If you see a couple — either an interracial heterosexual couple or an interracial gay/lesbian couple — there's a reason for it. Cupid hit them with an arrow, and they fell in love. It's just going to happen."

Because of the scarcity of white infants and an ever-increasing availability of nonwhite children, more white families are also choosing to adopt Asian, Hispanic, and African American children. Bob Denig, bishop of the Episcopal Diocese of western Massachusetts, was living in Germany with his wife, Nancy, a landscape architect, when, after seven years of infertility, their adoption social worker asked them if they would be open to parenting nonwhite children.

"In the best sense, we didn't care one way or the other," Bishop Denig says. "We just wanted kids, and I really love the two children we have. The fact that they are African American is an important part of who they are; hence, by extension, it becomes an important part of who we are as a family. But what really stands out is that we are these four individuals who, by God's grace, or by serendipity, or by dumb luck, are thrown together. Somehow that seems more important than the racial issues. I'm not being color blind — we are who we are — but the best thing about our family is that *we are together.*" Eleven-year-old Nick maintains a droll sense of humor about his family. For a long time, Nick's standard compliment whenever his dad did something good was, "Not too bad for a white guy."

Lisa Miller, of Amherst, a labor and delivery nurse, specifically wanted a child of another race. "When I couldn't get pregnant with a second child," she says, "I went to an adoption meeting and saw a woman carrying a Korean baby. I held the baby, looked at my husband, Jedd, and said, 'This is it.'"

Like mixed marriages, transracial adoptions, particularly of biracial and African American children by white families, have stirred up private and public debate. When Freda Sbar, a single parent, first brought her adopted African American daughter home to Northampton, her parents did not call her. "They already considered my being a lesbian a tragedy. When I finally called them," she says, "they asked me minimal questions, such as 'Is the baby OK?' Clearly, they were not excited."

When teachers Debbi Friedlander and Eric Goldscheider, of Belchertown, were about to adopt Joshua, a two-year-old Jamaican, they told Eric's father about their plan and were angered by his response. "Wouldn't you want to consider adopting an Asian child?" he asked them. "Because the child's IQ would probably be much higher."

The National Association of Black Social Workers opposes these adoptions, too — for vastly different reasons. During 1972, the group issued its landmark position statement, calling transracial adoption a "form of genocide." The statement had a sweeping effect across the country, with many state and private agencies subsequently banning these adoptions. Although the number of adoptions of nonwhite foreign children has remained fairly steady for many years, the estimates of white parents adopting African American children fell sharply.

In an opinion piece in *The Springfield Union* in 1992, Annie Johnson, vice president of the local chapter of the black social workers' association, said, "I am firmly opposed to multicultural or transracial adoptions. These children experience special problems with personal and racial identity development. I think that white parents would have difficulty in teaching the black child to cope with the injustice and social realities of racism against people of color which exist in our system. Sameness gives one a sense of belonging and acceptance. To ignore the importance of race, ethnicity, and culture would be detrimental to the emotional stability of our children."

In 1993, Wade Henderson, the legislative director of the NAACP, told a reporter with the National Public Radio program *All Things Considered* that such adoptions not only scar the children involved but also hurt the African American people as a whole. "It's the pain of losing the fruit of our community," he said. "And it's the pain of losing one's children to the very culture that has historically been the source of so much suffering for African Americans."

Elizabeth Bartholet is a Harvard professor of civil rights law, the biological mother of a grown-up white son, and the adoptive single parent of two young Peruvian boys. In *Family Bonds: The Politics of Adoptive Parenting*, published by Houghton-Mifflin, she explains her disagreement with the National Association of Black Social Workers:

Adoption agencies throughout the land segregate children waiting for homes on the basis of race.... Black children are, as a result, condemned in large numbers to foster limbo, their lives put on hold while they wait for months, years, and often their entire childhood for color-matched families.... The studies of transracial adoptive families also provide an overwhelming endorsement of transracial adoption. They show that black children raised in white homes are doing as well in terms of achievement, adjustment, and self-esteem as children raised in same-race families. In a society torn by racial conflict...these studies show parents and children, brothers and sisters, relating to one another as if race were no barrier to love and commitment.... And this seems a positive good to be celebrated. The government should not be in the position of discouraging the creation of such families.

Sandi Ililonga, who is biracial, spent ten years in and out of foster homes and institutions because her adoption agency refused to place her with a white family. She was finally placed with a white family when she was twelve and believes that whites should be allowed to adopt blacks. To promote transracial adoption, she has become the spokeswoman of the National Coalition to End Racism in America's Childcare System.

"Not placing children in available homes is wrong," she told a large audience at the Open Door Society's annual adoption conference in Massachusetts. "It's a very racist policy, and I think it's a dangerous policy for the children involved. I know what happens to those children, because I went through that and my white

208

parents had to undo all the bad ideas that I had collected about myself because of this ten-year wait. Ironically, it wasn't until I was living in my white parents' house that I grew up with a picture of the black Jesus on the living-room wall."

Currently, there are approximately 50,000 children of African American heritage in the foster-care system, and more adoption agencies are beginning to respond to this crisis by permitting transracial adoptions. The current policy of racial matching (black children to black families only) would, in fact, become illegal under a bill now before Congress, cosponsored by Carol Moseley-Braun, a black senator from Illinois. The Reverend Jesse Jackson calls the bill a reaffirmation of the Civil Rights Act, saying, "Transracial adoption, like marriage, must be protected by law and must be open as an option for everyone."

George Holland, the chief executive officer of the Chemical Finishing Corp., in Westfield, is a conservative Republican and proud of it. His wife, Susan O'Neill, a former nun from a Boston Irish family, is a feminist psychologist specializing in the treatment of incest victims. Married for eleven years, they still battle over their political beliefs, but one thing they never disagree on is their belief that adopting two African American children — Zack, now four, and Amanda, now seven — was the best thing they have ever done.

As a white man working in the traditional business world, Holland hears a lot of racist comments from business acquaintances, especially directed toward blacks. "Let me tell you about my family," he usually responds, taking out of his wallet photos of his children. Along with Zack and Amanda, he has three children from his first marriage: Chrissy, his twenty-one-year-old adopted African American daughter, and his two biological children, Gillian and Michael.

"You should see the looks on my colleagues' faces," Holland says. "Suddenly, the conversation changes direction." His opinion of the transracial adoption controversy is even more blunt. "Frankly, I get very angry at black social workers' not wanting whites to bring up black kids," he says. "Part of me wants to say, 'I've just got a family here, folks, *so bug off.*'"

It is no surprise that multiracial families often seek a sense of solidarity within their own growing community. Throughout the United States, many of these families have formed support groups to talk about their concerns in an atmosphere free of external judgment. In western Massachusetts, a large group attends monthly gatherings and an annual camping trip with their children. Every other month, the adults gather separately at evening potlucks called "Guess Who's Coming to Dinner," where they socialize and hold formal discussions.

At a recent dinner, Heather and Alex Hiam of Leverett arrived with their new baby, Noelle. When Heather, the intellectual, green-eyed daughter of a black father and a white mother, was growing up in the 1970s, she remembers reading countless articles presenting vivid arguments against interracial relationships. "They always said that the children would suffer so much," Heather recalls. "Since that was so far from my own experience, I kept asking my mother, 'What are they talking about? Because I don't feel as though I've been particularly damaged.' My mother kept telling me that those articles were written by people with their own warped views and not to pay any attention to them."

Now a trade consultant to China, Heather Hiam has formed her own "second generation" multiracial family. She is married to Alex, a white business consultant and author she met while they were both at Harvard, and they have three biological children ranging in age from six months to eight years — and ranging in skin color from pale pink to light brown. "You can't solve race problems through having multiracial children," Alex says. "In fact, you end up passing your ideals on without having cleared it with your children in advance. But I don't think that it's a problem. I think it's a strength."

Away from the scrutiny of their critics, the clear consensus among these families is that they *are* in the vanguard, preparing the way for the inevitability of a truly multiracial society. "After all," Alex says, "people have great difficulty getting along with each other, so any little pockets of harmony — amid all the discord — are foundations on which the future can be built."

Grade Seven to Grade Eight

Bless Me, Ultima

📖 Rudolfo A. Anaya ✒ Dennis Martinez

Hispanic, Mexican American

1994 (1992), Warner Books

An enduring hallmark of Chicano literature, this rites-of-passage tale combines insights into the spiritual side of Mexican American life with an exploration of adolescence. Antonio is a young boy growing up in rural New Mexico, where he struggles with questions he has about his ability to fulfill his parents' dreams for his future. Antonio finds spiritual solace when Ultima, a *curandera* or folkhealer, comes to live with the family. Ultima shares her knowledge of traditional folk medicine and ceremonies with Antonio, and she helps him find a sense of stability. Antonio's experiences with Ultima evoke a sense of magical realism when he encounters a golden carp while fishing, or exorcises an evil spirit from one of Antonio's uncles, who has been cursed by local witches. Eventually, he begins to interpret his cosmological existence within a dualistic tension of good and evil.

The spiritual evolution of a Chicano boy in this entertaining morality tale.

The spiritual experiences of Ultima and Antonio may seem particularly foreign to some readers, but many Mexican Americans will find Anaya's authentic interpretations familiar, and will recognize the common Spanish and Calo (a Mexican dialect of Spanish) phrases interspersed throughout.

There are some hints that indicate this may be an autobiographical piece and that may be part of why this entertaining story has been through over twenty printings since its initial publication in 1972. Because there is no glossary, monolingual English speakers may need help from Mexican American bilingual students to understand some of the passages, and perhaps the next edition could include a glossary. HERIBERTO GODINA

A Thief in the Village and Other Stories of Jamaica

📖 James Berry

Caribbean, Jamaican, Physically Disabled

1990, Puffin, 📖 Rochman, Hazel, *Somehow Tenderness Survives.*

Infused with lyrical language and Jamaican folklore, this collection of nine interrelated stories focuses on a Caribbean boy's childhood. Many of the themes in these stories are appealing to middle-school readers because their themes are familiar to adolescents. "Elias and the Mongoose" and "Tukku-Tukku and Samson" are stories that focus on boys labeled as misfits. Elias, who is physically disabled, is teased cruelly because of his physical condition and because of the care and attention he gives his pet mongoose. "Tukku-Tukku and Samson" also takes up the issue of bullies. The term Tukku-Tukku is a derogatory nickname which means little and fat. In this case, the protagonist eventually outgrows his tormentors. "Becky and the Wheel-and-Brakes Boys" examines a girl's determination to have her own bicycle, despite the fact that she risks being called a tomboy. Although her Granny-Liz is concerned that the girl wants to do these "boy-things," Becky remains unfazed.

In nine stories, the author blends imagination and memory to depict a Caribbean childhood.

The Jamaican dialect used liberally throughout these stories may require some explanation for those not familiar with the vocabulary and cultural practices. In the Jamaican dialect, for example, the repetition of key words is essential. In addition to introducing readers to this dialect, the stories also paint a broader picture of Jamaican culture, going beyond reggae, ganja, and gazing at the sea.

Hazel Rochman's *Somehow Tenderness Survives,*

which offers stories by South African writers, would be an excellent companion piece to use with Berry's book. The two books together could provide an intriguing experience in cross-cultural literary connections. DAPHNE MUSE

Charlie Pippin

📓 Candy Dawson Boyde

African American

1987, MacMillan

Charlie, a spunky young woman and budding entre-preneur, works hard to learn everything about the

An African American girl seeks to learn all about the Vietnam War to better under-stand her father.

Vietnam War to better understand her father, a bitter Vietnam veteran. Charlie tries to make sense of her father's turmoil, and to maintain her business, all the while she is undergoing the usual strains of adolescence.

Her cleverness and tenacity make Charlie an engaging character, and she rises both to the challenges of puberty and to her father's anger with real determination.

This novel is recommended reading for Vietnam vets, their children, and grandchildren. Also recommended is Ann Nolan Clark's *To Stand Against the Wind*, a wartime story about Vietnam involving an eleven-year-old refugee living in America.
DAPHNE MUSE

The Summer of the Swans

📓 Betsy Byars ✒ Ted CoConis

Mentally Disabled

1981 (1970), Puffin, Penguin

A dated but sensitive portrayal of a family that includes a developmentally disabled child.

Left in the care of her bossy Aunt Willie, four-teen-year-old Sara har-bors great resentment toward her father. Her anger and discontent spill over into her rela-tionship with her older sister Wanda, who Sara feels is prettier and seems to "have it all together," and her developmentally disabled brother Charlie. She clearly loves Charlie, but she feels put upon for having to watch him all the time.

One night, Charlie gets lost in the woods near a lake where he loves to watch swans. Volunteers from the small town in which they live come together and search for him. The radio station announces his dis-appearance and refers to him as a "mentally handi-capped child who couldn't speak."

Published in 1970, *The Summer of the Swans* con-tains dated language. But the portrayal of Charlie is sensitive, accurate, and compassionate. He has a wide range of emotions and feelings, and the illustrations do not depict him as a loner or pitiful in any way.

Through her relation-ship with her brother, Sara gains new insights into herself and her fami-ly. Byars uses an analogy that depicts life as a series of huge uneven steps. In one scenario, Sara sees herself in a prison shirt, taking a big step out of the shadows; in another, there are steps in front of her that will enable her to rise to the sky. Charlie is depicted on a flight of small yet difficult steps, but steps nonetheless.

Byars provides fully developed characters whose feelings are always present on the page and whose fears are apparent to the reader as well.
BARBARA A. KANE

The Shadow Brothers

📓 A.E. Cannon

Native American, Navajo

1992 (1990), Dell Publishing Company, Inc.

A somewhat unrealistic treatment of tensions in a Mormon family with an adopted Navajo son.

Identity conflicts intrude on the relationship be-tween Marcus Jenkins, a Mormon, and his foster brother, Henry. Henry is a Navajo Indian, the son of a friend of Marcus's father. Henry has lived with the Jenkins family since the age of seven when his mother died. During their junior year, a newcomer at school, an Ute Indian, arouses anxi-eties in Henry about his ethnicity.

Although some aspects of the relationship are

believable and the pain experienced by Marcus as he observes the changes in Henry seems real, it does seem unusual that the question of heritage should surface so late. It's also hard to assume that Henry has not had more contact with his Indian family before these pressures arise. Still the story could spark enough interest among older teens to produce some interesting and worthwhile discussion, including changing Mormon attitudes toward Native Americans. BINNIE TATE-WILKIN

Dive

📖 Stacey Donovan

Gay/Lesbian/Bisexual

1994, Dutton Children's Books

Dive's vibrant heroine, Virginia Dunn, or V as she's called by friends and family, has a compelling voice that plunges readers immediately into her story. At the novel's opening, V's dog is hit by a car and her mother chooses not to spend the money to revive it. Immediately thereafter, her father's hospitalization with an obscure fatal disease provokes a variety of responses. V's brother is

Virginia deals with her dysfunctional family and discovers the love of another young woman.

drugged and distant, her mother sinks even deeper into a bottle of Scotch, V's best friend is remote, and V is left trying to hold everything together for her younger sister.

Surrounded by confusion and betrayal, V meets Jane, and finds a love more satisfying and spiritually reviving than any she's known. She's ignited, hopeful, and fulfilled in a way that makes questioning her choice of a female lover seems like a small issue. The novel escapes being a romantic trauma-drama through the author's lyricism and her ability to point extraordinary word pictures. Her vivid language evokes the horror of internal and external realities and "days that end without answers." SUSIE WILDE

The Boy Who Drank Too Much

📖 Shep Grene

Dysfunctional

1980 (1979), Dell Publishing Group, Inc.

Narrated by a fifteen-year-old nameless boy, this novel's central focus is alcoholism. Buff Sanders, a heroic high school hockey player, befriends the

Buff, a teenage hockey player, develops a drinking problem.

narrator and helps him hone his skills. The boy is eager to make his first goal and hopes Buff will be instrumental in helping him do so. He observes Buff carrying small bottles of liquor and asks why he drinks. Buff replies, "It helps me to relax, play better and gives me self-confidence." The narrator seeks a neighbor's advice about Buff and Buff's dad, who also drinks. This neighbor, Ruth, is a recovering alcholic.

After several episodes of drinking and subsequent beatings by his father, Buff disappears. Eventually, he is found by the narrator and his girlfriend Julie. Buff is drunk, so they take him to the home of Ruth. She convinces Buff to join a hospital rehabilitation program. Buff's father arrives at Ruth's house drunk and disorderly. Buff calls the police, then runs away. When the narrator finds him this time, he offers even more support and encouragement, proving his friendship and loyalty.

During one of the most important games of the season, Buff takes an alcohol-filled thermos from his bag, but manages to resist the urge to drink. Although the team loses the game that could have taken it to the playoffs and the narrator never gets to score his goal, the coach awards letters to every team member for their valiant effort. Buff realizes that living at home will only exacerbate his problems and moves in with Ruth. Buff's friends join him in his rehabilitation process and go to the center with him twice a week.

Buff has to deal with the fact that his father killed his mother while driving drunk and that their move to this new town has been difficult and disconcerting as both his father's drinking and his own have gotten worse. Buff and his dad are not portrayed as wild drunks, but as people who suffer from a disease. The author stresses the importance of support systems and shows how victory is not always in winning the game. What comes through most clearly in the writing is the love of the game and the strong feelings for the players. BARBARA A. KANE

Edith Jackson

Rosa Guy

African American

1995 (1993), Puffin, ✳ Series, ▥ Rosa Guy, *Ruby*.

Seventeen-year-old Edith Jackson has worked hard to keep her family together. She and her three younger sisters are orphaned and always fighting for more—more respect, more attention, more love. Edith hopes one day to get a job, factory work perhaps, so that she can take care of her siblings and they can stay out of foster and group homes. At first, nothing else—not school, her own needs, or boys—matters.

A poor African American orphan faces hard choices and tries to keep her siblings together.

Edith is wise, giving, and smart, even though she doesn't believe in her own intelligence. She can sense phony and spiteful people as easily as she can tell genuine, caring folks. Back at The Institution, their foster home, Edith helps with toddlers and babies in the nursery and truly enjoys it. Mrs. Bates, a retired lawyer who was also an orphan, sees the girl's heart and intelligence and bluntly tells her, "Unless YOU decide that you are a person who can make choices and fight for them —you will never begin to count." Edith hates Mrs. Bates' assessment but she sees how her life has been set up as if she is invisible. Is it because she is poor, black, orphaned, and alone? Where are her dreams and opportunities? It is then that Edith decides to take control because she sees that only people who demand attention get it. She begins to make choices to control her own life.

Because Edith tells this story, readers get a strong sense of her personality and the clear, guileless way she views people and situations. Edith makes mistakes but comes to see how important having choices and making wise ones are. The story touches on loneliness, poverty, teen sexuality, and abortion. ALISON WASHINGTON

No Promises in the Wind

Irene Hunt

Irish American, Polish American

1993 (1970), Berkley Publishing Group

Poverty, unemployment, and homelessness are often perceived as the fault of the people trapped in those conditions. In Irene Hunt's novel, *No Promises in the Wind*, the author underscores the role that society plays in contributing to these conditions.

Through the voice of fifteen-year-old Josh we see how the Depression impacts the lives of a family struggling with a

Two Depression-era brothers run away from an abusive home to try to survive on their own.

father's rage and subsequent abusive language and violent behavior. His frustrations and sense of defeat are taken out on his eldest son.

Joey, Josh's younger brother, idolizes Josh. When Josh finally decides to run away from home and all of negative things going on there, including his sense that by eating his meager food allotment he is depriving his family, Joey goes with him. In the end, Josh finds himself emulating many of the ugly behaviors he so hated in his father. But finally the boys reconcile, and they return home to a less dysfunctional family.

The author writes movingly of the horrible conditions poor people endured in those times. Unfortunately, many of her graphic depictions could be describing the reality of poor, unemployed, and homeless people today. Josh and Joey are fortunate enough to encounter people who care for them and literally save their lives.

Their abusive father believes that hard work and the desire to work will overcome the country's economic troubles. Unfortunately, he is proven wrong. Hunt's novel examines social realism in much the same way the contemporary authors Virginia Hamilton, Gary Soto, and Robert Cormier do in their work. This is an excellent selection to support children in discussing the "American Dream" and its implications for poor people. MASHA RUDMAN

Deliver Us from Evie

📖 M.E. Kerr

Gay/Lesbian/Bisexual

1994, HarperCollins (Trophy)

Deliver Us from Evie is told by Parr, the youngest of three farm children. He's been dying to escape rural life for as long as he

When a young boy's older sister comes out as a lesbian, he faces prejudice.

can remember. His brother's gone off to college and become a frat brat who plays down his rural roots to impress his city-slicker girlfriend. Parr still has hope for his sister Evie, a large-hewn girl who's always loved the farm and farm work. Then suddenly, Evie is swept up in a turbulent relationship with rich, beautiful Patsy Duff.

This book dares to face real issues honestly. For example, the mother, fearful for her daughter's future, points out that Patsy's wealth and good-looks will protect her from mockery, while Evie, poor and from a lower social economic status, fits a common lesbian stereotype and will be far more susceptible to prejudice.

Kerr courageously takes on stereotyping, parental fears, rural intolerance, religious narrow-mindedness, all with a plot that moves so fast that these elements become part of the story rather than issues bundled together. Kerr, always a fictional forerunner, has placed real-seeming characters in a setting that highlights the complexities of coming out in a small community. SUSIE WILDE

Now That I Know

📖 Norma Klein

Gay/Lesbian/Bisexual

1988, Bantam

Nina's parents are divorced and have joint custody of her, splitting their time each week. Nina is concerned that her mother Jean isn't interested in dating—other divorced mothers she knows have

Nina, the daughter of divorced parents, discovers that her father is gay.

active social lives. She decides to buy her mother a personal ad for her birthday. But Nina is also concerned that if each of her parents remarries, she will no longer have a prominent place in their

lives. Her friend Dara's father has remarried and never wants to see Dara again. When Nina's father comes out to her as his lover Greg is about to move in, a combination of fear of rejection, competition, and discomfort with gayness sets in. Nina is particularly upset that her father had kept his relationship a secret and wonders if this is part of how he will freeze her out of his life.

This book is particularly remarkable for its explicit addressing of Nina's thoughts about the sexual aspect of Duncan and Greg's relationship, sparked in part by her growing interest in Damian. Nina realizes that she just doesn't find the idea of sex appealing—homosexual or heterosexual. Her initial reaction is to leave her father's home and not go back.

Her mother encourages her in this decision and voices a strong dislike for homosexuality, assuming that this is the only issue for Nina. When her mother begins to accept her ex-husband's relationship, she remarks to Nina that Duncan is lucky that he has two people in his life that he loves. Duncan and Greg are the only stable couple in the book. Nina decides, with the help of Damian, who has a gay brother, that her father's lack of honesty wasn't meant to hurt her and that he has difficulties too.

In the end, she returns to the old joint-custody arrangement. The strength of the book lies in how it follows the initially homophobic reactions of characters through to the realization that their objections to Duncan and Greg generally have other sources in the characters' own insecurities. Homophobia then becomes something that can be overcome with thoughtful reflection. The fact that Damian also has a gay brother shows that homosexuality is relatively common. Moreover, the tales of dysfunctional heterosexuality make the characters' attempts to see gayness as unnatural all the more false. CHRIS MAYO

214

Cantora

📖 Sylvia Lopez-Medina 🖋 Various Sources
Hispanic, Mexican

1992, Ballantine Books, 🏛 Ana Castillo, *So Far from God*; Helena Maria Viramontes, *The Moths and Other Stories*; *Under the Feet of Jesus*.

A wonderful multigenerational novel of the Latina experience.

Based on the oral history of her own family, Sylvia Lopez-Medina's *Cantora* makes us wonder what inspiration may be hidden in our own pasts.

In *Cantora*, Amparo's family chronicle resides in the stories her great-grandmother, grandmother, and mother have told her. As she pieces the stories together, she sees not just a picture of the women in her family but of herself as well. The women in this novel are strong and resilient and they are bound to each other by love and history, not obligation.

The novel is well written. It begins in 1978 with Amparo keeping her Aunt Pilar company. Aunt Pilar has become a victim of Alzheimer's and travels back to the past often, taking her niece with her in memories. The reader is invited to join:

"My name is Amparo. Join me here with my aunt. Sit here beside us. Cover yourself with this quilt. My Grandmother Rosario made it. Warm yourself with it. The mystery of our lives are to be found in its varicolored threads. I will share the tears and the triumphs of these lives. I will show you how to survive anything. We will show you how to survive everything." And they do.

Thoughtful readers in seventh and eighth grades might enjoy this journey to the heart of Amparo's family, and be encouraged to listen closely to their own families' stories. JANIS O'DRISCOLL

A Teacup Full of Roses

📖 Sharon Bell Mathis
African American
1972, Puffin

Paul is a twenty-four-year-old aspiring artist addicted to heroin. Joe, his younger brother, is determined to escape from the dysfunction of his family, and to marry Ellie, his high school sweetheart. This once-intact family is torn asunder by Paul's addiction, and the mother's obsessive love for her oldest son.

Mathis does not shy away from graphic scenes of drug use, which some young readers may find disturbing. While bolder and even more heart-wrenching novels have been written since this one was first published in 1972, Mathis took a daring and forthright stance when she wrote about drug addiction in the early 1970s. *Teacup* is a prime example of how Mathis, Virginia Hamilton, and a few other authors were pioneers in dealing with social realism in young-adult fiction. DAPHNE MUSE

A story of the tragedies that befall an African American family ravaged by drug addiction.

Shizuko's Daughter

📖 Kyoko Mori
Asian

1993, Holt, As Series, 🏛 Sue Ellen Bridgers, *Notes for Another Life: A Novel*; Eve Bunting, *Face at the Edge of the World*; Stella Pevsner, *How Could You Do It, Diane?*.

As a result of her mother's suicide, all the light and color have been taken from twelve-year-old Yuki's world. Yuki becomes silent, and cut off from almost everyone, longing for the loving and creative relationship she shared with her mother, Shizuko. Her stepfather remarries all too soon after her mother's death and Yuki's stepmother Hanae systematically removes all traces of Shizuko from the house.

After her mother's suicide, an Asian must make her way through adolescence feeling alone and isolated.

Yuki reenters the world through the memories of her mother's art and running. The love of her grandmother and her precious Aunt Aya keep her connected to her mother. The story follows Yuki through her last year in college, when Yuki finally starts to believe that life will be all right, and her healing begins.

In a culture where people are taught to hold on to their feelings, Yuki rebels in small ways. The compelling writing evokes the overwhelming loss felt by Yuki, her grandmother, and her Aunt Aya.

Set in Kobe, the story provides readers with a look at the details of daily life in Japan. Accompanying notes provide further information on the setting, and a glossary defines Japanese

215

words used in the story. *Shizuko's Daughter* was listed on the 1994 American Library Association's list of Best Books for Young Adults. It also won the Elizabeth Burr Award given by the Wisconsin Library Association to a Wisconsin author for distinguished achievement in children's literature.

PAM CARLSON

April and the Dragon Lady

Lensey Namioka
Asian American, Chinese American
1994, Browndeer Press

Lensey Namioka half-jokingly told me during a visit with her that this story was about "revenge." April, the second child in the family, fights back against gender-bound expectations from family members. Being honest to her love of rocks, she chooses to attend the Colorado School of Mines after high school. She does not purposely look for Caucasian boys; it just happens that the boy who understands her and who shares her interest is a Caucasian. Since her mother's death, she has assumed the burden of taking care of the family, including her aging grandmother. However, April refuses to be trapped by the sense of honor and duty and attends an out-of-state university that offers a program in her field of interest.

An Asian American teenager deals with cultural differences regarding family obligations of a daughter.

The author portrays the conflict between the obligations of a daughter and the sense of individualism belonging to one who was born and raised in the United States. *Situations presented in the story can be used as case studies for cross-cultural understanding of values and problem-solving strategies. The setting and April's problems are familiar to many teenagers. They can compare their thinking and action when caught in similar situations.*

Most of all, I love the author's humor, which sparkles between the lines. For example, April's grandmother hides among a group of Japanese tourists in order to play a trick on the family during an outing to Mount Rainier. She starts a conversation with a Japanese tourist by offering her advice on buying Navajo rugs, with limited means of language on a topic about which she knows nothing. Yes, life may be overwhelming; but there are lighter sides to many of its pressing demands. This young adult novel demonstrates that so well.

BELINDA YUN-YING LOUIE

When I Was Puerto Rican

Esmeralda Santiago   Megan Wildon
Hispanic, Puerto Rican
1994 (1993), Addison-Wesley, ✱ Spanish

Esmeralda Santiago's memories of her childhood in Eisenhower-era Puerto Rico are clear and vividly drawn. Nicknamed "Negi," she grew up in the rural village of Macun, where metal roofs cover one-room houses and chickens roam the front yard among tropical fruit trees. Her youthful struggle on the island is not about poverty and want, but about a search for peace of mind and stability in the family life dominat-

A woman's memories of growing up in Puerto Rico and New York City.

ed by her parents' tumultuous relationship. Mami and Papi love each other, but they have a hard time making a life together on a daily basis. They argue bitterly, hurling insults and accusations at each other.

This biography begins when Negi is about four or five years old. She is the oldest of a growing number of children. Whenever village life becomes too much for Mami, she moves the children into the city or a suburb for weeks or months at a time before a reconciliation with Papi.

Helping her mother with the younger children and moving back and forth disrupts Negi's schooling and makes it difficult for her to develop friendships. She learns early on that her mother's yearnings for the proverbial "better future" require hard work and trade-offs. At one time, Mami is the only mother in Macun who works outside the home. Mami and the children are suddenly viewed with suspicion and shunned by neighbors.

When Mami moves her brood to New York City, tremendous adjustments are required, including getting used to the seasons and having to stay inside where it's safe instead of being able to play outdoors. Negi, now a teenager, is bewildered by racial division and prejudice at school while she struggles to become fluent in English. But she proves to be a strong and determined individual.

216

When Mami is laid off from her factory job where she sews brassieres, Negi accompanies her to the welfare office to translate when she applies for public assistance. Negi soon begins to translate for other people at the office. At home, she entertains her family for hours on end in their crowded apartment with fantastic tales that make them forget their suffering.

Her efforts to excel academically pay off when a guidance counselor encourages her to seek admission to the High School of Performing Arts. The book's epilogue is set ten years after that audition, as Negi pursues her studies at Harvard.

What's pleasing about the book is that Negi comes through as a whole person. She is neither a paragon or a cliché. While her mother features prominently in her life, Negi has also established a special, loving relationship with her father. Each chapter begins with a Spanish homily and its English translation. A glossary at the back of the book helps the reader understand Spanish words and phrases. LESLIE ANDERSON MORALES

The Well: David's Story

📖 Mildred D. Taylor

African American

1995, Dial Books for Young Readers, ✳ Series

Anyone familiar with Mildred B. Taylor's books will be well acquainted with the Logans. *The Well* is another Logan family saga told in the voice of David, whom readers of Taylor's previous books (*Roll of Thunder, Hear My Cry; Let the Circle Be Unbroken; The Road to Memphis*) will recognize as the father of Cassie, Stacey, Christopher-John, and Little Man.

A subtle portrayal of racial conflict in the deep South.

This story focuses on a well in Mississippi, the only well in the immediate area that has not gone dry and that happens to be on the property of the relatively prosperous African American Logans. Although the Logans are glad to share the well with their less-fortunate black and white neighbors, one white family finds this situation particularly galling.

Taylor introduces complexity into what could have been a stereotypical standoff between black and white, creating real-life multidimensional characters and situations. David's brother Hammer is proud, but he is also maddeningly self-destructive and typically narcissistic about the impact of

his actions on the rest of his family. The text is further enriched by minor characters such as Mama Rachel, and her story about the loss of her name to her former white owners, and David's father, whose light skin makes him able to pass for a white

man but whose own story is a cautionary tale about caste and color "in this white man's world." Not all of the white characters are evil on a grand scale; most are caught in a web of the banality of racism.

Taylor demonstrates that white man's truth can never reside in the stories of black folks in this time and in this place; however, David's story testifies to a deeper truth, a history, as Taylor avers, "not then written in textbooks." With all of the eloquence of this truth and this history, Taylor's books, and this one is no exception, demand to be read. MARY FROSCH

Maya's Divided World

📖 Gloria Velasquez

Hispanic, Mexican American

1995, Arte Publico Press

Maya's Divided World is the story of a Mexican American girl living in a predominately Anglo middle-class neighborhood in southern California. The book begins with Maya, a seventeen-year-old high school junior, starting the school year trying to hide the fact that her parents divorced over the summer. Maya is an only child who has spent her life in the comfort and security of an upwardly mobile family. Early on

A Chicana girl reacts to her parents' divorce by getting involved with the wrong peer group.

in the story, the reader learns that Maya's mother is a college professor, her father is an engineer, and Maya, an honor student, is the only Chicana member of the school tennis team. In the Catholic Chicana community: "Divorce is something shameful, always the woman's fault, and something only gringos do." Maya herself is very attached to her father, Armando, who has moved to San Francisco, and very angry at her mother, Sonia, for "making him leave." Maya begins to lose interest in school

217

and to act out by lying to her mother and teachers, pushing her friends away, joining a new peer group, and dating an Anglo boy.

As Maya struggles along, she closes herself off from her friends and family. In spite of her unfriendly attitude, her old friend Juanita refuses to abandon her, and eventually enlists a psychologist, Ms. Martinez, to help. But Maya, Juanita, and Sonia enter therapy too easily; given the Mexican American Catholic attitudes expressed earlier in the book, it doesn't seem real. Ms. Martinez herself has divorced and is now remarried to a Caucasian man.

Once Maya agrees to meet with her, Ms. Martinez begins to take up more narrative space. The second half of the novel is as much about Ms. Martinez and her personal emotional problems surrounding her first marriage and divorce as it is about Maya's recovery process. On the positive side, by showing Ms. Martinez's struggles, a new dimension is added to the reader's understanding of the complexity of marital relationships.

Juanita's role is small, essentially serving as the catalyst for Maya's growth as she works to recreate her identity as the daughter of divorced parents. With Juanita's help, Maya finds that she can develop loving relationships with both her mother and father, and that she does not have to choose one over the other or lose herself in the process. It is refreshing to see teenage women portrayed as loyal to each other during a crisis, instead of stereotyped as flighty girls easily divided over boyfriends and social status.

An added plus in this book is the brief glossary of Spanish words and phrases, many of which are used only in casual family conversation. ROSA E. WARDER

Child of the Owl

Laurence Yep
Asian American, Chinese American
1990 (1977), HarperCollins

Casey, the story's protagonist, has never stayed in one home for very long. When she moves in with her grandmother, Paw-Paw, in Chinatown, she recognizes that Chinatown is a unique environment, blending elements of both Chinese and mainstream American culture. At first, she feels as if she does not fit in.

Casey and Paw-Paw live in a cold, tiny apartment, and they often do not have enough food, but this relationship provides Casey with a sense of stability that she has never had before. The traditional Chinese stories Paw-Paw tells captivate Casey. When Casey sees her friends — especially those who are American born — dismiss these stories, she feels that these individuals are missing out. The stories help provide her with a sense of identity: she is a "Child of the Owl," according to the family stories, and this helps give her a context for dealing with her feelings.

In a further attempt to find out about her family, Casey asks Sheridan, an old friend of her father's, to tell her what her parents were like when they were young. Both did well at school, he says, but when they graduated during the Depression, her father was unable to find a job. Her mother easily found secretarial work according to Sheridan, because "most American bosses are men who'll hire a pretty Chinese girl like that. But to hell with some uppity Chinese boy. Let him stay a houseboy." After years of frustration, Barney began gambling, feeling that something was owed to him.

An Asian American girl goes to live with her grandmother in San Francisco's Chinatown in the 1950s.

Casey is sympathetic toward her father until he breaks into her grandmother's house to steal her owl charm, injuring Paw-Paw in the process. Although Paw-Paw recovers and the charm is eventually returned, her anger at her father remains. She does forgive him, but ultimately sees him as limited in many ways. He is unable to see past his personal pain, something that Paw-Paw and her stories have helped Casey to do.

Child of the Owl deftly explores the power of stories and describes what life was like for many Chinese Americans during the 1950s. Explanations of Chinese and Chinese American culture are vivid and clear. The characters are well drawn and believable. Laurence Yep's examination of Casey's connections to their family and culture is both thorough and complex. LISA MOORE

Bread Givers

Anzia Yezierska

Jewish

1975 (1952), Persea Books, Inc., Anzia Yezierska, *Hungry Hearts and Other Stories; Red Ribbon on a White Horse.*

Sara, the youngest of four daughters, in a turn-of-the-century Jewish household, grows up watching her father, Reb Smolinsky, tyrannize her family. He

A Jewish girl at the turn of the century is caught between her father's traditions and her own life-choices in this powerful book.

drives away her sisters' suitors and exploits his wife's loyalty and sense of duty. Following a violent argument, Sara leaves her father's house and strikes out on her own. She lives alone in a dark and squalid basement apartment and is often hungry. At the end of a twelve-hour workday, she goes to night school for two hours. Eventually, she graduates from college and goes back to the old neighborhood as a schoolteacher. Still not free of her father's influence, Sara struggles to maintain her sense of self and meet the obligation she feels as a dutiful daughter when her father, now an old man, becomes ill.

Outside the family, Smolinsky is lionized as a learned man, one who reads and protects the Torah, and by extension defends his people. They don't know that in his haste to marry off his daugh-

ters with the help of a matchmaker, he greatly misjudges the characters of the young men he selects; or that his get-rich-scheme to buy a corner grocery store fails.

Yezierska writes powerfully about poverty, Americanization, family tensions, and the ambiguity of success. She captures the language and culture of immigrant Jews at the turn of the century. She explains the complex dynamics of a traditional society challenged in its new circumstances. Smolinsky is not a tyrant in a vacuum. A woman's virtue at that time was measured by how well she helped her husband or — depending on the circumstances — her father. The religious pursuits of certain male heads of household placed economic burdens on many women. At the same time, exclusion from most religious activity forced women to develop skills useful in the larger world.

Sara's early years are vividly described. The story of Sara's childhood is rich in detail. By comparison, the book races through her college years and the months of her first job. Still, we are left with a sense of having gone back in time and lived the experience so often romanticized in historical accounts of Ellis Island immigrants.

LESLIE ANDERSON MORALES

219

CHAPTER 3

COMMUNITY/ FRIENDSHIP

One of the most important roles children's books can play is to teach young people how others live. The process children go through in developing friendships with others quite different from themselves can be greatly eased by having children read books about those once thought unimaginably foreign. The true multicultural reader learns to see similarities in every community, and in this way new opportunities for friendship and understanding among different people become possible.

Focusing on the importance of using books to foster friendship and community, this chapter covers a wide range of issues and themes, including: community service, cooperation, gangs, conflict resolution, and homelessness. Central to the chapter is the idea that reading—and young readers—can have a tremendous impact on our social relationships. Vignettes and sidebars offer practical advice on getting a library card, starting a literary club at school, and making your own library.

DAPHNE MUSE

Kindergarten to Grade Three

Who's in Rabbit's House?

📖 Verna Aardema   ✒ Leo D. Dillon & Diane Dillon
African, Masai
1979 (1977), Dial Books for Young Readers

Rabbit returns to her home one evening only to discover that she cannot get in. Her house is occupied by a threatening "bad animal" that calls itself The Long One. The larger animals of the region offer to help, but to no avail. Finally, a clever frog saves the day by tricking The Long One, who turns out to be only a caterpillar, into leaving.

This satisfying story, told with repetition of key phrases so that young listeners may speak the lines along with the reader, is based on an old Masai folk tale. These phrases, along with the inclusion of

An African folktale about a "bad animal" who keeps Rabbit out of her house.

Masai ideophones (such as "kpidu, kpidu, kpidu" for the sound Jackal's feet make when he runs) lend this book a delightful rhythm, making it ideal for reading aloud. The story also lends itself easily to dramatization. The wonderful illustrations encourage this, by presenting the story as a play being acted out by a troop of Masai actors wearing clever, expressive animal masks.

This story, sure to be a favorite of young children, makes an excellent addition to a collection of folklore, and would also be appropriate for a teaching unit on Kenya or Tanzania. As the preface explains, the Masai hairstyles, jewelry, and housing, as well as the terrain, are authentically portrayed, though the masks are the illustrators' invention. JODI LEVINE

Tiger

📖 Judy Allen   ✒ Tudor Humphries
Asian, Southeast Asian
1994 (1992), Candlewick, 📖 Tsuchiya, Y.,
The Faithful Elephants.

Beautiful illustrations place this story in a village in south Asia where the people believe a tiger is in the vicinity. Though the villagers know it is illegal to kill tigers, they want this one killed so they can sell its skin. A young boy, Lee, listens to the gossip and

hopes the tiger will not be killed. But the news is out and soon a big hunter arrives. He agrees to stalk and shoot the tiger but insists on going alone. The illustrations follow his hunt and his confrontation with the tiger. The double-page illustrations of the tiger are very impressive. When the hunter returns, the villagers discover that he did shoot the tiger—but with his camera! Lee is happy the tiger is safe.

Illustrations of a Southeast Asian village frame a story about hunting a tiger and shooting it— with a camera!

The art, in muted shades, is very realistic, full of vibrant colors and cultural and geographic details— clothing, transportation, scenery from life in the bush. The features of the people are not stereotypical. There is a lovely full-page spread depicting the young hunter with handsome Asian features, fatigue pants, and backpack. He is not the stereotypical "big white hunter"; instead of guns he carries a camera in his pack.

The environmental message is quite clear. At the end of the story are two pages giving information on why tigers are an endangered species and what efforts are being made to save them. A companion picture book to read to older children might be *The Faithful Elephants* by Y. Tsuchiya (Morrow, 1988), which is a moving story about the effect of war on animals in the zoo. GLORIA D. JACKSON

The Children's Book of Virtues

📖 William J. Bennett (editor)   ✒ Michael Hague
Multicultural
1995, Simon & Schuster, 📖 Kohl, Herbert, *A Call to Character.*

Based on Bennett's popular collection, *The Book of Virtues, The Children's Book of Virtues* is intended to teach self-discipline, compassion, loyalty, faith, and honesty. Selections include excerpts from the Bible, Aesop, The Brothers Grimm, and Hans Christian Andersen. Promoted as a tool for parents and children in Bennett's "moral education" movement, this book seems better suited to another century and another country. While stories, poems, and fables are important tools to help parents introduce their children to the essentials of good character, these selections fail to reflect the sound values of many Americans whose voices are not represented in this collection. The Bible is the only spiritual or religious text represented. One apparent nod to multicultural reality, "The Indian Cinderella," presents stereotypes of women. No contemporary African American, Latino, or Asian American literature is represented in the collection at all.

Seeking to teach virtues to young readers, this stereotype-ridden collection fails to represent this country's multicultural children.

Alicia Aspinwall's "There Was a Little Girl" reeks of sexism and scolds girls for misbehaving (i.e., acting like boys):

Her mother heard the noise,
And she thought it was the boys
A-playing at a combat in the attic;
But when she climbed the stair;
And found Jemima there,
She took and she did scold her most emphatic.

A more inclusive and substantive collection of stories of this type can be found in Colin Greer and Herb Kohl's *A Call to Character*. Bennett's book fails to address the challenge provided by the complex society in which we live. DAPHNE MUSE

The Elders Are Watching

📗 David Brouchard   ✒ Roy Henry Vickers
Multicultural
1990, Eagle Dancers Enterprises, Ltd.

The Elders Are Watching is a plea for preserving our world for future generations. Alternating beautiful illustrations of nature with text that calls for a change in how we treat the environment, the authors, a Canadian educator and an Indian artist, combine their passion for ecology and art.

A plea for the environment, beautifully presented in verse and image.

The book features an unidentified narrator who reminds the reader that "the elders are watching" and they expect humanity to care for the only world they have:

They told me to tell you the time is now.
They want you to know how they feel.
So listen carefully, look toward the sun.
The Elders are watching.

In the first part of the book, readers are reminded by the messenger that their ancestors entrusted them with the earth, the water, the air, the animals, and the trees—the essence of life. The Elders are disappointed and angry that humanity has misused and wasted so many resources. Mining has left pits and scars in the earth. Wanton killing of animals for sport has destroyed many buffalo, bear, fish, and other sea life.

The warning softens to a message of encouragement toward the end of the book when the narrator says that the Elders are seeing some things that make them smile. They are happy to see the green returning to the land, and they appreciate the efforts of those who sacrifice to save even one ancient tree. The last part of the book admonishes the reader to save the beauty of the earth by watching and caring for it.

The urgency of the warning is as powerful as the brilliant colors and the unique designs superimposed on the scenes. Forms and faces appear as shadows and spirits within each full-page painting. Roy Henry Vickers uses silhouettes most effectively. The stark blackness of forms stand out against the layers of intense blues, reds, yellows, and oranges of the sky. SHIRLEY R. CRENSHAW

Smoky Night

📗 Eve Bunting   ✒ David Diaz
African American
1994, Harcourt Brace and Company

Smoky Night graphically depicts the Los Angeles riots through the innocent eyes of a child. From his apartment window he watches his neighborhood crumble and burn like a war zone. He asks his mother why this is happening. "It can happen when people get angry. They want to smash and destroy. They don't care anymore what's right and what's wrong." As night falls, the boy's mother tucks him into bed.

A powerful look at the L.A. riots as seen through the eyes of a child, but lacking any analysis.

She is stoic, calm, a safe haven in an otherwise tumultuous storm. Later they are jolted out of their beds and made to evacuate their building. The boy loses his cat in the shuffle and worries about it until a firefighter arrives at the shelter, holding the cat and their long-time neighbor Mrs. Kim's cat. The two cats, who usually fight, put aside their differences and drink milk from the same bowl. The boy and his mother decide to do the same, and befriend Mrs. Kim.

This story takes place in a multicultural L.A. neighborhood. Prior to the riots, the boy and his mother refused to shop at Mrs. Kim's store, preferring to "buy from their own people." However, upon seeing the devastating effect that prejudice can have on humanity, the boy and his mother rise above the chaos and confusion to befriend Mrs. Kim.

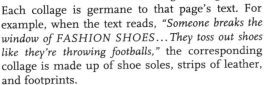

This book is simply yet powerfully written, and the illustrations are brilliant and striking. Vivid acrylic paintings are set against collage backgrounds. Each collage is germane to that page's text. For example, when the text reads, *"Someone breaks the window of FASHION SHOES...They toss out shoes like they're throwing footballs,"* the corresponding collage is made up of shoe soles, strips of leather, and footprints.

This book makes a powerful statement against racism and injustice. But nothing is said about why people rebel, and there is no discussion of the economic conditions that lead to rebellion.

BARBARA SMITH REDDISH

Fly Away Home

📖 Eve Bunting   ✏ Ronald Himler

Dysfunction

1993 (1991), Clarion Books

Fly Away Home is a sober depiction of a real-life problem facing many families: homelessness. A young boy named Andrew, whose mother has died, lives in the airport with his father because they're homeless. The book describes the problems they face, such as sleeping in a different place to avoid getting caught, and having to blend in with the crowd. On weekends, Andrew stays with another "airport family" because his dad works as a janitor. His father is always looking through the newspapers for a better job. Andrew and his father both talk about saving their money and someday living in an apartment, as they did before Andrew's mom died.

Broaches the subject of homeless families but describes an unrealistic scenario.

One day Andrew sees a bird fly in to the airport terminal. It tries to escape, but cannot find its way out, until one day it manages to slip through an open door and fly off. Andrew is inspired by the bird's determination to free itself and go home, and hopes that he and his dad will do the same some day.

This book deals with a serious problem in our society, yet leaves many questions unanswered, and perhaps paints an unrealistic picture of homelessness. The book does not explain why Andrew and his father are homeless. Also, Andrew is barely five years old. He has no home, no toys, and no security. He is forced to carry people's bags and hail taxis to earn money. He lives an arduous and dangerous life, yet he never cries or complains. He maintains a cheerful outlook and is hopeful for the future.

By Eve Bunting · Illustrated by Ronald Himler

The book does not discuss any resources for Andrew and his dad like a public welfare system or a homeless shelter. It also raises questions about his mother which really should be addressed. Are young readers led to believe that they could become homeless if their mother dies? These issues need to be discussed. BARBARA SMITH REDDISH

Recommended Titles on Homelessness
LEA DELSON

FOR PRESCHOOL CHILDEN AND YOUNG READERS

A Rose for Abby *by Donna Gunthrie*
(Abingdon Press 1988, Ages 4-8)

At the Sound of the Beep *by Marilyn Sachs*
(Dutton 1990, Ages 8-12)

Fly Away Home *by Eve Bunting,*
illustrated by Ronald Himler
(Clarion Books 1993, Ages 5-8)

Home: A Collection of Thirty Distinguished
Authors and Illustrators of Children's Books
to Aid the Homeless *edited by Michael Rosen*
(Zolotow/HarperCollins 1992, Ages 3 and Up)

Home Boy *by Curt and Gita Kaufman with
photos by Curt Kaufman*
(Atheneum 1987, Ages 5-8)

Seeing Eye Willie *by Dale Gottlieb*
(Knopf 1992, Ages 5-8)

Sophie and the Sidewalk Man
By Stephanie Tolan, illustrated by Susan Avishai
(Four Winds 1992, Ages 7-9)

Space Travelers *by Margert Wild*
(Scholastic 1993, Ages 5-9)

Uncle Willie and the Soup Kitchen
by DyAnne DiSalvo-Ryan
(Morrow 1991, Ages 6-8)

We Are All in the Dumps with Jack and Guy
by Maurice Sendak
*(Michael di Capua Books/HarperCollins 1993,
Ages 5 and Up)*

FOR OLDER CHILDREN AND TEENAGERS

The Beggars Ride *by Theresa Nelson*
(Orchard 1992, Ages 12 and Up)

December Stillness *by Mary Downing Hahn*
(Clarion Books 1988, Ages 11 and Up)

Dew Drop Dead *by James Howe*
(Atheneum 1990, Ages 8-12)

Dicey's Song *by Cynthia Voight*
(Atheneum 1982, Ages 9 and Up)

Edith Jackson *by Rosa Guy*
(Viking 1978, Ages 12 and Up)

The Family Under the Bridge *by Natalie Carlson*
(Harper & Row 1958, Ages 8-12)

The Fastest Friend in the West *by Vicki Grove*
(Putnam 1990, Ages 10-12)

Maniac Magee *by Jerry Spinelli*
(Little Brown 1990, Ages 8 and Up)

Missing Gator of Gumbo Limbo: An
Ecologocial Mystery *by Jean Craighead George*
(HarperCollins 1992, Ages 9-13)

Monkey Island *by Paula Fox*
(Orchard 1991, Ages 10 and Up)

Mop, Moondance, and the Nagasaki Knights
by Walter Dean Myers
(Delcarote 1992, Ages 8-12)

The Paper Bag Prince *by Colin Thompson*
(Knopf 1992, Ages 5-9)

Street Family *by Adriene Jones*
(Harper & Row 1987, Ages 7-10)

Way Home *by Libby Hathorn*
(Crown 1994, Ages 8 and Up)

Giving Thanks: A Native American Good Morning Message

📖 Chief Jake Swamp   ✒ Erwin Printup Jr.
Iroquois, Native American
1995, Lee and Low

Rooted in the ancient Haudenosuanne Thanksgiving Address, *Giving Thanks: A Native American Good Morning Message* acknowledges and celebrates Mother Earth and all the universe. While this idea is embraced by many Americans once a year, it is part of the daily teachings and practice of the Iroquois, recited at all gatherings of the Six Nations—Mohawk, Oneida, Onondaga, Cayuga, Seneca and Tuscarora.

A wonderful Thanksgiving Address used by six nations to celebrate Mother Earth.

The text is taken from a Thanksgiving Address by Chief Jake Swamp (Tekaronianeken) who has been a Chief of the Mohawks for over twenty-five years. The language is simple and eloquent.

The illustrator, Erwin Printup Jr., has done an excellent job of illustrating the printed word. His subjects and landscapes are well defined within the context of the environment. The colors are bold and lock your eyes onto the page. Peace-filled reverence resonates from each page.

Teaching children to be at peace with the physical world can promote peace between humans. In accepting and appreciating the natural things given by the Creator, people become more accepting of differences and strive harder to live in harmony. People who accept these natural gifts do not lack self-confidence and need not resort to violence to survive. This is an excellent book for all children.

YOLANDA ROBINSON-COLES

The Boy Who Didn't Believe in Spring

📖 Lucille Clifton   ✒ Brinton Turkle
African American, Hispanic
1988 (1973), Dutton

For anyone who needs a boost on a gloomy day, *The Boy Who Didn't Believe in Spring*, by Lucille Clifton, should do the trick. The two main characters, a boy named King Shabazz and his best buddy, Tony Polito, hear a lot of talk from adults about spring, but they see nothing in the world around them that matches the rhetoric. Their parents' and teachers' talk about crops and bluebirds leaves them questioning the adults' grip on reality, and they both conclude that spring is probably a myth. But curiosity gets the better of them, and one day, King says,

Two boys set out to find signs of spring's arrival in their urban neighborhood.

"I'm going to get me some of this spring." He and Tony go out into their neighborhood to search for signs of spring. When they don't see anything unusual on their block, they decide to risk crossing the street together to investigate new sections of their neighborhood.

The book follows them as they explore, marveling at all the strange new things they find, with no adults around to tell them what to think, or what things are. The charming illustrations, provided by Brinton Turkle, (best known for his award-winning books *Deep in the Forest*, *Do Not Open*, and *Thy Friend, Obadiah*), capture the awe of being a little boy in the big city. His attention to detail, from city fire hydrants and chain-link fences to the boys' well-used sneakers, brings the story to life and clarifies things for the youngest readers. The friendship between King and Tony is portrayed as natural and comfortable, a good example of the relationships that can occur in a multiethnic neighborhood.

As King and Tony pass a church, a bakery, a restaurant, and the busy commotion of the city streets, they continue to look for signs of spring. Their search leads them to a vacant lot behind a high-rise apartment complex, where they find a stripped and abandoned car. As they approach, the boys discover a little patch of pointed yellow flowers growing out of a crack in the cement. "Man, I think you tripped on these crops!" King laughed. "They're comin up," Tony shouted. "Man, the crops are comin' up!" As they look at the plant in amazement, they hear the sound of wings flapping in the air above them and watch as a pair of birds fly away from the abandoned car. When King and Tony reach the car, they find a nest with four light-blue eggs, and they decide that spring is real after all.

The boys are caught off their block by Tony's older brother, and as the book ends they know they will get into big trouble for crossing the street alone, but their discovery of spring seems worth it. Readers will agree. ROSA E. WARDER

Sadako

📘 Eleanor Coerr ✏ Ed Young

Asian, Japanese

1994 (1993), Hodder & Stoughton

Dedicated to "the children of Hiroshima," this exquisitely illustrated book tells the story of Sadako Sasaki, a little girl who died as a result of the bombing of Hiroshima. Sadako's letters and writings

A Japanese girl discovers she has leukemia as a result of the bomb dropped on Hiroshima.

have been previously published. This picture book makes Sadako's story available to a new generation of younger readers.

The story opens when Sadako makes the mistake of calling the memorial day for victims of the bomb a "carnival," and her mother corrects her, reminding her that her own grandmother died during the bombing. When Sadako is diagnosed with the "atom-bomb disease," her best friend, Chizuko, remembers an old folktale, and urges her to fold one thousand paper cranes to become well again. Tragically, she doesn't get well.

Details such as relay races, holidays, and bean soup, make it easy for a reader to identify with Sadako's world and care about what happens in her life. In no way do Sadako or her family seem like people who could have been our "enemies" or anybody's "enemies." Children reading *Sadako* turn the pages slowly, and they return to it again and again. Young's pastel illustrations are potent and evocative.

Coerr and Young are to be commended for this testament to one of the worst tragedies of the twentieth century. *Reading it, each reader will want to add his or her own folded paper crane to the base of the peace monument.* NAOMI SHIHAB NYE

Donovan's Word Jar

📘 Monalisa DeGross ✏ Cheryl Hanna

1994, HarperCollins

Donovan loves his family and especially likes visiting with his grandmother, who lives in a senior citizen's complex. Donovan also loves words: the size and shape of them, their sound, and the way they feel in his mouth. He delights in "collecting" words that evoke some kind of special response within him. Donovan has an opportunity to use his words on a visit to his grandmother.

Donovan loves to collect words and shares these with a group of senior citizens.

Unfortunately, the seniors are at odds with each other on this day. Donovan attempts to create a more harmonious setting by sharing his words with the seniors; they in turn share them with others. Soon the seniors are talking and laughing.

This is an easy-reading book that will appeal to readers intrigued by the title. The chapter format will encourage beginning readers who wish to exhibit "older reader" behaviors. The book can also be used to encourage young children to value words and their meanings and power. The writing is somewhat pedestrian, but the short chapters and simple text are appropriate for beginning readers. VIOLET HARRIS

Tonight Is Carnaval

📘 Arthur Dorros ✏ Club de Madres Virgen del Carmen of Lima, Peru

Hispanic, Peruvian

1995 (1991), Dutton Children's Books

This is a delightful story of a little boy who is anxiously awaiting the village festival in Peru because he is to play his *quena* (flute). The book would stand well

A Peruvian boy anxiously waits for the village festival.

enough on its own, but the addition of photographs of *arpilleras* (hand-quilted and embroidered pictures) makes it a total joy. *Arpilleras*, originally made to express political frustration, here enchant the reader with their color and intricacy. *Teachers will be pleased at the glossary of Peruvian terms at the back of the book and with the photos showing the women of the Club de Madres Virgen del Carmen of Lima, Peru, actually making the arpilleras.* NAOMI WAKAN

Adopted by the Eagles: A Plains Indian Story of Friendship and Treachery

Paul Goble

Lakota Sioux, Native American

1994, Simon & Schuster Children's, ✱ Series, Goble, Paul, *The Girl Who Loved Wild Horses*; *Star Boy*; *Buffalo Woman*; *The Great Race*.

This Lakota Indian story was told by Chief Edgar Red Cloud, one of the last great Lakota storytellers. White Hawk and Tall Bear are "kolas," special friends who share a sacred bond. Returning from an unsuccessful raid with his friend, White Hawk suggests they bring back two young eagles they have spotted nesting on a ledge. Once he has lowered Tall Bear down to the ledge, however, White Hawk runs off, abandoning Tall Bear. Tall Bear, realizing he has been left to die so that White Hawk can marry Red Leaf, the woman they both love, Tall Bear calls upon the Great Spirit for help.

An engaging Sioux tale of the betrayal and the honor of a friendship.

He is adopted by the eagle family and is eventually returned to his village. Once there, he refuses to seek vengeance against White Hawk, saying, "He is my kola." Instead, Tall Bear marries Red Leaf, and they return together to the eagles, bringing gifts in fulfillment of his promise to them.

Children will respond to the betrayal in this story. They can be helped, if necessary, to see its more subtle message: friendship should be honored and renewed. Excellent illustrations celebrate nature and evoke Native American design. Indian people are depicted in traditional attire and practicing traditional activities. Lakota words are explained in the text or in the footnotes. JACKIE LYNCH

Reading As an Attitude: A Child's Transformation from Non-reader to Writer

ROSA E. WARDER

I am reading a wonderful storybook. It is a simple story of a young boy who daydreams through his daily activities, and it's illustrated with colorful paintings, collage, and pencil drawings. It has a full twelve pages of text describing the boy's adventures as his daydreams mingle with his "real" life. What makes this book special, though, is that it was written and illustrated by a child who doesn't "know" how to read. The story line was dictated to an adult, who then typed it up verbatim. The author, a first grade-student, apparently didn't feel that not knowing how to read was the slightest obstacle in "writing" a picture book.

The child's quality of tackling a job and carrying it through simply because he has a vision of what he wants to create is not unusual among his classmates, many of whom have "written" books via dictation or their own invented spelling systems. Early elementary schoolteachers will no doubt recognize this as a typical attidue amongst many kindergarten through second-grade students. For many young learners it comes down to trusting their own abilities and the belief that one can do whatever one puts one's mind to, and that one can rely on adults to guide and assist when asked. Clearly, with this spirit at heart, children become the learning "sponges" they are so often termed.

So, what happens to this sensibility as we grow older? Why do we all know so many talented people who just can't seem to get their paintings down to a gallery, or their manuscript off to a publisher? When I speak with this young writer and his friends, I am struck by their confidence, their boisterousness, their cockiness. They haven't learned the social lessons of humility, capitulation, and shame. They believe they can accomplish anything. They go in and out of their fantasy life grabbing at clues and picking up lessons as easily as we adults change our shoes. They are not afraid of failure, for it has no shame attached to it yet. They jump in and do things when the feeling strikes them; they have accidents and make mistakes, and often enjoy the results of these unplanned events. These children don't take no for an answer easily. They haven't heard "Don't give me any attitude" a thousand times yet.

Illiteracy has reached frightening proportions in this country. A recent study released by the Department of Education estimates that ninety million Americans over the age of sixteen, almost half that category's total population, are functionally illiterate. When I compare the energy of the first-grade author and his classmates with these statistics, I can only guess about the series of spirit-breaking events that resulted in a population of adults without the skills to obtain employment, let alone the ability to fulfill their childhood dreams. I know they will have to develop a serious "attitude" to overcome the obstacle of illiteracy.

Attitude can be a wonderful thing. In the spirit of my first-grade friends, it is a sense of clarity, confidence and, yes, audacity. It is the faith that a dream can become something tangible, and that mistakes are just part of life. It is a way of being full of yourself and loving it, a quality that gives the typical first grader the demeanor of a champion. My first-grade friends who aren't reading yet don't say, "I can't read." Instead they refer to themselves as "new readers, beginning readers and pre-readers."

To look at the seemingly random pattern of lines and spheres and translate them into something you want to know requires an attitude. An attitude of trust that those squiggles actually stand for something real and faith that it will someday, somehow, make sense to you. This kind of attitude is sorely needed in our society. We could all learn a great deal by observing the littlest learners amongst us and trying to recapture a little attitude ourselves. By the way, the book written by this young man, The Boy Whose Dreams Come True, was entered into a local contest and won a "Reading Rainbow Exceptional Qualities Award and Certificate." The young author/illustrator is currently writing poems and painting illustrations for his second book "about nature and pollution" and seeking a publisher. Oh, yes, he is still a "pre-reader" and it's not stopping him for a second.

Rose E. Warder is an artist and writer living in Oakland, California.

My Friends

📖 Taro Gomi   ✏ Various sources
Asian American, Japanese American
1995 (1990), Chronicle Books, 📖 Gomi, Taro, *Bus Stops.*

This boardbook, with simple text accompanied by striking watercolor graphics, offers a message on the value of friendship. Each of the little girl's friends has taught her something, including animals, people, and books. "I learned to explore the earth from my friend the ant." In a wonderful combination of art and words, young children are inspired to think about the ways they are connected to the world. Readers will be encouraged by the girl's friendship with books to read more.

This boardbook for very young readers introduces a diverse set of friends.

JANIS O'DRISCOLL

A Family in Singapore

📖 Bridget Goom   ✏ Jenny Matthews
Asian, Chinese, Singapore
1986 (1984), Lerner Publications Company,
✳ Series

This book depicts the life of a twelve-year-old girl, Chor Ling, and her family in Singapore, a tiny country off the tip of Malaysia. About the size of Chicago, Singapore's geographical location in East Asia has brought both disasters and prosperity. Three-fourths of the people in Singapore are of Chinese descent, as is Chor Ling. This book focuses on the lives of Chinese immigrants even though groups from India, Malaysia, and elsewhere live there.

The life of twelve-year-old Chor Ling and her family, Chinese residents of a town in Singapore.

Chinese immigrants in Singapore maintain many of their cultural traditions. Chor Ling's father prefers chopsticks to a fork and spoon saying, "My food doesn't taste right when I eat with a fork and spoon." Chinese customs have become part of mainstream life in Singapore.

From this book young readers can learn about the history, geography, economics, and culture in Singapore.
LI LIU

Me and Neesie

📖 Eloise Greenfield   ✒ Moneta Barnett
African American
1984 (1975), Thomas Y. Crowell Company, ✳ Series

Janell's best friend, Neesie, is daring, mischievous, and funny. She teases Janell into wriggling as her mother plaits her hair.

The adventures and eventual parting of an African American girl and her imaginary best friend.

She lures Janell from her household tasks. She sneaks down on the sofa behind Aunt Bea just before she sits down. But no one else can see her because she is Janell's imaginary friend. When, much to her parents' dismay, Janell mentions Neesie to Aunt Bea, the elderly woman assumes that Janell is seeing a ghost and, clutching the arm of the sofa, she tries to chase it away. "Did I get it, Janell? Did I get it?" she asks, as Janell and Neesie flee the room before the giggles break loose.

But the friendship between the two girls—the one real, and the one imagined—begins to change as the start of the school year approaches. Neesie grows

somber, as if anticipating that she will be displaced by friends made of flesh and bone rather than imagination. Sure enough, when Janell goes off to school alone, she doesn't give much thought to Neesie—not with her new friends and new teacher to think about. When Janell comes home from school, Neesie is nowhere to be found. Happy memories comfort Janell, as does the idea of going to school the next day and playing with her new friends. "And I wouldn't never tell them about Neesie," she says. "Cause she was mine. Just mine."

Although this is one of Greenfield's older books, it is timeless for its humor and for it's vivid portrayal of one of the more unique and vivid figments of so many children's imaginations. Moneta Barnett's pencil illustrations fill each page, and while evocative of a mid-1970s milieu, they are sensitive portrayals of African American family life.
LINDA JOLIVET

Night on Neighborhood Street

📖 Eloise Greenfield   ✒ Jan Spivey Gilchrist
African American
1991, Dial Books for Young Readers, 📖 Bryan, Ashley, *Sing to the Sun*; Hudson, Wade, *Pass It On: African-American Poetry for Children.*

The short, realistic poems and reassuring illustrations in this attractive picture book are a reminder that in a world of erupting violence there are still loving families worshiping together and nurturing their children. There are still neighborhoods where children play street games together in safety and adults work out community

Realistic and reassuring short poems celebrating the love, support, and family life of African Americans.

problems at meetings. Yet the simple words and lyrical phrases also realistically tell of a child afraid of the night and young men resolutely turning away from "The Seller." Colorful and positive illustrations of African American adults and children enhance the mood. This is a book of hope and beauty. *Many poems are easy for children to learn and recite.*

There are many good books of African American poetry, but especially good are the picture books *Sing to the Sun* by Ashley Bryan and *Pass It On: African-American Poetry for Children* by Wade Hudson. GLORIA D. JACKSON

Jamaica and Brianna

📖 Juanita Havill   ✒ Ann Sibley O'Brien
African American, Asian American
1993, Houghton Mifflin & Company, ✳ Series

Jamaica and Brianna is a lovely picture book/early reader for young girls. The book centers on the friendship of two girls who are about five or six years old. Jamaica is African American and Brianna is Asian American. The two girls are in the same class in school, and they live in the same neighborhood.

The story takes place during the winter when Jamaica is given her brother's outgrown boots to wear until her parents can purchase new ones for her. The boots fit her just fine but Jamaica hates them and feels they are boyish and ugly. When Jamaica heads off through the snow to school, her friend Brianna says, "Jamaica, you're wearing boy boots!" Brianna is wearing pink boots with fuzzy white cuffs, and Jamaica feels embarrassed. She decides to hasten the demise of her hand-me-down boots by working her finger through a little hole in the toe and ripping it wide open. She is scolded for being careless with her boots, but her actions do force her mother to take her to buy new boots. When they get to the shoe store, even though Jamaica sees boots for sale just like the pink boots Brianna has, she decides to get cowgirl-style boots instead, "So Brianna won't think I'm copying her."

Jealousy threatens the friendship between an African American girl and an Asian American girl.

When Jamaica wears her new boots to school the next day, Brianna tells her they aren't "in" and Jamaica feels sad and unsure about her choice. Later, she remembers that despite thinking pink fuzzy boots were cool, she chose this cowgirl style herself because she liked it. With her boots keeping her feet dry and warm, she enjoys a day in the snow, feeling good about her choice.

As it turns out, Brianna was just upset because the pretty pink boots Jamaica had admired were really Brianna's sister's hand-me-downs, and Brianna was jealous of Jamaica's new boots. Once the girls are able to say how they really feel, and apologize for their mean remarks, they put their friendship back on track.

The charming illustrations by Anne Sibley O'Brien add a great deal to the book, making it very easy for young readers to follow the story. She captures Jamaica's and Brianna's conflicting emotions with her colorful paintings, and brings their neighborhood and school environments to life.

The relationship between Jamaica and Brianna is simple and realistic. The ease with which their friendship moves back and forth between love and hate over little things is typical of the age group depicted. The book shows readers that they can make decisions on their own despite their friends' opinions. Jamaica and Brianna would be an excellent addition to a classroom library collection for young elementary school-children. ROSA E. WARDER

Jamaica Tag-Along

📖 Juanita Havill   🖌 Ann Sibley O'Brien
African American
1989 (1984), Houghton Mifflin, ✳ Series

Jamaica has nothing to do. All her friends are busy. Her brother Ossie is going out to play basketball, he tells her she's too young to play. Jamaica follows him on her bicycle and secretly watches the boys on the court where she sees that one of them is shorter than she is.

Dashing onto the court, she dribbles, shoots, and almost makes the basket. Now she's sure the boys will let her play. Instead, they tell her to go away and play on the swings. She starts to swing, but a little boy named Berto keeps walking in front of her. She goes to the sandbox. The same little boy wants to help. When his mother tells him that "big kids don't like to be bothered by little kids," Jamaica remembers that is what her brother says to her. It hurts her feelings.

An African Amerian girl is snubbed by her older brother.

Jamaica invites Berto to help her build a sand castle. Just as they are finishing, Ossie's game ends and the other boys go home. Together they work on the castle, and Jamaica doesn't mind if Ossie tags along.

The story uses the "turning the tables" device to make its point. Ossie's rejection of Jamaica is typical of the on-again off-again nature of siblings separated by age and gender. It's natural for children to want to have their own friends and activities, and hurt feelings are inevitable. This story has a nice, safe ending. LESLIE ANDERSON MORALES

One Fine Day

📖 🖌 Nonny Hogrogian
Armenian
1974 (1971), Simon & Schuster

In this 1971 Caldecott Honor Book, a thirsty fox has his tail chopped off when he drinks milk from a woman's pail. The woman agrees to sew the tail back in place if the fox agrees to replace the milk. In his search, the fox finds he must strike many bargains before he is able to refill the container and regain his tail.

Nonny Hogrogian's illustrations portray lovely expressions on the fox's face during his deal-making with a cow, a field, a stream, a maiden, a peddler, a hen, and a miller. The soft, muted style shows the traditional Armenian clothing as a natural part of the landscape. The story and pictures are appealing to young children who will delight in the fox's escalating predicament, and will cheer him on as he makes amends.

A lively Armenian folktale about a fox's negotiations with others.

232

Cumulative bargaining to solve a problem is a familiar motif in folklore. The best-known example is probably *The Old Woman and Her Pig*, available in many versions. JANIS O'DRISCOLL

What Kind of Babysitter Is This?

Dolores Johnson

African American

1991, Macmillan Press

An African American boy, Kevin, refuses to accept a babysitter while his mother goes to school. She does not say anything, but her face shows what she feels. He whines and demands that she take him with her. At that moment, the babysitter arrives and we are introduced to Lovey Pritchard, an elderly African American woman with snow-white hair. After Kevin's mother leaves, he attempts to do the same—but only for attention—for he steps back into the house after he notes that the babysitter will not chase him.

An African American boy must deal with a new babysitter while his mother goes to school.

As he grumbles about his situation, Kevin hears her turning on the television and assumes that "now, she will be glued to her soap operas." To his amazement, she is watching a baseball game. He is pleasantly surprised, yet insists on wanting to dislike her.

He writes her off, declaring that she must not know a thing about baseball. As the game is ending, Ms. Pritchard begins to pull out objects from her purse. Kevin again assumes the worst: "Here it comes now, her telephone numbers, her nail polish, those kissy kissy books that babysitters read." Instead, Ms. Pritchard pulls out a baseball cap that she plops on her head and a pennant that she begins to wave around frantically to root for her team. Kevin is shocked.

After the game is over, Ms. Pritchard does pull out a book, and Kevin is assured that he was right, that it is a "kissy kissy book." He is lured in by curiosity and to his surprise, it is a book about baseball that she is reading. He becomes excited and draws in closer to his babysitter. He becomes so engrossed with what Ms. Pritchard is reading that he does not even hear his mother come in the door.

Upon his mother's return, he asks if Lovey can move in with them. His mother inquires about his change of heart, to hear her son reply, "She's not a babysitter, she is my friend." The readers are exposed to a young boy who, although initially resistant to this older woman, proves that although there is a vast age difference, there can still be some mutual common interests. He also proves to himself that his prejudgments were wrong.

This book would allow a mother and child to be able to talk about the necessity that a babysitter may play in their lives. MARTHA L. MARTINEZ

Coconut Kind of Day

Lynn Joseph   Sandra Speidel

Caribbean, Trinidadian

1990, Lothrop, Lee & Shepard Books

Coconut Kind of Day is a collection of poems written by Lynn Joseph to remember her childhood in Trinidad. These poems are rich with description, filling the reader's senses with sights, sounds, and scents. Joseph includes poems about snail races at school, coconut drives with her daddy, boys playing cricket, fishermen pulling in their nets, music playing, and the sounds of the island.

The author's childhood memories inspire this collection of evocative poems about Trinidad.

Each poem is illustrated with a soft pastel drawing by Sandra Speidel. Speidel chooses dark background paper and uses warm shades to create a lush, warm feeling. The combination of words and pictures in this book are a feast for the senses as well as an appreciation of the culture of Trinidad.

Joseph includes a note from the author. It describes why she was inspired to write the book and offers definitions for words in the poems that may be unfamiliar to readers. DEBORAH PATTERSON

Pepita Talks Twice

📖 ✒ Ofelia Dumas Lachtman

Hispanic, Mexican American

1995, Arte Publico, ✳ Bilingual English/Spanish

In this brightly illustrated bilingual book, a young girl named Pepita finds herself challenged by her ability to speak two languages. Frustrated at being constantly asked to translate for relatives, neighbors, and classmates, she decides to stop speaking Spanish. When asked why she is not going to speak

A Hispanic girl is challenged by the demands of being a bilingual child.

Spanish anymore, she says to her mother, "I'm tired of talking twice." But she soon realizes this means she can no longer share tender moments with her grandmother, sing special songs, or call her dog in for supper. A threat to her dog Lobo's life results in her fully appreciating the value of her bilingual gift. Both her family and her teacher impress upon her the importance of being able to speak two languages.

The story line features Pepita's decision-making process, something not often seen in books focusing on girls, and the characters are portrayed as brown-skinned Mexican Americans, which is rare in children's books with Mexican or Latina characters. Very young children may be drawn to the cartoon-like illustrations. The book is well designed and the graphic symbols used to separate the English text from the Spanish are attractive. The drawings also create a real sense of the community in which Pepita lives and goes to school, as well as the life at home she shares with her parents, brother Juan, and beloved dog. DAPHNE MUSE

Can't Sit Still

📖 Karen E. Lotz ✒ Colleen Browning

African American

1993, Dutton Children's Books, 📚 Jonas, Ann, *Color Dance.*

In Karen E. Lotz's *Can't Sit Still*, the reader meets a wonderful and vivacious African American girl who is both curious and fascinated by the changing environment surrounding her. The book focuses on her reactions to those changes and her own discoveries about herself and her relationship to them.

Her high energy and need to explore, combined with her inability simply to "sit still," are reflected

in her everyday routine experiences. From riding her bike through homework to helping her mom, she displays a keen sense of longing to be in the world and finding much happiness there. That sense of childhood happiness remains all too rare in much of children's literature.

A child observes her environment and interacts with what's around her.

The poetic narrative and simple vocabulary make it a great book for those who are relatively new readers. The author introduces each season and provides activities to go along with each. During winter, we see the young girl playing in the snow. In summer, she jumps in and out of the water from a hydrant, and come spring, she dances in the rain. The vivid and lively illustrations make the reader "feel" each season. *Can't Sit Still* provides a special look at the meaning, appreciation, and power of the small things in life. MARTHA L. MARTINEZ

Yagua Days

📖 Cruz Martel ✒ Jerry Pinkney

Caribbean, Hispanic, Puerto Rican

1976, Dial

Set in New York's Lower East Side and Puerto Rico, *Yagua Days* tells the story of a boy's first trip to his parents' homeland. One rainy day at the beginning of summer vacation, the young protagonist, Adan Riera finds himself trapped in his parents' New York bodega with nowhere to play. The mailman, a jovial character well-known in the neighborhood, arrives and tells Adan that what seems

Life in a Puerto Rican neighborhood in New York City is compared to life in Puerto Rico.

like a washout is actually a "yagua day." Before Adan can learn what this means, Adan's father opens a letter from his brother inviting the Riera family to his *finca* (plantation) in Puerto Rico for two weeks.

The story shifts suddenly to Puerto Rico, where Riera meets his Unclue Ulise and his family at their mountainside home, shares feasts with them, explores the bountiful plantation, and finally learns the meaning of the mysterious term everyone has

234

mentioned to him: "yagua" is the large outer covering of a palm frond. On rainy days, children and adults alike use these huge surfaces as sleds, sliding down wet, grassy hills. When Adan returns to New York, he tells the mailman all about his "yagua days."

This engaging story will resonate for any child who has "returned home"—that is, traveled to the country where their parents were born. Cruz captures the sensations of meeting family members for the first time, enjoying huge meals, and discovering a way of life that is at once new and yet somewhat familiar. There are a few flaws to the book. The sterile dialogue detracts from the otherwise enjoyable story, and adults may want to alert young readers that the life depicted is idyllic and should not be taken as a representative Puerto Rican experience. The black-and-white illustrations by the acclaimed Jerry Pinkney evoke both New York streets and the rural, mountainous Puerto Rican landscape in loose, varied strokes. Together with the text, they convey a sense of the communtites in Puerto Rico and New York. The book includes a useful glossary of the Spanish terms sprinkled throughout the story. DAPHNE MUSE

The Woman Who Outshone the Sun

📖 Alejandro C. Martinez 🖋 Harriet Rohmer, David Schecter, and Fernando Olivera
Hispanic, Mexican
1991, Children's Book Press, ✴ Bilingual English/Spanish

This is a beautifully written and illustrated bilingual book based on a poem by Alejandro Cruz Martinez. Martinez was a promising young Zapotec Indian poet who spent many years collecting the oral traditions of his people, including the story of Lucia Zentano upon which this folktale is based. He published his own version of the story as a poem. Martinez was killed in 1987 while organizing the Zapotecs to regain their lost water rights.

A beautiful and instructive tale about a mysterious newcomer to a Mexican village.

One day a beautiful and mysterious woman, with long flowing hair, arrives in the village wrapped in nature and surrounded by butterflies and flowers. Many of the villagers are utterly fascinated by Lucia; others are afraid of her. The river that runs through the village loves Lucia and clings longingly to her

each time she washes her hair. Each day she combs the water back out into the river.

While the elders in the village respect Lucia, some of the younger people are cruel. They tease her and call her names. She ignores their taunts, which only makes them angrier. Their treatment of her becomes increasingly cruel and hostile until she's finally driven away from the village. But the water from the river clings to her and will not let go, so she takes it with her. The loss of water brings about great suffering amongst the people in the village and they go in search of her, begging forgiveness. Lucia consents to their request only if they agree to be kind to those who are different.

There are many lessons embedded in this tale, including the need to respect human differences and nature. The combination of the environmental and acceptance themes underscores those lessons. *It is also nice to present children with the opportunity to teach history and cultural traditions. The parallel between Martinez's efforts to organize his people and the legend of Lucia could open a deeper discussion with children about the history of Mexico, and about current political conditions.* DEBBIE WEI

Nettie Jo's Friends

📖 Patricia McKissack 🖋 Scott Cook
African American
1994 (1989), Alfred A. Knopf Books for Young Readers, ✴ Series, 📚 Lada, Josefa Kratky, *Homes.*

Nettie Jo's cousin is getting married, and just as the finishing touches are being made on her flower girl's dress, she learns that she won't be able to take her most beloved doll, Annie Mae—not with her looking "all tattered and such." But Nettie Jo, with Annie Mae in hand, begins a quest for a needle. The quest yields a red feather, a ribbon, a penny, but no needle. Nettie Jo asks Miz Rabbit for some help, but Miz Rabbit has no time for such concerns. Her ears have flopped so that she won't be able to hear fox as he comes after her. Nettie Jo takes the ribbon she's found and ties up Miz Rabbit's ears and she is happily on her way. Nettie Jo continues her search and turns up an empty spool, a hat, a button, a comb and a thimble, but no sewing needle. She and her doll next encounter Fox, and she asks him if he can help her, but he replies that he'd be of no help—he's been blinded by the sun. Nettie Jo offers him the hat she's found and he, too, is on his way. And so the story goes until Nettie Jo eventually loses hope of ever finding a needle. Neither she nor Annie Mae will be going to any wedding. She sits beside a window until drawn outside by a loud racket. A parade of her animal friends come to thank her and present her with the needle she so needs.

In a delightful fable of friendship, an African American girl is rewarded for helping her animal friends.

This is a fairly predictable and straightforward tribute to the Golden Rule that many young readers will undoubtedly absorb quickly and enthusiastically. The illustrations, a warm mix of watercolor and colored pencil steeped in rich golds and oranges, are sure to appeal to almost any reader of this delightful tale in the African American folklore vein.

CHRISTINE PALMER

Heroes

📖 Ken Mochizuki ✎ Dom Lee

Asian American, Japanese American

1995, Lee & Low Books

A Japanese American who was born and raised in Seattle's large Asian community, author Mochizuki describes some of the key events in Japanese American history for children. In his fine previous picture book, the award winning *Baseball Saved Us* (1993), he narrated the experiences of a Japanese American boy placed in an internment camp during World War II. In his new picture book, *Heroes*, he describes what it was like to be a Japanese American boy growing up in the United States at the height of the Vietnam War.

A Japanese American boy faces racism from his classmates during the Vietnam War.

Donnie is a typical American kid who loves football and hanging out with his friends, but he's tired of seeing Japanese people portrayed as the bad guys in the movies. Actually, with the Vietnam War on, simply being Asian is bad enough. Kids who don't know him point their fingers at him at school and make shooting noises.

His (non-Asian) friends, who brag about what their fathers did in World War II and love to play war themselves, insist that he has to play the bad guy. When Donnie says that his father fought for the United States during World War II and that his uncle served in Korea, the other kids don't believe it and their teasing increases. Worse still, neither his father nor his uncle will talk about their military experiences or let him borrow any of their medals to show the other kids.

They don't even want Donnie playing war or watching war movies. As Uncle Yosh says, "Real heroes don't brag. They just do what they are supposed to do."

Eventually Donnie's father realizes that his son is in pain and in need of heroes. One day he and Uncle Yosh pick Donnie up after school wearing their old military uniforms covered with the medals they'd won. Donnie's father, we discover, was a member of the 442nd Regiment, one of the most highly decorated units in U.S. Army history. Needless to say, the other kids are impressed, the teasing stops, and Donnie, his self-respect restored, leads everyone off to the playground to play football.

There is still a significant amount of prejudice against Asian Americans in the United States, but, until recently, it received relatively little press. Books like *Heroes* are important because our children, whatever their ethnic and racial background, need to be aware of the major contributions that Asian Americans have made to American society. Beyond its value as a teaching tool, however, Ken Mochizuki's *Heroes* is also an excellent story, and Dom Lee's illustrations, many of which have the look of sepia photographs, ably support that story. This book is strongly recommended. MIKE LEVY

236

A Promise to the Sun: A Story of Africa

Tololwa M. Mollel Beatriz Vidal

African, East African

1992, Joy Street Books

Children love fanciful stories about how things came to be, and every culture seems to have its own fable about how the sea became salt or how poison came into the world or why the possum has a naked tail. This book tells a traditional East African story of why the bat sleeps during the day and flies at night, and why the sun seems to linger a while at the horizon before finally setting.

A story of why bats sleep during the day and fly at night.

"Long ago, when the world was new," it begins, "a severe drought hit the land of the birds." Beatriz Vidal's intricate watercolor illustration perfectly captures the sense of dryness: the wilting maize plants and shriveling trees. Yet we know from the start that there are magical possibilities in this dying land, because in the limbs of the tree that spreads across the page are dozens of colorful birds. Vidal has done her homework; the birds are weaver birds, peacocks, guinea fowl, whydahs, lovebirds, and other magnificent creatures that really do live in East Africa.

The birds hold a meeting and decide to send a representative to go look for rain. In an odd twist, the bat ("their distant cousin") is chosen to go. She visits the moon, the stars, the clouds, the winds, and finally the sun, crying, "Earth has no rain, Earth has no food, Earth asks for rain!" The sun agrees to help if the birds will promise to build it a nest in the treetops so that it does not have to travel all the way to the horizon each night.

The bat agrees; she herself does not know how to build a nest, but she is sure the birds will gladly do this simple thing in exchange for rain. What happens next is fairly predictable, but charming nonetheless.

Tololwa M. Molle is a gifted writer, with a keen sense of the simple detail that will make an image click in a child's mind. Here, as in *The Orphan Boy* and in other Molle renderings of traditional tales, the language is lilting and evocative. His sentences are languid and dreamy, easy on the ear and full of images.

The vocabulary is more extensive than in some picture books, making it a difficult book for young readers, but even the youngest listeners will get the sense of what is happening and understand the bat's actions and feelings.

There are many stories available that tell how the world came to be the way it is. *A Promise to the Sun* deserves inclusion in a collection because of its rich text and illustrations, because its hero is female, and because it is simply a good story.

CYNTHIA A. BILY

Mrs. Katz and Tush

 Patricia Polacco

African American, Jewish

1992, Bantam, Audio Cassette

A Jewish widow, an African American boy, and a Manx cat named Tush ("she has no tail—all you can see is her tush")—form an unlikely familial alliance in this sentimental tale. Larnel and Mrs. Katz spend most of their afternoons together. She tells him stories of her native Poland and invites him to share Seder with her. She explains Passover to him; how her people, the Jews, were slaves like his ancestors. She also teaches him to say kaddish for her husband and to lay a rock on his headstone for remembrance.

An African American boy and a childless Jewish woman develop a life-long loving relationship.

As the years pass, Larnel grows up and gets married, but Mrs. Katz remains an important part of his life. When she dies, he has the following inscribed on her headstone: "Mrs. Katz, our bubee...such a person."

Patricia Polacco draws on her own Eastern European heritage as the basis for this story. It focuses on relationships rather than action. As a result, warmth and love flow from the book. Polacco's painted illustrations reflect this and give the book an old-fashioned flavor. The characters' features are exaggerated—Larnel's head is too big for his body, but this does not detract. One page shows Mrs. Katz, Larnel, and Tush joyfully dancing. The artwork is so lively it seems as if they will dance right off the page. *This book would be a wonderful read-aloud as the language is just as lively.* PAM CARLSON

Dragonfly's Tale

Kristina Rodanas
Native American, Pueblo
1995 (1991), Houghton Mifflin

This cautionary tale from the Ashiwi Zuni people of New Mexico tells of the dangers of squandering wealth, and boasting to one's less fortunate neighbors, and also demonstrates the rewards of generosity. A prosperous village decides to impress its less fortunate neighbors by staging a mock battle in which all the weapons are made of food. The invited neighbors are puzzled by this vulgar waste of precious resources. During the festivities, the harvest goddesses known as Corn Maidens appear disguised as old beggar women. Two kind children, brother and sister, offer them bread, but are quickly scolded by an elder who considers that act more wasteful than the food fight in

An Ashiwi Zuni tale about the dangers of squandering wealth and boasting to one's less-fortunate neighbors.

progress. The Corn Maidens, appalled by the terrible waste and greed, send mice and insects to the village that night to deplete the grain stores. Undaunted, the villagers continue to live wastefully in anticipation of another great harvest. Instead, however, the Corn Maidens inflict a terrible drought on the village, and the humbled villagers go to their neighbors to seek help, inadvertently leaving the two generous children behind. In an effort to comfort his sister, the brother fashions a toy insect out of corn husks, which comes magically alive and acts as a messenger to the Corn Maidens. Remembering the past kindness of the children, the Corn Maidens relieve the drought. The insect made by the boy becomes the first dragonfly, which hovers near corn stalks to this day. In today's greedy society, this story poignantly illustrates the consequences of waste and ostentatiousness.

The author's richly detailed illustrations beautifully capture many details of pueblo life, from the dance to summon the Corn Maidens to the traditional dwellings and clay bread ovens to the geometric designs on the pottery. This engaging traditional story, first recorded in 1884 and here adapted by the author, is well told and also contains many universal folkloric elements. *It could be used as part of a unit on folktales equally well as one on Native American Pueblo culture.* JODIE LEVINE

My Friend Leslie: The Story of a Handicapped Child

Maxine B. Rosenberg   George Ancona
Physically Disabled
1983, Lothrop, Lee & Shepard

Using strong black-and-white photographs to bring the reader into the story, Rosenberg portrays the relationship between a kindergarten child with multiple handicaps and a classmate who befriends her.

Leslie is one of the more than two million special needs children who have been mainstreamed effectively into public schools. It takes her a little longer to do things, but she demonstrates her own level of

This picture book presents a multi-handicapped kindergarten child who is accepted by her classmates.

competency in taking on and completing assignments. She has an outgoing personality and proves to be popular among her classmates.

Using the voice of the sympathetic narrator Karin, the warm book conveys the intelligence and endearing qualities of this particular girl. But while some strides have been made in accepting children with disabilities, there remains a real need for them to be included as a natural part of our lives. While Leslie is friendly and popular, other special needs children may have demanding personalities, much like their nondisabled counterparts. The picture of disabled children has been painted far too narrowly in this book; their personalities and needs are as varied as those of other children.

Young children just learning to read or struggling to develop their pre-reading skills will find this book accessible. MEREDITH ELIASSEN

237

Carolina Shout!

📘 Alan Schroeder ✏ Bernie Fuchs

African American

1995, Dial Books for Young Readers, 📖 Logan, Judith, *When the Ragman Sings*; Nye, Naomi Shihab, *The Tree Is Older Than You Are*; *This Same Sky: A Collection of Poems from around the World*.

Early in the century, street vendors used "short, rhythmic songs to call attention to their wares." *Carolina Shout!* pulls together some of those songs, or "shouts," as background to the story of Delia, who lives in Charleston, South Carolina. Her sister can't hear a thing when she goes outside, except maybe a train whistle or a mosquito. But Delia tells her sister, "You're just not listenin'. There's plenty of music, if you wanna hear it."

The book is a collection of the musical shouts Delia hears each day in the streets of Charleston, South Carolina.

There's music in the raindrops on tin roofs, in Mama's laughter, in the wheels of the milk wagon and the clink of the milk bottles—and in the chants of the workers. The carpenters sing, "Whomp, bidda-bay!/Whomp, bidda-bay!/ Come six o'clock,/we quit our day!" The Waffle Man cries, "Get 'em hot,/Piping hot,/Get 'em while they're/good 'n hot!/Waf—fffles here!" Hopscotchers and rope jumpers make up the craziest rhymes, but Delia's favorite is the Charcoal Man who comes down the street every evening with coal dust in his throat and buckets of coal in his hands.

The author's note points out that no real attempt has been made to collect the vendor's calls, but that "tantalizing scraps appear here and there." The opera Porgy and Bess includes three. *Several books that Schroeder cites have collections of shouts. Students may want to try to hunt down some of the "wonderful shouts" the author says he was unable to include, such as the Watermelon Vendor's Cry or the Cry of the Ah-Got-Um Man.*

Though there's no conflict in the story, the language is poetic and strong, a real celebration of "an authentic bit" of America's cultural history. Fuchs' faces and street scenes shine with light and reflections, pulling the reader right into Charleston at the turn of the century. The faces in these pages are warm and lively. Each person is individually drawn and each looks like he or she has great life stories to tell.

Carolina Shout! can be used with many age levels. Young children will be captivated by the sheer sounds of the words. Students of all ages can go on "listening hunts" for the everyday music they hear around them. Older children can collect or make up their own street rhymes and interview grandparents and others to research playground and community lore.

In *When the Ragman Sings*, a middle grade novel by Judith Logan, Dorothea, a young girl in Baltimore, associates the cry of the ragman—"Rags, rags! Old iron and bags"—with the death of her mother. *Carolina Shout!* can also be used to introduce the idea that people everywhere create poetry. Naomi Shihab Nye has selected poems for *The Tree Is Older Than You Are* (Simon and Schuster, 1995), and poems from Mexico with paintings by Mexican artists in *This Same Sky: A Collection of Poems from around the World* (Macmillan, 1992). JANE KURTZ

Town Child

📘 Mary Carter Smith ✏ Sylvia James George

African American

1976, Nordika

In *Town Child*, Mary Carter Smith uses her experiences as a school librarian and professional storyteller to recreate the poetic voices of city children. The collection includes poems about children at home and at school, during all seasons, and all around town. While there is a positive tone throughout the book, there are a few poems about some of the serious problems that worry children.

From the opening poem, "Our Town" until the end of the collection, the reader is treated to the special highlights of city life, especially Baltimore, the author's hometown. "Crab Time," "White Steps," and "Haiku Baltimore" share images of this East Coast town.

Poetry brings to life the sights and sounds of a city and the African Americans who live there.

Other poems such as "Tiger" and "Window Garden" remind us of the many cities where there are zoos and flowerboxes in the windows. Some of the negative aspects of city life are viewed in the City Sounds section. The noisy city has ambulance screams, dogs barking, and garbage trucks that go "chomp, chomp, chomp." Even a city child's view of rural areas is shared in the section on "The Country." "My Brother and Me" relates the thoughts of one child who likes the city and one who likes the country. Another poem describes the experience of using an outhouse.

The strength of the collection is the sensitive way in which racial issues are handled. High self-esteem and pride in the African American heritage mark the poems in the "Colors" section. Two of the most well-known poems, "Colors" and "Black is," promote brotherhood and celebrate the differences in African-American people. The sadness a child would feel following the riots in cities after the death of Martin Luther King Jr. is the subject of the poem "Saturday, April 6, 1968." The description of the looting, fires, and soldiers in the street may remind today's children (born after the 1960s) of their emotions during the recent Los Angeles riots. The "Untruths" section has poems about the verbal abuse children experience.

Though first published a quarter-century ago, *Town Child* still is meaningful for today's young people and the adults who work with them. The line drawings that are interspersed throughout provide a visual highlight to some of the poems. Some of the slang is outdated (there should be footnotes for phrases like "I dig it" and dances called the hustle and the bump) but the book documents the speech of the sixties. Even though this collection is small, an index of the poems would have also been a helpful research tool. *Children enjoy sharing selections from this volume for their school projects, church programs (there is a section entitled "Church"), and other oral presentations. Most of the poems are short enough to memorize. Individually or as a group, children can give a dramatic presentation of these poems.* MARTHA RUFF

The Last Princess: The Story of Princess Ka'iulani of Hawaii

📖 Fay Stanley ✒ Diane Stanley

Hawaiian, Pacific Island

1994 (1991), Four Winds Press

This biographical story is a picture book for children up through the fifth grade. It tells the sad but revealing facts of the betrayal of the Hawaiian people by the early American settlers.

The pictures and writing of the first few pages read like a fairy tale. A beautiful princess grows up in comfort adored by all. But then the author relates the conspiracy to annex the islands to the United States. The king dies suddenly, there is an abortive native revolt, and Queen Liliuokalani is dethroned and impris-

A picture book about the takeover of Hawaii by the U.S. and Princess Ka'iulani's fight to keep her land.

oned. Princess Ka'iulani is in school in England during most of these tragic happenings. When she returns to the islands and realizes that the country is being taken over by the United States, she goes to Washington to intercede on behalf of her people. She meets with President Coolidge, who seems sympathetic to her cause but is unable, or unwilling, to curb the actions of the white settlers and the U.S. Navy. Soon after Coolidge leaves office, Congress votes to annex Hawaii (1897). The princess dies at the young age of twenty-three after catching a fever.

The text of the story is dramatic and emotional, supported by the many colorful illustrations. Princess Ka'iulani is portrayed as an intelligent, courageous, and loyal young woman. GLORIA D. JACKSON

The Park Bench

📖 Fumiko Takeshita (translated by Ruth A. Kanagy) ✒ Mamoru Suzuk

Asian, Japanese

1989 (1988), Kane Miller Book Publishers

Especially popular with primary school students, this delightful book chronicles a day in the life of a special park bench. In this park, there is one worker who takes especially good care of this rather intriguing, almost magical, bench to ensure that it appears clean and welcoming. The caretaker keeps an eye on all the comings and goings and well-being of the bench. From his first friendly pat

This delightful Japanese picture book observes a day in the life of a park bench.

in the early morning to his good-night wishes, the caretaker demonstrates tremendous pride in his efforts to maintain this bench. While the story line itself is not unique to any one culture, the setting provides the reader with a small but interesting visit into urban Japan, and the story shows how one worker in this country takes special pride in what he does to make the surroundings beautiful for everyone. NAOMI WAKAN

Fox's Dream

Keizaburo Tejima

Asian, Japanese

1990 (1985), The Putnam Publishing Group

Winner of the *New York Times* Best Illustrated Children's Book Award, *Fox's Dream* includes five-color woodcut illustrations that bring to life the lovely beauty of the vast, silent, wooded mountains. The illustrations, more than the text, convey the mood and visions of the lonely fox, as the branches of the snow-covered trees become long-horned deer-like companions and then four large white birds in the fox's imagination.

But the story also commands attention and appreciation. On a cold night when "the bears and chipmunks are asleep for the winter," one small, brown fox moves through the forest. The fox has the unattainable visions of deer and birds mentioned above, then a vision of a vixen with three pups, sparks the memory of "leaping with his brother and sister in the warmth of the gentle sun."

In this Japanese tale, a lonely fox finally finds a real friend to replace his imaginary ones.

The visions fade. The fox wanders on through the lonely forest until finally he sees a real vixen with her fur shining in the morning light. The story closes with the two foxes nuzzling each other, with the promise of companionship, new life, and spring.

Keizaburo Tejima has written and illustrated a number of outstanding picture books, all of them about the wildlife and native people of his homeland, Hokkaido, the northern island of Japan. We are fortunate to have English translations of a number of his books to introduce children to a little-known and very beautiful area of Japan which does not conform to our stereotypes. It is noteworthy that the last indigenous people of Japan, the Ainu, make their homes on the island of Hokkaido. *This book would be an excellent vehicle for opening a discussion on diversity within Japanese culture.* ANNA PEARCE

Literary Trick or Treat

ROSA E. WARDER

In an effort to upgrade and support the literary health of her community, for the past fifteen years "The Book Lady" of Oakland, California, has treated young children to books instead of candy at Halloween. Only one recipient has refused. A twelve-year-old boy responded to a book about to go into his hands by saying, "I don't want no book." Twenty minutes later, he was back with his curiously wide-eyed six-year-old brother. Slightly embarrassed and definitely wearing the look of having been chastised on his face, he said, "My mamma told me I'd better come back and get a book. Can I have one for my little brother, too?"

Pulling from the hundreds of review copies she receives annually, selections donated by supporters and those found in second-hand stores, the Book Lady has introduced young children to the works of Tom Feelings, Ed Young, Virginia Hamilton, Candy Dawson Boyd, Sundairia Morninghouse, and many others. Her literary treat has become a such a highly anticipated tradition in the community, some of the trick-o-treaters return during the year to read their stories and ask for more books. Parents have even begun to request books for themselves.

In the fifteen years she's been tricking them with her literary treats, the Book Lady estimates that she has donated more than 5,000 books to two generations of children who live in her working class neighborhood.

Rosa E. Warder is an artist and writer living in Oakland, California.

What a Wonderful World

George David Weiss and Bob Thiele

Ashley Bryan

Multicultural

1995, Simon & Schuster

"What a wonderful world!" These words resonate in my head often, and I was delighted to see one of my favorite songs adapted as a children's book. I was also excited by Ashley Bryan's illustrations, which serve as the visual accompaniment for the lyrics. The naive

Depicts children from many backgrounds in a puppet show that brings Louis Armstrong lyrics to life.

style of the brightly colored illustrations and the puppet-like characters should prove especially appealing to very young children. It is somewhat curious and feels stereotypical, however, that the only child who appears in costume is the Native American girl.

This memorable song by George David Weiss and Bob Thiele with its simple, yet touching, expression of beauty and harmony, was made famous by the great jazz trumpeter and vocalist Louis Armstrong. *Along with playing a recording of the song, I would encourage teachers to incorporate biographical information on Armstrong with the use of this book.*

With the shared hope of the lyrics vividly portrayed through the illustrations and the spirit of the song rather contagious, *What a Wonderful World* should be welcomed in any class of young children.

DAPHNE MUSE

Music, Music for Everyone

Vera B. Williams
Multicultural
1988 (1984), William Morrow

Music, Music for Everyone is the third story Vera B. Williams has written and illustrated about Rosa and her family. In the first book Rosa, her mother, and her grandmother save up to buy a comfortable chair. In the second story they use the money they've collected in a jar to buy an accordion for Rosa's birthday. As this story begins the chair is empty and so is their jar.

Rosa and her friends start a band to raise money and inspire everyone in the neighborhood to dance and sing.

Grandma is ill and there is no money to spare for the jar. To refill it, Rosa decides to start a band with her friends Leora, Jenny and Mae. The girls practice together and name themselves the Oak Street Band. Leora's mother gives them their first job, inviting them to play for the fiftieth anniversary of the opening of their family store. This party is a neighborhood event and grandma is well enough to attend. The girls are a hit, inspiring everyone to dance. After the party the girls share the money equally. Rosa immediately puts her share into the jar.

Williams uses brightly colored paintings to illustrate the story adding to the festive feeling throughout much of the book. Each page has a decorative border which the illustrator uses to show images from the earlier stories or to further this story along.

As in each of the other stories it is clear that Rosa is part of a community. Her family, her friends, and her friends' families all play a role in helping her to achieve her goal of contributing to the family jar. Rosa shows readers how to set a goal and the steps she goes through to reach it. She is a thoughtful, hardworking, strong female character.

DEBORAH PATTERSON

The Junior Thunder Lord

Laurence Yep Robert Van Nutt
Asian, Chinese
1994, BridgeWater Books

241

Adapted from a seventeenth-century Chinese fable by Pu Songling, *The Junior Thunder Lord* centers on a young boy named Yue who has trouble learning his school lessons. He is helped by Xia, the smartest boy in class, who says, "Those at the top should help those at the bottom." Yue remembers these words into adulthood. One day he meets a man whom the townspeople call "Bearface," because they think he is stupid and ugly, when actually he is just unfamiliar with their ways. Yue, remembering Xia's words, buys Bearface a meal, and later Bearface saves Yue from drowning. They become friends and travel the countryside together. One day they return to Yue's village only to find that it has been ravaged by drought. To Yue's surprise, Bearface begins to summon the rainclouds, explaining that he is actually a Junior Thunder Lord who has been banished to the earth for insulting a Dragon King. Having served his three-year sentence, he returns with Yue to the sky to show Yue how to squeeze rain from the clouds. He showers Yue's village with rain, and returns Yue safely home. From that day on, each time it rains, Yue and his family look up into the sky and give thanks to the Junior Thunder Lord.

A seventeenth-century Chinese fable about a boy rewarded for his compassion.

Yue is rewarded for his compassion, for not judging Bearface on his looks or his unusual ways, and for remembering his friend's advice: "Those at the top should help those at the bottom"— a profound message for those who have risen to great heights and fail to look behind them.

This book is brightly illustrated depicting the Chinese people in traditional clothing.

BARBARA SMITH REDDISH

Making Books Your Business

Daphne Muse

Every Tuesday and Thursday at 7:45 A.M., three cashiers, three security guards, and three stocks clerks appear at the back door of P.S. 121, an elementary school in New York City's Bronx borough. The employees quickly start unstacking tables and setting up a display rack. By 8 A.M., they have transformed a small, drab entryway into The Children's Bookstore.

During the next thirty minutes, they assist forty to fifty customers and take in $60 to $100. Then these nine employees, all fifth-graders, leave for class. So do their supervisors: Robin Cohen, a reading teacher, who created this thriving bookstore; and her partner, Veray Darby, a fourth-grade teacher.

Cohen explained how the bookstore started: "Students wanted to read outside of class, but they had no books. There were no bookstores in this part of the Bronx, and the local library's hours had been severely cut. The children were begging for books, and we had nothing for them."
Like many teachers at P.S. 121, Cohen had a classroom library, but she knew her students needed more. "It's vital that students read and be read to at home, so their reading skills grow stronger and they learn to enjoy books," she said.

Using her own money, she bought enough books to fill two large buckets, then let students borrow the books to read at home. There was a $2 replacement fee for lost or damaged books.

Soon, many students were reporting books lost and paying the fines. Cohen thought the children were being irresponsible—until she noticed some of the "lost" books in their book bags and desks. But when she told students they could return the books and she would refund their money, they refused. They wanted to keep the books. That's when Cohen realized that the students were "buying" their favorite books.

Could something be done to help students own books to read for pleasure? Cohen decided to start a bookstore right inside the school. The idea was a gamble. "We couldn't envision how it would work," recalled Dianne Dewwerreau, president of the P.S. 121 Parents' Association. But the leaders of the 500-member group were impressed by the enthusiasm of the two teachers. With the parents' support—as well as that of the school's principal, Virginia Fiore, and a $1,300 start-up grant from the New York City Teachers' Consortium—Cohen and Darby bought book racks, a cart, plastic baskets, and about $500 worth of books.

The two teachers put up fliers seeking students to work as everything from clerks to book critics to advertising executives. Students had to fill out a job application, stating their qualifications and why they wanted the job. They also needed a teacher's recommendation and a parent's permission. Other applicants were interviewed during lunch hour. Then the new employees were trained.

Store clerks learned how to organize display tables and help students make selections. Cashiers learned how to use calculators and make change. Security guards studied how to direct customer traffic and check that all books purchased had been stamped.

Cohen and Darby also hired students as book critics who read store selections and wrote reviews. Advertising executives made posters to promote the store. The student employees were paid with certificates redeemable for free books—two certificates a month for employees who arrived on time on the mornings they had selected to work.

Parents devised an inventory system for the bookstore. Except for those with tapes, all books sold for $1.50.

The bookstore opened in the fall of 1991 in an alcove by the school's back door. At first, business was slow. But soon posters, announcements at the school, and fliers mailed to homes drew customers. In three months, the bookstore made back its initial investment. It has been operating on its profits ever since.

"We even develop a layaway plan," Cohen said, "because kids can't pay for a book all at once. The whole thing has become a learning experience. For example, teachers use the critics' reviews as examples of how to write a summary, and the job application as examples of how to fill out forms."

A majority of the customers at The Children's Bookstore was aged five to eleven. The books are all for children ranging from classics like *Charlotte's Web* to biographies and books on sport figures. But the bookstore also has attracted adults who come to buy books for their children. "And many parents like being able to spend an extra ten or fifteen minutes with their kids in the morning browsing in the bookstore," said Dianne Dessereau. "Parents bring in other parents to the bookstore. People talk about the books. The senior kids also get a sense of leadership, a sense of how to relate to people in a workplace."

"When they buy books, the kids are more eager to read them," said Brian McFaden, father of a second-grader, Brian Jr. "My son picks out what he likes, and we sit down and read the books together at home. He also brings his books to school to share with his class."

One morning found Aja Ortiz, a fourth-grader, prepared to purchase a book of mystery stories. "They have a nice selection—books with pictures and also a lot of words," she said. Ian Spence, a second-grader was examining several books. "I have $1 with me, so I'll put one on layaway," he said, showing four quarters. "I like to look at the books first."

"I'm good with math, and now I'm learning to be good with money," said fifth-grader Tamika Brown, a cashier.

"I like to help the kids," said Jennifer Piña, a security guard. "It's fun working in a bookstore. I think I might want to do this when I grow up."

As The Children's Bookstore grows, Cohen and Darby face new challenges. "The hardest part is just getting the books," Cohen said. They now have ordered from book clubs' clearance catalogs, bought books from flee-market vendors, and driven to a publisher's warehouse sale in search of low-cost books. But more sources are needed. Last summer, Cohen wrote to children's book publishers across he country, seeking to purchase books. Not one replied.

"To keep prices down, we have to keep our average cost to $1 per book," she explained. "Any profits are used to buy new books, and we have also given some money to the school." Last spring, the bookstore helped the school buy a tripod and a video recorder.

Reading always has been important at P.S. 121. "Communication skills—reading, writing, speaking, and listening—are the most important set of skills you can give children in elementary school," said Principal Fiore. Twice a day, every teacher reads a literature selection aloud in class, and there are also select reading periods, when both students and teacher read books. "Instead of reading textbooks, we use books of literature, such as *Call of the Wild* and *The Diary of Anne Frank*," Fiore added. "I even give parents a homework assignment: Read to your child at least fifteen minutes a night. A child who is read to will do much better."

She's thrilled that students are still excited about the store—students like Loretta Jackson, 10, a critic who stated on her job application that she wanted to be an undercover detective and a poet. "If I ever stopped reading," Loretta said, "I don't know what would happen to me."

For more information, write to: Robin Cohen, P.S. 121, Dept. P, 2750 Throop Ave., Bronx, N.Y. 10469. (Include a self-addressed stamped envelope.)

243

Grade Four to Grade Six

Sometimes I Think I Hear My Name

📕 Avi

Dysfunctional

1995 (1982), Avon

Thirteen-year-old Conrad Murray lives in St. Louis with his aunt and uncle because his divorced parents are not capable of caring for him. For spring vacation, he sets his sights on going to England, but has

A boy and a girl become friends and set out to find their estranged families.

a change of heart and decides to visit his parents. When he goes to get his airline ticket, he meets and befriends Nancy, a girl who also lives apart from her parents. Conrad finds that his parents have no room for him in their lives. Upon his return to St. Louis, he receives a letter from Nancy that states that she has been sent to Switzerland because her parents felt he was a poor influence.

The lack of parental support and bonding is clearly demonstrated in the relationships that both Nancy and Conrad have with their parents. While Conrad has supportive relatives that nurture and care for him, Nancy depends solely on her friendship with Conrad to sustain her. Although Conrad's parents do not meet his expectations, he comes to appreciate the love and support provided by his aunt and uncle. On the other hand, Nancy blames herself for her parents' problems and withdraws into herself. Both Nancy and Conrad have access to resources that provide for their material needs.

While both characters accept the realities of their situations, what will happen to them in the future is left to the reader's imagination. The depth of their pain remains unclear, and it appears as though Nancy is dependent on this young boy to carry her through this difficult time of transition in her life. This open-ended, unrealistic approach also prevents the readers from understanding more about the parents and why the divorces resulted in the children being set so far apart from their parents.

BARBARA A. KANE

Leaving for America

📕 Roslyn Bresnick-Perry ✏ Mira Reisberg

Jewish

1992, Children's Book Press

Of the many books dealing with the immigrant experience, most approach the subject from the perspective of the recently arrived immigrant, focusing on the journey over or the first encounter with a new home. This is one of very few to look at what precedes the journey— the decision to leave and the last days in one's old home.

In this bittersweet story, the author recounts of her girlhood emigration from a Jewish shtetl (village) in Russia to join her father in the United

A rare look at the author's last days in the Russian shtetl of her youth before emigrating to America.

States. Told from the young girl's perspective, the story focuses on her last days in Russia, many painful good-byes, and the memories she will keep all her life. She is sad to know that she will most likely never again see many of the people she leaves behind, and fearful about entering a new, unfamiliar culture. But she is also filled with excited anticipation. Details such as her mother's decision to take her feather bed and embroidered underwear because it might be impossible to get anything so nice in America, or the grandfather asking the narrator if she will

remember to be a true Jewish daughter when she's gone, illuminate the range of emotions surrounding the family's difficult decision to leave their family and community behind.

The bright, beautiful paintings that illustrate the text makes use of collage techniques, featuring photographs of the real-life families of the author and illustrator on the walls of the houses. Yiddish words are used in the text. JODIE LEVINE

The Fred Field

Barbara Hood Burgess
African American
1995 (1994), Dell Yearling, ✳ Series, 📖 Burgess, Barbara, *Oren Bell.*

The Fred Field is a sequel to Burgess' first book, *Oren Bell.* Oren, his sisters LaTonya and Brenda, and friends attempt to solve the murder of their friend, Fred Lightfoot. Fred was a young teen who was a foster child, brilliant musician, and exceptional mathematician. Unfortunately, he succumbed to the attractions of the "street," and circumstances led to his untimely demise. Oren and company cultivate a vacant lot in his memory which becomes a place for children and adults to enjoy sports, music, and flowers, and they dedicate themselves to finding the murderer.

A friend's death moves a multiracial group of teenagers to create a play field in his memory.

The book retains *Oren Bell*'s original characters and all of their quirkiness: the ever optimistic Mama, her good-guy fiancé Jack, recovering alcoholic Granddaddy, little sister Brenda (a brilliant artist and mathematician), Oren's twin sister LaTonya with her knack for sunny optimism and organization, busybody Aunt Grace, and cousins Dink and Dede. Oren's best friends return, as well as a new nemesis

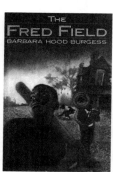

Goon Eye/Dooley. Their offbeat adventures take readers on a roller-coaster ride as the friends spook the murderer.

The novel succeeds as a mystery but there are some jarring elements. Although set in the "inner city" of Detroit, the children seem slightly naive. The inclusion of some distinctly urban language would have added a great deal more veracity to the setting. One might, however, label the characters, their language, and actions as tongue-in-cheek or urban tall tale. The book will capture the interest of readers because of its quick pace, unusual events, and the likability and intelligence of its characters.
VIOLET HARRIS

The Most Beautiful Place in the World

Ann Cameron   ✎ Thomas Allen
Guatemalan, Hispanic
1988, Alfred A. Knopf

Juan lives in San Pablo, a Guatemalan mountain town, perched on the lush rim of a lake. Although the seven-year-old boy remembers a time when he lived with his father and mother together, his father "wanted to go out with his friends...the way he did when he was single," and before long, he had abandoned his wife and son. Juan's mother has moved the two of them in with her mother, and for a time it seems that there is a small measure of togetherness—after cleaning houses during

Struggling against poverty and his mother's departure, a Guatemalan boy seeks an education.

the day, Juan's mother takes him for long walks through the bustling night-time streets. Soon a man joins them regularly, and before long, Juan learns that while this man wants Juan's mother to be his wife, he does not want Juan. Juan's mother marries this man and, with little explanation, and seemingly less care, she too abandons her son. He is allowed to stay with his grandmother, but soon must help to make ends meet. He begins by shining shoes outside the town tourist office, and lucrative though the work is, Juan finds himself lonely, envious of the children who passed him each day, "neat and clean, with their pencils and their notebooks, going to school." He, too, longs for an education. At first, he learns to read signs with the assistance of his customers, them to read passages in the newspaper, and finally, he summons the nerve to ask his grandmother if he might go to school. Expecting her to say no because she needed his contribution to the household, he is startled by her enthusiasm for the idea. It is only a matter of time before Juan becomes a star pupil, quickly catching up and then surpassing his classmates.

The title, *The Most Beautiful Place in the World*, comes from a tourism poster that Juan reads to his grandmother, who cannot read. And while the poster might refer to Guatemala, while Juan's grandmother might say that it is "where you love somebody a whole lot, and you know that person loves you," a reader might say that it is the place

Juan gets to on his own after overcoming the sad obstacles that have been put before him.

Readers of Ann Cameron's other acclaimed books for young readers, the Julian stories, may be a little disappointed in *The Most Beautiful Place in the World*—it has none of the exuberant humor that those stories have. In fact it is a relatively modest, straightforward story—a very real sort of story —about just how hard life can be for children in other parts of the world. Some readers may be disoriented by the fact that Cameron doesn't flesh out the pain of abandonment more fully; the pain is acknowledged simply, not dwelt upon. And given who Juan seems to be, this seems like an honest treatment. BINNIE TATE-WILKIN

Taking Care of Yoki

Barbara Campbell
African American
1986 (1982), Harper & Row, ✳ Series

Taking care of Yoki is a funny, charming, plausible tale of an active, independent young African American girl who successfully copes with difficult situations and makes realistic decisions to which readers can relate. Eight-year-old Barbara Ann, called Bob, cannot believe all the trials and tribulations she must endure. With her father in the Pacific fighting in World War II, Bob has to deal with insensitive teachers, cranky Mrs. Beene who lives downstairs, and her sometimes difficult best friend Chuckie. Bob worries about her father being killed, about being baptized, and about forgetting her Easter speech. Worst of all, Bob's friend Yoki, the horse who pulls the milk truck, is soon going to be "put out of his misery." It's all too much to take, but Yoki's trouble is the last straw. Bob's decision to steal, hide, and take care of Yoki motivates Bob to make other selfless choices and helps her discover support and friendship unexpectedly in Mrs. Beene.

A charming story set during War World I about an African American girl and a horse.

The story also gives a glimpse into 1940s ideas, fashion and hairstyles, war rationing, and everyday life. Bob acts when she feels wronged but relents and seeks help when her actions could make the situation worse. She loves her family, friends, and the horse Yoki, and she works hard to make wise and good choices even if those choices turn out muddled.

Even without pictures, the descriptions are vividly written and clear enough to let readers see what is happening in Bob's world. Taking Care of Yoki *makes a wonderful read aloud or group read story.* ALISON WASHINGTON

The Secret Grove

Barbara Cohen ✏ Michael J. Deraney
Arab American, Jewish, Middle Eastern, Palestinian
1985, Union of American Hebrew Congregations

Beni is short and always the last one to be chosen to play soccer. One day in frustration he runs away from the schoolyard and finds himself near an Arab village. Though it is just across the road from his own village, there has never been any association between the two communities. The time is the mid-1960s, and Beni is well aware of the hostilities in which his country has been involved; his own father has lost an arm in war.

When an Arab boy comes along, Beni is apprehensive—but soon sees that the other seems to feel the same way. They break the ice, talk briefly, and agree to meet again. The second time the two boys meet, the Arab boy shows Beni a school text with an ugly drawing of a Jewish soldier. Beni objects to it, and the boy agrees that it is not fair. Then Beni remembers hearing his teacher say that only an Arab would steal money from his mother. For a moment he thinks of mentioning it, but decides not to. "I knew such a question would make him as angry as the picture had made me," he reasons. The two boys understand each other. Then, after sharing an orange and planting some of its seeds, they part, knowing they probably will not meet again.

An Israeli boy and an Arab boy meet by chance and realize that stereotypes are unfair and harmful.

Twenty years and two wars later, Beni returns to the village of his childhood and finds an orange tree growing in the spot where he and the other boy planted the seeds. He remembers that brief but significant friendship between two children who could see past the barriers of cruel stereotypes to the qualities they had in common as human beings.

It's a very simple story, simply told, but all the more powerful for conveying an idea that adults may spend a lifetime avoiding.

The story should prove conducive to lively classroom discussion, even among early grades, about such topics as intolerance, stereotypes, and twisting of information. For older children, it could open the way to frank consideration of the prejudices that students are aware of in themselves and the stereotypes that they believe other groups hold about them. Essentially, this story is about imagination: the ability to put oneself in someone else's shoes and understand how he or she feels. This idea, too, would lend itself to fruitful discussion in the classroom.

Readers can discuss why only the Jewish character is named and whether or not the illustrations seem realistic, but as a whole, the book comes across very fairly, with both clarity and gentleness.
ELSTON MARSTON

Next-Door Neighbors

📖 Sarah Ellis
Multicultural
1990, McElderry

Next-Door Neighbors is a story about a new child in town and her unexpected path to self-esteem. Peggy, a clergyman's daughter, seeks acceptance in her new town by telling a lie. When the lie is exposed, she is ostracized by the other girls.

A new girl in town befriends two other outcasts, and the threesome together gain self-esteem.

Because of her isolation, Peggy forms a friendship with a lonely immigrant boy named George. The two outcasts spend time with the Chinese gardener who lives in the basement of the house next door to Peggy. Together, all three—Peggy, George, and the gardener—discover their inner strengths and gain courage to overcome the barriers facing them.

In this case, loneliness leads to unlikely alliances that are supportive and provide sustenance for each character's growth. BINNIE TATE-WILKIN

Barrio Teacher

📖 Mayra Fernández, Introduction by Alma F. Ada
Hispanic, Mexican American
1992, Sandcastle Publishing

In sharing her poetry with us, Mayra Fernández allows us into the world of her students and her own children. "Each poem is a vignette, a complete story, the fullness of a life captured in the brevity of a poem of verse both terse and deep, firm and tender," notes Alma Flor Ada in her introduction.

As a fifth, and sixth, grade teacher in East Los Angeles, her poems convey insights for understanding how the world and the community impacts their day-to-day lives. In "The First Day," she describes the confidence and pride with which she enters her classroom, only to be confronted by the true reality of her student's world. "Barrio Principal" details a principal's outrage at and determination to do something about the lack of books about the Latino experience in the United States.

A teacher from an East Los Angeles public school shares poems she wrote from her experiences working with inner-city children.

The content, focus, and fertile writing style of the poetry will encourage young readers to speak about the power and value of the written word.
MAGNA M. DIAZ

The Answered Prayer and Other Yemenite Folktales

📖 Sharlaya Gold ✒ Mishael Maswari Caspi and Majory Wunsch
Jewish, Yemenite
1990, The Jewish Publication Society

Arabs and Jews lived in peace in Yemen until the seventh century, when the Jews were deprived of citizenship because they refused to accept Islam. Most occupations were closed to them, so they became potters, jewelry-makers, or charcoal or wood-sellers. They were extremely poor, and were forbidden by law to ride a horse, carry a weapon, wear new clothes, or to travel freely.

In 1949 and 1950, almost the entire Jewish population of Yemen, forty thousand Yemenite Jews, were permitted to enter Israel. Dr. Michael Caspi, a

24

Yemenite Jew fluent in Arabic and Aramaic (an ancient conversational language which persists today as a common language in Arab lands), collected stories from the new arrivals in order to preserve their oral tradition. It is important to capture the heritage of any group, but these immigrants, in particular, are not as well known as their European counterparts.

It is interesting to note that men are the storytellers in the Yemenite tradition. They reveal much of the Yemenite way of life and the culture of the people. But the content of the stories focuses more on the men's perspective. One of the stories, "Ya'ish and the Protector" is an exception. It features a woman who serves as a protector to the Jews. Her amazing prowess with the bow and arrow and with the sword, as well as her intelligence and peace-making skills, help her to rescue the Jews of San'a from a wicked king who wants to banish the Jews from the safety of the walls enclosing San'a. She fulfills all the king's requirements and forces him to live up to his promises of safety for the Jews. Another story, "The King's Three Questions," has a similar theme. It concerns a king who threatens to exile the Jews unless someone can answer three questions. When the Jews send a young boy to respond to the challenge, the king is affronted, but he soon learns that the boy can indeed answer his questions wisely, and once again, the Jews are saved.

Eye-opening stories from the oral tradition of Yemenite Jews, who have faced oppression throughout history.

Most of the stories in this book exemplify the hard life and struggle for daily existence faced by the Yemenite Jews. Many also deal with simpletons, wise men, and greedy men. The book goes a long way toward dispelling some of the more commonly held stereotypes about Jews in general. *Children might also compare these stories with those of other oppressed peoples.* MASHA RUDMAN

Paris, Pee Wee, and Big Dog

📖 Rosa Guy ✒ Caroline Binch

African American

1988 (1984), Macmillan Press Ltd.

Almost twelve-year-old Paris has planned to spend Saturday with his mom, but when she has to work and gives him a list of chores, he thinks his day is

Literary Club
DEBBIE ABILOCK

For many years I have organized and run a successful program at my school called Literary Club. Operating in a middle group between student-run and teacher-run literature discussions, we break the kids into small (6-12 students) groups of mixed ages (3-4 and 5-6). They stay together for the whole year reading books, poems, short stories. Each group's discussions are facilitated by two parents who have been trained to ask questions and to teach students to think critically about what they read. Responses are sometimes enacted through drama, sometimes through drawings, often through discussion and writing. There are no vocabulary lists. Reading is sometimes chosen by the parents, sometimes by the group members, and there is always some give and take in what the group reads. All responses are not "equally correct," but all are equally respected and considered.

The most important parts of the program are:

1. Asking questions, questioning answers

2. Shared negotiation of meaning

3. Involving parents (the third member of the team including the teacher and the child in the decision-making aspects of the program)

4. Involving children in the decision-making aspects of the group

ruined. It is Pee Wee, Paris's small, undisciplined, adventurous friend who apparently saves the day. Pee Wee promises to help Paris clean if he'll just go skating down Dead Man's Hill. Along the way, the boys run into Paris's nine-year-old cousin, Big Dog. Paris and Pee Wee sometimes envy Big Dog because his father is a part of Big Dog's life, but they hate how Big Dog's smart mouth sometimes gets them all into trouble. The three of them set off on a day of skating, fishing, eating hot dogs, and trying to avoid Marvin, the neighborhood bully. The trouble begins when Paris causes an accident when he's almost hit by a car, Pee Wee is injured skating, and Big Dog falls into the Hudson River.

Three African American boys spend an adventurous Saturday in New York.

Paris realizes that Pee Wee will lead him astray if Paris lets him.

In the end, Paris faces his tormentor Marvin, acts selflessly, and decides to follow his own instincts instead of being led by his friends. The culmination of events makes Paris think about how he clings to his neighborhood, how much he takes for granted, how important his mother and friendships are, and how he misses his father. Paris decides that he will have to one day leave his neighborhood, but for now, he just wants the security of the familiar.

With its beautiful, intricate, black-and-white illustrations, this story is adept at capturing the genuine feelings of a boy in the midst of change. Paris's words and thoughts don't appear to be those of an adult writing as a child but a boy's actual dialogue and ideas. ALISON WASHINGTON

The Gift-Giver

📖 Joyce Hansen
African American
1989 (1980), Houghton Mifflin, ✳ Series

This novel describes the friendship that develops between Doris and Amir, two African American fifth graders living in the South Bronx. At the beginning of the book, Amir has just moved into the neighborhood. He's quiet, serious, and studious, with big eyes. Shifted from foster home to foster home, he has developed a keen insight into human behavior.

A highly engaging rendering of a boy and girl's friendship, life in fifth-grade, and an African American neighborhood in the Bronx.

"Every time I went to a new family, I had to study the people hard, so I'd know how to act in that house." His ability to look inside is what attracts Doris. She has always been protected by her parents and is beginning to resent the fact that she has to come home right after school, while her friends hang out in the park. With Amir's encouragement and example, Doris is able to help a troubled classmate and accept added family responsibilities when her father suddenly loses his job.

Although he is a nonconformist, Amir is accepted by the other kids on 163rd Street. When he is moved to an upstate group home at the end of the book, everyone misses him. "All we talked about was Amir. We couldn't think of anything else. I couldn't figure out how somebody who didn't play basketball, hockey, talk about other people, lie, cheat or do anything we did, leave such a big emptiness when he wasn't around. How could somebody who only smiled and looked like he was always seeing the inside of things, make a bunch like us feel so strange when he wasn't there?"

A warm story about family support and friendship, *The Gift-Giver* makes the fifth-grade world of kids on 163rd Street come alive with school tests, basketball games, double dutch contests, and summer excursions to the country. The sometimes violent realities of urban life are described too, but Hansen provides a diverse and well-balanced view of an urban African American community. Written in Doris's voice (modified black vernacular English), the dialogue is believable and readable. The story of this Bronx neighborhood continues in the sequel. LAURI JOHNSON

Yellow Bird and Me

📖 Joyce Hansen
African American, Mentally Disabled
1986, Clarion Books, ✳ Series

This sequel to *The Gift-Giver* revisits Doris's South Bronx neighborhood a year later. Now in the sixth grade, she has lost her closest friend Amir, who was placed in a group home in upstate New York when his foster family moved. Doris is despondent and determined to visit Amir, so she defies her parents and takes a secret part-time job at Miss Bee's Beauty Hive to raise money for the trip.

Paralleling the theme of Doris's burgeoning independence is her growing friendship with Yellow Bird, the class clown. In a series of letters to Amir interspersed throughout the book, Doris mentions that Yellow Bird has been bugging her about helping him with his homework. Amir urges Doris to look *As Doris helps Yellow Bird with his schoolwork, she discovers he has dyslexia.* "inside of Bird to see who he really is" and assist Yellow Bird in whatever way she can.

Despite Doris' diligent tutoring, Yellow Bird falls further behind in class, his acting out increases, and he is eventually placed in a special education class for children with behavioral problems. Fortunately, a visiting drama teacher recognizes Yellow Bird's dramatic talents and casts him as one of the leads in the school play. As a result of this teacher's intervention and Doris's advocacy, Yellow Bird's dyslexia is diagnosed and he is placed back in the regular classroom with supportive services.

In one of the few books to depict an African American protagonist with a disability, the author has created a rich, vibrant urban neighborhood and complex, memorable characters the reader cares about. When Yellow Bird triumphs in the school play and is able to help Doris with her part, we cheer too. This is a well-written, life-affirming tale about the importance of friendship and a perceptive teacher in a child's life. LAURI JOHNSON

Sami and the Time of the Troubles

📖 Florence Parry Heide ✒ Ted Lewin

Arab American, Lebanese, Middle Eastern

1992, Houghton Mifflin & Company

Sami, age ten, has never known a time when there was not fighting in Lebanon. Night and day, his family hides in the basement of their apartment building. His younger sister, Leila, and his mother are with him, but his father has been killed. When the shooting is bad, Sami finds comfort in his grandfather's calm presence—yet he also feels that Grandfather is looking for something from him.

Memories of the past and hope for the future sustain a boy and his family throughout the war in Lebanon.

The days of insane violence and destruction drag on, days of waiting and wondering and, somehow, still hoping. (The time of the troubles lasted from 1975 to 1991.) Sometimes the shooting ceases for a while, and Sami's mother may let him go out to play. He recalls a time when something amazing happened during such a lull. The children of the city, hundreds of them, marched through the streets, waving the Lebanese flag and carrying signs demanding an end to the senseless war.

But then the bombardment starts up again, and back to the basement Sami runs. This time his uncle has managed to buy a peach from one of the vendors who always appear as soon as things are safe. It reminds Sami of his father's peach orchard outside the city. Somehow he knows the trees are still there—and suddenly he knows what Grandfather is waiting to hear from him. Yes, he tells his grandfather, the children will keep calling for peace, and someday it will come.

One of the authors, Judith Heide Gilliland, spent time in Beirut during the Lebanese war. She creates an utterly authentic atmosphere of impotence and bafflement and disbelief when "the night rocks with noise, the air shudders." Sami tells us the story of civilians caught in an event over which they have no control, just managing to live from day to day. Yet they do so with reminders of beauty, such as the carpets that Sami's uncle has brought from the apartment to brighten their basement home. Illustrations by Ted Lewin are equally authentic, with dramatic contrast between the scenes of everyday life outdoors (even a wedding party) in the midst of bombed-out rubble and the darkness of the basement.

Because of the subject matter and the subtle way that the experience of war is conveyed, this book is appropriate for readers older than the central character's age. It would lend itself to discussion, in a seventh- or eighth-grade class, of war's impact on civilians, such as the striking note of realism in the boys' "war" play.

While there is no real plot, the story holds the reader's attention because of the extreme conditions under which Sami's family is living. The reader is led into what will be for many children a new experience, one that strengthens imagination and compassion. Along with a sense of the universality of war, we get a colorful and specific glimpse of another culture. ELSTON MARSTON

Eating Crow

📖 Lila Hopkins

African American, Jewish, Physically Disabled

1988, Franklin Watts

This zany celebration of friendship between two very different boys begins when a mute Jewish boy arrives at an all black school, along with his talking crow. Add to this the character of Old Miss Sophie, who everybody knows is an oddball and who (the kids believe) may be a root doctor or conjure woman, and readers are hooked.

Croaker Douglas is asked by his teacher to "eat crow" and make friends with Zeke, who lost his voice from the trauma of losing his mother and father in an airplane accident. Zeke has come to live with his aunt in a small town in North Carolina, where he is placed in Croaker's class. Fascinated by Zeke's circumstance and even more intrigued by his pet talking crow, it is easy for Croaker to get over his first feelings of hostility toward the white intruder. Thus the tentative friendship begins and the events that follow are entertaining, sure to capture the interest of the most reluctant reader. In one irresistible scene, when the boys have gone fishing together, Croaker's labrador retriever and the crow fight over a fish caught by the boys. The truce between the pets is symbolic of the growing friendship between Croaker and Zeke. Their relationship is sealed when they both confront local bullies and Croaker saves Zeke, and then later when Zeke regains his voice to save Croaker. BINNIE TATE-WILKIN

This zany tale celebrates the friendship between two boys, one black and the other Jewish and mute.

Over the Green Hills

📓 ✒ Rachel Isadora
African, South African, Transkei
1993 (1992), Greenwillow Books

If children of picture-book age have heard of South Africa at all, they are likely to think of it as only a land of conflict. *Over the Green Hills,* the story of a loving family in the former black homeland Transkei, shows that South Africa is also a land of beauty and warmth.

This book tells the story of the boy Zolani, who walks from his home in Mpame over the green hills with his mother and sister Noma to visit Grandma Zindzi. To prepare for the trip, Zolani gathers a sackful of mussels at the shore and loads it on the goat's back. His mother carries Noma on her back, a box of dried fish on her head, and a basket of mielies (corn) under her arm. Along the way, they greet friends, help a stranger stuck in the mud, and add a pumpkin, some firewood, and a chicken to what they are carrying. After several hours of walking, they come to Grandma Zindzi's village, and Zolani and

A young boy and his mother travel across the Transkei homeland of South Africa to visit his grandmother.

Grandma Zindzi play their penny whistles together as the sun goes down.

Isadora spent several years living in South Africa, and she has a good eye for the small, yet important, items in the background of daily life—foods, animals, music, buildings. The text and the beautiful illustrations are full of detail, although, as is the case with most picture books about Africa, many things are just a little cleaner and in better repair than in reality. As in her *At the Crossroads,* the author effortlessly includes plenty of nouns that evoke Africa: mango, guava, pawpaw, monkeys, aloes, ostrich, mielies. The text, however, is somewhat flat and stilted; it does not carry the warmth that we are meant to feel between Zolani and his family.

The helpful author's note (printed just above the copyright information) defines some of the local terms used in the story and explains what and where the Transkei is. CYNTHIA A. BILY

Lift Every Voice and Sing

📓 James Weldon Johnson ✒ Elizabeth Catlett
African American
1994 (1993), Walker and Company

The song "Lift Ev'ry Voice and Sing" was written in 1900 by J. Rosamond Johnson and his brother, James Weldon Johnson, for schoolchildren to sing at a birthday celebration for Abraham Lincoln. Catlett's illustrations make this version of the song the most appealing of the many that have been published. Catlett is a well-known artist, a civil rights activist, and the granddaughter of North Carolina slaves. Her linocut prints, produced in 1946 and 1947, capture the agony and dignity of the African American struggle for freedom.

The book includes a transcript of the lyrics as well as sheet music for "Lift Ev'ry Voice and Sing," an expression of African American pride and hopes that has been sung in the White House, at baseball openings, for Black History Month celebrations, and in classrooms and homes all over the country. DAPHNE MUSE

Dramatic linocut prints illustrate the lyrics to the Negro National Anthem.

25

If It Hadn't Been for Yoon Jun

Marie G. Lee
Asian American, Korean American
1993, Houghton Mifflin

From a decidedly Eurocentric perspective, Lee presents the reader with some of the conflicts facing a young Korean American girl adopted by a European American family. While the book relates one girl's experiences, it reinforces gross stereotypes throughout its 134 pages.

Seventh-grader Alice Larson is the adopted Korean daughter of the Reverend and Mrs. Larson. The Larsons also have a biological daughter, Mary, who is Alice's blond-haired sister. Alice frequently expresses her feelings about her "dilemma." She says to her mother, "I know I look Korean...but I don't feel Korean at all. I feel totally American, like you, and Dad and Mary."

An uninteresting conventional look at Korean American children of immigrant families.

Alice is a popular young woman. She makes the junior high school cheerleading squad, and the star football player of the school likes her. She has a group of friends and is well-adjusted as long as she doesn't need to think about issues of race. Alice's story takes place in Minnesota where, apparently, the only other people of color are "Indian kids."

Alice's wall of protection is challenged when a newly arrived Korean immigrant, Yoon Jun Lee, joins her class. Yoon Jun also wears glasses, speaks broken English, and constantly looks at the floor. Alice tries to avoid Yoon Jun because she doesn't want to be reminded of being Asian, yet she occasionally has to work with him. In preparing for "International Day," Alice has to take Jun as a partner.

By the end of the story, Alice's orbit of friends includes Julie and Yoon Jun, and Alice is learning Korean from Yoon Jun. I kept hoping that harder issues would be raised, and that Lee would do something meaningful with them. Alice's eyes are opened to class issues when she visits both Julie's and Yoon Jun's homes. However, other than finding out that people of color are generally poorer, we learn nothing about sociopolitical reasons for inequities. Why are all the "Indian kids" the ones in detention? What does it mean for children of color to be adopted into white families? What are young people to do about the self-hatred they feel? And why are Asian Americans always supposed to find their identity from things "over there"—that is, from Asia. What about an Asian American identity? This story line provides no answers, nor is it particularly interesting. We learn that Asian girls are cute and desirable, Asian boys are geeky, Indian kids are bad, and Eurocentric standards of beauty and behavior are the norms toward which we should all aspire. There is a token missionary in the form of Alice's father, who goes around dispensing good deeds and helping other people. Finally, Alice, when visiting Yoon Jun's house, hears Mrs. Lee say a grace. She asks Mrs. Lee where she learned the grace and Yoon Jun's mother replies, "Our family always good Christian...I learn this from a nice missionary lady." DEBBIE WEI

The Village That Allah Forgot: A Story of Modern Tunisia

Norris Lloyd   Ed Piechocki
Arab American, Middle Eastern, Tunisian
1973, Hastings House (Eagle Publishing Corp)

It's the early 1960s; Tunisia is newly independent and expectations are high. But an isolated little village seems to have been overlooked in the country's development plans. Though near a main road to Tunis, the capital, it has only a donkey path connecting it to the highway, and it stagnates. The old men sit around and complain all day; the children, with no school, are at loose ends. Ali, the ten-year-old hero of the story, has lost his father in a confrontation with the former colonial power, France. His family is very poor.

A Tunisian boy struggles to provide for his family in this out-of-print title worth finding.

He has a plan, though. By selling flowers on the roadside, he earns enough to buy a funny-looking hen, whose eggs he sells to drivers on the Tunis road. When a passing artist stops to make a sketch of him, and notices the boy's own drawings in the roadside dust, he gives Ali some paper and crayons. Now Ali has something else to sell, and people actually buy his pictures. With the money, Ali realizes his dream of buying a sheep, traditionally demanded by the Muslim "big feast." Just as important, he proves his ability to provide for his family like a man.

There's more going on in Ali's life. Envious of his relatively rich uncle, Ali squabbles with his

52

cousin. Almost by accident, the two boys make up rival teams from among their friends and start building a road. Before long, Ali's jealousy subsides —and the old men have something else to do besides complain: give advice. Meanwhile, a university student, whose father came from the village, stops by one day for a visit. He agrees to return weekly and start a small school. Hearing the young man's stories about Tunisia's long history, Ali gains not only a greater appreciation of his country but also a keener sense of his own identity.

A small book, written with humor and grace, Ali's story has a great deal packed into it in a natural, flowing way. We learn something about the countryside and Tunisia's fascinating ancient history, about Islam, about the position of women and their desire for education, about traditional village life and mentality, and about a society in transition. We can share in Ali's efforts to make a living and in his struggle for self-realization. Not least of all, we observe the villagers' discovery that Allah has not forgotten them; indeed, Allah helps those who help themselves. The illustrative sketches are appealing.

This out-of-print book will probably be rather hard to find (interlibrary loan may help), but locating it is well worth the effort. Not only does it introduce an unfamiliar country in an accessible, enjoyable manner, but it also speaks to the universal emotions and trials of growing up. The Village That Allah Forgot *would be an excellent choice for classroom reading aloud.*
ELSTON MARSTON

The Village Basket Weaver

📖 Jonathan London   🖊 George Crespo

Belize, Caribbean, Central American, Garifauna

1996, Dutton

The Garifuana are black Caribs living along the Caribbean coast of Central America. They are descendants of the Carib people and Africans who originally inhabited the island of St. Vincent in the Lesser Antilles. Tavio and his grandfather are Garifuana people living in a small Carib village in Belize.

Carpio is the village basket weaver and knows the secrets of the patterns passed on through generations. He is now the only remaining person in the village who knows how to make a cassava basket. Tavio is quite concerned about his grandfather's ability to continue this tradition. Carpio has become older, weaker, and tired from decades of

weaving baskets and being a village leader. The muscles and veins in Carpio's long, thin arms have become "twined and twisted like strands woven into a basket." But his tired and bent fingers continue to weave new cassava baskets.

Carpio is dismayed that the village young people now move to Belize City to work for big companies that destroy the trees in the forest. Like the others fleeing to the city, Tavio has dreamed of leaving the village. But he could not bear leaving behind his grandfather.

A young boy in Belize makes a life-changing decision when he realizes the role traditions play in people's lives.

One day he comes to their regular spot under the cashew tree, but his grandfather is not there. Tavio's uncle takes him out to sea to explain that grandfather is now too ill to continue the basket-making tradition. Tavio, who has watched his grandfather make baskets all of his young life, cannot let the tradition die. He asks his grandfather to tell him how to finish the cassava basket.

Indigenous people living in Central and South America are not often portrayed in contemporary children's books. Jonathan London treats these people as breathing, living beings and not as some exotic artifacts to be studied and catalogued. The relationship between Tavio and his grandfather Carpio is a precious one, and the writer honors the mutual respect they have for one another.

Through this story, young children will come to know that there are still people who live contentedly in this world much as they did hundreds of years ago. The illustrations are endearing and celebrate a sense of respect for the Garifuana's and their traditions. DAPHNE MUSE

So Sings the Blue Deer

📖 Charmayne McGee

Hispanic, Mexican

1994, Atheneum

Still living in quiet isolation in the mountains of Mexico, the Huichol Indians have committed themselves to doing something to preserve the earth before it is too late.

The Huichols have been given twenty deer from the Mexico City Zoo, and they have chosen thirteen-year-old Moon Feather to oversee the deers' return to the mountains. The deer, sacred to the

Huichol's, are an endangered species at risk of becoming extinct. Moon Feather's father accompanies him on the trip to Mexico City, but he understands that on this journey his son must stand on his own feet.

Mexico's Huitchol Indians are featured in this book on environmental protection.

Moon Feather is filled with excitement and honored to have been chosen by his grandfather, the grand shaman, to make the journey. One shaman feels it will be a wasted journey and discourages all efforts related to the journey. Moon Feather descends from mountains filled with clean air, blue skies, and pure water into the throat-choking smog of the city, where people live in run-down dwellings on treeless boulevards. The land where the Aztecs once lived is no longer majestic.

With her deft writing, McGee brings us into the sacred world of the Huitchol. The purity of the water, the beauty of the deer, and the pollution of the city are captured very realistically. But most importantly, the power, presence, and commitment of Moon Feather resonates throughout the book. His love and high regard for the earth support him in trekking hundreds of miles to secure these precious deer for return to the mountains where they had dwelled for centuries. This story might well inspire others to get involved with environmental causes. MAGNA M. DIAZ

Rio Grande Stories

Carolyn Meyer (editor)
African American, Hispanic, Native American
1994, Harcourt Brace, Meyer, Carolyn, *Where the Broken Heart Still Beats; Voices of South Africa; White Lilacs.*

Seventh graders at Rio Grande Middle School in Albuquerque, New Mexico, needed to raise money for their school, so they decided to write this book.

Produced by a group of seventh-graders in New Mexico, a collection of stories from various ethnic groups.

From stories, traditions and recipes, these young people created something beautiful and in the process came to a better understanding of themselves, their families and each other. The lives of these Native American, Hispanic, African American, and Anglo children are

linked by common threads in stories like Tony Martinez's "The Great-Great-Great-Great-Who?," Franklin Cox's "Estebanico, Black Explorer," and "Miracle Dirt," by Peter Kingston and Joseph Baca.

For "The Hidden Jews of New Mexico," Jeremy Steinberg researched his family and learned the untold story of Jews in New Mexico. He interviews Naomi Luna, who was raised Catholic, but learned she was Jewish as a teenager. She goes on to tell him how Jews had come from Spain to the New World in the fifteenth century because Spain required that Jews convert to Christianity or leave the country. Franklin Cox writes about Estebanico, a black explorer who came to the New World with the Spaniards in the sixteenth century. Ricky Begay's "Navajo Code Talker" tells how Navajo Indians created a code during World War II that was never broken by the Japanese army.

Helpful pronounciation guides for names, places and foreign words are included at the end.

Editor Meyers is the author of *Where the Broken Heart Still Beats* (A.L.A. Best Book, 1992), *Voices of South Africa* (An NCSS-CBC Notable Children's Trade Book, 1986), and *White Lilacs* (1993). MAGNA M. DIAZ

Felita

Nicholasa Mohr ✒ Ray Cruz
Caribbean, Hispanic, Puerto Rican
1990 (1979), Bantam Books Inc., ✳ Series

Family solidarity, intergenerational communication, and racial prejudice are featured strongly in this story of a young Puerto Rican girl growing up in New York City. As the book opens, Felita's family is packing up to leave their friends and neighbors in El Barrio to move to a new neighborhood where her parents say the "schools are better." Felita is reluctant to move and resists helping

An eight-year-old Puerto Rican girl experiences prejudice in her new neighborhood.

the family pack. In her words, "A sinking feeling was making me feel sick inside. I could hardly climb the two flights of stairs. Each step was taking me farther away from my friends. It wasn't fair, nobody had asked me if I wanted to move."

Told in a series of vignettes, the story becomes most riveting right after the family has settled into the new neighborhood. When Felita's mother suggests she go outside and make friends, the implications of being the first Puerto Rican family in an all-white neighborhood become apparent.

Felita begins to play hopscotch with a group of girls, but they push Felita, tell her to "go back to your own country," hurl racial epithets, and rip her new

dress. After comforting her, Felita's mother echoes the message of the book: "Understand these people are wrong, but you must not hate them. Instead you must learn to love yourself . . .that is the real victory." But those well-meaning words do not translate so easily when hate becomes a part of "the daily diet." After other family members also experience harassment, the parents decide it is too dangerous and move back to the old neighborhood.

In the remaining vignettes, Felita experiences a fire that destroys a neighborhood store and a falling out with her best friend Gigi. Her close relationship with Abuelita, her grandmother, sustains her and serves as her connection to her heritage and Puerto Rico. Abuelita's death at the end of the book sets the stage for Felita's journey to Puerto Rico in the sequel, *Going Home* (Mohr, 1989). Ray Cruz's energetic black-and-white drawings pulsate with the sights and sounds of city streets and help create an authentic mood. LAURI JOHNSON

Mojo and the Russians

📗 Walter Dean Myers

African American

1977, Viking Press

Dean has big problems: suspicious-looking Russians seem to be prying top-secret information out of Willie, a man on Dean's block. Worse yet, Willie's strange girlfriend, Drusilla, might put a *mojo* on

In this playful story, a group of African American friends try to figure out what Russian spies want with a neighbor.

Dean. His friends tell him that a *mojo*—a powerful spell used to get even with someone—will work if you believe, and Dean definitely believes Drusilla could send him to the Great Beyond in the shape of a one-eyed frog. So with the help of his friends, Dean devises a plan to find out what secrets

Willie is giving the Russians in hopes of convincing him to stop jeopardizing national security. Also, it wouldn't hurt if they could convince Willie to calm Drusilla down so she won't put a mojo on Dean. Thus begins Operation Brother Bad, a series of actions that will stop Willie and the Russians and keep a spell off of Dean. Leslie even helps by trying to put a counter-mojo on Dean and an atomic mojo on the Russian embassy. Once the connections between Willie, the Russians, Drusilla, and mojos is made, Dean and his friends refrain from any more investigative work.

This story about friends coming together to help one another is peppered with comic encounters and explanations that rely more on belief than logic. The kids support each other when necessary, risking their own comforts to keep a friend mojo free. The kids have fun, use their imaginations, and come up with a variety of ways to solve their problems.
ALISON WASHINGTON

Malcom X:
By Any Means Necessary

📗 Walter Dean Myers 🖊 Various sources

African American

1994 (1993), Scholastic, Inc.

Myers chronicles the life of Malcolm X from his impoverished beginnings, to his rise to prominence as one of the most influential black leaders in America, to his assassination. Myers details Malcolm's everyday life, his prison term and conversion to Islam, and his changing ideas about race in America. Much of the

An accessible biography of this influential figure.

information here is not new, but it is clearly presented and Myers is not afraid to touch the ugly parts of his life, giving a rounded picture of its subject.

He was born Malcolm Little in Nebraska in 1925 to parents who were supporters of Marcus Garvey, black unity, and independence. After his father was mysteriously killed, his mother struggled to support her seven children. But she became sick, and was put into a sanitarium in 1939. Malcolm's siblings were separated and he moved from home to home. A teacher discouraged him from being a lawyer because that is "no realistic goal for a nigger," and Malcolm turned his intelligence to life in the streets as a numbers runner, thief, and drug dealer. At twenty, he was sentenced to prison for a burglary conviction, and Malcolm's transformation began.

56

In prison, Malcolm educated himself and was exposed to the disciplined lives of black Muslims. After initially rejecting their teachings, he later embraced the philosophy and was noticed by Nation of Islam leader Elijah Muhammad. Eager to enlighten others about the black Muslim faith, and with his intelligence, knowledge of the streets, and gift for speaking, Malcolm quickly began to fill temples. Malcolm's fervor, eloquence, and controversial statements propelled him to national recognition, sometimes overshadowing Elijah Muhammad. Malcolm split from the Nation of Islam in 1964 because of changing personal views and schisms with the leader. He visited Mecca and began to accept whites, angering many former followers. His family was threatened, his house firebombed, and he was put under surveillance by both the government and the Nation of Islam. He was assassinated in 1965 while giving a speech in Harlem. However, Malcolm's message of black interdependence, moral fortitude, and Muslim unity was not quelled by his death, but grew stronger.

His legacy touched many poor, voiceless blacks who looked to him for inspiration. Myers presents a broad, favorable picture of Malcolm's ascent to worldwide recognition. Malcolm X *provides a chronology that shows the global social and political context of Malcolm's own life, gives information about Malcolm's contemporaries, and covers key periods in American history such as the black literary movement, the Depression, and the civil rights movement. Hence, the book could be used as a historical reference. With the many pictures, details, bibliography, index, and easy reading style, this book is accessible to anyone wanting to learn about Malcolm X and the world around him.* ALISON WASHINGTON

Diego Rivera: Artist of the People

🖋 Anne E. Neimark   ✏ Various sources
Hispanic, Mexican
1992, Harper Collins

Diego Rivera was born in Guanajuato, Mexico, in 1886 and grew up during the politically dynamic times of the Mexican Revolution (1910-1920). As a three-year-old, he displayed a strong artistic ability. In the early twenties, he left for Europe and settled in Paris, where he studied cubism, impressionism, and fauvism. By 1925, he had gained significant fame for his colorful and highly political murals. His work, however, also brought him criticism and scandal. From the Ministry of Public Education in Mexico City to the National Palace, from the Ford Motor Company at the River Rouge plant in Michigan to the RCA building in New York City, Rivera's work reflected his sentiment and desire to help the poor, especially in Mexico. The mural on the RCA building was later destroyed because in it Diego had painted the face of Vladimir Lenin, the chief leader of Russia's 1917 revolution and a Communist.

A thorough portrait of the dramatic life, politics, and art of Mexican artist Diego Rivera.

Active in Mexican and world politics, Diego's sometimes volatile and often complex relationship with Frida Kahlo, an artist in her own right, is discussed. The reproductions of his works provide a representative sense of his work. *This biographical work provides middle and junior high school students with an opportunity to examine the work of this controversial artist, as well as a chance to discuss how communism in its formative stages affected his work and the world.*

The book includes an index, bibliography, and a list of his murals in the United States.
MAGNA M. DIAZ

The Bee Tree

🖋 Patricia Polacco
Jewish
1993, Philomel Books

"I'm tired of reading, Grampa...I'd rather be outdoors running and playing," Mary Ellen sighs to her grandfather in the opening line of *The Bee Tree.* And Mary Ellen's grandfather takes her at her word. Run she will, as granddaughter and grandfather set off to find that special kind of tree where bees store their sweetest honey. In

A Jewish girl's grandfather teaches her about the sweetness to be found in books.

the garden, they collect several bees in a jar, then grampa frees one and he and Mary Ellen chase it through the Michigan countryside as it flies back to its hive. Along the way, they meet their neighbors — Mrs. Govlock, Einar Tundevold, Olav Lundheigen, the Hermann sisters, and Bertha

Fitchworth, to name a few—all of whom join in the exuberant chase, along with a number of goats and geese, and a trio of musicians, too. Destination reached and honey collected, the parade of bee chasers returns to Mary Ellen and her grandfather's for a celebratory feast of biscuits, tea, and, of course,

honey. In a quiet moment, Mary Ellen's grandfather spoons some honey on to the cover of one of her books—one of those books she didn't want to read.

"Taste," he tells her. "There is such sweetness inside of that book too!... Such things...adventure, knowledge, and wisdom. But these things do not come easily. You have to pursue them. Just like we ran after the bees to find their tree, so you must also chase these things through the pages of a book!"

Like so much of Patricia Polacco's other work, *The Bee Tree* has a distinct European flavor to it despite being so clearly set in the American landscape. This is accomplished in part by characters whose names and dress suggest the diverse places they may have emigrated from—Eastern Europe, Scandinavia, Germany, to name but a few—and in part by Polacco's delightful full-spread illustrations which further evoke the "old world" with women in babushkas and men in traditional caps and hats. Both contribute to this book's value as a portrait of the "melting pot" aspect of the midwest in the later years of the last century and the earlier years of this one. BARBARA GOLDENHERSH

Children of the Fire

📕 Harriette Gillem Robinet

African American

1991, Atheneum

Set in Chicago in the 1870s, *Children of the Fire* details the effects of the Great Chicago Fire on an eleven-year-old former slave from Mississippi named Hallelujah. Initially, Hallelujah is a somewhat spoiled, snippy girl who cajoles, charms, and blackmails her foster family, the LaSalles, for a variety of privileges. She manipulates Mr. LaSalle into allowing her to watch the fires despite Mrs. LaSalle's opposition. Hallelujah goes to watch the fire with Edward Joseph and, in a fit of pique, argues with him. Harsh words are exchanged between the

two; Edward Joseph criticizes her for being a former slave and an ungrateful orphan. She sputters a retort, kicks him, and runs away to watch the fire on her own.

Hallelujah's mischievous streak is unleashed as she ventures throughout the burning city by herself. She also encounters a variety of Chicagoans, primarily European immigrants and native-born whites who are variously helpful or hateful. She is called "nigger" more than once and questions her value. She starts to grow up quickly as she witnesses the reactions of Chicagoans to the destruction. Eventually, she and a wealthy white girl, Elizabeth, whose family had previously scorned her as a "nigger," become friends as they make their way through the turmoil to Hallelujah's house. Hallelujah's home is a hubbub of multiracial cooperation as individuals of all races left homeless seek shelter and food. Hallelujah wonders whether this comraderie will outlast the fires.

A young black girl experiences racism and classism, but also cooperation, during the Great Chicago fire of 1870.

Hallelujah is a complex character who embodies many of the contradictory impulses of a formerly enslaved person who must confront racism and self-doubt. Although the novel takes place over a few days, Robinet captures the feelings, sounds, and frustrations that catastrophes cause. Most of the characters, even the minor ones, are depicted with such skill that the reader immediately has a feel for who they are. Robinet does not interject an anachronistic modern sensibility into her historical fiction. She depicts the social milieu in an authentic manner; there are no pat solutions to the racial or class animosity, just a realistic depiction of the time period. Robinet does, however, leave the reader with some sense of hope. VIOLET HARRIS

Aplauso!

📕 Joe Rosenberg (editor) ✏ Hispanic Children's Theater

Hispanic

1995, Piñata Books, ✳ Bilingual English/Spanish

Compiled by Joe Rosenberg, the award-winning director of Bilingual Theater who has developed bilingual theater companies and staged works by Hispanic writers, this is an excellent anthology of plays focusing on Hispanic cultures. Ranging from pure fantasy to social realism, the anthology includes plays in English, Spanish, and bilingual

An anthology of plays focusing on Hispanic culture. formats by leading playwrights such as Alvin Colon, Jose Gaytan, Lisa Loomer, and Hector Santiago. Most of the writers are from two cultures and have been enriched by their dual heritage. *There is a preface to each play that serves as a guide for staging it.* Unfortunately, the book does not include a glossary or a map. DAPHNE MUSE

The Chichihoohoo Bogeyman

Virginia Driving Hawk Sneve
Nadema Agard-Smith
Dakota, Mentally Disabled, Native American, Physically Disabled
1993 (1975), University of Nebraska Press

This enticingly titled book offers an interesting picture of contemporary Native American girls in an adventure story that is universal, yet culturally specific. An author's note explains that, like the imaginary bogeyman created by white parents to discipline their children, many Native American tribes have also created similar spirits. Historically, Sioux children learned to keep quiet by being threatened with a "chichi," an invisible spirit who represented

While visiting their grandparents, three cousins are convinced they've found the real bogey man. the enemy. Amongst the Hopi people, the hoohoo appears at certain times of the year in the form of a kachina, a costumed and masked Hopi man who checks on children's behavior.

The three spirited cousins in this story begin to believe in the "chichi hoohoo bogeyman," so named by them because, although all three girls have one Sioux parent, Lori is half Hopi and Mary Jo is half white. A summer visit to their Dakota grandparents who live on the Big Sioux River in South Dakota leads to a series of adventures when the girls set off on their own without telling their parents. They decide to wade across the river to explore an old fort because, as Cindy, the boldest of the three, states, "if we were boys we could go wherever we wanted along the river and nobody would tell us not to." When they reach the other side they see a disheveled man with a "crab-like" gait emerge from

an old shack. The girls decide that maybe they've found their own "chichi hoohoo bogeyman." When they venture back in a canoe the next day the strange man confronts them and runs after them. Cindy swears the other two girls to secrecy, but her two cousins have nightmares that awake the rest of the family, and Cindy suddenly runs away, thinking it's her fault.

It all works out in the end, when the girls find out that the man is the developmentally disabled and deaf brother of a neighbor who came to visit when his sister was away and is trying to fend for himself in the old family cabin.

The three protagonists are spunky and likable, and their dialogue on target. There are even a few humorous moments, including the girls cheering for the Indians attacking a wagon train during an old Western at the local theater. Unfortunately, the portrayal of the disabled adult is somewhat stereotypical and unbelievable, and the author resolves everything a little too neatly in the end. LAURI JOHNSON

The Ojibwa

Helen Hornbeck Tanner and Frank W. Porter III (editors) Various sources
Native American
1992, Chelsea House Publishers, Series

Eddie Benton-Banai was fortunate to have grown up in a family and community where he could came to know many of the Ojibway tribal elders and learn from them. There are several aspects about this book that set it apart as a distinctly Indian approach to history. First, Benton-Banai does not omit the spiritual aspects of daily life. For example, Benton-Banai states, "I hope you take what I seek to put down and use them in a good way. Use them to teach your children about the way life has developed for the native people of this country. Use them to redirect your life to the principles of living in harmony with the natural world." Second, the value of

An innovative and accessible introduction to Ojibway culture.

women is clear. "The earth is said to be a woman. In this way it is understood that woman preceded man on earth. She is called Mother Earth because from her come all living things."

In the final chapter, entitled "Stepping into Modern History," Benton-Banai shares the impact of colonization upon tribal history and culture. He takes us through missionaries and government policy to the present period.

There is a minority of Indian people today that seem to be trying to take control of their own lives and the destinies for their children. They are pushing for recognition of the hunting and fishing rights guaranteed through treaties with the United States. They are seeking payment for and restoration of stolen land. They are trying to reestablish native religious ceremonies as a day-to-day source of strength and way of living. They are protesting the existence of corrupt, BIA-controlled tribal governments, and seeking recognition for traditional forms of Indian government. They are forming their own schools to balance the knowledge of modern survival with the knowledge of native culture and philosophy.

It is the author's belief that learning about these Ojibway teachings can help restore the strength and continuity of indigenous communities. The lessons develop in complexity as the book goes on and rarely have I seen a children's book explain as clearly this book does. Every page of this text is illustrated with clear line drawings printed in brown ink on textured tan paper. Maps are included. Ojibway language is used throughout along with pronunciation guides, so that it becomes easy to understand and learn the words presented. LORIENE ROY

Front Porch Stories at the One Room School

📚 Eleanora E. Tate ✒ Eric Velasquez

African American

1992, Bantam

Twelve-year-old Margie and her seven-year-old cousin Ethel spend a hot summer night swatting mosquitoes, following noises in the dark, and listening to Margie's father Matthew tell stories. Margie's narration frames her father's tales about his family, friends, and adventures in their hometown of Nutbrush, Missouri. Matthew intrigues the girls with stories of specters both imagined and real; opossum and floods in the town's one-room school;

259

Using Your Local Library
ROSA E. WARDER

Libraries are our greatest source of free information, entertainment, and amazing stories, and getting a library card is easy. Here are some tips:

* *Set aside an unhurried morning or afternoon to take your child to the local library. Bring something that shows you have residency within your county or city. Children just need to be able to print or sign their first name and they can have a card of their own.*

* *Make sure you have checked the hours of the library.*

* *Ask if the library has a children's librarian or children's room.*

* *Adults should have a driver license, employee or student ID, or passport.*

* *Present your ID and proof of residency.*

* *Fill out the simple form.*

* *Most libraries take 10-15 minutes to process your application and present you with a temporary or permanent card, useable immediately.*

* *Go over the library's rules regulations with your child so that they understand their new responsibility as a library patron.*

* *Take the time to explore the library leisurely and then select your books.*

* *Checkout those books, tapes, records, CDs, and don't forget to return them.*

* *Be sure to read the bulletin board for the many community events your library sponsors, such as storytelling hours, film screenings, workshops, readings and book signings by local and nationally known authors.*

* *When you get home, note what you checked out and the due date on a calendar so you won't run up library fines.*

Rosa E. Warder is an artist and writer living in Oakland, California.

Matthew's stern, demanding Aunt Daisy who takes part in a potato-and-walnut throwing melee; and Matthew's unforgettable meeting with First Lady Eleanor Roosevelt. The girls enjoy Matthew's tales, sometimes doubting the plausibility of a few but always finding out new trivia tidbits and history about Nutbrush. The stories show the supportiveness and solidarity of Matthew's family and community and reveal the town's flavor as Matthew tells of the many important people in his life.

Two African American girls listen as a father tells stories about his childhood in their town.

The last two tales are told by Margie and Ethel. Margie speaks of the Gentle Giantess Ella Ewing who, at eight feet four inches, was the world's tallest woman. Ella led a relatively normal life and traveled around the world, but Margie feels Ella might have felt lonely sometimes because of her differences. Ethel tells a fairy tale that parallels her own life. A mother and daughter live an idyllic life until the mother goes away and doesn't return. The little girl goes to live with a nice family who loves her, but she still misses and waits for her mother to return. Margie recognizes the story as Ethel's own experience and sees that "everybody has a story to tell."

Front Porch Stories is an easy reading, light-hearted look that melds fantasy, history, and legends. The author's note at the end describes the town, church, school, experiences, and the factual evidence on which the stories were based. Eric Velasquez's detailed, realistic, and beautiful drawings accent the text well, giving faces to the folks mentioned in the stories. ALISON WASHINGTON

Secret of the White Buffalo: An Ogala Legend

C. J. Taylor
Native American, Ogala Sioux
1993, Tundra Books, ✷ Series

Spring has come to the Ogala Sioux nation and Black Knife, Blue Cloud, and others in the village realize that the buffalo have not returned and there is no sign that they will come. There is much strife and discord in the village. As the best scouts in their nation, Black Knife and Blue Cloud are sent to find out why no buffalo have arrived.

In the early stages of their journey, they meet up with a sacred woman. Thoughts of capturing this woman and taking her back with him whirl through Black Knife's head. But as quickly as thoughts form in his mind, the sacred woman knows what he is thinking. She admonishes him not to take her captive, but Black Knife lunges at her and she makes him disappear. She then sends a message forward with Blue Cloud: "Tell your people what you have seen here. Tell them that the arguing and fighting must stop. They must prove that they can work together. They must build a great tipi in the center of the village. When it is finished, I will come."

The Ogala Sioux people devise a plan when they realize that the buffalo will not return this spring.

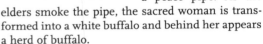

Blue Cloud takes the message back to his people. True to her word, the sacred woman comes when the tipi is completed and she brings them the gift of a peace pipe. As the elders smoke the pipe, the sacred woman is transformed into a white buffalo and behind her appears a herd of buffalo.

Along with the benefits of unity and collective effort, readers get to see a powerful sacred woman calm a bickering and divided nation. The beautiful illustrations are treasures in and of themselves. MARTHA L. MARTINEZ

The House That Crack Built

Clark Taylor, afterword by Michael Pritchard
Jan Thompson Dickson
African American, Dysfunctional, Hispanic
1992, Chronicle Books

Using the popular chidren's rhyming book *The House that Jack Built* as the framework, author, Clark Thompson, and illustrator, Jan Thompson Dickson, have written and illustrated a book about crack and its effects on our communities.

The book begins by showing profits from the drug trade. The book's first line, "This is the house that crack built," is accompanied by a picture of a mansion in a pristine setting.

A look at all aspects of the drug trade, and how it destroys neighborhoods.

The story unfolds to show the power of the owner of the mansion, his private army, and the farmers in the field who are forced to grow "plants that people can't eat."

Children learn quickly that the tragedy of drug addiction begins with the oppression of the peasants in countries where the drug originates. Illustra-  tions make clear that large amounts of money exchange hands in this trade, but neither the farmers nor the residents of "the street of a town in pain" will see the benefits. The book quickly draws in all the affected elements—the gangs, the police, the children, the "girl who's killing her brain, smoking the crack that numbs the pain." It ends with the image of a crack baby and the lines "and these are the tears we cry in our sleep that fall on the baby with nothing to eat."

This book is incredibly important. It faces hard issues head on. Its images and words are not pretty or soft, but it reflects the reality of the world in which many of our children are forced to live. The political analysis evident in the story is especially important for children. The authors are clearly angry with America's response to the drug crisis. Telling children to "just say no" is not enough when we deny oppurtunity and hope for any kind of future. As Michael Pritchard points out in his afterword, "Where there is no hope, there is no choice."

By addressing the drug trade, the creators of this book have attempted to carve out a niche of hope for the children who read this story. While disturbing and unsettling in its contents, the ultimate message of this book is one of power and choice. DEBBIE WEI

The Yellow Leaf

📖 Hasan Terani ✎ Mahasti Mir

Arab American, Middle Eastern, Persian

1995 (1994), Mage Publishers

"One Big Tree stood near a stream. The Leaves changed from green to red, then orange, then yellow and one by one they let go of their branches."

But the last yellow leaf on the tree does not want to fall. He thinks that when the spring returns, he will be able to turn green. The tree, the breeze, the birds, the rain, and even the river fly try to persuade him to join the other leaves, but their efforts are in vain. Finally, the gardener, an old and wise man, patiently explains the life cycle and nature's rebirth to the yellow leaf.

Through a simple story, the author presents a perspective of inevitable natural changes of life, and the fact that with every ending there comes a beginning. A sensitive and rather complicated subject is portrayed in a comprehensible way for children. The adventure of the yellow leaf unfolds in gemlike illustrations that perfectly match the text. Young readers will treasure this wise Persian tale. SHAHLA SOHAIL GHADRBOLAND

A Persian tale about the life cycle and rebirth in nature.

261

City Kids in China

📖 Peggy Thomson ✎ Paul S. Conklin

Asian, Chinese

1991, HarperCollins

Peggy Thomson's *City Kids in China* represents children's life, studies, habits, and hobbies in the city Changsha in China during 1980-90s. The book focuses on children who study martial arts and music, though most Chinese children do not receive this special training.

A description of life in the Chinese city of Changsha for the children who live there.

A high value is placed on education in Chinese society. Many parents want their children to excel in the arts and send them to evening schools to gain advanced skills. But most children have to stay at home and do their homework and study hard every day. "Playtimes, children say, are counted out in short snatches before supper and in Saturday nights and parts of Sundays. Through the weeks before exams, the playtimes are shorter yet".

Chinese people value education above all else because, they believe, knowledge can change a person's life. As the example in the book, "In the father's own life, school opened new worlds and freed him from the bleak toil of his ancestors. He was the first ever in his family to read. Now he teaches over the radio. At night he writes."

Having spent time in the city of Changsha, Peggy Thomson and Paul S.Conklin offer an accurate depiction of life in the city. This book is beautifully illustrated with photographs and the text is enlivened with humor. LI LIU

262

The Best Bad Thing

Yoshiko Uchida

Asian American, Japanese American

1993 (1983), Aladdin Books

Told from the perspective of a young Japanese-American girl named Rinko Tsujimura, this story takes place in California during the late 1930s. Rinko's parents are worried about their widowed friend, Mrs. Hata, who lives on an isolated farm with her two young sons. Mrs. Hata's husband has recently died, and she is trying desperately to continue supporting the family. Rinko's parents graciously volunteer Rinko to live with and help Mrs. Hata during the last month of her summer vacation. Rinko is less than enthusiatic about the prospect of staying with Mrs. Hata, but reluctantly agrees to go.

Young Rinko Tsujimura learns that what looks like a "bad thing" can turn out to be good.

Thus unfolds Rinko's summer where the obligation of staying with Mrs. Hata becomes a memorable experience which she comes to treasure. Uchida uses Rinko's experiences to portray glimpses of the lives of Japanese American families during this time. The tensions created by economic pressure and prejudice in California during the 1930s are clear, but we also see the strength of the Japanese American community. Rinko is a classic character in children's literature. She has the clear identity and voice of a young person in early adolescence faced with decisions and complexities, which are recognizable as universal struggles by young readers today. She says,

"Actually I guess I'm about five different people depending on who I am with. With Joji, I can be mean and bossy. With Mama and Papa I can be stubborn and ornery. With Mrs. Sugar I can be cheerful and sweet. And with the big bully, I really tried to be strong and brave, the way my Aunt Waka told me to be. The trouble is, I can't seem to stay that way. The minute I go to school, I am Rinko, the meek and mild, and I don't like myself when I'm like that. In fact, I never feel like my own true self at school. But sometimes, I'm not exactly sure which is the real true me."

Before she goes to stay with Mrs. Hata, Rinko is told by her friends that Mrs. Hata is crazy. But she quickly learns that people are not all that they seem. She learns to respect Mrs. Hata's tenacious will to keep her family together and her farm intact. Rinko also discovers a mysterious old man, Mankichi Yamanaka, living in Mrs. Hata's barn. Rinko sets out to uncover the old man's secrets, and she learns the pain and loneliness faced by undocumented workers. Surely these lessons ring as true today as they did for Rinko in the 1930s.

There are many tender and bold messages in this book, including the dignity of working people, the ugliness of prejudice, and the strength of community and family. Rinko's voice and and vision are both unique and universal—a sure confirmation of Uchida's powerful presence and fine writing skills. DEBBIE WEI

Finding the Green Stone

Alice Walker Catherine Deeter

African American

1991, Harcourt Brace and Company

This book is the second collaboration on a children's book between Alice Walker, Pultizer Prize-winning author, and Catherine Deeter, an award-winning painter and sculptor. The book is a favorite read-aloud story for children of all ages because of the clear, descriptive language and the stunning paintings on each page. The story centers on a pair of African American siblings, Johnny and Katie, who have a competitive and loving relationship.

The people of a magical village help a boy discover the value of love and forgiveness.

They live with their family in a village that is brought to life by Deeter's paintings. It is a pretty community of green hills, comfortable homes, free-roving animals, and happy, cooperative people, primarily of African descent, but representing every race. In this special place everyone owns a sparkling green stone that seems to be the source of a powerful joyfulness that suffuses their lives.

One day Johnny loses his stone, and begins to covet Katie's green stone. It seems to be bigger and brighter than his was. His frustration makes him mean to his sister, and he accuses her of having taken his stone. He tries to take it from her, and as they fight

"even the memory of his own stone vanished." Johnny's pain soon turns to anger directed at people around him who still possess their green stones. Finally, he asks his sister's help and forgiveness and begins to search for a way to get his stone back.

Johnny realizes that his stone disappeared about the same time he had been rude to an elder in the community, calling him a "bad name," and that his actions since had kept him from finding his stone. He goes to the elder, Mr. Roseharp, apologizes and explains his dilemma. Mr. Roseharp understands and urges him to seek his family's help. It is important to note here that Mr. Roseharp is an older man of African descent with snow-white dredlocks. He is seen tending an abundent garden in front of his well-kept home. This is not an image of black men that is seen frequently in children's books or other media.

Eventually, the entire villlage is brought together to help Johnny find his stone. They all search for hours, collecting rocks. In the presence of so many people who care about him, Johnny finds himself overcome with emotion and "begins to feel as if a giant bee were buzzing in his chest. It felt like all the warmth inside himself was trying to rush out to people around him." As his "warmth" spreads he discovers that what was only a plain rock a moment before is in fact his green stone.

The illustrations for this book are an essential complement to the story. Vibrant paintings illustrate the richness of the setting, and the many expressions on the faces of the townspeople are painted in such authentic detail that the reader feels a familiarity with the book's characters and perhaps a desire to live in the town of the green stone, too. ROSA E. WARDER

To Hell with Dying

📖 Alice Walker 🖌 Catherine Deeter

African American

1993 (1988), Harcourt Brace and Company

To Hell with Dying is Pulitzer Prize-winning novelist Alice Walker's second children's book. (*Langston Hughes, American Poet*, published in 1974, was her first.) It is a collaboration with painter and sculptor Catherine Deeter, whose colorful illustrations grace every page and bring the story to life. It is the story of an unlikely friendship between Mr. Sweet, "a diabetic and an alcoholic and a guitar player," and a neighboring young girl and boy. Based on a childhood memory, the setting is in a poor rural

area of cotton farms and African-American share-croppers.

The story is not a typical one for children's books. The language is as gritty as the poverty of the characters, but the theme of unconditional love for a friend and neighbor, despite his many shortcomings, is inspiring to readers young and old. Whenever Mr. Sweet yearns to give up on life, and take to his deathbed, the children's father calls him back by saying, "To hell with dying, man. These children want Mr. Sweet." Then the children throw themselves on Mr. Sweet's bed and kiss him and tickle him until he just has to keep on living. The story tackles some of the hard facts of black American life. Mr. Sweet, for example, was once a talented and ambitious boy who wanted to be a doctor or a lawyer or a sailor, only to find that as a black man he could not achieve his dreams. Now he is best known for his drinking, fishing, and guitar playing, as well as his patience and kindness with the children in his community.

The special relationship between an old man and a young girl who inspires him to stay alive.

Deeter's illustrations are a perfect match for the text; this book is truly a partnership between author and illustrator. The colorful paintings emphasize the sharp contrast between the richness of the people's lives and the poverty of their surroundings, set against the vast landscape of the South.

This book is not for very young children. However, it does serves as a wonderful bridge for young readers who still enjoy picture books yet require more mature subject matter. ROSA E. WARDER

The Butterfly Seeds

📖 🖌 Mary Watson

European American

1995, Tambourine Book

Mary Watson was inspired to write and illustrate *The Butterfly Seeds* by her grandfather's story of how he first came to New York from Manchester, England.

The story begins with Jake, sitting atop an over-stuffed trunk in an empty house and staring out the window, missing his beloved grandfather. Jake's grandfather has brought presents for the family, and for Jake there's a tin box filled with seeds that grandfather promises will become hundreds of butterflies.

The seeds comfort Jake on his journey across the sea and through the inspection at Ellis Island. But when he's situated in his urban home, he wonders how and where he can plant the seeds. Newly arrived immigrants from all over the world come to his aid when Jake decides to make a window box. Mr. Gargiulo gives him a crate that he lines with burlap from Mr. Lingchow, the fish peddler. Mr. O'Malley, the blacksmith, donates metal hangers, and all the neighborhood children help him gather dirt and carry the box up to his window. And one day, in the midst of a summer storm, blossoms and butterflies burst forth to gladden the hearts of Jake and his entire neighborhood.

A new immigrant in America, Jake plants his grandfather's butterfly seeds to remind him of home.

Using this book with mid- to upper-elementary students, we have launched a number of rich discussions. Illustrations, so marvelous at depicting the era, help children distinguish historical differences. We've talked about how Jake was made welcome in the new country and why those newly arrived understood his feeling overwhelmed. We've talked about sense of community, and how Jake reestablishes his relationships even though he's moved an ocean away from his first home. SUSIE WILDE

Early Black Photographers, 1840–1940

📖 Deborah Willis　✎ Archival photographs

African American

1992, The New Press

Early Black Photographers is a postcard book of twenty-three rare photographs selected form the photographic archives of the New York Public Library's Schomburg Center for Research in Black Culture. This collection testifies to the dedication of a century of African American photographers. Individually, each photograph is a record of African American history in both rural and urban settings. Although some photographers gained national recognition, most produced their works not for fame or fortune, but to serve and preserve their communities and the memory of the individual people who made these

Twenty-three rare photographs taken by pioneering black photographers in America.

communities strong and vibrant. These cameramen captured the diversity of African Americans throughout the north and south and the developing west as they photographed families, private moments, classrooms, churches, workplaces, and leisure activities, making portraits of both the celebrated and the humble.

The unique format of these photo cards, including the

early black photographers

brief biography of the photographer and the title of the event or person photographed on the reverse of each card, provides a springboard for innovative teaching. One could research the life, achievements, and contributions of African American photographers; discuss the historical, social, and political implications of the subjects and times of the photographs; creating classroom or library displays; or even devote a unit of study on the collections of the Schomburg Center for Research in Black Culture. These are only a few possibilities for these nicely printed, oversized photo cards.

This important visual collection of the work of pioneering black photographers in America should be part of every multicultural collection.

MELVINA AZAR DAME

Between Madison and Palmetto

📖 Jacqueline Woodson

African American

1995 (1993), Delacorte, 📚 Woodson, Jacqueline, *Last Summer With Maizon.*

Maizon is a bright, somewhat idiosyncratic, and intense young girl who leaves an exclusive boarding school because she is unwilling to conform to the expectations and various cliques. *Between Madison and Palmetto*, set in New York City, depicts her neighborhood and her grandmother, who is her emotional anchor.

The story follows Maizon's friendship with Margaret, as each faces personal dilemmas that test their love for each other. Maizon becomes friends with a white girl, enters into a relationship with her returned father, and seems to box out

A sensitive and realistic portrayal of puberty, anorexia, and interracial friendship between two girls.

Margaret. Margaret is undergoing puberty and feels uncomfortable with her body changes; she feels too big and resorts to anorexic behavior and attitudes.

Each girl must find her way back to the other in order to support each other through crises.

Woodson does not resort to easy solutions or simple happy endings. The reader is left with the feeling that these girls' lives will always be fluid and changing. Some hints are given: Margaret is interested in establishing a relationship with a male; Maizon seems less inclined and is more comfortable with her female friendships. Indeed, a group of males tease Maizon and Margaret about their public displays of affection and their sexuality. Maizon's father wants more involvement in her life; her Native American grandmother recognizes that she will not be around to serve as a buffer for Maizon much longer. Margaret's mother and brother have slowly recovered from the sudden death of their husband and father. All of this is presented sensitively and in believable fashion with crisp writing.

VIOLET HARRIS

Tamika and the Wisdom Rings

📖 Camille Yarbrough ✎ Anna Rich

African American, Dysfunctional

1994, Random House/Stepping Stone Division

As in her earlier novel, *The Shimmershine Queens*, Camille Yarbrough in this book depicts pre-adolescent girls coming of age. This novel tackles a difficult subject matter, the senseless violence bred by poverty and drugs in the inner city.

An African American girl living in a community plagued by drugs and violence finds strength in her family.

Tamika lives in an urban apartment complex, where life with her parents, sisters, and the community center is full and happy. She belongs to a group called Sweet Fruit of the African Family Tree Club, and with her friends in the building she learns African dances, writes poetry, and produces works of art.

When the club room is trashed by "drugged up kids," however, Tamika's father, the building superintendent, decides he'll have to close it for good.

Tamika's parents are portrayed as loving and hard-working people who believe in rearing their children with respect, and who take a stand against injustice in their community. After Tamika and her sister have a confrontation with some older kids in the building, the family gathers together to give the girls wisdom rings. Each ring stands for something important to guide them and to remember: to love yourself, for instance, or to carry yourself with dignity.

Unfortunately, the "drugged up kids" have no respect for anyone. One day, following the wisdom ring ceremony, one of them shoots and kills Tamika's father. Fearing further violence, her mother moves them to a new neighborhood. The new neighborhood has its own set of problems, but Tamika and her family must learn to make it their home. From this point on, the story centers on the family as they discover their ability to live and grow despite tragedy, and the sad truths of what one cannot just move away from.

The novel's power lies in the realistically portrayed problems of urban life, the perspectives of Tamika and her sisters, and the family's tenacity. One problem in the book, however, is the lack of time spent on the emotional and financial impact of the father's death. The mother takes on two jobs, the apartment the family moves to is smaller than the previous one, the girls cry occasionally, but the importance of this transition period feels like an aside to the main plot of moving on and being strong.

With the novel directed at an age group that is just moving from the fantasy stage to the acutely passionate pre-adolescent stage, there should be some concerns about the absence of authentic emotion given the frightening story line. It appears as if the feelings Tamika and her family would have experienced were sacrificed in the quest to show strength and resolve. ROSA E. WARDER

265

Virginia Hamilton and the Dillons: A Cross-Cultural Collaboration

Daphne Muse

*"My father always said that if he were the sun around which we, his five children, revolved,
then our mother was the universe. I agree with him; I think that was so.
Mother had a quiet determined way about her. She held the household and all of us together.
She never tried to tell us which way to go or which road to take.
To her way of thinking, it was up to us to find out and pursue and we did."*
—Virginia Hamilton

I FEEL AS THOUGH I HAVE COME TO KNOW Virginia Hamilton through her more than thirty creatively compelling and profoundly written young adult novels, riveting biographies, and comprehensive collections of folktales. For the past twenty-five years, I have read, reviewed, and used Hamilton's work in my role as a parent, educator, editor, and curriculum consultant. Her skill and creative power as a writer and consummate storyteller are most clearly demonstrated for me in works like *Zeely* (1967), *The Planet of Junior Brown* (1971), *MC Higgins, The Great* (1974), *Paul Robeson: The Life and Times of a Free Black Man* (1975), *The People Could Fly* (1985), and more recently *Anthony Burns: The Defeat and Triumph of a Fugitive Slave* (1988) and *The All Jahdu Storybook* (1991).

Her first published young adult novel, *Zeely,* had a major impact on the horrendously stereotypical image of Africans in children's literature. It is the story of how a young girl uses her imagination to recreate and reinvent a sense of herself and those around her. Though an encounter with her imagination, the protagonist Elizabeth renames herself Geeder and forms an intriguing relationship with Miss Zeely Tayber, her uncle's neighbor. But most importantly, Geeder comes across a photograph of a Watusi queen who happens to look just like Miss Tayber and Geeder dreams that Miss Zeely Tayber is really the Watusi queen in the photograph.

At a time when black people, especially girls, were seriously beginning to struggle with self-acceptance and self-worth, this bold and imaginative book was indeed revolutionary. Hamilton's description of Zeely reflects a turning point as demonstrated through Geeder's ability to embrace and accept the beauty of Zeely's dark skin color and African features:

"She is thin and stately in a long smock that reaches her ankles, she is over six feet tall, her expression is calm and filled with pride, she is the color of rich Ceylon ebony, and she has the most beautiful face Geeder had ever seen."

Along with creating an intelligent female character who could dream about something other than boys or finding her prince, this ground-breaking book resoundingly celebrated the beauty of black girls and women in ways that I had never before read or seen acknowledged. As an elementary schoolteacher and an employee of Drum and Spear Bookstore trying to develop a children's literature section that reflected the strength and dignity of black people as well as the contributions people of color had made to world civilization, the arrival of Hamilton's visionary work signaled a reclamation of self-acceptance that had been overwhelmingly excluded from children's literature. The pride that Hamilton feels in her people, our history, and her own acceptance of self continues to be reflected consistently in the voice and characters of her most recent works as well, including *The Magical Adventures of Pretty Pearl* (1983) and *Cousins* (1990).

Now after almost thirty years as a writer, Hamilton's contributions have nurtured and impacted the critical thinking of two generations of young people all over the world. While much is made of the tumultuous pathology driving our communities into despair, still too little acknowledgment is given the profound impact that black, Asian, Latino, Native American, Pacific Island, gay and lesbian writers have had on shaping the consciousness and characters of many of our young people. Her works, and those of several other contemporary writers, including Gary Soto, Diane Bauer, and Jospeh Bruchac, have also played a pivotal role in the literary pedagogy that serves as the centrigual force for some of the more progressive educational movements in the country.

Through her memorable readings at schools, libraries, and community centers, Hamilton also brings her voice, compassion, and creative spirit directly to her readers. Hamilton also has the astute ability to create the "power and presence of character" in her work in much the same way that her fellow Ohioan Toni Morrison does in her novels, and she possesses the same kind of power to examine class and racial issues quite extraordinarily. Her focus on the "Billy Tomorrow's"—communities of homeless young people caring for one another and living in abandoned buildings in New York—in *The Planet of Junior Brown* (1972)—was a strong indicator of her ability to understand, early on, the relevance of social issues and their impact on the lives of young people. Through her writing and role as an editor, she also continues to make seminal contributions to the literature and has been a moving force in making multicultural children's a powerful and sustaining presence in our children's education and literary enrichment.

Hamilton remains a visionary who stands in her power and honors her truth resoundingly and continues the tradition begun by some of our earliest black griots and writer's of children's literature, including the nineteenth-century author and editor of the children's magazine *The Joy*, Mrs. A.E. Johnson. Along with Johnson, early

twentieth-century authors of children's literature, Charlemae Rollins, Langston Hughes, Shirley Graham, Yoshika Uchida, Lorenz Graham, and Arna Bontemps forged innovative paths as well.

As the winner of scores of the most prestigious awards in children's literature including the John Newbery Medal, Coretta Scott King Award and the Gustav-Heinemann-Friedinspreis fur Kinder und Lugendbucher, Hamilton has surpassed most writers in her field. Highly acclaimed critics, scholars, and educators, including Masha Rudman, Sterling Stuckey, and Violet J. Harris have also focused on her work in their own writings. It is equally important for her to continue her work without the fiscal challenges and constraints that often suffocate or impede creative work.

While I sometimes toil to read some of her more complex works, her work supports me in feeling that outside of oppression, people can really maximize their human potential and deliver the power of their being in the most affirming and creative ways imaginable. She has established a literary legacy that I have passed on to my now twenty-three-year-old daughter, who is now passing the legacy on to her three-year-old daughter. It is a legacy that I also have had the privilege of sharing with hundreds of teachers in training, students, and scores of children and young adults who live in my East Oakland community. As a 1995 recipient of a MacArthur Fellowship, Hamilton will go forward with a yet-to-be realized dream; a dream that would inevitably enrich the intellectual, cultural, and literary lives of millions of children in the twenty-first century.

"Black children are the children that fairy tales forgot."
—*Leo Dillon,* ABA Show Daily *Interview*

Where Virginia Hamilton takes us with her powerful and imaginative storytelling, Leo and Diane Dillon create the visual images for the journey. For more than three decades beginning with their first fully illustrated children's books *The Ring in the Prairie: A Shawnee Tale* (1970), Leo and Diane Dillon have created some of the most beautiful, engaging, and endearingly thoughtful illustrations to be found in children's books. As two of the most highly respected and recognized contem-

porary illustrators in the world, they have played a major role in moving children's literature away from its often one-dimensional and stereotypical portrayal of people of color into a more compassionate, compelling, and graphically sensitive rendering of their spirit and physicality.

Hamilton and the Dillons serve as a fine example of people building bridges across cultures to bring about the boldest sound of our voices and the richest images of ourselves. Both Hamilton

268

and the Dillons realize just how important it is for people of color to read our own words and see ourselves beautiful and spirited in images that will nurture many from across the calming waters of childhood into the often turbulent waters of adolescence. Their illustrations have played an integral role in bringing multicultural children's literature to the forefront and in creating healthy and physically as well as spiritually elegant images of African American peoples.

Over a period of the last twenty-five years, they have collaborated on several projects including *The People Could Fly, Many Thousand Gone,* and *Her Stories: African American Folktales, Fairy Tales and True Tales.* This literary and artistic choreography results in a dance that nourishes our intellect, enriches our minds, and endears our hearts to their stories, their works.

Awarded the Caldecott Medal twice for *Ashanti to Zulu* and *Why Mosquitos Buzz in People's Ears: A Western African Tale,* their list of honors also includes four Boston Globe Horn Book Awards, the Society of Illustrators Gold Medals, Two Coretta Scott King Awards, and three *New York Times* Best Illustrator Awards. Both also hold honorary degrees from the Parsons School of Design.

With each new book project, the Dillons conduct extensive research and collect information about the dress and customs of each culture. There is no ethnocentric presumptuousness or cultural insensitivity. In order to insure authenticity for *Northern Lullaby,* they studied the cultural and artistic styles of the native peoples of Alaska, including the Tlingit and Haida groups. In formulating ideas, they experiment with materials and techniques. The process often results in the creation of new techniques.

While each book seems more exquisite than the previous one, they all have a very distinct style and exemplify a kind of dignity of character that is at times simply magical. The rich skin color in *Aida* and the variation in skin tones brings an aura of excitement. The combination of the chocolate childlike images combine with the soft black pencil drawings in *Honey, I Love and Other Love Poems* to create some of the most tender and love-filled illustrations I've yet to see. While some have dreamed a world, I have dreamed the worlds that these illustrations have taken me to since the first time I saw them in 1973. Now, having shared so many of their books, I know that there are bound to be several generations of young children whose dream worlds will be shaped by the profound, bold, and truly endearing images created by Diane and Leo Dillon. In their own lifetime, they've created and imagined legacies that are certain to serve as the foundation for better living, working, and understanding one another across the cultural and gender divide.

A Chronological Listing of U.S. Editions of Books by Virginia Hamilton

TITLE	PUBLICATION DATE	PUBLISHER
Zeely	1967	Macmillan
Time Ago Tales of Jahdu	1969	Macmillan
The House of Dies Drear	1970	Macmillan
The Planet of Junior Brown	1972	Macmillan
W.E.B. DuBois: A Biography	1972	Thomas Y. Crowell
Time Ago Lost: More Tales of Jahdu	1973	Macmillan
M.C. Higgins, The Great	1974	Harper & Row
Paul Robeson: The Life and Times of a Free Black Man	1974	Macmillan
The Writings of W.E.B. DuBois	1975	Thomas Y. Crowell
Arilla Sun Down	1976	Greenwillow Books
Justice and Her Brothers	1978	Greenwillow Books
Dustland	1980	Greenwillow Books
The Gathering	1980	Greenwillow Books
Jahdu (Read-Alone)	1982	Greenwillow Books
Sweet Whispers, Brother	1982	Philomel Books

The Magical Adventures of Pretty Pearl	1983	Harper & Row
Willie Bea and the Time the Martians Landed	1983	Greenwillow Books
A Little Love	1984	Philomel Books
Junius Over Far	1985	Harper & Row
The People Could Fly: American Black Folktales	1985	Alfred A. Knopf
The Mystery of Drear House	1987	Greenwillow Books
Drear Chronicle	1987	Greenwillow Books
A White Romance	1987	Philomel Books
Anthony Burns: The Defeat and Triumph of a Fugitive Slave	1988	Alfred A. Knopf
In the Beginning: Creation Stories from Around the World	1988	Harcourt Brace Jovanovich
The Bells of Christmas	1989	Harcourt Brace Jovanovich
Cousins	1990	Philomel Books
The Dark Way: Stories of the Spirit World	1990	Harcourt Brace Jovanovich
The All Jahdu Storybook	1991	Harcourt Brace Jovanovich
Drylongso	1992	Harcourt Brace Jovanovich
Plain City	1993	Scholastic/Blue Sky Press
Many Thousand Gone: African Americans from Slavery to Freedom	1993	Alfred A. Knopf
Jaguarundi	1995	Scholastic/Blue Sky Press
Her Stories: African American Folktales, Fairy Tales and True Tales	1995	Scholastic/Blue Sky Press

269

Picture Storybooks Illustrated by Leo and Diane Dillon

1964	*Hakon of Rogen's Saga* by Erik Christian Haugaard (Houghton Mifflin)
1965	*A Slave's Tale* by Erik Christian Haugaard (Houghton Mifflin)
1967	*Claymore and Kilt* by Sorche Nic Leodhas (Holt, Reinhart, Winston)
1968	*Shamorock and Spear* by Francis Pilkington (Holt, Reinhart, Winston)
1968	*The Rider and His Horse* by Erik Christian Haugaard (Houghton Mifflin)
1971	*The Untold Tale* by Erik Christian Haugaard (Houghton Mifflin)
1971	*The Search* by Murray/Thomas (Scholastic)
1974	*Burning Star* by Eth Clifford (Houghton Mifflin)
1985	*The People Could Fly* by Virginia Hamilton (Knopf)
1988	*Sing A Song of Popcorn* by Beatrice Schenk de Regniers (Scholastic)
1989	*Moses' Arc* by Alice Bach/Cheryl Exum (Delacorte)
1991	*Miriam's Well* by Alice Bach/Cheryl Exum (Delacorte)
1992	*Many Thousand Gone* by Virginia Hamilton (Knopf)
1993	*From Sea to Shining Sea* by Amy L. Cohen (Scholastic)
1995	*Her Stories* by Virginia Hamilton (Blue Sky Press)

Picture Books Illustrated by Leo and Diane Dillon

1970	*The Ring and The Prairie* (OP) John Bierhors (Dial)
1972	*Honey, I Love* by Eloise Greenfield (Viking)
1974	*Whirlwind Is a Ghost Dancing* by Natalia Belting (Dutton)
1974	*Songs and Stories from Uganda* by W. Moses Serwadda (World Music Press)
1974	*The Third Gift* by Jan Carew (Little Brown)
1975	*The Hundred Penny Box* by Sharon Bell Mathis (Viking)
1975	*Song of the Boat* by Lorenz Graham (Crowell)
1976	*Why Mosquitos Buzz in People's Ears* by Verna Aardema (Dial)

Grade Seven to Grade Eight

Big Man and Burn Out

Clayton Bess

Gay/Lesbian/Bisexual

1985, Houghton, Mifflin

Jess Judd has lived with his grandparents on their farm ever since his mother left him there when he was very young. He gets along very well with Sid, his grandfather, but every interaction with his grandmother, Hannah, is prickly and combative. Meechum, an older boy in his class at school, has flunked eighth grade a number of times and now just sits in the back of the room doing nothing. Most of the teachers at the school ignore him, neither requiring nor expecting any work from him. As Jess gets to know Meechum better, he realizes that Meechum is an intelligent, sensitive, curious person who has given up on himself. With the assistance of Mr. Goodban, the English teacher, Jess convinces Meechum to pass eighth grade and go on to high school with him.

One day, Jess invites Meechum over to his place and they spend the day running around the farm

A boy's friendship with an older classmate features complex protagonists but a caricatured supporting cast.

and going fishing. They end the day skinny-dipping in the pond and are laying on the bank naked when Hannah comes up to them and starts yelling. She furiously tells Meechum to go home and is about to start in on Jess when Sid comes up and tells Jess to leave while he talks to Hannah. Sid informs Hannah that the boys are just exploring and playing, and that if it isn't "just play," then they'll have to accept that as well or they'll drive Jess away.

While Clayton Bess has written an engaging story of friendship and growing up, only a few of his characters are allowed to be whole people. Jess, his grandparents, and Meechum are shown as generous, petty, confused, sad, and happy, but the other characters are either all good or all bad. The teachers at the school, with the exception of Mr. Goodban, are all caricatures of bad teachers: mean, ignorant, and narrow-minded. Mr. Goodban, on the other hand, is portrayed as caring, interesting, and intelligent. The fact that Mr. Goodban is in a gay relationship is handled matter-of-factly, not as a central piece of the story.

SUE FLICKINGER

The Moves Make the Man

Bruce Brooks

African American

1996 (1984), Trophy Book

This novel is set in the 1950s, when Jerome Foxworthy, an African American teenager with exceptional moves on both the basketball court and in the classroom, is the first and only African American student to integrate the biggest high school in Wilmington, North Carolina. Intelligent and adaptable, he thrives in this new situation, he finds it difficult to establish a friendship with Bix Rivers, a European American teenager who prefers baseball to basketball and academic studies. Bix is not easily faked out by any "move," and so it takes "many moves" to form the bonds of friendship between the two.

Two high-school friends — one white, one black — discover that racial differences prove less important than personality traits.

The backdrop for this book is the 1954 landmark case *Brown v. Board of Education of Topeka*, which outlawed segregated schools in the United States. Brooks successfully and realistically represents the integration of public schools throughout the South. Ultimately, Jerome and Bix discover that racial difficulties prove less important than their common personality traits.

Both boys are loners and frequent a secluded basketball court where Jerome teaches Bix how to play the game. Bix picks up "hoops" in six weeks, but he draws the line at learning "moves," as he sees them as a falsehood. He somehow relates them back to his own domestic situation and his mother's nervous breakdown. He swears he will have no lies or "moves" in his life. But Jerome notices the inconsistencies in Bix's personality, such as the time he brings Jerome a Mock-Apple pie — a fake that looks and tastes like apple pie. For Jerome, moves are the only way he knows how to play; they are his self-expression and means of survival in the many new situations that confront him.

The story is narrated by Jerome, using a flashback technique. This gives the reader an understanding of why Bix has run away and "got out of his life." The importance of this story goes beyond the interracial friendship between the two boys; it has much to say to both adults and young adults. A passage from the book states, "remember that things you start and stop so neatly by yourself do not always end on the spot. If you are faking — somebody is taking. If no one else is there to take a fake — then, for good or bad, a part of your own self will follow it. There are no moves that you truly make alone." MARILYN ANTONUCCI

Children of the Longhouse

Joseph Bruchac

Mohawk, Native American

1996, Dial Books

Good writing and rich storytelling can often transcend the historical chasms young people find difficult to overcome. That is exactly what Bruchac accomplishes in *Children of the Longhouse*. Although there is a need for

An eleven-year-old Mohawk boy and his twin sister fight off bullies — during the late 1400s.

more Native American fiction set in contemporary settings, this novel, set in the 1400s, has strong parallels to many of the issues and challenges facing young people in communities across the country.

Eleven-year-old Ohkwa'ri and his twin sister are two of the most admired young people in their village. But they are also the object of an older boy's spite and hatred. The twins get caught up in a "gang rivalry" when Ohkwa'ri thwarts Grabber's plan to raid another village by telling the clan leaders. When Grabber learns what Ohkwa'ri has done, he uses the upcoming game of lacrosse (a sport known in the Mohawk language as Tekwaarathon) to seize revenge.

Territorial imperatives, gang mentality, and petty jealousy serve as the basis for this mysterious novel which takes young readers through the world of Mohawk traditions and clan rituals.

Along with a glossary and pronunciation guide, the book also contains a suggested reading list and an afterword on the evolution of the story upon which the novel is based. Bruchac talks about the recovery of a sacred place, and how the fields once planted with corn are flourishing again and life has come full circle. DAPHNE MUSE

271

The House on Mango Street

Sandra Cisneros
Hispanic, Mexican
1984, Vintage

Young Esperanza tells about her life in the little red house she hates to call her home. She wishes that her name were more lyrical or eccentric, she wishes that her house was pretty and open, her neighborhood beautiful and happy, but mostly she wishes to be free of the many restrictions that she and other girls her age have to deal with. Minerva, a poet, is always unhappy because her husband left her; talented Ruthie, who is considered "off" by many other adults; beautiful Sally's father beats her for talking to boys; and Esperanza's own mother, who fears her daughter's intelligence is being wasted. Esperanza sometimes has no words for the intense feelings she experiences, but she knows that someday she will go far beyond the boundaries of Mango Street. She is admonished, however, to never forget that it is a part of her, and that she must return "for the others.... For the ones who cannot leave as easily as you."

A girl recalls her life through powerful stories about the people and places in her Hispanic community.

In poetic prose, Esperanza gives glimpses into the lives of the people on Mango Street in vignettes that deal with love, friends, school, relationships, home and neighborhood life, and budding curiosity about puberty and sexuality. She explores the variety of emotions she and those around her experience, as she comes to realize her desire to write and move away. Cisneros accurately captures the feelings and voice of a young girl as she struggles to integrate her days on Mango Street with her sense of who she will be one day. Although most of the men and boys in Esperanza's stories are often brutal and harsh with women, some are caring and friendly, tenderly sharing their happiness or sadness with the ones they love. ALISON WASHINGTON

Teenage Tokyo:
The Story of Four Japanese
Junior High School Students

Jo Duffy and Takashi Oguro
Asian, Japanese
Kodansha Ltd./Boston Children's Museum

Teenage Tokyo is an outstanding contribution to children's literature about Japan. Created by a Japanese and American team to accompany the exhibition, "Teen Tokyo: Youth and Popular Culture," at The Children's Museum in Boston, it is brilliantly designed to expose American readers to many aspects of contemporary Japan.

The four stories are presented in Japanese *manga* or comic book-style. Not only is this the format read widely by Japanese children, but it is also a popular vehicle for adult literature. An estimated two billion manga are sold in Japan yearly.

The setting of the stories is an urban junior high school and it is full of details about school life in Japan. American readers can be encouraged to compare their routines, physical plant, principal, teachers, social groups, clothing, hairstyles, and after-school activities to those of the characters in the stories.

This comic book-style book shares the stories of four junior high school students in Japan.

The characters, four very different early adolescents, are presented with remarkable depth in this slim, fifty-six-page comic. Readers are sure to identify with shy and studious Mika Hoshino, whose closest friend tries to get her to be more fashionable and to hang out with friends, while her family expects her to come home to help with their traditional Japanese restaurant. They are also likely to enjoy Mika's thirteen-year-old best friend, Akiko Ando. Akiko loves to shop and is both teased and admired because she has dared to break the rules and perm her hair. She did this while visiting her father, whose corporation sent him to America on business.

Kenji Yamamoto is a fourteen-year-old boy whose mother is a housewife and his father an accountant. He is the class clown and is on the soccer team, which is preparing for the important upcoming school-wide sports competition, the *kyugitaikai*. Yuichi Okazaki, the fourth protagonist, is a fifteen-year-old who is popular, handsome, and also a fine athlete. His parents, however, are pressuring him constantly to study for the enormously challenging high school entrance exams. Their expectation, directly stated in Yuichi's presence by his mother at a meeting with the principal, is that Yuichi not shame the family by being admitted to any but the top high school. Yuichi is having a hard time giving up his hobbies and fun-loving ways to concentrate on his studies. In a small-print aside he reveals to the reader, but not to his mother or the principal, that he is afraid that he isn't good enough.

Thus, as the foreword says, this is "a comic book with a serious purpose.... *Teenage Tokyo* is designed to help youngsters better understand how growing up in contemporary, urban Japan is both similar to and different from life in the United States.... The four main characters encounter many of the challenges familiar to American early adolescents:

-learning to identify one's central values
-finding a place within the school community
-recognizing diversity of family and social class

While the issues are universal, the setting and ways in which they are resolved are distinctly Japanese. In examining the visual and narrative details of the story, readers will discover some of the many ways in which Japanese young people differ from their American peers." ANNA PEARCE

Shimmy Shimmy Shimmy Like My Sister Kate: Looking at the Harlem Renaissance Through Poems

Nikki Giovanni
African American
1996, Henry Holt

For more than twenty years, Nikki Giovanni has written and taught about the Harlem Renaissance. This collection, inspired by students in a ninth-grade class, includes poems by twenty-three African American poets. Giovanni uses works by some of the greatest twentieth-century African American writers, including Arna Bontemps, Robert Hayden, Sonia Sanchez, Ntozake Shange, and Langston Hughes. Giovanni makes selections to affirm the joy and address the pain of being African American. Honoring great writers of the past and celebrating contemporary voices, the collection is also testimony to the range

Twenty-three of the greatest poets of the Harlem Renaissance.

of styles, visions, and voices in the black community.

Gwendolyn Brooks' "Riot," Waring Cuney's "No Images," and Margaret Walker's "For My People" are some of the more than seventy-five poems included in a book that offers young readers a better understanding of the Harlem Renaissance and the role it continues to play more than seventy years later in shaping African American life.

At the end of each selection, Giovanni provides insightful commentaries that teachers and parents will find helpful. The book also contains biographical notes on each poet and a bibliography for further readings.
DAPHNE MUSE

New Guys Around the Block

Rosa Guy
African American
1995 (1983), Puffin, ✳ Series

One summer in Harlem, all seventeen-year-old Imamu Jones wants to do is paint his apartment for his mother's homecoming and stay out of trouble. But tasks are hindered by a series of burglaries in the area and the police's continual harass-

A young African American man tries to solve mysterious burglaries in his neighborhood.

ment of anyone in Imamu's neighborhood. His mother, a recovering alcoholic, will be home from the hospital soon. The Phantom Burglar runs rampant, and the police relentlessly haul in anyone who has had a run-in with them or is young, male, and black. Imamu's friend Iggy is out of prison and crazier than ever. To top it off, two new guys, Olivette and Pierre Larouche, enter the picture and create an entirely new perspective for Imamu.

Olivette is well traveled, intelligent, articulate, calm, and controlled. He fearfully rules fourteen-year-old Pierre, trying to make him strive for perfection, but Pierre is drawn to the street-schooled, dangerous Iggy. Imamu is intrigued by Olivette's knack for endearing himself to others and disarming them with his intelligence and cool demeanor, and accepts his help painting Imamu's apartment. They decide to team up to discover who the Phantom Burglar is. All trails point to Iggy, but much is still unexplained.

When Iggy is arrested and the arrows and clues prematurely sentence him to death, Imamu is sure he was not the only culprit, although he may have been involved. Imamu discovers that Olivette is the

27

angry mastermind behind the crimes and that he gets away with it because of his handsome, controlled exterior, and intelligence.

Guy develops the mystery slowly, perhaps to round out the characters, motives, and to explain Olivette's philosophies, so some students may become bored with the pace. Olivette and Imamu's conversations sometimes seem more mature than the young men's years. Overall, however, the characters are drawn realistically. Guy accurately captures the intense feelings of a young man struggling to break out of a mold and trying to find control in seemingly uncontrollable situations. ALISON WASHINGTON

Zeely

📖 Virginia Hamilton ✎ Symeon Shimin
African American
1986 (1967), Simon & Schuster

Zeely is a beautifully written, evocative, and accessible novel about a girl's summer, strongly focused on issues of identity. Elizabeth, or Geeder as she wants to be called for the summer, is a precocious pre-adolescent, eager to experience and observe all that goes on around her. Soon after she reaches her uncle's farm, she sees Zeely and is entranced by her grace and beauty. Portrayed in the illustrations as slightly awkward, just moving toward adolescence, Geeder sees qualities in Zeely that she does not yet possess; strength and serenity evident in her proud carriage.

An African American girl believes the young woman she's just met is a Watusi queen.

Although Hamilton writes about African American experiences, race is never presented as an explicit issue. In *Zeely* as in her other novels and stories, the characters' race is one aspect of their complex, individual personalities. Indeed, what Geeder admires in Zeely is the latter's assurance and self-esteem.

Geeder begins telling the townspeople that Zeely is a Watusi queen. When Zeely finds out, she tells Geeder two stories, one a Watusi legend and one a childhood experience. With Zeely's kindness and strength as her guide, Geeder learns how she herself would like to grow up.

Hamilton incorporates vivid, well-drawn characters, lyrical descriptions of nature, and poetic and humorous language in a novel about a young girl's

coming of age. By the end of the story, when Elizabeth sheds her summer nickname, she has developed a clearer idea of who she wants to be: a strong, independent person who is true to herself. LISA MOORE

The Harlem Renaissance

📖 Jim Haskins ✎ Archival illustrations
African American
1996, Millbrook Press, 📖 Fauset, Jessie Redmond, *There Is Confusion*

From 1916 to 1940, black America celebrated and championed an artistic and intellectual revolution. Bold, new literary voices emerged, the powerful faces of African Americans appeared on canvases that hung in prestigious museums and art galleries, and salons flourished. Although the movement was based in Harlem, its ramifications were felt throughout the nation. The literary and artistic legacy of the Harlem Renaissance became the foundation for many of today's writers, artists, entertainers, and thinkers.

Chronicles one of the most important periods in African American culture.

Author Jim Haskins introduces the reader to the central figures of the Harlem Renaissance, including Bearden, Blake, Burke, Hughes, Hurston, DuBois, Toomer, Douglas, and Cullen. Haskins covers not only the deep artistic and literary inroads made by artists and writers during that period but also the political forces driving the movement. He rescues lesser-known figures from obscurity. Although Jessie Redmond Fauset often fails to appear on reading lists in African American literature, she is credited as the first African American to publish a Harlem Renaissance novel. Fauset's ground-breaking novel *There Is Confusion* (1924) focuses on educated, middle-class African Americans who moved in elite circles of society.

In many ways, the book functions as a cultural map to that period, with Haskins serving as the guide. The power and energy of the movement is also brought alive through a series of photographs and portraits, and quotes; vignettes, and sidebars enhance the book's design. DAPHNE MUSE

Hey, Dollface

📖 Deborah Hautzig

Gay/Lesbian/Bisexual

1978, Greenwillow Books

Hey, Dollface traces the growing relationship between tenth-graders Val and Chloe, from initial friendship to thoughts about homosexuality. As they become friends, Val marvels at Chloe's ability to be physically affection-

A complex story of two teenage girls who encounter homophobia and decide against developing a relationship.

ate. She simply is not used to a friend touching her or holding her hand so easily. Val begins to daydream about holding Chloe while she sleeps and begins to wonder if there is more to her feelings than just friendship. She uneasily wonders if Chloe feels the same as she does but is reluctant to talk about it with Chloe for fear that it is one-sided. Val's mother answers her questions about homosexuality, noting that although she doesn't know much about it, she does know gay couples who are happier than married couples. But when her mother admits that she can't quite bring herself to believe that homosexuality isn't perverted, Val is reluctant to tell her about her feelings for Chloe. Instead, Val talks to a favorite teacher who assures her that homosexual fantasies are normal and that even heterosexuals can be attracted to a person of the same gender. Miss Urdry hedges on whether or not homosexuality is unnatural. Thus ambivalently fortified, Val decides to talk to Chloe. The issue is forced when Chloe's mother sees them embrace in bed. The fact that their physicality has been observed eventually brings them to confront each other. They decide that what they feel is stronger than typical friendships, but Chloe decides she does not want to become lovers.

Hey, Dollface is a complicated exploration of ambivalent desire and intense friendship. The uncertainty with which each girl approaches the question of a potentially sexual aspect to their relationship is handled well. Val's discussions with authority figures provide some information, but their unwillingness to give untroubled positive support for homosexuality doesn't allow Val to fully discuss her concerns. One wonders what the girls' decision would have been had they received different advice. On the other hand, the story also breaks

with a notion of clear and stable sexual orientation by showing some degree of homosexual attraction between girls who decide not to be homosexual.
CHRIS MAYO

The Man Without a Face

📖 Isabelle Holland

Gay/Lesbian/Bisexual

1987 (1972), Trophy

Fourteen-year-old Charles is desperate to get away from his older sister who constantly puts him down. He decides to spend the summer studying for the entrance exam at St. Matthew's boarding school. He realizes he will need some help and gets up the courage to ask Justin McLeod, a retired teacher, to tutor him. Justin is an older man who is a mystery to his neighbors. He has a disfigured face and stays

In this slightly dated but engaging story, a boy develops a friendship with his tutor and worries about being gay.

by himself, never socializing with anyone. Over the course of the summer their friendship grows and Charles begins to worry about what his feelings really mean. Justin helps him to understand that friendship and love are important and do not necessarily mean that Charles is gay.

Charles's feelings are dealt with sensitively and as a normal part of life. Justin does not take advantage of him, making very clear to Charles that their relationship is a friendship and nothing more. The book stresses that it is important to love another person. Most of the references to either character's being gay are oblique or implied. The book also does not address a gay relationship, but rather focuses on the developing feelings of an adolescent boy. This reflects the time period in which the book was written—the early 1970s, when gay issues were becoming public but it was not yet acceptable to be too overt about them. The fact that the gay man dies at the end of the book neatly removes him from being an ongoing part of Charles's life.

The language and attitudes within the book are also representative of the late 1960s and early 1970s, and may seem dated to many readers. However, the book is engaging and easily holds the attention of the reader. While Justin and Charles are portrayed as complicated characters with both admirable and questionable qualities, most of the

275

other characters in the book are one dimensional. Few of the issues raised in the book are resolved by the end, but the reader is left with the assurance that Charles has grown over the summer. SUE FLICKINGER

B-Ball: The Team That Never Lost a Game

📖 Ron Jones
Disabled
1990, Bantam Books, 📖 Greenfield, Eloise, *Alesia.*

Here is a wonderful book that celebrates the best of the human spirit and does not pander to people with disabilities. Set around the California Special Olympics, this sensitive and insightful young-adult novel offers a refreshing and realistic view of mentally and physically challenged young people and the emotional and social challenges they face everyday.

A spirited basketball team dispells many myths about people with disabilities.

For this basketball team, winning means playing the best you can. Written with warmth, humor, and understanding, this coach tells of his ten-year special relationship with a group of people who learn to appreciate each other, basketball, and the strengths that can be found in their physical and mental disabilities.

Out of a sea of color comes Coach Jones, Michael, Joey, Eddie, and the other members of a basketball team of mentally and physically disabled people. Their ethnicities and disabilities vary. Coach Jones describes the physical and mental "barriers" that differentiate these players from Magic Johnson or Larry Bird. The characters face the same fears, hopes, and aspirations of non-disabled people, and personal difficulties are revealed as springboards for their achievements.

This book is imbued with humor and makes those of us who are not disabled examine our priorities in life. It could be used in tandem with Eloise Greenfield's *Alesia.* DAPHNE MUSE

A House Like a Lotus

📖 Madeleine L'Engle
Gay/Lesbian/Bisexual
1985 (1984), Farrar, Straus & Giroux

As with all her books, the characters in Madeleine L'Engle's book *A House Like a Lotus* are complex, interesting people. The story is written in the first person from the viewpoint of Polly, the seventeen-year-old daughter of Meg and Calvin (from *A Wrinkle in Time*).

Polly is spending three weeks in Greece working at a conference and puzzling through the events of the previous year. Her uncle had introduced her to Max and Ursula, a lesbian couple, who lived on the same island as her family. When Polly first finds out they are lesbians, she's upset and moves into denial. Later she talks with her father about it, and he encourages her to not let it matter but rather to think about Max and Ursula as people. Their lesbianism is not a central part of the book and is dealt with as only one piece of information about Max and Ursula. Their relationship is pictured as strong and loving.

This book features well-drawn characters and a strong lesbian couple, but maintains a reluctant attitude toward accepting homosexuality.

Much of the book deals with Polly coming to terms with that reality. While this approach to gay and lesbian people is needed in young adult books, there is a hint of the "don't ask, don't tell" attitude, particularly from Polly's parents. They treat the discussion about Max and Ursula as gossip and admonish Polly's brother for bringing it up. Polly later assures her father that she is not a lesbian and they are both relieved to hear it. The message is that while it's okay for people to be gay or lesbian, it's not something to be discussed openly, and there's still relief when a person is not gay/lesbian. SUE FLICKINGER

Madeleine L'Engle
A House
Like a Lotus
A Novel

Now Is Your Time!: The African American Struggle for Freedom

📖 Walter Dean Myers

African American

1992 (1991), HarperCollins, ✳ Braille, Series

How does one decide what events should be culled to chronicle a group's history and struggle for freedom? For writer Walter Dean Myers, the task called for incorporating his family's story with extensive examples of Africans and African Americans from centuries past and the present who strived to experience the full range of American rights. In its early chapters, *Now Is Your Time!* gives faces, histories, families, and feelings to people who were regarded as property. Via photos of documents, reproductions of letters, and pictures or drawings, Myers traces the journey of Abd al-Rahman Ibrahima, an African enslaved and brought to the New World. Ibrahima represents many for whom there are no records.

An interesting book on the achievements of African Americans in various fields.

Other chapters explain important events concurrent with the stories Myers tells, like the colonists' struggle against British rule and the creation of the Declaration of Independence. Men and women who dared to defy or change the status quo are represented in the life of George Latimer, who escaped the South in the prow of a boat, or Cinque, who succeeded in a ship rebellion and won his freedom. More importantly, however, Myers shows the effect of generations of oppression and rights denial on a race and how people still dreamed and fought to be released from their shackles.

The tone of this book is hopeful and encouraging. Myers speaks of people who continued to try even if the odds were not in their favor. He tells about his great-grandmother, Dolly Dennis, and his own family history, passed down orally for generations, at The Bower plantation in West Virginia. Myers' account rolls on to the civil rights movement of the 1960s, showing how the move toward freedom began the moment the first captive set foot in the Americas.

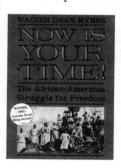

The strengths of the book are its easy reading style, the many pictures and documents, and the personal accounts of the ordinary people, artists, scientists, activists, and writers highlighted. *With its bibliography and detailed index, it is an interesting and engaging reference for learners of any age.*

ALISON WASHINGTON

The Young Landlords

📖 Walter Dean Myers

African American

1989 (1979), Puffin Books

When fifteen-year-old Paul and his friends are challenged to do something with their lives one summer, they form the Action Group and look for ways to change the world. They decide to convince a landlord to change the decrepit conditions of his building. As a way of legally dumping The Stratford Arms, the owner, Mr. Harley, sells the building to an unaware Paul for $1, and all the kids embark on being landlords. Two shortly fall to the wayside, leaving the rest with responsibilities they never expected. The building houses a variety of characters—the Robinson sisters who always need something fixed, Mrs. Brown who believes a dead former heavyweight champion lives with her, and Askia Ben Kenobi, a martial arts enthusiast who cavorts in costumes.

A group of African American teens learn responsibility and caring while they run a business in their urban neighborhood.

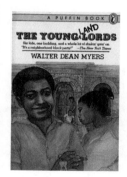

For the remaining members of the Action Group the business is soon hard work, especially when the tenants don't take them seriously. But their financial worries are lessened when a quirky accountant, Mr. Pender, aids them, and the group learns about compassion through running the building; to help a sick tenant, for instance, they throw a street party that raises $400.

The Action Group makes a difference through commitment and concern for their neighbors and later are asked to manage another building. As Paul reflects on the summer, he sees that he didn't understand the difficult choices ahead. He learns that "answers were a lot easier to come by when you stood across the street from the problem... And when there weren't good answers you had to make do the best you could."

Myers writes this book with a sense of community accountability and loyalty, fun, and a tongue-in-cheek detective style. Because we care about the group, we believe the situation is possible. Paul is astute and honest as he tells about being discouraged, scared, and disheartened with his friends and The Stratford Arms. Thus, he's trustworthy when he relates the excitement they experience. ALISON WASHINGTON

Scorpions

📕 Walter Dean Myers

African American, Hispanic, Puerto Rican

1990 (1988), Harper & Row, ✳ Video

Twelve-year-old Jamal and his best friend Tito hope to one day leave Harlem and sail on clear blue waters into a relaxing sunset. When Jamal's brother is jailed and asks him to take over the Scorpions gang he leads, Jamal is afraid to get involved. Mack, his brother's crazy friend, believes Jamal is "heir to the throne" as the leader's brother, and Jamal unwillingly complies. Soon others in the gang, particularly two members named Angel and Indian, challenge Jamal. Tito joins the Scorpions to help Jamal out, and the guys realize they've made a life-threatening mistake. Mack gives Jamal a gun for protection even though Tito and Jamal think having a gun is dangerous and wrong. Meanwhile, Jamal tries to keep his annoying sister Sassy out of his business, help his mother with the bills and the cooking, and avoid bad grades. Jamal also has to avoid Dwayne, a bully who wants to fight him. Fed up with Dwayne's threats, Jamal takes the gun to school and scares the bully off. But afterwards, Jamal feels he has changed because he has pulled a gun on another person, and he's actually more afraid now because he is unsure of what he would do with the gun.

A realistic fictional portrayal of gang violence, peer pressure, and friendship.

Jamal gets a job at a store but Angel and Indian make trouble for him there, and he is asked to leave. Jamal feels powerless to fight Dwayne, Angel, and Indian, and useless in trying to help his mother and brother. Angel challenges Jamal for the leadership of the Scorpions, and Jamal brings Tito and the gun to back him up. When Angel and Indian, both high on drugs, harass and beat Jamal, it is Tito who pulls the trigger, shooting Angel. Tito, gentle, nonviolent, and caring, is forever changed by the incident. Jamal finds out that Angel has died, and Tito confesses to the police because his guilt makes him sick. Tito's grandmother takes him to Puerto Rico, and, sadly, the friendship ends.

Scorpions is a frightening and tragic story about two boys who lose all hope for a better life thanks to poor and misguided choices. Myers explores the powerless young and the desperate choices they sometimes make. ALISON WASHINGTON

Fast Sam, Cool Clyde, and Stuff

📕 Walter Dean Myers

African American

1995 (1975), Viking Press

Twelve-year-old Francis moves to a new neighborhood and hopes to make friends. He meets Clyde, Sam, and Gloria, as well as neighborhood kids who support one another during difficult times in their lives. Francis, nicknamed Stuff, becomes a guide as he shows us his life with the group called "116th Street Good People," stopping to detail what they experience together. Stuff tells of basketball games and hanging out, fights, dance contests, and school. He talks about his feelings for girls, discussions about sex, marriage, and faithfulness, the group's first big party, and dreams. Along with the lighthearted tales and comedy, Stuff discusses how the group tries to help Clyde after his father is killed and Gloria when her father leaves the family. They encourage Sam to take academic classes and shoot for college.

An African American boy speaks of influential friends and events in his new neighborhood.

The 116th Street Good People look out for one another in times of peril or when others try to diminish an individual's value. When a neighborhood acquaintance becomes a drug user and almost overdoses, the 116th Street Good People get help and try to save him. Even then, however, the group realizes that not everyone has hope or can fix their problems just by talking to others who care. As Stuff recounts these amazing, mundane, curious, joyous, and painful stories, he explains his bond to his friends: "I just hope I'll always have people to care for like that and be close to. And I'd like to be able to teach someone else that feeling." Stuff grows emo-

tionally and intellectually with his friends and neighbors and is made better through knowing them. He believes everyone should have a group that allows him or her to be real, and supports, encourages, and sometimes hurts along with him or her.

Myers takes typical kids, puts them in average and extraordinary situations, and tests their mettle. They are compassionate and sensitive, willing to be scared or sad in front of each other as easily as they joke or show happiness. Myers's characters struggle to figure out their place in the world, and, for a while at least, they face its challenges knowing they are not alone. ALISON WASHINGTON

The Righteous Revenge of Artemis Bonner

Walter Dean Myers
African American, Native American
1994 (1992), HarperCollins, ✳ Series

This Western adventure focuses on fifteen-year-old Artemis Bonner, who sets out to avenge his uncle's murder and find his hidden treasure in the 1880s. The quest takes him from New York to the American "Wild West"—Arizona, California, and Alaska. Along the way, Artemis makes a lifelong friend in half-Cherokee Frolic Brown, and they both endeavor to catch the evil and brutal Catfish Grimes and his lovely and cunning accomplice, Lucy Featherdip.

A rollicking, action-packed parody of the Old West, featuring two teenage friends, one black and the other Cherokee.

Through Artemis's journal account of "the whole story, and the truth as well," we watch him fight for honor, duty, and love as he crosses a gritty and foreign early America. The story's fanciful, outrageous text (Artemis and Frolic fight off bears, escape burning cabins, work on barges to and from Alaska, and meet Wyatt Earp) works as a tall tale in

which the heroes crusade to redeem souls amid rampant wickedness.

In vivid, humorous language, Myers releases an action story in which the characters depend on their personal beliefs, intelligence, and sensitivity, not just the codes of the Old West, to persevere. Unlike typical tall tale prototypes, however, our heroes are decidedly human, crying when hurt or sad, fearing dangerous situations, and complaining in foul or adverse circumstances. All the while, they follow through to a satisfactory resolution. The story line does contain some slapstick violence, but the reader will recognize it for the Western spoof and parody that it is. ALISON WASHINGTON

Motown and Didi: A Love Story

Walter Dean Myers
African American
1987, Dell Publishing

Living in the midst of Harlem with her drug-dependent brother and out-of-touch mother, Didi dreams of going to college in this complex and optimistic tale. In spite of unexpected obstacles, Didi and her friend Motown muster courage and hold on to their hopes.

Didi recognizes her family's problems yet remains high spirited throughout the novel. Motown, with only the wisdom of an elder brother to guide him, also remains optimistic and focused in his life. Dealing with emotional, familial, and material deprivation, Didi and Motown strive to live in worlds beyond their everyday lives. DAPHNE MUSE

Two strong African American teens struggle to survive life in the inner city.

Make Your Own Library
DAPHNE MUSE

In an earnest effort to make reading a priority in their community, members of the Community Involvement Committee of the Sam K. Hailey Elementary School in the Woodlands, Texas, created the Hailey Book Share. Established in a rent-subsidized apartment complex near the school, this leading library has created a love of reading among the Hailey students living in the complex. It also serves as a real source of encouragement and support for getting preschoolers and their parents interested in storytelling and reading.

279

280

Under the Blood-Red Sun

Graham Salisbury
Asian American, Japanese American
1995 (1994), Delacorte Press

Hawaii, at the time of the Pearl Harbor bombing, is the setting for this gripping novel about heritage, patriotism, and family relationships. The small house where Tomi Nakaji lives with his parents, younger sister, and grandfather, is on the property of a much larger home where his mother works as a maid. Although Tomi is sometimes embarrassed by his family's inferior social status and the bullying of neighbor Keet Wilson, the Japanese American boy is generally content with his life, which includes his baseball team and friends from eighth grade. His best friend Billy, a *haole* (white boy), shares Tomi's interest in baseball. One of their most memorable experiences from that fall of 1941 is the day the boys spend on Mr. Nakaji's fishing boat. However, there are subtle warnings that their idyllic existence is coming to an end, such as newspaper stories of overseas battles, and racial remarks from Keet. When Grampa unfurls his Japanese flag, Tomi immediately reacts, knowing that their neighbors will not be pleased.

A gripping novel about a Japanese American family living in Hawaii after the bombing of Pearl Harbor.

One Sunday morning as Tomi and Billy play catch, planes began to soar overhead and bombs begin to fall. The bombing of Pearl Harbor changes Tomi's life forever. The family's racing pigeons are killed, suspected of being messenger birds. Tomi's father is arrested, and his fishing partner killed, when they sail into the harbor without flying the American flag. Later, Grampa is also taken away. Tomi makes a daring journey to the island where his father is being held under arrest. Although he is unable to change his father's fate, Tomi is at least able to see his father one last time before he is sent to the mainland for internment. The novel covers only a few months in Tomi's life, but it is a time of growth and change. The reader feels assured that Tomi, his mother, and sister will be able to survive the years until his father and grandfather return from internment. Their friends—a group composed of Japanese, Portuguese, Hawaiian, and Caucasian people

—continue to support the family and each other. This portrait of a specific time and place in the American experience is brought to life by strong characters and vivid historical detail. *The book would be especially useful when taught in conjunction with a twentieth-century history unit because it personalizes a dark era in America's past.* Although the characters may judge each other by their ethnicity, a teacher points out that the war is actually about the abuse of power. At the conclusion of the novel, Tomi continues to voice his support for the American government while honoring his Japanese heritage, as symbolized by a family heirloom sword which he holds for his grandfather. The book is among the few novels for children that looks at World War II from the Japanese American perspective. PETER D. SIERUTA

Off the Streets and Into the Books
DAPHNE MUSE

"Our press is devoted to the preservation of Negro culture by building unique containers for the words of my peoples. Experimenting with letterpress printing, bindings, printmaking, and calligraphy, we build books about our culture. These books reflect the pleasure we receive from the crafts of bookbuilding."

—Amos Paul Kennedy, Publisher of Jubilee Press

Determined to teach young people to appreciate the power and beauty of the word, Amos Paul Kennedy has spent more than twenty years teaching young people in Chicago and throughout he country the fine art of bookmaking. Kennedy has gotten hundreds of young people to come in from the streets. With them they bring their worn and weathered jeans, from which Kennedy teaches them to make paper. The handmade paper in turn becomes wonderful and spiritedly designed books.

There are books shaped like snakes, others go in circles and some come with beautiful handmade boxes with sliding tops. Some are charm books to be worn for "positive energy." The pages of the charm book of African proverbs are handcut in the shape of a snake, a symbol of wisdom in some African cultures. There are stories about baseball, Harriet Tubman, and lots of African proverbs. Devoting himself to crafting beautifully formatted and wisely written books, Kennedy is saving lives and passing on a rich literary and artistic legacy.

Trying Hard to Hear You

📖 Sandra Scoppettone

Gay/Lesbian/Bisexual

1991 (1974), HarperCollins

When sixteen-year-old Camilla falls in love with Phil, she has no idea what the rest of the summer will bring. The negative reaction from her best friend, Jeff, toward Phil seems a bit odd to her, but Jeff soon changes his tune and she doesn't think much about it. Then the Fourth of July party comes and Jeff and Phil are found kissing in the bushes. The group reacts with jeers and abuse, which takes various forms over the next few weeks, escalating to a potentially violent incident. Camilla is hurt and confused about how to think about both Jeff and Phil. She gradually begins to understand that how Jeff feels about Phil is similar to how she feels about Phil.

A forthright but uneven book about teenagers confronting homophobia and prejudice.

The book raises a variety of subtle and complex issues. The author draws on an interesting parallel between society's reaction to interracial dating and its reaction to gay relationships. The group of friends also has to deal with the deaths of their peers. The gay relationship between Jeff and Phil is not dealt with in depth; the focus of the story is on the group's reaction to Jeff and Phil.

Many myths about gays are addressed, though very briefly and a bit too didactically. The gay relationship in the story is never given a chance to be explored in the same way as Camilla's and Phil's relationship. In the end Phil dies, neatly removing the possibility of the group having to deal with an ongoing relationship between the two boys. Nonetheless, this book is an important one for young people to read. It points out some of the stereotypes and difficulties gay teenagers face, both from their friends and in forming and maintaining intimate relationships. SUE FLICKINGER

The Alfred Summer

📖 Jan Slepian

Physically Disabled

1982 (1980), Macmillan

Written in 1980, The *Alfred Summer* uses some pejorative language specific to disabled people, yet remains a moving story about friendship, using the characters' disabilities as the common bond which unites them against a hostile world.

Lester, a bitterly sarcastic fourteen-year-old, resents his mother's persistent nagging as much as he resents his own cerebral palsy, a disability that interrupts his fluency and denies him grace and ease of movement. His friends are Myron, who is overweight, unkempt, self-conscious, and generously pimpled, and Alfred, who is developmentally delayed, a condition seemingly exacerbated by his mother's overprotective nature. Lester's mother vehemently disapproves of both of Lester's friends because of their "differentness." When in public, the three boys are invariably subjected to awkward stares and whispers. Lester feels that they "leave a trail of silence in their wake" and refers to the group as the "Cripple Parade."

A candid story of four friends who call themselves the "Cripple Parade" because of their disabilities and "differentness."

One particularly poignant chapter depicts Lester and his mother at Coney Island. A circus barker is enticing people to visit his "Freak Show," and Lester describes his distress and discomfort with the scenario. "They filled me with horror…I was frantic…all too close to the bone…" Lester is repulsed by this commercial venture to reap profit from another's misfortune.

One day Myron confides that he is building a boat in his basement. The boat is Myron's avenue to freedom, his liberation from torment and ridicule. Alfred and Lester are intrigued, for they can barely imagine such independence. In a surprising twist, the boat serves to liberate the group, not by carrying them away, but by building their importance, self-worth, and sense of self.

Shortly before the boat's completion, Claire—an intelligent yet irreverent girl who befriends the group—enters the basement. Myron comments that she "flunks the girl test," meaning she is unattractive. Claire actually refers to herself as "the man of the house" since the death of her father. It is implied that her "misfit" status is her common bond to this ungainly group, an interesting commentary on women. (The other female characters are portrayed as either overprotective mothers, incessant naggers, or martyrs.)

This book can serve as a valuable tool for young people, one that can open up dialogue about disability, about adolescence, about gender, and about friendship.
BARBARA SMITH REDDISH

The Cay

📖 Theodore Taylor

Caribbean, African American

1994 (1969), Heinemann Educational Publishers,
✳ Series

This very popular, well-written adventure story tells of Phillip, a young white boy, and Timothy, an elderly Caribbean sailor, who are shipwrecked together on a tiny cay in the Caribbean. Set in the early 1940s, the story begins in Curacao where Phillip and his family live because of his father's employment with a local oil refinery. Phillip's mother wants to return to the States for reasons of safety, but, ironically, their ship is torpedoed by German U-boats on the journey home. After his ship sinks, Phillip finds himself on a raft with Timothy. He notes how ugly Timothy is and, in the process of getting to know each other, he asks for Timothy's name, which, it turns out, is his only name. Phillip muses, "My father had always taught me to address anyone I took to be an adult as 'mister,' but Timothy didn't seem to be a mister. Besides, he was black."

This story of a white boy and a black man shipwrecked together promotes a condescending view of blacks.

The author clearly is prejudiced against black people then and now. But the reader is, perhaps unconsciously, drawn into an attitude of superiority over Timothy, partly because this talented man is depicted as an illiterate, subservient, kind protector of the young white boy. Stereotypes are unintentionally strengthened when Timothy calls Phillip "Young bahss" and when Phillip makes a judgment about Timothy's features as being ugly. Over the course of the novel Timothy helps Phillip, who is blinded because of a blow he received when he was hit in the head during the process of escaping from the ship. Phillip is totally ignorant of how to survive, while Timothy is a master at it. It does test credibility when Timothy cannot spell "help," and must ask Phillip to spell out the word with rocks.

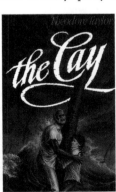

Phillip thinks, "I felt good. I knew how to do something Timothy couldn't do. He couldn't spell. I felt superior to Timothy that day, but I let him play his little game, pretending not to know that he really couldn't spell."

Again, the intent is honorable, but the effect is less than constructive. Phillip does save Timothy's life by nursing him back to health when Timothy has a fever. And the two characters do establish a strong bond of affection. But in the end Timothy sacrifices his life for Phillip, thus affirming a stereotypic literary device of having the "good black servant" die in the process of saving his young white master. What is more, the author raises the flag of colorblindness when he has Phillip ask, after having been with Timothy on the island for two full months, "Timothy, are you still black?" This is meant to be an affirmation of the universality of human beings, and an indicator that Phillip is losing his prejudices. But it seems to affirm that it is less positive to be black than to be white, and that being black is something to overcome rather than a distinctive and positive feature of a human being.

In the story, Phillip survives and mourns the loss of Timothy, who has not only saved his life, but has taught him how to survive on his own. In the end he is a somewhat chastened and changed boy. His eyesight is restored, but he now no longer enjoys the company of his peers. He prefers to talk to the black people on the pier and at the market.

The story is moving, and evokes great sympathy. He is a great character. The problem is that white readers may be affirmed in their condescending attitudes toward "ignorant blacks." And black readers may feel uneasy at the stereotypes in this otherwise entertaining and well constructed book. *Teachers may want to find other books in which there are strong black male characters, or have their students go on a search for books that present a different image of black people. Some good choices are Roll of Thunder Hear My Cry, or any of Mildred Taylor's* books. MASHA KABAKOW RUDMAN

Taste of Salt: A Story of Modern Haiti

📖 Frances Temple ✏ Leonard Jenkins
Caribbean, Haitian
1992, Orchard

Haitian folklore says a taste of salt is what a zombie needs to break away from servitude. Such were Jean-Bertrand Aristide's sermons against the corrupt political machinery in Haiti—a country-wide wake-up call to overthrow those in power and to create a new humane society. This deftly crafted first novel traces the events leading up to Aristide's first election, as seen through the eyes of two young characters with direct ties to Aristide.

The book is set up in three sections, with the first and last two being told through the view of Djo, a poor boy to whom Aristide provides housing and education. Djo's tale of living on the streets, his impressions of the young Aristide, his education and his enslavement on a Dominican Republic cane farm conveys the inner strength of young Haitians,

Two young Haitians tell their stories about their personal involvement with Jean-Baptiste Aristide's rise to power.

and their desire at all costs to bring back respect and honor for Haiti. The middle section is told through the eyes of Jermie, a young Haitian girl whose job is to record Djo's story after he is hospitalized trying to save children's lives during the bombing of Aristide's homeless shelter. In the process Jermie realizes she has her own equally powerful story to tell: she was on hand at the bombing of an election site, and saw the Haitian secret police march toward Aristide's church to kill its parishioners. Djo and Jermie felt helpless and ineffectual until they met each other. By sharing their respective stories, they gain insight into their contributions to the revolution.

While the two characters are fictional, Temple expertly puts them at the center of real events, giving keen insight into the rocky road to democracy in Haiti. Readers will gain a true sense of the turmoil in Haiti while enjoying a fine example of young-adult literature. The offerings on children's literature on Haiti are so few, it is welcome to see such a powerful work. LISA FAIN

Marked by Fire

📖 Joyce Carol Thomas
African American
1982, Avon Books, ✳ Series

Abyssinia Jackson was born in a cotton field, surrounded by the women of Ponca City. Her auspicious birth makes her special to the community, particularly the women, who all take care of Abby and believe she is destined for greatness. Abby grows happily under the community's watchful eye. To Abby this is both a blessing and a curse, because she can't get away with any mischief. Her security and happiness are whisked away, however, when a tornado rips through the town. Abby's father's barbershop is reduced to rub-

An African American girl discovers strength and purpose in a small community.

ble, and her defeated father just walks away from the family. A woman named Sally becomes crazed after the storm and views Abby as a foe to be vanquished. Worst of all, Abby is raped by a man in the community. That incident quiets her melodious voice, sends her to bed for months, and ends her belief in a benevolent and just God. Once again, it is the women of Ponca City—Abby's mother, Patience, and the healer, Mother Barker—who bring Abby back to her vital, song-filled, and faith-led life. Abby regains her courage and voice, decides to continue to help her community by becoming a doctor, and, along with the other women, passes on knowledge, fortitude, and hope to a new generation of girls.

Marked by Fire treats the delicate subjects of losing faith, rape, death, and physical abuse with care and sensitivity. One caveat, however, is the portrayal and role of the men in Abby's life. Her father's eventual return and its effect on Abby is not covered; Brother Jacob is jailed but leaves deep emotional and mental scars on Abby; Abby's friend Lily is almost beaten to death by her husband. The only other clearly defined male presence is Mother Barker's elderly husband. The story is decidedly female-centered, but the men on the fringe are mostly negative, making a springboard for discussion about abuse, stereotypes, and images.
ALISON WASHINGTON

283

CHAPTER 4

CULTURAL TRADITIONS

We are a country of Muslims, atheists, Jews, Christians, Hindus, and devout spiritualists without a specific religious affiliation. We celebrate the winter solstice, Hanukkah, Christmas, Kwanzaa, and Ramadan. We brought long-standing cultural traditions and rites of passage from Haiti, Laos, Ghana, El Salvador, France, Germany, England, and Samoa, among countless others. Many of our children are taken through rites of passage that include bar mitzvahs, inceneros, debutante balls, and gang initiations.

Social upheaval, immigration, greater cultural awareness, and historical benchmarks all influence what becomes a rite of passage in our society. There are a growing number of curiosity kits, dolls, puzzles, cookbooks, and cultural calendars being produced and marketed to correspond to celebrations and rites of passage such as National Coming Out Day, Tu B'Svat, Kwanza, and the Day of the Dead—many holidays that did not exist before or were formerly excluded.

But it is too simplistic, and at times very dangerous, to equate interesting foods, festive clothing, and rituals with the essence or spirit of these celebrations. All too often people see the intent and significance of holidays and celebrations based on standards and values of their own culture, a view that frequently results in offending other cultures rather than honoring them.

A culture's traditions, rites of passage, religion, spirituality, and cosmology (that branch of philosophy dealing with the origin and general structure of the universe) are rooted in deeply held beliefs, which can be perverted by outside interpretations, analysis, and commercialization. To add yet another complication, many of these traditions and celebrations are problematic. While many are sexist to the point of ritualizing the denigration and abuse of women and others devalue children, there remains a number of rituals and rites of passage that serve as significant milestones in human evolution and progress. As new rites of passage emerge, some of them displacing sexist and scarring ritualistic practices, many of them will lay the foundation for new standards and values. Eloise Greenfield's "Writing for Children: A Joy and a Responsibility," written in 1979, is as compelling now as it was almost twenty years ago.

MASHA KABAKOW RUDMAN AND
DAPHNE MUSE

Masha Kabakow Rudman is a noted critic of and commentator on children's literature with a focus on combating stereotypes and promoting social justice. Her Children's Literature: An Issue Approach *(Longman, 1995) has become a classic in the study of children's litera-ture. She has contributed to and coauthored numerous books, and written monographs and hundreds of articles.*

Kindergarten to Grade Three

The Gold Coin

📖 Alma Flora Ada (translated by Bernice Randall)
🖌 Neil Waldman

Cuban, Hispanic

1991, Atheneum, ✳ Spanish

This original story set in Central America has elements of a folktale and follows a "journey-quest" model. The exquisite illustrations provide an authentic Latino flavor.

In the story, Dona Josefa is an old woman who willingly spends time helping her neighbors in need. One night Juan, a thief, watching through his window, sees her with a gold coin and hears her exclaim: "I must be the richest person in the world." Believing this, he determines to come back the next day to steal her wealth. She is not at home, and he tears up the house looking for the money, but there are no gold coins to be found.

He starts to follow the path she took, expecting the coins to be on her person. He is directed by kind neighbors but is always too late to catch her, as Dona Josefa is constantly on the move helping friends in need. In the process of his pursuit, this silent, angry habitue of darkness is forced to talk with other folk, ask and receive help, and work each day helping them in their fields. As a result he becomes healthier and has better changes. When he eventually catches up with Dona Josefa, he has no thought of stealing from her, but instead offers to fix the roof of her house so that she can continue on her errands of mercy. The sensitive paintings reflect the gradual change in the thief.

In Central America, a thief chasing after a gold coin is changed for the better.

Alma Flora Ada is a well-respected proponent of multicultural and bilingual education. Her book, Language Arts through Children's Literature *, written in collaboration with R. Zubizarreta (Children's Book Press, 1989) provides a unique and practical guide to using multicultural literature with students.* GLORIA D. JACKSON

Nadia the Willful

📖 Sue Alexander 🖌 Lloyd Bloom

Middle Eastern

1992 (1983), Dragonfly Books,

📖 Reynolds, Jan, *Sahara.*

Though Arab people stereotypically live in tents in the desert, few people in the Arab world still follow these nomadic Bedouin ways. This vanishing traditional culture provides a background for *Nadia the Willful.*

Nadia is a quick-tempered young heroine whose mercurial moodiness is soothed by the attention of Hamed, her eldest brother whom she loves and admires. When Hamed disappears into the desert one day, Nadia's world falls apart. Hamed does not return; he has died in the harsh desert sands.

Tarik, the children's father and leader of his clan, is grief-stricken. Desperately wanting to forget his loss, Nadia's father forbids anyone to mention the name of his beloved son. Tarik believes that by forgetting his son, the pain of his anguish will pass.

Overcome by her brother's death, a Bedouin girl finds comfort in his memory.

Nadia thinks of her brother constantly, but as she is forbidden to mention his name, she cannot share her loss. She becomes sad, temperamental, and lonely, throwing temper tantrums that alienate her friends and family alike.

Her father is also consumed with misery. Tarik's unhappiness makes him bitter and cruel. Unable to discuss his son by his own decree, he grows angry and withdrawn.

One day Nadia finds her other brothers playing a game that Hamed taught them. But they are not playing the game correctly. They have forgotten Hamed whose name they cannot speak. Nadia teaches them to play the game correctly, and as she speaks of Hamed, she remembers him and somehow this memory eases her pain. In spite of her mother's warning, Nadia continues to talk about Hamed. She retells the funny stories he told. She speaks about the kind things he did and tells the shepherds how Hamed trained his favorite little lamb.

As Nadia talks to her friends and family about Hamed, their grief lessens also and soon everyone is remembering him except his father. Tarik still does not share his grief about his son, the joy of his life.

One day a shepherd boy speaks Hamed's name by accident in Tarik's presence. For his unwitting crime, the boy is banished by Tarik.

Nadia goes to her father to protest this injustice. "You will not rob me of my brother Hamed!" she cries. Nadia asks her father point-blank if he can remember his son anymore. Tarik admits that he cannot. Gently Nadia begins to speak of her lost brother, telling her father the details she remembers. And as she speaks, Tarik begins to recall his son.

Tarik calls the people together. "From this day forward, let my daughter Nadia be known not as Willful, but as Wise. And let her name be praised in every tent, for she has given me back my beloved son."

And from then on, Hamed lives in the hearts of the people who loved him.

This is a good book to introduce children to the life of the Bedouin people, but it is a better book for exploring the universal feeling of loss at the death of a loved one. SANDRA KELLY

The Piñata Maker

📖 🖊 George Ancona
Hispanic, Mexican
1994, Harcourt Brace and Company,
✴ Bilingual English/Spanish

Originating in the cultures of Mexico, Central and Latin America, piñatas are now commonly found at birthday parties and other celebrations throughout the United States. These gaily decorated papier-mâché figures filled with toys, candy, and sometimes even books, are often used to engage youngsters and challenge their ability to burst open this treasure trove while blindfolded. Much like the preparations

An elderly Mexican crafts-man makes piñatas for the whole village.

that go on for Carnival or Mardi Gras, piñata making is held in high-esteem. In this story, seventy-seven-year-old Don Ricardo is a celebrated piñata-maker in his village in southern Mexico. Using simple and easily found materials, Ricardo makes exquisite and exciting piñatas, masks, and puppets. *Bold color photographs and step-by-step instructions guide children in making their own unusual piñatas. Ricardo shows how to transform cardboard boxes, inflated balloons, and other materials* into the wonderful and spirited toys. *His creativity and energy are plainly apparent giving young readers the opportunity to see an active and vital older person. Suggestions are also made for filling the piñata so as not to make it too heavy or unwieldy.*

While the photographs show that this is by no means a wealthy village, the surroundings are not bleak and dismal, and people go about the business of making a livelihood for themselves. These richly colored photographs also picture the weathering and texturing of Ricardo's deep brown skin against the bright colors of the pinatas. Through Ricardo's work as an artist and through the bold color photographs, students also get to see how resourceful Ricardo and the people in his village are. *The Spanish/English text makes this book very useful in* ESL *or heritage language classes.*
NAOMI WAKAN

Where the Buffaloes Begin

📖 Olaf Baker 🖊 Stephen Gammell
Great Plains, Native American
1989 (1981), Viking Children's Books

The pencil drawings by Stephen Gammell will haunt you long after you've read this tale of Little Wolf. From a misty legend retold by Olaf Baker, he evokes an ancient dreamy vision of shaggy buffaloes rising and raging. Nawa, the oldest member of the tribe, keeps the legend alive over campfires.

In *Where the Buffaloes Begin* curious, courageous Little Wolf steals away one early dawn to seek the great lake of the south to discover for himself the truth of the legend. On horseback,

Little Wolf discovers how buffalo came to his people in this beautifully illustrated retelling of a Native American legend.

he travels alone and finds nothing at first but the stillness of the prairie. Unnoticed, a party of Abssiniboins passes Little Wolf on their way to a surprise raid on Little Wolf's village. Further away from his village than he has ever ventured, Little Wolf spots the lake of legend and waits silently, watching from a hill. The mysterious murmur of night falls.

"...Do you hear the noise that never ceases? It is the Buffaloes fighting to get out upon the prairie. They are born below the water but are fighting for the air, in the great lake in the southland where the Buffalo begin!"

Little Wolf's courage, curiosity, and patience are rewarded by a great vision: a herd of buffalo slowly rising and swiftly charging from the lake. They are headed in the direction of Little Wolf's village. A wild spirit whispers and Little Wolf leaps on his horse in strength and delight. Accompanied by the raging ancestors, Little Wolf sweeps across the lonely plain and tramples the enemies of his people, saving his village from death. After the buffaloes disappear into the night, Little Wolf himself becomes part of the legend of where the buffaloes begin.

Olaf's Baker's use of sensory details brings this legend to life. You can almost hear and smell the buffaloes. You can feel the stirring in Little Wolf's heart when he finally sees them. Along with the majestic drawing of Stephen Gammell, this tale of long ago becomes a vivid experience, not soon to be forgotten. FAITH CHILDS-DAVIS

I'm in Charge of Celebrations

📖 Byrd Baylor   ✏ Peter Parnall

Native American

1995 (1986), Simon & Schuster

Byrd Baylor's lyrical prose, written in the first person, and Peter Parnall's stunning illustrations, transport the reader to the Southwest desert of the United States, to explore and respond to the wonders of nature with a young Native American woman. In an effort to offer an alternative to typical American celebrations, the narrator proudly proclaims that she has created for herself one hundred and eight celebrations, "besides the ones they close school for." The young woman chooses to celebrate many events. The Time of the Falling Stars happens in the middle of August, "when every time a streak of light goes shooting throught the dark, I feel my heart shoot out of me." The Rainbow Celebration Day marks the time she and a jack rabbit stood and watched a triple rainbow over the canyon and a "real New Year is the day spring begins," and she celebrates it with horned toads, ravens, and quail.

A Native American woman celebrates the many wonders of the U.S. Southwest desert.

This book focuses the reader's attention on the fact that a sense of celebration is within a person, rather than only happening to a person on predetermined holidays. Holidays that are put "on" a person come with all the attached baggage and often lose their zest and individuality. For many young children, celebration is not a personal time, but rather a time when there are certain expectations required in order to make it successful regardless of family circumstances.

Baylor's new viewpoint also reminds us that it is the spiritual, not the material, things that are necessary for personal development. Baylor writes that "once you make the decision your whole life opens up and you begin to know what really matters and what does not."

Byrd Baylor has collaborated with Peter Parnall before, and all three collaborations have been Caldecott Honor Books. This book is as strong as the others as Parnall and Baylor capture the pulse of desert life. *It will inspire any age reader to seek out the events in life that really are important and to celebrate them in one's own way. Baylor invites each one of us to grab a notebook and begin to write about celebration.* MARILYN S. ANTONUCCI

Teaching Respect for Native Peoples

BEVERLY SLAPIN AND DORIS SEALE

* DO *present Native peoples as appropriate role models with whom a Native child can identify.*

* DON'T *single out Native children, ask them to describe their families' traditions, or their people's cultures.*

* DON'T *assume that you have no Native children in your class.*

* DON'T *do or say anything that would embarrass a Native child.*

* DO *look for books and materials written and illustrated by Native people.*

* DON'T *use ABC books that have "I is for Indian" or "E is for Eskimo."*

* DON'T *use counting books that count "Indians."*

* DON'T *use storybooks that show non-Native children "playing Indian."*

* DON'T *use picture books by non-Native authors that show animals dressed as "Indians."*

* DON'T *use story books with characters like "Indian Two Feet" or "Little Chief."*

* DON'T *organize activities that trivialize Native dress, dance, or ceremony.*

* DON'T *use books that show Native people as savages, primitive craftspeople, or simple tribal people, now extinct.*

* DON'T *have children dress up as "Indians," with paperbag "costumes" or paperfeather "headdresses."*

* DON'T *sing "Ten Little Indians."*

* DON'T *let children do "war whoops."*

* DON'T *let children play with artifacts borrowed from a library or museum.*

* DON'T *have them make "Indian crafts" unless you know authentic methods and have authentic materials.*

* DO *make sure you know the history of Native peoples, past and present, before you attempt to teach it.*

* DO *present Native peoples as separate from each other, with unique cultures, languages, spiritual beliefs, and dress.*

* DON'T *teach "Indians" only at Thanksgiving.*

* DO *teach Native history as a regular part of American history.*

* DO *use materials that put history in perspective.*

* DON'T *use materials that manipulate words such as victory, conquest, or massacre to distort history.*

* DON'T *use materials that present as heroes only those Native people who aided Europeans.*

* DO *use materials which present Native heroes who fought to defend their own people.*

* DO *discuss the relationship between Native peoples and the colonists and what went wrong with it.*

* DON'T *speak as though "the Indians" were here only for the benefit of the colonists.*

* DON'T *make charts about "gifts the Indians gave us."*

* DON'T *use materials that stress the superiority of European ways, and the inevitability of European conquest.*

* DO *use materials that show respect for, and understanding of, the sophistication and complexities of native societies.*

* DO *use materials that show the continuity of Native societies, with traditional values and spiritual beliefs connected to the present.*

* DON'T *refer to native spirituality as "superstition."*

* DON'T *make up Indian legends or ceremonies.*

* DON'T *encourage children to do Indian dances.*

* DO *use respectful language in teaching about Native peoples.*

* DO *portray Native societies as coexisting with nature in a delicate balance.*

* DON'T *portray Native peoples as the first ecologists.*

* DO *use primary source material—speeches, songs, poems, writings—that show the linguistic skill of peoples who come from an oral tradition.*

* DON'T *use books in which Indian characters speak in either "early jawbreaker" or in the oratorical style of the "noble savage."*

* DO *use materials that show Native women, elders, and children as integral and important to Native societies.*

* DON'T *use books that portray Native women and elders as subservient to warriors.*

* DO *talk about lives of Native peoples in the present.*

* DO *read and discuss good poetry, suitable for young people, by contemporary Native writers.*

* DO *invite Native community members to the classroom and offer them an honorarium. Treat them as teachers, not as entertainers.*

* DON'T *assume that every Native person knows everything there is to know about every Native nation.*

Doris Seale, who is of Santee and Cree descent, and Beverly Slapin are co-editors of *Through Indian Eyes: The Native Experience in Books for Children.* They are cofounders of Oyate.

289

The Woman Who Fell from the Sky: The Iroquois Story of Creation

📖 John Bierhorst ✏ Robert Andrew Parker

Iroquois, Native American

1993, Morrow, 📖 Hamilton, Virginia, *In the Beginning*; Anderson, David A., *The Origin of Life on Earth.*

According to the Iroquois, as recounted by John Bierhorst, the creation of the world was an accident. When one of the woman-of-the-sky-people becomes pregnant with twins, her husband, out of jealousy, uproots the tree whose flowers give light to the sky country and drops her down the resulting hole. As she falls toward the water far below, other sky people turn into ducks to cushion her fall, and into water animals, who gather mud to create the Earth. The mud is then placed on the turtle's back. Landing on the turtle, the sky woman expands the Earth to its present size, creates the stars and sun, and gives birth to her children, the gentle Sapling and the hardhearted Flint. The boys grow rapidly to adulthood. Sapling takes over the creation of all the good things of the Earth, while Flint creates all of the Earth's troubles. For example, Sapling makes fish, but Flint puts small bones in them for people to choke on. Sapling makes spring, but Flint creates winter. Sapling also makes people and shows them how to build houses and fires. Their work completed, the sky woman and her sons return to the heavens. The book concludes with a prayer of thanksgiving, not just for, but also to, the Earth, the rivers, the plants, the animals, and the stars.

An Iroquois creation story that serves as a fascinating counterpoint to creation stories from other cultures.

This lovely creation myth is particularly fascinating for the ways in which it differs from the standard Judeo-Christian accounts found in Genesis. It might be used to great effect in any ecumenically oriented religious or public school classroom. Robert Andrew Parker's delicate gouache and pen-and-ink illustrations, though not particularly Native American in style, add considerably to Bierhorst's highly readable text.

Among the differences between the Iroquois and the Judeo-Christian accounts of creation that might be explored are the possibility that the creation of our world was essentially accidental, the role of woman as primary creator, and the balance between good and evil as exemplified by the twins Sapling and Flint. Particularly worthy of discussion is the Native American belief, brought out in the final prayer, that the natural world was not, in fact, created for humanity's exclusive use, and that such things as rivers, trees, and animals have, in effect, a status equal in importance to that of humankind. These same ideas, however, could be troublesome to parents or religious schoolteachers of a more conservative bent.

A number of other multicultural picture book accounts of creation have been published in recent years. Among the best of these are Virginia Hamilton's collection of creation stories from around the world, *In the Beginning*, and David A. Anderson's retelling of the Yoruba myth, *The Origin of Life on Earth*. Bierhorst's *The Woman Who Fell from the Sky* might easily be used in conjunction with these books or others. MIKE LEVY

Fox Song

📖 Joseph Bruchac ✏ Paul Morin

Abenaki, Native American

1993, Philomel Books

Inspired by a story from Joseph Bruchac's family, this tale of Jamie Bowman and her grandmother describes a fun, strong, and loving intergenerational relationship. Jamie and her grandmother pick berries, sing songs, taste maple syrup just tapped from the tree, and tease one another about putting on their snow boots. One of Grandma Bowman's favorite pastimes involves looking for fox tracks in the snow. "Sometime," Grandma Bowman says, "when you are out here and I am not here with you, you keep your eyes open. You might see her and when you do, you will think of me."

A story of a loving intergenerational relationship between an Abenaki girl and her grandmother.

Along with tracking the fox prints, Jamie's grandmother tells great stories about the French side of the family's learning from, and developing relationships with, the Abenaki. Grandma Bowman also teaches Jamie songs, including one for greeting each new day: "When you sing it, you will not be alone."

After Grandma Bowman dies, Jamie remembers both the special and the mundane things they used to do together. In her room, Jamie spots a birch basket they made together. She feels so sad. She quietly gets up and goes to the woods where she and her grandmother had spent so much time. In the woods she leans her back against a tree and starts to sing the song her grandmother taught her. A fox appears and sits to hear the end of the song. Jamie remembers her grandmother's words about the fox and realizes she will never really be alone. Without hitting the reader over the head, Bruchac's story lets us know that death is natural and can have honor and meaning.

Bruchac includes the words of an Abenaki greeting song in the text. Although the book is not bilingual, Abenaki words are an integral part of the text throughout and are immediately explained.

Many children's books about indigenous peoples are highly stylized or romanticized. But the subtleties of Paul Morin's realistic illustrations flesh out the realities of contemporary daily Indian life. Traditional artifacts such as birch baskets intertwine with new lace doilies. Paintings of tree trunks become particularly three dimensional. You can feel the warmth of the sun or the coolness of a stream in Paul Morin's paintings.

This book would well prepare children for a discussion about grief or loss. It is also a good model of a close, loving family. Finally, the book might also be used in a unit on the natural world: the seasons, wildlife, and walking in the woods. NOLA HADLEY

All Night, All Day: A Child's First Book of African-American Spirituals

Ashley Bryan (editor) and David Manning Thomas (musical arrangements)

African American

1991, Simon & Schuster

Spirituals, rather than the creations of single individuals, are the outcry of a whole people, their condition so powerfully expressed that the songs continue to speak to us through the centuries. The songs preserve the thoughts and attitudes of African American slaves expressed in their own voices, the poetry of their language a perfect match with the syncopated rhythms and simple melodic structure. These songs sit easily even in the untrained voice; almost anyone can sing and enjoy them. Today's prevalence of gospel, soul, rap, and many other related black musical styles sometimes eclipses the fact that spirituals have a special place in African American music history.

An appealing selection of twenty African American spirituals.

The songs in this collection, selected by Ashley Bryan, include familiar pieces such as "He's Got the Whole World in His Hands" and "This Little Light of Mine," a perfect song for children and adults to affirm ourselves and our talents, and lesser-known pieces such as "Rocks and the Mountains," which promises a new hiding place for sinners, seekers, and mourners, or "Open the Window Noah." Simple accompaniments for piano or guitar enhance the melodies.

Colorful illustrations bring us brown-skinned night and day angels, a tropical paradise of flowering trees and flowing rivers, and a multigenerational black family gathered to "Eat at the Welcome Table." There are black flute players, madonnas and children, gray-bearded men, shepherds, and many boy and girl angels set against the rhythm of African-inspired batik patterns. Though black children will find special identification with this book, it does not exclude others; neither is it solely for Christians. These songs and drawings are inclusive in that they keep a part of our common history alive, they honor our ancestors, and they nourish us in the ways particular to art. MARY MOORE EASTER

Uncegila's Seventh Spot: A Lakota Legend

Jill Rubalcaba   Irving Toddy

Lakota, Native American

1995, Houghton Mifflin Company,

Jones, Jennifer, *Heetunka's Harvest* ; Goble, Paul, *Adopted by the Eagles*; Goble, Paul, *Flying with the Eagle*; Bruchac, Joseph, *Racing the Great Bear* ; Bruchac, Joseph, and London, Jonathan, *Thirteen Moons on Turtle's Back: A North American Year of Moons*; Pohrt, Tom, *Coyote Goes Walking.*

Uncegila is an evil, serpentlike creature from Lakota legend. She can be killed by sending an arrow into her seventh spot, but few warriors try. "One look at Uncegila and a warrior's eyes boiled in their sockets. Then came madness,/ then death." In *Uncegila's Seventh Spot: A Lakota Legend*, Jill Rubalcaba offers a version of this Native American story that captures the flavor and poetry of the oral storytelling tradition.

Cottonwood trees whisper Uncegila's secret to two brothers, Blind-Twin and First-Twin, who then set out to find Ugly-Old-Woman, the shaman, "maker of magic arrows that always find their mark." Ugly-Old-Woman gives them the arrows in exchange for "the comfort of arms circled around me." Since Blind-Twin cannot see her ugliness, he is happy to put his arms around her to warm her. In his hug, a witch's spell falls away and she becomes Beautiful-Young-Girl. She gives them what they will need to survive Uncegila's powers.

The two brothers succeed in their quest and take Uncegila's heart with them. Although their village, afterwards, never knows hunger, danger, or fear, the heart demands many ceremonies. The people become tired of "the heart's endless whims." The brothers finally choose to destroy the heart so the people can grow strong and resourceful. Beautiful-Young-Girl then comes to live with the people.

The slaying of a ferocious beast, told in a Lakota legend that high-lights the story-telling tradition.

While Rubalcaba was working on this book, she went to sleep listening to Native American story-tellers on tape, "trying to 'feel' the nuances of their speech and the manner in which they phrased things."

Teachers who use storytelling in the classroom will find this book helpful to give the sense of the storytelling tradition where stories are "handed down generation to generation, polished with each roll of the tongue, like a pebble caught in the ocean wave."

Illustrator Irving Toddy, who lives on a Navajo reservation in Arizona, decided he needed to get a cellular phone while he was working on the book, but he couldn't get good reception unless he climbed to the top of a mesa. Rubalcaba says she likes to think of him thinking about the story as he stood on the mesa, "facing the wind—cellular phone in hand."

Other tellings of Lakota legends include Heetunka's Harvest by Jennifer Jones, many of Paul Goble's books, including *Adopted by the Eagles, Flying with the Eagle, Racing the Great Bear* by Joseph Bruchac, *Thirteen Moons on Turtle's Back: A North American Year of Moons* by Joseph Bruchac and Jonathan London, and some of the Coyote stories such as *Coyote Goes Walking*, a retelling of four Coyote stories by Tom Pohrt. JANE KURTZ

Northern Lullaby

🦅 Nancy White Carlstrom   🖌 Leo & Diane Dillon
Multicultural, Native American
1992, Philomel

Teaching a child about respect requires diligence. When they learn about respect, they are better able to accept differences in others. One of the easiest ways to communicate this value

A child says goodnight to the natural world in this engaging book.

is by teaching children to respect their environment.

In *Northern Lullaby*, each night a child performs a ritual of saying goodnight to the natural elements, i.e., the moon, the stars, the river, the snow, etc. With each "goodnight" the child remembers the role each element plays in life.

The layout and watercolor illustration of this book make it quite easy for children to become absorbed. The words appear in poetic form on the left border and the illustration covers a page and a half. Each illustration looms larger than life, with the child's house always neatly tucked away in the bottom corner of the picture.

While the setting is a wintry one, the book exudes warmth and each element is given a human face while retaining its natural properties. The book will help children foster respect their environment. YOLANDA ROBINSON-COLES

My First Kwanzaa Book

📖 Deborah M. Chocolate   🖌 Cal Massey
African American
1992, Scholastic, Inc., 📖 Brady, April A., *Kwanzaa Karamu: Cooking and Crafts for a Kwanzaa Feast.*

The African American holiday of Kwanzaa, a harvest celebration, is being practiced by more and more people every year. Beginning on December 26 and lasting seven days, Kwanzaa celebrates the shared life and history of black people. The name Kwanzaa comes from a Swahili word meaning the first fruits of the harvest. Young children and their families can be introduced to this holiday by reading *My First Kwanzaa Book*. The preparations and family activities of one household are vividly illustrated and simply related in this picture book by Deborah Chocolate. A one-page introduction, for adults, describes the author's enjoyment of Kwanzaa and sets the tone for reading the story to children. She explains that the African language Swahili is used for sharing the seven principles or beliefs of Kwanzaa. A pronunciation guide for some of the Swahili terms is included at the end of the book. A footnote suggests that readers get more details from *The African American Holiday of Kwanzaa*, a book by Maulana Karenga the "Father of Kwanzaa."

A warm introduction to the African American harvest celebration of Kwanzaa.

The story opens in the home of a family including a mother, father, and young son. As the little boy joyfully shares his Kwanzaa experience, each page highlights the many ways that the extended family participates in the holiday. "When mama says, 'It's Kwanzaa time,'" is the cheery refrain that gives the story a poetic rhythm. A festive atmosphere is created as the boy and his family put on African clothes, cook special foods, and decorate their home. Other family members arrive and share in the special holiday activities for the seven days of Kwanzaa. They enjoy lighting the candles, making music with African instruments, reading African folktales, and giving gifts to relatives from far and near.

The full-color illustrations capture the warmth and love shared by this African American family. The text on each page appears in a bottom border, and most of the spreads include a small inset picture of the Kwanzaa candles and candle holder. As the story is read, children can see the order in which the seven candles are lit during the week-long  celebration. The African American flag, the Kwanzaa candle holder, a map of Africa, and other items for the celebration are depicted throughout the story. The Kwanzaa display itself (the mat, candle holder, unity cup, fruits, and vegetables) appears only on the title page. This display is usually the center of a family's Kwanzaa celebration and should have been included in at least one picture in the story.

Nevertheless, this book is a special treat for story time and holiday gatherings. The glossary and guide at the end will be helpful for people who are beginning to learn about Kwanzaa. MARTHA RUFF

Legend of the Bluebonnet: An Old Tale of Texas

Tomie de Paola

Comanche, Native American

1983, Putnam, de Paola, Tomie, *The Legend of the Indian Paintbrush.*

Anyone who has ever been in the Texas hill country in the spring knows the magic of the bluebonnet flower. They transform ordinary green mounds into rolling, undulating blue waves. Author and illustrator Tommie de Paola was intrigued by the flower on a visit to Texas, and a friend of his shared with him the Comanche's tale of how this flower came to decorate the state. De Paola's

A beautiful Comanche tale about a girl's sacrifice to end a drought.

version, while enhanced for young readers, remains true to the heart of the original tale.

Legend has it that there was once a great famine in Comanche country. Many had died, including the parents of a young girl. She had a prize possession, a doll that her parents had made for her. Her mother sewed the doll to resemble her daughter, and her father brought blue feathers from far away to put in its hair. Now that her parents were dead, the girl's doll was her only link to them.

One day, the great shaman said the spirits wanted the tribe to sacrifice its most valued possession, and then the rains would come. The other members of the tribe hemmed and hawed about burning their things for the sake of rain, despite the debilitating heat. However, the young girl knew that her special doll was the object to burn. So one night she went and offered her doll to the Gods, and the next morning the hills were blanketed with blue flowers, much like the feathers in her doll's hair. Then the rain fell, and the famine was over because of the young girl's sacrifice.

This beautiful story shows the Comanche's respect for the earth, aspects of their religion, and their respect for the integrity of the young. The beauty of the text is surpasses only by the softness of de Paola's signature illustrations. This book is a true treasure. LISA FAIN

293

Spirit Child: A Story of the Nativity

📖 Bernardino de Sahagun (translated by John Bierhorst) ✏ Barbara Cooney

Hispanic

1990 (1984), Mulberry Books

This story of the Nativity was written in Nahuatl by Fray Bernardino de Sahagun in 1583 and was translated from the original text by John Bierhorst. The story combines the gospels of Matthew and Luke with the Aztec tradition. "The story of the spirit child was recited by Aztec chanters to the accompaniment of the upright skin-drum called huehuetl and the two-toned log drum called teponaztli." In keeping with the essence of the story, the illustrations combine the European and Aztec traditions. BYRON RUSKIN

An English translation of the Aztec version of the Nativity.

Las Navidades: Popular Songs from Latin America

📖 ✏ Lulu Delacre

Caribbean, Hispanic, Puerto Rican

1992 (1990), Scholastic, Inc., ✶ Audiocassette, Spanish

Born in Puerto Rico of Argentinean parents, Lulu Delacre has compiled a collection of popular Christmas songs from Latin America and Puerto Rico. Beautifully illustrated by her own hand, she uses a variety of symbols and images to illustrate the themes and messages conveyed in the songs.

Because much of Latin America and Puerto Rico is Catholic, many of the songs reflect those religious beliefs. But some also speak of nature and the seasons. Special annotations have been added to explain the customs noted in many of the songs. The musical arrangements are simple and can be followed easily. The book is also available with a cassette. While the English version of the songs is good, more care is needed to place the Spanish accents correctly. The mispronunciation of Spanish words on the tape is inexcusable and insulting.

A bilingual collection of Christmas songs from Puerto Rico and Latin America.

In an effort to make the book more inviting, Delacre has hidden a series of fourteen lizards throughout the book. *Teachers, librarians, and young readers themselves will also find the book's bibliography useful.* MAGNA M. DIAZ

Vejigante Masquerader

📖 ✏ Lulu Delacre

Carribean American, Hispanic, Puerto Rican

1993, Scholastic, Inc., ✶ Bilingual English/ Spanish, Videocassette

Even outside of Latin America, the West Indies, and New Orleans, Carnival has become a very well-known celebration, embraced by non-Catholics and people from a broad range of cultures from around the world. The costumes, festivities, and grand parades have become a part of urban communities from New York to San Francisco and from Rio de Janerio to Ponce.

In *Vejigante Masquerader*, a young boy named Ramon lives in Puerto Rico, known for having one of the best Carnival celebrations anywhere. He works hard, saves his money, to buy his Vejigante mask. A store owner offers to let Ramon work off money advanced to him in order to buy his mask. Ramon is also faced with a challenge from some older boys with whom he longs to associate.

A Puerto Rican boy works hard in order to afford a mask for Carnival in a beautifully illustrated bilingual book.

Brightly and beautifully illustrated, the book includes instructions on how to create your own Vejigante from papier-mâché. Written in Spanish and English, and a winner of the Book of Americas Award, the book includes Vejigante chants, a glossary, and bibliography. Also available is a twenty-five-minute VHS video in English entitled The Legend of the Vejigante. MAGNA M. DIAZ

Arroz con Leche: Popular Songs and Rhymes from Latin America

📖 ✏ Lulu Delacre

Hispanic

1989, Scholastic, Inc., ✶ Bilingual English/ Spanish, Videocassette

This collection of chants and songs from Latin America, many of which are remembered from the author's own childhood in Puerto Rico as the daughter of Argentinean parents, includes selections from Puerto Rico, Mexico, and Argentina. Some, such

A colorful bilingual collection of songs and rhymes from Latin America.

as "Que linda manito" ("A pretty little hand") and "Aserrin, asserin" ("Sawdust song") are fingerplays for infants or toddlers. Others, such as "Naranja dulce" ("Orange so sweet") and the title song "Arroz con leche" ("Rice and milk") are circle games played by older children. All appear in both the original Spanish and loosely translated English. Footnotes describing the games are included, as is sheet music for many of the selections.

"¡Qué llueva!" ("It's Raining!") celebrates the brief, sudden downpours so common in Puerto Rico and other tropical places:

¡Qué llueva! ¡Qué llueva!
la virgen de la cueva,
los pajaritos cantan,
las nubes se levantan,
¡Qué si! ¡Qúe no!
¡Qúe caiga el chaparron!

It's raining! It's raining!
The cavern maiden's calling.
The little birds are singing
All the clouds are lifting.
Oh yes!—Oh no!
Oh! Let the downpour fall.

Soft, colorful illustrations, show authentic details of life in Latin America, such as food vendors in Mexico and a view of Old San Juan Cathedral in Puerto Rico.

Young readers may wish to start a collection of songs and rhymes from many cultures. Older children may examine the diversity of Latin America by noting similarities and differences among the selections from the different cultures represented. JODIE LEVINE

Grandma's Latkes

📕 Malka Druker (edited by Eve Chwast)
✒ Eve Chwast
Jewish
1992, Harcourt Brace & Co., 📖 Kimmel, Eric A., *Hershel and the Hanukkah Goblins.*

For Molly, being chosen as Grandma's helper for making latkes is an honor in the preparation of the many latkes needed for the Hanukkah party. Molly

learns many things from her grandmother, including the recipe passed on from Grandma's Grandma and Grandma's secret hints for cooking. Molly and the reader also learn the history of Hanukkah, including why latkes are eaten. The passing on of traditions is emphasized as Grandma tells Molly, "Now you know enough to teach your own grandchildren."

The story of Hanukkah is told amidst the process of sharing an important experience between these engaging characters from differing generations. The story also provides parents and teachers with the tools to understand this holiday as commemorating a fight

Making latkes with her grandmother, Molly learns the origin of Hanukkah.

for religious freedom. The book includes Grandma's recipe for latkes so families and classrooms can experience the preparation of latkes for themselves. And with the cooking hints shared in the book, the process will be an easy and joyful one.

The woodcut and watercolor illustrations further enhance the richness of the story. The text is placed both beside and within the illustrations, generating continued interest in the story line.

The Chanukkah Guest by Eric Kimmel is another book that emphasizes the tradition of latkes while sharing, through a humorous storyline, the traditional activities enjoyed during the holiday such as playing dreidle and lighting the menorah. Using these two books together can provide a comprehensive picture of this holiday.

It may be noted that the holiday is often spelled in various ways. The holiday name is Hebrew and has been transliterated into the various spellings. This is a point that should be clarified for children. BARBARA GOLDENHERSH

Little Eagle Lots of Owls

📕 Jim Edmiston ✒ Jane Ross
Native American
1993, Houghton Mifflin Company

Little Eagle Lots of Owls is the tale of a young North American Indian boy with a long name—so long his grandfather, the chief, shortens it to Little Eagle. To ensure that he will never forget his true name, the chief gives Little Eagle a gift: a strange creature, fast asleep. The boy travels to the river forest and the plains, and even performs a rain dance in an attempt to arouse the sleeping creature, but nothing works. Finally, when the sun goes down, the creature

295

296

awakens and Little Eagle discovers that it is actually three owls huddled together. The boy's grandfather, who is on another mountain, states, ". . . you have the sharp eyes of the eagle and you are as wise as the owl. Now you know your true name."

A book riddled with stereotypes of Native American culture.

Nothing about this story reflects authentic Native American culture, traditions, or folklore. The text is limited and fragmented, making the story difficult to follow. Little Eagle is represented as a generic "Indian," with a stereotypical name and costume.

Illustrator Jane Ross's unique silk painting illustrations are visually pleasing, but only reinforce the Native American Indian stereotype portrayed in the story. Children should only be presented with the best quality literature we have to offer them. There are too many other works of genuine Native American Indian literature worth reading.

DENISE JOHNSON

The Star Maiden: An Ojibway Tale

📖 Barbara Juster Esbensen ✒ Helen K. Davies
Native American

1991 (1988), Little, Brown and Company,
📖 Copway, George, *Chief of the Ojibway Nation, The Traditional History and Characteristics Sketches of the Ojibway Nation.*

In 1847, George Copway, or Kahgegwagebow, published a work that, in later editions, came to be known as *The Traditional History and Characteristic Sketches of the Ojibway Nation*. In addition to his writing, Copway is remembered as a Methodist missionary as well as a proponent of the preservation of native culture, especially his own Ojibwa/Anishinaabeg culture. The first of the legends he reported was that of "The Star and the Lily," which is satisfactorily retold by Esbensen and illustrated by Helen K. Davies as *The Star Maiden*. Copway defined three types of Ojibway legends: the humorous, the historical, and the moral or educational. He classified "The Star and the Lily" as an historical tale that relates Ojibway beliefs about the origins of a flowering plant.

A somewhat flawed retelling of the Ojibway legend that explains the origin of water lilies.

In *The Star Maiden*, a woodland people live happily and well in a time of plenty and peace. Then one night a star draws close to the people. Several young men are sent to investigate. One of them dreams that the star appears to him as a silver maiden who expresses her desire to live with his community. She is welcomed and, after taking on the shape of several living plants, is transformed, along with her sisters, into a water lily.

This retelling carries the essence of Copway's story, but it overlooks several important aspects. References to native religious belief are omitted—for instance, the Anishinaabeg were in the habit of gazing at the stars because they believed that is where the spirits of good people resided after their death. The young men also honor the star with an herb-filled pipe. A second shortcoming is in Esbensen's occasional use of somewhat antiquated language. Finally, Esbensen neglects to provide background on the role of storytelling in the Anishinaabeg culture.

Illustrations impart images of the flora and fauna of the Anishinaabeg woodland and prairie and elements of Anishinaabeg culture, including wild rice, blueberries, wigwams, and puckered-seam moccasins. Each illustration is shown as a panel framed by geometric and floral quillwork and beadwork designs.

LORIENE ROY

Uncle Noruz (Uncle New Year)

📖 Fareedeh Farjam ✒ Farsheed Mesqali
Iraniam, Middle Eastern

1983, Mazda, ✳ Series, Spanish

Just before the beginning of the Iranian new year, Noruz, the Old Woman (symbol of winter), does her spring cleaning and decorates her house with flowers and special Noruz decorations. After working hard for a few days, she puts her best dress on, arranges her delicious homemade cookies on a plate, makes orange blossom tea, and sits on her veranda awaiting Amu Noruz.

A story about the Iranian New Year that celebrates the beginning of spring.

Amu Noruz, or the Iranian Santa Claus (symbol of spring), comes to town on the first day of spring and visits the people's homes to bring freshness and happiness. But when he enters the Old Woman's house, he finds her asleep.

This Iranian folktale portrays some of the traditions of Noruz interwoven into a beautiful story. It is retold in a fine yet simple text. Children will enjoy and learn about a different tradition and a new year's celebration in a culture where rejuvenation of nature is still an important annual event.

The color illustrations, a combination of painting and cloth collage by a renowned Iranian artist, harmonize with the text. SHAHLA SOHAIL

Moja Means One: Swahili Counting Book

📗 Muriel Feelings ✏ Tom Feelings

East African

1994 (1971), Puffin Books, 📖 Prior, Jennifer, *The Games of Africa.*

This is a traditional counting book, proceeding from one to ten with a simple English sentence for each number. The English names for the numbers do not appear; Arabic numerals are accompanied by the Swahili names, with a pronunciation guide.

Each number is covered in a two-page spread, largely taken up by the glorious black-and-white illustrations of rural East Africa. The number eight (nane), for example, has the text "Busy market stalls

An appealing counting book with Swahili numbers and images of East African culture.

are stocked with fruits, vegetables, meats, fish, clothes, jewelry, pottery, and carvings." The scene is of a marketplace in a coastal village.

The text and illustrations are simple and clear. "Nane means eight, count the eight market stalls; tano, five, count five animals." There are children in many of the scenes, shopping with their mothers, playing games, and listening to stories. Children as young as one- or two-years-old will find the pictures and the game of counting interesting, and can learn the numbers in English and Swahili at the same time.

For older children and willing teachers, the illustrations offer the opportunity for much more discussion and learning. The fruit stall in the market scene, for example, has twenty-five pieces of fruit : bananas, mangoes, passion fruit, pineapples, a melon, and more. Another stall has nine pieces of pottery in different shapes for different uses. Women carry things on their heads and on their backs. Men and women dress in traditional clothing. *There is a lot to talk about here, as an introduc-*tion to African life and culture, or to reinforce what some children already know.

Teachers will also find the author's introduction and closing note helpful. A map of Africa shows the countries where Swahili is spoken, and Muriel Feelings gives some basic information about the language and how she came to learn it.

Tom Feelings's proud, bold, dignified illustrations are a nonstereotypical look at East Africa. The people in his scenes are strong and beautiful, somber and proud. His buildings are straight and symmetrical, his fences in perfect repair. Clearly, his intention is to show rural life at its best, and to demonstrate pride in his people.

The book is dedicated to "all Black children living in the Western Hemisphere," and the introduction stresses the importance for children "of African origin" to learn about their African heritage. This book and the companion, *Jambo Means Hello* by the same author-illustrator team, can be a welcoming and respectful introduction to East African life for interested children of any ethnicity. CYNTHIA A. BILY

Spin a Soft Black Song

📗 Nikki Giovanni ✏ George Martin

African American

1987 (1971), Farrar, Straus & Giroux, Inc.

How do children feel about everyday things such as going to the store, going outside, or watching the man who sits on the corner? *Spin a Soft Black Song* is a collection of poems that reveal children's thoughts. George Martin's illustrations empress the innocence with which children view life.

What makes this volume of poetry so good for children is that they can read it themselves. It doesn't have a lot of large words but it has large feelings. These feelings can be spun into a song for life, a song which children can whisper or shout from rooftops.

In "poem for ntombe layo (at five weeks of age),"

An ingenious book of poems from an African American child's perspective.

three short verses allow us to hear a baby's thoughts about being laid down. In "let's take a nap," a child muses at his mother's preparations to put him to sleep—which results in her falling asleep.

There is much love in this ingenious, empathetic book. YOLANDA ROBINSON-COLES

Iktomi and the Buzzard: A Plains Indian Story

📖 ✦ Paul Goble
Native American, Plains Indian
1994, Orchard Books, ✳ Series

298 ▷

Goble continues to communicate his growing knowledge and understanding of Native American storytelling with his fifth book about the incorrigible Plains Indian trickster, Iktomi.

This time, Iktomi is walking to powwow, dressed in his finest eagle feathers, when he comes to a river that is too wide to cross. In need of a lift, he talks Buzzard into flying him across but can't resist making rude references to Buzzard's bald head. Buzzard takes revenge by dumping Iktomi head-first down a hollow tree. As usual, Iktomi does not feel he deserves what has happened to him. Finally, he tricks two girls looking for firewood into saving him. This humorous story is accompanied by Goble's beautiful India ink and watercolor illustrations.

An entertaining tale of the Plains Indian trickster, Iktomi.

Unlike Goble's earlier volumes, this book includes passages set off in gray type that are meant to "encourage listeners, young and old, to make comments." Goble also includes tips for oral readings.

Though the vocabulary is a bit difficult, elementary children will still enjoy this entertaining tale.
KAREN ROBERTS STRONG

The Bells of Christmas

📖 Virginia Hamilton ✦ Lambert Davis
African American
1989, Harcourt Brace, 🏠 McKissack, Patrick, *Christmas in the Big House.*

An African American family in Springfield, Ohio, celebrates Christmas 1890 with a holiday season made memorable by visiting relatives, plenty of gifts, and an eagerly anticipated snowfall. Narrated by twelve-year-old Jason, the story concerns the interminable wait as the days before Christmas slowly tick down. Jason and his siblings decorate the tree, discuss the upcoming church recital, and wish for snow, while dreaming about the arrival of the Bells, their cousins from West Liberty, Ohio. Jason's friend Matthew is particularly enthusiastic about seeing Cousin Tisha, the long-time object of his affections.

When Christmas morning arrives, the tree is piled high with trains, dolls, clothes, and books for the children—and outside the window snow has begun to fall. The Bell relatives arrive bearing even more gifts, including a special, mechanized wooden leg that Uncle Levi has created for Papa, whose leg had been amputated after an accident. The marvelously descriptive story tells of a satisfying Christmas dinner, a sleigh ride to church, and the holiday program, in which all of the children perform. Christmas night ends with Jason, Tisha, and Matthew taking a quiet

A highly illustrated book wonderfully imagining Christmas 1890 for an African American boy's family.

sleigh ride through the snow, reflecting on the holiday and dreaming about the future. As Tisha exclaims before they head for home, "We're sleighing toward 1990!"

The thin, oversized volume is particularly well-suited for reluctant readers, who will be pleased to see a rather brief story for intermediate readers well broken-up by the profuse number of illustrations. Each color picture is captioned with a line of text, giving the illustrations a stately, old-fashioned appeal. There is much warmth in the family relationships depicted in both the illustrations and text. Hamilton has done a masterful job of recreating an historical Christmas, writing with evocative language and a keen eye for detail. Readers will enjoy comparing the similarities and differences between Christmases of yesterday and today. Candles on the tree, bathtubs in the kitchen, and horse-drawn sleighs may be part of the past, but the long wait for Santa Claus, the joyous time with relatives, and the excitement of Christmas morning are still the same. The book makes perfect holiday fare, but is also quite suitable for black history units. Contrasting the prosperous 1890 holiday of the Bell family with the 1859 African American celebration in Patricia McKissack's *Christmas in the Big House* would be especially interesting, as would be comparing Hamilton's story with contemporary novels of Christmas and Kwanzaa.
PETER D. SIERUTA

The Voice of the Great Bell

📖 Lafcadio Hearn (retold by Margaret Hodges)
🖌 Ed Young

Asian, Chinese

1989, Little, Brown & Company

This folktale comes from the collection of ghost stories, *Some Chinese Ghosts*, by Lafcadio Hearn. This is a mystical story about a great bell which finally was molded with a pure girl's sacrifice of her life. The girl's father, "a worthy man," has been commissioned by the emperor to oversee the construction of a gigantic bell. But twice the most famous bell makers of the empire fail in making the various metals hold together in the form of the bell. The emperor is angry and threatens Kouan-Yu with death if for the third time the bell fails to be built.

A somewhat flawed retelling of a Chinese folktale.

Kouan-Yu's daughter, who loves her father dearly, consults an astrologer who tells her that the bell will not be built unless "a pure maiden" is melted in the crucible with the metals for the bell.

When the third attempt is under way, the daughter throws herself into the crucible, much to her father's agony. One of the daughter's shoes remains behind, having come off when a servant girl tried to restrain the daughter from leaping.

After reading the book, readers will ponder the content and the plot of the book, because they will be moved by the little Chinese girl's great spirit of sacrifice, and shocked by the system of the ancient society which is reflected in the story that the father has to die if he fails in fulfilling the emperor's command. They may also be amazed by the mystical astrology, and confused by the girl's shoe at the end of the story. All the points above are the attractions of the book. However, some problems exist.

First, words and phrases of a particular regional or ethnic group are important features of that group; literature should reflect the linguistic richness of culture. Words that come from different regions also make language richer and more colorful. There are some particular terms in the book, but as these terms are placed apart from other words or sentences that would support their deep meaning, so sometimes it is difficult for readers to realize the real meaning. For instance, it says in the book: "Nearly five hundred years ago the Emperor of China, Son of Heaven, commanded a worthy man, Kouan Yu, to have a bell made so big that the sound..." Here the "Son of Heaven" sounds like Heaven's son or a person's name, but actually "Son of Heaven" is a respectful title for Emperors of China. Another example is the phrase, "worthy man." "Worthy man" is a common traditional address to a male who has a certain social position, even if he only has one servant. A more correct translation would be "Master Sir" rather than "Worthy Man." In this book, the emperor sends his message to the Worthy Man. Judging from that, the "Worthy Man" must be a high government official or a high ranking military officer, because traditionally the emperor would not directly contact a common "worthy man" or a bell maker. It is wonderful to present the specific words of the ethnic group in the book to show its way of expression, but here it fails to make readers understand the exact meaning of the particular words.

Second, the end of the story is confusing, because the girl's shoe has no causality with the story. It says in the story that the tones sounds: "like some vast voice uttering a name, a girl's name the name of Ko Ngai!" Since the tones of the bell sounds the girl's name, why at the last page of the book does it say "And still when Chinese mother hear the voice of the great bell...they whisper to their little ones Listen! That's Ko Ngai crying for her shoe!..." Readers will be confused over whether the tones of the bell sound the girl's name or is Ko Ngai crying her name or crying for her shoe?

Finally, while the story has beautiful illustrations, they are too abstract. Can it help young readers get a clear idea about China and Chinese culture from the story? This kind of art style may be better used in books that describe a story or situation that young readers are familiar with. However, since most young readers have no previous knowledge of the story or even about ancient China, these pictures can't help children imagine what they don't know, or what they have never seen. But it is worthwhile reading the book to gain more ideas about China, Chinese culture, and Chinese people.

LI LIU

Joseph Who Loved the Sabbath

📖 Marilyn Hirsh   ✒ Devis Grebu

Jewish

1988 (1986), Puffin Books

The Sabbath is the most important sacred day of the week for observant Jews. It is considered a high act of holiness to observe the Sabbath regularly. It is a day when even poor people can feel like royalty as they wear their best clothes, prepare special meals, and praise God for the bounty of the spirit.

A light-hearted story celebrating the honoring of the Jewish Sabbath.

This story is about a very poor man, Joseph, who saves all of his meager earnings to celebrate the Sabbath each week, sometimes alone, more often with friends. His employer, a rich and very greedy man named Sorab, does not appreciate Joseph's hard work, or his pattern of spending his hard-earned money on the Sabbath observance. No matter how hard Joseph works, Sorab gives him only a pittance for wages.

One night Sorab has a dream in which a genie appears and announces that before the month is up Joseph will rightfully claim all of Sorab's wealth and possessions. Sorab becomes so obsessed by fear that his dream will come true that he sells his house and lands to a rich merchant and trades all of his money for a gigantic ruby. Then he sails away to a faraway land to escape Joseph. The ship sinks, Sorab drowns, and a large fish swallows the ruby. When Joseph goes to the market to purchase his food for the Sabbath, he spends his last coin for a wonderful fish, which turns out to be the one that swallowed the ruby. He redeems the ruby for enough money to purchase Sorab's house and land and spends the rest of his life working hard and sharing his good fortune with many friends and strangers, and his house is always filled with joy.

While this story is a celebration of the practice of honoring the Sabbath, it does not apply to all Jews. But it does reflect the importance of the Sabbath for many Jews, especially those who are observant. It also provides a basis for discussing rituals and their significance in any religion. The story also provides some sense of how traditions become an ongoing part of a religion or spiritual practice.

The stylized illustrations contribute a light touch to the story, preventing it from becoming too ponderous. MASHA RUDMAN

The Boy Who Loved Morning

📖 Shannon Jacobs   ✒ Michael Hays

Native American

1993, 📖 Wisniewski, David, *Rainplayer*

As a young boy plays his flute to awaken the morning, he is joined by a coyote, a crow, and a snake. They all praise his talent. On his way back home, he encounters his grandfather praying to the Great Spirit, pleading that the buffalo return to their hunting grounds. Boy understands that his grandfather is preoccupied with the survival of the tribe.

A Native American boy learns the difference between honoring nature and showing off.

Reflecting upon the survival of his people, Boy belittles his gift of playing the flute for the morning, and considers it insignificant. Although his grandfather takes interest in him, and asks if he continues to greet the morning, Boy longs to greet the morning with his grandfather in the way they had done before. Grandfather mentions that Boy's naming will be soon. Boy tries not to think of the naming ceremony that is two moons (roughly two months) away; yet as it approaches, he imagines names that may be fitting as he plays for the mornings.

On this particular night, he is unable to sleep and goes to the mesa to play. He does so with great excitement—not peacefully, as is his custom. This provokes the morning to come early, and Boy is ecstatic. He shouts, "Wakes Morning Early," and asks his animal companions what they think of the name. They do not respond, and Boy fails to note their hesitation and concern over Boy's power. He is excited and pleased with his ability to bring on morning early and wants to show his grandfather at his naming ceremony. Boy decides that he wants to call for a full sunrise at midnight! Here he is no longer honoring the morning, but is now driven by his ego.

With Boy having lost sight of the real significance of his gift, Boy's grandfather is angered by his arrogance and abruptly stops him. Humiliated and hurt, Boy runs to the mesa, where he meets up with his animal friends. They question how his performance went, and it is here that he realizes for himself that he was vain and forgot that honoring the morning was his purpose. Having achieved adultlike insight, he realizes that he must apologize to Grandfather.

Grandfather finds him asleep on the mesa, and

Boy apologizes for his inconsiderate actions. As they greet the morning together, Boy wonders what his name will be, and with great care, chooses what he thinks would best describe him: "Morning Song." As the sun rises, Grandfather blesses the name, and Morning Song's animal friends are content as well. Readers witness that animals, nature, and harmony play an important role in Native American life.

The ways in which we relate to one another can both change and upset the sacred harmony of the earth. This story clearly demonstrates that, and gives readers an opportunity to gain a greater understanding of the relationship between people and nature. The vivid illustrations fill each page and are just as integral to the book as the narrative.
MARTHA L. MARTINEZ

The Chanukkah Guest

📕 Eric A. Kimmel ✏ Giyora Carmi
Jewish
1990 (1988), Holiday House, 📖 Kimmel, Eric A., *Hershel and the Hanukkah Goblins*

Ninety-seven-year-old Bubba Brayna is making potato latkes for her guests including the Rabbi. When there is a knock at the door, Bubba Brayna, whose sight and hearing are not very good, believes it to be the Rabbi, and she begins the Chanukkah celebration, lighting the candles, playing dreidel and eating latkes. But in fact, her guest is not the Rabbi, it is a hungry bear, awakened from hibernation. When the villagers arrive, the bear has left, having eaten all that was prepared. With the help of her guests, however, Bubba Brayna makes more latkes and a happy Chanukkah is had by all–including the bear.

A playful story featuring a slapstick Chanukkah celebration.

The book includes a glossary of terms to clarify the Chanukkah celebration for the reader but lacks a recipe for latkes. The bright and colorful illustrations portray an elderly woman who is still quite capable, despite her poor vision and hearing.
BARBARA GOLDENHERSH

Let's Celebrate

📕 Lada Josefa Kratky
Multicultural
1995, Hampton-Brown Books

Young people from different American cultures come together to learn about, enjoy, and celebrate various holidays. The photographs might lead one to believe that non-Americans also celebrate these holidays and subsequently can be interpreted as misleading.

While the Dancing Dragon is a unique and honored symbol in Chinese culture, the book does not convey this. There is a photograph of a Dancing Dragon, but there are no words to explain it. *When used in classrooms, the teacher should supplement it with additional information.* HSIU-FENG TSENG

Photographs without explanatory text illustrate various ethnic groups celebrating certain holidays.

Baseball Bats for Christmas

📕 Michael Arvaarluk Kusugak
✏ Vladyana Krykorka
Inuit, Native American
1993, Annick Press Ltd.

In 1955, fewer than one hundred people lived on the treeless shores of Repulse Bay at the north end of the Hudson Bay. That Christmas, the local bush pilot, Rocky Parsons, delivers six Christmas trees to his stop at the Hudson Bay Store.

While the people of Repulse Bay exchange gifts and attend Catholic services on Christmas Eve, they know nothing of Christmas trees. One child, Yvo, comes up with a brilliant idea: to carve the trees into baseball bats.

Children from all over Repulse Bay come to play ball in the snow. The following autumn, all the bats are broken from so much use, and the children anxiously await the arrival of the next delivery of raw material for their baseball bats. This is a marvelous story of cultural adaptation. It also shows how some rituals, like baseball, can become universal.

The Native American people of Repulse Bay, Canada, devise a creative alternative to Christmas trees.

Illustrator Vladyana Krykorka traveled to northern Canada and stayed with the Kusugak family in order to photograph and paint the people of Repulse Bay in their own environment. NOLA HADLEY

The Flute Player, an Apache Folktale

📖 ✎ Michael Lacapa
Apache, Hopi, Native American
1991, Northland Publishing Company

The Flute Player tells of a young man and woman who fall in love at a hoop dance. He tells her that he plays the flute; she vows to place a leaf in the local river if she likes his song.

The next morning he plays a song so beautiful, "People working in the canyon in the cornfields said, 'Listen, that sounds like the wind blowing through the trees.'" Later, he finds a leaf in the river. He plays again for her the next morning, and the next morning he again finds a leaf in the river. Unfortunately, the following morning the young man must leave on a hunting trip with his uncle. The young woman does not know that he is gone, and she waits in vain to hear his flute.

A romantic love story that captures the spirit of Apache storytelling.

After a few mornings, the young woman decides he doesn't like her anymore and she becomes very sad. Eventually the young woman becomes so sad she becomes ill. Her family takes her to a medicine man, but she does not get well and dies.

The young man returns from the successful hunt and immediately runs to play his flute for her. He looks in the river for a leaf from her but doesn't find any leaves. Again the next day he plays for her but doesn't see any sign of a leaf in the river. The following day he finds out from the girl's brother that she has died. The young man goes to play his flute at the young woman's burial site. Soon afterwards he disappears. Even today in the canyon you can hear the beautiful flute songs in the wind and you can see leaves floating in the river. "But we smile and know that the girl still likes the flute player."

Both characters, who are never named in the story, take on a mythical quality. The sadness of this story is softened by the vibrant and bold color illustrations of Michael Lacapa, which carry the youngest reader easily into the wistful fabric of this tale. The story hits a universal note that will appeal to most adults, who can relate to the enormity of grief that we have felt at the first suggestion of unrequited love. *This book could be used in a unit about the history and cultures of the American Southwest.* NOLA HADLEY

Climbing Jacob's Ladder: Heroes of the Bible in African-American Spirituals

📖 John Langstaff (editor), John Andrew Ross (piano arrangements) ✎ Ashley Bryan
African American
1991, Margaret K. McElderry Books

Climbing Jacob's Ladder is organized around spirituals about Biblical heroes. Each song is preceded by a brief story that identifies the hero and pictures him. Illustrator Ashley Bryan gives us black Noah ("Didn't It Rain"), black Abraham ("Rock-a My Soul"), black Jacob of the title, black Moses, black Joshua in the Battle of Jericho, little black David playing his harp, black Ezekiel's wheel in a wheel, black Daniel in the lion's den, and a black Jonah being tossed to the whale. Sadly, this book has no female "heroes."

In the piano accompaniments, the simple harmonic structures, characteristically suggested by spiritual melodies, are not always retained. Sometimes the arrangements get jazzy with unexpected chromatic chords ("Ezekiel Saw the

An illustrated collection of African American spirituals about Old Testament heroes, sadly no heroines.

Wheel"), and sometimes they offer gospel-tinged bass lines, as in "We Are Climbing Jacob's Ladder," which suggests the late twentieth century rather than the past. Instructions for guitar accompaniments are provided with simpler and more appropriate chording. In any case, the slaves originally sang these songs wherever they were working or worshipping so no accompaniment is necessary to hear and appreciate them fully. In addition to great enjoyment, the music in this collection brings whole eras to life. MARY MOORE EASTER

Daddy's Chair

📖 Sandy Lanton ✏ Shelly O. Haas

Jewish

1991, Kar-Ben Copies, Inc.

After his father's death, Michael attempts to reserve a place for him: daddy's chair. His mother explains that his father will not return, and will not sit in his chair ever again.

A boy, supported by his family and Jewish ritual, accepts his father's death

Michael asks questions about the Jewish ritual of shiva, the seven-day period of mourning, and he is comforted by interacting with other members of his family. They try to compensate for some of the sadness he feels over the loss of his father, but they in no way suggest that Michael should not think about and mourn his father. Michael is comforted by his family members' concerns and their acknowledgment of his

grief. Some Jewish rituals related to death are explained within the context of the story.

This story can help young children to compare different cultural customs of mourning and dealing with death. The book can help children come to terms with a death that has occurred in their family, and to examine the universal as well as unique customs with respect and awareness. The simplicity of the text serves to underscore the power of Michael's feelings for his father.

MASHA RUDMAN

Georgia O'Keeffe

📖 Linda Lowrey ✏ Rochelle Draper

European American

1996, Lerner, ✱ Series

Georgia O'Keeffe sensualized art in a way that brought much controversy into her life. Moving from painting what pleased her teacher to painting what moved her soul and inspired her spirit, O'Keeffe found beauty in the vitality of living flowers and the bones of dead animals, and she painted things no one else ever thought of painting. Her work often confused people and challenged them to think beyond the narrow boundaries of their lives.

Author Linda Lowrey tells how O'Keeffe overcame her frustration and found her own way of seeing the world. For very young children, the book explores the many dimensions of O'Keeffe's life and the challenges that come with being a creative person. O'Keeffe pursued and honored her creative passion, and this certainly was no easy task for a woman during the earlier part of the twentieth century. This book also introduces young people to some of the inner

An unimpressively illustrated biography of an important, highly independent artist.

workings of the art world and show, how O'Keeffe's husband, who was a world-renowned photographer, supported her growth and development as an artist.

Unfortunately, Draper's illustrations do not capture the strength, dignity, and beauty of O'Keeffe and clearly reflect the work of someone relatively new to the field. But readers will still be intrigued by the life and work of one of America's greatest artists. The book also includes a brief "Afterword" and a list of important dates that highlight some of the major events in O'Keeffe's long and productive life. DAPHNE MUSE

Latkes and Applesauce: A Hanukkah Story

📖 Fran Manushkin ✏ Robin Spowart

Jewish

1992 (1989), Scholastic Inc., 📖 Diamond, Barbara Golin, *Just Enough Is Plenty*; Singer, Issac Bashevis, *Zlateh The Goat and Other Stories.*

In Eastern Europe, the Menashe family is looking forward to celebrating the miracle of Hanukkah with the traditional feast of latkes (potato pancakes) and applesauce, but an early blizzard covers the potatoes and apples before they can be gathered. The family begins the eight nights of celebration anyway, even sharing their dwindling supplies with a stray kitten and a lost dog. Before the festival ends,

A family of Russian Jewish emigres shares a warm story about preserving traditions.

the family's generosity and good cheer are rewarded with a miracle feast of latkes and applesauce.

This is a warm, sweet story enhanced by soft colorful illustrations. Each illustration is a subtle study in light that draws the reader to the story. The glow that appears in each drawing reflects the love in the Menashe family, and the miracle of Hanukkah, the festival of lights.

For very young children, this book is a good introduction to some basic elements of this Jewish holiday. Children whose own families celebrate Hanukkah will identify with the book's evocative illustrations. This is highly recommended for young children and artists of all ages. JANIS O'DRISCOLL

Coyote: A Trickster Tale from the American Southwest

 Gerald McDermott (translated by Aida E. Marcuse)

Native American, Zuni

1994, Harcourt Brace and Company,
 McDermott, Gerald, *Arrow to the Sun*; Troughton, Joanna, *Who Will Be The Sun?*; Bierhorst, John, *Doctor Coyote*; Johnston, Tony, *Tale of Rabbit and Coyote*; Stevens, Janet, *Coyote Steals the Blanket*.

The trickster Coyote romps through countless Native American stories. Sometimes he is clever and cunning, and other times he is a prankster. In this Zuni-derived tale, he is a fool.

Blue Coyote wants to laugh, dance, and fly like the crows. For a while, the birds humor him and let him try; but Blue Coyote's boastfulness angers the crows, and he ends up the color of dust.

Simplified to appeal to preschoolers, this coyote story differs from traditional coyote tales because Blue Coyote seems to be a victim. The crows appear haughty and mean-spirited, leading the reader to feel some sympathy for Blue Coyote.

A somewhat inauthentic retelling of traditional Native American coyote trickster vignettes.

In the art, Blue Coyote seems more hapless than egotistical, and the crows appear arrogant. Offering us a character reminiscent of Wily Coyote, author-illustrator McDermott's illustrations are bright and humorous, and show Blue Coyote as a simple buffoon. Although the book works well enough as a picture book, it is not representative of the coyote in traditional Native American tales. This interpretation is best suited for very young readers. JANIS O'DRISCOLL

The Always Prayer Shawl

 Sheldon Oberman Ted Lewin

Jewish

1994, Boyds Mill Press

Illuminated by remarkable illustrations, this is the story of a young boy who emigrates from Russia with his family to the United States. Simply turning the pages gives the reader a vivid picture of the characters, their loving and respectful relationship to each other, their strong sense of tradition and community, and the hardships they endure, both before and during their emigration. The first set of illustrations is in black and white, reflecting the almost photographic sense of memory in the old country, where Adam grew up. The pictures become paintings in color to indicate contemporary times and an older Adam.

A colorful introduction to Hanukkah for very young readers.

The text adds the poignancy of small details of the relationship between Adam and his grandfather, who remains in Russia. The story of this Jewish family is the story of many immigrant families from all over the world. The grandfather gives Adam a prayer shawl that his own grandfather had given him long ago. Adam cherishes his "always prayer shawl" as something that will never change, but everything else in Adam's life changes, like growing up and moving to a new home. The shawl becomes an integral part of Adam's life, and he even learns how to repair its fraying edges. When Adam grows old he tells his grandson about his life as a child in Russia, and about the importance of the continuity of the prayer shawl. Even though the fringes, the collar, and the cloth have changed, it is still the same prayer shawl it has always been, and will always signify the heritage of this family.

Through its evocative words and pictures, this story brings up some important issues of what happens to people and traditions over time. It raises the question of how to avoid melting into the larger community while still accepting change. *It invites discussion of which changes may be damaging and which ones may be beneficial and which can be the foundation for discussions about other cultures and their traditions.* MASHA RUDMAN

The Hundredth Name

📖 Shulamith Levey Oppenheim ✏ Michael Hays
Arab American, Middle Eastern
1995, Boyds Mill Press

An Arabic folksaying tells us that Allah has one hundred names—such as the Merciful, and the Wise—but human beings only know ninety-nine of them. The camel alone knows the last and most important name, and that accounts for its haughty, proud expression. Perhaps we can read in this a reminder that our knowledge will never be perfect.

A sensitive portrayal of Islam and one Arabian boy's family.

Around the notion of the hundredth name the author has woven a gentle story of a village boy in Egypt and his camel Qadiim. The boy, Salah, wonders why the camel always looks so woebegone. Trying to cheer the boy, Salah's father reminds him of the camel's great privilege in knowing the ultimate name of Allah, who cares for all creatures. He reminds Salah, too, of the importance of prayer. That night Salah prays—and in the morning he notices a difference in Qadiim. The camel's head is held higher, and Salah feels sure that Qadiim now knows the hundredth name of God and will be contented.

There are many important qualities that commend this book. The telling of the story is particularly graceful, and meaning can be found much deeper than its plot. Salah is an unusually tender-hearted child who expresses the sensitivity to life that should be encouraged in all children.

The story also conveys a warm and trusting relationship between boy and father. Further meaning comes in the sym-

pathetic interpretation of Islam, with emphasis on the goodness of Allah. In this respect the book is a valuable contribution to children's literature—especially these days when, seen through the clouded glass of current political disorder, the image that most Americans get of Islam is harsh and gravely distorted.

Like the author, the illustrator has chosen a soft, idealized representation of Egyptian village life, depicted in muted colors and simplified forms rather than the brilliant greens and earth hues of reality. Yet his pictures do give a view of "eternal Egypt" both informative and evocative, which will attract children and adults alike; and they are exquisite.

A needed illustration of present-day rural life in the Middle East, this book can add to classroom discussion of values such as the importance of both religion and folklore in people's lives, the universality of family love, and the relationships of humans with animals.
ELSTON MARSTON

The Chippewa

📖 Alice Osinski ✏ Various sources
Native American, Ojibway
1987, Children's Press, ✳ Series

The A New True Book Series is intended to introduce elementary school students to American Indians. Osinski, a non-Native writer, spent seven years teaching on reservations in South Dakota and New Mexico, although these tribal groups vary greatly from the

A brief, somewhat simplified history of the Ojibway people and their customs and traditions.

Anishinaabeg (Ojibwa or Chippewa). The 1,800-word text of *The Chippewa* portrays Anishinaabeg life in nine short chapters. Osinksi selects details that would interest a young audience, such as the construction of wigwams, canoes, and snowshoes, and decorative arts including beading and dental pictographs. She also effectively depicts a sense of the traditional seasonal calendar from maple sugaring to wild ricing and winter trapping and fishing.

Her renderings of some historic events is somewhat simplified. While it is true that the Anishinaabeg did live near Sault Sainte Marie, Michigan, traditional belief holds that they previously lived along the northern Atlantic coast.

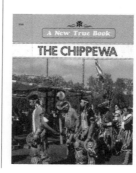

The process of finishing rice is also abbreviated; neither husking nor winnowing is mentioned. Finally, Osinski's word choice is somewhat antiquated. The Chippewa are now more frequently referred to as the Ojibwa or the Anishinaabeg. "Hunting grounds" denotes the stereotypical

Native afterlife, "the happy hunting grounds." *Still, the incomplete nature of* The Chippewa *may prompt young students to question and lead them and their adult teachers and caregivers to seek out more detailed supplemental sources.* The book is indexed and has a glossary, although some glossary words (gathering, lumber, profession) are curious inclusions. LORIENE ROY

The Magic Weaver of Rugs: A Tale of the Navajo

Jerrie Oughton   Lisa Desimini

Native American, Navajo

1994, Houghton Mifflin Company

This beautifully told tale explains the origins of Navajo rugs, and underlines the importance of self-sufficiency.

According to legend, the Navajo people were once sad, defeated by cold and hunger. "Even when winter had come and gone, it stayed winter in their hearts because the white wolf of fear crept among them. Fear that they would not survive." One day, two women decide to leave the camp intending to pray for help and encounter Spider Woman. Spider Woman is a being of inordinate strength, depicted by Desimini in a velvet green gown, her white-gray hair standing on end. The two women are terrified. However, they are desperate for help for their people, so when the Spider woman makes a loom and commands them to weave a rug they do so, in fear for their lives. Once the rug is finished, the women are free to go and they return to their camp convinced that Spider Woman has refused to help them and that they have failed their people. But Spider Woman has given them the gift of independence. The women share their new skill, and henceforth the Navajo people are able to weave rugs for themselves and to barter rugs for food. They are cold and hungry no longer.

A legend of the origins of Navajo rug-weaving.

This simple legend shows a people's movement from poverty to prosperity through learning a skill that can be shared throughout the community and passed down along the generations. The Navajo people draw on natural resources — wood, wool, and plants and berries for dyes — for the raw materials to make their rugs, and invest them with patterns drawn from their imaginations. As Spider Woman says, "Weave with your very souls."

Another strong motif is the important role of women — the empowering Spider Woman, and the two brave women who wanted more for their people and gained the key to freedom from the worries of survival. Equally significant is Spider Woman's demand that the Navajo people recognize their homeland, and use the riches it offers to make a life there. "Perhaps we need to go to a land that is kinder, where we can find food and warmth." "You are of this place." Spider Woman's voice echoed back and forth in the canyon walls."

Oughton tells the story with an eloquence that makes it perfect for reading aloud, and Desimini's artwork captures both the bleakness and the beauty of the desert lands. This beautiful book is a useful teaching tool. LINDSEY TATE

¡Viva Mexico! A Story of Benito Juarez and Cinco de Mayo

Argentina Palacios, Alex Haley (editor)

Howard Berelson

Hispanic, Mexican

1993, Steck-Vaughn Company, ✳ Series

The growing popularity of the Mexican holiday Cinco de Mayo, in the United States, makes this book, which explains the holiday's origin, a timely one. Benito Juarez is truly one of the most remarkable figures in Mexican history. He was a Zapotec Indian whose hard work and humble beginnings led him to become a lawyer who championed the rights of poor Indians. Through his work and commitment, he also became the President of Mexico in 1861. This biographical account of Benito Juarez also focuses upon Mexico's confrontation with France when it briefly held colonial rule. Emperor Maximilian of Austria briefly ruled Mexico while Juarez's government went into exile and ruled from the northern borders of Mexico.

A biographical account of the Mexican hero Benito Juarez, an enduring model of perseverance.

Cinco de Mayo, or the fifth of May, marks the Battle of Puebla between Mexico and France on May 5, 1862. This was a decisive battle in which the French had superior military power, yet lost to the determined Mexican army. This holiday commemorates the resilience of Mexicans in the face of great odds — much like the character of Benito Juarez, who is an enduring model of perseverance in the face of adversity.

The text is colorfully illustrated by Howard Berelson. Though *¡Viva Mexico!* does not go into detail about why or how the French were ultimately defeated in Mexico, it does focus upon a very central character, and the text is suitable for beginning readers. *Since the holiday is quickly becoming a recognizable, but seldom understood event in the United States, this story should have a strategic place in the multicultural classroom.* HERIBERTO GODINA

Itse Selu: Cherokee Harvest Festival

📖 Daniel Pennington   ✒ Don Stewart

Cherokee, Native American

1994, Charlesbridge Publishing Inc.

Itse Selu offers an interesting and apparently authentic alternative for those who wish to explore the tradition of harvest festivals without focusing on the celebration of Thanksgiving. "Itse Selu" is the name given by contemporary Cherokee people to the festival celebrated at the harvest of the corn. Both hunters and farmers, the Cherokee used the celebration to offer thanks for their harvest and to symbolize the beginning of a new year.

A Cherokee village boy tells of the importance of traditional harvest festivals.

This background information is offered by the author before he begins his story of a special day in the life of a Cherokee boy, Little Wolf. Pennington follows Little Wolf as he becomes caught up in the excitement of preparations for the celebration. The story focuses on the child's growing anticipation and enjoyment of the festival, while at the same time providing information about Cherokee traditions and their way of life.

Little Wolf rises in the morning, eats breakfast, bathes, plays with his friend, watches his grandmother making him a pair of *dilasulo* (footwear), and listens to his grandfather tell a story reminiscent of a Brer Rabbit tale. He and his sister fall asleep and are awakened in time for sunrise and the green corn dance. Children often are struck by the similarities of the events of Little Wolf's day to their own experiences on a holiday.

The story emphasizes the importance of family and the value of each member. Particularly noteworthy are the contributions made by the grandfather as a storyteller for the village, and Little Wolf's older sister Skye, whose work is that traditionally performed by women and is depicted as being important and of great value to the family and the village.

Cherokee terms are used throughout the story, with pronunciation guides and definitions provided at the bottom of each page. These aides add to the authentic flavor of the story and help those reading the story aloud to avoid making inaccurate guesses as to correct pronunciation. An additional page at the end of the book discusses how Cherokee was originally a spoken language. In addition, information is provided about how Quoyah, a Cherokee, created an alphabet or syllabary so that the Cherokee language could be written and read.

For children who are only familiar with the story of Thanksgiving, Itse Selu offers an example of how harvest festivals were an important part of the lives of peoples who were farmers. Discussion and investigation of why various cultures mark the beginning of the New Year at different times may also be pursued. It is an enjoyable story that depicts a people in a strong, positive light. DONNA GAGNON

Little White Cabin

📖 ✒ Ferguson Plain

Native American, Ojibway

1992, Pemmican Publication, Inc., 📚 Benton-Banai, Edward, *The Mishomis Coloring Books.*

A young Ojibwa and an elder, Danny, develop a friendship, and the elder gives the young man a special braid of sweet grass for his prayers. A series of signs including

The growth of the friendship between a young Ojibway man and an elder.

the appearance of an owl, indicate that Danny's death is imminent, and one day the young man goes to visit and finds only an empty porch signaling the death of Danny.

The narrator remains nameless, making the story awkward to follow at times. Also the use of Ojibway words in the earlier dialogue will make the book more challenging for non-speakers of Ojibwa. Danny's death may also leave some readers troubled. As in Plain's earlier book, *Eagle Feather, an Honour,* the intergenerational male relationships are rendered in a tender and respectful way. The elder is valued for the culture and wisdom he imparts. The youngster develops pride because he is treated with respect and appreciation, as when he receives the gift of sweet grass. In remarkable, monochromatic acrylic, graphite, and pen-and-ink illustrations, the main characters are broadly drawn against a background that looks like tanned hide. Images of the spirit world are drawn with the same realism as those of more mundane reality. Drawings may not be bright enough to be shared with a large group, but are easily visible to a small group sitting in a tight circle. NOLA HADLEY

Tikvah Means Hope

Patricia Polacco

Jewish

1994, Doubleday

Patricia Polacco has written a biographical picture book about the 1992 fire in Oakland, California, in which more than 3,000 homes were destroyed.

Preparations are being made for the Jewish harvest holiday of Sukkot, while Tikvah the cat watches. Mr. Roth and his young neighbor, Justine, decide where they are going to build the sukkah—

A Jewish family endures the devastating California fires of 1992.

a hut made out of sticks and hung with brightly colored cloth, fruit, and palm branches. The sukkah commemorates the time when the Jews wandered the desert and had no place to live, and also is a time to give thanks for their homes and the harvest.

The next morning after having slept in the sukkah, Justine and her best friend, Duane, are at the store, when they hear that a fire has started in their neighborhood. They are unable to get home because the fire fighters are evacuating the neighborhood and residents are being sent to the school gym. Everyone is there except for Tikvah the cat. With the end of the fire, the families return to their homes. Mr. Roth cries, "If only I could find something, anything that would prove I had a life here." And at that moment, they find the sukkah still standing. All the neighbors

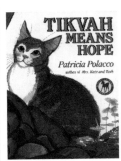

gathered there to give thanks for "good food, friends, and our lives." Suddenly, they hear Tikvah, who has survived the fire, and they all celebrate. Mr. Roth says, wiping away his tears, "Tikvah, in Hebrew, means hope."

In the illustrations that very vividly express the details of the story, Polacco also has what appears to be authentic photos of her family situated in various illustrations.

The author's note at the end gives the details of the fire, explaining the losses of lives, homes, and wildlife. She also tries to explain the feelings held by people who have experienced such a loss and the "sense of community that has welded our spirits together." They still share their memories and, most of all, hope. DORIS COSLEY

The Keeping Quilt

Patricia Polacco

Jewish, Russian

1988, Simon & Schuster, ✳ Audio Cassette, Series

In this first-person narrative, the author relates the story of her Jewish family from their emigration from Russia to the present, using a treasured quilt as a symbol of their continuity. Her great-grandmother's childhood dress and shawl, worn on the trip from Russia, along with other articles of clothing from the family, all go into a quilt to remind them of the Old Country. Passed through generations, the quilt becomes in turn a "huppa" at several weddings (which change with the times), a receiving blanket for several generations of babies, a tablecloth for birthday parties, and a covering on a deathbed. The story ends with the author, the quilt's current keeper, wrapping her own infant daughter in the precious heirloom.

A treasured quilt is passed down in a Jewish family from generation to generation.

Though the narrative is a bit dry, this is an excellent portrayal of family continuity and the importance of tradition in this one family. Teachers may wish to use the book as an introduction to this theme with their students, perhaps then asking them to compile family trees or histories or discover if their families have any heirlooms akin to the quilt. Perhaps they would even like to create some of their own.

The illustrations are in black and white except for

the quilt, which is shown in full color. This book received the Sydney Taylor Award from the Association of Jewish Libraries. JODI LEVINE

Just Plain Fancy

📖 ✎ Patricia Polacco
Amish
1994 (1990), Dell Publishing Company Inc.,
📖 Foster, Sally, *Where Time Stands Still*.

In language suggesting the speech of the Pennsylvania Amish, *Just Plain Fancy* is a vignette about Amish life that contradicts the frequent mis-

An Amish girl discovers a "fancy" peacock egg.

perception that it is a life without pleasure or color. Naomi is a young Amish girl, proud of the way she handles her responsibility of tending to the chickens, but who also would not mind something "fancy" in her life. Naomi's wish comes true when a peacock egg fortuitously hatches among the chicken eggs. Naomi wonders whether the peacock is too fancy to be Amish. Naomi's dilemma is settled by an elder: "This be one of God's most beautiful creations. He is fancy, child, and that's the way of it."

Just Plain Fancy is one of only a handful of picture books on Amish life. Most books for young people on this subject are nonfiction and are best suited for middle-school readers. This book, however, will appeal to preschoolers and primary-grade students.

Polacco's illustrations re-enforce the message that this life is simple but not drab. The illustrations are large drawings accented with color and wonderful facial expressions. *The text is generally clear, but children will probably need explanations of Amish traditions to appreciate fully the significance of shunning and of the new white organdy cap.* JANIS O'DRISCOLL

Dumpling Soup

📖 Jama Kim Rattigan ✎ Lillian Hsu-Flanders
Asian American, Hawaian
1993 (1991) Little, Brown and Company

Dumpling Soup is a delightful book that celebrates the family and is a wonderful introduction to the kinds of family traditions that shape so much of the local culture in Hawaii. Based on the author's childhood memories of growing up on the island of Oahu, the book begins as the main character, Marisa, tells us about her family and describes her eagerness to take part in

An Asian American girl learns to make dumplings for her family's traditional New Year soup.

the preparation for the big New Year's celebration.

Every year on New Year's Eve, Marisa says, her whole family goes to Grandma's house for dumpling soup. Most in her family are Korean, but there are some Japanese, Chinese, Hawaiian, or Haole (Hawaiian for white people). Grandma affectionately refers to the family as chop suey, which means all mixed up in pidgin.

This year, however, Marisa will help Grandma make the dumplings. "Everybody in my family loves to eat, so we have to make lots and lots of dumplings," she says.

While New Year's Eve parties on the mainland United States are typically associated with adults and champagne, New Year's in the Hawaiian Islands is very much a family affair, complete with fireworks. *Dumpling Soup* provides its readers with a description of the food, fun, and festivities surrounding a significant celebration for the people of Hawaii. *In addition, the book can be used as a springboard for students to consider the variety of ways people across the United States and around the world celebrate events such as the new year. Students might also share and investigate the different traditions and celebrations significant to their own families.*

The artwork in the book is full of color and warmth. Though not completely authentic in depicting the people and their dress, the illustrations do vividly capture particular aspects of the local lifestyle, such as the collection of shoes and slippers outside the front door, the sky full of fireworks, and the dining table laden with *ono* (delicious) foods.
KARLEEN H. TANIMURA MANCHANDA

Dinner at Aunt Connie's House

Faith Ringgold
African American
1993, Hyperion

Melody loves to visit the beautiful beach home of her Uncle Bates and Aunt Connie. This summer, she finds two surprises: Lonnie, her aunt and uncle's newly adopted son, and twelve magical paintings by Aunt Connie. Each painting is the portrait of a courageous African American woman who offers a short history of herself to Melody and Lonnie, when they find the paintings hidden in the attic. "I am Fannie Lou Hamer, born in 1917 in Mississippi," says one painting, "I was a civil rights activist and public speaker. I worked with Martin Luther King for voters' rights in the South. I helped thousands of people register to vote."

Two African American children find portraits of twelve famous African American women in an attic and learn their histories.

Activist Sojourner Truth, film star Dorothy Dandridge, opera singer Marian Anderson, and writer Zora Neale Hurston are but a few of the women who relate their stories and, in so doing, give the two children who listen to them great pride in being African American and inspire them toward accomplishing great things themselves.

Dinner at Aunt Connie's House takes its title from a story quilt of the same name, and true to other Ringgold works, like *Tar Beach,* the full-page illustrations are bold and vibrant. *While the book is certainly sufficient unto itself, it is also a wonderful starting place for further and deeper stories of the important African American women included in it. And, surely, the actual story quilt (shown on the last pages of the book) is an ideal model for a culminating activity representing the histories of any number of related individuals, be they members of a family, or participants in history.*
DORIS COSLEY

Tar Beach

Faith Ringgold
African American, Hispanic
1994 (1991), Crown Books, ✳ Series

Faith Ringgold's powerful imaginative, storytelling and illustrative gift are the rich mainstays of this beautifully illustrated tale of family history, identity, and love—a tale that has become a contemporary children's classic. Set in New York City's Harlem during the 1930s, the story begins on an apartment building rooftop. Here, on this "tar beach," eight-year-old Cassie Louise Lightfoot, her mother, father, baby brother BeBe, and neighbors, find a cool respite on hot summer nights. According to Cassie, "sleeping on Tar Beach was magical. Lying on the roof at night, with stars and skyscraper buildings all around me, made me feel rich, like I owned all that I could see." Indeed, lying on the mattress under the stars is the first step toward Cassie's imagined flights around the city—to the George Washington Bridge in the distance, "a giant diamond necklace," which Cassie's father helped to build, and which opened the day she was born in 1931; and to the Union Building that her father is working on from perches high above the city—the building whose union won't allow her father join because of his African American/Native American heritage.

An African American girl narrates the special things she dreams of for her family and self.

From her fight over the Union Building, Cassie goes on to imagine a better life for her family—a time when her father "won't have to stand on twenty-four-story-high girders and look down"; a time when her mother "won't cry all winter when [her father] goes to look for work and doesn't come home"; a time when she and her family "can have ice cream every night." Through her imagination, Cassie, portrayed as a strong, self-confident girl, claims power and freedom for herself and those she loves.

Combining autobiographical and fictional narrative with radiant illustrations and the strong central character of Cassie, Ringgold transports young readers to another time and another place. Through her evocation of flight, she taps not only a child's imagination, but also, as she comments in her autobiographical an African American oral tradition. MARTHA L. MARTINEZ

The Tie Man's Miracle: A Chanukkah Tale

📖 Steven Schnur ✎ Stephen T. Johnson

Jewish

1995, Morrow

Steven Schnur writes Chanukah story for older children, *The Tie Man's Miracle: A Chanukah Tale.* The story begins when Seth, eager to light candles on the last night of Chanukah, is interrupted in his holiday thoughts by an encounter with the somber tie man. He is mysterious, wearing neither an overcoat nor boots in the snow, and when the boy questions him about the cold, he answers, "I've been colder." The tie man is evasive when Seth asks him why he does not celebrate. He seems strangely taken with the happiness of this young family in the midst of Chanukah. Presently, he reveals that his own family was lost in the war.

A salesman who interrupts a Chanukkah ritual has a special story to tell about the Holocaust.

The tie man is persuaded to stay for candles, dinner, and a conversation that evokes painful memories in him. Rather than leave the family in sadness, he relates an old tale of a miracle; when all nine candles are extinguished at the same time, a wish is carried right to the ear of God. Seth, lingering over the dying candles, beholds this Chanukah miracle and wishes, not for himself, but for the tie man; that he could have his family back. The nine candles extinguish at the same time and "Suddenly the room grew bright. I heard voices shouting 'Papa, Papa!' Shadows danced on the ceiling, feet scurried across the floor, laughter filled the air. And then all was silent and dark." The young boy never saw the tie man again.

Schnur relates the story gently, respectfully leaving room for family discussion about the Holocaust and miracles, preserving a quiet tension between telling the truth and leaving room for wonder. Johnson's watercolors are reserved, but there is a wealth of emotion in the faces he paints.

SUSIE WILDE

The Sabbath Lion: A Jewish Folktale from Algeria

📖 Howard Schwartz and Barbara Rush
✎ Stephen Fieser

Jewish, North African

1992, HarperCollins

In this adaptation of an Algerian Jewish folktale, a young boy, Yosef, has an amazing experience in the desert. The oldest son of a very poor, widowed mother, Yosef works hard to help feed his six brothers and sisters. When Yosef's mother receives a letter informing her that an uncle has died and left his money to her, Yosef must travel to Cairo to retrieve the fortune. His mother pays a caravan leader a great deal of money to ensure that he will stop the caravan and rest while Yosef observes the Sabbath. But when the time comes, the caravan leader refuses to stop, and Yosef is abandoned in the desert. While he waits alone, a huge lion comes to sit with him, and Yosef realizes that this lion is an embodiment of the Sabbath spirit. After the Sabbath ends, the lion cares for Yosef, accompanying him to Cairo and back to Algeria, and Yosef is rewarded for his religious observance.

A Jewish boy risks his safety in order to observe the Sabbath.

In the simple cadences of the folktale, the authors of this book provide a detailed explanation of the purpose of the Sabbath and of many of its rules. These explanations are presented in clear, comprehensible language that is neither cloying nor presumptuous. No prior knowledge of the Jewish Sabbath is expected, but the tone of the book ensures that almost any reader will appreciate and respect the religious and cultural traditions. An added benefit is the explanatory "commentary" provided at the end of the story. Although the book is certainly not didactic, it does not shy away from placing a value on observance and freely assumes the existence and power of God.

The lion protects and transports Yosef, but he is also a symbol of the Jewish people and thus has a very resonant power. He provides a welcome antidote to the ubiquity of Disney's version of the lion figure.

Relying on the sweeping, swirling patterns of desert sands, flowing clothes, and billowing clouds, the lovely illustrations of this book effectively convey the grandeur of the lion and enhance the fairy-tale element of the book. Because of the allegorical

311

tone, the characters are somewhat one dimensional (the evil caravan leader, the dutiful son). This is not necessarily a bad thing; children will benefit from exposure to the conventions of the folktale. The text is quite densely worded, but the story needs this level of detail to be effective. Readers will learn about an ancient culture rooted in a specific and compelling time and place, as well as about religious practices that are still observed today. Whether used to reinforce the same religious values or simply to introduce uninitiated readers to customs that may be new to them, *The Sabbath Lion* will be interesting to all audiences. And the enduring values of close family connection, keeping one's word, and belief in the power of trust are relevant to anyone at any time. JUNE CUMMINS

Too Many Tamales

📖 Gary Soto 🖊 Ed Martinez

Hispanic, Mexican

1993, Putnam

While preparing the tamales for a Christmas dinner, Maria's mother takes off her wedding ring. Eager to be an adult, Maria puts it on. Without realizing it, she leaves her mother's ring on and it ends up somewhere in the middle of the maize.

A festive, colorful, nonstereotypical portrayal of a Mexican holiday.

Puzzled and panicked, Maria enlists the aid of her cousin to eat the tamales until they find her mother's ring before her mother discovers that the ring is lost. They stuff themselves and do not find the ring, so Maria deduces that they must have swallowed the ring unknowingly. Understanding that being an adult means taking responsibility for your actions, Maria decides to confess to her mother. As she begins to tell her what happened, Maria notices that her mother is wearing the ring. She then tells her

mother that they have eaten all the tamales while trying to find the ring. Maria's mother calmly states that they will simply make another batch. At the mention of more tamales, all the children groan and all of the adults laugh. The story clearly demonstrates that Maria learns

from her mistake.

The illustrations illuminate the festivity and harmony that exist in this home. They also capture the spirited and colorful artifacts that are very much a part of the holiday season in Mexican American culture. It is truly refreshing to see a book that does not portray Mexican Americans in the stereotypical sombreros, sarapes, and huaraches. MARTHA L. MARTINEZ

Building an Igloo

📖 🖊 Ulli Steltzer

Aleut, Eskimo, Inuit, Native American

1995 (1981), Henry Holt & Company, Inc.,

📚 Arvaarluk, Michael, *Baseball Bats for Christmas*; Ekoomiak, Normee, *Arctic Memories.*

Most of us have been fascinated at one time or another by igloos. Even among those of us who grew up in colder snowy climates, there are still few who know how to really build one. Author/photographer Ulli Steltzer traveled to the northern Arctic to photograph Tookillkee Tiguktak and one of his sons, Jopee, building an igloo.

The Tiguktak family now lives in a house (like most Inuits) in Griese Ford, the most northern settlement in Canada, on Ellesmere Island. But when Tookillkee was a young boy, he learned to build and live in an igloo. He still builds one when he goes hunting for a musk ox or a polar bear, and he has taught his sons the skill as well. This book details each step of the building process, showing how the site is picked, the blocks cut, and the walls built. After the final top block is placed, Tookillkee is trapped inside and must carve a doorway to crawl out.

An Eskimo family demonstrates how to build an igloo in a book that does not explore larger cultural issues.

Steltzer's black-and-white photographs of the building process are remarkable. It is easy to be impressed with this effective technology when you see pictures of two grown men standing and walking upon the snow brick walls.

While the book does not provide details about Tookillkee's life or culture, the building of the igloo tells a great deal about the tenacity and survival strategies of the Inuit.

Other recommended books about the Inuits are Michael Arvaarluk's *Baseball Bats for Christmas* and Normee Ekoomiak's *Arctic Memories.* NOLA HADLEY

The Path of Quiet Elk: A Native American Alphabet Book

Virginia Stroud

Native American

1996, Dial/Division of Penguin, Jean, Georges, *Writing: The Story of Alphabets and Scripts*; Clifton, Lucille, *Black A B C's*.

Drawn from diverse Native American teachings and based on a philosophy loosely shared by Plains Indians, Cheyennes, Arapahos, Kiowas and other native people, *The Path of the Quiet Elk* teaches a world view that emphasizes the interrelatedness of all things. The author, a Cherokee-Creek adopted into a Kiowa family, earned the wisdom of The Path from a medicine woman.

A lyrical Native American alphabet book about the interconnectedness of people and nature.

Each letter of the alphabet is highlighted by a box and accompanied by a parable-like vignette, such as the following one for the letter "b":

"Butterflies are everywhere.
'Humans are like butterflies,' Wisdom Keeper remarked. 'The butterfly is always changing. You will change and take flight when you learn the secrets of the Path of the Quiet Elk."

There are, however, some problems with the book. The surrealistic artwork, while colorful and intriguing, may be disturbing for some readers. And while the idea for this alphabet book is good, the reading level of the text is too advanced for the format. Alphabet books generally appeal to very young children, but this text is written for those with reading skills at the third- to sixth-grade level.

Other notable alphabet books include Georges Jean's *Writing: The Story of Alphabets and Scripts*, a fascinating journey into the history of writing, and Lucille Clifton's *Black A B C's*. DAPHNE MUSE

The Big Tree and the Little Tree

Mary Augusta Tappage Terry Gallagher

Native American, Shuswap

1986, Pemmican Publications, Inc., National Film Board of Canada, *Mary Agusta* (film).

Mary Augusta Tappage tells an instructive tale of the natural world that celebrates both the power of youth and the value of taking care of and honoring our elders. Living in the forest, Big Tree doesn't like having a smaller, younger tree growing near him. But Little Tree can't move. Big Tree constantly speaks of his importance: "Later on, you might grow up to be a big tree and then you might be of some good, but right now you're small and useless and nobody seems to care for you. Later on, you might be like me. You might be somebody."

The little tree is eager to grow up and be useful, and he does. The squirrels begin to eat his fat pine cones, birds start nesting in his strong branches, and people gather pine needles and branches for their beds.

A Native American story of two trees addresses issues of power, youth, and respect for elders.

As the Little Tree grows larger and stronger, Big Tree grows older. He also grows less strong and productive. But as Little Tree grows in strength, he also becomes more humble and displays real appreciation for, and gratitude toward, Big Tree: "Without you, I wouldn't be here. I am one of your children. I am part of you. My cones are your cones. My branches are your branches. When I was small, you spread your branches over me so the snow wouldn't break me down. You got scorched when the forest fire went by, but you protected me. You scared away the deer when it wanted to nibble my tender shoots." Little Tree comforts his elder with reassuring words, reminding him that together, their cones will start new forests.

Despite the treatment Little Tree received from Big Tree, he respects what Big Tree has provided, and he reveres his elder. In this way the tale addresses some complex concepts about elders, youth, leadership, and power.

The bold black-and-white illustrations of northern trees and squirrels, moose, deer, owls, and butterflies bring a vitality to the story. NOLA HADLEY

The Luminous Pearl: A Chinese Folktale

Betty L. Torre Carol Inouye

Asian, Chinese

1990, Orchard Books, Chinese Minford, John, *Favorite Folktales of China*.

The moral of this adaptation of a Chinese folktale is that virtue is rewarded and mean actions are punished. Issues of who is elite and who is lowly are explored.

31

The daughter of the dragon king chooses her perfect suitor from two brothers after testing their morals. The theme of the tale is commonly found in other folktales from around the world. Who is the perfect suitor for the female to love? And how can he demonstrate his fitness? Each different community has its specific culture and different standards of matchmaking.

Two Chinese brothers set out on a quest for a luminous pearl to win the hand of a beautiful princess.

In ancient China, a woman had no right to choose her spouse. Generally this was done by her parents or other relatives. Many tragic stories are depicted in Chinese literature when families used such criteria as the suitor's family background, social position, and economic situation rather than his moralities. This mythical tale instructs people to understand that strong morals are more important than anything else when judging a suitor.

The illustrations in the book represent the main ideas and events in the story, but they do not accurately represent traditional Chinese culture. The dragon king has no imperial crown, and his daughter's hairstyle is not a princess's hair style. Nevertheless, the tale is a familiar one, and probably has its origins in Asia. LI LIU

Buffalo Dance: A Blackfoot Legend

📓 Nancy Van Laan (foreword by Bill Moyers)
✒ Beatriz Vidal

Blackfoot, Native American

1993, Little, Brown & Company 📖 Goble, Paul, *Crow Chief: A Plains Indian Story*; Goble, Paul, *The Gift of the Sacred Dog*.

For generations, the Blackfoot people have venerated the buffalo with a performance of the sacred Buffalo Dance before and after a hunt. The dance is a ritual of thanks to the animals for sacrificing some of their own so that the Blackfoot may survive. *Buffalo Dance* is a retelling of the legend of the dance's origin. A young woman's courage to bargain with the buffalo honors the dignity of both her people and the great animals who share the plains with them.

The origins of a Blackfoot ritual for giving thanks before the buffalo hunt.

A young Blackfoot woman agrees to live with the buffalo in exchange for food for her people. Her father tries to reclaim her, but is trampled to death by them. The buffalo chief tells the woman that her grief is equal to their own grief when a buffalo is killed.

The buffalo chief also presents a challenge: if she can bring her father back to life, they can both return to their people. A magpie finds a piece of her father's backbone, which the woman covers with her robe. As she sings prayers over the robe, her father is restored to life.

The young woman gives the robe to the buffalo chief and the buffalo chief says, "In turn, we will teach you our dance. When your people kill our kind, have them do this dance and sing this song. That way, we will come back to life, just as your father has done."

The story is simply and directly told, and is supported by Beatriz Vidal's colorful illustrations, using traditional Blackfoot patterns, designs, and symbols. *The language is poetic, and the illustrations are well matched with the text so that readers in grades 3 through 6 can appreciate the significance of the myth: the sacredness of all life and the gifts of the natural world.* JANIS O'DRISCOLL

Yo, Hungry Wolf!: A Nursery Rap

📓 David Vozar ✒ Betsy Lewin

Multicultural

1995 (1993), Dell Publishing Company Inc.

Vozar has leaped into uncharted waters by taking classic tales and setting them to rap verses. While some teachers, librarians and parents may be repulsed by rap,

Classic nursery rhymes are retold to appeal to those who like rap music.

many children will be enthusiastically engaged by the slang and contemporary rhythms with which these tales have been infused.

Now the wolf ain't fakin'…
And his stomach is achin'…
He's got to have pigs…
to slice into bacon.

Not only are the words profanity-free, but also the rhymes abound with humor and Vozar succeeds in connecting the tales structurally and morally. The wolf, who is unsuccessful in capturing one of the pigs to eat, goes into the "Little Red Riding Hood" caper to try his luck. Again he is thwarted, but this time by "Little Red Rappinghood." She threatens:

Wolfie you better change your diet
Eat anything else, steam it or fry it.
'Cause girls and Grannies aren't meant to be eaten.
If you try again, you'll just get a beatin.

The strong and whimsical sense of improvisation makes for an interesting approach to these otherwise traditional, sometimes morally compelling, and at times very frightening tales. *Yo, Hungry Wolf!* is a great opportunity for young children to discuss the positive side of rap music and the various ways in which people communicate information and ideas. These innovatively written stories are bound to be an interesting departure from the usual, often predictable stories read by many children. MARTHA L. MARTINEZ

The Fourth Question: A Chinese Tale

📖 Rosalind C. Wang ✏ Ju-Hong Chen

Asian, Chinese

1991, Holiday House, Inc., ✲ Spanish

The content and structure of this folktale is similar to several other Chinese as well as Western folktales. Readers may be familiar with the construction of the plot, but they may not be familiar with this specific content and characters.

Yee-Lee journeys to Kun-Lun Mountain to seek advice from the Wise Man.

In this story the major character leaves home to find a better life, to gain knowledge and experience, and to get good advice from a wise man. Yee-Lee, the poor young man, goes to Kun-Lun Mountain to get answers and advice from the Wise Man. He wants to know why he is still poor even though he works very hard. The reason he seeks advice is commonplace, but the geography leading to the destination, Kun-Lun Mountain, is comprehensible only to readers who are familiar with Chinese literature and culture. Sometimes it is really difficult for young readers to understand certain terms because the particular term contains deep or abstract meaning. Kun-Lun Mountain is a high mountain in Xinjiang province in the west of China. Kun-Lun Mountain does not only mean a mountain, sometimes it implies something else. In this folktale it is related to Buddhism. As Kun-Lun Mountain is near India which is the birthplace of Buddha, Kun-Lun Mountain is regarded as the place nearest heaven in which many supernatural beings, immortal beings, and wise men live.

Kun-Lun Mountain often relates to Buddhism, and Hua Mountain relates to Taoism, one of the chief religions in China. Young readers may need help from others to understand the particular meaning of the terms.

On Yee-Lee's way to the mountain, he meets three characters who also want answers to their questions. The dragon is one of the three. Maybe young readers know that dragons relate to China, but they may not know that the dragon is an imaginary creature like a crocodile or snake with wings and claws. The dragon is the symbol of power, but it is controlled by the emperor in heaven. It has the strong power to control thunder, lighting, and rain.

The dragon in this tale says it has behaved properly for thousands of years, and yet it still can not fly into the sky. Young readers can learn that in Chinese folklore, many supernatural beings originally were common creatures. They cultivate themselves for thousands of years, and they become supernatural beings with strong power and magic like snake or fox superwoman, wolf or tortoise superman. They may need help understanding why the Wise Man lives in Kun-Lun Mountain. Otherwise, from the Wise Man's long white hair, long white beard, and his mystic advice, they can judge for themselves that the Wise Man is an immortal being who has certainly endured for many years.

Yee-Lee generously asks the Wise Man the questions on behalf of the dragon, the old man, and the old woman, even though he is permitted only three questions. In the end, as a reward for his generosity, Yee-Lee receives not only his answer, but a good and successful life.

Although some of the elements of the story are similar to other tales from other cultures, it provides rich Chinese culture, history, and religion through its written language and in its beautiful pictures. With help, readers will gain much knowledge of Chinese culture from the story, and will enjoy the accurate pictures in the book. LI LIU

315

316

White Bead Ceremony

Sherrin Watkins, ✎ Kim Doner
Native American
1994 (1981), Council Oak Publ. Co., ✳ Other
Language, 📖 Howard, James H., *Shawnee: The
Ceremonialism of a Native American Tribe and Its
Cultural Background.*

Author Sherrin Watkins is a Shawnee/Cherokee lawyer and writer from Oklahoma. The theme of this book, her first for children, is how Native Americans are striving to preserve their traditions by passing them on to their children. Watkins also emphasizes the value of family among Native Americans. Her portrayal of the naming ceremony is both accurate and authentic, although variations are to be expected, given the diversity of Shawnee peoples.

A family throws a Shawnee Indian girl a traditional naming ceremony.

The central character of White Bead Ceremony is four-year-old Mary Greyfeather, a Shawnee Indian child who likes Barbie dolls and prefers English to the Shawnee language, which her mother insists she study. Grandma decides that giving Mary a Shawnee name will pique the child's interest in her heritage. A traditional naming ceremony is arranged, in which Mary will be given a white bead necklace to wear with her new name.

Family and friends arrive on the big day for the naming ceremony and feast. But oops...the person bringing the necklace has car trouble! Grandma Greyfeather saves the day by devising a suitable replacement. While her great-aunts suggest animal names that have come to them through prayers and dreams, Mary imagines the playful creatures coming to life in her kitchen. Finally, Mary's name is repeated for all to hear, while the elder women solemnly put the homemade necklace—a string of white buttons—around her neck. Mary's extended family welcomes her anew with gifts, a festive breakfast, and some expected teasing.

Although it is wordy at times, Watkins's narrative is lighthearted and sincere, presenting warm, believable characters. Mary wiggles and giggles like any healthy child; Momma expresses the impatience of a modern woman; and Grandma holds appropriately old-fashioned ideas. A one-page Shawnee history, included at the close of the story, contains basic information understandable to young children.

Mary's character is displayed primarily through Kim Doner's mirthful but realistic full-page illustrations. Doner, an award-winning artist of Cherokee descent, used bright watercolors and pencil to paint Mary and her family as handsome people, imbued with individual characteristics and emotions. Her animals are cute and playful, yet respectfully portrayed.

Doner's illustrations also appear on the thirty-two English/Shawnee word cards that appear throughout the text. The cards are reprinted at the end of the book, to be cut and used as flash cards. Teachers and librarians may want to cut, laminate, and keep the cards in an envelope. A pronunciation guide at the beginning of the book helps readers pronounce Shawnee words on the cards and in the text.

The first in a planned series about the Greyfeathers, *White Bead Ceremony* is a delightful way to introduce young children to some aspects of contemporary Shawnee family life and traditions. *Since Mary is a young character, and the Fry readability is high (10.2), this book is recommended as a read-aloud selection for pre-K through second grade. Have a map handy to show the children the location of Oklahoma and present-day Shawnee lands. For additional background* on Shawnee names and naming, adult readers may consult James H. Howard's comprehensive work, *Shawnee: The Ceremonialism of a Native American Tribe and Its Cultural Background.*
MELISSA HECKARD

The Crane Wife

Sumiko Yagawa (translated by Katherine Paterson)
✎ Suekichi Akaba
Asian, Japanese
1993 (1981), American Printing House For The
Blind, ✳ Japanese

An elegant translation of this Japanese folktale, *The Crane Wife* offers children a flavor of the traditional tales of Japan. The story reflects the value of kindness, gratitude, and selflessness that characterizes many Japanese customs and traditions. A young peasant, Yohei, saves the life of a wounded crane. Soon afterwards, he is visited by a beautiful stranger who begs to become his wife.

An exceptionally moving Japanese folktale about a peasant who receives a great fortune for saving a wounded crane.

The delicate young woman has a mysterious gift for weaving the most exquisite fabrics. She and her husband sell them for a handsome price. Tempted by greed and curiosity, Yohei breaks his promise never to look at his wife while she is weaving. To his disbelief and horror, he discovers that the young woman is the very crane whose life he saved and that the fabric is woven with her own feathers. With the promise broken and her secret discovered, the crane must leave Yohei and flies away into the distance.

Through this tale, readers are captivated first with the mystery and, finally, with the devotion of the crane wife.

From somewhere Yohei heard the whisper of a delicate, familiar voice. "I had hoped," the voice said sorrowfully, "that you would be able to honor my entreaty. But because you looked upon me in my suffering, I can no longer tarry in the human world. I am the crane that you saved on the snowy path. I fell in love with your gentle, simple heart, and, trusting it alone, I came to live by your side. I pray that your life will be long and that you will always be happy."

Akaba's paintings have been described as "haunting" and "exquisite." They are exceptionally moving and capture the simplicity and solitude of Yohei's mountain village and delicate elegance of the story's heroine. The muted tones of the paintings seem especially appropriate for the story's appreciation of humility and wariness of extravagance.

The universal nature of the themes in The Crane Wife, *and its interesting plot, make the book versatile for use in the classroom. In addition to incorporating this tale into a study of Japanese culture, it would be wonderful to compare and contrast with traditional tales from other countries (for example, in a folktale unit). The significance and symbolism of the crane in Japanese culture could be investigated, drawing upon additional relevant literature. Additionally, a "Note to the Reader" at the end of the book includes a brief background of the folktale's significance in Japan as well as a pronunciation guide to the Japanese words used in the story's translation. This note mentions that the tale "has been made into plays, movies, and even an opera." Consequently, children may use their artistic, dramatic, and linguistic talents to recreate the story as a puppet show, drama, or song. Students might also retell this folktale in the setting of present-day Japan or America to gain a deeper appreciation for the timelessness of stories in this genre.*

KARLEEN H. TANIMURA MANCHANDA

Roses Sing on New Snow: A Delicious Tale

Paul Yee Harvey Chan
Asian American
1992 (1991), Simon & Schuster Children's Books

Maylin cooks in her father's restaurant in the New World. Her food is wonderful, but her father gives the credit to her lazy brothers.

A young Chinese American girl's remarkable cooking stirs trouble.

The Governor of South China comes to the New World for a visit, and he, too, is delighted with Maylin's cooking. When Maylin's brothers are given credit for a dish called Roses Sing on New Snow, however, they cannot recreate it, and Maylin's father is forced to admit that his daughter is the true creator. She is presented to the Governor, who wishes to offer the dish to the Emperor in China, but Maylin

helps him see that even with the same ingredients, the chef's artistry cannot be duplicated. The true pleasure of Roses Sing on New Snow can be produced only by her hands.

Maylin's father and brothers' discrimination against her is clearly demonstrated by the author but never addressed directly. Instead, the author offers a tale reflecting nineteenth-century Chinese American values, allowing the reader to draw his or her own conclusions. Children will have no problem seeing that Maylin is a capable woman and that the men in her immediate family are fools. The Governor, on the other hand, does not seem surprised that a woman could be such an accomplished chef, but he has to learn lessons about cooking ingredients and artistry. Maylin teaches him these lessons with the same patience she shows her family.

Calm pervades the illustrations, which look like oil paintings. Maylin never proselytizes but she shows us how women stood up for themselves in spite of restrictions of the time. The story is a successful recreation of another century whose values may irritate us but offer an interesting starting point for broad discussion. JANIS O'DRISCOLL

The Riddle of the Drum: A Tale from Tizapan, Mexico

Verna Aardema Tony Chen

Hispanic, Mexican

1979, Four Winds Press

A king in Tizapan wants to find a worthy man to marry his beautiful daughter Fruela. He hires a wizard to make a strange drum. A palace guard carries the drum throughout the land, chanting a strange riddle about the drumhead, which is made of a mysterious material. Whoever guesses what the drumhead is made of will win the princess.

Suitors to the king's daughter tackle a riddle in this instructive Mexican story.

The drum gives off a thunderous sound. The handsome Prince Tuzan hears the drum and sets out to solve the riddle. On his way to Tizapan, he meets some unusual people: a runner, Corrin Corran; an archer, Tirin Tiran; a blower, Soplin Soplan; a hearer, Oyin Oyan; and an eater, Comin Coman. With his friends' help, the prince solves the riddle and outmaneuvers the crafty king.

The book packs in a lot of instructional elements. The names of the chief characters have their roots in the characters' unique strengths, e.g., Corrin Corran is from the Spanish verb, correr, meaning "to run." *Useful vocabulary words appear in Spanish. Pronunciation guides are embedded in the text and a glossary appears at the back of the book. Aardema also uses a cumulative refrain to keep track of the many characters and to keep the momentum of the story going.*

The graceful illustrations feature a variety of peoples from time periods over Mexico's long history. Black-and-white double-paged spreads alternate with full-color spreads. LESLIE ANDERSON MORALES

Writing for Children— A Joy and a Responsibility

Eloise Greenfield

IT IS A JOY TO WRITE FOR CHILDREN. IN addition to the satisfactions that derive from creative activity, there is a sense of sharing the world with someone who has not been in it very long. And yet, there are times when I wonder why anyone would want to write, to suffer the pain and frustration of trying to trigger a flow of words that will not come and to be racked by the fear that a door has slammed and locked the words inside forever. At those times I have to say to myself, "This has happened before. I've had this terror before. The words will come; they'll come." I try to remember that although words do sometimes flow unbidden from their source, it is often just this suffering, this tension, that awakens my African muse.

Almost every writer has experienced this terror and the rush of relief and gratitude that accompanies, finally, the rush of words. It is not easy, therefore, to admit that the muse is not infallible, that she must be continually challenged as to the validity of her offerings, but we must have the courage to face that fact. Our audience is too vulnerable, too impressionable, for us to entrust our art entirely to this force that lies somewhere in the subconscious mind, that repository of accumulated knowledge, attitudes, and emotions. Both the rational and the irrational, the healthful and the harmful, reside there as the result of a lifetime of conditioning.

In this society, our conditioning has been, to a great extent, irrational and harmful. This country was built on a foundation of racism, a foundation that is only slightly less firm after centuries of black struggle. Attitudes toward women, toward men, attitudes regarding age, height, beauty, mental and physical disabilities have been largely of the kind that constrain rather than encourage human development. To perpetuate these attitudes through the use of the written word constitutes a gross and arrogant misuse of talent and skill.

Librarians, no less than writers, have a responsibility to challenge their own conscious and subconscious beliefs, as well as the validity of the books they select. Standing as they do between authors and children, they are the conduit through which book messages flow. The importance of their role as selector cannot be overemphasized. Nor can the importance of the question they must ask: What is the author saying?

There is a viewpoint which denies the relevance of this question, that holds art to be sacrosanct, subject to scrutiny only as to its aesthetic value. This viewpoint is in keeping with the popular myth that genuine art is not political. It is true that politics is not art, but art is political. Whether in its interpretation of the political realities, or in its attempts to ignore these realities, or in its distortions, or in its advocacy of a different reality, or in its support of the status quo, all art is political and every book carries its author's message.

In the area of black-oriented literature, much of what is communicated is venomous. Considerable attention has been devoted by sociologists to the study of the targets of racial abuse and oppression. The trauma, the damage to the spirit, the stifling of creativity, the threat to mere physical survival, have all been well documented. Not enough attention, however, has been given to the study of those who, because of their conditioning, manifest delusions of grandeur, delusions that the whiteness of their skin makes them somehow special. The need to keep these delusions well nourished, to fortify them against any invasion of reality, makes these people menaces to society. Some of them are writers. They wield word-weapons, sometimes overtly, sometimes insidiously, yet they disclaim all responsibility for what they say, being merely "objective observers of the human scene," or "secretaries transcribing the dialogue of characters over whom they have no control." Is it the writer's fault that the characters just happen to be racist?

Children need protection from these word-weapons. They need protection in the form of organizations such as the Council on Interracial Books for Children, and black literature journals, such as *Black Books Bulletin*, and they need librarians who care. The library can and should become the center for regular and systematic education of children in the dynamics of racism as it occurs in literature. Even the youngest school-age child can be told: "There are some people in the world who are very sick. Some of them are so sick that they don't want you to know what a wonderful being you are."

Until children are knowledgeable enough to defend themselves, racist books must be kept out of their reach, as any other deadly weapon would be. To say this is not to demean the intelligence of children, but to recognize the power of communication to influence the thought, emotions, and behavior not only of children, but also of adults. Tens of billions of advertising dollars effectively spent each year attest to this fact.

The books that reach children should authentically depict and interpret their lives and their history; build self-respect and encourage the development of positive values; make children aware of their strength and leave them with a sense of hope and direction; teach them the skills necessary for the maintenance of health and for economic survival; broaden their knowledge of the world, past and present; and offer some insight into the future. These books will not be pap; the total range of human problems, struggles, and accomplishments can be told in this context with no sacrifice of literary merit. We are all disappointed when we read a book that has no power, a story that arouses no emotion, passages that lack the excitement that language can inspire. But the skills that are used to produce a well-written racist book can be used as well for one that is antiracist. The crucial fact is that literary merit cannot be the sole criterion. A book that has been chosen as worthy of a child's emotional investment must have been judged on the basis of what it is—not a collection of words arranged in some aesthetically pleasing way, but a statement powerfully made and communicated through the artistic and skillful use of language.

We are living now in a period of rapid growth comparable to that one year in the life of adolescents when they have trouble keeping up with the changes occurring in their bodies. We are struggling to keep up with our new understanding as we unlearn myths that have existed for hundreds—in some cases thousands—of years, and as we challenge the concepts that have defined us and our goals.

Webster's New World Dictionary, for example, defines the word *success* as: "The gaining of wealth, fame, rank, etc." I am incensed each time I read it. To take beings who have the potential for infinite growing, for infinite giving of their ideas and talents, of their caring, and to commend for their greatest efforts aspirations that glorify two of the basest of human attributes—greed and egotism—and not be ashamed to set it down in print, is a harsh indictment of the society in which we live.

But we are learning. Though few of us here today will live to see it, there will come a time when positive attitudes will be so ingrained in the fabric of our society, so pervasive, that constant examination of our artistic expressions will no longer be necessary. Our art will reflect us, and we will be in a state of health. For now, though, we have work to do. We will make mistakes sometimes. We will have periods of conflict and confusion. But we owe it to children, we owe it to posterity, and we owe it to ourselves to persevere. Our place in history demands it. *Used by permission of author.*

Ebony Visions and Cowrie Shell Dreams: Black American Classics in Fiction and Poetry for Young Readers

Daphne Muse

I AM BOOK
I am Book. Open me. Read me.
Secrets I do unfold!
Share me. Dream with me.
Visions I do behold.

AS A PEOPLE TORTURED BY THE HORRORS OF slavery and the ongoing struggle to overcome racism, African Americans have often been fueled, nurtured, and sustained by the ancestral legacy of storytelling. As in many other cultures, storytelling has also allowed African Americans to honor the past and work to secure a future for ourselves in this society. This powerful legacy inspired late nineteenth century and early twentieth-century writers such as A. E. Johnson, Arna Bontemps, Lorenz Graham, Ellen Tarry, and Ann Petry, who passed their tradition on to African Americans now writing for children and young adults. Virginia Hamilton, Walter Dean Myers, Eloise Greenfield, Tom Feelings, Patricia McKissick, and scores of other writers have become powerful and passionate witnesses who look beyond the illusions of denial and examine the hard social realities underlying the fabric of our lives.

They have also created stories that reveal the pulse of our passions, examine the vitality of our visions, and chronicle our ongoing quest for freedom and self-determination.

With the support of a formidable oral tradition, the path to creating black classics in American children's literature was paved during the late nineteenth century when fables, folktales, and short stories for young readers were published in African American newspapers and Sunday school texts. In 1887, A. E. Johnson published a monthly magazine for children called *The Joy.* That same commitment to African American storytelling and literary traditions was reaffirmed in 1920, when Jesse Fauset and W. E. B. DuBois founded *The Brownie's Book*, a monthly magazine of black fiction and poetry for young people.

When framing a context for literary standards that identify our classics, Dr. Candy Dawson Boyd, author and professor in the department of education at St. Mary's College in Moraga, California, passionately notes, "African American theorists, scholars, educators, parents, librarians, authors, illustrators, and publishers have to define for themselves what makes a book about African Americans a classic. I don't think that we can use definitions from whites." Boyd is adamant in expressing how offended she is by the fact that Joel Chandler Hariss's *Uncle Remus Stories* and Ezra Jack Keats's *A Snowy Day* are considered milestones in black children's literature. "Why are they distinguished? What kind of new ground did they break? The browning of the characters in *A Snowy Day* is what made that book. What about Lorenz Graham's *South Town* series and Virginia Hamilton's 1974 Newbery Award-winning book, *MC Higgins the Great*?" These groundbreaking works represent the willingness of writers to incorporate tough social issues into their fiction and poetry.

"Their stories take us into the core of our humanity, the chasms of our rage and boldness of our intellect, and the brilliance of our imaginations," notes Boyd. "Publishing, distribution, advertising, networking are still areas to which we have limited access. We have very little decision-making power regarding who sits on the major committees to award prizes. In mainstream children's literature that determines the route to 'classic' status."

But despite frequent exclusion from the route, many African American books have earned "classic" status based on a strong tradition of literary excellence, a loyal readership that has passed these books on from one generation to the next, and the indomitable spirit of ancestral griots still longing to be heard. Our classics also resonate with rich imagery and bold literary innovations found in literature from the most highly regarded traditions and cultures. There is something within the people with which you can identify. It is so strong that it is unforgettable. "You might forget the plot, but the character remains memorable," says Effie Lee Morris, former coordinator of children's services for the San Francisco Public Library. Having served on both the Newbery and Coretta Scott King awards committees, and as a veteran with more than forty years of experience, Morris looks forward to the emergence of Greenfield's *Nathaniel Talking* as a classic. "It is one of my favorites. I love the rap rhythm that carries the story." Capturing the essence of popular black music in the 1990s and a strong sense of community, *Nathaniel Talking* contains rap lyrics and poems that affirm black urban life honoring long-held values and traditions.

While Paul Lawrence Dunbar, Lorenz Graham, Ellen Tarry, and Langston Hughes were pioneers in celebrating brown and black children in American literature, Mildred Taylor, Sharon Bell Mathis, Tom Feelings, Elizabeth Howard, and John Steptoe have touched the hearts, spirits, and minds of *today's* children with stories that capture their imagination, nurture their intellect, and encourage self-acceptance and self-reliance.

John Steptoe's *Mufaro's Beautiful Daughters*, a Caldecott Honor Award-winner and a Cinderella-type African tale, evokes some strong feelings for Tatiana Small and Thembi Hates Williams, both twelve-year-olds at Montera Junior High in Oakland, California. "Everything in *Cinderella* is so pink and the women have ugly faces filled with warts. The pictures in *Mufaro's Beautiful Daughters* are so beautiful; they really make me feel good," says Williams. "I remember reading a book about black people putting charcoal on their faces as a sign of beauty. But so many of us were taught that dark skin was not beautiful," states Small. "*Cinderella* just doesn't seem like a classic to me anymore," she says matter-of-factly. "It was just something that was passed on to me, but doesn't hold much meaning for me now."

Small and Williams find these books entertaining as well and want to see them on the big screen. In the hands of astute filmmakers such as Julie Dash or John Singleton, Walter Dean Myers's gripping novel *Scorpions*, June Jordan's remarkable love story *His Own Where*, and Virginia Hamilton's *Zeely* would make excellent films for young audiences.

"These books really do tell our stories and they have taught me so much about history, slavery, and what it's like living now," says Williams, whose home has wall-to-ceiling shelves filled with books by black authors. "I really feel like I can stand up to my teachers and I can argue with other people because I'm learning so much from these books."

"From books by these authors, I'm also learning that Africa is more than Somalia and South Africa," says Small with a definite tone of adolescent indignation in her voice. "I get a big picture of a continent filled with lots of countries and different kinds of people. When I go to the library, I still have to look for black books. They don't stay on display like Beverly Cleary's books do. But you better believe, I have started to look for them now. When I have children, these are the books I want to read to them and want them to read as well."

This is a generation of young people who have been sent off to dreamland with Nikki Giovanni's "poem for rodney" or Eloise Greenfield's "Way Down in the Music":

I get way down in the music
Down inside the music
I let it wake me
Take me
Spin me round and make me
Uh-get down

Inside the sound of the Jackson Five
Into the tune of Earth, Wind, and Fire
Down in the basses where the beats comes from
Down in the horn and down in the drum
I get down
I get down

I get way down in the music
Down inside the music
I let it wake me
Take me
Spin me round and shake me
I get down, down
I get down

—ELOISE GREENFIELD, from *Honey, I Love and Other Poems*

They have also grown up with a sense of pride and knowledge of themselves found in characters such as Jeeder from Virginia Hamilton's 1967 groundbreaking novel, *Zeely*. In my own household, the poems from Eloise Greenfield's *Honey, I Love* became my daughter's mantra, her lunchtime companion, and her bedtime reading. No other book held her interest for as long a period. Now that she's a parent, it has become part of my four-month-old granddaughter's rapidly growing library.

Sixteen-year-old Malik Wilson, a student at Montgomery Blair High School in Silver Springs, Maryland, and his eight-year-old brother, Rodney, a student at Pincrest Elementary School in Silver Springs, grew up nurtured by black literary treasures. "Now Rodney is read-ing the books that I read when I was younger," says Malik. He especially likes Eloise Greenfield's books. Novels by Richard Wright and Toni Morrison are becoming literary staples for Malik as a young adult, but he still holds on to some fond memories of works by Virginia Hamilton and considers Mildred Taylor's *Let the Circle Be Unbroken* one of his all-time favorites. "I'll never forget the Logan family, their struggles in Mississippi," he notes with a tremendous sense of gratitude.

These literary treasures also nurture the minds of our young readers and prepare them intellectually and culturally to embrace the adult fiction of Paule Marshall, Gwendolyn Brooks, James Baldwin, Audre Lorde, John Edgar Widerman, and Marita Golden. "The ability to appeal across time is what makes a book a classic. It doesn't feel dated. It also deals with the questions that we ask ourselves over and over again regarding our identity, relationships with one another, and finding our place in the world," according to Dr. Rudine Sims Bishop, professor of education at Ohio State University and author of *Shadow and Substance*. During the past thirty years, books by African American authors have become an integral part of public library collections, home libraries, and literature-based curricula in many schools throughout the nation. "The all time favorite in my classroom is *Roll of Thunder, Hear My Cry*. The students ask for it year after year," notes Julia Williams, chair of the English department and teacher at Calhoon County Public High School in Edison, Georgia. "Even the boys who hate to read, read this book and often more than once. I have also found that some of Zora Neale Hurston's short stories appeal to those who have real resistance to or challenges with reading." For the past two decades, teachers have been receiving book reports focusing on works by Joyce Carol Thomas and Myers. Students are writing about Hamilton, Feelings, and Taylor in both public and private schools around the country.

According to Ken Smikle, publisher of *Target Market News*, a Chicago-based newsletter covering black consumer marketing news, black people spent $178 million dollars on books in 1992. Of that figure, $163 million was spent through book clubs and retail outlets. The remaining $17 million went for encyclopedias and reference books.

While precise sales data on black children's books has been difficult to secure, more than 81,000 books for children and young adults published in the United States remained in print last year and 5,000 were published in the United States in 1992, according to the Cooperative Children's Book Center in Madison, Wisconsin. Ninety-four of them were by black authors and/or illustrators and represented works by seventy-eight individuals. With less than 2 percent of the books published in 1992 authored by African Americans and with the lion's share of marketing resources still going to European American authors, black books simply don't receive the benefits derived from the consistent massive marketing campaigns that must also generate ancillary products including television shows, mugs, T-shirts, posters, and buttons. The launching of Malcolm Jamal Warner's *CBS Story Break*, however, with Warner's astute awareness of our culture and history, may possibly have significant impact on bringing this body of literature to an even larger audience.

Even so, word of mouth marketing, tenacious librarians, and loyal readers have made it possible for veteran authors such as Boyd, Taylor, Hamilton, Myers, and Greenfield to realize sales of more than 100,000 copies for some of their books. According to Karen Johnson, the thirty-four-year-old manager of Marcus Books in San Francisco, "Some of our best-sellers include Walter Dean Myers's *18 Pine Street* and Brenda Wilkinson's *Loudell*. But *Roll of Thunder Hear My Cry* and *Let the Circle Be Unbroken* have sold steadily at record levels since they were published in 1976 and 1981 respectively."

These "shining stars in our black sky" owe a tremendous debt of gratitude to the organizers of the Freedom Schools during the Civil Rights movement of the 1960s as well. Former activists such as Charlie Cobb, Jeniffer Lawson and Julius Lester created Freedom primers to help young people better understand how racism suffocates their dreams and lives. Their work with young children sparked a renewed interest in books that chronicled self-acceptance, achievement, and vision in the black community. The past efforts of independent publishers such as Associated Publishers, Drum and Spear Press, and Third World Press have made it possible for new companies such as Just Us Books, Black Butterfly Press, and Black Classic Press to continue to support the expanding arena of culturally vital and historically compelling literature for young readers.

These books and their characters have helped in confirming our beauty, our intellect, and our contributions to world civilization. They also allow me to revisit my childhood as an adult, to fill major gaps in my own cultural illiteracy, and to honor the power and dignity that have made us such a resilient people. That is the substance of which our classics are made.

A FEW NOTED CLASSICS

This list is based on more than twenty-five years of responses from librarians, teachers, parents, and young readers themselves. There are several other outstanding works of nonfiction, fiction, biographies, anthologies, art, and picture books by African American authors that deserve a place on a list of classics, but more than anything, books for young readers written by African Americans deserve the broadest readership possible for they often represent some of the most wonderfully spirited and compelling moments in the human experience.

Moja Means One by Tom Feelings and Muriel Feelings (Dial, 1971, ages 4-8). Having gained an eager readership for some three decades, this picture book introduces numbers and Swahili with gracious illustrations and pride in African people.

Stevie by John Steptoe (Harper, 1969, ages 4-9). While his mom and dad go to work, Stevie is left in the care of Robert's family. In this loving and nurturing environment, Stevie forms a bond with a new friend. The strength of community is apparent in this sweet story.

Spin a Soft Black Song by Nikki Giovanni (Hill and Wang, 1985, ages 4-10). In a series of exquisitely crafted selections including "poem for rodney," Giovanni raises profound questions, shares some tender moments, and brings forth the spirited vitality of youth.

Zeely by Virginia Hamilton (MacMillan, 1967, ages 8-14). Hamilton's touching first novel brings an African American girl together with an imaginary Watusi princess from her ancestral world.

323

The People Could Fly by Virginia Hamilton (Alfred A. Knopf, 1985, all ages). In this extraordinary collection of fantasy, folktales, and slave narratives, Hamilton uses the power of her historical voice to share humorous, mind-boggling, and spine-chilling tales that capture the will of a people and their quest for freedom.

The Everett Anderson Series by Lucille Clifton (Holt, Rinehart and Winston, 1970, ages 4-10). Centered around nine poems about a boy who likes to play in the rain, is not afraid of the dark, but sometimes feels lonely, *Some of the Days of Everett Anderson* is the first book in this delightful series of poems and stories focusing on the life of a young black boy growing up in urban America during the 1970s and 1980s.

Honey, I Love and Other Poems by Eloise Greenfield (Crowell, 1978, ages 4-10). A small black girl's warm, precious, and often spirited response to the world around her is reflected in sixteen incredibly wonderful poems. This book was also produced as an album with the poems read to the accompaniment of a jazz quartet.

The Hundred Penny Box by Sharon Bell Mathis (Viking, 1975, ages 6-9). Truly understanding how important old things are to her, young Michael just loves to hear his one-hundred-year-old great great Aunt Dew tell a story for each year of her life based on souvenirs she keeps in her special box. This is one of the few African American stories for young readers available on video.

Roll of Thunder, Hear My Cry by Mildred Taylor (Dutton/Dial, 1976, ages 9-15). Set in 1933 in rural Mississippi, the Logan family holds fast to their independence and pride despite night riders, burnings, and constant humiliation.

Mufaro's Beautiful Daughters by John Steptoe (Lothrop, Lee and Shepard, 1987, ages 5 & up). Nyasha and Manyara are Mufaro's two beautiful daughters. Nysasha is kind and considerate, while Manyara is selfish and spoiled. When the king announces that he is looking for a bride, the entire family makes the journey to see if one of Mufaro's daughters will be chosen.

Cornrows by Camille Yarbrough (Coward, 1979, ages 5-12). With lulling voices and gentle fingers, Mama and Great Grammaw weave a tale as they braid Sister's hair and little brother Me Too watches.

Peaches by Dindga McCannon (Lothrop, Lee and Shepard, 1974, ages 8-14). The desire and longing of a young black girl growing up in Harlem combined with her love of family is revealed in this spirited story.

Circle of Gold by Candy Dawson Boyd (Scholastic, 1984, ages 8-12). This 1985 Coretta Scott King Honorable Mention book is the endearing story of friendship and a young girl's quest to find a place in her family, especially in her mother's heart.

The Dream Keeper and Other Poems by Langston Hughes (Alfred A. Knopf, 1932, ages 6 & up). A marvelous collection of fifty-nine lyrical poems and songs exploring the black experience.

The Soul Brothers and Sister Lou by Kristin Hunter (Avon, 1968, ages 10-16). In this exciting story, fourteen-year-old Louretta Hawkins takes us through her tough and often militant world during the 1960s. Somewhat surprisingly, she becomes a voice of moderation and evolves as a confident young woman guided by pride in her heritage.

Scorpions by Walter Dean Myers (Harper and Row, 1988, ages 12 & up). The acquisition of a gun tragically changes the lives of twelve-year-old Jamal Hicks and his running buddies when he takes over the leadership of his older brother's gang. But the real protagonist in this novel is the Street.

Christman Gif by Charlemae Rollins (Morrow, 1993, all ages). Originally published in 1963, this is a fantastic collection of stories, poems, songs, and plantation recipes giving us deeper insight into the celebration of Christmas during slavery. Included are selections by Frederick Douglass, Booker T. Washington, Zora Neale Hurston, and Gwendolyn Brooks.

His Own Where by June Jordan (Dell, 1971, ages 12 & up). A deeply complex and moving love story set in a cemetery examines how we love each other and ourselves.

324

Golden Slippers: An Anthology of Negro Poetry for Young Readers by Arna Bontemps (Harper & Row, 1941, ages 6-12). In a collection of lyrical and profound poetry, Langston Hughes takes us to "Havana," Ariel Williams Holloway sends us "Northboun'," and Georgia Douglas Johnson lets us visit "My Little Dreams." Bontemps also includes selections by other venerable writers including Countee Cullen, William Stanley Braithwaite, and Sterling Brown.

Bronzeville Boys and Girls by Gwendolyn Brooks (Harper, 1956, ages & up). This collection of poems by the Pulitzer Prize-winning author reflects day-to-day life and dreams of young black Americans living in Chicago during the mid-twentieth century.

South Town, North Town, and Return to Southtown by Lorenz Graham (Crowell, ages 10-16) In this saga, David Williams migrates North with his family in search of a better life. He later returns to the South in order to share his talents as a doctor with his home community.

Jackie by Luevester Lewis (Third World Press, 1970, ages 5-10). Jackie moves into a new neighborhood and has a very interesting gender-related adventure.

A Hero Ain't Nothin' But a Sandwich by Alice Childress (Avon, 1973, ages 10-16). In this incredibly rich novel, the reader experiences the complex world of Benjie, a thirteen-year-old, drug-addicted African American male.

SOME CLASSICS IN THE MAKING

Aunt Flossie's Hats (and Crab Cakes Later) by Elizabeth Howard (Clarion, 1991, ages 6-12). Two young sisters' visit to an aunt's home becomes an opportunity to learn about the history of black people as a result of rummaging through a series of hatboxes. This book is important because it is one of the first to show an African American home in which shelves are filled with books.

Pass it On: African American Poetry for Children by Wade Hudson and Floyd Cooper (Scholastic, 1993, ages 4-10). In keeping with the tradition, Hudson and Cooper keep the vitality and spirit of the black community alive with a collection of poems that focus on strength, joy, and pride.

Uncle Jed's Barber Shop by Margaret King Mitchell (Simon & Schuster, 1993, ages 7-12). In the segregated South of the 1920s, Sarah Jean's Uncle Jed, the only black barber in the county, overcomes obstacles to pursue his dream of saving enough money to open his own barbershop.

The Patchwork Quilt by Valerie Flournoy (Dial, 1985, ages 5-12). With scraps from the family's old clothing, a Halloween costume, and a new party dress, Tanya helps her grandmother make a beautiful quilt reflecting the three generations of her family.

Tar Beach by Faith Ringgold (Crown, 1991, ages 7-12). In 1939, as eight-year-old Cassie Lightfoot lies on the "tar beach" roof of her building in Harlem, she dreams of flying over the George Washington Bridge and of owning it one day.

Brown Angels: An Album of Pictures and Verse by Walter Dean Myers (HarperCollins, 1983, all ages). Through pictures from the dusty corners of an antique shop and words from a truly brilliant writer, we get to visit with African American children living around the turn of the century.

Sing to the Sun by Ashley Bryan (HarperCollins, 1992, ages 5 & up). In this wonderful collection of poems and paintings that celebrate the ups and downs of life, we hear the spirited voices of our ancestors as well as the joyous jive of jazz.

Habari Gani? What's the News? A Kwanzaa Story by Sundaira Morning House (Open Hand, 1992, ages 6-12). Seven-year-old Kia Edwards and her family celebrate Kwanzaa, the African American holiday that takes place between December 26 and January 1. Kia also experiences the seven principles of Kwanzaa woven into the fabric of her family and community life.

The Music of Summer by Rosa Guy (Delacorte, 1992, ages 12-18). The question of intraracial color conflict arises when eighteen-year-old Sarah Richardson is confronted with the "hinkty" and hurtful attitudes of her light-skinned, upper-

325

middle-class African American friends who want nothing to do with the poorer, darker Sarah.

Fallen Angels by Walter Dean Myers (Scholastic, 1988, ages 12-18). In this harrowing and heroic coming-of-age Vietnam era novel, Richie Perry and his fellow teenagers find themselves in the middle of a war, the goals of which were never fully understood by the soldiers nor the folks at home.

Nathaniel Talking by Eloise Greenfield (Black Butterfly Books, 1989, ages 7-12). In a series of eighteen rap poems, nine-year-old Nathaniel

B. Free talks about friendship, the recent death of his mother, his relationship with his father and extended family, and the dreams he has for himself.

Soul Looks Back in Wonder, by Tom Feelings (Dial Books, 1993, all ages). With brilliant artwork, Feelings joins thirteen major poets including Alexis DeVeau, Maya Angelou, Walter Dean Myers, Eugene B. Redmond, and Margaret Walker to celebrate the magic, creativity, and endurance of the African American spirit.

Grade Four to Grade Six

Festivals of Egypt

Jailan Abbas   Abd el Wahab Bilal and Tim Loveless

Egyptian

1995 (1993), Amideast

All over the world, festivals provide an opportunity for people to celebrate beliefs or traditions that they hold in common. This book enables American children to learn about, and even experience, some of the special occasions celebrated by Egyptian children.

A useful guide to the origins of Muslim, Christian, and secular holidays.

Published in Cairo, *Festivals of Egypt* describes the origins, historical development, and contemporary observance of the most significant Egyptian holidays: Moulid el-Nabi (Prophet Muhammad's birthday), Ramadan (Islamic month of fasting), Eid el-Fitr (feast at the end of Ramadan), Eid el-Adha (feast commemorating Abraham's willingness to sacrifice his son in obedience to God), moulids (birthdays to show respect for religious people of the past), Christmas, Epiphany (baptism of Jesus), Palm Sunday, Easter, Sham el-Nessim (celebration of spring), and Nile festivals modeled after those celebrated by ancient Egyptians.

Readers may be surprised to learn that several of these occasions are Christian. Christians constitute approximately ten percent of the Egyptian popula-

tion; most are Coptic, but some are Greek Orthodox, Catholic, and Protestant as well. During the Fatimid Dynasty (969-1172), Christian holidays became national celebrations in which even the caliphs (leaders of Islamic dynasties) joined, demonstrating an ecumenical tolerance that remains characteristic of most Arabs even today.

Useful supplementary material includes a brief introduction to the various calendars used in Egypt, including the Gregorian, Higra, and Coptic calendars. A short excerpt about Ramadan from the novel Khan el-Khalili *by Nobel laureate Naguib Mahfouz conveys the excitement that accompanies the approach of Ramadan.*

Particularly valuable are the sidebar notes which provide additional details, including historical information, definitions, songs, and other items of interest. Recipes enable children to participate in preparations and celebrations for some key Muslim holidays. In a few cases, additional information is wanting. For example, fasting is cited as a common practice in Judaism, Christianity, and Islam alike, but the significance of the practice is not explained. The songs are written in transliterated Arabic as well as English, but since Arab and Muslim non-Western music use tuning systems, the musical notation is not provided, so American children will not be able to actually learn the song. For the most part, however, the level of detail and length of the entries are appropriate for young readers. The extensive illustrations and photographs will help maintain children's interest, although the quality of the photographs themselves is inconsistent.

Festivals of Egypt *can be a useful tool for helping to explain unfamiliar holidays celebrated by an Egyptian, Muslim, or Eastern Orthodox friend or classmate (the book describes how these holidays are observed in Egypt in particular, but their religious significance is universal). Children can also contrast and compare the way they celebrate certain holidays with the way the same occasions are celebrated in Egypt. And, of course, in elementary classes where students already study or celebrate national and religious holidays from different parts of the world and for different religions, this book makes it possible to broaden the experience to include Egyptian and/or Islamic festivals.*
LESLIE S. NUCHO

Hanukah Money

📖 Sholem Aleichem ✒ Elizabeth Shub and Uri Shulevitz

Jewish

1991 (1978), William Morrow & Company, Inc.

Hanukkah Money is a holiday story focused on the custom of giving children money as a Hanukkah gift. Although they participate in the candle lighting and dreidel playing, the two young brothers in this book are most interested in how much money they will receive from their relatives.

As the children anticipate how much money they'll gather, we see how the family observes the holiday. It is difficult, however, to escape the preoccupation with cash. The other aspects of the Hanukkah celebration are mostly conveyed through the illustrations, and have little or no mention in the text.

A look at Hanukkah customs that focuses too much on money.

The illustrations are simple line drawings which are more appealing than the story.

The humor and characters will be primarily appreciated by readers with some knowledge of Russian Yiddish life. Other Hanukkah books with broader themes are better suited to the general reader. JANIS O'DRISCOLL

The Remarkable Journey of Prince Jen

📖 Lloyd Alexander

Asian, Chinese

1992 (1991), Dutton

Lloyd Alexander's works of fantasy for children are widely lauded. In this novel, he creates a character who, with his loyal friends, sets out on a quest and meets nearly impossible challenges along the way.

Unlike much of Alexander's work, this novel is set not in a fantasy world but in ancient China. The story follows an emperor who would like to improve his kingdom: his subjects are hungry, governed by corrupt officials (all of which, unhappily, is true of Chinese history). But the royalty hides in the palace and knows little of conditions on the outside.

The emperor has heard of a utopian land called Tien Kuo which is said to be so well-ruled that the "subjects thrive and prosper, the land yields harvests in abundance, the arts flourish as richly as the orchards. The laws are just, but seldom enforced, since the inhabitants deal with each other as they themselves would wish to be dealt with. Thus, few officials are needed, but they serve their monarch and the people well." The emperor would like to discover the means of ruling so well. Lacking anyone more loyal to his cause, he sends his son, Prince Jen, to find Tien Kuo and study the methods of its rule.

The son of an ancient Chinese emperor is sent by his father on a seemingly impossible mission.

Prince Jen sets out with loyal comrade and royal retainers, but he meets with one mishap after another. He is beset by weather and terrain, by thieves and rising revolutionaries calling themselves the Yellow Scarves and intending to take over the kingdom. Prince Jen has been given six gifts to present to Yuan Ming, the ruler of Tien Kuo. Seemingly old, rusty, and insignificant, each of the six gifts turns out to have some magic property. One by one, the gifts are lost, stolen, or given away to someone in need. So too are each of his comrades lost, until Prince Jen finds himself alone, penniless, and in jail, unable to prove his identity.

Reminiscent of the Arabian Nights tales, as well as of traditional Chinese fiction, the reader is kept glued to the pages of the book until the very last, when all ends surprisingly and happily. We watch Prince Jen grow from a pampered, spineless boy into a resolute, determined young man who knows a good deal about his own empire and has gained the spirit and wisdom to rule it well. In fact, Tien Kuo might be closer at hand than we thought.

The details reflect many aspects of Chinese culture, literature, and history, and the story is told in a distinctly Chinese style (mixed with a lot of the delightful magic of Lloyd Alexander). GINNY LEE

Powwow

🔖 📝 George Ancona
Native American
1993, Harcourt Brace and Company, 📖 Braine, Susan, *Drumbeat...Heartbeat: A Celebration of Powwow*; King, Sandra, *Shannon: An Ojibway Dancer*.

Feathers, beads, bells, and paint; fry bread, Indian tacos, corn soup, cotton candy, and french fries; Turquoise and silver jewelry, miniature headdresses hanging from rearview mirrors, and sweet-grass braids; high-pitched singing, steady drumbeats, flute music, a wonderful diversity of languages, and most of all, laughter—these are the sights and smells and sounds that bombard a spectator at a Native American powwow. But what does it all mean?

A photographic essay of a powwow held on Montana's Crow Reservation.

Photographer Ancona has provided an introduction to the modern powwow that adults and children alike will find valuable. Focusing on the biggest powwow today, the Crow Fair in Montana, he takes the reader through standard events that one can see at almost any powwow across the country, whether on a reservation, on a college campus, or in the city. A time of visiting friends and being with other Indian people, powwows are also a chance for dancers to "strut their stuff" and compete against their peers.

We watch young Anthony Standing Rock play with friends and then get dressed in his traditional dance outfit. We then join him in the festivities, beginning with the opening "parade," called the Grand Entry, and on through the standard dances seen at any powwow—the intertribal, men's and women's traditional dances, men's and women's fancy dances, men's grass dance, women's jingle dress dance, and the tiny tots' competitions. As Ancona describes each style's dance outfit and manner of dancing, well-placed, full-color photos clearly reflect the text.

Other recent books on contemporary powwows include *Drumbeat...Heartbeat: A Celebration of the Powwow*; text and photographs by Susan Braine; Lerner, 1995; *Shannon: An Ojibway Dancer* by Sandra King; photographs by Catherine Whipple, Lerner, 1993. *Powwow* is highly recommended for all public, school, and tribal libraries. LISA A. MITTEN

The Origin of Life On Earth: An African Creation Myth

🔖 David Sankofa Anderson
📝 Kathleen Atkins Wilson
African
1991, Sights Productions

This myth from the Yoruba religion has been transformed into an award-winning picture book. Storyteller David Anderson, who is known as Sankofa, has written a children's version of a Nigerian creation myth which explains how the world began. *The Origin of Life on Earth* has a brief introduction providing basic information about the development of the Yoruba religion.

Even though the explanation can be understood by a child, it is not necessary to read the introduction in order to enjoy the story. However, before reading the story aloud,

A beautiful picture book that revives a unique Nigerian creation myth for children.

teachers and parents should read the preface and the glossary, which includes a pronunciation guide.

As the story opens, the world doesn't exist and Olorun, God, lives in the sky with the people of his kingdom, the Orishas. In this myth, it is Obatala, one of the Orishas, who receives permission from God to create the world. He wisely gets advice about creating the earth from an elder Orisha. He soon has formed the land called Ife, which is the name of the Yoruba's holy city. Obatala uses the rich brown soil to form creatures that looked like him. His attempt to create people almost fails until God aids him. God forms the sun, makes the earth rotate, and breathes life into the people. According to the Yoruba, these were the first people in the world, and they were the Yorubas' ancestors.

The entire design of this book, (the dust cover, the end papers, the illustrations) is an explosion of color. Each page of text is framed by a thin gold border, and the initial letter on the page is a large colored letter. The illustrator received the Coretta Scott King award for the outstanding full-color illustrations which appear on half of each spread. The opening scenes are excellent replicas of the burst of color created by the colorful African clothing worn by the Orishas.

Since there are few picture book versions of African myths, this book is a must for every school and public library. This unique African myth can be used in mythology units, African history projects, and storytelling activities. The text has a smooth flowing style which is perfect for reading aloud. This story is a welcome introduction for studying the people of Nigeria, one of Africa's wealthiest nations and the African country with the largest number of immigrants in the United States. MARTHA RUFF

Aztec, Inca, and Maya

📖 Elizabeth Baquedano 🖊 Michel Rudkin, Zabe Rudkin, and David Zabe

Aztec, Hispanic, Incan, Mayan

1993, Alfred A. Knopf, ✳ Series

Structured around twenty-nine, two-page chapters, this book contains a photographic collection of classical artifacts associated with Meso-American and Andean societies. Using maps at the beginning of

A picture book that presents artifacts associated with Aztec, Inca, and Mayan civilizations.

the book proves to be a good strategy. The world was and looked different geographically at that time. It is important to illustrate how the world once looked, for there were numerous nations that did not exist.

All too often, artifacts are seen as pieces solely made to place in museums or special collections. Their role in the daily lives of people is not placed in context. The book clearly explains how the artifacts were used in agriculture, hunting, the arts, sports, and religious life. It also helps young people in understanding that some of these societies were highly sophisticated, and that some of their technologies were quite advanced for the times. The book is certain to support critical inquiry in young minds. BYRON RUSKIN

Katie and the Lemon Tree

📖 Esther Bender 🖊 Joyce Dunn Keenen

Amish

1994, Herald Press

Katie travels with her husband from Germany to America. There she plants a lemon tree to symbolize the promise of a new land on which to build a home. Months turn quickly to years and suddenly it's twelve years later. The lemon tree has flourished with Katie's patient care.

This is a story is about hope and about waiting: Waiting patiently for the day when fruit will appear on the branches of the lemon tree. Waiting for there to be enough money in the tin box to send for Mother. The book's main theme is expressed in Mother's words to Katie before she departs for America: "Keep the Faith, and Milk the Cow." In other words, Be patient and

A somewhat didactic story of the perserverance of an Amish couple travelling from Germany to America.

work hard all the while. Unlike most Amish and Mennonite books, the focus is not on the detailed traditions of this way of life. The characters of the story are not as important as its message.

The book suffers somewhat for this choice. It's a short book, and it may read a bit like a rough draft. At the very least, the author could have elaborated on Katie's husband and family. Nonetheless, the story is energetic and delivers a clear message about persistence and patience. NANCY PAQUIN

This Place Is Crowded: Japan

📖 Vicki Cobb 🖊 Barbara Lavallee

Asian, Japanese

1993 (1992), Walker Publishing, ✳ Series

This Place Is Crowded: Japan by Vicki Cobb, is a rather skewed look at life in contemporary Japan presented from a mainly urban and Eurocentric perspective.

A superficial and generalizing look at contemporary Japan.

The back cover of the book states, "Can you imagine living in Japan? The first thing you would notice is that it is crowded. Very crowded. But the Japanese people don't mind." These are incredibly superficial statements about a very complex country. Certainly, the largest Japanese cities are infamous for packed subways, tiny apartments, and stop-and-start traffic, but there are other areas, particularly in Hokkaido and Kyushu, that are much more sparsely populated, where people live in multi-floored homes, and where roads are not continually congested. Cobb seems to focus primarily on urban life in Japan, as if it characterizes all life in Japan.

Cobb also lays out blankets of generalities regarding the psyche of Japanese people. Cobb writes, "Just as school is the center of children's lives, the company is the center for working adults." It is unfair to generalize in this way, especially these days, when studies show that more and more Japanese men regard their families as a higher priority than their work. Another problematic statement is "Children must go to school until they finish high school." This is untrue and feeds off the prevailing attitude about the severity of the Japanese education system. There is, in fact, a drop out rate in Japan, and there are numerous examples of children leaving school to work to support their families. There are plenty of other examples and statements Cobb makes that she presents as universal truths about Japan, yet they are subject to exception and modification.

Lavallee's illustrations are beautiful. The bright colors she uses and the borders she places around the text are eye-catching, yet the content of the illustrations also paints a simplistic picture of Japan. In the part where Cobb discusses automation in Japanese farming, for example, the primary image in Lavallee's illustration is of traditional, back breaking farming. In fairness, she does include a small tractor in the corner. Most of Lavallee's illustrations feature traditional and stereotypical aspects of Japanese culture. Pages are taken up by illustrations of squatting Sumo wrestlers, clone-like children posing for photographs in front of national landmarks, bathers relaxing in hot springs, and kimono-clad adults participating in festivals and tea ceremonies. While these images are still a major part of Japan's national identity, there are also many societal changes that would provide a more representative picture of Japan today. *This Place Is Crowded: Japan* feels like a slightly off-the-mark social studies text, for Cobb fails to show the growing diversity in attitudes and life-styles that characterizes contemporary Japan. KATHY COLLINS

A Kwanzaa Fable

📖 Eric V. Copage
African American
1995, William Morrow, ✴ Audio Cassette

When his widowed father dies suddenly, thirteen-year-old Jordan is torn between his responsibilities to his family and his rebellious friends. Jordan's grandmother has come to rely upon him to take care of his rambunctious eight-year-old twin siblings. But Jordan is devastated by his father's death. Although he is surrounded by people who love him, Jordan feels alone and abandoned by his father—the most important influence in Jordan's life.

A troubled African American teenager learns how to apply the principles of Kwanzaa to daily life.

Jordan finds his way to Snackman, a neighborhood shopkeeper, who becomes an unlikely hero to Jordan. Filled with questions, Jordan is gently guided by Snackman's patience and wisdom. The shopkeeper introduces the seven principles of Kwanzaa to Jordan, who learns how to apply them to life's everyday challenges and demands.

Through self-determination and faith, Jordan weathers the first semester of high school and discovers that losing his father also brings something vital and affirming into his life. The novel ends with a huge Kwanzaa feast and an opportunity for Jordan to reflect on the meaning of faith, unity, purpose, and responsibility.

Copage's book is bound to become a standard and an inspiration for future generations of African American boys. His "Kwanzaa Music: A Celebration of Black Cultures in Song" serves as a wonderful musical companion to this novel and includes selections by Aretha Franklin, Mahlathini & the Mahotella Queens, and James Brown. DAPHNE MUSE

The Buffalo Hunt

📖 Russell Freedman 🖌 Various Artists
Native American
1988, Holiday House Inc.

This fine picture book, by the award-winning author Russell Freedman, transcends age and reading levels. As with all picture books, the illustrations play the primary role in telling the story. The words expand the story but are not intrusive. The sparse text explains the record of Native Americans on the plains, as captured by artists George Catlin and Karl Bodmer, whose paintings are included. These artists recorded the daily lives of the Plains in their paintings and journals. These paintings and text entries are judiciously selected for impact and clarity. The result is a surprisingly artistic, yet accessible book that offers something for all age levels.

A revealing pictorial history of the buffalo hunts of the Plains Indians.

Freedman makes excellent use of this historic record of a vanishing traditional way of life. The sacred aspects of the buffalo and the rituals surrounding the buffalo hunt are thoroughly explored in both illustrations and text. Freedman describes the way in which the Native Americans utilized every part of the buffalo. The robes, tents, and paintings made from buffalo hides are depicted and described in detail. This kind of authenticity fascinates children and provides teachers with comprehensive information for lesson plans. *I have used this book with first and second graders to present the buffalo and horse cultures of the Plains.*

The illustrations can be enlarged with the aid of an opaque projector to enable the students to see details in the paintings. The accompanying text can be read aloud by the teacher or a student. Students themselves may create a presentation using the text and illustration in a presentation for younger children or peers.

BUFFALO HUNT

RUSSELL FREEDMAN

Scenes of the buffalo hunt as depicted in the movie Dances With Wolves, *can be shown to contrast the efficient methods of the Native Americans versus the wanton destruction of the buffalo by white hunters who followed them. The whites deliberately decimated the buffalo populations in a successful attempt to starve the Native Americans so they would be more manageable and not a threat. Historic footage of the buffalo hunt can be found in the catalogue of the Native American Public Broadcasting Consortium and used to demonstrate the differences between white and Native American perspectives on the use of utilizing renewable resources.*

Freedman describes the buffalo shirts and buffalo dances and ceremonies of the tribes of the Plains in the nineteenth century using the authoritative text and paintings of the two artists. The represen-

tation is authentic, sensitive, and revealing. The paintings and explanatory text allow reader to peer into the minds of traditional peoples and see the world from their perspective, thus giving us a new appreciation of this culture. ELAINE P. GOLEY

From a Child's Heart

Nikki Grimes 🖉 Brenda Joysmith

African American

1993, Just Us Books

In their innocence, children can appeal to the greater good in any adult. In this volume of poetry, one child shares her prayers to God. The language is simple, the requests are straightforward, and the results create a stronger bond.

What kinds of things do children pray about? They pray for love, caring, a parent, a parent's health, strength, unity, and peace in their homes and in the world. They pray to say thank you. They pray to be understood.

The prayers exhibit humility not in the face of the world but in the face and presence of God. There is little need to pretend here and children know it. The child admits to mistakes but promises to try to do better. The child prays when she feels the need, not when instructed to by an adult. As a result, the prayers come directly from the heart and reflect the inner workings of the soul.

The first prayer, "A Credit," asks God for help to be somebody. There is no special question as to what would be the right profession. Rather, it is request is to be the best that the child can be.

Two other prayers — "Sideyard" and "One More Year" — are requests for Grandma. In "Sideyard," the child talks about the beauty of nature

An African American child shares her conversations with God in a story that addresses children and religion.

and how her grandmother has taught her to appreciate it. In "One More Year," the child explains to God why she needs her grandmother. She acknowledges that God needs her grandmother too, but right now her need is great and she would like to keep her one more year.

The prayers are not complex. They are not planned for perfection. These two simple facts make them exactly what prayer should be: a humble conversation with God. Children need to understand the existence of a creator in words they understand. They need to understand omnipotent power and strength. They need to understand that while they may be small and their voices tiny, they can still be heard.

In a world where moral and religious values have reached an unhealthy decline, it is extremely important to know that there is a source that can and will calm all fears, wash away all tears, and replenish all needs. This book of prayers is for all children regardless of religious orientation. The book will help the light at the end of the tunnel to shine brighter and perhaps make the tunnel itself a little shorter. YOLANDA ROBINSON-COLES

Her Stories: African Folktales, Fairytales & True Tales

Virginia Hamilton ✏ Leo and Diane Dillon
African American
1995, Blue Sky Press

Virginia Hamilton's most recent collection of African American folktales, after *The People Could Fly* and *Many Thousand Gone*, is the richest yet. This striking collection of seventeen tales, all featuring a female protagonist, spans the width and breadth of the African American experience. *Her Stories* includes true stories, such as Lettice Boyer's recollections of the days of slavery in "From Way Back"; folktales, such as a story about the relative status of the sexes called "Woman and Man Started Even"; and twists on classic fairy tales, such as "Catskinella," a Cinderella story.

Seventeen refreshing, non-dogmatic African American folktales featuring women protagonists.

There are stories here for every interest and a wide range of age levels. "Little Girl and Buh Rabby" and other animal tales will amuse young children, while the downright spookiness of a southern Louisiana tale about a she-vampire, "Lonna and Cat Woman," will catch the attention of junior high-level readers. The collection attempts to redress the gender imbalance often found in folktales in a refreshingly nondogmatic way—these women are not one-dimensional "positive role models," but real human beings of every character type.

As she explains in her afternote, these stories hold special meaning for Hamilton. "When I was a child, I heard stories told by women." They retain some of the idiom and rhythm of the sources from which she retold them and flow as smoothly as readers of her earlier volumes will expect. Printed on heavy paper and bound in a sturdy cloth casing, these tales are to be read and read out loud, over and over again. The book itself is a pleasure to hold with lush, detailed full-color illustrations that reward prolonged inspection.

First and second graders will enjoy listening to Her Stories. For upper grades, it makes a useful addition to any study of African American culture and history. HAROLD UNDERDOWN

Pueblo Storyteller

Diane Hoyt-Goldsmith ✏ Lawrence Migdale
Cochiti, Native American, Pueblo
1994 (1991), Holiday House

Told from the perspective of a young girl from the pueblo of Cochiti, one of the eight Northern Pueblos in New Mexico, this nonfiction work provides ample information about contemporary American Indian culture.

April is a happy child with a sense of her pueblo's history and with an obvious pride in her heritage. The book takes us through various aspects of life in Cochiti. There are numerous photographs in a modern pueblo setting. Many elements of traditional Indian culture are

An informative and much-needed guide to contemporary pueblo life.

present: the baking of bread and the making of pottery and drums. April and her grandfather also enjoy playing golf on the golf course that the tribe owns and operates.

Author Hoyt-Goldsmith portrays April and her family with respect. The author made a number of visits to the Trujillo Emily. In addition, she consulted with experts in the pueblo and council members of the Eight Northern Pueblo Council. *Addresses are included for anyone interested in obtaining more information about storytellers, drums, or the Cochiti Dance Group. Also included in the book are the pueblo legends of "How the People Came to Earth," a glossary, and an index.*

More works of this quality and nature are necessary additions to the collections of all public libraries. It is important for other authors to be aware that there are gaps in materials on American Indians, but books such as *Pueblo Storyteller* certainly help fill those holes. JUDITH CASTIANO

In the Month of Kislev: A Story for Hanukkah

📖 Nina Jaffe ✏ Louise August

Jewish

1995 (1992), Puffin Books, 📖 Sherman, Josepha, *Rachel the Clever and Other Jewish Folktales, The Uninvited Guest and Other Jewish Holiday Tales,* and *While Standing on One Foot: Puzzle Stories;* Jaffe, Nina, and Zeitlin, Steve, *Wisdom Tales from the Jewish Tradition.*

Set in a Polish town during a Hannukah celebration, this story focuses on the values of tradition.

The citizens of a Polish town celebrate Hanukkah in this simple "wisdom story" with the feel of a traditional Jewish folktale. Mendel, a peddler, lives in a small house with his wife and their three daughters, Leah, Gittel, and Devorah. The family struggles to make ends meet, unlike their neighbor Feivel, an uncharitable lumber merchant who lives in great wealth with his wife, children, and servants. During the celebration of Hanukkah, Mendel's family cannot afford to buy potatoes with which to make the traditional potato pancakes, called latkes. On the first night of the holiday, Leah, Gittel, and Devorah pass Feivel's home and smell the latkes being prepared inside. They go to bed with nothing to eat, yet are satisfied that they were able to smell the Hanukkah treat. This continues for seven nights, but on the last night of Hanukkah, Feivel catches them outside his home. He takes Mendel's family to the rabbi, demanding that they be forced to pay him eight rubles for smelling his latkes. The wise rabbi asks the townspeople to contribute their Hanukkah *gelt* (money), places it in a bag, and shakes it up, telling Feivel that the fair payment for the smell of the latkes is the sound of money. Seeing the error of his ways, Feivel is a changed man and thereafter known for his charity. And from that point on, the two families celebrate Hanukkah together.

The "wisdom story" is a tradition in Jewish literature and folklore involving a dispute settled by clever thinking. Because the "message" is more important than characterization, the people in the story are usually not drawn in depth. Mendel and Feivel are essentially stock characters; their children are not differentiated at all. Through simple words and colorful woodcut illustrations, the story presents an entertaining picture of how Hanukkah is celebrated. An afterword explains the historical significance of the Jewish holiday, and describes some of its traditions, such as the lighting of the Menorah, the playing of dreidel games, and dining on customary foods. Stories and riddles are part of the celebration. *This book hinges on a riddle: how will the conflict between the two families be resolved by the rabbi? Children may enjoy suggesting other clever ways in which this dispute could be settled.* Other interesting folktale collections that would supplement this text include *Rachel the Clever and Other Jewish Folktales* by Josepha Sherman, *The Uninvited Guest and Other Jewish Holiday Tales,* and *While Standing on One Foot: Puzzle Stories* and *Wisdom Tales from the Jewish Tradition* by Nina Jaffe and Steve Zeitlin.

PETER D. SIERUTA

Maria Molina and the Days of the Dead

📖 Kathleen Krull ✏ Enrique O. Sánchez

Hispanic

1994, Macmillan Publishing Company

In many cultures, the dead are celebrated and honored through regular rituals and traditions. Kathleen Krull offers young readers the chance to learn about the customs and traditions of another culture in *Maria*

A girl guides us through the Mexican celebration of Day of the Dead.

Molina and the Day of the Dead. This is the story of a young Mexican girl and her family who, along with the other members of their community, honor the deceased with a large celebration. The Day of the Dead, though similar in some respects to the American Halloween celebration, has marked differences that are highlighted in Krull's story. With Maria as the guide, young readers will discover the history of the celebration as well as its importance to those who engage in it. Krull accomplishes this by engaging the characters in the celebration in Mexico, then transplanting them in the United States, where Maria anxiously awaits Halloween thinking that it is the same as the Day of the Dead. When Maria learns that in the United States she will have candy instead of

pan de los muertos, she begins to worry about her family's ability to honor the dead in their newly adopted homeland. However, it is through this conundrum that Maria learns that cultural traditions change—that she and her family can celebrate the Day of the Dead and Halloween, creating their own unique Molina tradition.

Not only does *Maria Molina and the Day of the Dead* provide an interesting and entertaining story, but Krull also includes a more academic rendering of the history of the celebration, coupled with suggestions for further reading on the custom. Of interest to some will be the recipes for a few of the traditional Day of the Dead treats, such as the *pan de los muertos* that Maria loves. A *unique celebration of family history and cultural appreciation, Krull's piece provides teachers with many avenues of exploration into the concept of multiculturalism.* CHRISTINE PALMER

A Great Miracle Happened There: A Chanukkah Story

📖 Karla Kuskin   ✎ Robert Andrew Parker

Jewish

1993, HarperCollins

The story of Hanukkah is told as a modern Jewish family celebrates with friends.

A young Jewish boy invites a friend to his family's celebration of the first night of Hanukkah. He explains to his friend, and by extension, the reader, that Hanukkah, or the Festival of Lights, commemorates a miracle that took place when the Jews recaptured the Temple of Jerusalem from the Greeks. One day's supply of lamp oil continued to burn for eight days, until fresh oil could be brought.

The friend's presence provides a pretext for an explanation of the origins of Hanukkah, and shows that non-Jews are welcome at their Jewish neighbors' celebrations. The holiday is treated with appropriate respect. *A Great Miracle Happened There* can serve as an introduction to Hanukkah for children of any background.

Illustrations show the modern family's holiday preparations and the miracle of the first Hanukkah story. LYNN EISENHUT

Cultural Alladay: A Celebration of Our Nation's Diversity

TRAVIS E. JACKSON, ED.D

Named by a group of students from two middle schools in Ridgewood, New Jersey, Cultural Alladay provides participants with a way of honoring diversity in our communities and society. The students recognized that although we have plenty of holidays to celebrate individual cultures (St. Patrick's Day, Kwanzaa, Cinco de Mayo, Yuan Tan), we have no one holiday celebrating our multicultural nation.

The students drafted a proclamation declaring the Friday before the official observance of Columbus day as Cultural Alladay, and they secured the approval of the Ridgewood board of education, the mayor, the village council, and the chamber of commerce. Since the first year, the observance has spread to other places in Bergen County.

Although they never told anyone how the day should be celebrated, they did suggest some guidelines. Students came up with the slogan, "Strength in Diversity: Get Connected." They helped design a logo, and they helped to put together a diversity packet, which was distributed to the town's high school, two middle schools, and six elementary schools. When other schools and school districts sought help, they were encouraged to use any of the lesson plans or projects—beyond the familiar sharing of native food and costumes—designed to help students learn to respect individual and cultural differences. Most importantly, they advised those choosing to observe the holiday to do so in a way that responds to their particular situation. In Benjamin Franklin Middle School, the students invited a speaker—a Bergen County executive—the first year. During the second year they watched and discussed a movie—Separate But Equal—on Thurgood Marshall and the famous 1954 Supreme Court ruling. And for the third year, they tackled a topical problem: "Why are the Yankees thinking about leaving the Bronx?" These activities were designed by a group of people sitting around and brainstorming, and were refined by teachers and students. Each of the days got a little closer to the goal for Cultural Alladay: to help students and staff to understand the differences among people and how those differences affect the way we get along and learn together in school and in the larger society.

Travis E. Jackson is the unit administrator of Benjamin Franklin School, 335 North Van Deen Ave., Ridgewood, NJ 07451.

Native American Rock Art: Messages from the Past

📖 Yvette La Pierre   ✎ Lois Sloan

Native American

1994, 📖 Hobbs, Will, *Kokopelli's Flute*; MacGill-Callahan, Sheila, *And Still the Turtle Watched.*

Who created the mysterious works of art found in canyons, on stone outcroppings, and on cave walls across North America? Why did these early artists create the petroglyphs and pictographs? And, perhaps most intriguing, what do the pictures mean?

An interesting examination of early Native American art such as cave drawings and pictographs.

Native American Rock Art: Messages from the Past is a beautiful nonfiction book that attempts to answer all of those questions.

Each chapter in the book starts with a vignette that sets the scene. The text then moves into information on six different topics: Who were the first Americans? How did they create the rock art? How were the locations chosen, and how did the place affect the creation of the art? How do scientists date rock art? What's the process archaeologists use as they try to interpret the meanings of certain pictures? How can we stop the destruction of rock art? The book ends by listing rock art sites on public land that can be visited.

La Pierre, a freelance editor and writer who specializes in environmental issues, grew up in the California desert, where she became intrigued with rock art as a child. This book is illustrated with detailed and intriguing photographs of rock art and with illustrations by Lois Sloan, who has illustrated for the national Geographic Society and the Smithsonian.

Looking at the images from the past and talking about what they might mean is interesting in itself, but students may want to do rock paintings. Commercial rock art kits are available. Teachers can also simply collect their own rocks and have students create symbols for things that matter to them and paint the symbols on their rocks.

Two novels that can be used in connection with *Native American Rock Art* are *Moon Dancer* by Margaret Rostkowski, in which fifteen-year-old Miranda goes rock climbing in Utah and finds a connection with the people from the past who created some rock art, and *Kokopelli's Flute* by Will Hobbs, a novel set in New Mexico. Thirteen-year-old Tepary Jones is convinced that the petroglyphs on the cliff wall hide something important. When he finds a bone flute that pot hunters have left behind, he falls under the power of magic from the distant time. In order to survive, he must find the secrets of Kokopelli, the flute player from Hopi legend "who brought the seeds from village to village, whose journeys are remembered on rock walls from Peru to Colorado."

And Still the Turtle Watched by Sheila MacGill-Callahan with pictures by Barry Moser, tells of a turtle carved on a rock over the Hudson River, watching the changes human beings have brought over the years. *Students could use it as a model to create their own picture books.* JANE KURTZ

Antelope Woman: An Apache Folktale

📖 ✎ Michael Lacapa

Apache, Native American

1995 (1992), Northland Publishing

In *Antelope Woman: An Apache Folktale*, Michael Lacapa retells and illustrates a traditional folktale explaining why the Apache won't hunt antelope. Lacapa begins with an elder explaining to his son the traditions of their people before they spend the day hunting.

His story starts with a young, beautiful, and highly skilled woman who is not interested in the young men of her village. The gifts they constantly bring her fail to move her. Then one day a young man comes to the village who teaches the people to honor all things great and small. He teaches an elder how to improve his bow. He teaches a woman how to carry water and honor it. Every night the young man disappears, and no one knows to where.

A Native American tale that explains why the Apache won't hunt antelope.

The young woman becomes intrigued and follows him into the brush. She sees him jump through four hoops and change into an antelope. He motions for her to follow him and she does, changing into an antelope herself.

She joins the young antelope's family and learns many things. But she wants to take these messages back to her family. The young couple return through the hoops, changing back into people. The

335

young man carries many gifts to give the young woman's parents, for he wants to marry her. At first, the people are glad to have them return, for they teach many things that improve the quality of life throughout the seasons.

The young couple marry, but their first children, who are twins, are not accepted. The couple eventually decide to move back with the antelope, where they and all other things are respected. They return through the four hoops with their children and are never seen again by the villagers.

This brief, gorgeously illustrated story emphasizes one basic theme, which the narrator states:

"Since then we have learned to honor all things great and small. So today, my son, we honor the antelope by never hunting or killing them. For out there among the antelope are Antelope Woman and her children and they are a part of us. Now as we hunt, my son, we must be thankful to the Creator, who gives us all things great and small and who teaches us to honor them all."

All characters take on a mythical quality, as they are never named in the story. The vibrant and bold color illustrations of Michael Lacapa can carry even the youngest reader into the heart of this tale. *This book could be used in a unit about ecology and the history and cultures of the American Southwest.*
NOLA HADLEY

Crow and Weasel

📖 Barry Lopez   ✏ Tom Pohrt

Eskimo, Native American

1990, Farrar, Strauss & Giroux

Written with a consideration for Native American values, but not deriving from any specific tradition, this modern myth of two young braves, Crow and Weasel, highlights much of what has been respected of Native American cultures in the United States.

An imaginative tale in which two men of an Indian tribe leave home on a journey.

The artist, Tom Pohrt, has immersed himself in a study of specific tribal costume, both Inuit and Plains, and has tried to incorporate those designs as truly as possible, still leaving room for his own wonderful individual creativity and skill.

In the world of the book, the line between human and animal is blurred. Crow has the head of a crow and Weasel has the head of a weasel, and they have appropriate appendages where visible, but other

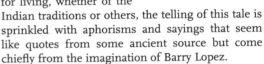

than that, the two young braves are quite human. Their clothes hide much of any other indication of animal or human nature. The shaman who blesses their journey is a mountain lion, and in their travels they meet humans as badgers and a grizzlies.

Full of good wisdom for living, whether of the Indian traditions or others, the telling of this tale is sprinkled with aphorisms and sayings that seem like quotes from some ancient source but come chiefly from the imagination of Barry Lopez.

Crow and Weasel have an idea that they would like to go farther north than anyone of their tribe has ever gone before. At first their families pooh-pooh the notion. It sounds foolish and full of danger. But the mountain lion's dream indicates they should go.

On their way, they meet a mouse from another tribe. In discussing journeys and quests, Crow says, "...our older people tell us that without a dream you do not know what to do with your life. So it is a good thing [to follow one's dream]." Mouse replies, "To be a good hunter, to be a good family man, to be truthful instead of clever with people, to live in a community where there is much wisdom, that is what all of us want." We hope our own communities are listening.

At one point, Crow has great difficulty crossing a river. He struggles to understand it. Weasel tells him, "What is there to understand? You just get away from something like that. You don't live in the water. A river, that's not your place." Crow comes to this understanding, "... with some things in life you don't try to fight. A young man wants to fight everything, it is in him to do that. A grown man knows to leave certain things alone. Some things you don't answer. It doesn't mean you have no courage."

The two braves discuss storytelling. Crow tells him to "put the parts together in a good pattern, speak with a pleasing rhythm, and call on all the details of memory."

Badger tells them to take good care of their stories and give them away when they are needed. "Sometimes," she says, "a person needs a story more than food to stay alive."

Later, when they lie starving, a grizzly bear brings them food and tells them of a similar situation in which he himself saw the beauty of a flock of geese against the sun and was inspired to go on.

"Sometimes it is what is beautiful that carries you," says Weasel. "Yes," replies Grizzly, "It can carry you to the end. It is your relationship to what is beautiful, not the beautiful thing by itself, that carries you."

As they approach home, Weasel suggests mischievously that it would be nice to arrive well dressed and fancy, but Crow says seriously, "I think we look good. And we are alive." After the telling of their stories and what they learned, they are given a place of respect in the tribe. They reflect, "It is good to be alive, to have friends, to have a family, to have children, to live in a particular place. These relationships are sacred. This is the way it should be." GINNY LEE

Magid Fasts for Ramadan

📖 Mary Matthews ✒ E. B. Lewis
Arab American, Egyptian, Middle Eastern, Muslim
1996, Houghton Mifflin

As the world of multicultural children's literature continues to grow, young readers come to learn about highly held traditions and practices that have been sustaining forces in various cultures. In Mary Matthews' *Magid Fasts for Ramadan*, we meet an eight-year-old boy living in Cairo, Egypt, who is determined to fast during Ramadan, despite the protests from family members. Ramadan is one of the high holy periods during which Muslims fast between sunrise and sunset each day. Magid simply does not want to wait, and feels his age has nothing to do with his faith. But he soon discovers how difficult it is to go without food or water for an extended period of the day. He tries to keep his secret from his family, while struggling to maintain his vow to Allah. Realizing the pressure that the family has placed on the twelve-year-old sister Aisha, the father proposes a way in which both can honor Allah and stand tall in their faith.

Although family members protest he is too young, an eight-year-old Egyptian boy fasts during Ramadan.

The story is well written and strongly conveys the family's closeness and the depth of their spiritual beliefs. In light of the fanaticism and ignorance often associated with Islam, this book is a step forward in correcting some of the misunderstandings of this religion.

Illustrator E. B. Lewis avoids caricature. None of the stereotypical trappings that often accompany Muslims appear in this story. Much like any other family, we see Magid's parents hugging and reassuring each other. There is also an illustration of the family praying together in their home.

At the end of the book is "A Note on Islam" and a "Glossary and Pronounciation Guide." The note on Islam provides a brief but useful overview of Muslim culture. In the glossary, the author also explains the fact that some sounds in Arabic have no English equivalent and that the pronounciations of some terms are approximate. DAPHNE MUSE

Star Tales: North American Indian Stories About the Stars, Moon, and Sky

📖 ✒ Gretchen Will Mayo
Native American

1987, Walker and Company, 📕 Caduto, Michael J., *Keepers of the Earth.*

Star Tales is a collection of tales from Native Americans about the origins of constellations and the sky spirits' relationships with mankind. Each story is prefaced with a one-page introduction that makes general comments about the animals or people depicted, and the tribe from whom the tale originated. The book ends with a "Where the Tales Began" section that lists who first collected these tales. The book also includes a research note that details the history and acquisition of the designs and illustrations by the Milwaukee Public Museum. The glossary covers people, places, and objects mentioned in the tales and important in Native American culture.

An illustrated collection of Indian legends about the stars, moon, and sky.

Many of the stories are ironic in tone, and we see that irony skillfully conveyed in "Morning Star Takes a Wife." *The tales would work well with* Keepers of the Earth *by Michael J. Caduto (1988). That book provides spin-off activities with a section on the moon and constellations for teachers (and parents) interested in Native American culture.*

For example, these tales would translate well into a dramatic production, with some students acting out parts as a narrator reads the story. ANDREA L. WILLIAMS

337

338

Christmas in the Big House, Christmas in the Quarters

Patricia McKissack ◆ Fredrick McKissack and John Thompson

African American

1994, Scholastic, Inc.

A rich account of Christmas, 1859, from the perspectives of slave and owner on a Virginia plantation.

It's Christmas, 1859, on a Virginia plantation. In the Big House, everything is elegant and abundant, but there is an undercurrent of unease. There is talk of abolitionists, the Underground Railroad, and secession. In the slave quarters, conditions are wretched, but the slaves do celebrate. Their songs and stories tell of their hope for freedom. This hope is the book's main theme. But readers must understand that the relationship between those who lived in the Big House (the master and his family) and those who lived in the quarters (slaves and overseers) was by no means an amiable one, nor were most slaves ever invited to celebrate anything in the Big House. The lines were clearly drawn and the relationship depicted in this book was the exception and not the rule.

Beautiful, full-color illustrations bring the characters to life, and will help children to identify with them. By the end, children will feel they know the twelve-year-old girl who learns that she has been "hired out," away from her family, and the boy who tells his mother that next year he is "gon' run away to freedom."

This readable, well-researched book uses primary sources to paint an accurate picture of the South on the eve of the Civil War. Period recipes, poems, songs, toys, riddles, and games are included, as well as references to Dickens's A Christmas Carol and John Brown and Harper's Ferry. The resulting account is rich with possibilities for further discussion. DAPHNE MUSE

The Indian Way: Learning to Communicate with Mother Earth

Gary McLain ◆ Michael Taylor and Gary McLain

Native American

1994 (1990), Peter Smith Publisher Inc., ✳ Series

Thirteen moons mark the progress of the year and the cycle of the seasons. For each of these thirteen moons, Gary McLain shares with us one of the special full moon stories he heard as a child from Grandpa Iron, a Northern Arapaho Medicine Man. Like many grandfathers, Grandpa Iron was fond of telling stories to the children, who were as eager to listen: "All us kids would sit in a circle around the old potbelly stove in Grandpa and Grandma Iron's long house and listen intently to the stories of wisdom the old man had to tell." Adhering to a familiar ritual, he would burn a few small pine needles for a purifying smoke. Then he would begin one of his full moon stories.

The stories Grandpa Iron tells are rich in traditional Native values concerning the proper relationship of human beings with the earth and all living creatures. From the story for the time of the "Moon When the Snow Blows Like Spirits in the Wind," Grandpa Iron "told us we should respect everything that is alive. He taught us we should realize that our Mother, the Earth, is alive and that if we respect her, she will respect and take care of us."

Each of Grandpa Iron's stories inspires the listener to recognize the simple, but profound truths of our delicate bond with the earth and all who live on her. If we truly hear these stories, we gain a new respect for much of what we all too often take for granted—food, clothing, shelter, water, and the very air we breathe. Such poetic images as water being "the blood of our Mother Earth" without which no life can exist remind us of the fragile web of Life. In "Moon of Frost Sparkling in the Sun," Grandpa Iron tells of the excesses of those who do not honor this "Circle of Life" and how dishonoring this Circle leads to spiritual and physical illness, as it does for the greedy hunter who takes more deer than he needs.

Traditional moon stories, accompanied by activities, convey Native American values about the environment.

The concepts presented in these thirteen full-moon stories are given more concrete expression through a series of twenty activities included with this collection. Especially valuable for younger readers, these recommended projects allow one to put into practice the values shared by Grandpa Iron. Respect for the ecosystem includes raising plants, being aware of where our food comes from, respecting our parents and our elders, learning about the earth, treating nature with respect when going camping, sharing our time and talents with others, making a medicine wheel, and even participating in a sweat lodge ceremony and experiencing a vision quest.

A bibliography of reading materials for learning more about Native American beliefs supplements the

stories and the activities. The atmospheric painting s by McLain and illustrations by Michael Taylor complement the tone of the book, which, true to its environmental theme, has been printed on recycled paper. VICTOR SCHILL

The Princess Who Lost Her Hair: An Akamba Legend

📘 Tololwa M. Mollel ✐ Charles Reasoner

African, Akamba, East African

1992, Troll Associates, ✳ Audio Cassette, Series

An African tale about kindness that provides much helpful background material. This story is retold by Tololwa M. Mollel, a Maasai from Tanzania, who has made a name for himself setting traditional African folktales into lyrical English prose. It tells of a princess who is beautiful but haughty and too proud of her lovely hair. One morning, a bird asks for a few strands of hair to line her nest, and the princess rudely refuses. The bird warns that she will regret her unkindness.

A drought comes and when the winds blow, they take away the princess's beautiful hair. She is ashamed to be seen without it, but none of the king's magicians or wise men can help her. Muoma, a beggar boy, has dreamed of a magical bird who can restore the princess's hair. When Muoma approaches the king, he is angrily sent away.

Muoma sets out anyway to follow his dream bird. Along the way, he shares his last food with a hungry ant, his last water with a thirsty flower, and his last energy with a desperate mouse. But it is not until he helps the princess learn kindness herself that her hair returns and the two are married.

Charles Reasoner's stylized illustrations are like elaborate cartoons with simple shapes and vivid, airbrushed colors. The faces are solemn and proud, the beggar's no less than the king's. The clothing and other small details are colorful, evoking Africa without strictly depicting the styles of any particular people. The scenes are believable, with just a touch of magic.

The story offers elements that will be familiar to children who have read several folktales: the haughty princess, the boy who is poor but wise, the shape-changing spirit. *Teachers may want to use this story to* open discussion about how different people often reach similar conclusions about the world, and how they tell stories that are at once global and local.

An afterword gives information about the Akamba people of Kenya and the importance of rain to their way of life. It includes a map showing where on the continent of Africa the Akamba live, a description of the calabash, and the beginnings of a discussion of the meaning of the tale. Troll Associates' Legends of the World Series offers folktales from Native American, Hispanic, Asian, and African cultures in colorful paperbacks. CYNTHIA A. BILY

Dancing Rainbow: A Pueblo Boy's Story

📘✐ Evelyn Clarke Mott

Native American, Pueblo

1996, Cobblehill Books, ✳ Series

The powerful and clarifying lens of photographer Evelyn Clarke Mott offers young readers a chance to visit a traditional Tewa Indian Feast Day celebration honoring St. John. It is a day of dance, dinner, and fun. Curt, a young Pueblo Indian, and his grandfather, Andy, lead us through the various rituals, dances, and ceremonies of this celebration, and the distinct features of the Tewa tribe within the larger Pueblo nation are highlighted. For example, Tewa terms appear in the text and, in the beginning of the book, the grandfather's name is written in the Tewa alphabet.

A powerful, revealing photo essay about a Tewa Indian boy and his grandfather sharing a traditional Feast Day Festival.

The reader also learns that Tewa children are taught to dance as soon as they learn to walk. Curt's pride in being Tewa, in the knowledge passed on from his ancestors, and his choice to travel the path of his grandfather, speak eloquently about a people determined to honor the best of their spirit in order to celebrate "The Great Spirit."

Their rituals, which include pouring salt on people's heads to keep away bad spirits, and face painting, are discussed in a very straightforward manner. The photographs capture the dignity and poise of the elders, the vibrant and colorful costumes of the dancers, and the beauty of Pueblo country.

Although Curt's ancestors were farmers who instilled a reverence for Mother Earth in his family, most of them now work at businesses outside the

339

pueblo. With too few books focusing on contemporary Native American life and traditions, this is an important book for teachers to bring into the classroom. However, although *Dancing Rainbow* brings us another step closer to a better understanding of contemporary Native American culture, there remains an urgent need for books that portray Native Americans as the bankers, teachers, writers, artists, architects, and tradespeople many of them are today. DAPHNE MUSE

Come On Into My Tropical Garden: Poems for Children

Grace Nichols   Caroline Binch
Caribbean American
1990, Lippincott,   Nichols, Grace, *A Caribbean Dozen: Poems from Caribbean Poets.*

This provocative collection features twenty-eight poems on issues many of us must deal with every day. Set largely in the Caribbean, these poems touch on developmental issues of identity, self-confidence, abuse, and parental neglect.

One of the most powerful poems in the book, "The Fastest Belt in Town," argues against corporal punishment. Many of the poems are about the interdependence of humans, animals, and the rest of nature. *There should be some discussion regarding abuse before this poem is read. Some of the poems are written in dialect. Many of the poems are environmentally focused, and I would recommend using the book in tandem with others on the need to rescue, restore, and preserve our planet.* DAPHNE MUSE

In this collection of twenty-eight Caribbean poems, children explore pressing social issues.

The Hummingbird King: A Guatemalan Legend

Argentina Palacios   Felipe Davalos
Hispanic, Mayan, Native American
1993, Troll Associates, ✳ Audio Cassette, CD-ROM, Series, Spanish

Kukul (beautiful feather) is destined to be chief of his city-state. Protected from danger by a feather from a guardian hummingbird, Kukul becomes a compassionate and successful chief. But his jealous uncle, who wishes to become chief, steals the feather.

Unprotected without the feather, Kukulis killed by an arrow from his uncle's bow.

Kukul's body is changed into a beautiful quetzal bird, the symbol of freedom. This colorfully illustrated picture book brings young readers into the Mayan world and culture. The colorful illustrations enhance the understanding of Mayan nobility, physiognomy, dress, and appearance. The author's note at the end of the story describes the mystical and spiritual importance of the quetzal bird to the Mayan people of Guatemala. BYRON RUSKIN

A chief is killed and is transformed into a quetzal bird—a Mayan symbol of freedom.

Fun With Chinese Festivals

Tan Huay Peng   Leong Kum Chuen
Asian, Chinese
1991, Heian International, Inc.

A perfect book for an introduction to Chinese festivals for children ten years old and up. Whether it is the lunar New Year Festival, the Lantern festival, the Dragon Boat festival, or the Seven Sisters festival (among the many listed), the reader will find out all sorts of fun facts about the beliefs and customs of the Chinese culture. The book includes the added bonus of introducing many Chinese words and the puns associated with them. While the writer uses the Cantonese dialect, the festivals are, of course, common to all Chinese, wherever they may be living. There are also many witty illustrations.
NAOMI WAKAN

A great introduction to Chinese festivals.

Piñatas and Paper Flowers: Holidays of the Americas in English and Spanish

Lila Perl   Victoria De Larrea
Hispanic
1985 (1983), Houghton Mifflin Company,
✳ Bilingual English/Spanish

This bilingual (English-Spanish) book compares festival beliefs and practices in English-speaking and Hispanic countries in the Americas. Whether the holiday is specific to one place, as, for example, El Dia de San Juan Bautista in Puerto Rico, or is celebrated by

340

people everywhere, such as the New Year Festival, readers will enjoy the accounts of the preparations and practices of eight popular holidays. While the festivals are mainly of Christian origin, native religions with such festivals as *Inti Raymi* in Peru are touched on. The line drawings, tinted in orange, are very attractive but do make the Americas seem to be one single ethnic group. This is a classic, still in print because of its unique coverage. NAOMI WAKAN

A classical bilingual explanation of how Spanish-speaking and English-speaking people of the Americas celebrate holidays.

The Spring of Butterflies and Other Chinese Folk Tales of China's Minority People

📖 Neil Philip (editor) (translated by Liyi He)
🖌 Pan Aiqing and Li Zhao
Asian, Chinese
1985, Lothrop, Lee & Shepard

The fourteen tales in this book come from minority groups, such as Tibetan, Tahi, Uighur, and Bai, living in China. First translated into Chinese and then

Fourteen tales from the Tibetan, Thai, Uighur, Bai, and other people living in China.

translated into English by Liyi He, the tales presented here are full of creatures, real and magical, including monkeys, cranes, dragons, winged horses, witches, wizards, and a magic golden fish. At the same time, the cultures and customs of the various cultures are illuminated in these traditional stories.

In "The Spring of Butterflies," a couple in love escape from Tyrant Wang by jumping into the Bottomless Pond. In "Green Dragon Pond," the Dragon King of the Dali Lake tries to capture the little daughter of the Dragon King of Dongting Lake. In "The Tibetan Envoy," Princess Wencheng's father sets impossible tasks for the envoys of the prince who wants her hand in marriage.

The stories are set against the dramatic and majestic Chinese landscape of towering mountains and magnificent palaces. The colorful illustrations also enhance the timeless beauty of the stories. Created by two Chinese artists who live in Beihai City, the paintings accurately reflect the origin of the stories. The readers of He's stories will get a glimpse into the

rich diversity of China, a country often thought of as monoethnic in nature. CATHY Y. KIM

Kwanzaa

📖 A. P. Porter 🖌 Bobby Van Buren
African American
1991, Carolrhoda Books, Inc., ✳ Series, 📕 Brady, April A., *Kwanzaa Karamu: Cooking and Crafts for a Kwanzaa Feast.*

In this outstanding book, A. P. Porter describes the origins of the African American holiday Kwanzaa, explains the seven principles or goals, and provides a great deal of insight into the

An insightful look at the history and culture surrounding Kwanzaa.

African heritage of African American people. It also provides a brief history of the early struggles of African Americans.

Colorful pencil sketches depict the African people who came to the United States as slaves. Other illustrations depict children making items used in the Kwanzaa celebration, other Kwanzaa articles, and families and friends taking part in the celebration.

A glossary of Swahili words used in the text and a separate listing of the seven principles are provided. Description of the items needed to celebrate Kwanzaa is included at the end of the book. The text is attractively laid out and easy to read. LINDA JOLIVET

Aida

📖 Leontyne Price 🖌 Leo and Diane Dillon
African American
1996 (1990), Harcourt Brace Jovanovich

This beautiful picture book adaptation of Verdi's opera *Aida* captures all of the grace, courage, and nobility of its eponymous Ethiopian princess. It is exceptional for Leontyne Price to write this book, for she is the most famous Aida in history; she notes in her afterword that Aida is part of her inner self, her closest character because, she says, "My skin was my costume." However, rather than read between the lines and lament the paucity of African roles in the operatic tradition, this book is a true celebration of one amazing woman.

Aida is an Ethiopian princess captured by the Egyptians. The two countries are at war, and many Ethiopians have been taken prisoner. While Aida

341

A masterful picture book adaptation of Verdi's opera about an Ethiopian princess.

does not reveal her true self to the Egyptians, they still sense a difference about her and give her an honored position of waiting on the Egyptian princess. Aida performs her duties well, gaining the respect of her master and of a handsome soldier. The soldier and Aida fall in love; not only is this forbidden because of their feuding countries, but the Egyptian princess also has her eyes on the soldier. After the Egyptians capture Aida's father, the King of Ethiopia, the war escalates, and both Aida and her lover have to choose either their love or their country. They both opt for their countries, and the soldier is sentenced to be buried alive. Aida sneaks into his crypt, and they die together.

Aida's courage and regal bearing are inspiring throughout this book. She is extremely ethical, grapples with difficult issues, and maintains loyalty to all throughout the story. Although an ancient Ethiopian, she is a truly modern woman and a won-

derful role model for young women, as she was for Ms. Price. The art captures all of her beauty and adds its own musicality and regality to this well-written book. Luminescent acrylics are used on marbleized paper to create an Art Deco effect. Every other page has smaller drawings in the upper margins that show sequential details of the unfolding plot. Overall, this book is masterful. Readers young and old will enjoy this story of a very strong woman. LISA FAIN

The Sacred Harvest: Ojibway Wild Rice Gathering

⬛ Gordon Regguinti and Carly Bordeau
✏ Dale Kakkak
Native American, Ojibway
1992, Lerner Publications Company, ✳ Series

Eleven-year-old Glen Jackson Jr. goes with his father to gather wild rice, the sacred food of the Ojibway in the Leech Lake reservation. Glen learns to push the boat gently through the dense stalks of wild rice. His father carefully shows his son how to choose the rice that is ready for harvest, telling him that the grain becomes dark brown when it is ripe.

The next day, with Glen Jr. guiding the canoe through the tall grasses with his long pole, the two go out. Using two wooden knockers, Glen Sr. fills the bottom of the canoe with rice from the ripened stalks. They finally stop and clean some of the grain from dry, loose leaves and stems. They see Glen's uncle, Steve, and his ricing partner, Tony, and they speak of past ricing seasons.

As they start again the next day, Glen Jr. tries to harvest the rice while his father guides the boat. It takes him some time to learn to use the wooden knockers well. They bank their canoe, unload their equipment, and bag their rice. They have harvested over 100 pounds. At landing docks further down the river, people stop their rice bagging to visit with old friends and share "ricing" lore. Many of the ricers have been coming to the area for generations, often driving more than four hours to gather the sacred grain.

An Ojibway father helps his eleven-year-old son experience his first wild rice harvest.

Glen Jr. and his father head to Grandmother Susan's house to parch the rice in order to loosen the grains from the husks. While others are tending to this stage of the process, Glen Jr. will get to play with his cousins. Part of the process involves jigging or dancing on the rice in moccasins.

The author provides clear cultural and historical details illuminating how the Ojibway harvest and process the rice, and how important this tradition is to the Ojibway people. Dale Kakkak's photographs capture the strong family ties and the extraordinary beauty of the environment. NOLA HADLEY

Kinaalda: A Navajo Girl Grows Up

⬛ ✏ Monty Roessel
Native American, Navajo
1993, Lerner Publications Company, ✳ Series,
📖 Braine, Susan, *Drumbeat Heartbeat: A Collection of the Powwow.*

Thirteen-year-old Celinda McKelvey is preparing for her Kinaalda, a Navajo coming-of-age ceremony that usually takes place when a girl has had her first menstrual period. The Dine believe that the Kinaalda ceremony was given to them by the Holy People so that women could have children. During this two- to four-day event, a girl learns about her culture and the responsibilities of a family.

The story reflects the respect shown females in

contemporary indigenous societies. Menstruation, for example, is considered powerful and important, making a young woman a central figure within a family for a few days.

This photographic essay takes the reader through Celinda's process of preparing for and experiencing her Kinaalda. Celinda lives in Bloomfield, New Mexico, but her family returns to their grandmother's house on the reservation for the ceremony. Guests arrive, prayers are sung, and Celinda is dressed in a traditional "rug dress." She wears turquoise necklaces and buckskin moccasins that wrap around her calves.

A photographic essay of a Navajo coming-of-age celebration believed to mold girls into women.

Ceremonially, Celinda's mother "molds" her into a beautiful, strong woman. When the molding is finished, Celinda runs out of the hogan to the east, where the new day begins. She must run every day of the ceremony. After the first run, Celinda must prepare a cornmeal cake which is baked in corn husks. As the cake is cooking through the night, Celinda must stay awake to hear prayers that introduce her to the Holy People who will protect her throughout her life. She must sit still with a straight back throughout the prayers. In the morning, she runs again at dawn.

When Celinda returns, it is time to cut her cake. The author writes, "It is believed that if the cake is still gooey when the sun rises, the young girl will have a hard life." Celinda is relieved to find out that her cake is perfect, and she cuts it into large pieces for the guests. After she is "molded" for the last time, she can eat and finally rest. The ceremony complete, Celinda says "I know I don't look any different, but I feel different. I feel like a Navajo. Just like my mom and my aunts and my grandmother."

This book is a vital addition to the Native Americans Today: We Are Still Here Series. It teaches about respect between generations and passing on community customs and spiritual traditions. *It is highly recommended for teenage and pre-teen girls of all cultures who are working to develop a positive identification with their changing bodies as well as for Native American girls who are interested in learning more about their roles in indigenous societies.* NOLA HADLEY

Day of Delight: A Jewish Sabbath in Ethiopia

▢ Maxine Rose Schur ✎ Brian Pickney
Ethiopian, Jewish
1994, Penguin Books/Dial Books

This enjoyable and informative picture book follows the story of a family as it prepares for the Jewish Sabbath. Maxine Rose Schur writes the tale from the point of view of Menelik, a young Ethiopian boy who lives with his family in the hills of Ethiopia in a traditional Jewish village of farmers and blacksmiths.

The detailed text and Brian Pickney's exquisite illustrations introduce the reader to the villagers' daily tasks. The farmers, for instance, must cope with drought and locusts the blacksmiths forge sickles over a hot flame and each family maintains a home

An enjoyable picture book chronicling the celebration of the Jewish Sabbath in an Ethiopian village.

with no running water, a horsehair broom, and a dung cookfire. Ms. Schur weaves many Ethiopian words into the story, helping to evoke a culture in which soap for the bath is made from a plant called "soapwort," a fire is grown with a "bellows," and a "ragball" is used for play.

The book provides a look at an intriguing mingling of cultures we might not ordinarily associate with each other. ROSA E. WARDER

Hanukkah: The Festival of Lights

▢ Maida Silverman ✎ Carolyn S. Ewing
Jewish
1987, Simon & Schuster Children's,
▥ Greenfield, Howard, *Chanukah.*

This is a recounting of the events in Ancient Jerusalem that the holiday of Hanukkah commemorates. When the army of King Antiochus destroys the Temple of Jerusalem, it sets in motion three years of violence between the invaders and the Jews who worshipped there. Undaunted by the larger numbers of soldiers, Mattathias and Judah the Maccabee lead the resistance until finally Judah manages to lay siege to

A clearly written and well illustrated book about the origins of Hanukkah.

343

the city. The siege is successful; the temple's menorah is recovered and rekindled. Somehow the flames burn for eight days though there is only oil for one day. This is the miracle of Hanukkah.

Most books about Hanukkah spend little time on the holiday's origin, concentrating instead on its celebration. Here, however, the story is told in clear language that captures the sadness of the defiled temple, and the anger that fuels the violence that follows. The emotion of the event is clear even if some details are vague. Antiochus is not identified (he was Greek), but he and his soldiers are simply "the enemy." Besieging a city is not described in the text , and young readers will need to have this military tactic explained to them in order to understand how the Jews were able to reenter Jerusalem and reclaim their place of worship.

Carolyn S. Ewing's illustrations are evocative, each framed by pillars suggesting the temple and several depicting the violence only alluded to in the text. The struggle for the temple was harsh. *This retelling is appropriate for grades 4-6.*

Chanukah (1976) by Howard Greenfeld, also interprets the events that led to the miracle of the menorah, but without illustrations. Its language is clear, but the book's layout lacks appeal. JANIS O'DRISCOLL

When Thunders Spoke

🖐 Virginia Driving Hawk Sneve   🖋 Oren Lyons-Onandaga

Dakota Sioux, Native American

1993 (1974), University of Nebraska Press

Fifteen-year-old Norman Two Bulls collects agates on sacred Thunder Butte to trade for candy at the local trading post on his Dakota reservation. When Norman's grandfather has a dream that something good will happen if Norman searches on the dangerous west side of the butte, Norman makes the hazardous climb to appease the older man. After falling down a steep embankment, Norman discovers a sacred coup stick that was used by Dakota warriors in the old days to touch their enemies in a courageous act of valor. His grandfather insists that the stick is *wakan*, or holy, and urges Norman to hang it up on the wall and not disturb it. The coup stick proves a continuing source of contention, however, as Norman's mother, a recently converted Christian, disagrees with his

A Dakota boy discovers an ancient relic and affirms his Native American identity.

father, who believes in the power of the relic.

There is a strong supernatural element in this story as the coup stick's appearance changes with each passing day and unexplained things begin to happen. Norman finds some large agates and the courage to stand up to the trader he works for, insisting on being paid in cash. Norman's father is promoted to foreman on the reservation's ranch. But when the trader tries to involve the Two Bulls family in an agate-mining scheme that will destroy the sacred butte, Norman learns the power of being able to "honor the old ways even as you live in the new."

Sneve has written a timeless story that successfully captures the flavor of life on a Dakota reservation and emphasizes the theme of the elder as culture bearer, passing on the old ways to a younger generation. Sneve is also one of the few writers who brings the contemporary world of Native Americans to young readers. Dakota phrases and explanations for traditional practices are scattered throughout the book, creating an authentic insider's perspective. The greedy trader and insensitive white tourist are one-dimensional, but their failure to understand the importance of sacred land is certainly plausible.

Although the writing is sometimes stiff and the story ends rather abruptly, this novella effectively conveys how the past reaches into the present and the role of tradition for many Native peoples. The black-and-white pencil drawings are rich with cultural details and illuminate the spirit of the story. LAURI JOHNSON

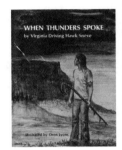

Red Eggs and Dragon Boats

🖐 Carol Stepanchuk   🖋 Various sources

Asian, Chinese

1993, Pacific View Press

This very accessible book covers five major Chinese festivals, their customs, beliefs, and recipes. The layout, with explanatory sidebars, is attractive, and the facts are clearly stated. This book's major attraction is its splendid illustrations done by Chinese folk artists, which reflect the local life of the region

This accesible illustrated book observes five Chinese festivals.

from which the artists come. While the book can be read with pleasure by ten-year-olds and up, the younger readers will respond to these childlike paintings. Dragon boat dumplings, long life noodles, and almond and sesame cookies are a few of the mouth-watering recipes provided. This book, with its readily available information, will appeal to teachers and students. NAOMI WAKAN

Doesn't Fall Off His Horse

🔲 ✒ Virginia A. Stroud
Cherokee, Kiowa, Native American
1994, Dial Books for Young Readers

In recording the story of her great-grandfather's daring boyhood horse raid on the Comanche, Virginia Stroud, a Cherokee author and illustrator, gives us a picture of life for the Kiowa on the southern plains at the turn of the nineteenth century. The story starts as Saygee, a young girl, waits to ask her grandfather Steve for a story. Rather than interrupt his reflections upon the earth, she waits patiently, thinking about his age and experiences as well as all that has happened to the Indian people. Grandpa Steve welcomes her and pulls out a leopard-skin quiver and states his Indian name, Doesn't Fall Off His Horse. The quiver was a prized possession and very rare, but it didn't help him make a coup. He explains to his granddaughter that coup is a very serious and dangerous form of playing tag. The purpose is to embarrass or dishonor an enemy by catching him off guard. Saygee's grandfather goes on to tell a story of a daring boyhood raid to steal horses from the Comanche camped south of his Kiowa encampment.

An exciting tale based on the true story of the Cherokee author's great-grandfather's daring boyhood raid on the Comanche.

Despite the silence and skill of the young men, they are discovered — Saygee's grandfather is wounded but manages to make it back to his camp. Grandpa Steve is taken to the medicine woman's tent for healing where he gradually recovers. The young men are admonished by the elders. Their deed, although very brave, could have put the whole encampment at risk. Because Grandpa Steve was able to remain on his horse and return home, however, he was given his Indian name.

The illustrations are action-packed, full of activity, and the story is suspenseful and exciting. The text also conveys Kiowa values and culture in both the present and the past. Stroud has won many awards for her paintings and has been featured in numerous magazines. Her bright pastel paintings move the reader clearly through the drama of this story. Of her illustrations, Stroud says, "Art is a way for our culture to survive . . . perhaps the only way. More than anything, I want to become a visual orator, to share the oldest of Indian traditions." She certainly has succeeded. NOLA HADLEY

Portraits of Native Americans: Photographs from the 1904 Louisiana Purchase Exposition

🔲 The Chicago Field Museum ✒ Charles Carpenter
Native American
1994, The New Press

Portraits of Native American Indians is a postcard book of twenty-three photographs selected from the Chicago Field Museum's collection, taken from the 1904 St. Louis exposition commemorating the centennial of the Louisiana Purchase. The exposition presenters recreated an

A rich set of postcards portraying Native American people and culture at the time of the 1904 Louisisana Purchase.

Indian reservation that housed hundreds of Native Americans representing about twenty tribes. Indians went about their daily lives among the teepees, and there were elaborate exhibits depicting Native American culture, way of life, occupations. Dressed in traditional clothes, Native American women beaded floral designs on looms, wove baskets, and demonstrated day-to-day activity characteristic of an Indian reservation. Charles Carpenter, at that time the chief photographer for the Field Museum, set up a makeshift studio where he photographed the Indians, who posed dressed in full regalia. He also did photographic studies of tribal arts and crafts.

Carpenter's invaluable photographs document the diversity and complexity of Native American tribes; the history of the Native American experience at the beginning of the twentieth century; the structure of Native American self-rule on the reservations, with emphasis on the social, religious, educational, and daily life of the Indians; Native American artifacts; and much more. This sampling

345

of Carpenter's rich collection provides an engaging historical experience and a valuable addition to any collection of multicultural, artistic, photographic, or historical material. MELVINA AZAR DAME

African Art Portfolio, An Illustrated Introduction: Masterpieces from the Eleventh to Twentieth Centuries

Carol Thompson   Various Sources
African American
1993, The New Press,   Penney, David, *North American Art Portfolio*; The Brooklyn Museum, *Egyptian Art Portfolio*.

To coincide with "Africa 95," The Royal Academy of London assembled an unprecedented exhibition of African art representing the continent as a whole from prehistory to the present. This portfolio comes with twenty-four unbound color plates of African masterpieces from the eleventh to the twentieth centuries and a booklet. The selected images, drawn from exhibition catalogues published by the Center for African Art (now the Museum for African Art) in New York City, represent nine of the fifty-three countries on the continent of Africa. The collection includes ceremonial masks of cloth, wood, gold; figures of wood, ivory, bronze, terracotta; furniture; and portraits. The booklet provides background information on each image in well-illustrated essays, and is divided into four broad areas: 1) works of art linking the past, present, and future; 2) art of Africa's ancient cities and kingdoms; 3) forms and uses of African masks; 4) African artists' use of materials, technology, abstraction, and naturalism. Extensive footnotes and references are provided for further research and study.

An illustrated introduction to African American masterpieces from the eleventh to the twentieth century.

It is necessary to understand the spiritual, practical, and historical meaning of African art in order to appreciate it. This portfolio will surely change the way we look at African art. It will persuade the reader to accept African art on its own terms rather than according to the standards of the Western art world, to recognize and appreciate these objects for the masterpieces they are.
MELVINA AZAR DAME

Sunpainters, Eclipse of the Navajo Sun

Baje Whitethorne
Native American, Navaho
1994, Northland Publishing Company

Kii Leonard and his grandfather witness a solar eclipse. As the world of the Navajo reservation darkens, Kii Leonard hears his grandfather tell him the story of Na'ach'aahii, also known as the Little People or children of the rainbow—those mythical creatures who come from the Four Directions with their ladders, pots of paint, and brushes to repaint the colors of the world. Eventually the hogan brightens and Kii Leonard can see that the whole world is indeed brightly awash with vivid color. He gives thanks to the Na'ach'aahii for their beautiful colors and to Pipa, his grandfather, for the story of the little painters.

The character of Kii Leonard is a composite of author / illustrator Whitethorne as a child and his own son, Blaine. Through the text of the story Whitethorne is remembering a similar incident that he experienced with his grandfather. Both plot and text

An imaginative book set on a Navajo reservation that features the story of Na'ach'aahii, the children of the rainbow.

lend realism to a very imaginative story. They explicitly describe life on the Navajo reservation from family relationships, the hogan, clothing, and foods, to the physical environment around the main characters' hogan.

Kii Leonard learns the value of sitting, observing, and waiting quietly with his own thoughts and imagination. He learns to respect the earth, and learns about balance and harmony as he gives thanks and prayers at the end of the eclipse.

The vivid paintings by Whitethorne are playful and dramatically illustrate the engaging text. The subject matter is good for those with established reading skills and is well suited for reading aloud.

This book would be nice to add to a unit on southwestern history, Indian culture, or ecology of the southwest. It would also be very effective for art students or children who are just learning to recognize colors. The illustrations will quickly activate young imaginations. In fact, this book would be a wonderful way to add cultural diversity to a unit on physical science about the solar system and eclipses, or to teaching very young children about colors. Older children will also enjoy looking for the hidden miniature Navajo village hidden in each illustration.

I would recommend combiniong this very imaginative book with another story for young readers about the Navajo, Red Ribbons for Emma, *which presents contemporary tribal struggles over land rights and the role of Emma Yazzie in that struggle. Sharon Burch's audiotape recordings* The Blessing Ways *and* Yazzie Girl *would make excellent background for the unit. Both are available from Canyon Records (4143 N. 16th Street, Phoenix, Arizona 85016).*
NOLA HADLEY

Ininatig's Gift of Sugar: Traditional Native Sugarmaking

Laura Waterman Wittstock, Foreword by Michael Dorris ✒ Dale Kakkak

Native American, Ojibway

1993, Lerner Publications, ✳ Series,

Braine, Susan, *Drumbeat Heartbeat: A Collection of the Powwow.*

To help the Ojibway survive the end of a harsh winter, Ininatig, "the man tree," gave people the gift of his sweet, dark, thick syrup. He taught them how to cut his skin and to collect the syrup. Families "now had enough food to keep them strong until the ice on the lake broke and there would be fish. The man tree had saved their lives." Now, every spring, the Anishinabe elders give thanks to the maple tree.

Ininatig's Gift of Sugar: Traditional Native Sugarmaking is a picture book that tells of one contemporary elder, Porky, who runs a sugarbush camp by Lake Independence in Maple Plain, Minnesota. Before camp starts Porky must check to see that he has enough metal taps, plastic bags, filters, and storage and boiling barrels. The trees must be thanked before the tap-

In a highly recommended book, an Ojibway elder gives thanks to the maple trees for the syrup that helps his people survive the winter.

ping begins. Once the trees are ready to be tapped, people begin arriving at the camp. Porky invites a busload of students from the city to learn how to take care of the woods and how to tap trees.

The students also learn how to make syrup and sugar. To make sugar, a thick syrup is boiled in a smaller bucket and then poured into a small hand-hewn wooden trough where it is stirred until it changes into pure maple sugar. Before the syrup is quite ready to be poured into the sugar-making trough, it is used to make candy.

Eventually, it is time for the children to return to their bus and go back to the city. When at last the sap stops running, Porky gives gifts of sugar to his many helpers and they hold a feast in their camp. They thank the trees once again for their gifts.

This book is highly recommended. Photographs included in the book illustrate in detail the entire process. The book complements other recommended books about the Ojibway. *This book would work well in a unit with other spring ecological or naturalist activities.* NOLA HADLEY

American Indian Tools and Ornaments

Evelyn Wolfson ✒ Smithsonian

Native American

1981, David McKay Company, Inc., Freedman, Russell, *Buffalo Hunt;* Whitney, Alex, *American Indian Clothes and How to Make Them;* Wolfson, Evelyn, *American Indian Utensils;* Wolfson, Evelyn, *American Indian Habitats.*

This is a history of Native American tools and jewelry making as well as a hands-on, how-to book for children. Chapters on using traditional implements and methods to craft these items are the second part of the book. Photographs of ancient tools and jewelry as well as photos of modern Native Americans actually crafting these items will be of interest to children. A bibliography is included listing other books on Native American crafts and bead work.

A useful book about how to make Indian tools and jewelry with bone and shell.

Wolfson presents diagrams and archival photographs of Native Americans using these implements and wearing the ornaments described. Other photographs depict Native Americans using tools for traditional tasks. Further chapters include how to find and clean bones and shells to make these projects. Wooden dowels can be substituted in place of bones.

These books can be used along with books on sign language and body painting for enjoyable hands-on activities that give students a sense of participating in the cultures of Native American tribes. Russell Freedman's book, Buffalo Hunt, *can also be used to find motifs and examples of painted buffalo hides used for clothing and dwellings. These can be used as backdrops for a display of Native American crafts made by children using the traditional tools and methods. This gives the children the feel of actually participating in the cultures of these peoples. These items can also be used as props and backdrops for Native American storytelling.*

Wolfson has written two other books: American Indian Utensils *and* American Indian Habitats, *also for children. These books also give instructions for making items using traditional materials and tools. These books would make interesting classroom or home projects for history fairs. Another book by Alex Whitney,* American Indian Clothes and How to Make Them, *would be useful for projects with younger children.*
ELAINE P. GOLEY

A Boy Becomes a Man at Wounded Knee

Ted Wood and Wanbli Numpa Afraid of Hawk

Native American

1995 (1992), Walker Publishing, Keegan, Marcia, *Pueblo Boy.*

Written in collaboration with an eight-year-old Native American, *A Boy Becomes a Man at Wounded Knee* tells a story of mending the tragedy of Wounded Knee, South Dakota. Wanbli Numpa Afraid of Hawk is an Oglala Lakota who lives with his family on the Cheyenne River Reservation in South Dakota. He has grown up hearing stories of how his great-grandfather was present at the horrible massacre of Wounded Knee. He has learned from medicine men that this horrible battle broke the sacred hoop of

Wanbli journeys with other Lakota to Wounded Knee seeking tribal unity.

unity for the Lakota and can be mended only when the Lakota have traveled the path once traveled by their ancestors five times in five years, ending on the hundredth anniversary of Wounded Knee.

Wanbli Numpa joins his father in this difficult trial. The book is based on Wanbli Numpa's journal and recounts the difficult journey he insisted he take with his people, the pain through which he passes to accomplish his goal. Although few children

will have shared this experience, they will find it fascinating. They also will understand Wanbli's mother's concerns as she fusses over his keeping warm, getting enough sleep and eating well.

It is essential that these books be available to children, for too often their reading is limited to myths and legends from the Native American past. By discovering the lives of contemporary Native Americans, readers find their stereotypes of Native peoples challenged. NANCY HANSEN-KRENING

Five Heavenly Emperors

Song Nan Zhang

Asian, Chinese

1994, Tundra Books, Inc.

"Children's Books as Works of Art" is the slogan for Canadian publisher Tundra Books, Inc. The publisher's commitment to elegance in children's literature is evident in *Five Heavenly Emperors.*

Author Song Nan Zhang's first book for Tundra, *A Little Tiger in the Chinese Night: An Autobiography in Art*, told of growing up in China. It won Canada's Mr. Christie's Award for best children's book (ages 8-11) in 1994. *Five Heavenly Emperors*, Zhang's second book, is a beautiful picture book which is also geared to children ages eight and up. This Canadian willingness

Simple retellings of thirteen ancient Chinese creation myths.

to develop picture books for older children contrasts with American publishers who tend to lump all beautifully illustrated books together and call them K-3 picture books regardless of content. It is a shame that so many American publishers throw beauty out the window for readers over the age of eight.

In *Five Heavenly Emperors*, Zhang shares the creation myths of his homeland. The simple retellings of these complex myths make the text easily understandable by children. A "Who's Who in Heaven" is appended to the stories for ready reference. The book also features a Tai Chi map and a short glossary that shows the historic development and modern use of Chinese writing.

All this aside, the best part of the book is Zhang's incredible artwork. His paintings, inspired by ancient Chinese pottery, sculpture, and paintings, are lovely. Curved lines in the shape of swirling ribbons, contorted mythological creatures, billowing cloud formations, coiled snake tails, and gnarled tree branches add a sense of graceful movement to the illustrations. An underlying tension in the art makes each picture look as if it has only stopped for a moment and will soon flow off the pages. SANDRA KELLY

Ethnic and Gender Stereotyping in Recent Disney Animation

A. Waller Hastings

ENORMOUSLY POPULAR AMONG CHILDREN, yet reviled by many adults for its effect on children's literature, Disney animation remains a dominant force in the popular culture of today's children. Love them or hate them, it is impossible to ignore the books, films, and associated merchandising that confront us in fast food restaurants and department stores, on television and bookstore shelves, as well as in the movie theater. Disney's pervasive, integrated marketing of its product and high production values make its choices about what to depict, and how to depict it, a particular problem. From *Snow White* (1937) through *Beauty and the Beast* (1991), Disney's versions of fairy tales have become the "original" versions for millions of children, and more people today probably associate *The Jungle Book* and *Winnie the Pooh* with Disney rather than Kipling or Milne.

The advent of the video recorder in the early 1980s significantly raised the stakes in the battle for children's minds. Carefully managed video releases more efficiently recycle older "classic" Disney products into homes, where easy availability promotes multiple exposures to each film. Disney dominance was further cemented by an aggressive new creative team, which developed a string of hits beginning with *The Little Mermaid* (1989).

Having been challenged by members of the Arab American, African American, Native American, and feminist communities, Disney seems to be trying to be somewhat more sensitive to blatant sexism and racism, which were very much apparent in its earlier films, books, and merchandise. Disney insiders told the *New York Times* that the company "is making a concerted effort to address many different racial and ethnic themes" (Sharkey, 22). While the Native Americans of *Pocahontas* are still not as demeaning as the stereotyped red men of *Peter Pan* (1953), Disney still needs to work a more accurate portrayal of people of color into its products.

Many critics and educators are hostile to Disney films because of past distortions of history and literature. The films' commercial success also works against attempts to address multicultural concerns. But as the dominant force in a major segment of the culture industry, Disney carries too much influence to allow offending depictions to go unprotested.

Perhaps the most egregious ethnic stereotyping in modern Disney animation is the depiction of the Arab world in *Aladdin* (1992). Criticism of the film on these grounds is justified, as it employs most of the cinematic clichés about the Arab world that Hollywood has developed over the years. *Aladdin* hit American theaters with an opening number that said inhabitants of the fictional city of Agrabah would "cut off your ears / If they don't like your face / It's barbaric, but hey, it's home." The lyrics were judged so offensive to Islam that the film was withdrawn from distribution in at least one Moslem country, Indonesia (Sharman, 13), and drew protests from the Arab American Anti-discrimination Committee. The words to the song were modified prior to *Aladdin*'s video release in the United States. Astonishingly, lyricist Alan Menken had already prepared alternate lyrics because he was concerned about the potentially offending lines, but the studio had gone with the original version (Hajari and Hardy).

Even the revised lyrics retain the reference to the land being "barbaric," but shift the reference for the barbarity from the people to the intense heat and sand. However, merely cleaning up the opening lines was not enough to eliminate Arab stereotyping from *Aladdin*. The merchant who sings those lyrics and frames the story is a con artist, eager to cheat the unsuspecting customer. As such, he is reminiscent of the Middle Eastern trader of the earlier Disney short, *The Small One* (1978). Jafar, the evil vizier, employs Gazeem, "a humble thief who comments that he "had to slit a few throats" to get the magic scarab that leads to the lamp. The palace guards chasing Aladdin through the marketplace boast, "I'll have your hands for a trophy." The hero himself is a petty thief. In short, Arab society is presented as violent, cruel, corrupt, and exotic.

The marketplace is peopled with just about every strange "Oriental" performer known to Hollywood convention: a fakir on a bed of nails (aren't magic-making fakirs supposed to be Hindu, anyway?), another walking on hot coals, a sword swallower, and a fire eater. Fascination with the harem manifests itself in Jasmine's complaints of luxurious captivity, as she plays with her "pet" in lush gardens by a dancing fountain. This pattern, alternating negative depictions of cruelty and violence with the exotic, is characteristic of Western cultural imperialism.

Such depictions of the East as "irrational, enchanted, and medieval" do not invite the viewer to attain a more genuine understanding of that culture but may support severe political measures against Arab culture (Sharman, 15). This becomes a more than significant concern when one reflects that *Aladdin* was in development against the background of the Persian

Gulf War, when Western powers united to bomb one of the most important cities of historical Islamic culture.

Disney's next feature, *The Lion King* (1994), seemed unlikely to generate complaints about stereotyping. It was, after all, a movie about the African plains, with no human characters. Even the inevitable anthropomorphism involved in the beast fable genre was at a minimum; unlike the "animal" characters of *Robin Hood* (1973), the lions and hyenas of *The Lion King* walk on all fours and eat other animals. While the film proved enormously popular, becoming Disney's highest grossing film ever, it still came under attack for its politics. Christian fundamentalists questioned a New Age environmentalism that they saw underlying both *The Lion King* and *Pocahontas* (Roberts). At the other end of the political spectrum, Katha Pollitt challenged the film's "weirdly sincere defense of feudalism, primogeniture, and the divine right of kings."

It seems unlikely that Disney seriously proposed a return to the bad old days of the Middle Ages; rather, the film's echoes of Shakespearean tragedy—Klass called it "Hamlet with fur," (1) and the villainous Scar owes a great deal to Richard III—may account for this seemingly retrograde ideology. *The Lion King*'s emphasis on each individual's place in a naturally ordained hierarchy, the violation of which threatens the very survival of the society, however, does open it to conservative political interpretations.

When one adds the fact that the usurping forces appeared to some viewer to reflect racist and homophobic assumptions, the scene was set for another controversy over Disney stereotyping. The false king, Scar, bears the marks of the effetely intellectual, while his hyena henchmen have been seen as underclass denizens of "the jungle equivalent of the inner city" (Schwartz). To save the lion society and prevent ecocatastrophe, these undigestible elements must be destroyed or banished.

To accept allegations of racism and homophobia in *The Lion King* requires that one accept that certain stereotyped characteristics sufficiently identify a character as black, Latino, or gay, even in the absence of any visual racial characteristics or overt homosexual behavior. This seems rather circular reasoning, since it means accepting that the stereotypes are valid in the first place. Allegations of negative stereotyping seem even less credible when one reflects that the film uses prominent African American actors to voice the admirable king, Mufasa, his wife, Sarabi, and the baboon holy man, Rafiki (James Earl Jones, Madge Sinclair, and Robert Guillame, respectively). Further, the film was scored by the openly homosexual Elton John. It thus appears stereotyping hardly depends on intent; indeed, the most insidious part of a negative stereotype is its capacity to affect depictions of certain groups without conscious thought.

Differential treatment of various characters does suggest that some stereotypical behaviors have found their way into the film despite some attempts to be culturally sensitive. Among the lions, the royal family all lack discernible accents, whether they are voiced by black or white actors. Only the languid, upper-class British tones of Scar (voiced by Jeremy Irons) depart from this norm. Years of *Masterpiece Theater* and other middle-brow cultural products have accustomed American audiences to see European accents as a mark of intellectual superiority, if not snobbery, sustaining complaints that the film may be anti-intellectual (Pollitt); it is possible that some viewers associate intellectualism with homosexuality, but surely this does not mean that any intellectual character must inevitable be gay.

The case for gay-bashing in the characterization of Scar seems to be this: He has an upper-class accent, is an intellectual, and has no mate. He taunts Mufasa early in the film by saying in a somewhat effeminate voice, "Oh, I shall practice my curtsey" and responds to Simba's innocent statement "You're so weird" with the rejoinder "You have no idea." A great deal of Scar's brooding persona reflects recent trends in depicting Shakespeare's Richard III, in which the king is played as a gay fascist. Could the character be gay? No doubt he could, if a creation of paint and light can be said to have sexuality. But in the absence of overt sexual behavior of any kind, it is unlikely that most viewers—child or adult—will perceive him as such. Anyone who can pick up on the alleged "gayness" already understands enough about the subtler indicators of sexual preference to

have made up his or her own mind, and is unlikely to be influenced either way by the film.

One other scene in the film may suggest a homophobic attitude on the part of the animators. In the climactic battle, Timon decoys the hyenas by performing a hula in full dress—a scene that was calculated as "the gag virtually guaranteed to bring down the house" (Daly, 20). That cross-dressing remains a major source of humor in our society may well reflect our own general unease with gender norms.

Similarly, the association of gang violence only with blacks and Latinos may say something about our cultural discomfort with race. The hyenas in *The Lion King* exhibit patterns of behavior consistent with gangs early in the film, when they torment the cub Simba who has wandered beyond the edge of his father's kingdom. While the African American voices of Mufasa and Sarabi are essentially deracinated, the hyenas Shenzi (voiced by Whoopi Goldberg) and Banzai (Cheech Marin) do exhibit certain ethnically specific speech patterns. At one point, for instance, Banzai says "¿Que pasa?" to cover for his accidental naming of Mufasa to Scar. It is certainly possible, then, for viewers to interpret the hyenas as members of an ethnic underclass.

To the extent that stereotypes operate in *The Lion King*, they reflect the ubiquity of such ideas in our society. Stereotyped behaviors appear ready-made to serve various characterization purposes here, in part, because the animators, working with characters they did not perceive of as belonging to a minority group, don't really have guidelines for understanding stereotypes and how they are created.

In *Pocahontas* (1995), on the other hand, awareness of the cultural minefield was present from the beginning. Studio animators were "in sensitivity training from the onset of production" (Sharkey, 22). Russell Means, the former Native American activist who voiced the film's Powhatan, told the *New York Times* that he initially found the film's script "full of stereotypes" and objected to some of the music (Sharkey, 22), but says of the finished picture that it "is the finest feature film ever done about American Indians in the history of Hollywood" (Lockhart and Smith, 25).

Reaction to the film among less obviously

self-interested Native Americans was mixed. Some found positive things to say, while retaining some suspicion of Disney stereotyping. For instance, Native American scholar and writer Paul Gunn Aleen said, "At least the little one will learn that this group of people had an effect on colonial life" (Connell). Native American journalist Cheryl Red Eagle noted that the film "didn't quite manage to avoid all of the stereotypes" but has "come a long way from the Peter Pan Indian characterization."

Other Native American commentators greeted *Pocahontas* with open hostility. Laura Waterman Wittstock called the film's heroine "that Frankensteinesque Disney creation" and Lakota journalist Time Giago objected strenuously to the film's repeated use of the word *savage*.

From the outside, there appear to be positive images in this film's depiction of Native Americans. The details of Powhatan Indian life were carefully researched and, within the limits of a popular medium directed at children, are reproduced in the film. Details of village life, including material objects such as houses and canoes, the men's hairstyles, and the division of agricultural labor, are all rendered with meticulous accuracy. The major exception in this attention to detail is that the Indians are more fully clothed than is consistent with the record of seventeenth-century Powhatan culture, when young people of Pocahontas's age typically went about naked. But it is perhaps inevitable that the studio which had to add flowery bras to the originally topless centaurettes of *Fantasia* would draw the line at naked bodies in a G-rated film.

Attention to historical accuracy is abandoned when it comes to Pocahontas herself, who is aged about a decade to support the romance with John Smith (who is correspondingly made younger and more handsome than his historical counterpart); even her hairstyle has been modified in accord with "white" ideals of beauty. The long, flowing hair is consistent with the Barbie model, but not with the recorded descriptions of Powhatan female hairstyle. Furthermore, while the Indians whose culture is so carefully drawn avoid the demonization of previous cinematic "red men," they may simply reflect the other pole of white culture's exploitation of the Native American: the Noble Savage.

The "film Indian" has always reflected white concerns rather than Indian perceptions; even "sympathetic" portrayals of Indians can usually be attributed more to political or social trends in white society than to a genuine interest in Native American peoples (O'Connor, 25). In the supercharged climate of the 1990s culture wars, it is evidently not going to be enough to simply take particular care to get facts right.

Pocahontas runs afoul of another on-going Disney problem: the depiction of female characters in its animated films. Elsewhere I have argued that the 1989 adaptation of *The Little Mermaid* reduced Andersen's heroine from an individual capable of choice to a sentimentalized object of manipulation by others, and imposed an obligatory "happy ending" on the tale (Hastings, 1993). Beginning with *Beauty and the Beast* (1991), however, Disney's heroines became steadily stronger and more independent. Belle, the beauty of the title, is a reader, seemingly calculated to win back the alienated legions of teachers and librarians who had cringed at Disney's previous fairy tale films. She loves to read and fantasize about escaping her provincial life, and—true to the fairy tale on which it is based—volunteers to stay with a truly scary beast in order to save her father. She stands up to the bullying Gaston, who wants to marry her and father half a dozen children with her. The Disney film has been praised as "a fairy tale that's vividly aware of contemporary sexual politics" with "a heroine of spirit who finds romance on her own terms" (Warner, 10). On the other hand, some contend that the exception of Belle as a positive heroine is false, that her character fades into the background as the real action involves her beastly suitor. The film ultimately offers the same old story, a romance plot that robs female characters of self-determination and individuality.

Belle appears to be an advance on previous Disney heroines, but remains subject to the romantic convention that dictates the film must end with the heroine marrying the hero. Jasmine, the princess of *Aladdin*, shares Belle's desire to escape her present life but is more active on her own behalf. Rather than waiting for a prince to rescue her, she slips out of the palace on her own. In marked contrast to previous Disney heroines, she emphatically does not want to marry a prince and consistently drives off various suitors offered to her under a law that requires her to marry someone of noble blood. She protests against being regarded as "a prize to be won" by her father and the disguised Aladdin.

But Jasmine, too, ends the film requiring rescue by the hero, and finds her most significant role as reward to Aladdin for his virtues. In *Pocohontas*, Disney offered for the first time a heroine who is the rescuer rather than the rescued, and who rejects marriage to the handsome hero because she is needed for other work —to develop peaceful relations between her people and the English colonists. In many ways, Pocohontas is the strongest heroine the studio has ever offered, and should have won praises from feminist critics.

That it did not reflects both Disney's past sins, which cause many people to view its films with a skeptical eye, and the controversial decision to depict Pocahontas as a young woman, rather than the twelve-year-old girl of historical record. Not only was she shown as an adult, she was given a Barbie-esque figure that needlessly eroticizes the film. The maturing of Pocahontas supports a love story superimposed on her relationship with Smith; as in other films, Disney altered a traditional story—here a historical legend rather than a fairy tale—to create an unnecessary romantic interest. The result, in this case, was to divert attention from a potentially strong, independent woman to her sexualized image. Pocahontas might say, echoing Jessica Rabbit (*Who Framed Roger Rabbit?*, 1988), "I'm not bad—I'm just drawn that way"—but then, in animation, drawing is everything.

The firestorm of protest that greeted *Aladdin* seems to have sensitized the studio to multicultural concerns, as efforts to "get it right" in *Pocahontas* suggest. That even those efforts failed to avoid questions about the depiction of women, people of color, and gays suggest that it may be impossible for a major representative of the culture industry to put such concerns to rest until some seriously sustained attention is given to the unlearning of stereotypes throughout society.

A. Waller Hastings is the Associate Professor of English at Northern State University

353

WORKS CITED

CONNELL, JOAN. "Disney's Version of Pocahontas Untide the Historical." *Cleveland Plain Dealer* (June 27, 1995), 6-E.

CUNNINS, JUNE. "Romancing the Plot: The Real Beast of Disney's *Beauty and the Beast.*" *Children's Literature Association Quarterly* 20:1 (Spring 1995), 22-28.

DALY, STEVE. "Mane Attraction." *Entertainment Weekly* (July 8, 1994), 18-25.

GIAGO, TIM. "Weighing in on Disney Version of Pocahontas." *Aberdeen American News* (July 1995).

HAJARI, NISID, AND JAMES EARL HARDY. "Aladdin Stirs Arab Gripes." *Entertainment Weekly* (February 5, 1993), 12.

HASTINGS, A. WALLER. "Moral Simplification in Disney's *The Little Mermaid.*" *Lion and Unicorn* 17:1 (June 1993), 83-92.

KLASS, PERRI. "A Bambi for the 90s, via Shakespeare." *New York Times* (June 19, 1994), 2:1, 20-21.

LOCKHART, KIM, AND LIZ SMITH. "Voices in the Wind." *Disney Adventures* (July 31, 1995) 20-25.

O'CONNOR, JOHN E. "The White Man's Indian." *Film and History* 23 (1993), 17-26.

POLLITT, KATHA. "Subject to Debate." *Nation* (July 3, 1995) 9.

RED EAGLE, CHERYL. "Pocahontas: Give Disney Credit for Trying." *Aberdeen (SD) American News* (June 30, 1995).

ROBERTS, JOHN. "Pocahontas Kidnaps History: Disney Preaches Nature Religion." *AFA Journal* (August 1995), 12-13.

SCHWARTZ, PAULA. "It's a Small World...And Not Always P.C." *New York Times* (June 11, 1995), 2:22.

SHARKEY, BETSY. "Beyond Tepees and Totem Poles." *New York Times* (June 11, 1995), 2:1,22.

SHARMAN, LESLIE FELPERIN. "New Aladdins for Old." *Sight and Sound* 3:11 (November 1993) 12-15.

WARNER, MARINA. "Beauty and the Beasts." *Sight and Sound* 2:6 (October 1992), 6-12.

WITTSTOCK, LAURA WATERMAN. "Add Pocahontas and Ethnic Blend to List of Disney's Animated Lies." *Minneapolis Star-News* July 1995.

Images of Arabs in American Children's Literature

Elsa Marston

WHEN AMERICANS HEAR THE WORD *ARAB*, distorted images often come to mind: handsome princes and vapid maidens of Disney films, or camels, tents, and concealing head scarves. Far worse is the all-too-prevalent notion of "terrorist," an irrational man of violence acting from unfathomable motives. Much of this oversimplification and inaccuracy can be attributed to political bias in the United States: media, novels, and films that consistently put the Arab in the role of outlaw. Some Leon Uris novels and such films as *True Lies, Jewel of the Nile,* and *Protocol* fall into that category.

The injustice and danger of promoting such a view is obvious to anyone concerned about the attitudes children absorb. Even though many Americans may be indifferent to or suspicious of the "foreign," most of us can trace our roots to other countries. As the circumference of the global village changes, each generation will need to know more, not less, about other parts of the world. This is particularly true regarding the Arab countries because of their contributions to world culture.

The negative attitudes of most Americans regarding the Arab world are all the more ironic because of the success of the Arab community in this country. Arabs first started coming to the United States in the 1880s, mostly Lebanese Christians from mountain villages that could no longer provide a livelihood for a growing population. Though some men emigrated to avoid military conscription or religious tensions, by far the greatest pull was the promise of a better life. Typically, the immigrants—including many women—worked at first as peddlers, eventually settling down to start shops; before long they could be found all over the United States, from the large eastern cities to remote western towns. Followed later by Arabs from other countries, many of whom headed for factory work in Detroit, Arab Americans proved themselves exemplary citizens—hard-working, law-abiding, and enterprising.

Arab Americans have risen to the top of fields as varied as banking and professional sports, science and manufacturing, art and scholarship. Nationally known names (to mention just a few), include entertainers Marlo and Danny Thomas, Casey Kasem, Callie Khouri, and Paul Anka; consumer advocate Ralph Nader; U.S. Secretary of Health and Human Services Donna Shalala; White House correspondent Helen Thomas; pioneer heart surgeon Michael DeBakey; and space scientist Farouk el Baz.

Americans must bear in mind, too, the cultural, ethnic, economic, and religious diversity among the peoples who live in the vast expanse known as the Arab world. Their diversity exists in historical background, dress, social mores and attitudes, religion, and other aspects of culture. The extremely conservative Arab of a Gulf state, for example, has little in common with the sophisticated professional woman or man of Tunisia.

Currently, a few books do exist in America for children and young adults that focus on Arabs, Arab Americans, and their contributions to American society and world civilization. Countries of the Middle East and North Africa are adequately and, on the whole, fairly represented in several nonfiction books. Fiction, however, has an extremely powerful and lasting impression and there is a severe shortage of fiction for young readers on Arabs or Arab Americans.

Among the many different Arab peoples, Palestinians are undoubtedly the group most present in U.S. children's literature. This is because books about Israel are numerous (more than equaling those about all the Arab countries combined) and books about Israel almost inevitably make some reference to Palestinians. While some of them are disparaging and stereotypical, others are revealing, clarifying, and sympathetic. But in many of the books, such as *Joshua's Dream* and *Becoming Gershona*, the Arabs of Palestine simply don't exist; they're ignored completely. In others, such as *Aviva's Piano* and *Alina, A Russian Girl Comes to Israel*, the Arabs are referred to indirectly as unexplained, faceless terrorists—the bogeyman in political guise. These books for young children are simplistic and don't even attempt to address the complexities of the culture. Nonetheless, by omitting any meaningful reference to the Palestinians, they reinforce two common themes in Zionist ideology that reflect negatively on the Arab inhabitants: that Palestine was simply there for the taking ("a land without a people"), and that Israelis live under constant threat from "others."

Much worse are those books that take an unequivocally hostile approach to the Palestinian Arab population. To varying degrees, all of the following books indulge in anti-Arab slurs and untruths that can be intended only to confirm prejudice—hardly a justifiable mission for children's literature today. In *The Boy from Over There*, the Arabs are viewed as vicious, ignorant, and selfish in their unwillingness to "share" the country. An earlier novel for teenagers, *The Year*, produces the epitome of negative stereotypes: "There we saw our first Arab, complete with flowing headdress and three wives following him on foot as he rode a tiny donkey." *Alina, A Russian Girl Comes to Israel* and many biographies of Golda Meir, the only woman Prime Minister of Israel, also reflect negative attitudes toward the Palestinian Arabs.

The majority of children's books set in Israel, fortunately, are much less hostile, offering an image of Arabs that admits good qualities on a personal level. In *Smoke Over Golan* and *Lori*, the Arab characters, such as a captured Syrian officer, are treated with respect, while the focus of *The Muckhtar's Children* is on the people of an Arab village near a kibbutz. Even so, a patronizing attitude creeps in. The *mukhtar* (chief official) and his villagers may be dignified and likable, but they are also conservative, backward, even childish, clearly in need of the enlightened views and advanced technology offered by the Israelis. Historical background on the Arabs' resistance to the Jewish

state is ignored.

More thoughtful books, raising questions about the basic dilemma of the conflict, include *When Will the Fighting Stop?*, *The Secret Grove*, and *One More River*. Here we see Arab characters as human beings with their own valid needs, rights, and emotions. A photo essay entitled *Gavriel and Jemal: Two Boys of Jerusalem* goes farther in presenting a meticulously balanced, positive view of both Arab and Jew, equally peaceable, capable, and admirable.

The most sympathetic approach to the Arabs appears in two outstanding books for teenaged readers: *My Enemy, My Brother* and *The Accomplice*. Since both protagonists are non-Arab—a young Jew who has survived a concentration camp and an American teenager on an archeological dig in Israel—Arabs are secondary characters. Nevertheless, the overwhelming threat facing the Arab villagers in the two stories and the pathos of their predicament comes across clearly. In these novels we see Palestinians as worthy and intelligent people, caught by forces beyond their control. Sad to say, these gripping books have been out of print for some time, and nothing has replaced them.

Besides the books about Israel, there are some other novels for young people that might be expected to convey a decidedly negative image of Arabs—stories about terrorism, specifically hostage-taking. In addition to *Captives in a Foreign Land*, *After the First Death*, *Call Back Yesterday*, and *Zed* are hostage stories. Here, too, the reader may be in for a surprise. In all four novels, the aims of the extremist group are, for the most part, comprehensible, and at least one of the men emerges as a believable, even sympathetic human being. Thus the reader can better understand the frustrations and anger that lead people to violent strategies.

A second striking characteristic in each book is the emotional connections that develop between hostage and captor. In *After the First Death*, a poignant attraction grows between the emotionally starved young terrorist and the courageous American girl he is holding at gunpoint. The two most admirable individuals in *Zed* are the guard assigned to the English boy

356

being held hostage and a Saudi Arabian captive. Though dealing with a sensational subject that, in a typical adult thriller, would arouse antipathy toward the Arabs, these books have largely avoided the stereotyped image of terrorists.

Most of the recently published children's fiction about the Middle East seems to be either picture books or novels about non-Arab ethnic groups. They present warmly sympathetic images which hint at the great variety of life and subcultures found in the region: Egyptian peasants in *The Hundredth Name*, city dwellers of war-torn Lebanon in *Sami and the Time of the Troubles*, and picturesque Palestinian village life in *Sittit's Secrets*.

What's missing are novels about contemporary Arab youth—especially stories written from the "inside" by Arab or Arab American authors—that would appeal directly to American readers in the middle grades and up. One young adult novel, however, does fit this description—a remarkable book, successfully published in Germany before appearing in this country. *A Hand Full of Stars* vividly describes a teenaged boy's years in Damascus in the early 1960s, when Syria was sliding under the political oppression that has held it ever since. The Arab author presents a compellingly authentic view of ordinary people as they struggle with the demands of everyday life and try to find ways to resist the police state.

This is the kind of story, along with the picture books mentioned above, that most honestly and effectively represents the complexities of Arab culture. They bring humanity to the characters, often missing in works focusing on Arab peoples and their cultures. By drawing on shared experiences and emotions, these books contribute to a sense of commonality and lessen the impression of difference, strangeness, and exoticism.

Until very recently, the publishing climate in the United States did not encourage books focusing on Arab culture or portraying Arab or Arab American characters in a positive light. Books with settings in unfamiliar foreign countries, we're often told, won't sell—and the Arab countries are so *very* "foreign." The lack of books, especially by authors from within the culture, may also be due to small supply. While

Arabs have an extraordinarily long and rich tradition in scholarship (such as Edward Said) and literature (such as novelists Vance Bourjaily and Diane Abu-Jaber), thus far there seem to be few Arab and Arab American writers ready to turn their talents to children's literature.

One of the most essential purposes of children's literature is to open young minds, broaden young people's understanding of the world, and nurture a sense of empathy and compassion for others. Multicultural awareness seems already to have produced a few books that help meet the need for a view of present-day Arab people as they are, in all their complexity and variety—not prepackaged in long-outworn stereotypical images. For that we can rejoice, while hoping for more in the near future.

There remains a dire need for books that bring Arab Americans to the forefront and herald their contributions to this society and the world. Many themes and topics beg for treatment in stories for young people about the Middle East: confrontation between tradition and modern ideas, the changing roles of women, relationships between the sexes, youth rebellion, the effect of rapid technological development on people's lives. We also need books that document the more than one-hundred-year presence of Arabs in America and that present Arabs as individuals engaged in a range of activities from sports and music to education and politics. By focusing on similarities, while noting differences, we— and our children—can learn to be receptive to *people*, rather than reacting blindly to stereotypes.

Elsa Marston is an award-winning author who writes fiction and nonfiction for young adults and children, with particular focus on the Middle East.

WORKS CITED

DAVID ADLER, *Our Golda: The Story of Golda Meir* (New York: Viking, 1984)

BRENT ASHABRANNER, *Gavriel and Jemal: Two Boys of Jerusalem* (New York: Putnam, 1984)

TAMAR BERGMAN, *The Boy from Over There* (New York: Houghton Mifflin, 1988)

MIRIAM CHAIKIN, *Aviva's Piano* (New York: Clarion, 1986)

ROBERT CORMIER, *After the First Death* (New York: Pantheon, 1979)

MARGARET DAVIDSON, *The Golda Meir Story* (New York: Scribner's, 1976)

JAMES FORMAN, *Call Back Yesterday* (New York: Scribner's 1981)

GLORIA GOLDREICH, *Lori* (New York: Holt, Rinehart and Winston, 1979)

ROSEMARY HARRIS, *Zed* (London: Faber, 1982)

MOLLIE KELLER, *Golda Meir* (New York: Franklin Watts, 1983)

SUZANNE LANGE, *The Year* (London: S.G. Phillips, 1970)

KAREN MCAULEY, *Golda Meir* (New York: Chelsea House, 1985)

MIRA MEIR, *Alina, A Russian Girl Comes to Israel* (Jewish Publication Society of America, 1982)

URIEL OFEK, *Smoke Over Golan: A Novel of the 1973 Yom Kippur War in Israel* (New York: Harper, 1979)

ADRIENNE RICHARDS, *The Accomplice* (New York: Little Brown, 1973)

RAFIK SCHAMI, *A Hand Full of Stars* (New York: Dutton, 1990)

SHEILA SEGAL, *Joshua's Dream* (Union of American Hebrew Congregations, 1985)

NAVA SEMEL, *Becoming Gershona* (New York: Viking, 1990)

SALLY WATSON, *The Mukhtar's Children* (New York: Holt, Rinehart and Winston, 1968)

OTHER FICTION AND NONFICTION ABOUT ARAB AMERICANS

BRENT ASHABRANNER, *An Ancient Heritage: The Arab-American Minority* (New York: HarperCollins, 1991)

ELSA MARSTON, "Rima's Song," in *Join In: Multiethnic Short Stories for Young Adults,* Donald Gallo, ed. (New York: Delacorte, 1993)

ALIXA NAFF, *The Arab Americans* (New York; Chelsea House, 1987)

JANIC SHEFELMAN, *A Peddlar's Dream* (New York: Houghton Mifflin, 1992)

357

Grade Seven to Grade Eight

A Fruitful Vine

📖 Carrie Bender ✒ Susan E. Haas
Amish American
1993, Herald Press, ✳ Series

Miriam has lived all of her forty years with her parents. An only child, with no other close ties in the world, she finds herself alone after her parents' death. Until now, she has always been too busy with chores from sunrise to sunset to find time for herself. But now, she begins a journal.

What will Miriam do with her life? What will seem unnatural is the emphasis that emanates over a forty-year-old "child." The obvious? In the real world, a woman of forty is no longer a child. The flip side of this is that the young adult reader can identify with Miriam's loss as we all experience loss at one time or another.

Miriam becomes Nanny first to one widower's fam-

Through her journal, an Amish woman reveals her struggle with the death of her parents.

358

ily and then another. Although the possibility of marriage to either of these young men looms in the background, Miriam's inexperience hampers her relationships. As the different possible life situations materialize, the reader may wonder impatiently, "so when will she find a man to marry," which is the theme for most of the book. Again, the young adult of today's world may not be able to relate to Miriam's priorities.

Nevertheless, there is still much to learn in reading *A Fruitful Vine*. And while the reader may become impatient with the book's portrayal of the role of women, the book may also stimulate some interesting class discussions. NANCY PAQUIN

Sweet Fifteen

Diane Gonzales Bertrand
Hispanic, Mexican American
1995, Arte Publico Press

Trying to find good fiction for older teens can be frustrating, and finding young adult works with strong cultural themes is nearly impossible. However, Diane Gonzales Bertrand's novel, *Sweet Fifteen*, is a rare gem that will appeal to young Hispanic readers as well as a general audience. Traditions, family, and friends lie at the core of this novel.

Two Mexican American girls deal with loss as they prepare for a traditional rite of passage.

The story is about two young women, Stefanie, a fourteen-year-old Mexican American girl whose father has recently died, and Rita, a Mexican American woman struggling to make a success of her dressmaking shop and to find happiness in her personal life. The two meet when Rita is hired to make the gown for Stefanie for the traditional rite of passage for young Hispanic girls into womanhood on their fifteenth birthday. During the fittings, Rita discovers the girl and her mother, Iris, are still crippled by grief. They are lost without Stefanie's father to guide them, leaving Iris's brother Brian to take over as the padrino (godfather). Rita, who lost her father as a teenager, decides to help the family through the process of moving on with their lives, taking advantage of the upcoming celebration. Much to her surprise, Rita finds herself involved with the family in many different ways. She becomes friends to Stefanie and Iris and finds love with Stefanie's uncle Brian.

History and tradition are accented in the dia-logue between Rita and her grandmother, Abuelita. Rita, in turn, takes these conversations as an oppurtunity to examine her own life and to guide her relationships with Stefanie and her family. The ritual of the birthday celebration manifests a universal desire to be respected in our families and communities, and to publicly honor important transitions and events in our lives.

The narrative is steeped in the simple gestures and expectations of Mexican American culture, complete with the inherently paternal family dynamics. Even a reader who has no knowledge of Mexican American culture will understand the characters, and the tension they all feel between their personal problems and their rich heritage and traditional values.

This novel is of particular interest because of the detail and the thought-provoking scenarios given to Rita's character as a woman in her twenties. This period of life where young women are making vital choices about education, career, relationships, and family is rarely given the time and consideration that Bertrand has taken here. This angle is seamlessly woven into the format of a romance novel, keeping the reader on his toes, allowing him or her to grow and learn along with the characters.

This novel would be an excellent gift for any girl of fourteen years and older, the language is descriptive and clear, the romance format appealing and thoroughly enjoyable. ROSA E. WARDER

Rites of Passage: Stories About Growing Up By Black Writers from Around the World

Tonya Bolden (Editor)
African/African American
1994, Hyperion Books

In this volume about growing up black, Bolden has brought together voices from Australia, Costa Rica, Ghana, South Africa, and the United States, including works by established writers like Ama Ata Aidoo, Toni Cade Bambara, and J. California Cooper. There are also works by emerging authors including Charlotte Watson Sherman, Martin J. Hamer, and Quince Duncan.

Focusing on family relations, school life, friendship, betrayal, and the world of work, these stories offer insight into the black experience and reveal the common ground on which many young black people stand. In Toni Cade Bambara's "Raymond's Run," a young girl with a squeaky voice, skinny arms, and the ability to run as fast as the mythical Mercury learns that winning isn't everything. Ghanaian writer Ama Ata Aidoo's "The Late Bud" provides an interesting lesson in the sometimes destructive nature of pride. In "Big Water," Charlotte Sherman Watson deals with the onset of menstruation and the terrifying as well as celebratory feelings it brings about.

Seventeen coming-of-age stories by such black authors as Toni Cade Bambara and John Henrik Clarke.

The adolescents in these stories are richly drawn and their stories offer grounding life lessons and inspiring moments of reflection. While some of these stories shatter illusions, others provide compelling examples of the struggles young people must face in order to pass forward into adulthood.

The range of writing styles and the varied experiences drawn upon make this a memorable collection that is certain to be read by young people around the world.

Teachers and parents will find many of the stories especially useful in promoting discussions around adolescent issues and concerns. The awkward moments parents and teachers sometimes find difficult to address serve as bridges to greater understanding in so many of these stories. The collection can also serve as a creative approach for incorporating geography, literature, and history into the teaching of writing.

Bolden has compiled a fine literary adventure through adolesence and collected stories that broaden the all-too-narrow view of who black people are. DAPHNE MUSE

The Gaia Atlas of First Peoples: A Future for the Indigenous World

📘 Julian Burger ✒ Various sources

Multicultural

1991 (1990), Penguin Books, ✳ Series

We all have a stake in preserving our environment and saving our rain forests, rivers, and other aspects of the natural world. The demise of the environment ultimately means our own demise. Indigenous peoples of the world are particularly at risk because their habitats are threatened. Development has destroyed much of the rain forest and polluted the land, air, and water, and even remote Antarctica. These resources are only renewable and sustainable to a certain point. They are not infinite resources as the West once believed.

This books includes photographs and maps that give us a sense of the lives and challenges of original peoples worldwide. The book includes a general index as well as an index of peoples covered in the text. *This is an excellent resource for the exploration of multiculturalism, racism, civil rights, and environmental and survival issues.* The problems of modern colonization and the exploitation of these peoples is thoroughly examined. Part one of the book explores the cultures of original peoples in a sensitive manner. Part two outlines the environmental and political crises they face. Part three explores the unique vision of these peoples and the progress they have made toward self-determination and survival.

An encyclopedic look at indigenous peoples of the world.

Many of the marginalized peoples included in this atlas are not mentioned at all in textbooks. Too often, materials are sanitized to eliminate discussions of political and environmental issues affecting indigenous peoples. Textbooks are often dishonest, since they do not explore the realities of these people's lives. There are books about Haiti for children that do not address the problems of grinding poverty and child labor that the Haitian's face. When Nelson Mandela became the president of South Africa, there were few children's books about him and the problems of apartheid.

Their struggles are relevant to us and should be explored by children. This book can be used with some of the excellent biographies of minorities published by Chelsea House. ELAINE P. GOLEY

359

Why I Write about Africa for American Children

MARGARET MUSGROVE

As I worked through Murdock's encyclopedia of African peoples, I was thrilled to find that there were many African ethnic groups whose English phonetic spellings began with the letter x. I needed an x entry for my alphabet book assignment for my children's literature writing class, and I chose the Xhosa. I wanted to write for children about African culture, and the alphabet book seemed the perfect starting place. Using my own experience of living, teaching, and studying in West Africa, I wrote my first picture book about Africa, Ashanti to Zulu: African Traditions.

Growing up in Plainville, Connecticut, I had never studied African history or culture except for the Egyptians, who were not considered Africans in the 1950s. I did not identify with them at all, but I did identify with a black image I was exposed to in an elementary school classroom: Little Black Sambo. I did not know that he was a boy from India. I knew only that I felt some connection to his dark skin, and that I unequivocally and thoroughly despised him and my uncomfortable connection to him. I did not understand why I felt embarrassed by this image, because as a child I could not really understand the inherent difficulties presented to me by this negative image and my sense of identity as a "Negro" child growing up in the white racist schools of New England in the 1950s. Being associated with or identified with black images or even chocolate ice cream was bad in those days, but I still felt the need to defend my identity. Once when my white friend Bobby Short declared that Africans had no languages and only spoke "mumbo jumbo," I tried to argue. But like Bobby, I had heard "African" only in Tarzan movies, where in fact the "natives" did speak "mumbo jumbo," and always behaved like children who looked to Tarzan for guidance. I had no knowledge then of Twi, Ewe, or the hundreds of African languages or the people who spoke them. I did not have the information that could free Bobby and me from the blatant stereotypes that portrayed Africans as subhuman.

My knowledge of Africa, like that of most American children in the fifties, began with slavery. Africans had been renamed Negroes and reduced to a people who were not even associated with a homeland. Negroes were an American invention— a people stripped systematically of language, culture, politics, history, and family to serve the white plantation system in America.

American myth and culture created a fiction about Africans that made the term slave and African synonymous. Negro slaves were a fragmented people without a collective cultural memory or history. Children sometimes ask me if there are still slaves in Africa when I talk to their classes about Ashanti to Zulu. Even in these supposedly more enlightened times, children have gotten the message that black skin and slavery are synonymous, and that Africa is the land of slaves. Works such as Roald Dahl's best-seller Charlie and the Chocolate Factory, with its pygmies from Africa forced to work in a locked chocolate factory, unapologetically reinforce this myth.

So I write about Africa because I know that we African Americans must reclaim our image and our peoplehood within the American myth. I know that to accomplish this, I must go back beyond slavery to a time of regal ancestors who had sophisticated judicial and political systems, and great cultural traditions and style. We must begin at the beginning of our story when Africans defined Africans in an African context.

In the movie Sankofa, the sankofa bird is the symbol that represents the concept of reaching back to move forward. I want to offer American children a more honest, expanded image of themselves and of their history. I want to help awaken their collective African memory, for without this they cannot really know who we were and who we can be.

In her acceptance speech for the Nobel Prize for Literature, Toni Morrison said that language allows us to make sense of our existence. I hope that by making African history available to American children and by resurrecting a positive image of a whole people, that my words will help children to make sense of their existence. That's why I write about Africa.

Margaret Musgrove is a professor of writing at Loyola College in Baltimore, Maryland, and the author of the 1977 Caldecott Award-winner, Ashanti to Zulu: African Traditions.

From The Black Aesthetic (Garden City, New York: Doubleday & Company, Inc. 1971), pp 303-307.

Dance on My Grave: A Life and Death in Four Parts

📕 Aidan Chambers
Gay/Lesbian/Bisexual
1995 (1982), HarperCollins

Written as a series of journal entries by Hal, the main character, and reports by a social worker assigned to his case, this book relates the events of a few weeks one summer. Encouraged by his English teacher to keep a journal, Hal gradually works through his thoughts and feelings.

He meets Barry Gorman at the beginning of the summer and falls in love almost immediately. Near the beginning of their relationship, Barry insists that

An engaging story about two male lovers that avoids a meaningful consideration of gay relationships.

they make a pact that when one of them dies the other would dance on the other's grave. Hal agrees, without thinking much about it.

Barry is constantly looking for new adventures and more excitement. After a few weeks he is no longer as interested in the relationship with Hal; he's beginning to feel hemmed in. He has a brief fling with a girl he and Hal meet on the beach. When Hal finds out, they have a fight. Hal leaves in anger and a short time later finds out that Barry was killed on his motorcycle as he was, presumably, heading toward Hal's house. Hal is devastated by Barry's death and upholds the pact they made by dancing on his grave late one night. He is caught in the act and charged with damages.

The format the author used to relate the story is very engaging. The combination of journal entries, the social worker's reports, and a few newspaper articles provide a sense of authenticity and depth to the story. The relationship between the two boys is treated as normal, though they are understandably wary about having other people find out about them. The character of Barry is somewhat flat; since the story is written from Hal's perspective, the reader learns very little about Barry other than what Hal sees.

Barry's death removes the possibility of having to deal with an ongoing relationship or the conscious decision to end the relationship. The death of a loved one is a topic that many readers will be able to identify with, while the reality of an ongoing gay relationship is less familiar or comfortable. While the fact that Hal and Barry fought over a girl

may help some readers accept the relationship between the two boys, this device may suggest that the attraction between the two boys was temporary, only a phase they were passing through. Although this is one of only a few books written from the perspective of a gay character, it does not invite the reader to consider a gay relationship seriously.
SUE FLICKINGER

The Fall of the Aztec Empire

📕 Jane Stevenson Day 🖊 Keith Henderson
Aztec, Native American
1993, Denver Museum of Natural History & Roberts Rinehart Publishers

This is a beautifully illustrated history of the final days of the Aztec civilization before it capitulated to Spain. The illustrations used for this picture history book originally appeared in a 1922 two-volume edition, by W. H. Prescott, entitled *The Conquest of Mexico*. The sharp graphic style of Keith Henderson is effective in conveying both the symbolic value and physical attitude of historical figures. Few details escape this artist's eye. Henderson used the codices at the British Museum as a visual source for his drawings. Of special note are the shields of the Aztec warriors emblazoned with large Aztec glyphs. The illustrations are fanciful, but they never distort the cultural artifacts used in that period. Although this is a picture book intended for young readers, the ini-

Beautifully illustrated snapshots of the final days of the Aztec civilization.

tial pages contain a comprehensive history of the Aztecs and include several maps of Mexico at the time of the conquest. This pictorial history details the arrival of Cortes and the influence of Malinche, the young Indian girl who learned Spanish and was his translator and mistress.

What makes this book an important contribution to understanding this pivotal moment in North American colonization is the even-handed manner in which the text presents information. Jane Stevenson Day, chief curator of the Denver Museum of Natural History, has written an admirable introductory essay that describes pre-Hispanic Central Mexico, and a detailed description of the Spanish conquest accompanied by maps tracing the march of Cortes. The distinct portraits of the different participants in the conquest of Mexico include Catholic missionaries, conquistadors,

361

and Aztec warriors. Instead of emphasizing one orientation, the entire text reads like a snapshot of a historical moment that changed the fate of an entire civilization. Accompanied by excellent illustrations, this book is intriguing reading for children of all ages. HERIBERTO GODINA

Grand Mothers: Poems, Reminiscences, and Short Stories about the Keepers of Our Traditions

Nikki Giovanni
Multicultural
1994, Henry Holt and Company

Grandmothers are keepers of traditions. The women who contributed to *Grand Mothers* were fortunate enough to have shared with their grandmothers special relationships that have sustained them throughout their lives.

Loving tributes from twenty-seven women to their grand-mothers.

This is an anthology of tributes to the women who have lived before us. The book includes essays, poems, short stories, and reminiscences by a diverse and talented group of writers, including award-winning writer Nikki Giovanni, the editor.

Grand Mothers includes tales of love, family, and commitment, as well as the difficult times that many of these women confronted. Nikki Giovanni's grandmother recalls the murders of Emmett Till and the four little girls in a Birmingham, Mississippi, church, and what those events meant to her then and now. Erin Khue Ninh remembers the stories her mother told about her grandmother, who worked on a farm from the time she was twelve.

The twenty-seven splendid contributors include, among others, Gloria Naylor, Maxine Hong Kingston, Daryl Cumber Dance, Virginia C. Fowler, and members of The Warm Hearth Writers Workshop. All of the stories in this anthology reflect the value of grandmotherly advice and the way our elders can serve as models for us. Some of the lessons are difficult to accept; others, as gentle and reassuring as the many recipes that figure so prominently in the majority of these stories.

The grandmothers in this collection are a varied bunch. Some are strong and authoritative career women; others are withdrawn and haunted wives or widows. Their collective memory spans the globe and reaches back in time as far as the American Revolution. In a short poem contributed by Gwendolyn Brooks, titled "My Grandmother Is Waiting for Me to Come Home," the simple unconditional love of the grandchild-grandmother relationship is brought forward for all of us to appreciate:

My grandmother is waiting for me to come home.
We live with walnuts and apples
in a one-room kitchenette above The
Some Day Liquor Gardens.
My grandmother sits in a red rocking chair
waiting for me...
I love my grandmother.
She is wonderful to behold
with the glory of her coal-colored skin.
She is warm, wide and long.
She laughs and she lingers.

The image of grandmother is a comforting one, even when the grandmother belongs to someone else. As contributor Mildred Bolinger Andrews puts it, "Grandmothers are the ones children go to for love, for stories, for comfort when they've been scolded, for guidance, and of course, for treats." ROSA E. WARDER

Bat Mitzvah: A Jewish Girl's Coming of Age

Barbara Diamond Goldin   Erika Weihs
Jewish
1995, Viking

This book about Bat Miztvah provides an insightful look into Jewish women's history. First created in 1922, the Bat Mitzvah is a ritual for twelve- or thirteen-year-old girls to mark their place in their spiritual and social community, and their new responsibilities as Jewish adults.

Girls' and women's stories from across the globe trace the diverse Jewish tradition of the Bat Mitzvah.

The book includes the stories of over twenty girls and women around the world who have honored this tradition. One such story features Yiling Livia Chen-Josephson, the first girl in China's history to have a Bat Mitzvah ceremony. In 1990, she journeyed from New York to Kaifeng accompanied by her family, a rabbi, cantor, and Torah scroll. Chen-Josephson was eager to acknowledge and honor her

Chinese-Jewish heritage, which dates back to the eighth century, when Persian Jews came to China as traders along the Silk Road. Chen-Josephson's stories, and others in this volume, illuminate an ethnic diversity in Jewish culture that often goes unacknowledged.

Along with exploring the powerful role that Jewish women have played in history, this book looks at the learning of the Hebrew alphabet, an integral part of the practice and the reading of sacred texts. The book also contains an excellent glossary that includes terms like Reform Judaism, Tallit, and Shabbat.

This well-researched book is another example of how more and more cultures are reaching back into their history to revise old traditions and bring new ones forward. Organized in two sections focusing on "The Women's Story" and "Ceremony and Celebration," Goldin's writing is clear, and easy to follow. Each of Erika Weihs' black-and-white scratchboard drawings is thematically appropriate, capturing the compassion, spirit, and tenacity of Jewish women throughout history.

Teachers, librarians, and parents interested in doing additional research will find the following titles most useful: *Four Centuries of Jewish Women's Spirituality* by Ellen M. Umansky; *Written Out of History: Our Jewish Foremothers* by Sondra Henry and Emily Taitz; and Dianne Ashton; and *Jewish Women in Historical Perspective* by Judith R. Baskin.
DAPHNE MUSE

In the Beginning: Creation Stories from Around the World

📕 Virginia Hamilton   🖌 Barry Moser

Multicultural

1992 (1988), Harcourt Brace and Company

Creation myths that explain the birth of the human race and the origins of the world we live in are universal. Virginia Hamilton does a superb job of retelling twenty-five of these myths for young readers in *In the Beginning*, a Newbery Honor Book that has received wide acclaim.

Twenty-five creation myths from around the world.

The book is recommended for children aged twelve and up, not because of the difficulty of its language but because of the content. Hamilton does not write for the timid or slow reader. Younger children may become confused if they are not able to comprehend the cultural background of these stories. The myths are better understood by older children, who may be more secure in their own spirituality and who have gained some familiarity with ancient cultures.

Hamilton tells the myths in a simple abbreviated form, using dialogue to move the stories along. Her style makes the tales attractive as read-aloud selections for teachers who are seeking to add detail and authenticity to their classroom study of various cultures. After each story Hamilton includes a useful "comment" section which explains the origins of the myth and additional information about the religious background of the people. These remarks might be more effective if they had been placed at the beginning of each story.

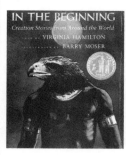

The myths retold by Hamilton include the Chinese story of Phan Ku, who came from a cosmic egg and died to become the earth; a Mayan creation myth taken from the Popol Vuh, the sacred history of the Maya people; the Hebrew story of Yahweh the Creator; and three Greek myths, which include the story of the creation of the earth, heaven, and underworld.

Individual myths are illustrated in color with dreamlike, and sometimes eerie, paintings by Barry Moser. Though the paintings are lovely, they do occasionally lack some authentic detail. The illustration of the ancient Egyptian sun god, Ra, shows the divinity with a bird's head that looks more like a hawk or eagle than the falcon head given the god in ancient depictions, and Ra's foe, the serpent Apophis, looks more like St. George's dragon than the evil snake-god depicted on Egyptian papyri. This confusion may be due to Hamilton's use of the culturally loaded term "dragon" to conjure up this creature. She also describes the appearance of dragons in a Mesopotamian tale. Unfortunately, this word brings images of European knights and large fire-breathing lizards to the minds of most children.

These small criticisms aside, the book is well-researched and includes an extremely useful three-page bibliography. However, it should be mentioned that the works of E. A. Wallis Budge, cited as a source, are so dated as to no longer be considered useful by many Egyptologists. SANDRA KELLY

363

American Indian Voices

📖 Karen D. Harvey and Lisa D. Harjo
✏️ Various sources
Native American
1995, The Millbrook Press, ✳️ Series,
📚 Harvey, Karen, *Indian Country: A History of Native People in America*; Riley, Patricia, *Growing Up Native American: An Anthology*.

This anthology of Indian writing is organized into four broad themes—beliefs, traditions, change, and survival. Editor Harvey has prefaced each section with an introduction explaining what each of these themes means. Although many recent books on Native cultural history take this approach, this collection speaks to the subject through Native voices rather than through anthropology.

A good anthology of historical and contemporary literary works by Native Americans.

The arrangement is roughly chronological, as "beliefs" and "traditions" contain more historical voices, while "change" and "survival" focus on contemporary writers. But those categories are by no means exclusive; indeed, Harvey's arrangements of modern poetry, speeches, prayers, short stories, and autobiographical essays within each chapter convey the timelessness of Native beliefs and traditions, as well as the fluidity of change and survival.

The thirty-eight selections contain some surprises, such as Buddy Red Bow's lyrics to his rock and roll song "Black Hills Dreamer," and Jack Forbes's satirical piece on which Indians are eligible to play in an all-Indian basketball tournament, "Only Approved Indians Can Play: Made in USA," as well as contributions from some more familiar writers (Black Elk, Louise Erdrich, N. Scott Momaday). Black-and-white reproductions of the paintings of Native artists are unobtrusively scattered throughout the book. Sources for each poem or prose are given, as is a further reading list and an index. A succinct work that accomplishes its goal.

Because the authors here write primarily for adults, two additional books are recommended that focus on the experiences of Native children and their writings: *Growing Up Native American: An Anthology*, edited and with an introduction by Patricia Riley, and *Rising Voices: Writings of Young Native Americans*, selected by Arlene Hirschfelder and Beverly R. Singer. LISA A. MITTEN

Barrios and Borderlands

📖 Denis Heyck
Hispanic
1994, Routledge

Designed as a textbook for use in high school and college classrooms, *Barrios and Borderlands* looks at a full and rich spectrum of Mexican American life. Featuring excerpts from Sandra Cisneros' *House on Mango Street*, Danny Santiago's *All Over Town* and Roberta Fernandez's *Raining Backwards*, the book will engage adept young readers with its look at culture and history. Readers will find Rosario Morales' "I Am What I Am" a great piece on cultural identity and clarification.

A timeline presented at the beginning of this collection of short stories, essays, interviews, songs, and poems orients the reader to the historical evolution of

An innovative textbook/anthology of Latino writing, notable for its inclusion of women writers.

the different Latino groups, and the introduction by Heyck invokes the reader to consider the diversity within Latina/o culture. Heyck edits a fairly comprehensive collection of works by prominent Latino authors, playwrights, and poets, and also includes other voices such as community organizers, artists, a refugee from Central America, an executive, and a migrant worker.

This anthology principally covers Mexican American, Puerto Rican, and Cuban American ethnic groups. A brief biographical sketch accompanies each of the contributiors, whose pieces are categorized under six general themes: family, religion (mostly dealing with Catholicism), community, the arts, (im)migration and exile, and cultural identity.

Heyck casts a wide net in this multifaceted overview of Latino culture that also includes photographs, music lyrics, folklore, and cooking recipes. A glossary translates some of the unfamiliar words for non-Spanish readers. There are many reasons to include this text in the multicultural classroom, but probably the most important is the integration of female voices within this anthology. In addition, *Barrios and Borderlands* achieves Heyck's stated goal of presenting a pluralistic Latino mosaic that will help develop multicultural understanding. HERIBERTO GODINA

ANPAO: An American Indian Odyssey

📖 Jamake Highwater ✒ Fritz Scholder

Native American

1992 (1977), HarperCollins

This unusual modern legend is the story of Anpao, a young Native American man who is a compilation of all of the heroes in traditional Native American folklore. Highwater has woven a modern

Traditional tales from Native American tribes woven into a boy's coming-of-age adventures.

legend, or odyssey, of traditional Native American folkloric motifs. Anpao personifies people struggling to survive in a world which is strange to them. Tales of the first encounter with whites are some of the stories included in this legend. Stories about the horses, diseases, and other elements introduced by whites to Native American society are also included here.

The traditions of the storyteller are employed by Highwater as he weaves old and new stories into a ritual tapestry that is, like a Navajo blanket, the sum of its elements. Anpao travels through the dawn of

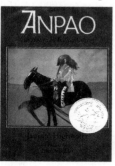

the world, the creation myths of Native peoples, and through the "Lessons of Heaven and Earth" or Native American mythology and cosmology. He also travels through time and the world just as Odysseus traveled about the ancient world. Another tale, "The Invasion From the Sea," tells the story of the first encounter Native American culture had with the white world and its disastrous results. The book can be used with older readers who need the challenge of a new literary form entwined with themes of the ancient peoples of North America.

This book won a Newbery Award for older readers given by the American Library Association each year for exemplary fiction and nonfiction books.

ELAINE P. GOLEY

The Royal Kingdoms of Ghana, Mali and Songhay: Life in Medieval Africa

📖 Patricia McKissack and Fredrick McKissack
✒ Various sources

West African

1994 (1993), Henry Holt and Company

Veteran authors Patricia and Fredrick McKissack have done an incredible amount of research to produce this history of medieval Africa. The book deals specifically with the West African empires of Ghana, Mali and Songhay (sometimes spelled Songhai in other works).

The Royal Kingdoms of Ghana, Mali and Songhay is a treasure trove of history from a region that has previously received little notice. The book's pages are jam packed with historical facts, poetry and legends from the oral tradition, a time line, seven pages of notes on the text, and an extensive bibliography. Illustrative material is in the form of black-and-white photographs and detailed maps.

A challenging history of medieval West African empires from 500 to 1700 A.D.

The book begins by discussing the untrue beliefs about African civilization that held sway in Europe and America for many years. The McKissacks take a firm stand that "The purpose of all these erroneous theories was simply to justify slavery and attitudes of racial superiority," and set out to set the historical record straight.

Along the way, the authors do not shy away from discussing controversial theories about African civilization that abound today. As they point out, archeologists, anthropologists, historians, and linguists are still working to unravel the threads of time that

Patricia and Fredrick McKissack

stretch back to medieval Africa. And as these scientists study the past, they at times disagree. The McKissacks are to be commended for reasonably discussing many historical points of view and giving the various historians' rationale and source materials. The McKissacks ask readers to take big delicious bites of the historical record instead of an approved history "baby food" of bland information that lacks texture or flavor.

Slight criticism is not meant to decry the worth of this book. As the McKissacks are anxious to dispel misinformation about African civilization, it is a shame that some misinformation about Islam, a religion practiced by many West African people in the middle ages and today, appears here. Twice, the authors repeat that Muhammad, the Prophet of Islam, wrote the Koran (sometimes spelled Qu'ran), the holy book of Muslims. This statement would be blasphemy to a Muslim, and is also historically inaccurate as Muhammad himself was illiterate. The revelations he received were not written down in final form until some years after his death. There are other minor mistakes in the sections of the book that deal with Islamic history and the use of the Arabic language that would not have made it into print if the publisher had asked an expert in these areas to read the manuscript before publication.

The sheer scope of the 1500 years of history presented in *The Royal Kingdoms of Ghana, Mali, and Songhay* makes this a difficult book to use in its entirety in a classroom. *Teachers will find that some of the most valuable sections of the book are the excellent primary source materials from both oral and written sources. These accounts beg to be read aloud and shared. They are a time travel ticket for students to view history through the eyes of the people who made it. Students could be assigned various sections of the text that contain primary source materials, and asked to read and memorize these sources, then to present them to the class, following the tradition of the griots, oral historians of West Africa.*

It goes without saying that *The Royal Kingdoms of Ghana, Mali and Songhay* would be a valuable addition to any school library. SANDRA KELLY

Gold: The True Story of Why People Search for It, Mine It, Trade It, Steal It, Mint It, Hoard It, Shape It, Wear It, Fight, and Kill for It

📖 Milton Meltzer   ✏ Various sources

Multicultural

1993, HarperCollins

Beginning with the Andean legend of El Dorado, the author takes us into the various cultures where gold has played a role in developing and destroying the society. Meltzer examines the ancient worlds of Egypt, Greece, and Rome; the brutal search for gold by the Spanish in the New World; the American Gold Rush; and finally the use of gold in the modern world. On this journey all over the world—spanning 5,000 years—we learn about mining, slave trades, the use of gold in art, rituals, money, and exploitation. Whatever pleasure or wealth gold has created, it "has been a nightmare for the native peoples."

The story of gold and our unrelenting and often exploitative search for this precious metal.

Meltzer points out that whether the gold rush was in California, Australia, or South Africa, native peoples and low-status immigrants lost land or performed hard labor for little pay, and greed dominated miners, laborers, bankers, and merchants equally. Disgusted by the gold frenzy in the United Stated, Thoreau wrote: "It makes God to be a moneyed gentleman who scatters a handful of pennies in order to see mankind scramble for them. Going to California is only three thousand miles nearer to hell." And the gold rush continues even today. Now encouraged by the Brazilian government, native peoples in Columbia, Venezuela, and Peru see their young children sacrificed to the pursuit of gold, working for low wages and ravaged by the promise of great wealth.

Meltzer sets this sobering description of the pursuit of gold against its truly glorious use as a medium for artists since the time of the Incas. He also discusses its uses in health care and in manufacturing.

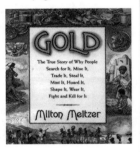

Meltzer makes these connections in clear, interesting, well-documented language. The history is good reading, but it looks like a dry textbook. Many illustrations are from original sources, but they have little visual appeal. Because the text is superior, one wishes more effort had been put into the layout as an enticement to students. The book also includes a table of weights, a bibliography, source notes, and an index.

This is an excellent example of thematic history and it is quite accessible to students in sixth-eighth grades. JANIS O'DRISCOLL

366

Ben's Wayne

📖 Levi Miller

Amish

1989, Good Books

This story about an Amish boy's coming-of-age reveals much about Amish culture and life-style, revealing its larger portrait through the characters (including Ben, Wayne, and Wayne's wild brother Roy) and their day-to-day activities. Readers learn, for instance, about what it's like to be a Buve (a young unmarried man) growing up in an Old Order Amish Community, and many

An Amish boy struggles with traditions and the temptations of the outside world.

other aspects of Amish life through various sub-plots. The story is filled with conflict and challenges, and will appeal to young adults between twelve and fifteen years of age. The book introduces and affirms what will seem to many young readers like a whole new world. They will identify with Ben's questions and doubts about how he is to live. NANCY PAQUIN

Growing Up Muslim in America

📖 Richard Wormser 🖊 Archival photographs

Arab American/Middle Eastern, Multicultural

1994, Walker and Company

Despite the fact that almost six million Muslims live in the United States and with more than 1,000 mosques in the country, Islam remains one of the most misunderstood and seriously maligned religions in America. Islam was the religion slaveowners forced slaves to abandon in favor of embracing Christianity.

Using interviews with Muslim teenagers, Richard Wormser takes us beyond the stereotypical headlines to provide an important look at this segment of our society. The book includes a historical overview of Islam, an examination of the Koran, and a look at the

An important introduction to Muslim life in America, featuring first-hand accounts.

steady growth of Islam in African American communities. However, the need for some real historical detail around the long-term presence of Muslims in America is needed. Enriched by a series of first-person accounts of daily life, this is one of the

few books for young readers that introduces them to the Muslim world in America. It also provides a much more comprehensive picture of who Muslims are, what beliefs they hold, and the roles they play in shaping this society.

Nathmia, a Muslim teenager from the Middle East, tells of being physically attacked by a fellow student when the United States bombs Iraq. But I must take exception to the author's statement that the attack on Nathmia "was an exception to the way Muslims are treated in America." They often are portrayed as terrorists and religious fanatics in newspapers, books, and movies. However, Muslim

young people hardly appear at all. This book brings a face and a real identity to these young people. Many of them wear baseball caps, play basketball, and eat fast-food. Others wear the traditional *hejab* (head scarf) and contribute to correcting the textbook and general misperceptions about Islam. Wormser also speaks to the various Islamic sects and provides a brief history of black Muslims. Through an examination of the Koran, he also does a credible job of examining Muslim beliefs.

Ayeshia Kezmi, a Muslim high-school student, speaks to her process of evolution into her Muslim identity; "I did not cover my head until I was in high school. Although I felt myself a sincere Muslim, I did wonder about the kind of life other students were living. Interestingly, it was my non-Muslim friends who encouraged me to assert my identity as a Muslim. I strongly believe that you can't stay to yourself. You have to have both non-Muslim and Muslim friends." When she was about to enter high school, Tehani El-Ghussein felt a great deal of anxiety about covering her head. But she too found real support from her best friend, who was not a Muslim.

Along with exploring some of the rituals and traditions, the book also focuses on sex education, women and Islam, and the warring history between Christianity and Islam. The book also touches on Muslim-Jewish relations and how Islam has impacted the prison movement. The young people we meet along the way provide us with a real sense of the diversity in Islam and how this religion centers their lives. DAPHNE MUSE

367

CHAPTER 5

FOLKTALES, FAIRY TALES, AND LEGENDS:

fantasy and the imagination

hroughout the history of multicultural children's literature, the portrayals of other cultures available to young readers usually come in the form of folktales. A substantial body of this work exists in this country, a testament to the rich cultural traditions of the world's people.

ne of the many ways that folktales can be used constructively is to take a story such as *Cinderella* and explore other versions across different cultures. There are countless versions of this tale, each of them containing something culturally specific that can serve as an entry point for learning about other cultures. The earliest Cinderella story known is *Yeh Shen*, a Chinese tale in which a non-Western concept of beauty is strikingly evident. In *Mufaro's Beautiful Daughters*, by John Steptoe, two gorgeous young women from ancient Zimbabwe represent another type of beauty not stereotypically drawn. Not every "Cinderella" story has exactly the same elements, but a cross-cultural comparison reveals a great deal about our common humanity. This chapter includes reviews of multiple versions of the Cinderella story as well as an Afro-centric *Goldilocks and the Three Bears* and a Korean Brer Rabbit tale.

t is, however, vital that people of different colors or lifestyles appear not only in folktales but also in other genres. Being able to see people of different races doing everyday, mundane tasks — and not only in exotic or esoteric circumstances — is critical for children if they are to get a balanced view. Currently, it is difficult to find indigenous peoples from any continent in contemporary and realistic stories. While it is enriching and informative to read folktales of different peoples, an unfortunate by-product of this is that stereotypes are perpetuated, with children believing that these people are either extinct or are part of a world that is unlike the contemporary world. A classroom should contain as many books that reflect the multicultural nature of the world as possible.

MASHA KABAKOW RUDMAN

Masha Kabakow Rudman is a noted critic of and commentator on children's literature with a focus on combating stereotypes and promoting social justice. Her Children's Literature: An Issue Approach *(Longman, 1995) has become a classic in the study of children's literature. She has contributed to and coauthored numerous books, and written monographs and hundreds of articles.*

Kindergarten to Grade Three

Bringing the Rain to Kapiti Plain: A Nandi Tale

📖 Verna Aardema 🖌 Beatriz Vidal

African American

1992 (1981), Puffin ✳ Audio Cassette

This Kenyan folktale was "discovered" more than seventy years ago by the famous anthropologist Sir Claud Hollis, who once camped near a Nandi village. Verna Aardema has put in a cumulative refrain that gives the story the rhythm of "The House That Jack Built."

A Kenyan folktale explains how rain was brought to the arid Kapiti Plain in a powerful read-aloud book.

One year, there is a drought so severe on Kapiti Plain that the grass dies and the large animals migrate away looking for more food. An eagle feather falls near Ki-pat, the cowherder, as he stands on one leg watching his cattle. He fashions an arrow and shoots it into the huge black cloud shadowing the plain whereupon thunder crashes and rains pour. Not only is the drought broken but, "The grass grew green and the cattle fat / And Ki-pat got a wife and a little Ki-pat / Who tends the cows now, and shoots down the rain / When black clouds shadow Kapiti Plain."

The story moves along in a straightforward manner with a satisfying resolution. The rhythm of repetition allows complicated concepts to be conveyed in an entertaining and memorable fashion: the interdependence of animals and the environment; the harmonious relationship between humanity and nature; and the value of passing tradition from one generation to the next.

The book is a powerful read-aloud as reader and listener are soon able to commit the story to memory. Selected as a "Reading Rainbow Book," it includes pictures that are lush and vividly drawn. More fanciful than realistic, they contribute a lightness and energy to the story that make it complete.

LESLIE ANDERSON MORALES

The Fortune-Tellers

📖 Lloyd Alexander 🖌 Trina Schart Hyman

African, Cameroon

1992 (1992), Dutton Children's Books

In a comic case of mistaken identity, a young carpenter takes the place of the fortune-teller in a village in Cameroon. He prospers, dispensing the sort of meaningless advice he once received from the "real" fortune-teller, such as, "You shall wed your true love if you find her and she agrees."

A controversial retelling of a Persian fairy tale about a farmer who becomes rich by buying a dancing tiger.

The wise fool is a common folkloric element used effectively here. *Teachers and readers may wish*

to compare and contrast this story with fools tales from other cultures, or perhaps look at a diverse selection of folklore and identify other common elements and themes. Also appropriate for discussion in the classroom is the author's portrayal of the villagers, who happily pay a fee in exchange for common-sense advice and could easily be construed as gullible.

JODIE LEVINE

The Cajun Gingerbread Boy

📖 🖌 Berthe Amoss

Cajun

1994, Hyperion Books

"Way down on the Bayou Lafourche, there lived a sweet Cajun mawmaw so lonely for the sight and sound of a little one that she baked for herself a child made of gingerbread." The gingerbread boy makes his way off the cookie sheet, out the kitchen door, and down to the shrimp boats

A Cajun version of a familiar European tale offers a window onto a little-known culture.

where a man is playing Zydeco (a type of Cajun music). He smells so good that wherever he goes, he must escape people who want to eat him.

He finally dozes in the sun at Bayou Teche, where he is tricked by the clever M'sieur Cocodrie (crocodile). After offering him a ride on his back, M'sieur Cocodrie captures the gingerbread boy in his "big-as-a-swamp jaws."

Although the story and its moral are familiar, this version is enriched by the Louisiana setting, and encourages young people to interact with the story. This imaginative design enhances this tale tremendously. There is also a delightful recipe for Cajun gingerbread boys at the back of the book.

Author Berthe Amoss's able storytelling and witty illustrations make for a wonderful retelling of this tale through the lens of Cajun culture. DAPHNE MUSE

The Devil's Storybook: Stories and Pictures

Natalie Babbitt
Hispanic
1994 (1974), Farrar, Straus & Giroux * Spanish

The Devil is always looking for trouble and for ways to make you fall into his traps, but sometimes those same ways trap him. Can the Devil be outsmarted?

This collection of "devilish" stories brings a sense of much-needed humor to children's literature. In "La Hermosa Dama," a beautiful young girl is bombarded by suitors asking for her hand in marriage. She refuses, showing no interest in any of them. She also remains saddened by the fact that it is only her beauty that brings these men to her.

Humorous stories about the Devil from classic children's author Natalie Babbitt.

Hearing her lament that she will never marry, the Devil decides to intervene, causing her more grief. But in the end, she defies him.

All ten of these stories are cleverly written, and young people are bound to enjoy hearing them. The illustrations serve the stories well, reflecting the humorous tone of the contents. Several of Babbitt's books have been translated into Spanish including this one and *Tuck Everlasting* (Tuck Para Siempre). MAGNA M. DIAZ

Crocodile! Crocodile!: Stories Told around the World

Barbara Baumgartner   Judith Moffatt
Multicultural
1994, Dorling Kindersley

An accomplished storyteller, Barbara Baumgartner has taken a series of her favorite stories, giving us regional selections from the United States and nationally treasured tales from China, India, and Puerto Rico.

In "Crocodile! Crocodile!," an East Indian tale, monkeys and a foolish crocodile engage in a contest of wills. "The Squeaky Old Bed," a story from Puerto Rico, focuses on a little boy who finds a whole world under the bed where he plays. There's also "The Grateful Snake" from China and a Native American tale, "How the Chipmunk Got His Stripes." From Appalachia comes "Sody, Sody, Sody Saleratus," about a ferocious bear.

Children will find the beautifully colored, cut-paper illustrations appealing. *The book includes a section called "Bringing the Story to Life with Stick Puppets." It provides instructions for parents and teachers on how to make stick puppets*

Stories from around the world retold with colorful illustrations and instructions for making puppets.

and use them to encourage children to expand the ideas and themes of these stories. There is also a section called "Folktale Resources." These often spirited stories are wonderful for read aloud and are sure to bring hours of enjoyment to any child. MAGNA M. DIAZ

The Nightingale

Michael Bedard   Regolo Ricci
Asian, Chinese
1992 (1991), Houghton Mifflin Company, * Chinese

The nightingale of this story is a beautiful bird who lives happily in the woods in China, bringing pleasure to all who hear its sweet song. The king hears of this magnificent creature and orders his servants to capture the bird who, at first, is honored to sing for such a distinguished audience, but who eventually misses its freedom. The greedy king replaces

The Chinese emperor comes to appreciate the value of the real nightingale only after a mechanical reproduction fails him.

the nightingale with a mechanical version who never tires of singing. Ultimately, however, the king learns that only the real nightingale can truly soothe him, and with the bird's forgiveness, is saved from an illness.

This rich fairy tale introduces to young readers many ideas about the nature of generosity, authenticity, and pleasure. The book also offers a glimpse at traditional Chinese customs. Experts on the subject may find that while the hair and clothing styles are distinctly Chinese, the illustrator seems to have combined styles from different historical eras. LI LIU

Ma'ii and Cousin Horned Toad: A Traditional Navajo Story

Shonto Begay
Native American, Navajo
1992, Scholastic, Inc.

This traditional Navajo story is one of the "Coyote-out-walking" stories used to teach children ways of appropriate behavior or explain natural happenings. In this tale, Ma'ii (Coyote) was hungry and decided to pay a visit to his cousin. Cousin Horned Toad was a hard worker who weeded his cornfield and took good care of his property. His work was interrupted when Ma'ii suddenly appeared and asked for a meal of corn. Being a gracious host, Cousin stopped his work, gathered some corn, and roasted it over the fire. Ma'ii ate it all and asked for more. Again Cousin Horned Toad went to the field, gathered corn, roasted it, and served it to his cousin. Ma'ii did not even thank him.

A Navajo Coyote story that includes a glossary of Navajo words.

Nearing the end of his patience, Cousin Horned Toad told Ma'ii that if he wanted to continue eating there, he would have to work for his keep. Instead of working, Ma'ii rested and began plotting how to get his cousin's property. He began to yell with pain, and when Cousin Horned Toad ran to help, Ma'ii snapped his mouth shut, swallowed his small cousin, and then claimed his farm.

After another meal, Ma'ii contentedly fell asleep. He was awakened by a voice repeating, "My cousin, my cousin." Ma'ii ignored it and went back to sleep, but the voice persisted. Ma'ii began to fear that Cousin Horned Toad's spirit had come to haunt him and he ran away to a quiet spot under a juniper tree.

The voice continued and was more distinct. This time, Cousin Horned Toad identified himself, and said he was comfortable inside Ma'ii's stomach but would rest better if he could pull out Ma'ii's ribs. The thought of this led Ma'ii to beg Cousin Horned Toad to come out, but he refused. Ma'ii tried to drown him out by drinking a huge quantity of water. Next, he tried to burn him out, but succeeded only in burning his own hair and skin.

Finally, Ma'ii tried to negotiate with his cousin by promising his farm back if only he would come out. Cousin Horned Toad frightened Ma'ii so much by grabbing his heart that Ma'ii fainted. Then, Cousin Horned Toad crawled out of Ma'ii's mouth and gave his tongue a jerk, which awakened him. He screamed and ran off, never to return.

Shonto Begay's soft-toned backgrounds provide a contrast to the frightening forms of the coyote and the menacing presence of the horned toad who resembles a small gargoyle. Some of the illustrations, especially the sharp teeth and the open mouth of the coyote, might frighten younger children.

The author explains in the afterword that whenever he comes upon a horned toad, he gently places it over his heart and greets it with "Ya ateeh shi che" (Hello, my grandfather). Navajo people believe that the horned toad gives strength of heart and mind, and it must always be treated with respect. The book also includes a glossary of Navajo words with pronunciations and translations in the back of the book to help the reader understand some of the language in the story. SHIRLEY CRENSHAW

Iroquois Stories: Heroes and Heroines, Monsters and Magic

Joseph Bruchac   Daniel Burgevin
Iroquois, Native American
1985, The Crossing Press

Joseph Bruchac is one of the foremost scholars of Native American folklore and culture in the world. In his introduction, he describes the history as well as the cultural and political contributions of the six Iroquois nations. The Iroquois confederacy first included five nations: the Mohawk, the Oneida, the Onondaga, the Cayuga, and the Seneca. Later, the confederacy included the Tuscarora. This confederacy gave us the wisdom of Hiawatha and the notions of democracy embodied in the Iroquois confederacy, later adopted by the original colonies. The Iroquois were powerful militarily. They were instrumental in the British victory in the French and Indian wars. They were also a tolerant people who invited non-Iroquois peoples to sit under the tree of peace with them.

Iroquois tales retold by a leading Native American scholar.

Bruchac describes the "Long House" and the structure of the tribes who lived within it. In the Long House, storytelling was an integral part of daily life. The stories the Iroquois tell today around the kitchen table are just as compelling as they were long ago when told by the campfire. The oral tradition is still important in these cultures in conveying traditional culture and wisdom. For this reason, folktales and legends remain important to these peoples. We have lost many stories through the decline of storytelling. Bruno Bettelheim theorized that over ninety percent of European folklore has been lost for the same reason. This loss of cultural richness diminishes our heritage. The Iroquois have preserved the art of storytelling as entertainment, instruction, and sacred ritual.

This book can be used in the classroom as part of a unit on comparative folklore. The Iroquois tales can be compared to European folktales and legends. The differences in philosophy, spirituality and world view can be discussed after reading these stories and comparing them to familiar European folktales. What are the values held in common by Native American and European cultures? Which values are different? How are the folktales used by each culture? It is only through the knowledge and appreciation of other groups that we can understand, accept, and tolerate the views of others. Too often, even today, this is not the thrust of multicultural storytelling in the classroom. By learning about others, we learn about ourselves. This concept is not always apparent to children unless it is discussed and studied in the classroom and at home. ELAINE P. GOLEY

Native American Animal Stories

Joseph Bruchac, Introduction by Vine Deloria Jr.

John K. & David K. Fadden

Native American

1992, Fulcrum Publishing

The oral tradition of Native North American cultures enriches this collection of animal stories retold by Joseph Bruchac, a nationally known storyteller and author of *Abenaki, English, and Slovak Ancestry.* These tales about creation, celebration, vision, and survival are drawn from various tribal cultures, including the Seneca of the Eastern Woodland, the Choctaw of the Southeast, the Hopi and the Zuni of the Southwest, the Miwok of the West Coast, and the Cree of the Subarctic. They first appeared in *Keepers of the Animals: Native American Stories and Wildlife Activities for Children*, which Bruchac coauthored with Michael J. Caduto.

Twenty-four profound tales that present Native American tribal values concerning the association between people and animals.

Each story presents Native values concerning "our relations, the animals." The animals, birds, and reptiles in these stories are presented as brothers and sisters with whom people are joined in the great Circle of Life. The stories teach that our association with our animal relatives should be marked by honor, respect, and a thankful attitude for their contribution to the survival of mankind.

Bruchac retells them in language familiar to modern readers, and his storytelling background is apparent in the natural flow of language that allows us to "hear" each story as we read it. He uses the rhythm of the storytelling voice to lull the reader into a mood receptive to the simple but profound messages of these tales. They are perfect for reading aloud.

A glossary and pronunciation key of Native American words, names, and brief profiles of each Native people add to the reader's knowledge and understanding of Native beliefs. Vine Deloria Jr. contributes an introduction that elaborates on Native American perceptions of the order and balance in all existence. Striking black-and-white illustrations by Mohawk artists John Kahionhes Fadden and David Kanietaheron Fadden, plus the use of thick, cream-colored paper and bold typeface, contribute to a quality production — physically as well as textually. VICTOR SCHILL

373

Sh-Ko and His Eight Wicked Brothers

Ashley Bryan ✒ Fumio Yoshimura
Asian, Japanese
1988, Simon & Schuster

This story, originating from Japanese myth, was first recorded in Kojiki in the early eighth century. The Kojiki is written in three parts beginning with the creation of Japan by the gods and goddesses. The second part details the relationship of these gods with humans. The third segment recounts historical facts about Japanese culture, which was a verbal heritage until the emperor commissioned a scholar to record each family's heritage.

A non-Japanese retelling of a Japanese myth that supplements but shouldn't replace other versions.

Sh-ko travels to meet the princess. He is later joined by his brothers, and on their journey they encounter a rabbit in pain from the loss of his fur—a punishment for deceiving the crocodiles. Of the nine brothers, only Sh-ko treats the rabbit with kindness. He is subsequently rewarded when the princess recognizes his compassionate nature and chooses him as her husband.

For some reason, Bryan changes Sh-ko's name (meaning ugly) from the original Ohkuninus no Kami (meaning a god of a country) and changes the sharks to crocodiles (which actually translates the same). Additional changes are made to the text by Bryan. For example, in the original version, Sh-ko's brothers kill him out of jealousy, but he is reincarnated by the gods at his mother's request. He is then sent to a far-off land where he marries yet another princess against her father's wishes.

Although myths have a variety of versions with varying perspectives, the names Bryan uses do not appear in any other versions of the story. The illustrations are the only element consistent with the original. They are warm and reflect physical and ethnic characteristics well. Bryan, outside the culture, decides to make changes while not necessarily understanding the breadth or scope of a given culture and its traditions. Read together, traditional versions of this story plus Bryan's version offer some interesting opportunities for comparison. CHIEKO YAMAZAKI-HEINEMAN

The Third Gift

Jan Carew ✒ Leo & Diane Dillon
African American
1974, Little, Brown & Company

Long ago, Amakosa, the leader of the Jubas, began to feel the approach of Death. Knowing he needed a successor, he summoned the Elders of his clan. He told the Elders that they had to move to greener pastures. So move they did to a fertile green valley they named Arisa, at the base of a mountain they called Nameless.

Once again Amakosa saw Mantop, the Messenger of Death. He called the Elders together and told them that they should choose a leader who would climb the mountain and return with a gift he found there. Twice, new leaders brought new gifts from the mountain. The third leader, however, did not return as had the others. The villagers searched for him to no avail. Many days passed. Then one morning he came running through the village. He described snow, and how it felt, and how it melted each time he attempted to bring it from the mountain. He had brought to them the gift of fantasy, imagination, and faith.

An enduring collection of twelve African American poems beautifully illustrated by the Dillons.

The Third Gift reflects the rituals people perform to insure order in their lives. The power to imagine the unknown is a most important gift.

Children need to know that their world is only a part of a larger one waiting to be discovered. Leo and Diane Dillon have provided illustrations that capture the awe and appreciation that accompanies the receipt of a gift. YOLANDA ROBINSON-COLES

Afrotina and the Three Bears

Fred Crump
African American
1991, Winston-Derek Publishers, Inc.

Afrotina's father returns from a trip to the city with presents for his daughter: a frilly pink dress, a flowery parasol, and shiny, black patent leather shoes. The next Sunday after church, Afrotina tells her parents she wants to take a walk to show off her new clothes. When she gets to a cave in the woods, she smells something good. Without so much as a knock of "hello" she goes in. We know how the story goes: the chairs, the soup, the beds.

When the bears return, they are angered to find their home broken into, their food eaten, and their furniture damaged. They threaten to eat her; Afrotina negotiates. She promises to make things right. She will make the beds, take the chair home to be fixed, and bring back Sunday dinner.

An Afrocentric retelling of the classic Goldilocks and the Three Bears.

Afrotina then confesses her bad manners to her parents and asks for their help. Daddy repairs the chair and Mother packs a lunch basket. The little girl goes back to the cave and has lunch with the bears, all the while remembering her manners. They invite her to visit again.

While this is an updated tale, it is not really a modern one. Some traditional values are trotted out: the father works in the city and brings home presents, the family goes to church together on Sunday, and good manners are pitted against bad. There is a market for stories that emphasize traditional family roles and prescribed behavior. Parents who educate their children at home, librarians who are asked for material that teaches moral development, and teachers who want to instill certain behaviors in their students are likely to find that this book has great appeal.

The drawings are cartoonish but cute. The reader expects Afrotina to start walking across the page. The creator has done something very interesting with the book design. A detailed text appears on one side of the spread and a captioned four-color illustration appears on the other.

There are notable differences in Crump's treatment of this classic folktale. The parents are depicted as much older than one usually expects the parents of young children to be. The father is balding, has gray hair, and wears glasses. What's also different is that the young girl negotiates her terms of freedom when the bears threaten to have her for dinner. Some readers might find the moralizing a bit heavyhanded. Others might welcome the opportunity to focus on those details that make this story unique from other retellings.

LESLIE ANDERSON MORALES

C.L.O.U.D.S.

Pat Cummings
African American
1986, Lothrop, Lee & Shepard

Chuku excels at his new job as a junior artist in Creative Lights Opticals and Unusual Designs in the Sky. He is given responsibility for the sky over New York City. Chuku soon realizes that no one else wants the assignment, but he is determined to do his best.

A young African American is hired to paint the skies of New York City in a brightly illustrated book.

He consults his manual on his job responsibilities before visiting the city. He doesn't see much of an opportunity to show his creativity because hardly anyone ever looks up. Each day his supervisor passes his work on for production, yet Chuku is not satisfied. Thinking that his ability is being wasted, he comes up with a plan which surely will make him known. However, he must weigh his desire for constant notice against breaking many rules. What choice will he make?

Chuku's story is about making choices, standing firm in one's beliefs, and achieving goals. While he wants to do his best, he still needs reassurance and motivation. While Chuku is African American, all young people will appreciate his talents and understand his dilemma. They will understand the need to be appreciated while learning that one should not allow this need to adversely affect others.

The author's vibrant illustrations make us believe in Chuku's talents. YOLANDA ROBINSON-COLES

Clean Your Room, Harvey Moon!

Pat Cummings
African American
1994 (1991), Aladdin Books

One Saturday morning, Harvey is happily ensconced before the television set. Munching toast, trusty remote control in hand, he's looking forward to the morning lineup of cartoons. Then, much to his horror, at ten minutes to nine—ten minutes before the programs are to begin, his mother appears in the doorway with garbage bags

An African American boy faces a universal task in an appealing story.

and cleaning utensils at the ready. "Today, young man, is the day you clean your room!" she declares. Harvey's room probably should be declared a disaster area and a health hazard. His excavation turns up debris worthy of a whole landfill: broken toys, sticky comic books, wrinkled posters, unmatched shoes, dirty clothes, moldy food, a dead grasshopper, several small, unrecognizable fuzzy objects, and some mysterious pink goo. While Harvey's pet cat could, if cats could speak, attest to his Herculean effort to bring order to the chaos, it turns out that Harvey's mother doesn't believe that sweeping everything under the rug really qualifies as "putting things away."

While Harvey is an African American boy, *Clean Your Room, Harvey Moon!* is not so much about multiculturalism as about cleaning rooms. As such, it is about and for any and all children who have had to face the seemingly hopeless archeological task. Pat Cummings's amusing and bright illustrations, the rhyme, and, above all, the humor with which Harvey's saga are conveyed will only draw children further into the already appealing story. LESLIE ANDERSON MORALES

La Isla

📖 Arthur Dorros ✏ Elisa Kleven

Caribbean, Hispanic

1995, Dutton Children's Books

A Latina girl and her grandmother use their vivid imagination to travel to the Caribbean.

Isla is the destination of Rosealba Abuela's imaginary evening excursions. On the wings of Abuela's stories, off they fly over the Atlantic, south from New York to a Spanish-speaking Caribbean island. Like giant birds, they float past bridges and buildings, boats and markets, to the colorful, inviting home of Tio Fernando. Home there is filled with hugs, stories, and magic. Rosealba learns of family history through the stories and artifacts that fill the home in which Abuela once lived. Ethnic and family identity are nurtured for the tan-colored protagonists.

The watercolor and collage illustrations are full of surprising details. An amazing variety of colors, patterns, shapes, and sizes are represented in this children's adventure story. Some may think the illustrations are too busy; others will relish them. FAITH CHILDS-DAVIS

Myths, Legends, Folktales, and Fairy Tales
RUTH STOTTER

MYTHS *are stories from prehistory, sacred to the people who told them. They often feature supernatural heroes, gods, and goddesses. Myths have been called: "sacred narratives explaining how the world and man came to be in their present form" (Alan Dundes), day dreaming of the human race" (Sigmund Freud) "picture language" (Claude Levi-Strauss) "autobiographical ethnography" (Bronislaw Malinowski), "other people's religion" (Sam Keen).*

LEGENDS *are usually told in a reminiscent manner as true happenings, often associated with a geographic landmark, a person, or event. "The legends of a given period...reflect the main concerns and values, tensions and anxieties, goals and drives of that period."—Richard Dorson*

FOLKTALES *are stories that were reflecting the culture — foods, clothing, customs, and beliefs told before the availability of books. "Folktales are the prose fiction of oral literature." — Jan Brunvand*

FAIRYTALES *take place in a timeless, enchanted world, with human beings as the main characters. Fairytales are symbolic — events and objects representing inner emotions and feelings. "A soothing and healing power can emanate from fairytales" — Max Luthi*

From A Storyteller's Calendar, 1988-ongoing. Reprinted with permission of Ruth Stotter.

How the Sun Was Born

📖 ✏ Third Grade Class of Drexel Elementary, Tuscon, Arizona

Hispanic, Mexican

1993, Willowisp Press Inc. ✳ Spanish

This is a perfect book to introduce children to Aztec mythology. It consists of a myth created by third-grade students. The text is illustrated with drawings by the children in bright primary colors that resonate with the repetitive patterns of Huichol and Aztec art. Each illustration is accompanied by an explanatory sentence.

Creating the book allowed the authors to delve into the prescientific world to ponder how the suns came into being. Readers become immersed in explaining their surroundings in terms that they may not have been exposed to before. *How the Sun Was Born* also affirms the work of children as significant. This could possibly encourage young children to become authors at an early age.

An Aztec-inspired legend told and illustrated by third-grade students in an inspired, unique book.

This book is an inspiring example of children's learning. The authors were allowed time in class to create their work and therefore had a tangible product at the end of their learning experience.

This project allowed children not only to learn of pre-encounter or pre-conquest civilizations but also to have the space to create and use their imaginations to re-create and re-form ideas. The project was simple, but not simplistic.
MARTHA L. MARTINEZ

Moon Rope: A Peruvian Folktale

Lois Ehlert (translated by Amy Prince)
Hispanic, Peruvian
1992, Harcourt Brace and Company

A mole and a fox try to climb to the moon in this bilingual Peruvian folktale.

According to the author's note, this story is "an adaptation of a Peruvian tale called the Fox and the Mole." Written in both English and Spanish, Fox entices Mole to go to the moon with him by telling him that "there are big worms up there." Fox and Mole braid grass to form a rope, but Fox, unable to place the rope around the crescent moon, convinces the birds to carry the rope to the moon for him. Mole and Fox begin their ascent, but Mole falls off and is rescued in space by a bird. Embarrassed, he forever stays in his mole hole except to come out at dark. The Fox makes it to the moon and the birds say that on a clear night they can see him in the moon.

The collage illustrations for this book are spectacular, with modern, brilliant colors and abstractions of ancient Peruvian motifs from textiles, ceramics, and jewelry. BYRON RUSKIN

Why Cats Chase Mice: A Story of the Twelve Zodiac Signs

Mina Harada Eimon
Asian
1993, Heian International, Inc. ✳ Series

The first thing you'll notice about *Why Cats Chase Mice: A Story of the Twelve Zodiac Signs*, is the singsong quality of its narrative. Words are strung together like notes in a musical composition. It's definitely meant to be read out loud.

"What does a cat do when he sees a mouse? He chases it, of course! Everybody knows that cats and mice do not get along. But does anybody know why?"

Thus begins the author's entertaining retelling of this folk legend about the origin of the zodiac and how the animals in it were chosen.

Eimon gives details about the animals' race to Kami-sama's palace. Nezumi-san, the mouse —a mischievous little fellow—tricks the cat by giving him inaccurate information about the rules of the contest. He tells the cat that the competition will begin a day later than scheduled, so the feline relaxes for a few more hours.

A charming Japanese explanation of the origins and meanings of the zodiac.

Meanwhile, the sneaky mouse hops onto the back of an unsuspecting ox, Ushi-san, for a free ride to the palace.

"Finally, after three nights and two days of endless walking, the ox arrived at Kami-sama's palace," Eimon writes. "He rejoiced to see that he was the first one to arrive, and he proudly proceeded down the Grand Hallway to the foot of the Heavenly Staircase. But "just as he was about to enter through the door...out jumped Nezumi-san from the bundle on his back. The mouse ran up to Kami-sama and loudly proclaimed, 'I am first!' Imagine how surprised the ox was!"

He is not the only animal fooled.

Children should find *Why Cats Chase Mice* amusing and charming. Eimon puts a different spin on a story with hundreds of variations. The book's vivid colors, clear lines, and detailed illustrations make it a visual treat as well. CHRISTINA ENG

37

The Green Lion of Zion Street

Julia Fields ✏ Jerry Pinkney
African American
1993 (1988), Aladdin

Each morning, a group of African American children wait for their school bus beneath a streetlight. One wintry morning, "ten times colder than a roller skate," when the bus is late, the children wander across a bridge and into the eerie fog, seeking adventure. A murky figure lurks in the mist—"a green, green lion./Fierce. Mighty./ Proud./ Fierce./ Smirky./ Vain." The closer the children get to it, the faster their imaginations race toward exuberant and harrowing scenarios, and finally, courage gives way to flight, and the children speed toward the safe brightness of a park, where they collapse in a heap, breathless, in the morning light, until the fog clears and their nerve returns. They begin a wary journey back across the bridge, looking for the source of their terror. The lion is still there, impervious as ever, but they discover that he is made of stone, keeping permanent, lonely watch over the Zion Street bridge.

Conveyed in African American English set in a mesmerizing free verse form, and with Jerry Pinkney's typically beautiful watercolors capturing the crispness in the air and the children's thrilled panic, *The Green Lion of Zion Street* is a delightful rendering of the exhilaration children take from testing their fears and the bemused disdain with which they regard the object of their fear when they've summoned their courage. This being said, this prose poem is probably not for all children of kindergarten to third-grade age—the story is relatively abstract and may be hard for many to follow.

The stone lion on Zion Street instills fear and admiration in some young African Americans in an abstract but delightful tale.

YOLANDA ROBINSON-COLES

Anancy and Mr. Dry-Bone

Fiona French
African American, Caribbean
1991, Little Brown

This is an original story based on characters from Jamaican and African folktales. The artwork consists of black cut-outs against brilliant backgrounds. The idea for the Caribbean setting came from a book of photographs of brightly painted houses found on the islands.

An original, brightly illustrated story based on Jamaican and African folktales.

Anancy and Mr. Dry-Bone try to win the hand of the lovely Miss Louise by making her laugh. Mr. Dry-Bone lives in a big house at the top of the hill. He is rich and wants to marry Miss Louise. Anancy lives in a small house at the foot of the hill. He is poor and he wants to marry Miss Louise. Miss Louise, who lives on the other side of the hill, is neither rich nor poor; she is clever and beautiful. She has never laughed. The first man who makes her laugh is the one she will marry.

Mr. Dry-Bone dresses up in his very best clothes and works all his powerful conjuring tricks, but Miss Louise never even smiles. Anancy, determined to do better, goes to his friends—Tiger, Dog, Alligator, Monkey, and Parrot—to borrow different items for an outfit to impress the lady. None of their best clothes are available, so Anancy ends up with a weird-looking outfit. From Tiger, he borrows a jogging suit; from Dog, a hunting hat. He borrows shoes from Alligator, a tie from Monkey, and feathers from Parrot. By the time he gets to Miss Louise's door to show her some of his conjuring tricks, he's quite the fellow. Miss Louise takes one look at Anancy and laughs and laughs until tears run down her face. He doesn't even have to perform his magic tricks and stunts. Even Mr. Dry-Bone laughs. Everyone laughs. Anancy and Miss Louise marry and they all live happily every after.

The "happily ever after" ending might not appeal to adults, but it should be pointed out that the story focuses on the power of friendship and humor. Without the generous support of his friends, Anancy would not have made any impression at all on the desirable Miss Louise. Further, Miss Louise chooses a suitor on the basis of her relationship to him, not his wealth or good looks. Mr. Dry-Bone is a likeable skeleton. He might frighten very young children but not grade school children.

French has illustrated many books for children. She read many Jamaican Anancy stories but thought them too long and complicated for a picture book. She pairs Anancy with Mr. Dry-Bone and draws on Anancy's trait of borrowing from an African folktale. LESLIE ANDERSON MORALES

The Mountains of Tibet

Mordicai Gerstein

Asian, Tibetan

1987, Harper & Row

Inspired by the Tibetan *Book of the Dead*, this original tale has the aura of ancient wisdom. Although it could be set in any culture, the clothing, the kites, and the style of living portrayed in the intricate miniatures all evoke Tibet.

The story begins with a boy who loves to fly kites. In a few pages we follow him through his long life, in which he longs to see other countries but ends up staying home. At his death, the small square pictures representing his life suddenly bloom and become great swirling circles of alternatives. Within these circles are illustrations of all the animals, the various peoples, the different countries, all the possibilities of the universe.

A young Tibetan boy dies, and is reborn, in a provocative book with simple but effective illustrations.

He is given a series of choices regarding his next life. First, does he want another life at all? Then, in what part of the universe? On what planet? As which animal? In what country? As a boy or girl? Remembering his last life only hazily, he makes each choice as it seems good to him at the time. By the end we are not really surprised to find that the story is about to begin all over again with a little girl who loves to fly kites. We are inclined to exclaim, "Why, he's become the same thing all over again!"

The always interesting question for us is: What would we do with our lives if we could start all over? Would we avoid the pitfalls and mistakes that we have made? Would we be more virtuous, ambitious, kind, wise, healthy, or wealthy? Or is there something in us that would direct us to become the same thing all over again? We gain some real insight into how Tibetan culture handles this question. For older groups, this can become a really introspective exercise, but interesting discussions can also ensue with younger children.

At the end, as the spirit materializes into a worldly being once more, the paintings are again contained within a small square. The drawings are simple and childlike, but colorful and effective. GINNY LEE

The Chinese Mirror

Mirra Ginsburg　　Margot Zemach

Asian, Korean

1991 (1988), Harcourt Brace Jovanovich

This story, adapted from a traditional Korean tale, hails from a time in Asian history when China considered itself surrounded by unrefined barbarians. The story depicts the country bumpkin ambience of an isolated Korean village, with a lack of worldly wisdom.

A humorous tale from Korea about villagers who see themselves in a mirror for the first time.

A man goes on a journey to China and brings back a mirror. No one in the village has ever seen a mirror or knows what one is. Everyone looks into the mirror and sees a different person. The man himself sees a laughing stranger. His wife, however, sees a beautiful young girl and is jealous. The mother sees an old crone and can't understand why her daughter is so jealous. The son sees a boy who appears to have stolen a pebble, and is angry. A neighbor sees a big bully, and, appropriate to his own unconscious estimation of himself, smashes the mirror.

Although everyone who looks into it misunderstands the mirror, nevertheless, it reflects something true about the character of each person. It is amusing and revealing to go around a class and ask children to describe the "strangers" they would see in the mirror if they had lived in that village; they come up with some interesting interpretations of themselves.

The simple line drawings in Chinese ink and color wash evoke Korean rural lifestyle, accurately depicting clothing, houses, and other cultural accoutrements. Margot Zemach, though not an expert on Korean culture, has extensively studied Korean genre paintings for this work, and her knowledge and appreciation of Korean culture is evident. GINNY LEE

379

Her Seven Brothers

📖 🖊 Paul Goble

Cheyenne, Native American

1993 (1988), Aladdin, 📕 Goble, Paul, *The Girl Who Loved Wild Horses, The Gift of Sacred Dog, Star Boy, Buffalo Woman, The Great Race.*

Paul Goble has captured the universal experience of gazing into the night sky and viewing the constellations. A majority of the world's population has probably thought about the most recognizable formation of all—the Big Dipper. *Her Seven Brothers,* is an artistic rendering of a Cheyenne legend about the creation of the Big Dipper.

Goble's illustrations are known for their authentic detail and colorful style. In this book, his striking images also beautifully evoke the very method of storytelling. In the first few pages, the eye is treated to teepees, plants, and deer set against a dark night sky with brilliant star formations. White lettering on the black page remind the reader that "stories were told after dark when the mind sees most clearly."

A strikingly illustrated Cheyenne Indian legend of the creation of the Big Dipper.

An unseen storyteller shares the tale of the creation of the Big Dipper. A young Indian girl, an only child, learns to embroider beautiful designs on fabric with porcupine quills. Envisioning that she has seven brothers living alone in the far north, she devotes her days to making and decorating men's shirts and moccasins with intricate patterns of quill work. One day she sets off to find the trail that would lead her to the seven brothers.

After many days, the girl finds the brothers' tipi, meets her brothers, and gives them her gifts. They take her in, protecting and providing for her. One day, while escaping a buffalo stampede, the little brother shoots an arrow straight up into the air. It miraculously becomes a pine tree that reaches the star world, where the girl and her brothers are safe from the buffalo. The girl and her seven brothers are still there today, in the shape of the Big Dipper.

Adjacent to the dedication page, the author has included some informative notes about the historical significance of the Cheyenne designs and identifies the museums where the original artifacts are available for viewing. SHIRLEY R. CRENSHAW

Africa Dream

📖 Eloise Greenfield 🖊 Carole Byard

African, African American

1992 (1977), HarperCollins

All children dream of traveling to magical places and, for the African American girl in this book, that magical place is the home of her ancestors. In her dream, she shops in a marketplace, understands ancient languages, and is welcomed home by her long-ago relatives. They feed her, play music for her, and rock her back to sleep. On each two-page spread, the dreamer describes something she sees or does in two to four short, first-person lines. The repetition of "I" and "me" keeps the child herself always in the forefront.

The text is simple and lilting, a pleasure to read aloud to young children, who enjoy the cadences and alliteration of Eloise Greenfield's poetic lines.

Carole Byard's black-and-white illustrations invite comparisons with Tom Feelings's, especially since both artists

An African American girl dreams about ancient Africa, a land that may seem overly idealized in the book.

have captured many of the same images. Byard's images lack the richness and vitality of Feelings's, and the haze at the edges of the images, meant apparently to suggest the dream state, adds more chaos than atmosphere. These are not illustrations that invite the reader to linger and examine the dreamworld. Still, the faces of the long-ago granddaddy and the new "old" friends are haunting and resonant.

While some adults may hesitate over the book's image of Africa as unwaveringly glorious and gleaming, a place of pearls, perfume, and towering buildings of stone, this is about a young girl's dream. At some point African American children also need to learn that part of the beauty of Africa lies in its peoples' strength in the face of hardship. But children dream of magical places, and for young readers of all backgrounds this is a fine introduction to the idea of a heritage, and a cultural home. CYNTHIA A. BILY

Tortillitas Para Mama and Other Nursery Rhymes

📖 Margot C. Griego, Betsy L. Bucks, Sharon S. Gilbert, and Laurel H. Kimball ✎ Barbara Cooney

Hispanic

1988 (1981), Henry Holt and Company,

✳ Bilingual English/Spanish

Children play hand games and recite nursery rhymes in every culture and in every language. These simple rhymes are often the first introduction to literature and poetry that children learn. *Tortillitas Para Mama* is a spirited book of this oral and literary tradition. The four editors collected nursery rhymes from Spanish communities all across the Americas, resulting in a book of classic verbal antics for young children. The subject matter, like the tales from Mother Goose, revolve around the simple daily tasks that make up the life of a young child: eating, bathing, dressing, playing, and exploring nature.

A useful collection of Spanish nursery rhymes and hand games.

Each rhyme or game is given a page of its own and is written in English and Spanish for ready translation. "El Beso De Mama" ("Mama's Kiss") gives voice to a small child's love for its mother: "Every morning, I dream at dawn that an angel from heaven will come to kiss me. When I open my eyes, I look around and in the same spot, I see my Mama." *Many of the rhymes have directions for accompanying finger plays or other activities.* To soothe bruises and scrapes, "Colita De Rana" ("Little Frog Tail"), is recited while "rubbing the hurt away with a circular motion: "Get well, get well, little frog tail. If you don't get well now, you will get well tomorrow."

The illustrations by Barbara Cooney lovingly portray many aspects of Hispanic culture in Mexico, in South and Central America: a grandmother dressing a little girl for

church, a mother making hot chocolate while her children stand impatiently nearby, a family fishing from a small boat, an old man and a little girl walking down a cobblestone street, and of course the making of tortillas.

The format would be very useful in multilingual school settings, or for early introduction to a second language. The lyrical sound of the rhymes are often lost in the English translation, but this book is a wonderful opportunity to learn a few simple Spanish phrases. The text has been "child tested" for generations, and has universal appeal. ROSA E. WARDER

Hot Hippo

📖 Mwenye Hadithi ✎ Adrienne Kennaway

African

1986, Little Brown

Hippo is hot! He thinks how wonderful life could be if he lived in the water. He goes to the mountain to find Ngai God of Everything and Everywhere. Ngai tells the animals where to live and what to eat.

Hippo begs to be able to live in the rivers and streams. Although he promises not to keep eating grass, Ngai is not convinced. He wants to be sure that the hippopotamus will not eat all the little fishes. Hippo promises that he will open his mouth whenever Ngai likes so that he can see for himself. When he also promises to stir the water with his tail to show that he is not hiding any bones, the deal is on.

An African tale explains why one hippopotamus lives in water in an engaging book for beginning readers.

Back home, Hippo jumps into the river. He can't swim, so he holds his breath and runs along the bottom. Occasionally, he comes to the top and opens his huge mouth so that Ngai can see that he's kept his promise.

The banter between the hippopotamus and the mountainous supreme being is engaging. This book works well for story hour and for beginning readers.

Many of the watercolor illustrations include large dark subjects, yet they don't look "heavy." There is a translucent quality to the artwork that is pleasing to the eye. The bold renderings of Hippo and the other animals are balanced by the gentle impressionistic quality of the background.
LESLIE ANDERSON MORALES

38

The Rabbit's Judgment

📖 Suzanne Crowder Han   ✏ Yumi Heo

Asian, Korean

1994 (1991), Henry Holt and Company, ✱ Bilingual English/Korean, 📖 Han, Suzanne Crowder, *Let's Visit Korea.*

In the tradition of the Brer Rabbit folktales, *The Rabbit's Judgment* shows how a clever rabbit comes to the aid of a man cornered by a ferocious tiger. Throughout children's literature and in various cultures, rabbits have endured as symbols of ingenuity, creativity, and spirited energy. In this book, the rabbit's cleverness saves his skin.

While this book has no Korean content in either its story (although traditional, it is really just a funny animal story) or its illustrations, the Korean/English text makes it useful for new immigrant students who speak little English. It is also excellent for families, who want to share a story with children but who may speak no English. In the introduction, Suzanne Crowder Han gives a little information on the Korean writing system and background on the story itself. The author lives in Seoul, and the illustrator was brought up in Korea. *The story is clearly told and would be suitable for reading to all primary school students. The vocabulary for reading is at the upper elementary school level.* The

A bilingual (Korean and English) Brer Rabbit tale that is a favorite of young readers and useful for new immigrant families.

illustrations are wildly popular with students, rendered in a sophisticated but childlike manner. In the background of each large illustration are amusingly stylized animals and insects, while the main characters — the man, the rabbit, and the tiger — are cartoon-like. This is a charming book and a great favorite with K-3rd grade students.
NAOMI WAKAN

All the Magic in the World

📖 Wendy Hartmann   ✏ Niki Daly

African American

1993, Dutton Children's Books

Seen as an eccentric and quirky old man by many, Joseph shows the neighborhood children how some of the simple things surrounding them can become magical. He chooses Lena, a shy and awkward girl, to witness the magic. Lena becomes entranced when she learns to do a few tricks with a simple piece of string. Often teased by the other children for being clumsy, Lena is now teased for paying attention to the old man. But the children's

An older African man's "magic" helps children accept difference in this useful if simplistic book.

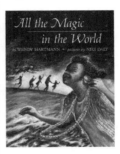

curiosity wins out when they see him transform old can pop tops into a necklace for Lena. They become fascinated with the old man's powers, but he won't take any credit. He helps them to see that magic is a matter of imagination and perception. He guides them into another dimension of creativity — where "junk," for instance, is a medium for artistic expression — and introduces them to another way of playing in the street. A strong element of this story is the emphasis on reverence for elders. Initially, the children have a guarded, almost fearful relationship with the old man, but through his patience and penchant for magic, he teaches them many lessons without preaching.

Joseph's creative hand guides the children into a greater acceptance of things that are new and different. *Books like* All The Magic in the World *can help teachers, librarians, and parents lay the foundation for an appreciation of more controversial books that deal with differences.* MARTHA L. MARTINEZ

Aki and the Fox

📖 ✏ Akiko Hayashi

Asian, Japanese

1991, Doubleday and Company

Each page of this warm tale is filled with playful images depicting a stuffed fox sent to Aki (the main character) by her grandmother. One day, Kon, the fox, is accidently torn, so the two set off on an adventurous train journey to Grandmother's house to fix Kon's arm. The story insightfully describes the landscape and modern life in Japan. The illustrations conjure vivid images of Japan. The illustrations depicting Aki taking a hot bath at her grandmother's house and buying a lunch box at the train station are both common scenes in Japan. Hayashi recalls these childhood feelings with delicate drawings.

A rare and warm tale of a young girl and her grandmother in modern-day Japan.

Aki and the Fox is a valuable work because of its attention to detail. Of all the Japanese folktales introduced in the United States, few accurately depict contemporary Japanese life. The abundance of old folktales contributes to the stereotyping of Japanese culture. *Aki and the Fox* is a valuable work for its realistic depiction of modern life in Japan and Asia in general. CHIEKO YAMAZAKI-HEINEMAN

The Mapmaker's Daughter

M.C. Helldorfer Jonathan Hunt
Feminist
1991, Bradbury Press

Suchen, the adventurous mapmaker's daughter, longs to travel to Turnings, a far-off place under the spell of an evil witch. Her father forbids the dangerous journey until the King threatens to kill them both for giving the Prince directions to Turnings.

An adventurous young woman rescues a prince from an evil witch and is rewarded for her bravery in this feminist tale.

Suchen offers to travel to Turnings to rescue the Prince if the King will spare their lives. She takes along her mother's white cloak, a map, and a lock of her father's hair, which all turn into animals who help her along the way. She valiantly rescues the Prince from the witch's castle and is rewarded, in the end, with gifts from the King: a gold medal, a red cape, and a fine horse.

The end implies that Suchen will continue her exciting and adventurous lifestyle versus the more traditional ending where the female marries the Prince and lives happily ever after. It is interesting to note that Suchen wears her mother's white cloak as she sets off on her first adventure. The white is perhaps symbolic of purity. Yet she receives a red cloak as a reward for rescuing the Prince. The red is perhaps symbolic of her prowess and valor. Suchen is the hero of this folktale, but she is not the only female character. The witch who rules Turnings is female, as is the goatherder who helps her across the mountains. This story successfully portrays female characters in a wide variety of roles, not just hero or witch. The image of the one-dimensional woman does not prevail in this unusual tale. BARBARA SMITH REDDISH

Two of Everything

Lily Toy Hong, Edited by Judith Mathews
Asian, Chinese
1993 (1993), Albert Whitman & Company

In Lily Toy Hong's *Two of Everything* magic can bring good fortune, but it can also bring trouble. When Mr. Haktak's wife falls into his magic pot, he rescues her immediately. But when Mr. Haktak looks at the pot again, he sees another pair

A delightful Chinese folktale about a magical pot that can duplicate anything.

of legs sticking out of it—belonging to a second Mrs. Haktak! This spirited retelling of a comic but wise Chinese folktale finds its perfect complement in the author's lustrous and vibrant illustrations. Children will find it easy to appreciate the humor and irony in the story.

Although the story is predictable, children will enthusiastically volunteer a guess that a second Mrs. Haktak is in the making, and that the original Mr. and Mrs. Haktak will share their good fortune with the second Mr. and Mrs. Haktak. As the first Mrs. Haktak says, "It is good that the other Mrs. Haktak has her own Mr. Haktak. Perhaps we will become the best of friends…With our pot we can make two of everything, so there will be plenty to go around."

The theme of sharing is highlighted in this story. *Two of Everything* offers opportunities for young children to be introduced to or reminded of concepts appropriate for their age level. For example, throughout the story, two is repeated over and over —two purses, two hairpins, two coats. The story also furnishes great opportunity for teaching conflict resolution. What if the first Mr. and Mrs. Haktak don't get along well with the other Mr. and Mrs. Haktak? Who should keep the magic pot? How can it be a win-win situation?

This delightful and funny story will appeal to children of all ages and to younger children in particular. Teachers will appreciate this rich source for literacy learning for children. HELEN R. ABADIANO

How Sweet the Sound

Wade Hudson and Cheryl Willis Hudson
Floyd Cooper
African American
1995, Scholastic, Inc.

The Hudsons have compiled twenty-three songs representative of many African American musical traditions in this attractive volume. These include spirituals, traditional folk songs, work songs, gospel, jazz, and chants. Familiar songs include "Kum Ba Ya," "Go Down Moses," "Take My Hand, Precious Lord," "Take the 'A' Train," "Say It Loud, I'm Black and I'm Proud," and "Happy Birthday." The collection provides good material for discussions about unsung innovators who changed music in fundamental ways or those who pioneer in musical areas not typically identified with African Americans, such as opera. The Hudsons succeed in their intent to provide an historic overview of African American music in the United States. Rap, however, is not included. This could serve as the starting point for spirited discussions about the cultural, political, and economic importance of rap as well as the criticism directed against it.

A compilation of songs reflecting crucial aspects of African American history.

This volume is important because it documents African American music for an audience that increasingly does not have access to formal music instruction in public schools and because it validates the importance of black music to U.S. culture. The inclusion of a music score for voice, piano, or guitar along with historical notes for each song are quite useful.

Floyd Cooper's oil-on-washboard illustrations demonstrate a boldness of line and shape, vividly conveying the mood evoked by each song. The colors range from muted browns, tans, and yellows to intermittent sections of bold, contrasting colors. The cover is especially joyful and engaging.
VIOLET HARRIS

Little Fingerling

Monica Hughes   Brenda Clark
Asian, Japanese
1992, Hambleton-Hill Publishing Inc.   Norton, Mary, *The Borrowers*; San Souci, Robert D., *The Samurai's Daughter*; White, E. B., *Stuart Little*.

In Japan, the story of a teeny, tiny fellow named Issun Boshi is famous in folklore. There have been quite a few retellings of this story for Western children, including *Little Fingerling*. This book, originally published in Canada, is notable for its attention to details of historic Japanese life in the Edo period.

The watercolor art by Brenda Clark is done in a style reminiscent of Japanese art. "If I had strictly followed the Japanese woodcut style, the characters wouldn't have any expression," Clark said, explaining how she adapted a traditional art style to illustrate a children's book. "So in this book they're semi-stylized, but with expression. I wanted the faces to have personality."

In this Japanese folktale, a tiny hero defeats evil monsters and wins the hand of his sweetheart.

In the story, Issun Boshi, also called Little Fingerling, is born to the classic childless peasant couple of folklore. His mother is granted a son after she prays at a local shrine for "even a little child, no bigger than the tip of my finger." Little Fingerling's parents are delighted with their son, and he proves to be a help and comfort to them even though he grows no larger than his father's finger.

When he is fifteen years old, Issun Boshi decides to leave home to seek his fortune in the world. With a sewing-needle sword in a scabbard at his side, he sets off for the capital city of Kyoto.

When Issun Boshi arrives in Kyoto, he finds work in the marketplace decorating combs. One day a noblewoman comes to the stall to buy combs and meets Issun Boshi. She is delighted with him and asks him to join her household. Issun Boshi is getting rather tired of comb decorating, so he agrees to go home with the lady.

The noble lady and her husband and children become fond of Issun Boshi and treat him like a member of the family. Before long, Issun Boshi has fallen in love with Plum Blossom, the noble family's daughter. She shares his feelings, but due to their differences in size, the relationship seems doomed.

Plum Blossom decides to visit the temple of Kanzeon, the goddess of mercy, to pray for help. Issun Boshi offers to go with her and guard her from danger, though no one believes he will be much of an escort. Plum Blossom cannot bear to hurt her beloved's feelings, so she accepts his invitation and together they set off for the temple.

On their way, they are waylaid by two horrible three-eyed blue giants, the Oni of Japanese folklore. Issun Boshi proves his bravery and ability to use his sewing-needle sword and saves the day. When the monsters flee, they leave behind a lucky mallet that will grant a wish when struck on the ground. Issun Boshi is too small to wield the mallet, so Plum Blossom gives it a swing and wishes for them both.

Her fervent yearning turns Issun Boshi into a mighty full-sized samurai warrior. The two marry and live happily ever after.

As a follow-up to this story, ask children to imagine that one day they woke up to discover that, like Issun Boshi, they were only the size of a man's finger. Have them write creative stories detailing the challenges, adventures, and perhaps even some funny situations they would face. After youngsters complete their writing, they can revise and edit their stories, then self-publish them in miniature illustrated books. Stuart Little by E.B. White and Mary Norton's The Borrowers as well as some classic fairy tales might be read in conjunction with Little Fingerling for comparison.
SANDRA KELLY

Swamp Angel

📗 Anne Isaacs ✐ Paul O. Zelinsky

Feminist

1994, Dutton Children's Books

This modern-day American folk tale tells the story of Angelica Longrider, a formidable "woodswoman" born to an unsuspecting Tennessee couple in 1815. At birth she is as tall as her mother. She builds her first log cabin at age two. By the time she is twelve she has earned the nickname "Swamp Angel" by plucking the settlers' covered wagons from the mire in Dejection Swamp.

A modern-day feminist folktale depicting "The Greatest Woodswoman in Tennessee."

Her most fearsome foe, however, is a bear called Thundering Tarnation. No man in the land has succeeded in trapping the bear, and they all ridicule Swamp Angel for even attempting to capture it. "Hey, Angel, shouldn't you be home mending a quilt?" they sneer. "Quiltin' is man's work," she counters, confident in her bear-trapping abilities. Eventually Swamp Angel defeats the bear, but not before a long and arduous battle.

Angel and Tarnation, the story goes, stir up so much dust fighting in the hills that they're now called the Great Smoky Mountains. Tarnation's pelt, which covers Montana, is now called the Shortgrass Prairie; when Swamp Angel throws Tarnation into the air, "he crashes into a pile of stars," which is now called Orion, the bear constellation.

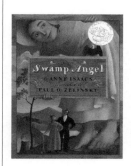

Unlike typical American folktales, Swamp Angel is a modern-day heroine: capable, intelligent, and female. When her male counterparts suggest that she give up bear hunting and go bake a pie, she replies with great aplomb, "I aim to. A bear pie."

Swamp Angel's parents have high expectations for her from the beginning. They name her Angelica Longrider, implying that she is angelical and will go far in life. They appear throughout the story, always in the background, but ever mindful of Swamp Angel's well being and always there as moral support. Swamp Angel does go far. She grows up to be "the greatest woodswoman in Tennessee." BARBARA SMITH REDDISH

Ben's Trumpet

📗✐ Rachel Isadora

African American

1991 (1979), Greenwillow

✽ Audio Cassette, Video Cassette

With simple pen-and-ink drawings and a few words this picture book is a tribute to creativity and individuality.

Ben lives in Harlem during the 1920s. Every evening, he listens to the jazz music coming out of the Zig Zag Club, and plays air trumpet along with the band, sometimes falling asleep on the fire escape in order to

In love with jazz, an African American boy in 1920s Harlem learns to play the trumpet in this Caldecott Honor-winning classic.

stay as close to the music as possible. He is impressed by all of the musicians, but it is the trumpeter to whom he is especially attracted. Eventually, Ben meets the trumpeter, who teaches him how to play a real trumpet.

Rachel Isadora's Caldecott Honor-winning drawings capture the glamour of Harlem during this colorful era. The hardships of life there are not glossed over. Ben's family is not supportive. His apartment looks hot, his baby brother is naked, his grandmother stares forlornly out the window, and his father drinks and plays cards. When Ben plays his trumpet for his family, they are not attentive. This disturbing portrait of family life may trouble some children, and Ben's rescue by a benevolent stranger is problematic. Nevertheless, *Ben's Trumpet* remains a masterful book, full of life and energy. LISA FAIN

The Dream Stair

🔲 Betsy James ✎ Richard Jesse Watson

Hispanic, Mexican American

1990, Harper Collins

All children understand what it is to feel alone and a little afraid in the dark of night, even when they know they are safe in their own beds. The granny in *The Dream Stair* deals with this fear by setting a candle beside her granddaughter's bed, telling the girl, "This candle keeps you safe in the dark, safe in my heart. Go up the stair, go down the stair, and tell me all about it in the morning." In her dreams, the child takes the candle to light her way as she climbs up the Dream Stair to her cellar room, where she plays until it is time to return to her own room and awaken to share her adventures with her grandmother.

A Mexican American girl climbs the "dream stair" among familiar objects in her home, overcoming her fear of the dark.

The universal theme of overcoming childhood fear of the dark is handled sensitively, if a little obscurely. Many children will take the concept of a "dream stair" literally, thinking the girl really is wandering about her house—perhaps sleepwalking—all night, until it is explained to them that traveling the Dream Stair is really a way to direct one's dreams toward pleasant memories and away from nightmares. What makes *The Dream Stair* unusual is that the unnamed narrator is depicted as a Mexican American child, and her dreams are filled with images from her two cultures: a painted clay bird plays soccer; a plastic bear-shaped honey bottle marches across her kitchen table. Chili peppers share space with cartons of lowfat milk; there are tortillas and cornflakes for breakfast. Human characters, recognizably Latino without being stereotypes, are realistically portrayed.

A growing number of children's picture books acknowledge the multicultural nature of America's population. However, it is still rare to find a story not based upon a traditional folktale that features characters with non-European backgrounds but does not treat race or ethnicity as an issue. Children need to find themselves in the books they read. If every time they encounter a child like themselves, they are somehow called upon to validate their cultural background, they cannot be expected to feel a part of the whole. Books like *The Dream Stair* include, rather than exclude, these children as equal participants in American culture. LYNN EISENHUT

Rain Feet

🔲 Angela Johnson ✎ Rhonda Mitchell

African American

1994, Orchard Books

Who would not relish sticking his feet in a cool puddle of water? In *Rain Feet*, Joshua relishes the rain. He wears a bright yellow slicker, hat, and galoshes while jumping, hopping, and splashing through the neighborhood. The poetic text captures the sheer pleasure of enjoying nature with figurative language such as "plop!" and "splash!"

An African American boy dances in the rain in a poetic, brightly illustrated book.

Rhonda Mitchell's soft colors alternating with the bright yellow of Joshua's clothing evoke images of a light spring or summer sprinkle or shower rather than the torrents of a storm. The cover depicting Joshua with raised pant legs and bare feet squiggling in water invites the reader to share a similar weather interlude. The back cover with its bright yellow galoshes creates a familiar image of childhood for many. VIOLET HARRIS

Goha

📖 Denys Johnson-Davies ✏ Nessim Girgis
Egyptian, Middle Eastern
1993, Hoopoe Books

It is often said that humor does not translate, but the stories of Goha are an indisputable exception. Goha, as he is called in Egypt ("Juha" or "Joha" in other Arabic dialects), is known and loved throughout the Arab world. He is thought to have originated over a thousand years ago, and ever since, he has provided *Twenty-seven vignettes featuring Goha, the well-known Egyptian fool.* a mechanism through which ordinary people could poke fun at their rulers, customs, and the inevitable pitfalls of life. Goha plays the fool, but time after time, he outwits cheats and robbers and exposes the pompous and pretentious. He has been the subject of plays and films, and his escapades have been translated into numerous languages. This collection of twenty-seven vignettes was compiled in Egypt by noted translator Denys Johnson-Davies. The illustrations by an Egyptian artist convey an additional element of humor, albeit with a less-than-favorable caricature of Goha himself and some of his protagonists.

Many of the stories related here are about justice, and Goha always manages to ensure that justice is served. Some have other morals, and some, no doubt, carried a political or social commentary at the time they first appeared. There is little here to inform the reader about the Arab people or culture, but in its own way Goha sends an important cross-cultural message: Americans and Arabs can share a laugh, and at this basic level, humor serves as a bridge between people that endures beyond the ebb and flow of political tensions. LESLIE S. NUCHO

Anansi and the Talking Melon

📖 Eric Kimmel ✏ Janet Stevens
African American
1994, Live Oak Media ✱ Audio Cassette, Series

A clever spider tricks Elephant and some other animals into thinking the melon the spider is hiding in can talk. The animals set out to visit the King so that they might present the talking melon to His Highness. Hidden in the melon, Anansi taunts the King until the ruler is so angry he kicks the melon a long distance away where it breaks into pieces. Anansi is hungry from all the excitement. He's hiding in a bunch of bananas and eating when Elephant returns to his garden and takes the melons to task for getting him into trouble. From his new hiding place, Anansi calls out to Elephant: "We bananas should have warned you. Talking melons are nothing but trouble."

This picture book is lively and fun. The whimsical artwork depicts a fantasy rain forest where Warthog cuts flowers in his garden and Hippo relaxes with a book in an umbrella-covered patio chair. Certain details are tremendously effective. The melon rind has such dimension, it begs to be touched. Illustrations that place the observer at the spider's point of view —just inside the melon and looking into the face of the curious animal—are stunning. *A clever spider tricks Elephant, in a fanciful, strikingly illustrated picture book set in Africa.*

The story's creators should be commended for depicting the king of the jungle as a gorilla rather than the traditional lion. This shift in characterization shakes up the reader and forces a reconsideration of traditional images. *This depiction invites discussion about assumptions, roles, and appearances.* LESLIE ANDERSON MORALES

The Three Princes: A Middle Eastern Tale

📖 Eric A. Kimmel ✏ Leonard Everett Fisher
Middle Eastern
1994, Holiday House

Author Eric A. Kimmel first heard the story of the three princes from some Saudi Arabian students in his storytelling class at Portland State University. Enchanted by the tale, he tracked down versions of the story in Egyptian, Moroccan, and Persian sources. *A princess promises to marry one of three princes in this retelling of a Middle Eastern tale.*

Kimmel begins his own retelling with a tradiional Middle Eastern beginning that is more poetic in the original Arabic, but still forms a nice introduction in English. "Once there was and once there was not a princess who was as wise as she was beautiful." Though the three princes who court the princess get top billing in the title, the princess is really the story's central character. She proves to be a worthy heroine, intelligent, charming, and romantic.

Many seek the hand of the lovely princess, but she is most smitten with Prince Mohsen, a handsome young man with flashing eyes and a dearth of material goods. In spite of Mohsen's poverty, the princess is determined to marry her love. She sends Mohsen and his cousins (who also wish to marry the princess) on a quest, promising to marry the one who brings her the greatest treasure. After

a year of adventures on the quest trail, Mohsen and his cousins meet to compare the wonderful magical gifts they have brought back.

The first prince has found a crystal ball that will show the viewer what is happening anywhere in the world. The second prince has returned with a flying carpet; Prince Mohsen has a single orange. The orange, however, is no ordinary fruit: It can cure any illness.

The prince is anxious to get home and look in the crystal ball, to see how the princess is doing. To their horror, they find that she is gravely ill. Quickly they hop aboard the magic carpet to rush to her side. Prince Mohsen feeds his beloved princess the healing orange and almost instantly she becomes well. Now it is up to the princess to decide which prince truly saved her, for he is the one she will marry. Was it the first prince? If he had not seen her so ill in the crystal ball no one would have even known she was sick. Was it the second prince? If his magic carpet had not been available to rush the princes back to the palace, the princess would surely have died. Was it young Prince Mohsen? After all, his magic orange cured her.

At this point in the story, teachers reading the book can stop and ask their students to think about what decision the princess should make. As a writing activity, students can follow the writing prompt, "The princess should marry..." explaining which prince they think the princess should marry and why. Have students read their persuasive arguments to the class, and then conclude the story.

Which prince does the princess choose? Take a guess, and then read the book to see which of her suitors the princess marries. Rest assured that the story says they "lived together in joy and delight to the end of their days." SANDRA KELLY

The Witch's Face: A Mexican Tale

Eric A. Kimmel ✏ Fabricio Vanden Broeck
Hispanic, Mexican
1993, Holiday House 📖 Hinojosa, Francisco, *The Old Lady Who Ate People: Frightening Stories*.

While traveling to Mexico City, Don Aurelio Martinez spends the night in a house owned by three women. He is curious as to why the youngest warns him not to drink the beverage they offer him. He pretends to sip it and fall asleep. To his horror, he discovers that the three women are evil witches. He peers through a keyhole and is repelled to see them eating cockroaches and lizards while drinking blood. Shocked, he falls and knocks himself out, spoiling his chance to escape.

In this eerie Mexican tale, a man becomes involved with witches when he spends the night at their house.

He awakes to find himself in a cage. Emilia, the youngest, has not yet taken the final vow to become a witch. She offers him a way out if he will rescue her. To save her, he must take the beautiful witch mask she wears and destroy it. He should then make another to replace it. He escapes by using an extra pair of witch's wings to fly away while the witches are out. When he arrives home, he makes a crudely stitched face of leather but cannot bring himself to destroy the beautiful one. His mistake results in tragedy for both himself and Emilia.

Adapted from a tale from Central Mexico, the story is just spooky enough for middle graders. Spanish words are scattered throughout the story but no glossary is included. The illustrations are well matched to the story. Spots of color splattered on the pages give the whole book an eerie appearance—faces appear unreal, like the masks the witches wear. The somber tale has danger, love, even grossness. There is no happy ending, which makes it very different from more pat folktales. One drawback is small, dense print. PAM CARLSON

Jaha and Jamil Went Down the Hill: An African Mother Goose

📖 Virginia Kroll ✏ Katherine Roundtree

African

1994, Charlesbridge

Kroll offers verses that Mother Goose might have written if she had lived in Africa. The forty-eight poems correspond to a list at the front of the book of Mother Goose rhymes. Matching the adaptations to the less familiar rhymes such as "My Sister and I" and "How Many Miles to Babylon" is challenging, but most of the verses are based on familiar rhymes like "London Bridge" and "Pat-a-cake." The reader might have to flip back and forth from this list to the text until he or she is more comfortable with the cadence of the newer poems.

A lively but disorganized collection of verses that Mother Goose might have written had she visited Africa.

These poems are about various aspects of life including food, clothing, and customs in modern and traditional Africa — "Bend a Wire" describes coppersmithing; "Little Ahmed Has Lost His Goats" describes goat-herding. Others describe family relationships, geography, and wildlife. "Pangolin, Pangolin" and "Where, Oh Where?" mention animals that most of us couldn't begin to imagine without the benefit of the accompanying illustrations. Most of the poems are specific to an event or activity, but several cover general topics. "All Around Africa" is a counting rhyme that introduces the reader to a dozen tribes.

The bright illustrations use up every available square inch of the page. They are full of color but don't look crowded. They work well as a background for the text. Each page of the book is distinguished by the name of an African nation; twenty-eight African countries are included. The country's name is overlaid on a "textile" border unique to the country.

There is a map of the African continent at the back of the book. A pointer connects each of the twenty-eight represented countries to a thumbnail-sized version of the page where the rhymes appear in the body of the book.

The book's lack of organization keeps it from being as convenient to use as one might hope. There's no order to the rhymes or the countries selected. It is neither alphabetical nor geographical. Same-page pronunciation guides are included on some pages, but a glossary complete with phoneticized spelling would have been helpful. There is no mention made of abstract political and historical concepts like independence and colonialism.

LESLIE ANDERSON MORALES

Eyes of the Dragon

📖 Margaret Leaf ✏ Ed Young

Asian, Chinese

1987, Lothrop, Lee & Shepard

Margaret Leaf retells a story based on a Chinese legend about a Chinese dragon painter. In the legend, the painter, Chang Seng Yung paints four dragons on the wall of the Tung-ang temple in Chin Ling. The two dragons come to life and break loose when the painter adds their eyes. The other two dragons, who do not receive eyes, remain to this day on the temple walls. There is also a proverb based on this legend, which, when translated from its symbol, means Paint-Dragon-Put-Eye. This symbol is included on the back cover of the book by Ed Young, the illustrator.

A thoughtful, masterfully illustrated folktale celebrating the traditional symbol of the dragon in Chinese culutre.

Leaf was inspired to adapt this tale because of her fascination with the dragon in Chinese culture and art. She first encountered Ch'en Jung, a thirteenth century dragon painter, in the Nine Dragon handserver that he painted. She attempts to help the reader understand the harmonious principles of dragon painting and the task of the dragon painter through the retelling of the folktale about a Chinese magistrate, his grandchild, Little Li, and the dragon painter, Ch'en Jung.

In Leaf's story, the magistrate decides to have the famous dragon painter, Ch'en Jung, decorate the unadorned wall that surrounds and protects their small Chinese village with a portrait of the Dragon King. Ch'en Jung agrees to paint the Dragon King on the condition that he can paint the dragon in his own manner and that it will be accepted as he creates it. The magistrate eagerly accepts, and Ch'en Jung begins to paint. When the painting is completed, the magistrate discovers that , though magnificent, it lacks eyes. The painter explains that it would be dangerous to paint eyes on this dragon. But the magistrate is a prideful person who places having his own way ahead of honoring his word. He insists that Ch'en paint the eyes. Ch'en does as he is told and then flees from the wall, as he knows that giving eyes to the dragon will give the dragon life. The dragon rises into the midst of a great storm cloud, leaving the wall crumbled behind him.

Ed Young's masterful use of pastels fills the paintings with an energy that is in accordance with the principles of dragon painting. The reader will gain a better understanding of the importance of tradition in the Chinese culture through a thoughtful look backward into a time in China when dragon-painters were as much sought after as computer system engineers are today—a time when honor and respect for one's word was given and most often returned.

Ed Young evokes the wisdom of the Chinese Ming painter T'ang Yin, who said, "You must paint with a sweeping brush...so to bring out the life of the muscles and the bones...but you must give him awe-inspiring eyes in order to express the essence of the spirit of the dragon." Young's illustrations are awe-inspiring and will transform the reader's imagination to an essence close to the spirit of the dragon. MARILYN ANTONUCCI

Into This Night We Are Rising

Jonathan London G. Brian Karas
Multicultural
1993, Viking Children's Books

A journey above the earth teaches children to accept people's differences.

As a metaphor for discovery, the dreamlike vision of this book can be read in both literal and symbolic ways. As children from a range of cultures float above the earth, they discover that their world contains many different customs, traditions, and peoples in its lands. While symbolically holding hands, the children express a consciousness of harmony and peace among peoples. The author explains that there should be "no fear" as they journey through the various stages of their explorations. While the challenges of diversity are often daunting for those working with young chidren, the tone of the book is happy and upbeat.

Showing young children examples of how to attain peace and harmony in their day-to-day lives is crucial. The childlike quality of the illustrations encourages young children to explore their own creativity. *Teachers and librarians will find this book especially useful for children placed in a diversified setting for the first time.* MARTHA L. MARTINEZ

Fire Race: A Karuk Coyote Tale About How Fire Came to the People

Jonathan London Sylvia Long
Karuk, Native American
1993, Chronicle Books

In the beginning, the animals had no fire. They are cold, their food is uncooked, and they have no light at night. But one day, Wise Coyote hears that fire exists at the end of the world, jealously guarded by three Yellow Jacket Sisters. He organizes the animals to steal the fire. Wise Coyote, the trickster, cons the Yellow Jacket Sisters into closing their eyes while he snatches their fire. They discover his crime and chase after the fire as it is passed from animal to animal. Finally, Frog swallows it and hides underwater until the Yellow Jacket Sisters give up the chase. When Frog comes out of the water, he spits the hot coal onto the root of a willow tree. The animals then rub two willow sticks together to get a fire going.

An engagingly told Coyote tale with detailed, accurate illustrations.

This Karuk story from Northern California shows how fire comes from wood. In his afterword, Julian Lang states that the Karuk are a "Fix the Earth People." He explains that they gather to clean sacred places and their prayers seek to preserve a healthy earth. This story emphasizes the Karuk respect for animals and the earth. It also demonstrates peo-

ple's dependence on nature. Author Jonathan London's tight, deft, story-telling keeps readers interested in the unfolding events. Illustrator Sylvia Long's depiction of the animals is not at all cartoonish, and she adds details from Karuk culture, giving the bear an *Ishpukatunveech iikiv*, or money necklace, and the mountain lion a *Yuxchananach iikiv*, or abalone-chip necklace. LISA FAIN

Yeh-Shen:
A Cinderella Story From China

Ai-Ling Louie Ed Young
Asian, Chinese
1988 (1982), The Putnam Publishing Group
Perrault, Charles, *Cinderella*; Perrault, Charles, *Little Glass Slipper*.

Told with a poetic simplicity very much in keeping with the Chinese literary tradition, *Yeh-Shen* is a book of classic beauty and charm for all children. The story is at least a thousand years older than the earliest known Western version of Cinderella. One of the manuscripts on which the story is based was written during the T'ang dynasty (A.D. 618 — 907). This manuscript is reproduced at the beginning of the book.

A Chinese variation of the Cinderella story emphasizing positive values.

Although there are more than five hundred versions of "Cinderella" stories throughout the world, *Yeh-Shen* contains unique details. Unlike some versions, *Yeh-Shen* features only one ugly stepsister. Rather than a fairy godmother, Yeh-Shen has a fish whose bones later serve as her magical ally.

Among the dominant themes in *Yeh-Shen* are kindness, generosity, patience, endurance, and gratitude. Ed Young's Chinese panel art depicts themes from Chinese culture and folklore. Yeh-Shen is delightfully pictured in a costume that honors her magical mentor. "At once she found herself dressed in a gown of azure blue with a cloak of kingfisher feathers draped around her shoulders. Best of all, on her tiny feet were the most beautiful slippers she had ever seen. They were woven of golden threads, in a pattern like the scales of a fish and the glistening soles were made of solid gold." The illustrations in glowing pastels and shimmering watercolors bring life to the text.

Children who are introduced to Yeh-Shen *will wonder how stories that grew out of ancient cultures widely separated from each other can be so very much alike. This is a good opportunity to do a cross-cultural study of folktales using the Cinderella theme.* The Cinderella tales also reflect how sexism is institutionalized throughout the world. HELEN R. ABADIANO

Tortoise's Flying Lesson

Margaret Mayo Emily Bolam
Multicultural
1995, Harcourt Brace

This book is an ideal introduction to the fascinating world of folklore for primary readers. The eight easy-to-read stories in this collection have been freely adapted from various sources.

The lively language of *Tortoise's Flying Lesson* makes this a great read-aloud book for parents and teachers. The theatrically inclined will particularly enjoy making the various animal noises scattered throughout. When we field-tested this book with our favorite lap "pets," aged five and seven, there was plenty of wheedling and cajoling for "Just one more story."

The stories selected by Mayo, like many folk stories, are didactic in the most pleasant way. They remind children not to believe everything they hear, that kindness is

A multicultural selection of delightful folk stories complmented by brightly colored illustrations.

greater than fear, that brains will triumph over brawn, and that being small is not bad at all.

Emily Bolam's delightfully bold paintings will capture the most reluctant young reader. The bright colors and sense of movement truly complement Mayo's animated text. And somehow in this magical world where blue and orange trees grow on yellow grass beneath blue clouds that dance in a white sky, everything looks just right.

As an introduction to Tortoise's Flying Lesson, *teachers or librarians might want to adapt one of the stories as a puppet play. Standard animal hand puppets would serve well, as would traditional shadow puppets.*

To make a shadow puppet theater, start by cutting off the top and bottom of a cardboard box. Cover one side with a thin white paper screen. Decorate the box to resemble a stage. You can attach paper scenery to the screen (tissue paper attached to the inside of the screen will glow when the screen is backlit). Cut puppets out of black construction paper so that you have a silhouette of the animal desired. *Attach a popsicle stick or bamboo skewer to each puppet.*

On performance day, put the stage on a table that is covered with a skirt to hide the puppeteer. Back-light the stage with an overhead projector or slide projector. If you are using a slide projector, you can get a color screen by projecting an out-of-focus slide. Act out the scene by manipulating the puppets between the light source and the screen.

Students could also read and perform the stories, making their own shadow puppets. They might also design and create puppets out of paper bags or socks.
SANDRA KELLY

The Stonecutter: A Japanese Folktale

📓 🖊 Gerald McDermott

Asian, Japanese

1995 (1975), Harcourt Brace & Company

📖 McDermott, Gerald, *Arrow to the Sun.*

This folktale has been told and retold in many versions and attributed to a number of cultures. This simple but powerful version is from Japan.

A lowly stonecutter, hacking away at a mountain, longs to be more powerful than he is. He envies the wealth of a prince, the power of the sun, the obscuring might of a cloud, and the steadfast imperviousness of a mountain. The spirit of the mountain finally grants his wish to be the most powerful of all.

A well-told Japanese folktale about the folly of power, with bold, abstract illustrations.

In each position, he flaunts his power, wreaking havoc and ruin upon the people. But each time, his opponent proves more powerful. Finally, the more powerful entity is a stonecutter, hacking away interminably at the mountain.

Some versions have the "mountain" request to become the stonecutter once again, completing the circle of wish fulfillment, with the hero returning to himself. In this version, however, the last scene shows the "mountain" trembling at the obvious implication that eventually he will be removed from existence by the patiently insistent stonecutter. On a deeper level, perhaps he is trembling at the revelation that there is no such thing as absolute power.

An interesting story to read alongside this one is the fable *The Lion and the Mouse,* in which the seemingly more powerful being is rescued by the seemingly smaller and weaker one. The timeless hope in both these stories is that when those who lust after power have destroyed themselves, the meek—the patient stonecutters—will inherit the earth. The connectedness of all things is emphasized; one being cannot act selfishly without adversely affecting others, and eventually himself also.

The illustrations in *The Stonecutter* are abstract geometric cutouts in bold primary reds, blues, yellows, as well as greens and purples. *Before reading this story to very young children, it is helpful, to introduce the idea of abstract illustration by showing them the cover without actually talking about it. The cover is an abstraction of a red palace with a green prince standing at the door.*

Ask the children if they can see the prince. Can they see that he is standing at the door of his palace? What color is the prince? Someone is likely to answer "Green," so that even those who were not sure earlier can see that this is a prince.

If some seem still unsure, you can go further and ask, "How many windows are on the second floor of the palace?" and have a student point out the six windows.

As you go through the story, ask, "What are these green things?" (Blocks of stone.) "Do you see the spirit of the mountain?" "Where is the prince in the procession?" These questions can be asked quickly, almost as an aside, but they will draw the children's attention to the use of abstract design as symbol.

After the story, as a follow-up activity, you might have a lot of geometric forms cut out of colored paper squares—rectangles, circles, half circles, triangles of different kinds and sizes —and ask children to paste them onto a background paper to make their own illustration, either for this story or for a story of their own.

Gerald McDermott has also done another indigenous tale, this one about southwest Native Americans, using the same concept of bold geometric design for illustration, with perhaps even greater effect, in his *Arrow to the Sun.* GINNY LEE

Mirandy and Brother Wind

📓 Patricia McKissack 🖊 Jerry Pinkney

African American

1988, Alfred A. Knopf ✳ Audio Cassette

The story of Mirandy is based on a family picture of Patricia McKissack's grandparents as teenagers with the prize cake they had just won at the junior cakewalk. A traditional southern event and a popular social activity that was introduced in America by slaves, the cakewalk was a dance competition for an elaborately decorated cake.

Mirandy is an active young girl who loves to dance and is eager to enter her first cakewalk. She tells her mother that she wants Brother Wind as her partner. There is a local belief that if anyone could catch the wind, they would have their wish granted.

Mirandy seeks advice on how to catch Brother Wind. The grocer tells her to put black pepper in the wind's footprints to make him sneeze, and then throw a quilt over him. Mirandy tries the pepper mill and quilt strategy, but Brother Wind escapes. Mirandy goes to see Mrs. Poinsettia, "conjure woman," who gives her an old book with a spell to catch the wind. Following her directions, Mirandy prepares the cider-filled crock bottle and sets it down on the

The evocative story of an African American girl's first cakewalk, based on a family photograph of the author's grandparents in 1906.

north side of a large willow tree. Brother Wind smells the cider and jumps into the bottle, but escapes before Mirandy can capture him. Later, Mirandy watches Brother Wind slip into a barn. She slams the door and orders Brother Wind to obey her. She then puts on her finest dress and leaves for the cakewalk without a partner.

At the dance, Mirandy chooses Ezel, a partner no one else wants. The crowd is amazed that Ezel and Mirandy dance so well and everyone agrees that the couple is the best and deserves the prize cake.

This imaginative tale, grounded in historical detail, skillfully captures this period and community. Hopefully, it will encourage young readers to explore the stories in their own families' past. Jerry Pickney's illustrations evoke rural life for southern black Americans in the early 1900s. Pickney's art blends impressionistic and representational styles. The initial two-page illustration introduces Brother Wind dressed in a silvery-blue coat, a top hat, a flowing cape over silvery-blue checked trousers, a vest, a polka-dotted tie, and high-button shoes. The outdoor scenes include a variety of patterns in clothing, rugs, food, wood floors, and furniture. The large double-page illustrations have just enough space to incorporate the text within the scene, so text and the setting are one.

SHIRLEY R. CRENSHAW

Getting Dressed

📖 Dessie Moore   ✏ Chevelle Moore

African American

1994, HarperCollins ✳ Series 📖 Moore, Dessie, *Good Morning*; Moore, Dessie, *Good Night*.

Some children love the predictability of actions repeated day after day. *Getting Dressed* gives the reader the impression that the young boy featured in the book puts on his clothing and plays the same games daily. The author skillfully incorporates lessons on counting and ordering actions sequentially, introducing the use of words such as "first," "then," and "next." Buttons are counted as his sweater is buttoned. In

An African American boy goes about his daily dressing rituals.

between, the boy pretends he is a cowboy. (Thankfully, the author does not have the boy play "cowboys and Indians.")

As with *Good Morning*, the illustrator—Chevelle Moore—uses scratchboard techniques along with bold primary colors and patterns to create realistic illustrations. The boy's race and ethnicity are not addressed. *Objects are easily identifiable and the person sharing the book can engage the child in identification activities.* VIOLET HARRIS

Let's Pretend

📖 Dessie Moore   ✏ Chevelle Moore

African American

1994, HarperCollins ✳ Series 📖 Moore, Dessie, *Good Morning*; Moore, Dessie, *Good Night*.

Television and movie characters abound in the creative play of many children. School-yard chants about Teenage Mutant Ninja Turtles, the Power Rangers, and Barney abound. Some parents are concerned that these electronic images fail to

An African American girl uses her imagination to play creatively.

foster the same kind of imaginative play as books. *Let's Pretend* encourages readers to use various objects such as pots and pans, toy cars, and Mommy's clothes in their play, as the main character does. She has fun and uses her solitary time to entertain herself. The pretend play leaves her tired, and she cuddles in Daddy's lap for a nap.

The text rhymes and the language is simple

enough that repeated readings should foster memorization. The language flows and is not stilted. The bold, scratchboard illustrations with clearly identifiable objects enhance the text for readers and listeners. VIOLET HARRIS

The King's Equal

📖 Katherine Paterson ✏ Vladimir Vagin

Feminist

1996 (1991), HarperCollins

A greedy and narcissistic young prince whose father decrees that he cannot inherit the crown until he meets and marries a woman equal to him, is furious at the king's edict. He cannot imagine a woman as beautiful, intelligent, and wealthy as he. His servants search high and low, parading princess after princess before him, but no one meets the prince's impossibly high standards. Meanwhile, a peasant woman travels to the castle on the advice of a wolf, to meet the prince. The prince finds her very beautiful, but questions her intelligence. She responds by saying, "I know one thing that you don't, that you are very lonely."

An intelligent peasant woman teaches a prince the meaning of true happiness in this feminist fairy tale.

The prince is impressed. How could anyone know one more thing than he? And besides, he is very lonely. Having passed the tests of beauty and intelligence, he asks the woman if she is wealthy. She responds with a question of her own, "Is there anything you desire that you do not already have?" The prince's mind races with thoughts of vast lands, diamonds, ships, and of course, the crown. "Yes," he replies. The woman responds by saying, "There is nothing that I want that I do not already have, so perhaps I am wealthier than you." At this the prince realizes that the woman actually surpasses him in beauty, intelligence, and wealth, and begs her to marry him. She refuses, telling him to go and live as a peasant for one year, while she rules the castle. He does, and is changed for the better because of the experience. He returns to marry her, and together they rule the kingdom fairly and compassionately.

In this cleverly told, well-written story, the woman is portrayed in a positive light. She is able, intelligent, and compassionate. Her primary goal is not to marry a prince but to rule their domain just-ly. She succeeds in these goals, and marries the prince only after he's changed his ignorant ways.

When using this book in the classroom, a good activity is to compare this folktale with other more traditional folktales in which the "happy ending" results in the female marrying the prince. A thought-provoking question to ask the class is "How is this marriage different?" Teachers may then want to discuss the concept of values and priorities and pose the question "What is important to the Prince?" "What is important to the peasant woman?" and "How do they compromise?"
BARBARA SMITH REDDISH

The Tale of the Mandarin Ducks

📖 Katherine Paterson ✏ Leo and Diane Dillon

Asian, Japanese

1995, Puffin Books

Japanese folktales are filled with people who turn into animals and animals who turn into people. Sometimes the motive is mischief, sometimes malice. But often, as in this story, the purpose is to return a favor.

A retelling of a japnese folktale in evocative wood block prints.

There are two couples in this tale: two mandarin ducks, who represent conjugal bliss, and the people, who help them and are helped by them in turn.

The drake is captured by a cruel lord, and put into a cage to show off his beautiful feathers. He begins to mope for his mate. He droops. The lord loses interest, and Yasuko, a kitchen maid, takes it upon herself to release the duck, whereupon the lord, who cannot bear the notion of someone else taking charge, sentences her and Shozo, a one-eyed Samurai, now fallen from favor, to death for their presumption.

Yasuko laments her foolishness in letting the drake go free, but Shozo consoles her: "It is not foolish to show compassion for a fellow creature."

The happy ending, cleverly brought about by the two ducks in disguise, prompts the moral: "Trouble can always be borne when it is shared."

The illustrators, while not Japanese themselves, have done a masterful job of researching the Japanese wood-block prints known as Ukiyo ("paintings from the floating world"). About a hundred years ago these prints inspired Western poster artists and became so popular worldwide as to have become nearly synonymous with Japan itself.

The full-page paintings in the Ukiyo style certainly evoke old Japan of an undefined time in the past. There is no mistaking these paintings for Chinese or Korean. Details such as hairstyles and fashions of clothing are all taken straight from wood-block prints. Even the muted Japanese color and the all-important flow of the definitive black line are exactly evocative of the art of the wood-block print.

Potential classroom discussions around this book can run from asking students how life would be different if everyone was as compassionate as Shozo and Yasuko, to whether or not children can understand the story from the lord's point of view. The book clearly offers up a moral. GINNY LEE

The Turkey Girl: A Zuni Cinderella Story

Retold by Penny Pollock   Ed Young
Native American, Zuni
1996, Little Brown

Caldecott Award-winner Ed Young's pastel and oil crayon drawings easily entice readers into this mystically illustrated and thought-provoking version of Cinderella. The vivid colors of the Southwest, combined with this intriguing drama about humankind's bond with nature, make this story about a failure to keep a promise come to life in new ways.

In the shadow of Thunder Mountain at the edge of her pueblo village, Matsaki, the Turkey Girl, must eke out a living by herding turkeys, valued for their black-and-white tail feathers, used for decorating Native American prayer sticks and ceremonial masks. Her tattered shawl and torn dress prevent her from joining the others in feasting, dancing, and celebrating at the Dance of the Sacred Bird Festival.

A highly appealing Native American version of Cinderella.

Although she has talked to the turkeys during all her years of tending them, they have never spoken to her. On this particular day, however, a huge turkey steps forward and says, "Maiden Mother, do not water the desert with your tears. You shall go to the dance." Gathering around her, the turkeys reveal some of their sacred secrets and turn her tattered dress, ragged shawl, and yucca sandals into a doeskin dress with rare shells dangling from the hem. Bejeweled and amazed, the girl asks how she can possibly thank them. They ask her not to forget them.

In her loveliness, the Turkey Girl dances every dance and is admired by feather-wearing braves. The music keeps going until she realizes that she has broken her trust with the turkeys: by forgetting them "her dress [becomes] rags, her shawl tatters, and her sandals [become] worn yucca fibers."

The portrayal of the much-maligned turkey as a smart and loyal bird is refreshing and, in the end, friendship and trust are valued most. With an intriguing story line supported by fine and, at times, almost poetic writing, this book will have tremendous appeal to young readers and may even appeal to older readers sharing stories with their younger siblings. DAPHNE MUSE

Sukey and the Mermaid

Robert D. San Souci   Brian Pinkney
African American
1996 (1992), Simon & Schuster

This story is based on a brief folktale from the Sea Islands and is one of the few tales of African American origin that involves a mermaid. The piece was combined with a West African tale for additional story elements, resulting in a fresh and original

In this unusual Sea Island folktale, an unhappy African girl is given kindness and wealth by a mermaid.

telling that still feels authentic. The plot is unpredictable, presenting unusual choices and decisions.

In folktale tradition, the story begins with the words, "Storyteller say." Sukey, a young girl, lives with her ma and step-pa, a "bossy, do nothing man" who gives her endless chores. Sneaking off to the shore one afternoon, she sings a song: "Thee, thee, down below? Come to me, Mama Jo!," and a brown-skinned mermaid appears. At day's end, Sukey remembers her unfinished work, and the mermaid gives her a gold coin to appease her parents.

Sukey gets one coin daily until her greedy step-pa tries to capture the mermaid, so the mermaid stops coming. Sukey becomes ill from overwork and grief at the loss of her friend, but she is visited by the mermaid in a dream and asked to live with her. Although she has declined to live with the mermaid before, Sukey now goes to her underwater cave where she is happy and secure.

After a time, she pleads to return home. The mermaid acquiesces, giving Sukey a bag of coins and the name of the man she should marry. Sukey, now a grown woman, meets this man and loves him for his honesty and kindness. Her plotting step-pa kills him and steals the coins, but is drowned escaping. One final time, the mermaid appears and offers Sukey a painless life below, but Sukey asks her to revive her fiancé. Happily married, the couple discovers the buried bag of coins.

The plot is inventive; the language is rich and descriptive. The characters talk in an easy, pleasing dialect. The words weave a tale that is perfectly matched with the illustrations, done on black scratchboard and colored with oil pastels. Their fine, swirling lines create the impression of movement and the feeling of the sea and island life.

Framing the tale, the narrator says, "I step on a thing, and the thing bend," perfectly synthesizing the twists and turns of the tale. One's path is not always straight, with everything concluding as expected. You make your choices, but then other things happen. And it is not riches, but love, that brings harmony. JACKIE LYNCH

The Feather Merchants & Other Tales of the Fools of Chelm

Steve Sanfield ◆ Mikhail Magaril
Eastern European, Jewish
1993, William Morrow

Chelm is a special place in Eastern European Jewish folklore. It is a town in which all the inhabitants are fools. They are simple people, not greedy or nasty, but they are all fools. Some of the stories included in this collection are: "A Beginning," "The Shul," "The Rabbi," and "Oyzar the Scholar." In "A Beginning," the townspeople want to transport logs to their town, but cannot decide which end should be the one to enter the town first. They resolve this dilemma by knocking down some houses at the side of the road, widening the road enough to carry the logs in horizontally.

In "Yossel and Sossel," one of the men of Chelm writes a letter to his uncle, making very large letters on the page. When he is asked why, he explains that his uncle is deaf, and whoever reads the letter to him will know to speak loudly if the words on the page are extra large. In "Berish the Shammes," the caretaker of a synagogue builds a roof to cover the new sundial so the dial won't get ruined by the rain. In this same story, the

A collection of Eastern European Jewish folklore about Chelm, a town of fools and simpletons.

caretaker is given the responsibility of breaking the news to a man's wife that her husband has died in an accident. He is admonished to break the news gently, so he asks the woman if "the Widow Rifke lives here." When she responds that she is not a widow, he retorts, "How much do you want to bet?" In another story two brothers set out to capture the moon in a barrel. When they have the moon in the barrel, they seal the barrel shut and try to rent the moon to people in the town. But they notice that there is a moon in the sky, and considering that this moon is an impostor, they check to make sure their moon is still in the barrel. Lo and behold, it is gone, and the brothers loudly complain that someone has stolen the moon from them.

There are hundreds of stories about the fools or "wise men" of Chelm. Although the stories gently mock the characters, they are, especially in Sanfield's versions, very respectful of the culture. The foolishness is always explained in terms of logic and previous understanding. It is often an intellectual challenge to follow the thread of the Chelm people's thinking. *If a unit on fools in folklore is undertaken in the classroom, children will be able to see that foolishness is universal, and not stereotypic of any one group or culture.* MASHA RUDMAN

The Magic Horse

◆ Sally Scott
Middle Eastern, Persian
1985, Greenwillow Books

The lively retelling of a Persian fairy tale about a flying horse.

In ancient Persia, a wizard brings before a king and his son a flying horse made of ebony and inlaid with gold and jewels. The wizard offers the horse in exchange for the princess's hand, but she angrily refuses the offer. Quite impressed with the horse, the prince leaps into the saddle and flies off to faraway lands where he finds and falls in love with another beautiful princess. They return to his land, whereupon she is stolen by the ruthless wizard. Angered and saddened by the loss of his beloved, the prince vows to find her.

The author offers a lively retelling of a Persian fairy tale simplified from Sir Richard Burton's *Arabian Nights*. The refined full-page acrylic illustrations, in the tradition of Persian miniatures, bring the story to life. Young readers will treasure this trip to the land of flying carpets. SHAHLA SOHAIL

The Enchanted Storks: A Tale of the Middle East

📖 Aaron Shepard and Nina Ignatowicz
🖌 Alisher Dianov

Middle Eastern

1995, Houghton Miflin Company

The mighty Calif of the glorious city of Baghdad and his trusted Vizier disguise themselves as merchants to roam the bazaars. Listening to the talk of the Calif's subjects, they hear insider information to help them govern judiciously. One fateful day, the Calif buys a jeweled snuff box from a wrinkled old peddler. Underneath the lid, he finds a piece of parchment that reads: "A sniff of snuff, for wings that soar. Casalavair for hands once more." Intrigued by what appears to be magic snuff, the Calif and his Vizier inhale the pungent powder and before a second breath can be taken, they are transformed into a "flurry of wings, beaks, and feathers." Two storks stand where a ruler and his closest advisor once stood.

The Calif of Bagdad and his Vizier are turned into storks.

This enchanting tale reflects its Middle Eastern origins from the first sentence to the last. "Favor now should greet my story," the teller begins, "Allah must receive the glory." And glory follows this tale of good versus evil from the bejeweled front cover to the gold-encrusted back jacket in the lustrous illustrations of the Russian artist Alisher Dianov. Dianov endows his palette with the richness of a ruler's treasure. Lush tapestries drape the pages, framing the story in gold and turquoise. A stork's-eye view of the magnificent city sets the scene with narrow, tiled streets weaving between domed towers and vessels sailing along the wide, green Tigris river at the city's edge. Palm trees sway in the distance, while high overhead the Calif and Vizier snap and clatter their beaks, talking in a language only other storks can understand, as they soar above Baghdad.

At first, the Calif greets his transformation into a stork as an advantage. Surely the storks know more of the city than he can ever know. But when the Calif tries to use the "magic" word penned on the parchment to regain his natural form, he finds that he has been tricked. "Casalavair" is not the magic word; it is as false as any "castle of air" could be. Forced to exist on slugs and grubs and worms like ordinary storks, the Calif and Vizier resolve to uncover the plot that has led to their enchantment.

Like many folktales, *The Enchanted Storks* provides a dash of history, a sprinkling of culture, and a large serving of morality as good triumphs over evil in the end. The Calif and Vizier discover that the plot to enchant them has been instigated by the Calif's covetous brother, Omar, and carried out by Khadur, the greatest of sorcerers. Disenchantment seems impossible at first, but the Calif reveals his greatness, even in the awkward form of a stork. When he comes to the aid of a weeping woodpecker who had also been enchanted by Khadur, he finds the clue that will transform him once again. He overhears the enchanter bragging about switching two letters in the magic word: Casalavair should have been inscribed as Calasavair. As soon as he regains his form, the Calif frees the woodpecker from her enchantment by asking her to become his wife.

The Enchanted Storks evokes the mystery and majesty of the Middle East. *The tale would provide a vivid opening for a unit on the history of the Islamic empire of which Baghdad was once the capital. Shepard's author's note provides a brief outline of the historical period of this vast empire which spread from India to Spain. Other ideas for classroom use include comparing cultures through folktales from around the world and making a folktale map with a picture of a book jacket pinned to each country of origin.* KIM GRISWELL

Momotaro, The Peach Boy: A Traditional Japanese Tale

📖 🖌 Linda Shute

Asian, Japanese

1986, Lothrop, Lee & Shepard

Momotaro is a well-known tale and song in Japan. Momotaro, born from a peach and raised by an elderly couple, grows into a brave man who battles the evil Onis (spirits) that steal from his parents and the villagers. Along his journey, he meets a monkey, a dog, and a pheasant with whom he shares his food. In exchange, the animals help him to return the stolen treasure to the villagers.

A classic Japanese tale, unevenly rendered, with stereotypical illustrations.

Shute successfully adapts this Japanese folktale to English, introducing several Japanese words with

English translations and fostering a greater awareness of cultural and linguistic diversity.

The fundamental theme of the story is the son's desire to pay his filial respect to his adoptive parents, an important aspect of Japanese morality. Shute distorts the ending, making the Peach Boy into a Robin Hood-like hero, discrediting the authenticity of the original tale. Although Shute states that she consulted Japanese narrative picture scrolls of the twelfth through fourteenth centuries, her illustrations suggest otherwise. Unfortunately, some of the illustrations are stereotypical images of Japanese people. CHIEKO YAMAZAKI-HEINEMAN

The Leopard's Drum: An Asante Tale from West Africa

Jessica Souhami
African
1995, Little Brown

Osebo the leopard, a master drummer, has the most magnificent drum ever seen or heard in the kingdom, and he will not let anyone else have it. Osebo even refuses Nyame the Sky-God's request for the drum. Nyame sends decrees that he will give a big reward to whomever brings him the drum.

A brightly illustrated retelling of an African folktale.

Onini the python and Esono the elephant try to take the drum, but they fail. Asroboa the monkey hides behind a mask in an attempt to get the drum, but he fails too. Clever and persistent, Achi-cheri the tortoise, the smallest of the animals, devises a plan for getting the drum. Her plan succeeds and in return she asks Nyame to turn her soft shell hard so as to protect herself from other animals. The victory of the soft-spoken and gentle animal makes others in the forest jealous, but Achi-cheri's prudent request keeps her safe.

With brilliantly colored illustrations adapted from her own shadow puppets, author Jessica Souhami retells the story of how a tortoise outwits a boastful leopard. The geometrical cutouts give the book the feel of an animated film, and the illustrations match the spirit of the story. Souhami, who studied textile design at the Central School of Art and Design in London, performs folktales from many cultures using brightly colored puppets, storytellers, and musical accompaniments. *The story lends itself to adaptation, and children could easily create a version of this tale and mount a production.* DAPHNE MUSE

Mufaro's Beautiful Daughters: An African Tale

John Steptoe
African American
1987, William Morrow & Company, Inc. ✳ Series

Inspired by a folktale in an 1895 anthology, *Kaffir Folktales*, this story comes from a people who lived near the ruins of Zimbabwe in southern Africa. In this version, a man named Mufaro lives in an African village with his two beautiful daughters, Manyara and Nyasha. Bad-tempered Manyara dislikes her sister because she is so kind and loved by everyone. She warns Nyasha that one day she will be queen and Nyasha will be a servant in her household.

Eventually a messenger arrives in their village with the news that the king is in search of a wife. Although Manyara tries to convince her father that Nyasha would be happier staying at home, he is determined to bring both of them before the king. During the night, Manyara leaves for the capital because she is so desperate to be first to see the king. As she travels, she encounters a young boy who asks for food, and a wise woman offering advice. Manyara rebukes both of them and hurries on.

The next morning, there is a great commotion when the villagers realize that Manyara is missing. They follow her footprints, which lead to the capital. Nyasha encounters the same boy and wise woman—when the boy asks for food, she feeds him, and when the wise woman stops her to give advice, she listens. Then, as they enter the city, Manyara runs out of the king's chamber screaming that she has been attacked by a five-headed snake. Nyasha enters the palace anyway and sees a small garden-snake which she once had welcomed into her garden. As it turns out, the snake is actually the king in disguise. In fact, he was also the little boy and the wise woman along the road. As a result of her kindness, the king knows that Nyasha is worthy to be his wife. Nyasha becomes queen and Manyara becomes her servant.

This African folktale warns against selfishness, but perpetuates an image of passive women.

This is a beautiful moral tale about the self-defeat of greed and selfishness. The illustrations are derived from the architecture of Zimbabwe, and the regional flora and fauna. While this is def-

398

initely a story from a specific cultural and historical time, the story conveys its message in a simple and straightforward manner that can be understood by all readers.

One drawback of the tale that reflects its cultural specificity is the way in which the girls are given passive roles. For all her ambition, greed, and manipulativeness, Manyara is simply trying to win the approval of a man, either her father or the king. The mother of the girls has no role at all in the story, and the only other female characters are the king's mother and sisters, who prepare the wedding feast. The girls themselves are reduced to simple tropes such as "beautiful and kind" or "beautiful and evil." Although the lessons this story teaches are universal, the restricted roles of the female characters undermine the multicultural approach of the author. MICHELLE GARFIELD

The Story of Jumping Mouse: A Native American Legend

John Steptoe
Native American
1984, Lothrop, Lee & Shepard

In this moving retelling of a Native American legend, a young mouse hears the stories of the elders, and his desire to visit the Far-Off-Land begins to

A Native American legend about a tiny mouse who exhibits enormous courage.

dominate his life. There is only one thing he can do: he must journey there. His travel is perilous. He both gives and receives help from other animals along the way, and his sacrifices are profound. But his steadfastness is rewarded as he is transformed from one of the humblest creatures to one of the most grand.

"Hold fast to your dream": Steptoe's tender text and gentle pencil drawings turn an almost too-familiar admonition into a poignant insight. The art is large, and detailed in terms of scienctific illustrations.

John Steptoe's *The Story of Jumping Mouse* was a Caldecott Honor Book in 1985. It is a deeply personal retelling of an ancient Native American legend. It is the story of dreams and hopes made real by challenge, sacrifice, and compassion, accessible to all children. KAREN ROBERTS STRONG

Coyote and Little Turtle: A Traditional Hopi Tale

Herschel Talashoema, Eugene Sekaquaptewa, and various sources, including Hopi children
Hopi, Native American
1994 (1993), Clear Light Publishers,
✳ Bilingual English/Hopi

Coyote and Little Turtle: A Traditional Hopi Tale and *Coyote and the Winnowing Birds: A Traditional Hopi Tale* feature the language and culture of the Hopi Indians, one of the best known of the Southwest Native American Nations. Part of Clear Light Publishers' Orig-

A fun tale that teaches lessons about respect for others and helps preserve Hopi culture and language.

399

inal Language Series, these books are a collaboration between the Institute for the Preservation of the Original Languages of the Americas; the Hopi Tribe Cultural Preservation Office; the Elder Storytellers; the children, staff, and board of the Hotevilla Bacavi Community School; and the Bureau of Applied Research in Anthropology at the University of Arizona.

Coyote, who is forever getting into or causing trouble, is once again the focus of these stories. They are meant not only to teach children moral lessons but also to entertain them.

In one such tale, Coyote schemes to catch some birds for his meal. However, the industrious and clever birds have a plan of their own. They get Coyote to suggest that he should fly with them, and the birds give him some of their feathers in order to do so. Once Coyote is aloft, the birds take back their feathers and Coyote falls from the sky. Not to worry, Coyote will rise again to cause more trouble in future tales.

These simple tales, familiar to many cultures around the world, are accompanied by delightful illustratrions by thirty-two children (in grades K-6) of Hotevilla Bacavi school. *Along with a bilingual text, the book includes a section for parents and teachers explaining Hopi grammar and a Hopi-English glossary.* Such bilingual books—especially those dealing with Native American languages—are fairly rare. Coyote and Little Turtle is an important tool in preserving native languages and cultures of the Americas. JUDITH CASTIANO

Addy's Theater Kit

📖 Valerie Tripp, et al.

African American

1994, Pleasant Company Publications ✳ Series

A spinoff of the book Meet Addy, *an innovative kit including a script, tips for actors, and a director's guide.*

This innovative kit offers children a way to expand on the book *Meet Addy,* a book about a young slave girl who with her family escapes from North Carolina in 1864. *The kit includes four copies of a twenty-nine-page script, "Friendship and Freedom," written for six characters and adapted from the book. At the end of the script is a section entitled "Tips for Actors." The Director's Guide provides instruction on a host of topics related to putting on a dramatic production such as planning the play, props, costumes, and playbills.*

For each section, there are helpful hints, color and black-and-white photographs of actual artifacts, and anecdotes that provide a historical context for the story. This innovative kit includes clear directions that children in grades two through five should be able to follow independently. It is an interesting companion to the book, and introduces many basic elements of theater and drama. JOAN PRIMEAUX

Darkness

📖 Mildred Pitts Walter 🖊 Marcia Jameson

Multicultural

1995, Simon and Schuster

Mildred Pitts Walter's *Darkness* is a poetic work exploring the wonder of blackness in our lives. Walter's text asks "Are you afraid of the dark?" and then launches into a lyrical celebration of darkness in the natural world. Walter starts with the "fiery falling star and pinpoint lights" that can only be seen in the night sky. She says, "babies begin in the darkness of the mother's womb," and goes on to list miracle after miracle from gems grown inside the earth to the "dark clouds that bring refreshing rain."

A poetic celebration of dark things that puts darkness in a whole new light.

Having described the world, Walter brings in the human element. She describes the magic of a shadow, the dark insides of our minds that produce all our creative and secret thoughts, and dusk when family and friends gather for laughter and talk."

In a lovely circular structure Walter ends her story with night and says the "darkest hour just before dawn is dreamtime." Walter dispels the fear of dark as well as its undeserved bad reputation. For her, darkness gives life and inspiration, encouraging new modes of thought. The book is a great departure for children from traditional portrayals of darkness pointing out how darkness is important in their lives.

Illustrations by St. Croix artist Marcia Jameson have a vibrant, glowing quality. Even amid her dark landscapes, she places light accents, praising darkness with the contrast. SUSIE WILDE

How Many, How Many, How Many

📖 Rick Walton 🖊 Cynthia Jabar

Multicultural

1993, Candlewick Press

This book exposes the young reader to a panorama of different faces representing many cultures and to the numeric system through the use of riddles.

There are a number of riddles illustrating each number. For example, for the number seven, the riddle reads, "Rainbows follow storms in March, How many colors in the arch?" A rainbow is illustrated with the seven colors, in addition to seven children and seven hats. Each page has a good deal of information for young children to grasp.

Children of many different ethnic backgrounds answer riddles and practice counting in this colorful picture book.

The author also includes characters from other stories: "Here Goldilocks sleeps all alone. How many bears are coming home?" While an older reader knows that there are three bears, the younger reader can count the bears and possibly link it to the story if he or she is familiar with it.

At the end of the story, the reader is informed that there are sets of things that can be counted other than the set that answers the riddle. Thus the reader is encouraged to pay attention to details, or else he or she could miss something.

Children can return repeatedly to this book perhaps finding something new each time. Counting becomes an active visual process that is sure to entertain almost any child. MARTHA L. MARTINEZ

400

Everyone Knows What a Dragon Looks Like

📖 Jay Williams ✏ Mercer Mayer

Asian, Chinese

1984 (1976), Four Winds Press 📖 Wolkstein, Diane, *Magic Wings: A Tale from China*; Yep, Laurence, *The Boy Who Swallowed Snakes*.

Han is the poor, kindly gate sweeper for the city of Wu. One day a messenger arrives to warn the city that an enemy army is planning to attack. The Mandarin asks his advisers for advice. They decide to ask the great sky dragon for help. The next day a short, fat man appears at the city gate. He announces that he is the dragon and has come to save the city. No one believes him except Han. For Han's sake, the man turns himself into a fierce dragon and frightens away the attackers.

In this wittily illustrated Chinese tale, only Han knows not to judge on appearances alone.

The arrogance of the Mandarin and his advisers contrasts with the humility of Han and the dragon, who convey the message that people shouldn't make assumptions based on appearances alone. Williams uses vivid language—"lightning sizzled" and "the dragon was the color of sunset shining through the rain." The dragon's hidden identity will surprise and delight readers. Witty pen-and-ink drawings and paintings make effective use of shadow and light. Illustrator Mayer is a stickler for details, from expressive faces down to the wrinkles on the bottoms of people's feet as they bow down to pray. Readers will see something new each time they view the pictures. PAM CARLSON

Galimoto

📖 Karen Lynn Williams ✏ Catherine Stock

African

1993 (1990), Lothrop, Lee & Shepard

✶ Audio Cassette, Series

Karen Williams's *Galimoto* is about a seven-year-old African boy named Kondi. In Malawi, *galimoto* means car and refers to push toys made from wires or sticks, cornstalks and yam pieces indigenous to the region, the kind of toys that Kondi decides he wants to make. In search of the necessary materials, Kondi trades with friends, asks for packing wires from an uncle who is a shopkeeper, interrupts the miller grinding maize to see if he has any to spare, and is mistaken for a thief when he climbs a fence surrounding a trash heap to collect spokes from broken bicycles. After collecting enough wire, Kondi settles upon making a pickup truck. All day long, he bends the wires to form the vehicle. Then, by the light of the moon, he leads his friends on a *galimoto* parade through the village.

Through the text and Catherine Stock's lovely watercolor illustrations, *Galimoto* offers insight into African village life, from the women waiting to have their maize ground, to customer buying fabric at the village dry goods store, to children playing with wheelbarrows. And the ever resourceful Kondi will certainly inspire other children to create their own toys from found objects. (In fact, Kondi's *galimoto* is so vividly

An African boy makes his own galimoto, or push toy in this joyful book.

drawn, with each wire bending and joint clearly outlined that it could serve as a model for children who want to make their own *galimotos*.) But the real joy of this book is in the way it conveys one child's devotion to creating something to play with—surely a kind of devotion that many children will recognize. DEBORAH PATTERSON

Rain Player

📖✏ David Wisniewski

Mayan, Native American

1996, Houghton Mifflin Company

A Maya village is threatened by a drought. Pik, one of the young men in the village, boasts that, if he were ruler, he would demand that Chac, the rain god, bring rains. Chac hears his bold pronouncement: "Is it right for such a small creature to bear such a large tongue?"

Realizing that his arrogance has caused him to forget his place in the order of life, Pik suggests that he and Chac play a game called pok-a-toc, so that Pik can earn the god's forgiveness. Pik realizes that he cannot take on

A Mayan boy challenges the rain god to a game of pok-a-toc in an accessible but inauthentic book.

the task alone, and asks the jaguar and the quetzal to come to his aid (both animals are held sacred by

the Mayan). With the assistance of the animals, Pik wins, and Chac keeps his promise and provides rain.

David Wisniewski uses artistic license in the retelling of this Maya legend. The result is less "authentic," but also more accessible to young American readers, than other versions of the tale.

Wisniewski's geometrical cutouts and colorful illustrations will also help children relate to this story. MARTHA L. MARTINEZ

Nine-In-One, Grr! Grr!: A Folktale from the Hmong People

📖 Blia Xiong and Cathy Spagnoli 🖌 Nancy Hom

Asian, Hmong

1989 (1989), Children's Book Press

The Hmong are a minority group in Southeast Asia primarily from Laos. Thousands of Hmong people have come to America as political refugees.

In the afterword to this children's book, the edi-

An excellent animal tale, and one of very few Hmong children's books in the U.S.

tors write: Blia Xiong heard *Nine-in-One, Grr! Grr!* when she was a small child living in the mountains of Laos. Blia was one of the first Hmong to come to Seattle in 1976, fleeing a war that had killed many of her people in Laos. She quickly learned English and helped the many Hmong families who followed from the refugee camps in Thailand. Adapting to a very different lifestyle here was hard for many, especially the elders who missed their old life in Laos. Many Hmong families also felt new tensions as their children grew up here as Asian Americans in a very different social climate. So, in 1978, Blia helped form a Hmong Association to preserve traditional music, dance, crafts, and stories.

A testament to the creativity of Hmong culture and to the Hmong in America who are even now struggling for cultural preservation, this charming folktale explains why tigers only have one cub every nine years. Tiger lives in a land of bamboo and wild banana trees. One day, she decides to visit the great god Shao to find out how many cubs she will have. Shao pronounces that Tiger will have nine cubs each year and Tiger is thrilled. But Shao warns

Tiger to remember his words, for they alone will determine the number of Tiger's cubs. Tiger walks off happily reciting "Nine-in-One, Grr! Grr!" A clever black bird, the Eu bird, overhears Tiger and quickly understands that if Tiger has that many children each year, tigers will overrun the land. She flies to Tiger and distracts her so she forgets the rhyme she is singing. When Tiger complains, Eu tells her that she remembers the rhyme—"One-in-Nine, Grr! Grr!" Then Tiger happily continues on her way and "that is why, the Hmong people say, we don't have many tigers on the earth today!"

There are few Hmong children's books in America, and this one will be valuable for children from the Hmong tradition as they seek validation of their traditional cultural forms, as well as a good introduction to those forms for other children. *The text is rhythmic and makes an excellent read-aloud selection for young children.* The bright colors of Nancy Hom's stylized illustrations, patterned after the Hmong appliqued art form of "story cloths," will capture children's imaginations and hold their interest. DEBBIE WEI

The Mask of the King

📖 Jwing-Ming Yan, Edited by Alan Dougall

🖌 Li Xieu-Liu

Asian, Chinese

1990, YMAA Publication Center ✳ Series

Part of a series of Asian folktales retold by the author, this volume includes one South Asian and three Chinese folktales. After each story, the author

Four Asian folktales describing how to solve problems with wisdom and wit.

discusses the main themes and poses questions to help young readers understand them.

In "Blessing in Disguise," an old man's beloved horse cripples his only son. While neighbors blame the incident on bad luck, the old man reflects that the situation may not be bad after all. Later, his son is exempted from serving in a devastating war because of his physical disability, while most neighbors' sons are killed in fighting. At the end of the story, the author encourages readers not to give up if an unlucky event happens, nor to be overjoyed because of a lucky event.

These stories are instructional but not overly didactic. The themes and lessons, while subtly presented, are usually explicit and easily extracted from the stories. BELINDA YUN-YING LOUIE

Butterfly Boy

📖 Laurence Yep 🖊 Jeanne M. Lee
Asian, Chinese
1993, Farrar, Straus & Giroux Inc. 📚 Yep, Laurence, *The Boy Who Swallowed Snakes*; Yep, Laurence, *The Ghost Fox*; Yep, Laurence, *The Man Who Tricked a Ghost*; Yep, Laurence, *Tree of Dreams: Ten Tales from the Garden of Night.*

Based on the writings of Chuang Tzu, the 4th Century B.C. Butterfly Philosopher, this is the story of "a boy who dreamed he was a butterfly, and, as a butterfly…dreamed he was a boy." Often the boy's confusion led him to do things that amused those around him, but their laughter meant nothing to him. Sometimes he would try to explain his perspective to people, but no one could understand the beauty he saw in an "ugly world." He continued to fly as a butterfly and dance as a boy," and he was never sure which he liked better."

An adept retelling of an ancient Chinese philosophical paradox that works best supplemented by background information.

Yep's story of the Butterfly Boy is supported by detailed, colorful paintings that show the reader how the world of a boy can intersect with the world of a butterfly.

Yep has adeptly retold several Chinese folktales in addition to this one. As many students in sixth grade study ancient civilizations, this book could be a useful addition to such classes. The tale is an allegory in Chinese philosophy, which Yep does not explore beyond this story. *Teachers will need to introduce more background information or guide discussions in order to add the book to the curriculum.* Younger readers may find the philosophical paradox posed too puzzling for fruitful reading. ROXANNE FELDMAN HSU

The City of Dragons

📖 Laurence Yep 🖊 Jean Tseng and Mou-Sien Tseng
Asian, Chinese
1995, Scholastic, Inc.

People ought to be judged by their accomplishments, not their appearances. That's the lesson of Laurence Yep's *The City of Dragons.*

Set in a small Chinese town, this compelling fantasy centers on a young boy, Chung Kuei, who has the saddest face in the world. "Even when he was happy," Yep writes, "everyone who saw him thought he must be sad, and they became sad, too." Unable to see past his expression, they avoid him altogether.

When some of the village elders ask Chung Kuei to stay home from the harvest festival because he'll ruin the party, the outcast runs away from home. But he soon learns that he can't ever "run away from this face."

On the road, Chung Kuei meets a caravan of giants, "each in a helmet and armor of rhinoceros hide, and with hair so long that it tapped the heels of their boots." Together they travel to an underwater city of dragons looking for pearls. That magical realm is brought to life through Jean and Mou-Sien Tseng's impressive, vibrant watercolors.

Pearls in the city, however, are scarce now because the dragon maidens, who magically can shed tears of pearls, can't seem to cry anymore. They've heard enough depressing stories about disasters, lost loves, deaths, and other cruelties. They "yawned and politely covered (their) mouths with (their) paws. 'We've already heard that one.'" Nothing else and no one else can draw any more sympathy from them— no one, that is, except Chung Kuei.

When the dragons see the little boy's sad face, they're convinced that

A Chinese boy with the saddest face in the world teaches his village not to judge people by their appearances.

something tragic has happened to him, something they believe he won't reveal. Overwhelmed by emotion, they once again begin to cry tears of pearls.

The people in Chung Kuei's village are thrilled with the riches he carries back to them. The face that once caused him great shame brings him honor instead.

Everyone realizes that they "should have judged the boy by what he did and not by the way he

403

looked." This clever story teaches that, more than anything else, beauty is about acceptance and respect. CHRISTINA ENG

Lon Po Po: A Red-Riding Hood Story from China

Ed Young
Asian, Chinese
1989, Philomel Books ▯ Grimm, Jacob, *Little Red Cap*; Hyman, Trina Schart, *Little Red Riding Hood*; Perrault, Charles, *Little Red Riding Hood*; Regniers, Beatrice Schenk, *Red Riding Hood*.

Ed Young's pastel and watercolor illustrations, rendered in ancient Chinese panel art technique, add drama to this Chinese variant of the Little Red Riding Hood story. In *Lon Po Po* (grandmother in Chinese) there are three sisters—Shang, Tao, and Poatze—rather than a single girl. The wolf decides to disguise himself as their grandmother, knowing that the children love and respect her and would willingly be of service to her. Under the leadership of the clever eldest daughter, the three sisters join forces and succeed in thwarting the wolf's evil intentions.

Lon Po Po is a rich resource for discussions of cultural differences and their expressions in folktales. Children can identify other versions of Little Red Riding Hood and relate them to Lon Po Po. Further, Shang, Tao, and Poatze's success against the wolf conveys a positive message about the value of working collectively.

Ed Young has done justice to an oral tradition that is over a thousand years old, and this book was justly awarded the Caldecott Medal.
HELEN R. ABADIANO

A Chinese version of Little Red Riding Hood that won a Caldecott medal.

404

Let Me Tell You a Story: Storytelling in Multicultural Children's Literature

Joseph Bruchac

"LET ME TELL YOU A STORY." FEW WORDS are more magical than these. With these words, a door unlocks, allowing the listener to walk into another, different world. The most successful approaches in children's literature involve the telling of stories. Stories are as old as human language itself and may have been one of the primary reasons for the development of language. Wherever I have traveled or lived—from West Africa to Baffin Island, from the Mayan highland rain forests of Mexico to the volcanic slopes of Hawaii to my current home in the Adirondack mountain foothills of New York State—I have seen the same attentive response to those words.

Once, long ago, something happened to a man or a woman who wished to share a particular experience with others. And so a story was told. It was so long ago, the story was told without words. Perhaps it was danced, mimed, or sung. Then, because that story had such meaning, those who saw and heard remembered it — and later told it themselves. Through storytelling people could share those experiences which, without a story, no one would have remembered beyond one generation or beyond one person's lifetime. Memory and story are also, it seems inextricable. By turning the events of history into story, they become more memorable. Stories, then, allow us to remember more.

Storytelling, rather than presenting a flat, lifeless canvas, involves all of the senses and may be so deeply somatic that people hearing (or reading) a story find themselves physically moving with it. A good storyteller brings texture and presence to a tale. Good storytelling is also as natural to human beings as breathing and seems to be almost as necessary. While not exclusive to any particular culture or class of people, it is as inclusive as the shape of the listening circle that seems to form instinctively around the storyteller.

Unlike watching television or a movie, listening to storytelling is not a passive experience. Not only do many storytelling traditions include some kind of call and response, many stories, songs, and even dances include those who are listening. The Iroquois storytellers of North America's eastern woodlands punctuate their talks with the word "Honh" to which "Heng" must be responded or the storyteller will stop telling! The use of interactive videos and CD-ROMs may well play a key and innovative role in taking storytelling to another level.

Stories are frequently used to convey cultural values and can offer deep insights into other cultures. They tell us how others see the world in ways that are similar to or different from our views. Stories such as "Jack and the Beanstalk" and other European tales of finding one's fortune, often in the shape of gold, help us see that the attainment of personal success through overcoming obstacles and even monsters, is an important cultural value in European traditions.

Many Native American stories have, as a central theme, doing things for the good of the people. In the story "Gluskabe and the Four Wishes," which comes from the Abenaki Indian people of New England, four men seek to gain their greatest wishes. The three who seek individual gain achieve dubious success. The one who wishes to be taller than all men is changed into a tree. The one who does not wish to grow old and die becomes a boulder. The one who wants more possessions than anyone is given his wish while in a canoe and the weight of all those possessions sinks the boat and he drowns. Only the man whose wish was to be able to do more for his people is given his wish in a way that is not personally destructive. In contrast to Jack, this Abenaki hero succeeds only when he thinks of others, thus giving us insight into a culture where communality is of great importance.

Because storytelling often works on many lev-

406

els, it is especially well-suited for children. A story that seems simple on the surface may have different meanings for the same people at different times in their lives. Those different meanings do not cancel each other out but add to the richness of the story over the years. Thus, a child hears a story and remembers it for its wonderful, exciting, or funny moments, only fully appreciating its other teachings with age.

"The Boy Who Lived with the Bears" is an Iroquois story with precisely that kind of depth. It tells of an orphaned boy who is left with his uncle. The uncle grows tired of caring for him and abandons the boy by trapping him in a cave. Instead of despairing, the boy remembers lessons taught by his deceased parents and sings for help. The boy is then freed from the cave by the animals—a symbolic rebirth. He is adopted and cared for lovingly by a mother bear. Observing the bear's behavior, the uncle also suffers a change of heart and takes on his proper role as caregiver for his nephew. An Iroquois child, on hearing this story, might hear the reassuring lesson that even hopeless situations may work out for the best if you maintain faith and courage. Even if you lose your parents, the story says, somewhere there will be someone who will love and care for you. The story takes on a further meaning for that same Iroquois child upon reaching adulthood. Now, the story says, you must remember that it is the responsibility of all adults to care for children. You must show as much responsibility and love for all children as did the mother bear in "The Boy Who Lived with the Bears." The lessons of this story are more poignantly true today for a society in which, all too often, children are not rescued when they are abandoned, and where far too many adults show neither love nor responsibility toward children.

The structure of the average story was outlined 3,000 years ago by the Greeks. It has a beginning, a middle, and an end. The start of a story is almost always signaled by such words as "Once upon a time," or "I will now tell a story." And a similar formulaic ending releases us, through such phrases as "They all lived happily ever after," or "So the story goes." Thus, there is a clearly defined space within which a story takes place and the listener or reader knows when the

story is over. The story is a kind of journey in which the storyteller allows us to share. It also may be seen as a four-part structure. It begins when the protagonist sets out from home. We see this when Jack goes out to seek his fortune; when Odysseus sets sail for Troy; and when a Yoruba girl in West Africa falls in love with a handsome stranger and leaves her parents to go with him. It then comes to a point when the main character is faced with great danger or difficulty. Jack is confronted by a giant, Odysseus is shipwrecked, the Yoruba girl discovers her handsome man is really nothing more than a skull wearing borrowed body parts. The story then continues with the protagonist overcoming those challenges. Finally, it ends with the hero or heroine returning home—wiser and perhaps sadder from what has been learned. This home - journey - home pattern is easy for children to recognize once it has been pointed out to them.

CRITICAL THINKING

The nature of stories makes them useful tools in developing critical thinking. When a character in a story makes a wrong decision, the results are often so clearly portrayed that a child may find it easier to make better decisions of his or her own. One of the trickster heroes of Abenaki stories is Azeban, the Raccoon. (In the Abenaki language, Azeban—the name for the raccoon—literally means "Trickster.") Azeban invariably ends up getting into trouble when he makes wrong decisions. In one memorable tale, Azeban finds a big rock on a hill and decides to push it so that it will roll down hill. Then Azeban tries to see if he can run faster than the rock. He manages to get ahead of the rock, but then stumbles and the rock rolls over him. It is still common for Abenaki parents to say to their children, "Don't be like Azeban!"

In most Native American cultures and in many other parts of the world, storytelling has a dual purpose: entertainment and instruction. Instead of striking, shouting at, or ridiculing a child who did something wrong, Native elders tell the child a "lesson" story, a moral tale that shows why such behavior is wrong. A contemporary Mohawk story, "Akonwara," tells how two children are left with their grandmother who lives in a cabin in the woods. The little boy grows bored because he has no television to watch and he begins to bully his smaller sister. The grandmother warns him three times that a terrible monster called Akonwara, "The Ugly Face," is waiting outside. This monster eats little boys who do not obey their elders. When he misbehaves a fourth time, the grandmother thrusts him out into the darkness and shuts the door tight. He begs to come back in, but the grandmother refuses to open the door. She waits until he stops banging on the door, determined to teach him a lesson he will not forget. However, the grandmother waits too long. When she does finally open the door, the little boy is gone—taken by Akonwara, never to be seen again.

This use of stories reflects the Native belief that physical abuse and verbal abuse lead only to more abuse; violence creates violence. A lesson story goes into the heart and remains there. The person who remembers that teaching story is not only made wiser, but also morally and spiritually stronger. As people move from childhood to adulthood to being elders, the firm and gentle guidance of stories is always with them.

All storytelling is a part of "multicultural" storytelling. Such archetypal characters as the wise elder, the young man or woman going out to find his or her way in the world, the lost child who is adopted or saved by animals, are found in virtually every storytelling tradition but are told in many different and interesting ways. Best of all, we may learn lessons from stories in a non-threatening and memorable way. Even those who seem least likely to hear may be touched by the right story.

John Stokes teaches traditional survival skills through The Tracking. How to make a fire with a bow drill, how to follow the tracks of an animal, how to track our own dreams and understand our roles as human beings are all part of his teaching. Stokes uses storytelling as a central part of his teaching, storytelling he has learned from many years of living and working with indigenous elders in Australia, Hawaii, and North America. Two years ago, Stokes went to make his yearly visit to the Zuni Indian High School. The principal informed him that things were not good. There were now youth gangs at

Zuni and there had been a drive-by shooting. He doubted that Stokes would be able to reach these tough kids.

At his first assembly, John stood on the stage and looked out at Native American teenagers who were wearing sunglasses and dressed like gangbangers. He asked them about the drive-by shooting.

"They deserved to get shot," someone yelled from the audience.

"Why?" John asked.

"Because they flipped off the guys who shot them."

"Ah," John said, "let me tell you a story."

As the room became quiet, he told them the story of a young American man who became an expert in Aikido. He went to Japan to study that martial art and began to think of himself as a master. Late at night, he was on a bus when a big Japanese man got on. The big man was drunk and began swearing at the other passengers and pushing them. The American man who knew Aikido was waiting for the big drunk to reach him. He was going over in his mind all the things he would do to that drunk.

Just then, though, a small elderly Japanese man stood up. He walked right up to the big drunk and put his hand on the man's shoulder. "My son," the old man said, "tell me what is troubling you." The big drunken Japanese man sat down on the floor of the bus and began to cry. "It's my wife," he said, "she is in the hospital, and I can't help her."

And as the old man patted the drunk on the back, comforting him like a child, the American who knew Aikido felt very foolish. He understood that he was far from being a master. The old man was the master.

When Stokes finished that story there was complete silence in the room. He looked out and said, "Anyone who wants to can come to my workshops tomorrow. But they must promise that they will do everything I tell them to do."

The next day, every one of those young people who had been dressed like gangbangers was in John's workshop. They did everything he asked them to do. All because of the power of the story.

The interest factor remains just as strong in stories that are written down. Reading skills can be strengthened through storytelling. When an adult reads an interesting story to a child, that child is much more likely to want to read further stories on his or her own. It is important for us to have stories written by people who have lived those stories. Authenticity is critical. Native Americans are not the only ones who can write down Native American stories. But insiders are more likely to know about their cultures and their stories and thus be able to tell the stories well.

It takes a long time to learn not only the story but the culture and the language from which that story springs. Clarity comes, I believe, from an awareness of complexity. It was because of a lack of knowledge that Longfellow's epic poem "Hiawatha" was misnamed. It is really a story about the Chippewa culture hero Manabozho. Hiawatha was a historical leader of the Iroquois, one of the founders of their League of Peace, which brought together five formerly warring nations a thousand or more years ago. Similar kinds of renaming happened to European immigrants when they came to Ellis Island and were confronted by Americans who did not speak their languages and gave them new names as a result. My father's mother came from Slovakia, and I always thought her first name was Pauline. I only found out when she was in her eighties that her real name was Appolina, but the immigration officer did not know how to spell that and wrote "Pauline" instead. There is a Jewish American story that tells how one immigrant from Poland became named "Sam Ding." He spoke a little English and, by accident, the man in front of him had the same name. When it was his turn, the immigration officer asked for his name. "Same ding as him," said the man. "Sam Ding," said the immigration officer and wrote it down.

From 1966 to 1969, I lived and taught high school to young men and women of the Ewe nation in Ghana, West Africa. Through hearing my students' stories, I learned at least as much from them as they learned from me. I have many stories to tell of my experiences in those years, and I learned a number of traditional Ewe stories of Yiyi the Spider Trickster (who is known as Anansi to the neighboring Akan peo-

ples). I also realized that I was not the one to tell those stories. However, those African stories did help me look with new eyes at the stories of Native Americans and helped me become a better storyteller of the tales from my own traditions as a result.

Not long ago scholars of European heritage believed that neither black Africans nor Native Americans had any storytelling traditions at all. Considering the fact that Aesop's fables are actually traditional African tales — "Aesop" comes from "Ethiop," a person from Ethiopia — this is especially ironic. Regarding the Native people of the Americas, some writers in the eighteenth century went so far as to state that American Indians had no real language at all, but gave speeches the way birds sing, by instinct, without any intellectual understanding of what they said. Those scholars actually stated that when they were at home with their families, American Indians did not speak but growled and grunted like animals. In the words of Immanuel Kant, in a 1772 lecture delivered at the University of Konigsberg, "The American Indians are incapable of civilization ... and having no motive force, for they are without affection and passion." In fact, Kant went on to say, they "hardly speak at all, never caress one another, care about nothing and are lazy." The research of Henry Rowe Schoolcraft began to change that view. Schoolcraft was an American writer of the mid 1800s who carefully studied the cultures of many of the Native American nations, especially those in the Great Lakes region and the Northeast. Schoolcraft's own wife was a Minnesota Ojibway. She aided him greatly as he wrote down a number of the great stories of the traditions of the Algonquin peoples, including the epic of Manabozho, the hero later misnamed by Longfellow. With the publication of *Historical and Statistical Information Respecting the History, Conditions and Prospects of the Indian Tribes of the United States* in 1857, Schoolcraft helped begin a new awareness of the intellectual greatness of Native American culture. He did it in large part through telling stories.

Storytelling is one of the finest tools we have to reach other human beings. It is a wonderfully effective way to present and understand the complexity of human experience we now call multi-culturalism. Much of the best children's literature either uses storytelling as a central device or is storytelling, pure and simple. Written stories are most effective when they reflect the spoken word. For that reason, I am convinced that one of the best ways for children to encounter these written examples of storytelling is through reading aloud to them. Thereafter, whenever they read that story on their own, they have the memory of a real human voice telling the tale. Reading a story aloud may also be a way of testing its efficacy with children. If it seems stiff or incomplete, that may be a sign that the writer failed to catch the rhythm and the shape of the story. When a story truly flows, it can shape a circle that encompasses a whole world, allowing the listeners to see and imaginatively experience things they may never have considered before, to welcome and better understand new ideas and old, much-needed truths.

THE BEST STORIES EVER TOLD?

There are so many stories told by so many wonderful storytellers that any list of the "best" stories must either be very long or very incomplete. Some stories, in fact, may best be described as cycles of tales, which taken as a whole add up to more than the sum of their parts and which have been told and retold by innumerable tellers. In terms of Trickster tales alone, I think of the Jack tales of Appalachia, the High John, the Conqueror stories of the African American South, and the Ananse the Spider tales of Ghana in West Africa which became the Anancy tales of Jamaica. Jane Yolen's landmark *Favorite Folktales from Around the World* (Pantheon Books, 1986), *Homespun: Tales from America's Favorite Storytellers*, edited by Jimy Neil Smith (Crow Publishers, 1988), and *Ready to Tell Tales*, edited by David Holt and Bill Mooney (August House, 1994) are three excellent volumes that can be used as an introduction to the best stories.

Here is a brief list of some of my own favorite tales from the Native American traditions of the Northeast. These are stories that I frequently tell, stories that combine the elements of delight and instruction and are of particular relevance to today's world. In each case I give the origin of the story, a brief summary, and indicate where a written version may be found.

1. THE CREATION STORY
Haudenosaunee (Iroquois), Northeastern Woodlands of North America
There are many versions throughout Native North America of this tale in which the earth is created on the back of the turtle who floats in the great ocean. The story is so widespread that North America is called "Turtle Continent" by many American Indian nations. The Iroquois version remains my favorite, with such powerful images as the woman falling from the sky-world to be caught between the wings of the geese, and the animals diving to bring up earth to give her a place to stand. It is a tale of cooperation and caring, a story in which we are shown the importance of women and in which we see the living earth as our mother.

There are dozens of written versions of this story. Some of the best include those in *Tales of the Iroquois* by Tehanetorens/Ray Fadden, Iroqrafts Books; *Traditional Teachings* by Mike Myers and Michael Kanentakeron Mitchell, North American Indian Travelling College; and *Seneca Myths and Folktales* by Arthur C. Parker, University of Nebraska Press.

2. THE GREAT LEAGUE OF PEACE
Haudenosaunee (Iroquois), Northeastern Woodlands of North America
The Iroquois League was formed from five related nations, the Seneca, Cayuga, Ononodaga, Oneida, and Mohawk after a long period of violent warfare and bloodfeuds between them. A messenger referred to as The Peacemaker was sent by the Creator to bring peace back to the people. The tale of how this was accomplished is a true epic. With the help of Hiawatha (not Longfellow's character, but an historical figure who was a great orator) and the woman known as Jigonsasah (sometimes called "The Peace Queen"), The Peacemaker succeeded in his great mission. Each time I think I have heard the whole story, I hear another part of it. I was told by Oren Lyons, an Onondaga Faith Keeper, that every part of the story has other stories connected to it. The beauty and importance of peace, the way that seemingly

409

evil people can be transformed into good and useful members of society, and the power to be found in union are the extremely important messages that this great story conveys.

Written versions can be found in *The White Roots of Peace* by Wallace; *Tales of the Iroquois* by Tehanetorens/Ray Fadden, Iroqrafts Books; *Traditional Teachings* by Mike Myers and Michael Kanentakeron Mitchell, North American Indian Travelling College; and *Seneca Myths and Folktales* by Arthur C. Parker, University of Nebraska Press.

3. THE WIND EAGLE
Abenaki, Northeastern Woodlands
This is one of a cycle of stories told about the transformer and trickster hero known variously as Gluskabe, Glooskap, Koluskap, and Odzihozo. After forming himself from the earth where Ktsi Nwaskw, the Great Mystery, let fall some of the dust of creation, Gluskabe goes about the world, guided by Grandmother Woodchuck. Gluskabe's job is to learn to understand the world and also make it a better place for the human beings still to come. Part of what he must learn is when not to change things, as in this story when he finds out that tying the wings of the Wuchowsen, the great eagle whose wingbeats create the wind, disrupts the natural balance of the world.

My own telling of this tale may be found in *Native American Stories from Keepers of the Earth*, Fulcrum Press, and on the audio tape *Gluskabe Stories*, Yellow Moon Press.

The next major milestone for this planet is the welcoming of the millennium. At the start of this century, many thought that storytelling was a thing of the past. In fact, the survival and the growing strength of storytelling indicate its importance as one of the most vital ways to learn and preserve our personal, cultural, and natural histories. Through storytelling we learn to understand ourselves in relation to others and see the diversity of the world around us. In the millennium to come, there will be many new stories to be told, as well as old ones to remember. If the voice is true, if the story sings with the power of a human voice, when those words "let me tell you a story" are read or spoken, our children will continue to listen and, most importantly, to learn.

Born of Abenaki descent, Joseph Bruchac is a scholar of Native American culture, an internationally known author, poet and storyteller. His book, A Boy Called Slow, *received a 1996 Mountains and Plains Book Award. He lives with his wife in upstate New York.*

Grade Four to Grade Six

The Wonderful Story of Zaal: A Persian Legend

📖 Mohammad Batmanglij and Najmieh Batmanglij
✒ Franta
Ancient Persian, Middle Eastern
1985, Mage Publishers 📖 Picard, Barbara Leoning, *Tales From Ancient Persia.*

This ancient Persian legend, which first appeared in *Khodai Nameh: The Tales of Kings*, in the sixth century, reappeared in Shahnameh four centuries later. What Saam, the powerful hero of seven lands, longs for more than anything else in the world is a son. But when Zaal is born, his hair is all white, like an old man's. Confused and angry, Saam has Zaal taken away and exposed on a hillside.

Seemorgh, a giant bird (a popular figure in Persian mythology), who lives on top of a high mountain, finds Zaal and raises him to be a fine young man. Meanwhile, one night, Saam dreams of Zaal and, ashamed of what he has done, decides to find

A fine retelling of a Persian legend about the mighty hero of Shahnameh.

him with the help of his flying carriage.

Unlike many heroes of legend, Saam is not flawless. He commits an offense that he later regrets. *As a teaching tool, this story can be a lesson in Persian mythology and can also prompt moral questions for class discussion.*

The story is retold in fine language that retains the essence of the original legend. SHAHLA SOHAIL

The Naked Bear: Folktales of the Iroquois

📖 John Bierhorst (editor) ✎ Dirk Zimmer
Iroquois, Native American
1987, William Morrow

John Bierhorst is one of the most noted folklorists specializing in Native American folktales and mythology. These sixteen stories are from the Six Nations of the Iroquois who live in New York and Canada. They were among the first folktales to be collected in North America. Here they are retold for children. The black-and-white illustrations, are humorous without being stereotypical and depict traditional Iroquois folklore motifs.

Traditional folktales of the Iroquois provide an excellent introduction to Native American culture.

Bierhorst's introduction offers a brief overview of Iroquois life before and after contact with the white world. Bierhorst relates that the nineteenth-century Iroquois who told these stories were thoroughly Europeanized in their dress, housing, and enterprises. The stories, told by the elders to children in front of the campfire, brought to life another place, another time. Bierhorst describes the Iroquois storytelling skills and traditions which are still practiced today.

The stories included in this collection are about children, ghosts, animals, and traditional Iroquois life, which will appeal to children. One of my favorites, "Chestnut Pudding," tells of magic and a boy's clever manipulation of powerful witches in order to save his grandmother. Daily family life is also depicted, along with scenes of magic, talking animals, and beings with superhuman powers. The traditional language of these tales is maintained in the translation, though the tales are simplified for younger readers. *The print is large and accessible to third or fourth graders, although the stories can be read to younger children.*

The book contains a bibliography of references and an explanation of motifs common to certain geographic areas. This book is an excellent way to introduce young children to Iroquois culture, and a good way to begin a presentation on Native American stories, music, food, and crafts. ELAINE P. GOLEY

Peach Blossom Spring

📖 Fergus M. Bordewich ✎ Yang Ming-Yi
Asian, Chinese
1994, Green Tiger Press, Inc.

Schoolchildren in China are familiar with this story in the same way children in the West know Heidi, Peter Pan, and Alice in Wonderland. There have been many versions, and it has been the subject of poems and paintings since the fourth century A.D., when a popular poet, Tao Chien (also called Tao Yuan Ming), wrote this tale of a life of few possessions and simple pleasures.

In ancient China a poor fisherman discovers a secret land in a classic Chinese tale told here with period illustrations.

This picture book tells of a poor fisherman who, having wandered farther than he intended, finds himself on a stream flowing with peach blossoms. Through a small cave, he happens upon another world where people from an ancient time live quietly and at peace with one another. Farming and leading an idyllic life, they are far removed from the modern, bustling, fast-paced world of self-seeking, greedy people eager for riches and material goods. (Of course, the "modern world" of the story is the fourth century and the "ancient time" is several hundred years earlier.)

Impressed by his new friends, the fisherman decides to stay with them, returning home only to fetch a few things. (*At this point in the story, it is fun to ask your audience whether they think going back, even briefly, is a good idea. Fattened on fairy tales, they will usually respond with a resounding NO! But the tale goes on, and their fears of his botching his return prove well grounded.*)

He is warned to tell no one of this utopian land, but, cannot hold his tongue. The mass of people who end up accompanying him cause so much confusion that he cannot find his way back. And no one else has found it since, though many have looked.

The illustrations, one full page facing each page

of text, are done in the style of the *Mustard Seed Manual*, the ancient handbook of Chinese painting in ink and watercolors, with a bit of artistic embellishment. The costumes accurately portray the time represented (as not all picture books on China do), lending both color and life to the characters in the story.

This tale provides a good opportunity for a fun exercise of imagination. When asked to think about what to bring along if they were going forever to live in a very different place, like China or ancient times, children must choose the one item they would miss most from their normal lives. How might they adjust to the new place? (How might a child manage to bring along something like ice cream?)

After discussion, you can take a vote. Who would choose to stay in the modern world (with family, friends, and modern attractions), and who would choose to go with the fisherman to a world in some manner perfect? GINNY LEE

Hoang Breaks the Lucky Teapot

📖 Rosemary K. Breckler   🖌 Adrian Frankel

Asian, Vietnamese

1992, Houghton Mifflin

Hoang is a Vietnamese boy with a vivid imagination. One day, he imagines that a teapot (*gia truyen*) is a steaming dragon and throws his ball at it, breaking it into pieces. He tries to repair the teapot because he knows that it brings good luck and good fortune to his family. Try as he may, he cannot repair it, but manages to paint an old teapot to resemble the cherished *gia truyen*.

A Vietnamese boy tries to repair a teapot he has broken in this symbolic story of contemporary Vietnam.

The lucky teapot symbolizes the history and culture of Vietnam, and was passed from father to son over many generations. War and political events ravaged Vietnam, damaging their heritage, just as Hoang damages the lucky teapot. The author hopes that people like Hoang have the desire to rebuild their country as Hoang has carefully rebuilt the *gia truyen*. The author expresses her love for her country and feelings about the troubles there. This book will help young readers to gain some knowledge about Vietnam, and reading it with an adult, they can gain a deeper understanding of the symbolism. LI LIU

The Jolly Mon

📖 Jimmy Buffett, Edited by Savannah Buffet

🖌 Lambert Davis

Caribbean, West Indian

1988, Harcourt Brace Jovanovich   ✳ Audio Cassette

This adventure story was inspired by songwriter/performer Jimmy Buffet's experiences sailing in the Caribbean Sea. One morning the Jolly Mon goes to the beach to sing for his breakfast. He discovers a beautiful guitar floating in Snapper Bay. The moment he touches it, he knows how to play. When Good King Jones hears what has happened, he orders a boat built so that the Jolly Mon can share the happiness of his music with other islands.

A fisherman finds a magic guitar in a somewhat misleading portrait of the Caribbean by songwriter Jimmy Buffet.

The dreadlocked hero crosses the bay and travels to Pumpkin Island, Parrot Key, Mango Bay, and Lemonland. He has been on Coconut Island for a while when news reaches him that the king is dead. The Princess Marigold needs Jolly Mon to return home to cheer the people up with his music.

On the way back to Bananaland, he is captured by One-Eyed Rosy and her pirate gang. Angry when

they can't pull the gems off the guitar, they push the Jolly Mon into the sea. As he sinks to the bottom, he sees a dolphin—the same white dolphin painted on the back of the guitar. It untangles and frees the Jolly Mon, identifies himself as Albion, and explains that he's come to take the Jolly Mon home.

Recovered at Bananaland, the Jolly Mon is led by Princess Marigold to his boat and the magic guitar. The painting of the white dolphin has disappeared but Albion, splashing in the bay, explains that it's time for Jolly Mon to be the new king. At the end of the Jolly Mon's long and happy life, he is taken away by Albion. They disappear into the sky, headed toward Orion.

Loaded with fantasy, this fairy tale risks confusing young readers about what is fact and what is fiction in terms of life in the Caribbean. Most West Indians do not really live in thatched huts as depicted in this book. Caribbean women do not wear

412

flowers in their hair and men do not wear coconuts on their heads. It's important to note this is a mishmash of tropical cultures. The book is likely to gain attention on the basis of the author's name.
LESLIE ANDERSON MORALES

Where Angels Glide at Dawn: New Stories from Latin America

📖 Lori M. Carlson and Cynthia L. Ventura
🖌 Jose Ortega
Hispanic
1990, Lippincott, Harper & Row

An excellent collection of stories from Latin America and the Caribbean.

This is a funny, fascinating, frightening, and touching collection of stories from Latin America, with an introduction by the highly acclaimed Chilean novelist Isabel Allende. Allende's introduction reads like a story in itself and notes that "Story-tellers haven't disappeared completely from the city, but now they are called writers." Before coming to the printed page, many of these stories were part of the oral tradition familiar to children throughout Latin America.

These sometimes clever and thought-provoking tales reflect a range of characters and moods as broad as the political and cultural landscape of Latin America. Magical rabbits, millionaires, mobsters, an endless civil war, and snow falling in the tropics are all intertwined. In "The Day We Went to See Snow" by Alfredo Villanueva-Collado, the author recounts the day his family took a trip to San Juan, Puerto Rico, to see the snow that fell on the tropical island. A funny kind of reassuring laughter arose when I read that story, because my grandmother once told us a story about Felisa Rincón, a former mayor of Puerto Rico, bringing snow from San Juan to New York. Things we often think of as mere folklore are sometimes true.

Ariel Dorfman, a Chilean author and human rights activist, Jorge Ibarguengoitia, a Mexican writer who was also the author of several children's books, and Reinaldo Arenas, a Cuban-born American writer, also contributed to this fine collection of short stories. *While broad in focus and interest, the high literary quality of these stories makes them most appropriate for readers with very adept reading and analytical skills.* The book also includes a very helpful glossary. MAGNA M. DIAZ.

The Painter and the Wild Swans

📖 Claude Clement 🖌 Frederic Clement
Asian, Japanese
1993 (1986), Puffin Books

Ice blue paintings and the majestic elegance of swans are the initial attraction of this picture book. The story is about Teiji, a painter of some excellence and renown who wants to capture the beauty of wild swans in his paintings. In fact, he is so captivated by their beauty that to seek them out, he forsakes all his friends, his clients, his life in town, and even his art.

A Japanese painter gives up all his material assets to follow wild swans in an attractive picture book.

Farther and farther north he pursues them, to the icy cold. In despair he regards their beauty, frustrated at not being able to capture it before he dies. Then he realizes that it is not necessary to capture it; it is enough to be a part of it. "It doesn't matter if an artist never paints this. Such real beauty is rare and impossible to capture. At least I have seen it before I die," says the painter in a moment of inspiration, whereupon he transforms into a swan. In his life afterward as a swan, he thinks of his human life as a dream. Or, perhaps, the man is dreaming he is a swan as he dies of the cold in the wilderness of the north.

The illustrations are so subtle that at first glance one does not even realize that there are transformations from one picture to the next. Throughout the book the illustrations seem to be part one thing, part another, akin to Escher's ability to turn a school of fish into a flight of birds in a single painting.

Seemingly simple and clear enough to read to children, the tale is nonetheless of a profound nature beyond the level of the nursery room story hour. It remains uncertain whether the poem at the end is dedicated to the (real-life) photographer Teiji, or whether Teiji himself wrote it. Also, the beautiful (and accurate) Japanese calligraphy accompanying the paintings line by line, one line of the poem per page, and repeated at the end, is not attributed to anyone. Did Teiji himself do it? Or did the illustrator, Frederic Clement, become so proficient at Japanese calligraphy that he did the lettering himself?

Although Japanese and Chinese brush writing requires a special brush and other accoutrements, it

413

might be an interesting exercise to see how close to the Japanese one might come even without knowing any Japanese. Or perhaps a Japanese lesson book or even a calligrapher might be found to offer instruction.

Japanese haiku—brief poems of three lines with a specific number of syllables per line—are popular with some English teachers. Another exercise might be to write haiku (or other forms of poetry) with similar subjects (beauty, desire, cold, the life of an animal versus the life of a person) as themes. This beautiful and haunting book may end up appealing more to adults than to children, but with a compassionate presentation, older children can relate to these distinctly Japanese emotions, which also touch something universal. GINNY LEE

Charlie and the Chocolate Factory

📕 Roald Dahl ✒ Richard George

Multicultural

1992 (1964), Buccaneer Books ✳ Series

When the publishers first received the manuscript for this book (so the story goes), some of the editors were aghast at the blatant racism they detected in it, particularly the inclusion of pygmies, imported from Africa, who work and live in the chocolate factory

A classic from the 1960s with an insidiously racist text, despite the appeal of its candy-laden setting.

and are paid in cacao beans and chocolate. The little chocolate-colored people, called Oompa-Loompas, sing all day, are very happy, and have no names. Further, they are experimented on from time to time by the dictator of the chocolate factory, Willie Wonka. Sometimes they are injured by this experimentation, sometimes they disappear. When Dahl was confronted with the issue of racism he is reputed to have said, "Nonsense! I wrote this book for my son after he had had an accident. I wouldn't write a racist book for him." And the book was published as is, with the illustrations clearly depicting little chocolate-colored pygmies.

The book was revised in 1973, evidently in response to public outcry, so that the Oompa-Loompas are no longer black, no longer pygmies, no longer from Africa but, rather, are "Imported direct from Loompaland." But all other details remain. They are still nameless, experimented on, sing and are happy all day and night, even though they must always remain in the chocolate factory.

Although their color is now white and their hair is sandy colored, they are still slaves, and the behavior of Mr. Wonka is still cruel and dictatorial.

The plot of this very entertaining and popular book revolves around Charlie, an innocent, poor, obedient boy, who, along with some other children not nearly as well behaved as Charlie, wins a ticket to tour the magical, mysterious chocolate factory. It soon becomes clear that Charlie will inherit the factory. The other children, because they are not as obedient or well behaved as Charlie, are punished in several cruel and humiliating ways. This, for some people, adds to the humor of the story.

This book is an example of insidious racism that children must be taught to detect and respond to with clear refutation of the ideas contained within the pages. The book is, indeed, very entertaining, especially to children who are not African American, rich, fat, gum chewers, or excessive TV watchers. To those children who are, this may be a frightening story because these characteristics are not favored in the story. The overriding virtue in this book is unquestioning obedience to the authority of Willie Wonka. When racism and other hateful messages are cloaked in such attractive garments, the racist ideas become internalized without young readers' knowing it. It is all the more important for caring adults to bring these stereotypes and behaviors to children's attention, so that they may be armed for critical reading rather than disarmed by charming language and images. MASHA RUDMAN

Hero of the Land of Snow

📕 Sylvia Gretchen ✒ Julia Witwer

Asian, Tibetan

1990, Dharma Publishing ✳ Series 📖 Gernstein, Mordicai, *The Mountains of Tibet*; Timpanelli, Gioia, *Tales from the Roof of the World*.

The Gesar epic is to the Tibetans what the Mabinogian is to the Irish, the Gatiloke to the Cambodians, the Kalevala to the Finns, and the Ramayana to the Indians. It is the national tale retold time after time and in many versions in song, story, poem, dance, and painting.

This book is a relatively simple retelling, without the lengthy passages or florid flourishes that characterize epic tales. Although this tale is an excep-

An inexpert retelling of the Tibetan national epic.

414

tional one, this version is inexpertly written. There are many examples of legendary tales told in simple, elegant language for children. *Hero of the Land of Snow*, however, reads too much like a high school essay on the subject.

The drawings are somewhat childlike—colorful and culturally accurate, but a little awkward nonetheless.

The story follows Gesar, a young man who through magic and supernatural power must overcome an evil ruler to become a great king. A torturous race is announced in which all the lords (including the evil king and Gesar himself—who at that point takes on the guise of a dirty beggar) are to race on horseback to see who will be king. During the course of the race, Gesar overtakes several people. He tests their character and thus wins his first loyal supporters. With his supernatural steed, Gesar wins.

A beautiful girl is chosen to be his queen, but before she is deemed worthy, she must learn that beauty itself is a poor thing without dedication and humility. "Her pride in her beauty was foolish! Her youth would fade, one day she would be old. Only her deeds and the goodness of her heart truly mattered."

This book is only the beginning of a long epic tale in which Gesar and his bride, Brougmo, have many adventures. Hopefully, more adventures will be forthcoming. Readers have little material on Tibet. (One other slim book of folktales is Gioia Timpanelli's *Tales from the Roof of the World*. Also, Mordicai Gernstein has written a brief and sweet tale about the powers of reincarnation entitled *The Mountains of Tibet*.) A note in the back with Tibetan pronunciation is very helpful, although it doesn't go far enough. For instance, we do not know whether the G in Gesar is meant to be hard or soft. GINNY LEE

Drylongso

📖 Virginia Hamilton ✒ Jerry Pinkney

African American

1992, Harcourt Brace and Company

Little Lindy has lived with drought so long, she doesn't recall when the land was green and growth was plentiful. Everything is covered with gritty red dust, and Lindy and her parents have little hope that the weak, thirsty plants will produce. When a wall of dust blows in with a spindly young man trying to outrun it, Lindy can sense the changes coming. The boy was separated from his family by the dust storm and stays with Lindy's family; she accepts him as the brother she always wanted. Because drought had stayed so long, people thought it was a common, everyday occurrence and called the long, dry period Dry-Long-So. The boy was named Drylongso in reference to the long drought his mother dreamed would come after his birth, but he knows that "life will grow better" wherever he goes.

Drylongso has the gift of divining water and helps Lindy's father start a new garden with seeds the boy brings. Lindy watches as Drylongso searches for water and seems to make it appear out of the earth. Her family enjoys some of the sweetest spring water they've ever had and watches their seedlings grow with the life-giving flow. Sadly for Lindy, however, Drylongso leaves to find his family without saying good-bye. She realizes that he made her life better and believes he'll return when it's cool again.

In *Drylongso*, Hamilton creates a legendary and mystical philanthropist in the boy who makes 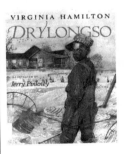 the lives of others better. The author surmises that, based on weather patterns, droughts would occur west of the Mississippi in the 1970s, where and when Drylongso takes place. This way, she revives the "Dust-Bowl" era in American history. Pinkney's swirled, primarily brown illustrations reinforce the dry and arid feel the story gives. Drylongso subtly touches on people's misuse of the environment as well as their constant hope for a better tomorrow. ALISON WASHINGTON

The All Jahdu Storybook

📖 Virginia Hamilton ✒ Barry Moser

Multicultural

1991, Harcourt Brace and Company

In this highly imaginative collection of African American folktales, Jadhu is a trickster on The Mountains of Paths. According to the well-known

A graphic recreation of Mississippi's Dust Bowl era from the powerful team of Virginia Hamilton and Jerry Pinkney.

African American children's author Virginia Hamilton, he was born in an oven with two loaves of bread—one baked brown, the other black, but Jadhu didn't bake at all. Jadhu came out covered with a magic dust that makes others sleep when he sprinkles it on them and wake up when he lifts it off. In *The All Jadhu Storybook*, Jadhu journeys around the world stirring up the lives of the forest creatures. For example, Jadhu runs into the ugly giant, Trouble, who keeps people and animals in a barrel. Jadhu puts Trouble to sleep and helps the others escape, then he warns them to stay out of that barrel of Trouble's.

As helpful as Jadhu can be, he can also aggravate others on The Mountains of Paths. At one point only the chameleon trusts him, and Jadhu has to stop playing tricks until he has redeemed himself. On some of his travels, Jadhu becomes Lee Edward, a little boy in Harlem; later he runs into the far woods and meets Hansel and Gretel, Little Red Riding Hood, and Cackle Giant, a colossal red chicken who, until meeting Jadhu, has no story. Jadhu becomes a boy in the East and meets Yin, the keeper of long gray time, and Yang, the keeper of warmth and light. Jadhu helps Yang become balanced with Yin so the world has equal time of light and dark.

> *Virgina Hamilton's imaginative collection of African American tales about Jahdu, a mythical trickster.*

The mythical characters and creations in Hamilton's sprightly text stretch the imagination and tease reason. Moser's illustrations are bright, vivid, and sometimes frightening. Combined, the artists bring out Jadhu's impishness and caring.
ALISON WASHINGTON

Willie Bea and the Time the Martians Landed

🎴 Virginia Hamilton

African American

1989 (1983), Greenwillow Books

Willie Bea is convinced she saw a Martian one Halloween night. Halloween is her favorite time of year, and her entire family gathers to celebrate. But this is October 31, 1938, the date of Orson Welles's infamous War of the Worlds broadcast. Twelve-year-old Willie Bea, some of her family, and many of the townspeople get caught up in the hysteria, believing that a Martian invasion is actually underway. Could Martians really be attacking, and would they reach the family farm? Willie Bea knows that the report sounds strange, but how can she disbelieve the authoritative voice on the radio? She was planning to dress up as a hobo or a pirate, but what would it matter if the world was coming to an end?

When Willie Bea's Uncle Jimmy says something strange has been sighted on a nearby farm, Aunt Leah is frantic. Aunt Lu talks about jumping down the well, Uncle Jimmy wants to stand watch with a shotgun, but Willie Bea thinks she can communicate with the Martians. Her mother refuses to panic, but is cautious and won't let the kids go begging for treats. Willie Bea must see the Martians, so she sets out on stilts to the farm where "the creatures" were sighted. When she runs into an oddly illuminated farm machine in a dark field, Willie Bea thinks it's something from another planet. The next day the family realizes they've been hoaxed, but they'll never forget that Halloween night.

> *An African American girl and her family are fooled by Orsen Welles' famous radio broadcast about Martians landing on Earth.*

Hamilton blends the familiar theme of family love with thoughts on the influence and power of media and mystical workings of machines—in this instance, the radio. ALISON WASHINGTON

This Home That We Have Made

🎴 Anna Hammond and Joe Matunis (translated by Olga Mendell) ✏ Joe Matunis

Multicultural ✳ Bilingual English/Spanish

1993, Crown Books

Drawing on a mural developed by formerly homeless Latino and African American children in New York City, the author provides us with a sense of the concerns of these children for safety, shelter, and happiness. Emphasizing the importance of working together, the story and the mural clearly depict the children's ongoing needs and concerns related to creating community.

> *A bilingual exploration of homelessness based on a New York City mural.*

Visual representations of their concerns serves

as a way for others to understand and better support the efforts of these homeless children. Written in both Spanish and English and focusing on the pain and confusion of being homeless, this book explores the self-determination of these children and their hope for a future under a roof they can call home. MARTHA L. MARTINEZ

Read, Learn, and Fly
DAPHNE MUSE

There are many venues for introducing multicultural children's literature to an even broader audience. In 1995, the Bureau of Exhibitions, Museums, and Cultural Exchange of the San Francisco International Airport mounted an exhibit of original artwork from multicultural children's books. This exhibit was mounted in the airport's international terminal. In the past, the Bureau of Exhibitions had curated exhibits that included taxicabs from around the world, radios, hats, shoes and African masks.

Along with original art by Leo and Diane Dillon, Dom Lee, Enrique O. Sanchez, Vo-Dinh Mai and Joe Sam, several of the illustrations were accompanied by pages from the original manuscripts, photographs of authors and illustrators, and in one case, the pen with which the stories were written. The project came about as a result of a collaborative effort between the exhibitions division of the airport, the San Francisco Public Library, and children's literature advocates in the San Francisco Bay area.

For the six months that the exhibit ran, teachers, parents, children, and millions of travelers had an opportunity to see the artwork and read excerpts from works by Kimioko Saki's Sachiko Means Happiness, *Angela Johnson's* When I Am Old With You, *Lorenz Graham's* South Town, *Sundaira Morninghouse's* Nightfeathers, *and more than fifty other titles featured in the exhibit. As a result of its popularity, the exhibit was extended twice.*

Such exhibits provide additional opportunities to introduce these books to an audience who might otherwise never come to know that a broad and rich array of cultural experiences exist in poetry, biographies, storybooks, anthologies, and young adult fiction.

The River That Gave Gifts: An Afro-American Story

◧ ✎ Margo Humphrey
African American
1995 (1979), Children's Book Press, [Series

The River That Gave Gifts is a story about four young African American children paying their respects to an elderly woman.

As the story begins, the children have come to realize that Neema is old and is going blind. Because of their love and respect, they decide to give her gifts now while she can still see them.

In this African American story, four children each make their own special gift to the beloved elder woman of the town.

Each child sets out to find a gift. Jey makes a chain of gold buttons, Kengee makes ribbon bows, and Orande builds a small box to hold Neema's gifts. Meanwhile, Yanava sits by the river, pondering what her gift should be. Soon she notices the river sparkling like diamonds. It lulls her to sleep, chanting "Take me into your hands."

When Yanava awakens and washes her face she notices that her hands glow brighter as she washes. It is then that she understands what her gift should be.

The River That Gave Gifts emphasizes the love and respect due our elders. It also teaches that all human faculties are fragile and diminish over time.

Each gift that Neema receives is important but Yanava's gift of light outshines what the others have brought. This gift allows her to see clearly what the others have brought. It is a gift that comes from the heart and spirit, requiring faith. It cannot be bought or sold. YOLANDA ROBINSON-COLES

Aesop: Tales of Aethiop the African, Volume 1

◧ Jamal R. Koram ✎ Demba Mbengue
African
1989, Sea Island Information Group,
✳ Audio Cassette, Series

The fables of Aesop are well known for their ingenious animal characters and the eternal truths found in the stories' morals. In *Aesop: Tales of Aethiop the African,* storyteller Jamal Koram has

417

retold the stories and placed them in an historically correct context. Even though Aesop lived in Greece, Koram acknowledges Aesop's African heritage and gives an African setting to the tales. The full-color cover shows Aesop as an African griot, or historian, who is wearing African clothing. He is accompanied by a musician playing the *kora*, a large stringed instrument. The reader will be attracted to the warm colors of the cover and the fine artwork, which is different from the book's illustrations.

The author has retained the original format of the fables. The moral at the end of each story has also been included in the table of contents. Readers can choose stories by their title (which might not identify the theme) or the moral, which is listed with the title. All of the characters and places have African names. The glossary and pronunciation guide are valuable aides for reading aloud and sharing African culture.

An evocative retelling of Aesop's fables, set in Africa.

The African animal characters, including the civit, caracal, forest hog, and topi, are seldom found in other children's books. A glossary provides the reader with definitions of uncommon terms used in the book. The civit, a member of the cat family, uses flattery to trick a crow out of a piece of food. In another tale, "The Lion and the Forest Hog," the forest hog is not intimidated by the lion and prepares to fight him. Clearly, the forest hog is a ferocious animal. In these tales, the actions and dialogue of the personified animals demonstrate the moral of the story.

The characters in the stories also offer glimpses of life in certain regions of Africa. The wise men and elders of the village share character-building advice with the young people. An old farmer tricks his children and helps them discover what's really important in life. An elderly woman successfully argues her case against a thieving physician. Children in the stories also learn valuable lessons about life. The sad ending of "The Boy Who Cried Wolf" is softened by a poetic chanting style. *These fables can be used for discussions in ethics classes which have recently been added to curriculums in some states.*

This collection and others by Jamal Koram have a similar style; they are simple stories which can be embellished for storytelling. The illustrations are only fair line drawings, which leave a lot of room for imagination. The dynamic storytelling style of the author is featured on an audiotape, which includes some of the stories from this book. This cassette provides an example of how these stories can be developed into a delightful treat for the ear and for the imagination. MARTHA RUFF

Fire on the Mountain

📖 Jane Kurtz and Wolf Leslau 🖌 E. B. Lewis
African American
1995 (1994), Henry Holt & Company, Inc.

Against the backdrop of Lewis's luscious watercolor tapestry, Kurtz reconstructs a folktale she heard as a child in Ethiopia. Introducing her readers to Alemayu, a young Ethiopian boy, who dreams of one day being a rich man, Kurtz offers a tale of challenge, wit, and perseverance that will capture many a young mind.

Hoping to find work in the house of the rich man who employs his sister, Alemayu, a clever young shepherd, travels to his sister's home after the untimely death of their parents. Alemayu encounters the rich man, a boastful and mean-spirited figure who challenges Alemayu to spend a night alone in the cold wilds of the neighboring mountains. Alemayu accepts the challenge as he has accomplished this feat many times as a shepherd, and returns triumphantly the following morning to collect his prize: four cows and a bag of gold coins. However, the rich man reneges on his wager, and it is up to Alemayu, his sister, and the rest of the servants to demonstrate to the man the level of his ignorance and dishonesty. In the end, Alemayu and dignity prevail, as he becomes a wealthy man from the riches of his prize. As our society shifts away from a strong sense of morality, tales like these become even more important.

A collection of folktales from Ethiopia and Eritrea that span the categories of folktale types.

A timeless tale, Kurtz' *Fire on the Mountain* is sure to delight young readers. CHRISTINE PALMER

The Flame of Peace: A Tale of the Aztecs

📖 ✒ Deborah Nourse Lattimore

Aztec, Hispanic, Mexican

1991 (1987), Harper & Row

Two Flint, a young Aztec boy, lives in Tenochtitlan, the capital of the Aztec empire. While he has known peace in his short lifetime, the appearance of the army of Tezozomoc in the hills is about to change that. Seeking to avoid war, the Aztec emperor sends a party bearing gifts to Tezozomoc. But Tezozomoc's warriors attack the peace party and Two Flint's father is killed.

Two Flint asks his mother if the Aztecs were always at war with the peoples who live along the shores of Lake Texcoco. "No," replies his mother, "there was peace in the past until the light of the Morning Star began to die. With no New Fire from Lord Morning Star, there can be no peace, only war." Two Flint is determined to find Lord Morning Star. The lord appears to Two Flint in his dreams and warns him of the "nine evil demons of darkness who rule the road" to the hill of the star.

The story of a young Aztec boy that can be the basis for compelling classroom discussion.

Predictably, Two Flint is successful in his journey to reach Lord Morning Star and returns with the New Fire. Two Flint places the New Fire on the altar of the great temple and peace reigns. As a young man, Two Flint learns to value struggle early in his life. *Many of the rituals and traditions of Aztec culture are revealed in this story. The book also introduces interesting concepts of Aztec calendrics, including the New Fire ceremony, the significance of the twenty days of the ritual calendar, and the nine lords of the night. All make for compelling classroom discussions.*

The illustrations simulate those that appear in Mixtec-Aztec codices. The book includes a pictographic glossary to help young readers interpret the illustrations. BYRON RUSKIN

The Knee-High Man and Other Tales

📖 Julius Lester ✒ Ralph Pinto

African American

1972, Dial Press

Julius Lester's *The Knee High Man and Other Tales* is a delight for readers of all ages. Featuring familiar "characters" from the natural world—Mr. Bear, Mr. Rabbit, the Snakes, Mrs. Wind, and Mrs. Water— these parables were derived from the interactions between slaves and slave owners.

A delightful collection of six traditional African American folktales originally told among slaves.

The tales come out of the rich oral tradition of black American folktales. Some stories are moralistic tales, used to pass on family and community values to children in an amusing manner; some are simply for the fun of telling. A bonus in this book is Lester's prologue, in which he discusses his love of good stories, his own research on their historical background, the symbolism, and layers of meaning.

This slim volume holds only six stories, but they are full of adventure, thanks to the expert work of Lester and illustrator Ralph Pinto. In "What Is Trouble," Mr. Rabbit shows lazy Mr. Bear what trouble means. In "Why Dogs Hate Cats," we learn the "real" reasons behind dog and cat fights: a dispute over a smoked ham. Snakes' true nature is revealed to an overly trusting man in "The Farmer and the Snake." "After all," the snake says, "I'm a snake. You knew that when you picked me up."

These simply told folktales are fun to read and leave a lesson in history for the young reader. Their range and humor make them ideal for reading out loud to young adults as well. ROSA E. WARDER

The Mouse Couple: A Hopi Folktale

📖 Ekkehart Malotki ✒ Michael Lacapa

Hopi, Native American

1988, Northland Publishing Company

📖 Kwon, H., *The Moles and the Mireuk.*

A mouse couple so value their adopted daughter that they want the most powerful being in the universe to marry her. After consultation with the sun, clouds, north wind, and the spirit of the butte, they finally

419

find a perfect, if seemingly unlikely, husband.

This traditional Hopi tale is richly illustrated with stylized drawings and geometric designs. Hopi values, such as an emphasis on hard work and a willingness to care for one's elders in their old age, are clearly communicated. Though a bit awkwardly written in places, the story is nonetheless engaging.

A traditional Hopi folktale somewhat awkwardly told.

Perhaps one of the most interesting things about The Mouse Couple *tale is its similarity to a Korean folktale retold by H. Kwon in* The Moles and the Mireuk. *Though they come from opposite sides of the world, the two stories are nearly identical. This provides an excellent opportunity for an entertaining exercise in comparative folklore. Children can compare the two stories, then go on to look at other folktales which have variants from all over the world. Versions of the Cinderella story, which appear in places as diverse as China, Africa, and the Americas, may also be used for this activity.* JODIE LEVINE

The Dark-Thirty: Southern Tales of the Supernatural

📖 Patricia McKissack ✎ Brian Pinkney
African American
1993 (1992), Knopf 📖 Lester, Julius, *The Tales of Uncle Remus.*

This collection, winner of both a Newbery Honor Book and a Coretta Scott King Awards, consists of ten tales inspired by actual events in African Ameri-

Ten fantastic tales based on southern black legends and myths.

can history in the South, where author Patricia McKissack grew up. Spanning well over a century, from the days of slavery to the civil rights era, the stories offer a bouillabaisse of history and culture. Whether or not actual ghosts appear, all the tales have some element of the supernatural to keep the reader in suspense.

The first story dramatizes the cruelty of slavery. Henri, a mulatto slave, is sold by his heartless master (also his jealous half-brother), and becomes a legendary hero when his escape takes on supernatural dimensions. In other stories, we see how many strove to help the fugitive slaves, for their fate is recorded in the diary of a noted abolitionist and conductor on the Underground Railroad. The introduc-

tion to another tale describes how African American folk histories were preserved by a Library of Congress project in the 1930s. Inspired by a narrative from this 10,000-page manuscript of *The Slave Narratives* is a poem called "We Organized," telling, in dialect, how slaves outwitted Massa to be free even before President Lincoln signed the Emancipation Proclamation. Decades later, blacks survived in the workplace by organizing, and "The 11:59:" refers to the Brotherhood of Sleeping Cars Porters, the first all-black American union, founded in 1926. In this suspenseful tale, a retired Pullman porter tries to beat the phantom Death Train (the 11:59 in porters' jargon). Other stories from history relate to the Ku Klux Klan's reign of terror ("Justice"), the successful 1955-56 Montgomery, Alabama, bus boycott that proved to be a pivotal event in the American civil rights movement ("The Woman in the Snow"), and the turmoil at home and abroad plaguing America in 1968 ("Boo Mama").

Among those tales inspired by African American folklore are "The Sight," about babies born with their faces covered by a caul and the special psychic powers they have, and "The Conjure Brother," about the root doctors who concocted magic potions or cast spells for good luck or good health. Each story is placed within its historical or cultural context before the author works her spell-binding narrative magic.

McKissack explains in her preface that as a child, she and her friends called the thirty minutes before nightfall the "dark-thirty"—the brief time allotted to her and her friends to return home safely before the monsters took over. Inspired by her grandmother, who spun hair-raising ghost stories, McKissack carries on the family tradition. Her narratives take us past reality into the twilight zone when "shapes and shadows play tricks on the mind" and where anything can—and does—happen.

Even more important than this momentary spine-chilling delight are the beneficial knowledge and human emotions derived from the tales. Suitable for middle-school grades, this anthology would work well in teaching units on folklore, history, and storytelling. *The stories can be read aloud, adding to many other class activities.* Among the many books that can accompany this highly recommended collection are Julius Lester's four volumes in *The Tales of Uncle Remus* series, illustrated by Jerry Pinkney. Brian Pinkney (his son) provides the scratchboard art that perfectly complements *The Dark-Thirty*, heightening each tale's suspense with his surrealistic impressions. LAURA M. ZAIDMAN

The Orphan Boy: A Maasai Story

Tololwa M. Mollel ✒ Paul Morin

East African, Maasai

1996 (1990), Houghton Mifflin Company

As a boy, Masai author Tololwa M. Mollel spent his school holidays on his grandfather's coffee farm in Tanzania. While working on the farm, he listened to his grandfather tell marvelous stories. Drawing on this childhood heritage, Mollel retells the story that explains why the planet Venus is known to the Masai as Kileken, the orphan boy.

In this legend, a lonely old man spends his evenings stargazing. One night, he notices that a star is missing from the sky. As he searches the sky for the lost star, he hears the footsteps of a stranger. His visitor proves to be a young orphan boy in search of a home. As he is childless and alone, the old man offers to take the boy in.

The captivating story of why the planet Venus is known to the Masai as Kileken, the orphan boy.

Kileken becomes a great help to the old man. He milks the cows and takes them to pasture, leads the donkeys to the spring, and performs countless other chores. Even when the land is threatened by drought, Kileken manages to take the cattle out to dry pasture and bring them home well fed.

The old man becomes curious about how the boy manages to complete his chores so quickly and how he keeps the cattle so fit and well fed when there is no grass or water. When the man asks the boy how he performs such seemingly impossible tasks, Kileken says that he must keep his secret. To share his secret will mean the end of the old man's mysterious good fortune.

Overcome with curiosity, the old man secretly follows Kileken one morning. What he sees is amazing. Unable to contain his surprise, the old man lets out a cry. In dramatic fashion, Kileken disappears, leaving the old man even lonelier than before.

After Kileken's strange disappearance, the missing star that had vanished from the sky reappears. Not really a star, it is the planet Venus—and perhaps it is also the orphan boy.

Mollel's retelling of this story is more than just a rehashed traditional tale. It is a window through which young readers can view the nomadic pastoral lifestyle of traditional Masai people of Kenya and Tanzania. Illustrator Paul Morin traveled to Masai country to research the land and lifestyle of the people. His artwork is captivating in its attention to detail and its beauty. Black-and-white and color illustrations blend harmoniously. Morin's illustrations are part of an attractive graphic package that includes borders featuring traditional African beadwork.

Teachers will find The Orphan Boy *a rich mine for creative-writing projects.* SANDRA KELLY

When I'm Alone

Carol Partridge Ochs ✒ Vicki Jo Redenbaugh

African American

1993, Carolrhoda Books Inc.

Using her imagination to explain to her mother why her room is such a mess, the girl in this story rationalizes:

When I'm alone, with only me
And no one's here to disagree,
That's when the strangest things I see
And wonder can they really be?
It's enough to make me groan,
What happens here when I'm alone.
Such troublemakers I have known,
Those beasts who come here on their own.

The girl claims that a series of mischievous animals—ten aardvarks, nine lions, eight turtles—have made a mess of the house. As she goes about her chores, dutifully cleaning up as instructed by her mother, the animals follow right behind, and just as dutifully, make the mess.

An African American girl uses her vivid imagination to justify the mess in her room in this humorous book.

The girl's wonderful imagination carries the storyline. The book reveals creative ways in which both parents and children deal with issues like messy rooms. While the girl in this book is African American, she could be from any culture. A messy room has everything to do with being a child and nothing

to do with culture or color. Books like this show the commonalities that exist across cultural and gender divides. The humorous tone of the writing and poetic imagination of the child make for a fun and easy read.

MARTHA L. MARTINEZ

The Long-Haired Girl

📖 Doreen Rappaport ✏ Ming-Yi Yang
Asian, Chinese
1995, Dial Books for Young Readers

Doreen Rappaport's *The Long-Haired Girl—A Chinese Legend* is a tight, well thought-out, and moving story filled with remarkable drawings about a young woman, Ah-mei, and the sacrifice she must make for the sake of her village. It is set in a town below the Lei-gong Mountains during the middle of a drought. The crops are withering. People are exhausted, desperate even for water.

A Chinese woman challenges the God of Thunder in this engaging classic with exquisite watercolors.

One day, looking for herbs on a mountainside behind her house, Ah-mei pulls out a long, white turnip from a crevice in a rock. To her surprise, water begins to trickle out of the hole. She has accidentally unearthed a spring!

This, however, is only the beginning of her adventure.

The girl is immediately swept up to the top of the mountain where the wicked and selfish God of Thunder, Lei-gong, lives. He threatens her.

"So you have found my secret spring. If you tell anyone about it, I will kill you."

With that warning, he sends Ah-mei back home.

"I can change life for everyone in the village," she thinks. "But to do it I will have to give up my life."

How will she solve her dilemma? Fortunately for everyone, Ah-mei is just brave and clever enough to challenge and fool the merciless thunder god. With help from her family and a few villagers, she is able to trick Lei-gong.

Ming-Yi Yang's illustrations in *The Long-Haired Girl* complement Rappaport's retelling of this engaging classic. Yang, who grew up near Shanghai in China, was an award-winning artist by the time he was ten. He is also the youngest painter invited to show his work in the National Museum of China.

His exquisite watercolors resemble traditional Chinese paintings. Ah-mei's hair is dark and luscious, her expressions spellbinding. The landscapes—with mountains and birds in the background—are absolutely beautiful. CHRISTINA ENG

The Faithful Friend

📖 Robert D. San Souci ✏ Brian Pinkney
Caribbean
1995, Simon & Schuster

San Souci sets the tale in Martinique of the last century. Clement and his faithful friend Hippolyte set out to meet Pauline, the woman Clement intends to marry. Hippolyte cautions Clement to beware of Pauline's uncle, Monsieur Zabocat, who is reputed to be a *quimboiseur*, or wizard. Angered by Pauline's acceptance of Clement's proposal, Zabocat banishes them all from his home and enlists three zombies to kill them. Only the friends' loyalty saves them and allows Clement and Pauline to marry.

An exciting tale set in 19th-century Martinique about a great test of friendship.

San Souci presents an exciting tale that maintains some of the traditional motifs of folktales from this region such as curses and symbolic numbers. Although there are elements of the supernatural, it is not the stereotypic "mumbo-jumbo" of movies. The characters retain human qualities, act in expected ways, and hold universal values. Wisely, San Souci does not mimic island patois but skillfully blends in authentic dialect words and phrases. San Souci includes a glossary and a note about the origin of the tale.

Brian Pinkney's scratchboard illustrations, brightened with purples, blues, yellows, tans, and reds, replicate the lushness of Caribbean islands. Pinkney uses swirling lines to denote movement and action, and creates brown and tan faces full of personality. VIOLET HARRIS

The Legend of El Dorado

📖 ✏ Beatriz Vidal, Adapted by Nancy Van Laan
Hispanic, Native American
1991, Knopf

"Long ago, before any creature lived on the Earth, the pale Moon, blinded by the light of the Sun, shed a single tear. Round like the Moon, the teardrop became Lake Guatavita, the holiest of all lakes." Such is the poetic and highly visual language of this moral and movingly mysterious legend. The queen and princess of the Chibcha people, a Native American people from South America, made the mistake of walking near Lake Guatavita. There they are entranced by a beautiful ruby-eyed serpent, who lures them into the lake.

The king is grief stricken and overcome by the loss of his wife and daughter. He loses both the will and strength to remain the leader of his people. With the king in such despair, the Chibchas are concerned about the fact that their "nation" is ripe for conquest. The tribal priests decide they must hear the serpent speak in order to solve this dilemma. The king is told that he must offer up his riches to the serpent every year until the serpent decides it is time to reunite the king with his family. Loving his family more than his nation, the king is willing to give up his riches to be reunited with them.

An elegantly illustrated adaptation of a Native American legend of a mythical golden lake in South America.

The king fears that the serpent will forget its promise, so he creates a special ceremony. Once a year, the Chibchas anoint their king with fragrant oils, then cover his body with gold dust. He becomes El Dorado, "The Gilded Man," for he is golden like a god. Seated upon his throne, the king is carried to the edge of Lake Guatavita. When he has no more riches, he throws himself into the lake. To this day, these mysterious riches remain hidden in the depths of Lake Guatavita.

With elegant illustrations in strikingly beautiful colors splashed across the page, the artist re-creates some of the incredible beauty found in the landscapes of South America.

Many parents and some teachers may have a difficult time using stories grounded in mysticism and ritual. Nevertheless, there can be tremendous benefit in learning more about the origins of myths and why they continue to be passed on through the generations, for myths often have an inherent moral message that helps children establish values and standards in their lives. MARTHA L. MARTINEZ

Public Libraries: Cultural Repositories for Everyone's Stories

Rosa E. Warder

THE PUBLIC LIBRARY HAS LONG BEEN A CULtural and informational repository; however, for the past few decades the library has become much more than the caretaker of our written culture. Libraries are now one of the primary bridges between individuals and community resources, serving as outreach centers providing homework assistance, extensive cultural programming, and collaborative projects with public and private schools.

Whether it's the storytelling hour, the homework tutorial, or the availability of special needs resources, collections and events at many public libraries across the country reflect the cultural and ethnic diversity of America. At a library in Oak Hill, West Virginia, the library was recently turned into a rain forest for the state's summer reading program "Reading is Natural." During

Black History Month, several San Francisco Bay Area branch libraries become veritable museums filled with decades of documentation that reflect the struggles and accomplishments of African Americans. At branches from Berkeley, California, to New York City and Birmingham, Alabama, to Beloit, Wisconsin, book displays provide young people with a look at a range of human rights issues. During Children's Book Week, libraries across the country come alive with the favorite characters from books by Jan Spivey Gilchrist, Alma Flor Ada, and Joseph Bruchac.

Through the public library, many children and young people get their first introduction to computers, and they are able to find information in a non-threatening and helpful setting. Despite the drastic cuts in government monies, public libraries, spearheaded by dedicated librarians and their staffs, have continued to expand the scope of their services to meet the changing needs of an increasingly diverse and often multilingual patronage. Librarians have been working diligently to develop their collections to include the information and cultural awareness needed for their respective communities. Collections now often include many bilingual titles, audio tapes, and periodicals. Programs range from story hours that may include sign language or languages other than English, and community outreach services to assist parents, teachers, and new immigrants to negotiate the sometimes overwhelming bureaucracy in seeking social services.

Children and young people can discover places and people they never knew existed, and they can also learn to exercise their rights. Our libraries are truly national treasures that need our continued patronage and support.

Following is a list of libraries that have outstanding multicultural children's literature collections and exceptional services for families in urban and rural communities. This is by no means a comprehensive list, as there are many more library-based programs for children and young adults that do an exceptional job of serving as a solid resource in their respective communities.

The Akwesasne Cultural Center
R.R. 1
Box 14C
Hogansburg, NY 13655-9705
Ph. (518) 358-2240
Fax(518) 358-2649

This public library, museum, and cultural center was developed to inform the public about Native Americans in an educational, research, and cultural environment. A particular focus of the center is to dispel the movie images and myths surrounding native peoples, and to enrich the understanding of Mohawk culture specifically. The large collection of books on Native Americans is housed separately from the general collection and includes many oral history/story tapes. The museum collection has tours and lectures available on Mohawk life.

The Asian Pacific Resource Center
Los Angeles County Public Library
1550 W. Beverly Blvd.
Montebello, CA 90640
Ph. (213) 772-2650
Fax (213) 722-3018

This branch of the Los Angeles County Public Library system was developed to serve the large Asian community of Southern California and to provide information to the community as a whole about Asian culture. The materials throughout the library and in the children's collection focus on Asian Pacific countries with emphasis on the heritage of people from China, Japan, Korea, the Philippines, and Vietnam. The collection includes books, magazines, newspapers, films, and videos in both English and many Asian languages. The Los Angeles system has many branches specifically developed to serve the Asian community including: The Chinatown Branch, Little Tokyo Branch, and Pico Pico-Koreatown Branch.

Atlanta-Fulton Public Library
1 Margaret Mitchell Square
Atlanta, Georgia 30303
Ph. (404) 730-1700
Fax (404) 730-1989

This Library boasts a number of special features, including an extensive collection of children's literature and reference materials for students. A number of children's authors including Patricia McKissick and Eloise Greenfield have conducted readings in conjunction with events organized by the staff. The Special Collections department has an extensive collection of African American materials as well as good oral histories and genealogical references.

The Berkeley Public Library
Central Branch
2090 Kitteredge Street
Berkeley, CA 94704
Ph. (510) 644-6100
TDD No. 548-1240

Situated in the heart of downtown Berkeley, this library is a literary and cultural center of diverse communities throughout the East Bay. The Berkeley system includes four community branches that share many services and programs with the Cen-

424

tral Branch. The Central Branch has a large children's room complete with a separate story/activity room, and is fully staffed by children's librarians who provide help with school projects, read stories, act as research assistants, and process children's library cards. Their extensive collection of children's books has been carefully developed to reflect the multicultural population of the community. A highlight of this branch is the reference section on children's literature, which includes information on disability, special needs, and ethnic/cultural titles and programs. Services include story hours, movies, homework help, concerts, readings, and holiday events.

The Boston Public Library
Central Branch
666 Boylston Street
(617) 536-5400

This extensive library system has 25 local branches and a business services branch. The Boston Public Library has a network of children's rooms throughout the system and an extensive collection of multicultural children's literature. The individual branches regularly publish annotated bibliographies including books of interest to teens, folktales from around the world, and ethnically or culturally specific selections. Some of the services at this library are book mobiles, lap sits, disabled services, homework clubs, readings, lectures, and film and video screenings.

The Cesar Chavez Public Library
615 Williams Road
Salinas, CA 93905
(408) 758-7345

Named after the powerful Chicano farm workers' leader, this library has a program focused on the rural community that surrounds it. As well as a substantial Spanish language and bilingual collection, their program includes bilingual story hours, arts and crafts classes, and assistance for students with school projects.

The Chicago Public Library
George Cleveland Hall Branch
Charlemae Hill Rollins Children's Room

Charlemae Hill Rollins was an author and librarian who dedicated over thirty years to this branch of the Chicago Library System. She was admired

for her tireless crusade against the stereotypical characterization of African American children in books. As well as this room dedicated in her honor in 1989, a decade after her death, there is an annual Charlemae Hill Rollins Colloquim.
The Cleveland Public Library
Central Branch
325 Superior Avenue
Cleveland, OH 44114-1271
Ph.(216) 623-2800
Fax (216) 623-7015

This 26 branch library system has a commitment to multicultural literature and services. The reference and educational support centers, research centers, and community activities centers reflect the diversity of Cleveland and the world. Their foreign language collection includes over 225,000 volumes in over 40 languages. The individual branches have excellent multicultural children's collections and services, including classes and activities.

The Washington, DC, Public Library Services
Main Branch
901 Street North West
Washington, DC 20001
(202)727-0321
Deaf Services (202) 727-2142

This branch of the DC public library system is known as a model for deaf outreach services. They have an extensive collection of materials for deaf patrons, and many staff members are trained in sign language. The children's collection has a multicultural emphasis, particularly Vietnamese, Latino, and African American. Their services include story hour, homework clubs, and events with accessibility for disabled children and adults.

The East Los Angeles Library
Chicano Resource Center
Los Angeles County Public Library
4801 East Third Street
Los Angeles, CA 90022
(213) 263-5087

The Los Angeles County Library system has a number of ethnically specific branches throughout the county. The center of the Spanish language supported branches is the Chicano Resource Center. This center has a massive collection of children's books in Spanish language and bilingual text. An emphasis on historical and cultural information can be seen in the many programs and activities developed at the center for patrons of all ages. The library services also publish regular pamphlets and annotated bibliographies focusing on different aspects of their extensive collection.

The Library of Congress
The Children's Literature Center
Thomas Jefferson Building
Washington, DC 20540
(202) 707-5535

Founded in 1963 as an information center within the Library of Congress, the Children's Literature Center received the mandate to serve those organizations and individuals who study, produce, collect, interpret, and disseminate children's books, films, television programs, or other forms of materials destined for children's information and recreation use. This center does not directly serve children; however, they benefit indirectly from the assistance given to teachers, librarians, parents, and others who work with youth. The collection of children's books, including approximately 190,000 titles and related items, such as games, sound recordings, maps, and illustrations, can be retrieved by accessing the Library's data base. The library can be visited in person, but inquiries can also be made by telephone or letter. The center also publishes reference sources about children's literature.

The Newark Public Library
The Multilingual materials Acquisition Center
P.O. Box 630
5 Washington Street
Newark, NJ 07101-0630
(800) 645-0068

The Newark Public Library system has had extensive multicultural materials for many years; however, they have taken their commitment to multicultural education to a new level with the development of the Multilingual Materials Acquisition Center. The Newark Public Library was awarded a federal Library Services and Construction Act grant to establish this program. The program specifically works to develop multicultural and multilingual collections for every branch's children's rooms. Materials include non-fiction, fiction, reference materials, and periodicals aimed

at assisting students, parents, and teachers and at encouraging and fostering a greater awareness and understanding of one's own culture and that of others. The main branch is home to the James Brown African American Room and the Sala Hispanoamericana.

The New York Public Library
The Office of Branch Libraries
455-5th Ave.
New York, NY 10016

The New York Public Library system is the most extensive public library system in the nation. With over 80 branches spread throughout the five boroughs. System-wide multicultural and multilingual collection development has made this system very accessible to the diverse population of New York City. Readings, films, and workshops for children and adults are an integral part of the public access programs. As well as local branches, the system includes a number of specialty library centers that have extensive book collections and also serve as living museums and showcases for past and current cultural exhibitions. These centers include: Center for the Humanities, The Library for the Performing Arts, Fordham Library Center, Schomburg Center for Research in Black Culture, Spuyten Duyvil Branch, Andrew Heiskell Library for the Blind and Physically Handicapped, St. George Library Center, Todt Hill-Westerleigh Branch and the Ottendorfer Branch. The branch libraries division also runs a mail-order catalog that features specific information about the branch libraries, available publications, posters, and film and video catalogs.

The Oakland Public Library
Main Branch
125-14th Street
Oakland, CA 94612
(510) 238-3432

This urban library system has branches throughout the city of Oakland. The main library coordinates programs such as family literacy and Partners for Achieving School Success (PASS) that serve families at library branches and community centers. Branches have children's collections specifically developed to reflect the ethnicity of the surrounding communities, including an Asian collection in the downtown Chinatown branch and a Native American collection at the

426

Diamond/Fruitvale branch. The main branch has a separate children's room with extensive multicultural materials.

Queens Borough Public Library
Central Branch
89-11 Merick Boulevard
Jamaica, NY 11432
(718) 990-0894

The Queens library system has a commitment to the multicultural population in its communities. In 1977, the system put into place The New Americans Program specifically designed to address the fact that more than one in three Queens residents is born outside of the United States, creating a population that includes over 100 nationalities. Services include English-as-a-Second-Language Classes, Mail-A-Book (mailing books to Queens residents in Chinese, French, Greek, Italian, Korean, Russian, and Spanish), Coping Skills Workshops and Support Groups, and Cultural Programs (literary, performing, and folk arts). The Spanish Language collection includes over 75,000 items housed at 21 branches; the Chinese Language collection encompasses 28 branches and over 70,000 items. Most library branches in the system also have Korean language and Multi/Bi lingual collections.

The Saint Paul Public Library
Central Branch
90 West Fourth Street
St. Paul, MN 55102
(612) 292-6311

The Saint Paul Library has had a long commitment to its youngest patrons. The children's rooms throughout the system are known for their extensive collections and children's programming. The main branch services include story hours and puppet shows. The library has published numerous pamphlets specifically showcasing multicultural children's literature under the heading "Experience the World," which include suggested readings and activities for every age level.

The San Francisco Public Library
Main Branch
Civic Center
San Francisco, CA 94102
(415) 557-4400

This system has twenty-six branch libraries to serve the cultural needs of the diverse Bay Area community in the Spanish language Mission District, Chinatown, and Japantown, as well as extensive services for deaf and blind patrons. The collections at the branches system-wide have been developed to include multicultural materials at every reading level. The individual branches provide enrichment classes with sensitivity to culture and languages. Librarians at the Mission, Chinatown, and Japantown branches, in particular, focus on multilingual collections and services.

The San Jose Public Library
Biblioteca Latino Americana Branch
690 Locust Street
San Jose, CA 95110
(408) 294-1237

Situated in one of California's fastest growing cities, this branch has an impressive collection of Spanish language and bilingual materials for children. Most staff members are Spanish speaking and provide assistance to young patrons and their families in a culturally supportive atmosphere. Spanish/Bilingual story hours, homework assistance, and community programs are part of this branch's services.

The Seattle Public Library
Washington Center for The Book
1000 Fourth Avenue
Seattle, Washington 98104-1193
(206) 386-4184

The Seattle Public Library system is a model of what multicultural libraries can become. The librarians have developed an extensive children's collection of books, videos, and audio tapes with authors and illustrators representing virtually every ethnicity. Services include: story hours, homework helpers, services for disabled patrons, and a series of pamphlets featuring recommended books that explore and celebrate various ethnic heritages.

427

National Library Resources
Ethnic Materials and Information Exchange
Round Table (EMIE)
American Library Association
ALA/EMIERT
50 East Huron Street
Chicago, IL 60611

EMIE Roundtable serves as a national information exchange for librarians, teachers, and other parties interested in multicultural literature and curricula materials. The EMIE reviews books and materials, publishes essays and debates, and reports on conferences and workshops in the EMIE Bulletin.

Libraries for the Future
521 Fifth Avenue, Suite 1612
New York, NY 10175-1699
(800) 542-1918

Libraries for the Future is a national non-profit organization that gives voice to the interests of active and potential users of America's public library system. LFF initiates and supports grass-roots organizing, demonstrations, research, and public awareness activities to focus attention on the resources and services that public libraries now offer and on those needed in the next century for a diverse civic community and a strong democracy.

CD-ROM Technology in the Multicultural Classroom:

Using CD-ROM to Educate English As a Second Language Students and to Introduce American Students to Other Cultures

Linda A. Singer

In her article "CD-ROM and At-Risk Students" in the October 1992 issue of *School Library Journal*, Roxanne Baxter Mendrinos states "CD-ROM technology is a great equalizer, bringing success to all students, regardless of their prescribed ability levels." A CD-ROM is a software package that contains text and sometimes interestingly rendered images. Many CD-ROM's are set up in such a way that users can interact with the images, ideas, concepts, and text, often creating their own stories. Many have been produced to encourage problem-solving skills and creative new learning strategies. My experiences using CD-ROM programs with students matches Mendrinos's conclusion. I have observed students at computer monitors manipulating text and characters in a CD-ROM story book to meet their own needs and interests; students who were not able to have this interaction with canned programs on videotapes or filmstrips. As each form of storytelling changes or supplements the previous presentation, so have CD-ROM story books added dimensions to the printed and audio visual mediums. In fact, CD-ROMs may be transforming the way people learn to read as well as the way reading is taught.

CD-ROM INNOVATIONS

Combining CD-ROM text, pictures, motion, and sound, CD-ROM story books are versatile learning tools that make it possible for students to learn and remember the story from several presentation modes. Students may look at graphics, watch videos, and listen to music, speeches, and narrated text. Most CD-ROM story books are accompanied by a print version of the same story, allowing students to read

428

the stories when away from the computer. Students' ability to read the print version is enhanced by the features they used at the CD-ROM workstation. Students tend to remember what they have seen or listened to more readily than they remember what they have read.

CD-ROMs also facilitate research by making more resources available and accessible. Instead of looking through one of many indexes for a topic being researched, students may type in a key word to access information in a matter of seconds from many different sources. In most cases, students can then print out this information and take it with them.

CD-ROMS IN E.S.L. CLASSROOMS

The impact of CD-ROM technology can be seen in bilingual or E.S.L. classrooms. Imagine students in a classroom where the teacher speaks and presents materials in a language they do not understand. What do the students do? Most likely they tune out. What if, on the other hand, students are given activities and tools they can control and interact with at their own pace, reviewing a section until they feel they understand the concept or information? This is the genius of the CD-ROM.

While working at a high school with a large English As a Second Language student population, I was able to observe their use of CD-ROM programs. Students were asked what they liked about this technology. Finding out more about their home countries and printing out material to take with them was one of the things that topped their lists. The print-out allowed them to highlight pertinent information without the laborious task of taking notes. When taking notes, these students often found themselves trying to copy, letter by letter, words they did not understand, a process which often resulted in error-filled work that demoralized the student instead of providing incentives to learn.

MULTICULTURAL CD-ROM PROGRAMS

The CD-ROM innovations already mentioned above are extremely valuable in a multicultural education. For example, hearing languages and music from several countries and clicking on a word to hear it pronounced repeatedly, are obvious advantages to learning with CD-ROMs.

A growing number of CD-ROM story books are available in English and Spanish. This is true of the Random House/Broderbund Living Books Series, which includes *Aesop's Fables: The Tortoise and the Hare.* Bringing Aesop alive on CD-ROM may also result in revitalizing the way in which history is taught as well. These emerging readers can actually travel back centuries and gain an even better understanding of how the morals of such stories apply to today's society. Students can interact with history through this technology and, one day, may be able to be in the same room with great and challenging moments in U.S. and world history.

More and more multiethnic themes and children's books are slowly beginning to make their way onto CD-ROM. The Center for Media Education, a Washington, D.C.-based public policy think tank, theorized that the lack of multicultural software may also have something to do with the small number of people of color who use home computers. Although it may be a while before we see books by Tom Feelings, Donald Crews, Laurence Yep, or Pat Cummings on CD-ROM, or a breadth of materials that bring forward more information about the contributions women have made to building this country, some exciting materials are beginning to appear.

Microsoft's *How the Leopard Got His Spots* by Rudyard Kipling provides some insights into historical and contemporary Africa. There is a short book within the program about South Africa and the background music is by the highly praised, world-renowned group, Ladysmith Black Mambazo. The artwork for the story is very beautiful and gives a feeling different from the cartoon-like illustrations in most story books. Words like "high velt" and "Ethiopian" are not only pronounced but there is an illustrated definition and explanation of each. The frequent opportunity to hear words from other languages pronounced slowly and correctly may do a lot to demystify some of the prejudice instilled in children about other languages, especially those from African countries. They can eventually learn that these lan-

429

guages don't "sound funny." Students are also taught to play an African game, Mancala, popular throughout many regions of Africa. Danny Glover's captivating narration adds to the feeling and power of the story. This story book is a wonderful supplementary tool for students (grades 4 & up) studying folktales and African cultures.

500 Nations: Stories of the North American Indian Experience, produced by Microsoft as a part of its Home Series, is an excellent work. This CD-ROM is based on *500 Nations,* a Jack Leustig film, produced by Jim Wilson and Kevin Costner. The program is interactive, featuring many graphics and film and video clips. Although Costner narrates a part of this CD-ROM program, the most interesting narrations are done by Native Americans who tell stories passed down through the family. Amongst them is Celane Not Help Him, the daughter of Dewey Beard, the last survivor at Wounded Knee.

500 Nations provides both a historical perspective and a look at contemporary Native Americans. Students learn about tribal history and culture, about individual Native Americans and their struggle to maintain their culture and way of life. Some teachers who used *500 Nations* with me were concerned that the word "Indian" was applied more frequently than "Native American." In the section "Living Nations," Tall Oak, a Narragansett from the northeastern part of the United States, tells us that it was Columbus who called Native Americans "Indians." He said that they refer to themselves as "the people, the human beings." I feel that the use of "Indian" is overcome by the information and understanding students can gain from this program.

Microsoft Encarta '96, produced by Microsoft Home, has a section called "InterActivities." One of the features of this section is Ellis Island, which begins with a brief tour of the island. The student can then go to a map of the world and click on a small square representing a country. When a country is selected in this manner, information about the immigrants from the country and when they immigrated to the United States appears on the monitor. My favorite section includes audio interviews with immi-

grants or their children. One man tells of the inhumanity of the physicals given at Ellis Island, and the daughter of an immigrant tells how the judge "winked" as he swore her mother in as a citizen even though she couldn't read English.

1995 Time Almanac, produced by SoftKey, has a special feature on "Diversity," which emphasizes how America's face has changed dramatically. It is the CD-ROM version of the December 2, 1993 special issue of *Time* Magazine called "New Face of America." The woman's face on the controversial cover was created by *Time* to show how Americans might look as various races and ethnic groups intermarry.

There is a slide show, "Changing Face of America," which shows how immigrants are changing our society. "Immigration" is a series of photographs showing immigration from Ellis Island to the Haitian refugees on overcrowded boats. "New Face of America" employs a morphing device to show how America will look in the future as couples intermarry and have children. There are charts about immigration and many articles about immigration and immigrants.

In StarPress Multimedia's *Material World: A Global Family Portrait,* narrated by Charles Kuralt, we meet thirty families from around the world. What is unique about this CD-ROM program is its emphasis on material things. We learn a lot about people through their belongings and what they consider important in their lives. Through their answers to a sixty-item questionnaire, families relate how much time they spend at work and play and discuss their religions, what they value most, and what they think their children's futures will be. We see video and still pictures of the families and their belongings.

Microsoft World features the culture and daily lives of real people. In addition to being an atlas, it includes thirty-one families from around the world. We meet these families through photographs, videos, and audio clips. We see the families' kitchens, we learn about their meals, what they do on a busy day, what their workday is like, and what the children's schooling entails. We go on shopping trips and discover what they do during their leisure time. Besides the family portraits, there are culturgrams about the countries, information and illustrations about the countries' modern architecture, musical clips, and a detailed world atlas.

Middle-school students may learn about the history, culture, and life of African Americans, Asian, Hispanic, and Native North Americans by using Gale Research's *DISCovering Multicultural America*. This CD-ROM program contains over 2,100 biographies, more than 2,500 essays, 500 landmarks, a time line with over 3,000 events, a list in excess of 4,600 organizations, over 500 full-text periodical articles from ethnic news sources, and more than 350 significant documents. Included are biographies of Harriet Tubman, Amy Tan, and Cesar Chavez. The NAACP and AMERIND (American Indian Movement for Equal Rights in Native American Development); essays on Japanese in the United States: Pre-1885; and Hispanics in American Sports: An Historical Overview; documents such as the Civil Rights Act of 1964, the Tydings-McDuffie Act, and Martin Luther King Jr.'s "I Have a Dream" speech are all included in *DISCovering Multicultural America*. *DISCovering Multicultural America* is multimedia with videos, audio clips, photographs, and other graphics.

Art Speigelman's *Maus: A Survivor's Tale* and *Maus II: And Here My Trouble Began* were written as a pair of books about his parents' daring survival of the Holocaust. Told in a comic strip format with the Nazi's portrayed as cats and the Jews as mice, an often gut-wrenching view of life before, during, and after the death camps is presented. The drama of the *Maus* story is magnified in the CD-ROM format and includes a commentary on the making of *Maus*. Produced by the Voyager Company, this provocative story is certain to produce some vital responses.

The success of students using multicultural themes in stories they create using the CD-ROM writing programs, *Davidson's Story Club Express* and MECC's *Storybook Weaver,* depends on how well their teachers use and explain the folktales.

Davidson's Story Club Express differs from all previous CD-ROM programs cited in that it is a language development curriculum with many components for elementary schools. The pur-

pose of this program is to "build English language development and multicultural awareness among all students, including mainstream, Chapter 1, At-Risk and English as a Second Language (ESL)." It uses fifteen CD-ROMs for "self-paced practice and learning." Videodiscs are presented by teachers, and there are cooperative learning activities for oral and written language development. The CD-ROMs include folktales which highlight French, African, Jamaican, and Japanese peoples and reveal interesting points about their cultures.

MECC's *Storybook Weaver Deluxe* is a fairly effective program that promotes student writing and critical thinking skills as well as helping students illustrate stories they produce. It would be hard to write and illustrate multicultural stories with this product given the limited number of pictures which clearly present people from other cultures. There is a teacher's guide that has a section on "Suggestions for Writing Activities," "Drawing on the World Around Me," and "Drawing on the Traditions of Folklore and Folktales." Although a useful bibliography is included, the teacher must locate the folktales to read to the students.

Lyn Miller-Lachmann, editor-in-chief of *Multicultural Review*, states in her article "Bytes & Bias: Eliminating Cultural Stereotypes from Educational Software" (*School Library Journal*, November 1994) that "in the case of *Storybook Weaver*, teachers will need to go beyond the teacher's guide to help students understand the distinct themes, motifs, and characters in folklore from across the world." I am also convinced that the teacher is the important ingredient in the success of students using *Davidson's Story Club Express*.

When I first began my research, very few CD-ROMs existed which would enhance a student's knowledge of other cultures. There were world atlas CD-ROM programs which had photographs, videos, snippets of languages and music, but none could give students a real understanding of other cultures. I agree with Lyn Miller-Lachmann's concern that there has been a lack of in-depth treatment of different cultures on CD-ROM programs. Most of the CD-ROM programs cited in this chapter were

431

released after her article appeared in the November 1994 issue of *School Library Journal*; each program meets some or all of her criteria. "We need more accurate illustrations; greater depth, variety, and substance in dialogue; better roles for people of color; and multiple perspectives," says Miller-Lachmann.

I hope more CD-ROM programs will be developed with the purpose of effectively introducing students to other cultures and peoples. Students need to know the history of other cultures and how their backgrounds affect today's world. They must have tools like the CD-ROM programs in this chapter to help them feel more at home and to help them share their cultures with others.

According to Daphne Muse, "With a rich literary tradition having been established in multicultural children's literature during the past thirty-five years, it is critical for the technology to reflect the institutionalization of the literature in the curriculum, library collections, and the overall understanding of the literary scope and breadth of this nation. CD-ROM can most certainly reflect the rich cultural and literary legacies that have been established."

Muse shares my concern that access to CD-ROM programs for students of limited means also must be improved. Government bodies supporting the budgets of schools and public libraries must provide funding for the acquisition of CD-ROM hardware and software as they funded the purchase of films, videos, and recorded materials. Strategies must also be developed to insure that access to this technology is more widely and reasonably available. According to the Software Publisher's Association, a software industry tracking orgnization based in Washington, D.C., schools spent $2.1 billion on computer hardware and software in 1993, and that figure was projected to grow to $2.24 billion in 1994. During the first three quarters of 1994, SPA noted that CD-ROM software sales had already exceeded $151 millon.

Programs can be set up outside these government agencies by forming public-private partnerships. One such model is a program called Northern Virginia Community Computer Center Partnership (NV3CP), which is setting up computer centers with CD-ROM capabilities in housing complexes where students with limited means live. The partnership includes community organizations, government offices, and local businesses. This model is one which makes it possible for students from all cultural and economic backgrounds to have access to this technology and be supported as emerging skilled readers, writers, and researchers.

As we move into the twenty-first century, we can continue to explore what this technology will mean in terms of the development of solid reading and critical thinking skills for children. This technology may also help students sort through and gain a better understanding of the complex social issues surrounding and fueling our lives. But it is clear CD-ROM technology has the potential for igniting a renewed interest in learning to read, write, and think. While we have yet to see the real impact that CD-ROM can have on the literacy and culture of this country, the potential is clear.

CD-ROM PROGRAMS CITED (All were produced in 1995. Release date for some may be 1996. Some titles are updated annually.)

DAVIDSON'S STORY CLUB EXPRESS, Davidson & Associates. Macintosh. $1,600.

DISCovering MULTICULTURAL AMERICA, Gale Research. Windows. $500.

500 NATIONS: STORIES OF THE NORTH SMERICAN INDIAN RXPERIENCE, Microsoft. Windows. $39.95.

HOW THE LEOPARD GOT HIS SPOTS, Microsoft. Windows. $49.95.

MATERIAL WORLD: A GLOBAL FAMILY PORTRAIT, StarPress. Macintosh and Windows. $39.95.

MICROSOFT ENCARTA '96, Microsoft. Windows/ Macintosh. $99.95. Updated annually.

MICROSOFT WORLD, Microsoft. Windows. $69.95.

STORYBOOK WEAVER DELUXE, MECC. Windows/Macintosh. $79.00 (school version), $46.00 (home version).

TIME ALMANAC, SoftKey. Macintosh/Windows. $49.95.

THE COMPLETE MAUS CD-ROM, Voyager Company. $49.95.

Linda Singer writes a column called "The Jewel Box" for MultiMedia Schools *and is on its editorial board.*

Grade Seven to Grade Eight

The Devil's Storybook: Stories and Pictures

📖 ✒ Natalie Babbitt

Hispanic

1994 (1974), Farrar, Straus & Giroux ✳ Spanish

📚 Babbitt, Natalie, *Tuck Everlasting.*

The devil is always looking for trouble and for ways to make you fall into his traps, but sometimes those same ways trap him. Can the devil be outsmarted?

Humorous stories about the devil from classic children's author Natalie Babbitt.

This collection of "devilish" stories brings a sense of much-needed humor to children's literature. In "La Hermosa Dama," a beautiful young girl is bombarded by suitors asking for her hand in marriage. She refuses, showing no interest in any of them. She also remains saddened by the fact that it is only her beauty that brings these men to her.

Hearing her lament that she will never marry, the devil decides to intervene, causing her more grief. But in the end, she defies him.

All ten of these stories are cleverly written, and young people are bound to enjoy hearing them. The illustrations serve the stories well, reflecting the humorous tone of the contents. Several of Babbitt's books have been translated into Spanish including this one and *Tuck Everlasting* (*Tuck Para Siempre*). MAGNA M. DIAZ

Stories from Costa Rica: The Children of Mariplata

📖 Miguel Benavides (translated by Joan Henry)

Hispanic

1992 (1989), Forrest Books ✳ Spanish

Using animal allegories to address issues of poverty, injustice, greed, ecocide, and war, the author mixes poetry, ironic tales, and magical myths in eleven simple stories.

Originally published in Spanish under the title *Los Hijos de Mariplata*, the stories stand up well in translation, as Joan Henry accurately captures the spirit of each story.

Much like George Orwell's *Animal Farm*, "The Children of Mariplata" —one of the books best stories— uses fish to illustrate the oppressive ways in which people hold power over one another. *Together, these stories can serve as a viable platform for discussing moral and ethical issues.* They are also the kind of stories that encourge and challenge the critical thinking skills of young people. MAGNA M. DIAZ

Eleven challenging Costa Rican animal allegories that address human foibles.

A Brush with Magic

📖 Williams J. Brooke ✒ Michael Koelsch

Asian, Chinese

1995 (1993), HarperCollins 📚 Bang, Molly, *Tye May and the Magic Brush.*

In this clever retelling of a traditional Chinese folktale, Liang, a young artist, is able to bring his drawings to life with a magic brush. Author William J. Brooke, noted for the insight he brings to his renditions of traditional tales, has expanded this story, usually offered as a picture book, into novel form.

Liang is amazed and perplexed by his ability to give life to his drawings. He uses his ability to create a creature with a human's head and a monkey's body, which he names Monk-Li. Monk-Li is loyal to his creator, but is not accepted by either human beings or monkeys. Ultimately, like Frankenstein, his life is a responsibility Liang would rather not accept.

In this traditional Chinese folktale, an artist brings creatures to life with his paint brush.

The book captures the essence of the artist's struggle: being different, aching to be recognized, loving and fearing his gift. Liang, the people who care about him, the people who try to use him, and even the painted creatures he brings to life must all consider whether the magic is in Liang, the brush, or both.

The story is written simply, with humor and drama. *It is a good entry point for discussions of motifs in folklore, particularly those that are unique to certain cultures. Another useful exercise is to have students*

434

look at picture books addressing the same story to see how Brooke conveys ideas and images in novel form. JANIS O'DRISCOLL

The People Could Fly: American Black Folktales

📖 Virginia Hamilton ✏ Leo Dillon and Diane Dillon
African American
1985, Knopf, ✳ Audio Cassette, Series

The People Could Fly is a compilation of twenty-four tales, primarily from black folklore, that teach, moralize, amuse, and sometimes scare the reader. Tall tales, stories of tricksters, devils, and people, and tales of freedom were passed down orally. Hamilton captures the spirit of the oral tradition marvelously, in colloquial language, as if the stories are being spoken. The four sections are divided the-

Twenty-four classic folktales about slavery, trickery, and freedom in America in an award-winning classic.

matically: the first contains "Brer Rabbit" stories, in which the weaker, but smarter, rabbit outwits the predators; part two consists of fairy tales and tall tales; the third section includes chilling, cautionary stories of the supernatural; part four focuses on tales of slaves taking, or, in rare cases, winning, their freedom. The final story, for which the book is titled, tells of slaves who have magic words that enable them to fly away from brutal oppression. Although they must leave behind the ones who don't have the words, they also leave behind the memory of their flight, and the dream of freedom, the story of their escape. After each story, Hamilton provides information about the characters, history, or people who retell the legend, encouraging us to remember the voices of the past while passing on the stories.

Hamilton has brought together familiar themes in *The People Could Fly*, noting the alterations made by individual tellers. The Dillons' bold black-and-white illustrations evoke the more intense feelings in each story, in turn frightening, comical, fanciful, or mournful. While younger children might find the combination too intense, middle-grade youth will most likely enjoy them. The bibliography cites other versions of the fables recounted.
ALISON WASHINGTON

The Dark Way: Stories from the Spirit World

📖 Virginia Hamilton ✏ Lambert Davis
Multicultural
1990, Harcourt Brace Jovanovich, 📖 Lyons, Mary, *Raw Head, Bloody Bones.*

Banshees, witches, devils, and tricksters—all travel the dark way. This collection of twenty-five stories from Italy, Kenya, Ireland, Russia, Wales, America, and other countries, warns, scares, befuddles, and amuses readers. Some of the stories are familiar, some less so—

A collection of folktales, myths, and stories from around the world involving spirits and the supernatural.

"Medusa," "The Flying Dutchman," a Banshee tale; "One-Inch Boy," "Baba Yaga, the Terrible," or "The Argument." At the end of each story, Hamilton comments on the story's origin, some of its meanings, and the characters involved. In the Japanese tale

"One-Inch Boy," a couple prays for a child and receives a teeny boy. The boy sees the world, saves a princess from a horrible demon, and is magically "wished" to full height by the princess out of gratitude and love. At the end, Hamilton explains how the demon in this story is an "oni," a Japanese devil who is easily fooled and a comic foil in stories involving humans.

Some of the stories, like "Manabozo," involve animals who save themselves through cunning; others, like "The Horned Women," involve humans who outwit deceptive spirits or evil, supernatural beings. A final group of fables warns listeners not to be cruel, vain, stubborn, foolish, or disobedient, for he or she could end up just like the people in "The Witch's Boar" or "The Magician's Fellow." Primarily, the tales are not excessively frightening; even milder souls will be able to handle the stories and vividly beautiful pictures without becoming too upset. Some of the tales will be familiar enough for children to imagine other outcomes and versions. The bibliography lists five full pages of sources for further reading. ALISON WASHINGTON

Author Shares Research Techniques for Making Books Authentic

JANE KURTZ

Last year, I met with a group of teachers who had invited me to come into their classrooms to talk about my experiences as an author. We wanted to think of useful ways for the students to connect with my picture books, which are set in Ethiopia, far from the prairies of North Dakota where I now live. One of our ideas turned out to be the best connector I've ever used.

Before my visit, I provided a typed version of a story called Pulling the Lion's Tail, *which was being illustrated by an artist named Floyd Cooper and would not be out until the following fall. Teachers read the story aloud to their classes and pointed out that no one, not even the author, knew what the pictures would look like when the picture book was finished. Then the students did their own illustrations for the story.*

It was a great exercise in listening, in choosing pivotal moments in scenes, and tying art to language. In the case of one sixth-grade class, it was also a great exercise in research. They took the time to study Ethiopia so their pictures would be informed. That sixth-grade class had the best questions about Ethiopia of any group I've ever addressed; they had struggled with getting the details right and they wanted to know about things they had been unable to track down. Their one inaccurate illustration—of the new mother seated at a spinning wheel—has prompted me to talk about the importance of illustrators doing their homework and getting the cultural details right.

Illustrators have a tough job when they have to provide the visuals for a place they've never been. Let me share a few of the experiences of Earl Lewis, illustrator of my first Ethiopia-connected picture book. He started by contacting an Ethiopian family in Philadelphia, where he lives, and taking pictures of a brother and sister who served as models for the children in the story. An Ethiopian restaurant owner was the model for the rich man. I sent him a packet of pictures to help him fill in the background; he saw baskets, and clothing, and other Ethiopian items in the houses of the people he met.

When he was finished with the preliminary art, he showed it to one of the women who had been helpful. "Oh no," she said, "A man in Ethiopia would never eat with his hat on." Unfortunately, Earl hadn't taken any pictures of the rich man with-

out his hat on. The solution? "I gave him my own hair line," he told me on the phone much later. "When he saw the finished illustrations, he was definitely surprised."

Fire on the Mountain (Simon & Schuster, 1994) was Earl's first book. Since then, he has applied the same painstaking research to a book set in Madagascar and one set in Tanzania. It was a relief, he says, to work on his book Down the Road *(Harcourt), set in the United States. His hardest task for that book was getting three people up into an apple tree so he could take some pictures for the ending of the story. "I kept hoping the branch wouldn't break," he says, "at least not until I got my photograph."*

Hard as those details are to come by, they are what he wants for his art. As a young African American boy growing up in Philadelphia, he started attending Temple University's Saturday morning Student Art League in sixth grade. According to an interview in Philadelphia Magazine, *by the time his work was being exhibited in art galleries, he had come to see himself as "a documenter of places in time and space. I want to stop the world, to hold it still."*

Because of Earl's way of working, he was not sure if he should tackle my next book. My brother had come back from teaching in Addis Ababa to tell me about the street kids who had taught him to raise pigeons. I was struck by the way kids who have literally nothing still find ways to be playful, to care for life, to dream. Together, my brother and I wrote Only a Pigeon *(Simon & Schuster, 1997). Earl loved the story, but he wasn't sure he could get the illustrations right. The solution? He and my brother used their own money to travel to Ethiopia this spring. With my brother as Amharic translator, Earl found the brothers he wanted to use as models and took photographs of the boys with their pigeons. It wasn't easy. But the book will now offer a real look at scenes few people in the U.S. have seen. And luckily, research— as I hope increasing numbers of students will discover—has its own rewards.*

Jane Kurtz is the author of four children's books including Fire on the Mountain.

The Maid of the North: Feminist Folk Tales From Around the World

📖 Ethel Johnston Phelps ✒ Lloyd Bloom

Feminist

1982, Henry Holt and Company

An uneven collection of twenty-one fairy- and folktales meant to focus on spirited, courageous heroines.

This collection of twenty-one fairytales and folktales, reshaped by author Ethel Johnston Phelps, attempts to portray what the author calls "spirited, courageous heroines." Rather than evincing meekness and docility, these heroines are resourceful, often know magic, possess self-confidence and a clear sense of their own self-worth, and often act with moral or physical courage. Though the author claims that seventeen cultures are represented, most of the stories come from northern Europe and Britain. The reason Phelps offers for her choices is not very convincing; that colder climates produced a more rugged, "early" life and therefore, more challenges for women who lived there. Her storyteller's privilege to edit some of the stories to best suit her purpose, highlighting the heroine, does not always serve her well, and the stories are not as beautifully told as one might wish.

Best among the stories are several that do not hail from northern Europe. "The Monkey's Heart,"  an African folktale, extols the cleverness of a female monkey who makes one mistake in allowing herself to be tricked into traveling on the back of a wiley and hungry (male) shark (in most other versions of this folktale, the predator is a crocodile), but then tricks the shark into returning her home safely. "The Tiger and the Jackal," a Punjabi folktale, presents a farmer and his wife exchanging roles when the farmer makes the mistake of promising a hungry tiger his wife's cow instead of his own oxen (and so valuing his work above hers); in order to release her husband from his foolish promise and scare away the tiger, the wife dresses up as a hunter, offering the tiger's bones to the jackal while the husband nervously awaits the outcome at home. In the Zuni folktale "The Hunter Maiden," an Indian girl, the sole survivor among her siblings, finds herself having to provide for her aged parents during a particularly harsh winter. She must break a tribal taboo and hunt, or else her parents will starve. She not only brings home a string of rabbits, but she also confronts and sustains herself (with only a little help from admiring war gods) against the terrifying Cannibal Demon. "The Old Woman and the Rice Cakes" is a Japanese tale about the value of even a few grains of rice and an old woman's desire to keep hold of her rice cakes, a metaphor for her life. Through her ingenuity, the woman escapes from a cave of ogres, taking with her a magic stirrer that will keep her in rice cakes forever.

Only a few of the northern European folktales stand up to these in their depiction of a heroine's resourcefulness. Although it is in the nature of folk-telling to reflect the values of a particular culture, in pushing her heroines, Phelps has too often taken away the original focus, destroying the tension of a story such as in the case with her retelling of "Gawain and the Lady Ragnell" and "East of the Sun and West of the Moon." Expressing a partiality for lighthearted tales, Phelps also peppers her anthology with silly stories, such as "Daffy and the Devil," a Cornish-peasant version of Rumplestiltskin, and "The Giant's Daughter," a Scandinavian tale of greed and envy. Other stories lack distinction, and one wonders whether Phelps strains to include them because she can make them reflect her theme.

MARY FROSCH

Multicultural Folktales: Stories to Tell Young Children

📖 ✒ Judy Sierra and Robert Kaminski (Translated by Adela Allen)

Multicultural

1991, Oryx Press, 📖 Sierra, Judy, *Flannelboard Storytelling Book.*

This collection of twenty-four folktales from Europe, Asia, and the United States are both familiar ("The Three Little Kittens" from the United States, and "The Stonecutter" from Japan) and not so well known ("See for Yourself" from Tibet). An introductory section explains the importance of folktales as "commentaries on social relationships and behavior." *The book also offers instruction on analyzing folktales as a reflection of a particular culture. Advice on choosing stories is offered, and storytelling techniques.*

436

The stories are divided into two sections: those recommended for ages two-and-a-half to five and those for ages five to seven. Most stories are presented in the same format: a short history of the story, the story itself (one or two pages in length), line drawings, specific examples for use in creating a flannelgraph version of the story, ideas for audience participation, and a list of related stories. Some also have ideas for using puppets. Three of the stories contain both English and Spanish versions. A bibliography of individual and collected folktales is included at the end of the book, along with a detailed index. The only culture missing in the main text is Eastern European, although three such tales are listed in the bibliography.

This anthology of spirited folktales from around the world includes techniques for storytelling.

This is a unique and easy-to-use resource for teachers, librarians, and anyone interested in telling stories, whether they have experience or not. They are also tales young people can read on their own. PAM CARLSON

Dragonwings

Laurence Yep

Asian American, Chinese American

1975, Harper & Row

Inspired by newspaper accounts of the young flier Fung Joe Guey's twenty-minute biplane adventure in the hills of Oakland, California, on September 22, 1909, author Laurence Yep has written an ambitious historical novel about Chinese immigrant life at the turn of the century. The story is narrated by Moon Shadow, a young Chinese boy whose father, Windrider, and grandfather have already immigrated to the "Land of the Golden Mountain." Moon Shadow has only his father's magnificent kites with which to identify this mystery man, but within the first ten pages, he is whisked off to join his father by a business associate cousin, despite his mother's attachment to him and his grandmother's grave misgivings.

Moon Shadow and his father face poverty and discrimination in this accurate historical novel about early Chinese immigrants in America.

From the moment that Moon Shadow arrives in California from China, the Land of the Golden Mountain becomes the Land of the Demons. Yep cleverly climbs inside the shoes of his narrator, allowing the reader to encounter the strangeness of a new country through his child's eyes. The smells, colors, shapes, and sounds of San Francisco come to life as completely foreign and often alarming to Moon Shadow, who compares these experiences to their Chinese counterparts. While Windrider's "Company" (a group of business partners in a Chinese laundry) welcomes and provides a familiar context for Moon Shadow, "Tang Town" (or Chinatown) is clearly not a wholly safe environment. Subject to unpredictable and violent attacks from the white community, from which it can expect little protection, Tang Town also harbors its own hostile brotherhoods and fraternities —and even within the close-knit family of men who surround Moon Shadow and his father, Black Dog's opium habit nearly destroys Windrider's dream to fly.

There is much to commend about this novel. It rarely stoops to stereotyping and includes many authentic historical details. The renovated stable has one of the latest inventions: electricity; Windrider gains a reputation for repairing "horseless carriages"; Windrider corresponds with Orville Wright, who shares blueprints with him; and the San Francisco earthquake and fire are described vividly. Chinese acceptance of adversity as a test of strength and will is contrasted against the American notion of greed and opportunity. The novel's greatest strength is its bow to the power of storytelling itself; from Windrider's interpolated account of his encounter with the Dragon King in a dream on his first night in America, to a later scene where Windrider and Miss Whitlaw share different stories of how the constellations came to be, Yep layers the novel with cross-cultural exchanges in the form of these stories.

But the novel is not without its weaknesses. Some characters seem too good to be true. Windrider allows his wife to languish back in China, until he achieves his moment as a flyer and suddenly realizes the importance of his family in the final pages of the novel.

Still, Yep sets out to counter various stereotypes set forth by the media, as he claims in his afterword. Nowhere in these pages will one encounter Dr. Fu Manchu and his yellow hordes, Charlie Chan and his fortune-cookie wisdom, or the laundry men and cooks of movie and television. This is the story of early Chinese Americans as they really were—hardworking and lazy, practical minded and dreamers, old and young, and womanless. MARY FROSCH

CHAPTER 6

NEWCOMERS
ESTABLISHING ROOTS

nly Native Americans can claim to be indigenous inhabitants of the United States. The rest of us are either immigrants or the descendants of immigrants. Even those not rightly called immigrants because they did not come here voluntarily—e.g., enslaved Africans who were forcibly removed from their land, and Mexicans whose lands were taken over by the United States in the nineteenth century—have nonetheless all been newcomers. Yet, in spite of our largely immigrant heritage, until recently, the world of children's books maintained a curious silence about who we really are and about the past that has shaped us.

hat does it mean to be a newcomer or immigrant to the chaos, turmoil, and isolation of beginning anew? These issues are rarely considered in children's books, except in cases where newcomers are presented as success stories on the road to becoming American. The result is that assumptions about what it means to be an American are generally mired in notions of the need to shed one's former culture, language, and history in order to be accepted.

ue in part to the tremendous demographic changes in our society during the past two decades— changes that promise to be even more

dramatic in the next century—inexorably, children's books are beginning to reflect the real lives, anxieties, and experiences of more young people. Nowhere is this more evident than in the renewed interest in issues such as immigration, acculturation, and cultural accommodation, and in the crucial question of what it means to be an American.

 he section that follows includes a series of essays and reviews that focus on how these issues are being reconsidered and renegotiated in our society, and in the world of children's books. This chapter explores the myriad ways children confront such issues as isolation and language barriers and looks at how these issues can be incorporated in the classroom. Recent books also present different models of acculturation that include maintaining native language and customs, and accommodating to new culture in creative ways. Lourdes Dia's essay, "Behind the Golden Door" addresses how immigration has been treated in children's literature and film.

SONIA NIETO

Sonia Nieto is a professor of education at the University of Massachusetts, Amherst. She has published widely in the areas of multicultural and bilingual education, the social and cultural context of learning, and the education of Latino students.

Kindergarten to Grade Three

How Many Days to America?: A Thanksgiving Story

📖 Eve Bunting ✒ Beth Peck

Caribbean, Hispanic

1990 (1988), Houghton Mifflin Company

Illegal immigration is a major topic of controversy in America today, a political football for politicians in need of an issue that they can carry to an election victory. This is particularly true in California, Texas, and Florida, though the repercussions of illegal immigration, not to mention the sometimes Draconian measures being proposed to halt it, are beginning to be felt throughout the United States. Eve Bunting's treatment of immigration in *How Many Days to America?* is indirect. She avoids any explicit discussion of the politics of illegal immigration. For example, we are never even told whether her characters are Haitian, Mexican, or Cuban. Rather, she wishes us to see the human side of the story and the very real suffering that poor people go through when they risk their lives and those of their children on a dangerous voyage across the Caribbean.

A powerful, somewhat somber tale about a group from a Caribbean island who risk their lives trying to immigrate to America.

The narrator, a boy of about ten, knows little of the political situation that causes his parents to flee their comfortable home, just that soldiers have come in the night and his parents are opposed to whatever it is that the military represents. That same night the boy, his younger sister, and their parents, along with many other people, board fishing boats, carrying little but the clothes on their backs and enough money to buy passage to America. The boat is overcrowded, its engine breaks down, there are storms, and the immigrants run out of food and water. Another boat approaches filled with armed men who steal their few valuables. When they approach land the first time, a few men swim to shore. But soldiers return the swimmers to their boats, warning the people off at gunpoint and giving them just enough food and water to survive a few more days. Eventually, however, the immigrants do reach America, where they are warmly welcomed. By coincidence, it is Thanksgiving and a grand meal has been prepared.

For refusing to condemn illegal immigration and portraying the immigrants sympathetically, Bunting's book has been deemed controversial, particularly in those places where illegal immigration is a major issue. Bunting's decision to have the immigrants land on Thanksgiving day and the comparison she draws between them and the pilgrims is a brilliant reminder of how the fact that, with the exception of the indigenous people and descendants of African slaves, most people who immigrated came across the water fleeing adverse and repressive political and religious circumstances. By centering her tale on the human issues, particularly those effecting a ten-year-old boy and his younger sister, Bunting has created a powerful, somber tale of survival in the face of adversity. Illustrator Beth Peck uses her equally somber trademark palette of brown and gray pastels with considerable success in support of Bunting's story. MICHAEL LEVY

Halmoni and the Picnic

📖 Sook Nyul Choi ✒ Karen M. Dugan

Asian American, Korean American

1993, Houghton Mifflin Company

This charming book struggles to carry a nice message about tolerance and acceptance, while carefully avoiding the reality of children's experiences. Yunmi is a young Korean American whose grandmother, Halmoni, has recently come to America to live with her. The cover of the book itself is a dead giveaway that the book will try hard to be multicultural. Halmoni is pictured wearing a *ch'ima* and *chogori*, the traditional Korean skirt and top. Throughout the book, even on the class picnic, Halmoni faithfully wears her ch'ima and chogori. Yet, in 1995, even in Korea, one would be hard pressed to find women dressed this way, except on special, traditional occasions. In the United States, the *ch'ima* and *chogori* would almost

A Korean American girl asks her grandmother to chaperone a school picnic in this unrealistic, saccharine story.

certainly be worn only for very special occasions, not to walk children to school. Perhaps the author is remembering how her own grandmother dressed, but the book would not ring true for most young Korean Americans.

The book goes on to show a saccharine Yunmi and her equally saccharine friends concerned about Yunmi's grandmother's feeling of isolation. Again, while they convey an important message, the children's expressions of concern do not ring true. How much better this book would have been if Nyul had chosen to show these conflicts as they really exist. Most children of Yunmi's age would probably be embarrassed by having to walk to school everyday with a grandparent or by having a grandparent acting as chaperone for the class picnic. There would also be feelings of shame and guilt about the embarrassment. When clearly and realistically articulated, these type of conflicts would give children much more insight into the experiences facing young Asian Americans.

Despite its faults, I would recommend this book for a number of reasons. *I believe it could be used to help children read critically. We can ask children if they think that children in real life would say and do the things that children in this book do. We can ask them to figure out how they would respond to what children would really say. We could even ask our children which response is better. In fact, Nyul's world is a nicer world. Can children think of ways to bring reality closer to it?* As has sometimes been the case with literature from other cultures when there is a dearth of culturally representative literature, recommendations are sometimes made based more on scarcity than on quality. DEBBIE WEI

Molly's Pilgrim

📖 Barbara Cohen   ✏ Michael Deraney

Jewish

1990 (1983), Lothrop, Lee & Shepard,
✳ Film, Video Cassette, Series

In the early part of this century, Molly's family fled the Cossacks in Russia and traveled to the United States. They used to live in New York, where they were surrounded by other Jewish people, and, although life was difficult, Molly felt at home. But now she and her parents have moved to a small town where children taunt her for her differences. When Thanksgiving time comes, Molly's teacher asks each child in the class to make figures for a classroom Thanksgiving scene. The children can make either Native Americans or pilgrims. Molly describes her assignment to her mother when she gets home from school, and informs her mother, who is unfamiliar with American history, what a pilgrim is. "Pilgrims came for religious freedom," Molly tells her.

Molly's mother promises to make a doll for Molly, and the next morning, Molly awakes to find a beautiful doll, not of a Plymouth pilgrim, but of a girl whose bright clothing evokes the traditional dress of Eastern Europe. "But Mama, she doesn't look like the pilgrim woman in the picture in my reading book." This, of course, is the point. Molly's mother has followed the definition of "pilgrim" that Molly provided her, and created a doll in the image of herself as a child, her family having fled Eastern Europe in the name of religious freedom. But such an explanation doesn't prevent Molly from feeling misgivings as she draws the doll from its bag and places it upon her desk at school, just as it doesn't prevent the jeering of her classmates. Molly's well-intentioned teacher intervenes in the jeering, and soon sets things straight with the class by confirming that Molly's mother is indeed a pilgrim and placing the idea of Thanksgiving in the context of the Jewish festival of Sukkoth. And, finally, she reminds everyone that pilgrims are still coming to America.

While this book might be a strong candidate for early independent reading followed by group discussion, and while it attempts to address some aspects of stereotyping, a teacher should be prepared to address some of the thornier accompanying issues. For example, the nature of the teasing that Molly withstands has a decidedly racist tone. There are also the questions surrounding the stereotyping of "Indians" and "pilgrims." Clearly, such stereotyping was allowed in the time being portrayed and, as such, merits discussion. These flaws, however, aren't addressed in the book. Lastly, there might be some question about whether the book inadvertently perpetuates a sort of facile understanding of historical stereotype by suggesting that the pilgrims came to America only in pursuit of "religious freedom." History, it seems, is more complicated. VICKI MERRILL

> *During Thanksgiving, a Jewish girl learns the true meaning of "pilgrim" in this ingenious but somewhat problematic book.*

441

442

Incorporating Immigration Into the Curriculum

ALYCE HUNTER

Allen Say's Grandfather's Journey *is a wonderful story that can be used to challenge sixth to eighth-graders to think, talk, and write about a variety of ideas and themes related to immigration. Using this book as a read aloud for a reading/writing workshop class, I have found that the simple text and beautiful illustrations encourage students to consider the journey and feelings of their ancestors as they came to America. This book can be used to spark a multigenerational dialogue in which students interview their oldest living relative. Students are often surprised to find that, as in Say's book, many family stories are about crossing the ocean and the feelings of homesickness and alienation that bond the young and old. These interviews can be developed into short stories or character sketches that continue to help middle-level learners appreciate the richness of their own roots and the heritage of others.*

Grandfather's Journey *can also be used in conjunction with other young adult literature [such as Lawrence Yep's* The Star Fisher *(1991) and Yoshiko Uchida's* A Jar of Dreams *(1981)] as a core text about the themes of immigration, alienation, identity, and internal conflict. Journal entries can be centered around responses and reactions to such poignant lines as "So I return now and then, when I cannot still the longing in my heart" (p. 31) and "I think I know my grand-father now" (p. 32). Children can also trace the course of American history immediately prior to and following World War II by being asked to explain and research this book's illustrations.*

Grandfather's Journey *can be used to help recently immigrated students with limited English ability to share their "journey" stories. These students are often quick to giggle at the picture of the dapperly dressed young grandfather crossing the choppy sea. They are then prompted to tell the story of their own journey or draw a picture of what mode of transportation brought them to America and how they looked when they arrived. These illustrations can be posted proudly on the class bulletin board.*

Immigrant Girl: Becky of Eldridge Street

📖 Brett Harvey ✏ Deborah K. Ray

Jewish

1987, Holiday House

Readers are immediately drawn into this story of an immigrant Jewish family who came to America to avoid the pogroms—the organized massacre of Jews in Russia during the first few years of the twentieth century. Becky, the narrator, tells of the nine people who live in the three-room flat on New York City's Lower East Side. She tells of the chores each person is

A girl and her family, emigrants from Russia, settle in New York in this somewhat idealized story.

responsible for, and of what she learns in school. She also shares her embarrassment when children laugh at her because she mispronounces words.

Young Becky's narration paints a portrait of the Lower East Side at the turn of the century, with its sweatshops and child labor. Becky also informs the reader about Jewish customs and values of cleanliness, love of learning, honoring the Sabbath, loyalty to family, and reverence for freedom.

The story is somewhat idealized: even though Becky tells of the hardships, they seem almost cosmetic. The author's language does not directly uncover the hardship and oppression of poverty; however, the truth may be communicated when teachers add historical information and invite the children's personalized responses. The reader cannot help admiring the fortitude and strength with which this family and others like it managed to survive. MASHA RUDMAN

I Hate English!

📖 Ellen Levine ✏ Steve Bjorkman

Asian American, Chinese American

1989, Scholastic, Inc.

Mei Mei has just moved to America, and she refuses to learn English. She wants to write, speak, and think only in Chinese. In this deceptively simple story, author Ellen Levine shows a new immigrant's difficult integration into American culture.

Mei Mei's biggest fear is losing her cultural identity by assimilating in American society. She understands English, but hates everything about it—its sounds, its letters, and its radical difference from Chinese. She is happier when she goes to a community where everything looks almost like China; she can speak her language, and she can tutor other children. She feels secure in this environment, and forges strong friendships. It is a tutor there who persistently but gently insists she learn English. He succeeds despite Mei Mei's obstinate behavior, and their final breakthrough is cathartic and rewarding.

A Chinese girl living in New York accepts her bilingual education.

This unassuming book teaches children that it is fine to value one's own culture while embracing the new one. This lesson is, of course, applicable to all immigrants. When Mei Mei makes the decision to speak English, it is not a capitulation but a positive choice that will enrich her new life in America. She realizes that she will still be Mei Mei: a new Mei Mei who can speak both Chinese and English. LISA FAIN

In America

📖 ✏ Marissa Moss

Jewish

1994, Dutton Children's Books

Personal history opens doors to understanding in Marissa Moss's *In America* as a young boy learns about the immigration of his Lithuanian grandfather. It begins when they look at pictures in a photo album, and continues as Walter and his grandfather go to mail a package back to grandfather's friend in Lithuania. Grandfather tells how he left Pikeli because he wanted to have the same freedoms as others did in the United States. When the boy questions him further, he states his view simply: they were bothered a lot because they were Jewish and therefore considered different. "But everyone is different," said Walter. "Who wants to be the same?"

A warm story about a young boy who learns how his Lithuanian grandfather came to America.

His grandfather explains, "Smart question, Walter, but people aren't always so smart. Sometimes they're scared of what they don't understand. And when they're scared, they can be mean."

The story unfolds throughout with similarly caring dialogue. Walter's grandfather discusses what freedom has meant to him in his life, the novelty of coming to a new country, the courage of taking risks, and the importance of remembering one's heritage.

It turns out that they are mailing prunes to grandfather's friend, letting each other know that things across the sea are not as different as one might expect.

As the small boy listens, he applies his grandfather's teachings to his own life and crosses the street for the first time by himself, learning about fear and independence in that vivid way only a story can teach. SUSIE WILDE

Grandfather's Journey

📖 ✏ Allen Say

Asian American, Japanese American

1993, Houghton Mifflin Company

Allen Say's *Grandfather's Journey* is warm, poignant, intimate, memorable, and personal. The cross-cultural experience of two generations of a Japanese family is told from the grandson's perspective. The first part tells of the grandfather's immigration to California and his trip to Japan many years later to visit the land of his youth. The second part tells of the grandson's journey to his grandfather's land—California, and his own longing for his motherland, Japan.

A classic story about a Japanese American man and his grandfather bridging cultures and generations.

The thrill and excitement the grandfather experiences on his first journey to the New World are vividly conveyed. He is amazed by the Pacific Ocean, "deserts with rocks like enormous sculptures," "huge cities of factories and tall buildings," and "towering mountains and rivers as clear as the sky." Powerful imagery allows the reader to journey with the grandfather and experience his delight in his new life and his longing for what he has left. Impressionistic illustrations complement the text well.

HELEN R. ABADIANO

I Speak English for My Mother

📖 Muriel Stanek ✒ Judith Friedman

Hispanic, Mexican American

1989, Albert Whitman & Company

Lupe, a Mexican American girl, must speak English for her mother, who speaks only Spanish. Most of the time, this makes Lupe feel grown up and important, though she occasionally resents having to drop everything to accompany her mother to an

A sensitive portrayal of a young girl who must speak English for her mother, who speaks only Spanish.

appointment and act as translator. When Lupe's mother receives a pay cut at work, she knows that she must find a better job to support her family. This is the incentive she needs to begin the difficult task of learning English as a second language. Lupe helps her mother with her homework and is proud of her efforts, but confesses that she might miss the responsibility when her mother is able to speak fluently on her own.

This story presents a wonderfully strong single-parent family and a supportive, loving community. All characters are portrayed extremely respectfully and sensitively. The story line is realistic, one which many bicultural children experience, and is presented authentically through the perspective of the child narrator.

Children in Lupe's situation will certainly identify with the protagonist's predicament, and hopefully their classmates and teachers will learn from the model presented here as well. JODI LEVINE

Angel Child, Dragon Child

📖 Michele Maria Surat ✒ Vo-Dinh Mai

Asian American, Vietnamese American

1983, Raintree

Ut is a little girl, newly arrived from Vietnam, trying to honor her mother's request to be an "angel child" and be happy in her new American school. But the other kids tease her and she doesn't know how to tease back.

She is homesick for Vietnam and for her mother, who had to stay behind. She tries to be brave, to be a "dragon child," but the dragon comes out in anger, and she fights with a boy who teases her. A

wise principal puts the two of them in a room together, commanding that Ut tell her story and that Raymond write it down. As a result of this scheme, the two come to a deeper understanding of one another, and the school holds a Vietnamese fair to raise money to bring the mother to America.

A young home-sick Vietnamese girl tries to adapt to her new American school.

In the bright pastel-colored pencil-and-scratch drawings, the family of Vietnamese girls is first shown wearing traditional Vietnamese dress. As the story progresses and the girls become more Americanized, they begin wearing jeans and T-shirts and spring dresses. By the time their mother appears, on the last page, they look almost as American as the red-headed boy.

With the growing number of multiethnic classrooms in America in recent years, this story stimulates a couple of novel ideas. If there are children in your class of a certain ethnicity, holding a classroom fair based on the food, language, story, song, dance, dress, and other customs of that country is a way to help those children feel welcome and significant (especially if they are encouraged to be the authorities on the subject). A fair also offers insight into other ways of thinking, doing, talking, eating, and being—a mind-expanding exercise at any age.

Another activity is to pair kids off one on one (preferably mixing cultures or attitudes or possibly only genders—whatever provides an intriguing alternate point of view) and have them write each other's stories. One talks, the other writes. Not a make-believe story, but the story of their lives. This could include an important event, a major move, how it feels to be new, tall, short, lonely, invaded, surrounded, bored, scared, wide-eyed with wonder, or any of a multitude of other emotions or situations a child might already have had.

A brief afterword in this book explains the legend behind the angel and the dragon from which the nation Vietnam is said to have descended and also gives us an understanding of the system of Vietnamese names. GINNY LEE

The Little Weaver of Thai-Yen Village

📖 Tran-Khan Tuyet ✒ Nancy Hom

Asian American, Vietnamese American

1987, Children's Book Press, ✳ Bilingual English/Vietnamese, Series

Hein is a young Vietnamese girl who lives with her mother and grandmother in a small village in Vietnam's countryside. The time is the early 1970s.

A Vietnamese girl's life is torn apart by the Vietnam War in this slightly simplistic bilingual book.

The U.S. is waging a war against Vietnam. This story depicts how the war reaches Hien's village, killing her mother and grandmother and seriously injuring Hien. She is then brought to the U.S., where she recovers and struggles to adjust to this new country and to reconcile her feelings of separation and loneliness for her country and people.

While this book realistically recounts the wartime experience, it fails to deal adequately with the devastating traumas of losing one's family and the subsequent uprooting and relocation to another country. It asks hard questions which the author then does not attempt to answer or explain ("Why were they killed so brutally?" "After all...wasn't it these foreigners who killed my mother and grandmother and bombed our villages?" The writing is simple but not well-crafted.

Similarly, the illustrations are simple and flat with little detail, imparting a one-dimensional perspective. The illustrator employs bright colors but no soft shading, and the resulting impression is one of harshness.

The book does, however, relate some of the rich history and values of Vietnamese culture, and it incorporates a biligual translation on each page.
LYNNE LIJIMA

445

Whose "Culture" Are We Talking About Anyway?

Priscilla H. Walton

DURING THE LAST TWENTY YEARS, NEW social and political issues have forced us to think beyond homogenous cultural categories. It has become harder to speak of African Americans, Asians, Eurocentric whites, or Latinos as if each group were an undifferentiated mass. Those terms serve us poorly as we try to describe the United States today. Each of these categories encompasses diverse groups. Although such terms may have been useful in the early development of multicultural education, they no longer work.

Today, new and varied "Latino" communities are formed of Haitians, Dominicans, Cubans, and Jamaicans in New York and Florida. Growing communities made up of Guatemalans, Salvadorans, Nicaraguans, Mexicans, and other indigenous populations from those countries have spread across the nation in cities like Los Angeles, San Diego, and Chicago. The category "Asian" cannot begin to capture the complexity of languages and cultures of the peoples from India, China, Vietnam, Laos, Cambodia, Japan, the Philippines, and the Pacific Islands now settling in this country.

These cultural differences fueled by the Immigration Act went largely unnoticed during the civil rights movement of the 1960s. Multicultural debates were directed at specific historical populations that demanded redress. But important changes were taking place: First, with growing divisions along social class lines; and second, the addition of new and disparate groups to American society that did not fit the previous categories (black-white, brown-white) of race relations—e.g., Hispanic blacks from the Caribbean, poor whites from underdeveloped countries of Eastern Europe, Hispanic whites and indigenous peoples from a variety of

Central and South American countries.

This cultural transformation has vast implications for the way we think about multiculturalism and multicultural education. It complicates the concept of affirmative action. It makes the task of developing the "canon" in our institutions more difficult. It highlights the complexity of implementing inclusive pedagogical practices. It forces us to enlarge our understanding of ethnicity, race, and citizenship. What holds us together with all this diversity? How do we represent all these cultures equitably in our educational institutions?

Cultural changes should prompt a closer look at renewed controversies over affirmative action and immigration. In this culturally complex society, who is most deserving of affirmative action? Should social class be given more emphasis than race? Should only those who meet the criterion of historical redress in United States society be entitled to affirmative action? Should the states subsidize schooling and health services for non-citizens while the availability and quality of both decline for citizens? Are national boundaries a thing of the past in an interdependent world order where capital and labor know no borders? What are the implications for equity and social mobility of the influx of linguistically and culturally diverse peoples in America?

These issues require serious debate. Conservatives have been setting the agenda because liberals have held to old ideas about who "we" are, despite a changing cultural landscape. I challenge you to debate these issues with colleagues, parents, and members of your own community.

First published in Multicultural Education, *Summer 1995.*

Behind the Golden Door: The Latino Immigrant Child in Literature and Films for Children

Oralia Garza de Cortes

ALTHOUGH MEXICAN IMMIGRANTS HAVE been in this country since the turn of the century as a consequence of the mass migrations brought about by the Mexican Revolution, novels that portray the immigrant experience from the Americas have appeared only in the past several decades. The genre began with Ernesto Galarza's autobiography, *Barrio Boy*, published in 1971. Since then, a body of work about the immigrant experience and the child's role in that experience has slowly emerged, including several films as well as scores of books. Themes range from the experience of immigrants as legal residents to the fate of the "illegal," a derogatory term that conjures stereotypes about criminal activities. The literature also explores a variety of themes common to the immigrant experience including friendship, heroism (especially female heroism), the role of children as caretakers, children as translators, unaccompanied children, separation from the family, fear of deportation, racism (including white on brown and brown on brown), the crossing-over experience, the inevitable role of the *coyote* (middleman), and the abuse of immigrants at the hands of these *coyotes*. While the majority of novels are intended for upper elementary and middle-school readers, a few titles are available for younger children. Three films are also available. These books and movies began to reveal the myriad American experiences anticipated by the poem inscribed on the base of the Statue of Liberty evoking the "golden door" to this country. *I Speak English for my Mother*, by Muriel Stanek, is a book for younger readers that explores family life with a single mother. Lupita is a bright elementary age girl who has a close, loving relationship with her mother, who knows no English. Thus, Lupita's mother comes to rely on Lupita as her primary translator. Lupita's work consists of helping her mom understand everything from teacher's notes and conferences to telephone calls and doctor's prescriptions. Her chore is a common experience among Spanish speaking children whose parents have yet to cross the language barriers that stand in the way of successful citizenship. That responsibility, however, takes its toll on young Lupita who sometimes has to choose between work and play.

"You will have to come and speak for me," Mom said. *"I must go to the clinic and see a dentist right away!"*

"But I want to play," I told her.

"Necesito que vengas ahora!" my mother said, which means, "I need you to come now!"

I wished I didn't have to go with her that day. Lupita's mother, however, recognizes her language deficiency and attempts to correct it by enrolling in English classes, an important step toward lessening Lupita's responsibility.

Ginger Gordon's *My Two Worlds* explores the two versatile cultures of a young Dominican American. Kirsy Rodríguez lives in New York City, but her extended family—consisting of her grandmother, grandfather, and numerous cousins—lives in the Dominican Republic. Readers travel with Kirsy via the highly attractive color photographs, designed to juxtapose the climate and the lifestyle of the two places that are home to Kirsy. Kirsy herself is portrayed as a "tourist" soaking in her extended family's culture while visiting the island and then returning to her everyday life in New York City. The book allows little room to explore Kirsy's background, family history, or personal feelings about her co-existence in two cultures. But with its colorful portraits of children in the Dominican Republic, the book provides an opportunity to view everyday island life as experienced by some of the children who live there.

Over Here It's Different: Carolina's Story, by Mildred Leinweber Dawson, is a juvenile book that offers a more thorough interpretation of life for Dominican American children, as expressed by an eleven-year-old, Carolina Liranzo. George Ancona's sharp black-and-white photos capture Carolina and her family in their present-day setting, while Dawson's eloquently convey a comparison of daily life on the two islands—the Dominican Republic and Manhattan.

Another picture book that portrays the Caribbean immigrant experience is Eve Bunting's *How Many Days to America?* Although it is unclear which specific cultural group is being portrayed, the poignant story is a family's flight from a repressive government. The frightful journey in a small boat affects even the youngest one, who measures the journey by the number of days it will take to reach shore. The story reflects a modern-day pilgrim family's yearning for freedom.

An unusual and controversial picture book for younger readers is Gloria Anzaldúa's bilingual *Friends from the Other Side/Amigos Del Otro Lado*, set along the Texas-Mexican border in Brownsville, Texas, the author's hometown. In the story, a young boy, Joaquín, emerges from the alleyways, on a shimmering hot summer's day, wearing a tattered, long-sleeved shirt, protection for the embarrassing sores that cover his body. Joaquín is a child from the "other side," a common term used by border residents to describe the newly arrived people from Mexico.

In Anzaldúa's story, the neighborhood kids call Joaquín a "wetback" and yell: *"Hey man, why don't you go back where you belong? We don't want any more mojados here."*

The book shows how young Mexican American males learn to bully new and recently arrived "illegals" or "wetbacks" as undocumented people are also called.

Illustrator Consuelo Méndez employs various media to provide a sensitive backdrop for the story, using watercolors with graphit and colored pencils and collage to present a realistic, highly detailed look at the everyday reality of the poorest of America's children. Méndez's illustrations, including dignified depictions of many of the shacks that line the

447

streets along the border, combined with Anzaldúa's text, evoke deep feelings. A recent book discussion of *Friends from the Other Side* among undergraduate Latino migrant students enrolled at a private Catholic college in Texas elicited mixed emotions. While a few of the students praised the picture book for its honesty and courage
in portraying a mostly neglected group in children's literature, many of them were disturbed by the accurate, all-too-real depiction of extreme poverty. If students all-too-familiar with these deplorable living conditions do not enjoy seeing the dark side of poverty, it is because poverty is not pleasant, and it is a chapter in many people's lives that they wish they would never have to revisit. To recall poverty is to recall a painful experience and prior deprivation that newly arrived citizens to the middle class would just as well see remain buried. Regardless of these mixed relations, the story can serve as a springboard for talking about the impoverished living conditions under which many people continue to live.

Another book for older readers that provokes deep emotional responses is Gary Paulsen's *The Crossing*. Paulsen juxtaposes two central characters, an alcoholic Vietnam veteran stationed at the air base in El Paso, Texas, and Manny Bustos, a fourteen-year-old street kid from Juarez. *The Crossing* is a classic example of stereotyping because it maintains the good (white) vs. bad (black) paradigm and depicts impoverished Mexicans as the instigators of crime. In the novel, the young Mexican kid is portrayed as a streetwise, conniving thief capable of robbing and killing a white man for cash and a chance to escape to the other side. The Vietnam veteran meets Manny several times and observes his behavior, but the two cannot communicate due to language barriers. Ultimately, the veteran is killed by other Mexicans in a gang fight. In his dying moments, he reaches out to Manny and hands over his wallet, offering Manny his cash and financial means to cross over.

Gary Paulsen's juxtaposed white/brown protagonists are once more visited in female form in his recent *Sisters/Hermanas*. In much

the same vein as his male protagonists in *The Crossing*, his two contrasting characters in *Sister/Hermanas* are a wealthy Anglo teenager and an undocumented Mexican girl who works as a prostitute at night. The two fourteen-year-olds meet by accident one day while they are in the same department store. Rosa is trying to escape from the authorities as Traci is trying on some clothes from the rack where Rosa is hiding. For one brief moment in time, their paths intersect.

Several other authors also relate the Mexican immigrant experience, documenting the journey that many young people take in their effort to make a better life for themselves. José Maldonado in Theodore Taylor's *The Maldonado Miracle* is a case in point. The twelve-year-old protagonist must cope with the death of his mother; he has little choice but to make the journey to the United States in the hope that he can be reunited with his father, a migrant farm worker toiling in the California fields. José's journey involves a trip in the hands of Gutierrez, the *coyote* or middleman charged with delivering undocumented workers to their American destination. Unforseen circumstances prevent José from being reunited immediately with his father, but he and his dog, Sánchez become part of a miracle that rejuvenates a dying town. By adding a humorous element to an otherwise heavy theme, Taylor effectively presents the pain, struggle, and sometimes joy in the lives of undocumented children. *The Maldonado Miracle* takes an unusual plot twist in that the parish priest goes beyond his call of duty and develops a friendship with José, helping him to find his father and volunteering to return the family to their native town.

A similar theme is to be found in Irene Beltrán's *Across the Great River*. Fourteen-year-old Katrina and her family wade the dangerous waters of the Rio Grande, losing track of their father in the process. The family continues the treacherous journey, making their way to the border town of Eagle Pass, Texas, where the struggle to survive is made difficult by *coyotes* and other robbers who beat and rape Katrina's mother. Beltrán's novel shows Katrina and her

448

mother ultimately returning safely to their home in Mexico, where they are reunited with the father, who had been deported in the course of the crossing.

Another female heroine shows great courage and leadership by taking on the role of the primary wage earner for her family. The book's fourteen-year-old heroine in *Lupita Mañana*, by Patricia Beatty, leaves her small fishing village near Enseñada, Mexico, near the California border, to try to make a living for herself and her family. Lupita wants to support herself and her brother (who crosses over with her) as well as her recently widowed mother and her siblings who have stayed behind. The lure of a better life is fostered by Lupita's aunt, who writes home from Indio, California, and reports on the wonderful life she leads. Lupita and her brother, Salvador, evade immigration authorities at every step of their journey, walking many miles on dangerous roads and highways, always fearful that they will be captured and returned. When they finally do connect with their relatives, they are amazed to discover the bleak poverty and miserable conditions that their aunt hid from them. Lupita proves to be the stronger character as she struggles with her brother's newfound obsession with a consumerist lifestyle. In the end, Lupita's brother is captured during a raid at a local party. He is unable to save himself because, unlike his friends, he does not possess a sufficient command of English to fake his citizenship. Lupita remains, hoping to learn enough English to avoid deportation, get an education, and attain a better life.

It should be noted that this book was written before a key Supreme Court decision gave undocumented children the right to public schooling and before legislation in California threatened these rights of immigrnat children. Neither Lupita nor Salvador are able to attend school in the United States, and their long-term prospects are dim without education.

Older students will find Ernesto Galarza's autobiographical *Barrio Boy* a fascinating story. Galarza barely recalls the intimate details of daily life in the rural villages of Mexico and his family's eventual settlement in the barrios of Sacramento. Victor Villaseñor's *Rain of Gold* provides high drama in his rich autobiographical family history. Regarded as the *Roots* of Mexican American literature, the story gives readers an intricate look at the immigrant journey to California during and after the Depression. Both *Barrio Boy* and *Rain of Gold* place the migration to the United States within its proper historical context, examining the Mexican Revolution and its long-term effects on the uprooting and displacement of families.

On a lighter note, middle and high school students will enjoy noted essayist and writer José Antonio Burciaga's humorous story "Weedee Peepoo," in his collection of short essays by the same title. In this story, the author recalls his parents' diligent efforts to help each other sound out the complicated English syntax while learning to recite the Preamble to the Constitution of the United States, a prerequisite for American citizenship.

The Central American immigrant experience in children's literature is perhaps the most poignantly told. Frances Temple's *Grab Hands and Run* is an eloquent testament to the plight of the Central American refugee. The story is told from the point of view of twelve-year-old Felipe, who enjoys a comfortable life with his younger sister, Romay, his mother Paloma, and Jacinto, her *companero* (life-long companion). Felipe enjoys his modest urban lifestyle as well as the visits to his mother's rural village, but from the book's beginning, there are signs of trouble. Young rebel soldiers linger around Felipe's grandparent's home. When Jacinto disappears mysteriously one day, it becomes evident to Felipe's mother that they are in danger and must flee. Felipe's mother is firm in her desire to fulfill her "disappeared" *companero's* wish for them to "grab hands and run" and embarks upon a treacherous journey with Canada as her final destination. In the harrowing process, she must ward off overzealous *coyotes* eager to take a cut from the latest batch of war victims. Paloma and her two children make four border crossings, only to be captured by immigration authorities in the Rio

Grande Valley in Texas. The authorities take Paloma, Felipe, and Romy to "El Coralon," the detention center for undocumented persons requesting political asylum from Central America. Temple's sensitive novel depicts the family's temporary stay with a kind and loving family in Wisconsin. That family serves as a modern "underground railroad," providing a safe harbor and passage for Salvadoran refugees on their way to political asylum in Canada.

Another fine novel for young adult readers on the Central American immigrant experience is *Journey of the Sparrows*, by Fran Leeper Buss. Trying to escape the war in El Salvador, Marie and her two siblings, along with other refugees, barely survive their passage to America nailed shut inside a crate in the back of a truck. Once in Chicago, the hardship takes on yet another dimension as Maria searches for food and work while at the same time trying to evade detection. With no English and no skills, she turns to the Catholic church, where she finds a warm soup kitchen and a sympathetic priest who helps her recross the Rio Grande into Mexico in an effort to locate her baby sister. *Journey of the Sparrows* is a poetic, hopeful novel that profiles the resilient spirit of immigrant children, many of them unaccompanied by parents, who continue to suffer in their effort to adjust to their new environment.

The Cuban exile experience of the early 1960s is told from a child's point of view in Hilda Perera's *Kike* and Maria Armengol Acierno's *Children of Flight Pedro Pan*. *Kike* depicts the lonesome adventures of an eight-year-old and his brother, who along with 21,000 other unaccompanied Cuban children, are sent to the states via jumbo jets, armed with visa waivers provided by the Catholic church. Their parents fear that they would be otherwise indoctrinated into the Cuban army. Soon after their arrival, Kike and his older brother become wards of the state when their sickly, aging grandfather can no longer care for them. For four years Kike and his brother float through foster homes; Kike feels disillusioned and abandoned. At his last foster home, Kike begins to adapt to his wealthy Anglo family's culture and lifestyle, but his stay is interrupted when his parents arrive suddenly

in Miami. Rather than experiencing a happy welcome, the confused child resents his parents for their lack of material possessions and their inability to be successful. This book, written by a Cuban immigrant author and translated into English, portrays the complexities of the immigration experience and parent-child relationships disrupted by political turmoil, years of separation, and the strains of adapting to a new culture.

Maria Armengol Acierno's recently published *Children of Flight Pedro Pan* is also the story of the unaccompanied Cuban children who were sent by their parents to the United States to escape Communist indoctrination. While many Cubans, including the parents of the two child protagonists, initially supported Fidel Castro against the dictatorship of a ruling tyrant, their disappointment with the new government is immediate and dramatic. The parents of ten-year-old María and her eight-year-old brother José make arrangements for the two children to live in Miami with family friends until they themselves can make definite plans to join them. The two children board a jumbo jet filled with many similarly unaccompanied children. Upon their arrival in Miami, the children must deal with their new life in a small apartment, a stark contrast to their spacious plantation. What began as a short separation extends into a year-long wait as María and José recognize that they are in Miami for the long haul and that they will not be returning to their beloved land. They begin the grueling process of adjusting to their new life in Miami Beach without their parents.

Unfortunately, *The Children of Flight Pedro Pan* is a lackluster attempt to present an important historic event in literary terms. The short novel sweeps through the major events in the lives of the two children and minimizes their circumstances by stringing one-liners together into sweeping paragraphs.

As literature, the novel is thinly guised. Both it and *Kike* lack the drama and suspense of Sonia Levitin's *Journey to America*, which portrays a parallel immigrant experience, a family's parting in the wake of the Nazi persecution of the Jews. *The Children of Flight*

Pedro Pan is important, though, because it portrays an often ignored part of the Cuban child's immigration experience. In comparing both novels on the Cuban experience, one finds common threads. The resentment of the young characters toward their parents is a result of their feelings of abandonment. In addition, both writers describe the humiliation of the adults in the story as they witness how they are relegated to menial service jobs for their inability to function professionally in a new language.

Immigration themes also predominate in various fiction films produced by independent Latino producers and made available to schools and public libraries through National Video Resources and the MacArthur Foundation Library Video Project. These films have special appeal to a generation of young people raised on the images of television and Hollywood movies. They provide a visual dimension to the portrayal of immigrant life and are especially useful for reluctant readers and students who are learning English. The three films described below are highly recommended; their stories and characters are as compelling as those in the best novels on the subject.

Among the most notable films is *Sweet Fifteen*, produced by Richard Soto for the highly-acclaimed *Wonderworks* series. Although the purported theme is a young girl's plans for her *Quinceanera*, the underlying theme becomes the future of her family as her father's citizenship status is called into question. The setting for *Sweet Fifteen* is East Los Angeles in the early eighties when more stringent laws requiring employers to demand proof of citizenship were enacted. Although Marta de la Cruz's father has lived in California for over twenty years, he cannot prove his citizenship. Mr. de la Cruz's undocumented status makes him a likely candidate for deportation. Overcome by the trauma of losing his job, coupled with his loss of pride, Mr. de la Cruz cannot bring himself to ask his former employer to verify the necessary paperwork needed for the amnesty program. With a little ingenuity, Marta embarks on the quest.

Maricela is the story of a Central American girl's effort to adjust to a new language, culture, and country while, at the same time, trying to understand the horrifying events that have made her an exile in the first place. Maricela's mother finds work in the Malibu home of an affluent California family, and Maricela goes to live with her mother in this wealthy family's home. Although the employer is an understanding, empathetic woman who genuinely cares for Maricela, her teenage daughter is far from loving. This selfish, crude youngster deliberately hurts Maricela and embarrasses her in front of her equally snooty friends. In both these films, the conflict is resolved when the girls take action on their own behalf.

Another film on the immigrant experience is *Esperanza*, the story of a girl who finds herself responsible for her younger brother when her mother is abruptly taken one morning during a raid on her way to the local laundromat. An observant Anglo neighbor, thinking she has done the right thing, calls the police to report the unsupervised children. But Esperanza eludes the police in her determination to be reunited with her father, a migrant farm worker working somewhere in the California fields. Following a sketchy clue from a letter her father once wrote, Esperanza sets out to find him. But Esperanza lacks the maturity and social skills necessary to function properly, and so she runs into trouble several times.

As immigration continues to consume popular opinion, raising doubts and fears in people's minds, we must recall the words of Emma Lazarus in her famous pooem "The New Colossus," inscribed on the Statue of Liberty:

> …*Give me your tired, your poor*
> *Your huddled masses yearning to breathe free,*
> *The wretched refuse of your teeming shore*
> *Send these, the homeless, tempest-tossed, to me:*
> *I lift my lamp beside the golden door*

These well-known words have served immigrants well in the one hundred years since the poem was written. The indelible words have served as a source of pride and inspiration to the millions who have passed through the "golden doors" of liberty. The challenge for our younger generation will be to discover if they will continue to provide light for the new huddled masses, the poor who find their way to America through a different shore, yearning for liberty even if they cannot enter through the golden door.

It is unfortunate that the mean-spirited nature of the immigration debate and the accompanying media hype have played to people's worst fears for their safety and security. The message Latino children are hearing is a sad commentary—that undocumented persons, who may share their heritage, are not wanted here, they do not belong, and the United States will go to any legal means to insure that they are kept out. And it should be noted that this debate affects an increasingly diverse and growing population of immigrants in this country from across the world.

In all of this, what are young people to think about the issues that confront them in daily newspaper headlines and on prime-time news? How can young people begin the educational process that will enable them to become more empathetic, rational, and reasonable about such a complex issue as immigration? How can they begin to develop an understanding of the struggles and human suffering of immigrants and of undocumented persons who have no legal stature in this country but who wish to participate more fully? Hopefully books like this guide will aid that process.

Oralia Garza de Cortes is a children's librarian for the Austin Public Library. She authored Hispanic Americans: For Our Family, Our Friends, Our World: An Annotated Guide to Significant Multicultural Books for Children and Teenagers *(Bowker, 1992) and is a juvenile editor for the* Multicultural Review.

Reprinted with permission of Greenwood Publishing Group, Inc., Westport, Conn.

Grade Four to Grade Six

An Ancient Heritage: The Arab American Minority

Brent Ashabranner Paul S. Conklin
Arab American, Middle Eastern
1991, HarperCollins, Naff, Alixa, *The Arab Americans.*

Quick! Pop quiz! What do these people have in common? Comedian Danny Thomas, radio personality Casey Kasem, teacher and astronaut Christa McAuliffe, consumer advocate Ralph Nader, heart surgeon Michael DeBakey, and Oscar-winning actor F. Murray Abraham?

If you don't know, it's not surprising: according to author Brent Ashabranner all of these people belong to one of America's least known and understood minorities, Arab Americans. In *An Ancient Heritage*, Ashabranner discusses the cultural inheritance of America's approximately three million people of Arab descent.

The book begins with a historical overview of Arab civilization, then focuses on the two main waves of Arab immigration to the United States. The first of these occurred prior to World War I, when about 100,000 Arabs came to live in America. This massive migration slowed to a trickle after a discriminatory law designed to limit non-European immigration

Interviews and a brief history provide a good overview of Arab American life and culture.

to America was enacted in 1924. The law unfairly restricted immigration to the United States according to discriminatory racial and ethnic quotas. Arab immigration to the US. rose again after World War II, with the majority of the people in this second group arriving after the revision of America's immigration laws in 1965.

With the historical background set, Ashabranner then begins a series of interviews of a diverse group of Arab Americans. Men and women, Muslims, Christians, and Druze share their stories and those of their families. They speak of their love for their culture, the prejudices they have encountered, and the hope they have for their future and that of their children in America.

Many of these stories are inspiring and others are shameful examples of prejudice, some on the part of well-known American politicians who refused to accept campaign contributions or endorsements from supporters with Arab ancestry. The stories are told in a loose conversational style using many direct quotes that let the interview subjects speak for themselves.

An Ancient Heritage is illustrated with black-and-white photographs by Paul S. Conklin. The illustrations include family portraits, historic photographs, and scenes of religious and cultural events. SANDRA KELLY

Dia's Story Cloth: The Hmong People's Journey of Freedom

📖 Dia Cha ✒ Chue and Nhia Cha

Asian American, Hmong

1996, Lee & Low Books in Cooperation with the Denver Museum of Natural History.

With innovative books like *Zora Neale Hurston and the Chinaberry Tree*, *Joshua's Masai Mask*, and the highly acclaimed *Baseball Saved Us*, Lee and Low has established itself as an important publisher of children's books in the few years since its founding. Now it brings us a book that is bound to become an immigration and artistic classic.

Dia's Story Cloth: The Hmong People's Journey to Freedom provides an engaging and powerful vehicle to teach history, often deemed as one of the most boring subjects in school.

Emerging as a bridge between the past and pre-

Dia's aunt and uncle stitch a story cloth to chronicle the Hmong people's journey to the United States in this excellent book.

sent, Vietnamese and Laotian story cloths have become a new narrative form in the American artistic and literary landscape. As a result of the war during the 1960s in Vietnam and Laos, many Hmong people, like Dia Cha and her family, were displaced.

Dia Cha and her family fled to Thailand, where they spent four years in a refugee camp. When the Communist regime took over after the Americans pulled out of Laos in 1975, fifteen-year-old Dia and her family came to the United States. Stitched by her aunt and uncle, the story cloth tells about the Hmong people's enduring search for freedom, which began centuries before in China and continued throughout their settlement in Southeast Asia. Although the needlework required for the story cloths was once solely done by the women, detention in the refugee camps resulted in men learning the craft as well. The story cloths are made without patterns, or measurements, and are similar to handstitched quilts and tapestries found in many other cultures around the world.

The book is beautifully designed and the story cloth tells a complex and at times painful story. In one section of the story cloth, "yellow rain" (Agent Orange) falls from an airplane. The most minute details are included in the story cloth, and each time young children are bound to find something in it. The book also includes an overview of Hmong culture, history, traditions, and some of the stitchery techniques. DAPHNE MUSE

The Lotus Seed

📖 Sherry Garland ✒ Tatsuro Kiuchi

Asian American, Vietnamese

1993, Harcourt Brace Jovanovich, 📕 Schmidt, Jeremy, *Two Lands, One Heart*; Temple, Frances, *Tonight by Sea*.

In an understated text and delicate illustrations, Garland and Kiuchi tell a story of "how a family's heritage is passed down from one generation to the next, and how hope, like the lotus seed, can survive through the worst of circumstances." *The Lotus Seed* opens with a mysterious and intriguing sentence: "My grandmother saw the emperor cry the day he lost his golden dragon throne."

The narrator's grandmother, wanting some-

An inventive fable about immigration and passing on tradition, loosely based on the Vietnamese experience.

453

thing to remember the emperor by, "snuck down to the silent palace, near the River of Perfumes, and plucked a seed from a lotus pod that rattled in the Imperial garden." She hides the seed and carries it with her—on her wedding day, on the day the bombs fell and soldiers "clamored door to door," on the day she scrambles into a crowded boat and says good-bye to Vietnam. She takes it with her to the strange new land of blinking lights and speeding cars, where she and her relatives live together in one big house. She cries when her grandson steals the seed and plants it in a place he later can't remember.

But in the spring, a lotus blossom unfurls its petals, and the grandmother calls it a "flower of life and hope." She gives a seed to each of her grandchildren. The narrator hides hers in a secret place so she can someday give seeds to her own children "and tell them about the day my grandmother saw the emperor cry."

The faces are indistinct in much of this beautiful book, emphasizing the fact that the story of loss and reborn hope is the story of many. Garland's author's note gives a brief background about Vietnamese history and the approximately one million Vietnamese people who fled by boat to the United States. But Vietnam is not mentioned by name in the text, so older students could be encouraged to become sleuths and unlock some of the mysterious references for themselves.

Since there are few words on each page, this book is a pleasure to read aloud to children as young as kindergarten. Older students can collect bits of their own family history and stories, perhaps discovering something that has been treasured for generations as the lotus seed was.

Many books on the immigrant experience also connect. In *The Butterfly Seeds* by Mary Watson, a grandfather gives a young European boy some seeds to take with him to the new land. *I Was Dreaming to Come to America* by Veronica Lawlor is a collection of quotes from the Ellis Island Oral History Project, illustrated with whimsical handpainted collages. A nonfiction book, *Two Lands, One Heart* by Jeremy Schmidt, illustrated with photographs by Ted Wood, shows a mother and son's recent visit to Vietnam, years after the mother fled with her younger brother and sister. A novel, *Tonight by Sea* by Frances Temple, captures the experience of fleeing Haiti in the early 1990s. JANE KURTZ

The Friends

📖 Rosa Guy

African American, Caribbean American, West Indian

1995 (1973), Puffin Books, ✳ Video Cassette, 📖 Guy, Rosa, *Ruby*.

Fourteen-year-old Phyllisia (Phyl) Cathy has moved from the West Indies to Harlem and hates everything about New York. There is no place to play, the city is dangerous, the people all seem cruel and hateful. The kids at school make fun of Phyl's accent and the way she dresses, so Phyl reacts to them with loathing and disgust, although she desperately wants a friend. She believes the other children wouldn't bother her so much if she had a companion, so she latches on to Edith Jackson, a poor, flighty, but genuine person.

Recently arrived from the West Indies, a teenaged girl learns to appreciate her one friend in a touching story.

Phyl and Edith become close. Edith helps Phyl out with the problems she has at home—a domineering father, an ailing mother, and a bubble-headed sister—and Edith asks only for friendship in return.

Phyl sees the disparity between her life and Edith's poverty, but money is not an issue at first. When Phyl brings Edith home for a visit, Mr. Cathy berates Edith for her appearance, and Phyl, suddenly ashamed of her friend, does not defend her. Phyl doesn't want to believe she looks down on the poor blacks around her but, in that respect, she is just like her father. Phyl's pride and maltreatment of Edith because of her shabby dress and poverty leads to their estrangement, and it takes time for Phyl to realize the value of her friend's honesty, caring, and inner beauty.

The Friends is both sad and gratifying because it shows how friendships can be sources of support even when people take their friends for granted. The book honestly depicts Phyl's feelings through the first-person narrative and addresses the important theme of bigotry within communites of color. Indeed, Phyl's cruelty to Edith is an unsparing example of class consciousness, one that kids can learn from. ALISON WASHINGTON

Hector Lives in the United States Now: The Story of a Mexican American Child

📘 Joan Hewett ✒ Richard Hewett

Hispanic, Mexican American

1990, HarperCollins, 📖 Howlett, Bud, *I'm New Here*; Gordon, Ginger, *My Two Worlds*.

Hector Almarez is a ten-year-old Mexican-American living with his family in Los Angeles. This book is a photographic essay on his life and assimilation into American culture. There are two primary strands to the story. His parents are in the midst of preparing for citizenship classes. Hector is preparing for his first Holy Communion. The book makes many references to Hector's two cultures. Frequently, customs associated with holidays, various foods, or even people, such as the *padrinos* (or godparents — important in his communion), are casually mentioned. The author's note discusses the Immigration Reform and Control Act of November 1986 and how it provided amnesty for previously undocumented aliens. There is a brief reading list. The black-and-white photographs give a gritty feel to the story. Hector and his family come through as real, vibrant people in both picture and text.

A useful story about the impact of the 1986 immigration legislation on one Mexican American family, and on U.S. immigration in general.

Although this book focuses on the immigration experience of a Mexican American, it would be useful to teachers discussing with students the immigrant experience in general. Activities stemming from this book might be preparation of foods or objects discussed in Hector's story. Also students might be assigned research projects to find further historical background as they discuss immigration. The results can be displayed on the bulletin board along with a photo of the student. ANDREA L. WILLIAMS

New Faces of Liberty

📘 Karen Jorgensen-Esmailli ✒ Cynthia Stokes Brown

Multicultural

1988, Many Cultures Publishing, 📖 Jorgensen-Esmailli, Karen, and Brown, Cynthia Stokes, *New Faces in Our Schools*.

Many Cultures Publishing has created two guides by teachers for use in the multi-ethnic classroom. *These guides contain a series of interactive lessons that use primary sources to lead students to an understanding of the reasons for immigration. The lessons and materials are collected in a loose-leaf binder for easy reproduction.*

An innovative teacher-student guide describing the immigration experience, past and present.

New Faces of Liberty, written for grades five through eight, begins with student interviews as a way to explore the roots of our immigrant experience. Throughout the twelve lessons, students construct an understanding of the early immigrant experiences of the Irish, the Mexicans, and African slaves, and of the recent immigrant experiences of people from Cambodia and El Salvador.

An important feature of *New Faces of Liberty* is its three-part approach, combining research, student-conducted interviews, and conflict resolution techniques to bring students to an historical and an active understanding of the cultures in their classrooms. This high school guide focuses on recent immigration from Afghanistan, Mexico, Vietnam, and Haiti. *San Francisco teachers have used these units in social science and language arts classes.* GRACE MORIZAWA

Onion Tears

📘 Dianna Kidd ✒ Lucy Montgomery

Asian, Vietnamese

1994 (1991), Puffin Books, ✳ Series

Nam-Huong arrives alone on the shores of Australia after fleeing Vietnam by boat with her grandfather. Nam-Huong and Grandfather flee after her parents and siblings are taken hostage by soldiers. The journey across the Atlantic Ocean is too strenuous for Grandfather. When he passes away, still holding Nam-Huong's hand, her heart is broken. No family. No country. What will become of Nam-Huong?

455

A Vietnamese girl adjusts to life in Australia, in a heartwarming but difficult story that may require adult guidance.

Onion Tears is the poignant story of young Nam-Huong's adjustment to life in a new land and her struggle to come to terms with the mysterious disappearance of her family and the death of her grandfather. Nam-Huong lives with Auntie and young Chu Minh, a Vietnamese foster family. She attends a local elementary school but is teased by her white classmates, who cannot pronounce her name and poke fun at the Vietnamese food she eats at lunchtime. But Nam-Huong finds solace in the letters she writes to little yellow canary, a bird she raised as a pet in Vietnam. Nam-Huong recalls memories of cooking meals with her family, harvesting crops, and sharing music with her grandfather. Each letter ends with the same question: "Have you seen my Dad, my Mom, Lan, Tri, and Son?" Auntie also sends letters to authorities in Vietnam. But there is no reply.

Miss Lily, Nam-Huong's teacher, becomes her best friend. When Miss Lily falls ill, Nam-Huong goes to her home and shares soup, fruit, and custard. She wears some of Miss Lily's perfume, tends to her garden, and takes care of Samson, Miss Lily's dog. But one day, Miss Lily is taken to the hospital. Nam-Huong takes Samson home, but the dog runs away. Nam-Huong's frantic search for Samson becomes her own search for peace of mind and social acceptance. Will Nam-Huong find Samson? Will Miss Lily get well? Will Nam-Huong find her family and return home to Vietnam?

Onion Tears is a heartwarming story. But the book's sequence of events are difficult to follow. Kidd is not successful in helping young readers make the transition from life in Vietnam to the present. We know Nam-Huong is confused about what has happened to her. But readers also are confused. Characters are mentioned, but their relationship to Nam-Huong is not fully explained. Events are described, but we don't know when they take place. To keep up with Nam-Huong, readers must return to previous chapters for clues—hard work!

The cover illustration and black-and-white sketches by Lucy Montgomery are simple and touching. Onion Tears *is promising but should be read in the classroom with a teacher's guidance. If the book is assigned for independent reading, some youngsters may find the plot too frustrating to enjoy.* LISA RHODES

The Truth About Columbus

📓 James Loewen ✒ Various sources
Native American
1992, The New Press, 📖 Loewen, James, *Lies My Teacher Told Me.*

The voyage of Columbus was a momentous event in history; we celebrate a holiday in his name and even use the date 1492 to divide history. However, Columbus and his voyages

A poster book that dissects myths about the Christopher Columbus story.

are now viewed with mixed feelings as we become aware that American history books sometimes don't tell the truth and much of what our schools teach is more legend than fact. *The Truth About Columbus* examines what the textbooks say, and what they don't say, about Columbus and the discovery of America. Here is a much needed work which by teaching students to separate legend from fact critically, leads to seeing America from a different perspective. Loewen's examination of Columbus, the voyages and discoveries, the myths and legends, is substantiated by eighty-one footnotes and sources. The centerfold of this book contains an exciting, color pull-out poster of text and attractive illustrations to bring history more vividly into the classroom.

The potential uses to which teachers can put this multifaceted 20" x 32" poster are limitless. As a tool for understanding the role of primary sources and critical thinking, the poster compares wrong or distorted statements about Columbus from fifteen American textbooks with more accurate information, and points out several key facts that history books routinely omit. As a springboard for research, and to facilitate further reading, a bibliography of ten important sources is provided. A thorough index is also included.

This is a valuable supplement and much needed alternative to the textbooks used in any class covering the explorers, Columbus, and the discovery and exploration of America. It is a must, not only for collections providing research material on curriculum topics, but also on the general issue of critical thinking. MELVINA AZAR DAME

Presenting Cultures Through Maps and Posters

Maps can serve as great visual aids when reading and discussing literature. They are especially useful in creating a sense of place. The creative use of posters, both artistic and historical, also enriches the learning experience significantly.

Peters Projection World Map *presents all countries according to their true size. (Traditional Mercator Projection maps distort sizes, making Europe appear much larger than it actually is.)* A New View of the World *by Ward Kaiser is a handbook on the Peters map. Map/$18 and handbook/$3.95 available from Northern Sun Merchandising, 2916 E. Lake St., Minneapolis, MN 55406.*

Asante, Molefi K., and Mark T. Mattson, Historical and Cultural Atlas of African Americans *(MacMillan, 1992). Excellent reference book.*

Waldman, Carl, Atlas of the North American Indian *(Facts on File, 1989). Maps and illustrations by Molly Braun. $16.95.*

Turnabout Map of the Americas *presents South America on the top and North America on the bottom. Available in English, Spanish, or Portuguese. $6.95. Laguna Sales, 7040 Via Valverde, San Jose, CA 95135.*

A variety of progressive posters are available from Syracuse Cultural Workers, Box 6367, Syracuse, NY 13217. (315) 474-1132; Donnelly/Colt, Box 188, Hampton, CT 0647. (800) 553-0006; Northern Sun Merchandising, 2916 E. Lake St., Minneapolis MN 55406; and Northland Poster Collective, P.O. Box 7096, Minneapolis, MN 55407. (800) 627-3082.

A collection of eighty-four maps and charts on Native American history is available from Historic Indian Pub., 1401 Sunset Drive, P.O. Box 16074, Salt Lake City, UT 84116, (801) 328-0458.

Women of Hope Poster Series *by Bread and Roses Cultural Project is a beautiful set of twelve full-color posters highlighting the achievements of women, their courage, compassion, and contributions in shaping American life. The posters come with study guides, which include biographical information about the women and suggestions on how to use the posters to teach multiculturalism and economic and social justice. The series also includes a twenty-seven minute, closed-caption video. Bread and Roses Cultural Project, Inc. 330 West 42nd Street, New York, NY 10036; (212) 631-4565/ (212) 695-0583.*

From: "Rethinking Our Classrooms: Teaching For Equity and Justice." A special issue of Rethinking Schools.

In the Year of the Boar and Jackie Robinson

Bette Bao Lord Marc Simont

Asian American, Chinese American

1984, HarperCollins

In 1947, the Year of the Boar, Bandit Wong and her mother move to Brooklyn, New York, to join Bandit's father. Although sad about leaving the Wong clan in China, Bandit looks forward to her new life in *Mei Guo,* the "Beautiful Country," with excitement. However, even with her new American name, Shirley Temple Wong, assimilating into the new culture

An intriguing story of a Chinese girl's Americanization in Brooklyn.

turns out to be more difficult and lonelier than anticipated. Although she willingly faces many new cultural challenges in her new fifth-grade class, the piano lessons with Señora Rodriguez, and the English language, Shirley feels discouraged and disappointed with her inability to belong.

Everything begins to fall into place, however, when she is befriended by the toughest girl in the class, who invites her to play stickball and nicknames her Jackie Robinson after the popular Brooklyn Dodgers baseball player. Shirley Temple Wong finds and secures her place in a new country as her love of baseball grows.

Readers will find the Chinese way of life described in the book intriguing. They will also become sensitive to the difficulties of adjusting to a new life as they share the stories of Shirley Temple Wong. CATHY Y. KIM

Yang the Third and Her Impossible Family

📖 Lensey Namioka ✒ Kees De Kiefte
Asian American, Chinese American
1995, Little, Brown & Company, ✷ Series

The Yang family's adventures continue as they learn to be "American" in *Yang the Third and Her Impossible Family*, the sequel to *Yang the Youngest and His Terrible Ear*. In this story, the family has been living in Seattle for a little less than a year. The Yangs are all talented and dedicated musicians, except Fourth Brother (also known as "Sprout"), who has a tin ear. The family home is filled with music. Instruments and sheet music are lying around, and anyone can pick up an instrument and play whenever the mood strikes. Yingmei plays the cello, Second Sister plays viola, Eldest Brother and Mr. Yang play violin, and Mrs. Yang is a pianist. Yingmei, known as Third Sister by her family and Mary by her new American friends, is trying desperately to fit in with a group of girls at her school. She keeps a notebook of English words and meanings so that she will never make a mistake and embarrass herself by saying the wrong thing. But she finds that learning English is much more difficult than just remembering new words, and that many words and phrases have more than one meaning, which can be very tricky.

A Chinese immigrant to the U.S. tries to fit in, even if it means breaking family customs.

In Chinese culture, family hierarchy is reinforced by variations in naming; for example, each of the children's names are presented to the reader in three different ways: a Chinese name that is used at home, an American name that is used in school, and a "birth-order" name that establishes the child's rank in the family. Reading this book provides more than a cultural lesson to the reader, it also amplifies some of the difficulties immigrant children must face in an alien culture.

The story, narrated by Yingmei/Mary, revolves around her quest to become like Holly, the girl she admires at school. Confident and authoritative, Holly looks like a princess from a candy tin Yingmei had in China. Unfortunately, Yingmei feels her family is forever embarrassing her in front of Holly and her other school friends, primarily because of the differences between Chinese and American culture. In an amusing scene at the Yang's first Thanksgiving dinner, Mrs. Yang tries to compliment Holly's mother and show her respect by telling her how much older she looks than her age, and how nice and fat she is, while Yingmei, who has learned that Americans want to be seen as young and thin, cringes.

Determined to find a way into Holly's elite circle of girls and become her special friend, Yingmei decides to adopt a kitten from her, the last of a full litter of kittens. Yingmei knows that she shouldn't bring a cat into her home because it would shred sheet music and damage musical instruments all over the house, but when she sees the smallest of the litter fighting for a spot among her litter mates, she immediately identifies with it. With the help of her youngest brother, she decides to save it from the pound and hides it in the basement.

For young readers, many of the antics Yingmei and Fourth Brother go through to hide the kitten will make for a fun read. To develop a code to call the kitten to eat, Fourth Brother pretends to take up violin again, despite his terrible ear, and the family is more than willing to let him "practice" in the basement.

The racism children learn from their parents is subtly intertwined with Yingmei's narrative as she examines her family and friendships and overhears her new friends' reactions to her family's customs. Eldest Sister, for example, refuses to assimilate, proudly wearing her Chinese clothes and playing Chinese folk music. Eldest Brother is not afraid of being called a wimp when he won't risk his fingers to play sports with the other boys. In the end, their resolve to be themselves sets an example to Yingmei and her new friends.

Namioka has created an easy-to-read chapter book for young readers that gives a glimpse of Chinese culture and has a happy ending for Yingmei and her kitten. She also presents the idea that it is possible to be different and yet earn respect from people if you respect yourself. Anyone who has ever felt out of place in an unfamiliar setting will enjoy this story. ROSA E. WARDER

Yang the Youngest and His Terrible Ear

📖 Lensey Namioka ✒ Kees De Kiefte
Asian American, Chinese American
1994 (1992), Dell Publishing Group, Inc.

Yingtao Yang and his musical family move to Seattle from Shanghai. Despite the fact that Yingtao is tone deaf and does not share the family love of

A Chinese American boy and a new school friend exchange cultural knowledge and help each other with family problems.

music, his father has high expectations for him to play his part as second violin in the family quartet with his three siblings.

Yingtao's father was once a violinist in the Shanghai Philharmonic Orchestra and is now a member of the Seattle Symphony Orchestra. His mother is a pianist. The family is utterly baffled by Yingtao's lack of talent and assumes that he isn't trying. They push him even harder. The pressure comes to a climax as the family quartet prepares for a recital.

When Yingtao befriends Matt, a boy in his class, he discovers that Matt has a similar problem with his father. Matt's father has high hopes for him to be an excellent baseball player; Matt, however, prefers to play the violin. As their genuine and caring friendship grows, Yingtao and Matt exchange deeper understandings of one another. They also try to come to terms with the pressures felt from their fathers and devise a plot to "challenge their fathers' authority." The plot peaks as Matt "bow syncs" for Yingtao's second violin part in the family quartet during the recital. When their little plan is discovered, they also manage to convince their fathers to appreciate and support their interests and talents. CATHY Y. KIM

A Peddler's Dream

Janice Shefelman Tom Shefelman

Arab American, Lebanese American

1992, Houghton Mifflin Company

How many Arab immigrants came to the United States before World War I? Take a guess. If you based your estimate on the amount of coverage that most history books give to immigration from

A Lebanese boy leaves his small village in the mountains for the United States in this highly recommended story.

the Arab world during America's peak years of immigration, you might have guessed "zero," a word which comes to us from the Arabic language.

The number? Over 100,000. The story of one of these almost forgotten immigrants is told for young readers in *A*

Peddler's Dream. Husband and wife, author and illustrator Janice and Tom Shefelman based this work of historical fiction on the true experiences of their neighbor's Lebanese ancestor.

Solomon Joseph Azar is the hero of the tale. His journey to the United States begins in a small village in the mountains of Lebanon. Looking for a better life, and perhaps a little adventure, Solomon leaves

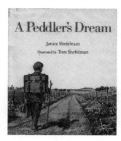

his homeland on a ship, promising to send for his fianceé, Marie, when he is settled. As other passengers on the ship succumb to sea sickness, Solomon credits his seafaring Phoenician ancestors for a hereditary immunity to nausea on the ocean.

Once he arrives in the United States, Solomon starts work as a peddler, traveling from farm to farm on foot selling his wares. He dreams of some day owning his own store. Disaster strikes when Solomon is attacked and robbed of his pack and his purse. Kindly fellow immigrants, a German farm family, comfort Solomon. Despite his loss, Solomon still believes in his dream and works hard to achieve it.

As the story continues, Solomon finds work as a clerk in a store. He travels back to Lebanon to marry Marie and bring her to the United States. Solomon is made partner in the store and Marie blends the traditions of her Arab heritage with her new life in America to make a home for them both. Three children later, it seems they have achieved their dream. Solomon's partner has retired and he is sole owner of a prosperous store. Again disaster strikes. This time it takes the form of a fire that destroys everything Solomon and Marie have worked so hard for. With the same toughness and tenacity that had brought them so far, they vow to rebuild better than before. The ending is a happy one.

This well-written book is beautifully illustrated and provides a unique look at the lives of early Arab immigrants. *Simple language makes the book easy to read to the smallest child, but the complex issues that form the background to the story will provide plenty of discussion with older children.*

This book is highly recommended as an addition to school and classroom libraries. It will prove particularly useful to teachers who are teaching about historic immigration, since it is one of the few books for children that focuses on non-European immigration during the early twentieth century. SANDRA KELLY

460

They're All Named Wildfire

Nancy Springer
African American
1989, Atheneum

They're All Named Wildfire is an extraordinary work that tackles a difficult subject with integrity. What makes a book about racism as seen by two fifth-grade girls notable is the growth of the main character, a European American girl named Jenny. When an African American family moves into the other side of Jenny's family's duplex, many of the people in the rural Pennsylvania town react with bigotry. Jenny's mother is the exception; she is a mechanic and used to "doing the opposite of what people expect." The African American family has five children, including a girl Jenny's age named Shantery. Jenny initially feels very uncomfortable about being "so close to black people." Her life is further complicated when her mother takes a housewarming gift over to the new family and volunteers Jenny to walk to school with Shantery when the semester starts.

In the week before school starts, Jenny and Shantery get to know each other and realize they share a love of horses. They both dream of some day owning their own horses and being able to ride whenever they like. Like Jenny, Shantery has a large collection of toy horses and has named them all

A remarkable book about an interracial friendship threatened by the community's racism.

Major Legislative Milestones in U.S. Immigration History

CHINESE EXCLUSION ACT (1882)
* *Suspends immigration of Chinese laborers for ten years*
* *Bars Chinese naturalization*
* *Provides for deportation of Chinese illegally in United States*

IMMIGRATION ACT OF 1891
* *First comprehensive law for national control of immigration*
* *Establishes Bureau of Immigration under Treasury*
* *Directs deportation of aliens unlawfully in country*

IMMIGRATION AND NATURALIZATION ACT OF JUNE 27, 1952
* *Continues national origins quotas*
* *Quota for skilled aliens whose services are urgently needed*

IMMIGRATION AND NATIONALITY ACT AMENDMENTS OF OCTOBER 3, 1965
* *Repeals national origins quotas*
* *Establishes seven-category preference system based on family unification and skills*
* *Sets 20,000 per country limit for Eastern Hemisphere*
* *Imposes ceiling on immigration from Western Hemisphere for first time*

IMMIGRATION AND NATIONALITY ACT AMENDMENTS OF 1976
* *Extends 20,000 per country limits to Western Hemisphere*

REFUGEE ACT OF 1980
* *Sets up first permanent and systematic procedure for admitting refugees*
* *Removes refugee as category from preference system*
* *Defines refugee according to international, versus ideological, standards*
* *Establishes process of domestic resettlement*
* *Codifies asylum status*

IMMIGRATION REFORM AND CONTROL ACT OF 1986
* *Institutes employer sanctions for knowingly hiring illegal aliens*
* *Creates legalization programs*
* *Increases border enforcement*

IMMIGRATION ACT OF 1990
* *Increases legal immigration ceilings by 40 percent*
* *Triples employment-based immigration*
* *Establishes temporary protected status for those in the U.S. jeopardized by armed conflict or natural disasters in their native countries*

Sources: Immigration and Nationality Act of 1992; Immigration and Naturalization Service 1991, Statistical Yearbook

"Wildfire." By the time the first day of school rolls around, Jenny is more comfortable with Shantery and begins to think of her as a possible new friend. Jenny's friends, however, shun the two of them. Later in the day Shantery is called "nigger" and Jenny "nigger lover." At this point, Jenny decides that to keep her friends at school, she must side against Shantery.

Jenny very quickly reaches a point where she realizes that she doesn't feel good about what she's doing, nor does she like what she is seeing in her "friends." It takes time, but Jenny realizes that Shantery deserves to be treated like everyone else. In a scene where some kids are taunting Shantery, she jumps in and calls them "a bunch of snot-nose, half-baked bigots!" along with a few other choice epithets. This action marks her as a full-fledged "nigger lover," but opens a door for Jenny and Shantery to develop their friendship and be honest about what is going on around them.

One unusual aspect of this story is that the adults are not portrayed as saviors or even necessarily very smart. The school principal tells Shantery she should "try to fit in better," as if her difference causes other kids' behavior. When their neighbor Mr. Seitzel buys a palomino horse and puts it in the pasture behind their house, Mr. Seitzel says to them "Jenny, you're welcome to come see this horse anytime....But I don't want no nigger on my land or messing with my horse." Shantery is humiliated, and Jenny finds herself torn between her desire to ride and her disgust with Mr. Seitzel.

Eventually, Jenny and Shantery sneak a ride on the horse. They are caught, and Mr. Seitzel presses charges against Shantery for trespassing. With the help of Jenny's parents, the charges are dropped, but both families suffer. The girls are harassed even more at school, their homes are sprayed with racist graffiti, and their families receive violent threats. Finally, the girls are pulled out of school and Shantery's family decides to move away. Before they leave, Mr. Seitz's horse is found in the pasture with its throat cut and the words "Here's your horse nigger gal" spray-painted across its golden hide.

After the family moves away, things return to normal for Jenny at school and at home, but Jenny is acutely aware that she has changed. This is a sometimes graphic book that does not shy away from the ugly facts of racism. What makes the book remarkable is the way the author depicts Jenny's internal thought processes about what she sees in herself and others. ROSA E. WARDER

The Storyteller

📖 Joan Weisman   ✏ David Bradley
Chippewa, Native American, Pueblo
1993, Rizzoli Books

Rama's family has moved in order to be closer to their father, who has recently been hospitalized. Rama is often responsible for taking care of her younger sisters and brothers. In the new city, she meets Ms. Lottie, an elderly woman who is also ill. Rama feels drawn to Ms. Lottie and gives the elderly woman a story-telling doll. The doll has a mouth shaped as if poised to speak, and her arms are filled with scores of baby dolls listening attentively.

A storytelling doll sparks a friendship between a Native American girl and an elderly woman in this heart-warming book.

Both share stories with one another, and Ms. Lottie emerges out of her shell of illness and eventually finds herself feeling strong enough to venture out of her apartment. As the friendship grows, Ms. Lottie grows stronger. Rama's dad also recovers and, eventually, Rama and her family return home. Although it is difficult to say goodbye, Rama is comforted by the fact that Ms. Lottie will continue to tell stories to other children in the apartment building.

This intergenerational story clearly demonstrates how love, compassion, and the thoughtful sharing of time can serve as a healing force. MARTHA L. MARTINEZ

Goodbye, Vietnam

📖 Gloria Whelan
Asian American, Vietnamese American
1993 (1992), Random House

The time has come for Mai and her family to leave their home in Vietnam. The police are angry because her uncle's family has escaped successfully. Now they are keeping close watch on Mai and her family. They earn passage on a boat sailing to Hong Kong.

Emigrating from Vietnam to the United States, Mai and her family face a long, difficult journey in this poignant, instructive book.

461

There is trouble on the way—a faulty engine, lack of food, and sickness. Their boat even picks up a survivor of a pirate attack.

Upon reaching Hong Kong, they are herded into a warehouse where hundreds of refugees are living. The officials locate her uncle in America and he agrees to act as a sponsor for Mai's family. Mai's final words are "Everything we were leaving behind would grow small, but not so small we would ever forget it."

The language in the book is simple, as if reflecting Mai's limited English. The author explains Vietnamese customs such as Tet (the Vietnamese New Year celebration) and the work of Mai's grandmother, who practices traditional medicine. The author weaves these elements into the story in a manner that is instructional but never pedantic. Each character's feelings—fear, uncertainty, hope—are poignantly portrayed. The author's description of the sea voyage is particularly effective. An important afterword discussing the plight of Vietnamese refugees as of 1992 places the story in context. PAM CARLSON

Tales from Gold Mountain: Stories of the Chinese in the New World

Paul Yee ✦ Simon Ng

Asian American, Chinese American

1990 (1989), Macmillan Publishing Company

This wonderful book of modern folktales combines the author's knowledge of Chinese history with a respect and knowledge of Chinese folktale traditions.

Yee succeeds in creating a series of tales which profoundly echo the voices of history. His stories are spooky, funny, romantic, and full of the down-to-earth presence of the working-class immigrants whose lives they reveal. Chinese Canadian history closely parallels Chinese American history, so these tales are a good reflection of the Chinese immigration experience in North America.

Eight wonderful stories about Chinese people in North America, emphasizing resilient optimism.

In "Spirit of the Railway," Yee integrates familial separation and longing with a depiction of the harsh working conditions facing Chinese railway workers to create a classic ghost tale that honors the memory of those Chinese pioneers. Farmer Chu leaves his family in China to find work in Gold Mountain, but he disappears and his wife frets, awaiting word from him. Farmer Chu's son then journeys to the Americas in search of his father. He encounters other workers who tell him, "Search no more, young man! Don't you know that too many have died here? My own brother was buried in a mud slide. My uncle was killed in a dynamite blast. No one warned him about the fuse. The white boss treats us like mules and dogs!"

Young Chu finally encounters his father's ghost in a tunnel the workers are attempting to blast through a mountain. His father's ghost tells him, "A fuse exploded before the workers could run. A ton of rock dropped on us and crushed us flat. They buried the whites in a churchyard, but our bodies were thrown into the river, where the current swept us away. We have no final resting place." Young Chu helps give his father and the other workers a proper burial and the workers are able to complete the tunnel. This simple tale incorporates much of what Asian American historians have been able to discover about the working and living conditions of early Chinese immigrants.

In "The Friends of Kwan Ming," Kwan Ming is hired as a houseboy for a greedy, selfish boss. The boss abuses him, and after tripping on the floor which Kwan Ming is scrubbing, he orders Kwan Ming to bring him a suit which won't tear, a pair of leather boots that won't wear out, and forty loaves of bread that won't go stale. Kwan Ming's friends come to the rescue to provide these things. The greedy boss so enjoys his bread that he cannot stop eating, but as his body expands, the suit and boots hold fast and finally the boss explodes. Again, Yee creates a story with traditional folktale elements that teach young readers about the type of mutual support which was necessary for workers to survive in the hostile environment.

One of the book's best stories is "The Revenge of the Iron Chink." In this story, Lee Jim works as a foreman in a cannery. The boss, Chimney Head, buys a machine to replace all the workers. He calls the machine the Iron Chink. Lee Jim is angry. He has worked for Chimney Head for twenty years and his dismissal is his reward. On the day the final load of salmon arrives to be canned, the workers must watch as the Iron Chink does all the work they previously did. As Lee Jim and the workers wait to board the boat to take them away, he holds up his bloody bandaged hands to the boss and says, "I wanted to send a gift to the Queen, too. In two of the tins, she will find my baby fingers! I think she will find them as sweet as any salmon meat we have canned!" As the boat pulls away, the fuming Chimney Head believes the entire shipment is spoiled, but Lee Jim unbandages his hands for the workers to see: "There were his baby fingers, still attached to his hands, as pink and healthy as any man's!"

Although these spirited stories focus on the past, the themes are timeless. Accompanied by beautiful, and sometimes funky illustrations by Simon Ng, these tales are quite memorable and reveal an important dimension of Chinese American history and culture. DEBBIE WEI

The Star Fisher

📖 Lawrence Yep

Asian American, Chinese American

1992 (1991), Puffin Books, ✱ Bilingual Chinese/English

Based on the author's family's experiences, a beutiful book about a Chinese American family in West Virginia in the 1920s.

The Star Fisher is a beautifully written and sensitive portrayal of a Chinese American family's experience as new arrivals to West Virginia in the 1920s. In his preface, author Yep writes, "West Virginia has always been more real to me than China. That's because my grandmother, mother, aunts, and uncles spoke more often of West Virginia than of China . . . I should also say that my own family's trek was not unique. Though their numbers were small before the changes in the immigration laws in the 1960s, Chinese families refused to be confined to the Chinatowns on the two coasts and searched for a place in America for themselves even before the 1920s."

The Star Fisher is essentially an oral history of Yep's family, focusing on the experience of a young girl named Joan Lee. Born in America, she, her immigrant parents, and her younger siblings moved to Clarksburg, West Virginia, in 1937 so her father could start a laundry business. While chron-

icling the family's experiences, Yep also deftly interweaves information about Asian American life and history that are seldom addressed.

He begins by recognizing and honoring bilingualism. Throughout the book, conversations in Chinese are presented in plain type while those in English are set in italics. This typographic technique seamlessly demonstrates the linguistic shifts which the Lee children must make in negotiating their lives between the world of her parents and the world of mainstream American culture.

The reader also learns something of the obstacles faced by immigrants. Joan's father, the laundry worker, is a highly educated man. Joan explains to the startled West Virginians who admit to not having seen "many of your kind around here" that her family was allowed to immigrate because of her father's status as a scholar. The irony that scholars were allowed to enter the United States only to become manual laborers will not escape the critical reader.

Yep writes of prejudice with an honest voice, neither overdramatizing nor underestimating its impact. He also provides a sympathetic portrayal of the situation faced by the oldest child of immigrant parents. Joan must watch over her younger brother and sister and serve as navigator for her parents in the uncharted waters of Clarksburg. This predicament will be familiar to many young readers.

This book is highly recommended for anyone interested in the complexities of living as a member of a marginalized group in America. DEBBIE WEI

463

World's Languages Dying at Alarming Rate: Shrinking Linguistic Diversity Mourned;

State's Native Tongues Especially Hard Hit

Steve Connor

Most of the world's 6,000 languages will either be extinct or on the road to extinction by the end of the next century, linguistic experts say.

The loss is especially acute in California, which has been called the world's third most linguistically diverse region, after New Guinea and the Caucasus. According to Leanne Hinton of UC-Berkeley, about 50 of North American's 250 native languages are in California, and all of them are in trouble. The latest extinction occurred last month with the death of the lone speaker of Northern Pomo, woman in her eighties.

Twenty Native American languages have died in the state this century, according to Hinton, and none of those still spoken is being learned widely by children or used in daily commerce: "There are still 50 Native American languages being spoken in California but not a single one of them is spoken by children. The vast majority are spoken by fewer than 10 individuals all over 70 years old."

Native American languages were suppressed until the 1960s. Indian children sent to boarding schools were punished for speaking their parents' language. Now, a movement exists among California Indians to learn the elders' tongue before it's too late. Some tribes have set up summer language camps for youngsters.

"Despite the desires of the language activists, the outlook is somewhat grim," according to Hinton. "There is no chance any of these will be first languages. But those who are trying to keep them alive are determined they will at least have a future as second languages."

Michael Krauss, a language researcher at the University of Alaska, warns that the rate at which native tongues are dying will cause irreparable damage to human civilization:

"I call this a catastrophe—the rate of loss of mankind's linguistic diversity." Between 20 and 50 percent of the world's languages are no longer being learned by children, he said. "For the next century, up to 95 percent will either become extinct or become moribund and headed toward extinction."

The pressures leading to language extinction stem from encroachment on the territories of indigenous peoples, mass migration, and the desire to learn the dominant languages of the world—notably English. Even surviving languages are becoming more homogeneous as more prestigious dialects replace their less prestigious relatives.

"Why should we care? The first argument is that the world would be a less interesting place to live in," Krauss argues. The second reason is that "mankind's way of thinking in different ways is reduced." For instance, some medicinal plants are known only to certain native peoples, so cultural knowledge is lost with a language. Krauss identifies medicinal plants such as curare and quinine that are unlikely to have come to prominence without understanding the South American languages that gave the plants their names. "The last argument is that we do not yet realize that we are living in an ecosystem of human diversity which is essential to our survival. Do we know what we are doing when we eliminate that diversity? We do not have the right to make that decision for posterity."

Reprinted by Permission from The London Independent, *One Canada Square, Canary Wharf, London HI4 5DL.*

Affirming Languages and Cultures

Lourdes Diaz Soto

In the Lehigh Valley, where my family and I reside, only three members of the Lenne Lanape tribe (Delaware Indians) speak their home language. The loss of home languages and cultures is a national trend proving costly to families and to society as a whole.

How can educators help alleviate barriers to linguistic and cultural education? First, we can help dispel misconceptions about bilingualism and biculturalism. Decades of research in the field of bilingual education point to the cognitive, linguistic, and the social advantages of raising children bilingually. As educators we can emphasize the need for higher levels of language learning. Young children who are more adept at their home language will actually learn a second language more readily and easily.

Second, we can implement high-quality bilingual and bicultural programs capable of maintaining home languages. Our ability to provide an education that is respectful of languages and culture can help to halt the tide of language loss. Children who perceive that their home language and culture is appreciated and respected by others will internalize positive, affirming messages. We can help change existing educational deficit models to enriching and affirming learning environments.

Third, we can require universal second language (and cultural) learning as an integral part of the educational process, for both learners and educators. Children deserve an opportunity to add languages and cultures to their repertoire of skills and to learn firsthand about the historically diverse strength of our nation and the world. An education that is bilingual and bicultural will make possible a society capable of communicating with many people in many languages. Our concerted effort can help to shift existing educational agendas from teaching shame to instilling pride.

Lourdes Diaz Soto is an associate professor of education at Lehigh University in Bethlehem, Pennsylvania. She teaches graduate courses in bilingual and multicultural education. Her research has focused on early educational issues affecting culturally and linguisticallly diverse young children. Reprinted with permission of Kappa Delta Pi, an international Honor Society in Education.

465

Grade Seven to Grade Eight

West Indians in America

📘 Alexandra Bandon   ✐ Various sources

Caribbean American, West Indian

1994, New Discovery Books, ✳ Series

West Indians in America focuses on immigrants from the Caribbean regions. Like many who leave home looking for a better life, these immigrants from Haiti, Trinidad, Tobago, and other island nations have stories to tell that go beyond sociological data and political causes.

A section titled "Personal Narratives from West Indian American Immigrants" contains immigrants' personal stories. We also hear the voices of second- and-third-generation West Indian immigrants.

These stories focus on their departures, the journey north, and the difficulty of settling in a new country. For some, the decision to come to the United States has been a dream come true; for others, a nightmare. Readers learn about socio-economic and political conditions the immigrants left behind and about the religious and cultural traditions that they have brought with them. Black-and-white photographs accompany the stories. MAGNA M. DIAZ

Focusing on the Caribbean, instructional personal narratives of immigrants.

Lupita Mañana

📖 Patricia Beatty
Hispanic, Mexican
1992 (1981), Beech Tree Books

Lupita's father dies in a boating accident. As he was the sole provider for Lupita's family, his death brings tremendous emotional and financial turmoil. Her brother Salvador tries to get his father's job, but the owner of the boat dislikes him because he had once shown some interest in the boat owner's daughter.

After their attempts to find meaningful employment fail, Lupita's family decides that she and Salvador should cross the border into the United States and find jobs there. Along the way, they find that the road to the new land is laced with enormous dangers from thieves and many hungry people like themselves. Being caught by the Mexican border patrol could result in death. But remaining in Mexico simply is not a viable option.

A poignant story about a girl's dangerous and illegal journey from Mexico to the United States.

What follows is a painful, heartrending, and sorrow-filled story that eventually turns on a thread of hope. This is an inspiring story for children who need to learn more about all of America's immigrants and their motivations for leaving their homes to come to America—sometimes to end up even worse off than they were before. MAGNA M. DIAZ

Journey of the Sparrows

📖 Fran Leeper Buss with Daisy Cubias
El Salvadoran, Hispanic
1993 (1991), Dell Publishing Company, Inc.

This young adult novel opens with Maria, the fifteen-year-old protagonist, squeezed into the blackness of a crate on a truck traveling from Mexico to Chicago along with her older sister, Julia, and her much younger brother, Oscar. Maria and her family have been fleeing from one danger to another ever since the day they watched their father and Julia's husband

A valuable book about a Salvadoran girl determined to save and protect her family while illegally crossing the Mexican border.

being killed by the Salvadoran *guardia*. And now, the travelers have dwindled to three, as they've had to leave their mother and baby sister, who is too sick to travel, behind in Mexico. Maria and Julia hope to save enough money to send for them, but life in Chicago turns out to be far from secure, let alone even remotely profitable. Although there is the solace of a network of fellow immigrants, nothing can protect Maria and her siblings from the dangers of the vigilant immigration patrol who collude with mercenary employers, nothing can ease the burdens that fall upon Maria's shoulders when Julia is unable to work, nothing can take away the nightmares of the *guardias* and their hateful campaign. Then, as if to prove how easily things can go from bad to worse, Maria receives a letter notifying her that her mother was deported back to El Salvador where she is bound to face the same fate that her

husband and son-in-law faced. But baby sister Teresa remains in Mexico and Maria, using the money she's made and the profoundly generous gift of a friend, makes the terrifying solo journey to Mexico to retrieve her sister.

Journey of the Sparrows is a valuable addition to the few books that address the truest adventure of seeking refuge in America. Fran Leeper Buss and her collaborator, Daisy Cubias, do not spare readers the often tragic details which touch upon Maria's life—the possibility that her sister may be bearing not her husband's child but that of one of the *guardias* who raped her, the dangers of the immigrant experience, the permanent partings, and the poverty. And yet, this is also a portrait of tremendous courage and tremendous compassion, and there are the transcending dreams of beautiful quetzals in flight. MAGNA M. DIAZ

The Girl from Playa Blanca

📖 Ofelia Dumas Lachtman
Hispanic, Mexican American
1995, Pinata Books

Elena and her little brother, Carlos, leave their seaside Mexican village to find their father, who has vanished while struggling to make a living in Los Angeles. Elena is hired by a wealthy Hispanic family and supports her brother and herself while searching for her father.

The search leads her on a frightening path filled with crime and intrigue. But the journey also helps her to find friendship, love, and the confidence she needs to grow into her own cultural and personal identity.

A delightful adventure story and mystery novel addressing immigration and biculturalism.

Elena's background is an important theme in the novel, but not necessary to the plot. A light, fast-paced page turner, this young-adult mystery may find its way into the hearts and backpacks of legions of young readers eager to explore new literary territory.

With relatively few Hispanic/Latino/a novels for young readers, *The Girl from Playa Blanca* helps to fill a void and to bring new thematic possibilities in this growing body of literature. DAPHNE MUSE

Through Our Eyes: A Journal of Youth Writing

⚑ Many Cultures Publishing

Multicultural

Many Cultures Publishing, 📖 Jorgensen, Karen, and Brown, Cynthia Stokes, *New Faces in Our Schools.*

Through Our Eyes brings readers into the worlds of young immigrants who are in high school or who have graduated recently. Their stories are of struggle, hope, family, courage, loneliness, and love.

Reflecting the diversity we now find in our classroom, the young immigrants are from places around the world including Sarajevo, Cambodia, Haiti, and Vietnam. Students will see themselves and their cultures reflected in the stories, poems, and screenplays. These pieces address themes important to all teenagers. A Sephardic Jew from Iraq compares his social life on a visit to Israel to his social life in Marin county. An immigrant from El Salvador tells how the break-up of his family after escaping from El Salvador led him to turn to a gang "to have somebody to advise me, somebody to look up to and people to hang out with." An African

A diverse collection of stories written by young immigrant students in the United States.

American interviews his friend, a Korean immigrant whose father was African American. The writer concludes. "We're both poor, young, and have broken families. We are both struggling and searching for the promised land."

Not only do these stories address questions important to high school students but they provide models for their own writings. Teachers who have read the Background Essays *published by New Faces of Liberty will find these stories add another layer to their understanding of immigrant students.*

The teacher guide focuses on ways to motivate students to write, lists specific questions for each story and followup activities that can be used for all of the stories. There are also suggestions for integrating these stories in English and language arts, social studies, and foreign language classes. GRACE MORIZAWA

Chinese American Portraits: Personal Histories 1828-1988

⚑ Ruthanne Lum McCunn

Asian American, Chinese American

1988, Chronicle Books, 📖 Young, Judy, *Chinese Women in America: A Pictorial History.*

This collective biography is a testament to Chinese Americans who have fought the odds and endured. McCunn has compiled seventeen profiles of men and women from all walks of life and organized them into three sections: Pioneers, Generations, and Contemporaries. Written in a lively narrative style, profiles include people like China Mary, an Alaskan frontierswoman; Harry Lee, a "cowboy" who became Louisiana's first Chinese American sheriff; Li Khai Fai and Kong Tai Heong, a husband and wife doctor team who diagnosed and fought the bubonic plague in Honolulu at the turn of the century; Lue Gim Gong, developer of frost-resistant strains of oranges; and Arlee Hen, a black Chinese woman from Mississippi.

Relevant historical information is interwoven throughout the stories, and an extensive bibliography is provided at the back of the book to place individual lives in a historical context. Each profile is illustrated liberally with rare archival photographs and detailed cap-

An enlightening, accessible history of the Chinese experience in America revealed through profiles and a wealth of background information.

tions which tell the compelling stories of the struggles and triumphs of ordinary and extraordinary Chinese Americans. Chronicling both the diversity of inter-racial backgrounds in different geographical loca-tions and the depth of discrimination in the Chinese experience helps to dispel stereotypes and set the record straight. This is an enlightening work of scholarship, easily accessible to an upper middle school audience. LAURI JOHNSON

468

This Migrant Earth

📖 Tomas Rivera (translated by Rolanda Hinojosa)
Hispanic, Mexican
1987, Arte Publico Press, ✳ Spanish

Few works of young adult literature broach the topic of agricultural migrant labor. Readers may find these stories intriguing because of their insightful descriptions of topics, such as death and lost love. However, the stories are poorly connected other than by the common theme of migrant life.

A collection of underdeveloped stories organized around migrant life in America.

One section in the middle of the book lapses into thir-teen one-page narratives. Stories like "The Paling Time and Fading Year," "Burnt Offerings," and "This Migrant Earth" most-ly describe the oppressive conditions associated with migrant labor. These are snapshots of migrant life, brief glimpses that do not develop into a sustained story or plot.

Although Rolanda Hinojosa tries to accurately translate the text first written in Spanish by Tomas Rivera, this translation does not convey the creative literary flow of the original. This is a common prob-lem in some translations; however exacting the attempt, what results is an awkwardly structured text that places itself outside of the sphere of the ethnic group it attempts to describe; in this case, Mexican American farm laborers.

HERIBERTO GODINA

Immigrants

📖 Martin Sandler ✐ Various sources
Multicultural
1995, HarperCollins

A former television writer with a flair for captivating writing, Martin Sandler in *Immigrants* adds to his text photographs and doc-uments from the Library of Congress. *Immigrants* has few words per page, making it accessible to a younger elementary-aged child. The pictures speak as loudly as the words. Photographs, paintings, and engravings show people crowded on ship decks, wait-ing at Ellis Island, working and living in new apart-ments. Families play, learn, and earn livings in their new country, whether as workers in urban factories or as farmers tilling new soil.

A thematic history of immigration, featuring photos, drawings, and stories from the Library of Congress.

The book is punctuated with wonderful quota-tions from both famous and more unknown per-sons. Golda Meir writes, "I can remember only the hustle and bustle of those last weeks in Pinsk, the farewells from the family, the embraces and the tears. Going to America then was almost like going to the moon."

There's a wonderful, touching story of how immigrants brought balls of yarn with them, one end of which they left with someone on land. "After the yarn ran out, the long strips remained airborne, sustained by the wind, long after those on land and those at sea had lost sight of each other."

Whether in picture or story, the emotion, excite-ment, and struggle explored in this book make his-tory seem immediate and alive to young readers.
SUSIE WILDE

Macho

📖 Victor Villasenor
Hispanic, Mexican
1991 (1973), Arte Publico Press

The critical success of Victor Villasenor's *Rain of Gold* prompted the second printing of this earli-er work originally published in 1973. Villasenor concedes that Macho is a product of the sixties, but maintains that his book's importance has not diminished.

Macho is a migration story whose elements are familiar to many Mexican Americans. The sixteen-year-old protagonist Robert Garcia leaves his native Mexico to search for a better life in the United States, confronting, in the process, the many hardships of life as an undocumented immigrant. There is a tone of pathos throughout the story as Roberto faces one challenge after another while maintaining his moral resilience.

This story of a young illegal Mexican immigrant takes an insightful look at machismo.

Villasenor successfully captures Mexican *machismo*, the exaggerated masculinity that is a facade for more complex human emotions. At the same time, the book may alienate female readers by concentrating on exclusively male characters. Readers will find an insight-ful and perhaps unflattering representation of labor leader Cesar Chavez, who condemned the hiring of Mexican nationals to replace striking union workers. HERIBERTO GODINA

So Far From the Bamboo Grove

Yoko Kawashima Watkins

Asian, Japanese, Korean

1986, Lothrop, Lee & Shepard, ✳ Series,

Choi, Sook Nyul, *Echoes of the White Giraffe*; Choi, Sook Nyul, *Year of Impossible Goodbyes*; Day, Frances Ann, *Multicultural Voices in Contemporary Literature*; Hautzig, Esther, *The Endless Steppe*; Reiss, Johanna, *The Journey Back*; Reiss, Johanna, *The Upstairs Room*; Siegal, Aranka, *Upon the Head of the Goat*; Uchida, Yoshiko, *The Invisible Thread*; Uchida, Yoshiko, *Journey Home*; Uchida, Yoshiko, *Journey to Topaz*; Watkins, Yoko Kawashima, *My Brother, My Sister and I.*

1945 was an extremely dangerous time for a Japanese family to be living in northern Korea. More than ever the Koreans resented the Japanese, who had overrun their country and ruled it as their own. Stationed in North Korea, Watkins and her family led a peaceful life until the North Korean communist army started to advance. Suddenly, just before midnight on July 29, 1945, when her father and brother were not at home, Watkins, her mother and her sister, Ko, were forced to flee for their lives. They fled at night, crowding into railroad cars, short of food and water, afraid.

The memory of their nightmare escape is obvi-ously etched deeply in Yoko's mind as she describes scenes of war, death, rape, and other atrocities. During an air raid attack, she suffered a shrapnel wound on her chest and the fragments of metal embedded in her right ear resulted in permanent hearing loss. Searching through garbage for food, guarding their sparse belongings, disguising themselves as men so as not to be molested by the soldiers, the three exhausted, terrified refugees trudged forty-five miles to Seoul. Often they left messages carved on walls in trainstations for their father and brother. Through sheer

The author's escape as a young girl with her family from Korea to Japan during World War II.

determination and ingenuity, they finally reach Japan and settle in Kyoto, but illness and hardship continued to plague them. Heartbreakingly, Yoko's mother dies at the train station. Watkins and Ko are later reunited with their brother.

Years later, Yoko Kawashima Watkins gives a poignant gift to her readers by reliving this harsh time through writing about it. Now living in Massachusetts, she describes the personal victory that enabled her to write the book: "I competed with life and death when young. And I won." When I met Watkins in 1992, I saw her as a rare human being who is truly able to celebrate each person she meets. She does not take any of life's gifts for granted. She enjoys the simplest things and gives of herself in the most genuine, loving, and unselfish ways. Busy writing and speaking, she remembers the hard-earned lessons of her childhood. Highly acclaimed and much in demand as a speaker, she remains unspoiled and real. She recently finished the sequel, *My Brother, My Sister, and I*, which is the harrowing story of how she and her siblings survived as refugees in post-World War II Japan. Watkins' books are beautiful examples of how people are sometimes able to assuage and transcend the pain of traumatic experiences through writing.

So Far from the Bamboo Grove was selected as an American Library Association Notable Book. It also received the Parents' Choice Award Book for Literature, the Teacher's Choice Book of the National Council of Teachers of English, the School Library Journal Best Book of the Year, and the Judy Lopez Memorial Award for a Work of Literary Excellence. So Far from the Bamboo Grove *might be used in a study of World War II. Parallels can be drawn with books such as* Year of Impossible

Goodbyes *and* Echoes of the White Giraffe *by Sook Nyul Choi;* Journey to Topaz, Journey Home, *and* The Invisible Thread *by Yoshiko Uchida; as well as Holocaust survival stories such as* The Endless Steppe *by Esther Hautzig;* Upon the Head of the Goat *by Aranka Siegal, and* The Upstairs Room *and its sequel,* The Journey Back, *by Johanna Reiss. These books attest to the fact that vivid autobiography is one the most forceful forms of history; teachers searching for ways to enliven their history classes might consider using books such as* So Far from the Bamboo Grove.

The structures of So Far from the Bamboo Grove *might also be analyzed for the way the suspense is developed through the use of parallel structure in which the author alternates her personal story with accounts of her brother's corresponding struggle.*

This book along with her other books which include her book of folktales, might be used in a study of the author. When Yoko Kawashima Watkins visited my school, she did a beautiful job with the students, gearing each presentation to the age of the children and giving of herself tirelessly.

Another interesting study of So Far from the Bamboo Grove *would be an analysis of the way Watkin's classmates treated her. This approach would fit into an examination of peer pressure and/or social and economic class. Role playing, writing activities, and discussions about the heartbreaking cruelty of the students and Watkin's responses afford insight into group dynamics, as well as enabling youngsters to learn strategies for coping with similar situations and helping them become more understanding and welcoming of those who are different from themselves.*

FRANCES A. DAY

CHAPTER 7

JUSTICE, HUMAN RIGHTS, EQUITY

n providing our children the skills that they need to succeed, too often we—whether parents, teachers, librarians, or neighbors—neglect the equally important task of teaching our children that they should be an integral part of recreating the world for themselves and their children. We need to nurture in our children the vision of a better future and to encourage them to fight for that vision. Literature can play a central role in nurturing and encouraging our children.

have found that nothing stimulates discussions of equality and justice better than a well-crafted story. One can talk of racism, sexism, classism, or homophobia, but students rarely learn from abstract lectures. As a fifth-grade teacher, I have found that literature is such a powerful tool that I use it not only as the basis of my reading and writing instruction, but also for social studies, history, and geography.

eading quality literature, such as Mildred Taylor's *Roll of Thunder, Hear My Cry*, Milton Meltzer's *The Chinese Americans*, and Barbara Lewis's *Kids with Courage: True Stories about Young People Making a Difference*, is also at the core of the intellectual, cultural, and socially responsible lifelines of our children. Children also need to learn how to critique bias within books, research information, and analyze data. Being able to understand who speaks and who does not speak in a book, or whose perspective is being presented and whose omitted, provides children with important keys to enhancing their critical thinking and analytical skills.

n his illuminating and instructive retelling of the Rosa Parks story included in this chapter, Herb Kohl demonstrates how the passive voice and vague language are often used to avoid unpleasant or harsh realities. Kohl also shows how even so-called good books can be used to distort history and channel the legacy of social movements, uprisings, and rebellions into safe terrain.

iolet Harris's essay "Why Are You Always Giving Us that Black, Latino, Asian, Gay, Woman's Stuff?" offers specific advice for incorporating "issue-oriented" materials into the curriculum. It also explores hostility on the part of students who may feel singled out, implicated, embarrassed, or seemingly disinterested by books addressing topics in the history of "their" ethnic group.

riters such as Diane Bauer, Walter Dean Myers, Yoshiko Uchida, and Jacqueline Woodson have come forth with bold voices to chronicle the injustices, confront the issues, and tell the untold stories, and some of their books are reviewed in this chapter.

BOB PETERSON

Bob Peterson teaches fifth grade at La Escuela Fratney School in Milwaukee, Wisconsin, and was selected as the 1995 Wisconsin Elementary School Teacher of the Year. He is also an editor of Rethinking Schools.

Kindergarten to Grade Three

Rebel

📖 Allan Baillie ✏ Di Wu

Asian, Burmese

1994, Ticknor and Fields

A general drives into a small village in Burma and has his tanks destroy playground equipment at a school while the children watch.

The general informs the children that he is in charge of the land now. Half of their family's earnings are to go to him. His exploits are to be lauded in the schools. As he speaks, a thong is flung through the air, hitting the general on the head and knocking his hat off into the dust. Furious, he demands to know which child is wearing only one thong. To his disgust, he sees that everyone in the crowd, students and teachers alike, is barefoot, and that behind them there is a great pile of thongs. In effect, the whole village threw the thong. They stand together as a single entity against this representative of tyranny, opposing him with one will. Foiled, the general drives away, leaving the whole town in an uproar of laughter.

A warmly told Burmese folktale eerily reminiscent of recent events in Burma.

This little folktale takes on ominous undertones when considered in the light of the events of the past decade in Burma, where the military really did take over the government in a violent coup. One woman, Suu Kyi, daughter of Burma's national hero, Aung San, returned to Burma from England in 1988 to protest the military takeover. Continuing in her father's tradition, she traveled the country, giving lectures and encouraging the people to stand up for themselves. For her efforts, she was placed under house arrest by the military, not released until July of 1995. (Aung San Suu Kyi was awarded the Nobel Peace Prize in 1991. Her book *Freedom From Fear and Other Writings* is available from Viking.)

Aung San Suu Kyi and the people of the village in this story have much in common: their love for their country and a sense of duty to their people, their self-reliance, and their hatred of tyranny.

The illustrations in this picture book are full of character, warmth, and humor. The children and the people of the town are all drawn as distinct individuals, each with a determined look. The clothing, the architecture and the temples of the village, the vegetation, the landscape of rice paddies, and even the saffron-colored robes and begging bowls of the monks, are all most evocative of Burma. GINNY LEE

The Rajah's Rice

📖 David Barry ✏ Donna Perrone

Asian, East Indian, Feminist

1995, W. H. Freeman and Company

In this folktale from India, a young girl becomes a heroine because of her mathematical prowess. Through her efforts, she rescues her village from starvation and outwits the mighty Rajah.

In her small village in India, Chandra is a girl who loves elephants and numbers. She works as the bather of the Rajah's elephants, and maintains a system — keeping track of the number of toes, tusks and so forth — that helps her take care of them. With one exception, Chandra lives a happy life. On rent collection day, she sees that the villagers must pay a lot of rice to the Rajah since they farmed on his land. "The Rajah has enough rice to cover 256 Manhattans, seven stories high in rice." While the Rajah hoards rice, the people of the village go hungry. This makes Chandra angry, but she feels helpless in the face of tradition.

A young Indian women uses her skill in mathematics to help her villagers against the Rajah.

One day, the Rajah's elephants become sick. He calls in many doctors to treat them, but the elephants just get sicker. Finally, Chandra asks if she can examine her beloved elephants. She finds that their ears are infected and carefully cleans them. After the elephants recover, the Rajah offers Chandra a reward of her choice. Faced with a roomful of glittering jewels, Chandra turns her attention instead to the Rajah's chessboard. She says:

"The villagers are hungry, Rajah. All I ask for is rice. If your Majesty pleases, place two grains of rice on the first square of this chessboard. Place four grains on the second square, eight on the next, and so on, doubling each pile of rice till the last square."

The villagers shake their heads sadly at Chandra's request. The Rajah is delighted. She has made what appears to be a simple request that should cost the Rajah no more than a few ounces of rice. But as the Rajah's servants begin honoring Chandra's request, it becomes apparent that two grains of rice rapidly become tons. A little more then half the chessboard is completed when the Rajah runs completely out of rice. He asks Chandra what he can do to be released from his promise. Chandra wisely replies, "You can give the people of the village the land they farm, and take only as much rice as you need for yourself."

Had the Rajah actually fulfilled his vow, Chandra would have been given enough rice to fill the Ganges River. This young female heroine and mathematician brings justice to her village by redistributing wealth and living the power of her principles. At the end of the book, the author provides a chart that explains how the powers of two increase rapidly. DEBBIE WEI

The King's Chessboard

📖 David Birch   ✒ Davis Grebu

East Indian

1993 (1988), Puffin Books

Here's a book you can count on. *The King's Chessboard* is a wonderful tale that teaches mathematical concepts in the most painless fashion.

The story is set in ancient India, where a wise man has done a favor for a foolish king. The king orders the man to accept a reward, but the man demurs. Serving the king is reward enough, he protests. But the king's royal ego demands that the man accept his majesty's largesse.

His hand is forced. The man points to the king's chessboard and requests an unusual reward. "I ask only this: Tomorrow, for the first square of your chessboard, give me one *A wise man out-* grain of rice; the next day, *smarts a foolish* for the second square, two *king in this tale* grains of rice; the next day *set in India.* after that, four grains of rice; then the following day, eight grains for the next square of your chessboard. Thus for each square give me twice the number of grains of the square before it, and so on for every square of the chessboard."

The king does a little mental calculation, trying to figure out how many grains of rice the total will be. As he is unable to reckon the final quantity, the queen suggests they ask the wise man. Still, that would show that the king doesn't know, so his majesty remains proud and mute. Finally, to cover his ignorance, the king grants the man's request.

Well, no one seems to realize how quickly things double, and before long the palace granaries are in danger of losing all their rice. The king looks out his window one day and sees sixteen ox carts, each carrying a ton of rice, roll down the road to the wise man's house. He summons the royal mathematicians who tell him that in order to keep his promise the king will have to come up with 274,877,906,944 grains of rice.

Now this is totally off the topic, but previous editions of this book listed incorrectly the amount of rice as 549,755,830,887 grains. (In no way should imparting this information reflect the fact that the reviewer spotted the mistake or that she has any knowledge of math. In fact, she counts all numbers over 100 as simply "big.") It seems we as a nation need more books like *The King's Chessboard* that combine math with literature, and teach us all the computational literacy we are lacking.

Before this digression takes up all the words the editor has allowed for this review, rest assured that the proud king who didn't study his math lessons is humbled in the end. May this be a warning to all the innumerate. SANDRA KELLY

Berchick

📖 Ester Silverstein Blanc   ✒ T. N. Dixon

Jewish American

1989, Volcano Press Inc.

It is rare that books portray Jews as farmers or dwellers in rural areas. This story depicts a Jewish family living on a homestead in Wyoming. The mother finds an orphaned colt, which the family names Berchick ("little bear" in Yiddish,) because his coat is so furry. Although Berchick is everyone's pet, he particularly belongs to the mother of the family. He understands her commands in Yiddish, and she takes very good care of him.

After a time the family must give up the homestead because of hard economic times, and they sell Berchick. He keeps coming back home until, finally, the mother has a long talk with him and encourages him to run loose into the wild. He does so and is occasionally seen by former neighbors happily and freely running with a herd of wild horses. The family now lives in town, where the father is a tailor. Everyone misses the homestead, but they are glad that Berchick has his freedom.

This family was successful at farming, but the economy was such that no one bought their wheat. It is hard to tell why they gave up after only one bad season, but this is not discussed in the book. The father of the family decides to go back to being a tailor, and the family moves into town, but the stereotype of Jews exclusively as city dwellers is challenge. The stereotypes may have arisen because in many countries in Europe Jews were not permitted to own land. There were a number of Jewish settlers that homesteaded land in America's Midwest and West, some of them sponsored by a philanthropic fund.

A Jewish family moves from their homestead to the city in a book that challenges stereotypes.

This book can raise discussions about preconceptions of different people and their work. It can also spark some historical research about what jobs were permitted and which ones prohibited to certain populations, as well as why. MASHA RUDMAN

Terrible Things: An Allegory of the Holocaust

📕 Eve Bunting ✏ Stephen Gammell

Jewish

1989 (1980), Jewish Publication Society

The animals in the forest live in peace and serenity until the Terrible Things arrive one day to take away all the animals that fly. The remaining animals of the forest are glad they do not have wings and, although these creatures of the forest miss the birds' songs, they note how much quieter it is now that the birds are gone and go on with life as usual. But the Terrible Things return again and again, each time taking another type of creature: those who swim; those who have bushy tails; those with quills. Only the little rabbit wonders why the animals don't stick up for each other. Finally only little rabbit is left. Little rabbit believes that if the forest creatures had only stuck together, they might have survived. And so, little rabbit decides to leave the forest to tell other forest creatures about the Terrible Things in hopes that someone will listen.

In this thoughtful Holocaust allegory, the animals of the forest are carried away one by one.

In a foreword, Eve Bunting notes that in World War II, people allowed their neighbors to be taken away. Bunting uses this allegory of the forest creatures to illustrate the terrible things that can happen if we do nothing. *Terrible Things* is illustrated with black-and-white pencil sketches. Though lacking the vibrancy of many current picture books, these illustrations are appropriate for the book's message. There is no brightness here.

This allegory provides a thoughtful approach to the start of a study of the Holocaust. It offers a basis for discussion from which young children can begin to understand the horrors that can occur, and to learn to stand up for each other and for what they believe is right. The story can be used to discuss the idea of standing up for one's classmates, friends, or siblings, without touching on the Holocaust and its consequences.
BARBARA GOLDENHERSH

The Artist and the Architect

📕 ✏ Demi

Asian, Chinese

1991, Henry Holt and Company

The Artist and The Architect is based on a Chinese ethnic folktale. Designed to point out the dangers of trickery, its moral is, "Lift a rock only to drop it on one's own feet."

Envying an architect's talent, an artist plots to frame him. The trap the artist sets for the architect finally backfires on him and he loses his life. His fate seems fair, if not merciful. This folktale helps children distinguish between right and wrong as they condemn the artist's selfishness and admire the architect's talent, cleverness, and wisdom. The story ends with an old Chinese proverb: "The small man harbors an envious spirit; the great man rejoices in the talents of others." Demi suggests that maybe, at the last moment, the architect relents and saves the life of the wicked artist. This sort of question encourages children to think about the kind of people they want to be.

A classically illustrated Chinese folktale.

The wonderful illustrations done in the style of classical Chinese art, provide fascinating images of the ancient buildings and lifesyles. LI LIU

475

The Empty Pot

🎲 🖊 Demi

Asian, Chinese

1991 (1990), Henry Holt and Company, ✳ Chinese

A classically illustrated Chinese folktale stressing the virtue of honesty.

The Empty Pot, retold and illustrated by Demi, emphasizes that honesty will be rewarded.

The Chinese emperor needs an heir. He proclaims, "Whoever can show me the best flower grown in the pot I will give you, will succeed me to the throne." Young Ping is one of the candidates. However, the emperor has tricked the children — all of the seeds have been cooked and therefore cannot grow. Of all the children, Ping is the only one who brings his empty pot to the emperor. Like the other

children he wishes to be the next Emperor, but honesty is more important to him than success. As a result, the emperor chooses Ping to be his successor.

Beautiful illustrations are largely faithful to the style of Chinese classical art. LI LIU

Teammates

🎲 Peter Golenbock 🖊 Paul Bacon

African American

1992 (1990), Harcourt Brace Jovanovich

At a time when baseball was rapidly becoming the nation's national pastime, racism prevented many skilled and talented African American players from entering the field. While they had a league of their own, black players were not allowed to play in major-league baseball until 1947. Author Peter

An engaging picture book version of the story of the first African American major league baseball player.

Golenbock makes it clear that only his great courage and control enabled first baseman Jackie Robinson to "break the color line" during his outstanding career with the Brooklyn Dodgers.

The pain that accompanied the challenge of break-

ing the racial barrier is dealt with in the story, as well as the solidarity of friends and colleagues that made it possible. In the face of hatred and criticism, Robinson's teammate, shortstop Pee Wee Reese, stood beside Robinson during a particularly vicious encounter at Cinncinati's Crosley Field. Reese placed his arm around Robinson and declared his support. The team owner, Branch Rickey, is also portrayed as a man of compassion and honesty. Both Robinson and Rickey were pioneers in the field of sports and race relations.

Although baseball is the framework for the story, the author uses Robinson's life in baseball as another example of how people have struggled and continue to struggle for social and racial justice. Writing skillfully and with a knowledge of the sport and its history, Golenbock crafts a good story. The characters are complex and multidimensional, portrayed with some emotional depth.

The picture-book format and engaging writing make this story work across a range of reading, age, and interest levels. Illustrator Paul Bacon's watercolors are interestingly juxtaposed with reproductions of photographs that document some of Robinson's painful and illustrious career in baseball. VICKI MERRILL

Mei Li

🎲 🖊 Thomas Handforth

Asian, Chinese

1990 (1938), Doubleday and Company, ✳ Chinese

Mei Li is not a traditional Chinese tale, but a story written in the 1930s by Thomas Handforth, who spent several years in China.

Mei Li is a common girl's name in China, meaning beautiful. This Mei Li lives in a village in the north of China, near a city resembling Beijing. She does not want to stay at home all the time, as her family expect. She wants to go to the fair

An unusual girl's adventure story from 1930s China.

like her brother, so when he leaves, she sneaks out behind him. She buys firecrackers, joins one of the female circuses for the day, has her fortune told, and returns home.

Filled with details, such as typical food and clothes for the Chinese New Year Celebration and the New Year City Fair, *Mei Li* accurately and successfully represents the social values, traditional culture, and customs in the North of China in the 1930s.

This excellent book, with its beautiful writing and pictures, is not only a readable story book, but also serves as a reference book for Chinese culture and custom. It can help young readers gain accurate ideas and impressions about China in the 1930s. It is also a delightful girl's adventure story. LI LIU

Freedom's Fruit

📕 William Hooks ✒ James E. Ransome

African American

1995 (1975), Alfred A. Knopf, Inc.

In *Freedom's Fruit*, accomplished storyteller William Hooks rewrites a conjure tale he first heard as a child. Mama Marina is well-known for her conjure talents, and her master pays her a gold piece to put a spell on his grapes to keep the slaves from eating them as soon as they ripen. Mama Marina is saving to purchase the freedom of her daughter, Sheba, and her daughter's beloved, Joe Nathan.

Fall comes and the slaves leave the conjured grapes alone. Though they are angry with Mama Marina, they know better than to mess with a conjure woman.

The autumn is followed by a steamy summer and the horrible news that Joe Nathan is to be rented to other plantations. Joe knows that will mean cruel

A conjure woman frees her daughter and her daughter's beloved from slavery.

masters and, worst of all, little time to see Sheba. When the couple shares the dilemma with Mama Marina, she walks among the grape rows until thunder strikes and "lightning slashed through the vineyard, turning the vines to silver," and then, suddenly, Mama Marina knows what she will do.

The following night she commands Joe and Sheba to eat the enchanted grapes. After the fall harvest, when the grape leaves wither and die, the couple begin to age rapidly until, by mid-winter, they lie close to death. It is then that Mama Marina strikes a second bargain, trading in all her gold coins for two dying slaves. The master takes her for a fool, but when spring comes and the grapevines are ready to bud, Joe and Sheba recover and gain their freedom.

James Ransome's illustrations eloquently reflect the many changes of land and moods throughout the story. SUSIE WILDE

Sweet Clara and the Freedom Quilt

📕 Deborah Hopkinson ✒ James Ransome

African American

1995 (1993), Random House, ✳ Series

This is a tale of the resourcefulness of a young girl in the face of what appears to be a nearly insurmountable social injustice. We know from history that the Underground Railroad made it possible for some slaves to escape to the North and to freedom, but Sweet Clara and the Freedom Quilt places the past in a perspective through which young readers may begin to understand the horrors of slavery and the never-ending will of the enslaved to survive and to be emancipated. *Sweet Clara and the Freedom Quilt* is the story of how one young girl's ingenuity brought freedom and happiness to many for years to come.

The marvelous story of a young slave girl's creative effort to bring happiness to others.

Anxious to return to her mother on North Farm Plantation, Clara quickly pieces together bits of cloth she collects from her sewing job in the main house, and scraps of conversations from other slaves about the geography of the land, to create a quilted map. It is the painstaking stitches, woven by Clara's nimble fingers, that eventually lead Clara to her mother and to freedom. The wonder of this tale is in its ability, in such a limited space, to entice the reader to identify so closely with Clara and her mission. Thus, it is with joy, rather than with sorrow, that we bid farewell to Clara when she leaves the plantation, because we know that she is journeying to a safe haven. Clara leaves the quilted map, her legacy, behind so that other slaves may follow the stitches to freedom, and it is their hope that becomes our own in this marvelous tale of the inventiveness and tenacity of Sweet Clara. CHRISTINE PALMER

See next page for classroom suggestions.

477

Using *Sweet Clara* in the Classroom

DEBORAH HOPKINSON

One of the most surprising things about having a book published is to see your story take on a life of its own. That has certainly been true with Sweet Clara and the Freedom Quilt, *which I wrote before I had ever done a single school visit! I never imagined the creative ways teachers would use it in their classrooms—from kindergarten through sixth grade.*

Having the author collaborate with teachers can also help teachers appreciate the many ways in which the book can be used as a learning tool.

Here are some of the inspiring ideas I have learned about:

* *Math. The first teacher who ever invited me to visit her classroom had discovered my book in a math workshop. Making a quilt in the classroom means learning what makes a square "square" and how to measure.*

* *Geography and Mapping. Where might Sweet Clara and Jack have started from? How close to the Ohio River were they? Can you map a trail to Canada? Can the class make a map of their neighborhood?*

* *Quilts. Children in a classroom in Honolulu showed me their own "Freedom Quilt," with illustrations of what freedom meant to them, accompanied by a separate written narrative for each quilt square. The same class did a "Love Quilt," combining activities for Valentine's Day and Black History Month. Children in Maine sewed their own replica of James Ransome's depiction of Sweet Clara's quilt, and a quilt guild in Irvine, California, made twenty quilts as gifts for local elementary schools.*

* *History. A first-grade class in Bellingham, Washington, transformed their school into an underground railroad journey. They dressed in dark clothes, learned songs like "Follow the Drinking Gourd," and mapped an escape route that took them through their school into the "freedom" of the playground.*

Deborah Hopkinson is the author of several children's books including *Pearl Harbor* and *Sweet Clara and the Freedom Quilt.* Reprinted with author's permission.

Wheels: A Tale of Trotter Street

Shirley Hughes

Multicultural

1992 (1991), Walker Books Ltd.

Carlos's and Billy's friendship is suddenly disrupted when Billy gets a new bike and Carlos resents the fact that his mother cannot afford to give him one for his birthday.

Readers are presented with a diverse community including names such as Sanjit, Lal, Harvey, Barney, Pete Patterson, Carlos, and Billy. The children are shown playing around on their bicycles during their vacation. Both Carlos (Hispanic Latino) and Billy (African American) are racing and see a new bike. They both state that it would be nice to own a new bike. Unfortunately, only Billy's family can afford one. Carlos is hurt, and Billy knows this. Billy lets Carlos ride his new bike, but it is not the same; Carlos still desires one of his own.

A lightheared story of friendship between boys of different ethnicities.

Carlos's birthday is a few days away, and he begs his mother for a new bike. She calmly and sadly explains that they cannot afford one. Carlos is still excited about his birthday and silently hopes he will receive a bike. On the day of his birthday, his mother gives him a big hug and prepares cake and other goodies. He also receives, "a jigsaw puzzle, a new jacket in dazzling red and green like the big boy bikers wear, and a toy car with a remote control." He appreciates the gifts and thanks his mother, yet he still hopes for a bike.

Since he resents Billy for getting a new bike (especially on his birthday) Carlos chooses to spend the day with his mother at the bakery, rather than showing his new toys to Billy. At the end of the day, Marco, his older brother, comes into the house and asks Carlos if he would like to see his present. They walk to the shed where Carlos finds a bright red go-cart. Carlos is overwhelmed and thanks Marco. He understands that Marco's gift exceeds all of his expectations.

In an effort to get the friendship back on course, Carlos invites Billy to enter the "Non-Bicycle Race" with him and compete with other children on skates, skateboards, and go-carts. As friends and partners, Carlos and Billy win the race. Both come to understand that teamwork is better than individ-

ual effort. The illustrations reflect a culturally diverse neighborhood filled with children who play together and struggle with growing up together.
MARTHA L. MARTINEZ

Harriet and the Promised Land

Jacob Lawrence

African American

1993 (1968), Simon & Schuster

For more than sixty years, Jacob Lawrence has been one of America's foremost painters. His rich artistic vision has helped capture the history of black Americans. But when I first read *Harriet and The Promised Land* in 1968, I was simply appalled. I wondered how young children would relate to the cruel and scary pictures. After reading the book two more times, I began to understand that Lawrence had used rhythmic verse and horrific pictures to highlight the urgency of Tubman's mission.

Through his powerful paintings and rhythmic verses, Lawrence portrays the life of Harriet Tubman.

Lawrence felt that softly rendered pictures would not portray adequately the horror of slavery. The people in the illustrations have enormous hands, and it took people with big hands to do the demanding and often back-breaking work required to chop cotton, till mile after mile of hard Georgia clay, and hold the confidence of freedom firmly enough in their hearts to escape the ravages of slavery. The big hands also serve as a metaphor for the generosity Harriet and the abolitionists extended in offering the gift of political freedom to slaves.

Harriet Tubman's larger-than-life hands and body convey her bold magnificence and unwavering presence. While some of the paintings/illustrations feel deeply personal, others convey a sense of the history that words simply cannot. In some of the illustrations, Lawrence juxtaposes the beauty of nature against the terror of the escape. The verse also reveals some of the clever ways runaway slaves would disguise themselves:

> Good people gave
> Them food to eat
> And a chance to rest
> Their weary feet.
> They gave Harriet chickens
> To disguise

> The runaway slave
> From spying eyes.

Lawrence provides a compelling and unsettling visual story that answers so many of the questions young children are bound to have about slavery, Harriet Tubman, and those who chose leadership roles in helping people escape to freedom. I would recommend that young children read this with someone older.

The simple line border used in the design element of the 1993 edition tends to take away from the free floating form of the same illustrations used in the 1968 edition. While I wish the designers had maintained the integrity of the 1968 edition of the book, the reissuing of this story is a most important step in continuing to tell the story of freedom fighters like Harriet Tubman for generations to come. DAPHNE MUSE

Now Let Me Fly: The Story of a Slave Family

Dolores Johnson

African American

1993, Macmillan Publishing Company

While still a very young girl, Minna is kidnapped by slavers and taken from her African village. It doesn't make her captivity any easier to know that a member of the village, recently banned by Minna's father for dealing in slaves, is responsible for her enslavement. Few children's books focus on the role that Africans sometimes played in the slave trade. Sold to a plantation owner in America, she is forced to work long hours in the fields, forbidden to use her own name or speak her native language. Still, she resolves to remember her African heritage and pass it on to the four children she bears with a young African man the master gave her permission to marry. He is later sold without a thought for his wife.

In a picture book for all ages, a kidnapped woman tells of her family's experiences as slaves in 19th century America.

Minna's older son is sold only a year later. She arranges for her two middle children to join other slaves in "stealing away" to freedom.

A subtle message of one oppressed people helping another is present in the news that Minna's younger son was accepted into a Seminole Indian family in Florida and moved with them to Oklahoma when the

Seminoles were relocated by the U.S. government in 1842. Minna and her youngest daughter remain on the plantation until the 13th Amendment to the Constitution in 1865 sets the slaves free. Taken from the name of an old hymn about slaves finding a promised land in heaven, the title *Now Let Me Fly* also brings to full circle Minna's freeing of a small bird in Africa, and her yearning to fly free in the United States.

The biggest difficulty in using this book with students will be getting past the format. Vivid oil paintings by the author bring the people and activities of one-hundred-and-fifty years ago to life, but the book's picture book design makes it appear, at first glance, a book for preschoolers. We all know that picture books can be designed for any age, but the popular assumption is that these materials are for very young children. Commissioned by the Children's Museum of San Diego to create paintings and a story for a Black History Month celebration, *Dolores Johnson has created a fictional tale solidly rooted in fact that is an excellent supplementary title for American history units in grades three through five, when children have the educational background to appreciate the real meaning of slavery and the hardships endured by slaves in the American South.*
LYNN EISENHUT

Seminole Diary: Remembrances of a Slave

🎨 ✏ Dolores Johnson

African American, Native American

1995 (1994), Macmillan Publishing Company

Seminole Diary begins with Gina finding her mother sitting by a trunk in their attic reading a book. Gina's mother explains the book is "a gift one of our ancestors handed down to us—a slave named Libby. We're lucky she could read and write because she left us this treasure. She recorded a time when there was a special relationship between two groups of people."

A beautiful, thoughtful story featuring a diary written by a young slave girl.

As a young girl, Libby escaped with her father and her younger sister from a southern plantation. Her diary records her experiences as they are taken in by a group of Seminole Indians. Delores Johnson creates an especially moving story out of a little known aspect of African American history. She portrays Libby with sympathy and understanding. Through her words we experience what it's like to be a slave and the courageous dignity of her father who escapes the plantation with his daughters because, "My girls will never live another day as slaves. I'm a man and I aim to live as one!" Libby wonders why they fled south instead of following the North Star. She worries about her younger sister Clarissa, who is not as strong as she is. She records how the Seminoles offer them food and water and invite the family to live with them as slaves, so that white plantation owners won't dare try to capture them. Though at first they are treated as refugees, they gradually become participating members of the Seminole village. Clarissa is even adopted by a Seminole woman. When the Seminoles are forced off their land, Libby and her family must decide whether they will leave their homeland and be moved to the Oklahoma Territory or resist, moving farther south to preserve their freedom.

Libby's story is enhanced by Ms. Johnson's vibrant oil painting illustrations, which capture the terror of escaping and the joys of living in freedom. They also capture the subtleties of the Seminole culture and the colors of southern Florida.

The diary format personalizes this historical story and makes it especially powerful and accessible for young children. *My group of eight- and nine-year-olds identified with Libby's struggles and discussed the scenarios in the book—living in slavery versus living among the Seminoles, relocation versus staying to fight for one's rights and land.* This book offers a beautifully told story that presents provocative issues in a thoughtful, respectful, manner. DORIS FINKEL

Baseball Saved Us

🎨 Ken Mochizuki ✏ Dom Lee

Asian American, Japanese American

1995 (1993), Lee and Low Books, Inc.

One often neglected reality of the internment experience is the effect it had on family structures and interactions. This is a beautifully written and illustrated account of the Japanese American internment experience from a young boy's perspective. Through the narrator "Shorty," and his brother Teddy, Mochizuki provides children with a realistic and engaging pic-

A young boy's realistic, wonderfully engaging account of the Japanese American internment experience.

ture of camp life, rich in detail while remaining true to the perspective of a child. Beginning with the chaos of the internment process, Mochizuki takes the reader into the camp and shows how the destruction of family life continued within the confines of the camps themselves. The simple act of  a family dinner becomes an impossibility in the camps. Mochizuki goes on to present an image of formerly productive older people now having nothing to do but "stand or sit around." When Teddy responds to his father's request to bring him a cup of water with "Get it yourself," the picture of the fracturing family becomes starkly clear.

Shorty's father then decides that one way to preserve the family relationships is to form a baseball league. The building of the fields and sewing of uniforms allow the adults to see beyond the daily miseries and fears of camp life and to be productive. Playing of this quintessential American sport brings back a sense of family and community. That they are playing it behind barbed wires in an internment camp is an especially poignant irony. Baseball becomes a tool for regaining pride and a sense of self.

While most books dealing with the internment experience end with the closing of the camps, Mochizuki takes the story beyond the barbed wire and shows how virulent racism raged for years after the end of World War II. Any attempt to deal with this difficult period in ways that present both the historical framework and the subtle details of life as they were experienced by the interned is difficult. Mochizuki has succeeded in this effort and done a tremendous service to the field of children's literature by providing young readers with a realistic look at how some Japanese Americans who were interned dealt with their lives in painful circumstances. DEBBIE WEI

Pink and Say

📖 🖊 Patricia Polacco

African American

1994, Philomel

Patricia Polacco tells a true story from her family's history that has been passed down through the years. This is the deeply moving story of Polacco's great-great grandfather's role in the American Civil War.

Wounded fifteen-year-old Sheldon Russell Curtis, also known as "Say," comes out of a strange sleep to see another young bluecoat, "the color of mahogany." It is Pinkus Aylie, known as Pink. Pink carries the wounded boy to his mother, Moe Moe Bay, at the old plantation. She nurses him back to health over a period of time, and the boys get to know each other. When Say finds out that Pink is able to read, he feels ashamed and counters by telling them that he has shaken hands with Abraham Lincoln. Eventually, Say recovers and the mother feels great sadness when Pink tells her that they must go back to war. But marauders come, kill Moe Moe Bay, and take the boys to Andersonville, where Pinkus is hanged. Say survives, goes home, marries, and tells the story to his daughter, who tells it to her children. The story is passed through the generations. In each family, the hand that touched Lincoln touches each generation down the line. The author gently dedicates the book to "Pinkus, who left no descendants."

The story is narrated by Say, whose voice makes for a very touching tale of war, slavery, and friendship. Detailed information about the times is interwoven in the story. Vibrant, realistic illustrations reach out to the reader's heart. DORIS COSLEY

A touching, true Civil War tale describes the friendship between two soldiers, one white and one black.

The Journey of Meng: A Chinese Legend

📖 Doreen Rappaport 🖊 Yang Ming-Yi

Asian, Chinese

1991, Dial Books for Young Readers

The first emperor of China is remembered for being the first emperor to unite the many warring states into one nation. He standardized the coins, the system of writing, and the axle length between the wheels of carriages so the ruts in the roads would fit all vehicles. He also joined together all the regional walls that small princes had built to protect their domains, connecting them into the one Great Wall stretching a thousand miles, and offering protection from the fierce barbarian tribes to the north.

A moving fairy tale about building the Great Wall of China illustrated in comic-book-style drawings.

He was also noted for his cruelty. He sent thousands upon thousands of conscripted citizens to work on the Great Wall under barely survivable conditions. Many men died and were buried in the wall, their bones becoming part of its structure.

This story is about one of those men, a scholar not fit for such heavy manual labor. His wife, at first nobly bearing her burden as was proper for Chinese wives to do, finally could not bear the injustice any longer and, in the middle of winter, set out to look for her husband.

As is typical of Chinese fairy tales, the evil emperor sees her and wants her for his own. She exacts promises from him to have her husband buried with gold and jade and honor, but then, in defiance and in loyalty to her husband, she throws herself into the sea, where she becomes schools of silvery fishes, which can be seen there to this day in her remembrance.

The illustrations are large versions of Chinese comic-book-style drawings, rendered in ink and brush and watercolor washes. They will be attractive and refreshing to American audiences, evoking and illustrating a Chinese lifestyle of two thousand years ago. GINNY LEE

Faithful Elephants: A True Story of Animals, People, and War

Yukio Tsuchiya   Ted Lewin
Asian, Japanese
1988, Houghton Mifflin Company

Faithful Elephants, by Yukio Tsuchiya, is the true story of three elephants in World War II Japan. The narrator visits the Ueno Zoo, just outside Tokyo, on a spring day, and comes upon a memorial honoring the animals that have died there. A zoo employee, tenderly polishing the monument, shares the story of three elephants, John, Tonky, and Wanly, who are buried there.

The moving, true story of what happened to the animals in the Tokyo Zoo during World War II.

He reveals that during the war, as bombs rained on Tokyo day and night, Japanese government officials decided all the zoo animals must be put to death. They reasoned that the animals could become dangerous if the bombs broke their cages, allowing them to escape and run wild through the streets. All the zoo animals were poisoned, but the three performing elephants managed stubbornly to

cling to life, rejecting the poisoned food. The zookeepers were forced to starve them to death. "Seeing his beloved elephants dying this way, the elephant trainer felt as if his heart would break," Tsuchiya writes. Our hearts break right along with the elephant trainer's as we read this poignant account of the peripheral atrocities of war.

Tsuchiya's writing is understated; the story unravels gently rather than bombarding the reader with despair. The moral struggle of the zookeepers charged with killing the elephants is clearly evident, yet the text doesn't spell out the issue or the arguments.

The vibrant and colorful watercolor illustrations by Ted Lewin draw the reader into the story. As the zoo-keeper begins to reveal the tragic story of the elephants, the illustrations become dark and moody. As they watch their beloved elephants creep closer to death, the zookeepers' facial expressions and body language suggest great regret and sadness. One particularly moving illustration depicts a keeper looking away from the starving elephants, his fists clenched and his gaze downcast.

Although the setting of most of the story is Japan during World War II, *Faithful Elephants* has a universal and timeless quality. The human characters are nameless, and the illustrations do not exclusively suggest Japan. In fact, it is easy to imagine this story taking place anywhere, any time. *It is a story that will facilitate family talks and classroom discussions on many issues of importance, such as war and peace, life and death, obeying authority, animal rights, and searching out alternatives in difficult situations.*

The subject matter of Faithful Elephants *could be upsetting for younger children. Older children (seven years and up) will be just as moved by the story as younger kids, but will be able to look at the story in a more sophisticated way. As kids develop a sense of justice and of their own place in history,* Faithful Elephants *will likely provoke deep thinking and intense conversation.*

Most children's books about Japan during World War II focus on the bombing of Hiroshima or Nagasaki. They usually outline atrocities in an impersonal, factual way or tell the story of a particular family or child. The different lens on World War II that *Faithful Elephants* provides will lead children and adults to think about previously unexplored effects of war. KATHY COLLINS

Nettie's Trip South

📖 Ann Turner ✎ Ronald Himler

African American

1987, Simon & Schuster

Based on the author's great-grandmother Nettie's diary, *Nettie's Trip South* chronicles a trip that she, her sister, and her brother, a reporter, made to Richmond, Virginia, just before the American Civil War. Nettie is only ten, but her father wants her to see what the South is like. Her brother is sent to cover the condition of slaves in Richmond. Somber pencil illustrations are a fitting complement to the text, which, though spare, still manages to give emotional color to this chapter of African American history. Nettie "reports" her impressions in a letter to her friend, Addie, writing, "Julia told me slaves are thought to be three fifths of a person. What were they missing? Was it an arm, a leg, a foot, or something inside?" With the clarity of a child, she reports on the living conditions of slaves, the fact that they have only one name, "like a cat or a dog," and, worst of all, the horror of a slave auction. She goes home understanding that only an accident of birth has spared her a similar fate. She writes to Addie, "I have bad dreams at night." Nettie grew up to be an abolitionist. VICKI MERRILL

An historical novel based on a real diary account of a young girl's trip to the south before the Civil War.

The Bracelet

📖 Yoshiko Uchida ✎ Joanna Yardley

Asian American, Japanese American

1993, Philomel Books

Yoshiko Uchida's *The Bracelet* artfully weaves the themes of friendship and human spirit together with the internment of many Japanese Americans during World War II. The story's main character, seven year-old Emi, is a Japanese American girl whose family is forced to leave their California home for an internment camp. She wears a bracelet that is a treasured gift from her best friend. As she leaves behind all that is familiar, Emi believes that the bracelet will serve to help her remember her friend. When the bracelet is lost at an imprisonment station, Emi comes to realize that such cherished memories reside not in objects, but within the heart.

A poignant, child's-eye view of a Japanese American internment camp during WW II.

Told from a child's point of view, the book expresses, with poignant simplicity, the disbelief and disappointment of this painful part of Japanese-American history. We learn that "Emi and her family weren't moving because they wanted to. The government was sending them to a prison camp because they were Japanese Americans, and America was at war with Japan. They hadn't done anything wrong. They were being treated like the enemy just because they looked like the enemy. The FBI had sent Papa to a prisoner-of-war camp in Montana just because he worked for a Japanese company. It was crazy, Emi thought. They loved America, but America didn't love them back. And it didn't want to trust them."

Uchida's afterword includes brief historical anecdotes of the unjust imprisonment of Japanese Americans during the war. It is a powerful complement to the story, and reveals the author's personal commitment, ensuring that such injustices are remembered so that they may never happen again.

This book could be a valuable part of units of study on topics such as friendship, memory, and personal heritage, as well as a useful supplement to American history curricula. All children can relate to Emi's desire to remember her best friend.

KARLEEN H. TANIMURA MANCHANDA

Two Moms, the Zark, and Me

📖 Johnny Valentine ✎ Angelo Lopez

Gay/Lesbian/Bisexual

1993, Alyson Wonderland Publications, Inc.

As two women become engrossed in a conversation, their child becomes impatient and wanders off to look at the Zark at the zoo. He finds a good time playing with the Zark, but he realizes after awhile that he is lost.

When an elderly couple offer to help him, they also accost him for not having a "normal" family. As the young boy attempts to defend himself and his two mothers, he is told that he will be placed with a new and better family.

The boy knows he does not like the sound of that, so rather than taking their help, he runs off.

As the boy loses the McFinks, he finds another family willing to help him. Initially he is apprehensive. But then he realizes that this family looks nothing like each other. One child is brown, another one has blue eyes, and one looks like neither of the two parents. The illustrations clarify the visual differences in the characters.

A simplistic but valuable contemporary story about non-nuclear families.

In teaching how value judgments can damage others, the story encourages young children to accept differences and keep open minds. While the storyline is rather simplistic, there remains a real need for books that illustrate that non-nuclear families are a viable part of our society. MARTHA L. MARTINEZ

Uncle What-Is-It Is Coming To Visit!!

📖 ✒ Michael Willhoite

Gay/Lesbian/Bisexual

1993, Alyson Wonderland Publications, Inc.

Tiffany and Igor's mother tells them that their Uncle Brett is coming to visit. The children don't know who he is and ask all sorts of questions about him. The mother tells them that Uncle Brett is gay, but before she can explain what that means, she has to run to the kitchen to rescue the burning brussels sprouts.

A fun, useful book about a visit from a gay uncle.

Igor and Tiffany go out to play, wondering aloud what "gay" means. They run into two older boys, Shelby and Waldo, who give them different descriptions of gay men. Shelby says they dress like women and shows Tiffany and Igor a picture from a Gay Rights parade. Waldo tells the children that gay men wear leather and chains, like Hell's Angels. Igor and Tiffany go home with mixed-up pictures in their heads, very wary of meeting their uncle the next day. When Uncle Brett comes, he doesn't look anything like these stereotypes, and Tiffany and Igor have a great time with him.

Michael Willhoite has created a fun story with illustrations that highlight and then dispel some of the stereotypes of how gay men look. The clear message in the book is that most gay men look and act like everyone else, they just happen to love other men. At the same time, the author makes clear that some men do indeed wear dresses or leather, and that that is also acceptable.

One aspect of the book that is not believable is that Tiffany and Igor, eight- and nine-year-olds, do not know that they have an Uncle Brett. Some explanation is needed as to why their parents had not talked about him before. *This book offers ample opportunity to discuss with children how and why stereotypes are made as well as ways of responding to people who hold those beliefs.* SUE FLICKINGER

Follow the Drinking Gourd: A Story of the Underground Railroad

📖 ✒ Jeanette Winter

African American

1992 (1988), Alfred A. Knopf, Inc.,

✳ Audio Cassette

This story is a fictional account of the career of a conductor, Peg Leg Joe, on the Underground Railroad during slavery. Joe was a white sailor who helped slaves escape. He would work for a slave holder on the plantation during the day, and at night, he taught slaves a song that gave them instructions on how to escape to freedom. Once the slaves had learned the song, Peg Leg Joe would leave for another plantation where he would do the same thing.

A fictional account of a conductor on the Underground Railroad that is an excellent supplement to other books on slavery.

One day when a family was about to be split up because the husband was being sold, they decided to use the information in the song in order to escape. That night the couple left, along with their son and two other people. They ran all night and crossed a stream so that the master's dogs would lose their scent. The song told them to follow the drinking gourd, which was actually the constellation of stars known as the Big Dipper. The group of runaways walked by night and slept by day. They followed the directions given to them in the song. After weeks of uncertain travel and constant danger, they found Peg Leg Joe waiting to transport them across the Ohio River. Joe told them about a path of houses that would lead them to Canada and freedom. They were then taken to a safe house so that they could sleep, eat, and rest. From there, the group went to several houses along the route, until they finally boarded the steamship that carried them over to Canada.

This story does an excellent job of describing what the Underground Railroad was and how it operated. It begins with an historical note about the story that explains what happened to slaves as they attempted to escape to freedom.

The story is informative for young minds because of the way in which it helps them understand how and why an entire family might make the decision to escape. The initial escape is not only a dangerous move, but also places the fugitive family in constant danger.

The story ends with the lyrics and music to the slave song that instructed them to "follow the drinking gourd." The story is simple and informative enough to adequately convey what is actually a complex part of our history. The illustrations are colorful reminders of the uncertainty and fear that is implicit in the story line. *The author does not provide a political or moral indictment of slavery, but begins from a position of assumed moral outrage and slave resistance. Therefore, this book cannot stand alone as a teaching tool, but is an excellent accompaniment to a larger lesson on slavery in the United States.* MICHELLE GARFIELD

Encounter

Jane Yolen ✒ David Shannon

Hispanic, Taino

1992, Harcourt Brace and Company

Ignore the old adage to "begin at the beginning," and start reading *Encounter* by beginning at the end. The author's and illustrator's notes found on the last page are best read before the story that forms the body of the book.

These notes give concise background information on the culture of the Taino, people who lived in the Caribbean before the arrival of Christopher Columbus, in 1492. Just over fifty years after the arrival of the first Europeans in the Taino homelands, the estimated native population on the islands had dwindled from 300,000 to less than 500. Taino society had been decimated by foreign disease to which the people had no immunity.

The arrival of Europeans to the Americas, as told by a Taino boy.

Jane Yolen is one of a handful of children's authors who chose the Columbus quincentenary to present young readers with a book about the Taino people. *Encounter* is a picture book, but it is not a cheerful tale for the very young. This powerful publication, which tells the story of Columbus's arrival from the point of view of a young Taino boy, is the story of the extinction of a people.

Yolen's tight poetic prose is perfect for reading aloud. In addition to the historical lesson found in Encounter, *the author's writing provides an exceptional model for aspiring student authors.* Encounter *offers fine examples for teaching the use of adjectives, dialogue, simile, and metaphor, and particularly personification.* In the book, canoes give birth to baby canoes that in turn spit out strange creatures. Bells are hollow shells with tongues that sing, and a spear bites cruelly until a hand bleeds and the vital fluid of life cries out in pain.

David Shannon's thought-provoking illustrations provide a perfect complement to the text. Many are dark and menacing, offering a foreshadowing of things to come. Several of them slip into fantasy, providing an opportunity to discuss with children which pictures portray actual happenings and which are imaginary.

Encounter *is an effective tool for introducing indigenous Caribbean civilization. It is also a useful selection to read during a classroom unit on the Age of Exploration and will help children rethink what is termed "the discovery of America."* SANDRA KELLY

485

Why Are You Always Giving Us That Black, Latino, Asian, Gay, Woman's Stuff?

Violet J. Harris

LIZ, A MIDDLE-SCHOOL TEACHER, RAISED THE issues in a graduate course I was teaching devoted to multicultural children's literature. We were discussing several nonfiction books about various parallel cultures.[1] Among the books discussed were *The Door of No Return* (Barboza, 1994), *An Indian Winter* (Freedman, 1992), *Now Is Your Time!* (Myers, 1991), and *I Am an American: A True Story of Japanese Internment* (Stanley, 1994). Previously, Liz had written a journal entry about her commitment to multicultural education. Her commitment, however, was tempered by the realities of the classroom. Some of her students rejected the insistence upon "multicultural" perspectives or the attempts to categorize them in one group or another.

She shared two classroom experiences and her attempts to reconcile them with her commitment to multiculturalism. One thoughtful journal entry captured the conflict and her concerns regarding what to do about it:

> I was reminded of an incident last year when a student looked into my class and said, "Oh white students, black students, even a Chinese student." The Chinese student happened to be a Cambodian American who considered herself American, period, since she was born in America. She ended up in tears. I am also reminded of an African American student who was not interested in watching a factual video about the 54th Regiment because it made him totally angry. How does my view of the importance of parallel cultures impact these students? What right have I to force students to find out about a heritage that they don't view as theirs? Many years ago I was put in my place by an African American student who asked why I always had my classes read books about blacks. Go figure. Do I have the right to be disappointed when a student does a superficial reading of a biography about Ida Wells-Barnett because her life doesn't interest him. His main con-

> cern as an eighth grader is to get as good a grade as possible without having to do the hard part of reading. How do we teach students about the contributions of many cultures without offending individuals? I just don't know enough yet. Maybe we simply, or not so simply, teach them to be lifelong learners who have open minds and accepting hearts.

In my response to her about the student who did not want to read about the 54th Regiment or questioned the inclusion of books about blacks, I suggested she keep in mind that these students have been brought up on the same negative images as everyone else: "No one wants to claim a status that is denigrated. Young people often have these types of responses, especially if they feel they are being singled out. I think that part of the great tragedy of America is that we have not acknowledged the extent of oppression that continues today and the benefits that some people derive from that oppression." I also talked about engaging children in meaningful discussions about the literature. But my response to Liz's dilemma — one shared by thousands of educators, librarians, and parents across the country—seemed inadequate.

She shared the comments in our weekly class session, and some spirited and self-revealing discussions ensued, as we began to discuss our own feelings about racial classifications and the sociopolitical consequences of those categories. The African American students decried the images that depicted African Americans and their cultures as monolithic and pathological. They expressed concern about those whose roots were West Indian, Latino, or reflective of different geographic regions such as the "West" rather than the Deep South or large urban areas in the Midwest or East. Two Native American students clarified the vast differences between their two groups, which provided a hint of the variations among the other 298 Native American nations.

The European American students did not favor the label "white" because it obliterated their national and ethnic origins. The lone international student spoke about ethnic differences in Taiwan. Emotions ranging from humor to anger and frustration were apparent. Each of us recognized the need for comparable discussions with children if we are to move beyond the celebratory and somewhat safe food and festival approach to multiculturalism, an approach that often ghettoizes and diminishes the pedagogical power of the work. Clearly, such intense but sorely needed conversations will not be comfortable. We must prepare for the raw emotions that some of us, and some of our students, are bound to share.

In an article, author Walter Dean Myers addresses the reluctance of some African American students to respond favorably to literature depicting images of people like them. He notes the mixed feelings that are often evoked:

> I've been to schools and would try to get black kids to read books about blacks. Many of them stood straight up and said they did not want to read black books. Kids don't want to stand out. So when they get to a book about blacks where there are roaches running around the living room, people turn and look at them and ask, "Oh my goodness, are there roaches running around the living room?" It's embarrassing. So kids don't want to read that. (Sutton, 1994, p. 178)

Such reactions are not unique or limited to this decade. Philosopher, scholar, writer, and former director of the NAACP, W. E. B. Du Bois wrote of similar concerns for children in the 1910s and 1920s.[2] Du Bois's response to the dilemma was to create a children's magazine, *The Brownies' Book* (1920-21), that would challenge the pejorative images of African Americans in children's literature, periodicals, and textbooks. The reasons cited for creating *The Brownies' Book*—entertainment, countering racist images, and apprising children of their heritage—remain valid; indeed, a volume containing selected excerpts, photographs, and illustrations from the magazine was published by Oxford Press.

I understand the feelings of Liz's students and the reactions Walter Dean Myers discusses. It is often difficult to bear the burden of one's race or ethnicity, gender, religion, language, or other element of difference. Oppression, racism, sexism, ignorance, and other forces exacerbate the problem. In addition to fighting a range of "isms," groups must confront, critique, and combat the formidable power of popular culture. Pocahontas's aerobicized and "Nordicized" visage from the Disney movie sells a mind-boggling array of products, from candy and sleeping bags to shoes and notebooks. How many Asian Americans cringed at stereotypes of the "model minority" son who attends medical school or the exotic sex siren Margaret who taunts her parents with "bad boy" white guys in the sitcom "All American Girl"? As many observers have noted, the prevailing image of African Americans on television is one pathology after another. For the most part, the multidimensional, complex, often interesting lives of people of color are missing from television and movies.

Where are the stories about young black girls who want to be cartographers and oceanographers; Native American boys living in urban regions and taking rap music to a whole new level; Asian youth eager to build intra-Asian alliances to heal historical hurts that go back more than two centuries; and where is the humor and where are the stories that focus on "really cool" things about being a girl or a person of color? We lose sight of the fact that not all lives are lived pathologically; that there really are people who work hard to sort through the confusion and live their lives beyond the constraints of racism, sexism, classism, and homophobia.

One has to search print and electronic media diligently to find exceptions. One of my favorite examples is a series of two Coca-Cola commercials that subvert some popular notions. One commercial features an attractive, dark-skinned African American woman with short, natural hair confidently responding to an advertisement seeking "an All-American beauty." The second features a skateboarding, light-brown African American male with red dreadlocks and freckles responding to an advertisement seeking "the boy next door." These were brilliant campaigns but they appeared primarily on Black Entertainment Television. Imagine the conversations that could have resulted with widespread airings of the commercials during European American shows such as "Friends," "Seinfeld," or "Frasier."

487

The burden of difference becomes additionally bothersome if you are the token representative of difference. The life of late nineteenth- and early twentieth-century African American poet and writer Paul Laurence Dunbar is instructive in that regard. He faltered, occasionally, under the weight of his European American audience's demands for poetry written in dialect. Dunbar wanted to share his poetry written in standard English more often than allowed. From time to time, Dunbar's poetry for children still manages to find its way into some anthologies. The most comprehensive collection of his children's poems appeared in a book entitled *Little Brown Baby: Paul Laurence Dunbar Poems for Young People*, by Bertha Rodgers (Dodd, Mead and Company, 1940). Harlem Renaissance poet and writer Countee Cullen's plaintive poetic lines, "Yet do I marvel at this curious thing, to bid a poet black and make him sing" aptly capture Dunbar's travails.

Likewise, in "Bootsie," Ollie Harrington's spiritedly satirical cartoons of the '40s and '50s capture a brilliant moment reflective of the stereotypical view, still held, "that all black people can sing." The cartoon depicts an African American physicist preparing to make a presentation at a prestigious meeting of his professional peers: "Doctor Jenkins, before you read us your paper on interstellar gravitational tensions in thermonuclear propulsion, would you sing us a good old spiritual?" (Harrington, 1958). Contemporary authors echo Dunbar's and Cullen's desire to write about whatever they wish, without solely reflecting their race or ethnicity, gender, language, sexual orientation, class, or other aspect of difference.

Walter Dean Myers also writes of the difficulties involved in convincing an editor to pitch him non-black stories:

> You know, I've written somewhere around fifty books...but no publisher has come to me and said, "Walter, why don't you write a book about, say, the politics of New York?" They'll come to me and say, "Why don't you write a book about some aspect of black life?" So what I'm suggesting is that when a black person approaches a publisher, the ideas that are accepted are normally ones that the editor can see as recognizably black.... I've had people say to me, "This character is not particularly black. Why did you write about this?" The publishing world touts itself as very liberal, but I keep challenging people to name five books written over the last 20 years by blacks that are on non-black subjects. So when you have a black writer who says, "I've got this great idea about space monkeys that talk," he or she is turned down (Sutton, 1994, p. 179).

Poet Lucille Clifton accepted the challenge to write on any topic with her novel, *Sonora The Beautiful* (1981). As Myers argued, Clifton's book is unique among those by African American authors because it takes place in the Southwest and the characters are European American. I suspect that a similar straitjacketing of other authors of color exists to a lesser degree.

Myers's consternation about being placed in an "authorial black box" is a serious concern. Many European American authors write about cultures other than their own. An underlying assumption seems to be that European American authors possess some abilities that enable them to transcend significant cultural barriers (ironically enough barriers they have had a primary hand in sustaining). They can enter into the world of the "Other" and extract basic universal truths or present cultural specifics in a clear, convincing manner. In contrast, ethnic authors are not encouraged to experiment. They are perceived as being inextricably linked to one identity and unable to enter another's culture or worldview.

Conversely, one cannot expect a child to read a book simply because the author's demographic features or those of the character's match the reader's. I learned this lesson in a most striking manner when, a few years ago, I worked with African American third, fourth, and fifth graders in an after-school program. One aspect of the program was sustained silent reading with a focus on African American children's literature. I surveyed the children in order to determine their reading interests. Their responses were as expected: they wanted fun books filled with humor, adventure, animals, and mystery.

Aware of the different reading interests and abilities, I offered books such as *The Chocolate Touch* (Caitling, 1979); *The Gold Cadillac* (Taylor, 1987); the Julian series, authored by Ann Cameron; *Paris, Pee Wee and Big Dog* (Guy, 1984); *The Lucky Stone* (Clifton, 1979), and several others. To my surprise, many of the books featuring

African Americans were not selected. Stunned, I searched for reasons why the children did not select those books. Were they too difficult? Did the covers seem unappealing? Did the other books seem more fun? I decided to use the books that were not selected as read-alouds. I "sold" the books to the children with pre-reading activities such as sharing many examples of the authors' work, briefly describing the books' content, or asking students to predict content or discuss how the books reflected their lives. More positive responses to the books resulted.

This experience taught me some valuable lessons. Our job is to guide childrens' selection and broaden their choices by offering new reading experiences. Given a choice, children select books that entertain with thrills, chills, and humor. But a politically or culturally medicinal approach to literature or forced lessons about multiculturalism are only causes for rejection.

The next time I worked with students — middle school in this case — I fared much better. The emphasis was on multicultural literature at the request of the teacher in whose class I conducted research. Mindful of children's interests, my selections included fun, serious, scary, and adventurous books such as *Crystal* (Myers, 1987), *Stories from El Barrio* (Thomas, 1992), and *The People Could Fly* (Hamilton, 1985). Read-alouds, creative dramatics, and theater books increased the appeal of the literature. Most importantly, however, initial selections shared were not about slavery, internment camps, racism, or role models. But these more difficult stories came later, and intense discussions accompanied them. I do not suggest that a "Don't Worry, Be Happy," philosophy determine the selection of multicultural or multiethnic literature. And I do argue that fiction and nonfiction about oppression require research, preparation, and thoughtfulness because children will feel anger, hurt, pain, guilt, fear, helplessness, pride, and numerous other emotions. Preparation on the part of the teacher, librarian, or parent will assist young readers in understanding and sorting through their own emotions around these often tension-filled and volatile topics. When a child asks why he or she has to read books about black people, Asians, women, or lesbians, that child is seeking an honest answer and may be expressing mistrust about your intentions

or the book's content, displaying anger toward or curiosity about the group, or testing your feelings about the group. You can respond in terms of the book's literary or entertainment value. If additional discussion is warranted, you might focus on the ability of the literature to transport the reader to a new community, affirm the validity of the child's culture, or the author's attempt to tell a human story.

I was reminded of the continuous nature of the struggle to write, publish, and disseminate multicultural literature when I met a former doctoral student who had been teaching in New York City. Her students were African American and Latino/a. Her initial attempt to share ethnic literature with her students had been rejected and she, too, sought advice about selecting literature that would appeal to these students. We talked, shared strategies, and I gave her several titles, heartened to see that she would not allow the students to reject the literature without reading at least some of it and discussing their feelings. Perhaps some of the students found words that grabbed their hearts, minds, or imaginations.

It seems so simple, but the task is often daunting. Sharing multiethnic and multicultural books seems so logical, but it is an ongoing struggle that will continue as long as society stratifies individuals and groups on the basis of differences.

Violet J. Harris is an associate professor at the University of Illinois.

NOTES
1 "Parallel cultures" is a term attributed to author Virginia Hamilton. She uses the term "to describe groups formerly called minority, to suggest to you that so-called minorities — those blacks, browns, and yellows — make up a vast contingent in the worldview.

It seems fitting to acknowledge that all peoples stand as equals side to side. Thus, parallel culture is a more apt term than minority, which imposes a barrier and a mighty majority behind it." Virginia Hamilton. "Everything of Value: Moral Realism in the Literature for Children," *Journal of Youth Services in Libraries,* 6 (993): 363-77.
2 W. E. B. Du Bois was one of the original founders of the NAACP and the Pan African movement. His seminal works include *The Philadelphia Negro* and *The Souls of Black Folks* among his hundreds of writings. He is regarded as the prototypical African American public intellectual.

489

WORKS CITED

BARBOZA, S. *The Door of No Return.* New York: Cobblehill Books, 1994.

BERRY, J. *Ajeemah and His Son.* New York: HarperCollins, 1992.

CAITLING, P. *The Chocolate Touch.* New York: Morrow,1979.

CLIFTON, L. *Sonora the Beautiful.* New York: Dutton, 1981.

CLIFTON, L. *The Lucky Stone.* New York: Delacorte,1979.

CULLEN, C. "Yet Do I Marvel." *Color.* New York: Harper and Brothers, 1925.

FREEDMAN, R. *An Indian Winter.* New York: Holiday House, 1992.

GUY, R. *Paris, Pee Wee and Big Dog.* New York: Delacorte, 1984.

HAMILTON, V. "Everything of Value: Moral Realism in the Literature for Children." *Journal of Youth Services in Libraries,* 6 (1993): 363-77.

————. *The People Could Fly.* New York: Knopf, 1985.

HARRINGTON, O. *Bootsie and Others: A Selection of Cartoons.* New York: Dodd, Mead & Company, 1958.

JOHNSON-FEELINGS, D. *The Best of the Brownies' Book.* New York: Oxford Press, 1995.

MYERS, W. D. *Crystal.* New York: Viking Kestral, 1987.

————. *Scorpions.* New York: HarperCollins, 1988.

RODGERS, B. *Little Brown Baby: Paul Laurence Dunbar Poems for Young People.* New York: Dodd, Mead & Company, 1940.

STANLEY, J. *I Am an American: A True Story of Japanese Internment.* New York: Crown Publishers, Inc., 1994.

SUTTON, R. "An Interview with Walter Dean Myers." *School Library Journal,* 6(40) (June 1994) 24-28.

TAYLOR, M. *The Gold Cadillac.* New York: Dial, 1987.

THOMAS, P. *Stories from El Barrio.* New York: Knopf, 1992.

Grade Four to Grade Six

Something Upstairs: A Tale of Ghosts

Avi

African American

1990 (1988), Avon Books

Moving is usually an unsettling experience for older children. They will have to make new friends, go to a new school, and become familiar with the neighborhood. Their fears are compounded by their desire to be liked. When they move across the country, they have to learn the regional nuances as well, quite a task for a child just reaching puberty.

A young California boy tries to help the ghost of a young slave to find his murderer.

Kenny Huldorf is such a person. Living in Los Angeles, Kenny, is used to Christmas picnics at the beach, watching the evening sunsets, and playing baseball every day. When his parents announce that they are moving to Rhode Island because of their new jobs, he is disappointed.

Preparing for the inevitable, he investigates Rhode Island through books. He finds, to his amazement, that the city of Los Angeles is larger than the entire state. He also discovers that it snows quite frequently there, a phenomenon that Kenny has observed only on distant mountain peaks. Nothing that he has read prepares him for his new house or its former occupants.

The Huldorfs have leased The Daniel Stillwell House. The house is located in a historic area of Providence. From the time Kenny first steps into the house, he feels a certain strangeness. His parents give him the top floor. While checking the room, he comes across a brown stain on the floor. Instantly, he feels that someone has died there.

Kenny's feelings are confirmed that night when he sees a ghost. Coming from sunny California, he is not aware of New England's haunts. He does not know if he should believe his eyes or believe his parents who do not believe ghosts exist. Each night thereafter, the ghost, Caleb, climbs through the stain in the floor and begins searching for an exit. Kenny, astonished and afraid at the same time, tries to discover what Caleb wants. However, each young man bears the burden of ancestors and societal norms, and trust is very difficult for them both. Eventually, Caleb explains to Kenny that he is trying to get out to find his murderer before the murder actually occurs. To Kenny, this seems impossible—but then again talking to a ghost is suspect, too. How can Kenny help Caleb and at what cost?

Something Upstairs is unique because it is a story told to the author by a young man who says that he actually experienced it. He relates his story to Avi because he thinks that Avi might understand and be able to help him to understand. Avi investigates Kenny's story and finds many of the reference points still as Kenny described them. If Kenny did not dream them, and he had no knowledge of the house and its previous inhabitants until he arrived there, then why is everything where he remembers it to be in his time travel? In addition, the activities of slaves were seldom in the public record. However, there is a reference to the slave boy that Kenny says he met.

The experience has left Kenny with many unanswered questions, none of which, surprisingly, "how" or "why him". The most important question to Kenny is, did he actually help Caleb to escape to freedom or is he trapped in another house still trying to escape?

In the twentieth century United States, there are no human slaves. In Caleb's world, slavery is the center of great controversy. The house itself is a focal point of a mysterious unsolved murder with supernatural inferences. When Kenny descends into the past, he is more uncomfortable than afraid. He is never sure of how he can right the wrongful death of Caleb. Caleb has tried unsuccessfully with previous residents to make this journey, but each one has betrayed him in the end.

Kenny's experience with Caleb reinforces an old saying: "Those who do not know their past are destined to repeat its mistakes." Will the personal knowledge of the injustice that Caleb has faced change Kenny's perspective on the past? How much will this experience determine the path that Kenny takes in the future? Only time will tell.
YOLANDA ROBINSON-COLES

Only the Names Remain: The Cherokees on the Trail of Tears

📖 Alex W. Bealer ✏️ Kristina Rodanas
_____
Cherokee, Native American
_____
1996 (1972), Little Brown
_____

In 1837 and 1838, thousands of Cherokee Indians, who had lived peacefully along Georgia's Chottahoochee River for hundreds of years, were marched from their homelands in Georgia to exile in Arkansas by white men from England, Scotland, Germany, and France whom they had befriended. The "Trail of Tears," as their route has come to be known, cuts across the Appalachian Mountains. and continues through Tennessee and Kentucky, across the southern tip of Illinois, through Missouri, and on to the western part of Arkansas. Although author

Alex W. Bealer fails to mention it, some Cherokees were "resettled" in Oklahoma as well. Fighting bitter cold and unbearable heat, one out of every four died on this physically and psychologically treacherous journey, and a culture was virtually destroyed.

Along with providing an insightful look into the Cherokee and this atrocity visited upon them, Bealer uses language to create a very visual sense of the conditions and terrain that supported this once-thriving culture. He provides a picture of a highly advanced society with its own government, language, and alphabet rather than the usual "savages" portrayal still found in many books. He offers background information on their relationship with other indigenous nations, but stops short of romanticizing the Cherokee, and chronicles the Cherokee's relationship with the British and the founding of America.

A balanced and insightful (if slightly inaccurate) book about the removal of Cherokee Indians from their homelands.

Kristina Rodanas's illustrations at the beginning of each chapter, especially the rendering of the _Cherokee Phoenix_ newspaper at the beginning of the section entitled "Sequoyah and the Talking Leaves," provide young readers and teachers with a sense of how technically and artistically advanced the culture was.

Contrary to what Bealer states in the book, small but stable Cherokee communities did exist in Southwest Georgia near towns such as Cuthbert, Shelmound, and Albany. A map identifying the areas where the Cherokee lived and the route of the Trail of Tears would also have been helpful. Though flawed, the book will help young readers to ask questions about genocide that occurred long before the internment of Jews in concentration camps and right in the midst of slavery. DAPHNE MUSE

When Justice Failed: The Fred Korematsu Story

📖 Steven Chin ✏️ David Tamura
_____
Asian American, Japanese American
_____
1993, Raintree Steck-Vaughn, Series
_____

Fred Korematsu was just one of 72,000 United States citizens of a total of 112,000 Japanese and Japanese Americans interned during World War II. At first, he, like the other citizens interned, refused to believe that the U.S. government would take families from their homes and confine them in barren

492

wastelands. He was wrong. After successfully evading internment by assuming the identity of a Chinese American, Korematsu was caught and sent to a camp. *When Justice Failed* tells the story of his internment and later struggle to obtain an apology from the government. Readers will be impressed by the courage Korematsu and his fellow Nisei and their Sinsei children demonstrated in speaking out against the government's mistreatment of them. The impact of the length of time between his internment and the resolution of the Korematsu case (1941-1983) will further impress students with the injustice of the internment and responsibility of all citizens to guard the civil rights of all people living in the United States. NANCY HANSEN-KRENING

The story of Fred Korematsu, the Japanese American whose case about his WWII internment was heard by the Supreme Court.

The Foot Warmer and the Crow

📖 Evelyn Coleman   ✒ Daniel Minter

African American

1994, Macmillan Publishing Company

In a book readers will not soon forget, Evelyn Coleman tells the story of Hezekiah, an enslaved man. Forced to live on Master Thompson's plantation, he longs to be free like the birds with which he communes.

One night, a wise old crow lands on Hezekiah's shoulder and tells him a story. The crow also tells Hezekiah that he must learn all he can about his master so as to be able to use Master Thompson's weaknesses against him.

When Hezekiah learns his master talks in his sleep, he offers to become Master Thompson's foot warmer. Snuggled under the covers on those bitterly cold nights, he listens to the master's rantings and ravings. Later, he bets that he can tell the master what most scares him.

Master Thompson says that nothing scares him and wages a full night's head start toward his freedom for Hezekiah.

Hezekiah tells the master the story the crow had related to him and the master "threw up his hands

A memorable fable with striking illustrations about a cunning slave who gains his freedom.

and covered his face." Indeed, Hezekiah had voiced his worst fear.

Hezekiah slips away. With wit and cunning, he has won his freedom.

Daniel Minter's bold art enhances the text with wood carvings in striking colors. Facial expressions that are sometimes surreal help to convey the pain, the cruelty, and also the hopefulness of this story.

Role-playing might be used with this book. There are lessons here in perseverance, sensitivity, strength, and survival. BETTYE STROUD

Mother Jones and the March of the Mill Children

📖 Penny Colman   ✒ Archival illustrations

Feminist

1994, Millbrook Press

"Pray for the dead and fight like hell for the living" were the words by which she lived her life. Born Mary Harris Jones in Cork County, Ireland, on May 1, 1830, Mother Jones would leave a legacy as a fighter for the rights of American miners, railroad workers, mill and factory workers, and particularly the rights of children. Illustrated with archival photographs, posters and cartoons, *Mother Jones and the March of the Mill Children* is an excellent way to introduce young readers to this inspiring woman and to generate interest in this period of history.

An excellent introduction to Mother Jones and her fight for American workers, particularly children.

Colman's book provides a carefully documented look into one of most important struggles ever launched to gain rights for workers and abolish child labor.

During the first half of the nineteenth century, industrial workers lived extremely harsh lives often working twelve hours a day, six days a week for wages as low as $1.00 a day (approximately $12.00 a day in today's dollars).

This book chronicles the story of the historic 1903 demonstration led by Mother Jones to reform child labor and secure workers' rights. The demonstration took the form of a twenty-day, 125-mile protest march, the final destination of which was a meeting with then-President of the United States Theodore Roosevelt. Jones was joined by mill children and adult workers. Newspapers carried stories about this historic march almost every day. Jones brought forward children whose hands had been mutilated trying to manage heavy machinery. She spoke of children being "sacrificed on the altar of profit."

Despite the fact that Roosevelt ultimately refused to see her, Jones's efforts brought about real changes in child labor laws and the workforce in general. Colman aptly chronicles both Mother Jones's public efforts and her private tragedies, including the loss of her entire family to yellow fever, and her subsequent death in by Chicago's Great Fire of 1871. Unfortunately, some of the same issues faced by Mother Jones are back on the table today: workers' rights are as fragile as ever, and factories and fields full of immigrant children toiling next to their weary parents. This book is then timely as well as educational. DAPHNE MUSE

What I Had Was Singing: The Story of Marian Anderson

📘 Jeri Ferris 📷 Archival photographs

African American

1994, Carolrhoda Books

Divided into ten chapters that cover everything from her formative years to the legacy she left, author Jeri Ferris's well-documented biography of Marian Anderson admirably presents Anderson's life and details both the discrimination and the opportunities she encountered.

Anderson was born February 27, 1897, in South Philadelphia, Pennsylvania. From the age of six, she knew that she wanted to sing. Even at two years old, Anderson was singing at the top of her voice to the colorful flowers on the wallpaper in the living room while pounding out tunes on her imaginary piano.

A thoughtful biography capturing the singer's brilliant voice and commitment to human rights.

Although she grew up in a racially mixed neighborhood, the lines of demarcation were brutally clear. While the obstacles were at times formidable, Anderson had support early on in her singing from her family, Dr. Lucy Wilson (the principal at South Philadelphia High School), and tenor Roland Hayes. Hayes was the first black American singer

to achieve international success.

Hayes heard Anderson sing in her church and was so stunned by her voice that he made arrangements for her to take voice lessons with his own teacher. Although Anderson's grandmother opposed the arrangement and momentarily deferred Marian's dream, other opportunities continued to present themselves. With each one came the recognition that Anderson had the potential to become a major presence on the stage.

She would come to master the lyrics of Giuseppe Verde's "Un Ballo in Maschero" (The Masked Ball) as easily as she did those of the spirituals rooted deep in her soul. Her legacy opened up the doors for other great black opera singers, including Jessye Norman, Leontyne Price, Kathleen Battle, and many more.

While Anderson never spoke publicly against discrimination, her dignity, grace, and commanding voice at times were enough to disrupt the bigotry surrounding her. In 1939, The Daughter's of the American Revolution, an organization of white women directly descended from participants in the American Revolution of 1776, refused to allow her to perform at Constitution Hall in Washington, D.C.; unfazed, she moved her "concert" to the steps of the Lincoln Memorial where she sang on Easter morning before 75,000 people.

Ferris writes clearly and in a manner that thoughtfully engages young readers into asking why anyone would deny Anderson the chance to share her gift with the world. The language used to describe Anderson's evolution is clear and evocative. The details about her life are never gratuitous, but give readers a full sense of her journey and the challenges she faced in a magnificent career that would bring her to the White House and to some of the most celebrated opera houses and concert halls in the world. Ferris has also included a bibliography, very useful notes, and an index. The use of archival photographs further enhances the biography.

Although she died on April 8, 1996, Anderson lives on through her memorable voice, distinguished career, and unwavering dignity. Ferris truly captures Anderson's life and provides readers with an opportunity to visit a part of history they may have heard of but about which they may know little. DAPHNE MUSE

Ten Mile Day and the Building of the Transcontinental Railroad

Mary Ann Fraser
Asian American, Chinese American
1993, Henry Holt

In 1862, Theodore Dehone Judah traveled to Washington, D.C., to convince Congress to finance the transcontinental railroad. His request resulted in the Pacific Railroad Act, which, in turn, led to the building of the first railway across North America. Of the approximately 13,000 men hired to build the Central Pacific Railroad, 11,000 were Chinese. The railroad contracted with a firm in San Francisco who brought the men in directly from Asia. On one particular day, April 28, 1869, Chinese laborers were instrumental in laying ten miles of track on the Central Pacific Railroad.

A flawed, if evocative, account of the role of Chinese labor in building the first railroad across North America.

Anti-Chinese sentiments ran high during the early 1860s. The white men working for Central Pacific did not believe the Chinese were strong enough to do the work and strongly resented them for working for less money and for their ability to stay healthy (by working in teams) on the job.

Along with detailed sidebars that appear on several pages, author Mary Ann Fraser's acknowledgments reveal the decision-making process related to the research she had to conduct in order to bring real authenticity to the book. Along with obtaining archival photographs to use in conjunction with the development of her illustrations, she visited the actual sites of the Ten Mile Day and the joining of the rails.

Fraser has chosen to focus very specifically on the role the Chinese played in building the railroad, but little information is provided on the impact this new culture had on their lives. The author includes some fascinating details in this well-researched text. But little attention is paid to the frighteningly harsh conditions under which these men labored. While anti-Chinese sentiments are mentioned, no real details are provided regarding the racial hostilities that Chinese laborers had to endure on a regular basis.

There is nothing especially unique about the illustrations, which are also done by Fraser. She provides distinct features for the Euro-Americans in the book, but the Chinese laborers tend to look alike, and there is no variation in height or body shape. This is an important factor in moving away from stereotypes that all Asians look alike.

The book also includes a small list of suggested readings. This book does not stand alone and should be used in conjunction with other sources focusing on the Chinese laborers and the building of the railroads.
DAPHNE MUSE

You Want Women to Vote, Lizzie Stanton?

Jean Fritz Dy Anne DiSalvo-Ryan
Feminist
1995, Putnam

Refusing to be addressed as Mrs. Henry Stanton, Elizabeth Cady Stanton emerged during the 1850s as a controversial leader in the fight for women's rights. In this well-documented and engagingly written biography for young readers, author Jean Fritz provides an insightful profile of a woman who, among other things, rebelled against her parents' traditional rearing, became an abolitionist, and, at twenty-four, eloped with a man ten years older.

A well-documented and engaging biography of a leader in the fight for women's rights in the 1850s.

While her husband went on to become a state senator, Stanton raised their seven children and refused to be silenced either by her husband's insistence that she not speak out on women's issues, or by her father's threats to disown her. Stanton spoke at the first Women's Rights Convention in Seneca Falls, New York, in 1848, went on to make speeches on behalf of her friend and fellow suffragette Susan B. Anthony, and continued to speak and write for fifty more years before she died in 1902. She lived long enough to see some women enter college and vote in local elections, but did not live to see women win full suffrage with the 19th Amendment in 1920.

Dy Anne DiSalvo-Ryan's simple black-and-white illustrations complement the well-written text.

494

Even without being assigned, some young readers will enjoy finding their way into one of the many great stories about women gaining rights as citizens in equal partnership with men. DAPHNE MUSE

The Middle of Somewhere: A Story of South Africa

Sheila Gordon

African, South African

1992 (1990), Bantam Books, Inc.,

Gordon, Sheila, *Waiting for the Rain.*

In 1913, the all-white parliament in South Africa (composed of Afrikaans and English-speaking whites) passed the Native's Land Act. This act divided South Africa's land mass between the black and white population and established the principle of territorial segregation. Africans (67%

A simple yet profound story of a 1950's black family in South Africa struggling to keep their land.

of the population) were allotted only 7% of the country's land mass, while whites received the balance. In 1950, the white parliament enacted legislation that greatly extended territorial and residential segregation. Africans were stripped of their South African citizenship and declared citizens of ethnically-based territories (the infamous Bantustans). Land and homes owned or occupied by blacks in white South Africa were often declared black spots. Efforts were undertaken by the government to remove blacks from the land and resettle whites. The forced relocation of people of color in South Africa (the legislation also affected people of mixed backgrounds and Indians) constituted one of the largest forced removals of people in human history.

Author Sheila Gordon, who was born in Johannesburg, does an excellent job of personalizing this period of South African history in the novel *The Middle of Somewhere.* She reveals the inequities, complexities, and realities of life engendered by apartheid. The main character of the story is nine-year-old Rebecca, a member of an African family determined to resist removal and maintain its land. Gordon contrasts Rebecca's impoverished material life with the lives of affluent whites. But she is careful to show the warmth and sense of community that is typical in Rebecca's township. One of the most important messages she conveys is the power

of united resistance and protest. Rebecca's family and most of the people in her community stand together against forced removal. Their united action makes it more difficult for the government to act against them as families and individuals. Another significant factor that Gordon emphasizes is the role the international community can play in fostering justice and peace.

Throughout the novel, Gordon is clear in her denunciation of apartheid. However, she is careful to distinguish between whites who support the policy (or quietly benefit from it) and those whites who take active steps to abolish apartheid. Her vision of South Africa's future is demonstrated most clearly through the symbolic use of dolls. Rebecca cherishes the tattered white doll given to her by her mother's employer. She rails in protest when her militant brother John castigates her for keeping the doll: "Why do you play with that stupid white doll?" John retorted. "Those whites are the cause of all our trouble. They put Papa in jail. They want to chase us out of our homes. How can you play with one of their dolls, Rebecca. You haven't got any sense." Later, when a friend of the family gives her a beautiful black doll, Rebecca refuses to part with the white one. As the story ends, Rebecca is pushing both dolls in a pram side by side.

Gordon has produced a simply written yet profound story that offers rich avenues of research and discussion. In many ways, *The Middle of Somewhere* is a more successful work than Gordon's earlier novel, *Waiting for the Rain* (Orchard Books, 1987). The latter is a powerful introduction to apartheid, but the second half of the story seems contrived, and Gordon is not always on firm footing in her retelling of South African history. Fortunately, *The Middle of Somewhere* avoids these problems. *Teachers, however, need to understand the economic realities facing South Africa today.* Forced removals ceased with the end of apartheid and the institution of a democratic political system. Unfortunately, South Africa's wealth is still concentrated in the hands of a wealthy white few. The new government is faced with the daunting challenge of devising policies that ensure a more equitable distribution of the country's wealth while maintaining peace and stability.

BRENDA RANDOLPH

The Captive

Joyce Hansen
African, Ghana
1995 (1979), Scholastic, Inc., Berry, James,
Ajeemah and His Son; Cameron, Ann,
The Kidnapped Prince: The Life of Olaudah Equiano;
Rupert, Janet, *The African Mask*; Sterne, Emma,
The Slave Ship.

Named 1995's best book on Africa for older children by the African Studies Association, *The Captive* is a sensitive and well-written novel. The main character Kofi, a boy of twelve "seasons," is the son of an important Asante leader in what is now Ghana.

Inspired by a true story, this fine novel is one of very few available on the slave trade in West Africa.

During a trip to the capital city of Kumasi, Kofi's family is betrayed by Oppong, their household slave. Kofi is sold into slavery and eventually shipped across the Atlantic, where he is bought by a New England family. The book was inspired by the life of Olaudah Equiano. At the age of twelve, Equiano was captured in what is now Nigeria and sold several times before being transported to the U.S. and sold to a Virginia planter. Equiano's autobiography was recently adapted for children by Ann Cameron under the title *The Kidnapped Prince: The Life of Olaudah Equiano* (Knopf, 1995.)

More than half of *The Captive* takes place in Ghana or on board the ship bringing Kofi to the Americas. Author Joyce Hansen uses the British term "Ashanti" instead of the preferred Ghanian term Asante, but she does an excellent job of recreating eighteenth-century Ghana. She describes a stratified Asante society with royalty, commoners, servants, and slaves. However, it is also a society where enslaved people were permitted to marry into their owners' families.

The novel provides teachers with an excellent opportunity to explore similarities and differences between African systems of involuntary servitude and those in the Americas. Both systems denied full freedom to the enslaved and demeaned the individual. Kofi comes to understand this after he himself is enslaved. As he puts it "we were slaves—Master Browne's property.... I began to think of Oppong. I understood him now. Though my father treated him like a son and not the way Master Browne treated me, Oppong probably hated being a slave.... one human being could never own another."

However, the primary and very important difference between slavery in Africa and slavery in the Americas was the way in which slave labor was utilized. The Americas were characterized by plantation slavery, while in Africa domestic slavery was the norm. Plantation slave systems (and mining systems) used large-scale labor to produce a high volume of goods for trade. The desire for large profits fostered brutal and inhumane methods of production. In African societies where enslaved people performed primarily domestic and military functions, the workload was much lighter. Generally, the enslaved performed the same tasks as their owners. Slavery in Africa should not be called benign, but slaves did have selective rights and privileges that were rarely seen in plantation slave systems in the Americas. Over time, African slaves or their descendants were usually incorporated into the communities in which they lived. The stigma of slave origins could remain with a family for generations, but the condition of slavery usually did not.

Hansen also does a good job of recreating the Middle Passage. Her descriptions make this forced migration come alive in all its horror. Using Equiano's experiences as a guide, Hansen continues the story of Africa in America by portraying America through Kofi's eyes. When the awful voyage ends in New England, Kofi finds himself in an unbelievably cold land he describes as "a dead world with no brightly colored flowers or robes." He is puzzled when he sees a woman carrying a basket in her hands rather than on her head "like any sensible person would." He longs for the "red clay walls and warmth" of his mother's sitting room and is disappointed to find gloomy New England houses with wooden walls and floors similar to the planks on the slave ship. In the final segment of the book, Hansen weaves Paul Cuffee, the African American shipowner and abolitionist, into Kofi's life.

There are few novels written for children on West Africa and none that gives the insight Hansen provides for this historical period and setting. *Ajeemah and His Son* by James Berry (HarperCollins, 1992) explores a similar time and place, but West Africa is peripheral to the major events of the story. Emma Sterne's older and very fine book, *The Slave Ship* (Scholastic, 1953) describes the period of slavery,

but it too has little African content. The focus is on the tribulations of Cinque, the courageous man who was captured in Sierra Leone, led a mutiny aboard the *Amistad*, and won his freedom in the Supreme Court of the United States. *The African Mask* by Janet Rupert (Clarion, 1994), which was named a Notable Book by the African Studies Association this year, focuses completely on West Africa (the Yoruba to be specific) and includes a discussion of indigenous slavery but the events take place centuries before the Atlantic slave trade.
BRENDA RANDOLPH

Up in the Air: The Story of Bessie Coleman

📓 Philip S. Hart 📷 Archival photographs
African American, Feminist
1996, CarolRhoda Books, Inc.

Combining solid historical research with good writing, author Philip S. Hart has given young readers a real treasure in this book, which documents Bessie Coleman's journey to become the first African American woman pilot. Poverty, an inferior education, and prejudice did not keep Bessie Coleman from realizing some of her dreams. Coleman was born into a large family in Texas in 1892 and grew up to be an interested and hard-working student. But because she was responsible for the care of her younger siblings, Coleman attended high school sporadically. She did well enough, however, to go on to college, where one of her professors assigned a paper that led her to learn of the Wright brothers and Raymonde de Laroche, a French woman who became the first licensed female pilot. Coleman was intrigued to learn that women flew airplanes.

The well-told story of the first black woman to earn a pilot's license.

Money problems meant that eventually Coleman had to return home and work as a domestic. She continued to nurture her interest in flying and later accepted her brother Walter's invitation to come to Chicago and try living up North.

Coleman was able to make a living barnstorming. Often called flying fools, barnstormers would take brave souls up in the air for a fee or seek out short-hop passengers and deliveries. Coleman also wanted to open an aviation school, but found that children were more receptive to the idea than adults. Although this dream was never realized,

Coleman resisted society's boundaries for women and blacks. She was killed in 1926, when she was thrown from the seat of her plane during the Negro Welfare League's air show.

In 1987, Hart and his wife produced *Fliers in Search of a Dream*, a documentary film about black aviators. In 1995, the U.S. Postal Service issued a Coleman commemorative stamp. Using archival photographs and documents to illustrate the book, Hart brings the zeal of a serious researcher and solid writer to this book. The results are interesting and inspiring, and are bound to encourage a new generation to realize their dreams.
DAPHNE MUSE

The Tainos: The People Who Welcomed Columbus

📓 Francine Jacobs ✏ Patrick Collins
Native American, Taino
1992, Putnam

The Taino were an ancient people who were not a single tribe but a diverse family of Native Americans. They spoke a common tongue—Arawakan—which differed from the language of other South Americans. They inhabited the grassy plains and lowland rainforests of the northern coast of South America about three thousand years ago and thrived in their hunter-gatherer society.

Francine Jacobs writes about these people sensitively, respectfully portraying them as the gentle and caring population who welcomed Columbus and his men with curiosity and hospitality. Columbus and his men responded in kind initially, with small gifts and friendliness, but quickly began thinking of the ease with which they could conquer and enslave these peaceful people.

A sensitive look at Taino civilzation at the time of Columbus' arrival.

The Spaniards' insatiable appetite for gold led to the oppression and eventual demise of the Taino. The Taino, ironically, were puzzled by the fact that the white men so desperately sought gold because they themselves had prospered and lived contentedly for ages without placing any great value on the yellow substance.

By the summer of 1494, "The ancient Taino civilization and the simple farming economy on which it depended were being destroyed by the Europeans, who, for all their advantages and arro-

497

gance, failed to understand the disastrous consequences of their greed."

The book notes many historical facts, taking the perspective of the Tiano over the more conventional Eurocentric perspective of Columbus's voyage to the new world, which can encourage meaningful classroom discussion. ELIZABETH CAPIFALI

I am Regina

📖 ✒ Sally M. Keehn

Native American

1993 (1991), Dell Publishing Company Inc.,
📖 Beatty, Patricia, *Wait for Me, Watch for Me, Eula Bee*; Richter, Conrad, *A Light in the Forest*.

Regina is ten years old when she and her sister Barbara are kidnapped from their home by Allegheny Indians. Though their mother and one brother are away at the time, their father and another brother are killed. The Indians divide their captives between them. Tiger Claw takes Regina and a toddler named Sarah. He is a cruel master, beating Regina and forcing her to carry Sarah in a makeshift backpack. They travel for weeks to reach his village and then live with his mother, Woelfin, an old, bitter woman. She treats Regina not much better than Tiger Claw does.

An engrossing novel based on a true 18th-century story of a young white woman held captive by Allegheny Indians.

Fortunately, Regina is befriended by Nonschetta, who teaches her the Indian ways and language. The Indians trade fur with White men, but usually Tiger Claw brings home rum rather than the food and blankets that are needed. After Nonschetta and her baby son are killed by White men, Regina almost loses hope. She is almost twenty when a smallpox epidemic decimates the tribe. Tiger Claw is one of the victims. It is after this that White soldiers arrive to bring Regina and Sarah back "home." Although Regina has taught Sarah hymns and told her Bible stories, by the time she is freed, she no longer remembers how to speak English. When the girls are taken with other captives to be reunited with their families, Regina doesn't recognize her mother. It is only when a white-haired woman begins to sing a favorite hymn that she remembers that her name is Regina, not Tsinnak.

This is a story that doesn't hesitate to portray the harsh life and cruel treatment sometimes suffered by captives. It also reveals complexities in the relationship between Native Americans and White settlers. The story is based on fact—Regina Leininger was held captive from 1755-64. Knowing it is true makes the ending even more poignant. The author includes an afterword on the actual Regina and a bibliography of twenty-two titles. The story is a fast read, moving between tragedy and times when Regina is almost content. She is a powerfully-written character. None of the characters remains static. Relationships change, as when Woelfin takes Regina's side against Tiger Claw after he tries to rape her; by the end of the story, she looks upon Woelfin almost as a second mother. The depth of the author's research is reflected in the tone of realism achieved throughout the book. Incredibly, this is her first book. Readers are involved from the first page in what Voice of Youth Advocates calls a "moving and thoroughly credible book."
PAM CARLSON

The Return

📖 Sonia Levitin

African, Ethiopian, Jewish

1987, Fawcett Juniper Books

Set in the early 1980s, *The Return* is the story of an adolescent Ethiopian Jewish girl who makes a trek by foot from Ethiopia to Israel. Accompanied by her younger brother and sister, Desta is determined to leave her war-torn nation to seek her spiritual heritage. In the midst of this journey, Desta contends with many of the issues teenage girls deal with around the world.

Ethiopia has a large population of Fulasha Jews, and although they have a presence in Israel, it is often an uneasy one. Desta's family is among those few thousand Jews still living in the mountains of Ethiopia, and they refuse to convert to Christianity. The novel covers the traditions of this unusually mixed cultural heritage, and the difficulties they encounter. This novel also broadens the picture of contemporary Africa and its people and makes a solid point of departure for discussing Jews of color around the world.

A compelling novel about an Ethiopian Jewish girl's search for her heritage.

Realistic and compelling, this intricately written novel, steeped in the complex history of the Middle East, is for the well-read young reader. Although the circumstances are quite different, 14-year-old Lesley in Lynne Reid Banks's *One More River to Cross* faces some similar issues of resettlement when her Canadian businessman father decides to uproot his family and take them to live on a kibbutz in Israel. Both young women must come to terms with issues faced by most adolescent girls, as well as move through deep spiritual experiences that test their resolve. DAPHNE MUSE

The Sad Night

Sally Schofer Mathews

Aztec, Native American

1994, Houghton Mifflin Company

To the victor belong the spoils; to the victor also belongs history. The winners of wars are the ones who write the books that tell the tale for future generations.

This truism is no more apparent than in the case of the Spanish conquest of Mexico. Though the Aztecs were a literate people, very few of their bark-page books, called codices, have survived. Nearly all were destroyed by the victorious Spaniards. According to author and art educator Sally Schofer Mathews, fewer than twenty of these rare documents exist today and, of these few, none dates to before the arrival of Hernán Cortés and his Spanish soldiers in 1519.

A striking picture book account of the Aztecs' last victory in their war against the Spaniards.

The Sad Night is a striking picture book that pays homage to the Aztec codices. The book's vibrant illustrations are done in the style of Aztec art, with rich colors and interesting detail that invite youngsters to linger a while over each page.

Mathews's *The Sad Night* takes its title from the name the Spanish gave to the night of the Aztec's last victory in battle. The book begins with a short overview of Aztec history and the founding of the island city of Tenochtitlan. The main action takes place during the year 1519, called *1-Reed* by the Aztecs. During this year it was foretold that the god Quetzalcoatl would arrive in the guise of a man. By coincidence, this was also the year that Hernán Cortés and his soldiers of fortune arrived in Tenochtitlan.

Mistaken for the god in human form, Cortés was welcomed by the Aztec ruler Moctezuma. After Cortés and his men moved into the Aztecs' island capital, they took Moctezuma hostage. The Aztec king surrendered all the gold objects in his treasury, which the Spaniards melted down into small bars that they could carry easily.

Ironically, when the Spaniards tried to escape from the city following the death of Moctezuma, it was the stolen gold that was their downfall. As they left the city under cover of darkness, an Aztec sentry sounded the alarm. The Spaniards fled with the Aztec warriors close behind. The two sides engaged in battle on a wooden bridge that led to the mainland. Vastly outnumbered, many Spaniards were killed. Other Spanish soldiers fell into the water, where the heavy gold hidden in their clothing pulled them down to a watery death.

As an interesting final note to the story, Mathews describes the accidental discovery of some of these historic gold bars—they were found a few years ago when workers were digging a new subway.

The Sad Night includes a section entitled "More About the Aztecs and Cortés" and an explanation of the Aztec calendar.

A perfect follow-up to this book would be to make replicas of an Aztec calendar disk and a codex. ISANDRA KELLY

Harriet Tubman: Slavery and the Underground Railroad

Megan McClard ✏ Archival illustrations

African American

1990, Silver Burdett Press, ✳ Series

Harriet Tubman rescued over three hundred people from slavery during the mid-1800s. In recognition of her importance in leading people to freedom, she became known as Moses. She escaped from slavery in Maryland in 1849 and made nineteen trips back to the South, becoming more daring every time. Though she never learned to read, her advice was sought by such luminaries as abolitionist John Brown and women's rights leader Susan B. Anthony.

An easy-to-follow biography of the woman who dedicated her life to rescuing slaves.

Tubman worked as a cook to finance her trips to the South. She also served as a nurse and spy for the Union army during the Civil War, even helping to recruit blacks as soldiers. She established schools for freedmen and a home for the elderly.

Despite all that she accomplished, the government never paid her, as they did all men who did the same work. When she died, however, she was given a military funeral.

The text is easy to follow and generously peppered with quotes from Tubman and other well-known figures of the time, such as Frederick Douglass. Maps, black-and-white photos, and colored illustrations are also included, as well as timelines of her life and the Civil War, suggested titles for further reading, a list of sources used by the author, and a detailed index. Harriet Tubman is the only African American featured in the series on the American Civil War and influential people from that time. PAM CARLSON

The Bobbin Girl

Emily Arnold McCully

Feminist

1996, Dial Books

In this well-written story, author Emily Arnold McCully recalls an era when American women stunned the world by proving their independence as wage earners and then by standing together in the courageous fight for workers' rights. Ten-year-old Rebecca Putney is a bobbin girl in a cotton mill in Lowell, Massachusetts. The mill is hot and noisy, and the damp, lint-laden air has made one of the girls sick. Rebecca needs to help her struggling family. When the workers hear that their pay is to be lowered, some decide to protest. Knowing that troublemakers will be dismissed, Rebecca finds herself faced with a very difficult decision.

A well-written novel loosely based o the true story of an 1830's girl involved in the fight for workers' rights.

Although this story is set in the 1830s, the circumstances and conditions are not so different from those in thousands of sweatshops and factories throughout America more than 150 years later. Like many of today's CEOs, mill owners then employed ruthless measures to increase productivity and profits: clocks were slowed, machines were speeded up, wages were lowered. Although the girls in today's factories have names like Trinh and Carmelita, the conditions are frighteningly similar to those Rebecca encountered in the 1830s. According to McCully, "The heroines of America's industrial age were its factory girls. I've always admired their insistence on fair and equal treatment; their stories still resonate today."

McCully's "Author's Note" provides a context for the story and discusses Harriet Hanson Robinson, the woman on whom her character Rebecca is loosely based. This book is a valuable contribution to women's history, illuminating the role women played in the Industrial Revolution, and how they worked to change conditions for women workers. DAPHNE MUSE

Escape from Slavery: The Boyhood of Frederick Douglass in His Own Words

Michael McCurdy, Introduction by Coretta S. King

African American

1993, Alfred A. Knopf, Inc.

Escape from Slavery: The Boyhood of Frederick Douglass in His Own Words, is a shortened version of Douglass's spare and powerful autobiography for the juvenile reader. In order to arrive at a fast-moving story for the younger reader, Michael McCurdy has eliminated detailed descriptions of the land, information about distances from one place to another, and involved discussions of family relationships and friendships. He has added short, italicized sections that skillfully set the excerpts in context and connect them chronologically.

A skillfully abridged version of Frederick Doulass's powerful autobiography.

Sections that deal with the sexual crimes of slavery have also been omitted. What is left is certainly sufficient to follow the story Douglass tells of his own life. In McCurdy's book we see that Douglass's triumph is his escape, his marriage, and the beginning of his work for the abolition of slavery. I highly recommend this book.

MARY MOORE EASTER

A Long Hard Journey: The Story of the Pullman Porter

📕 Patricia McKissack and Frederick McKissack

🔖 Various sources

African American

1995, Walker & Company, ✱ Series

Through words and pictures, *A Long Hard Journey* examines the struggle of the first major black labor union. When rail travel first became accessible to the masses, it was a dirty, uncomfortable, miserable mode of transportation.

An account in words and pictures of the Brotherhood of Sleeping Car Porters, the first union in America to include black members.

This changed when George Pullman built the first expensive, luxurious sleeping cars in the 1860s. His business, which used a large pool of former slaves as a workforce, became profitable with the advent of cross-country rail travel. Pullman cars were known for their beauty, comfort, and the excellent service of their all-black porters. Many minimally educated blacks were anxious to have such steady paying jobs that provided the freedom of travel, respectability, and security within the black community. For fifty years, most porters were grateful and happy to have their jobs despite the poor wages, servility, and many restrictions of the porter's position. Attempts to unionize or obtain better benefits were squelched by the Pullman Company. Despite this, the porters formed an informal organization that acted as a network for news, stories, jokes, and camaraderie. Slowly, this organization turned its attention to how the Pullman porters might garner better working conditions.

In 1925, a frustrated porter named Ashley Totten enlisted the help of social and labor advocate and newspaper editor A. Philip Randolph. With others willing to risk their jobs, Totten and Randolph founded the Brotherhood of Sleeping Car Porters and took on one of the most powerful corporations of their time. The Brotherhood was routinely attacked by the Pullman Company—management tried to sabotage the Brotherhood's leadership, attacked it financially, threatened and intimidated workers, and used spies to infiltrate the group. Many Brotherhood meetings were held secretly, and wives often represented their porter husbands.

In addition, much of the black community resented the Brotherhood's "rocking the boat." Through twelve arduous years of demoralizing setbacks, stalled negotiations, and wavering morale, Randolph fought to keep the Brotherhood viable despite the Pullman company's negative campaign. Finally, in 1937, the brotherhood settled on a contract with the Pullman Company, becoming the first black union to sign a labor contract with a major corporation. The Brotherhood gave the porters dignity, better wages, lighter workloads, and job security. Members also backed civil rights causes and supported black laborers around the country. The Brotherhood existed independently until 1978, almost ten years after the advent of air travel put a huge dent in the luxury rail business, when it merged with a larger organization.

The Brotherhood of Sleeping Car Porters emerges as a strong force in both the labor and civil rights movements. Its success did not come fast or easily but was achieved by diligent people willing to sacrifice. A bibliography tells where to find more information and an index makes the book an easy reference. ALISON WASHINGTON

Taking A Stand Against Racism and Racial Discrimination

📕 Patricia McKissack   🔖 Fredrick McKissack

African American

1990, Franklin Watts, Inc., ✱ Series

In this much needed book, the McKissacks outline the history of racism and the fight against it. They also examine the different forms racism takes and analyze where it can lead if left unchallenged.

A provocative examination of racism in the United States including excellent anti-racism activities for students.

While the history of racism in the United States cannot be boiled down to ten simple points, the authors have done a respectable job of presenting a basic history of racism in this country. Along with an overview of relevant court cases, boycotts, and protest, the authors include an intriguing selection of interviews and group discussions with students and teachers. The latter deal with such complex issues as denial, condescension, euphemism, and internalized oppression.

Moving and well-researched profiles of famous

501

civil rights activists, such as Rosa Parks, W. E. B. Du Bois, Jesse Jackson, and Marcus Garvey are presented alongside equally stirring portraits of unsung heroes. These include Beulah Mae Donald, whose landmark victory against the Ku Klux Klan in 1987 sent a clear message to racist organizations that they are not above the law, and high school senior Portland Birchfield, who bravely wrote and directed a play about racism at her school in a midwestern suburb. Portland's story will undoubtedly inspire some students to write plays of their own.

The final chapter presents excellent ideas for getting involved in the struggle against racism in schools and communities, with practical suggestions that are appropriate for both students and adults. Included also are a thorough index to facilitate research, and a bibliography for further reading. Important information about organizations such as B'nai B'rith, the Urban League, the National Association for the Advancement of Colored People, and People United to Save Humanity is also given. An appendix provides their addresses for individuals or groups of students who want to write to any of the organizations.

This is a very readable book that will encourage readers to re-examine personal beliefs and take a stand against racism. Students and educators who are implementing James Banks's Social Action Approach to Multicultural Curriculum Reform, in which students make decisions on important social issues and take action to help solve problems, may want to start their own Partners in Achievement Group as described in the book. Another option is to incorporate activities into existing groups such as the student council. Drama, writing, discussion, music, and art may also be used to respond to issues presented in the book. FRANCES A. DAY

Underground Man

📘 Milton Meltzer

African American

1990 (1972), Harcourt Brace & Company

In 1832, seventeen-year-old Josh Bowen can't figure out what to do with his life. The son of a New York farmer, Josh tries to farm but knows it is not his strong suit. He tries preaching but knows that's not his calling, either. He stumbles into the abolitionist movement when he helps a slave cross the Ohio River. Josh strongly agrees with the principles behind the movement and decides his life's work will be to help free slaves from bondage. Josh meets with many famous and influential abolitionists of the time such as Levi Coffin, Salmon P. Chase, and William Lloyd Garrison. Josh encounters resistance from Northerners as well as Southerners buts finds friends in a variety of places.

A noteworthy novel about a white abolitionist based on a real figure.

While helping a family cross the Ohio, Josh is betrayed by his accomplice and apprehended. He is sentenced to fifteen years in prison, where he must endure harsh mistreatment. He teaches during his jailing, nurses others and lives through a raging cholera epidemic, and is freed because of the efforts of his father and Josh's powerful friends. Josh vows that he "won't do what I did that brought me in here," but he soon returns to his job as an active, risk-taking abolitionist. He is caught and imprisoned again just before the Civil War.

Meltzer's *Underground Man* is noteworthy for its use of actual events, court records, personal accounts, news reports, advertisements, and experiences of fugitive slaves and people from the period. Josh's character, based on a real person, shows the principled struggle of some whites sympathetic to the plight of slaves. The abolitionist movement was a multicultural and multiclass movement, and the people in this story explain the powerful reaction some Northerners had against slavery. Underground Man *could work well with nonfiction accounts of slavery and the abolitionist movement.* ALISON WASHINGTON

The Hispanic Americans

📘 Milton Meltzer 🖊 Morrie Camhi and Catherine Noren

Hispanic

1982, Thomas Y. Crowell Junior Books

This book presents Hispanic American history through individual stories that show the struggle of a people looking for better education, improved finances, and better lives in the United States. Meltzer focuses primarily on Mexicans, Cubans, and Puerto Ricans, but stresses the differences among Hispanic groups, cautioning readers to avoid lumping them all together.

The Hispanic Americans looks at a variety of families and their lives in the United States. Many came here because of opportunities and freedoms unavailable to them in their native lands. Once in this country, however, many encounter racism, housing discrimination, few jobs and poor pay, and ill-treatment from employers exploiting immigrant and migrant labor. The Vinas family emigrated from the Dominican Republic to get away from the unemployment, oppression, violence, and natural disasters that robbed them of a peaceful and comfortable life. In New York, the Vinas have found some security and have ambitions to keep moving ahead. Some stories are not as positive as the Vinas's; great numbers of immigrants start poor and remain poor, running into conditions they tried to escape in their homeland. Many Mexican immigrants will take work as seasonal day laborers, earning some of the lowest salaries in America. Readers learn that, because of those conditions, some of those exploited workers have banded together to form unions to fight oppression. Their struggle for basic rights and benefits, and against racism and fear, continues today.

> *A clear, easy-to-read series of portraits of Latinos in the United States.*

Meltzer's clear, easy-reading text is complemented by photographs that show the variety and history of Hispanics throughout the United States, the cohesiveness of their neighborhoods, and the impact of unions on the working conditions of many farm and industry laborers. *With a bibliography and index, students and teachers can use this as an introduction to and reference for learning about one of the fastest-growing populations in our multicultural society.* ALISON WASHINGTON

The Glory Field

Walter Dean Myers

African American

1994, Scholastic, Inc.

This sweeping historical saga focuses on the young people of one black family as they struggle through times of sadness, change, and progress in the United States. The novel begins with the harrowing story of eleven-year-old Muhammad, who is abducted from his West African home and brought to the New World as a slave. His descendent, Lizzy, breaks the bonds of slavery when she escapes from a southern plantation in 1864. At the turn of the twentieth century, Elijah helps save his family's South Carolina land—known as the Glory Field—but, in doing so, is forced to leave the home he loves. In Depression-era Chicago, Luvenia sees her dream of a college education shattered, but continues her quest for success. Tommy has the chance to integrate a white university if he'll avoid joining the 1964 civil rights demonstrations but, in one of the novel's strongest scenes, chains himself to a racist sheriff with the shackles that once enslaved his ancestor Muhammad. The final section of the book concerns contemporary teenager Malcolm, who accompanies his crack-addicted cousin from Harlem to a Lewis family reunion at the Glory Field. All told, there are six generations of the Lewis family—and six powerful stories—in this ambitious volume.

> *Six generations of an African American family fight for freedom and equality in a powerful if lengthy novel.*

Reminiscent of Roots *in its scope and breadth, the novel is a natural for study during Black History Month.* Each historical period is accurately portrayed, and the characters are not racial archetypes for their era, but skillfully delineated individuals, so well-drawn that a full-length novel could easily have been created around each one. *At nearly four hundred pages, the length of the novel may be daunting for some readers, especially since the extraneous subplots and characters that provide so much historical flavor to the stories sometimes slow the progression of the overall narrative. Introducing the book via one of the individual stories may be helpful, as would be dividing a classroom into six teams, each assigned to read and present a different segment of the novel.* Many readers, however, will find the stories so engaging that the length of the book will not be a problem. Instead, they will be moved by the mothers and fathers, children, grandparents, and cousins of the extended Lewis family as they celebrate the freedom, pride, and unity that has endured for over two hundred and forty years. As the eighty-year-old Luvenia reminds her gathered relatives at the conclusion of the novel, "We can look forward and we can look back, too." PETER D. SIERUTA

503

Red Ribbons for Emma

📗 New Mexico People and Energy Collective Staff
Native American, Navaho

1981, New Seed Press, 📖 Hendershot, Judith,
In Coal Country; Rappaport, Doreen, *Trouble
at the Mines.*

Red Ribbons for Emma depicts the life of a woman
struggling to maintain control of her land and the
quality of life for her people. Collectively authored
by three individuals from the New Mexico People &
Energy organization, the book was written as one
of several projects to educate the public about
the impact of energy development projects in
the Southwest.

The story traces Emma Yazzie's everyday life,
depicting her struggle to protect her land in the
Navajo reservation from exploitation and undesired
development by local power companies, such as the
Four Corners Power Plant. The reader sees the
impact the power plant and the coal mine have had
on the Navajo reservation. The plant belches dirty
smoke that pollutes the air, and Emma's sheep are
no longer allowed to graze in traditional areas
because the plant-treated water released into their
watering holes makes it too hot for them to drink.

*A somewhat
simplistic but
timely story
of a Navajo
woman's fight
against an
energy develop-
ment project.*

While the coal mine delivers
thousands of tons of coal
to the power plant, many
Navajos don't even have
enough fuel to burn in
their stoves.

The title of the book
comes from one of several
tactics Emma uses to try and
keep the power plant from
being built. "The company
men had marked the spot
with ribbons tied on wooden stakes called survey
posts. Emma smiles now when she remembers the
way they [the Navajos] would yank up those markers." Emma later dreams about the ribbons for
these markers decorating the land where her sheep
are grazing. But markers aren't her only tactic.
Emma Yazzie takes the power plant and mine to
court, charging that they are polluting Navajo air,
land, and water.

Although Emma loses her court case, she doesn't
give up her fight for the land. "Indian people have a
different way of thinking about the land than the
companies do. Their big shovels nose their way into

the ground to take the minerals out and they tear up
the grass roots. Once the grass is gone, the land just
blows away in the wind. The Indians believe that if
you treat the land badly, the land will die. The energy companies can find
someplace else to go, but
the Navajos have no place
to go when their land dies."

Black-and-white pho-
tographs lend realism and
depth to the text, which at
times is overly simplistic.
Yet this book manages to
convey the reality of the
economic exploitation of
Indian peoples and the reasons for their resistance,
courage, and persistence. This book remains timely, serving as a clear example of how we are contributing to our own ecological destruction.

*Red Ribbons for Emma would work well with other
books on the Navajo, including Doreen Rappaport's*
Trouble at the Mines, *about the mining industry.
Also recommended is Judith Hendershot's* In Coal
Country, *a picture book about growing up in an
Appalachian coal mining town. All address how we are
abusing and misusing the land.* NOLA HADLEY

Sing Down the Moon

📗 Scott O'Dell
Native American, Physically Disabled
1992 (1970), Dell Publishing Group Inc.

O'Dell's skill as a storyteller is evident in the spare,
lean prose of this historical novel. The strongest of
the young warriors of a Navajo tribe, Tall Boy, is
seriously injured by white soldiers while trying
to protect his people.

Despite pleas from
friends and family not
to marry a "crippled"
man, the young heroine,
Bright Morning, follows
her heart and marries
Tall Boy. While others
see Tall Boy as defective
and incomplete, Bright

*A Native American
woman struggles
to keep her com-
munity together
in a compassionate
historical novel.*

Morning sees him as no less of a person than he was
before. For her, he is still whole, and Bright
Morning wants others to see that as well.

Filled with compassionate insight, this novel
examines a very personal aspect of the removal of
the Navajos from their homelands. O'Dell, a white

writer known for his careful research on Native Americans, allows young readers to feel the heartbeat and pulse of history. MEREDITH ELIASSEN

Nightjohn

📖 Gary Paulsen

African American

1995 (1993), Dell Publishing Company Inc.,
✱ Audio Cassette

Nightjohn is strong stuff: a brutal depiction of the horrors of slavery. Some may view it as "white bashing," others may feel that blacks appear too much as victims, and some may see a little of both.

A controversial brutal novel of slavery for older children. In this unsubtle account, nary a white person demonstrates any kindness. The story begins as Sarny, a female slave on the Waller plantation, recounts how she came to meet Nightjohn, a slave who escaped to the North and then returned to the South to teach other slaves how to read. Throughout the story, all liberation comes at a price. Nightjohn is captured and reenslaved, although his will is never broken. At the book's end, Sarny is willing to sneak away and join Nightjohn's school.

This book is appropriate for the upper grades and should be read in conjunction with other books on slavery. It would work well for units combining American history with literature/reading study. Booklink's September 1995 issue includes a useful bibliography of fiction and nonfiction on this subject. A number of activities and discussion ideas are useful in looking at the issue of slavery. Examples include research on wage labor during the era of slavery, writing a diary from literary characters' points of view, discussing United States presidents who owned slaves, and locating the Big Dipper and discussing its importance for the Underground Railroad. ANDREA L. WILLIAMS

Women of the Wild West: Biographies from Many Cultures

📖 Ruth Pelz 📷 Archival photographs

Feminist

1994, Open Hand Publishing Inc.

Their names are Sacajawea, Biddy Mason, Mary Bong, Juana Briones de Miranada, Mother Joseph, May Arkwright Hutton, Kate Chapman, and Sarah Winnemucca. Sacajawea was a Shoshone Indian who traveled with the explorers Lewis and Clark. Juana Briones de Miranada was a Spanish American woman who became a wealthy landowner and important community leader. Biddy Mason was among a handful of black women who blazed the Oregon Trail. Kate Chapman was an African American writer who grew up in Yankton, in Dakota Territory, and chronicled life in her town and the accomplishments of other African Americans. Mary Bong was one of the few Chinese women who lived on the Western frontier. Mary Hutton came West after the railroads were built and became a successful business woman. Sarah Winnemucca was a Paiute Indian who fought for the rights of indigenous people. Mother Joseph was a Christian missionary, who traveled to the West to spread her religion and way of life specifically among Native Americans.

By providing short biographical stories about each woman, author Ruth Pelz has provided us with *A rare examination of eight brave women who made contributions to early American history.* a rare look into the history of women and the Western frontier. Her long-standing interest in uncovering hidden histories is apparent, and the book's bibliography demonstrates the breadth of her research. Unfortunately, although the bravery and courage of each woman is discussed, the book lacks overall historical context or discussion of how this Western expansion continued to wreak havoc on the lives of Native Americans.

In some instances, Pelz has included information that enhances the reader's understanding of the terms used, and each story is introduced by a brief biographical sketch. With few books available that explore the roles women played in early American history, *Women of the Wild West* is an important addition for libraries and classrooms. The archival photographs provide information for young people and are bound to spark interest in this period of American history. DAPHNE MUSE

Dear Benjamin Banneker

📖 Andrea Davis Pinkney 🖌 Brian Pinkney
African American
1994, Harcourt Brace & Company, 📖 Haber,
Louis, *Black Pioneers of Science and Invention.*

Benjamin Banneker was an early American scientist noted for his expertise in mathematics, surveying, and astronomy. He is also noted for having published a widely-read almanac for which he did all the complex calculations and for having designed and built the first clock ever made in America, painstakingly carving each piece of wood.

All his scientific accomplishments aside, Banneker is best known for his correspondence with then Secretary of State Thomas Jefferson on the issue of slavery. Banneker was of English and African descent, and though born free himself, had experienced the horrors of this institution firsthand. Both his father and grandfather had been slaves, and when he was twenty-eight, Banneker unsuccessfully tried to help the woman he loved escape from slavery.

A short picture book introducing one of the first African American scientists.

In 1791, Banneker began his famous letter to Jefferson, pointing out the hypocrisy of slaveholder Jefferson's statement in the Declaration of Independence that "all men are created equal."

Excerpts from Banneker's letter and Jefferson's response appear in *Dear Benjamin Banneker*, a short picture book that offers a brief biographical overview of Banneker's life. The book focuses on Banneker's role as a champion of human rights and his status as one of the first African American scientists. *Dear Benjamin Banneker* features full-color illustrations by Brian Pinkney. The double-page spread that shows Banneker standing outside his cabin on a snowy night contemplating the stars is particularly striking.

This book is a gentle introduction to a fascinating and important man, but its short length leaves no room to discuss Banneker's achievements in city planning, his incredible memory, his promotion of pacifism, his support of free public education, and his opposition to capital punishment.
SANDRA KELLY

Captives in a Foreign Land

📖 Susan Lowry Rardin
Middle Eastern
1984, Houghton Mifflin

To many Americans, the Middle East is synonymous with terrorism. This novel about hostage-taking is a remarkably sensitive, perceptive, and sympathetic portrayal of both captors and victims, a story that will shake preconceived ideas, open minds, and touch hearts.

Six American kids, visiting Rome with parents who are attending a conference on nuclear disarmament, are kidnapped and taken to a secret spot in the mountains of North Africa. They are treated somewhat roughly and harangued for their "soft American ways." The two girls are subjected to the seemingly contradictory cultural rules of their Arab Muslim captors: they should be "protected" but nonetheless do the "dirty work" and remain silent. The young Americans rise to the challenge—not without a few realistic scraps among themselves—and prove that they can take whatever comes their way, winning their captors' grudging respect.

At the same time, they come to respect their captors' motives. This group, rather than seeking ransom money or release of prisoners, wants to force the United States to lead the way in nuclear disarmament.

A first-rate adventure story with complex portraits of extremist Arabs who kidnap six American children.

While not entirely credible, this does allow the reader to see that some extremists are motivated, not by destructive madness, but by urgent needs that have, for them, a compelling logic.

The young Americans do contrive a way to get word of their whereabouts to the outside world, and they are rescued by a commando-type operation. Safely back in "civilization," they are far from sure that their rescue was a simple matter of the "good guys overcoming the bad." Nothing is that clear, they have learned, and they have all grown remarkably in understanding, self-reliance, and the ability to have confidence even in someone who appears to be the enemy. The youngest child, a timid boy of seven, actually grieves that his adventure has come to an end. He had discovered unsuspected strength and resourcefulness in himself, had found a kind surrogate "father" in one of the older men of the Arab group, and had won the respect of others.

506

As an adventure story, this book ranks with the best, but its value is far deeper. The setting is vivid, and characterization strikes this reviewer as superb. The captors, as well as the children, develop individual personalities and voices. Rather than leaning on stereotypes, the author treats the Arab men with respect. Though one character, unbalanced in his bitterness, is cruel to the children, he is eventually disciplined. Insights into the ways relationships develop and prejudices are overcome by necessity, give the reader much to think about.

One critical note: the bland jacket art does little to attract attention to this excellent novel.
ELSA MARSTON

The Memoirs of Chief Red Fox

📗 Chief Red Fox, Edited by Cash Asher
📷 Archival photographs
Native American
1971, McGraw Hill, 📖 Freedman, Russell, *Indian Chiefs*.

Drawn from the journals kept over seventy-five years by Chief Red Fox, this is a first-person account of the life of a Native American chief who lived to be over one hundred years old and whose life spans two centuries. Born on June 11, 1870, Red Fox recalls hearing guns blasting during the battle in which his uncle, Chief Crazy Horse, defeated General Custer's cavalry and leaving the reservation to travel the world with Buffalo Bill Cody's Wild West Show. During his lifetime, Chief Red Fox met many great historical figures, such as Thomas Edison, the King of England, the Kaiser of Germany, and Theodore Roosevelt.

The fascinating and accessible autobiography of a Native American chief.

Red Fox describes his boyhood on the reservation where his teepee was made of buffalo hides, as well as details of traditional Native American children's lives in the nineteenth century. However, everything he knew in his boyhood is gone. He says, "The blood of 20,000,000 buffalo has been spilled into the Western plains. The wild horse has been enslaved behind the plow, the vast primeval forest cut down, the eagle shot from the sky, the clear rivers, streams and lakes have been polluted and the air changed into poison."

This book is as valuable as a record of a prominent Native American in his own words, that is accessible to children. As a bonus, the chief's spectacular life—traveling the world with Buffalo Bill's Wild West Show and meeting leading figures of the day—appeals to children and adults. His colorful life is fascinating to students and provides an excellent entry into a unit on the traditional Plains cultures of Native Americans. Red Fox is eloquent and writes with great honesty and humility. His words make the lives and traditions of Native Americans come alive.

An appendix containing entries from Chief Red Fox's journal in his own hand is included, as are archival black-and-white photographs and some sepia-tone photos from the nineteenth century. *The book can be used with Russell Freedman's excellent* Indian Chiefs *to teach a unit on Native American leaders and traditional cultures.*
ELAINE P. GOLEY

Words By Heart

📗 Ouida Sebestyn
African American
1983 (1979), Bantam Books Inc., ✳ Audio Cassette, Series, Video Cassette

Lena, a young black girl, is determined to excel in the narrow-minded, bigoted community in which she lives. And she plans to do it by winning the spelling bee. Facing ignorance and racism, the family members are unflinching in their struggle to get ahead. They succeed, but at a terrible price: Lena's beloved father is murdered.

Lena's courage is the most powerful aspect of this award-winning and controversial novel. Her father's patience in coping with the mistreatment of his daughter and himself is unbelievable. The extremes of action and emotion wrought by racism are evident. Lena's family is placed in a situation where there is no resource available to them but themselves. While this is clearly an example of an author's ability to evoke feelings in the reader through actions, the characters do not provide the necessary understanding of human feelings. BINNIE TATE-WILKIN

An African American girl stands up to racism and violence in a controversial, award-winning novel from the 70s.

Minty: A Story of Young Harriet Tubman

📖 Alan Schroeder   ✏ Jerry Pinkney
African American
1996, Dial Publishing

This touching, brilliantly illustrated and well-told story of Harriet Tubman's childhood offers a look at the little girl whose later efforts as a freedom fighter would bring her worldwide honor and recognition. As a young child on a Maryland plantation Tubman was called "Minty" and considered a "problem" slave. Tubman's mistress sent the strong-willed child from the house to the fields in an effort to break her spirit.

Author Alan Schroeder provides an engaging account of Tubman's youthful dedication to freedom: "The first two traps were empty, but inside the third, a fat, glossy muskrat was struggling to get free. Squatting down, Minty pulled apart the steel jaws of the trap. She glanced back to make sure Sanders was out of sight. Then, happily, she let the muskrat go, releasing it downstream."

An engaging, brilliantly illustrated account of Harriet Tubman's childhood.

Illustrator Jerry Pinkney captures the drama of each tense moment as well as the tenderness and care lovingly heaped upon Minty by her mother, Old Rit, with powerful renderings of the characters' physicality. Pinkney has demonstrated similar skill and sensitivity in books like *John Henry* by Julius Lester and *The Patchwork Quilt* by Valerie Flournoy. The result is visually engaging and memorable. Although the language is geared to grades four and up, in the hands of a good storyteller, younger children are sure to find the story enthralling.

For teachers, librarians, and parents not familiar with the life of Harriet Tubman, this book is a good introduction to the life of a remarkable woman. For young children, it is a way to understand how the seeds of freedom are planted and nurtured. DAPHNE MUSE

Brother Eagle, Sister Sky: A Message from Chief Seattle

📖 Chief Seattle   ✏ Susan Jeffers
Duwamish, Native American
1993 (1991), Dial Books

Brother Eagle, Sister Sky, is a dramatic representation of Chief Seattle's response to the U.S. Government's offer to buy his exhausted and defeated people's land in the mid-1850s. He responded in his native language, in the poetic style of his oral tradition. The words were transcribed by Dr. Henry A. Smith, who knew Chief Seattle well, and they have been interpreted and rewritten many times since. In this telling, Susan Jeffers, an extraordinary artist and illustrator, adapts the tale again to bring his wisdom to the youth of today in the midst the world's worst environmental crisis. Jeffers's intent is "to deliver a message from Chief Seattle."

A somewhat stereotypical but enjoyable presentation of Chief Seattle's response to the U.S. government's attempt to buy Native land.

She first depicts Native American lifestyles prior to the arrival of European settlers. The native peoples are shown gathering wood, building dwellings, riding horses, canoeing, and enjoying the beauty of the land. Jeffers uses her artistry to give as much prominence and detail to the plants and animals in her illustrations as she gives to the people, reinforcing the message that each facet of life is dependent on all others and that all life is equally precious.

Chief Seattle's words are recreated here in clear and accessible language. The text reads as a wonderful story with anecdotes from his mother, father, grandparents, and ancestral spirits. "The voice of my grandfather said to me, 'The air is precious. It shares its spirit with all the life it supports. The wind that gave me my first breath also received my last sigh. You must keep the land and air apart and sacred, as a place where one can go taste the wind that is sweetened by the meadow flowers.'"

As the message goes on to talk of the destruction of the earth and the folly of those who think they can possess it, Jeffers's illustrations become stark reminders of the environmental degradation that continues to plague the land. However, this message is one of hope and renewal, a call for action. As the illustrations show a forest decimated by

508

clear-cut logging and a family of European Americans planting seedlings there, Chief Seattle says, "All things are connected like the blood that unites us. We did not weave the web of life. We are merely a strand in it. Whatever we do to the web, we do to ourselves."

The book is an engaging opportunity for discussions about the environment and Native American history. However, this should not be the only text on Native Americans children read; the images offered here of Native Americans as the noble caretakers of the earth and European Americans as both destroyer and last hope are somewhat stereotypical. ROSA E. WARDER

The Year They Walked: Rosa Parks and the Montgomery Bus Boycott

Beatrice Siegel Archival photographs
African American
1992, Four Winds Press

Rosa Parks, a modest black woman, was the catalyst for the civil rights movement of the sixties. Though this is not a biography as such, it provides background information about her life and explains the growing political awareness that resulted in her refusal to give up her seat to a white man on an Alabama bus. It was this action that detonated the frustration of a community denied their civil and human rights.

An informative introduction to the story of Rosa Parks and non-violent activism during the civil rights movement.

The book follows the ensuing bus boycott from its first uncertain days, through its gathering strength, and final victory when the Supreme Court declared the segregation laws of Alabama to be illegal. This is a dramatic story of an oppressed people aroused, wielding power through nonviolence, careful organization, and plodding perseverance. They were inspired by the rallying cries of Martin Luther King Jr., who rose to prominence as their charismatic leader.

The book is factual, well-written, and simple enough to be read and comprehended by children ages ten years and older. It concludes with information on the life and work of Ms. Parks, and the recognition she received after these events. It has accompanying news photographs from various sources, an excellent index, and a reading list for young people. Its acknowledgments and lengthy resource bibliography show that the author not only researched historical sources but also interviewed many African Americans in Alabama. For more information on Rosa Parks, be sure to read "The Story of Rosa Parks and the Montgomery Bus Boycott Revisited," an essay in Herbert Kohl's *Should We Burn Babar?*. GLORIA D. JACKSON

Just Listen to This Song I'm Singing: African-American History Through Song

Jerry Silverman Archival photographs and reproductions
African American
1996, Millbrook Press

Writers are devising some truly wonderful ways to connect today's young people to history. In *Just Listen to This Song I'm Singing*, Jerry Silverman uses black spirituals, worksongs, blues, and jazz to invite young people to journey from the days when this country was a slaveholding society up to the Civil Rights Movement of the 1960s. Each song becomes a chapter title for the book.

Using well-documented information on the period out of which the song came, Silverman explains the meaning of the song. "Michael Row the Boat Ashore" reflects the quiet

An innovative history of African American experience through song.

rhythm of the people who live on Folly, Edisto, Tyebee, Wassaw, Sapelo, and Amelia, a series of islands off the southeastern coast of the United States. The song also tells the dramatic story of an escape from slavery to freedom.

This "lyrical history" concludes with the song "We Shall Overcome," an adaptation of a hymn entitled "I Shall Overcome." This song would go on to become the anthem for the civil rights movement, labor struggles, and scores of human rights movements around the world. Silverman, who is a professional folksinger and guitarist, teaches and performs in schools all over the country.

Along with the song "Casey Jones," the author also includes a short play. Casey was a legendary train engineer about whom millions of America's school-age children have sung for decades. Sim Webb, the black fireman who served with Casey, spent his life telling the story of Casey Jones and taking us through the mesmerizing world of freight train lore.

Handsomely and thoughtfully designed, this wonderfully illustrated collection includes musical notations and works especially well in interdisciplinary programs using music and history. The archival illustrations were carefully selected and serve to reiterate each song's theme. Other songs include "Joe Turner," "Don't You Leave Me Here," and Scott Joplin's "The Ragtime Dance Song." There is a recommended listening feature at the end of each section that includes works by Roland Hayes, Mahalia Jackson, Paul Robeson, Pete Seeger, and Louis Armstrong. The book also includes further readings, notes, and an index.

Teachers will find this book an engaging approach to a subject that often is not done justice by traditional teaching materials. DAPHNE MUSE

Onkwehonwe-Neha, Our Ways

📖 Sylvia Maracel Skonaganlehera ✏ Carlos Freire
Iroquois, Native American
1994, Sister Vision, Black Women and Women of Color Press

This publication is about the history of the Haudenosaunee, the Iroquois Confederacy and their way of life—Onkwehonwe-Neha. The book documents more than a century of Canadian legislation that disrupted Indian communities, and describes Indian resistance to the policies.

A flawed picture book attempt to present Canadian Indians' struggle for rights.

In 1867, Indian Law was passed in Canada establishing an assimilationist policy and sending government agents onto Canadian Indian reserves. The act determined who was Indian and who was not. In the 1920s, the federal government of Canada outlawed many traditional Indian religious ceremonies. The Canadian Royal Mounted Police raided a longhouse to prevent the people there from practicing their religion. In 1946, Ontario revised the Education Act, insisting that all children ages six through sixteen attend provincially recognized schools. Native children were once again removed from their communities.

Change arrived in the 1950s as British Columbian chiefs organized themselves into First Nations organizations. Through the 1960s and 1970s, many Indian communities experienced revitalization efforts. In 1971, Native elders wrote a publication entitled, "Indian Control of Indian Education." By the 1980s, Canada witnessed a conference on aboriginal rights. The author indicates that the Canadian government still wants to run Indian affairs, but indigenous peoples are now insisting on having a voice in policies that affect their communities.

Although this book manages to present an aspect of Iroquois history succinctly, it is an odd mixture. The text is too adult for a picture book format. The pictures do little to support or enhance the text. Based on Canadian history, with no real focus on Iroquois living within U.S. boundaries, this book may not prove to be of great interest to U.S. students who are not already motivated to explore Indian history. NOLA HADLEY

Down in Piney Woods

📖 Ethel Footman Smothers
African American
1992, Random House

Author Ethel Footman Smothers has written an exceptional first novel with *Down in the Piney Woods.* Set in the rural South, the book draws the reader into the world of Annie Rye, a spunky girl full of questions and mischief. Annie Rye lives on a small farm with her parents and a younger brother and sister. Her world is turned upside down when her "half-sisters," whom she barely tolerates during their occasional visits, arrive to live with her family permanently. Annie Rye hates sharing her family with the older girls, and makes up her mind to drive them away. Instead, she finds herself in trouble with her new siblings, her old siblings, and her parents and grandparents.

An excellent novel about an African American share-cropping family in the South.

The difficult lives of sharecropping families are wonderfully portrayed in this novel. Annie Rye and her family are depicted as hard-working, loving people who are committed to their home and their way of life. The description of their living conditions and the excellent use of Southern black American speech convey a strong sense of place. The children are full of silliness and mischief, and have a sense of duty to the farm; the parents and grandparents are firm and affectionate with them. A secondary theme of racism and white supremacy is also present. The new family that has moved onto the landowners' property is violently racist and dangerous. Smothers handles the growing tensions between the two families with intelligence, including a portrayal of the property owners, as Caucasians who are not overtly racist and find themselves embarrassed by these newcomers. *For children who may have no experience with Southern history this multifaceted work serves as an excellent cultural introduction.* ROSA E. WARDER

Elena

Diane Stanley

Hispanic, Mexican

1996, Hyperion Books for Children

Elena is the story of a young woman's quest for personal and social freedom and a portrait of one of the most fascinating periods in Mexican history.

Mexico had been ruled by Porfírio Díaz for thirty years, and while he had brought great stability to the country, the gap between the rich and the poor was great and growing wider. Millions of Mexican Indians had become landless serfs, and fewer than a thousand families controlled the land. As the misery of the nation grew, so did the fervor and passion of men such as Emiliano Zapata and Pancho Villa. By 1911, the rebels drove Díaz out of office, and for ten years Mexico remained locked in a civil war. Many of the refugees fled to the United States, and Elena's family eventually found their way to El Paso, Texas.

A memorable novel for very young readers of a young girl during the Mexican Revolution.

Diane Stanley's story of a young woman who dreamed of an education, spent her money on books, and longed for a life beyond sewing, singing, and a husband makes a strong impression. The book is handsomely designed. It contains a map of Mexico that highlights the areas discussed in the story, a glossary, and a detailed historical note about the Mexican Revolution. There remains a real need for novels for very young readers, and this story has all the components of becoming at least a twice-read tale. DAPHNE MUSE

I Am an American: A True Story of Japanese Internment

Jerry Stanley Personal and archival photographs

Asian American, Japanese American

1994, Crown Publishers, Inc.

Executive Order 9066, signed by president Franklin D. Roosevelt on February 19, 1942, gave the military authority "to remove enemy aliens and anyone else suspected of disloyalty." Although the document never mentioned the Japanese, everyone knew that it was meant for them. All Japanese, regardless of citizenship, were evacuated from the West Coast and put into relocation camps in such places as Utah and Wyoming.

Jerry Stanley's *I Am an American* offers a compelling lesson on the internment of Japanese Americans during World War II. "These citizens had committed no crime, broken no law, and when their rights were taken away, they were charged with no offense," Stanley writes. "Their only crime was that they were of Japanese ancestry."

One family's story interwoven with a broader history of the Japanese American internment during World War II.

Based on interviews and personal recollections, the book is an account of Shi Nomura's family's internment during the war. Nomura, a high school senior, was just about to propose to his girlfriend, Amy Hattori, when their families were forced into camps. Nomura and his family lost their home and business, and spent nearly three years behind barbed wire fences at Manzanar, a camp in the California desert. "One of the largest internment camps, Manzanar held over ten thousand men, women, and children guarded by eight towers with machine guns. No area within the camp was beyond the reach of a soldier's bullet."

Stanley sets the family's story in the larger context of Japanese immigration to America, racial hostility towards the Japanese, and political events that occurred before and after the bombing of Pearl Harbor. Photographs in *I Am an American* enchance the text. Some are personal family snapshots taken by Nomura; others are culled from archives. They help give faces to the thousands of families whose lives were altered forever by the camp experience. CHRISTINA ENG

511

Song of the Trees

📖 Mildred D. Taylor   ✒ Jerry Pinkney

African American

1984 (1975), Bantam Books Inc.

The Logan family—eight-year-old Cassie, her brothers Stacey, Christopher-John, and Little Man (Clayton Chester), their grandmother Big Ma, and their parents, David and Mary—is surviving the Depression, poor, but not as destitute as some. Unlike many families, black and white, the Logans live on land they own, and that is very important to them. The father works in another state, and the women struggle to make do at home.

One day, as the kids are gathering berries in the nearby forest, Cassie sees that white men have marked the trees on Logan land to be cut down for lumber. Mr. Andersen, in charge of the project, offers the Logans $65 for all of the wood he takes, but the women don't take the money. Mr. Andersen threatens, but the women stand firm. They are afraid however, and send eleven-year-old Stacey to Louisiana to bring back the father. The children see their father as the ultimate protector; if he had been there, the white men would not have attacked the trees.

The award-winning African American writer's first novel based on her father's recollections of growing up in the Depression.

As the men continue to chop down the trees, Cassie laments how the trees once sang songs of long ago to her but now lay silent on the ground. Cassie and the boys, despite their mother's warnings to stay away, go down to the lumber site. Mr. Andersen yells at them to go home and, in his haste to get rid of them, starts a ruckus in which Little Man hits Mr. Andersen with a stick, Christopher-John kicks him, and all three must prepare for a whipping from Mr. Andersen because "they need teaching how to act."

David Logan and Stacey arrive just in time to stop the whipping. They had been planting sticks of dynamite all over the forest, planning to destroy it if the loggers persisted. The father returns and convinces Mr. Andersen that the family would not hesitate to blow up the forest, with them in it, if they did not leave the land exactly the way it was, not even removing the trees already cut down. The loggers leave, but the trees remain silent.

In her writings about the Logan family, Taylor blends fiction with her own family's stories. *Song of the Trees* is Taylor's first published recounting of the stories her father told to her about his life as a boy in rural Mississippi during the Depression. This story highlights family cohesiveness, interdependence, and pride, as well as the importance of land ownership. Emphasizing the defiant spirit and love for nature Cassie inherits from her father, it also reinforces the idea of father and family as protectors and providers of sanctuary against the world for the children. ALISON WASHINGTON

Mississippi Bridge

📖 Mildred D. Taylor   ✒ Max Ginsburg

African American

1992 (1990), Bantam Books Inc. ✷ Braille

Mississippi Bridge is told from the viewpoint of Jeremy Simms, a white boy who desperately wants a friendship with the African American Logan family but knows that the racist attitudes of those around them, and black people's wariness of whites, prevents it.

Jeremy sees racial injustice repeatedly. He hates to see others humiliating blacks, and does not take part in it. Jeremy knows that what the whites do is wrong but does nothing to stop it.

On a rainy day, the Logan kids and their grandmother are planning to take a bus trip. The bus arrives, and seven-year-old Cassie does not understand why Big Ma chooses a seat in the back when there are open seats near the front. Ten-year-old Stacey explains that those seats are reserved for whites. As the bus fills, Jeremy sees the bus driver make the black passengers, including the Logans, get off the bus to accommodate more white passengers. One man refuses and is literally thrown off the bus by the driver. Jeremy apologizes to him for the incident and is smacked by his father for "snivelin' after niggers." His father goes on to explain that blacks have a different place in the world, not alongside white people.

A boy wonders about fairness after witnessing a bus accident.

As the bus crosses a bridge Jeremy sees it slide and career into the swollen Rosa Lee River. As he runs to get help, Jeremy meets some members of the Logan family and tells them what happened. So that they won't worry about their grandmother, an embarrassed Jeremy tells them about the seating incident and assures them that Big Ma was not on the bus.

At the river, Jeremy sees that good, decent people were drowned, and he asks, "if the Lord was punishing, how come Grace-Anne and Miz Hattie? They ain't hurt nobody." He says that he understood nothing about that day, such as why certain people were on the bus and not others.

Jeremy Simms represents a reasonable and open-minded voice in a closed society. As Jeremy gets older, he better understands that friendships between whites and blacks were usually aloof and potentially dangerous. This depiction of the strained but definite rules regarding interracial relationships is repeated in Taylor's novels.

ALISON WASHINGTON

The Gold Cadillac

📖 Mildred D. Taylor ✒ Michael Hays

African American

1987, Dial Books for Young Readers

It is 1950, and Lois and her sister Wilma have not encountered much racism until their family takes a trip in a flashy and expensive car to visit relatives in Mississippi. The girls have a typical childhood in an Ohio house near many relatives. The story begins when their father drives home a beautiful gold Cadillac. Everyone loves it except Lois's mother, and the car causes a rift between the parents. The father wants to take a trip south in the car, but the other adults advise against it, saying some might take offense at a northern black man flaunting such a fine possession. The father defends his decision by saying that he worked hard and honestly to buy that car and that "it meant something to me that somebody like me from Mississippi could go and buy it. The entire extended family goes along in order to watch out for one another on the possibly dangerous trip. For the

Two sisters learn about family unity and racism when their family takes a trip down South.

girls, the adventure is fun-filled until they leave Ohio and enter Kentucky, where the father tells the girls not to speak when white folks are around, and the two see signs that say "White only, Colored not allowed" on buildings and public facilities. Lois suddenly feels like an alien in her own country.

Later, the family is stopped by the police. The father is accused of stealing the car, arrested, and jailed. He pays his bail, and the family continues until the father is too exhausted to drive. He decides that it is unsafe for them to travel any farther in the car and returns to a nearby city to borrow a cousin's older, less conspicuous car.

The trip changes things for Lois. Now, she's full of questions about the events and why things are this way. Her father explains that because of slavery, ignorance, and racist laws, many whites treat blacks as subhumans. He eventually sells the car, however, because it pulls the family apart.

For Lois, the Cadillac starts her on the road to awareness about racism and family unity. This book may do the same for many youngsters.

ALISON WASHINGTON

The Friendship

📖 Mildred D. Taylor ✒ Max Ginsburg

African American

1987, Dial Books for Young Readers

Nine year-old Cassie Logan narrates this story about the touchy Southern issue of names and the decorum of titles. The text also compels readers to examine the qualities of loyalty and obligation, friendship and pride.

A neighbor sends the Logan kids to the Wallace store, even though their parents do not want them around the shop. Outside, they encounter Mr. Tom Bee, an elderly black man. In the store, Cassie notices that the white storekeeper's son shows Mr. Bee no respect. Mr. Bee then asks very loudly to see John, the store owner, and Cassie knows something is wrong. No black could call a white adult by his first name. The owner's son is aghast at the old man's impertinence, but Mr. Bee continues his requests for "John," and, finally, the store owner solemnly complies. John Wallace impatiently tells Mr. Bee that the old man cannot forget his place, but Mr. Bee continues to call the owner John.

Friendships and race relations are tested when a black man calls a white storekeeper by his first name.

Mr. Bee then tells the story behind his actions. Many years before, Mr. Bee saved young John Wallace's life and took him in as family. As the teen became older, Mr. Bee expected their relationship would have to conform, but the young man promised that he would never make Mr. Bee call him "Mister" because he owed so much to him. Mr. Bee was merely holding John to his promise.

The trouble begins when Mr. Bee returns to the store for chewing tobacco. Now, other white men are present when Mr. Bee asks repeatedly for John to give him tobacco. Everyone in the store reacts to the old man's "insolence" and demands that Mr. Wallace take charge. Mr. Wallace does not seem to react, but as the old man is leaving, the storekeeper shoots him in the leg. Mr. Wallace rationalizes the act by saying that, as a Christian, he didn't want to kill Mr. Bee, but "this here disrespectin' me gotta stop. You gotta keep in mind you ain't nothin' but a nigger." Mr. Bee neither relents nor repents; instead, he reminds Mr. Wallace of his earlier promise. The old man continues to rail against the "ungrateful soul," yelling the white man's name until no other sound exists.

The children see the injustice of the segregated system and way of thinking, in which something as seemingly innocuous as how a person is addressed can provoke violence. The author draws from the bounty of stories about the South that her father told her, saying that through these stories, she "learned a history not then taught in story books, a history about the often-tragic lives of black people living in a segregated land." ALISON WASHINGTON

Esther's Story

📖 Diane Wolkstein ✒ Juan Winagaard

Jewish

1996, Morrow

Diane Wolkstein's *Esther's Story* brings alive the Biblical heroine celebrated during Purim. The book takes the form of Esther's diary, given to her by her uncle Mordecai, a Hebrew judge in the Persian court. The story begins when she is eleven. She carefully sets out her life with her uncle Mordecai, her guardian since her parents' death, and describes the times in which she lives, including a three day banquet where guests "lay on silver couches in the courtyard," drinking from golden goblets in the perfume of blossoming trees, viewing "colored stones in the floor formed in the shape of roses."

A retelling in diary form of the life of Jewish Queen Esther from the Bible.

Eventually, Mordecai comes home and announces that the queen has been banished, and a new queen must be selected. Mordecai tells his niece that she must change her name from Hadassah to Esther, which means "secret" or "concealed." A year later, Esther is taken to the palace with other beauties from whom the King will chose his bride. Esther is homesick, humble, and a sister to the others, all the time confused as to why she must hide her Jewish heritage.

When the King sees Esther, he is taken with her good humor and forthright manner and asks her to be his bride. Esther is content as queen, though she distrusts the new prime minister, Haman. When Haman announces a plan to kill the Hebrews and seize their wealth, Mordecai tells Esther she must reveal who she really is. Esther courageously and wisely exposes her true identity in a way that undoes Haman's plot and saves her people. As a result, her uncle becomes the new prime minister.

Realistic illustrations by Juan Winagaard show his dedication to research and historical accuracy. He has carefully selected images of Esther, this dark-haired beauty. His illustrations also record with care the emotional tones of all the characters in this dramatic story. SUSIE WILDE

Tongues of Jade

📖 Laurence Yep ✒ David Weisner

Asian American, Chinese American

1991, HarperCollins

Retold by award-winning author and master storyteller Laurence Yep, this is a fascinating collection of Chinese American folktales. Using a historical voice and poetic vision, Yep brings us a beautiful collection, told with great skill and insight. One of the most valuable aspects of the collection is Yep's framing of the pieces within important themes to Chinese American history.

In his introduction, Yep writes, "In ancient times, the Chinese covered their dead with pieces of jade. In those days, the Chinese believed that jade had the power to preserve the body. Beyond that, though, every storyteller speaks with a tongue of jade, preserving an entire time period. " He goes on to explain the role of stories in the Chinese-American community. Initially, the stories were meant to remind them of home and to teach lessons about "how a wise man could survive in a strange, often hostile land." But, later, as the Chinese began to set-

An expertly told collection of folktales about the Chinese American experience.

tle permanently in America, these stories were used to educate the younger generation about "the China they had left or perhaps never seen."

In the opening section, entitled "Roots," Yep depicts Chinese immigrants, mostly peasant farmers, who worked to develop the agricultural economy of the West Coast. (The "roots," then, are both figurative and literal.) Yep talks about the immigrants' connection to the land, and of the "fruit" which is born of the land: both the "fruit" the peasants brought from China, in the form of ideas and technology; and the "fruit" reaped in America as a result of new ideas and lessons learned.

In "Family Ties," Yep pays homage to the many Chinese men who labored in America, prevented by the country's harsh immigration policies from reuniting with their families. Of one story in this section, Yep writes, "Finally, I think of 'The Phantom Heart' as a kind of parable for a homecoming. At best, many of the guests (Chinese immigrants in America who would return to their families in China) would have depended upon letters to communicate with their families. In some cases, this tenuous link might last ten, twenty years. What was it like for these emotional strangers to return home after so many years? What was it like to leave a bride of sixteen and come back to a wife of thirty-six? Even five years of seperation can create an emotional distance between a husband and wife. In some cases, it must have taken all of the wife's patience, strength, and resourcefulness to transplant a phantom heart into a returned guest."

Yep credits Jon Lee with collecting the bulk of the stories in the 1930s. Lee's stories were published in a collection entitled *The Golden Mountain*. What makes this book special is Yep's insight into the mutiple purposes folktales serve within communities. All too often, folktales simply become a pat solution for the introduction of multicultural content into a curriculum. And too often, they are presented out of context. Folktales evolve from the need to tell stories, to teach lessons, and to preserve traditions. They are a map of people's experiences and views of the world. Yep understands this and treats these folktales with the reverence, deeper complexities behind these "simple" tales. This is a wonderful collection, expertly told and expertly contextualized. DEBBIE WEI

The Devil's Arithmetic

Jane Yolen

Jewish

1990 (1988), Viking

Hannah reluctantly attends the seder (Passover celebration meal) at her paternal grandparents' house. She and her brother, Aaron, are much more comfortable with their maternal grandparents because they do not pressure the children to remember or think about the events of the Holocaust. Her father's family, who are survivors of the concentrations camps, bear the numbers tattooed on their arms as constant testimony. Hannah is named for a dear friend of her great-aunt Eva's, who was killed in the Holocaust.

A difficult but extraordinarily moving story of a modern Jewish girl's connection with the Holocaust.

When the time comes at the seder for the Prophet Elijah to be welcomed into the house, Hannah opens the door to perform the ritual and finds herself transported back in time and place to a small village in Poland just before the Jews are to be sent to concentration camps. She has become Chaya, the person for whom she was named. She is fully aware of who she really is, but she also cannot escape this experience of being in the midst of the Holocaust. She learns about her family, and she experiences first hand what it means to be a part of the community of the concentration camp. In the end she, as did her real namesake, sacrifices her own life to save her friend Rivka. She walks willingly into the oven and emerges back at her grandfather's seder, where she realizes that Rivka is her great-aunt Eva.

One of the messages in this extraordinarily moving book is that we are part of the past and must learn about it in order to involve ourselves fully in the present. The Jewish heritage of the shtetl emerges clearly, and the reader identifies with many of the characters. The insanity of the Holocaust also becomes obvious, and the graphic scenes of oppression are made very personal because the reader identifies so strongly with the protagonist: Hannah/Chaya.

This is a hard book to read, but children from fifth grade and up have taken it to their hearts and have used it as a springboard for more study and for active participation in peace education and education for understanding. MASHA RUDMAN

The Story of Rosa Parks and the Montgomery Bus Boycott Revisited

Herbert Kohl

Upset by the way the story of Rosa Parks is told to children, educator Herb Kohl wrote "The Story of Rosa Parks and the Montgomery Bus Boycott Revisited," an essay that appears in his book *Should We Burn Babar?* (The New Press, 1995). The following are two versions of the Rosa Parks story, the first a composite "generic" version created by Kohl from dozens of existing children's books and textbooks, the second Kohl's own suggested retelling, incorporating changes he discusses in his essay.

"ROSA WAS TIRED: THE STORY OF THE MONTGOMERY BUS BOYCOTT"

Rosa Parks was a poor seamstress. She lived in Montgomery, Alabama, during the 1950s. In those days there was still segregation in parts of the United States. That meant that African Americans and European Americans were not allowed to use the same public facilities such as restaurants or swimming pools. It also meant that whenever it was crowded on the city buses, African Americans had to give up seats in front to European Americans and move to the back of the bus.

One day, on her way home from work, Rosa was tired and sat down in the front of the bus. As the bus got crowded she was asked to give up her seat to a European American man, and she refused. The bus driver told her she had to go to the back of the bus, and she still refused to move. It was a hot day, and she was tired and angry, and became very stubborn.

The driver called a policeman, who arrested Rosa.

When other African Americans in Montgomery heard this, they became angry too, so they decided to refuse to ride the buses until everyone was allowed to ride together. They boycotted the buses.

The boycott, which was led by Martin Luther King Jr., succeeded. Now African Americans and European Americans can ride the buses together in Montgomery.

Rosa Parks was a very brave person.

"SHE WOULD NOT BE MOVED: THE STORY OF ROSA PARKS AND THE MONTGOMERY BUS BOYCOTT"

It was 1955. Everyone in the African American community in Montgomery, Alabama, knew Rosa Parks. She was a community leader, and people admired her courage. All throughout her life she had opposed prejudice, even if it got her into trouble with European American people.

In those days, Alabama was legally segregated, which means that African American people were prevented by state law from using the same swimming pools, schools, and other public facilities as European Americans. There also were separate entrances, toilets, and drinking fountains for African Americans and European Americans in places such as bus and train stations.

The facilities African Americans were allowed to use were not only separate from the ones European Americans used but were also very inferior. The reason for this was racism, the belief that European Americans were superior to African Americans and that, therefore,o European Americans deserved better facilities.

In those days, public buses were divided into two sections. One at the front for European Americans, which was supposed to be "for whites only." From five to ten rows back, the section for African Americans began. That part of the bus was called the "colored" section.

Whenever it was crowded on the city buses,

African American people were forced to give up seats in the "colored" section to European Americans and move to the back of the bus. For example, an elderly African American woman would have to give up her seat to a European American teenage male. If she refused, she could be arrested for breaking the segregation laws.

December 1, 1955, on her way home from work, Rosa Parks took the bus as usual. She sat down in the front row of the "colored" section. As the bus got crowded, the driver demanded that she give up her seat to a European American man and move to the back of the bus. This was not the first time that this had happened to Rosa Parks. In the past, she had refused to move, and the driver had simply put her off the bus. Mrs. Parks hated segregation, and along with many other African American people, refused to obey many of its unfair rules. On this day, she refused to do what the bus driver demanded.

The bus driver commanded her once more to go to the back of the bus but she stayed in her seat, looking straight ahead and not moving an inch. It was a hot day, and the driver was angry and became very stubborn. He called a policeman, who arrested Mrs. Parks.

Mrs. Parks was not the first African American person to be arrested in Montgomery for refusing to move to the back of the bus. In the months before her refusal, at least three other people were arrested for the same reason. In fact, African American leaders in Montgomery were planning to overcome segregation. One way they wanted to do this was to have every African American person boycott the buses. Since most of the bus riders in the city were African American, the buses would go broke if they refused to let African Americans and European Americans ride the buses as equals.

From 1949 right up to the day Mrs. Parks refused to move, the Women's Political Council of Montgomery prepared to stage a bus boycott because of how African Americans were treated on the bus. They were just waiting for the time to be ripe. Nineteen fifty-five was the time.

However, none of the people who were arrested before Mrs. Parks was a leader. She was a leader, and the day she was arrested the leadership called a meeting at the Dexter Avenue Baptist Church. They decided to begin their refusal to ride the buses the next morning. They knew Mrs. Parks had the courage to deal with the pressure of defying segregation and would not yield even if her life was threatened.

The next day the Montgomery bus boycott began.

There was a young new minister in Montgomery in those days. His name was Martin Luther King Jr. People in the community felt that he was a special person and asked him to lead the boycott. At first, he wasn't sure. He worried about the violence that might result from the boycott. However, he quickly made up his mind that it was time to destroy segregation and accepted the people's call for him to be their leader.

The Montgomery bus boycott lasted 381 days. For over a year, the African American people of Montgomery, Alabama, stayed off the buses. Some walked to work, others rode bicycles or shared car rides. It was very inconvenient for them, but they knew that what they were doing was very important for all African American people in the South.

The boycott succeeded, and by the end of 1956, African Americans and European Americans could ride the buses in Montgomery as equals. However, the struggle for the complete elimination of segregation had just begun.

We all owe a great deal to the courage and intelligence of Rosa Parks and the entire African American community of Montgomery, Alabama. They took risks to make democracy work for all of us.

Herbert Kohl is director of the Costal Ridge Research and Education Center in Point Arena, California and the author of a range of books, including Should We Burn Babar?, 36 Children, Reading: How To, The Open Classroom, *and* Growing Minds.

Grade Seven to Grade Eight

Sounder

William H. Armstrong

African American

1989 (1969), HarperCollins, ✳ Series

This award-winning story revolves around a desperately poor black family of sharecroppers in Mississippi during the 1930s. Sounder, the family coonhound, is the only character in the book who is named. One day, the father steals a ham in order to feed his family. When the white sheriff and his deputies come to take the father away, Sounder is shot by the men and disappears into the woods. The remainder of the story details how the man's son searches for his father and for Sounder, and discovers a rural school with a very

A classic, New-bery Award-winning book about a poor southern black family in the 1930s.

kind teacher. In the end, both Sounder and the father, maimed beyond recovery, die. In many ways, Sounder becomes a symbol of the family and of the father in particular.

The one ray of hope is that the boy goes to school, and there is a sense that schooling will help him to a better life. At the beginning of the book, the author explains that he was told this story by an elderly black man, a teacher, who also worked for the author's father on weekends and after school and attended the white church (the only black man to do so), sitting alone in the balcony. Armstrong clearly feels great affection for this man. Unfortunately, the book is written from the perspective of a white man who, while pitying the condition of the family, never manages to imbue the black characters with strength and self-worth. The mother is passive, accepting of her fate, never questioning the injustices and the mean-spiritedness of white society. The father is a victim. The entire family has quiet courage, but what is emphasized in the story is the degradation and beating of the human spirit. The white characters are uniformly evil. This story does not celebrate anyone's heritage, but it does focus on the historical reality of the treatment of black people by many whites.

Mildred Taylor's series of books about the Logan family, set in the same time period and geographic area, provides a fitting contrast. Any of the series, particularly *Roll of Thunder, Hear My Cry*, which, like Sounder, won the Newbery Award for excellence in writing, can serve as a counter-example representing the same era from a perspective that emphasizes the spirit of the African American characters. MASHA RUDMAN

Ajeemah and His Son

James Berry

African, Caribbean, Jamaican

1994 (1992), HarperCollins

James Berry's *Ajeemah and His Son*, is a challenging story of changes in the lives of an African father and son following their capture into slavery. This short novel begins with

A short, rich novel of a father and son's experiences as slaves in Jamaica.

the reader in the preparations for the betrothal of Ajeemah's son, Atu, in Africa. The story moves through their capture by slave traders, their experience of the Middle Passage, and their subsequent lives of separation and bondage on an island in the Caribbean. This parent and child never see each other again, though they live out their days on plantations only miles apart. Because of the difference in

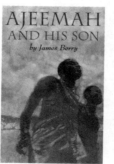

their ages and circumstances, and the different choices they make, their lives take different paths, each one full of grief.

The situations presented here are relevant to many contemporary situations. Atu's development into an angry young slave—his isolation and rebellion and the nasty turn his personality takes in response to the intolerable system he faces—offers a parallel to contemporary life. The father's patience, rewarded by freedom—which he buys at the cost of decades of his life and the loss of his son and his past—offers a thought-provoking contrast. Together, the charac-

518

ters' stories offer rich material for a discussion of the ways fate, the times, choice, luck, and community interact to shape a life under oppression. Young adults will be caught up in the story and relate the complex choices of the characters to dilemmas in their own lives. MARY MOORE EASTER

CityKids Speak on Prejudice

CityKids Foundation ✎ Leah Teweles and Bobbie Crosby
Multicultural
1994, Random House

Bold, varied graphics, photographs, and illustrations provide a dynamic background to the media clips, quick facts and statistics, poetry, and interviews that make up this book. CityKids, a foundation-supported youth group, explains: "We've written this book for and about young people like us. We don't pretend to have all the answers, You might notice there is no all-knowing narrator or voice." CityKids are described as "Blacks, Whites, Yellows, Reds, of all different religious, educational, and economic backgrounds."

Through statistics, poetry, and interviews, young people speak about prejudice.

Information on hate crimes includes statistics about anti-gay and lesbian violence, but otherwise the treatment of sexuality issues is sparse. In all, however, the combination of facts and individual voices makes this a compelling look into the explorations of an introspective and open group of young people. CHRIS MAYO

Black Stars in Orbit: NASA's African American Astronauts

Khephra Burns ✎ William Miles and archival photographs
African American
1995, Gulliver Books

In *Black Stars in Orbit: NASA's African American Astronauts*, Khephra Burns and William Miles discuss the contributions African Americans have made over the years to the development of space flight, despite veiled threats and resistance from, as well as discrimination by, colleagues, the military, and the U.S. government. The book focuses on the lives of such unsung pioneers as Colonel Guy Bluford, the first African American to venture into space; Colonel Fred Gregory, the first African American to pilot a space shuttle; and Dr. Mae Jemison, the first African American woman to travel in space.

The authors trace our fascination with flight back to Greek mythology, as well as African American folklore. One story tells of Africans captured and forced to work on plantations in the American South. One day, the decide they've had enough and throw down their tools. The overseer gets out his whip to flog them, but, before he can strike, they rise up into the air like birds and fly back to Africa and freedom.

Flying has always meant freedom. Yet only in this century

A compelling look at the contributions of African Americans to the development of space flight.

have we actually been able to do it. The Wright brothers flew a plane in 1903. The United States established NASA in 1958 and eleven years later, sent men to the moon. But it took decades more and the effort of thousands of people for the first African American astronaut to go into space.

What was the view from up there? For Colonel Gregory, who piloted the space shuttle Challenger in 1985, two years after Colonel Bluford's adventure, it was incredible:

"You get a marvelous view of the world from space," he says. "And the thing that impressed me was that you could see Houston, and then you'd see how really close Houston was to Mexico City, and how close Mexico City was to South America, to Africa, to Russia. Everything was right there.... There were no state boundaries. You kind of wondered from above as you looked down. . . how there could be any problems at all down there, because everybody was everybody's neighbor." The reader also learns of the contributions made by African Americans behind the scenes, on the ground. Dr. Robert Shurney, for example, helped design the moon buggy, and Dr. George Curruthers developed a combination telescope and camera used by astronauts on the moon to take pictures of the earth, the constellations, and other galaxies.

Black Stars in Orbit is based on years of research Burns and Miles did in the late '80s and features a number of historical photos. They visited NASA facilities in Texas and Florida, and interviewed African American astronauts and their families. The result is compelling and informative.
CHRISTINA ENG

Those Other People

Alice Childress
African American, Gay/Lesbian/Bisexual
1989, Putnam Publishing

A teacher attacks a female student in a cleaning closet and the act is witnessed by another teacher, Jonathan, and a student Tyrone. Jonathan, a young, closeted gay computer instructor, moved back to town when his lover, angered by Jonathan's refusal to admit that he is gay, called his parents and revealed the truth. His move home was an attempt to repair the damages, and to avoid the pressures of the urban gay environment.

African American Tyrone's story parallels Jonathan's to an extent. His family has moved to town to enjoy the benefits of their upwardly mobile father's hard work. But they find themselves the only African American family in town and un-wanted by many of the townspeople, particularly their neighbor.

An uneven novel about a gay, white teacher and a young black student.

When Jonathan and Tyrone witness the attempt-ed rape, they are confronted with aspects of their own and each other's identities that they hadn't intended to make public. Tyrone's family is initially supportive of his standing up for justice, but they pull back when they find out that Jonathan is gay, not wanting Tyrone too closely linked with him. As Jonathan observes, the story is "all about who we are and how unpleasing that may be—to other people."

Though Jonathan even-tually decides it is more important to come out than to keep his job, other politi-cal activism in the story is trivialized. Tyrone's uncle, Kwame, is ridiculed for speaking out against racism, even as Tyrone's family experiences such direct racism as having a cross burned on their lawn, dam-aging the house. While Jonathan's statement of pride in his identity is justly celebrated, it is unfortunate that Kwame's strength and convictions are parodied. CHRIS MAYO

The Rebellious Alphabet

Jorge Diaz (translated by Geoffrey Fox)
Olvind S. Jorfald
Hispanic
1993, Henry Holt and Company, ✱ Spanish

In a fictional place ruled by an illiterate dictator who no one understands, reading and the alphabet have been banned. The General blurts out non-sensical words and rules without reason or logic, demanding obedience to his every whim. The dicta-tor orders the town crier

A Latin American fable in which an illiterate general denounces the alphabet to protect himself from his educated detractors.

to lie and say that the world outside their village is "a mess" and to exhort the villagers to pay taxes.

One villager, Placido, defies him, devising an inge-nious system to print flyers denouncing the ideology of the General. The General has his soldiers look for

the culprit, and Placido is discovered. Enraged, the General commands that the alphabet be done away with. He also has all the signs and street direc-tions burned. Because of the resulting confusion and ignorance, the villagers come together and demand that Placido be released. With his release comes a magical rain, restoring peace and order. In the end, abandoned by his soldiers and left alone in his shame and ignorance, the General retreats to his castle.

Olvind Jorfald's illustrations employ dark, dreary colors and angular lines to set a dark mood for the story. MARTHA L. MARTINEZ

Damned Strong Love: The True Story of Willi G. and Stephen K.

Lutz Van Dijk (translated by Elizabeth D. Crawford)
Gay/Lesbian/Bisexual, Polish
1995, Henry Holt and Company

This book is based on a true story of the Polish author's experiences during World War II. Soon after the German occupation of Poland begins, the

The true and compelling story of a gay man picked up by the Gestapo during WWII.

narrator, Stephan, meets Willi, an Austrian soldier serving in the German army. They fall in love immediately and find a hideout where they can meet. They see each other as often as possible for the next few months, until Willi is called to the front. Stephan waits anxiously for a few months, relying on Willi's promise to write regularly. Finally, after not having heard from him, Stephan manages to find an address and write a short letter to Willi, saying how much he misses him and thinks about him.

About a month later, Stephan is arrested by the Gestapo, who have intercepted his letter. He is charged with homosexuality and sent to prison. For the next two and a half years, he is moved around to different prisons, enduring the abuse of guards and fellow prisoners. In the spring of 1945, he and a few other men escape and make their way to the British front. Stephan learns of Willi's death and fears that his letter may have caused it.

This book begins to fill the gap in information about the treatment of gays and lesbians during World War II. While Stephan makes no claim that his story is typical, it is nonetheless compelling. This book helps broaden young people's knowledge of how people were affected by the war and contributes to discussions of the effects of intolerance and violence. SUE FLICKINGER

Battlefields and Burial Grounds: The Indian Struggle to Protect Ancestral Graves in the United States

Roger C. Echo-Hawk and Walter R. Echo-Hawk
Archival photographs
Native American, Pawnee
1994, Lerner Publications Company

Pawnee brothers Roger and Walter Echo-Hawk present an excellent treatment of the exhumation of Indian graves by scientists, souvenir hunters, and others. Roger, an historian, and Walter, an attorney with the Native American Rights Fund, talk about the lack of legal protection given to Indian burial-grounds.

Beginning in the late 1700s with Thomas Jefferson, who dug up a burial mound in Virginia, and continuing through the 1980s, when privately-run museums displayed Indian bones, Native graves have been continually disrupted by amateurs and professionals alike, for reasons that would be laughed at were the graves those found in church-yards and cemeteries.

The authors give an informed and fair account of federal and state legislation on the issue. They also treat Native burial practices, military removal of the battlefield dead to the Army Medical Museum in Washington, museum excavations, tourist attractions, academic ethics, the 1906 Antiquities Act, and the 1990 Native American Graves Protection and Repatriation Act (NAGPRA).

The second half of this brief book details the long and bitter Pawnee struggle to reclaim the bones of their ancestors from the Nebraska State Historical Society Museum, the Army Medical Museum (now the National Museum of Health and Medicine), and the Smithsonian Institution. Clearly written, illustrated with appropriate photographs, and including bibliographic notes and an index, the Echo-Hawks' book is highly recommended for children and adults alike. LISA A. MITTEN

A highly recommended look at our society's attitude toward Native American burial grounds.

The Middle Passage: White Ships/Black Cargo

Tom Feelings
African American
1995, Dial, Hamilton, Virginia, *Anthony Burns*; Lester, Julius, *To Be a Slave*; Meltzer, Milton, *The Black Americans*.

Tom Feelings' visual depiction of the Middle Passage is both compelling and disturbing. This series of sixty-four narrative paintings is a tribute to the survival of the human spirit, yet the horror of the subject matter sears the soul.

The book tells the story of millions of women, men, and children torn from their homelands in Africa and forced to embark upon journeys on

521

disease-infested "death ships." Some of the pictures are graphic and can be deeply frightening to adults and children alike.

For example, there are scenes of bare-breasted women being dragged across the floor and raped, and rats nibbling into the armpits of dying men. The beauty of Feelings' artwork belies his horrifying subject. Using pen, ink, and tempera on rice paper, Feelings invests his work with an almost dreamlike quality. The illustrations sometimes have the feel of collage; at other times, they are mural-like. A brilliant introduction by John Henrik Clarke traces the roots of the Atlantic slave trade. Still, the images beg for additional explanatory text. While some children have a general understanding about slavery, the Middle Passage in itself remains unknown to most. In light of the fact that the book is being marketed for children as well as adults, the pictures alone may not suffice.

The horrific story of the Middle Passage of African slaves, that could use further explication. told through graphic paintings.

These pictures are bound to raise scores of difficult questions. While many African American authors chose to ignore or deny the role African rulers played in facilitating the slave trade, Feelings does not bypass this important part of that history. Along with a bibliography for older readers and adults, the book contains a map that shows the African diaspora in the Americas and the major slave routes, as well as a partial listing of islands in the Caribbean Sea where Africans were taken.

The Middle Passage is a powerfully illustrated narrative of one of history's many holocausts. Used with books such as Milton Meltzer's *The Black Americans*, Virginia Hamilton's *Anthony Burns*, and Julius Lester's *To Be a Slave*, it will provide older children with a deeper understanding of the horrors of slavery. DAPHNE MUSE

The Other 1492: Jewish Settlement in the New World

Norman H. Finkelstein ✏ Archival illustrations
Jewish
1989, Beech Tree Books

"Within three months there must not remain in my kingdom a single Jew." On March 31, 1492, King Ferdinand and Queen Isabella of Spain ordered all Jews to leave Spanish soil. According to *The Other 1492*, the irony of this edict is that there was hardly an aristocratic family in Spain that was not at least part Jewish. The Spanish Jews were forced to leave immediately and could take nothing of value with them. The only alternatives left them by what came to be known as the Spanish Inquisition were forced conversion to Catholicism or death. Many fled and found their way to the New World, some with Columbus. (Jewish cartographers charted the maps for his journey, and at least three Jews—including his interpreter, Luis de Tores— were part of the crew.)

The Other 1492 provides an excellent account of the causes and aftermath of the expulsion of Jews from Spain, as well as a fascinating description of the new lives many made in the New World. The book also contains archival documents and a very useful select bibliography. Illustrations include a painting of Rabbi Isaac Aboab da Fonseca, the first rabbi in the New World, and a copy of the title page of the Ferrara Bible, which was translated into Spanish for use by the *Marranos*—baptized Jews who posed as Christians in public, but who inwardly considered themselves Jews. The term, which literally means "pigs," was a disdainful term given to these "New Christians" by established Catholics.

A thorough and fascinating account of the expulsion of the Jews from Spain in 1492.

The book does not discuss the relations between Jews and the indigenous people in the "New World" they settled. It remains, however, a useful tool for discussing the real history of the settlement of the New World, as well as a fascinating account of a part of European history that will be unfamiliar to many students.
DAPHNE MUSE

The Eagle Kite

Paula Fox
Gay/Lesbian/Bisexual
1995, Orchard Books

Liam's father has AIDS. Liam's mother insists that he got it from a blood transfusion, although she's obviously furious with her husband. Liam knows his mother's story isn't true, but can't get her to say anything else about it.

A few years earlier, while on a family trip to the beach, Liam had seen his father embracing another man. His father had later tried to convince Liam that the man was just a friend. As the illness progresses,

522

Liam's father moves out to a small cabin a couple of hours away. Liam is angry with his father and scared about what will happen to him. He visits his father a few times, but the anger and fear do not go away. Just after Christmas they get a phone call saying Liam's father has gone into the hospital. Liam and his mother go to see him and are with him when he dies.

A vague novel about a boy struggling with the knowledge that his father is gay and is dying from AIDS.

No easy answers are presented in this book. The reactions of the different characters are understandable and taken seriously. The focus of the book is on Liam's reaction not just to his father's illness but also to his father's homosexuality. However, the reader is given very little information about what Liam is thinking and how he confronts his father's relationship with another man. The characters communicate very little with each other and often the dialogue is vague about the father's homosexuality and the other, characters' feelings about it.

SUE FLICKINGER

The Other Victims: First Person Stories of Non-Jews Persecuted by the Nazis

Ina R. Friedman
Multicultural
1990, Houghton Mifflin   Plant, Richard, *The Pink Triangle: The Nazi War Against Homosexuals.*

European Jews were not the only victims of Hitler and the Nazis. Around five million non-Jews were also murdered. Jehovah's Witnesses, Christians, homosexuals, gypsies, and blacks, as well as the mentally ill and physically handicapped, were systematically exterminated.

The Other Victims is an award-winning collection of first-person narratives about the Nazi horrors. Selections include "Grete: Dissenters Will Be Prosecuted," "Bubili: A Young Gypsy's Fight for Survival," and "Andre: The Slaves that Built the Rockets." The book also includes stories of some who resisted. In "Ondrej: A Czech Schoolboy Fights Back," we meet Ondrej Laska, the son of a Czech diplomat and one such resister. He was awarded a Medal of Valor for his bravery and went on to become an American citizen after the war. DAPHNE MUSE

Harrowing first-person accounts of Nazi persecution of gays, blacks, the disabled, and others.

I Am Joaquin

Rudolpho Gonzales
Hispanic, Mexican
1972 (1967), Farm Workers Press, ✳ Braille

Written in 1967, this poem has been mimeographed many times and distributed by teachers, student activists, farm-worker organizers, and theater groups. It was finally published in 1972. By then, 100,000 copies had already circulated.

Centered on the Chicano movement of the 1960s and 70s, this long and compelling narrative poem affirms self-respect and courage in the face of racism. Gonzales traces the history of Mexican Americans from their roots in Pre-Columbian

A powerful epic poem from the 1960s about the Chicano experience.

523

524

Mexico, through the Spanish conquest and Mexico's war of independence from Spain. It also addresses the United States takeover of half of Mexico through war in 1848 and the guerrilla resistance to that occupation. References are also made to the Mexican Revolution of 1910, to the contemporary exploitation of Mexican workers, and to the experiences of Mexican American soldiers being sent to fight in Korea and Vietnam.

Addressing the complexity of being rooted in two different worlds, the poem ends with the memorable words: "I am the masses of my people and/I refuse to be absorbed...I shall endure! I will endure!"

Unfortunately, the poem's power is diluted by its depiction of women as mere appendages to men. *It works better when paired with the works of highly respected women poets such as Gloria Anzaldua or Ana Castillo.*

This poem was written with mature readers in mind, but it offers powerful messages for younger readers. Accompanied by strong black-and-white photographs, this epic poem retains much of its power today and should be read by young people of all racial and ethnic backgrounds.

ELIZABETH MARTINEZ

The Journey: Japanese Americans, Racism, and Renewal

Sheila Hamanaka
Asian American, Japanese American
1995 (1990), Orchard Books

A moving account of an under-explored aspect of American history, *The Journey* combines details of a vivid mural with text to provide a view of World War II from the perspective of Japanese-Americans. Treating the injustices that Japanese-Americans

A valuable photographic essay about the Japanese American experience.

faced during this period, this book evokes compassion for those who were, like the author's family, subjected to prejudice and discrimination. Organized chronologically, the narration is easy to follow, and descriptions of the mural are often extended to include additional, related information.

Shared with children in a variety of ways, *The Journey* would be appropriate for a range of grade levels. At a very basic level, Hamanaka's exceptional artwork is accessible to young children.

The written information will encourage older children to think about the complex issues and blatant injustices addressed in the book. Some of the darker images, however, such as the depiction of the Ku Klux Klan and scenes of war, may not be appropriate for all children.

The artwork and text communicate both outrage and pride, and the depth of emotion here makes this a valuable alternative resource for better understanding of the United States and Japanese American history. While reference sources are not cited by the author, an alphabetical index of topics, people, and places mentioned throughout the book is included. *The Journey is an excellent supplement to traditional U.S. history textbooks, encouraging children to examine critically the effects of historical events and prejudice on the lives of all people.*

KARLEEN H. TANIMURA MANCHADA

On the Wings of Peace

Edited by Sheila Hamanaka 🖋 Various sources
Asian, Japanese
1995, Houghton Mifflin Company

On the Wings of Peace is dedicated to the memory of the people who died in Hiroshima and Nagasaki when the United States released atomic bombs on August 6 and 9, 1945. The book contains work by sixty writers and artists from across the globe commemo-

Sixty writers and artists commemorate the fiftieth anniversary of the Hiroshima bombing.

rating the fiftieth anniversary of the bombings. The result is intended to inspire a vision of peace in the world community.

The collection mixes memoirs, contemporary fiction, essays, poetry, and prayers, all centered on the theme of peace. The art includes collage, photography, painting, drawing, and posters. The

pieces are connected by their common theme only, so it is an eclectic grouping, with each piece reflecting in some way the artist's culture.

The book's layout is simple and the reproduction of the illustrations is of high quality. Each contributor is briefly identified and a bibliography of resource materials is provided. Royalties from the sale of the book go to Amnesty International USA, For Our Children's Sake Foundation, and the Friends of Hibakusha. JANIS O'DRISCOLL

Many Thousand Gone: African Americans from Slavery to Freedom

📖 Virginia Hamilton ✏ Leo & Diane Dillon
African American
1995 (1993), Alfred A. Knopf

These stories highlight both well- and lesser-known cases of people yearning for freedom and those who helped the cause of the oppressed. From dozens of sources, Hamilton chronicles the ravages of slavery and the often covert fight for freedom many slaves waged before the Civil War. In sections entitled "Slavery in America", "Running-Aways", and "Exodus to Freedom," Hamilton mixes personal accounts, individual profiles, and testimonies of how blacks and whites alike challenged, fled, and fought slavery. Part One examines the history of American slavery from the time the first black indentured servants were traded at Jamestown in 1619, zooming in on individual experiences. The reader learns, for example, of Olaudah Equiana who was kidnapped as a boy from Nigeria, but survived the Middle Passage and was repeatedly bought and sold until he ended up with a Quaker merchant. After earning enough money to buy his freedom, Equiana moved to England, where he worked to end slavery.

Strikingly illustrated personal accounts and profiles of people who fought slavery.

The second and third parts document the stories of many who risked their lives for freedom and some who preferred to die than return to bondage. These tales are complemented by stories of people who worked for freedom through the Underground Railroad, the court system, or outright resistance. Hamilton's accounts stop with the war between the states, but her afterword tells that, even after the war, slaves' struggles were far from over.

Many Thousand Gone gives names and histories to the faceless enslaved masses, making their stories personal and touching. It reminds us that the institution robbed so many of basic rights and shows the lengths to which people went in order to live free. Leo and Diane Dillon enhance the text with their striking, detailed illustrations. A useful bibliography and index are included for extended study and quick reference. ALISON WASHINGTON

Paul Robeson: The Life and Times of a Free Black Man

📖 Virginia Hamilton ✏ Various sources
African American
1974, Harper & Row

Robeson, a communist, a Phi Beta Kappa scholar, athlete, actor, and singer, struggled for equality for African Americans. This richly documented and thoughtful biography of Paul Robeson brings to life the beloved actor/activist in all his political and moral complexity.

Upon graduating from Rutgers College, Robeson became a lawyer, but then turned to the theater where his voice and acting talent earned him tremendous respect all over the world. He also became interested in communism and was an ardent supporter of the Soviet Union. His political beliefs cost him the support of the American public and made him the target of McCarthy-era political persecution.

An excellent introduction to this beloved African American's story for young readers.

While author Hamilton takes a sympathetic look at his life, she does not remain uncritical of communism or the Soviet Union. As she diligently documents his accomplishments and failures, Hamilton shows the paths that lead Robeson into so many worlds beyond his own. Born into a large, close-knit family, Paul loved, admired, and respected his father, who taught him to express his opinions with powerful ease. Early on in his life, hard work taught him purpose, and he would spend his life struggling on behalf of the working class.

Later, after his disgrace at the hands of political enemies, Robeson's name was banished from the encyclopedias and reference books that had lauded him prior to the infamous McCarthy era. In the 1960s, those same sources would begin once again to include information on Robeson. *Hamilton's discussion of these events provides an interesting and important lesson in how history is revised. With its excellent research and clear writing, this book will appeal to young people with strong reading skills.* DAPHNE MUSE

Between Two Fires: Black Soldiers in the Civil War

Joyce Hansen ✦ *Archival illustrations*
African American

1993, Franklin Watts, Inc., ✳ Series, 📖 Day, Frances Ann, *Teacher's Guide from Multicultural Voices in Contemporary Literature*; Hansen, Joyce, *Which Way Freedom*; Hansen, Joyce, *Out From This Place*; McKissack, Patricia and Frederick, *Taking a Stand Against Racism and Racial Discrimination*.

Most accounts of the American Civil War are written from the perspectives of northern whites who were struggling to save the Union and/or the white people of the South who were fighting to preserve their way of life. Here at last is the story of the Civil War told from the per-

A much-needed collection of primary documents about African Amrican soldiers in the Civil War.

spective of the African Americans for whom the war meant a chance to gain freedom and political rights for themselves and their descendants. The stories of the black soldiers who made up ten percent of the Union army during the Civil War are dramatically documented through primary source materials, including accounts by journalists and other observers, officers' reports, speeches, and the soldiers' own letters and diaries.

Part of the African-American Experience Series, which provides authoritative studies of various aspects of black history and the black experience, from the historic struggles of the nation's past to the social and political movements of today, this much-needed book brings to life the experiences of the uncelebrated, often unnamed African Americans who risked their lives for the Union. She points out that these soldiers braved two perils—enemy fire and the racism of their colleagues—in a valiant attempt to prove their loyalty and worth and to gain liberty and justice for themselves and their people. These courageous soldiers endured inadequate medical attention, recruitment restrictions, unequal pay, restrictions on promotion, extreme punishment, and unfair expectations.

The author notes that this is not so much a book about war as another chapter in the larger history of the struggle of a people for dignity and liberty. She adds that racism ultimately weakens a nation and makes victims of all its people. By personalizing this history, Hansen enables readers to experience the heartbreak and the triumph of her subjects. The art reproductions, engravings, maps, and black-and-white photographs are well captioned and augment the wealth of detailed information presented. An index, extensive source notes, and a bibliography of primary and secondary materials will assist readers who are interested in additional research.

In the classroom, teachers may want to use Between Two Fires *to supplement the information provided by history textbooks. An interesting individual or class activity would be to examine textbooks to see if information about the African American soldiers who fought in the Civil War is included. Teachers may want to discuss the impact of omission and exclusion on everyone, both the excluded and the included.*

Students might be encouraged to respond in writing to questions like these: How do you feel about being told only part of the story of your country's history? Why is it important to view history through multiple perspectives? How does viewing history from the perspective of the dominant group distort our view of what happened in our country? How do books such as Between Two Fires *help solve this problem? Joyce Hansen included the contributions of women during the Civil War. Who were these women and what role did they play? Does your history book mention them? How does racism and gender bias weaken a nation?* Taking a Stand Against Racism and Racial Discrimination *by Patricia and Fredrick McKissack is an excellent resource for further examination of these issues.* FRANCES A. DAY

The Scottsboro Boys

James Haskins
African American
1994, Henry Holt and Company

In *The Scottsboro Boys*, author James Haskins examines an important piece of American civil rights history in a format accessible for young readers.

This non fiction account of the infamous trial and conviction of nine African American men and boys accused of the rape and assault of two Caucasian women uses actual letters, interviews, and trial transcripts. In addition to these primary sources, Mr. Haskins provides a comprehensive overview of the poverty-stricken United States of the early 1930s, offering today's readers information essential to

A clear and concise account of the celebrated rape trial of nine African Americans.

an understanding of the case.

In clear and concise language, Haskins leads the reader through the events of the "day of the crime," the arrest, trials, and convictions, as well as an inquiry into the motives of the people and organizations involved. The conflicting stories of the "witnesses" are brought forth and compared side-by-side. The competition between the NAACP (National Association for the Advancement of Colored People) and the ILD (The International Labor Defense Organization of the Communist Party) to represent the accused is examined, illuminating the role of these powerful organizations in the trial.

The book concludes in 1976, when Clarence Norris, one of the accused "boys," is granted a pardon some forty-five years after the trial.

Haskins's ability to weave into his account the social and political changes that take place during the three-decade legal battle is what makes this text so valuable. The impact of the case on subsequent proceedings is also examined. The Scottsboro Boys *is an excellent introduction to the period preceding the civil rights movement, and its straightforward approach and comprehensive treatment will be appreciated by young readers and adults alike.*
ROSA E. WARDER

One More River to Cross: The Story of Twelve Black Americans

📕 Jim Haskins 📷 Archival photographs
African American
1994 (1992), Scholastic, Inc.

This award-winning author has written over eighty books for young people, many of them biographies of outstanding African Americans. This collective biography has been carefully selected and researched. The eight men and four women profiled are from many fields—science, exploration, business, art, aeronautics, sports, and politics. The biographies are each ten to sixteen pages long and are accompanied by photographs. The writing is fast-paced, easily comprehended, and factual. The stories contain enough adventure, courage, heartbreak, and success to serve a dozen fictional plots. The author emphasizes the courageous striving against prejudice

Short, fast-paced biographies of twelve African Americans who overcame considerable odds to achieve their goals.

and poverty, and the eventual achievements of each individual included.

Unlike many early multicultural biographies, this book deals honestly and fairly with episodes of racial injustice. The subjects are all excellent role models and include Ralph Bunche, Shirley Chisholm, Malcolm X, Fannie Lou Hames, Madame Walker (the first American woman to earn a million dollars), Charles Drew, and Ronald McNair, the space explorer. *The book will be a catalyst for honest classroom discussion and is an excellent supplement to social studies texts in middle and high school. There is a bibliography of resource books and articles, and also a good index. Interested students and adults can also turn to other of Jackson's many biographies.*
GLORIA D. JACKSON

Two Teenagers in Twenty: Writings by Gay and Lesbian Youth

📗 Edited by Ann Heron
Gay/Lesbian/Bisexual
1995 (1985), Alyson Wonderland Publications, Inc.

This shocking new book that raised my awareness and ought to be required reading for every adult working with young people, is actually a revision of a book written a decade earlier, *One Teenager in Ten.* Even a math moron like me can see the ratio hasn't changed, but Heron chose the new title to indicate that more teenagers are identifying themselves as homosexuals. She had also hoped that she'd find more support for gay teenagers. Instead, she found the level of support "hasn't kept pace with the number of teens who are confronting the issue of sexual orientation." She writes: "The sense of isolation and despair in the stories I received in 1993 was in fact even stronger than a decade ago." Witness the

A collection of poignant stories of teens dealing with gay/ lesbian issues.

fact that the author of one of the stories committed suicide before the book's publication, and, according to a 1989 federal study, gay and lesbian youth account for 30 percent of youth suicides annually.

Two Teenagers in Twenty unites individual voices for a profound effect. Their tones range across humor, sorrow, shame, and joy. A whole spectrum of experiences are represented. There are teens who feel freed by becoming themselves, who suffer the intolerance of their families, who are supported by friends, who find their friends deserting them, and more.

One young woman writes:

"I finally came out to my mother. She accepted it, but she told me that I have one hell of a life ahead of me. She told me it would be easier if I changed. But I can't change, and I don't want to change. I'm seventeen-and-a-half years old, and I have yet to meet another lesbian. I have my whole life ahead of me…if I don't go crazy."

And from a young man:

"We are not second class citizens, and we won't be treated like we are. Right now, I'm in the process of earning a high school diploma through a home-study course. I'm planning to go to college. I realize I'm gay, I'm proud, and I'm gonna get mine!"

This book ends with a helpful bibliography and an information about a pen pal service set up to meet the need for a sense of community and support among young homosexuals. SUSIE WILDE

The Girl with the White Flag: An Inspiring Story of Love and Courage in War Time

📕 Tomiko Higa (translated by Dorothy Britton)
Asian, Japanese
1995 (1991), Kodansha, Ltd., ✳ Japanese

The island of Okinawa lies south of the five main islands known as Japan. It was annexed by Japan in 1871 and was invaded by American forces in April of 1945, less than six months before the end of World War II. *The Girl with the White Flag* is the autobiographical story of Tomiko Higa, who was born in Okinawa and, at the age of seven, was part of the local population that was caught in the crossfire of the horrible seventy-three day campaign in which the Japanese Imperial Army and auxiliary forces lost 94,136 people and the American combined forces lost 12,281. More shocking, however, is the fact that 94,000 Okinawan civilians lost their lives. (Source: Okinawa Prefectural Welfare Support Association and U.S. Army publication *Okinawa: The Last Battle*.)

An inspiring autobiographical account of a young Japanese girl's experiences in WWII.

This, then, is the survival story of one seven-year-old child whose memories of that time were rekindled when she discovered a picture of herself. Now reproduced on the cover, the slightly blurred photograph shows Tomiko walking bravely toward American soldiers with a white flag in her hand. Behind her are Japanese soldiers who had been led to believe that they would be killed if they surrendered.

Four decades after her ordeal, Tomiko tells the story of those days, of her separation from her large family during her flight from the battles, of her search for food even among the dead, and her encounters with brutality, misery, fear, and, finally, with love and kindness. With great courage, Tomiko survived those terrible years, and her exciting and inspiring story is a great aid in giving both Japanese and American readers a broader understanding of this chapter in human history. ANNA PEARCE

Black Misery

📕 Langston Hughes, Introduction by Jesse Jackson, Afterword by Robert G. O'Meally
✎ Arouni
African American
1994 (1967), Oxford University Press, ✳ Series

Langston Hughes was invited to write a children's book, tentatively titled *Black Misery*, in 1967, to follow through on the landslide success of a series of books by Suzanne Heller with the word misery in their titles. It was planned as a series of forty-five illustrations with one-line captions by Hughes. Although Hughes died in 1967, finishing only twenty-seven of the captions, the entries stood complete as they were. They include: "Misery is when you can see all the other kids in the dark but they claim they can't see you": and "Misery is when you heard on the radio that the neighborhood you live in is a slum but you always thought it was home." It is a book about black children's feel-

A moving picture book from the '60s featuring illustrations on the theme of discrimination with witty captions by Langston Hughes.

ings, but also a footnote to the civil rights movement of the 1960s. Children should be guided as they read this book to reflect on things that make them "miserable" and to empathize with others for the misery imposed on them by prejudice and racism.

The 1994 edition comes with an introduction by Jesse Jackson and an afterword by Robert G. O'Meally. Together, they give the background and necessary context for today's readers to interpret Hughes's captions. BELINDA YUN-YING LOUIE

Night Kites

M. E. Kerr
Gay/Lesbian/Bisexual
1987 (1986), Trophy, ✻ Series

Erick's senior year in high school brings changes. He is attracted to his best friend's girlfriend, Nicki, and ends up losing both his best friend and his own girlfriend as a result. He finds out that his older brother, Pete, is gay and has AIDS. Erick is not bothered that his brother is gay; their relationship has always been open and comfortable, and it remains that way. But their parents have a much more difficult time. Harder for him is that he feels he can't tell anyone in his family about Nicki because he thinks they are overburdened with worry for his brother. He can't tell anyone outside of his family about Pete, because his father has ordered them to keep it only within the family.

A complex, thoughtful novel about a white teenager whose gay brother contracts AIDS.

The characters are all believable, though Erick is the only one whose thoughts and feelings are discussed. The parents' reaction is not surprising: They disapprove of their son being gay, but they believe very strongly that family is permanent, and are there for Pete when he needs them. The book's treatment of homosexuality and AIDS focuses on the family's and society's reaction to AIDS and not on the person who is gay or who has AIDS. The author does not necessarily make a point of giving out information about AIDS, but some of the myths about it are addressed through the reactions of some characters.

Pete's behavior as a gay man is, in many ways, a stereotypical one: He slept around, never creating and maintaining a long-term relationship, and in the end contracted AIDS. Pete discusses this openly with Erick, offering explanations, not excuses, for his behavior. The author does not present any easy answers and does not make everything "okay" in the end. The characters remain complicated, with difficult times still ahead of them. SUE FLICKINGER

The Primrose Way

Jackie F. Koller
Algonquin, Native American
1995 (1992), Harcourt Brace and Company, ✻ Series, Moore, Robin, *Bread Sister of Sinking Creek;* Speare, Elizabeth, *Sign of the Beaver.*

Sixteen-year-old Rebekah arrives in the New World in 1633 to be reunited with her father who left England after her mother's death. They are Puritans with strong beliefs governing behavior. Rebekah often finds herself in opposition to these beliefs, in part because her mother taught her to read and think for herself. She tries her best to adjust to her new life, although the settlement of Agawam is little more than a collection of hovels, and she must now do chores formerly done by servants.

Rebekah further sets herself apart from the others by befriending Qunnequawese, the niece of the local Algonquin chief. Rebekah wishes her friend to be "saved," but also finds much to admire in her friend's "heathen" beliefs. Rebekah finds herself thinking more and more of Mishannock, second in command of the Algonquin tribe. The other settlers believe him to be a witch, but Rebekah knows better. She respects the Indian men for the way they treat their women with dignity.

Puritan Rebekah finds her heart captured by "pagan" Native Americans in an involving work of historical fiction.

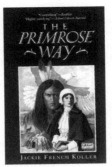

Whenever Rebekah is in trouble, Mishannock is there to save her. The "common sense" of the Indians is contrasted with the extremes of the Puritan's beliefs. Rebekah's educated mind is pitted against the ignorance of many of the settlers. Readers are caught up in Rebekah's turmoil in being torn between two cultures.

Rebekah seals her fate when she joins in the Indians' nikommo, or time of celebration, where she

529

dances with Mishannock publicly. Caught by her father and another elder, she is put in the stocks for three days. Even so, she cannot turn her back on her new friends. Even as she tries to deny her feelings for Mishannock, she goes to his village to help nurse the Indians through a smallpox epidemic. She commits the ultimate blasphemy by praying to both God and the Indian god Kiehtan. Qunnequawese dies, but Mishannock is among the survivors.

Rebekah decides to return to England. But as she begins the voyage, the captain conspires with her to stage her "death" at sea. She is then able to return to Mishannock and be truly free.

This emotion-filled, involving work of historical fiction is part of the excellent Great Episodes Series. The characters are portrayed very realistically, and the author puts great emphasis on historical accuracy. She includes notes on her research along with glossaries of Puritan and Algonquin terms, a pronunciation guide to Indian names, and a bibliography of thirty-seven titles. PAM CARLSON

Ishi In Two Worlds; A Biography of the Last World Indian in North America

▨ Theodora Kroeber ✎ Various sources
Native American, Yahi
1976 (1961), University of California Press,
▥ Kroeber, Theodora, *Ishi.*

This deluxe illustrated edition was from a classic by the wife of Albert Kroeber, the archaeologist who found and studied Ishi, the last Yahi Indian in California. Theodora Kroeber makes Ishi's story accessible to young people.

On August 29, 1911, dogs barked in a slaughter-house yard and awakened the butchers. In the dawn light, they saw a man crouching by the corral. This man was emaciated and unable to speak English. This was Ishi's first contact with the white world. The local sheriff put him in a jail to protect him from the curious local inhabitants of Oroville, California, where he was found. Alfred Kroeber, an anthropologist at the University of California, read a newspaper account of this man's capture and he sent a telegram to Oroville, taking responsibility for the man.

Ishi was to spend his last years in Berkeley

A classic that tells the compelling true story of the last Yahi Indian in California.

with Kroeber and his family. He learned to speak English, but most importantly, he taught Kroeber his language and the traditional culture and skills of his people, the Yahi, who had lived in California for thousands of years. Ishi was the last of his people to practice a traditional way of life in isolation from white society. He revealed to the anthropologist his knowledge of nature and animals, survival skills, and traditional arts that enabled his people to live in relative self-sufficiency for thousands of years. Because he had no previous contact with the white world, Ishi had no immunity to common diseases and died of pneumonia several years after he was found.

Many of the photos taken of Ishi before and after he was studied, and throughout his remaining years with Kroeber, are fascinating. Dr. Kroeber died in 1960, but his wife had already written this account of their years with Ishi and it received Kroeber's approval. This is a compelling, readable, and accurate account for children. *Some discussion should be raised regarding how anthropologists and others study dying civilizations.* ELAINE P. GOLEY

Alan and Naomi

▨ Myron Levoy
Jewish
1987 (1977), Harper Collins, ✳ Video

Against the backdrop of World War II, Myron Levoy's *Alan and Naomi* tells the story of a friendship between twelve-year-old Alan Silverman and Naomi Kirshenbaum. Alan is "just Alan," a sensitive young boy growing up in Queens, New York. He is forced by his parents to befriend Naomi, a French girl his age who has fled France with her mother after witnessing her father's death at the hands of the Gestapo. At the story's opening, Naomi is catatonic, trapped in a prison of terrifying images her mind cannot release. What begins as a burden for Alan is transformed into a beautiful friendship—ultimately, into his first romantic attachment. Through each other, Alan and Naomi discover the joys of friendship as well as the agonizing decisions that accompany the adult world of responsibility and commitment.

An incredibly powerful novel of a boy in 1940's New York who befriends a girl traumatized by Nazi brutality in France.

Like many literary heroes before him, Alan embarks on a quest to define himself in relation to himself, his fantasies, his friends and family. He must rescue Naomi using the only weapons at his disposal: his conscience, active imagination, and sense of humor. The monsters in this story breathe no fire but are even more terrifying: anti-Semitism and other prejudices, insanity, the horror and destruction of war, and the power of the human mind to heal or consume itself. Alan does not feel heroic all the time. He wavers, alternately wallowing in an adolescent lack of self-confidence and fantasizing about being a baseball or war-pilot hero who captures the newspaper headlines.

The theme of fantasy versus reality is reflected in the language Levoy chooses as a foundation for his story. Upon first reading, the fact that Levoy uses the word "crazy" or some variant of it on almost every page may not leap out at the reader, but a second look reveals how pervasive this term and notion is. What is crazy, of course, is the war. Levoy creates ingenious juxtapositions of action and fantasy in which the power, the pleasure, and the perils of the imagination are displayed to the utmost. French and Yiddish expressions are beautifully woven into the text and always defined in context, so readers come away from the book with a much expanded vocabulary in several languages, as well as some familiarity with topics from the poetry of Emily Dickinson to Jewish traditions and the effect of World War II on children and their families. As readers, we ride a roller coaster to the tragedy at the end, crying along with Alan, vainly asking "why" of the barren ground.

While it is unusual for a children's book to end on such a tragic note, by sixth grade most students are ready to explore what it means to lose a friend or relative, and many may have experienced the loss of a grandparent. Because the large issues of prejudice are played out between children of their own age, young readers become deeply engaged in this story, identifying intensely with the finely drawn and brilliantly developed characters, as well as the complicated issues and moral dilemmas the book presents.

One young reader's plea, "But there has to be a sequel," evokes perfectly the power of this book to move us. It was made into a movie in 1991. To attest to the universality of its themes, and the timelessness of its message, suffice it so say that *Alan and Naomi* has already been translated into eight languages—including German.

Teaching Alan and Naomi *is a richly rewarding experience. Parents may be invited to read the book along with their children, to discuss with them the complex questions raised by the text about racism, death, friendship, ethics, and values. For a complete classroom guide to* Alan and Naomi *including background information, bibliography, questions and answers for each chapter, plus writing exercises and activities, write to Bookwise, Inc. 26 Arlington Street, Cambridge, MA 02140.* ELLEN REEVES

Letters From a Slave Girl: The Story of Harriet Jacobs

Mary E. Lyons Todd Doney
African American, Feminist
1992, Charles Scribner's Sons

Harriet Jacobs, born in slavery in 1813, wrote her epistolary autobiography, *Incidents in the Life of a Slave Girl* in 1861. Jacobs's writing is weighed down by the conventions of Victorian style; she was, after all, writing for a largely white, female, decidedly middle-class readership, but author Mary E. Lyons has done a superb job of distilling Jacobs' story into a form accessible to junior-high-level readers.

The story takes place in a nineteenth-century North Carolina coastal town where a large, varied, freed black population mingled with urban slaves, many of whom were highly skilled craftsmen who enjoyed relatively good relations with local whites and a startling degree of apparent autonomy. This was the milieu that produced the fiery black abolitionist David Walker ("Walker's Appeal," 1831) as well as some of the most forceful black leaders of the Reconstruction Period. As a girl in an affectionate household, Harriet learned to read and write. Her letters are addressed to various key figures in her life, with no expectation that they would ever be read by those figures. Harriet writes to her dead parents, her beloved aunt and uncles, and her son. These letters span her life from 1825, when her mistress dies and Harriet is willed to a different branch of the family, until her escape in 1842. During these years, Harriet grows to young womanhood, becomes the unwilling object of her master's lust, falls in love with a free African American (whom her master will not permit her to marry), and bears two children to a white man she perceives

A superb distillation for junior-high readers of the autobiography of an escaped slave.

531

as kinder than her master. Through all this, her vicious, unprincipled master—the town doctor—harasses and threatens her, but never forces her into a sexual relationship. At the point when she believes such force is imminent, she runs from his plantation and hides in a cramped, crawl-space in her grandmother's house. She remains hidden in that tiny space for the next seven years until her escape North is arranged.

The epistolary device occasionally becomes awkward. In some ways, Lyons is more successful presenting Harriet's perceptions of her world than in showing Harriet as a complex human being. Despite this shortcoming, the book fascinates with an enormous amount of detail about the life, economy, and social and race relations in Harriet's small town.

An afterword summarizes Jacobs's life in "freedom"— a frequently terrifying ordeal because of the 1850 Fugitive Slave Law. The after-text material includes family trees, sketches, maps, and photos, a glossary of nineteenth-century words and their contexts, and an extensive bibliography. ROBIN BERSON

Lisa's War

🖊 Carol Matas

Jewish

1991 (1989), Scholastic, Inc.

This story tells of the heroic efforts of Danish Jews and Christians during World War II to transport Danish Jews to the safety of Sweden. In this very well-written book, each character is a real person with flaws as well as stellar traits: The book also tells of traitorous Christians and unheroic Jews, of some of the horrors of the occupation, and of the collaborative effort that made the evacuation from Denmark a success.

A well-written novel about a Jewish girl and her family that explores the reactions of Danish people to Hitler.

The story is narrated by Lisa, a bright Jewish adolescent living in Copenhagen. Lisa's father is a surgeon, and he has arranged safe places in his hospital for Jews to stay until they can be safely transported out of the country. Other Jews have arranged for their own private transportation. Some Danish fisherman risk their lives to rescue the Jews; some of them charge exorbitant prices for the rescue; others do it because of their convictions. Of the 7000 Jews in Denmark at the time, 474 are arrested and sent to concentration camps, and all of the others are transported safely to Sweden.

This book helps to reverse some strong stereotypes: the Jews did not all go as sheep to the slaughter, and, as a matter of fact, many were instrumental in their own rescue. The Danish people were, for the most part, heroic and altruistic, although some were scoundrels. Not all the Jews understood or believed the intent of the German government; some were arrested because they could not accept that they had been singled out for destruction just because they were Jews.

The story examines and unfolds the insanity and terror of the times, but it does not dwell on these. It is, essentially, a story of the heroism of ordinary people, and the possibilities that arise when people of good intent work collaboratively. MASHA RUDMAN

The Chinese Americans

🖊 Milton Meltzer 📷 Archival photographs

Asian American

1980, Thomas Y. Crowell

The Chinese Americans opens with a photo of Utah's Promontory Point on May 10, 1869, the day the first transcontinental railroad was completed. The photo does not include one Chinese face, although the sweat, skill, and muscle of Chinese workers was instrumental in making the impossible dream of the railroad come to fruition. The Chinese faced the same violence, anger, and discriminatory laws and practices that Native Americans, Mexicans, and blacks faced. Immigration acts restricted Chinese wives and families from coming to the United States, and a 1924 law kept out all Asian immigrants.

Despite such restrictions Chinese men worked to establish businesses and communities in the United States. Chinatowns were separated from the rest of the cities—the inhabitants recreated their homeland in America with distinct tastes, values, language, businesses, and news links because they wanted to retain Chinese ideals and were not allowed to live freely elsewhere. The Chinese faced riots in Denver, segregation in San Francisco, low wages in New York, and racism across the country. They continued to fight stereotypes, work for better conditions in low-skilled jobs,

A well-written introduction to Chinese immigration to the United States.

strive for equality in civil rights, and struggle to maintain their culture while becoming proud of their American heritage as well.

Meltzer's well-researched and documented text describes some of the hardships and triumphs faced by Chinese immigrants while they carved out a distinct piece of American society. While one book cannot encompass the experiences of the Chinese in the United States, this is a well-written, vividly illustrated, and easy-to-read beginning foray for youth and adults that includes an index and bibliography for reference and more information.

ALISON WASHINGTON

Frederick Douglass In His Own Words

📖 Milton Meltzer ✒ Stephen Alcorn

African American

1995, Harcourt Brace and Company

Many have written about Frederick Douglass, one of America's most powerful orators and champions of rights for blacks, women, and the poor, but Douglass's own speeches and writings reveal the strength and conviction of his vision. Meltzer deftly chooses a varied and illustrative cross-section of Douglass's recountings of his life as a slave and determination to be literate and free; his reflections on race relations, politics, and the Mexican American and Civil Wars; and his comments on economic freedom for blacks, unjust laws, and social reforms. Douglass discusses his escape to freedom, his trials in the north, and his initial exposure to the abolitionist movement and William Lloyd Garrison. After hearing Garrison speak, Douglass chose to tell others his own life story—despite the possibility of recapture—and devote his life to ending slavery and improving the lot of his people. Meltzer provides introductions to each selection, but it is Douglass's own clear, blunt, and truthful words that give insight into the man, the institution of slavery, and the country's unresolved racial and social conflicts.

A boldly illustrated collection of speeches, editorials, and letters from an early leader in the fight for black rights.

The book includes an index, bibliography, and biographical vignettes about Douglass's friends, mentors, and contemporaries such as William Lloyd Garrison, Susan B. Anthony, Ida B. Wells-Barnett, and Charles Sumner. What might be cause for discussion or controversy are Alcorn's bold, striking, and almost distractingly intense illustrations. Alcorn himself writes that the brown and black linocuts—prints made from designs cut into linoleum—provide "a dramatic visual backdrop... imbued with textures and patterns bursting with energy" and are "a visual equivalent to that elusive, indomitable spirit that could not be broken." Readers will not have lukewarm responses to the illustrations and must decide if they detract from or accentuate the text.

ALISON WASHINGTON

Rescue: The Story of How Gentiles Saved Jews in the Holocaust

📖 ✒ Milton Meltzer

Jewish

1991 (1988), HarperCollins

Meltzer has won many awards for his writing in the fields of history, biography, and social reform. His meticulous research is translated into works of nonfiction that read like novels. In this book, Meltzer first chronicles the history of anti-Semitism and then reports on Hitler's rise and the consequent oppression of Jews in Germany. He also tells of the collusion of most of the other countries of the world, who not only failed to oppose Hitler's actions, but also refused to accept Jewish escapees from Germany within their boundaries. Beginning with *Kristallnacht*, a nationwide pogrom against the Jews in 1938, it was clear that Hitler's intention was to murder all Jews. Systematic starvation, shooting, burning, and gassing of Jews were instituted, and few non-Jews had the courage or willingness to help.

A helpful book on Gentiles who risked their lives to save Jews from the Holocaust.

But, in this book, Meltzer tells of those brave and righteous few who did care and who did summon the courage to act. Depicting individuals such as Oskar

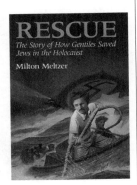

RESCUE
The Story of How Gentiles Saved Jews in the Holocaust
Milton Meltzer

533

534

Schindler, the Countess Marushka, and King Boris of Bulgaria; whole towns led by people such as Andre Trocme; and whole countries, such as Denmark, these stories help readers understand that bravery and virtue are possible in all instances, and that they make a difference in this world. Meltzer's book, written and published five years before Steven Spielberg's film *Schindler's List*, pays tribute to these individuals and nations.

The author gives many details about each of the rescuers and the way in which the Jews were rescued. He uses personal quotations and documents of the time to make each instance come alive. He demonstrates how important was each person's act of heroism, and how it is possible to combat even the worst forms of despotism. MASHA RUDMAN

Prejudice: Stories about Hate, Ignorance, Revelation, and Transformation

Daphne Muse
African American
1995, Hyperion Books

In the introduction to *Prejudice: Stories about Hate, Ignorance, Revelation, and Transformation*, Daphne Muse (the editor of this guide) reminds us that prejudice affects everyone. "In classrooms, on the playground, at home, and even in places of worship, prejudice invades almost every aspect of our lives," she writes. She encourages us to take another look at ourselves, and how we think about and treat other people.

Short stories and novel excerpts addressing bigotry and the way people unlearn hate.

The anthology is a collection of fifteen short stories or excerpts from novels by such writers as Marie G. Lee, Jacqueline Woodson, Flannery O'Connor, and Ntozake Shange. They examine racism, sexism and classism, pointing out that, as much as prejudice limits us and creates fear, it can also give us a false sense of power. More importantly, the stories highlight personal transformations. We soon realize that attitudes and beliefs can change and that people can always become more open and caring.

In Chris Crutcher's "A Brief Moment in the Life of Angus Bethune" Angus goes in the course of one evening, from being a fat teenager with a poor self-image to a fat teenager with a whole lot of fans.

"I'd sure be willing to go into the winter trade meetings and swap reflexes, biceps, and brain cells, lock, stock, and barrel, for a little physical beauty," Angus quips to himself.

Later that evening, though, he becomes the center of attention at a school dance. "A crowd gathers, and I'm trapped inside a cheering circle, actually performing the unheard of: I'm Angus Bethune, Fat Man Extraordinaire, dancing in the limelight with Melissa Lefevre, stepping outside the oppressive prison of my body to fly to the beat of Credence Clearwater Revival." CHRISTINA ENG

Songs That Promote Justice

BOB PETERSON

Following are a few songs that I use in my classroom:
"Bread and Roses," by Judy Collins
"Deportee," by Woody Guthrie
"Follow the Drinking Gourd" by The Kim and Reggie Harris Group
"Happy Birthday, Martin Luther King," by Stevie Wonder
"The Harder They Come," by Jimmy Cliff
"Harriet Tubman," by Holly Near and Ronnie Gilbert
"I Cried," by Holly Near
"Lawless Avenue," by Jackson Browne
"Lives in the Balance," by Jackson Browne
"On Monday," by Leadbelly
"Mr. Wendal," by Speech and Arrested Development
"My Country 'Tis of Thee My People Are Dying," by Buddy St. Marie
"The Letter," by Ruben Blades
"New Underground Railroad," by Holly Near and Ronnie Gilbert
"1913 Massacre," by Woody Guthrie and Jack Elliot
"Sambo Lando," by Seves/Manns
"The Secret Life of Plants," by Stevie Wonder
"Sister Rosa," by The Neville Brothers
"There But for Fortune," by Phil Ochs
"Unite Children," by The Children of Selma
"We Are the Champions," by Queen
"Where Have All the Buffalo Gone?" by Buddy St. Marie
"Why?" by Tracy Chapman
"You Can Get It If You Really Want," by Jimmy Cliff

Bob Peterson is an elementary school teacher at La Escuela Fratney, Milwaukee, Wisconsin.

If I Should Die Before I Wake

Han Nolan
Jewish
1996 (1994), Harcourt Brace Jovanovich

With hate crimes and anti-Semitism still prevalent in our society, this novel provokes the kind of reflection that can change lives. Sixteen-year-old Hilary Burkes hates Jews, finding her sense of group identity through participation in a neo-Nazi gang in her town. When she is critically injured in a motorcycle accident with her boyfriend Brad, she learns an extraordinary lesson that changes her life.

An extremely powerful novel about a neo-Nazi transported into the life of a Jewish teenager during World War II.

Deep in a coma in the Jewish Hospital, Hilary finds herself transported to Poland during World War II, where she is transformed into a young Jew named Chana. Forced from their home by the Nazis and marched off to the infamous Lodz ghetto, Chana and her family watch as people are driven to desperate acts. Those who survive life in the ghetto are shipped off to Auschwitz for mass slaughter.

Without sensationalizing the subject or writing sound-bite history, Nolan takes young people into a world they need to know and understand. The virulent hatred is seen in its contemporary form when Brad, Hilary's boyfriend, kidnaps Simon, one of the Jewish boys at school, in the name of "The Cause": "I hated Simon. I hated his stupid beanie, and his schoolbooks carried like silly treasures in his monogrammed backpack, and those squeaky leather shoes. I hated

that he enjoyed gardening. I hated hearing his voice through is living room window on those stinkin' summer nights, chanting in some spitty foreign language. And I hated his freakin' happy family where nothing ever went wrong."

The story is powerful, emotionally compelling, and unsettling in capturing the voice of bigotry. It is for those more mature readers equipped to endure the pain, and reach for some kind of understanding. DAPHNE MUSE

Addy's Surprise: A Christmas Story

Connie Porter   Melodye Rosales
African American
1993, Pleasant Company, ✳ Series

The third book in The American Girls Collection—stories about five American girls who lived long ago—is *Addy's Surprise: A Christmas Story* , about an African American girl's first winter in Philadelphia. It is 1864, and Addy Walker and her mother, Connie, have escaped from a Southern plantation to the North and freedom. But they also experience loneliness, hardship, and life in a freezing garret.

Author Connie Porter, wastes no time setting up contrasts between blacks and whites, and rich and poor, and building a plot around the dress that Addy wants and the

A happy if predictable story of an African American Christmas over 100 years ago with lovely illustrations.

kerosene lamp that her mother hopes for in this happy if predictable Christmas story. Porter's illustrations offers an historically accurate depiction of urban life after slavery. She deftly paints a city and a period where emancipation seems to be working in two ways. When Mrs. Ford, Connie's employer, defends her against a rich, white customer— the angry and irrational Mrs. Howell— we know that Mrs. Ford welcomes the chance to demonstrate her own liberalness after the Civil War; when Addy donates her savings to Reverend Drake's Freedmen's Fund rather than purchase a coveted red wool scarf for her mother's Christmas present, we know that she has understood the meaning of her family's sacrifice and the significance of her own freedom.

In addition to the lovely illustrations, part of the charm of this series can be found in the afterwords. In this case, "Looking Back 1864: A Peek Into the Past," provides an excellent context for the story. Here, Christmas's of North and South, and black and white are presented. Customs regarding gift-giving, food, and religious practices are described, drawing sharp contrasts between the practices of enslaved families and soldiers at the front, and the more fortunate Northern white families and Southern plantation-owning families. Especially valuable is the description of Philadelphia's Mother Bethel Methodist and Episcopal Church, the obvi-

535

ous model for Reverend Moore's church, and its role in providing help for newly escaped and, later, emancipated families. This section ends with a very useful account of black Christmas traditions and of the establishment of Kwanzaa to honor African American heritage. MARY FROSCH

Roll of Thunder, Hear My Cry

📖 Mildred Taylor ✏ Jerry Pinkney

African American

1995 (1976), Puffin, ✱ Audio Cassette, Series

This story, the first in a trilogy, introduces the Logan family and their struggle to keep up a boycott against a local store while trying to hold on to their land in Mississippi in the 1930s. It won a Coretta Scott King Award and helped to establish Mildred Taylor as one of the country's leading authors of books for young adults.

In an award-winning seminal work, a black child in the 1930s learns about injustice and pride.

The Logan children— Cassie, her older brother, Stacey, and younger brothers, Little-Man and Christopher-John—discover that the people in their community who are poorly educated are treated with little or no respect by most whites, and are, of necessity, cautious in almost all interracial interactions. They learn that for a black man to become angry or act violently against a white man inevitably ends in disaster or death for the former; this idea passes painfully through the Logans' lives when their friend T. J. is swept into crime with the white Simms boys but is the only one who pays for it. Cassie finds out that "how things are" is not always how they should be, and that knowledge brings about her tears for "those things which happened in the night and would not pass." Her education about life is an abrupt, harsh one, but it is tempered by the strength and wisdom she finds in her community.

The author uses her stories to educate young people about the emotions and events that helped drive the civil rights movement in later years. Her tales combine events in her own family's life with the collective experiences of other blacks. The Logans are a strong extended family that tries to understand racism while teaching the children that the status quo does not have to be accepted.

ALISON WASHINGTON

Bearing Witness: Stories of the Holocaust

📖 Hazel Rochman ✏ Darlene Z. McCampbell

Jewish

1995, Orchard, 📕 Feeling, Tom, *The Middle Passage*; Yolen, Jane, *The Devil's Arithmetic*; Zar, Rose, *In the Mouth of the Wolf.*

This is an outstanding collection of stories featuring a breadth of experiences and voices. In Hans Richter's "For Jews Only," for example a budding romance is almost destroyed when a yellow marker for Jews-only park bench becomes an issue between a man and his Gentile lover. Excerpts from Primo Levi's *Survival in Auschwitz* are bone chilling, but Ida Fink's "Splinter" is a more subtle tale.

As a separate issue, I long for more stories that focus on Jewish life beyond the Holocaust. My concern continues as more and more books on the Holocaust are published. I feel that all too often the Holocaust becomes the defining point for Jewish people and their culture. Relegating any group to an "historical ghetto" deprives those outside of the culture from really understanding the richer role they have played in civilization. I am also concerned that, with few exceptions, most books on the Holocaust fail to acknowledge the fact that gypsies, gays, and even some black people were forced into Nazi concentration camps.

This outstanding multi-genre anthology explores a wide range of Holocaust experiences.

There also remains a need for a comparative anthology examining slavery, the Jewish Holocaust, Native American removal, atrocities against women, the modern-day practices of slavery, and ethnic cleansing.

This is a collection that should be used with some real preparation. These stories are not easy to read, nor are they comfortable or comforting stories. They are explorations of what happens when prejudice festers and escalates to annihilation. Teachers, parents, and librarians might want to have Holocaust survivors come and share their stories first and talk about some of the selections in this anthology. A discussion that brings in comparisons with other historical atrocities might also serve to build a better bridge of understanding.

For additional reading on the Holocaust, Jane Yolen's The Devil's Arithmetic *and Rose Zar's* In the

Mouth of the Wolf *would further enlighten young readers. For a comparative examination of historical atrocities, Tom Feelings'* The Middle Passage *might serve as an interesting point for departure.*
DAPHNE MUSE

Somehow Tenderness Survives: Stories of Southern Africa

▣ Edited by Hazel Rochman
African, South Africa
1992 (1989), HarperCollins, ✷ Series,
📖 Laure, Jason, and Ettagale, Laure, *South Africa: Coming of Age Under Apartheid*; Naidoo, Beverly, *Journey to Jo'Burg: A South African Story.*

The spirit and resilience of South Africa are captured in this collection of ten stories by well-known and emerging South African writers. In spite of apartheid, economic deprivation, and a land scarred by terror, tenderness survives in South Africa, and these stories reflect that. They vividly illustrate how deeply racism affects personal identity.

Ten short stories by South Africans on how apartheid has shaped their society.

Some of the stories explore adolescent angst; the loneliness and self-hatred of mixed-race teenagers; how one young man violates the best in himself to fit in with white supremacy; and the radicalization of a traditional Indian woman who prints illegal political pamphlets to support an African worker's strike.

Nadine Gordimer's "Country Lovers" chronicles the ironic fate of two illicit lovers—a black woman and a white man—and the murder of their child. In Mark Mathabane's "The Road to Alexandra," a young black boy watches as the police break down the door of his home and drag his father to prison because his identification papers are not in order.

These stories reflect the ethnic and racial diversity of South Africa and the commonality of pain, even for the oppressors. The themes also focus on peer pressure and the emotional and intellectual bonding that occurs in a friendship. Editor Hazel Rochman has been judicious in her inclusion; five of the writers are black, and five white. Rochman also made selections that provide readers with a look into the lives of those who live in both urban and rural settings. But the themes reflect a broader and much more inclusive view of South Africa under apartheid.

Young readers and teachers may also find *South Africa: Coming of Age Under Apartheid* by Jason Laure and Ettagale Laure, and *Journey to Jo'Burg: A South African Story* by Beverly Naidoo interesting companion pieces to this collection. DAPHNE MUSE

Let the Circle Be Unbroken

▣ Mildred D. Taylor ✎ Max Ginsburg
African American
1995 (1981), Puffin Books, ✷ Series

Taylor's second novel about the fictional Logan family focuses on relations between blacks and whites in 1930's America. Young Cassie Logan narrates. The story opens with the murder trial of a family friend, T. J. Avery. The children must face

A southern Black family combats an unjust legal system during the Depression in a lengthy but compelling novel.

the brutal realities of a biased legal system that ignores the rights of blacks and forbids them even to serve on juries. Wade Jamison, a white lawyer and friend of the Logans, tries to keep T. J. out of jail, but he is unsuccessful.

After witnessing the trial, Stacey, the oldest Logan child, decides that there is little future in Mississippi for blacks, because whites can take away their livelihood and freedom, mistreat and degrade them, and use their influence to dominate the legal, and financial system to the detriment of black citizens. Stacey makes an ill-timed decision to run away to work in the Louisiana sugar cane fields, and his family is almost wrenched apart trying to bring him home.

Meanwhile, Cassie befriends Jake Willis, a black man whose spirit has been broken. He becomes, for her, an object lesson in the destructive efforts of self-hatred. Later, when landowners break up a developing interracial farm union by preying on the poor whites' tendency to look down on blacks, it becomes clear to her that racism is often the product of misplaced pride. Cassie shares her community's frustration when their rights are denied them—as in the case of an elderly black woman who yearns to vote, a sharecropper's son who wants to own the land he works, or a boy who wants to be treated with respect by his white peers. This story also contrasts Cassie's self-assurance and sense of identity with her half-white, torn-between-two-worlds cousin, Suzella. However, the story is not unremittingly negative in

537

538

its treatment of whites—a white boy, Simms, is very much a part of the Logans' life. They have a "slightly baffled and wary affection for this 'sport' who refuses to hate them," and realize that he has had a powerful influence on how they feel about whites. This well-written story, filled with descriptive detail, is lengthy but compelling, and the pages will pass quickly for readers. ALISON WASHINGTON

The Road to Memphis

📖 Mildred D. Taylor, Edited by Phyllis J. Fogelman
✒ Max Ginsburg
African American
1992 (1990), Puffin Books, 📖 Taylor, Mildred D., *Roll of Thunder, Hear My Cry.*

Set in Mississippi in the 1930s this prequel to *Roll of Thunder, Hear My Cry* is narrated by twelve-year-old Cassie Logan. T.J. goes on trial for murder and

A thought-provoking novel about an African American girl's life in 1941 Mississippi.

receives the death penalty from an all-white jury. This eventful book includes a number of thought-provoking episodes:

Sharecroppers are forced to plant less crops and receive less pay while landlords claim money from crops belonging to them. The union repeatedly tries to help the sharecroppers but are chased out of town by the landowners.

Miz Lee Annie laboriously studies the Mississippi Constitution, tries to register to vote, and is turned away. Eventually she is kicked off the land because

her attempt to register to vote is viewed as disrespecting her landlord.

Cousin Bud arrives to inform Mama that he married a white woman and now has a mulatto daughter, Suzella. Because Bud and his wife are having marital problems, Suzella spends six months with the Logan family. Initially, Cassie is jealous of the attention Suzella attracts. As they get to know each other, Cassie and Suzella grow close. Cassie is confused by Suzella's efforts to pass for being white so she will have a better life.

When Jeremy Simms gives each Logan child a photograph of himself, Uncle Hammer finds

Cassie's and flies into a rampage about never trusting a white man. Although Papa mistrusts white people, he tells Cassie he hopes she sees the day when things will change between the blacks and whites.

When Papa goes to Louisiana to work on the railroad, Stacey runs away with two friends to work in a sugar cane field, leaving behind no address. The family relentlessly searches for him while Stacey is badly mistreated and ends up in jail. After numerous attempts, Papa finally rescues Stacey and brings him home. "I done come home and it's the very best place to be." ALISON WASHINGTON

Red Tail Angels: The Story of the Tuskegee Airmen of World War II

📖 Patricia McKissack and Frederick McKissack
✒ Various sources
African American
1995 (1995), Walker and Company

Although they have long been recognized in the African American community, they have had to struggle to gain the widespread recognition

A fascinating story of the Tuskegee Airmen of World War II.

the Tuskegee Airmen deserved for their role in helping America to win World War II. Established in 1941 to train black pilots to fight in World War II, the 99th Fighter Squadron was expected to be a military failure. But this group of Tuskegee, Alabama, men shocked the army and the world by never losing a bomber and bringing home 150 Distinguished Flying Crosses and Legions of Merit. Based on their own stories, this book accompanies the airmen on their adventures, from training exercises to aerial acrobatics.

With their usual attention to detail, the McKissacks place the story in a well-researched historical context. Although more than 200,000 black men served overseas in World War I, and members of all-black units were honored by the French government, America paid little attention to those accomplishments. When World War II began, blacks in the armed forces were still treated with disdain and used in only the most menial positions. But, undaunted by racism and segregation, and determined to do their part to defend their country, men like Benjamin O. Davis Jr. and Wendell Pruitt went on to become legends in the field of military aviation.

While the book focuses primarily on the Tuskegee Airmen of World War II, the McKissacks include extensive information about the larger history of black men and women in aviation and the military. This may not be the kind of book young people will simply sit down and read from cover to cover, but it is filled with fascinating details and information that will bring them back time and again. Especially appealing are archival photographs that include pictures of women pilots and vintage airplanes.

A fine depiction of the role African Americans have played in the shaping of this country, *Red Tail Angels* is an excellent companion to such books as *The Civil Rights Movement in America From 1865 to the Present* and *A Long Hard Journey* for teaching units on the African American experience. DAPHNE MUSE

Journey Home

📕 Yoshiko Uchida ✒ Charles Robinson
Asian American, Japanese American
1992 (1978), Aladdin Books

A sequel to *Journey to Topaz*, this is a poignant and compassionate story of a Japanese American girl, Yuki Sakane, and her family's struggle for survival after they are released from Topaz, a World War II Japanese internment camp in America. Until the California exclusion order that prohibited Japanese from living on the West Coast was revoked, the family lived in a small apartment in Salt Lake City. When they finally returned to their home in Berkeley, California, the family faced anti-Japanese sentiment and other problems lingering from the war. Among these problems, the Sakanes have difficulty finding a place to live and a way to earn money to support themselves. Yuki's family combine their resources and strength with those of other Japanese Americans to begin reconstructing their lives. Eventually, they find new hope and strength in themselves, and Yuki learns the true meaning of home, discovering that coming home is "a matter of the heart and spirit."

A poignant novel of Japanese American family's struggles after their release from an internment camp.

The Sakanes' story is an authentic one based on the author's experience during this time period. Readers are offered a look into a tragic time in our history from the perspective of Japanese Americans. *This powerful story of the Sakane family evokes strong emotions and creates an opportunity to discuss such issues as racial prejudice and the impact of war on people's lives.* CATHY Y. KIM

Journey to Topaz: A Story of the Japanese American Evacuation

📕 Yoshiko Uchida ✒ Donald Carrick
Asian American, Japanese American
1995 (1971), Scribner, ✳ Braile,
📖 Uchida, Yoshiko, *Journey Home*.

Based on the true experiences of Yoshiko Uchida and her family, this story captures the bitter realities faced by Japanese Americans during World War II. When the Japanese bombed Pearl Harbor in 1941, eleven-year-old Yuki Sakane and her family were sent to live in an internment camp. Even though Yuki and her brother, Ken, are both American citizens, they are forced to leave their home in Berkeley, California. Because of their Japanese ancestry, Yuki and Ken's parents are forbidden by the laws of that time from becoming citizens. Declared enemy aliens, Yuki's family, along with other Japanese Americans, are sent first to a camp in California and then to a barren desert camp in Utah named Topaz.

A powerful 1970's novel based on the author's experience of an internment camp as a Japanese American girl.

Without their father, who is sent to a prison camp in Montana due to his active involvement in the Japanese American community, Yuki and her family adjust to the harsh conditions with their new-found friends in the camp. Although they face terrifying dust storms in the desert and inadequate facilities in the camp, the Japanese Americans in the camp remain hopeful about some day returning to their home on the West Coast. Interested readers can seek out Uchida's sequel to this book, *Journey Home*, which tells of the Sakanes' return to California after the war. CATHY Y. KIM

Mississippi Challenge

Mildred Pitts Walter ☎ Archival photographs
African American

1995 (1992), Simon & Schuster, 📖 Day, Frances
Ann, *Teacher's Guide from Multicultural Voices in
Contemporary Literature;* McKissack, Patricia,
and McKissack, Frederick, *The Civil Rights
Movement in America.*

This carefully researched book describes the determined struggle by African Americans for civil rights
in Mississippi, from the abhorrent days of slavery
to the signing of the Voting Rights Act of 1965.
With passion and clarity, Mildred Pitts Walter
writes about the Missis-
sippi Challenge, a strug-
gle that lasted more than
a century and that stands
out in history as testimony to the determination
and strength of a people
who eventually won their
right to vote.

*An in-depth
history of the civil
rights struggle in
Mississippi, with
accounts of legal
challenges,
personal testi-
mony and photos.*

Known for her ability
to speak directly to the
hearts of her readers,
Walter has taken an important segment of United
States history and brought it alive through the
authentic voices of activists, historians, volunteers,
and writers. Each chapter is prefaced with stirring
words from a freedom song, spiritual, poem, or
book. Black-and-white photographs of leaders such
as Fannie Lou Hamer and Bob Moses augment the
power of the written words.

Subjected to threats, harassment, violence and
the systematic denial of their political and economic rights for more than two centuries, the African
Americans of Mississippi continued to believe in
democracy and their rights as citizens. With chapter titles such as "Sit-Ins, Stand-Ins, Wade-Ins and
Kneel-Ins," Walter documents the perseverance
of a people determined to overcome their oppression. The sometimes complicated legal battles are

also personalized through the voices of the people
involved.

Part One deals with the uncertain status of African
Americans during the Civil War and the setbacks of
the Reconstruction Period, including the controversy
surrounding the Freedman's Bureau. Part Two
examines positive forces for change such as the
Mississippi Freedom Democratic Party (MFDP) and
the Student Nonviolent Coordinating Committee
(SNCC). The author documents the relentless hostility and violence encountered by those such as the
young freedom fighters James Chaney, Andrew
Goodman, and Michael Schwerner who worked to
register voters .

Mississippi Challenge, a Coretta Scott King Honor
Book, is chilling in its revelation of the incredible
lengths to which some white Mississippians were
willing to go to maintain their privilege. But it is
equally inspiring in its portrayal of black Mississippians who had the courage to fight back against
incredible odds. This is a compelling account of
heroes and heroines, both sung and unsung, who
worked together to make a difference. Mildred Pitts
Walter provides her readers with examples of people
who put their lives on the line for their beliefs.
Mississippi Challenge includes a bibliography and
extensive index for readers who are interested in
further research.

*Some readers might want to read the biographies of
the people highlighted in the books such as Fannie Lou
Hamer, Medgar Evers, and Ida B. Wells. Others might
be drawn to other books by Mildred Pitts Walter such
as* Because We Are *and* The Girl on the Outside;
additional books about civil rights are The Civil
Rights Movement in America *and* Taking a Stand
Against Racism and Racial Discrimination *both by
Patricia and Frederick McKissack. Students might
also be encouraged to analyze their United States textbooks to compare and contrast how the information in*
Mississippi Challenge *is treated. Class discussions of
omission as a form of bias that results in the distortion
of history might lead to further insights and, hopefully,
to recommendations for change.* FRANCES A. DAY

CHAPTER 8

BUILDING CROSS-CULTURAL RELATIONSHIPS

~~~~~~

For all the discussions of the importance of identifying bias-free literature and respecting cultural diversity, the most difficult task teachers face is incorporating new materials into already over-crowded classroom schedules, and using these materials to foster cross-cultural understanding among their students. In this chapter, Sara Simonson suggests ways to develop trust and turn the classroom into a community of learners; Patricia L. Marshall considers the obstacles and fears teachers confront in dealing with an ever-more diverse student body; and other essays offer practical tips to using multicultural materials effectively—and not just superficially—in the classroom. Key ideas include biracial/interracial relationships, second language acquisition, unlearning stereotypes, and sharing cultural traditions.

DAPHNE MUSE

Kindergarten to Grade Three

A Chorus of Cultures

📖 Alma Flor Ada, Edited by Violet J. Harris, Lee Bennett Hopkins, Morissa Lipstein, Jane McCreary, Christine McNamara, and D. J. Simison

Multicultural

1993, Hampton-Brown Books

This exceptional poetry anthology is a must for classroom teachers in elementary, middle, and high schools. Created specifically for use in school, the collection also includes twenty eight songs, music tapes, small books,

An excellent anthology of multicultural poems for every day of the year along with valuable teaching suggestions.

and charts (one for language development and a set for cultural heritage).

Arranged like a calendar, the book presents a poem for every day of the year. Within each month are poems reflecting a broad range of multicultural experiences from such writers as Nikki Giovanni, Langston Hughes, Wing Tek Lum, José Marti, and Gwendolyn Brooks. One of the most powerful and bold aspects of this anthology is the inclusion of children's voices, solicited from teachers around the country, with those of highly recognized poets. Rarely have I seen a book honor children's voices with the respect and dignity of this presentation.

The editors begin the anthology with a discussion of their editorial philosophy. The poems were selected for "literary merit and variety, appeal to children, representation of many different authors from a variety of cultures, cultural authenticity, significant themes, and instructional value." The introduction then explains the book's layout. Each month begins with a summary of noteworthy themes and days, and, for those holidays which do not fall on a consistent day, there is a page in the appendix with cultural and religous celebrations through the year 2003. (This index includes Chinese, Hebrew, Islamic, and Christian calendars.) *The daily selections are grouped around themes, and include teaching notes, additional notes on the text, and instructional activities for using poetry across the curriculum. There are also notes on activities to* help develop literacy. Footnotes for meaning and pronunciation of unfamiliar words are also provided.

There are indexes that outline poems appropiate for use with ESL *students and an index of poems for use across the curriculum (math and science, for example). The introduction alone is a wealth of information on pedagogy and multiculturalism. The anthology itself is carefully thought out and developed for teacher friendliness and useability.* But the most important thing about this anthology is the poetry. This is no fluffy mishmash of food, fun, and festivals. The anthology includes sophisticated poems, respects children's ability to deal with hard issues, and gives voice to timeless concerns. DEBBIE WEI

The Three Wishes: A Collection of Puerto Rican Folktales

📖 Ricardo E. Alegria ✏ Lorenzo Homar

Hispanic, Puerto Rican

1969, Harcourt, Brace, Jovanovich

Engaging children in the power and history of storytelling, these twenty-three Puerto Rican folktales highlight the rich African, Spanish, and indigenous folktale tradition that makes up this country's culture

"The Animal Musicians" focuses on aging. A donkey, goat, dog, cat, and rooster are going to be killed by their owners because they are "old and useless." They escape and form an orchestra to earn their living. Eventually they are able to stay together, living happily without the company of humans. In "The Rabbit and the Tiger," a manipulative rabbit always man-

Twenty-three mostly entertaining folktales depicting the Taino, Spanish, and African heritages of Puerto Rico.

ages to get his way at the expense of others; in this case, the tiger is the victim. Tricks abound in this playful story of trust and friendship.

The Juan Bobo tales feature a simple peasant boy who is not quite in touch with reality. These tales are sometimes quite disturbing to read because of how his mother treats him: she is both verbally and physically abusive. The particular tales included in this collection offer a somewhat demeaning portrayal of Puerto Ricans. In essence, we are presented with a teenaged boy who misinterprets everything his mother asks him to do. What is at first comical—the character of the Puerto Rican *jíbaro* (peasant from the countryside)—becomes degrading. Another book of Juan Bobo tales, retold by Carmen T. Bernier Grand, portrays the protagonist in a very different light.

Overall, however, this collection includes entertaining tales that both children and adults will enjoy. ELIZABETH CAPIFALI

All in a Day

▣ Mitsumasa Anno ✎ Ronald Brooks, et al.
Multicultural
1990 (1986), The Putnam Publishing Group

Conceived by Japanese author and illustrator Mitsumasa Anno to encourage peace and understanding among the world's children, *All in a Day* chronicles the same twenty-four-hour period in the lives of children in eight different countries, showing the differences but stressing the similarities. It features art by Anno and nine other internationally known children's artists: Raymond Briggs (England), Ron Brooks (Australia), Gian Calvi (Brazil), Eric Carle (United States), Zhu Chengliang (China), Leo and Diane Dillon (United States), Akiko Hayashi (Japan), and Nicolai Ye Popov (Russia). The stories can be read as one continuous narrative, or as a review of short stories. Subjects range from the triumphant return of a kitten, who rescues her mistress's purloined shuttlecock, to a family camping trip.

Nine internationally known children's artists follow one day in the lives of children in eight different countries in this alluring, if hard-to-follow, book.

Translated from Japanese, the text may be a little hard for children to follow without some adult help, but the idea that youngsters all over the world sleep, eat, and play in much the same way comes across clearly. Brightly colored illustrations, in distinctly different styles, create an alluring dynamic within the book. The breathtaking illustrations of Caldecott Award-winning illustrators Leo and Diane Dillon, for example, contrast with the rhythmic visual technique of Brazil's Gian Calvi.

A note addressed to parents and older readers briefly explains the author's intention in creating *All in a Day*. An explanation of international time zones, and of how a country's location in the northern or southern hemisphere determines the timing of its seasons accounts for why the children are simultaneously awake and asleep, playing in the snow, and swimming in the ocean. LYNN EISENHUT

Here Comes the Cat!: Siuda idet Kot!

▣ ✎ Frank Asch, Vladimir Vagin
Russian
1993 (1989), Scholastic, Inc., ✴ Bilingual English/Russian, ▥ Bunting, Eve, *The Terrible Things: An Allegory of the Holocaust*.

The publisher states that this almost wordless picture book, first published in 1989, is the "first book in the world designed by an American and painted by a Russian." The book is designed like a cartoon strip with word balloons that all bear the same message in Russian and English: "Here comes the cat." The colorful pictures show individual and groups of mice spreading this alarming message through the air, under water, in the towns, at entertainment centers, workplaces, and apartments. At the end, a crowd of fearful mice "persons" wait anxiously in the town square as the shadow of the cat looms on the opposite page. But what arrives is only a large grinning cat pulling an enormous cheese on a wagon. The final page shows a happily resting cat being groomed and fed by mice, while other mice are busy cutting up the cheese and joyously sharing it with everyone.

A town of mice dread the arrival of a cat, who turns out to be a lovable friend, in a colorful allegory co-produced by Russians and Americans.

Young children will enjoy the story, and adults and older students will realize how this cartoon serves as an allegory of two former Cold War enemies. Pronunciations of the Russian words are provided so that children can learn how to say "Here comes the cat" in Russian.

Another look at unknown fear—this time being realized—can be seen in Eve Bunting's picture book *The Terrible Things: An Allegory of the Holocaust*. GLORIA D. JACKSON

Where the Forest Meets the Sea

📖 📎 Jeannie Baker
Australian
1993 (1988), Greenwillow Scholastic, Inc.

Where the Forest Meets the Sea, is set in the rainforest of the Daintree Wilderness of Australia. A young boy and his father spend the day in the wild; the

A young boy and his father share their concerns about an Australian forest's survival.

father fishing while the boy explores. As the boy walks further into the forest, he imagines the history of the land by pretending it is a hundred million years ago. He mentions dinosaurs of long ago, kangaroos and crocodiles that used to live in the forest, and wonders if aboriginal children used to play in the hollow trees he finds. At the end of the day he shares fish his father has caught and wonders when, or if, they will return to the forest. The story ends by questioning whether the forest will still be there when they come back.

The story is accompanied by relief collages which Baker created from materials collected in the Daintree Wilderness and other assorted art materials. The richness of these collages draws the reader into the story and gives a feeling of being in the rainforest with the boy. She also uses shadowy drawings over some collages to further convey images from the past, such as the dinosaur and the crocodile. The drawing of the future shows the forest developed into highrises and vacation activity.

At the end of the book is a brief description of the Daintree Wilderness and an expression of concern for its survival. Rainforests around the world are currently the focus of many preservation efforts. *This book could be used to begin discussion about the value of and need for rainforests.* DEBORAH PATTERSON

Thirteen Moons on Turtle's Back: A Native American Year of Moons

📖 Joseph Bruchac and Jonathan London
📎 Thomas Locker
Native American
1992, Putnam Publishing Group, ✳ Audio Cassette

Known for his extensive volume of works on Native folklore, as well as his publishing company, The Greenfield Review Press, Abenaki storyteller and poet Joseph Bruchac offers authority and accuracy.

Bruchac teamed with poet Jonathan London to create this collection of poems that feature names used by Native Americans for the moons, or months, in a year. Artist Thomas Locker's richly-hued oil landscapes complement and enliven each of the thirteen poems.

In their notes, Bruchac and London explain that many Native peoples view the thirteen scales on Turtle's shell as "a sort of calendar," corresponding to the thirteen lunar cycles in each year. Since traditional Native Americans live closely in tune with nature, seasonal changes and other natural events influence their choice of moon names. Bruchac and London's selection expresses the diversity of moon names across geographic regions, and from nation to nation.

The poems are introduced through a brief exchange between a young Abenaki boy, Sozap, and his grandfather. While he carves a Turtle from a spruce log, Grandfather points out to Sozap the relationship between the scales on Turtle's back and the thirteen Abenaki moons. He explains that each moon has a unique name and story. Sozap asks, "…do other Native people have moons, too?" Grandfather's affirmative answer is embellished by the poems that follow.

Based on Native legends, the poems are rich with imagery from nature, imparting the variety and sensibility of Native beliefs and values.

A richly illustrated collection of poems that feature names used by Native Americans for the year's thirteen moons.

"Moon of the Popping Trees" (First Moon) retells the Northern Cheyenne story of how "Frost Giant" causes the cottonwood trees to "crack" with a blow from his club. Since only Coyote's howl can make Frost Giant sleep, Cheyenne children know better than to go out when the bitter cold has silenced all but the popping trees. The Cree story of how Frog was victorious in determining the length of winter, five months to match the five toes on his foot, is retold in the poem "Frog Moon" (Fourth Moon). Emerging from the poems are a variety of Native values, for example a respect for animals, an appreciation of Mother Earth's gifts, the rewards of hard work, the wisdom of peaceful discourse, and the importance of community.

Locker's page-and-a-half sized illustrations depict landscapes, animals, and people from a variety of perspectives. For "Moon of Popping Trees," he painted the coyotes and village from a distance, bathed in the frosty pinks and blues of a midwinter sunset. In contrast, the animals for "Frog Moon" are portrayed up close, darkened by shadows as the moon shines in the background. A few of the paintings include Native peoples, although in these scenes Locker is overly fond of painting Indian men in loincloths or without shirts. Ask an Ojibway man if he would go shirtless during "Maple Sugar Moon," or March, in the northern Great Lakes region! Locker overshadows this minor mistake with his ability to capture nature's beauty. Among his over a dozen other works for children are *The Land of Gray Wolf* (Dial Books, 1991) and *The First Thanksgiving* (Philomel, 1993), for which he created illustrations to accompany Jean Craighead George's text.

Thirteen Moons was selected for the International Reading Association's Teachers' Choices for 1993. *Readable at the third-grade level, it is an excellent starting point for exploring American Indian customs, legends, and values.* Other published materials about moon names are scarce. Manitoba storyteller Murdo Scribe retells a lengthier version of the Frog Moon legend in *Murdo's Story: A Legend from Northern Manitoba* (Pemmican Publ., 1985). Native American cultural or educational centers may provide additional local information. *Children should be encouraged to consider how months could be named to reflect seasonal changes in their own lives. Through this exercise, they will gain insight into the common sense used by Native peoples in marking the passage of time.*
MELISSA HECKARD

Cesar Chavez: Labor Leader

Maria E. Cedeno Various sources
Hispanic, Mexican
1993, Millbrook Press, ✱ Series

Despite being issued in 1993, this biography of Mexican American labor leader Cesar Chavez leaves out an important fact: Chavez passed away on April 22, 1992. Though Maria Cedeno provides a well-written description of Cesar Chavez's earlier life and contributions toward helping Mexican American agricultural workers in the United States, the exclusion of more contemporary information about him leads me to believe that this is similar to the other, older biographies on Chavez. *However, this easy-to-read version by Cedeno is an adequate introduction for elementary and middle-school students who are interested in the life of this unique labor leader.*

Chavez's popularity as a Mexican American cultural icon is both enduring and positive. Perhaps the most attractive features of this biography of Cesar Chavez are the many historical photographs interspersed throughout the text that include him posing with the likes of Robert Kennedy, Jesse Jackson, and his wife, Helen Chavez. Cedeno stresses Chavez's evolution and humble rise to power through nonviolent protest.

Cesar Chavez: Labor Leader should be a useful book for understanding this unique man's struggle for the rights of farm workers. *While reading and discussing the book teachers should integrate more current information related to his life, and be conscious of the fact that since his death, there has been some government support for commemorating Cesar Chavez through a national holiday.* HERIBERTO GODINA

An easy-to-read though uninspired introduction to the Mexican American labor leader and cultural icon.

Where I Came From

Victor Cockburn Judith Steinburg
Multicultural
1991, Talking Stones Press, ✱ Arabic, Audio Cassette, Chinese, French, Hebrew, Russian, Vietnamese

The combination of heart-warming sincerity, positive themes and joyful messages focusing on home, community, and family as well as nature, makes this a wonderful collection of songs and poems. Written in languages such as Arabic, Chinese, English, French, Hebrew, Russian, and Vietnamese, for each song or poem written in another language, there is an English version. Seeing so many poems and songs in so many languages is a stepping stone in assisting children to gain a better understanding of other alphabets and languages. Many of these wonderful poems and songs deal with exploring imagination, learning about worlds beyond your own, and developing friendships. Young children will be especially enamoured by whimsical poems like "Pour Ecrire un Petit Poem," "Family Tree," and "Lineage," will remind them of the importance of

A wonderful collection of over sixty multicultural songs and poems in different languages.

family. And the songs including "I Am Not Going To Jump In The Puddles," "Family Gifts," and "May There Always Be Sunshine," encourage children to have fun and explore the vast realms of their imaginations.

Using their more than ten years of experience in the classroom, editors Victor Cockburn and Judith Steinburg provide detailed, straightforward explanations and descriptions of some of the cultural artifacts and musical instruments noted in the text. Cockburn and Steinburg also include activities focusing on dancing, writing, and acting.

After a day of heavy skill drills and reading, these songs and poems would be an especially upbeat way to end the day for both teachers and students. This song and poetry book would be a great addition to any language arts program and would also work well in a home library. NAOMI WAKAN

The Legend of the Persian Carpet

📖 Tomie dePaola ✐ Claire Ewart
Middle Eastern
1993 (1972), Putnam Publishing Group

King Balash is beloved by his people and, in turn, he trusts and respects them. Every afternoon, his subjects visit the king in his palace where he keeps a fantastic diamond. Together the sovereign and his people watch as the beautiful diamond's light paints the walls with brilliant color. The kingdom's peace and tranquility ends when a stranger comes to the land to steal the diamond. As the thief is escaping across rocky terrain, he drops the diamond, which shatters into a million pieces.

A lovely picture book retelling of a Persian legend.

Grieving his loss, the king leaves his palace and goes to the place where the scattered diamond chips reflect the light across the rocky plain. He vows never to return to his dark, empty palace. The people are horrified that their ruler is planning to leave them forever.

His majesty is finally convinced to return to his throne for a year and a day by a young weaver named Payam. Payam promises King Balash that within that time, he and the other weavers will provide the king with a creation that will bring light and beauty back to the throne room. In a year and a day the carpet is finished. It is the most beautiful carpet in the world and the palace is once again filled with light. The kingdom has been saved by the young weavers.

Illustrator Claire Ewart spent a great deal of time studying the art of the Middle East and traveled abroad to research architecture and carpet making before completing her artwork. Together, she and DePaola have created a lovely picture book, of this Persian legend.

After reading the story, you can make your own Persian carpets. Take a piece of construction paper and punch holes along the short edges. Loop yarn through the holes to form a fringe for the carpet. Decorate the carpet with a collage of geometric shapes. This activity makes a good introduction to basic geometric shapes for younger children and can be used to introduce older students to tessellations and other geometric patterns found in Middle Eastern art. SANDRA KELLY

Everybody Cooks Rice

📖 Norah Dooley ✐ Peter J. Thornton
Multicultural
1992 (1991), The Lerner Group, 📖 Friedman, Ina, *How My Parents Learned to Eat.*

Young Carrie lives in a friendly neighborhood composed of families from many cultures. When it is time for dinner, her mom sends her out to find her little brother, Anthony, who is probably playing or sharing dinner in some friend's house.

An enaging look at the way nine families cook rice for dinner— a rare food book with a story line.

Using this interesting premise the author and illustrator provide a double-page spread for each of the nine homes that Carrie visits to find Anthony. Full-page illustrations of the adults and children and their dining areas show typical eating instruments and food, and depict adults and children with recognizable but nonstereotypical features. Carrie eventually finds her brother back in their own home.

The short text on each page identifies the country, the typical ingredients, and the tastes of the dishes being cooked. The people depicted are from Barbados, Puerto Rico, Vietnam, India, China,

Haiti, France, and Italy. The book ends with nine different rice recipes. Norah Dooley's book is one of the rare multicultural "food books" with an engaging story line and real substance.

This colorful book will be useful to children of different cultures and puts emphasis on the similarities among cultures. Children can observe the ethnic details in the pictures and relate positively to paintings resembling themselves. Good for classroom discussion and individual use, the book also encourages cooking projects in school or at home. Ina Friedman's How My Parents Learned to Eat *is a good companion book, as it humorously describes Japanese and American styles of eating.* GLORIA D. JACKSON

The Chi'i-lin Purse: A Collection of Ancient Chinese Stories

📗 Linda Fang ✒ Jeanne M. Lee
Asian, Chinese
1995 (1994), Farrar, Straus & Giroux, Inc.

Author and storyteller Linda Fang introduces young readers to classic Chinese literature, opera, and folklore in this fine collection. This book is an uncommon treasure that provides culturally authentic details with a really good read.

The stories come from an interesting variety of sources. During her Shanghai girlhood, Fang first heard some of the tales from her mother. Other stories are retellings of classic Chinese novels that Fang's father introduced her to when she was only eight years old. Some of these novels date back to the Ming Dynasty (1368 – 1644), though they are based on even older stories. Still more of the stories in *The Chi'i-Lin Purse* are based on classic operas, a Chinese tradition since the Tang Dynasty (618–907). Fang even includes a legend about a doctor known for developing surgical anesthesia during the Han Dynasty, over 1,500 years ago.

A fine retelling of nine classic Chinese tales that combines authentic details with a good read.

All these stories are lively and interesting to read and enjoy silently, but they are best read aloud. How could anyone resist sharing "Dog Steals and Rooster Crows," a delightful tale about one man who barks for a living and another who earns his keep crowing like a rooster? The potential for the reader to bark and crow and otherwise make delightful noises adds to the charm of the story.

The author includes a pronunciation guide, a glossary, and helpful source notes on each story. She also explains direct translations of Chinese expressions in context. Still, her use of Chinese words without translation in the stories may be confusing for some children, so teachers are advised to use the glossary to list definitions of Chinese words on the board for students to refer to as they enjoy the tales. The use of the Wade-Giles system to romanize Chinese names does not make for easy reading for those unaccustomed to this system. *Teachers, librarians, or others reading the stories aloud may want to pencil in the pronunciation of difficult words to make the reading smoother.*

The soft, dreamy pencil illustrations by Jeanne M. Lee in *The Chi'i-Lin Purse* offer an agreeable look at historic Chinese life. SANDRA KELLY

Moja Means One: Swahili Counting Book

📗 Muriel Feelings ✒ Tom Feelings
African, East African
1994 (1971), Dial, ✳ Bilingual English/Swahili,
📖 Prior, Jennifer, *The Games of Africa.*

This is a traditional counting book, proceeding from one to ten with a simple English sentence for each number. The English names for the numbers do not appear; Arabic numerals are accompanied by the Swahili names, with a pronunciation guide.

Each number is covered in a two-page spread, largely taken up by the glorious black-and-white illustrations of rural East Africa. The number eight (nane), for example, has the text "Busy market stalls are stocked with fruits, vegetables, meats, fish, clothes, jewelry, pottery, and carvings." The scene is of a marketplace in a coastal village.

The text and illustrations are simple and clear. "Nane means eight, count the eight market stalls; tano, five, count five animals." There are children in many of the scenes, shopping with their mothers, playing games, and listening to stories. *Children as young as one or two years old*

An appealing counting book with Swahili numbers and images of East African culture that won a Caldecott Award for its illustrations.

will find the pictures and the game of counting interesting, and can learn the numbers in English and Swahili at the same time.

For older children and willing teachers, the illustrations offer the opportunity for much more discussion and learning. The fruit stall in the market scene, for example, has twenty-five pieces of fruit—bananas, mangoes, passion fruit, pineapples, a melon, and more. Another stall has nine pieces of pottery in different shapes for different uses. Women carry things on their heads and on their backs. Men and women dress in traditional clothing. There is a lot to talk about here, to begin research about African life and culture, or to reinforce what children already know.

Teachers will also find the author's introduction and closing note helpful. A map of Africa shows the countries where Swahili is spoken, and Muriel Feelings gives some basic information about the language and how she came to learn it.

Tom Feelings's proud, bold, dignified illustra-

The Importance of Teaching Foreign Language Early
CLAUDIA MILLER

Claudia Schwalm remembers the first time she heard the lyrical notes of a foreign language, as a fifth-grader. Schwalm was translating songs into Spanish—as part of an experimental program to introduce languages to young students when she "just fell in love with the sound. I couldn't wait for high school, when I could take Spanish again."

Years later, she began teaching in Oakland's public elementary schools and realized that delaying language instruction until high school is too late.

"(In the United States), we introduce languages to students in high school, which is the worst time because kids are so self-conscious about making mistakes," she said. "But young children love languages. When you teach them how to count to ten in Japanese, they become fascinated with the different sounds."

After teaching for ten years, Schwalm left the profession in 1982 to start her own company, Claudia's Caravan, a mail-order business featuring multicultural and multilingual books and games. Today, her mail-order catalog is distributed to 5,000 school districts across the country; Schwalm has created language games for young children in 20 different languages and written Let's Count in Five Languages.

The Alameda resident is also publishing Being Bilingual Is Fun, a photojournal of local families raising their children bilingually, and has formed a nonprofit organization, Cultural Bridges, where teachers can rent artifacts from around the world to share with their students. For instance, teachers can order kits with Navajo weaver dolls, Kenyan stick drums, an audio tape of a Celtic harp, or a Vietnamese storybook, The Lotus Seed.

"Basically, I'd like to see an attitude change in young children. You can see how easy it is when they're young and how hard it gets when they're older," Schwalm said.

One day, Schwalm dreams of opening a multicultural library and resource center for teachers.

"It's important to start teaching multiculturally at an early age so kids develop an appreciation and respect for other cultures," she said. "Just teaching them a few words can change them from making fun to curiosity about language."

Schwalm describes herself as a reformed travelholic who has visited most of South and Central America, Europe, Africa, Japan, Thailand, and the Philippine Islands. Along the way, she collected items made by local artisans, many of which are now included in her Cultural Bridges kits.

"I know it's trite, but as we approach the 21st century, we are a global community," she said. "People ask me why we need multicultural and multilingual books in the schools. But multicultural education is everybody's culture — it doesn't mean only certain cultures."

Wendy Horikoshei, a 4-H youth development adviser who does training and research on diversity education for the University of California says that Schwalm began talking about teaching multiculturally to young children, "long before it became fashionable to talk about diversity."

"Research shows that from the time children are 3 years old, they notice differences. So the preschool age is definitely an important time to begin," Horikoshi said.

Claudia Miller is a staff writer for the Oakland Tribune.

tions are a nonstereotypical look at East Africa. The people in his scenes are strong and beautiful, somber and proud. His buildings are straight and symmetrical, his fences in perfect repair. Clearly, his intention is to show rural life at its best, and to demonstrate pride in his people.

The book is dedicated to "all Black children living in the Western Hemisphere," and the introduction stresses the importance for children "of African origin" to learn about their African heritage. This book and the companion, *Jambo Means Hello* by the same author-illustrator team, can be a welcoming and respectful introduction to East African life for interested children of any ethnicity.
CYNTHIA A. BILY

Jambo Means Hello: Swahili Alphabet Book

📖 Muriel L. Feelings ✏ Tom Feelings

African, Swahili

1992 (1974), Puffin Books, ✳ Series

Dozens of new alphabet books come out each year, and for good reason. The alphabet becomes the framework and construct for learning to read. In many alphabet books, though, the structure takes over and the information begins to feel forced and predictable. Not so with *Jambo Means Hello*. Children and adults will be drawn in by the welcoming African girl on the cover and held by the rich illustrations and interesting text. Authors Muriel and Tom Feelings use the traditional alphabet book here for an introductory lesson in the Swahili language and in East African life and culture.

An alphabet book introducing young readers to Swahili words and East African traditions.

Thus, A is for *arusi*, a wedding. The letter is given at the top of the two-page spread, followed by the Swahili word with pronunciation guide. The text is simple, but evocative: "When two people marry, it is an important event for their village as well as for their families. It is celebrated with drumming, dancing, and much food for all." The corresponding black-and-white illustration contains no fewer than forty-four figures, dancing, drumming, playing other instruments, or watching intently. A table bears an appealing array of fruits and drinks. A round hut and a hot sun complete the picture of the traditional rural village in East Africa.

Examples abound from *baba* (father) and *heshima* (respect) through *punda* (donkey) and *zeze* (a stringed instrument). Children whose knowledge of Africa is limited to what they saw in *The Lion King* will be delighted to learn that *rafiki* is the Swahili word for "friend." Swahili has no Q or X sounds, so the book is spared what are the two weakest pages in most alphabet books.

Muriel Feelings has an instinct for what children want to know and for what they need to learn. Many of the Swahili words she explains have to do with home and family, or everyday chores or school. But she also wants children—specifically "children of African ancestry"—to learn pride, self-respect, and respect for others. She seamlessly works in the ideas that "Children are taught early to show respect for adults," that "Africans worship God in many ways," and that "Beauty means different things."

Teachers and parents will find useful information in the author's introduction, which gives basic information about Swahili, including a map showing where it is spoken. Tom Feelings' engagingly beautiful illustrations draw the reader in easily. They also underscore a sense of respect and pride he has for the physicality of black people.

Jambo Means Hello *is an excellent introduction for children beginning an earnest study of Swahili, and for this purpose would work especially well with* Moja Means One. *But the book stands alone as an important resource for introducing the rich variety of rural East African life.* CYNTHIA A. BILY

Soul Looks Back In Wonder

📖 ✏ Tom Feelings, Contributions by Maya Angelou, Askia Toure, and Langston Hughes

African American

1994, Doubleday & Company, Inc.

Award-winning artist Tom Feelings, along with several renowned poets, celebrates the creativity of people of African descent in *Soul Looks Back in Wonder*; the first children's anthology of poetry by African American authors to win a Caldecott Illustration Award.

Powerfully illustrated works by well-known poets illuminate the creative past, present, and future of Africans around the world.

The coupling of Feeling's masterful sepia-toned paintings and the lyrical presence of words by Langston Hughes, Maya Angelou, Walter Dean

Myers, and Margaret Walker combine to form a powerful homage to the past, present, and future of Africans around the world and throughout time. Feeling's piece is a good introduction to African American literature and art, and is an artistic and compelling compilation that strikes at the chord of human existence, African or otherwise.
CHRISTINE PALMER

Tommy Traveler in the World of Black History

Tom Feelings
African American
1995 (1953), Black Butterfly Children's Books

When Tommy discovers that his local library doesn't have any books on black history, he turns to Dr. Gray, whose personal library becomes a living portrait of African American history for Tommy. As he reads about personalities from black history, Tommy falls asleep and dreams his way into the stories.

Originally written in the 1950s, *Tommy Traveler* includes such noted figures as Frederick Douglass, Joe Louis, and Crispus Attucks. Here also is the lesser-known Phoebe Frances, a woman who saved the life of general George Washington in 1776, during the Revolutionary War.

Reading about black history, Tommy dreams himself into the stories he has read in a comic-book style work that has endured since the 1950s.

Tommy Traveler's adventures, while published in hardcover, are depicted in comic-book style, which will make the book more appealing to children who are reluctant readers of biography. Period settings and clothing are authentic, and the book is well-researched and factually accurate. The note "To be continued" at the end of the book gives the impression that this author and illustrator may take Tommy on future time travels.

This book is an important addition to any collection serving children ages 7-12. It teaches one to take pride in one's heritage and makes the reader aware that a great deal has been left out of history text books. BETTYE STROUD

The Great Wall of China

Leonard Everett Fisher
Asian, Chinese
1986, Macmillan Publishing Company

Ten years of Chinese ancient history are condensed into this slim handsome book. Richly textured renderings in black, white and red of boldly contrasting images tell the story of King Chin Shih Huang Ti, the Fifth Supreme Emperor of China. His determination to protect the people of China from fierce Mongol invaders led to the historic building of the Great Wall of China. Packed with dates and facts, this historical picture book instructs young readers while it entertains. Deft character sketches of historical figures in Chinese history ring true. The plight of the common artisan and worker is portrayed in well-balanced images juxtaposing the military and royal authority with the obedient masses. Teachers, writers, and artists toil beside criminals, cheats, and trouble makers to build the 3,759 mile border of northern China. Those who protest are buried alive. After ten years, Chin Shih Huang Ti's vision is realized. The great wall has protected the people of China for at least a thousand years. Were the lives and labor of the people who built the wall worth the benefit of protection that the wall eventually afforded China? What historical consequences can be attributed to The Great Wall? *Either as thought provoking introduction to Chinese history for middle school students or as entertaining historical fiction, this story works and should be read to students interested in Chinese history.*

An expertly told brief history of the Great Wall of China and how it was built.

Chinese characters summarize each page with Mr. Fischer's signature. A translation of those characters are located on the last page of the book, along with the status of the wall as of the date of publication (1986). Even as the Great Wall lies in ruins, it remains a testament of China's past and present determination. Leonard Everett Fisher's straightforward telling of this historical event is expertly told and richly illustrated.
FAITH CHILDS-DAVIS

Spirit of the Maya: A Boy Explores his People's Mysterious Past

📖 Guy Garcia ✏ Ted Wood

Hispanic, Mexican

1995 Walker, 📖 Tutor, Pilar, *Mayan Civilization*; Schele, Linda, and Friedel, David, *A Forest of Kings: The Untold Story of Ancient Maya.*

Sheltered in the hot forests of Palenque, Mexico for more than nine-hundred years are scores of amazing pyramids originally built for King Pacal (pronounced Pah CAHL), who was only twelve-years-old when he first began to rule the city. *Spirit of the Maya* offers a sensitive photo portrait of contemporary Mayan life from the point of view of another twelve-year-old, Kin, a Lacandon Indian boy who is a direct descendant of the ancient Mayans.

A wonderful photo portrait of contemporary Mayan life through the eyes of a twelve-year-old Lacandon Indian boy.

Readers follow Kin as he goes to school, plays soccer, and asks scores of questions about his grandfather's wearing of traditional white robes, and about why his grandfather makes him wear his hair long in the Lacandon style. In a market near the majestic stone temples, pyramids, and other vestiges of this ancient culture, Kin's father, who sells traditional artwork is introduced.

Ted Wood's photographs capture both the beauty of the pyramids and the striking physicality of these descendants of the Mayans. The book also points out how diligently the Mexican government has worked to ensure that their archaeologists preserve the richness and integrity of these sites. The combination of Kin's story and the wonderful photos provides a rich cultural journey for young readers. DAPHNE MUSE

Reuben and the Fire

📖 Merle Good ✏ P. Buckley Moss

Amish

1993, Good Books, 📖 Lahman, Lois E., *A Teacher's Guide to Reuben and the Fire.*

Reuben and the Fire is truly an accurate portrayal in pictures and words, of life in the Amish communities in Philadelphia. The authors have combined incredible etchings of the Amish with an endearing story about a little boy named Reuben, and his five sisters.

Reuben copes with his bossy older sisters, raises rabbits with his grandfather, and rescues five puppies from a barn fire. At the end of the story, Reuben and his family uphold an old Amish tradition of building a barn together.

An endearing picture storybook about an Amish boy who lives on a farm with his large family.

This picture storybook written for children between the ages of 4 and 8 is a great read and a fine example of the cooperative spirit that fuels this culture. A teacher's guide is also available. NANCY PAQUIN

A Country Far Away

📖 Nigel Gray ✏ Philippe Dupasquier

African

1991 (1989), Orchard Books

Here is a delightful story of two boys, one in Africa, and one in a Western country, who have very similar lives despite living thousands of miles apart. Each page is divided into two sets of picture boxes, the top for the African boy, the bottom for the Western boy. Between the two sets of illustrations is text describing an activity. All of the pages cover essential activities to childhood: school, recreation, the birth of siblings, shopping with mom and dad, and

Adjacent illustrations compare and contrast two boys' lives — one African, the other Western — in a lively story.

family celebrations. For instance, one page says, "I helped my mom and dad. They were pleased." The top set of pictures shows the African boy chopping coconuts from a tree and milking a cow. His father gives him fruit as a reward. On the bottom, the Western boy is shown vacuuming and doing lawn work. His father roasts marshmallows with him. While their activities are worlds apart, each is helpful in their own culture. Also, the rewards are similar — a desirable food.

The setup of this book will make it easy for children to learn both the differences and similarities in the two cultures. Although their respective cultures appear far apart on the surface, the differences are merely material. As the book covers typical childhood activities, it also reflects typical

551

human emotions. The two families are shown as loving. The boys are both excited when the new sibling is born. They both relish free time with friends, the cool splash of water on a warm day, and late-night conversations with cousins. The book concludes with the two boys looking in a book and seeing the other, as they both dream of "a country far away," and the friend they could make. It is almost a circular ending as its premise takes readers back to the beginning of the story. Finally, the illustrations are lively and detailed, adding resonance and weight to the simple words. LISA FAIN

Ten Little Rabbits

Virginia Grossman   Sylvia Long
Native American
1995 (1991), Chronicle Books,   Baylor, Byrd
Hawk, *I Am Your Brother.*

A counting book that uses rabbits dressed in blankets of many Southwestern tribes instead of the stereotypical "10 little Indians".

This is a culturally sensitive and correct answer to those who are still tempted to use the song "Ten Little Indians" as a counting rhyme for children. This well-known rhyme is anathema to those who want to teach other cultures in a sensitive and nonstereotypical way.

The illustrations in *Ten Little Rabbits*, a counting book for younger children, are rendered sensitively and accurately by a Native American artist. The artist depicts authentic-looking rabbits instead of

cartoon-like rabbits with settings that are very realistic, much like Beatrix Potter's illustrations of animals. Sylvia Long's grandfather, Tatanka Sahdogan, captivated his grandchildren by telling stories and teaching them words in the Lakota (Sioux) language. This included teaching them to count to ten in Lakota.

Long draws on her experience living on a reservation to create some of the most captivating rabbits since Little Rabbit. The other strength of this book is that it relates authentic Native American dress and blanket motifs, which are explained at the end of the book, with the name of the tribe and information about the tribe from which the blanket

design originates. The illustrations also depict authentic totems and masks from the tribes of the Pacific Northwest, as well as traditional drawings and daily activities such as game playing, tracking, and hunting. Ten tribes are introduced and described for children. First, the artwork is described, then a description of the tribe is added at the end of the book. This is a wonderful book that details the subtle differences in the art and cultures of these tribes. ELAINE P. GOLEY

All the Colors of the Earth

Sheila Hamanaka
Multicultural
1994, Morrow,   Jenness, Aylette, *Families: A Celebration of Diversity, Commitment, and Love;* Rosen, Michael J., *Home: A Collaboration of Thirty Distinguished Authors and Illustrators of Children's Books to Aid the Homeless.*

In vibrant oil paintings and flowing verse, Sheila Hamanaka celebrates the diversity of the world's children. The colors and activities depicted by the author evoke the beauty of being alive. The children are varying shades of color; their families are as diverse as one can imagine. "Children come in all the colors of the earth/The roaring browns of bears and soaring eagles/The whispering golds of late summer grasses/And crackling russets of fallen leaves/The tinkling pinks of tiny seashells by the rumbling sea." Hamanaka creates images of hair, skin, shapes, and sizes. "Children come in all the colors of love/In endless shades of you and me/For love comes in cinnamon, walnut, and wheat/Love is amber and ivory and ginger and sweet/Like caramel, and chocolate, and the honey of bees."

Through her poetry, and vibrant art, the author brings pride to cultural diversity.

The children's playfulness thrums with joy and love and life. They are depicted arm in arm, swimming, combing one another's hair, jumping and playing together as a family. This is an imaginative introduction to the concept of multiculturalism and differences in society. NANCY HANSEN-KRENING

Count Your Way Through Japan

Jim Haskins ✒ Martin Skoro
Asian, Japanese
1987, Carolrhoda Books, ✳ Series

Using the Japanese characters for the numbers one through ten as a means of introducing Japanese culture has been widely used, and this book is a good resource for any facilitator wishing to expose children to that culture. However, authors should be careful to avoid stereotypic Japanese images.

Japanese characters for the numbers one through ten are used to introduce Japanese culture in a book that unfortunately, lacks authenticity.

Although Haskins's research on Japanese culture is vast, it is also biased in that there is no depiction of contemporary Japanese life. The No play, used to represent the number 10, is supported mainly by an affluent sector of Japan's population, and not representative of mainstream society. Therefore, the No play itself may be misleading to non-Japanese children. Images such as the kimono and traditional Japanese children's games are also misleading to the reader, as these images give the impression that Japanese people wear kimonos and play traditional games as part of their daily routines.

The illustrations in the book lack accuracy as they are more representative of Chinese culture, or possibly the illustrator's imagination, than they are of Japanese culture. For example, the chopsticks are not Japanese but Chinese, and the homes in Japan are not as sparsely furnished as the book would have us believe. These images foster stereotypes of all Asian cultures being interchangeable. In light of the fact that Haskins uses a bank of researchers to assist him with his books, it seems as though more attention might be given to authenticity and the kind of broadly sweeping stereotypes that appear in this book. CHIEKO YAMAZAKI-HEINEMAN

Mighty Mountains and the Three Strong Women

Irene Hedlund ✒ Various sources
Asian, Feminist, Japanese
1990, Volcano Press

This lively Japanese folktale is retold here in English from a Scandinavian version! Just that fact makes *Mighty Mountain and the Three Strong Women* a fascinating story, inviting a broad range of thinking about the nature of folktales and how they change and relate within different cultures. The tale also uses humor to encourage readers to question gender—role stereotypes, especially Japanese ideas of the subservient Japanese wife.

In this entertaining Japanese folktale, a Sumo wrestler meets three "strong" women.

The story itself is entertaining and engaging for readers of all ages. The protagonist, Mighty Mountain, is a substantial young man who wins his name by being the biggest and best Sumo wrestler in his whole village at the tender age of twelve. Certain that he can win the Emperor's grand yearly wrestling match, our hero decides to walk to the capital to compete.

Along the way he meets a pretty girl named Kuniko and takes the liberty of poking her in the side. Without spilling the water she is carrying, the young woman traps his hand under her arm. Not even his great strength can free him from her formidable grip, and she hauls him off to meet her Grandma.

Grandma too is an impressive character. Her ability to uproot great trees, combined with her daughter's habit of carrying the cow because "the poor cow gets sore feet," causes Mighty Mountain to faint. The humor of the text continues from there, stimulated by the three strong women's assessment of Mighty Mountain as looking "delicate" and in need of some proper food through his period of strengthening and training.

The story ends with humor too. Mighty Mountain reduces the land's greatest Sumo wrestlers to "blubbering and tears" and defeats the great Balloon Belly. When Mighty Mountain returns to marry

Kuniko, she "hugged him carefully, then picked him up and carried him and the heavy prize money halfway up the mountain. Then she put him down and let him carry her the rest of the way."

Strong-minded and able women are not often seen in traditional folktales but this exception proves to be interesting and humorously engaging as well as spiritedly written. ANNA PEARCE

Perez and Martina

📖 ✒ Marjorie Herrman

Hispanic, Puerto Rican

1992 (1991), Frederick Warne and Co., Inc.

A well-known Puerto Rican folktale depicting a cockroach and a rat who fall in love and unfortunately, reinforce gender stereotypes.

Perez and Martina is a traditional Puerto Rican folktale passed down orally for many generations. Martina is a cockroach who enjoys cooking and cleaning and is portrayed as a pleasant and contented domestic character. One day she finds a coin and purchases some facial powder, which enhances her beauty and desirability. She subsequently attracts numerous suitors and turns down all but one—Perez, the rat. She systematically rejects the others based on her question: "How will you speak to me in the future?" Perez and Martina marry and live happily until Perez suffers an untimely death. He accidentally falls into a pot of boiling rice, coconut milk, fruit and nuts (a favorite dish Martina has prepared for him) and drowns. Martina spends the rest of her days lamenting his death.

This folktale is an interesting commentary on gender roles. While Martina is quite conventional in her traditional domestic role, she is also quite resourceful and demonstrates an unusual assertiveness when evaluating her prospective suitors. She does not settle for any suitor but holds out for a particular one. You could assume that she is screening these suitors for a tendency toward future verbal abuse, but the story does not make that fact clear.

While Martina is nurturing, giving, and domestically oriented, Perez is represented as the hardworking, responsible male character. This opinion of the Puerto Rican woman may be questioned in today's society, but during the nineteenth century,

the woman's role was oriented toward being a homemaker, unlike the modern Puerto Rican woman who wears many hats, domestic and professional. ELIZABETH CAPIFALI

Girl from the Snow Country

📖 ✒ Masako Hidaka

(translated by Amanda M. Stinchecum)

Asian, Japanese

1986 (1984), Kane Miller, ✳ Japanese

Girl from the Snow Country depicts the life of a young girl, Mi-chan, and her own unique way of enjoying life in Japan's snow region, where families become isolated during the winter months. Mi-chan and her mother rarely get out, except to shop, and life in the village is monotonous. The village adults keep busy with the household chores, including preparations for spring farming, some light cottage industry, and tending to the cattle and the farm equipment, while the children help out or play outside.

A little girl enjoys winter in the isolated snow regions of Japan.

While anticlimactic, the story beautifully depicts the change of seasons, an important concept in Japanese culture. For example, the illustration depicting Mi-chan and her mother bowing and paying respect to a statue cloaked in snow of Jizo, protector of children and travelers, is a poignant example of Japanese folklore heritage and spiritual life-style.

The translation flows well, buts falls short of conveying the enormous respect and understanding that the Japanese have for the seasons.
CHIEKO YAMAZAKI-HEINEMAN

Pass It On: African-American Poetry for Children

📖 Edited by Wade Hudson ✒ Floyd Cooper

African American

1993, Scholastic, Inc., 📖 Miller, E. Ethelbert, *In Search of Color, Everywhere: A Collection of African American Poetry*; Sullivan, Charles, *Children of Promise: African-American Literature and Art for Young People.*

In his introduction, Wade Hudson sets a worthy and ambitious goal for this collection: to introduce children to a handful of great African American poets and their rich legacy. Poetry "holds a special place within African-American culture," he writes. Through poetry "history and traditions are kept alive and passed from one generation to another."

This collection in part meets the goal Hudson sets. There are some wonderful and challenging poets and poems here. Langston Hughes is represented by three poems, including "Dream Variation"; there's an appealing nonsense rhyme about peas from Henry Dumas; and the final spread features Lucille Clifton's poem "Listen Children," from which the title of this book is taken. But not all will speak to as wide a range of readers as "Dream Variation." Presenting poems that will be accessible to younger children and immediate to their world seems to have been of greater concern to Wade Hudson than offering the poems richest in history, memory, or literary strength. The book includes brief notes on the poets.

An illustrated collection of poems from Langston Hughes, Nikki Giovanni, and others that focuses more on accessibility than literary quality.

Floyd Cooper's art offers warm and inviting images of African American children and their families to accompany the poems. His paintings, however, are not always well served by the design of the book. Where two separate paintings appear on facing pages, the images seem to compete with one another and with the poems for our attention, to the detriment of each. Often the simplest paintings—Harriet Tubman seen against the night sky, a silhoutted mother or grandmother speaking to two attentive children—are the most successful.

Readers who are looking for a collection that offers a comprehensive introduction to the African American literary legacy would do better to turn to *Children of Promise: African-American Literature and Art for Young People*, edited by Charles Sullivan or the adult collection, *In Search of Color, Everywhere: A Collection of African-American Poetry*, edited by E. Ethelbert Miller. Those seeking an accessible introduction to the playful and careful appreciation of language possible in poetry and that hints at what more may be found in the rich heritage of African American poetry, may well be happy with what they find here. ANNE DAVIES

City Seen from A to Z

📖 🖎 Rachel Isadora, Edited by ALC Staff
African American, Multicultural
1992 (1983), William Morrow & Co.

Simple words are used to depict the interests of many of the individuals shown in this city-based alphabet book. Words such as "jazz" and "music" portray varied worlds of the children in these black-and-white illustrations. "Art" is illustrated by a picture drawn on an apartment building showing children of various cultures. And "zoo" is illustrated by pictures of animals children have drawn on a sidewalk.

The text is printed in a manner easily read by young children. The print is large and clear and placed in a white area of the page's illustration. The word is then represented by a picture. For example, one page shows two girls, one of whom has a hat representing the word "hat." *Very young children may not be able to use the picture directly to decipher the words, but the pictures represent the city culture well and provide a context for discussion. Despite some problems, this book is a good addition to a classroom collection of alphabet books and may well lead children to writing their own book of ABC's.*

A moderately successful alphabet book that uses a multicultural city as its background.

BARBARA GOLDENHERSH

John Henry, An American Legend

📖 🖎 Ezra Jack Keats
African American
1987 (1965), Alfred A. Knopf, ✳ Series

John Henry is usually depicted in song and rhyme as a full-grown man of heroic physical skill. Keats' decision to tell the character's story from his birth, through his youth, and into adulthood can be expected to have added appeal for young children.

The smiling bouncing brown baby grows up to work on farms and in cotton fields, but these activities are too tame for him. He goes on to get a job on a riverboat and swings a hammer on the transcontinental railroad. John Henry then

In the form of a ballad, this lively book retells the story of the African American folk hero John Henry.

556

begins working in a coal mine. During a cave-in, he saves lives by hammering out the burning fuse that leads to a pile of dynamite.

The tales of his strength grow with each re-telling. The story's climax takes place when John Henry has a fateful encounter with a steam drill. He competes against the drill as they tunnel through a mountain. John Henry is the first to emerge from the tunnel but he collapses and dies with his sledge hammer in his hand.

The illustration on the opening spread has a Van Gogh-esque quality that is reminiscent of "Starry Night." Keats' dark backgrounds provide an oily and gritty setting for the coal-mining, hammer-slinging John Henry. The punchy narrative succeeds with the effective use of alliteration, e.g., "sky swirled soundlessly…river roared…wind whispered and whistled and sang." The energetic text is well balanced with lively illustrations.

LESLIE ANDERSON MORALES

Talking Walls

Margy Burns Knight ✒ Anne O'Brien
Multicultural
1995 (1992), Tillbury House

Books containing universal themes exemplified across cultures are very helpful to classroom teachers who want to demonstrate a valuing of differences and an understanding of commonalities. This unusual book explores fourteen walls that are important exemplars of the beliefs, customs, and history, not only of specific people, but throughout the world.

A respectful and unusual exploration of fourteen walls as important monuments of world history.

The walls are the Great Wall of China, Aborigine art on cliff and cave walls, the paintings on the walls of the prehistoric Lascaux Cave, the Western Wall in Jerusalem, the bas-relief animals carved on the walls in Mahabalipuram in India, Muslim walls in Mecca and in Muslim homes across the world, the walls of Great Zimbabwe, the Incan walls of Cuzco, Peru, those of the Taos Pueblo, the murals on the walls in Mexico painted by great contemporary artists, the limestone walls of the Canadian Museum of Civilization, The Vietnam Veterans Memorial in Washington D.C., Nelson Mandela's prison walls in South Africa, and the Berlin Wall.

The endpapers of this beautifully illustrated book contain the word for "wall" written in thirty-six languages. Each of the pages contains some interesting information about the particular wall. The tone of the book is consistently respectful. None of the walls is viewed as "quaint" or "exotic." None of the people involved in worshiping at or visiting the walls is regarded as "strange" or "primitive".

The idea of taking a theme and spinning it out to its logical connections is a useful one for children of any age. Research into the literature as well as the history would prove informative and valuable.

MASHA RUDMAN

Masai and I

Virginia Kroll ✒ Nancy Carpenter
African, African American, Masai
1993 (1992), Hamish Hamilton, Ltd., ✳ Series

During a unit on East Africa in her elementary school classroom, a young African American girl learns about the Masai people and becomes intrigued by the kinship that she feels with them. Throughout the story, Linda compares different aspects of her life with what she thinks her life might be like if she were a Masai. Her life would change from living in a large urban apartment building, teeming with noise and enough people to make up ten villages, to a community surrounded by the natural sounds of animals and of the winds whirling through trees and by unobstructed views of miles and miles of open terrain.

As her family waits for her father to come home for dinner, Linda thinks about how the Masai men and boys eat together while the girls eat with the women. When her brother gets water from the faucet, Linda remembers how the Masai walk long distances to the water hole. Looking out across the busy city she imagines a Masai village where life is quieter, calmer, and simpler. The pet

An African American girl compares her everyday life in America to that of an Masai girl in Africa in an innovative, thoughtful book.

hamster she keeps in the apartment becomes a wild uncaged animal. As she gets into the car to go to her grandmother's birthday celebration, she thinks about the Masai walking even longer distances. There are some things that wouldn't change. That night as she prepares for bed, Linda looks in the mirror and realizes that if she were Masai she would look the same as she does now.

This is an excellent cultural comparison from a child's perspective. As Linda compares her life in the West with that of a young Masai girl, she educates the reader about everyday life among the Masai. The author is careful not to make any judgments or pronouncements concerning either culture. The comparisons emerge as simple facts of difference rather than positioning one culture as being more advantageous than the other. The illustrations aid the comparison in that one page will portray Linda performing a task while the facing page portrays a young Masai girl performing a similar task. One of the qualities of this story that differentiates it from others which address cultural differences is in how it portrays the similarities of each culture. Despite their differences, Linda and the Masai girl are doing basically the same things. The text ends on a slightly pan-African note by stating that the basic kinship Linda feels for the Masai is one of race and therefore ancestry.

The fact that many Masai still live the way they did hundreds of years ago allows young readers to look at some of the more traditional aspects of African cultures. But more needs to be done in terms of looking at how those cultures are redefining themselves and changing in accordance with the environment surrounding their lives and the demands of modern technology. MICHELLE GARFIELD

Jaha and Jamil Went Down the Hill: An African Mother Goose

🔖 Virginia Kroll   🖋 Katherine Roundtree

African

1994, Charlesbridge

The author notes that these are verses that Mother Goose might have written if she had lived in Africa. The 48 poems correspond to a list of Mother Goose rhymes which appears at the front of the book. Matching the adaptations to the less familiar rhymes such as "My sister and I" and "How many miles to Babylon" is challenging, but most of the verses are based on familiar rhymes like "London Bridge" and "Pat-a-cake." The reader might have to flip back and forth from this list to the text until she is more comfortable with the cadence of the newer poems.

This is a book that children can grow with. There are poems that teach about aspects of life in modern and traditional Africa. Some of the lyrics describe food, clothing, and customs. "Bend a Wire" describes coppersmithing and "Little Ahmed Has Lost His Goats" describes goatherding. Others describe family relationships, geography, and wildlife. "Pangolin, Pangolin" and "Where, Oh, Where?" mention animals that most of us couldn't begin to imagine without the benefit of the accompanying illustrations. Most of the poems are specific to an event or

activity, e.g., "Dance of the Tutsi," but a couple cover general otopics. "All Around Africa" is a counting rhyme which introduces the reader to a dozen tribes.

The bright illustrations use up every available square inch of the page. They are full of color but don't look crowded and work well as a background for the text. Each page of the book is distinguished by the name of an African nation; 28 African countries are included. The country's name is overlaid on a "textile" border and that fabric design is unique to that country.

There is a map of the African continent at the back of the book. A pointer connects each of the 28 represented countries to a thumbnail-sized version of the page where the rhymes appear in the body of the book.

The book's lack of organization keeps it from being as convenient to use as one might hope. There's no apparent order as to how the rhymes or the selected countries appear in the book. It is neither alphabetical or geographical. Same-page pronunciation guides are included on some pages, but a glossary complete with phoneticized spelling would have been helpful. There is no mention made of abstract political and historical concepts like independence and colonialism.

LESLIE ANDERSON MORALES

A somewhat disorganized collection of verses that Mother Goose might have written had she visited Africa.

557

My Little Island

Frané Lessac

Caribbean American

1987 (1984), J. B. Lippincott Company, ✳ Series, Video

My Little Island is an unnamed volcanic island in the Caribbean. The island is the place of birth of one of the boys and he has come to see his relatives, accompanied by his best friend, Lucca. For several days, he shows Lucca around the island. They see beautiful flowering trees and rare animals, eat fish and fruit and other local foods, shop in the city, snorkel in the ocean, and attend a wedding and a carnival.

A young black boy takes his white best friend to see the Caribbean island where he was born.

This book sends a clear but subtle message about cross-cultural understanding. The unnamed narrator tells us that Lucca is his best friend. Though the text never mentions race, the illustrations reveal that the narrator is black and Lucca is white. As he shows his friend around the island, the narrator, having lived in two worlds, knows which things are familiar and which seem strange to Lucca. As for Lucca, he gamely tries to learn as much as he can. At lunch, which includes pigeon peas and goat-water stew, "Lucca makes funny faces but eats it all."

The reader, too, is tantalized by the surrounding sights and sounds, from giant barking frogs in the countryside, and soursops and christophines at the fruit stand, to guava cheese, Picasso fish, and steel drums. The rollicking text is fun to read, full of short concrete sentences.

The illustrations are colorful and simplistic, based on author Frané Lessac's years of living on the Caribbean island of Montserrat. They are full of little details: dozens of people or fish, silly smiling iguanas, fanciful flowers. CYNTHIA A. BILY

A Button in Her Ear

Ada Bassett Litchfield ✎ Eleanor Mill

Physically Disabled

1976, A. Whitman, Houghton Mifflin Co.

Eight-year-old Angela decides she wants to overcome the fear of being different and alienated from others. Angela longs to hear the voices of her family and friends and share in their jokes and discussions. Her parents have her hearing examined and a determination is made that Angela needs a hearing device. The diagnosis and fitting of the hearing aid are portrayed forthrightly.

Initially she is afraid, until the doctor suggests that the hearing aid is a magic button that will enable her to hear everything. The button is indeed magical, allowing Angela to hear people

Angela receives a hearing aid which she calls her "magic button" in a realistic, helpful book.

and to tune them out selectively. The curiosity of the children is very much a part of the storyline. Even though some of the children are afraid of the hearing aid, they are eager to know how it works.

The author accurately and realistically addresses the fears a hearing-impaired child has as well as the prejudice children have toward disability.

Activities:
1. Bring in hearing aids and modern equipment for testing hearing loss.
2. Compare the old methods of testing to the new, and how improvements have been made.
BARBARA A. KANE

The Animals: Selected Poems

Michio Mado (translated by HRM Empress Michiko) ✎ Mitsumasa Anno

Asian, Japanese

1992, Macmillan, ✳ Bilingual English/Japanese

Japanese poetry, across the centuries is rich in imagery yet simple in form. Fortunately some of this heritage is accessible to children. While quite a number of books of haiku poetry are available, very little other Japanese poetry can be found in translation. A

An appealing book of descriptive poems about animals, with the original Japanese text accompanied by the English translation.

fine exception is *The Animals*, a beautiful book by eighty-three-year-old poet Michio Mado, winner of the prestigious Noma Award for Children's Literature. The book is translated by Her Majesty Empress Michiko of Japan, and illustrated by Mitsumaso Anno, a fine artist, beloved and honored both in the United States and his native Japan.

The Animals treats the reader to twenty short, sometimes humorous, sometimes poignant, poems whose fresh imagery invites the reader to see animals in new ways. For example, the poem Zebra reads: "In a cage/ Of his/ Own making." Occasionally we also come to see ourselves in a different light as in:

The Ant
Watching an ant
I often feel
Like voicing an apology
Toward this little being.
Life is life to any creature
Big or small.
The difference is only
The size of its container,
And mine happens to be so ridiculously,
Enormously big.

The design, illustration, and bilingual format (Japanese and English) add greatly to the appeal of the book. Each warm beige and white two-page spread features the Japanese text on the left and the English on the right, providing an opportunity for comparison by the reader. The bottom border is a lovely, delicate paper-cut frieze of intricately linked animals who seem to be moving across the page.

ANNA PEARCE

Rachel Parker, Kindergarten Show-Off

📖 Ann Martin ✒ Nancy Poydar
African American
1993 (1992), Holiday House

Olivia, an African American, and Rachel, a European American, must overcome feelings of competitiveness and jealousy in order to make their friendship work.

Olivia, an only child, narrates the story. The reader sees her class filled with the black and brown, cream, and sand-colored faces of her friends and classmates. Olivia is excited by the fact that her neighbor, Rachel, is also in her class. But she is also skeptical of a girl who has "a baby sister, a Grandfather that lives with them and two first names."

Olivia's mother tries to make things go smoothly for the two girls, yet they very much want to outdo each other.

After a spat, their antagonism toward one another becomes apparent to a teacher as well. She assigns a book for them to read together in front of the class. Realizing that there are certain words each does not know, they accept help from one another in order to read the book. Their cooperative effort results in their realizing that they both have strengths that are different but valuable.

An interracial friendship between two girls who initially are very competitive in school makes for a great beginning reader book.

Olivia must swallow her pride, but cannot quite manage to offer up an apology to Rachel for her rude behavior. But they both want the friendship. Along with learning respect for one another, Olivia and Rachel learn something about themselves and what they really know.

With illustrations that provide a high visual context for the story and a simple, straightforward text that emphasizes the importance of cooperation, this is a great story for beginning readers.

MARTHA L. MARTINEZ

Dancing With the Indians

📖 Angela Shelf Medearis ✒ Samuel Byrd
African American, Native American, Seminole
1993 (1991), Holiday House, ✽ Audio Cassette

During the eighteenth, nineteenth, and early part of the twentieth centuries, there were several Native American nations that befriended slaves; the Seminoles were one of these nations. Set in the 1930s, this is the heartwarming semi-autobiographical story of a young girl who visits her African American grandfather.

The young girl narrating the story describes how her grandfather ran away from a plantation and was taken in and treated like a brother by the Seminoles. Through majestic rituals that include the stomp, ribbon, and rainbow dances, she gains an abiding respect and deep appreciation for these people. Although initially the warrior calls frighten her, she becomes less afraid when asked to participate in the dances. She and her family dance until

A black family of the 1930s attends a Seminole Indian celebration in a tender, lovingly illustrated work.

dawn. Exhausted but excited, they return for another day of celebration with the Seminoles. The author, whose great-grandfather was a member of the Seminole nation in Oklahoma feels a strong kinship to the girl in this story. Medearis does a tremendous service to those in the African American community who are descendants of Native Americans or who have lived with them. There are too few stories that reflect on and document the fascinating and historically revealing relationships between African Americans and Native Americans.

Medearis's story also presents Native Americans as fully developed people and not mere artifacts or anthropological window dressing. There remains a tremendous need for many African Americans to embrace the other cultural and ethnic identities that stream through many of our veins.

In this tenderly written, lovingly illustrated book, the author has clearly made a significant contribution to clarifying and building stronger relationships between Native Americans and African Americans. MARTHA L. MARTINEZ

The Singing Man

Angela Shelf Medearis Terea Shaffer
African, West African
1994, Holiday House, Inc.

Adapted from a West African folktale, this story depicts the life of a Nigerian Praise Singer, or *Griot*, and explains how the Praise Singers came to be. A Praise Singer is one who preserves the history of the village by singing about the King's/Chief's ancestry and passing the songs from one generation to the next. In this story Banzar is the singing man and one of three sons who, after being initiated into manhood, must choose work that benefits the village. Banzar chooses to be a musician, unlike his brothers: one, a farmer; the other, a blacksmith. Banzar is ejected from the village because "music cannot fill the stomach" and has no practical use in the village. He travels from village to village and to other nations in Africa, eventually becoming the King's private musician, and returns to his village dressed in the finest robes. He finds his brothers very poor because the crops

A brightly illustrated adaptation of a West African folktale that explains how the Praise Singers came to be.

have failed, and they have no money to buy iron and forge tools. Banzar introduces himself as their long-lost brother and the whole village celebrates Banzar's good fortune. They realize that music is necessary after all. "Yams fill the belly and trade fills the pockets, but music fills the heart."

This is a beautifully illustrated book with colors inspired by the brightly printed textiles of Nigeria. The illustrations reflect the diversity of Nigeria's people and landscapes. Unfortunately, the author does not disclose the specific language spoken by the Yoruba tribe, the people in this particular village, but does, however, offer a pronunciation guide in the back to help with the names of the people and towns whose sounds have no exact match in English. For example, Banzar is pronounced BAHN-zar.

The villagers come to realize that music is an important part of their lives and serves the spirit and the soul. This book also celebrates the idea of working for the good of the village, not for personal gain. BARBARA SMITH REDDISH

Somewhere in Africa

Ingrid Mennen Niki Daly, Nicholas Maritz
African, South African
1992, Dutton Children's Books

In a subtle attempt to demonstrate that Africa is not one large jungle, this story follows Ashraf as he walks through a South African city to the big library. Along the way he encounters many of the things generally associated with urban settings: traffic lights, traffic, and several large commercial enterprises. The book that he is renewing at the library is his favorite book, which happens to be about that part of Africa that remains "wild and untamed." Ashraf has experienced this part of the continent only in books that he has read. In other words, his African experience is very similar to that of children in cities throughout the world. Yet, there are distinctly African elements to the city: for instance, Ashraf participates in an informal street dance.

A boy's life in an urban city in Africa dispells notions of a monolithic "jungle continent" in an accessible but somewhat simplistic book.

This book is an entertaining and easily accessible portrayal of a child in a non-Western society.

Ashraf's urban experience provides a theme through which other children are invited to relate to him. While the authors state that he lives in a city at the tip of Africa, they do not specify which city. Therefore, rather than being portrayed as a noteworthy exception, Ashraf's city could be anywhere in Africa. With busy downtown intersections, large buildings, highways, and helicopters, the illustrations contribute to the impression of urban life.

Although the text explodes the myth of Africa as a monolithic, savage continent, it does entertain the idea that such areas may exist in the countryside. There is a sense in the text that the authors are trying to create distance between city dwellers like Ashraf and more rural children in Africa. Phrases such as "wild and untamed" which are used to describe Ashraf's interest in other parts of the continent, encourage the idea of a savage Africa and, therefore, present Ashraf and his experience as an exception to what actually occurs in his country. In its portrayal of children from non-Western societies, the book emphasizes their similarity with Western children rather than cultural and regional difference. This is a oversimplified perspective, but it does suggest a way of overcoming difference. MICHELLE GARFIELD

Coconut Mon

📗 Linda B. Milstein 🖋 Cheryl Taylor
Caribbean
1995, Tambourine Books

This is a colorful counting book for very young children, whose object is to count from one to ten using coconuts sold by the "Coconut Mon." The scene is an unnamed Caribbean island, where coconuts are sold one by one to the people in the village. Linda Milstein's descriptions of the coconuts are full of smile-provoking adjectives that will delight young readers and color their speech. "O ten luv-ly coconuts, eight de-lic-i-ous coconuts, six crrr-unchy coconuts, three taaa-sty coconuts."

Set on a Caribbean island, this predictable counting book is full of stereotypical images and not recommended.

The island village is portrayed with bold eye-catching color illustrations by Cheryl Munro Taylor. However, I had some problems with the drawings: all of the people, with the exception of the "Coconut Mon," are oversimplified, with minimal features or in silhouette. The "Coconut Mon" has dreadlocks and somewhat more distinctive features, and he appears to be dancing and playing as he sells his wares. Unfortunately, the women are often portrayed as stereotypical "mammies Caribbean-style." They are pictured as overweight, with large, painted, smiling lips, floppy hats, shapeless dresses, and hands on the hips, or they are pushed into the background with no facial features at all. Everyone on this island is carefree, with nothing better to do than buy coconuts.

Coconut Mon ultimately has very little to recommend it. It is colorful and simple, with an easy-to-follow story, but there is very little challenge to even the youngest reader in the predictable flow of the text. Coupled with the troubling illustrations, the book may teach children more about Caribbean stereotypes than about counting to ten.
ROSA E. WARDER

The Song of el Coqui and Other Tales of Puerto Rico

📗 Nicholasa Mohr 🖋 Antonio Martorell
Hispanic, Puerto Rican
1995, Viking

These three stories weave a vibrant and colorful tapestry from the spirit of Puerto Rican folklore. Written with deep respect for the rich and complex ancestral traditions, the stories form a picture of a culture woven from a number of very different and beautiful threads.

"In the beginning there was no sound" is the opening line in "The Song of el Coqui." One day the great god Huracan looks down from his mountain with great sadness. His efforts to produce sound result in a fascinating journey through the natural and animal world.

In the parable "La Mula, the Cimarron Mule," La Mula is worked to near exhaustion by Spanish bandits. She is pushed, whipped, and told she's lazy. She is befriended by the slave Otilio and together they plan their escape. "La Guinea, the Stowaway

Three vibrant folktales that reflect the diverse Puerto Rican culture.

561

Hen" tells the story of a woman who tries to escape the bullets of African slave traders.

Rendered in fiery colors, the pictures, like the stories they illustrate, are sometimes frightening, vividly capturing the emotions of each story. DAPHNE MUSE

The Tiger and the Rabbit: A Puerto Rican Tale

📖 ✒ Francisco X. Mora

Caribbean, Hispanic, Puerto Rican

1991 (1965), Lippincott, ✳ Audio Cassette

According to Gloria Blatt in *Once Upon a Folktale*, "Folklore is a body of traditional belief, custom, and expression handed down largely by word of mouth …all are absorbed and assimilated through repetition and variation into a pattern which has value and continuity for the group as a whole." Folktales allow us to relive our ancestors' experiences — they are some of the most immediate cultural treasures we have.

Francisco Mora grew up in the rich oral tradition of Puerto Rico. She was the first Puerto Rican librarian in New York City and is known for her extensive knowledge of Puerto Rican folktales, which she describes as: "part of a folklore verbally preserved and enriched by the creative power of a people who drew from the hills, mountains, cities, and valleys."

A collection of witty and imaginative folktales from Puerto Rico.

In *The Tiger and the Rabbit: A Puerto Rican Tale*, we have eighteen short folktales that the author has heard all her life, like "The Shepherd and the Princess," a lovely story about a king who thought no one good enough to marry his daughter. He announces that he will only give her hand to the man who brings him all the waters of the world, all the flowers of the world, and a handful of hazelnuts. A kind and simple shepherd attempts to acquire these three things with the help of a strange boy he meets on the road. Eventually, the shepherd returns to the kingdom and presents himself to the king. The shepherd has all the waters of the world — a glass with waters from "the rain, the mountains, the hills, the valleys, the brooks, the springs, and the rivers, for it comes from the sea where all the waters flow" — all the flowers in the world — a honeycomb, in which the bees have condensed the essence of all flowers — and finally the hazelnuts.

The shepherd had placed tiny crabs into the bag of nuts, so that anyone reaching into the bag would get their fingers pinched and scream "ay-ay-ay" in pain. The shepherd marries the princess. The theme of royalty reflects Spanish influence on Puerto Rican culture. Cleverness and intelligence are emphasized as the best qualities to have, enough to win a princess for a shepherd.

"Casi Lampu'A Lentemue," is similar to Rumpelstiltskin. A young man named Paco is held captive by a witch who will release him only if he can guess her name (and this is where the similarity ends). It is interesting to see how Paco finds out her name. A crab plays a pivotal part in the story, and by the end the reader will have an insight as to why crabs run away when they see human beings.

"The Gluttonous Wife," is about an obese woman who marries a thin man who is so dedicated to her that, by eating with her, he soon becomes as fat as she is.

"The Three Magi," a typical Puerto Rican tale, shows the traditional rituals still observed by the people of this island. The "jealous horses" play a trick on the Three Magi. What happens next? January sixth, is a traditional holiday in Puerto Rico. Children excitedly await the arrival of the Three Kings, who will bring them toys and gifts. It is customary to use camels on this day, and not horses. The camels are bathed and prepared for the long voyage into the night on the eve of January fifth. The three camels, laden with toys, water, and food, depart and follow the star throughout the entire night, only to discover they have come full circle. They are perplexed as to what has happened until beetle tells them that the "star" they followed was actually a group of fireflies flying in star formation, who purposely lead them astray. The jealous horses convinced the fireflies to cooperate with their little scheme. Perez, the mouse, suggests they go and talk to Father Time. When they arrive at Time's house, they find him asleep and turn the clock back twenty-four hours. In the end, the children are not disappointed because the Three Kings arrive on time. Here we see the Christian influence of the Spaniards in this story. The sixth of January is as sacred a day as the twenty-fifth of December.

The rest of the folktales are enjoyable, wonderful, and varied in their themes of greed, friendship, and harmony. This selection should be read by elementary school children. The illustrations are colorful and well-detailed. ELIZABETH CAPIFALI

Bread, Bread, Bread

📖 Ann Morris ✎ Ken Heyman

Multicultural

1989, Scholastic, Inc.

Bread, Bread, Bread, combines simple text with color photographs to show that bread is a universal food. The photographs demonstrate bread in many shapes, sizes, and packages. They show bread mixed, shaped, baked, and then sold so that people may eat it. People from around the world enliven the pages, all eating, making, or selling bread. Morris concludes the text by joyously inviting readers to have a bite.

A lively photographic journey around the world showing how bread is made and eaten in other countries.

Included at the end of the book is an index which identifies the origins of each photograph and a brief description of the bread. The people and their breads included in this engaging book are from Peru, Guatemala, Israel, United States, Ghana, England, Indonesia, France, Portugal, India, Germany, Italy, Greece, Mexico, Ecuador, and Hong Kong.

This book has many possibilities for classroom use. The photographs offer a view around the world which gives readers a glimpse of different styles of dress, living, transportation, and architecture. Using bread as a unifying theme provides a potential springboard for exploring other common aspects of the many cultures represented. *Through discussion readers can be encouraged to examine similarities and differences among cultures. And, of course, readers can make bread, which involves their senses and is a concrete way to explore math and science.*

DEBORAH PATTERSON

Ashanti To Zulu: African Traditions

📖 Margaret Musgrove ✎ Leo Dillon and Diane Dillon

African

1992 (1976), Puffin Books

Young readers must constantly struggle to relate the letters of the alphabet to actual words, places, and people. *Ashanti to Zulu* is an alphabet book that links letters and common objects from twenty-six different African peoples. *Ashanti to Zulu* is well researched: Margaret Musgrove has lived and studied in Ghana, and has done extensive research there, as well as at the University of Massachusetts and Yale University; and the illustrators, Leo and Diane Dillon, studied authentic African designs and artifacts at the Schomburg Center for Research in Black Culture, the New York Public Library Picture Collection, the United Nations Library and Information Office, and the American Museum of Natural History.

The artwork for this book is truly extraordinary. The illustrations for each letter are as detailed as possible to represent each tribe accurately, depicting women, men, children, dwellings, artifacts, and animals native to Africa's different regions. Although twenty-six different tribes are represented, the artists depict the unique features of each tribe and keep them distinct from each other. Each image is framed by a design based on the Kano Knot (a woven

A marvelous alphabet/picture book for all ages that portrays twenty-six African tribes and their traditions.

design symbolizing endless searching, that originated in Kano [Ghana] during the sixteenth and seventeenth century). The final page of the book is a map of the African continent which shows the territory proper to each tribe.

In the text, each letter is represented with an African word and phonetic spelling, followed by a definition that is really a brief story about the land, its people, and their customs. Musgrove's approach gives a context for each word that is easily understandable. For the letter *C* the author writes, *Chagga,* (chah'-guy).

563

564

Children grow up in groups with other children of the same age and sex. Often a group takes a name that sounds brave or proud. The children work, play, and go to school together. In a special initiation ceremony they all become adults at the same time. Chagga priests perform this ceremony in traditional costumes, and sometimes the children's faces are painted. After a big celebration the children are considered adults."

Ashanti to Zulu is an alphabet book with a depth of information about African people and such attention to detail in the illustrations that it goes far beyond the age range normally considered for alphabet books. It can certainly be appreciated by readers from preschool through adulthood.

ROSA E. WARDER

Festival In My Heart: Poems by Japanese Children

Kawasaki Hiroshi (translated by Bruno Navasky)
Various sources
Asian, Japanese
1993, Harry N. Abrams, Inc.

Festival in My Heart is a virtual feast of poems written by elementary school students in Japan and originally published in the "Lifestyle & Culture" section of a Japanese newspaper. Kawasaki Hiroshi, a well-known Japanese writer who has published over sixty books, was their original editor. His affection for energetic, humorous subject matter and imagery is immediately evident and highly appealing. In his preface, Hiroshi writes, "there are children who still have soul enough to greet the natural world as a friend... I believe these are the ones who will write poems to make us adults gasp with wonder." Indeed, the whole tenor and tone of this book is one of gracious friendliness and invitation. This is unquestionably one of the best books of poems by children from any country ever collected.

A top-notch anthology of poetry written by Japanese children, enhanced by a selection of Japanese art.

The poems subject matter is tangible and compelling—working moms, baths, automatic ticket machines, garbage, and fireworks, as well as emperors, rivers, seeds, and school. A poem by Ishi Satoshi, a kindergartner (some of the poems were dictated to adults), called "Grandma's Wrinkles," is a guaranteed young-crowd-pleaser. "My grandmother's face/is covered with wrinkles./If you count on her forehead/there are twelve big ones./I drew a picture/of grandma's face—/I only drew a few wrinkles,/little ones so grandma/was very happy/and laughed. Then there were more wrinkles than before,/but I didn't tell her so."

Bruno Navasky, who translated the poems into elegant, natural English, lived in Japan for two years, doing research and teaching a class of first-graders. His translations bear none of the awkward lumpiness people sometimes associate with translated material. The stunningly beautiful illustrations represent the vast spectrum of Japanese art and include woodblock prints, scroll paintings, ink paintings, as well as screens, kites, and sculpture. A splendid fish swirls in a lively current on the cover.

For anyone needing material to cross the crucial cultural bridge between Japan and the United States, this book is IT. I'm pleased that most of the poems are longer than haiku, so teachers in the United States may extend their knowledge of "Japanese form." The poems could easily be used to stimulate children's writing on our side of the ocean. They lend themselves to immediate discussion and interaction.

NAOMI SHIHAB NYE

Heather Has Two Mommies

Leslea Newman / Diana Souza
Gay/Lesbian/Bisexual
1991 (1989), Alyson Wonderland Publications, Inc.

Textured and stylized drawings of happy, bouncing children and strong, confident women illustrate this story of a young girl with two mothers. The story explains, in plain and simple language, how Heather's Mama Kate and Mom Jane met, fell in love, and decided to have a child. Jane goes to a "special doctor" to make sure she's healthy, and then the doctor "put some sperm into Jane's vagina. The sperm swam up into Jane's womb. If there was an egg waiting there, the sperm and the egg would meet, and the baby would start to grow." The same even explanatory tone permeates

A classic, groundbreaking book that addresses the topics of same-gender parents and artificial insemination in an honest, positive, and touching manner.

the rest of the descriptions of Jane's bodily changes and childbirth. The pictures throughout this section of the book show Jane and Kate affectionately touching and looking at one another.

While the description of the process of artificial insemination stirred up controversy when the book was included in New York City's Children of the Rainbow multicultural curriculum, the rest of the book centers on Heather's ethnically diverse play group, illustrating and describing their wide variety of family units. When Heather hears that a playmate has a father, she feels bad that she is missing out on something. The play group leader Molly explains that Heather's family is special, as are the families of all the other children. They each share with Heather what makes their families special, including stepparents, nuclear families, families of adopted children, and other single-gender families. Interestingly enough, the words gay, lesbian, and homosexual do not appear, though the two mommies are shown in very affectionate and loving physical contact. CHRIS MAYO

Bein' With You This Way

🖩 W. Nikola-Lisa ✎ Michael Bryant
Multicultural
1995 (1994), Lee & Low Books, Inc.

Bein' With You This Way is unabashedly a book with a message. It begins with a young African American girl in the park, addressing an ethnically diverse group of children, along with one or two adults. "Hey, everybody are you ready? Uh-huh! Then snap those fingers and tap those toes, and sing along with me. All right! Here we go... She has straight hair. He has curly hair. How perfectly remarkably strange, Uh-huh! Straight hair. Curly hair. Different —Mm-mmm, but the same, Ah-ha! Now isn't that beautiful, simply unusual, bein' with you this way!" They make their way through the park, pointing out noses large and small, eyes blue and brown, arms thick and thin, legs long and short, skin light and dark, all "Different . . . but the same."

An idealistic, bouncy book about multiracial friendships and goodwill that is a natural for young readers.

Impressionistic watercolor and colored pencil illustrations depict characters from a variety of cultural backgrounds, all getting along harmonious-

ly as they climb on playground equipment, watch a family playing chess, chase birds, and play in the sandbox. Care is given to differentiate African, Asian, European and Latino physical characteristics, but there are no stereotypes; each person is portrayed as a distinct individual.

This is a world in which the reality of racial tension is acknowledged only indirectly: if there were no discord, there would be no need for a book stressing the essential similarities of all people. The bouncy rhythm and cheerful children of *Bein' With You This Way* will lead young readers easily and naturally to the happy conclusion that differences do not have to bring conflict.
LYNN EISENHUT

Indo-Hispanic Folk Art Traditions I

🖩 ✎ Bobbi Salinas-Norman
Hispanic, Mexican
1988, Piñata Books, ✳ Bilingual English/Spanish

This publication contains an extensive array of traditional and creative activities celebrating the Mexican holiday *Los Posadas*, a Christmas celebration marked by festive processions and visits to family, friends, and loved ones. The book includes numerous pages of black-and-white glossy photographs depicting a typical *Posadas*. Activities include the lyrics and music for songs, easy and comprehensive instructions for arts and crafts projects, historic recipes, and ideas for producing a *Posadas*, complete with ancestral costuming guidelines. The author also provides a wonderful discussion of the use of folklore in the classroom and provides significant historical descriptions for each activity, bringing a rich sense of the importance of heritage and culture.

An exceptional collection that offers a fun look at the Mexican Christmas holiday Los Posadas.

The text is replete with the customary vocabulary. An extensive glossary, a pronunciation guide, and a bibliography are located in the back. Line-drawn illustrations are simple in appearance but clearly demonstrate each action.

Now in its fourth edition, this book is one of the most comprehensive offerings on *Posadas*. It is appropriate for classroom and home use, with or without adult supervision. Because of the substantive cultural information, *Indo-Hispanic Folk Art Traditions* is also suitable for reports on Mexico and the Mexican-American experience. The Spanish and English versions of the text are bound together as a unit. An exceptional addition to any collection on Latino culture. PATTY WONG

Indo-Hispanic Folk Art Traditions II

📖 Bobbi Salinas-Norman ✒ Various Sources
Hispanic, Mexican, ✳ Bilingual English/Spanish

Celebrated the day before Halloween, *Dia de los Muertos* is a wonderful rite of passage, full of colors and pageantry, honoring the lives of dead loved ones. The festivities feature papier-mâché skeleton figures dressed in traditional clothing, graves decorated with bright orange and red flowers, and elaborate home altars, including a mixture of religious and indigenous artifacts: photographs of the deceased, beautiful papercuts, crosses, candles, and even toys.

Indo-Hispanic Folk Art Traditions II, beautifully captures the cultural richness of this traditional celebration. Like Indo-*Hispanic Folk Art Traditions I*, this book features several

The Mexican holiday Day of the Dead is brought to life in this collection of activities, lyrics, illustrations, and photographs.

arts-and-crafts and curriculum-related activities. The numerous pages of black-and-white and color photographs depicting typical *Dia de los Muertos* celebrations document this highly visual festival, and line-drawn illustrations clearly demonstrate each action in the activities section.

Indo-Hispanic Folk Art Traditions II *is the most definitive and comprehensive work to date on this subject for children and instructors. A map of Mexico, a bibliography on materials for children about death, and a glossary with pronunciation guide are also included. The text is suitable for reports on Mexico and the Mexican American experience. The Spanish and English versions of the text are bound together as a unit. This fourth edition is essential for any collection on Latino culture.* PATTY WONG

A Place for Grace

📖 Jean Davis Okimoto ✒ Doug Keith
Physically Disabled
1993, Sasquatch Books

Being too small to serve as a seeing-eye dog, Grace seems unable to find her place. But Charlie, a hearing-impaired man, realizes that this little dog can learn to become the ears for a person in need. With animals playing a greater role in supporting the emotional, psychological, and physical needs of people, this story reminds young readers that animals can help humans in turning disability into ability.

A warm story about a dog's role in the life of the disabled.

As has been noted in folktales and fairy tales, it is often easier for children to relate to animals than to people. The book becomes even more powerful because Grace is not simply dismissed because she can't serve as a guide dog for the blind. Her other strengths are recognized, and Charlie works with Grace to cultivate and support those strengths. Her inherent intelligence combined with the training to become a hearing dog, is clearly demonstrated in this story.

The warm style of the writing and illustrations convey the intelligence and endearing qualities that are required of hearing dogs. The book expresses the universal love and respect that often comes in relationships between dogs and people. MEREDITH ELIASSEN

Bitter Bananas

📖 Isaac Olaleye ✒ Ed Young
African
1994, Caroline House

Young Yusuf loves to drink palm sap, and he sells whatever is left at the market to help his family. One day, he discovers that baboons are stealing the sap. Despite his attempts to scare them off, the baboons keep coming

With the help of his family, a young African boy is able to stop baboons from stealing palm sap in a fun, popular book.

back. Finally, with the help of his family, he tricks the baboons into leaving him in peace.

The story is rich with playful onomatopoeia (The "bireep, bireep" of frogs, and the "urrp, urrp, grr-umph" of the baboons). Illustrations use vibrant colors and collage technique to evoke the lushness and energy of an African rainforest.

Bitter Bananas is fun to share and popular with children. Yusef's ingenuity and perseverance are appealing and set a positive example. He earns his sweet rewards. His family readily helps him when asked. He is industrious and independent, and he performs a job he enjoys that helps his family. JACKIE LYNCH

A Is for Africa: An Alphabet Book

▨ Ifeoma Onyefulu ✦ Ife Nii Owoo

African, Nigerian

1993 (1992), Cobblehill Books, ✳ Series

A Is for Africa is a useful addition to a collection of alphabet books. Written and illustrated by Ife Nii Owoo, this book uses a familiar format to present an accurate depiction of Africa and its people.

The words for each letter include more predictable items such as elephant and zebra as well as lesser-known items related to food, music, and work.

An alphabet book that helps enrich children's understanding of Africa.

Intermixed with the objects are concept words important to an understanding of Africa such as liberation, independence, and unity. The continent's diversity is emphasized. African people are depicted as looking and speaking differently and having different customs. In addition, there is an excellent balance between depictions of men and women in the illustrations. People of both genders are shown working, going to school, and fighting for independence. The vision of a continent that emerges from the book is both positive and realistic.

One unfortunate omission is a depiction of urban life in Africa. DONNA GAGNON

My Buddy

▨ Audrey Osofsky ✦ Ted Rand

Physically Disabled

1994 (1992), Henry Holt and Company

In this realistic and informative book, a young boy with muscular dystrophy finds a new friend in man's best friend. The boy has to rely on his family to perform a lot of the everyday tasks which his MD prevents him from doing. He feels uncomfortable, always having to ask people to assist him until, one day, he meets Buddy, a service dog who is trained to perform sixty commands. Buddy is not only a practical help with things like turning light switches on and off, but a good social ice-breaker for the boy. Together,

they take us through a typical day in their lives. We learn about the many useful ways that dogs can help people with disabilities, but also gain insight into the "disability-unfriendly" environment in which we live. *Children can discuss environmental changes that can be made to respond to many disabilities; wheelchair ramps, for example, alleviate the difficulty of entering buildings.*

Buddy and his master are more than just employer/employee; they are the best of friends who love and care for one another.

An informative story about a young boy with muscular dystrophy and his service dogs.

Activities:
1. Invite a physical therapist/occupational therapist to class. Bring equipment (wheelchair, prosthesis, etc.) for children to see and touch.
2. Take turns spending an entire school day in a wheelchair, or blindfolded. What does it feel like? Was it frustrating? What activities were you prevented form doing? What tasks did you rely on others to perform for you?
BARBARA SMITH REDDISH

Dreamcatcher

▨ Audrey Osofsky ✦ Ed Young

Native American, Ojibway

1992, Orchard Books

Ojibway dreamcatchers are willow hoops laced with a spider web of sinew, decorated with beads and feathers. Audrey Osofky's *Dreamcatcher* uses these artifacts as an occasion to tell a story and describe Ojibwa life in the process.

Osofsky describes traditional Ojibway life in a tissue of delicate, sometimes ominous, imagery. The story begins with a sleeping baby: "Dreaming

568

on a cradleboard, wrapped in doeskin soft and snug". Ojibway babies are strapped snugly to a cradleboard for the first two or three years of life to protect them and sharpen their senses. Osofsky's baby accompanies mother, sister, and grandmother as they go about their daily chores. Baby overhears a conversation between grandmother and big sister that was a routine part of Ojibwa education: "What did you see today that was beautiful... what did you hear that was pleasing?" asks grandmother.

The author traces the origins of a Native American artifact in a beautifully illustrated book that explores traditional Ojibway life.

As the day passes, baby watches and listens to the women working, the children playing, and his father paddling his canoe and, in this way, he is introduced to Ojibwa life.

Osofsky eloquently describes the dreamcatcher made by big sister "on a little willow hoop... like a small spider web, spun on nettle-stalk twine, stained dark red with the bark of wild plum." Nightmarish bears, owls, and "raggedy man in the dark" haunt the baby's sleep. The dreamcatcher traps them in its web, letting only good dreams pass through the hole in its center.

Ed Young's softly shaded illustrations convey the feel and rhythm of traditional Ojibway village life. Like the children in Young's 1990 Caldecott winner, *Lon Po Po: A Red-Riding Hood Story from China* (Philomel), the baby's eyes occasionally sparkle with character. Young interprets the baby's stages of sleep with different tones of color. He draws the baby dozing in blues and greens, deeply asleep in a wash of dark purple, and awakening in light-streaked coral. Each of Young's full-page illustrations is contrasted with a black border, on which Young has recreated an intricate pattern of flowers common in Ojibway beadwork.

Osofsky credits her inspiration for *Dreamcatcher* to the work of noted ethnomusicologist Frances Densmore (1867–1957). Densmore is best known for her extensive recordings of American Indian music. Her authoritative work, *Chippewa Customs* (1929), is still in print, although it does not include dreamcatchers. The scarcity of print materials about dreamcatchers makes Osofsky's treatment of the subject a welcome one. The National Council for the Social Studies selected *Dreamcatcher* as one of its Notable 1992 Children's Trade Books.

Children should be reminded that Osofsky is interpreting one version of the dreamcatcher legend out of many that exist. They should also be made to understand that *Dreamcatcher* idealizes Ojibway life, in contrast to reality then and now. *For information about Ojibway life and traditions, Minneapolis Public Schools publishes a wide array of curriculum materials for grades K-12. Although most crafts stores will have dreamcatcher kits or plans, I would not recommend encouraging non-Native people to make dreamcatchers, since they have a specific Native American function.* MELISSA HECKARD

Walk in Peace: Legends & Stories of the Michigan

Simon Otto, Edited by M.T. Bussey
Kayle Crampton
Native American, Ojibway
1992 (1990), Michigan Indian Press,
Benton-Banai, Edward, *The Mishomis Book: The Voice of the Ojibway.*

Michigan author Simon Otto retells eighteen Anishnabek legends and stories in this illustrated collection. *Anishnabek*, an Ojibway/Odawa word meaning the first, or original people, are Native peoples who migrated to the Great Lakes region from the Atlantic coast close to a thousand years ago. The name endures among contemporary Ojibway and Odawa peoples.

A fine picture book that retells eighteen Anishnabek legends and stories.

Son of an Ojibway father and an Odawa mother, Otto grew up surrounded by the traditions and stories of Northern Michigan's native community, and now devotes his time to writing and educating others about his heritage.

Through characters found in nature, such as the Turtle, Eagle, Moose, North Wind, and Cedar Tree, Otto writes about Anishnabek history and culture. His characters reflect the close relationship with nature held by Otto and his ancestors. Otto affirms this relationship in his preface, where he states that "being part of Mother Earth" led him to share these stories. Most of the stories also feature the character Nanaboozhoo, a supernatural being who is hero, trickster, and teacher to the Anishnabek. Beliefs, morals, values, cultural practices, and historical facts — these tales offer a little bit of everything.

Some of the tales explain the origin of natural phenomena. In the legend, "Turtle Gets a Shell," Nanaboozhoo apologizes to Mishekae (turtle) for stepping on her in a moment of foolishness. He gives her two shells and a special status among the Anishnabek, one that endures to the present. One story relates a more recent historical event, the arrival of the first Europeans. "The Council Meeting at Gitchi Wequeton" is the story of Chi-wee-bit (Big Tooth), who travels by canoe to meet with Anishnabek leaders and learns about the "tall strange men" exploring the big lakes region. Many of the tales deal with the theme of human faults, such as jealousy, pride, or selfishness. A young eagle's jealousy brings him disastrous consequences in "The Eagle Who Flew Too High."

Otto's selections are short, from one to three pages, and written in a direct, unpretentious style. Their simplicity makes them understandable to young children and easy to memorize for retelling. Otto is careful to remind readers and listeners that these are tales from a particular community and might be told differently elsewhere. His advice pertains to Native stories from any source. Kale Crampton's soft, realistic, black-and-white drawings of animals enhance many of the selections. Her drawings are small, which limits their value for large group read-aloud. Her simple style may inspire young readers to further illustrate these or other stories.

Walk in Peace *is suitable for read-aloud to lower elementary children and for independent reading by those at the upper elementary level. For older children or adults, Otto's stories complement research about Michigan's native peoples or the environment of the Great Lakes, and his writing rates with that of the best regional storytellers. An excellent companion to Otto's work is Edward Benton-Banai's* The Mishomis Book: The Voice of the Ojibway *(Red School House, 1979), a more in-depth treatment of Ojibway religion, history, and culture, written for young people from the Ojibway perspective.* MELISSA HECKARD

The Red Comb

📕 Fernando Pico (translated by Argentina Palacios) 🖋 Maria Antonia Ordonez

Hispanic, Puerto Rican

1994 (1991), Bridgewater Books, ✳ Spanish

The history of slavery in Puerto Rico has received relatively little attention. African slaves were brought forcibly to Puerto Rico or arrived on the island while fleeing from other countries. This book addresses this little known-history.

Greedy Pedro Calderon turns in runaway slaves to the Spaniards in exchange for large amounts of money. Rosa Bultron, an elderly woman, has compassion for the runaways and supports their desire to seek freedom. Señora Rosa reminds her fellow Puerto Ricans that their ancestors were slaves from Antigua who ran away from the English. This important connection links Puerto Ricans to a history of slavery and their black ancestry.

Señora Rosa's neighbor is a quiet, industrious young girl named Vitita, who lives with and takes care of her father and brothers. One day Vitita discovers a young woman who is a runaway slave under her house. She immediately shares this news with Señora Rosa, who encourages her not to tell her father but to leave plantains and sugar-cane juice for the runaway. After a few nights of leaving food, Vitita decides to leave the young woman a red comb given to her by her godmother.

The author Fernando Pico, an ordained Jesuit priest, is a history professor at the University of Puerto Rico. This book is full of the traditions and culture of the *jibaros* (peasants from the mountainside) who live in the interior of Puerto Rico. The illustrations are very realistic in their depiction of people, their villages, and the beautiful mountains surrounding them. This is a touching story that addresses aspects of a history rarely taught in classrooms. ELIZABETH CAPIFALI

A touching historical story of a Puerto Rican and a Spanish runaway slave that illuminates the history of slavery in Puerto Rico.

Stories for Free Children

📕 Edited by Letty Cottin Pogrebin
🖋 Various sources

Multicultural

1982, McGraw Hill

The visionary leadership that developed and published *Ms.* magazine, beginning in the spring of 1972, clearly understood the need for a feature focused on children. For more than ten years, "A Story for Free Children" was a regular feature in the magazineo and included pieces which have become literary treasures. Lois Gould's "X," for example, is a story about parents who refuse to name or reveal the gender identity of their child in order to prevent assumptions about who the child might become and what the child might do in life. Letty Cottin Pogrebin's article, "Baseball Diamonds Are a Girl's Best Friend," examines the sexist attitudes that prevent girls from having the same opportunities to excel in sports as boys have.

In collaboration with her son Slade Morrison, Toni Morrison wrote "The Big Box," a witty story-poem about adults admonishing free-spirited children.

> But you have to know how far to go
> So the grown-up world can abide you.
> Now the rules are listed on the walls,
> So there's no need to repeat them.
> We all agree, your parents and we,
> That you just can't handle your freedom.

Profiles of pioneering women doctors and abolitionists such as Dorothy Brown and Lucretia Mott are interspersed with fairy tales and fables. And some of the pieces are cleverly illustrated. In Shirley Camper Soman's "A Gun is No Fun," bullets are interspersed with the words and a submachine gun is positioned right through the middle of the story. While seasoned writers and skilled illustrators, including Julie Maas, Nancy Lawton, and Ray Cruz, are included, so is Catherine Petroski's thirteen-year-old daughter, who illustrated her own story "Beautiful My Mane in the Wind."

One of the earliest multicultural anthologies, a classic and endearing collection of short stories, fables, and fairytales.

Stories for Free Children is surely destined to become a classic in children's literature.
DAPHNE MUSE

Chicken Sunday

Patricia Polacco

Jewish, African American

1992, The Putnam Publishing Co., Luciow, Johanna, *Eggs Beautiful*; *How to Make Ukranian Eggs*; Polacco, Patricia, *Rechenka's Eggs*.

Polacco tells a spirited story from her own childhood. All the love she felt for the people in her life is poured into this book celebrating the richness diversity can add to our lives. The narrator, a young girl of Russian-Jewish heritage, tells how she and her friends, two African American boys, Stewart and Winston, wanted more than anything to buy the boys' grandmother a beautiful Easter bonnet.

Unfortunately when they go to ask the hat maker, an Orthodox Jew, if they can work for him to earn the bonnet, he thinks they are the children who once threw eggs at his shop.

A spirited story of a Jewish girl and two African American boys who break religious barriers to befriend an old Jewish man.

Miss Eula Mae, the boys' grandmother, tells them they must find a way to show the man that they are good children, so they make him a basket of *pysanke* eggs. On the Reading Rainbow episode that features her book, "Rechenka's Eggs," Polacco demonstrates how to make *pysanke* eggs by painting wax designs on them, dipping them in dye, painting more designs, dipping them in another color, etc., and then melting off the wax. *Children*

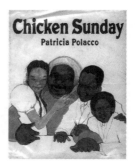

can partially experience this process by using watercolors and candle wax on paper outlines of an egg. The basket of *pysanke* eggs, brings Stewart and Winston a new friend and the coveted hat. Polacco's folk-art style of illustration is greatly enriched by the collage addition of photographs of the real Washington family and is a perfect tribute to Miss Eula Mae, with her "voice of Oslow thunder and sweet rain." VICKI MERRILL

The Tamarindo Puppy and Other Poems

Charlotte Pomerantz   Byron Barton

Hispanic

1993 (1980), William Morrow,   Bilingual English/Spanish

This is a bilingual book of thirteen poems about the love shared between family, friends, and pets. In "Hugs and Kisses," Maria's mother is going away for a month. Maria asks for and gets a kiss for each of those days—30 small kisses, *treinta besitos*. Then she asks for and gets a hug for each day—30 big hugs, *treinta abrazos*. Emboldened by her success, the little girl asks for a doll for every day that Mami

An illustrated collection of thirteen appealing poems about family and pets, with some text in Spanish.

is away. "No indeed, Maria!" says Mami.

"The Four Brothers" is a tongue twister about similarly named brothers. Two of them marry women whose names are similar to their husbands. The two couples have sons with derivative names and these sons also marry women with names similar to their husbands' names. Just when you think you've got it figured out, the other two brothers surprise you with something else.

The shorter poems are less complex, but still fun. The book assumes some knowledge of Spanish; no pronunciation guides are provided. The titular puppy looks like a Jack Russell terrier in search of an owner and the drawings look like those that might have been done by a child. It is an appealing book that will reassure and bring a laugh.

LESLIE ANDERSON MORALES

If I Had a Paka

📖 Charlotte Pomerantz ✏ Nancy Tufari

Multicultural

1993 (1982), Greenwillow Books, ✳ Multilingual

Twelve original poems by Charlotte Pomerantz, predominantly in English, incorporate words and phrases from ten other languages into the text. Usually the poem is printed once, with the non-English words translated in context, as in the title poem: "If I had a *pika*—meow, meow, meow, meow—I would want a *mm-bwa*—bow wow wow wow. If I had a *mm-bwa*—bow wow wow wow—I would want a *simba*—roar, roar, roar." Small children will enjoy guessing the meanings of the Swahili animal names by the sounds the animals make. Other poems rely on direct translation. "Lulu, Lulu, I've a lilo" presents two versions of a poem side by side, one in English alone, the other exchanging some English terms for Samoan.

A fun-to-read book of twelve original poems that introduce words and phrases from eleven different languages.

Sharing these poems with children will not result in a multilingual classroom, nor (since they are not drawn from traditional literature, nor composed by native speakers from the nations represented) will they necessarily help children to understand other cultures. However, they are fun to read and can pique a child's interest in learning about other languages.

Nancy Tufari's characteristic watercolor illustrations—large, deceptively simple flat blocks of color—effectively convey the mood created by the poems. The subjects depicted range from animals to people, vegetables to coffeepots, all portrayed in a manner relevant to a young child's experience. Human characters are appropriately chosen for the featured languages: an Asian child pensively chews a sandwich in "Toy Tik Ka" (Vietnamese), while a Latino boy explains that while he doesn't like rice and beans he's quite fond of "Arroz y Habichuelas" (Spanish). Imaginative framing (we see only the feet of one "lulu" flying off the page with the narrator's sololo) and vivid colors help capture readers' attention.

LYNN EISENHUT

Addy Learns a Lesson: A School Story

📖 Connie Porter ✏ Melodye Rosales

African American

1993, Pleasant Company Publications, ✳ Series

This book is divided into two sections. The first part tells the story of nine-year-old Addy Walker and her mother who arrive in Philadelphia to begin life in freedom. Everything is new to them in the big city. Addy finds a kind friend, Sarah, and she goes to school for the first time. Sarah's mother gets Addy's mother a job as a seamstress in Mrs. Ford's Dress Shop, and Mrs. Ford allows Addy and her mother to live in her garret.

When Sarah tells Addy they are only allowed to ride the streetcar designated for black people, Addy is confused and discusses the issue with her mother. "This where freedom supposed to be at," Addy tells her mother. "There ain't supposed to be things colored folks can't do." Addy's mother assures her that she is right, but "there's more to freedom than riding a streetcar." She goes on to say "There ain't nobody here that own us, and beat us, and work us like animals. I got me a paying job. You can go to school and learn to read and write. When you got an education, you got a freedom nobody can take from you."

After escaping slavery during the Civil War, Addy learns the meaning of freedom and true friendship in this book from the thoughtful Addy series.

In school, Addy sits next to Harriet (named after Harriet Tubman), who is smart, wealthy, and popular, and who has the life Addy thought freedom would bring her. Addy learns to read and write through the support of Sarah and Harriet. At the end of each school day, Addy rushes home to teach her mother what she has learned. Addy turns out to be a strong student and eventually wins the spelling bee. Addy wants both Sarah and Harriet to be her friends, but when she must choose between them, Addy learns some important lessons about friendship and real freedom.

The second part—the nonfiction section—describes how even though there were laws against educating enslaved African Americans, some secretly learned to read and write. Thousands of blacks knew education meant true freedom. Education opened the door to better jobs and better lives. JOAN PRIMEAUX

Where's Chimpy?

📖 Bernice Rabe 🖋 Kathleen Tucker and Diane Schmidt

Mentally Disabled

1988, Albert Whitman & Company

A young girl with Down's Syndrome takes the reader on a journey through her day in this excellent book for young children.

It's bedtime, and Misty wants her father to read her and her toy monkey a bedtime story. But Misty can't find Chimpy and must retrace her steps to locate him. Along the way, she finds other items that were misplaced during the day. Eventually, she finds Chimpy under a towel on the bathroom chair. Now that they're ready for the bedtime story, Misty's father discovers that he's misplaced his glasses. Misty finds the glasses under the storybook which has dropped to the floor. After the story, Misty counts all of the things that she found when retracing the steps of her day.

Although she has Down's Syndrome, Misty is portrayed as clever, creative, and capable. This book is an excellent tool for developing in young children an awareness about Down's Syndrome. Illustrated with photographs, the book depicts Misty dealing with the same kind of daily routine that many other children have. The book also emphasizes that looking different does not mean one is incapable of doing many of the same things other children the same age can do. It might take more time to do them and more patience, but Misty clearly shows that she is quite independent and competent.

Activities:
1. An excellent introduction to the congenital condition of Down's Syndrome is the book Our Brother Has Down's Syndrome. *This could be read aloud and discussed.*
2. After you have discussed the book and brought a certain level of awareness to the class invite a relative or friend of someone who has Down's Syndrome to talk about meeting the challenges of this particular disability.
BARBARA A. KANE

The Balancing Girl

📖 Bernice Rabe 🖋 Lillian Hoban

Physically Disabled

1988 (1981), Dutton Children's Books, ✳ Series

Margaret is a six-year-old girl who manages her mobility through the use of a wheelchair and crutches. This story focuses Margaret abilities, rather than her disabilities. She is adept at balancing objects—books, Magic Markers, blocks, cylinders, and dominoes—while moving along in her wheelchair. She can also balance herself while hopping on her crutches. She is self sufficient and capable of dealing

This fine book focuses on a disabled young girl's abilities rather than on her disabilities.

effectively with difficult situations. A classmate, Tommy, is jealous of her ability and all the attention she receives. He takes advantage of every opportunity he can find to destroy her creations.

A school carnival is planned to raise money for gym equipment, and the children are asked to come up with ideas for carnival booths. Margaret's idea is to set up domino blocks and sell tickets for the privilege of pushing down the first domino. Tommy wins the drawing.

Margaret's teacher has the same expectations for Margaret that she has for her other students, giving Margaret no preferential treatment.

The illustrations are beautiful. Margaret's wheelchair, crutches, and braces are depicted as devices that enable her to participate more fully in life's activities, rather than as obstacles to her participation. She appears to be determined and self confident when attempting something new.

Activities:
1. It might be interesting to bring to class devices that help disabled people, such as a wheelchair, crutches, braces, and slings so that the children can experience them firsthand.
2. You might even want to have children attempt to do everyday tasks using these devices.
BARBARA A. KANE

The Handmade Alphabet

📖 ✒ Laura Rankin
Physically Disabled
1991, Dial Books For Young Readers

In *The Handmade Alphabet*, Laura Rankin provides a handshape for the manual alphabet used in American Sign Language, and a corresponding letter of the written alphabet. The handshape then interacts with images shown in the book's artwork.

A superbly illustrated alphabet book in written form as well as in American Sign Language.

The superb illustrations, made with colored pencil on charcoal paper are both beautiful and dynamic. These manual alphabet signs which require movement are cleverly illustrated to indicate that movement. The illustration for the letter *J* simulates the motion of this letter by showing the little finger dipping into the jar of jam.

The selection of specific ideas or words are creatively chosen, offering the opportunity for thought and imagination. More colorful and inventive than most other books on sign language, this book offers an insightful connection between the letter and its manual alphabet sign. This book will offer classrooms a unique form of communication for both hearing and hearing-impaired children.

The hands pictured throughout the book are representative of various cultures and age levels. The hands chosen are appropriate to the object or idea shown; thus, a young child's hand shows *K* for a key rattle and a woman's hand shows *L* for lace. The cover illustrations are not repetitions of those inside, but provide additional concepts. These additional illustrations indicate the dedication of the author/illustrator to broaden the concept of this visual language. BARBARA GOLDENHERSH

Yo! Yes?

📖 ✒ Chris Raschka
African American
1993, Orchard Books

Two boys—one black, one white—meet. "YO!" says the first boy. "Yes?" replies the other sheepishly. Will they be friends? Can two people who look different be friends? The answer offered here is a resounding yes.

Author Chris Raschka masterfully portrays the drama of the boys' encounter against a simple background of color washes that shifts from cool, tentative blues at the beginning of the book to a warm, exuberant yellow at

Two lonely characters, one black and one white, meet on the street and become friends in a wise Caldecott Honor book.

the end. Perhaps to emphasize the universal nature of his tale—or to leave room for each reader's imagination—Raschka employs minimum narrative detail. His focus is on the boys; the slouches, the glances, the locked knees, and thrown up arms he captures are immediate and almost unnervingly familiar.

The text, composed completely of the boys' staccato dialogue of one- and two-word questions and answers, is as focused and telling as are the illustrations. Sometimes the boys' words are large, energetic, and affirmative; sometimes they are small. The hand-lettered words even shift from black to red on three of the crucial pages of the book—when with curved shoulders one boy reveals that he has "No friends"; when the other forcefully says "Look" and offers himself as a friend; and finally when the two join hands, jump up, and call out "Yow" together on the last spread. Like the wash backgrounds, the words themselves are attuned to the boys' emotions.

This is a wise book, well deserving of the 1993 Caldecott Honor it received. It reminds readers that strangers can become friends and that there's bound to be joy when a tentative "Yes?" becomes an exuberant "Yes!" ANNE DAVIES

573

Margaret and Margarita

▣ ✎ Lynn W. Reiser
Hispanic
1993, Greewillow, ✱ Bilingual English/Spanish

"There's nobody to play with" are words that parents often hear. For Margaret and Margarita, the language barrier prevents them from playing together —initially. While one speaks Spanish and the other English, their curiosity finally gets the best of them, and their shyness turns into an attempt at greeting one another in their respective languages, starting with hello.

Using the objects around them, they begin to name them and identify the colors in their respective languages. After a while, they speak with one another as though language isn't a barrier and it really doesn't matter.

Two young girls who speak different languages develop bilingual skills and a friendship in a quiet, helpful book.

When the girls' mothers decide it is time to leave the park, each child takes pleasure in introducing her new friend in a mixture of both languages. On their way home, both girls note that they want to return to the park tomorrow to meet their new-found friend.

When the girls speak with each other, the book moves into a bilingual mode. The ease with which the girls develop a communicative rapport could serve as a model for both children and adults. MARTHA L. MARTINEZ

Leagues Apart: The Men and Times of the Negro Baseball Leagues

▣ Lawrence S. Ritter ✎ Richard Merkin
African American
1995, Morrow, ▥ McKissack, Patricia, and McKissack, Frederick, *Black Diamond: The Story of the Negro Leagues;* Ward, Geoffrey C., Burns, Ken, and O'Connor, Jim, *Shadow Ball: The History of the Negro Leagues.*

Leagues Apart opens with a portrait of Babe Ruth and the question: "Who is the greatest baseball player who ever lived?" For many people Babe Ruth is the answer. But what about Hank Aaron and Willie Mays? And what about the veterans of the Negro Leagues who taught Aaron and Mays to play? Lawrence S. Ritter and Richard Merkin balance the portrait of Babe Ruth against portraits of two dozen superb Negro League athletes and show just how difficult it is to decide who was the all-time number one.

Leagues Apart is primarily a celebration of players and it is organized accordingly. Most pages feature an eye-catching portrait of one player done in oil pastel with the feel of a baseball card, and a brief summary of the player's career or special strengths. Red display type is used when a player's name first appears in the text and invites browsers to dip in and read whenever a portrait intrigues them. What readers find here are the players Babe Ruth never faced: Sluggers such as Josh Gibson or George "Mule" Suttles, whose fans chanted "Kick, Mule, Kick" when he stepped into the batter's box; versatile, all-around players such as Wilbur "Bullet Joe" Rogan or Cuba's Martin Dihigo; Rube Foster, who played as a pitcher, then organized the Negro National League in 1920; Cool Papa Bell, one of the fastest runners in Negro League history whose description of barnstorming is included; and Jackie Robinson and Satchel Paige, who finally joined the major leagues at age 42.

A marvelous picture book introduction to twenty-four of the Negro League's greatest baseball players.

As he tells the players' stories, Ritter also sketches in the background against which they played, offering an introduction to the history of the Negro League. But inquisitive readers will be left with questions. For a fuller account of the gentlemen's agreement that firmly closed major league baseball to black players until the late 1940s, the triumphs and trials of life in the Negro League, and the story of integrated baseball in Latin America, they will need to turn to longer books such as *Shadow Ball* by Geoffrey Ward and Ken Burns, or *Black Diamonds* by Patricia and Fredrick McKissack.

Even after exploring these longer histories, many readers will want to return to *Leagues Apart.* Richard Merkin's vibrant portraits will be enriched, but not replaced, by stories and statistics found elsewhere. Like an album of treasured baseball cards, this book should find a secure place in the hearts of fans. ANNE DAVIES

574

The Talking Eggs: A Folktale from the American South

📖 Robert D. San Souci ✏ Jerry Pinkney

African American

1989, Dial Books for Young Readers

In *The Talking Eggs*, San Souci, famous for his picture-book renditions of folktales, again presents us with a fictionalized version of an oral tradition. Found throughout Europe, as well as the American South, the story of the talking eggs was first collected among the Louisiana Creole and published by Alcee Fortier, a late nineteenth-century folklorist. Drawing from Fortier's version of the tale, San Souci presents a colorful, entertaining, and wondrous example of a classic tale. Coupled with Pinkney's dramatic watercolor and pencil drawings, this is a magical story in which children are able to discover the merits of kindness and patience.

An entertaining retelling of a Creole folktale, loosely based on Cinderella, featuring a virtuous African American girl and her evil sister.

The story focuses on an adolescent African American girl, Blanche, and her older sister, Rose. Rose is favored and spoiled by their vain mother. It is Blanche who works to provide for the family, and it is Blanche who is sent to retrieve water for a hot and thirsty Rose on a warm summer day. On the path to the well, Blanche encounters an elderly woman to whom she willingly serves a drink of water. In return for her kindness, Blanche is rewarded with a scolding from her mother, because the water she brought for Rose had turned warm along the way. Blanche escapes to the woods following her mother's tirade, where she again meets the elderly woman to whom she offered water.

The woman offers Blanche shelter for the evening if she promises not to laugh at anything she sees at the woman's house. Blanche agrees, and though she is surprised and at times wary of the things she witnesses (for example, a two-headed cow with spiral horns that brays like a mule), she manages to keep her promise to the woman. The following morning, the woman tells Blanche to go out to the barn and take only those eggs that do not plead with her to take them. Of course, it is the beautiful and jeweled eggs that Blanche cannot take, but she remains true to the old woman's instructions, and takes only the plain white eggs. She is rewarded by the jewels and dresses that fall from the eggs.

Elated by her discovery, Blanche shares this news with her mother and sister. Rose ventures into the forest in search of the old woman's house of wonder and, as befits a pampered and mean-spirited sister in many a fairy tale, she proves to be unable to hold to any of the woman's instructions. When she takes the jeweled eggs that spoke to her, she and her mother are chased by the wolves, snakes, and wasps that spring from their shattered eggshells. In San Souci's version of the tale, Blanche leaves for the city to live the life of a rich woman from the profits of her newly acquired jewels.

The Talking Eggs is a beautifully designed book that is sure to intrigue young readers.

CHRISTINE PALMER

Tree of Cranes

📖 ✏ Allen Say

Asian American, Japanese American

1991, Houghton Mifflin Company

Allen Say's *Tree of Cranes* introduces children to Japanese culture through a young boy's recollection of his very first Christmas. The young narrator vividly recalls experiences and feelings that children can relate to easily. "When I was not yet old enough to wear long pants, Mama always worried that I might drown in a neighbor's pond ... The last time I went there was a gray winter day, too cold for the fish to move around. They never came out from under the rocks, and all I caught was a bad chill ... Mama would be upset with me, I knew. She would know right away how I got my mittens all wet. But then, she might be happy just to see me." Knowing that Mother will find out and be upset, and feeling secure about Mother's love are emotions that children will be able to identify with.

A radiant tale of a young boy's first Japanese American Christmas.

The boy tells of the tree that was planted when he was born so that he might live a long life like a tree, and of the origami cranes his mother hangs on it at Christmas time. His mother also tells him about California—the place where she was born and lived until she met and married the boy's father. She also tells him about

575

Christmas time in California—the winking lights and small globes of silver and gold, the boxes of presents under each tree for friends and loved ones, giving and receiving.

This radiant tale appeals to the senses. Children can "see" the silver cranes hanging from the healthy branches of the boy's pine tree, the skin of an apple being peeled in a long strip like a red ribbon, and the fierce warrior depicted on the boy's kite. They can "smell" the scent of pine and of lighted candles. They can "taste" the sour plums and yellow radishes, and the hot tea in Papa's big cup. They can "hear" the boy's mother digging in the garden, or "listen" as she reads her son a story. And they can "feel" the joy in the boy's heart as he celebrates Christmas in a Japanese American style.

Glowing watercolor illustrations bring to life this cross-cultural celebration. HELEN R. ABADIANO

The Bicycle Man

📓 ✒ Allen Say
Asian, Japanese
1989 (1982), Houghton Mifflin Company,
✳ Video Cassette

Although told in the first person, the protagonist is actually a whole school. The location is a remote elementary school on a hillside overlooking a harbor in occupied Japan. The children have come with their parents, bringing lacquered, tiered picnic baskets full of "pickled melon rinds and egg rolls, spiced rice and fish cakes." The event is an annual, eagerly awaited sports day. Both the full-page drawings and the text offer details that underline the differences and the similarities between such an event as it is taking place in the East and in the West. For instance, in both there is a picnic, but one features sandwiches, and the other rice balls.

In occupied Japan, a group of school children and their families are entertained by American soldiers in a tender, humorous story.

It is a delight to see the parents and teachers throwing themselves so wholeheartedly into the events, hollering out encouragement. For prizes there were oranges, rice cakes, and pencils.

In the middle of the excitement, everything stops cold as the children notice a couple of American soldiers, one black and one with a shock of red hair, leaning over the fence, watching. At this time,

Americans would still have been a relatively rare sight, appearing to these children like monsters out of a Japanese fairy tale. But wait! These monsters are smiling. They wave. Timidly, the children gather. Politely, but equally cautiously, the principal welcomes the Americans.

Then, through some bumbling and humorous gestures, the strangers indicate they would like to try a bicycle. By this time, the children have begun to giggle. But their mouths fall open in astonishment as the black soldier demonstrates amazing prowess as a stunt rider.

By the time the visit is finished, there is warmth and friendship between the school and the soldiers. Told from the point of view of a small boy, we see how the suggestion of mistrust can turn into good feeling between peoples.

The almost cartoon-like characters of the illustrations exude personality and warmth. Even the American soldiers are drawn with an innocuous humor, but we can see how different they appear to the small children, who have been exposed only to other Japanese people. The drawings have been done with such tenderness that we can feel the author's poignancy in remembering his own childhood.

Ask the children to describe someone they know, or have seen, who makes them feel like hiding behind their mothers' backs. Does the superficial description seem to match an inner being? How do we choose our friends? Is it good to rely on outer details? What more might we do? GINNY LEE

Abiyoyo

📓 Pete Seeger ✒ Michael Hays
African
1994 (1986), Simon & Schuster Children's Books
✳ Video

Pete Seeger, a famous folk singer, musician, and storyteller, adapted this story from an old South African lullaby and story. He first told the story to his own children at bedtime as part story and part song. His children asked to hear it night after night, so he decided to write it down for other children to reread and retell in their own homes.

In Seeger's version, a ukulele-plucking boy and his magician father make too many objects disappear in their village. The townspeople are outraged, and the boy and his father are run out of town. Soon after, the townspeople awaken to find the great shadow of Abiyoyo, a giant thought to exist only in legend, in front of the rising sun. Everyone is greatly frightened, but they have no one to turn to for help.

Meanwhile the magician and his son, seeing Abiyoyo, plan to use their skills to help outwit the giant. The boy, plays a ukulele song about Abiyoyo to entice the giant to dance. Abiyoyo soon falls from exhaustion, and the musician uses his magic wand to banish the giant forever. The townspeople witness the entire act and declare the musician and the boy heroes of their village. They are, of course, invited to return to the town to live out their lives.

An American folksinger's lively retelling of a story based on a South African lullaby about a magician and his son who outwit a giant.

Michael Hays's illustrations of the townspeople show them as a very diverse group, representing many races and cultures, displaying a variety of dress. The reader will share a sense of community spirit when he or she joins in to sing the song of Abiyoyo. The themes of family values and the feasibility of a single-parent family are additional points for the reader to consider. A strong father-son relationship is a positive model for children who are in similar single-parent home situations. Magic is always a popular theme in children's stories, and it works well as a part of this story where it is a magic that comes forth from a spirit of cooperation constructed between a father and son, and eventually within a whole town.

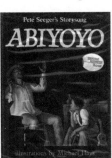

The magic of this story is also found in the direct and vivid voice of the storyteller, which is an integral part of the story. This story can be reinvented and told by anyone in their own way, just as Pete Seeger told this tale to his children in his own way. Seeger emphasizes that "there is no right way to tell a story." His message is that music, dance, acting, and art are all important tools to help all human beings have fun and enrich their lives. If the reader follows Seeger's example, there is no end to the stories that will be told in many different forms. MARILYN ANTONUCCI

Market Days: From Market to Market Around the World

Marti Shohef ✎ Madhur Jaffrey

Multicultural

1995, BridgeWater Books

The introduction reads in part, "Walking through any marketplace on this globe is a bit like opening a window and looking right into the heart of a country." Shohef and Jaffrey take us to Hong Kong, Egypt, Senegal, India, Italy, and Mexico as they describe the bright sights, clamoring sounds, and inviting smells of each unique marketplace. For example, we see ducks hanging by their necks in a Hong Kong market. The shopkeeper is cutting them up into small pieces with quick masterly strokes of

A colorful pictoral guide to marketplaces in Hong Kong, Egypt, Senegal, India, Italy, and Mexico.

a cleaver. In the Italian market we see red wine from Chianti, bread dipped in olive oil, olives with dull green flesh that has to be sucked off the pits, and huge portobello mushrooms that are grilled and doused with dressing. The Egyptian market offers one lane that specializes in copper pots, another devoted only to onyx, and a third that glitters with gold. As a break from buying and selling the local people enjoy a cup of thick Turkish coffee or sweet minty tea. While the marketplaces are not romanticized, an inclusion of some stories from the marketplace serves to enhance the book.

This colorfully illustrated book gives us a glimpse not only into the food and the wares sold in marketplaces around the world, but into the clothing, habits, traditions, and culture of the people. Taking a common theme and presenting it from a variety of cultures is one way to introduce mulitculturalism into the classroom. This is a food-centered book that provides a broader sense of the cultures, but is not an in-depth look at who produces the food, brings it to market, or who benefits most from its production. *Lessons can be devised to discuss how these foods get to market.*
BARBARA SMITH REDDISH

Lord of the Dance: An African Retelling

📖 ✒ Veronique Tadjo

African (West Africa)

1989 (1988), Harper Collins Children's Books, 📖 Haskins, James, *Black Dance in America: A History Through Its People.*

Dance is a creative medium through which a multi-cultural curriculum can be taught in the classroom. *Lord of the Dance* by Veronica Tadjo uses dance to tell its story. With illustrations that use bold colors to depict geometric move-

Boldly illustrated poems describe the colorful mask celebration of the Senufo people.

ment, West African artist Veronique Tadjo captures the history, lore, and spirit of the mask celebration of the Senufo people. This collection of creatively illustrated poems tells the story of the Senufo people who live in the north of the *Cote d'Ivoire* (Ivory Coast). Told through the Lord of the Dance, the book was inspired by Sidney Carter's hymn, "Lord of the Dance." As an interpretation of this African celebration of masks, the story winds through the traditional and contemporary aspects of the Senufos' lives.

Lord of the Dance provides teachers, librarians, and young people with an opportunity to learn more about African art, dance, and mythology. For those interested in examining curriculum that would work well with Tadjo's book, *Black Choreographers Moving Toward the 21st Century*, developed and prepared by John Henry in conjunction with San Francisco's *Project Artaud*, is a good beginning. BINNIE TATE-WILKIN

Subway Sparrow

📖 ✒ Leyla Torres

African American, Hispanic

1993, Farrar, Straus & Giroux, ✳ Spanish

Lyla Torres narrates in Spanish the story of a kind-hearted girl who attempts to capture a bird that has boarded a subway train. Realizing that there is little time before the next stop, she fears the bird will be trampled, unknowingly.

Despite the existence of cultural and language barriers, the girl manages to communicate with an English-speaking African American girl and a Polish woman. The woman whips off her scarf and throws it over the sparrow, capturing it before the train arrives at the next stop. The three of them take the bird outside and bid him farewell. The girl realizes that what the three of them did together, she could not have done alone. Through

In a wonderful book narrated in Spanish, a young Hispanic girl overcomes language barriers during an attempt to help a bird.

this fragile bird, three people who would not have normally come together find themselves achieving a common bond.

Instrumental in demonstrating that team effort can bring about powerful results, Torres's brightly-colored illustrations capture the teeming vitality of the New York subway setting. The wonderful yet simple and elegant panoramas give the readers a sense of the vastness of New York, while showing how people—even strangers—can come together in such a large city. MARTHA L. MARTINEZ

Annie—Anya: A Month in Moscow

📖 ✒ Irene Trivas

Russian

1992 Orchard Books

Five-year-old Annie accompanies her parents when they spend a month in Russia on business. She is initially terrified and confused by the cultural differences—even the alphabet isn't what she knows from home—and is not at all interested in the historical and cultural sights which interest her parents. The circus is a brief reprieve, but things get worse when she spends time in a Russian child care center. With the help of a kind teacher, Annie begins to overcome her fear, but it is

A well-told realistic story of two young girls breaking cultural barriers in Moscow.

the teacher's daughter, Anya, who finally breaks down the cultural barrier. Upon discovering that not only their names, but the names of their dolls (Katie and Katya) are similar, the two girls become fast friends. Soon, Annie is happy and engaged, and even learns a bit of Russian. She quickly learns that she and the Russian children are more alike than different.

This well-told and well-illustrated story paints an authentic picture of what a different culture might look like through a child's eyes. Young readers will learn a few words of Russian along with Annie as they visit a Russian park, holy city, ballet class, and home. *Annie—Anya* will help children to empathize with immigrant children in their midst. *This is also an excellent book to share with children planning on spending any time abroad and would be a welcome addition to any teaching unit focusing on Russia.*
JODIE LEVINE

The Rainbow Warrior Artists Series

Various artists, Foreword by Levar Burton
Multicultural
✻ Series

Traditional artists from around the globe share their talents with young readers in this three-volume series. Each of the books focuses on a diverse group of artists from a particular continent.

Each book profiles five artists. The individual chapters begin with a look at the land a particular artist lives in, plus background information on the history and traditions of his or her people. Next, a short biography of the artist is given; then, the story of his or her art is revealed. The artists freely discuss their inspiration, their spiritual connection to their art, and the challenges they overcame to become artists. These talented individuals close their stories with a message for young readers. In words that come from the heart, they encourage children to challenge themselves, respect their elders, care for the earth, discover their heritage, and nurture their own creative spirit.

This vibrantly illustrated three-volume series profiles traditional artists from around the world.

After each chapter, there is an activity page that features an art lesson courtesy of the artist profiled in the preceding chapter. Some of these activities include beading, weaving, music making, drawing, creativity with clay, simple carving techniques, dancing, basket making, and even yodeling.

Each book also has a glossary-index which explains unfamiliar words. The foreword to each volume is written by Levar Burton. Unfortunately, Burton's words are recycled in all three books, as are parts of the introduction to two of the books.

The *Rainbow Warrior Artists* series is illustrated with vibrant color photographs of the artists and the lands in which they live. The pictures of the artists show them at home, at work, and spending time with their families. The quality of the photographs is uneven, but all reflect the artists' joy in their creativity.

A portion of the proceeds from the sale of books in this series go to the Rainbow Warrior Fund for the preservation of native cultures and the environment. SANDRA KELLY

Little Stevie Wonder in Places Under the Sun

Sonja Wiley
African American, Physically Disabled
1995, Western Publishing Company, ✻ Braille

With too few resources available for blind children, I was excited to find *Little Stevie Wonder in Places Under the Sun*. The concept behind the book is quite wonderful: along with a "touch and listen" feature directly adjacent to the right margin, the book contains a shortened braille version of the story. The braille alphabet and numerical identification system appear in the front of the book.

Unfortunately, a series of flaws detracts from the book's potential. In a clear anachronism, for example, the book includes a cordless telephone, which did not exist when Stevie was a young boy. I was also dismayed to find a grammatical error. Although the story itself is charming, and very young children may well find it delightful, the introduction is poorly written.

On the positive side, the storyline clearly supports the building of cross-cultural relationships, truly enhanced by the "touch and listen" feature. Very young children will love the sounds, and even those who are not visually impaired will be intrigued by the inclusion of the braille text. The brightly-colored illustrations are well done and reflect the positive spirit for which Stevie Wonder is known. The illustrations are printed on coated stock pages, which can be wiped off with a damp cloth. The "touch and listen" feature is battery powered. There remains a real need

A flawed, if innovative, "sound story" biography, with braille, of young Stevie Wonder.

for interactive books, especially those that support the needs of children with disabilities.
DAPHNE MUSE

When Africa Was Home

Karen Lynn Williams   Floyd Cooper
African, Malawi
1994 (1991), Orchard Books

Many beautiful picture books set in Africa have appeared in the past decade. Their colorful market scenes or vibrant images of children playing and antelope running make any reader long to be there. What sets this book apart is the face at the center of it: the face of a young white boy with curly blond hair. As we become a more mobile society, more and more children are growing up in cultures different from their parents'.

A white boy in the United States longs to return to his former home in an African village in a story that will ring true for all expatriots.

Peter lives in Malawi with his parents; his father has a job there. The first illustration shows Peter as an infant, tied by a red cloth to the back of his *mayi*, his nanny, who has beautiful dark skin and hair bound traditional braiding and beadwork. The picture is startling at first, but soon it seems natural. This woman and child are calm, at peace, full of love. "When Africa was home," the book explains, "Peter had two mothers."

Although his parents are still tied to the United States, Africa is home for Peter. He has spoken English and Chichewa ever since he learned to speak, and his best friend is Yekha, the daughter of his *mayi*. He is used to falling asleep to the sounds of hippos mooing and to running barefoot in the soft dust.

His parents try to prepare him for their return to the United States, pointing out that in their real home people dress and eat differently—and cool off with popsicles. Peter thinks to himself, "That's not my home."

The family does fly home to a big American city, and Peter never stops missing Africa. When his father gets another job in Africa a few years later and is able to return to the same village, it does feel contrived. Yet this child so clearly needed to be back home, it would have been unsatisfying to have the story end any other way.

Karen Lynn Williams based her story on her own family's experiences in the Peace Corps, and Peter's story is a common one for children of expatriates around the world. The vibrant illustrations reinforce this central idea: Peter's white skin stands out against the colorful African scenes, and he looks out of place. But he is not out of place; he is home. *This book leads to interesting discussions about what makes a home, and what makes people friends.*

Undeniably, many people of all colors and ancestries feel drawn to Africa, and most anyone who has ever been there longs to go back. Maybe it's because the first people were African, because Africa is everyone's ancestral home. Whatever the reason, Peter's sense of belonging is strong and touching. And while the adults in the story may have a hard time understanding it, for the two children, one white—and one black—it's the most natural thing in the world. CYNTHIA A. BILY

Building Trust and Community in The Classroom

Sara D. Simonson

A CHINESE AMERICAN BOY IN SIXTH GRADE cuts school when the Chinese New Year approaches. Why? Not because he dislikes school or would rather be out celebrating. Each year since preschool, teachers have made a tremendous fuss over his knowledge of the Chinese New Year. They focus everyone's attention on him and ask him to recite once again his experience and family customs. Although proud of his heritage, the boy desperately wants to fit in with his middle school peers. Like many of his classmates, he prefers not to have attention drawn to his differences. His teachers, though well-intentioned, do not stop to consider how he might feel or the position they put him in as the outsider. They do not bother to ask him whether or not he wants to share. Rather than being in the spotlight one more time, the boy simply finds it easier to stay home.

Perhaps in a classroom where similarities and differences are celebrated throughout the year in all subject areas, this boy would not feel so conspicuous. However, in a classroom where multiculturalism is discussed and "added on" only during certain holidays, the safe environment has not been established. The freedom to share and to trust has not developed.

To develop a true community of learners in the classroom, educators must strive for integration of multiculturalism throughout the curriculum. Reaching this level of community involves a facet of unspoken trust. How does a community of learners evolve? How does one reach the point where students are interacting with one another and sharing their ideas through speaking, listening, reading, and writing? How do we instill within our students an appreciation of others and the awareness of similarities as well as differences?

What exactly is a community of learners? It is a supportive, caring environment that provides time, structure, and space for individuals as well as small groups. An "openness" is achieved through the sharing of reading, writing, and discussion—

teacher-to-students and student-to-student. Class meetings are scheduled on a regular basis to air concerns and questions or to celebrate new discoveries. Attending to one another's feelings with patience and understanding is necessary as well as a sense of humor. A genuine interest in diversity is required, plus the realization that there is a time to value similarities and differences. Students are active participants and researchers. And parents are viewed as valuable resources.

Within this community, one might also consider the implications of multiculturalism versus pseudo multiculturalism. Multiculturalism realizes the needs of *all* children in the classroom. Pseudo multiculturalism focuses on only the minority students represented in the classroom. According to Boutte and McCormick (1992), "authentic multicultural teachers realize that each child possesses different strengths, and that all people have weaknesses." (p. 144). Taking pseudo multiculturalism a step further, consider how some primary grade students are introduced to Indian units around Thanksgiving time. Some of the culminating activities are creating headbands with feathers. Students make fringed vests out of grocery sacks and cover the vests with animal pawprints and symbols. Then, they dance around a fake fire making war whoop noises with their hands and mouths. Is this a realistic portrayal of culture to instill in young children's minds? Similarly, when units on Japan are introduced in classrooms, how many students expect the streets of Tokyo to be filled with people dressed in silk kimonos? Although the introduction of a culture's history and customs are important, it is also imperative for students to be informed of a realistic view of culture. In another classroom, a teacher dusts off her curriculum guide only to find the addition of a multicultural component she is supposed to be teaching. She searches through her file drawer and finds an outline of a dragon surrounding some multiplication facts. With this

582

ditto in hand, she mentions the Chinese New Year to her class and checks off one more objective covered this year. A fourth teacher feels multiculturalism is not important to discuss this year since she does not have anyone in her class representing a different ethnic group.

How can we enhance multiculturalism within our classroom and build a sense of trust and community among our students? The discussion that follows considers how the integration of multiculturalism in daily routines will help to build a more thoughtful community of learners in grades four through eight.

DEVELOPING A COMMUNITY OF LEARNERS

This section reviews ideas and practices that encourage children from diverse backgrounds to open up and share their feelings. As Kawakami and Au write, "When [teachers] use students' strength as a starting point for instruction, they can view cultural diversity as a resource rather than as a deficiency" (1986, p. 79). These activities enhance the development of a community of learners and tap the resources available in diverse family traditions. Respect and genuine caring among class members are developed. Interest in other cultural traditions is generated.

One way to enhance classroom interaction and establish a sense of community is through the use of drama. Students may jot down on slips of paper cross-cultural situations which have offended them or made them feel uncomfortable. Partners or small groups then select one situation to portray with class members as their audience. Preparation time is provided for small groups to make decisions about the presentation: characters, setting, and an ending. After the dramatization, class members are asked to brainstorm other possible solutions. The drama may continue with the implementation of various solutions. Discussion is encouraged at each interval of the process. Drama allows participants to experience what their peers have felt frequently in day-to-day routines. The feelings shared and discussed help to bond students closer together through an increased understanding and identification with one another (Bhatty, 1991; Ritchie, 1991). If students lack the experience of interacting with other ethnic groups, teachers may use literature as a natural springboard for discussion and drama.

The students become the characters of the story and roleplay the situations, choices, and decisions made by the characters as well as other options the students create. Although drama is frequently implemented in the primary grades to help establish the concept of story and to encourage oral language development, students should be encouraged to dramatize situations and stories within the middle school grades to spur discussion, to reinforce the choices available to them, and to explore in-depth character analysis through higher thinking.

The sharing of recipes is a second method of bringing students closer as a community. Karen Selwyn (1991) describes how her students create a class cookbook each year. She asks each student to bring two recipes to school which represent a special family tradition. This activity sometimes involves students "interviewing and interacting with their elders; for example, to figure out an exact measurement that may have been passed down through generations as a "dash" or a "pinch." Selwyn also requests that each recipe be accompanied by an introduction explaining why this recipe was selected and the tradition it represents. The project becomes not only a class cookbook but also a collection of special traditions from various families, backgrounds, and cultures. According to Selwyn, the introductions to the recipes are the most widely read and valued among class members. During this unit, grandparents, aunts, uncles, or parents are invited to the class to share and prepare a recipe. The students enjoy sampling a speciality from one another's heritage. The link to another generation encourages the sharing of stories, history, and traditions among family members as well as class members.

A third way to get students sharing and interacting is through storytelling. Storytelling enhances cultural awareness, critical thinking skills, and enthusiasm for writing. Folktales, myths, and legends from various cultures can be introduced. These stories lend themselves to activities such as a trial analyzing different points of view or making comparisons between similar stories, such as *Cinderella* and *Mufaro's Beautiful Daughters*. Once students understand the format of these simple tales, they are eager to experiment with writing tales of their own. Storytelling can be performed through everything from simple enactment to puppets to finger plays to storyboards. Each method allows the students to create and to surround themselves with language (Zabel, 1991). These activities will enhance the speaking skills of students at a variety of grade levels. However, students in the middles grades can explore more in-depth issues—analyzing the characters' motives while practicing a performance to share with younger children.

LANGUAGES IN THE CLASSROOM
Another practice students enjoy is playing with language. By introducing simple words in different languages, students are exposed to a variety of linguistic experiences. Words and phrases such as "hello," "good-bye," "how are you?"and counting one through ten lend themselves easily to this practice. Students may become more involved by adding more words to the list representing slang, street talk, or dialectical differences. A simple "good-bye" may be stated with several substitutes in English without even considering other languages: "see ya," "bye," "later dude," "catch ya on the flip side," plus "adios" and "au revoir." Students will continue adding to the list, noting the exchange people share outside of the classroom, trying a variety of words among themselves, and beginning to value the other forms of the language that surround them daily (Boutte & McCormick, 1992).

Through observations of Martha Demientieff's Native Alaskan classroom, Lisa Delpit (1990) discovered several ways to integrate naturally an appreciation of languages—both formal and informal styles. Each day, students wrote and shared a newscast about upcoming events in school and in their community. The discussions that followed compared how news commentators may state the same message and how it might be shared from one member of their community to the next. Students create "bidialectical dictionaries" containing both forms of language. Students examined long, wordy statements in formal English and restated them in their own words. They tried to shorten the statements to a phrase and then posted them on small paper T-shirts hanging around the classroom. A bulletin board featured a column for "Our Heritage Language" and a column for "Formal English." Students contributed phrases and words to this bulletin board from reading books, newspapers, and magazines and from listening to conversations among peers and family members.

From time to time, the teacher set up the classroom as a formal dinner complete with the entire place setting of china and silverware. The students were invited to use only "Formal English" during this dinner. On another day, a picnic was created in the classroom. In this atmosphere, the students' "Heritage Language" was encouraged. Discussions regularly followed these activities for students to voice their feelings, frustration, and questions. These daily practices allowed the students to understand and respect the varying forms of the English language. Through the constant contrast of informal and formal degrees of usage, these middle school students became more receptive to and adept at using the English language.

James Lockhart shared how he integrated the issue of dialect and formal English throughout the year in his middle school classroom. Lockhart stated, "Unless speakers of nonstandard English, and for my situation that means primarily African American students, feel that their language and culture are respected, they will continue to feel alienated from the educational system and to resent what they perceive as attacks on their ethnicity" (1991: p. 57). He presented to his students poems, short stories, novels, essays, excerpts, rap music and videos exploiting the issue of dialect. He shared several examples of different types of dialects from a variety of authors. In this manner, Lockhart validated his students' speech patterns and backgrounds.

Lockhart promotes "bidialectism." He wants students to value who they are and to be proud of how they speak, but he also wants them to appreciate the need for formal English in certain real world situations.

ENCOURAGING CRITICAL THINKING
To encourage critical thinking skills, Crichlow, Goodwin, Shakes, and Schwartz (1990) suggested having students analyze and reconstruct certain paragraphs and sections in their social studies text to represent a more truthful look at history. These researchers referred to this as an emancipatory approach and were not concerned with the content coverage in a specific course or the number

of groups represented in a social studies text. Rather than struggle over the contents of a course, the researchers recommended having students research and build a more accurate picture of what the text is describing. Through this research and the use of multiple sources, diverse groups were considered and represented based on factual accounts. Students learned to question what they read and not simply to take it at face value. They developed research skills and a more precise way of stating factual information. This practice also involved the teachers taking a more critical look at suggestions and background presented in a teacher's guide.

Journals are another way to encourage students to express their thoughts and feelings. Nongraded journals let students know up front that their ideas are important—-not spelling, punctuation rules, or grammar. Teachers model effective writing practices when they correspond with the students in their journals. Conferences with students or mini-lessons in a "workshop" atmosphere can present the skills students are lacking. Journals are the place for students to air their feelings—- what makes them uncomfortable, what hurts or embarrasses them, what they would like to share with the class as well as when they would rather not be in the spotlight. Journals can be extremely flexible between teacher and student or student and student. A special closeness between writers and readers develops while sharing hardships, memories, and triumphs.

One teacher described how her class traded journals weekly with an ESL class in a neighboring school district. A special bond and renewed respect for diversity developed between the two groups of students. At the end of the school year, the teachers planned a party so each class could meet its writing partners. This project was a great success. The thrill and excitement of meeting new friends through writing and finally face-to-face added to the enjoyment of the assignment (McMahon: 1991).

The incorporation of multicultural literature into all areas of the curriculum moves children in new directions. In *Journey of the Sparrows* by Fran Leeper Buss, Maria is smuggled into the United States from Mexico with the hope of reuniting her family in a safer environment. Maria exclaims to her frail little brother:

...we made it. We're here in the North, where everyone gets so rich. We'll have lots to eat, and we'll send money so Mama and Teresa can join us. Mama'll be here soon. I promise. (pp. 17-18)

However, life in America is not so sweet: Maria struggles with immigration officials, lack of food, little money, and horrid working conditions.

In the picture book *Who Belongs Here? An American Story* by Margy Burns Knight, Nary also longs for the security of the United States, away from the fighting in Cambodia. When his grandmother finally brings him to America, his battle is one of acceptance:

Nary remembers his grandmother telling him that she had heard the U.S. was going to be better than heaven—full of food and peace. Nary wants to live in peace, so he doesn't understand why some of his classmates are mean to him.

Recently, as he was getting books out of his locker, two classmates said, "Hey, chink, out of my way."

"Yeah, get back on the boat and go home where you belong." (p. 15)

Through Nary's painful experience, the reader becomes more sensitive to the effects peers have on one another. A discussion following the reading aloud of this book can elevate the levels of awareness and communication among classroom members. It may lead to students role-playing or sharing similar situations and feelings. Other books such as *Amazing Grace* by Mary Hoffman, and *A Jar of Dreams* by Yoshido Uchida, portray characters who suffer from discrimination. The characters' strength and determination provide faith and optimism for the reader. The struggle for students to be proud of their heritage and who they are is in constant conflict with the treatment they receive from peers. Stories like *Dancing with the Indians*, by Angela Shelf Medearis, emphasize the proud traditions established within families. Books are a forum where students can experience, imagine, and take comfort in the actions presented. Books speak to young readers and reach them in ways that we adults cannot. Sharing special books and stories helps to create an understanding of diversity and strengthens classroom community.

Linda Blair (1991) put together a multicultural literature unit focussing on autobiographies to emphasize the narrative style of writing. The topics of alienation, assimilation, and acculturation are an integral part of this unit. Students are involved in discussion groups, reading logs, panel discussions, and finally, writing their own autobiographies. Blair believes, "We reaffirm our ancestral struggles through reading autobiographies and developing individual, narrative voices to reaffirm our own identities." (p. 28) Through the reading of student-selected autobiographies, students from different cultures begin to develop their own voices and their writing improves dramatically.

CONCLUSION

For a true community of learners to emerge, the teacher must promote recognition and appreciation of all cultural backgrounds. Similarities and differences should be acknowledged and discussed openly. Furthermore, a sensitivity to the individual needs of the students must also develop. A final example will illustrate this point. One teacher asked her students to bring to class a food item or dish that represented their family ancestry. This teacher was attempting to celebrate different cultures within the classroom. However, one African American girl became upset when she realized her teacher wanted her to bring a dish from Africa. The student did not know any African dishes to share. She kept saying to the teacher, "But I am an American. My family has lived here for generations." Overly enthusiastic for this culminating activity, the teacher refused to modify the assignment. She was pleased when students shared Swedish meatballs, English tea, and spaghetti. What did the African American student share? Her vote was for hot dogs; however, her mother appeased the teacher by calling a restaurant that served shark and placing an order to be delivered to the classroom. Was this an African dish? No, but the teacher did not know the difference in her quest for unusual foods. One might argue that Selwyn's class cookbook could lead to such a disaster. Notice, though, she is simply asking for a favorite recipe or special family tradition. Anything is acceptable. She is not going back to the "old country" for recipes. If a cultural dish is included, it is okay. If is not included, that is fine with her, too. Her students are in charge of selecting the recipes.

Family and cultural traditions of every student must be valued and recognized throughout the year. Through the classroom and activities described above, teachers can help build a sense of community among students at the intermediate and middle school levels, by knowing when and when not to focus on one particular child. By experiencing a variety of forums in their day-to-day routines, students have the opportunity to share, discuss, and learn about other class members in a trusting environment.

Multiculturalism should be embedded within the curriculum, occur naturally, and portray cultures realistically. Teachers need to re-examine their own practices. Every child in the classroom has something special to share, beginning with family traditions, backgrounds, and stories from grandparents. This is a natural place to start in the appreciation of diversity and the building of a community. As Giroux states:

Of course, more is at stake here than avoiding the romanticizing of minority voices, or the inclusion of western traditions in the curriculum. Multiculturalism in this sense is about making whiteness visible as a racial category; that is, it points to the necessity of providing white students with the cultural memories that enable them to recognize the historically and socially constructed nature of their own identities. (1992: p. 9)

Some of the ideas described above are activities or projects. They are not intended to be a quick shot in the arm or an answer to a multicultural objective of a school district. These ideas and practices are suggested as further ways to enhance the multicultural thread woven throughout the curriculum and to strengthen the bonds between the community members in a classroom.

Sara Simonson is Assistant professor of Elementary Education and Reading at Western Illinois University at Macomb, Ill.

Reprinted with permission from Rethinking Our Classrooms, Rethinking Schools, 1001 E. Keefe Ave. Milwaukee, WI 53212; (414)964-9646.

REFERENCES

BHATTY, R. "A developmental guidance approach to multicultural guidance." *Guidance Counseling* 7: 7-13, 1991.

BLAIR, L. "Developing student voices with multicultural literature.", *English Journal* 80: 24-28, 1991.

BOUTTE, G.S., & MCCORMICK, C.B. "Authentic multicultural activities", *Childhood Education*, 68: 140-148, 1992.

CRICHLOW, W., GOODWIN, S., SHAKES, G., & SCHWARTZ, E. "Multicultural ways of knowing: Implications for practice." *Journal of Education*, 172: 101-117, 1990.

DELPIT, L.D. "Language diversity and learning." In S. HYNDS & D.L. RUBIN (EDS.), *Perspectives on Talk & Learning* (pp. 247-266). (Urbana, Ill.: National Council of Teachers of English, 1990).

GIROUX, H.A. "Curriculum, multiculturalism, and the politics of identity." *NASSP Bulletin*, 76: 1-11, 1992.

KAWAKAMI, A.J., & AU, K.H. "Encouraging reading and language development in cultural minority children." *Topics in Language Disorders*, 6: 71-80, 1986.

LOCKHART, J. "We Real Cool: Dialect in the middle school classroom." *English Journal*, 80: 53-58, 1991.

MCMAHON, M. "New friendships through journals." In "Foreign students and recent immigrants in the English Classroom" (The Round Table). *English Journal* 80: 86, 1991.

RITCHIE, G. "How to use drama for cross-cultural understanding," *Guidance and Counseling*, 7: 33-35, 1991.

SELWYN, K.P. "Sharing food and stories." In "Foreign students and recent immigrants in the English Classroom" (The Round Table). *English Journal* 80: 85-86, 1991.

ZABEL, M.K. "Storytelling, myths, and folk tales: Strategies for multicultural inclusion." *Preventing School Failure*, 36: 32-34, 1991.

Addressing Concerns About Teaching Culturally Diverse Students

Patricia L. Marshall

The one word that best describes contemporary students, curricula, and school philosophies is *diverse*. This climate presents new challenges and demands on school personnel. Teachers should feel a definite need to develop a heightened sensitivity and cross-cultural awareness for teaching today's student populations.

Teachers who have concerns about teaching diverse student populations are often apprehensive about not being able to meet the needs of their students. Selecting the most appropriate teaching techniques and strategies involves constant vigilance on the part of every professional educator. Like other professionals, classroom teachers must constantly stay abreast of the latest interpretations of content and teaching techniques. One of the greatest tragedies is that many teachers simply have not had a formal professional opportunity to explore techniques and strategies more appropriate for their work with diverse student populations. In addition, the basic content knowledge that many teachers have studied while training to become teachers may not have included varying cultural perspectives. Consequently, these teachers should work to lessen or eliminate multicultural teaching concerns. When this is done,

teachers can redirect their attention toward those aspects of classroom interaction that will allow them to meet the needs of all students. Below are ways multicultural teaching concerns can be addressed:

* Make a concerted effort to learn more about the family structure of your students.

* Personalize contacts with students' parents by visiting homes and neighborhoods.

* Enroll in classes or workshops devoted to the past and more recent history of the ethnic or racial groups of students in your classes.

* Visit community centers, places of worship, civic events, or cultural or religious celebrations of members of nonmajority cultures.

* Begin a self-study project to read contemporary literature written by authors from diverse backgrounds.

* Subscribe to or borrow from a library monthly magazines published for ethnic populations.

* Explore research on individual learning styles.

* Involve students in unit planning.

* Enroll in a race-awareness or cross-cultural sensitivity workshop.

* Form professional collaborations with colleagues of a different race or ethnicity with whom you can share concerns and questions about working with diverse students.

The MCTS offers opportunities to explore the nature of teachers' concerns as they relate to diversity in contemporary schools. Cultural diversity in schools will continue to increase, resulting in significant changes in the way schools operate, but these changes need not cause major anxiety for teachers. Instead, diversity can be viewed as an opportunity for teachers to engage in analyzing their professional selves and as opportunities for professional—-and perhaps personal—growth.

RECOMMENDED READING ON MULTICULTURAL EDUCATION

Multicultural education is the most recent major schooling innovation in our country. Much of the writing on this topic challenges teachers to explore their own attitudes and behaviors toward culturally diverse students. The following books are excellent sources of information on this growing field of study.

Banks, J. A. and C. McGee Banks, eds. *Multicultural Education: Issues and Perspectives.* (Boston: Allyn and Bacon, 1993). Exploration of various dimensions of multicultural education including teaching about women and ethnic/racial minorities. Includes resource section and glossary list of culturally sensitive terminology.

Bennett, C.I. *Comprehensive Multicultural Education: Theory and Practice.* (Boston: Allyn and Bacon, 1990). Examines multicultural education as a "movement, curriculum approach, process and teacher commitment." Includes chapters on the role of individual learning styles in teaching and learning.

Grant, C.A. and C.E. Sleeter. *Turning on Learning: Five Approaches for Multicultural Teaching Plans for Races, Class, Gender and Disability.* (Columbus: Merrill Publishing Company, 1989). Provides a collection of lesson plans for various subjects (including art and mathematics) and grade levels using five different approaches to multicultural education.

Gollnick, D.M. and P.C. Chinn. *Multicultural Education in a Pluralistic Society.* (Columbus: Merrill Publishing Company, 1992) . Excellent introductory text on multicultural education. Includes one of the best all-around discussions on the basic tenets of multicultural education and the dominant culture in the United States.

Tiedt, P. L., and I.M. Tiedt. *Multicultural Education Teaching: A Handbook of activities, Information, And Resources.* (Boston: Allyn and Bacon, 1992.) Collection of activities and ideas for incorporating multicultural education into existing curricula. Especially appropriate for elementary school teachers.

REFERENCES

Fuller, F.F. "Concerns of teachers: A developmental conceptualization." *American Educational Research Journal,* 6(2): 207—26, 1969.

Gehrke, N. *On Being a Teacher.* West Lafayette, Ind.: Kappa Delta Pi, 1987.

Katz, L. G. "Developmental stages of preschool teachers." *Elementary School Journal,* 739(1): 50—54, 1972.

Marshall, P., S. Fittinghoff, and C.O. Cheney. "Beginning teacher developmental stages: implications for creating collaborative internship programs." *Teacher Education Quarterly,* 17(3): 25—35, 1990.

Patricia L. Marshall is an assistant professor at North Carolina State University where she teaches courses in multicultural education and elementary school curriculum. Her current research interests involve cognitive developmental theory within multicultural education in teacher education programs. Dr. Marshall is a member of Omicron Rho Chapter.

Grade Four to Grade Six

Child of the Warsaw Ghetto

▣ David A. Adler ✐ Karen Ritz
Jewish, Polish
1995, Holiday House, Inc.

A graphic story of life in the Warsaw Ghetto as seen through the eyes of a young Jewish boy.

We have no sanitized atrocity here. This is a sober and realistic depiction of life in the Warsaw Ghetto and, subsequently, the Nazi death camps as seen through the eyes of a young Jewish boy named Froim, born in Warsaw in 1936. Froim grows up in Poland, one of seven children. His father is a tailor and his mother sells candy and cigarettes to supplement the family's income. Much like people nowadays, Froim and his family pay little attention to the political climate of the day: Hitler's election, anti-Jewish laws, and so on. They concentrate instead on working hard and trying to make ends meet. After his father's death, Froim's mother can no longer afford their meager one-room apartment, and they move from place to place, eventually winding up in an attic.

Froim and his brothers are sent to live in an orphanage run by a kindly Jewish doctor named Henryk Goldszmidt. Soon after Froim moves to the orphanage, Germany invades Poland, and things get progressively worse for him. He begs for food in the streets, sees his neighborhood burn to the ground, and witnesses the slaughter of his neighbors. In 1940, a wall is erected enclosing seventy-three city streets. All Jews are ordered to live within the confines of the wall and little food or supplies are allowed through the gates. Thousands of people die of starvation, exposure to the elements, and disease.

In 1942, the Germans move the people out of the Ghetto and into Treblinka, a Nazi death camp. When the Germans empty Froim's orphanage, Henryk Goldszmidt is recognized by a Nazi soldier and offered his freedom. Mr. Goldszmidt refuses to leave his children. Froim escapes capture because he isn't wearing the armband which distinguishes him as a Jew, so the soldiers refuse to let him on the train. Froim and his mother hire a professional smuggler to take them to Plonsk, where they are caught in 1942 and taken to Auschwitz. His mother and sisters are killed immediately, but Froim and his brothers are sentenced to labor. Eventually Froim is liberated from the death camps by American soldiers, but not after some six million Jews are killed. One-and-a-half million of them were children.

This book is a powerful story of the atrocities of the Holocaust and an excellent tool for encouraging classroom discussion. Children can relate to the story because it is told through the eyes of a young boy. The material is graphic and honest and seems to respect children's right to accurate information. The illustrations are done in charcoal on gray paper and have the flavor of a very serious and important book, which encourages further discussion and critical thought. BARBARA SMITH REDDISH

Multicultural Cookbook for Students

▣ Carole L. Albyn ✐ Lois Sinaiko Webb
Multicultural
1993, Oryx Press

In classrooms across the country, children are frequently assigned to bring food from a country being studied in class. This cookbook, containing 337 recipes from 122 countries, has the potential to be very useful for those assignments.

Recipes are presented in sections roughly equivalent to the seven continents. Each section is introduced with an overview of the geography of the area, and of foods and recipes that are common to most of these cultures. Specific recipes are then listed by country, frequently with the recipe name given in the native language as well as in English. A variety of cooking techniques are presented, as are the ingredients' cost which vary widely. In addition, three important sections are provided: Safety, Common Sense, and Cleanliness Tips; Glossary; Index (including recipe names, major ingredients, and countries).

A book of hundreds of recipes from around the world, with disappointing design and little cultural context.

Although the directions are clear, the book has

several important drawbacks that should be noted. The book's design and layout are poor. The text is crowded, and there are no illustrations. Although the book is to be lauded for providing a wide range of recipes—some not found in any other source that I am familiar with—the disappointing format will not inspire anyone to return to the book again and again. One other problem is the book's narrow focus. No cultural context is provided to accompany the recipes, therefore limiting its usefulness as an educational tool. JANIS O'DRISCOLL

Children of the Maya: A Guatemalan Indian Odyssey

📖 Brent Ashabranner ✒ Paul Conklin

Hispanic, Guatemalan

1986, Dodd, Mead

An informative account of Mayans who fled violent political conditions in Guatemala in the early 1980s to settle in Florida.

Between 1980 and 1984, the Guatemalan army destroyed more than 440 villages in central and western Guatemala to keep them from becoming rebel strongholds. Some 30,000 Native Americans were killed, another 150,000 fled to Mexico, and a smaller number trekked through Mexico to the United States. The book opens with an introduction to the ancient history of the Mayan people. Using personal stories of families caught in the civil war, young readers will gain some understanding about how war destroys and sometimes leads to the extinction and reshaping of cultures.

Some of the families who have relocated to south Florida tell their stories and detail the adjustments they are struggling to make and their questionable future as refugees in south Florida. The strong black-and-white photographs complement the story, depicting a kind and gentle people caught in the web of a tragic civil war. BYRON RUSKIN

Extraordinary American Indians

📖 Susan Avery, Linda Skinner ✒ Various artists

Native American

1992, Children's Press, ✳ Series

Focusing on the United States, this extremely valuable book contains brief but thorough biographies of sixty prominent Native Americans from various nations and from the first Indian-European contact to the present.

More than a collection of famous chiefs and war leaders from past centuries, this readable book offers students a much-needed and well-rounded look at the diversity of Indian talents and achievements. Also included are sketches of seven organizations, events, or policies that the authors felt merited attention —the Iroquois confederacy, land allotment, the Sand Creek and Wounded Knee massacres, the Indian Reorganization Act and citizenship, Navajo Codetalkers, termination and self-determination, and the American Indian Movement.

Black-and-white photographs enhance most entries, although occasionally these photographs are somewhat peripheral to the subject, and at least one is mislabeled ("Sun Dance" instead of "Ghost Dance"). An excellent index is included, as is a lengthy but uneven further reading list which often inaccurately categorizes books as appropriate for either middle or upper grades. A valuable feature is the selection of videotapes available for purchase or rental from the Native American Public Broadcasting Consortium in Lincoln, Nebraska. This is a unique and essential title for all public, school, and tribal libraries, particularly for reference collections. LISA A. MITTEN

A unique and well-rounded collection of biographies of sixty prominent Native Americans.

Umm el Madayan: An Islamic City Through the Ages

📖 Abderrahaman Ayoub, Abderrazak Gragueb, Jamila Binous, Ali Mtimet, Heidi Slim ✒ Francesco Corni

African

1994, Houghton Mifflin, ✳ Spanish, 📖 Comes, Pilar and Hernandez, Xavier, *Barmi: A Mediterranean City Through the Ages*; *Lebek: A City of Northern Europe Through the Ages*; *San Rafael: A Central American City Through the Ages*

The long history of a North African city is brought to life for young readers in *Umm el Madayan: An Islamic City through the Ages*. Though Umm el Madayan (the name means "mother of cities") is a fictional place, its development parallels that of many Mediterranean cities in Tunisia, Algeria, Morocco, and Libya.

The reader is taken on a time-travel tour through

589

An intriguing illustrated history of a fictional North African city.

fourteen different time periods, beginning with the hunter-gatherers who first roamed the area and continuing through the first settlements, metropolitan growth, and on up to contemporary urban problems. Black-and-white drawings give a glimpse of a Phoenician house, a Punic warship, a Roman amphitheater, a Christian cathedral, an Arab market, a sixteenth-century bathhouse, and an Ottoman mosque. The illustrations also feature close-up pictures of artifacts, architectural details, and scenes of daily life. Double-page spreads, showing bird's eye views of a moment in the city's history, precede the description of each historical period. It is fascinating to watch the landscape change dramatically as buildings are raised and then razed, harbors constructed and deserted, and city walls built and demolished.

Brief informative summaries describe each historical period and place Umm el Madayan within the context of historical events around the world.

Umm el Madayan's final chapter finds the city at the dawn of the twenty-first century. Like many other cities in the world, it is facing the problems of population pressure, economic uncertainty, destruction of agricultural zones, and pollution of the environment. Its citizens cope with the dilemma of how to practice their religion in a world of modern temptations, and we learn that their attempts to preserve their past while looking to the future are not always successful.

Umm el Madayan *could be used by teachers as a model for class projects that highlight the history of their local area. Students could research the history of their own city, and then divide the city into time periods to be described and illustrated. Corni's detailed illustrations also provide good examples for lessons in pen-and-ink drawing. A section on Neolithic-era settlements is also useful for units on the origins of civilization.* SANDRA KELLY

Sitting Bull and the Battle of the Little Bighorn

Sheila Black, Edited by Nancy Furstinger ✎ Ed Le
Lakota, Native American
1989, Silver Burdett Press, ✳ Series

This biography is one of a series edited by Alvin M. Josephy, Jr., a noted ethnologist specializing in Native American studies. Sitting Bull was a great warrior who fought for his people's independence and tribal lands. This book honors a man regarded by all western Sioux, or Lakota, not only as a great warrior, but also as a holy man. The book also portrays the Sioux as caring people, correcting the erroneous image proliferated by films and traditional books of bloodthirsty savages.

A commendable biography of Sitting Bull, documenting his fight for his people's independence and tribal lands.

Particularly appealing to youngsters will be sections on Sitting Bull's childhood. The book describes Sitting Bull's childhood as a free individual and his subsequent incarceration at Fort Randall. Through learning about Sitting Bull's life, the reader also gains a greater appreciation for the general state of Native American affairs during his lifetime, particularly Native American culture and relations between Native Americans and whites. The book is to be lauded for its treatment of Native Americans, which humanizes the Sioux and presents their story sympathetically but not sentimentally. ELAINE P. GOLEY

Commodore Perry in the Land of the Shogun

Rhoda Blumberg ✎ Archival illustrations
Asian, Japanese
1985, Lothrop, Lee & Shepard

For over 200 years, during the strongest feudal era in Japan (the early seventeenth century), there was a policy of limiting foreigners who might want to enter Japan and limiting Japanese who might want to leave the country. Commodore Perry had come with a mission from the U.S. president —asking that Japan be open to Americans. The result was that Japan broke its policy of national isolation and began to follow Western-style imperialism. The book illustrates Commodore Perry and his delegation's arrival to nineteenth-century Japan and the mutual reaction between Japanese and Americans. The author includes a beautiful collection of illustrations from old Japanese community papers.

A sadly biased and incomplete account of Commodore Perry's seventeenth-century visit to Japan in an effort to "open" Japan to foreigners.

It is interesting to see an American author's perspective of how Japanese, amazed at Western materials and customs (for example, the large array of agricultural equipment and American clothing), reacted to Perry's arrival. Blumberg depicts how American gifts attracted the Japanese. Japanese people were so fascinated by American naval uniforms that they could not resist touching or putting their hand inside pockets or collars. The author describes these Japanese as somehow inferior.

In comparison, Japanese textbooks portray Perry as frightened and barbarous when he arrived. Blumberg should take more care to avoid an assumed cultural superiority of American over Japanese, but rather present elements from both perspectives in order to give a more balanced understanding.

Some historical information in the book tends to mislead the reader. For instance, the author does not mention much about Japan before Perry's arrival. Contrary to the author's statements, Japan was not a peaceful country without war. These pre-contact situations were the main reasons that triggered Japan's decision to sign the Kanagawa Treaty which opened the country to Americans. Actually, Perry's voyage was not a peace-making trip at all, but rather an extension of American imperial ambitions in Asia during, and after, the nineteenth century. Hiding this reality from children or illustrating the fact incorrectly does not properly prepare children for an understanding of the modern world. CHIEKO YAMAZAKI-HEINEMAN

Dee Brown's Folktales of the Native American, Retold for Our Times

| 📗 Dee Brown   📌 Louis Mofsie |
| Native American |
| 1993, Henry Holt & Company |

This anthology includes animal stories, allegories, trickster tales, and ghost stories. Told in the conversational style utilized by elders to tell stories around a campfire, these stories are told to children to introduce them to the religion and the culture of the tribe. These o stories include "How the Corn Came to Earth" and "How Day and Night Were Divided." Both serve as rich accounts of natural phenomena. There are also stories of the days when the animals were equals and they communicated with humans.

The story of how "Skunk Outwits Coyote" tells of a weaker animal using his cunning and wits to out-

smart a stronger animal. These tales contain lessons on behavior and the wisdom of the long cultural traditions of these tribes. Storytelling is a good way to introduce Native American culture to children.

After the stories are introduced, more information about the history, art, music, foods, and lifestyle of Native Americans can be introduced to students. The archaeology of various tribes can also be introduced to the student through stories and videotapes such as the National Geographic series on Native American tribes.

Storytelling can also be used as a vehicle to introduce Native American arts and crafts. Stories of traditional life can be followed with demonstrations on Native American pottery making, which can be engaged in by students. The pots and vessels necessary for everyday activities depicted in these stories can then be constructed using traditional methods. A demonstration of traditional sand painting can be useful in depicting Native American stories through a traditional art form. Sand can be purchased and dyed by students with food coloring and then applied with glue to

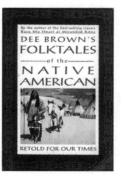

form traditional Native American motifs.

These stories can be a springboard to hands-on craft and food projects, which give the student the feeling of actually participating in the cultures the stories represent. Students can be asked to draw the stories and create their own stories based on these traditional Native American themes.

This book of folklore provides an excellent introduction to Native American cultures, preferably as part of a larger unit on various aspects of these cultures. The book helps the educator to present the material in a sensitive, accurate, and non-stereotypical manner. ELAINE P. GOLEY

Traditional folktales of Native American tribes, retold by Dee Brown that offer a good springboard for activities and further discussion.

591

Singing the Earth: A Native American Anthology

Joseph Bruchac, Diana Landau ✒ Frank LaPena
Native American
1993, Walking Stick Press

This is a beautifully crafted anthology of Native American poems, songs, stories, and art work that focus on nature and the environment. In his introduction, editor Joseph Bruchac quotes Chief Joseph, who said, "The earth and myself are of one mind. The measure of the land and the measure of our bodies are the same." This concept of the innerconnectedness of all things is central to Native American culture and beliefs, as is the sense of a mystical connection to the earth. Native Americans fought long and hard to maintain their traditional ways of life but were forced to sign treaties that separated them from their land and from their culture. The Indian view of the land is that it is sacred and cannot be subdivided and owned but must be shared and preserved for all the people and all future generations.

A beautifully crafted anthology of Native American poetry, songs, stories, and art.

The poetry of Native Americans, like their culture, is inextricably entwined with nature, as most of these poems, stories, and artwork demonstrate. They depict the wonder of nature, the divinity of the natural world that Native Americans perceive.

Native Americans can no longer share the wilderness they knew—it is gone. Ninety percent of North America's original forest is gone. Through their literature, Native Americans share with us all the wonders that nature holds for them. Their vision is still with us. It may be too late to reverse the destruction of nature, but the Native American's reverence for the earth might help us save what remains.

The story of "The Tree and the Corn" relates the sacred view of these plants held by Native Americans "of yellow corn and of white corn they made the flesh; of corn meal dough they made the arms and the legs of man. Only dough of corn went into the flesh of our first fathers, the four men who were created." Likewise, the poem of the Pawnee, "Spring Is Opening," records the wonder of nature. "Spring is opening, I can smell the different perfumes of the white weeds used in the dance." ELAINE P. GOLEY

Return of the Sun: Native American Tales from the Northeast Woodlands

Joseph Bruchac ✒ Gary Carpenter
Native American, Northeast Woodlands Indian
1989, The Crossing Press

The wisdom and practical knowledge of these ancient peoples is revealed in their folklore. As Bruchac tells us, "Stories are the life of a people. They tell the deepest hopes and fears of a nation. They reflect both everyday life and dreams. They affirm and help sustain the values of a culture." The stories he retells here are not available in other anthologies of Native American folklore written for children. They are creation myths and stories that answer our questions about the natural world and about life. The Tuscarora story, "Why the People Speak So Many Tongues," is the equivalent to the tower of Babel story in the Bible. "The Coming of Corn" tells the story of how corn came to earth to rescue the people when they were starving.

A compelling collection of Native American folklore from the Northeast Woodlands.

The Seneca legend of "The Storytelling Stone" demonstrates the Native American belief that even inanimate objects have a life and a spirit and contribute to the survival of people and nature. Most of these stories depict the interdependence of humanity and nature and reflect the Native American reverence for all life.

This anthology of folklore of the Native Americans of the Northeast Woodlands can be read by students in fourth grade and beyond. The print is large and the black-and-white illustrations are compelling. The language is consistent with the Native American oral tradition because Bruchac is a master storyteller, poet, and folklorist who is regarded as one of the foremost Native American scholars. His version of these traditional tales reflects a knowledge of and reverence for native peoples. ELAINE P. GOLEY

Keepers of the Earth: Native American Stories and Environmental Activities for Children

📖 Michael J. Caduto and Joseph Bruchac, Introduction by John Kahionhes Fadden & Carol Wood
🖊 N. Scott Momaday
Native American
1988, Fulcrum Inc., ✳ Audio Cassette, Series

Caduto and Bruchac have collaborated to produce a book of stories, lesson plans, and activities for children. Native American folklore is explored, and sometimes fascinating science activities relating to the themes of these stories are included. These activities link the stories to the modern world. Native American folklore contains blueprints for living our lives using the values and wisdom they impart to children and adults. *The introduction guides educators in the use of the stories and activities. Teachers are taught how to teach by example, use first-hand sensory experience, and ask creative questions. The activities help children to work cooperatively, to utilize problem-solving skills, and to discuss moral, environmental, and social ethics.*

A unique and excellent collection of Native American folklore and environmental activities that present Native American values.

There are also tips for telling the stories aloud effectively, as well as information on basic activities such as nature walks. The Onondaga creation myth, "The Earth on Turtle's Back," explores water and land habits for various creatures. When a woman dives into the water to get earth to put on turtle's back, the other animals realize that she cannot live in the water, but needs a land environment. *The activities that follow include a discussion of the story's themes and activities that explore land and water environments and the ways in which they support life. A study of the oxygen cycle is one activity suggested. The activities tie the ancient stories to real life, making the stories relevant to the child's experience.*

Each story is accompanied by a full-page illustration and followed by discussions of the themes in the story, questions, and activities. Each activity focuses on a scientific phenomenon explored in the legend. The lesson plans contain procedures, activities, materials, and goals. There are several lesson plans included for each story. Methods of tailoring the activities to various age levels are given in the introduction for teachers, and within the activities themselves. Legends about the sun, stars, and ocean are paired with environmental activities and scientific observations relating to these phenomena. They are not mutually exclusive but demonstrate a cultural vehicle for answering basic questions human beings have about the natural world.

The legends and illustrations reflect the dignity of Native American peoples. The illustrations themselves hold keys to the explication of the legend and the natural phenomenon they describe. There is also a glossary and pronunciation guide as well as an index of activities with a subject guide to activities. Each lesson plan also includes long-term projects and activities to extend the experience of the story and the activities. These include writing and other projects that elaborate on the lessons and themes. Some of the subjects covered in the chapters are earth, wind, weather, sky, water, seasons, plants and animals, life, death, and spirit. "The Legend of the White Buffalo" presents the concept of the unity of earth and the interdependence of all living things. This is an excellent text for teaching about Native American culture and values as well as ecology.
ELAINE P. GOLEY

Riel's People: How the Metis Lived

📖 Maria Campbell 🖊 David Maclagan
Metis, Native American
1978, Douglas & McIntyre Ltd.

The Metis of Canada are of European and Native American ancestry and have played a dynamic role in Canadian history. But only recently has their history been presented, mostly in films. In this book, Maria Campbell describes the life-style and tells some of the history of the Metis in Canada. The book covers the origins of the Metis, information about family life, culture, and economic subsistence, and the history of the Metis uprisings against the Canadian government.

In most literature, people of mixed races are presented as tragic figures. In this book, the author gives us a different picture which is graphic, realistic, loving, joyous, and full of pride. The Metis' dress, housing, religion, food, trans-

A graphic and realistic history of the Canadian Metis people, including their uprising against the Canadian government.

594

portation, and music reflect both their European and Native American origins. Campbell's passage on the education of the Metis reflects their strong sense of pride: "To attend such a school a Metis child had to live away from home for years. Many parents felt that the family was too important to be broken up, and kept their children with them to learn Metis skills instead of reading, writing, and memorizing from books. These children learned the settlement's history from the old storytellers, whose songs and legends had been passed down through generations, and so they grew up being proud of being Metis."

Historically, both European and Native American cultures looked down on the Metis. They had little protection of their lands and no real voice in the Canadian government.

By the mid-1800s, they began to organize to better their lives and to gain a political voice. Among other demands, they wanted a government in which they could be represented; the use of both French and English in courts and local governments; and a guarantee of their civil rights and customs. The Canadian government was not sympathetic to their demands and crushed both rebellions. The author is a descendant of one of the leaders of this Metis movement.

The Metis still struggle against racism and for protection of their civil rights and customs in Canada. But their culture still stands, a vibrant blend of very disparate cultures that continue to be at odds with each other. "They know who they are: 'Ka Tip aim soot chic'—the people who own themselves."

Black-and-white drawings by David Maclagan aren't exciting, but they are realistic and help in clarifying the text. NOLA HADLEY

Perihan's Promise

Helen Chetin 🖋 BulBul
Middle Eastern, Turkish
1992 (1973), New Seed Press

Perihan, a fourteen-year-old Turkish Canadian, has promised her father she would keep a journal during her visit to the old country. This is her story, in flip, funny language, and it reveals a thoroughly likeable girl. In part she is escaping: her divorced mother has recently remarried and Perihan's nose is out of joint. She is determined to find things in Turkey much better than things at home, and her enthusiasm never falters.

Perihan's observations of life in a conservative village of central Turkey center on the impending marriage of her cousin, who is only one year older than Perihan herself. Perihan is shocked at first, but determined to accept things as they are.

Perihan is fascinated by the house, the odd toilet, the village baths, a circumcision ceremony, the handsome man who fluffs up the cotton in mattresses, the problem of old attitudes versus modern medicine, competitions in oiled wrestling and ox-head throwing, and, of course, the five days of wedding festivities.

The drama is propelled by an earthquake, which strikes near the end of the merrymaking. This is a sign, says the village Imam, the Islamic religious leader, that the marriage must not take place—and that the "infidel," Perihan, is at fault. Perihan weathers the crisis and eventually returns to the United States, not only thrilled with her visit but also sufficiently mellowed to feel that she can make another start at accepting her mother's new husband and his family.

The book was first published in 1973 under the daunting title *Perihan's Promise, Turkish Relatives, and the Dirty Old Imam*. Though not a weighty book, it was well worth republishing, for it provides an unusually sympathetic introduction to a still quite traditional Middle Eastern culture in the course of a most enjoyable read. It also offers exuberant evidence of the benefits of approaching cross-cultural experiences with a positive attitude. What Perihan and the depiction of present-day Turkish village life may possibly lack in realism, they certainly make up in appeal.

A Turkish Canadian teenager visits the homeland and family of her father in an unusually sympathetic story about Middle Eastern culture.

One minor criticism can be made regarding the portrayal of the Imam. Though the "villain," embodying blind conservatism and resistance to progress, he appears almost a figure of fun, a pathetic old man, crazy enough to think, for a while, that Perihan might make a good bride for himself. A second religious leader, representing a more modern outlook, could have offered a constructive view of the religious life of the village in transition, with its conflicts between old ideas and new.

As a supplement to multicultural learning, *Perihan's Promise* offers an attractive approach with enough substance and to fuel a discussion of cultural values and practices. The new edition is illustrated by an artist who, like the author, knows the country well; like those of the earlier edition (by Beth and Joe Krush), the drawings are stylish and amusing. ELSTON MARSTON

Art of the American Indian Frontier Portfolio

📓 ✏ Detroit Art Institute
Native American
1995, The New Press

This portfolio reproduces twenty-four prints from the excellent Chandler-Pohrt collection of nineteenth-century American Indian art. These prints represent

Fine reproductions of Native American art from the Chandler-Pohrt collection, with an explanatory booklet in an affordable portfolio format.

a selection of the 200 objects featured in the award-winning catalog, *Art of the American Indian Frontier: The Chandler-Pohrt Collection*. They are accompanied here by an explanatory booklet for classroom or home use. This portfolio allows children to examine closely some of the objects from the original collection, and to see the continuity and change that characterize the visual creations of the Native Americans who lived during the nineteenth century. In an introductory essay, the collection's co-curator, Penney, describes the collecting adventures of collection founders, Milford Chandler and Richard Pohrt.

Objects from the collection are organized into three categories. The descriptive booklet is enhanced by nine black-and-white photographs. Two maps depict tribal locations and reservations during the nineteenth century.

This portfolio is highly recommended as an affordable way for school and public libraries to provide young people with superb examples of Native American art. DENISE JOHNSON

Indian America: A Traveler's Companion

📓 Eagle Walking Turtle 📷 Archival photographs
Native American
1995 (1991) John Muir Publications Inc.

This is a travel-guide-cum-history book of Native Americans, arranged geographically into nine regions, by state, and then by tribe within each state. The introduction gives us a brief history of Native Americans and their interaction with white society. The book lists the addresses of tribal councils within each state. There are also several pages of information on the major tribes who welcome visitors. This is information

A rare and comprehensive resource guide to Native American groups in North America.

that is rarely found in one place. Visitor information and the dates of public ceremonies are included in each entry. Black-and-white historic photographs are included throughout. The appendix includes the names and addresses of Native American museums, pow wow calendars, and a list of arts and crafts fairs with locations and dates. A glossary and bibliography are also included. *Teachers and students can write to tribal councils for information about the culture, educational programs, and folklore. Many tribes offer free or inexpensive publications, valuable resources for students who are writing reports, providing experience in gathering reference materials, a skill they will be able to use all of their lives.* ELAINE P. GOLEY

Iran

📓 Mary Virginia Fox ✏ Various sources
Iranian, Middle Eastern
1991, Children's Press, ✳ Series, 📖 Lengyel, Emil, *Iran*; Tames, Richard, *Take a Trip to Iran.*

Illustrated with color and black-and-white photographs, this book is from the *Enchanted of the World* series, which covers more than seventy countries from Europe, Asia, and Africa.

The book starts with regional history, explaining that the original name was Persia, an old name, coming from Pars, a province in the south. The new name, Iran comes from Aryan, the main ethnic group, as distinct from Semites and Torkamans. A few pages about geography and climate follow, then the next seventy-five pages cover in detail the history of Iran from the era of Cyrus the Great (500 B.C.) to the present.

A useful illustrated book about the land and the people of Iran.

The last three chapters of the book focus on natural resources, industry, agriculture, fishing, and life-style, and also take a close look at five major cities. The book closes with "Mini-Facts at a Glance" and important dates. Two maps are included.

This book, which provides a glimpse of different aspects of the country and its people, can be used as a useful teaching tool in geography, history, and courses in cross-cultural studies. SHAHLA SOHAIL

Indian Chiefs

Russell Freedman 📷 Archival photographs, Leonard Everett Fisher (map)

Native American

1987, Holiday House Inc., ✳ CD-ROM

In the nineteenth century, when white settlers made their way west to settle the country, leaders of the Native American tribes had to make a stand. The U.S. government actively waged war on the Indians and broke most of the treaties they made. President Ulysses Grant attempted to force Native Americans onto reservations, even though it meant starving and

Eloquent biographies of several nineteenth-century Indian chiefs, with full page black-and-white photos.

killing them in large numbers. Women and children were massacred in their villages. Not only land but the Indian culture and sometimes their very existence was at stake.

Indian chiefs faced overwhelming odds against the whites who came like locusts. Many chose to fight for what had been theirs for thousands of years. The book includes biographies of Red Cloud, Santana, Quanah Parker, Washakie, Joseph, and Sitting Bull. Full-page archival photographs of each chief are included. The book includes an index and a list of photographic resources.

Indian Chiefs addresses the demise of Native American peoples from their own perspectives and offers potraits of heroic Native American figures. Using materials from the Library of Congress, the National Archives, and other authoritative sources, Freedman eloquently tells these stories. Freedman does not revise history, but tells it accurately

with documentation and the dignity that Native Americans deserve. This book introduces the real lives of Native American leaders and addresses social and cultural history. It is written in an easy-to-read, clear style appropriate for fourth graders and up, and is one of the best books available on the subject. ELAINE P. GOLEY

Indian Signals and Sign Language

George Fronval, Daniel DuBois 🖋 George C. Hight and Jean Marcellin and George Catlin

Native American

1991, Random House Value Publishing

Since the Indians of North America represent many tribes and languages, Native Americans developed a system of communicating with their hands called sign language. This method of communication is still practiced in parts of the Americas.

The impact of sign language on daily life, government, trading, and other aspects of Native American culture are addressed in separate chapters. Photographs show Native Americans in full tribal dress, demonstrating the traditional signs and describing their uses.

A fun and interesting book on the Native American origins and practice of sign language.

Traditional sign language is an activity children find interesting and fun. The students can be divided into groups to practice various hand signals. The groups can then demonstrate their signs and meanings to the class. This method of participation increases enthusiasm for the traditional Indian cultures.

One chapter of the book includes photographs of Indian face and body painting, which I have used as an activity to teach Native American culture. Children love to do this. Use theatrical paints or cosmetics such as lipsticks, eyeliner pencils, rouge and eye shadow for this purpose.

As children are often intrigued by activities such as face-painting and using traditional clothing to create pageantry and dramas about other cultures, this book has great potential for inspiring innovative classroom learning . The book also contains an index and full-color tribal motifs on the end papers, which could be used for Native American craft projects. Although not available in stores, you can find this book in libraries and out-of-print book dealers. ELAINE P. GOLEY

Ancient Indians: The First Americans

📖 Roy A. Gallant ✒ Various sources
Native American
1989, Enslow Publishers, Inc.

Roy Gallant, a noteworthy nonfiction writer for children, has written a history of ancient cultures in the Americas. This book is an overview of archaeological discoveries of Paleo-Indians rather than an in-depth study for adults. The origins of these peoples, who some scholars believe came over the Beringian land bridge that connects Asia and Alaska, are explored. North American Indian ruins are pictured and described at the end of the book, which also includes an index, glossary, and bibliography.

A useful book on the origins of Native American groups and their cultures.

The author describes ways in which Paleo-Indians hunted migrating bison herds by chasing them off cliffs in mass kills. Photographs of bison remains and artifacts of Paleo-Indian cultures are included in the text. Gallant discusses many theories of the origins of Paleo-Indians as well as archaeological evidence for the ways in which they lived and hunted. The book contains two maps showing the migration routes of Paleo-Indians. It also details the way in which the Clovis and other Paleo-Indian cultures such as the Inuit tribe of the Southwest, the Plains tribe, and Native Americans of the Northwest migrated.

This book can be used to explore the origins of early man in America and the present-day tribes descended from these first Americans. The periods before and after the first contact are discussed and compared. The ruined cities and temples of these peoples are depicted in black-and-white photographs.

The chapters are short and the language is accessible for children in grades four and up. This is not a coffee-table book, but is a utilitarian history of man in America before Columbus.

This book can be used in the classroom and for research and discussion of these cultures and the archaeology of North America. Students can use this book for history projects about the cultures of the Americas before Columbus. The students can make charts of migration routes followed by Paleo-Indians, and use them as a springboard for more in-depth studies of Native Americans. ELAINE P. GOLEY

Tales From the African Plains

📖 Anne Gatti (editor) ✒ Gregory Alexander
African, Kenyan
1995 (1994), Dutton Children's Books,
📖 Courlander, Harold, Leslau and Wolf, *Harold The Cow-Tail Switch.*

Many readers are familiar with the Anansi tales from West Africa or variants found in the United States or the Caribbean. These tales emanate from East Africa, primarily Kenya. The collection consists of twelve tales, including four *pourquoi* or "why" tales such as "Why Hyenas Don't Wear Jewelry," and traditional tales that reinforce beliefs, values, or behaviors such as "The Poor Man's Reward" and "The Woman and the Bird." These tales stem from ethnic groups such as the Luo, Kikuyu, and Masai. Most involve animals, though a few feature supernatural beings. The writing is brisk and contains names, words, and phrases of various Kenyan dialects. The tales are entertaining, and they manage to educate the reader about the eastern region without being didactic.

One of the most intriguing tales is "Wacu and the Eagle." Wacu is a Kikuyu female. As such, she is only allowed to eat meat on feast days away from the males. Wacu defies tradition from childhood because her father treats her as a son and allows her to eat meat in public. All sorts of complications develop as Wacu violates tradition and causes a great deal of consternation among the community's males.

Folktales from the African Plains that educate the reader about East Africa, with breathtaking illustrations.

The illustrations are simply breathtaking. Alexander has captured the alternately intense and subdued colors associated with sunrise, sunset, moonglow, and daylight. The animals are realistic. The Masai are stunning. The long reddish locks of the men, the shaved heads of the women, the intricate beadwork and textiles leave you with the impression that you can step into the illustrations and find yourself herding cattle with the Masai, drumming, dancing in a procession, or battling an animal. The illustrations alone are worth the price of the book; the stories are an added bonus. Combined, they enrich our perceptions of East Africa. VIOLET HARRIS

597

Love Flute

📦 ✒ Paul Goble

Native American, Plains Indian

1993 (1992), Varsity Reading Services, ✳ Series, Audio Cassette, 📖 Goble, Paul, *Iktomi and the Boulder; Iktomi and the Berries: A Plains Indian Story; Iktomi and the Ducks: A Plains Indian Tale.*

A love flute, created from cedar wood, was used in "the old days" by young Native American men to tell the women they loved how they felt about them. Paul Goble retells the Plains Indian myth explaining the origin of this custom with his trademark clear prose and exquisite artwork.

The myth recounts the tale of "a shy young man who was given the very first love flute, long ago, by the birds and the animals." The young man is a brave hunter, always at the front of buffalo hunts, yet he cannot declare his feelings to the woman he loves. He watches as the other young men of the tribe whisper and banter with her. Deciding that his life is worthless without her love, he heads away from the camp. He travels for four days until he comes upon an aspen grove, where two Elk Men present him with a flute, saying "with the music of this flute you will speak straight to the heart of the girl you love."

A beautifully illustrated Plains Indian story explaining why young men serenade women with a cedar "love flute."

In his retelling, Goble emphasizes the importance of nature in Native American culture. The Elk Men have branching antlers, and in the blink of an eye, turn back into bull elk. They are the link between the natural world and the human world. As Goble explains in an introduction, the "courteous and magnificent" bull elk was understood to be dearly loved by the females in his herd and it was this success in love that the flute would bring.

The flute is made of cedar wood, the holes carved out by a woodpecker, and harmony infused into the instrument by all the birds and animals. As the young man plays the flute, he listens to and imitates the songs of birds and animals, weaving their rhythms into songs of his own until, again, his world and the natural world are entwined, "and so when a man played the flute, seeking to attract and create new life, he did so as an integral part of Creation.".

In Goble's beautifully-detailed illustrations, jagged mountain ranges merge in the distance with rippling clouds, aspen leaves form a golden canopy, and geese swing their long necks in rhythmic unison. His characters are clad in colorful buffalo skins with intricate designs; the majestic Elk Men wear shield-like masks and carry magical hoops with mirrors at their center. The text is broken up by a number of black-and-white drawings of love flutes, illustrating the variations in their markings and decoration.

As always, Goble is fascinating to read. An introduction to the text briefly explains some courtship traditions providing a larger context for the story of the love flute. He also provides references for other versions of the story and an address for those who wish to track down recordings of songs played on love flutes. LINDSEY TATE

Women in American Indian Society

📦 Rayna Green ✒ Various sources

Native American

1992, Chelsea House, ✳ Series

The author, a scholar of American history and a Cherokee woman, traces the history of Native American women from different nations from the time of early explorations to the present. Readers begin with the early portrayals of women as mere caretakers and soon are shown the many roles of women in the diverse Native societies —as healers, as keepers of stories, as educators, and many others. Readers learn that women, especially in the American West and Alaska, hold leadership roles within their own nations as well as within U. S. government and business. The remaining stories reveal the lives and power of Native women throughout the history of the United States, ending with modern-day women such as author Paula Gunn Allen and tribal leader Wilma Mankiller. Any reader who holds stereotypical views of women in general and Native American women in particular will be quickly and effectively disabused of these inaccurate images.

A stereotype-busting look at the contributions of Native American women throughout history.

NANCY HANSEN-KRENING

Shooting Back
From the Reservation

📖 Jim Hubbard   ✏ Native American children

Native American

1994, The New Press

In 1989, photographer Jim Hubbard founded Shooting Back, an organization that teaches "at-risk" children how to use cameras, and how to develop and process film. Shooting Back worked with children in a homeless shelter in Washington, DC. The photos these children took were assembled and shown at the Washington Project for the Arts and museums around the world, as documented by PBS and the book *Shooting Back: A Photographic View of Life by Homeless Children.*

Hubbard and Shooting Back take a similar approach with their second project. This time, Hubbard gave cameras to Native American children in different parts of the country. The resulting photos were displayed in Washington D.C., and are collected in *Shooting Back from the Reservation.*

A collection of snapshots taken by Native American children in reservations around the country that comprise an honest sobering book.

"Photographs have a way of preserving and complementing our memories," Dennis Banks, a Native American leader and teacher, writes in the foreword. "Memories may grow vague, but photographs capture moments in time, catch us just as we were. They are visual records of lives, places, and activities."

The black-and-white pictures are visual records of these children's lives on the reservations. They're paired with poetry written by children — giving us glimpses into their world, letting us see things through their eyes.

We get an honest, sobering, often tender look into everyday life on reservations in such places as Arizona, New Mexico, and South Dakota. The snapshots are candid and real, never posed.

Patrick Wichem's "Abandoned Mission," for example, taken on the White Earth Reservation in Minnesota, depicts an old, decrepit, abandoned building. It's nothing to be ashamed of or embarrassed about. That is just what a ten-year-old sees. In other photos, boys ride bikes, little girls dance in costumes, parents make funny faces.

Though these children live in barren, often remote surroundings, they still have a reverence for the past and for their communities. They may not have much money, but they're rich in other ways.

Thirteen-year-old Leann Slinky from Window Rock, Arizona, writes, "I would never want to see the people that are still going by the traditional ways decide to change."

Janelle Francisco, another teen in Window Rock, also appreciates what she has. "People in my community are nice to one another and know one another. We even care about our enemies no matter how much we hate them." CHRISTINA ENG

Come Home With Me:
A Multicultural Treasure Hunt

📖 Aylette Jenness   ✏ Laura DeSantis

Multicultural

1993, The New Press   ✳ Series, Spanish

This inaugural book of The Kids' Bridge Series is also available in a Spanish version, *Ven a mi casa: Una busqueda de tesoro multicultural. Come Home With Me* is based on a traveling exhibit originating at The Children's Museum in Boston, which examines the harmful effects of racism and discrimination and encourages children to accept diversity. This volume provides a perfect, fun-filled way to introduce the concept of cultural diversity to young children. With contagious enthusiasm,

A fun-filled book that encourages children to be curious and respectful of ethnic groups different from their own.

four youngsters from various ethnic backgrounds (Cambodian, Puerto Rican, African American, and Irish American) lead the readers on a journey through their ethnic neighborhoods and into their homes, shops, and museums, on a search for foods and other items rooted in their particular cultural traditions. Descriptions of related customs and legends are introduced in a spirited and accessible fashion. Colorful photographs render a convincing portrait of ethnic diversity in each of the four neighborhoods visited. *Although these neighborhoods are in Boston, this book can be used as a model in design-*

599

ing a tour of any neighborhood in the country. The activities, designed to foster an appreciation for the richness of neighborhood ethnic diversity in children, can also be adapted to different ages. Suggestions for exploring one's own neighborhood and other activities are a practical addition. *The glossary of foreign words that children might not know is useful.* This is an invaluable activity book for promoting cultural understanding. MELVINA AZAR DAME

The Best of the Brownies' Book

📓 Dianne Johnson-Feelings (editor)
✒ Various artists
African American
1996, Oxford University Press, ✳ Series

The Best of The Brownies' Book is a collection from the pioneering African American children's magazine of the early 1920s and a testament to the endurance of some of the great African American children's stories and books.

An exciting and inspiring 1920s compilation from the pioneering African American children's magazine published in the 1920s.

Published under the auspices of the NAACP, *The Brownie's Book* was edited by W.E.B. DuBois, Jessie Redmond Fauset, and Augustus Granville Dill. It brought the history and achievements of black people to a wide audience through poems and stories by writers such as Georgia Douglas Johnson, Nella Larson Imes, and Langston Hughes and biographies on figures like Phillis Wheatley and Frederick Douglass.

Also featured are articles about the accomplishments of young people from all over the world, as

well as artwork and photographs from some of the then-emerging artists of the Harlem Renaissance.

With an introduction by Marian Wright Edelman of The Children's Defense Fund, these stories, poems, articles, and letters will bring excitement and inspi-

ration to readers young and old. Even some of today's most hardened and cynical young people will have their curiosity piqued.

RELATED TITLES
Continuing their lifelong mission to seek out and preserve the very best books for children, Iona and Peter Opie's Library of Children's Literature brings a new generation an exceptional selection of children's books including *Popo and Fifina*, by Arna Bontemps and Langston Hughes, *The Book of Rhythms* by Langston Hughes, and *Black Misery* by Langston Hughes. DAPHNE MUSE

Pueblo Boy: Growing Up in Two Worlds

📓 ✒ Marcia Keegan
Native American, Pueblo
1991, Cobblehill Books

This photo essay follows a young boy as he goes about his daily life in the San Ildefonso Pueblo in New Mexico, one that combines using computers in school and learning ritual dances over 10,000 years old. Timmy is shown as having the same interests as any other ten-year-old boy: he rides his bike to school, listens to tapes on his Walkman, plays Little League baseball. At the same time, he is learning the ancient traditions of

An affirming photo essay that follows a modern Pueblo Indian boy as he goes about his daily life.

his people. His uncle carves *kachinas* (ancestral spirits), his aunt makes the distinctive black pottery of the San Ildefonso Pueblo.

The author has managed to describe Timmy's life in a manner that shows it as interesting but real, not exotic. Simple explanations of Pueblo Indian beliefs, customs, and rituals help young readers to understand Timmy's culture without pretending to provide an in-depth analysis. A visit to the Bandelier National Monument, the site of a pueblo abandoned since the 1,500s, lets readers build a mental bridge between the past and the lives led by Pueblo Indians today.

Although the final paragraph carries an obvious message, it is nevertheless a self-affirming one for American Indian children: "Timmy likes to belong to two cultures. He feels he has the best of both worlds." LYNN EISENHUT

Children Just Like Me

📕 Anabel Kindersley, Barnabas Kindersley,
Susan E. Copset; Foreword by Harry Belafonte
✒ Barnabas Kindersley
Multicultural
1995, Dorling Kindersley

Children Just Like Me is a collection of interviews and engaging photographs of children from thirty countries around the world. The photographic illustrations captivate with color and, while the child occupies center stage on each page, there are smaller pictures that show foods, pets, school books, or toys. There are pictures of topography and dwellings that give a real sense of how the children live.

Captivating interviews with children from thirty countries, accompanied by vivid color photographs.

Unlike many books that show children dressed in "traditional" costume, this book shows children dressed in everyday garb. They speak of family, home, food, games, and more. In addition to teaching us how others learn and believe, the book makes it possible for children to trace patterns of similarity and dissimilarity between cultures and to chart universal elements that transcend geographic boundaries.

There is also a wealth of information in profiles of individual children: Celina Tembe, who lives in Brazil's Amazon rainforest and mourns the destruction of the jungle; Tadesse Assefa, a nine-year-old Ethiopian who's lived in an orphanage since he was five and dreams of doing something good and important for people when he grows up; and Edgar, an eight-year-old from the Phillipines, who shucks 300 oysters before school and another 200 when he gets home, so that his parents can afford to send him to school.

Thoughtful in presentation, interview focus, and cultural diversity, this book shows children lifting their voices and telling stories to others around the world, building a wonderful symphony of lives.
SUSIE WILDE

How It Feels to Live With a Physical Disability

📕 ✒ Jill Krementz
Physically Disabled
1992, Simon & Schuster, 📖 Dwight, Laura, *We Can Do It!.*

Twelve physically challenged children between the ages of six and sixteen describe what it is like to live with a disability. Black-and-white photographs show each going about their daily routines with friends, families, and schoolmates.

For children who are not disabled and who have little contact with physically challenged peers, *How It Feels to Live With a Physical Disability* may be a real eye-opener. Some disabilities are hidden and others clearly apparent. The children's stories, told in the first person, reveal the same interests and dreams as any other group of young people.

Twelve physically challenged children from various cultural backgrounds describe life with a disability in an eye-opening work.

They also describe the courage and determination needed to overcome what sometimes appear to be, and at times are, insurmountable challenges. Most of the children mention experiencing periods of anger, depression, and embarrassment when their disabilities affect their ability to participate in activities with friends and at school. All cite the support of family and friends as being crucial to their success, but their own positive attitudes are obviously a significant factor.

Children of different cultural backgrounds are depicted, and the importance of involving disabled children in specialized sports programs is discussed at the end of the book. LYNN EISENHUT

Less Than Half, More Than Whole

📕 ✒ Michael Lacapa
Native American
1994, Northland Publishing

In *Less than Half, More than Whole*, Michael Lacapa tells and illustrates the story of a young boy of Native American and European ancestry who comes to terms with his multiple heritages with the help of his grandfather and a bundle of multicolored ears of corn.

601

Tony, Scott, and Will are skipping stones on a lake when they suddenly become aware of their physical differences. As the stones create pools of water, their reflections show Scott's yellow hair and blue eyes while Will's brown skin and black hair beam back at him. Will says, "You are not like me…I'm all Indian. I think you are only half, or less than half."

When the boys go home for dinner, Tony keeps hearing the words, "less than half" and is upset because the phrase implies inferiority. He questions his Grandmother Doris, his brother Daniel, and his Uncle about what it means to be part or half of something. Each provides him with an affirming image as they discuss his Anglo/Native American heritage. Through family pictures and a bundle of multicolored corn, his-grandfather Tada reassures Tony that he is a whole person.

A young boy of Native American and European descent comes to terms with his multiethnic heritages in a welcome addition to the literature.

With the corn in hand, Tony's grandfather says, "He [the Creator] did not give this gift in only one color but in many colors. I keep this bundle [of corn] here so that I will remember the gift the Creator has given me — my family of many colors. Some will see only the blue in this ear of corn, and others will only see the red; but I do not see anything less than six ears of corn and all that it means to our people. You are not a half a person because of your color, my son; you are a whole beautiful person."

This book is a welcome addition to the growing number of children's books that positively portray mixed-race children. *The attention paid to overt differences in physical characteristics should be a welcome opening for a discussion of race and ethnicity with all young readers or listeners.*

The vibrant and bold color illustrations of Michael Lacapa are even more remarkable than in his previous books. He has included a glossary of terms, concepts, and designs. Lacapa informs the reader which tribe each graphic design is from and the history or philosophy behind the book's design. NOLA HADLEY

Hopscotch Around the World

Mary D. Lankford ✒ Karen Milone
Multicultural
1992, Morrow Junior Books

Children play hopping games all over the world. While urban enclaves no longer teem with thousands of children playing hopscotch, the voices of young children can still be heard on playgrounds and city streets calling out old rhymes and making up new, sometimes rap-based, rhymes to accompany the hopping steps of the game. Played all over the world, from Nigeria (Ta Galagala) and Poland (Klassa), to Honduras (La Rayuela) and the United States (Hopscotch), the game involves drawing patterns in chalk or dirt, tossing an object into the

A variety of hopping games from around the world are presented in a well-designed book including illustrations, diagrams, and instructions.

pattern, then hopping through it without touching any lines. Without speculating on why the game is present in so many cultures, author Mary Lankford introduces hopscotch as an amusement practiced as far back as early Roman times. She then shares twenty versions of the game from sixteen different countries. Arranged alphabetically by country of origin with a map at the beginning of the book locating the areas where the games are played, each major variant of hopscotch represented in this well-designed book features a full-page color illustration of non-stereotypical children engaged in their form of the game. A pattern diagram accompanies a brief narrative describing what makes a particular version unique, and specific instructions for play follow.

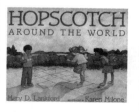

This book grew out of the author's own interest in the game of hopscotch, and her approach is more personal than scholarly. She did her research at the library and through interviews with friends and others who could tell her of their childhood experiences with the game. *While not exhaustive,* Hopscotch Around the World *is an excellent lead-in to a discussion of cultural similarities and differences. Not only does* Hopscotch Around the World *become*

an interesting way to launch a discussion centered on geography, it also becomes an engaging book for examining the variations on this game within the same country. LYNN EISENHUT

Learning To Swim In Swaziland: A Child's Eye-View of a Southern African Country

📖 Nila K. Leigh, Margaret Zoller Booth
✒ Various children's drawings
African, Swahili
1993, Scholastic, Inc.

This book was born when Nila K. Leigh's parents took her to live in Swaziland ("Smaller than New Jersey but kind of round") for an unspecified length of time, and she began writing letters back to her classmates in New York City.

Leigh tells her American friends the kinds of things they would be interested in—what the sky looks like at night, games and chores, school, fun, and food. Comments range from "There are no lions" to "The minute [Swazi children] see you they will want to be friends." Leigh even includes a Swazi folktale, "Why Some Animals Behave the Way They Do." The book concludes with a personal message to the reader: "You should not be afraid of what you have never done. You can do all kinds of things you never dreamed you could do. Just like swimming. Just like writing a book. Just like living in Africa."

A young New Yorker writes with excitement and respect about her new home in Swaziland in a story based on the author's own life.

This book is an important example for young readers, even those who have never traveled farther than down the block. Your experience can be written about. You, too, could make a book. Leigh's personable delivery pulls a reader into the story immediately and never lets go.

Children will love *Learning to Swim in Swaziland* for its exuberant graphics, its hand-lettered text, its intermingling of children's drawings and color photographs, and, of course, for its having been authored by an eight-year-old girl.

Nila tells her story with respect for African customs and people. It is a visitor's view and never claims to be otherwise, and nowhere does it degener-ate into a kind of "us and the other" document. *Learning to Swim in Swaziland* shares a personal world with feeling and affection—reading it, you will be inspired to pay better attention to where you are.
NAOMI SHIHAB NYE

The Magic Crossbow

📖 Alice Lucas ✒ You-Shan Tang
Asian
Voices of Liberty, ✳ Bilingual: English/ Vietnamese, Audio Cassette,
📖 Jorgensen, Karen and Stokes Brown, Cynthia, *Immigration Curriculum Guides; New Faces in Our Schools*; Lucas, Alice, *Four Champa Trees; Mountain of the Men.*

Reading folktales to children provides a way of teaching ancient history as well as explaining the realities of life. Voices of Liberty has published three bilingual folktales from Southeast Asia. Each of the folktales, simply and beautifully illustrated, comes with a

Three bilingual folktales from Vietnam, Cambodia, and Laos that share engaging themes of power, magic, and trickery.

guide for teachers and a tape cartridge in English and the original language of the culture represented. These folktales represent an intuitive understanding of their cultures.

The author, Alice Lucas, has maintained the voice of a storyteller in the translated tales. Like all folktales, the language is simple and the themes are universal. "The Mountain of Men and the Mountain of the Women" is part of a Cambodian legend about marriage customs and explains how it comes to be that the man proposes to the woman. The Vietnamese folktale, "The Magic Crossbow," tells the story of the battle for land, leading to betrayal and loss between the warring families. In the Laotian folktale, "Four Champa Trees," four young boys are saved from an evil queen. In each of the stories, it is the power of magic and trickery that transform and change the situation, thus drawing the reader into the folktale.
GRACE MORIZAWA

603

Handbook of American Indian Games

📖 Allan MacFarlan ✏ Paulette Mac Farlan
Native American
1985 (1958), Dover Publications, Inc.

Many children's games—from handball to lacrosse to relay races—are Native American in origin. This book explores these games and suggests ways to incorporate them in school settings. The introduction explains the purpose of the games, which is to develop physical agility and nature skills, to encourage thought and observation, as well as wood-crafting skills and discipline. Chapter introductions for each category of game give the reader the historical and cultural context in which the games were played. *The one- or two-page descriptions of these games sometimes feature diagrams and recommended grade level and include information on tribal origin, number of players, equipment required (many games require little or no equipment), and rules. In addition to games that feature physical activity, the book includes a number of guessing games that can be played in the classroom. These games can be used as a resource to follow storytelling and the study of Native American cultures. By learning and playing these games, students will acquire an appreciation for Native American culture and its contributions to our own culture.*

A nicely illustrated introduction to the origins and rules of Native American games that is unfortunately somewhat dated.

The book's illustrations, woodcuts with Native American motifs, greatly enhance the book. One drawback is the book's outdated treatment of cultural issues (the book was originally copyrighted in 1958). For instance, the books separates boys' and girls' games.

The book can be used as part of a larger unit on how our culture draws upon Native American culture in such areas as art, food, language, sign language, and other Native American skills. Tomie de Paola's The Popcorn Book, which covers the history of the use of corn, popcorn, and other food that originated in the Americas, would be a good complementary book.

In combination with units on Native American arts, crafts, and foods, the Handbook of American Indian Games can provide meaningful and enjoyable learning experiences at school and at home.
ELAINE P. GOLEY

A 16th Century Mosque

📖 Fiona Macdonald ✏ Mark Bergin
Arab, Middle Eastern
1994, Simon & Schuster, ✳ Series

This addition to the "Inside Story" series introduces young readers to an Ottoman mosque, provides background information on the Islamic faith and the history of Islam, and discusses who built mosques in Ottoman times. Both ends of the societal spectrum are included. Readers will learn about the everyday lives of workers and craftsmen as well as the exalted lifestyles of Sultan Suleyman II and his architect, Sinan Pasha.

The book is divided into illustrated two-page spreads that form independent essays on a variety of topics. Each short essay stands alone, making this an easy book for children to browse through and return to later. It also includes a glossary, an index, and an explanation of the Islamic calendar. As in all "Inside Story" books, special cutaway illustrations enhance and explain the text. The most fascinating section is an account of the architectural problems posed by the enormous mosque complex, which included round domes atop square buildings and minarets that towered over 200 feet in the air and were constructed by hundreds of workers from all over the Ottoman Empire.

A finely illustrated introduction to Ottoman mosques and the history of Islam.

Illustrator Mark Bergin, a specialist in historical reconstruction, provides attractive and accurate illustrations. His attention to the finest detail is evident in his depictions of clothing, calligraphy, and craft designs.

A 16th Century Mosque and its series companions would make fine additions to a school or classroom library. This particular volume could inspire a classroom project in which students design and make a model of an Ottoman mosque.
SANDRA KELLY

Aztecs and Spaniards: Cortés and the Conquest of Mexico

Albert Marrin ✐ Various sources

Aztec, Hispanic, Native American

1986, Simon & Schuster Children's Books

Marrin provides readers with his perspective on the Spanish conquest of the Aztec empire. Beginning with a description of Tenochtitlan, the capitol city of the Aztec empire, the author then provides readers with details that paint a picture of the daily life and beliefs of the Aztec people. Biographical details of the life of Cortés and his motives for journeying to the New World are presented. His trek from the modern city of Veracruz to the Basin of Mexico and his quest for gold are told in the goriest of details.

A sometimes gory portrait of the Spanish conquest of the Aztec empire.

The section describing the *Noche Triste* (Sad Night) is admirable, and the book concludes with the destruction of Tenochtitlan. The illustrations are redrawn from several codices, and include portraits of the main characters. *A bibliography for further reading is included, and the book should prove to be of interest to intermediate students studying the fall of the Aztec empire.* BYRON RUSKIN

Inca and Spaniard: Pizarro and the Conquest of Peru

Albert Marrin ✐ Various sources including Guaman Poma

Hispanic, Inca, Native American, Peruvian

1989, Atheneum

A clearly written historical account of Inca civilization and its conquest by Pizarro.

This book begins with a detailed history and discussion of the Inca civilization. The second chapter presents the story of Francisco Pizarro and his family. His brothers were later to play an important role in the conquest of the Inca empire. The narrative returns to the history of the Inca civil war between two royal brothers, Huascar and Atahualpa, which results in the weakening of the Inca empire and, ultimately, Pizarro's victory. The capture of Atahualpa, his ransom in gold, Spanish deceit, and the execution of Atahualpa follows. The story ends with the final battles between the Incas and Spaniards and the consolidation of power and wealth by Pizarro and his brothers. The narrative is clearly written, detailed, and thorough. The book contains numerous illustrations, mainly those of Guaman Poma from his *El Primer Nueuva Cronica y Buen Gobierno.* A suggested list for further reading is included.
BYRON RUSKIN

Going Home

Nicholasa Mohr

Hispanic, Puerto Rican

1989 (1986), Bantam Books, Inc., ✱ Series

In this sequel to the novel *Felita*, the protagonist has just turned twelve and is starting to resent her parents' newfound protectiveness. They let her brothers stay out late and go places by themselves, but Felita must

In a convincing and detailed story, the protagonist of the Felita series comes to terms with her heritage on a trip to Puerto Rico.

have a chaperone when she visits her friend Vinnie, a recent immigrant from Colombia. So when Tio Jorge invites her to spend the summer in Puerto Rico, she jumps at the chance. Felita has never been to Puerto Rico, but remembers her *Abuelita's* glow-

ing accounts of a beautiful island and close-knit communities. When she arrives for her visit, she finds that everything is not quite as she expected. Although she develops a close friendship with her neighbor Providencia, the small town where her uncle lives is quite a contrast to New York City and seems dull to Felita. In addition, some of the local girls make fun of her accent, call her a *Nuyorican*, and claim she's not really Puerto Rican.

Felita faces a dilemma and an identity crisis. If she doesn't belong in Puerto Rico, where does she belong? This book explores a common theme for Puerto Rican, Dominican, Mexican American, and other immigrant children who shuttle regularly between their family's home and the United States. Mohr convincingly presents the questions of grow-

605

ing up and cultural identity from a young Latina's perspective. The dialogue, incorporating English and some Spanish, is naturalistic, and the family and peer pressures are culturally specific yet universal. This is a book that raises questions for everyone about the meaning and importance of "going home." LAURI JOHNSON

The Arabs in the Golden Age

▣ Mokhtar Moktefi, (translated by Mary K. LaRose)
✎ Veronique Ageorges
Arab American, Middle Eastern
1992, Millbrook Press, ✷ Series, ▦ Meltzer, Milton, *The Amazing Potato; Cheap Raw Material; Who Cares?: Millions Do*.

This title is part of the Millbrook Press Peoples of the Past Series. Like all books in this series, it treats history as far more than a soporific sequential series of dates; the emphasis is on humanity, providing an historic look at the lives of everyday people and how they lived.

The time period covered in *The Arabs in the Golden Age* extends from the birth of the prophet Muhammad, in 570 C.E., to the fall of the Abbasid Dynasty, when the capital city of Baghdad was sacked by the Mongols, in 1258 C.E. During this period, which was roughly contemporaneous with the so-called Dark Ages and early medieval period in Europe, classical Arab culture flourished.

This excellent reference book is one of the few for children that details how people lived in the Middle East. The many topics covered include crafts and trade, scientific achieve-

A visually appealing reference book that details how people lived in the medieval Middle East.

ments, women's fashion and footwear, education, the *souk* (a Middle Eastern ancestor of today's shopping mall), religion, food and farming, warfare, and the postal system (swift delivery by an early "pony express" and air mail via pigeon post.)

The book features a time line of important events, a map of the Islamic Empire at its height, suggestions for further reading, a four-page index, and a glossary of Arabic words. Young readers will not find that they have to refer to the glossary often; when Arabic terms are used in the text, they are explained in English.

Visually, *The Arabs in the Golden Age* is appealing. Full-color illustrations, many in the style of classical Arab art, are spread throughout the book. Every page seems to contain at least a couple of pictures. Break-out boxes provide detail to complement the text. Unfortunately, at times the pages are a bit cluttered with all this artwork, making it difficult to follow the text which often breaks off in mid-sentence before a picture, leaving the reader to scramble to finish the thought after the illustration.

In spite of this one small criticism, the book is recommended, particularly for school and classroom libraries where it would be very useful as a research tool for students studying the medieval world.
SANDRA KELLY

When Will the Fighting Stop?: A Child's View of Jerusalem

▣ Ann Morris ✎ Lilly Rivlin
Jewish, Middle Eastern
1990, Antheneum

Any child who has ever been bored and lonely will understand how Mishkin feels—even though Mishkin, a Jewish boy of seven or eight, lives in one of the most fascinating and beautiful cities in the world. Jerusalem is his home and his family has lived there for generations. It's a wonderful place to explore and to play. But the lure of the city cannot quite compensate for the loss of a friend, and one of Mishkin's closest friends, a girl named Ala, is no longer

A simple but deep story of a Jewish boy in Jerusalem who wonders why there can't be peace among neighbors.

allowed to play with him. Tensions arising from the Palestinian-Arab uprising against the Israeli occupying forces in Jerusalem and the West Bank, it is implied, have separated these children.

So one warm day, Mishkin wanders through the city in search of a friend or something to do. The black-and-white photographs reveal to the reader the social and architectural landscape that Mishkin encounters, an intimate introduction to the byways of Jerusalem. Both writer and photographer convey enough information for the reader to experience Mishkin's day very much as he would, without dwelling on detail.

Mishkin's aimless path takes him past religious sites and sights of religious piety. It also takes him through unfamiliar quarters, where he does indeed meet some cold glances and a few hostile words. He

606

returns the hostility. But just outside the city, by a spring in an olive grove, he finds gentle kindness at the hands of an Arab man who gives him a drink. By the end of Mishkin's long morning on his own, we sense, he has acquired a richer store of experiences that will make him a more open, accepting person, better able to live peaceably in a mixed community when the fighting stops. This is a very simple story, but with deep and abiding significance.

What I admire particularly about this book is the unobtrusive balance and the nonjudgmental approach to the people who populate Mishkin's world and the issues that impinge upon it. The "peace" theme is handled with subtlety and sensitivity. In a scene where Mishkin engages in a little shoving match with an Arab boy, he shouts, "This is my home!" "This is everybody's home!" the boy answers. It is a story of human experience, universal and inclusive.

Students in upper elementary grades, even middle school, could analyze how the author and photographer have conveyed their views about people, place, and peace; younger children could appreciate the story on a simpler level. The scenes of the ancient stones of Jerusalem and the ongoing life in the old city will enhance the book for adult readers. ELSA MARSTON

Barefoot Gen: A Cartoon Story of Hiroshima

Keiji Nakazawa
Asian, Japan
1995 (1987), New Society Publishers,
✷ Series

This is a true account of life in Hiroshima during WWII. It is a tragic story of the atomic bomb attack and the people's suffering with a focus on the manipulation of the people by pro-war propaganda which prevailed at the time. Every aspect of Japanese daily lives was affected by the systematic belief in patriotism, in the emperor, and in the war.

The main character, Gen, and his family are peaceful people who struggle againt those neighbors who are opposed to their anti-war philosophies. This book affords young readers an opportunity to visualize how war affects people's minds and how people can be blinded by the system. It also highlights the discrimination by Japanese against Koreans, which continues to be a pressing contemporary issue.

Non-Japanese readers would benefit from more information on the historical background of Japanese imperialism which engendered military invasion of many Asian countries. This information would give the reader insight into the mindset of the people who lived in early twentieth-century Japan where the Emperor was deified, and people sometimes obeyed blindly. The goal of Japanese imperialism was for Japan to rise to a world power by whatever means it took.

Also helpful to the reader would be some explanation regarding the custom of punitive measures, ie., parents hitting children. This practice was an accepted societal norm at that time. This additional cultural information would be benefical in helping the reader more fully to understand the context of the book.

CHIEKO YAMAZAKI-HEINEMAN

A cartoon story of life in Hiroshima during WWII that would benefit from more cultural context.

The Incas

Shirlee P. Newman ✐ Various sources
Hispanic, Incan, Native American
1992, Franklin Watts, Inc., ✷ Series

This primer is the third in a useful series published by Franklin Watts. The narrative presents an organized and broad outline of Inca and pre-Inca civilizations. The story begins with the legend of the first great Inca, Manco Capac; the founding and construction of the Inca capital Cuzco; the fortress Sacsahuaman; and the magnificent road system that spanned the length of the Inca empire, some 3,000 miles. The next chapter discusses the pre-Inca kingdom of Chimor, the religious beliefs of the Incas, their astronomy, and their social and political organization. The third chapter presents a short history of the conquest of the Incas by Pizarro and the betrayal of Atahualpa by the Spaniards. The book concludes with a glimpse of modern-day Peru. A short glossary, a book list for further reading, one map, and twenty-one illustrations complete the book. The Franklin Watts series, *The Aztecs*, *The Maya*, and *The Incas*, is valuable because it offers a series of topics that can be developed by the teacher and student. BYRON RUSKIN

A broad overview of Inca and pre-Inca civilizations.

607

Singing America: Poems that Define a Nation

📖 Neil Philip (editor) ✒ Michael McCurdy
Multicultural
1995, Viking

In *Singing America*, readers are taken on a poetic journey that represents that breadth of the American cultural and historical experience. Interspersed with traditional spirituals, anthems, and Native American songs are poems by Walt Whitman, Gwendolyn Brooks, Edgar Allan Poe, Margaret Walker, Kitty Tsui, Allen Ginsberg, Robert Hayden, and many others.

The book is divided into five sections, covering (among other themes) the beauty of the landscape and the cultural diversity of America. Each poem is accompanied by the work of one of the nation's outstanding visual artist. Some of the pairings work exceptionally well; for example, Winslow Homer's "High Cliff, Coast of Maine" and Jean Toomer's "At Sea" stand together as a perfect artistic marriage.

A stimulating multicultural anthology celebrating the American experience that could have used more contemporary poems.

While no one book can contain all voices, it is a shame this anthology does not include more works by contemporary writers such as Lucille Clifton and Gary Soto. But the book does include some less-familiar works by well-known poets, such as Linda Hogan's "The New Apartment, Minneapolis" and Delmore Schwartz's "The True-Blue American."

While most of the poems will work best with readers in grades six and up, songs and traditional pieces such as "Casey Jones" and "Johnny Fill Up the Bowl" will be easily embraced by young children. As a stepping stone to *Singing America*, I suggest teachers, parents, and librarians use *Celebrate America in Poetry and Art* (edited by Nora Panzer and the staff of the National Museum of American Art, Smithsonian Institution).

For those teachers and parents eager to teach young people more about the history of America and the richness of its cultural landscape, these selections are bound to stimulate interest and generate real enthusiasm. DAPHNE MUSE

The Children of Egypt

📖 Matti Pitkanen, Reijo Harkonen, Matti A. Pitkånen
Middle Eastern, Egyptian
1991, The Lerner Group, ✳ Series

Like the other books in the Children of the World series, *The Children of Egypt* is a photographic essay of the people living in this region of the world. Numerous color photographs capture people doing the things they do every day: sailing a *felucca* on the Nile, making mud bricks, selling vegetables and eggs at the outdoor market, and giving horseback rides to tourists visiting the pyramids. Through the children's own experiences, various aspects of life in Egypt are introduced, including the country's population issue, common foods, the call to prayer from a nearby mosque, and the constant reminders of Egypt's ancient heritage—from the pyramids and sphinx to agricultural techniques that have changed little in thousands of years. The people looking back through the camera's lens convey a variety of emotions; some are smiling and friendly, while others appear preoccupied with the difficulties of daily life.

An inviting photographic essay of Egyptian children that covers a diverse geographic range but a misleadingly narrow socio-economic one.

The children featured come from many parts of Egypt. But despite this geographic diversity, only a narrow cross-section of Egyptian life is portrayed. Admittedly, Egypt's per capita gross national product is only $640 (compared with $23,240 in the United States), and the lifestyles depicted in *The Children of Egypt* are indeed typical of millions of Egyptians. However, there are millions of others, particularly in the major cities of Cairo and Alexandria, who dress like American children, live in high-rise apartment buildings, drive cars, are well educated, shop in stores, and work in the technological sector. These people are noted in passing, but we do not see any of them. Mention is made of the increasing number of people who wear suits and dresses, but only five peo-

ple in the entire book were photographed wearing Western-style clothing, and all are male and in the background; none of the featured children are so dressed. The two photographs of modern Cairo show high-rise buildings, but no people (except the policeman directing traffic), and in one of these scenes, camels being transported in a pick-up truck occupy center stage. Reference is made to the fact that many woman in urban areas work outside the home; unfortunately, we are not introduced to any of these woman.

The photographs are what generate this book's lasting impressions, and it is unfortunate that they do not portray the same diversity of lifestyle cited in the text. At the same time, the book's intimacy and realism help humanize and personalize the people it does depict in a way that few other books for young children do. *It is also a user-friendly way to introduce young Americans to traditional Egyptian life and culture. Teachers should be encouraged to use it, but urged to balance it with a discussion of Egypt's urban lifestyle and their many points of commonality with the lifestyle of American children.*

LESLIE NUCHO

The Bee Tree

📖 ✏ Patricia Polacco

Jewish

1993, Philomel Books

When Mary Ellen tires of reading, her grandfather decides it is time for a great adventure: finding a bee tree and the sweetest honey in the land. Together the two go to the garden and gather bees into a jar. Then Grandpa releases one of the bees and he and Mary Ellen begin to follow it. Along the journey through the Michigan countryside, they are joined in their search by various neighbors, immigrants from various European cultures whose diversity is evident in their names, their dress, their modes of transportation, and their interests.

An affirming story involving a young Jewish girl, her grandfather, and a group of immigrants to American's midwest.

After this group of characters reaches its destination, they all are invited back to Grandpa's for biscuits, tea and of course, honey. Amidst the "music, dancing, tall tales, and raucous laughter" they share the day's adventure. Grandpa then takes Mary Ellen to his study and spoons some honey on to the cover of one of her books. "Taste" he says. " There is such sweetness inside of that book too! Such things… adventure, knowledge, and wisdom. But these things do not come easily. You have to pursue them. Just like we ran after the bees to find their tree, so you must also chase these things through the pages of a book!"

Through colorful illustrations, Patricia Polacco depicts a farmland environment of the past, one with a diverse community of cultures, occupations, and interests. The pictures beautifully convey the text, enlarging and expanding the storyline.

BARBARA GOLDENHERSH

Meet Addy: An American Girl

📖 Connie Porter ✏ Melodye Rosales

African American

1993, Pleasant Company Publications, ✳ Series

📖 Porter, Connie, *Addy Learns a Lesson: A School Story; Happy Birthday Addy!: A Springtime Story; Addy Saves the Day: A Summer Story.*

One night in the summer of 1864, during the Civil War era in North Carolina, nine-year-old Addy Walker overhears her parents discussing a plan to escape slavery. But before Addy's family attempts it, they are seperated when Master Stevens sells Poppa and Addy's brother Sam to another plantation.

As a child slave, Addy is forced to work three jobs daily. She is a field hand worming tobacco plants, she serves lunch to Master Stevens, and she serves water to the other field hands. When the overseer notices Addy is not doing

An African American girl escapes from a cruel life of slavery in this fine book in the Addy Series.

an adequate job taking the worms off the tobacco plants, he storms toward her. "The overseer forced open her mouth and stuffed the still-twisting and wiggling worms inside. Addy began choking. 'Eat them!' the overseer growled. 'Chew them up— every last one of them. If you don't, I'll get some more.' Addy gagged as the worms' juicy bodies burst in her mouth."

Later, Addy expresses her hatred for white people to Momma, and is met with a compassionate response. "Honey, if you fill your heart with hate,

609

there ain't going to be no room for love. Your brother and Poppa need us to fill our hearts with love for them, not hate for white people."

Although their family is seperated, Abby and Momma carry out their plan to escape. Their hope is that the family will be together again some day in Philadelphia. Their plan involves disguising themselves as males and leaving baby sister Esther behind with Auntie Lula and Uncle Solomon, who remain on the plantation. Although Addy is confused, she has faith in her her family.

Their escape is suspenseful. The book ends with Addy and Mama at a safe house, being taken care of by an abolitionist. "'Momma, we done it, ' Addy said softly. 'Just like Poppa said. We took our freedom.'"

A nonfiction section, "Looking Back to 1864: A Peek into the Past," describes how and why slavery began, the slaves' lifestyle, the Underground Railroad, and the role of abolitionists.
JOAN PRIMEAUX

My Fellow Americans: A Family Album

📖 Alice Provensen	🖋 Various sources
Multicultural	
1995, Harcourt Brace	

Fearless women, inventive men, artists, writers, pacesetters, and groundbreakers are all part of the diverse America presented in this captivating book. Conflicting ideas, outlaws, and radicals as well as visionaries, reformers, and inventors have shaped the destiny of this nation. In this unique pictorial history of our heritage, Alice Provensen provides us with an album filled with the words, deeds, and challenges of fellow Americans, from "Rosie the Riveter" to Matthew Henson and Malcolm X to Cesar Chavez.

Using quotes from such figures as photographer Alfred Stieglitz, labor leader Eugene V. Debs, Martin Luther King Jr., and women's rights activist Susan B. Anthony, author Alice Provensen illustrates the great moments and contributions that have produced this country. None of the people portrayed are alive, but their contributions live on. This visual overview of who has shaped our thinking, provided our great literary treasures, built our enduring institutions, and forged our legacies is good way to induce otherwise reluctant young people to learn more about the history of our sometimes troubled, often incredibly inventive, and, at times, phenomenally prosperous country.

Provenson's work paints one of the fullest pictures of America from the brilliant geniuses of invention to the radical leaders of progressive movements, from the scoundrels of finance to some of our greatest literary legacies.

Provensen also includes a section on "American Expatriates." Grace Kelly, the Princess of Monaco; painter John Singer Sargent; writers James Baldwin; T.S. Eliot; and Gertrude Stein; and dancer Josephine Baker are profiled in this section. But I was struck by the fact that another section on writers omitted all traces of people of color as contributors to the early literary cannon.

The book ends with a section entitled "Observations & Reflections," which provides historical documentation and additional details about the lives of many of those portrayed in the body of the book. Provensen also includes such interesting information as: "The freed slaves (at least the males) became full-fledged citizens of the United States and legal voters when the Thirteenth, Fourteenth, and Fifteenth amendments to the Constitution were ratified, but they were powerless voters, robbed of many of their rights by local laws and mob action."

As both historical atlas and biographical journey, *My Fellow Americans* is a welcome contribution to the field of children's literature. DAPHNE MUSE

Interesting tableaux and portraits introduce a multicultural selection of influential people in American history.

Literatures of the American Indian

📖 A. LaVonne Ruoff	🖋 Various sources
Native American	
1992 (1991), Chelsea House, ✳ Series	

A professor of English at the University of Illinois, Chicago, author LaVonne Ruoff has compiled what may be considered the most comprehensive introduction to date to the genres and major authors of Native American literature, oral and written. Native American literatures are the oldest on this continent, yet they have not generally been included in American literature courses. In fact, few teachers are trained in this field. According to Ruoff, "The Modern Language Association has been in the forefront of encouraging scholars and teachers to study and teach American Indian literatures."

This book is divided into three sections: "An Introduction to American Indian Literature," "A Bibliographic Review," and "A Selected Bibliography."

The introduction provides an overview of the oral tradition, autobiographies, written fiction, and essays of Native Americana from the eighteenth century to the present. The bibliographic review also includes three sections: "Bibliographies and Research Guides"; "Anthologies, Collections, and Re-creations"; and "Scholarship and Criticism." Covered here are studies of oral literatures, including ritual dramas, songs, and narratives; studies of life histories, and autobiographies; general literary studies; studies of American Indian authors; teaching American Indian literatures; and background information. Also included is an extensive bibliography covering all of the works mentioned throughout the book as well as listings of relevant films, videotapes, journals, and small presses. The tribal affiliation of each Indian author mentioned in the text is also listed as well as a chronology of important dates in American Indian History.

A thorough bibliographic introduction to Native American literature.

This thorough volume is a major achievement and should serve as an invaluable resource for students and teachers on all levels. DENISE JOHNSON

Yanomami: People of the Amazon

David M. Schwartz, Victor Englebert
Native American, Yanomami
1994, Lothrop, Lee, and Shepard, Series

This book is part of The Vanishing Peoples Series. As the series title suggests, these indigenous peoples of the Amazon rain forests are in danger of xvanishing from the earth as their habitat is destroyed. This large-format photo-essay with full-page color photographs is a stunning book designed for children who are studying native peoples and ecology. The everyday lives of the Yanomami tribe who live on the borders of Venezuela and Brazil is depicted here in brilliant photographs of the people and their habitat.

The Yanomami are subsistence farmers of the rainforest. They plant fruit and vegetables, primarily manioc, in small forest clearings which occur naturally. They live in perfect harmony with their surroundings, taking only what they need from the environment. These people have been living this way—fishing, hunting and harvesting in the rain forest—for thousands of years. During the last few decades their habitat has been threatened. Settlers from the large cities and gold miners have cut down the forest, raped it of its natural resources, and left it polluted and uninhabitable.

This book can be used with the *Gaia Atlas of First Peoples* to explore the cultures of those who inhabited the land before Europeans invaded, and who live in traditional ways as did their ancestors for

A stunning photographic essay of an indigenous Amazonian tribe whose existence and habitat are threatened.

thousands of years. These people are excellent resource managers in their own environment. We can learn valuable lessons about flora and fauna of the areas these people inhabit from them, providing the people and the habitats survive long enough for scientists to study them. Most children know about the many species of rainforest life that have become and will become extinct because of the destruction of their ecosystem. In order to mine and farm the land, the rainforests of the world have been disappearing at an alarming rate. Many of the plants that are in danger might well lead to cures for illnesses such as cancer and AIDS. But even if they are discovered in time, these species may not survive the exploitation of the environment in which they grow.

The book is well worth using even with very young children who may not understand all of the text. Most of the text is simple and represents the daily lives of Yanomami children and their families as they harvest, fish and track. The way in which they build their dwellings from forest plant materials, utilizing modest amounts of renewable forest resources, is depicted. This is a lesson from which the industrial world has much to learn.
ELAINE P. GOLEY

Look What We've Brought You From Vietnam: Crafts, Games, Recipes, Stories, and Other Cultural Activities From New Americans

📖 Phyllis Shalant ✏ Joanna Roy

Asian, Vietnamese

1988, Julian Messner, ✳ Series

A three-paragraph introduction to *Look What We've Brought You From Vietnam* explains, without elaboration, that a large number of Vietnamese immigrants came to the United States during the 1970s and 80s because of a "long, terrible war between the governments of the north and south for control of the country. But they all brought along something very important—their culture."

A sampling of crafts, games, and recipes provide a brief introduction to Vietnamese tradition more appropriate for teachers than students

What follows are very brief descriptions of various selected customs, beliefs, and celebrations: two festivals (to celebrate the new year and the fall), three crafts, two pet suggestions (crickets and fighting fish), two games, two recipes, a folktale, and a puppet show. Although simply written, the information seems directed more at adults working with children than at the young readers themselves, and details are not always clear. It is very difficult to picture the Vietnamese water puppet theater from the description, and the pronunciation guide for four common English phrases translated into Vietnamese leaves room for several interpretations of how the Vietnamese words might sound.

There is no mention of how authentic the crafts and recipes are, although adults seeking multicultural activities for children will appreciate the use of easily obtainable materials. The only allusion to sources is in the acknowledgment, which states that "The information in this book comes from private individuals and public sources." Among the individuals mentioned are a Vietnamese college student, two UNICEF committee members, and an ESL teacher. No "public" sources are given. *Its brevity prevents this book from fulfilling the promise of its title, but it is a useful work for those seeking Vietnamese activities to include in a multicultural study unit.*
LYNN EISENHUT

I Live in the Music

📖 Ntozake Sange, edited by Linda Sunshine
✏ Romare Bearden

African American

1994, Stewart, Tabori & Chang

This book of poetry and art for children is a tribute to black music. It juxtaposes the playful, rhythmic poetry of Ntozake Sange with colorful, collage-like paintings on the theme of music *A colorful pairing of the art and music of two leading African Americans.* by her godfather, Romare Bearden, one of American's preeminent visual artists. Bearden's work, well reproduced here, sings on the canvas, calling you to listen. Complete with biographical sketches of the author and illustrator, this book is a fine way to introduce young people to these outstanding and powerfully creative artists.

A wonderful companion piece to the Shange/Bearden book is *The Block*, done in the vital collage style so much a part of Bearden's artistic identity. It also includes "Theme for English B," "Harlem Night Song," and "Stars," a series of fine poems by Harlem Renaissance writer Langston Hughes. *Teachers and librarians could create a wonderful unit on poetry and art using these two books as the foundation.* DAPHNE MUSE

The Aztecs

📖 ✏ Donna A. Shepherd

Aztec, Native American

1992, Franklin Watts, Inc., ✳ Series

Since the early 1940s, Franklin Watts has published a series of introductory books focusing on people from various cultures and countries from around the world. Along with introducing young people to the musical instruments from Latin America, artworks from China, and African American poets, these books help to bring new words and ideas to young readers.

With rather broad strokes, *The Aztecs* paints a

general picture of this rather complex and highly sophisticated civilization. But teachers should keep in mind that these books simply introduce basic information about a culture or a country. They are by no means meant to be comprehensive or definitive works. These books can pique the interest of young children and serve as an invitation for learning more.

A broad intro-duction to Aztec life and culture that should be supplemented by more compre-hensive books.

Well-illustrated with maps and pictographs from Aztec codices, this book should be supplemented with more in-depth information and videotapes. A glossary and short bibliography of further readings are included. BYRON RUSKIN

The Sioux: A First Americans Book

📗 Virginia Driving Hawk Sneve   ✒ Ronald Himler
Native American
1995 (1993), Holiday House, ✳ Series

Virginia Driving Hawk Sneve has been writing for Holiday House for a number of years. She has written some excellent works of fiction and poetry for young readers. This book is her most recent effort in non-fiction material.

A useful picturebook introducing the life and culture of the Sioux Indians.

Sneve focuses on the Sioux Indians of what is now North and South Dakota, Montana, and Minnesota. Sneve is Sioux herself and familiar with these tribes. As a Sioux, she writes from inside the culture with both a compelling creative, and authentic voice.

The book begins with a creation story—a shortened version of the creation myth—that explains how the Sioux came to be a part of the world and progresses forward in history. The various aspects of family, village, cultural, philosophical, military, and religious life are covered succinctly and interestingly. The artist, Ronald Himler, has done a good job of portraying scenes in the life of the Sioux people.

Sneve mentions some past leaders of the Sioux Nation and the advice one of those leaders, Sitting Bull, gave his people. In closing, the author briefly addresses the fact that Native Americans live today in modern society while still honoring their proud heritage.

This introductory series can be very useful to the young reader who may be interested in learning about the original inhabitants of the United States and can be helpful to teachers beginning to teach their students about other cultures and ethnic groups. JUDITH CASTIANO

Neighborhood Odes

📗 Gary Soto   ✒ David Diaz
Hispanic
1992 (1994), Harcourt Brace and Company, Scholastic

These playful and touching poems make us feel a part of the Hispanic neigh-borhood where Gary Soto grew up in Fresno, California. We learn not only of the community but also of the loving feelings these families have while they work and play. There is a glossary of Spanish words and phrases used in the poems. Readers will identify with these poems, even though they did not grow up in Soto's neighborhood.

Twenty-one evocative poems about growing up in Hispanic neighborhoods.

Other selections reflect the author's delight in everyday things such as the tortilla, *mi perrito* (my dog), or my library. The woodcut illustrations are gay and lively and enhance the writing.

These poems would work well with a study of the community and the family. Readers would see the similarities in all families and yet discover what

some of the Hispanic American traditions are in that area of California. Readers also would be able to identify with the children in the poems as they play and interact with their friends and families. The bilingual text makes it fun for students to learn words in a new language. It is important to note that the author and illustrator are both Mexican Americans. *Neighborhood Odes* also helps break the stereotypes of lazy Mexicans in sombreros. DORRIS COSLEY

613

Taking Sides

Gary Soto

Hispanic

1992 (1991), Harcourt Brace and Company

An entertaining, positive story about pressure on a Hispanic teen to assimilate.

Lincoln Mendoza, the main character in Soto's *Taking Sides,* refuses to take sides. The basketball coach at his new suburban junior high school advises him to abandon his pals in the barrio in favor of the middle-class white children at his new school. In a refreshing change from stories with Hispanic themes that focus on gangs, divorce, neglect, and either patronizing or just awful white people, Lincoln has good friends from the barrio, a a loving and intelligent mother whose Anglo boyfriend is a strong, sensitive man. The boyfriend is, in fact, one of Lincoln's strongest advocates. With the support of friends, his mother, and her friend, Lincoln is able to withstand pressures to assimilate. *Taking Sides* is entertaining, believable and well-written. NANCY HANSEN-KRENING

Baseball in April: and Other Stories

Gary Soto

Hispanic, Mexican American

1991 (1990), Harcourt Brace and Company

Enjoyable, but somewhat dated, short stories on the lives of adolescent Mexican Americans in California.

Gary Soto's collection of eleven short stories about Mexican American children growing up in California is written in a style that should be easily understood by young adolescent readers. Although the story's characters are Mexican American, Soto writes in a way that is familiar to mainstream monolingual readers. There is a glossary at the end of the text that explains the few Spanish and *Calo* (a Mexican dialect of Spanish) words that are interspersed throughout the collection, although most of the non-English words can be understood through the contexts in which they are used.

These stories center around assimilated, second- and third-generation Mexican American children and teenagers who usually shy away from an affilia-

tion with their Mexican heritage. Such a theme is expressed through the embarrassing and bumbling actions of a Mexican grandfather attempting to understand the real estate business in "Two Dreamers." In "Growing Up," young Maria comments about a lecture from her father: "Here it comes, Maria thought, stories about his childhood in Mexico. She wanted to stuff her ears with wads of newspaper to keep from hearing him. She couldn't wait until she was in college and away from them." These are Mexican American children who are distancing themselves from their Mexican roots and are trying to find their place among similarly-oriented peers, while encountering constraints, such as poverty, that can be found across all ethnic groups. The stories focus on children aspiring to appear on American Bandstand, such as in "The No-Guitar Blues," and struggling to learn karate as in "The Karate Kid."

Soto mostly describes events and relationships related to males, such as the title story "Baseball in April" which concerns two brothers' efforts to join a baseball team. However, four stories in the collection feature female characters. In "Broken Chain" and "Seventh Grade," girls are depicted as being elusive objects of desire for smitten boys. "Barbie" is an intriguing story of a young girl named Veronica who longs to own a Barbie doll. She is first given a "black-haired doll with a flat, common nose, not like Barbie's cute, upturned nose." Later, Veronica is given a real Barbie that, unfortunately, loses its head at the hands of one of Veronica's friends. In the end, Veronica reconciles herself when she takes both Barbies to bed with her.

The stories in this collection are simple moral narratives that should be enjoyed by most young adolescents who share similar growing pains and identity crises. However, at times, the datedness of Soto's references, such as the television program *American Bandstand* and the movie *Karate Kid,* make it difficult for some subsequent generations of children to relate. HERIBERTO GODINA

My Indian Boyhood

📖 Luther Standing Bear 🖋 Various sources
Native American
1988 (1931), University of Nebraska Press

In the late nineteenth century and early in the twentieth century, Native Americans were still able to practice traditional skills and culture. It is rare to have an authentic biography for children written by a Native American. *My Indian Boyhood* is such a book, and an important tool for introducing children to primary sources. The book can be used with biographical materials about Native Americans such as Russell Freedman's *Indian Chiefs* and the biographies of Native Americans published by Chelsea House.

A reissue of a rare autobiographical account of an early twentieth-century Native American boyhood.

Chief Luther Standing Bear wrote this book with the hope that it would lead children to a greater understanding and appreciation of traditional Native American cultures. The chief describes his boyhood on the great plains with his people, the Lakota. He discusses the daily life of his people. He also describes the origins of his people, bows and arrows, the Indian boy and his pony, hunting and fishing, plants, trees, games, how chiefs are made, medicine men, music, and killing the buffalo.

Other university presses, such as the University of Oklahoma Press, and various tribal councils also publish authentic materials about Native American cultures. Providing a series of biographies that span the centuries is so important for presenting a broad view of Native American cultures. ELAINE P. GOLEY

About Handicaps: An Open Family Book for Parents and Children Together

📖 Sara Bonnett Stein, Gilbert W. Kliman, Doris Ronald, Ann S. Kliman, Phyllis Schwartz 🖋 Dick Frank
Physically Disabled
1984 (1974), Walker & Company, ✳ Series

As part of the Open Family series, *About Handicaps* focuses on Joe, a young boy with cerebral palsy. Joe's crooked toes create a real challenge for him when it comes to walking. Initially, Matthew mimics Joe's special way of walking. Then, Matthew, who also has one crooked toe, wonders if his crooked toe could cause him to walk "funny" as well. Troubled by this thought, Matthew asks his father to buy him a pair of sunglasses, thinking they will prevent him for seeing too much of Joe's legs.

A young boy works through his feelings about his disabled friends in an enlightening story.

At one point, Matthew and his father meet a man wearing a prosthesis. Through the man's demonstration of his "support system" and a reassuring discussion about people with disabilities, Matthew begins to feel more comfortable about approaching Joe. Matthew and Joe build a toy car together, an activity that allows them to discuss disability.

Stein's book serves to assist children in developing an awareness about disabilities. It also enlightens adults about children's fears and provides viable suggestions for dealing with these fears. The book also emphasizes positive interactions between disabled and non-disabled people. The black-and-white photographs, showing disabled and non-disabled people interacting with one another, serve the focus and message of the book quite well.

A teacher might want to invite parents to share this book with children, using the text as a springboard for questions and discussions.
BARBARA A. KANE

Retold African Myths

📖 Eleanora Tate 🖊 Don Tate

African African

1993, Perfection Learning Corporation, ✳ Series

Africa's diverse cultural groups and rich storytelling traditions have inspired these stories, which represent eleven cultures—Ashanti, Bambara, Chagga, Ganda, Hausa, Kono, Mende, Sotho, Swahili, Yoruba, and Zulu. A map of the African continent identifies the location of each. The author retells eighteen myths, three each on six topics: creation, death, gods and mortals, tricksters, how and why, right and wrong. She previews each myth with a defined vocabulary list and cast of characters.

Rich retellings of myths about creation, death, gods, mortals, tricksters, and moral dilemmas that represent Africa's expansive cultural diversity.

Some tales focus on difficult moral choices, e.g., how should people act when asked to hide their true identity? Tales average four pages in length, with selected vocabulary highlighted. A concluding "Insights" essay briefly comments on the culture associated with each myth and offers ideas for class discussion. After reading "The Man Who Argued with God," for example, one learns that most Bantu languages have no gender identifying either females or males; instead, one deduces gender from the person's name.

Tate connects the diverse African cultures to oral tradition, explaining that African storytellers might pause in their narrative to ask listeners to decide what they think a character should do or say next. Tate former president of the National Association of Black Storytellers, gives a new twist to centuries-old tales with added characters and situations. Her versions pay homage to Africa's multicultural heritage and foster adolescent literacy. Several teaching aids help make these myths more easily understandable for classroom or extracurricular reading, and there are no negative stereotypes to mar the book's tone.

Tate's conversational style sparks independent critical thinking with interactive dialogue, such as "Now it's your turn. What do you think?" Don Tate II has contributed artful illustrations and graphic designs of African motifs that make the book visually appealing. On the cover, an African boy, wearing a traditional hat of gold, red, and green, proudly holds open his shirt to reveal a luminous moon and stars, suggesting the vast mythic universe of creation. Throughout the book, pencil sketches and graphic designs enhance the stories.

The family of humanity has a wealth of stories, and the Tates offer a cultural mosaic of Africa's different regions, languages, races, and religions. Such a varied ethnic spectrum teaches children to respect cultural diversity, to take pride in their cultural heritage, and to appreciate the universality of human values and character traits.

By engaging the readers' imagination and encouraging participation, the book could enhance a thematic unit on Africa or myths; it can be used in conjunction with other books in this series on Greek, Roman, and other world myths. Intra-curriculum ideas for reading writing, speaking, and listening, would work well for middle-school classes. One suggestion is to read myths aloud or act them out with sound effects. LAURA ZAIDMAN

Thank You, Dr. Martin Luther King, Jr.!

📖 Eleanora E. Tate

African American

1992 (1990), Bantam Books Inc.

After being bombarded with white images on television and elsewhere, many black children enter school with poor self images and confused ideas of beauty. This story attacks the problem directly, although with less didacticism than it might. When Gumbo Grove Elementary School prepares a President's Month play, Mary Elouise, who is black, doesn't relish her role as narrator of the black history section. She does not want to be different from her white peer and role model, Brandy. Mary's grandmother and a black storyteller help Mary Elouise improve her self image and learn about her heritage.

A useful story about an African American girl whose pride in her heritage increases when she receives a book about African history.

The message is obvious, but needed, and should be used for discussion of racial prejudice. This title could also be extremely helpful in parenting classes.
BINNIE TATE-WILKIN

Take a Walk in Their Shoes

Glennette Tilley Turner Elton C. Fax

African American

1992 (1989), Puffin Books

This well-written collection of biographies of fourteen important African American men and women will hold the attention of young readers. The subjects have backgrounds in a variety of fields, including politics, medicine, sports, and theater. Some, such as Frederick Douglass, Martin Luther King, Jr., and Rosa Parks, are well known, but others—such as organizer and school founder Mary McCleod Bethune or Dr. Charles Drew, who helped perfect blood transfusion techniques—are less renowned but deserving of greater recognition. The book notes that, ironically, Charles Drew died as a result of blood loss because he was apparently denied admission to an all-white hospital.

A well-written, illustrated collection of biographies of fourteen important African Americans professionals.

The text is well-written and includes a black-and-white portrait of each subject. The most unique feature of this book is the inclusion of skits about key events in each of the fourteen individual's lives. For example, the skit about Charles Drew has a group of children attending a school named for him. They are curious as to why their school is named after him. With the help of a former student of the doctor's, they, along with the audience and actors, learn about Dr. Drew's accomplishments. Because of their subject matter and brevity, the skits do tend to be a bit didactic; nevertheless, they are fun and educational for children to act out. JODI LEVINE

The Corn Woman: Stories and Legends of the Hispanic Southwest

Angel Vigil

Hispanic, Mexican American

1995, Puffin Books, ✷ Spanish

Here is a rich and varied collection of *cuentos*—or stories—reflecting the strong storytelling tradition of Spanish-speaking people in northern New Mexico and southern Colorado (the Rio Grande Valley). This is the area of the Southwest that was least changed by the U.S. takeover of Mexican lands in 1848.

Through extended travel in which he looked up many older people, Angel Vigil collected these stories. In doing so, he has given us, in his words, "a narrative arc of truth and beauty of a people and their continuing culture."

After a fascinating explanation of the origin of the oral tradition and its different forms—which include not only the story but also proverbs, riddles, and anecdotes—he begins with the Aztec legend of "The Five Suns." Then come a few tales from the first years after the Spanish invasion, which he calls "Stories from the Merging of Two Cultures." They include the famous "Legend of La Llorona (The Weeping Woman)."

The heart of the book is "the traditional *cuentos*" from the Southwest. It is followed by a grouping of ten contemporary stories. The book includes a glossary of Spanish words and a bibliography of twenty-eight related titles. Most but not all of the stories are presented in both English and Spanish.

The traditional *cuentos* consist of moral and religious stories, *chistes* (anecdotes, usually comical), tales of transformation, magic and wisdom, animal stories, and a group called *los dos compadres* (the two buddies) stories. The stories are populated with a universally appealing range of characters from stock characters such as Mr. Peanut (*Don Cacahuate*), to rich and poor men, tricky coyotes, village simpletons, old women with magical powers, and even, in one delightful tale, the real-life scientist Albert Einstein, who has to alter his theory about matter after learning, in a little Mexican restaurant, what happens to the weight of rice and beans when they are cooked together.

An entertaining and varied collection of stories that have been passed down by Spanish-speaking people in New Mexico and southern Colorado.

Occasionally, the point of a story seems elusive or something remains unexplained for no reason. Also, the layout of text on facing pages is unbalanced at times, which can be confusing or distracting. Although he does make it clear that the stories "contain roots of many world cultures," the author's introduction puts great emphasis on the Spanish and other European origins of most of the stories and little on their Mexican or Native

617

American roots. Vigil also points out that the stories draw much of their power from the fact that they have been an important part of family life for generations in the area—which anyone who has lived in northern New Mexico or southern Colorado can confirm.

This is a very useful, entertaining collection that tells a lot about the way of life and thinking in a magical part of this country—the Hispanic Southwest. ELIZABETH MARTINEZ

Beneath the Stone

📖 🖋 Bernard Wolf

Hispanic, Mexican

1994, Orchard Books, ✳ Spanish

Similar to Marcia Keegan's *Pueblo Boy: Growing Up in Two Worlds* (Cobblehill/Dutton, 1991), Beneath the Stone is a photo-essay that features a child influenced by dual cultures and traditions. Leo is a six-year-old Zapotec Indian boy, who inherits the Zapotec language and lifeways of his elders, but who also participates in the larger Mexican culture. Through Leo, author/photographer Bernard Wolf brings to life the customs and daily life of southern Mexico's Zapotec Indians,

An excellent photo essay featuring a Zapotec child influenced by dual cultures and traditions.

using vivid color photographs combined with an informative, storylike text. From the outset, Wolf emphasizes that the Zapotecs of Leo's community are an indigenous people who have endured for many centuries, still residing after 3,500 years in their ancestral village of Teotitlan del Valle, located in the Oaxaca Valley.

The period portrayed surrounds the Christmas season, a crucial time for Leo's family, who make their living as weavers. Weaving is a traditional art among the Zapotec, whose pre-Columbian ancestors flourished for two millennia prior to the fourteenth century. Wolf shows Leo's family as they prepare the wool, spin it, and weave it into intricately designed *tapetes*. His camera follows Leo and his father to Oaxaca City's busy weekend market, where he also captures the market's characters, action, and mood. The family will make much of their annual profit by selling *tapetes* to tourists at the lucrative holiday markets.

In addition to featuring the family's artistic heritage and livelihood, Wolf includes portraits of Leo's daily life. Leo is shown eating *atole*, a traditional corn soup, and playing with his friend. We see Leo at school learning to read Spanish, a second language to his native Zapotec. Turning his camera on the village, Wolf photographs a gold bust of Benito Juarez, Mexico's president from 1861-63 and its most famous Zapotec leader of the modern age.

Wolf illustrates common Mexican customs through photos of Leo's family participating in celebrations and worshiping during major holidays—the Day of the Dead, the anniversary of the Revolution of 1910, and Christmas. Leo's dual heritage is reemphasized in the book's final scenes, at the ruins of Monte Alban. Perched with Leo atop pyramid steps, dressed in modern casual clothes, the father tells his son about their powerful ancestors who built the magnificent city.

Ranging from the elderly to the very young, Wolf's lively subjects stand in stark contrast to the doll-like Oaxacan natives illustrated in *Saturday Market* (Lothrop, Lee, and Shepard, 1994). His narrative is compatible with his photographs, unbiased, and respectful of modern-day Zapotecs. Although the book lacks a bibliography, index, and

numbered pages, Wolf does include other useful research aids: a map showing the location of Teotitlan del Valle, a pronunciation guide for Spanish and Zapotec words in the text, and a short, frank history of pre-and post-conquest Zapotecs.

This book is recommended for independent research by children reading at the middle school level. Although Wolf doesn't address the issue, the topic of recent indigenous uprisings in southern Mexico is relevant to studying Mexico's Native peoples, especially since many of the revolutionaries are adolescents themselves. Younger children will enjoy Leo's upbeat story and photographs during read-aloud. Through Leo, children can gain a realistic understanding of who Mexico's Natives are today. For either purpose, this is an excellent source for exploring, comparing, and contrasting the experiences of contemporary Native children throughout the Americas. MELISSA HECKARD

From Abenaki to Zuni: A Dictionary of Native American Tribes

Evelyn Wolfson

Native American

1995 (1988), Walker and Company

Wolfson and Bock have produced a well-designed and well-executed reference book that should be welcomed by schools and public libraries. Parents of children who are interested in Native American life might consider giving this book as a gift.

The book opens with maps of "Major Cultural Areas" and "Dominant Language Families." Each entry gives a phonetic spelling of the tribal name and the meaning of the name if it is known. There are brief descriptions of the environment, villages, housing, food, transportation, clothing, mythologi-cal heroes, major ceremonies, and religious beliefs. The author also includes a brief historical review of what later happened to the tribe—reservations, treaties, and payment for tribal land claims.

The appendix consists of five substantive reference documents. The first is a list of major tribes of North America grouped by geographical area. This list is followed by a glossary in which each term is explained in two to eight sentences. In addition to a "Selected Bibliography," there is a list of supplementary material for curious readers in "Suggested Readings." The book closes with a helpful index. Tribes not listed in the Table of Contents may be found in the Index, where readers are directed to tribes that share a similar lifestyle.

Sixty-eight North American Indian tribes are described in this easy-to-use reference guide.

LESLIE ANDERSON MORALES

Boys (As Well As Girls) Should Meet Addy

Joan Primeaux

AS A CLASSROOM TEACHER, I'VE WITNESSED the power of multicultural literature in my fourth grade classroom. My school, located in a suburb of a midwestern city, is a monoculture. My class consists of 100% European Americans. So I use multicultural literature as a vehicle to broaden perspectives.

At the beginning of a recent school year, as I was planning a unit on African American history, I found myself searching for a novel to be used with a literature discussion group. The book I discovered turned out to be a treasure: *Meet Addy* by Connie Porter, book one of the American Girls Series. Ordinarily I offer options and allow the students to choose the novel that appeals to them. Because I wanted this particular group to include both genders, I arranged for it to include five boys and five girls. We met daily for forty-minute sessions over a period of six weeks. In order to further an understanding of African American history, we read and discussed *Meet Addy*. *Meet Addy* is a hybrid text set in the Civil War era. The for-mat is unique. The "Cast of Characters" section introduces the reader to the characters who appear in the novel and explains their relationship to one another. One sections of the book is a narrative based on historical events. The other section is a nonfiction account entitled, "Looking Back 1864—A Peek Into the Past" which serves to contextualize the narrative. The protagonist, nine-year old Addy Walker, overhears her parents discussing a plan to escape from slavery. Her family is separated when Master Stevens sells Addy's father and older brother to another slave owner. The suspense begins when Addy and her mother escape from North Carolina to Philadelphia hopeful that the family will be together again some day. The nonfiction section describes how and why slavery began, the slave's lifestyle, the Undergound Railroad, and the role of Abolitionists.

At the initial meeting of this group there was some resistance to *Meet Addy*. Comments like, "I think it will be too girly," and "I think it will be boring," concerned me. This group was literally judging a book by its cover. I knew we had work to do before we were ready to meet Addy. I decided we would read *Meet Addy* backwards, hoping that the historical context provided in the "Looking Back" section would help the students understand and even appreciate the narrative section. Our group discussions grew richer as the members' background knowledge on the Civil War era increased. Each group member researched and reported on an African American from the era. They presented their reports to the group, repeatedly referring to the "Looking Back" section by relating new information to the research previously done. With a solid understanding of the conditions and lifestyle of the Civil War era, we read the narrative section of *Meet Addy* independently. We met periodically to discuss the story, reactions, and elements of the culture. In the process, we grew attached to Addy. We empathized with her experiences and wanted to right the injustices. Most importantly, the narrative made the Civil War era come alive. The extent to which *Meet Addy* touched our hearts is evidenced by comments the students made. "I feel like I'm part of the story and I want to help Addy out. I would go into the fields and help her get her work done.," and "Master Stevens treated Addy like a dog. He said he trained her to do her job." "Forcing a human being to eat worms is the most cruel thing..." "Owning a human is wrong." *Meet Addy* motivated the students to read beyond what was required. At any given time someone was reading another Addy book independently. Plans for the future included, "I will recommend *Meet Addy* to my older brother," "I'm going to read all of the Addy books," and "I'm going to check out all six of them and read them with my mom." Everyone in our group viewed *Meet Addy* as an important component of our unit. "Addy books are not only for girls because you could put a boy in almost every situation," "The publisher should call it 'American Kids' because it's not just about girl stuff," and "Boys as well as girls should meet Addy."

Joan Primeaux is currently a doctoral student in Language and Literacy with an interest in Children's Literature at the University of Illinois. She is a Literacy Specialist in School District 25 in Arlington Heights, Illinois.

Using Pictures to Combat Bias

Ellen Wolpert

FOR MANY YEARS I SEPARATED MY POLITICAL work and my educational work. Politics was something I did before and after work. Education was what I did at my job at the daycare center. One of the benefits of the women's movement and educational awareness around multiculturalism is that they helped me bridge those worlds and better understand the politics of our everyday lives.

I gravitated toward pictures because I'm a visually oriented person and because young people are particularly sensitive to pictures. During the time they struggle to understand first spoken and then written words, they spend their lives "reading" images to understand the world. Through visual images, I wanted to integrate cultural diversity and challenge the dehu-manizing images that children receive.

At first I thought about using visual displays such as bulletin boards, but I found such displays unbearably passive. I wanted to create something the kids could play with, something that would become a part of their everyday activities. I began collecting pictures—from magazines, rummage-sale books, photographs of the children's families, newspapers, discarded library books—you name it. Then I used those photos and pictures to make games the kids already knew and enjoyed: bingo, lotto, rummy, memory/matching games. Catalogs are filled with such card games, generally using zoo animals, endangered species, numbers, or stylized graphics. I decided to save the money I spent on such games and use it toward my own picture collection.

I've developed three basic sizes of photos: 5 x 7, 7.5 x 8.5 and 7.5 x 11 (a full-page picture from National Geographic, for example.) The smaller photos lend themselves to games such as concentration and rummy, while the bigger ones are good for sorting and counting games. I try to collect two of each. I then mount the photos on a mat board and cover them with clear contact paper. While two copies are essential for games such as concentration, single copies may be used for rummy and puzzle-type games. Third, I try to organize the pictures around various themes: families, housing, sports, work, African Americans, Native Americans, women, food, transportation, ways of carrying things. The more photos I collect, the better I am able to mix and match and develop a variety of possibilities.

Here's an example of how I use the picture cards for a concentration/memory game using pictures of Native Americans. For a good game of concentration with young children, it is best to have two copies of at least 10 different images. I go through my card collection and pick out 10 sets of pictures that counteract the usual stereotypes of Native Americans. Some of the pictures I include: a young girl playing football, a man in a pin-stripe suit who heads a corporation, a family playing lacrosse, some kids. I also use some of the Native American photos in a concentration game with other themes.

The most important thing is to use the cards to spark discussion. I find this is particularly easy during some of the sorting, such as a form of rummy.

To make the rummy game, I use about 40 different images. I deal out three to a player, with a draw pile and a discard pile. The idea is to find something in common on three different cards. The player can determine the common attributes—whether it's food, men taking care of babies, women workers, people protesting injustice, housing. As we play the game, I try to get the kids talking about what is in the picture and how they determined the common attribute. This not only develops specific language skills, it also forces the children to focus on what is in the picture.

Because I concentrate on images that counter bias, this also indirectly challenges stereotypes. But I also interject comments. One of my children kept referring to "sitting Indian style" whenever I asked children to sit in a circle on the floor. When we played with my Native American cards, I specifically pointed out cards showing Native Americans sitting on couches or chairs.

It's important that teachers create activities that elicit children's comments in order to pick up on stereotypes and assumptions mentioned in casual conversations. I use those everyday comments as the basis for a game. If a boy repeatedly mentions that girls can't play baseball, I might pull out pictures that show girls playing sports.

When the movie Aladdin came out, I decided to collect photos of Arabs. An Arab man reading to his daughter, an Arab doctor, an Arab businessman in a "Western" suit. I used these cards to counter the movie's stereotypes of Arabs as hook-nosed, knife-wielding, turban-wearing "bad guys."

Finally, I think it's important to add your own photographs to such collections. I've taken pictures of kids on the playground, taking special care to show girls playing sports and climbing, and boys playing with dolls or playing "dress-up." I've also encouraged children to bring in pictures, which is particularly useful when we do a unit on families. I have found that such photos are the most "real" to kids and the most valuable part of my picture collection. They also provide a way for children readily to connect their family lives with their learning.

Pictures alone won't transform a classroom. But they become a key element in a classroom that encourages tolerance, understanding and self-respect. As children play with the pictures—as their own images are reflected back at them in positive ways, as their ideas and analytical thinking are encouraged, as they begin to understand that diversity exists everywhere—they will begin to develop pride, self-confidence, and respect for others.

Ellen Wolpert has been an educator and activist for more than twenty years. She is currently the director of the Washington Beech Community School in Boston, MA.

Reprinted with permission from Rethinking Our Classrooms, Rethinking Schools, 1001 E Keffe Ave. Milwaukee WI 53212; (414)964-9646.

Grade Seven to Grade Eight

Puerto Rico: America's 51st State

📖 David J. Abodaher   ✒ Various sources
Hispanic, Puerto Rican
1993, Franklin Watts, Inc.,   ✳ Series

An exceptional study of Puerto Rico's complex history and uncertain future.

In terms appropriate for young readers, David Abodaher explains the history of Puerto Rico, a commonwealth of the United States, and helps clarify the different scenarios for Puerto Rico's uncertain future. Will Puerto Rico become the fifty-first state in the United States? Will it become an independent nation? Or will it continue to maintain its commonwealth status? Abodaher discusses these various directions for Puerto Rico after providing a thorough backdrop of Puerto Rico's evolution beginning with the arrival of Columbus. Spanish colonial rule and exploitation of labor that decimated the indigenous population of Tainos led to the subsequent introduction of African slaves to this small island in the Caribbean. Not until the Spanish-American War, fought in 1898 between the United States and Spain, did Puerto Rico escape the tight bonds of economic control long helped by Spain. Despite attempts to "Americanize" Puerto Rico, this small country has maintained a strong drive for self-determination that is presently being challenged by political groups who want Puerto Rico to achieve statehood.

Abodaher presents an objective analysis of the political, historical, and social evolution of Puerto Rico and uses many historical photographs and drawings to help young readers understand the events and circumstances that have played an integral part in the development of this nation. On a lighter note, he also includes Puerto Rico's significant contributions to baseball. *Unique to this text is a pronunciation guide to help readers correctly pronounce words in the unique dialect of Spanish spoken in Puerto Rico. Also, there are suggestion for further reading. This is an exceptional text for students to examine the complex history and political situation facing Puerto Rico during this decisive period in its history.* HERIBERTO GODINA

George Washington Carver, Botanist

📖 Gene Adair, Introduction by Coretta Scott King
African American
1989, Chelsea House Publishers,   ✳ Series,
Video,   🎬 *Real McCoy* by Wendy Towle; *Outward Dreams* by James Haskins; *Shoes For Everyone* by Barbara Mitchell; *Man With a Million Ideas* by Virginia Ott

George Washington Carver, Botanist a title in the Black Americans of Achievement Series, is one of the freshest biographies written for young people. The author, Gene Adair, does not portray Carver as a purely virtuous man. Instead, he is brilliant in some respects, self-deluding in others. Adair emphasizes the importance throughout Carver's life of patronage from prominent or well-meaning whites. They, and some of his colleagues at Tuskagee worked together to create for the early 20th century the perfectly accomplished Negro icon. For whites, Carver became a symbol that anyone could make it (even in the Deep South) if they really wanted to succeed.

For blacks, Carver proved to (black and white) America what might be achieved if only one were given the opportunity.

A fresh and accurate biography of the famous African American scientist.

In written detail and photographs, Adair captures a sense of life for blacks from the end of the Civil War to the early 1930s. The first chapter begins with Carver testifying at the House Ways and Means Committee to persuade the federal government to put a tariff on imported peanuts. The reluctant white male Committee had planned to give Carver no more than ten minutes to speak. Slowly, with a combination of thorough knowledge of his subject and folksy charm, Carver won over his audience. Repeatedly, whenever Carver was underestimated, his humor, good manners, humility, and ability to captivate any audience, whether in the classroom or in the boardroom, made believers out of those who came prepared to dismiss him.

Adair provides information about Carver's professional career. Carver was an agriculturist who sought help struggling black farmers gain some sort of footing in an agricultural system that seemed determined to exploit their labors . He was not, however, an especially acute businessman in the commercial uses of peanuts and other products. Perhaps one of his most important roles was that of popularizer of information that could help both the farmer and the urban dweller recognize the interconnectedness of all living things.

The book includes a useful chronology, a further reading list, and a very detailed index. The reading list's titles are targeted towards an adult audience or to very mature younger readers. *Science teachers might look at the following titles to find other choices to encourage students to view scientists in full complexity: Real McCoy* (by Wendy Towle, 1993); *Outward Dreams* (James Haskins, 1991); *Shoes for Everyone* (by Barbara Mitchell, 1986); *Man with a Million Ideas* (by Virginia Ott, 1977).

ANDREA L. WILLIAMS

Maria, Mota and the Grandmother

📗 Stella Houghton Alico, Laura Ware (editor), Carol A. Penzotti ✏ Jan Young

Hispanic

1993, Sunstone Press

Set in colonial New Mexico at the turn of the century, *Maria, Mota and the Grandmother* tells the story of a young girl named Marta who goes to live with her grandmother and befriends a kitten named Mota. The easy-to-read text is accompanied by black-and-white photographs, making the story contextually easy to comprehend for upper-level elementary-school readers, yet sufficiently engaging for more proficient middle school readers. Some Spanish words are used to describe daily life and customs rural, colonial New Mexico, but a glossary is included at the end of the book.

A story of Latino culture in turn-of-the century New Mexico that does not adequately address Spanish colonialism.

Although this is a relatively simple story about Marta's special relationship with her grandmother, the setting makes this picture book unique. It covers a usually neglected region of Latino studies:

the Southwest. These New Mexicans acknowledge their colonial heritage with Spain. This is both intriguing and problematic for the text. It is intriguing because the book depicts daily life authentically, yet problematic because it articulates a colonial ideology (with constant references to Catholicism) that ignores the indigenous origins of cultural elements used by the settlers, such as cooking tools and folk medicine. The photographs are carefully staged, using human actors and a backdrop of adobe homes and the New Mexican landscape. *Used carefully, perhaps as a complementary text to illustrate differences between colonial and indigenous peoples of the Southwest,* Maria, Mota and the Grandmother *could add to a multicultural classroom.*

HERIBERTO GODINA

Steal Away

📗 Jennifer Armstrong

African American

1993 (1992), Orchard Books

Susannah, a recent orphan, moves from Vermont to Virginia to live with her uncle and his family. There a young girl named Bethlehem is given to Susannah as a slave. At the time, it was not uncommon for children to have their own slave servants. Susannah finds it difficult having someone her own age as a servant to meet her most intimate needs. She decides to try to make Bethlehem more her equal by teaching her to read. Soon she has an even more daring idea—to "steal away" back to Vermont. Bethlehem decides to go with her after Susannah's cousin Byron makes unwelcome advances to her.

An exciting if somewhat unrealistic story of a slave girl and her young master who escape to the North together in 1855.

The two make their getaway one morning by riding away on Susannah's horse. After traveling quite a distance, the horse runs away and the two must make their way north on foot. Disguised as boys,

623

624

they are almost exposed when a woman sees through their charade. They manage to get to Pennsylvania without being caught. It is there that Susannah cuts her hand on a knife. Infection sets in and they must seek help from a kind Quaker family. They help send Bethlehem to Toronto while Susannah returns to Vermont.

The two do not see each other for forty years. Bethlehem then asks Susannah to come to Toronto where she is dying of consumption. The two tell their story to their granddaughters, who have mixed reactions to it and to each other. Years later, Bethlehem's granddaughter sends the manuscript of the story to her granddaughter and so the unlikely friendship is not forgotten.

The story alternates between Bethlehem's and Susannah's first person accounts and also between the years 1855 and 1896. The use of first person is especially effective as each character's language reveals a different perspective. It is hard to believe that the two could get so far north without being caught, especially since Susannah's uncle has had "wanted" posters put up in all the towns. However, the interaction between the two girls is the backbone of the story. When the two are reunited, there is the awkwardness of their past relationship, but they see each other more as old friends now. This is a story of taking risks in dangerous times and going against the roles society had planned for two girls based on their color and gender. With people looking to understand more about those who are ancestors or descendants of slaves and those who are ancestors of slave owners, this may prove to be an interesting read. PAM CARLSON

The Ancient and Living Cultures Series

▨ Mira Bartok ✐ Christine Ronan

Multicultural

The fifteen books in the Ancient and Living Cultures Series are a wonderful resource for teaching children about various world cultures. Each book in the series focuses on a particular culture and explores it in a variety of ways.

The books all follow the same format, providing an introduction to the culture, a map showing its geographic location, a selection of myths and folktales, and a section about the religious life of the people. The resources at the end of each book feature a suggested reading list for children and their adult mentors, audiovisual selections, and a list of museums that house cultural artifacts. *The books also include a four-page tear-out center section which contains culturally relevant punch-out art stencils printed on heavy card stock. These stencils come with an explanation of their inspiration and symbolism. The stencils can be used to create the five art projects that are detailed in every book. For example, Ancient Egypt and Nubia features instructions for making a Nubian crown, an amulet necklace, a sistrum (a rattlelike musical instrument), an ersatz papyrus scroll, and a royal cartouche with your name written in hieroglyph writing inside the "royal ring" used to enclose the names of Egyptian royalty.*

Each book is illustrated with black-and-white photographs of museum artifacts and additional photographs of various monuments and cultural celebrations. Other illustrations feature drawings that show scenes from daily life, folklore, and technological innovation.

A series of fifteen books providing an interesting introduction to various cultures through art, folklore, history, and geography.

With purchase of any book in the Ancient and Living Cultures Series, the publisher grants permission to educators to reproduce certain valuable sections for classroom use. As an example, *Ancient Japan* allows reproduction of a map of Japan in the 1700s, two pages of illustrations of daily life in Japan during this period, a reading selection that retells the folktale of The Bamboo Princess, and project instructions for making a pilgrimage book, a samurai helmet, a wind-sock kite, a poetry fan, and a furoshiki (a decorative cloth wrapper used for wrapping gifts and carrying things).

The Ancient and Living Cultures Series has been used with great success at museum family-day events, schoolwide multicultural days, and in individual classrooms. The books also make terrific rainy-day activity resources for parents and children and would be useful for home-schoolers, too.

Portions of the royalties from the sale of books in this series go toward developing multicultural educational programs. SANDRA KELLY

Castro!

📕 Don E. Beyer

Caribbean, Cuban, Hispanic

1993, Franklin Watts, Inc., ✳ Series

"Fidel Castro may soon be the last major dictator in a world that seems bent on democratic reforms. He has vowed to stay the course and keep the socialist movement alive in Cuba against all odds. That he can do so as Cuba falls apart around him seems unlikely."

Beyer, a high-school teacher from Wisconsin, presents a comprehensive biography of one of the most interesting and controversial political figures within the Latino community and around the world. Beginning with Fidel Castro's family background, Beyer proceeds to describe Castro's school life and how the social environment helped to shape Castro's innate revolutionary spirit. This is not a sympathetic portrait of Castro, and Beyer describes the brutal warfare carried out by Castro, as well as his political cunning that resulted in his creation of a totalitarian society. Also highlighted is the dramatic confrontation with the United States' involvement with the Cuban Missile Crisis and the ill-fated Bay of Pigs Invasion.

A comprehensive biography of Cuba's controversial leader.

Castro! concludes with an analysis of Cuba's present depressed economic condition which threatens Castro's enduring more than thirty-year rule of Cuba. Beyer writes in a style that is accessible for younger students and includes many historical photographs and suggestions for further reading to aid students' understanding of one of the most controversial leaders of the western world. *While the book does not provide a complex examination of Cuba under Castro's leadership, it is especially useful for classroom analysis of the reasons some Cubans have immigrated to the United States under Castro's oppressive regime.* HERIBERTO GODINA

The Nubians: People of the Ancient Nile

📕 ✒ Robert Steven Bianchi

African, Nubian

1994, The Millbrook Press

There are plenty of excellent books for young readers on Ancient Egypt, but until now very few books have dealt with Nubia, Egypt's southern neighbor, which they called Kush.

A complex and rare history of the ancient Nilotic African civilization of Nubians.

In *The Nubians: People of the Ancient Nile*, Robert Steven Bianchi, a museum scientist, presents an over-view of the ancient history of this region for young readers. The book grew out of a series of lectures prepared at the request of a group of Nubians who were displaced from their homelands by Egypt's High Dam. According to Bianchi, "They were seeking ways to insure the survival of their history." After the lectures, Bianchi was honored by the Nubians. "They presented me with a karadj, a typical Nubian wedding gift, thereby marrying me in spirit to their community and their efforts to preserve their heritage. I then decided that a book for children, not only for Nubian children but for all the children of the world, would be a good idea."

This work is one of a very few books for children on the history of this region. It provides a solid introduction to Nubian history and culture. The book is illustrated with black-and-white and color photographs that show Nubian artifacts, now in various museums, and color photographs of sites in Nubia. The latter unfortunately, have a rather grainy quality and a yellowish cast. Also included are a map, a time line, an index, and a list of museums that house important Nubian artifacts. An epilogue entitled , "The Nubians Today," describes the displacement of the Nubian people by Egypt's High Dam and its impact on the archeological remains of Lower Nubia.

Because of its complexity, The Nubians is not an easy book to teach. It may be best approached using the "jigsaw method." Good research topics include: the geography of Nubia, the earliest inhabitants of Nubia, the Pan-Grave culture, the C-Group culture, the Kerma culture, the Nubian conquest of Egypt, the Kingdom of Napata, the Kingdom of Meroe, and the challenges facing the Nubian people today.

SANDRA KELLY

625

The Mythology of North America

📘 John Bierhorst
Native American
1986 (1985), Morrow Junior Books, 📖 Bierhorst, John, *The Mythology of South America; The Mythology of Mexico and Central America*

Part of the Bierhorst's work on the folklore and mythology of the Americas, this volume, covering the U.S. and Canada, joins volumes on *The Mythology of South America* and *The Mythology of Mexico and Central America*. Identified by geographic region and by tribe within those regions, the myths in this volume include creation myths, and the origins of cultures.

A valuable anthology of folklore of the North American Indians retold by one of our preeminenet folklorist.

Bierhorst is the most notable folklorist in North America. His work is well documented and well respected among scholars. Each section of the book is preceded by a discussion of the history of the tribes from the region and the unique characteristics of their mythology. The book can be read and understood by fifth or sixth graders. The real value of this book is that it is an accessible and reliable source of the authentic mythologies of North American Indians. The myths are not fictionalized or modernized as they are in many anthologies for children. They are presented in language which is understandable to students and consistent with the character of the oral traditions presented.

The significance of the myths as well as the life styles and beliefs of native peoples is thoroughly explored. *The book can be used for a unit on Native American cultures and folklore.* ELAINE P. GOLEY

If You Were There in 1492

📘 Barbara Brenner ✒ Various Sources
European American
1991, Simon & Schuster Children's

Beginning with the Moorish conquest of Spain, and the subsequent Spanish religious fervor and hatred of Islam, Meltzer provides young readers with a serious examination of Spain during the fifteenth century. From its rich artistic history to the primitive conditions under which many of the citizens lived. One chapter presents the fifteenth-century status of Jews and their contributions to Spanish society, as well as their expulsion from Catholic Spain in 1492. The role of cartographers in the society and Columbus's landing in the New World are presented for young readers to examine.

An illuminating and accurate account of Columbus' voyage and the expulsion of the Jews from Spain.

Meltzer remains a fine researcher and writer as is evidenced in this book. The illustrations consist of woodcuts, maps, and paintings from the period. This book fills a void and brings to light the real reasons Columbus made his first voyage to the New World. BYRON RUSKIN

The Rise of Islam

📘 John Child ✒ Various sources
Middle Eastern
1995,(1954) P. Bedrick Books Inc., ✳ Series, 📖 *Islam for Beginners* by N.I Mattar, *A Medieval Banquet in the Alhambea Palace* edited by Audrey Shabbas

The Rise of Islam could have provided a valuable introduction to Islam for middle-grade readers. Unfortunately, this book has too many errors and confusing statements to be recommended.

An error-ridden book on important Islamic people from around the world.

First published in England, *The Rise of Islam* was not updated for this American reprint. A map shows Yugoslavia as still one country and North and South Yemen, now unified as the Republic of Yemen, as two separate countries.

626

This book is divided into several sections, which include the early years of Islam, the Umayyad and Abbasid caliphates, and the Ottoman Empire. The time period, however, between the fall of the Abbasids in 1258 and the rule of Mehmet II, who became the first Ottoman sultan in 1451, is given only cursory treatment. The history of the Mongols, Seljuks, Ayyubids, and Mamlukes (who were not, as the book states, "Turks who captured Egypt"), Safavids, and Moguls is condensed into one rather incomprehensible page. The historic importance of Islamic Spain is almost entirely overlooked.

Scattered throughout the book, important sections of *The Rise of Islam* discuss Islamic art, medicine, mathematics and science, education, and trade during the middle ages. Due to the constraints of a sixty-four-page book, these sections are rather brief.

The emphasis in *The Rise of Islam* is on people and their role in historical events. This biographical approach is an interesting way to help young readers understand history through the lives of the people who made it. Break-out boxes give short biographies of many Muslims. Some of these have not been well researched. The biography of Muhammad's daughter Fatima states erroneously that Muhammad had no sons. Other biographies tend to dwell on strange detail, ignoring important information. Nowhere in the biography of Muhammad's wife, Ayesha, is it said that she was an important transmitter of the hadith, the oral tradition of Muhammad's words and deeds. Yet the author does write, "Despite Muhammad's position, she did all of the housework," and brings up the story that someone once accused her of infidelity.

The choice of biographical subjects is also hard to comprehend. For example, Libya's colonel Gadhafi is profiled, but Ibn Battuta, a medieval Moroccan scholar who was the most-traveled man of premodern times, is not.

Many of the illustrations in *The Rise of Islam* are well done. The combined use of maps, photographs, and reproductions of early Islamic art is to be commended. The illustrations are generally attractive and enhance the accompanying textual material. Break-out boxes also offer useful background material and some primary source documents.

Some of the illustrations and textual materials, however, overemphasize the strange and cruel in history at the expense of a balanced picture of society. The descriptions and illustrations of war, piracy, torture, drunkenness, violence, punishment, slavery, murder, and assassination support erroneous stereotypes of Islam as a warlike religion practiced by a society averse to pluralism and kindness of any sort.

It is a shame that *The Rise of Islam*, which could have advanced crosscultural awareness and understanding through education, was not more sensitively written and thoroughly researched.

(The reviewer would like to thank Elizabeth Barlow, Program Coordinator at the University of Michigan's Center for Middle Eastern and North African Studies, for her helpful comments and discussion.) SANDRA KELLY

Courage of Sarah Noble

Alice Dalgleish   Leonard Wiesgard
Native American
1991 (1954), Simon & Schuster,   *The New England Indians* by Kieth Wilbur, *A Unit About Woodland Indians* by Elaine Hansen-Cleary, *Dancing Teepees: Poems of American Indian Youth* selected by Virginia Sneeve

While traveling with her father through the Connecticut wilderness in 1707, Sarah Noble is frightened by what she hears about Native Americans; some children from a settlement she passes tell her that she will be skinned and eaten alive. When she first meets a Native American family, Sarah is frustrated by her inability to communicate with the children, and chides them for not knowing English. She quickly regrets her rudeness, however, and tries to teach the children English when they meet again. In return, the children show her where to find berries. Eventually, their fathers begin to trade and their friendship begins to deepen.

A European American girl from Colonial times with a Native American family in an endearing Newbery Honor book from the '50s.

When Sarah's father returns to Massachusetts, Sarah stays with her new "adopted family." At first, she is afraid of living with Tall John and his family, but soon immerses herself in their culture, learning how to grow corn, make baskets, and wear deerskin clothing. When her family returns, Sarah happily tells her mother about her experiences. She is glad to be back with her family, but

628

will remember her new friends.

Courage of Sarah Noble successfully portrays the contact between members of two cultures though the story focuses on the colonist's point of view, from Sarah's initial fear and ignorance to her gradual acceptance of Native Americans. Little information is presented about the particular group of Native Americans she meets, but this is primarily a story about Sarah's new experiences. This 1954 Newbery Honor Book is still a favorite of children today. LISA MOORE

Aztec: The World of Moctezuma

Jane S. Day
Native American, Hispanic
1992, Denver Museum of Natural History & Roberts Rinehart Publishers

Jane Day's colorful overview of the Aztec civilization integrates many photographs, maps, and illustrations to convey the complexity of Precolumbian Mesoamerica.

A colorful, but culturally biased overview of the Aztec civilization.

It draws mostly from historical accounts written by Spanish missionaries during the postcolonial occupation of Mexico. The intricate beauty of the graphics integrated throughout the text should be very attractive to students.

Many different aspects of Aztec life are covered, such as the advanced system of hydroponic gardening used to grow crops or chinampas. Aztec games are also examined, as well as daily life, medicine, social structure, sacrificial practices, and the confrontation with the Spanish conquistadors.

The book is problematic in the sense that it draws mostly from ideologically oriented sources that advocate colonial subjugation of indigenous peoples. Consequently, Day represents the Aztecs as an advanced civilized people, yet also refers to them as heathen cannibals. Nor does the text examine issues affecting the present condition of Mexico's indigenous populations. Consequently, a critical reading of the text is absolutely necessary to understand the complex interrelations between Mexico and Imperial Spain. *While, Aztec is an excellent text*

for examining the scope and breadth of Aztec civilization, as well as examining some of the interesting archaeological practices used to excavate Aztec ruins in the middle of Mexico City, its lack of critical perspective must be addressed if the book is used in classes. A glossary translates the many Nahuatl terms (the language of the Aztecs) used in the text.
HERIBERTO GODINA

Malinche, Slave Princess of Cortez

Gloria Durán
Hispanic, Mexican
1993, Shoe String Press

Through historical fiction, Gloria Durán attempts to make more familiar the life of one of Mexico's enigmatic figures, Malinche. Also known as Marina, she came from a Mayan ruling family and during the conquest of Mexico became part of Cortez's entourage, serving as his mistress and his translator. She quickly learned the Spanish language and could translate between Nahuatl and Mayan. Setting the tone for the book, the author poses an interesting question: "Did Malinche betray her people or did they betray her?"

Malinche has been vilified in Mexican folklore as a traitor, although some contemporary writers, such as Noble laureate Octavio Paz, have called for a reassess-

A portrayal of Malinche, Cortez's mistress and translator during the conquest of Mexico, that is overly sympathetic to the colonizers.

ment of Malinche's place in the Mexican consciousness. Durán offers his own interpretation, portraying Mesoamerican culture as something that Malinche has to rise above. Though Durán uses some primary sources—mostly the writings of Bernal Díaz del Castillo, who wrote his reflections fifty years after the fall of the Aztec empire—to give legitimate context to her fictional interpretation of events, many of these sources are themselves unreliable. Consequently, *Malinche, Slave Princess of Cortez* is a kind of historical fiction that is not well-informed, seems to favor colonial dominance, and denigrates Mesoamerican culture.

For example, Durán claims that Malinche was purchased by Cortez as a slave, and in one of the

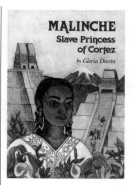

scenes Malinche and Cortez confront her mother for having originally sold Malinche into slavery. The mother is spared, but not before Marina offers her forgiveness.

It is somewhat perplexing to read a position that is so sympathetic to Cortez and Malinche, yet does not describe the oppressive rule of the Spanish upon the indigenous population of Mexico. Even when Cortez scolds Marina, there is flat-out racism subtly encoded in Duran's fictional dialogue: "You are acting just like an Indian. You are not yourself now"

I hesitate to recommend Durán's Malinche, Slave Princess of Cortez *because it does not make a sophisticated inquiry into an otherwise intriguing character, but rather clings to a colonial ideology that is not capable of transcending its very limited observations. That this text could be used in a classroom by Mexican American students to understand their history leaves me worried about its potential harm—not just for its treatment of ethnic identity, but for its gender stereotyping as well.* HERIBERTO GODINA

The Eternal Spring of Mr. Ito

Sheila Garrigue
Asian American, Japanese American
1995 (1985), American Printing House for the Blind, (Bradbury)

Sara Warren lives in Vancouver, British Columbia. She loves gardens and finds special joy in her association with Mr. Ito, a Japanese gardener, and his family. Mr. Ito gives her a bonsai of her own to nurture.

In a moving story, in honor of a interned Japanese American friend, a Canadian girl nurtures a bonsai plant during World War II.

When America and Canada declare war on Japan, everything changes for the Ito family. Not only does the government imprisons Japanese Americans, and Sara's family and friends turn away from the Itos and other Japanese Americans whom they at one point loved and respected. The Warren family's resentment toward all Japanese is compounded by the death of a relative in the war.

Mr. Ito, a proud and sincere man, flees to the mountains to escape the shame of internment. Sara finds him there, and she promises to take a large bonsai, kept in her garage, to the Ito family. After hiding the bonsai from members of her family who in their anger might destroy it, Sara carefully devises a plan. Managing to elude the authorities, she delivers the bonsai to the Itos at camp.

With the history, strength, and character of the Ito family symbolized by the aged bonsai plant, this is an intricate examination of the emotional conflicts of war. Although told mostly from Sara's point of view, the book offers a caring look at the trauma suffered by Japanese families during the World War II internment. BINNIE TATE-WILKIN

Ego-tripping & Other Poems for Young People

Nikki Giovanni George Ford
African American
1993 (1980), Lawrence Hill

In *Ego-tripping*, noted poet Nikki Giovanni explores the many nuances of African American culture. First published in 1980, *Ego-tripping* has been revised to include ten new poems and more contemporary illustrations.

The volume includes poems about dreams, communication, loneliness, intellectualism, funerals, black power, beauty and revolution. The title poem "ego-tripping" speaks eloquently to the strength and endurance of African American history and identity. Another poem offers a thoughtful consideration of revolution. Young people can feel the rhythm of change and they can observe its cost at a distance. They learn that change demands commitment, and can be a violent and chaotic process.

An eloquent and updated collection of poems on the African American experience from a leading poet.

Giovanni is a gifted poet with a special talent for creating memorable images. *Ego-tripping* rewards thoughtful consideration and will make young people pause at the mirror to check not only their appearances but also their beliefs.
YOLANDA ROBINSON-COLES

629

My First Book of Proverbs

Ralfka Gonzalez, Ana Ruiz
Hispanic, Mexican
1995, Children's Book Press, ✱ Bilingual
Spanish/English

Humorous illustrations bring to life a collection of proverbs written in English and Spanish.

"Dichos" or proverbs connect us with the wisdom of ancestors in a playful way. They remind us that "Experience is the mama of science" and "If you hang out with wolves, you will learn to howl." In *My First Book of Proverbs*, artists Ralfka Gonzalez and Ana Ruiz celebrate these word of mouth pearls in a humorous collection of richly colored illustrations.

Each proverb, printed in Spanish and in English, is animated by full-page color paintings. The folk art style in which they are rendered compliments the folkloric tradition of the dichos. Children of all ages can find fun and laughter in the artwork. *Critical thinking skills can be developed when young people are asked to discern the meanings of the folk sayings. Some are familiar, such as "Where there's a will there's a way." Others are surprising: "Pig out while you have a chance." In either case, students can have fun applying real life experiences to these proverbs in writing or discussion.*

Teachers may want to assign a proverb to each student. They must conjure their own illustrations and give personal interpretations of the proverb. Students enjoy sharing the wisdom of experience and the opportunity to draw and paint with humor. This book reminds us that "Lo que se aprende bien nunca se olvida." A lesson well learned is never forgotten. FAITH CHILDS-DAVIS

Frida Kahlo: The Paintings

Hayden Herrera ✎ Frida Kahlo,
Hispanic, Mexican
1993 (1991), Harper Collins

Art historian Hayden Herrera has put together a comprehensive collection of paintings and sketches by Frida Kahlo, the most prominent female Mexican artist of this century. In addition to the more than eighty paintings reproduced in the book, black-and-white photographs (including photographs of where she lived in Mexico) retell the passionate life story of this artist. Frida's husband, the famous painter Diego Rivera is also prominently featured in many photographs. This collection spans a lifetime and begins with family pictures showing Frida as a young child and concludes with pictures of her funeral. Throughout her life, Frida Kahlo was beset by pain due to an injury sustained in an accident. As a result, she had about thirty-five operations, mostly to her spine and right foot. Some of the photographs show Frida in bed or a wheelchair. The paintings include many self-portraits that reflect her physical and emotional struggle against debilitating conditions. These are marvelous works with a surrealistic and sometimes haunting qualities.

Eighty paintings retell the passionate life story of a leading Mexican artist in a valuable introduction to her work.

Herrera also describes the personal details of Kahlo and Rivera's turbulent relationship and insightfully connects the influence of the artist's personal lives upon their paintings. As an introduction to these dynamic artists, this is a valuable reference text for students. It provides both a Mexican and a female perspective on art. As a biography of a person who remained creative and active despite arduos physical conditions, this book stands as a steadfast reminder of the human spirit's ability to transcend adversity. HERIBERTO GODINA

Rising Voices: Writings of Young Native Americans

Arlene B. Hirschfelder and Beverly R. Singer
Native American
1993, Ivy Books

This collection of poetry and essays by young Native Americans is well intentioned but not entirely successful. Organized around six general areas of concern—"Identity," "Family," "Homelands," "Ritual and Ceremony," "Education," and "Harsh Realities"—it includes a superficial, cliché-ridden introductory commentary by the editors.

Although some pieces are memorable, especially given the age of their authors, most of the writing is (understandably) tentative, awkward, and amateurish. This raises a number of serious questions about the ultimate goals and uses of a collection such as this: What or who is the real intended audi-

630

ence? Do kids automatically respond more favorably to the writings of other kids? If we encourage kids to chop prose phrases and sentences up in unexpected places, is the result really poetry?

To be sure, there are gems of startling depth and quality scattered throughout this anthology. The "Identity" section is especially moving in its depiction of universal adolescent angst and bravado. The poem "Grandpa," by Shandin Pete, vividly portrays the dignity of an aged grandfather; Phil George's "Old Man, the Sweat Lodge" captures meaning of a sweat lodge in a young man's life. The section on education, consisting mostly of excerpts from the memoirs of young Native Americans forced into boarding schools, is particularly poignant. One young woman comments on returning to the tribal home from which she was taken at the age of six: "They greeted me kindly, but they and everything being so new and strange that I burst into tears. I could not eat for the lump in my throat and presently I put my head down and cried good and hard, while the children looked on in surprise …At last {my father] told me I had changed greatly from a loving child to a stranger." Other pieces in this section reflect varying degrees of compliance with the school's stated goal of assimilation and alienation from the children's original culture. It is impossible not to share the children's sense of betrayal and outrage with an alien government and society determined to demean, disparage, and distort them. There is no question that the young would-be writers represented here need to express themselves; further, there is no question that the larger society needs to hear voices such as these and to acknowledge the rights, needs, and hopes of contemporary Native Americans. In this context, *Rising Voices* serves a purpose. Ultimately, though, it is less than fully satisfying — a promise not quite fulfilled. ROBIN BERSON

A well-intentioned but amateurish collection of poetry and essays from young Native Americans.

Passport to Mexico

Carmen Irizarry, Hayward Art Group, Tony & Marion Morrison

Hispanic, Mexican

1994 (1987), Franklin Watts, Inc., ✳ Series

Passport to Mexico introduces young readers to the geography, industry, natural resources, and people of Mexico. This is an attractive book with many full-color photographs, maps, and diagrams. Despite having a lot of content information related to Mexico, this text has a format similar to a magazine that should appeal to younger students. This recent edition includes the latest information available on Mexico. Through the many photographs, a reader gains a sense of how people actually live in Mexico. There are photographs of people at a soccer match, a birthday party, and at the market.

An excellent and inviting introduction to the country and people of Mexico through photographs, maps, and diagrams.

What is especially appealing in this book are the sections called "Facts on File" where key facts about Mexico are presented, and the country is compared to other countries in the following categories: land and population, home life and leisure, economy and trade, and government and world role. Through tables and figures, readers develop an objective perspective on how Mexico compares comparison to other countries; the differences may be surprising for some. Did you know that the United States has a population density of about 70 people per square mile and Mexico has about 116? Or that the United Kingdom has an astonishing 614 people per square mile and that Australia has only 5? Such interesting facts and figures are creatively displayed for the reader in a comparative format that invites intellectual discussion and should spark the curiosity of many students.

I would highly recommend using *Passport to Mexico* in the multicultural classroom because it

631

makes the similarities and differences of various cultures more accessible for students without necessarily favoring a particular perspective. Too recent to have been included in even this updated edition, information related to the recent devaluation of the peso is not iincluded in the section on Mexico's economy and may have to be supplemented by the teacher. Yet, unless the classroom is focusing on economic issues, this should not detract from an otherwise excellent overview of Mexico. HERIBERTO GODINA

The Indian Heritage of America

📖 Alvin M. Josephy   ✒ Various sources
Native American
1991, Houghton Mifflin Company, ✳ Series

The book describes the cultures of the Incas, Olmecs, and Aztecs, tribes from Central and South America, that have greatly influenced the culture and development of the hemisphere but are often are often overlooked in favor of the Apaches and other tribes of the United States.

An accessible history of lesser-known Native American peoples of North and South America.

The book begins with chapters on the diversity of Native Americans, early humans in America, and white people's debt to the Native Americans. Much of what is great about America — government, agriculture, and the arts — is derived from Native American cultures. The Native Americans attempted to teach the Europeans how to hunt, fish, plant, harvest , cook native foods, and live in harmony with nature and other cultures.

Native American tribes often adopted whites and blacks as full members of their tribes. Their acceptance of other cultures and religions, is perhaps their undoing as well as their most valuable attribute. This book makes these complex cultures and histories understandable to older children as well as educators. *Reports and projects can be produced by students using this book. The book is a valuable resource in teaching about the cultures of Native Americans from North and South America.*
ELAINE P. GOLEY

Now That the Buffalo's Gone: A Study of Today's American Indians

📖 ✒ Alvin M. Josephy Jr.
Native American
1982, Alfred A. Knopf

Josephy's book examines the past, present, and future of Native American culture and shows that despite deliberate attempts to exterminate their culture, many of the tribes of the U.S. are thriving today. Josephy, a former editor of *American Heritage* magazine, president of the National Council of the Institute of the American West, and a trustee of the Museum of the American Indian, offers impeccable scholarship in this book. It is written for older readers, but it is accessible to grades six through eight in the classroom study of Native American cultures.

Contempory Native American society and culture explored for children in a valuable corrective to more skewed accounts.

One important section of the book addresses racial stereotypes which have plagued Indians since the Puritans thought them to be agents of the devil. This history serves as a valuable narrative from an Indian perspective and as a corrective to the often skewed accounts of Native American culture and history in American history textbooks.

This book can be used in the classroom along with selections from the authoritative documentary film on Native Americans produced by the Native American Public Broadcasting Company.
ELAINE P. GOLEY

Kiss the Dust

📖 Elizabeth Laird
Middle Eastern, Turkish
1994 (1992), Puffin, ✳ Series

Not everyone would agree that the Kurds, an ethnic minority in the Middle East, should have their own separate nation; the governments of Iraq, Turkey, and Syria, don't for instance. The very subject of this book, therefore, is controversial. By the end of it, nevertheless, most American readers will be persuaded of the justice of Kurdish claims. The title refers to the young heroine's witnessing a teenaged boy shot for reading a Kurdish nationalist leaflet in public, symbolically kissing the dust of a free "Kurdistan" as he dies.

Tara, age twelve at the start of the story, is the daughter of a well-to-do Kurdish factory owner in a northern city of Iraq. As the menfolk of the family become increasingly involved in supporting the Kurdish guerillas, Tara, her parents, and little sister have to escape to a mountain village. After a bombing raid on the helpless villagers, Tara's family flee again, over the mountains to Iran. There they live for a while in an internment camp, until they are moved on to Tehran where, fortunately, they have relatives who can provide some assistance.

A Kurdish girl flees with her family from Iraq to England in a nuanced book full of high adventure too.

That reprieve is short-lived. To avoid being sent to a worse internment camp, Tara's father manages to scrape up enough money for airplane tickets to London. The family makes it to Britain for the start of a new, safe, but hardly comfortable, life as penniless political refugees.

Tara grows in stature and strength as the story progresses, developing from a privileged schoolgirl into a resourceful, courageous young woman. Other characters are also credible, but what is most compelling about the story is the sheer drama and excitement. The nighttime escape from the family home just minutes ahead of the men coming to arrest them, the flight over the mountains, the hardships in the camp, the tension as the family prepare for their last flight, knowing that if anything goes wrong there will be no second chance; these episodes are high adventure, indeed, and all the more gripping because they are based on true-life stories.

Though the last part of the novel is quieter, it provides a different kind of tension in the clash of cross cultural expectations. Tara had assumed everyone in London would look like Princess Di, attractive and happy. Not so. The people she sees are dowdy and gloomy. The children at school seem shocking in their behavior; the cold stares of indifference almost harder to take than the outright hostility of the Iranians.

For seventh and eighth graders, Kiss the Dust would be a valuable resource for class discussions of nationalism, current events and world history, plus cross cultural experience. To be sure, the other side of the question —the considerations that make an autonomous "Kurdistan" *intolerable to governments in the area—is missing. It could hardly be otherwise, however; the author's presentation of her characters and their plight, as well as her obvious commitment to the cause, would not permit a balanced, objective approach. And undeniably, feeling the human drama behind the news is an important step in a young person's intellectual and emotional growth.* ELSA MARSTON

Tales from Home

📖 Judith Langer   ✏ Elba Herrero
Hispanic
1994, SUNY, Albany, ✱ Bilingual Spanish/ English

Judith Langer and Elba Herrero orchestrate an impressive collection of thirty-seven stories by bilingual middle-school students from Manhattan's lower east side. The book features a bilingual text with Spanish and English, on opposite pages and brief biographical sketches of the authors. This collection is unique because it focuses on Spanish-speaking students from the Dominican Republic, yet a few selections from Mexican, Venezuelan, and Puerto Rican students are also included. *Tales From Home* is made up of both personal narratives and imaginative fiction, with a compelling tone that is both sincere and candid. This collection of exemplary student writing from a Spanish-speaking group shares a common bond

An exemplary collection of student writings from bilingual Latino adolescents on a number of intriguing topics.

with other adolescents confronting a number of intriguing topics. "The Horrible Vacation" by Raquel Martinez describes a visit with her aunt in the Dominican Republic. Her sister gets burned when her father, who had been drinking kicks over a stove. As a result, he never drinks again. Nena Rivera's story, "The Intelligent Toad," is about a toad who is caught stealing and is thrown into a river as punishment. But, being a toad, he manages to escape, and decides to get a job to avoid another similar encounter.

These works transcends boundaries and are easily accessible for students from any culture. The bilingual format aids all readers in interpreting this particular dialect of Spanish. HERIBERTO GODINA

American Dragons: 25 Asian American Voices

Yep Laurence

Asian American

1995 (1993), Harper Collins

This sensitive, well-organized anthology includes poems, short stories, and excerpts from plays depicting the experiences of young Asian Americans whose families come from China, Japan, Korea, Tibet, Vietnam, and Thailand.

New voices are represented, as well as such luminaries as Maxine Hong Kingston, Darrell Lum, and Bill Wu. The selections are organized around six basic paths into what Laurence Yep calls "the vast psychological wilderness created by the American Dream": Identity; In the Shadow of Giants (parents); Wise Child; World War II; Love; Guides (grandparents). Yep's preface, afterword, and commentary on each section are imbued with deep compassion and awareness. The selections encompass a shifting equation of broadly shared adolescent experience, and uniquely Asian American experiences. (The internment experience in World War II is, of course, uniquely Japanese American.

Twenty-five well-written stories by Asian Americans about becoming "American."

"Yahk Fahn [eat rice], Auntie," by Darrell Lum, relates the struggles of a child who rejects his Chinese heritage—he resists education, is uninterested in Chinese customs, will not use chopsticks or learn to speak Chinese. These images are recalled by the child-become-adult, returned home after a seven-year absence to attend the funeral of the beloved aunt who represented the culture he has tried to deny. The story deals poignantly with his sense of loss and alienation from his family.

Lesley Namioka's "Who's Hu?" is narrated by a Chinese immigrant teenager, a brilliant mathematician who is set apart as much by her talent as by her alien culture and background. Her sole rival in an upcoming math competition, a self-important Caucasian boy, cruelly manipulates her anxieties and loneliness and almost succeeds in convincing her to "throw" the math exam in exchange for a date for the all-important prom.

Richard Haratani's "Attention to Detail" delicately captures the impact of Pearl Harbor on a Japanese American youth employed as a houseboy in the officers' club of a naval base. Peter Makota, who has left school because of rising anti-Japanese racism, is stereotyped and victimized on the base. Ironically, when Pearl Harbor is attacked it is a young white ensign who thinks of Peter, worries about his safety, and helps him get home safely.

Only occasionally does the quality of the selections slip. "Dana's Eyes," by Nicol Juratovac, deals with important issues of trust and betrayal when the young daughter of a divorced Chinese mother is molested by her baseball coach. The mother retreats into a culturally conditioned reverence for authority rather than defend her innocent daughter. Unfortunately, Juratovac's writing is awkward and didactic. Overall, however, *American Dragons* is an invaluable addition to any reading list multicultural or otherwise. ROBIN BERSON

Sacred River

Ted Lewin

Asian, East Indian

1995, Clarion Books, Yolen, Jane, *Letting Swift River Go*; Lewin, Ted, *The Reindeer People*; Fisher, Leonard Everett, *Ghandi*

The most sacred Hindu river, the Ganges, flows through Benares, one of the oldest cities in the world. In a nonfiction picture book, Sacred River, Ted Lewin offers glimpses and stories of that river and the pilgrims who come to Benares to bathe in its waters. He offers image after image in dignified language and colorful, detailed water-color paintings.

A fascinating depiction of the Ganges River, considered by Hindus to be the most sacred of all rivers appropriate for a range of ages.

"Across the mile-wide sacred river, the life-giving sun rises on a new day," the book begins. "The old boatman rows away from the dark stone steps called ghats." As the reader moves down the river, "Hooded pilgrims hunch in long boats that slide by on the dark river." When the sun rises, thousands of pilgrims step into the water, offering jai flowers. Later, the ashes of cremated Hindus are scattered on the water. When the book ends, "The souls of the faithful will continue onward, while their ashes join the jai flowers in the river on the long journey to the sea."

Primary students will be fascinated by the beauty of the scenes—the text is short, a sentence or two for each page. Older students can take a more in-depth look at India once their interest is sparked by this picture book. A longer nonfiction book about the most famous Hindu spokesman is *Gandhi* by Leonard Everett Fisher (Athenuem, 1995).

Fisher's black-and-white illustrations light up each page as he takes Gandhi's story from boyhood to the victory in the "long fight for India's freedom." An afterword explains about the nonviolent protestor's death from an assassin's bullet.

Students can also compare *Sacred River* with other Lewin books, especially *The Raindeer People* (Clarion, 1994), a look at the Sami people of Lapland. Some of the bright patterns and colors in the two books are similar, but the text in *Sacred River* is much shorter. JANE KURTZ

Mayan Vision Quest: Mystical Initiation in Mesoamerica

📖 Hunbatz Men, Charles Bensinger
✏ Cynthia MacAdams
Hispanic, Mexican
1991, Harper Collins

This book is a collection of black-and-white photographs of the major Mayan archeaological sites in Southern Mexico, Belize, Guatemala, and Honduras. The pictures and text also evoke the spiritual significance of these magnificent temples, ball courts, and pyramids. The book also seeks to explain the basic tenets of Mayan cosmology. The captions present detailed explanations of each of the photographs, and one's imagination is sparked by glimpses of the historical grandeur of indigenous culture before European colonization.

A photo collection of major Mayan archaelogical sites that sensitively introduces Mesoamerican culture and civilization.

Readers of all ages should enjoy this portrait of Mesoamerican culture and civilization. *Mayan Vision Quest* also could be useful in the classroom as an introduction to the esthetics of photography. HERIBERTO GODINA

This Same Sky: A Collection of Poems From Around the World

📖 Naomi Shihab Nye (editor)
Multicultural
1992, Simon & Schuster

This Same Sky is a wonderful collection of poems from all over the world selcted by Arab American poet Naomi Shahib Nye. Poets represented come from sixty-eight countries, ranging from Angola to Armenia, Ireland to Indonesia, Pakistan to Paraguay. Lively, unforced translations ease reading. Readers are rewarded with insights into ways of life that may seem exotic until one realizes, as Estonian Jaan Kaplinski, comments "that nothing at all is exotic in itself. There is no difference between digging potatoes in our Mutiku garden and sugar cane harvesting in Viti Levu [Fiji]."

Poets from sixty-eight countries show that we all live under "this same sky" in a wonderful collection.

Nye has done an outstanding job here of removing other cultures from the realm of the strangely romantic and giving them a human face. Whether browsing or reading the collection in its entirety, readers will find that we are all, indeed, connected by virtue of living under "this same sky." In "Under the Sky," for instance, Zia Hyder of Bangladesh writes "Fog hangs on the horizon—/ suddenly New York, Broadway, and Times Square / look dimly like Dhaka, Buriganga, and Laxmi Bazaar."

Entries are grouped in six broad categories—such as Dreams and Dreamers, Families, and Losses—each subtitled with an evocative quotation taken from one of the poems. Some selections are followed by notes explaining unfamiliar terms and place-names used, but there are no illustrations; readers must form their own mental images from the poets' words.

Brief notes provide information on the 129 contributors, while a map identifies the nation each calls home. There are suggestions for further reading that emphasize American poets. These are followed by two indexes: one to the countries represented, which should prove useful to teachers searching for material to include in a curriculum unit, and another to the poets themselves.
LYNN EISENHUT

635

636

Bright Star, Bright Dawn

📖 Scott O'Dell

Native American, Inuit

1988, Houghton Mifflin Company

Dedicated to those who have run the Iditarod, the grueling dog sled race across two mountain ranges and the Yukon River, from Anchorage on the Gulf of Alaska to Nome on the Bering Sea, this story is

An Inuit girl accompanies her father on a grueling Alaskan dog-sled race in an appealing if somwhat predictable adventure story.

narrated by Bright Dawn, an Inuit girl. Author Scott O'Dell quickly sketches a countercultural heroine in Bright Dawn as she accompanies her father, Bartok, on his seal hunts, even though according to the villagers a woman's place is in the home.

When Bartok is injured, he moves the family to a town where there would be greater contact with the white world. He also begins to race dogs as a hobby. Ultimately, Bright Dawn replaces her reinjured father as an Iditarod contender.

The story moves predictably toward a successful climax; Bright Dawn must prove herself to be brave and resourceful in the face of the enormous endurance test of the Iditarod. And O'Dell illuminates the conflict between the white-influenced world into which Bright Dawn has entered, and the Inuit world of legend and tradition, represented on the Iditarod by the veteran racer Oteg, whose Raven stories and trailside igloos save Bright Dawn on more than one occasion.

The reader learns about many aspects of Inuit culture, particularly those having to do with dog care and food. Although the book is fast-paced and exciting and does present a female heroine capable of traditionally male athleticism, nowhere in the story does Bright Dawn's gender become a characterizing feature of the way that she thinks and feels. O'Dell's use of the term "Eskimo" instead of "Inuit" also gives the book a dated feel. Still, as an adventure story that portrays the survival struggle of an old culture within the inevitable if intrusive context of a new one, this book is both useful and entertaining. MARY FROSCH

Canyons

📖 Gary Paulsen

Native American

1992 (1990), Peter Smith Publisher, Inc.,
📖 Patricia McKissak, *The Apache*; Gary Paulsen, *Night the White Dear Died*

Fifteen-year old Brennan lives alone with his mother, abandoned by his father when he was three. Now his mother has another man in her life — Bill. Brennan feels like a bit of an outsider in the world, and finds an outlet in running.

A solitary European American teen feels a kinship with a Native American in the nineteenth century, in this action-filled novel.

While on a campout with Bill's church's youth group, Brennan finds a skull with a bullet hole in it. From the moment he touches it, he has strange feelings, almost as if he knew the person.

After deciding to do some research to discover whose skull he has, Brennan learns that Dog Canyon, the place where he found the skull, was the site of battles between the U.S cavalry and the Apache Indians in the 1860s. He reads letters and papers from that time. He learns that the skull is that of Coyote Runs, a fourteen-year-old boy who was chased down and executed by soldiers in the canyon.

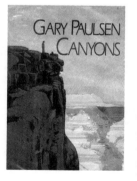

Brennan feels that Coyote Runs is urging him to return his skull to Dog Canyon. Meanwhile Brennan's mother and Bill are worried about his obsession with the skull. When he leaves home for the canyon, they call the police. Brennan runs nonstop for a day and a half. He reaches Dog Canyon and allows the spirit of Coyote Runs to guide him to the Indian's medicine place at the top of the mountain. As he lays the skull down, his connection with the other boy is broken.

The book alternates between the stories of Brennan and Coyote Runs. Sparse description conveys the grandeur of the canyon and surrounding scenery. As in *The Runner* by Cynthia Voigt, running is the chosen activity for a teen who feels isolated from the world. Paulsen skillfully blends history into this coming-of-age story. He also adds a mystic element as Brennan dreams and instinctively knows things that only Coyote Runs could have known or felt. Many will identify with Brennan's sense of accomplishment, as only he could find the proper resting place for the skull. Teen boys will be caught up in both the action and the emotional involvement between Brennan and Coyote Runs. PAM CARLSON

The Coming Home Cafe

Gayle Pearson
African American
1988, Atheneum

In this novel, an unlikely association forms between three people seeking work during the Depression brought about by accident. Elizabeth and Eddie meet after jumping the same freight trains to find work. Shortly thereafter, they meet up with Lenora, a young black woman. Reluctantly, at first, they travel together and work together in the fields. Eventually they settle down for a while in the abandoned Coming Home Cafe in Jacksonville.

An unlikely multicultural trio survives the Depression in a book that will help readers understand contemporary poverty.

Through the events that have caused Elizabeth to leave home in an attempt to save her family, the happenings on the road, and the conversation between the travelers, readers are offered a suspenseful picture of survival during the depression years. The struggle to find work and the hardships on the road will help young people understand the plight of today's homeless families. The book also conveys a sense of the racial prejudice of those times. This title could be used with others on the homeless and the depression years. BINNIE TATE-WILKIN

A Native American Feast

Lucille Recht Penner   Various sources
Native American
1994, Macmillan Publishing Company

This useful volume places information about American Indian cooking techniques, manners, customs, and recipes within a historical perspective. In the introduction, author Lucille Recht Penner explains how "Native American eating habits changed slowly over time and then changed rapidly with the Europeans' arrival." each of ten thematic chapters describes the eating habits and cooking techniques of Native American peoples, as well as how folklore, climate, geography, and the introduction of European plants and animals have influenced their diets. Each chapter contains fascinating and delicious recipes that "may seem strange to many of us today," such as hickory nut soup and squash blossoms. Other recipes, such as roasted corn on the cob, baked beans, and roast turkey, are familiar, proving, as Penner points out, that "We are heirs of Native American cooks who were the first to prepare some of our favorite foods."

A cookbook filled with delicious and authentic Native American dishes.

Some of the traditional dishes require items that are hard, if not impossible, to find, but common substitutes are provided. *With adult supervision, children can prepare all of these recipes: a unique and fun way for children to become involved with Native American heritage.* DENISE JOHNSON

It Happened in America: True Stories from the Fifty States

Lila Perl   Ib Ohlsson
Multicultural
1992, Henry Holt and Company

Filled with fifty-one exciting stories from each of the states and the District of Columbia, *It Happened in America* allows young readers and adults to enter the past and experience some defining moments in our country's history. There are stories of quiet courage, unbelievable failures, unrecognized accom-

A diverse and interesting compilation of true stories from each of the fifty states.

637

plishments, and bold defiance. The reader meets scores of historical figures, leaders, and cultural pioneers. The stories paint the landscape of the country with rich strokes of cultural diversity.

From Arizona comes "Hadji Ali and the Camel Experiment," one of the book's most intriguing stories. In 1856, hoping to carve out a wagon trail across Arizona for pioneers heading west, the U.S. army purchased a number of camels from Egypt and Arabia. Along with the camels came a handful of men from Egypt and the Arabian peninsula, including a devout Syrian named Hadji Ali. The idea to use camels was born out of necessity.

Although soldiers and prospectors knew very little about non-European nations or religious traditions other than Christianity, by October of 1857, the Camel Corp succeeded in helping to open up the trail. Ali then used the camels to carry fresh water along stretches of desert roads in Southwest Arizona, selling it to thirsty stagecoach passengers.

Ali remained in Arizona, and in 1880 he married and took the Spanish name Philip Tedro. In 1935, the Arizona Highway Department erected a pyramid shaped tombstone over his grave. Even in death, cultural ignorance prevailed—the pyramid is an Egyptian, not a Syrian monument. Some of the camels were sold to parks, zoos, and circuses; others were shot by ranchers because their appearance frightened the other livestock. Taken as a whole, this in many ways is a classic American story of cultural adaptation and misunderstanding, and the contribution and resourcefulness of the country's immigrants.

Other stories include Florida's "The Oranges of Lue Gim Gong," Hawaii's "The Farewell Song of Queen Liliuokalani," and Wyoming's "Where Women Came First."

Each state name serves as a chapter heading and the capital of each state appears beneath the name. After providing some background information on the state and the story's time period, the author poses a question, answers it, and then proceeds with a story specific to the state's history. *Teachers can have great fun developing geography, literature, and history units based on this wonderfully written, well-researched, and imaginatively formatted book.* The pen-and-ink illustrations are rather nondescript, but overall, *It Happened in America* paints a very comprehensive and interesting picture of who we really are. DAPHNE MUSE

Los Indios de Borinquen

Wilma J. Robles, Ph.D. (Translator)
Hispanic, Puerto Rican, Taino
1990, Producciones Anisa, Inc.

This is an informative book written in Spanish that introduces us to a young Taino child named Guati. Born on the island of Puerto Rico, Guati lives a typical life of the Taino Indian. Readers get an intimate look at Guati's family and learn about family life in general the different roles of the men in power, and the division of labor. Each chapter introduces us to pertinent vocabulary words used in this particular culture. After each lesson there are questions, which are not always effective in stimulating learning. *A creative teacher can work with cooperative groups that can use these questions as a guide. Some of the lessons also include maps. The illustrations present real-situations: people harvesting, the layout of the Taino villages, and the various roles of the men, woman, and children.*

This book is an excellent resource for elementary school teachers who want to introduce Taino culture to their classroom. Dr. Robles has tried to instill a sense of pride for the Puerto Rican child. They are able to see their culture and their ancestors as intelligent, hard working, caring people. This book dispels the myth that the Taino Indians were weak and lacked a well-developed culture. Hopefully, it will be translated into English, but if you have some knowledge of Spanish, do not hesitate to make it part of your teaching tools.
ELIZABETH CAPIFALI

Written in Spanish, this informative non-fiction book offers an intimate look at the typical life of a Taino Indian boy.

The Moon Bridge

📖 Marcia Savin

Asian American, Japanese American

1995 (1992), Scholastic, Inc., 📦 Daniel Davis,
*Behind Barbed Wire: The Imprisonment of Japanese
Americans During World War II*

Ruthie Fox meets Mitzi Fujimoto one week after the Japanese attack on Pearl Harbor. Both are in the fifth grade in San Francisco. Feelings against the Japanese are running high, but the two become friends. Ruthie feels both guilty and angry over the racist attitudes of her other friends. She is ostracized by them because of her friendship with Mitzi. The children's parents support them—Ruthie's parents even let her visit Japantown where Mitzi lives. But one day Mitzi and her family disappear without even saying goodbye. Months later Ruthie receives a letter from Mitzi who has been forced into an internment camp. Before she has a chance to visit the internment camp, Mitzi's family is moved again.

A lengthy but engaging novel of the friendship of a Japanese American girl interned during WWII.

Ruthie continues to write letters which she can't mail because she lacks an address. As time passes, she thinks of Mitzi less and less. After the war's end, she finally hears from Mitzi. Her family had been in Arkansas, but have returned to California. The two agree to meet at the Moon Bridge in Golden Gate Park. Mitzi shares what internment was like. She tells Ruthie, "my memories are the only things they let me keep." After an initial awkwardness, the girls hug and their friendship is renewed.

As the story focuses mainly on Ruthie, we get the barest glimpse of Mitzi's home life. The heart of the story, though, is a friendship in which neither girl pays much attention to skin color. The author has an eye for small details which add to the realism of the story. Woven throughout it are jump rope rhymes. billboard slogans, and the effects of war: food shortages, curfews, and the internment of an entire people.

Readers will get a good sense of what life was like for children of that era. Ruthie and Mitzi may appear innocent and unsophisticated compared to today's children, but their relationships with teachers and family reflect the time setting. The book is long for its intended audience, but determined readers will find the story involving and well worth the time.

An afterword speaks of the internment of the Japanese, the confiscation of their property, and the proposed legislation which would reimburse the internees who are still alive. PAM CARLSON

Pacific Crossing

📖 Gary Soto

Mexican American, Asian, Japan

1992, Harcourt Brace Jovanovich

Gary Soto continues to delight readers with his inspired writing and adventures that highlight cultural expectations in accessible ways. Pacific Crossing is one more book in a continuing series on protagonist Lincoln Mendoza, a Mexican American junior-high school boy from San Francisco. For those who have yet to meet Lincoln, this book will inspire them to seek out the others.

In this book, Lincoln leaves home for the summer and travels as an exchange student to Japan. He thinks he knows something about what awaits him, having studied kempo at Shoirinji kempo, a school for the martial arts.

A Mexican-American exchange student visits Japan for the summer in this authentic story.

Likewise, the Japanese family that hosts him has expectations about American boys. Through the shared adventures of Lincoln and Mitsuo, his Japanese "brother" of a similar age, expectations are challenged and a deeper understanding of people and cultures emerges. The boys learn the value of hard work by weeding the family farm. Lincoln learns to like ramen (noodle soup) and rice balls; the Ono family learns that Lincoln is less homesick for a hamburger than for tortillas and frijoles.

Many of Lincoln's experiences derive from his enrollment in a kempo dojo in Japan. He

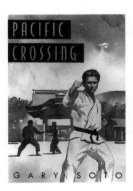

639

is initially surprised that although studying the martial arts is important to Japanese youth his age, baseball is the national passion. His own interest does not wane, and he works hard to earn a black belt, obeying all the traditions that are required: shaving his head is an example.

The adventures may teach lessons, but they are also authentic portrayals of boys. Lincoln and Shiguo go on a one-day exploration of Tokyo, which is bound to delight young readers for its zany edge and make adults a bit anxious about what happens when their children are out of their sight.

Author Gary Soto weaves both Spanish and Japanese words and phrases into the book in unintrusive ways. He also incorporates barrio slang, which provides some of the humor between the two cultural perspectives. Shiguo despairs that he will never master English with all its variations, but eventually learns that the meaning of "bad" can often be good and "being bad" can be a compliment. MICHELE SOLA

Independence and Revolution in Mexico, 1810–1940

🔖 Rebecca Stefoff ✏ Various sources
Hispanic, Mexican
1993, Facts on File, Inc.As Series

Independence and Revolution in Mexico covers what was probably the most turbulent historical period in Mexico's history. Rebecca Stefoff writes in a style that does not align itself ideologically, but presents the historical facts of each major conflict while explaining the political, economic, and social background of each country/region under study. These accounts begin with the struggle for independence from Spain; then a detailed description of the Mexican-American War explains how the United States acquired Texas, New Mexico, California, Arizona, Nevada, and parts of Colorado and Utah through the Treaty of Guadalupe Hidalgo in 1848.

An objective and useful historical study of Mexico's long, turbulent struggle for independence.

Stefoff explains how the United States killed over a thousand civilians when it bombarded Veracruz, Mexico, during this war. Such information is usually only covered briefly or not mentioned at all in many public school history books used in the United States. Stefoff proceeds to explain the strug-

gle for independence from France when Mexico was briefly ruled by a European monarch, King Ferdinand Maximilian of Austria who was overthrown by one of Mexico's most popular presidents, Benito Juárez. She concludes with a description of Mexico's internal struggle for independence from the dictatorship of Porfirio Dîaz—and describes the contributions of two famous revolutionaries, Pancho Villa and Emiliano Zapata. Independence and Revolution in Mexico contains many maps and historical drawings and photographs, as well as, a time-line, glossary, and suggestions for further reading. Also, the book has several offset inserts which describe the accomplishments of interesting people during the period under review such as the painter, Frida Kahlo, and the writer, B. Traven. *This unique history book should be valuable for students to analyze and inform themselves about events not usually covered in classroom texts, and is especially relevant considering the growing popularity of the Cinco de Mayo holiday in this country.* HERIBERTO GODINA

The Man Who Counted: A Collection of Mathematical Adventures

🔖 Malba Tahan ✏ Patricia Reid Baquero
Middle Eastern, Persian
1994 (1992), W.W. Norton

This most unusual book is authored by a Brazilian mathematician writing as a fourteenth-century Islamic scholar who is telling the tale of a Persian mathematician who lived a century before him. This mathematician in turn recounts stories and is himself regaled with tales by the people he meets. In the tradition of the famous Middle Eastern cycles of stories, such as "The Thousand and One Nights" and "Kalila and Dimna," *The Man Who Counted* is set up as a series of frame stories that nest neatly inside each other.

Set in medieval Baghdad, this story is a commendable classroom tool incorporating math and history.

The hero of these stories is Beremiz Samir, a youthful Persian mathematician known for his compassion and counting ability. Beremiz and an Arab friend journey to Baghdad to find their fortune. Along the way, Beremiz solves problems on the road and in the marketplace, shares his knowledge of the lives of great mathematicians in history, settles monetary disputes, and falls in love with an intelligent, charming young woman. Each chapter is a self-contained story, which instructs the reader on a particular aspect of mathematics. While some of the stories offer solutions to problems of logic, others give historic background on the game of chess, explain the charm of algebra and geometry, expound on the history of numbers and the usefulness of a base ten system, introduce magic squares, and show how to solve problems that involve the division of camels, melons, pearls, and gold dinars.

The book deftly weaves in some snippets of Islamic history, short selections of poetry by Omar Khayyam, a glimpse at medieval Arab trade, the Islamic lunar calendar, the medieval methods of measurement, and the use of weights and currency in the bazaar. There are a few historical inaccuracies in the book. For example, the Abbasid caliph who ruled during the sack of Baghdad in 1258 was not al-Mutasim, but rather the similarly named al-Muzta'sim. Also, some of the names used for characters in the book bear little resemblance to traditional Arab names. However, these mistakes are slight and do not detract from the work as a whole.

The book is illustrated with quirky black-and-white line drawings that appear at the beginning of each of the thirty-four chapters. These illustrations were prepared specially for the American edition.

It is an excellent book for teachers to use in a unit that integrates history and mathematics. At the seventh and eighth grade levels the teacher might read aloud certain chapters that offer problems to solve. Solving these problems in small groups offers a good opportunity for cooperative learning. SANDRA KELLY

Two Old Women: An Alaska Legend of Betrayal, Courage, and Survival

Velma Wallis Jim Grant
Native American, Inuit
1993, Epicenter Press

Ch'idzigyaak is eighty-years-old. She is so named because she reminded her parents of a chickadee bird. Sa', whose name means "star," is seventy-five. Both complain constantly of aches and pains and bemoan the loss of a past that never was. The two women's tribe decide to leave them behind one

day, the first time the tribe has made such a decision. The Chief is ashamed, but he doesn't feel he can oppose the sentiment of the people who have trusted their lives to him. Ch'idzigyaak has a daughter and grandson, but neither comes to her defense, as they are afraid of what would happen to them if they protested.

Left behind, the two women eventually realize that their constant complaints about their helplessness have convinced the others that they are in fact helpless. They decide to battle harsh weather, hunger, and despair. Drawing on skills and knowledge taught from early childhood — making snowshoes, gathering firewood from under the snow, snaring rabbits and birds—they rediscover self-confidence and physical vitality.

Two elderly women are abandoned by a migrating tribe and face starvation in a gripping novel based on Native American life a century ago.

Ch'idzigyaak and Sa' hadn't known each other well before their abandonment, but they both thrive on complaining and conversation about trivial things. Through harsh conditions and a shared goal of survival, their friendship grows.

Eventually the people return to the place where they abandoned the two women. They return to the tribe on their own terms. They have come to enjoy their newly found independence and the members of the band seek them out for their advice and knowledge.

This novel is based on a legend passed down from mother to daughter. It is a gripping story of human will and friendships, and describes a nomadic way of life that had begun to disappear by this century. By 1900, people began to settle in more permanent camps and villages. The author has lived off the land and this story rings of her firsthand experience. There's no glossary, but there is a map at the end of the book which shows probable trails followed by wandering bands of Athabaskans. LESLIE ANDERSON MORALES

641

Children's Book Awards

Rosa E. Warder

IN 1968, THE COUNCIL ON INTERRACIAL BOOKS for Children (CIBC) recognized the need to honor and support African American, Native American, Latino, and Asian American writers, in their often unrecognized efforts to bring new voices into the world of children's literature. Walter Dean Myers's children's book *Where Does the Day Go?* and Kristin Hunter's young adult novel *The Soul Brothers and Sister Lou* were the first to be honored. The awarding of this honor for unpublished manuscripts set a precedent and brought real attention to the need to recognize authentic voices in children's literature. While early twentieth-century authors including Yoshiko Uchida, Shirley Graham (DuBois), Arna Bontemps, and Langston Hughes had been honored for their contributions to children's literature, their works never received the support and recognition given their European American peers.

In 1975, Virginia Hamilton's compelling novel *M.C. Higgins, the Great* received the industry's Newbery Medal, an honor that in its 53 year history had never been awarded to a person of color. Since then, a growing number of Native American, African American, Latino, Asian American, gay, and lesbian authors and illustrators have been recognized for their outstanding and sometimes controversial contributions to the field.

CIBC was also instrumental in encouraging and supporting the early work of award-winning illustrators such as John Steptoe before the industry as a whole was willing to do so. In 1976, Leo and Diane Dillon were awarded the Caldecott Medal for the illustrations in *Why Mosquitoes Buzz in People's Ears* and they received the same honor in 1977 for the bold and innovative art in *Ashanti to Zulu*. They were the first illustrators of color to be awarded the Caldecott Medal, and it would be thirteen more years—not until 1990, when Ed Young received the award for *Lon Popo*—before another illustrator of color would be recognized by the Caldecott committee. David Diaz, honored in 1994 for *Smoky Nights*, is the most recent recipient of color.

The following is a list of children's book awards that have honored and supported creators and innovators in the field of multicultural children's literature. The criteria for many of the awards are similar: judges look for books that are well-written and/or illustrated, that inspire children and young adults. While each award has very specific submission criteria, many pay tribute to the bold creativity and challenging social realism portrayed in a growing number of books.

Along with major national and international awards, virtually every city and state in America now honors authors in the field of children's literature. Awards are often presented through local libraries, school districts, trade associations, and philanthropic societies.

AMERICAN BOOKSELLERS BOOK OF THE YEAR
American Booksellers Association
560 White Plains Road
Tarrytown, NY 10591

Known as the ABBY this award was established in 1991 to honor the book that American booksellers have most enjoyed handselling. Any book, regardless of reading level, is eligible to win. Booksellers from the ABA member stores nominate and then vote for the winning books. The award includes a cash award and an ABBY sculpture, and is presented annually at the ABA Convention. Although children's literature titles were awarded in 1991 and 1992, a separate children's category has been added.

AMERICA'S BOOK AWARD
Center for Latin America
University of Wisconsin
Milwaukee, WI 53211

In the last decade, an increasing number of junior and young adult books have appeared that portray Latin America, the Caribbean, or Latinos in the United States. To encourage and commend authors and publishers who produce these books, and to provide teachers with recommendations for classroom use, Consortium of Latin American Studies Programs (CLASP) initiated an annual children's and young adult book award with a recommended list of finalists. The 1994 Americas Book Award Winner was *The Mermaid's Twin Sister: More Stories from Trinidad* by Lynn Joseph, illustrated by Donna Perrone (Clarion Books 1994, ages 8 and up).

BOSTON GLOBE-HORN BOOK AWARDS
Children's Book Editor
The Boston Globe
P.O. Box 2378
Boston, MA 02107

This award is cosponsored by *The Boston Globe* and *The Horn Book* magazine. First presented in 1967, awards and honors are given for outstanding children's books published in the United States, written and designed to enrich the lives and imaginations of young readers. Over the years, the categories have changed from text and illustration to fiction, nonfiction, and picture books. Distinctive seals for book jackets are made available to publishers to honor and promote the winning books, and the books are displayed at *The Boston Globe's* annual book festival.

CARTER G. WOODSON BOOK AWARD
National Council for the Social Studies
3501 Newark Street, NW
Washington, DC 20016

This award was established in 1973 by the National Council for the Social Studies to honor Carter G. Woodson, a black historian and educator. The purpose of the award is to encourage the writing, publishing, and dissemination of outstanding social science books for young readers using subject matter that is related to ethnic minorities in a racially sensitive and accurate manner. Eligible books are nonfiction books with a U.S. setting, published in the U.S. during the preceding year.

CHILD STUDY CHILDREN'S BOOK AWARD
Child Study Children's Book Committee at Bank Street College of Education
610 West 112th Street
New York, NY 10025

Child Study Children's Book Award has been presented annually since 1943 to a book for children or young people which deals realistically

and in a positive way with problems in their world. Both fiction and nonfiction books are eligible. Books may be concerned with problems that are universal, such as war and poverty; personal problems such as family distress, divorce, or death; or problems with racism, classism, sexism, or disability. Books must also be realistic and written specifically for young readers. A committee of teachers, librarians, parents, authors, illustrators, and others experienced in working with children chooses the winning titles.

CHRISTOPHER AWARDS
The Christophers
12 East 48th Street
New York, NY 10017

The Christopher Awards have been presented since 1949, but a children's category was established in 1970. The annual award is given to authors and illustrators whose work is representative of the best achievements in the field. The criteria includes: affirmation of the highest values of the human spirit; artistic and technical proficiency; and a significant degree of public acceptance. Books are nominated by publishers with a panel of judges making the final decisions. Picture books, fiction, and nonfiction books are eligible.

CORETTA SCOTT KING AWARD
Social Responsibilities Round Table
American Library Association
50 East Huron Street
Chicago, IL 60611

The Coretta Scott King Award's purpose is to commemorate the life and works of the late Dr. Martin Luther King, Jr., to honor Mrs. King for her courage in continuing to fight for peace and social justice, to encourage creative writers and/or artists to promote the cause of brotherhood and peace through their work, and to inspire children and young adults to dedicate their talents and energies to help achieve these goals. The award was established in 1969 and is presented annually at the ALA conference. Since 1979, an additional award for illustration has been created. As part of the Coretta Scott King Award, the Genesis Award is given to authors of note who have published fewer than four books.

GOLDEN KITE AWARD
Society of Children's Book Writers and Illustrators
P.O. Box 66296
Mar Vista Station
Los Angeles, CA 90066

The Society of Children's Book Writers and
Illustrators has sponsored this annual award since
1973. Prior to 1977, the award was exclusively for
fiction works. In 1977, the competition grew to
include nonfiction titles and Honor Books. In
1982 a picture book/illustration category was
added. Members of The Society of Children's
Book Writers and Illustrators who have published
a children's or young adult title during the
preceding year are eligible to submit. Any work of
fiction or nonfiction for young readers that uses
art or photographs as a major part of the books is
eligible for the competition. Decisions are made
by a panel of children's book authors, illustrators,
editors, and librarians. The award is presented at
the Society's annual conference.

GOLD MEDALLION BOOK AWARD
Evangelical Christian Publishers Association
3225 South Hardy Drive, Suite 101
Tempe, AZ 85282

First presented in 1978, this award is given
annually to religious books in several categories,
including children's literature. Books published
during the preceding year are submitted by
publishers. The books are judged on the basis of
their relevance to Biblical truth in their content
and design, as established by the Evangelical
Christian Publishers Association. The winning
author receives the award at the annual CBA
International Convention.

HANS CHRISTIAN ANDERSON AWARDS
IBBY Secretariat
Nonneweg 12, Postfach
CH-4003
Basel, Switzerland

The Han's Christian Anderson Awards are given
biannually by the International Board on Books
for Young People (IBBY) and are considered to be
one of the most distinguished international prizes
for children's literature. Since 1956 the awards
are given to one writer and, since 1966, one
illustrator, who have made a lasting contribution
to literature for children and young people.
Originally, the prize was given for a particular

book. Since 1962, the prize takes into consideration an author's and/or illustrator's complete
works. The medalists are selected by an
international jury of children's literature experts.
Along with the medal winners, the jury may
also honor other candidates with a "highly
commended diploma."

HUNGRY MIND REVIEW CHILDREN'S BOOKS
OF DISTINCTION
Hungry Mind Review
1648 Grand Avenue
St. Paul, MN 55105

Established in 1991 by the *Hungry Mind Review*,
this listing honors outstanding books for young
readers from preschool age to young adults.
The titles are submitted by publishers and
recommended by booksellers, librarians,
educators, and others working in the field of
children's literature. Books must be published in
the U.S. for the first time in the proceeding year;
books must be compelling to children and adults;
should contain bold and fresh perspectives, be
sensitive to issues of culture and gender, and have
a lasting quality with special appeal to those
building a home library. Each year selections are
made in seven categories including fiction,
nonfiction, and picture books in three age/reader
levels. Poetry was added in 1995.

INTERNATIONAL READING ASSOCIATION
CHILDREN'S BOOK AWARD
800 Barksdale Road
Box 8139
Newark, DE 19714-8139

Established in 1975, this annual award is
presented to an author who has published no
more than two titles for a juvenile audience. The
winning book may be fiction or nonfiction for
children or young adults, and may be written in
any language. Starting in 1987, the award has
included two categories: one for a primary level
book and one for a young adult title. Books must
be submitted during the year of their publication.

JANE ADDAMS CHILDREN'S BOOK AWARD
Jane Addams Peace Association
77 United Nations Plaza
New York, NY 10017

This annual award was created in 1953 by the
United States section of the International League

645

for Peace and Freedom in honor of Jane Addams. The award's purpose is to give international recognition to a book that promotes the cause of peace, social justice, and world community. The awards also include Honor books. In 1993 a Picture Book category was added. The announcement of winning titles is made on September 6th, Jane Addams's birthday.

JANUSZ KORCZAK LITERARY AWARDS FOR CHILDREN'S BOOKS
Janusz Korczak Literary Award Committee
Anti-Defamation League of B'nai B'rith
823 United Nations Plaza
New York, NY 10017

Sponsored by the International Center for Holocaust Studies of the Anti-Defamation League of B'nai B'rith, this award was established in 1981. Books are judged on the way they exemplify the courage, humanitarianism, and leadership of Dr. Korczak, a Polish physician, educator, author, and orphan home administrator. Awards are given annually for books in two categories: fiction or nonfiction for young readers at the elementary or secondary school level, and books directed to parents and educators on the welfare and nurturing of children.

JEWISH BOOK COUNCIL NATIONAL JEWISH BOOK AWARDS
The Jewish Book Council
15 E 26th Street
New York, NY 10010

Of the nine categories of the Jewish Book Council Awards, two are for children's literature. Established in 1952, this award has been publicized under a variety of names depending on the donor of the funds for the award. The annual awards are given to books which combine literary merit with an affirmative expression of Jewish religious and/or cultural values. The author or translator must be a resident or citizen of the U.S. or Canada, although he/she may hold dual Israeli/U.S. or Israeli/Canadian citizenship. The book must be written and published in English.

JOAN FASSLER MEMORIAL BOOK AWARD
Association for the Care of Children's Health
7910 Woodmont Avenue, Suite 300
Bethesda, MD 20814

This award was established in 1989 to honor noted child psychologist and children's book author Joan Fassler. The award's purpose is to recognize outstanding contributions to children's literature that deals with hospitalization, illness, disabling conditions, dying, and death in a developmentally and age appropriate manner. The books submitted must be commercially published or released in English during the preceding two year period.

JOHN NEWBERY MEDAL
Association for Library Services to Children
American Library Association
50 East Huron Street
Chicago, IL 60611

Established in 1922, this award is named after the famous 18th-century publisher and seller of children's books, John Newbery. The Newbery Medal is presented annually to the author of the most distinguished contribution to American literature for children published in the United States in the proceeding year. The award is restricted to citizens or residents of the U.S. The recipient is chosen by a selection committee consisting of eight elected and seven appointed members from the ALSC.

MILDRED L. BATCHELDER AWARD
Association for Library Services to Children
American Library Association
50 East Huron Street
Chicago, IL 60611

This award was established in 1968 by the Children's Services Division, now known as the Association for Library Services to Children, of the ALA to honor Mildred L. Batchelder, an outstanding influence on children's librarianship and literature for over thirty years. The award's purpose is to encourage international exchange of quality children's books. The award is presented to an American publisher for the most outstanding English translation of a children's book that was originally published in a foreign language in a foreign country during the preceding year. A stipulation is that the translations not "Americanize" the book in either text or illustration. The award is presented annually on April 2nd, which is International Children's Book Day.

646

PARENTS' CHOICE AWARDS
P.O. Box 185
Waban, MA 02168
617/965-5913

First awarded in 1980, this children's literature award is sponsored by the Parents' Choice Foundation. The foundation selects the best and worst in children's toys, videos, books, TV programs, audios, movies, and video games utilizing a nationwide committee of over 3700 children, critics, parents, and pediatricians. The final selection is made by the Parents' Choice board.

SYDNEY TAYLOR BOOK AWARD
Association of Jewish Libraries
c/o National Foundation for Jewish Culture
330 Seventh Avenue, 21st Floor
New York, NY 10001

This annual award is sponsored by the Association of Jewish Libraries, and was established in 1968. It is awarded to the author and/or illustrator of a book determined to have made the greatest contribution in the field of Jewish literature for children published during the proceeding year. Fiction, nonfiction, and picture books for children and young adults are eligible.

RANDOLPH CALDECOTT MEDAL
Association for Library Services for Children
American Library Association
50 East Huron Street
Chicago, IL 60611

First awarded in 1938, the Caldecott Medal is given to an illustrator who creates the most distinguished picture book for children published in the U.S. during the proceeding year. The idea for the award was originated in 1937 by Frederic Melcher to honor Randolph Caldecott, an outstanding 19th century illustrator. The Section for Library Work with children of the ALA sponsors the program, and the Melcher family donates the medal. The Caldecott Medal Award and an Honor award are given for picture books in which the illustrations, rather than the text, are the heart and focus of the book. There are no age or reading level limitations on books submitted, however most illustrated picture books are intended for younger readers.

SKIPPING STONES BOOK AWARDS
Skipping Stones Magazine
P.O. Box 3939
Eugene, OR 97403-0939

Presented by *Skipping Stones Magazine*, an award-winning multicultural children's magazine, these awards have been presented since 1993 to authors and illustrators whose work addresses multicultural issues and/or environmental issues in children's literature. Books may also focus on global or social issues, non-violence, cultural and religious tolerance, community projects, environmental protection, ecology, conservation, etc. Books chosen have come from small and non-profit presses as well as well-known international publishers. A multicultural selection committee comprised of teachers, librarians, students, and *Skipping Stones* staff selects the winning titles.

THE WASHINGTON POST/CHILDREN'S BOOK GUILD NONFICTION AWARD
Established in 1977 by the Washington Children's Books Guild, this award for nonfiction children's literature is co-sponsored by *The Washington Post*. The award is presented to an author for the creation of a substantial body of outstanding nonfiction books. The winner is presented with a monetary award and a crystal cube at the Children's Book Week luncheon held annually in Washington, D.C.

UNICEF-EZRA JACK KEATS INTERNATIONAL AWARD
For Children's Book Illustration
(formerly USBBY-UNICEF Ezra Jack Keats Award)

This award, established in 1986, has been given in memory of the well-known children's author/illustrator, Ezra Jack Keats, to encourage outstanding artists to illustrate children's books. The biannual award is funded by the Ezra Jack Keats Foundation and administered by UNICEF. Any artist who has no more than five published children's books is eligible for this award, which is based on quality illustrations.

Resources

Compiled by Rosa E. Warder

We hope that the books, media materials, catalogues, and organizational references listed below will prove useful in identifying additional information and acquiring other resources.

CATALOGS

Arab World and Islamic Institute
Resources and School Services
(AWAIR) Catalogue
2095 Rose Street, Suite 4
Berkeley, CA 94709
(510)704-0517

A.L.A. Graphics - Catalog
American Library Association
50 E. Huron Street
Chicago, IL 60611
(800) 545-2433, (312) 836-9958

The Children's Book Bag
The Foundation for Children's
Books, Inc.,
30 Common Street,
Watertown, MA 02172
(617) 926-8190

The Children's Book Council Inc.
Materials Brochure & Summer
Reading and Incentive
Awards Program
568 Broadway, Suite 404
New York, NY 10012
(800)999-2160/(212)966-7509
FAX (212)966-2073

Continent Closeups - Map Discovery
Hammond Inc.,
515 Valley St.,
Maplewood, NJ 07040-1396
(201)763-6000/FAX (201)763-6558

Econo-Clad Books-Multicultural
Catalog
American Econo-Clad Services
P.O. Box 1777
Topeka, KS 66601
(800) 255-3502/(800) 628-2410

Ethnic Arts & Facts Catalog
Ethnic Arts & Facts

P.O. Box 20550
Oakland, CA 94620
(510) 465-0451/FAX (510) 465-7488

Knowledge Unlimited: Educational
Materials That Make a Difference
PO Box 52
Madison, WI 53701
(800) 356-2303/(608)836-6660,
FAX(608)831-1570
TDD (608)836-6767

The National Women's History
Project Catalog
National Women's History Project
7738 Bell Road
Windsor, CA 95492
(707) 838-6000
FAX (707) 838-0478

People of Every Stripe Catalog
P.O. Box 12505
Portland, OR 97212
(503) 282-0612

Special Needs Project: Good Books
about Disability Catalog
3463 State Street, #282
Santa Barbara, CA 93105
(800)333-6867-orders/(805)6834-
9633/FAX (805)683-2341

Teachers & Writers Collaborative
Catalog
Teachers & Writers Collaborative
5 Union Square West,
New York, NY 10003-3306
(212) 691-6590

The Whole Language Catalog by
Kenneth S. Goodman, Lois Bridges
Bird & Yvette Goodman
American School Publishers
1221 Farmers Lane, Suite C,
Santa Rosa, CA 95405
(707)578-3222

Women of Hope Poster Series
Bread and Roses Cultural
Project, Inc.
330 West 42nd Street, 15th Floor
New York, NY 10036
(212) 631-4565

MEDIA

Afro-Centric Black History
Video Program
24 Whittier Drive
Englishtown, NJ 07226
(908) 446-7218

Afro-AM Multicultural
Educational Materials
African American Images
1909 W. 9th Street, Dept. A-AM
Chicago, IL 60643
(800)552-1991/(312)445-0322
FAX (312)445-9844

Afropop! An Illustrated Guide to
Contemporary African Music
Sean Barlow & Banning Eyre
A Saraband Book
Book Sales, Inc.
114 Northfield Avenue
P.O. Box 7100
Edison, NJ 08818-7100
(908) 225-0530
FAX (908) 225-2257

Ashanti Publications
Afro-Centric Software Catalog
PO Box 2774
Antioch, CA 94531-2774
(800)757-5385/FAX (510) 757-6704

AudioFile: A Monthly Magazine of
Audiobook Reviews
37 Silver Street
POB 109
Portland, ME 04112-0109
(207) 774-7668/FAX (207) 775-3744

Children's Circle: Home Video
Based on Outstanding
Children's Books
389 Newtown Tpke
Weston, CT 06883-9989
(800) 243-5020
(203) 226-3355/FAX (203) 226-3818

Churchill Media
6901 Woodley Avenue
Van Nuys, CA 94106-4844
(800)334-7830/(818) 778-1978
FAX (818) 778-1994

Educational Video Center
55 East 25th Street
Suite 407
New York, NY 10010
(212) 725-3534/FAX (212)725-6501

The Family Video Guide
Terry & Catherine Catchpole
Williamson Publishing Co.
Box 185
Charlotte, VT 05445
(800) 234-8791

Film and Video Catalog - Published
Annually
Council on Foundations
1828 L. Street, NW
Washington, DC 20036
(202) 466-6512
FAX (202) 785-3926

First Run/Icarus Films - Films
and Videos
153 Waverly Place
New York, NY 10014
(800) 876-1710/(212) 989-7649

Highlander Collections
Highlander Center
1959 Highlander Way
New Market, TN 37208
(423)933-3443

Inter Image Video
PO Box 19951
Los Angeles, CA 90019-0951
(800) 843-9448

MECC: Educational Software
Catalogue
6160 Summit Drive

Minneapolis, MN 55430-4003
(800) 685-MECC/(612) 569-1640
(612)569-1551)

MPI - Video Catalog
16101 South 108th Avenue
Orland Park, IL 60462
(708) 873-3190
FAX (708) 460-0175

Multicultural Media Catalog
31 Hebert Road
Montpelier, VT 05602
(800) 550-9675/(802) 229-1834

National Educational
Media Network
655 13th Street
Oakland, CA 94612
(510) 465-6885/FAX (510) 465-2835

PARABOLA Storytime Series -
Audio Tapes
PARABOLA: The Magazine of
Myth and Tradition
656 Broadway
New York, NY 10012
(212) 505-6200/FAX (212) 979-7325

Read to Me! A Radio Book
Review for Kids
Featuring the Chenille Sisters
Produced by Borders Books
Check your local public radio sta-
tion for information.

Recorded Books Unabridged on
Audio Cassette
270 Skipjack Road
Prince Frederick, MD 20678
(800) 638-1304/FAX (410)535-5499

Recording for the Blind
20 Roszel Road
Princeton, NJ 08540
(800)221-4792

Resolution Inc./California
Newsreel - Film and Video
149 Ninth Street
San Francisco, CA 94103
(415) 621-6196/FAX (415) 621-6522

Videos for A Changing World
Turning Tide Productions
PO Box 864
Wendell, MA 01379
(800)557-6414

Videos for Understanding
Diversity: A Core Selection
and Evaluative Guide
American Library Association
50 East Huron Street
Chicago, IL 60611
(800)545-2433

Voyager Video Catalog
Voyager Video
P.O. Box 1122
Darien, CT 06820-1122
(800) 786-9248/(203) 655-1486

Wonderworks
WQED-TV
4802 5th Avenue
Pittsburgh, PA 15213
(800)262-8600/(412) 687-2990

ORGANIZATIONS

American Library Association
Publications Department
50 East Huron Street
Chicago, IL 60611
(312) 944-6780
FAX (312) 440-9374

Anti-Defamation League of B'nai
B'rith
Dept. JW
823 United Nations Plaza
New York, NY 11117
(212) 490-2525
FAX (212) 867-0779

Association for Supervision and
Curriculum Development
1250 North Pitt Street
Alexandria, VA 22314-9719
(703) 549-9110/(703) 549-3891

The Balch Institute for
Ethnic Studies
18 South 7th Street
Philadelphia, PA 19106
(215) 925-8090, ext. 224
(215) 925-8195

650

The Bay Area Global Education
Program (BAGEP)
312 Sutter Street, Suite 200
San Francisco, CA 94108
(415) 982-3263/FAX (415) 982-5028

California Tomorrow
Building B Ft. Mason Center
San Francisco, CA 94123
(415) 441-7631/(415) 441-7635

The Center for Media Education
1511 K Street, NW, Suite 518
Washington, DC 20005
(202) 628-2620
FAX (202) 628-2554

The Children's Book Council, Inc.
568 Broadway, Suite 404
New York, NY 10012
(212) 966-1990/(212) 966-2073

Children's Education Project
250 West 57th Street,
Suite 1527-130
New York, NY 10107
(212) 332-9675

The Children's Museum
300 Congress Street
Boston, MA 02210-1034
(617) 426-6500 ext.233
(617) 426-1944

CHIME (Clearinghouse for
Immigrant Education)
National Center for Immigrant
Studies
National Coalition of Advocates
for Students
100 Boylston Street, Suite 737
Boston, MA 02116
(800) 441-7192/(617) 357-8507
FAX (617) 357-9549

Consortium for Teaching Asia
and the Pacific in the Schools
(CTAPS)
East-West Center
1777 East-West Road
Honolulu, HI 96848
(808) 944-7768/(808) 944-7070

The Cooperative Children's
Book Center

4290 Helen C. White Hall
600 North Park Street
Madison, WI 53706
(608) 263-3720
FAX (608) 262-4933

Development Studies Center
2000 Embarcadero, Suite 305
Oakland, CA 94606
(800) 666-7270/(510) 464-3670

Educators for Social Responsibility
23 Garden Street
Cambridge, MA 02138
(617) 492-1764
FAX (617) 864-5164

ERIC Clearinghouse on Disabilities
and Gifted Education
The Council for Exceptional
Children
1920 Association Drive
Reston, VA 22901
(800) 328-2072

Everybody Wins Foundation, Inc.
165 East 56th Street
New York, NY 10022
(212) 832-3180/FAX (212) 832-3965

Facing History and Ourselves
25 16 Hurd Road
Brookline, MA 02146
(617) 232-1595

The Gay, Lesbian, and Straight
Teachers Network
122 West 26th Street, Suite 1100
New York, NY 10001
(212) 727-0135/FAX (212) 727-0254

International Reading Association
800 Barksdale Road
PO Box 8139
Neard, DE 19714-8319
(302) 731-1600/FAX (302) 731-1057

The Ms. Foundation For Women
141 Fifth Avenue, Suite 6S
New York, NY 10010
(212) 3535-8580/(212) 475-4217

National Association for
Multicultural Education
Multicultural Education Magazine

261 Bluemont Hall
Kansas State University
Manhattan, KS 66505
(913) 532-5797

National Black Child
Development Institute
1023 - 15th Street, N.W., Suite 600
Washington, DC 20005
(202) 387-1281/FAX (202) 234-1738

National Coalition Against
Censorship
275 Seventh Avenue
New York Ny 10001
(212) 807-6222
FAX (212) 807-6245

National Coalition of
Education Activists
PO Box 679
Rhinebeck, NY 12572 (Could not
find a number for them.)

National Library Service for the
Blind and Physically Handicapped
1291 Taylor Street, N.W.
Washington, DC 200542
(202) 707 5100
FAX (202) 707-0712

National Women's History Project
7738 Bell Road
Windsor, CA 95492
(707) 838-6000
FAX (707) 838-0478

National Writing Project
5627 Tolman Hall
School of Education
University of California
Berkeley, CA 94720
(510) 642-0963

Network of Educators on the
Americas (NECA)
Teaching for Change
Catalog/Newsletter
P.O. Box 73038
Washington, DC 20056-3038
(202) 806-7277
FAX (202) 806-7663

Primary Source
P.O. Box 381711

Cambridge, MA 02238-1711
(617) 661-8832/FAX (617) 661-6113

Project 10 (for Lesbian, Gay and
Bisexual Youth)
Fairfax High School
7850 Melrose Avenue
Los Angeles, CA 90046
(213) 651-5200

The REACH Center for Multicultural and Global Education
180 Nickerson Street
Suite 212
Seattle, WA 98109
(206) 284-8584/(206) 285-2037

Resources in Special Education
650 Howe Avenue, Suite 300
Sacramento, CA 95825
(800) 894-9799/(916) 971-7643
FAX (916) 641-5871

SEED (Seeking Educational
Equity and Diversity)
Wellesley College/Center for
Research on Women
Wellesley, MA 02181
(617) 283-2500

World Game Institute
3215 Race Street
Philadelphia, PA 19104
(215)387-0220/(215)387-3009 FAX

BOOKS FOR THE CLASSROOM
TEACHER

Librarians and parents may also find
some of these titles useful as well.

Affirming Diversity: The
Sociopolitical context of
Multicultural Education
Sonia Nieto
Longman Publishers
10 Bank Street
White Plains, NY 10606

American Indian Reference Books
for Children and Young Adults
Barbara J. Juipers
Libraries Unlimited
PO Box 3988
Englewood, CO 80155-3988

At the Essence of Learning:
Multicultural Education
Geneva Gay
Kappa Delta Pi
PO Box A
West Lafayette, IN 47907-1359

Basic Skills: Caucasian
Americans' Workbook
Beverly Slapin
Oyate
2702 Mathews Street
Berkeley, CA 94702

Becoming A Reflective Educator:
How to Build a Culture of
Inquiry in the Schools
John W. Brubacher and others
Corwin Press, Inc.
Sage Publication Company
2455 Teller Road
Thousand Oaks, CA 91320-2218

Books Alive: Using Literature
in the Classroom
Susan Hill
Peguis Publishers Limited
100-318 McDermot Avenue
Winnipeg, Manitoba
Canada R3A OA2

Building Communities of Learners:
A Collaboration Among Teachers,
Students, Families, and Community
Sudia Paloma McCaleb
St. Martin's Press, Inc.
175 Fifth Ave.
New York, NY 10010

Change/Education:
Issues in Perspective
Glenn Smith et al, Editors
LEPS Press
Northern Illinois University
Dekalb, IL 606115

Creating the Nonsexist Classroom:
A Multicultural Approach
Theresa Mickey McCormick
Teachers College Press
PO Box 20
Williston, VT 05495-0020

Culturally Responsive Pedagogy for
the 1990s and Beyond

Ana Maria Villegas
ERIC Clearing House on Teaching
and Teacher Education
One Dupont Circle NW, Suite 610
Washington, DC 20036-1186

Culturally Responsive Teaching
and Supervision: A Handbook for
Staff Development
C.A. Bowers and David J. Flinders
Teachers College Press
PO Box 20
Williston, VT 05495-0020

Diversity in Teacher Education:
New Expectations
Mary E. Dilworth, Editor
American Association of Colleges
for Teacher Education Publications
One Dupont Circle NW, Suite 610
Washington, DC 20036-1186

Diversity in the Classroom:
A Casebook for Teachers and
Teacher Educators
Judith H. Shulman and Amalia
Mesa-Bains, Editors
Research for Better Schools
444 N. Third Street
Philadelphia, PA 19123-4107

Drawing the Line: Tales of
Maps and Cartocontroversy
Mark Monmonier
Henry Holt and Company, Inc.
115 West 18th Street
New York, NY 10011

Educating for a Change
Rick Arnold, Bev Burke, Carl
James, D'Arcy Martin & Barb
Thomas
Between the Lines
394 Euclid Avenue
Toronto, Ontario
Canada M6G 2S9

Educating Teachers for
Cultural Diversity
Kenneth M. Zeichner
National Center for Research on
Teacher Learning
Michigan State University
116 Erickson Hall
East Lansing, MI 48824-1034

651

Embracing Diversity: Teachers'
Voices from California's
Classrooms
California Tomorrow/
Immigrant Students Project
Building B, Ft. Mason
San Francisco, CA 94123

Going Public: Schooling for A
Diverse Democracy
Judith Renyi
The New Press
450 West 41st Street
New York, NY 10036

Great Ideas in Education
Resource Center for
Redesigning Education
P.O. Box 818
Shelburne, VT 05482

Handbook of Research on
Multicultural Education
James A. Banks and Cherry A.
McGee Banks, Editors
MacMillan Reference
866 Third Avenue
New York, NY 10022

Julie and Brandon:
Our Blind Friends
National Federation of
the Blind of Idaho
1301 South Capitol Boulevard,
Suite C
Boise, ID 83706
(208) 343-1377

Multicultural America: A Resource
Book for Teachers of Humanities
and American Studies
Betty E.M. Ch'maj, Editor
University Press of America, Inc.
4720 Boston Way
Lanham, MD 20706

Multicultural Education,
Transformation and Action:
Historical and Contemporary
Perspectives
James A. Banks, Ed.
Teachers College Press
Box 20
Williston, VT 05495-0020

Multicultural Education: Strategies
for Linguistically Diverse Schools
and Classrooms
Deborah Menkart
Network of Educators
on the Americas
PO Box 73038
Washington, DC 20056-3083

Planning and Organization for
Multicultural Instruction
Gwendolyn C. Baker
Addison Wesley
2725 Sand Hill Road
Menlo Park, CA 94025

Ready-to-Use Multicultural
Activities for Primary Children
Saundrah Clark Grevious
The Center for Applied Research in
Education
Profession Publishing
West Nyack, NY 10995

Serving Linguistically and Culturally Diverse Students: Strategies for
the School Library Media Specialist
Melvina Azar Dame
Neal-Schuman Publishers, Inc.
100 Varick Street
New York, Ny 10013

Should I Go to the Teacher?
Developing A Cooperative
Relationship with Your Child's
School Community
Susan M. Benjamin & Susan
Sanchez
Heinemann
361 Hanover Street
Portsmouth, NH 03801-3912

Teaching to Transgress: Education
as the Practice of Freedom
bell hooks
Routledge
29 West 35th Street
New York, NY 10001

The Dreamkeepers: Successful
Teachers of African American
Children
Gloria Ladson-Billings
Jossey-Bass, Inc.
350 Sansome Street

San Francisco, CA 94104

MAGAZINES, NEWSPAPERS AND
PERIODICALS

BiRacial Child Magazine
Interrace, Inc.,
P.O. Box 12048
Atlanta, GA 30355
(404) 364-9690

Bookbird: World of
Children's Literature
Department of Foreign Languages
and Literatures
Purdue University
West Lafayette, IN 47907-1359
(317)494-0400/FAX (317)496-1700

Booklinks: Connecting Books,
Libraries and Classrooms
American Library Association
50 East Huron Street
Chicago, IL 60611
(800)545-2433

Children's Book Review
PO Box 5082
Brentwood, TN 37204-9767
(800) 543-7220

Creative Kids: The National
Voice for Kids
Prufrock Press
100 N. 6th Street, Suite 400
Waco, TX 76701
(800) 998-2208

Discovery
The Children's Book Council, Inc.
568 Broadway
New York, NY 10012
(800) 999-2160/(212) 966-2073

Educational Leadership Journal
Association for Supervision and
Curriculum Development
1250 North Pitt Street
Alexandria, VA 22314-9719
(703) 549-9110

Fast Forward: For Kids,
By Kids, About Kids
Opportune Press, Inc.,
232 E. Blithedale Avenue, Suite 210

652

Mill Valley, CA 94941
(415) 381-3463

Harambee: A Newspaper for Young
Readers That Focuses on the
African American Experience
Just Us Books, Inc.
301 Main Street, Suite 22-24
Orange, NJ 07050
(201) 6272-7701
FAX (201) 677-7570

Hungry Mind Review
1648 Grand Avenue
St. Paul MN 55105
(612) 699-2610
FAX (612) 699-0970

JAM: Junior America's Magazine
Children's Education Project
250 West 57th Street,
Suite 1527-130
New York, NY 10107
(212) 332-9675

Je Bouquine
(A French Literary Magazine for
Young Readers)
Bayard Press Juene
BP1 Cedex
Paris, France 99505

Lion and the Unicorn: A Critical
Journal of Children's Literature
Johns Hopkins University Press
2715 North Charles Street
Baltimore, MD 21218-4319
(800) 548-1784/(410) 516-6987
FAX (410) 516-6968

Multicultural Review
Greenwood Publishing Group, Inc.
88 Post Road W.,
P.O. Box 5007
Westport, CT 06881-5007
(203)226-3571

Native Peoples Magazine
5333 North Seventh Street,
Suite C-224
Phoenix, AZ 85067-6820
(602) 252-2236/FAX (602) 265-3113

Quarterly Black Review of Books
625 Broadway - 10th Floor

New York, NY 10012
(212) 475-1010

Rethinking Schools: An Urban
Education Journal
1001 E. Keefe Avenue
Milwaukee, WI 53212
(414) 964-9646

Show Me A Story: Family Literacy
Alliance Magazine
WGBH-TV
125 Western Avenue
Boston, MA 01234
(617) 492-2777

Skipping Stones: A Multicultural
Children's Magazine
P.O.Box 3939
Eugene, OR 97403
(503) 342-4946

Stone Soup: The Magazine
By Children
The Children's Art Foundation
915 Cedar Street
Santa Cruz, CA 95060
(800) 447-4569

Teaching Tolerance Magazine
Southern Poverty Law Center
400 Washington Avenue
Montgomery, AL 36104
(334) 264-0286

Through Our Eyes
A Journal of Youth Writing
Many Cultures Publishing
PO Box 425646
San Francisco, CA 94142-5646
(800) 484-4173, ext. 1073

Storytelling
Books and Other Publications
About Storytelling

About Story: Writings on Stories
and Storytelling 1980-1994
Ruth Stotter
Stotter Press
PO Box 726
Stinson Beach, CA 94970

Multicultural Folktales: Stories to
Tell Young Children

Oryx Press
4041 Central Avenue
Phoenix, AZ 85012-3397

The Parent's Guide to Storytelling:
How to Make Up New Stories and
Retell Old Favorites
Margaret Read MacDonald
Harper Collins (1995)
10 East 53rd Street
New York, NY 10022

New Handbook for Storytellers:
Stories, Poems, Magic, and More
Caroline Feller Bauer
American Library Association
50 East Huron
Chicago, IL 60611

Tales as Tools: The Power of Story
in the Classroom
The National Storytelling Center
National Storytelling Press
PO Box 309
Jonesborough, TN 37659

Tell Me Another: Storytelling and
Reading Aloud at Home, at School,
and in the Community
Bob Barton
Pembroke Publishers
538 Hood Road
Markham, Ontario
Canada LR3 3K9

Why are These Storytellers So
Happy? — A Catalogue of Story-
telling and Folklore
Books and Audio
August House
PO Box 3223
Little Rock, AK 72203-3223
(501) 372-5450/(501) 0372-5579

STORYTELLING ORGANIZATIONS
AND RESOURCES

National Storytelling Center
PO Box 309
Jonesboro, TN
(800) 525-4514/(423) 753-2171

Directory of California Storytellers
Bay Area Storytellers
1 Rochdale Way

Berkeley, CA 94708
(510) 525-1533

National Association of Black Storytellers, Inc
PO Box 67722
Baltimore, MD 21215
(410) 947-1117

1996 National Storytelling Directory
National Storytelling Center
PO Box 309
Jonesboro, TN
(800)525-4514/(423) 753-2171

Rabbit Ears Radio
Rabbit Ears Productions
131 Rowayton Avenue
Towayton, CT 06853
(203) 857-3760/(203) 857-3777

Storyline – A Publication of the Bay
Area Storytelling Festival
1 Rochdale Way
Berkeley, CA 94708
Storytime Books
A Series on PBS/Produced by KCET
4401 Sunset Boulevard
Los Angeles, CA 90027
(213) 666-6500

The Storyteller's Calendar: For
Lovers of Folk-Art and Folktales
Ruth Stotter
Stotter Press
PO Box 726
Stinson Beach, CA 94970
(800) 637-2256/(415) 435-
3568/FAX (415) 435-9923

24-Hour Talking Book Directory
1-800-BOOKS-PW

BOOKS ON CHILDREN'S LITERATURE

*A Guide to Non-Sexist Children's
Books, Volume II: 1976-1985*
Denise Wilms and Ilene Cooper,
Editors
Academy Chicago Publishers
425 North Michigan Avenue
Chicago, IL 60611

*Against Borders: Promoting Books for
A Multicultural World*

Hazel Rochman
American Library Association
50 East Huron Street
Chicago, IL 60611

*Alerta: A Multicutlural, Bilingual
Approach to Teaching Young
Children*
Addison-Wesley Longman, Inc.
1 Jacob Reading Way
Reading, MA 01867
(617) 844-3700/FAX (617) 944-
8243

*Appreciating Diversity Through Chil-
dren's Literature*
*Teaching and Planning Activities for
the Primary Grades*
Meredith McGowan, Tom
McGowan and Pat Wheeler
Teacher Ideas Press/Libraries
Unlimited
PO Box 6633
Englewood, CO 80155-6633

*Battling Dragons: Issues and Contro-
versy in Children's Literature*
Susan Lehr
Heinemann
361 Hanover Street
Portsmouth, NH 03801

*Behind the Covers: Interviews with
Authors and Illustrators of Books for
Children and Young Adults*
Jim Roginisk
Libraries Unlimited
PO Box 3988
Englewood, CO 80155-3988

*Beyond Dolls & Guns: 101 Ways to
Help Children Avoid Gender Bias*
Susan Hoy Crawford
Heinemann
361 Hanover Street
Portsmouth, NH 03801-3912

*The Black American in Books for
Children: Readings in Racism*
Edited with an Introduction by
Donnarae MacCann and Gloria
Woodard
The Scarecrow Press
Division of Grolier Education

Corporation
52 Liberty Street/Box4176
Metuchen, NJ 08840

*Books Without Bias: A Guide to Eval-
uating Children's Literature for
Handicapism*
Beverly Slapin
Squeaky Wheel Press
75 Desoto Street
San Francisco, CA 94127

*Children and Books I: African Ameri-
can Story Books and Activities for All
Children*
Patricia Buerke Moll
Hampton Mae Institute
4104 Lynn Avenue
Tampa, FL 33603

*Children's Literature: An Issues
Approach*
Masha Kabakow Rudman
Longman Publishers
10 Bank Street
White Plains, NY 10606

*Contemporary Spanish Speaking
Writers and Illustrators for
Children and Young Adults:
A Biographical Dictionary*
Greenwood Press
88 Post Road, West
Westport, CT 06881

*Cultural Connections: Using
Literature to Explore World
Cultures with Children*
Ron Joe
Pembroke Publishers
538 Hood Road
Markham, Ontario
Canada L3R 3K9

*Dealing with Diversity through Multi-
cultural Fiction: Library
Classroom Partnerships*
Lauri Johnson and Sally Smith,
Editors
American Library Association
50 East Huron
Chicago, IL 60611

*Experiences with Literature: A
Thematic Whole Language Model*

for the K-3 Bilingual Classroom
Sandra Nevarez, Raquel C. Mireles,
& Norma Ramierz
Addison-Wesley Longman, Inc.
1 Jacob Reading Way
Reading, MA 01867
(617) 844-3700/FAX (617) 944-
8243

*Fairytales and Fables from
Weimar Days*
Edited and Translated by
Jack Zipes
University Press of New England
Hanover, NH 03755

*Globalchild: Multicultural Resources
for Young Children*
Maureen Chech
Addison-Wesley Longman, Inc.
1 Jacob Reading Way
Reading, MA 01867
(617) 844-3700/FAX (617) 944-
8243

Guide to Multicultural Resources
1993/94
Edited by Charles Taylor
Highsmith Press
W5527 Highway 106
Ft. Atkinson, WI 53538-0800

*How to Tell The Difference: A Check-
list for Evaluating Children's Books
for Anti-Indian Bias*
Beverly Slapin, Doris Seale and
Rosemary Gonzales
New Society Publishers
4527 Springfield Avenue
Philadelphia, PA 19143

*Joyous Journeys with Books:
Multicultural Explorations*
M.A. Helshe and A.B. Kirchner
Teacher Ideas Press/Libraries
Unlimited
Po Box 3988
Englewood, CO 80155-3988

*Kaleidoscope: A Multicultural Book-
list for Grades K-8*
Rudine Sims Bishop, Editor
National Council of Teachers of
English
1111 W. Kenyon Road

Urbana, IL 61801-1096

*Immigrants in the U.S. in Fiction: A
Guide to 705 Books for Librarians
and Teachers, K-9*
McFarland and Company
PO Box 611
Jefferson, NC 28640

*Lift Every Voice: Guide to the 400
Best Children's Multicultural Books*
by Anna Dunwell
Multicultural and Minority Source
Materials Company
16 Park Lane
Newton Centre, MA 01259

*Light A Candle! The Jewish
Experience in Children's Books*
The New York Public Library
455 Fifth Avenue
New York, NY 10016

*Literary Maps for Young Adult
Literature*
Mary Ellen Snodgrass
Libraries Unlimited
PO Box 6633
Englewood, CO 80155-6633

*Multicultural Voices in
Contemporary Literature: A Resource
for Teachers*
Frances Ann Day
Heinemann
361 Hanover Street
Portsmouth, NH 03801-3912
(800) 541-2086/FAX (800) 847-
0983

*Multicultural Literature for
Children and Young Adults*
Ginny Moore Kruse and
Kathleen T. Horning
Cooperative Children's Book Center
University of Wisconsin-Madison
600 North Park Street
Madison, WI 53706
(608) 263-3720

Multicultural Projects Index
M.A. Pilger
Libraries Unlimited
PO Box 3988
Englewood, CO 80155-3988

*National Association for
Multicultural Education*
1993 & 1994 Proceedings
Edited by Carl Grant
Caddo Gap Press (1995)
3145 Geary Boulevard, Suite 275
San Francisco, CA 94118

*Our Families, Our Friends, Our
World: An Annotated Guide to
Significant Multicultural Books for
Children and Teenagers*
Lyn Miller-Lachmann
RR Bowker
121 Chanlon Road
New Providence, NJ 07974

*Public Library Services to Visually
Disabled Children*
S.G. Basu
McFarland Publishers
Box 611
Jefferson, NC 28640

*Reading About Japan: A
Bibliography of Japanese
Children's Literature*
Naomi Wakan
Pacific Rim Publishers
Box 5204,
Victoria, British Columbia
Canada V8R 6N4

*Reading Rainbow Guide to
Children's Books:
The 101 Best Titles*
Twila C. Liggett and Cynthia Mayer
Benfield
Citadel Press (1994)
600 Madison Avenue
New York, NY 10022

Signing
Elaine Costello
Bantam Books (1983)
666 Fifth Avenue
New York, NY 10103

*Silent About Us: An Annotated Bibli-
ography Focusing on Inuit Culture*
Paul Ongtooguk
University of Alaska
School of Education
PO Box 756480
Fairbanks, AL 99775-06480

656

Teaching Children's Literature:
A Resource Guide with A Directory
of Courses
Anne H. Lundin and
Carol W. Cubberly
McFarland & Company, Inc.
Box 611
Jefferson, NC 26840

Teaching Multicultural Literature
in Grades K-8
Edited by Violet J. Harris
Christopher-Gordon Publishers
480 Washington Street
Norwood, MA 02062

Telling Tales: The Pedagogy and
Promise of African American
Literature for Youth
Dianne Johnson
Greenwood Press
88 Post Road West
Westport, CT 06881

This Land is Our Land: A Guide to
Multicultural Children's Literature
for Children and Young Adults
Alethea Helbig and Agnes Perkins
Greenwood Publishers
88 Post Road West
Westport, CT 06881

Through Indian Eyes: The Native
Experience in Books for Children
Beverly Slapin and Doris Seale
New Society Publishers
4527 Springfield Avenue
Philadelphia, PA 19143

Today's Children's Books:
An Annotated Bibliography of
Non-Stereotyped Picture Books
Feminist Press
City University of New York
311 East 94th Street
New York, NY 10128

Understanding Abilities,
Disabilities, and Capabilities:
A Guide to Children's Literature
Margaret F. Carlin, Jeannine K.
Laughlin, Richard. D. Saniga
Libraries Unlimited
PO Box 6633
Englewood, CO 80155-6633
Venture into Cultures: A Resource
Book of Multicultural Materials
and Programs
Carla D. Hayden, Editor
American Library Association
50 East Huron Street
Chicago, IL 60611

Webbing with Literature: Creating
Story Maps with Children's Books
Karen D'Angelo Bromley
Allyn and Bacon
160 Gould Street
Needham Heights, MA 02194

Windows on the World:
Multicultural Festivals for
Schools and Libraries
Alan Heath
Scarecrow Press/Division of
Grolier Education Corporation
52 Liberty Street/Box 4167
Metuchen, NJ 08840

LEXICONS

Indian Terms of the Americas
Lotsee Patterson and Mary Ellen
Snodgrass
Libraries Unlimited, Inc.
PO Box 6633
Englewood, CO 80155-6633

The Dictionary of Bias Free Usage:
A Guide to Nondiscriminatory
Language
Rosalie Maggio
Oryx Press
4041 North Central Avenue,
Suite 700
Phoenix, AZ 85012-3397

Dictionary for Multicultural
Education
Carl Grant and Gloria Ladsing
Billings
Oryx Press
4041 North Central Avenue,
Suite 700
Phoenix, AZ 85012-3397

SOURCES FOR BOOK
TRANSLATIONS

Culturgrams
Kennedy Center Publications
PO Box 24538
Brigham Young University
Provo, Utah 84602-4538
(800) 528-6279/FAX (801) 378-7075

Index Translationum
UNESCO
Division de la Promotion
et des Ventes
7 Place de Fontenoy
75352, Paris 07 SP, France
FAX (331)42 73 30 07

Living Books Series
Broderbund
500 Redwood Boulevard
Novato, CA 94948-6121
(800)821-6263

Rosa Emilia Warder is an artist
and writer living in Oakland,
California. Her work centers on
issues of importance to women,
children, and bi-cultural peoples.
She is the writer and illustrator of
three children's picture books,
and is at work on a youth novel.

Special Library Collections

WE WANTED TO HIGHLIGHT A FEW OF THE private and academic libraries that house special children's literature collections. While we have not listed historical societies, do keep in mind that these often have a library or resource center worth using for research or for class field trips.

Avery Research Center for Afro-American
History and Culture
College of Charleston
66 George Street
Charleston, SC 29424-001
Ph. (803) 727-2009 Fax (803) 727-2017

Avery is primarily devoted to maintaining documentation on Africans and African Americans and the culture of South Carolina and the Sea Islands of Georgia. Along with extensive reference services to scholars and lay historians, the center provides special workshops, lectures, and outreach programs for children and young adults. Children and adults form the Sea Island communities also provide plays, programs, and events that reflect the rich history and ongoing cultural evolution of the area.

Center for the Study of Books in Spanish for
Children and Adolescents
California State University
San Marcos, California 92096-0001
Ph. (619) 750-4070 Fax (619) 750-4073

The Center serves educators, librarians, counselors, and publishers in the United States, Mexico, Spain, and Latin America. It also publishes special bibliographies, holds seminars, and conducts workshops. The Center sponsors a Cafes Literarios series, focusing on informal discussions about books in Spanish and books in English about Hispanics/Latinos for children and adolescents.

Education Resource Information Center (ERIC)
ERIC Clearing House on Rural Education and
Small Schools
P.O. Box 1348
Charleston, WV 25325-1348
Ph. (800) 624-9120 Fax (304) 347-0487

ERIC was founded in 1966 to collect, prepare, and preserve books, documents, and articles about American Indians, Alaska Natives, Mexican Americans, and migrant workers. They also maintain an electronic database on outdoor education programs and small schools, produce over 20 publications annually, and provide a toll-free bulletin board service. Primarily used by educators and educational agencies, the library does not serve children directly, but does provide essential information on multicultural education and resources nationwide.

The Kerlan Collection
Children's Literature Research Collections (CLRC)
The University of Minnesota
109 Walter Library
117 Pleasant Street S.E.
Minneapolis, MN 55455
(612) 624-4576

The Kerlan collection is named after Dr. Irvin Kerlan, an alumni of the University of Minnesota. Dr. Kerlan began collecting children's books in his home in 1946, and in 1949 donated the nucleus to the university to began his dream of a center of research devoted to children's literature. Upon his death in 1963, the balance of his collection became the property of the university and has since grown to approximately 40,000 volumes dating from the mid-1800s. Over 7,000 children's books are represented by original manuscripts and illustrations, donated by several hundred authors and illustrators. The carefully cataloged and preserved collection is often curated for traveling exhibits throughout the world. The CLRC also publishes a newsletter four times a year, highlighting recent acquisitions to the collection, coming events, exhibits, and information of interest about the field.

The Marguerite Archer Collection of Historic
Children's Materials
J. Paul Leonard Library
San Francisco State University (ASFSU)
1630 Holloway Avenue
San Francisco, CA 94132
(415) 338-1856

The Archer Collection was accumulated by a former teacher and librarian from Pennsylvania, who moved to San Francisco in the 1970s. In 1982, she gave SFSU over 3,500 items relating to children's literature spanning the period from the early nineteenth century to the 1980s. Since then, the collection has more than doubled in size. It is considered to be a major scholarly resource showing the progressive development and growth of children's literature. The collection also emphasizes materials which document or reflect the life, history, and culture of the San Francisco Bay Area. The collection includes a scrapbook produced by Japanese American school children interred at Posten, Arizona, called *Out of the Desert*.

The William Tucker Collection of Black Authors and Black Illustrators
North Carolina Central University
School of Library Information Services
Durham, North Carolina
Ph. (919) 560-5213 Fax (919) 560-6402

North Carolina Central University's William Tucker Collection of Black Authors and Illustrators is made up of eleven separate repositories. Named for William Tucker, believed to be the first black child born in America, the collection's emphasis is on

books written about black children. While each repository is unique unto itself, the overall collection consists of working drafts, sketches, typescripts, galleys, correspondence, and autographed books from authors and illustrators including Ashley Bryan, Alexis De Veaux, Elton C, Fax, Tom Feelings, Lorenz Bell Graham, Eloise Greenfield, Sharon Bell Mathis, and Charlemae Hill Rollins.

University of Oregon
Department of Special Collections
The Knight Library
1299 University of Oregon
Eugene, OR 97403-1299
Ph. (541) 346-1904 Fax (541) 346-1882

This collection contains original manuscripts, correspondence, production files, editorial materials, publicity materials, reviews, and ephemera from writers and editors including Yoshiko Uchida, Dorothy Sterling, Eva Rutland, and Barbara Nolen Strong.

Notable Bookstores

THE INDEPENDENT BOOK STORES LISTED HERE, and others in your community, should be applauded and supported for their heroic efforts to provide quality books in unique settings for their communities. The independent book store has long served as a gathering place and distribution point for ideas, culture, information, political discourse, and, of course, literature. In an era in which we commute to work and school, shop by catalog or warehouse, and spend considerable time in front of our TVs and VCRs, our sense of community and neighborhood have become fragmented. The small independent book stores can fill the vacuum left by the demise of the general store and the town hall.

Some of these stores are housed in community and cultural centers or affiliated with religious and/or spiritual organizations, museums, and schools. Others are clearly a part of business districts in African American, Latino, and Asian communities. Few enjoy the privilege of being housed in affordable facilities that provide enough space for books and events.

Since the early 1960s, independent bookstores have made their mark carrying self-published, controversial, politically radical, and ethnic books from small presses that the larger and chain stores often overlook. It was through the efforts of these small, often politically and culturally based stores that these books established a presence, gained a significant readership, and eventually secured recognition in the publishing world.

Many of the stores that sustained and nurtured the rich literary culture now available across the country have closed their doors over the past decades: Micheaux's and Liberation in New York City, Drum and Spear in Washington, D.C., and A Woman's Place Collective in Oakland, CA. Aquarius, a West Coast literary staple for more than three decades, was burned out during the 1992 rebellions in Los Angeles. While stores have closed due to a natural progression of the owners' interests and needs, many have been unable to survive financially next to the chain books stores that are springing up around them. Over one-third of the bookstores in existence when we started this project in 1993 are no longer in business.

The following stores carry a substantial selection of multicultural children's literature. While this is by no means a definitive list, it is a representative sampling of stores throughout the country that have been recommended by parents, teachers, librarians, and young readers.

AFIKOMEN: JEWISH BOOKS AND ARTS
3042 Claremont Ave.,
Berkeley, CA 94705
Ph. (510) 655-1977
Fax: (510) 655-3598

Storytelling time - *Yes*
Designated Area - *Yes*
Literary events include children's authors/illustrators - *Yes occasionally*
Book clubs and/or classes - *No*
Educational materials, games puzzles, dolls, etc. - *Yes*
Wheelchair accessible -*Yes*
Newsletter - *No*
CD ROMS, videos, books, and tape - *Yes*
Special Services bilingual staff - English/Hebrew/French/Spanish/Arabic

Afikomen features books that accent Judaism as a culture. They have a children's section with tables, chairs, and toys. Their youth collection includes books about where Judaism and other cultures connect in the world among all peoples of the Diaspora and on all continents. They also carry an extensive music collection.

BANK STREET BOOK STORE
610 West 112th St.,
New York, NY 10025
Ph. (212) 678-1654
Fax (212) 316-7026

Storytelling time - *Yes*
Designated Area - *Yes*
Literary events include children's authors/illustrators - *Yes*
Book clubs and/or classes - *No*
Educational materials, games puzzles, dolls, etc. - *Yes*
Wheelchair accessible - *Yes*
Newsletter - *Yes, Monthly*
CD ROMS, videos, books, and tape - *Yes*
Special Services - *No*

Known nationwide for its extensive collection of multicultural children's books. Bank Street prides itself on presenting a vast array of topics and cultures for their young readers. They also publish a monthly newsletter featuring new titles, classics, and reviews for kids by kids. Other features are an impressive collection of educational materials for parents and teachers, and their mail order catalogue service.

BLACKBIRD BOOKS
1316 East Pike St.,
Seattle, WA, 98122
(206) 325-3793

Storytelling time - *Yes*
Designated Area - *Yes*
Literary events include children's authors/illustrators - *No*
Book clubs and/or classes - *Yes*
Educational materials, games puzzles, dolls, etc. - *Yes*
Wheelchair accessible - *Yes*
Newsletter - *No*
CD ROMS, videos, books, and tape - *Yes*
Special Services: *No*

With a focus on books pertaining to "Black culture," Blackbird features an extensive children's selection including puzzles, games, cards, and workbooks. Their literary events include children's book authors and illustrators, poetry readings, and a class series on black history for older children and teens.

BLACK BOOKS PLUS
702 Amsterdam Ave.,
New York, NY 10025
(212) 749-9632

Storytelling time - *No*
Designated Area - *Yes*
Literary events include children's authors/illustrators - *No*
Book clubs and/or classes - *No*
Educational materials, games puzzles, dolls, etc. - *Yes*
Wheelchair accessible - *Yes*
Newsletter - *No*
CD ROMS, videos, books, and tape - *Yes*
Special Services - *No*

Black Books Plus specializes in African American, African, and African Caribbean literature and culture. Their comprehensive children's corner includes books, games, educational workbooks, tapes, and videos. The store regularly hosts author talks and book signings.

BLACK IMAGES BOOK BAZAAR
230 Wynnewood Village
Dallas, TX 75224
Ph. (214) 943-0142
Fax (214) 943-5451

Storytelling time - *Yes*
Designated Area - *Yes*
Literary events include children's authors/illustrators - *Yes*
Book clubs and/or classes - *Yes* (Writing, Journals, Drama)
Educational materials, games puzzles, dolls, etc. - *Yes*
Wheelchair accessible - *Yes*
Newsletter - *Yes*
CD ROMS, videos, books, and tape - *Yes*
Special Services: Britt Miller, storytell and author, conducts summer workshops here on writing and other forms of expression.

Specializing in African, African American, and African Caribbean literature and culture, their selection includes posters, greeting cards, music, videos, games and periodicals. The children's section is extensive for readers preschool through young adult. The store also hosts frequent lectures, slide shows and book signings by prominent and up-and-coming authors.

EDICIONES UNIVERSAL
3090 S.W. 8th St.,
Miami, Florida, 33135
Fax (305) 642-7978

Storytelling time - *No*
Designated Area - *Yes*
Literary events include children's authors/illustrators - *No*
Book clubs and/or classes - *No*
Educational materials, games, puzzles, dolls, etc. - *No*
Wheelchair accessible - *Yes*
Newsletter- *Yes, Children's Catalog*

660

CD ROMS, videos, books, and tape - *Yes*
Special Services - *No*

A bookstore and catalog distributor that exclusively handles Spanish language books, Ediciones Universal's selection represents authors from all Spanish speaking countries. Located in Miami, they feature many titles from Cuba.

EVERYONE'S PLACE BOOKSTORE
Afrikan Cultural Center
1356 W. North Avenue
Baltimore, MD 21217
Ph. (410) 728-0877
Fax (410) 383-0511

Storytelling time - *Yes*
Designated Area - *Yes*
Literary events inlcude children's authors/illustrators - *Yes*
Educational materials, games, puzzles, dolls - *Yes*
Wheelchair Accessible - *Yes*
Newsletter - *No*
CD ROMS, videos, books, and tape - *Yes*
Special Services - *No*

As an integral part of a thriving cultural center, Everyone's Place specializes in books by and about African, African Caribbean, and African American peoples. It boasts a collection of 1,000 titles for children. The store hosts many cultural and literary events in the community center. They also have an extensive selection of videos, story tapes, and games.

FOLKTALES
1806 Nueces St.,
Austin, Texas 78701
(512) 472-5657

Storytelling time - *Yes*
Designated Area - *Yes*
Literary events include children's authors/illustrators - *No*
Book clubs and/or classes - *Yes*
Educational materials, games, puzzles, dolls, etc. - *Yes*
Wheelchair accessible - *No*
Newsletter - *Yes*
CD ROMS, videos, books, and tape - *Yes*
Special Services - *No*

Known as "Austin's African American Literature Shop," Folktales is an all-encompassing book store. As well as a large children's book collection, they offer children's story hour, a teen "read-and-rap" group, a newsletter, open mic poetry readings, and numerous workshops.

HANEEF'S BOOKSTORE
911 Orange St.,
Wilmington, DE 19801
Ph. (302) 656-4193
Fax (302) 657-2106

Storytelling time - *No*
Designated Area - *Yes*
Literary events include children's authors/illustrators - *No*
Book clubs and/or classes - *Yes*
Educational materials, games, puzzles, dolls, etc. - *Yes*
Wheelchair accessible - *No*
Newsletter - *No*
CD ROMS, videos, books, and tape - *No*
Special Services - sign language, bilingual staff, housed in cultural/community center.

Housed in a culture center called Freedom Plaza 1, Haneef's features African American literature and periodicals. The children's section includes a wide array of books, puzzles, games, videos, and audio tapes.

HUE-MAN EXPERIENCE
911 Park Ave. W.
Denver, CO 80205-2601
(800) 346-4036/(303) 293-2665
Fax (303) 293-0046

Storytelling time - *Yes*
Designated Area - *Yes*
Literary events include children's authors/illustrators - *Yes*
Book clubs and/or classes - *Yes, for adults only*
Educational materials, games, puzzles, dolls, etc. - *Yes*
Wheelchair accessible - *No*
Newsletter - *Yes, quarterly*
CD ROMS, videos, books, and tape - *Yes*
Special Services - Special Kwanza story hours in December and gift making workshops for children.

Regularly hosts classes from the local schools at the store for story-hour and for African American cultural information sessions.

Known as the largest black bookstore, Hue-Man Experience has over 4,500 titles and carries an impressive selection of children's books, audio tapes, video tapes, and games that feature African, African American, and African Caribbean authors and illustrators. They also publish a newsletter, "*The African American Connection*" that features new titles and author interviews, and offers catalog purchasing.

MAMA BEAR'S BOOKSTORE
6536 Telegraph Ave.
Oakland, CA 94611
Ph. (510) 428-9684
Fax (510) 654-2774

Storytelling time- *No*
Designated Area - *Yes*
Literary events include children's authors/illustrators-*No*
Book clubs and/or classes-*No*
Educational materials, games, puzzles, dolls, etc. - *Yes*
Wheelchair accessible - *Yes*
Newsletter- *Yes*
CD ROMS, videos, books, and tape - *Yes*
Special Services - *Yes, Spanish bilingual staff*

A unique women's bookstore, coffee house, and gift shop, Mama Bear's is a gathering place for the East Bay women's community. It boasts a comprehensive and unusual children's collection. Many titles focus on family and social relationships, ethnic diversity, adoption, disability, and sexual preference. They also publish an informative newsletter including book reviews and notices for literary, cultural, and community events.

MARCUS BOOKS
1712 Fillmore St.
San Francisco, CA
(415) 346-4222

Storytelling time - *No*
Designated Area - *Yes*
Literary events include children's
authors/illustrators - *Yes*
Book clubs and/or classes - *No*
Educational materials, games,
puzzles, dolls, etc. - *Yes*
Wheelchair accessible - *Yes*
Newsletter - *No*
CD ROMS, videos, books, and tape - *Yes*
Special Services - *No*

Marcus Books was founded in
1960. Marcus specialize in books
"by and about Black people." Their
large selection of children's literature includes books for toddlers
through young adults. The store
regularly hosts authors' talks and
book signings.

PACIFIC WESTERN TRADERS
305 Wool St.,
Folsom, CA 95630
(916) 985-3851

Storytelling time - *No*
Designated Area - *Yes*
Literary events include children's
authors/illustrators - *No*
Book clubs and/or classes - *No*
Educational materials, games,
puzzles, dolls, etc. - *Yes*
Wheelchair accessible - *Yes*
Newsletter - *No*
CD ROMS, videos, books, and tape - *Yes*
Special Services: *Yes* - PWT also
serves as an art gallery for Native
American artists and as a craft
supplies store.

A resource center for Native American arts, traditional supplies, and
educational media, Pacific Western
Traders also has an extensive collection of Native literature. In the tradition of Native peoples, few books
are set aside as being simply for
children, rather all stories, myths,
folktales, and traditions are meant
for all members of the family and
community. This center carries

both "children's titles" and general
literature of native peoples. They
also display contemporary and traditional arts and crafts, and hold
demonstrations and exhibits.

ROOTS & WINGS CULTURAL BOOKPLACE
1345 Carter Hill Road
Montgomery, AL 36106
Ph. (334) 262-1700
Fax (334) 262-8498

Storytelling time - *Yes*
Designated Area - *Yes*, The Carter
G. Woodson Educational Theater
Literary events include children's
authors/illustrators - *Yes*
Book clubs and/or classes - *Yes*
"Freespirits Book Club"
Educational materials, games,
puzzles, dolls, etc. - *Yes*
Wheelchair accessible - *Yes*
Newsletter - *Yes, The African
American Connection*
CD ROMS, videos, books, and tape - *Yes*

Exclusively featuring literature from
the African Diaspora. Their children's section, known as "Anchor
Square" is a comfortable area with
tables, chairs, and an extensive collection of books featuring African
peoples. They also hold a number
of children's events throughout the
year, including storytellers, poetry
readings, and book signings by
children's authors/illustrators.

SHRINE OF THE BLACK MADONNA
13535 Livernois Avenue
Detroit, MI 48238
Ph.(313) 491-0777
Fax (313) 491-1320

Storytelling time - *Yes*
Designated Area - *Yes, as part of the
Art Gallery*
Literary events include children's
authors/illustrators - *No*
Book clubs and/or classes - *No*
Educational materials, games,
puzzles, dolls, etc. - *Yes*
Wheelchair accessible - *Yes*
Newsletter - *No*
CD ROMS, videos, books, and tape - *No*
Special Services - *No*

Along with its sister store in Georgia, Shrine of the Black Madonna is
affiliated with an African American
church community, and features a
children's collection of historical,
educational and spiritual titles,
including picture books, readers,
workbooks, and games that emphasize positive aspects of African
American culture.

OTHER SUGGESTED BOOKSTORES

*Although these stores did not respond to
requests for survey information, each
listing is followed by a brief description
of their inventory and interests.*

ASAHIYA BOOKSTORES
Little Tokyo Square
333 S. Alameda St., Suite 108
Los Angeles, CA 90746
(213) 626-5650

Asahiya's emphasis is on Japanese
literature and culture. The children's corner includes books, puzzles, origami kits, games, books on
tape, videos, and educational workbooks. The titles are primarily in
Japanese, and many books are bilingual, Japanese/English, or translated into English.

BONADEA ALASKA WOMEN'S
BOOKSTORE
2440 East Tudor Road, #304
Anchorage, AK 99507
(907) 562-4716

Specializing in feminist and
gay/lesbian literature, this store
makes a conscientious effort to feature a wide selection of multicultural and nonsexist children's books.

CULTURALLY SPEAKING
1601 E. 18th Street
Kansas City, MO 64108
(816) 842-8151

An Afrocentric book store and cultural information center, this shop
features an extensive collection of
books, games, workbooks, and story
tapes for children of color.

EACH ONE TEACH ONE
213 South Hyde
Columbus, OH 43215
(800) 860-KNOW

This African bookstore boasts an extensive collections of children's literature, educational workbooks, reference books, tapes, and periodicals. They also display their substantial collection on substance abuse, family healing, and African American history at conferences and workshops for social workers, teachers, and historians.

KINOKUNIYA BOOKSTORES OF AMERICA
123 Astronaut Ellison S. Onizuka, Suite 205
Los Angeles, CA 90012
(213) 687-4447

Kinokuniya specializes in books about Japanese culture. Their large selection of children's titles feature Japanese folktales and contemporary stories, and includes bilingual books, translated titles, videos, games, and CD Rom's.

Kinokuniya Bookstores also has stores in : Costa Mesa, CA; San Francisco, CA; San Jose, CA; Seattle, WA; New York, NY.

MEXICAN AMERICAN CULTURAL CENTER
3019 W. French Pl.
San Antonio, TX 78228-5197
(210) 732-2156

The MACC Bookstore specializes in Mexican and Mexican American and Native American culture. Their children's book section has titles for all ages, many in Spanish or bilingual Spanish/English, and includes traditional folk tales, novels, biographies, and educational materials.

MODERN TIMES BOOK STORE
888 Valencia St.,
San Francisco, CA 94110
(415) 282-9246

Now located in its new site, this community bookstore in San Francisco's Mission Delores district has been a gathering place for literary, community, and political discourse for years. The store features a children's collection that includes stories representing many different cultures and ethnicities. They also carry a large selection of Spanish language, bilingual, and translated Mexican folk tales.

OAKLAND CHINESE BOOK BTORE
710 Franklin St.,
Oakland, CA
(510) 465-9865

A little treasure of Oakland's Chinatown, this store features books about Chinese and Chinese American people. Their children's collection includes books in several Chinese languages as well as translated titles and bilingual books.

PYRAMID BOOKSTORE
2849 Georgia Ave., NW
Washington, DC 20001
(202) 328-0190

Founded in 1981, this store is considered to be the oldest African American book store in D.C. Their children's literature section includes an extensive collection of books for all age groups, puzzles, dolls, video and audio tapes, and educational workbooks. They also hold book signings and readings for their youngest clientele.

SAVANNAH BOOKS
858 Massachusetts Ave.
Cambridge, MA 02139
(617) 868-3423

Savannah book store, now located in its new site, features African American and African Caribbean literature. The children's section includes a large collection of picture books, readers and young adults' selections.

SHRINE OF THE BLACK MADONNA
946 Gordon St. SW
Atlanta, GA 30310
(404) 752-6125

Affiliated with an African American church community, this store features a children's collection of historical, educational, and spiritual titles including picture books, readers, workbooks, and games that emphasize positive aspects of African American culture.

BOOKSTORES VIA YOUR MAILBOX - CATALOG BOOK DISTRIBUTION

BOOKS FOR OUR CHILDREN
P.O. Box 1355
New York, NY 10028-0010
Ph. (212) 316-1255

This bookstore features an extensive selection of books by and about African American, African, and African Caribbean peoples. What makes this catalog store unique is the variety and scope of the titles offered. Their full color catalog includes original Black comic books, young reader series, biographies, romances, and a large selection of books for older children through young adults. Schools are eligible for a 25% discount on the catalog's titles.

CHINABERRY BOOK SERVICE
2780 Via Orange Way, Suite B
Spring Valley, CA 91978
Ph. (800) 776-2242
Fax (619) 670-5203

Chinaberry is a resource catalog of books, tapes, video, and "Simple Pleasures" for the entire family. They feature an in-depth assortment of multicultural books for all ages and have divided the catalog into sections based on reading levels. The stated goal of their collection is to provide items that "support families in raising their children with love, honesty, and joy to be reverent, loving caretakers of each other and the earth." Chinaberry ships within 24 hours of your order and has a special program for book fairs.

CLAUDIA'S CARAVAN
P.O. Box 1582
Alameda, CA 94501
(510) 538-5993

Claudia's Caravan is a multicultural and multilingual resource catalog providing curriculum materials, literature, activity books, film, video, games, audio cassettes, musical instruments, dolls, and cultural artifacts for use in the classroom or home. The catalog is detailed and comprehensive. The items they carry are stated as "carefully evaluated for their accuracy and positive imagery." The display rooms in Alameda, California are open every Saturday for the public to visit.

MULTICULTURAL PUBLISHERS EXCHANGE (MPE)
CATALOG OF BOOKS BY AND ABOUT PEOPLE OF COLOR
Highsmith
W5527 Highway 106
P.O. Box 800
Fort Atkinson, WI 53538-0800
(800) 558-2110

This catalog division of Highsmith includes a rare selection of multicultural publications for children and adults. Their inventory includes reference and resource books, activity workbooks, curriculum materials, audio/video selections, games, periodicals, and gift items. Their children's books, pre-school through young adult, feature positive, authentic stories from diverse cultures. MPE is a professional organization of African, Hispanic, Asian/Pacific Islander, Native and White American small press publishers of multicultural books. As well as this catalog, they also publish a bimonthly newsletter and conduct an annual conference.

NICK OF TIME
2063 Main Street #420
Oakley, CA 94561
(510) 754-7750

Nick of Time specializes in "Books about History and Culture for Young Readers." They offer a comprehensive collection of books by and about cultures world wide. They also carry curriculum materials called "Nick of Time Lesson Packets" designed to complement much of the literature available through Nick of Time. Their newsletter includes new titles, reviews, and recommendations --truly a history book store in your mailbox.

PAPYRUS BOOK DISTRIBUTORS
1114 4th Avenue
Los Angeles, CA 90019-3427
(213) 735-9071
(800) 484-6729, ext. 1114

Papyrus features a "Multicultural Children's Catalog" that includes books, audio tapes, and parent/teacher resources for children's education and entertainment. Their collection covers many topics: poetry, music, art, biographies, Spanish and bilingual titles, Rainbow Treasures, and special sections titled: "Khocolate Keepsakes, Hip Hop Reading (for older children), and the Langston Hughes Children's Collection. The company shares a commitment to educating today's children to be a part of the "global village" and to utilize literature to learn more about themselves and others. The annual catalog features newly published books primarily featuring African American authors; however, they also maintain an extensive backlist of books and can order any book that is still in print. Papyrus' services include "Bookwalk" seminars for teachers and in-service workshops for teachers and parents.

SPANISH BOOK CORPORATION
10977 Santa Monica Blvd.
Los Angeles, CA 90025
Ph. (310) 475-0453
Fax (310) 473- 6132

Established in 1967, this company is a family business located in West Los Angeles that publishes and distributes Spanish language and Bilingual titles. Their children's catalog includes more than 150 series with over 1,850 titles covering a vast range of interests and grade levels. All titles are selected on the basis of educational value, graphic presentation, and motivational content. Under the imprint of Bilingual Book Press, they have published: A Bilingual Dictionary of Mexican Spanish, The Best of Latin American Short stories, A Bilingual Dictionary of Latin American Spanish and California Missions. The company also hosts round table discussions for aspiring young Hispanic writers, and publishes a literary and cultural magazine: El Ateneo.
ujima expressions

OUR RAINBOW CHILDREN'S BOOKSHELF
P.O. Box 387
Marietta, GA 30061-0387
Ph. (770) 514-8793/8794
Fax (770) 514-1186

Our Rainbow Children's Bookshelf is a mail order bookstore specializing in African American literature for children pre-school through high school. Their selection is designed specifically to encourage African American children to read.

Their book club, "Pot of Gold," gives readers substantial savings for their purchases over a 12-month period. As well as new titles, they carry many classics that are difficult to obtain elsewhere.

663

Contributors

ABOUT THE CONTRIBUTORS

HELEN R. ABADIANO

Helen R. Abadiano is an Assistant Professor in the Department of Reading and Language Arts at Central Connecticut State University. Her academic and professional experiences include children's literature, teaching multicultural language arts, and literacy among linguistically and culturally diverse populations.

MARILYN S. ANTONUCCI

Marilyn Antonucci is a doctoral student at the School of Education, University of Massachusetts. She works full time coordinating a family literary program in western Massachusetts and makes much use of children's literature in her program.

SHERI BAUMAN

Sheri Bauman is a teacher and counselor at Centennial High School in Fort Collins, Colorado.

ROBIN BERSON

Robin Berson is the director of the Upper School Library at Riverdale Country School in New York City. She is the author of *Marching to a Different Drummer: Unrecognized Heroes of American History* (Greenwood, 1994). In addition, she has been a columnist for the *Wilson Library Bulletin* and a frequent book reviewer for the *School Library Journal*.

CYNTHIA A. BILY

Cynthia A. Bily is a writer and teacher living in Adrian, Michigan, who spends much of her personal time reading picture books and children's stories to her five-year old. Living in Kenya with her family, she developed a strong interest in Africa and African culture.

ELIZABETH CAPIFALI

Elizabeth Capifali is a doctoral candidate at the University of Massachusetts' School of Education. She has been a teacher in New York City and a teacher-researcher with Lucy Calkins. She draws on her Puerto Rican heritage to gain further perspectives on the literature.

PAM CARLSON

Pam Carlson is a Children's Specialist with Orange County Public Library, and currently serves as the librarian at Orangewood Children's Home, a shelter for children who are wards of the court system. Ms. Carlson is also a reviewer for *VOYA* and a former member of the California Young Reader Medal Committee.

FAITH CHILDS-DAVIS

Faith Childs-Davis is an artist, teacher, and parent and believes storytelling is a powerful tool in the development of values in young people. Through shared art and literature experiences, she encourages young people to be thoughtful, compassionate, and creative.

JUDITH CASTIANO

Judith Castiano was born in New Mexico and raised in Encinal. With her degree from the University of Arizona in Library Services, she is presently employed by the San Diego Public Library System.

YOLANDA ROBINSON-COLES

Yolanda Robinson-Coles is a freelance writer who often specializes in reading materials, toys, and games for children and young adults. Yolanda currently lives in Durham, NC with her spouse, David, and three of their daughters, Adrienne, Melantha, and Aiyana.

KATHY COLLINS

After teaching and traveling extensively in Japan, Kathy Collins received her MA in Teaching English to Speakers of Other Languages from Columbia University. She is currently a tutor, and is doing research on the teaching of reading in primary grades.

DORIS COSLEY

Doris Cosley has her BA in Education and Masters in Librarianship from The University of Washington. She is currently a librarian in the Bellevue School District.

SHIRLEY CRENSHAW

Shirley Crenshaw has a Ph.D. in Reading Education and an M.A. in Curriculum & Instruction. She has taught elementary school for many years; developed and taught college courses; conducted and presented workshops; been a Co-Editor and a review editor for *Missouri Reader*; served as a variety of professional organizations.

JANE CUMMINS

Jane Cummins is a freelance journalist specializing in children's television programming. She is also a graduate student at Columbia University, where her studies include British literature, women's studies, and children's literature.

MELVINA AZAR DAME

Melvina Azar Dame, a School Librarian Media Specialist and an ESL Instructor, is the author of *Serving Linguistically and Culturally Diverse Students: Strategies for School Library Media Specialists* (New York: Neal-Schuman, 1993). Her writing in the area of library services to ESL students have also been published in *ERIC Digest* and *Multicultural Review*.

ANN DAVIES
Anne Davies works as an editor of children's books at Harcourt Brace and Company.

CANDY DAWSON BOYD, PH.D.
Candy Dawson Boyd, Ph.D., is the first tenured African American professor at Saint Mary's College of California in Morago and recipient of the school's first professor of the year Award. She is the distinquished author of several children's books, including *Charlie Pippin* and *Breadsticks*.

FRANCES ANN DAY
Frances Ann Day is the author of a reference book and teaching guide to the works and lives of multicultural authors and illustrators. As a teacher, she was awarded for her excellence. She is currently pursuing a career as a writer, curriculum specialist, and educational consultant.

MAGNA M. DIAZ
Magna Diaz is a bilingual storyteller and has developed a bibliography of Latino books. Currently, she is a Bilingual Librarian, a Student Council Sponsor, the SEED (Seeking Educational Equity and Diversity) Leader for teachers at Kensington High School, and a member of REFORMA: a national association to promote library services to the Spanish speaking people.

MARY MOORE EASTER
As a poet/writer, Mary Moore Easter's work has appeared in many journals and anthologies such as *The Hungry Mind Review* and *Sing Heavenly Muse!* As a dancer/choreographer, her work has been presented nationally for more than 20 years with support from major foundations and arts institutions. She is a professor of dance at Carelton College in Northfield, Minnesota.

LYNN EISENHUT
Lynn Eisenhut is Coordinator of Children's Services at the Orange County Public Library in California. She revised and edited the *Children's Services Correspondence Course*, published in 1992.

HEATHER ELDRIDGE
Heather Eldridge spends her time pursuing flights of illustrative fancy, and she also works in the real world.

MEREDITH ELIASSEN
Meredith Eliassen is the curator of the Marguerite Archer Collection of Historic Children's Materials at San Francisco State University Library. She has an interest in children's books and has written articles about writers and illustrators of books for children and young adults.

MICHELE ELWOOD
Michele Elwood was a student at Eagle Point High School.

CHRISTINA ENG
Christina Eng is an entertainment writer and children's book reviewer with the *Oakland Tribune* and the *Alameda Newspaper Group*. She graduated with an English and American literature degree from Brown University in Providence, Rhode Island, and currently lives in Oakland, California.

LISA FAIN
Lisa Fain writes children's books surrounded by Cafe Bustelo cans in New York City.

ROXANNE FELDMAN HSV
Roxanne Feldman has her Masters degree in Children's Literature from Simmons College and is currently a Children's Librarian at the New York Public Library. She grew up in Taiwan and now lives in Manhattan with her husband and her cat.

SUE FLICKINGER
Sue Flickinger recently finished her doctoral program at the University of Massachusetts and is spending some time exploring employment options. She lives in Maryland with her partner.

MARY FROSCH
Mary Frosch heads the Department of English and Comparative Literature at the Spence School in Manhattan. She is also editor of *Margins: the Journal of English studies in Independent Schools*. She lives in New York.

DONNA GAGNON
Donna Gagnon is a first grade teacher at Mark's Meadow Laboratory School in Amherst, Massachusetts, and a demonstration teacher for the University of Massachusetts School of Education. Her interest in multicultural children's literature comes from her experience with diverse groups of children.

BARBARA GOLDENHERSH
Barbara Goldenhersh, Ph.D., has provided professional development opportunities nationally in areas of literacy, cooperative learning, portfolio use at the university level, hands-on mathematics, and school law. She has been a classroom teacher and is currently a visiting lecturer at Southern Illinois University at Edwardsville.

ELAINE GOLEY
Elaine Goley has a masters degree in Information Technology, another in Education, and is working on a masters in Linguistics. She is a prolific nonfiction writer and bibliography contributor, and currently teaches English as a Second Language.

666

KIM GRISWELL
Kim Griswell has an MA in Literature and an MA in Teaching Writing. She teaches composition, creative writing, and children's literature at Humboldt State University and College of the Redwoods in Northern California. A member of the Society of Children's Book Writers and Illustrators, her work has appeared in a wide range of national children's magazines.

MELISSA HECKARD
Melissa Heckard holds an MSLIS from Wayne State University. She has combined her experience as a teacher and librarian to work with American Indian parents, educators, and elders to improve the quality of literature about Native people.

CHIEKO YAMAZAKI-HEINEMAN
Chieko Tamazaki-Heineman was born and brought up in Japan where she received her B.A. in Anthropology from Nanzan University. While teaching, she received her masters degree in multicultrualism/bilingual education at the University of Massachusetts at Amherst. She currently resides in Japan with her husband and children.

GLORIA D. JACKSON
Gloria D. Jackson emigrated from India and has been a librarian with inner city schools in the U.S. for many years. She created and edited *The Mirror* , 1991-1993, a newsletter reviewing multicultural children's literature. She is currently a freelance reviewer and consultant in this field.

TRAVIS E. JACKSON
Travis E. Jackson is the unit administrator of Benjamin Franklin High School, Ridgewood, New Jersey.

DENISE JOHNSON
Denise Johnson is an Assistant Professor of Reading in the Department of Childhood and Special Education at the University of Central Arkansas. She teaches undergraduate and graduate courses in reading and children's literature.

LAURI JOHNSON
Lauri Johnson, a multicultural literature-based program developer with the New York City Board of Education, developed and coordinated Project Equal. She is the co-author of a curriculum guide and a monograph, and is currently in a doctoral program in Multicultural Education at the University of Washington.

LINDA JOLIVET
Linda Jolivet has a masters in Library and Information Studies, and a BA in Education, and is currently working with the Oakland Public Library systems in California. She previously worked as the collection development specialist for the Multicultural Children's Literature collection at Saint Mary's College in California.

BARBARA A. KANE
Barbara A. Kane is married, the mother of two sons, and is presently teaching sixth grade science in the Holyoke Public schools, Holyoke, MA. She received a Masters in Education degree from University of Massachusetts and enjoys painting, needlepoint, and fishing with her sons.

SANDRA KELLY
Sandra Kelly is the president of Nick of Time, a mail order company that specializes in books about history and culture for young readers. She was raised in England and California and has over a dozen years' experience working as a teacher in Egypt and the U.S.

CATHY Y. KIM
Cathy Kim is a third year graduate student in the College of Education at the University of Illinois at Urbana-Champaign. Her research focus is studying the lives, culture, and racial identities of Asian Americans and how they are represented in Asian American Literature.

NANCY HANSEN-KRENING
Nancy Hansen-Krening is a Professor at the Center for Multicultural Education at the University of Washington. Her interest in multicultural literature began with her first teaching job in a migrant labor camp and has extended over her thirty-four-year career.

JANE KURTZ
Jane Kurtz spent most of her childhood in Ethiopia. After ten years as an elementary and high school teacher, she began to write books based on her childhood memories, including *Fire on the Mountain* (Simon & Schuster, 1994), and *Pulling the Lion's Tail* (Simon & Schuster, 1995).

GINNY LEE
Ginny Lee has taught and worked in public libraries both in America and abroad. She has an MA in Asian Studies, an MLS, and a teachers certificate in both Spanish and Library Sciences. She is a freelance writer and has recently joined the *MultiCultural Review* magazine as a subject editor.

JODIE LEVINE
Jodie Levine has a Master's degree in elementary education from the University of Massachusetts where she worked in the Children's Literature office for two years. She works for the Massachusetts Audubon Society where she teaches environmental education to young children.

MICHAEL LEVY
Michael Levy is a professor of English at the University of Wisconsin-Stout. He is the author of the critical study Natalie Babbitt and numerous articles on children's literature and science fiction. Dr. Levy is married and has two children, one of them adopted from Korea.

LI LIU
Li Liu is a doctoral candidate at the School of Education at the University of Massachusetts.

BELINDA YUN-YING LOUIE
Belinda Yun-Ying Louie is an assistant professor at the Education Program of the University of Washington, Tacoma. She teaches classes on integrated curriculum, children's and young adult literature, and multicultural education.

JACKIE LYNCH
Jaqueline Lynch has had a longstanding interest in Children's literature. She graduated from Vassar College, 1966, and the Bank Street College of Education in 1969; both under-graduate and graduate theses were on childen's picture books. She taught kindergarten for four years and was an educational consultant to early childhoods programs in the New York City Public Schools for one year. After, she devoted herself to raising her three sons. She has been reviewing books for the Child Study Children's Book Committee at Bank Street College for the past 11 years.

DONNARAE MACCANN
Donnarae MacCann earned a doctorate in American studies at the University of Iowa, where she is now a Visting Assistant Professor in the African American World Studies program. Her published works include *White Supremacy in Children's Literature: Characterizations of African Americans, 1830-1900* (Garland, in press), and the coauthored books *African Images in Juvenile Lit-*

erature: Commentaries on Neocolonialist Fiction (McFarland, 1996), *The Black American in Books for Children* (Scarecrow, 1972, 1985), *The Child's First Books* (W.H. Wilson, 1973). She has been a children's librarian and has taught children's literature at UCLA, Virginia Tech, and the University of Kansa.

KARLEEN H. TANIMURA MANCHANDA
Karleen H. Tanimura Manchanda is a yonsei, a fourth-generation Japanese American, who was born in Hawaii and lived on the island of Oahu until she was twelve. She has taught second grade and is currently pursuing a masters degree in Language and Literacy at the University of Illinois at Urbana Champaign.

ADRIENNE MARSHALL
Adrienne Marshall is a part time community college English instructor. She grew up in Berkeley, and attended San Francisco State University and Holy Name College.

ELSTON MARSTON
Elston Marston writes fiction and nonfiction for young adults and children, with particular focus on the Middle East. She is an award-winning author.

ELIZABETH MARTINEZ
Elizabeth Martinez, a former editor of *The Nation* and a San Francisco-based editor of *CrossRoads* magazine, is currently a Chicana writer, teacher, and activist for social justice. Her most recent book is titled, *500 Years of Chicano History in Pictures.*

MARTHA MARTINEZ
Martha Martinez, a University of Illinois-Champaign graduate, writes extensively in her free time. She is the daughter of Mexican parents, and teaches Spanish in the Chicago area.

CHRIS MAYO
Chris Mayo is a Ph.D. candidate in the Department of Educational Policy studies at the University of Illinois at Urbana-Champaign and a teaching assistant with the Women's Studies Program.

VICKI MERRILL
Vicki Merill has an MLS and has worked as a children's librarian for the San Francisco Public Library and the Bellevue School District in Washington state. Her work has often centered around helping other librarians develop non-sexist and multicultural collections.

LISA A. MITTEN
Lisa A. Mitten is a librarian of Mohawk decent at the University of Pittsburgh. Active in the American Indian Library Association, she reviews books on Native Americans for numerous publications such as *Libraries Association Newsletter*, *Multicultural Review*, and *Library Journal.*

LISA MOORE
Lisa Moore, a graduate of Hunter college with a degree in Anthropology, has worked in various children's bookstores for the past six years. She currently works for Bank Street College Bookstore in New York.

LESLIE MORALES
Leslie Morales is the Senior Research Editor for a major magazine. She lives in Silver Spring, Maryland.

LESLIE S. NUCHO
Leslie Nucho is Vice-President for Information Services at AMIDEAST, a private, nonprofit organization that seeks to improve understanding, and cooperation between Americans and the peoples of the Middle East and North Africa. She has developed numerous educational materials for use in US schools, including the award-

668

winning video, *Introduction to the Arab World.* Ms. Nucho holds a master's degree in international relations form the Johns Hopkins School for Advanced International Studies (SAIS).

NAOMI SHIHAB NYE
Naomi Shihab Nye's most recent books are *Red Suitcase, Words Under the Words: Selected Poems, Benito's Dream Bottle,* and *Sitti's Secrets.* She edited *This Same Sky* and *The Tree is Older Than You Are* (bilingual poems & stories from Mexico, with paintings by Mexican artists.) She is part of The Language of Life with Bill Moyers series for PBS.

JANIS O'DRISCOLL
Janis O'Driscoll has both a BA and MA in literature and an MLS in Information Science. She has twenty years of experience as a librarian specializing in service to children and young adults and is currently the Coordinator of Youth Services in Santa Cruz City-County Public Libraries.

CHRISTINE PALMER
Christine Palmer is currently pursuing a doctoral degree in Socio-Cultural Anthropology at the University of California, Berkeley. Ms. Palmer's areas of research include the fields of folklore, ethnicity, and North America.

NANCY PAQUIN
Nancy Paquin, born in Mattapoisett, Massachusetts, is a graduate of Notre Dame College. She is the mother of three sons and author of a book of poetry, *A Clown Named She.*

JOAN PRIMEAUX
Joan Primeaux is currently a doctoral student in Language and Literacy with an interest in Children's Literature at the University of Illinois. She is a Literacy Specialist in School District 25, in Arlington Heights, IL.

BRENDA RANDOLPH
Brenda Randolph is director of *Africa Access,* a bibliographic service that publishes reviews of materials on Africa. Ms. Randolph has worked as a media specialist in schools in Virginia, Massachusetts, and Maryland.

BARBARA SMITH REDDISH
Barbara Smith Reddish is a doctoral student in the School of Education at the University of Massachusetts and the proud mother of a wonderful eight-year-old boy.

ELLEN REEVES
Ellen Reeves is a teacher, writer, and editor at The New Press in New York.

LISA RHODES
Lisa Rhodes is a freelance writer living in Maryland.

LORIENE ROY
Loriene Roy is an associate professor at the Graduate School of Library and Information Science at the University of Texas at Austin. Dr. Roy has written extensively in the area of librarianship and library services for children.

MARTHA RUFF
Martha Ruff is a storyteller and librarian, and currently a member of the National Association of Black Storytellers. She served on the Caldecott Award Committee.

BYRON RUSKIN
Byron Ruskin, MD is a retired, clinical associate professor of pathology, University of Illinois, Urbana-Champaign with an interest in juvenile literature.

VICTOR SCHILL
Victor Schill serves as public librarian in the Houston, Texas area. He is noted for being a knowledgeable reviewer of materials about American Indian people.

DORIS SEALE
Doris Seale (Santee/Cree) is a coeditor of *Through Indian Eyes: The Native Experience in Books for Children* and a cofounder of Oyate.

JESSICA SIEGEL
Jessica Siegel is both an educator and a journalist. She was a teacher at Seward Park High School in New York City for 10 years and is currently a freelance writer.

PETER D. SIERUTA
Peter D. Sieruta has published book reviews and critical essays in the *Horn Book Magazine, Children's Books and Their Creators* (Houghton Mifflin), *Writers of Multicultural Fiction for Young Adults* (Greenwood), and other reference volumes. He is also the author of *Heartbeats and Other Stories* (HarperCollins).

BEVERLY SLAPIN
Beverly Slapin is a coeditor of *Through indian Eyes: The native Experience in Books for Children* and a cofounder of Oyate.

SHAHLA SOHAIL
Shahla Sohail has an MLS degree and is currently a children's librarian. She is involved in the development of a Persian Children's Book collection and cultural activities for the Iran Cultural and Educational Center in Maryland, and is an award-winning translator of children's and young adult books.

MICHÈLE SOLÁ
Michèle Solá has been training teachers in second-language instruction, multicultural education, and gender equity as well as teaching Spanish (K-8th grade) at Manhattan Country School for 15 years. She is the author of *Angela Weaves a Dream: The Story of a Young Maya Artist* (Hyperion, 1997).

KAREN ROBERTS STRONG
Karen Roberts Strong is a Tlingit woman from Sitka, Alaska, and currently a doctoral candidate in Language and Literacy at the University of Illinois Urbana-Champaign campus. She is a published playwright and academic writer who has taught dance, English, and Indian Studies.

BETTYE STROUD
Betty Stroud is a full-time writer and former librarian. She is the Author of *Down Home at Miss Dessa's Dance Y'All* is forthcoming.

HAROLD UNDERDOWN
Harold Underdown is a children's book editor and former teacher. He maintains a WWW site dedicated to children's books at http://www.interport. net/~hdu/.

NAOMI WAKAN
Naomi Wakan is a partner at Pacific Rim Publishing House. She and her partner have written 22 children's books dealing with multicultural issues.

ALISON WASHINGTON
Alison Washington earned a Bachelor's degree in the teaching of English and a Master's in Education, focusing on curriculum and instruction from the University of Illinois at Urbana-Champaign. She currently works in the University of Cincinnati's Developmental Writing Department.

ANDREA L. WILLIAMS
Andrea Wiliams has an MLS from Texas Woman's University in Denton, Texas and has taught English and History to junior high students for 6 years. Currently she is a curriculum materials librarian at Midwestern State University in Wichita Falls, Texas.

BENNIE TATE WILKIN
Author, storyteller, and librarian services consultant, Ms. Wilkin is a former children's librarian and specialist in children's services. She recently published the second edition of her 1978 publication, "Survival Themes in Literature for Children and Young Adults."

PATRICIA WONG
Patricia Wong is a Branch Manager at the Berkeley Public Library in California and throughout her career has provided multicultural services and programming to the library community. She is a board member of the United States Board on Books for Young People and a juror for the Jane Addams Children's Book Award.

LAURA M. ZAIDMAN
Laura Zaidman, PhD., teaches courses in children's literature, composition, and literature at the University of South Carolina at Sumter. She edited *British Children's Writers, 1880-1914*, and is currently editing essays about children's literature.

ASSOCIATE EDITORS

ELAINE AOKI, PH.D
Elaine Aoki has been a classroom teacher, K-12 reading/language arts coordinator, and elementary principal, and is presently the director of the lower school at the Bush K-12 School. She is an award-winning educator and accomplished writer.

NOLA HADLEY
Nola Hadley, Ph.D. is an Appalachian/Cherokee woman who teaches American history and culture at Vista Community College in Berkeley, California. She has been a board member of the Indian Historian Press in San Francisco California and of Oyate, an American Indian educational resources project in Berkeley California. She leads faculty and campus trainings on diversity, and workshops and classes in peer counseling and leadership training for young people of color and their families.

VIOLET HARRIS
Violet Harris, an associate professor in the department of Curriculum and Instruction at the University of Illinois, teaches undergraduate and graduate courses in children's literature. She is an active member of the International Reading Association and the National Council of Teachers of English where she presents regularly on issues in children's literature.

MASHA RUDMAN
Masha Rudman is a noted critic of and commentator on children's literature with a focus on combating stereotypes and promoting social justice. *Her Children's Literature: An Issue Approach* (Longman, 1995) has become a classic in the study of children's literature. She has contributed to and coauthored numerous books as well aswriting monographs and hundreds of articles.

DEBORAH WEI
Deborah Wei currently works as a curriculum specialist in Asian/Pacific American Studies in the school district of Philadelphia. She is a founding member and on the Board of Directors of Asian Americans United, a grass-roots community organization advocating for rights of Asian Americans, and is currently on the steering committee of the National Coalition of Education Activities.

NAOMI CALDWELL WOOD
Naomi Caldwell-Wood is a school librarian media specialist at the Alan Shawn Feinstein High School for Public Service in Rhode Island. She has served as the president of the American Indian Library Association and is an accomplished writer of both books and magazine and journal articles.

CONSULTING EDITOR

DIANTHA SCHULL

Diantha Schull is Executive Director of Libraries for the Future, a national organization that represents the users of America's public libraries by promoting information and technology policy in the public interest. Ms. Schull is married to Walter B. Schull and has two college age children.

CONTRUBUTING EDITORS

SONIA NIETO

Sonia Nieto is a Professor of Education at the University of Massachusetts, Amherst. She has published widely in the areas of multicultural and bilingual education, the social and cultural context of learning, and the education of Latino students

NEHRU KELVH

Nehru Kelevh writes for 8th grade New York City history curriculum, and consults with the National Center for Reconstructing Education, Schools, and Teaching at Columbia University. He is presently working towards the degree of Doctor of Education at Teacher's College, in the Department of Curriculum & Teaching.

EDITORIAL COORDINATOR

ROSA E. WARDER

Rosa Emilia Warder is an artist and writer living in Oakland, California. Her work centers on issues of importance to women, children, and bi-cultural peoples. She is the writer and illustrator of three children's picture books, and is at work on a young adult novel.

EDITORIAL CONSULTANT

NANCY PEARL

Nancy Pearl is currently the director of the Washington Center for the Book at the Seattle Public Library, where she promotes books and reading through speeches, book reviews, and advising reading groups. She is married and has two grown daughters.

EDITORIAL AND ADMINISTRATIVE ASSISTANT

MOLLY GOULD

Molly Gould is Senior Acquisitions Editor at Peaceable Kingdom Press, which reproduces art from children's books. She is also a freelance writer who in San Francisco, California.

Index

673

674

677

686

Related Materials from The New Press

James W. Loewen
LIES MY TEACHER TOLD ME: EVERYTHING YOUR
AMERICAN HISTORY TEXTBOOK GOT WRONG
HC, $24.95, 1-56584-100-X, 384 pp.
*The best-selling, award-winning, iconoclastic look
at the errors, misrepresentations, and omissions
in the leading American history textbooks.*

James W. Loewen
THE TRUTH ABOUT COLUMBUS:
A SUBVERSIVELY TRUE POSTER BOOK FOR
A DUBIOUSLY CELEBRATORY OCCASION
PB with poster, $12.95, 1-56584-008-9, 48 pp.
*A provocative educational poster and booklet
that draws on recent scholarship to debunk the
myths and discover the man.*

Howard Zinn
A PEOPLE'S HISTORY OF THE UNITED STATES:
TEACHING EDITION
HC, $25.00, 1-56584-366-5;
PB, $13.00, 1-56584-379-7; 496 pp.
*An abridged edition of Howard Zinn's best-selling—
over 425,000 copies—history of the United States.*

Howard Zinn and George Kirschner
A PEOPLE'S HISTORY OF THE UNITED STATES:
THE WALL CHARTS
Portfolio, $25.00, 1-56584-171-9, 48-page booklet
with two posters
*Two oversized posters based on Zinn's best-selling
social history.*

Herbert Kohl
"I WON'T LEARN FROM YOU" AND OTHER
THOUGHTS ON CREATIVE MALADJUSTMENT
PB, $10.00, 1-56584-096-8, 176 pp.
*"One of the most important books on teaching
published in many years."*—Jonathan Kozol

Herbert Kohl
SHOULD WE BURN BABAR?: ESSAYS ON CHIL-
DREN'S LITERATURE AND THE POWER OF STORIES
HC, $18.95, 1-56584-258-8; PB, $11.00,
1-56584-259-6; 192 pp.
*The prize-winning educator's thoughts on the
politics of children's literature.*

Laurie Olsen
MADE IN AMERICA: IMMIGRANT CHILDREN
IN OUR SCHOOLS
HC, $25.00, 1-56584-400-9; 244 pp.
*An up-to-the-minute look at immigrant students
in American public schools, through a portrait
of one prototypical high school.*

Lisa D. Delpit
OTHER PEOPLE'S CHILDREN: CULTURAL
CONFLICT IN THE CLASSROOM
HC, $21.00, 1-56584-179-4;
PB, $11.95, 1-56584-180-8; 224 pp.
*A MacArthur Fellow's revolutionary analysis of the
role of race in the classroom. Winner of* Choice
*magazine's Outstanding Academic Book Award,
the American Education Studies Association Critic's
Choice Award, and one of* Teacher *magazine's
Great Books of 1995.*

Michele Foster
BLACK TEACHERS ON TEACHING
HC, $23.00, 1-56584-320-7, 240 pp.
*The first wave of black teachers in desegregated schools
speak out on the politics of educating black children.*

David Levine, Robert Lowe, Robert Peterson,
and Rita Tenorio, editors
RETHINKING SCHOOLS: AN AGENDA
FOR CHANGE
PB, $16.00, 1-56584-215-4, 304 pp.
*The country's leading education reformers propose
ways to change our schools.*

690

William Ayers and Patricia Ford, editors
CITY KIDS, CITY TEACHERS:
REPORTS FROM THE FRONT ROW
HC, $25.00, 1-56584-328-3;
PB, $16.00, 1-56584-051-8; 368 pp.
Classic writings on urban education from America's leading experts.

Anne E. Wheelock
CROSSING THE TRACKS: HOW "UNTRACKING"
CAN SAVE AMERICA'S SCHOOLS
HC, $22.95, 1-56584-013-5;
PB, $12.95, 1-56584-038-0; 336 pp.
A highly praised study of ways in which schools have successfully experimented with heterogeneous grouping in the classroom.

Suzanne Goldsmith
A CITY YEAR: ON THE STREETS AND IN THE
NEIGHBORHOODS WITH TWELVE YOUNG
COMMUNITY SERVICE VOLUNTEERS
HC, $22.95, 1-56584-093-3, 304 pp.
An honest account of the triumphs and setbacks faced by an idealistic and experimental social program in its infancy.

Gary Orfield and Susan E. Eaton
DISMANTLING DESEGREGATION: THE QUIET
REVERSAL OF BROWN V. BOARD OF EDUCATION
HC, $30.00, 1-56584-305-3;
PB, $17.95, 1-56584-401-7; 496 pp.
"A wise... authoritative book" (Jonathan Kozol) on America's return to segregation.

Ira Berlin and Barbara J. Fields, et al.
FREE AT LAST: A DOCUMENTARY HISTORY OF
SLAVERY, FREEDOM, AND THE CIVIL WAR
HC, $27.50, 1-56584-015-1;
PB, $15.95, 1-56584-120-4, 608 pp.
A winner of the 1994 Lincoln Prize, some of the most remarkable and moving letters ever written by Americans, depicting the drama of Emancipation in the midst of the nation's bloodiest conflict.

Ira Berlin and Leslie S. Rowland, editors
FAMILIES AND FREEDOM: A DOCUMENTARY
HISTORY OF AFRICAN-AMERICAN KINSHIP IN
THE CIVIL WAR ERA

HC, $25.00, 1-56584-026-9, 304 pp.
A sequel to the award-winning Free at Last, *moving letters from freed slaves to their families.*

American Social History Project
FREEDOM'S UNFINISHED REVOLUTION:
AN INQUIRY INTO THE CIVIL WAR
AND RECONSTRUCTION
PB, $17.95, 1-56584-198-0, 320 pp.
From the award-winning authors of Who Built America?, *a groundbreaking high school level presentation of the Civil War and Reconstruction.*

Beverly Guy-Sheftall, editor
WORDS OF FIRE: AN ANTHOLOGY OF AFRICAN
AMERICAN FEMINIST THOUGHT
PB, $20.00, 1-56584-256-1, 608 pp.
The first comprehensive collection to trace the development of African American feminist thought.

Mary Frosch
COMING OF AGE IN AMERICA:
A MULTICULTURAL ANTHOLOGY
HC, $22.95, 1-56584-146-8;
PB, $12.95, 1-56584-147-6; 288 pp.
The acne and ecstasy of adolescence—a multicultural collection of short stories and fiction excerpts that Library Journal *calls "wonderfully diverse from the standard fare."*

Joann Faung Jean Lee
ASIAN AMERICANS: ORAL HISTORIES OF FIRST
GENERATION AMERICANS FROM CHINA, THE
PHILIPPINES, JAPAN, INDIA, THE PACIFIC
ISLANDS, VIETNAM AND CAMBODIA
PB, $11.95, 1-56584-023-2, 256 pp.
A fascinating firsthand account of the diverse Asian American community.

Virginia Yans-McLaughlin and Marjorie Lightman,
with the Statue of Liberty-Ellis Island Foundation
ELLIS ISLAND AND THE PEOPLING OF
AMERICA: THE OFFICIAL GUIDE
PB, $15.00, 1-56584-364-9, 224 pp.
A primary source reader and resource guide to Ellis Island, a national landmark attracting over 3,000,000 visitors each year.

The Lorette Wilmot Library
Nazareth College of Rochester

ICELAND

Statute Miles

0   25   50

0   25   50

Kilometers

ICELAND

1. Abandoned farm on the southeastern coast, near Höfn.

2. Pinks alongside the road to Krísuvík, Reykjanes.

3. *Moss growing in volcanic cinders (deposited by the eruption of Mount Hekla in 1970) along a rivulet on the edge of Thjórsádalur.*

ICELAND

Photographs by ELIOT PORTER

Text by JONATHAN PORTER

Bulfinch Press

Little, Brown and Company

BOSTON · TORONTO · LONDON

FIRST EDITION

LIBRARY OF CONGRESS CATALOGING-IN-PUBLICATION DATA

Porter, Eliot, 1901–
    Iceland / photographs by Eliot Porter ; text by Jonathan
Porter. —1st ed.
      p. cm.
    ISBN 0–8212–1731–3
    1. Iceland—Description and travel—1981– —Views. I. Porter,
Jonathan. II. Title.
DL315.P67 1989
914.912—dc20   89–31568
                                                                  CIP

Four of the photographs in this book were previously
published in *Eliot Porter* (New York Graphic Society Books/
Little, Brown and Company in association with the
Amon Carter Museum, 1987).

BULFINCH PRESS is an imprint and trademark of
Little, Brown and Company (Inc.).

Published simultaneously in Canada by
Little, Brown & Company (Canada) Limited.

PRINTED IN JAPAN

GLOSSARY

Many Icelandic place names were derived from words that
describe the topographical features in those locations. Of the
descriptives listed below, some are used as complete names
(Höfn, Foss), others as prefixes or suffixes (Dettifoss,
Reykjavík, Vatnajökull).

dalur	valley
fell	hill, mountain
foss	waterfall, cascade
fjördur	fjord, bay
heidhi	heath, moor
hellir	cave, cavern, grotto
hlidh	gate, gateway, side
höfn	harbor, port, haven
jökull	glacier, icecap
laug(ar)	hot spring
nes	cape, point, headland, peninsula
reykja	smoke, steam
skógur	wood, forest, bush
vatn	lake
vík	inlet

ICELAND: *Notes on the Journey*

We drove through a landscape that at first seemed to defy topographical expectations; it was as if we had been transported to an alien world dreamed up by an imaginative armchair traveler. Around us luminescent green-velvet moss glistened in the gray drizzle. Ridges of hills and mountains—few conventional clues offered us any perspective— were scattered along the way, separated here and there by smooth beds of dull, gray-black volcanic ash. Among these beds were clumps of heather— small, bright white or pink flowers. Frozen in motion, congealed volcanic outpourings in lurid shades of green, red, yellow, black, and white appeared unexpectedly. There were no trees, nor even any bushes or large plants. Was this a world from the dawn of terrestrial creation, when the earth was cooling, only simple life thrived, and larger floral species had not yet appeared—or a world nearing its final days, when higher life forms had all disappeared, and the earth was declining into a cold twilight?

Iceland's landscape looks like those vivid, detailed scenes of imaginary planets depicted by science-fiction illustrators. The basic constituents —mountains, valleys, sky—are there, but the forms seem unfamiliar and exaggerated. There are enough indications to convince the observer that conventional physical laws apply, but it is clear that these laws have operated in conjunction with some very unusual geological processes. The colors are strange, the shapes odd and distorted. Perhaps it is no coincidence that American astronauts prepared for lunar excursions on Iceland's volcanic terrain. Iceland possesses a primordial quality,

something akin to what might be seen by a time traveler to an earlier, formative age of the earth. But at the same time it is a very old place.

*　　*　　*

Eliot had first conceived of going to Iceland in 1971 during a photographic trip to Greece and Turkey with his friend Paul Stein. They were, at the time, photographing the ruins of a Turkish temple covered with lichens. Paul liked to photograph lichens; he remarked that Iceland was famous for these striking plant forms, and that he and Eliot ought to go there. When Eliot returned home, he began to make inquiries of the Iceland Tourist Bureau. Beyond the attraction of the lichens, that Iceland was a product of great volcanic eruptions, that it possessed glaciers and hot springs, and that it was tantalizingly remote made the prospect of such an expedition quite appealing.

Although the trip was to be fairly long, Paul and his wife, Carol, planned to go along for a while. Eliot asked my wife, Zoë, and me if we would like to help out with the equipment, logistics, and driving. Joining our group were Mary Jane and Tad Nichols, old friends who had previously accompanied Eliot on photographic expeditions to unusual places, such as the Galápagos Islands. Tad had made a film of the eruption of the Parícutin volcano in Mexico. Joan and Bernt Matthias, also good friends, came along for a brief time.

We were drawn to Iceland not for its human history, but for its natural phenomena—and this remained our primary interest throughout the trip. The society of the island was not without its own interest, and man-made structures—farms, farmhouses, and churches—frequently attracted our attention as visual subjects. We were also interested in Icelanders and their sense of history, and in the sagas, the family chronicles of the Viking settlers.

The Vikings were a seafaring people; they came from the sea, made their living from it, and remained always oriented toward it. But for many years they sojourned in Iceland. As they settled down, they became farmers, constantly fighting among themselves and killing one another over territorial claims and family disputes. Ships, seafaring, and fishing; homesteads, farms, and livestock are all mentioned in the sagas. Oddly, however, the geographical references therein are mostly to place names—naming was a critical part of establishing the Vikings' claims to their settlements—and are important mainly as an anchor for the narrative of their deeds. They gave little explicit notice in their writings to the strange landscape that surrounded them and that must have repeatedly threatened their existence.

But to study the Icelanders and their history was not our purpose. So this journey was, above all, an exploration of the natural world of Iceland, a place of extraordinary geological interest, and one of unusual, and often peculiar, beauty.

Iceland is geologically both old and young. A product of the separation of geotectonic plates along the Mid-Atlantic Ridge, it began long ago as a seabed volcano breaking the ocean's surface to become an island, a process that is still active. However, the island also encompasses almost the entire range of geomorphic features and processes of the earth: sedimentary deposits, erosion caused by rivers and oceans, glacial leveling and scouring, effects of weather and temperature, and even the consequences of human settlement.

An island with an area of some 40,000 square miles encompassed by deeply indented coastline about 3,730 miles long, Iceland is located in the North Atlantic Ocean just below the Arctic Circle. It is largely a series of plateaus composed of layers of volcanic rock, with central regions dominated by elevated deserts, lava flows, snowfields, and glaciers, and coastal fringes pierced by deep fjords and valleys. Lowlands, where pastures flourish and most of the population is concentrated, constitute only about seven percent of the total area.

The formation of the island began in the mid-Tertiary period, approximately thirty million years ago. Sedimentary deposits of clay containing the remains of plants and trees from the Tertiary period reveal that extensive forests once grew on Iceland, and that it was considerably warmer than it is at present. During the Glacial epoch the island was completely covered by an ice sheet more than 2,300 feet thick which left its mark in extensive glacial scouring and moraines. Subsequently, a process of elevation occurred which changed the shape of the shoreline.

As much as one-eighth of the surface of Iceland is covered by vast snowfields and glaciers. The largest of these, Vatnajökull, spans an area of more than 3,000 square miles. Numerous glacial tongues flow outward from the edges of the snowfields, which are also the sources of rivers of great volume and power, some of which descend in spectacular waterfalls. Iceland is one of the most active volcanic regions on earth; such activity has been continuous since the island's earliest formation. Although some of the more than one hundred volcanoes have erupted only once, others have remained periodically active—including Mount Hekla, Iceland's most famous, if not its largest, volcano, which has erupted more than twenty times in recorded history. Hot springs, also generated by volcanic activity, are found throughout the island, especially in the southwest lowlands east of Reykjavík. The word *geyser* is borrowed directly from *geysir*, the Icelandic proper name for the Great Geyser, for which Iceland holds pride of place in the world regarding such phenomena. Earthquakes, yet another signal of the volcanic substructure of Iceland, have, like volcanoes, occurred frequently and caused much destruction throughout the historical era.

Although heavily forested before the Glacial epoch, Iceland is now virtually devoid of forests, and even of most large trees. In only a few places do stands of small birches or isolated trees remain, and the flora is otherwise confined to pasture grass, heaths, small flowers, moss, and lichens. Land mammals are apparently not indigenous to Iceland, and those that live there now were introduced by settlers. More than one hundred species of birds are native to the island, about half of them aquatic, and the surrounding waters abound with fish of many varieties, as well as with such marine mammals as seals and whales.

✳   ✳   ✳

We arrived in Iceland on June 15, 1972. During the first few days following our arrival in Reykjavík, we made preparations for our expedition, arranging for our transportation and acquiring provisions and equipment. We expected to stay some of the time in guesthouses, inns, and tourist huts, but also to do some camping. The huts provided only shelter and simple beds; we would need to cook our own meals whenever we stayed in them, and to eat lunch in the field as we traveled. Confronted with the unexpectedly cold and damp weather, we all purchased heavy Icelandic wool sweaters, which had a natural oil content that allowed them to be worn in the rain. With the sleeping bags, tents, and bulky camera equipment we had brought with us from home, and the boxes of food, utensils, and supplies we collected in Reykjavík, we soon had a considerable amount of baggage.

Because, in the beginning, our party numbered nine people, we had reserved two Land Rovers. Eliot had been assured that they would be new, but when we picked them up they proved to be anything but. We nevertheless found them to be very serviceable (only later did we experience a series of bizarre mechanical problems), and by carefully packing and loading the vehicles and their roof racks we were able to accommodate all of the people, equipment, and baggage. Fortunately, we did not intend to drive long distances without making frequent stops to photograph and explore.

In spite of its situation in the extreme northern latitudes of the Atlantic, Iceland has a relatively mild climate, owing to the northward sweep of the Gulf Stream. But the weather required some adaptation at first. It rained frequently and everyone complained of the cold—sooner or later we all caught colds. When the weather cleared, the summer sun, above the horizon for nearly twenty-two hours per day, warmed the air and land. We were surprised to discover that some Icelanders, inured to the cold, welcomed the sun by going shirtless, but we still found it cold, though at least somewhat cheering.

Our initial impressions of Iceland and its people, during the week or so we remained in Reykjavík, were mixed. At first we found people to be extremely taciturn and cheerless, which we took to mean that they were unfriendly, though that notion was soon corrected. We envied their stoic resistance to the dank cold. We were fascinated by the language and by the custom of using patronymics in place of surnames and of listing people by their given names—a source of considerable confusion to both natives and visitors.

Reykjavík seemed a forbidding place, and we were anxious to get on our way and into the country. Eliot had planned our itinerary well in advance of our arrival, as accommodations were

[13]

in demand, particularly for the inns, which were run by the Iceland Tourist Bureau in the summer, and which served as rural boarding schools in the winter. We would have to follow our schedule, and we had only a very rough preconception of what we might find of interest at any stopping place. Eliot had chosen our route—and the places we would visit at length—largely on the basis of sketchy advice, together with imaginative consultation of maps. Some areas looked promising or contained recommended sights; they did not always turn out to be as interesting as we had anticipated. Other places, seemingly less promising, offered unexpected rewards.

Our plan, then, was to cover as much of Iceland as possible in a two-month journey, while still giving adequate time to each region. At that time it was not possible to make a complete circuit of the island in one direction, as the great slough caused by runoff from the immense Vatnajökull on the southern coast had not yet been crossed by a road. But we were anxious to explore both ends of the coast on either side of the glacier, so we planned to drive first eastward, to the area north and east of Mount Hekla, to the west of Vatnajökull, and then along the southern coast to the end of the main coastal road. After this, we would double back through Reykjavík, and travel north and east around the northern side of the island, down the eastern coast, and west along the southeastern coast to the other end of the coastal road on the eastern side of Vatnajökull. Side trips would take us to the end of the western peninsula of Snæfellsnes, along the fjords of the northern and eastern coasts, and toward the center of the island, north of Vatnajökull.

We made several one-day excursions to the southwest, east, and northeast of Reykjavík in the first ten days. One of our preliminary ventures took us across the southwestern peninsula of Reykjanes, through Krisuvík and Grindavík

toward the extreme southwestern tip of Iceland; we stopped frequently to walk through the heath and the moss-covered lava fields. On the second of these short trips we encountered a sight that made a powerful and enduring impression on us of the immense forces that are active in Iceland. Near the tip of the peninsula is a hot spring that someone had once attempted to cap, presumably in order to harness its power. We had come upon another of these steam wells earlier, but this one was awesome in its force. A large pipe, about a foot in diameter, rose several feet from the ground and made an abrupt, ninety-degree bend, extending horizontally for perhaps fifty feet. From its orifice came a shocking, thundering rocket of steam that shook the ground and that could be heard as we approached it long before it actually came into view. The fan of steam shot out several hundred feet, wetting the nearby hillside. The pipe was secured against the backward thrust of the steam by concrete anchors. A valve that was no longer operable had evidently been placed in the pit surrounding the emerging pipe to shut down the flow; it was far from clear how such strength could be controlled. Here was a continuous and apparently inexhaustible blast of power.

The day before this journey to the hot spring, we had driven northeast to the great waterfall of Gullfoss on the Hvítá River. For all its impressive power, the waterfall seemed to pale by comparison with the hot spring we had seen rising from the subterranean furnace of the island's foundation. Yet, in a way, the two might be perceived as points along the spectrum of natural forces that have created and continue to shape Iceland.

Another trip northeast, to Thingvellir, offered a contrast to these violent scenes. Thingvellir is a now-peaceful green valley next to a lake called Thingvallavatn, though even here a huge lava fissure testifies to ancient volcanic upheavals. On this site the Althing, an open-air lawgiving assembly, first met in about 930 A.D. Often purported to be Europe's first "parliament," it was convened to settle disputes among the chiefs of ununited groups of Viking pioneers who had staked out claims on various parts of the island during the several decades following its discovery in the middle of the ninth century. Although the incipient commonwealth of the Althing was ultimately abortive, its site is revered by Icelanders as the cradle of their political culture, and it is now a national park. Perhaps because we were attuned less to the history of Iceland than to its natural scenery, we found Thingvellir disappointingly bland.

We packed the Land Rovers and left Reykjavík on June 25 for our tour of the island, heading east to Laugarvatn. From there we reconnoitered the route further east, where we would have to cross the Thjórsá River in order to get to the area east of Mount Hekla. In Thjórsádalur, the valley of the Thjórsá, the river washes over sandbars deposited by ash falls from the eruptions of the volcano. Bright chartreuse moss grows along the edges of small rivulets descending into the valley, cutting through the overburden of black ash and cinders to reveal underlying snowbanks preserved since the time of the last eruption. Oddly, Thjórsádalur reminded us of the desert landscape of our home in New Mexico.

After fording the Thjórsá, we traveled on very primitive roads approaching Landmannalaugar, through areas of the most strangely beautiful landscape we would see. Along the way we were learning, by trial and error (with plenty of the latter), the correct technique for navigating the crude tracks off the main roads. River fords, boggy fields, jagged and broken lava slopes: each required its own approach. At first, we were most adept in the desert-like terrain, as it most closely resembled our home environment. In a long, marshy valley on the way to Landmannalaugar,

the road became a flooded trench, the ruts caused by previous travel merging into a single canal. We could not determine how deep it was and therefore approached it with considerable apprehension. I was driving the lead Land Rover; Tad, who was more experienced with such conditions, urged me to keep going to the end of the road, but as the water rose above the floorboard, I tried to drive out of the trench, getting the vehicle stuck fast on the bank. We had to drive back in the other Land Rover to Landmannahellir to borrow a shovel (a significant omission in our equipment) with which to dig the car out, a very disagreeable task. A little farther on, the second vehicle suffered the first of what was to become a series of mechanical problems: the exhaust manifold actually broke off the engine, and the resulting racket made it very unpleasant to drive until we finally got it fixed.

It was soon apparent to us that Iceland is a place of startling contradictions. Peculiar juxtapositions of dramatic geological formations with contrasting textures, colors, and moods may be encountered almost anywhere: volcanoes and glaciers; ice and hot springs; hot and cold water running out of the ground side by side; soft, lush hummocks of moss alongside jagged flows of congealed lava; gentle pastures and bleak, featureless plains of ash. Much of the landscape looks very old, worn and mellowed by centuries of erosion by water, compression and abrasion by snow and ice, and the gradual chemical action of lichens and moss. The near-absence of wooded areas and even of lone trees, the result of deforestation by successive groups of settlers, enhances this sense of age. (Compare this to the rapid appearance of energetic new growth on the devastated slopes of Mount Saint Helens in Washington State following that volcano's catastrophic eruption.) Yet the appearance is deceptive—much of Iceland is, in some respects, very young.

We left Landmannalaugar on June 30, traveling southwest to Selfoss, where we had the ailing Land Rover repaired, and then east to Kirkjubæjarklaustur, near the end of the road south of Vatnajökull. It had begun to rain heavily at Landmannalaugar, and we were concerned that we might not be able to negotiate the swampy road by which we had come. A charming Icelandic family that was staying with us at the hut told us of a better route to the north, and when they left (the day before our departure) they kindly marked the way for us with cairns alongside the road. We packed the Land Rovers in miserably cold, driving rain and got across the ford as the river was rising.

We stayed several days at Kirkjubæjarklaustur in a school that had been converted into a comfortable inn for the summer; it had a very friendly and helpful staff. East of there, the road ended at a vast, rocky wasteland interlaced with innumerable churning streams that flowed out of Vatnajökull. An engineer assigned to the highway construction project, who was also staying at the inn, told us of plans to build a road across the effluent area, and of the immense obstacles the project would encounter. Thermal vents melt the ice under the snowfield, and every five to seven years the glacier is lifted by the water, and huge floods sweep out to the sea. The volume of one such recent flood has been estimated at one hundred thousand cubic meters per second.

We drove up into the highlands between Vatnajökull and Mýrdalsjökull. There, spattered on the rocks that were strewn across the wasteland between the glaciers, we found the multicolored lichens that had first prompted us to come to Iceland. The glaciers appeared vast on the horizon, but always far away and unapproachable. We forded many streams on successive attempts over the course of two days but were finally impeded by rivers too deep to cross. Still, we were able to approach the glacial tongues descending from

Mýrdalsjökull. The retreating glacier, riven by deep, ice-blue clefts and streams running through its convolutions and holes, had left behind isolated cones of ice covered with black cinders.

From Kirkjubæjarklaustur we began our clockwise circuit of the island, going by way of Selfoss and Reykjavík, and on July 8 reaching Varmaland, which became our base for several days' excursions. In Kaldidalur ("Cold Valley"), between Langjökull and a snow-covered mountain called Ok, and elsewhere along the way, we found many species of birds: plovers, whimbrels, snipes, gulls, terns, skuas, ducks, geese, and swans. Mary Jane was an avid bird watcher, and we had many discussions and arguments over the identification, markings, and habits of birds. These prompted Paul, in exasperation, to compose a limerick:

> Said the whimbrel while smoking his pipe,
> As a lover I have but one gripe:
> I find that one plover
> Is much like another.
> I prefer to consort with the snipe.

Mary Jane's enthusiasm, however, was always a source of cheer, even in the worst of conditions.

We drove from Varmaland on July 11, along the southern coast of Snæfellsnes to Búdhir, stopping at Hitardalur and Hnappadalur to examine spectacular volcano craters and collapsed lava tubes overgrown with silver-gray moss. Portions of the lava tubes had remained intact; in their cavelike interiors, untouched by the effects of weather, glossy red and orange formations looked as fresh as if they were still hot to the touch.

At Búdhir we were kept indoors for nearly two days by a strong gale that brought very heavy rain. Once the weather cleared, Eliot and Paul, inspired by the prolonged daylight, had the idea that it would be a novel experience to take daylight photographs at 11:00 P.M. So they went out late at "night" to photograph the gold sand and black lava stone beaches nearby. The following day, the Steins started for home, departing for Reykjavík in one of the Land Rovers.

We had unfortunately underestimated our need for the second Land Rover, and now we were required to return it to the rental agency. So Tad accompanied the Steins to Reykjavík, where he was able to rent a Volkswagen Beetle. He rejoined us at Varmaland, whence we continued east and north around the island beginning July 15. But new troubles with the remaining Land Rover forced us to hasten to Akureyri for repairs, and we were unable to make stops along the way. Akureyri, the second largest city in Iceland, turned out to be a very pleasant place. Using it for several days as our point of departure, we made excursions up both sides of the fjord as well as west through Öxnadalur, along the route by which we had come.

Mývatn, a lake filling a shallow depression surrounding many small volcanic cones on the road going east from Akureyri, is acclaimed as one of the finest scenic spots in Iceland. Although we found it less interesting than we had expected, it became our base for several trips to the north and south—to the great waterfall at Dettifoss, to the hot springs and mud pots just to the west of Mývatn, and along the road south toward Askja, Iceland's largest volcano, near the center of the island.

Car troubles continued to plague our journey. We had hoped to reach Askja, but near Herdhubreidh, a high, snow-covered, barn-shaped mountain south of Mývatn, the rear axle of the Land Rover began to make a terrible grinding noise. We turned around, fearing that it would break at any moment and leave us stranded in a remote area. The vehicle finally did collapse, barely two kilometers from our hotel at Mývatn. A mechanic was called from Akureyri on Sunday; he removed the rear drive shaft and drove the car back to Akureyri, returning it to us the next morning, after making what appeared to be only temporary repairs. The grinding noise recurred, convincing us that we should not make another attempt to reach Askja. When the rear axle indeed broke down again, I removed the drive shaft myself, and with only front-wheel drive available to us, we continued to Egilsstadhir, where more permanent repairs were at last accomplished. At least the weather had improved considerably, bringing many consecutive days of sun and warmth, and despite the afflictions of the Land Rover—which were beginning to achieve the proportions of a saga—Eliot found many interesting subjects to photograph.

We left behind the dramatic volcanic effusions of the north and west for the plateau of eastern Iceland. Here we found an altogether different landscape: long, smooth-sided, glacier-worn valleys and fjords, where thin tendrils of water fell from snowfields and icecaps atop the high ridges separating them. Shaped by processes that have long since ceased, these valleys have been abandoned to the almost imperceptibly gradual action of weather. Only the occasional massive talus of weather-fractured rock suggests the ongoing effect of alternate heating and cooling.

Cresting the last hill that overlooked Höfn to the west on the long drive from Egilsstadhir on July 30, we were presented with one of the most spectacular views of Iceland we had yet seen: an expansive vista of snowcapped mountains and glaciers, ranged one upon the next in recession toward the distant horizon, snaking down to the littoral. From Höfn, which we used as our base for a week, the road followed a narrow corridor between the jagged edge of Vatnajökull and the sea, ending at the eastern side of the great slough that we had viewed from the other end of the road, east of Kirkjubæjarklaustur. Here, where glacial fingers almost reach the sea, icebergs break off in small lakes from which melted ice flows out through short rivers to the sea, only about a kilometer away.

The saga of the Land Rovers had not yet been played to its conclusion. On July 31, on the way back to Höfn from a day trip, the transmission abruptly lost all but fourth gear. Thoroughly exasperated, we abandoned the vehicle after limping back, called Reykjavík, and demanded a replacement. It did not arrive by ship until August 4, and our pleasure at having a new vehicle was soon dissipated when, after driving it from the wharf to the hotel, the starter absolutely refused to work again. Henceforth on our return trip around the island, we would always have to park on a hill so that we could start the car by rolling it. By this time our problems with the vehicles had merged so completely with every other aspect of our journey that they had become simply another dimension of its conditions—just as the weather, something to be taken for granted and endured. Later we would look back on these experiences with a certain degree of amusement, and even nostalgia.

The Nicholses departed for home on August 6. The same day, Eliot, Zoë, and I began our return journey back around the island in the crippled Land Rover, retracing our route as far as Akureyri. From there we headed directly south across the center of the island, between Langjökull and Hofsjökull. By now we had become very experienced in traversing difficult terrain and in fording rivers. When crossing a deep, swift river near Bláfell, we towed two Renault sedans, whose drivers had been waiting on the bank for assistance, to the other side.

*   *   *

However unexpectedly the landscape changed from one mood to another in the course of our travels around Iceland, the compression of a variety of forces into this relatively small area was what we found most remarkable. It is as if Iceland were a self-contained exhibit, almost a microcosm (though at times its prospects seem dauntingly vast) of the stages of terrestrial genesis and transformation. Not only are the processes of geological formation and change visible and explicit in Iceland, they also occur in a strangely atemporal juxtaposition there. Primordial cataclysmic forces —volcanic eruptions, discharges of ash, rock, lava, and gas—are still occurring. Simultaneously at work are the slower and more gradual, but equally inexorable, forces of glacial scouring and erosion by rivers and sea. More subtle still are the transformations wrought by hot springs venting mineral deposits, by the corrosive effect of primitive vegetation, and even by the sculpting of the wind. And hidden from view are the unharnessed forces in play just below the sometimes-calm surface, only hinted at by the powerful jet of steam we encountered at the tip of Reykjanes. Equally, perhaps, the people of Iceland have themselves influenced the shape of the land. No doubt the land has also shaped them.

Jonathan Porter
Albuquerque, New Mexico
January 1989

ICELAND

4. *White flower growing on a black ash cliff at Langahlidh, near Kleifarvatn, Reykjanes.*

5. *Volcanic ash cliff near Kleifarvatn.*

6. *Moss growing in a lava cleft in Thingvellir, a national park.*

7. Sandbar of volcanic ash in the Thjórsá River, Thjórsádalur.

8. *Snowbank covered by ash fall from the eruption of Mount Hekla, Thjórsádalur.*

9. *Pinks growing among volcanic cinders in Thjórsádalur.*

10. *Stream near Landmannahellir, east of Mount Hekla.*

11. Snowbanks on the mountain road to Landmannalaugar, north of Mount Hekla.

12. *Fractured obsidian (volcanic glass) near Landmannalaugar, a hot spring.*

13. Lava and ash field near the mountain road to Landmannalaugar.

14. *Waterfall in a crevice below Mýrdalsjökull, on the southern coast.*

15. Lichens near Búdhir, western Snæfellsnes.

16. *Waterfall at Foss, on the southern coast, northeast of Kirkjubæjarklaustur.*

17. *Glaciated basalt columns near Kirkjubæjarklaustur, east of Mýrdalsjökull.*

18. *Columnar basalt formation in the highlands above Kirkjubæjarklaustur.*

19. *Cinder cones on the melting edge of Sólheimajökull, on the southern coast, near Skógar.*

20. *Moss growing on a cliff at the edge of Sólheimajökull.*

21. Small crevice in a glacier near Skógar.

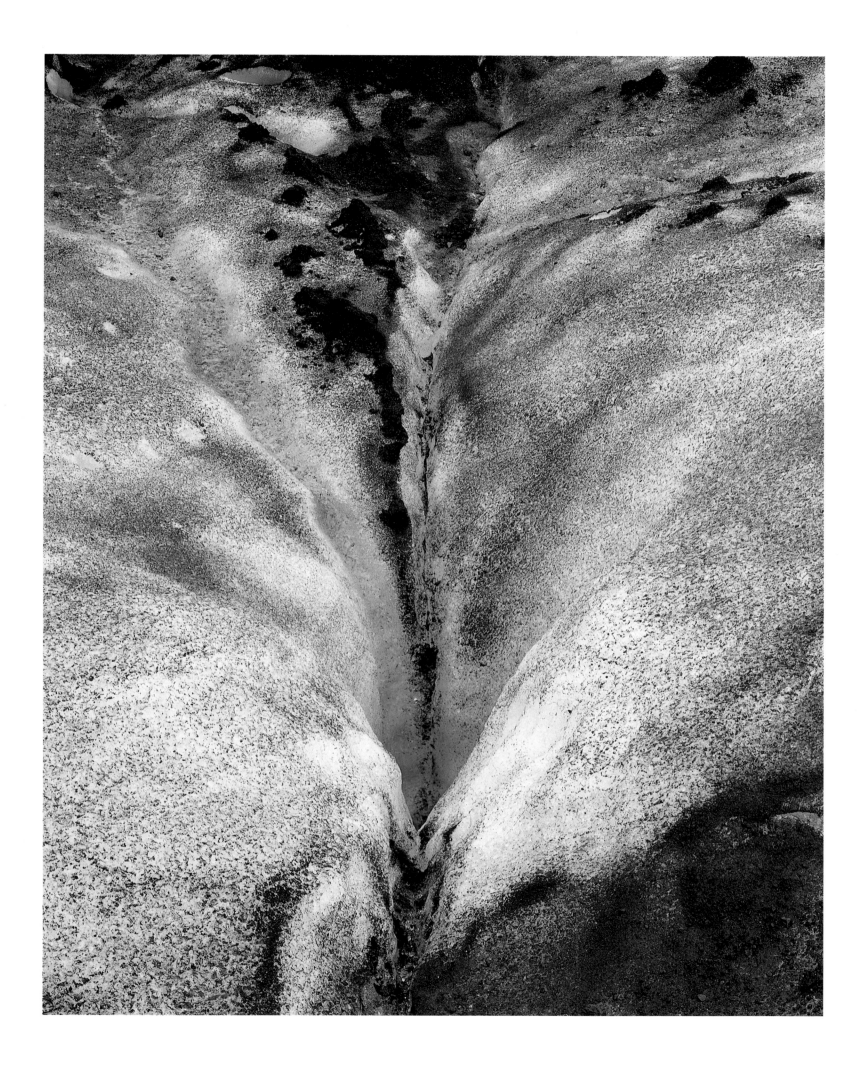

22. Lichens near Skógar.

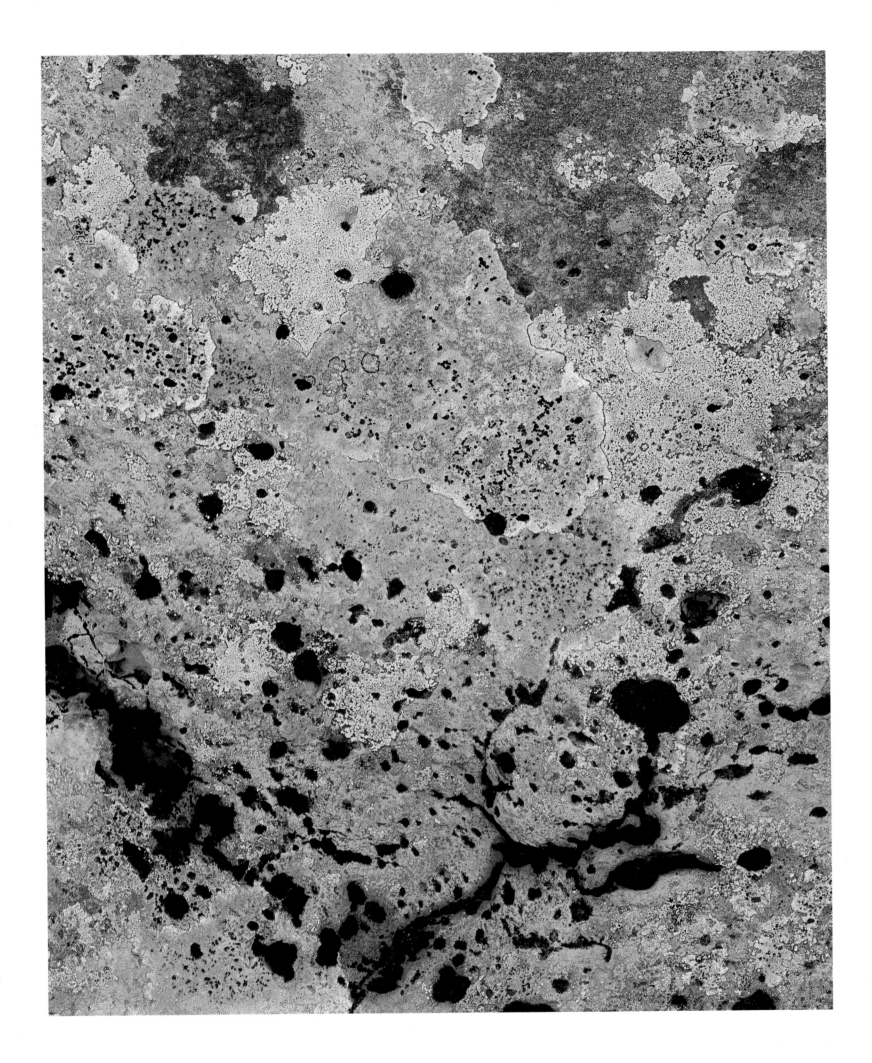

23. *Ice in a glacial lake on the northern edge of Eyjafjallajökull, near Thórsmörk.*

24. Cotton grass near Varmaland, at the base of Snæfellsnes.

25. Springs in a gorge near Húsafell, west of Langjökull.

26. *Pyroclastic lava in Hitardalur, eastern Snæfellsnes.*

27. *Red pumice field surrounding a volcano cone in Hnappadalur, eastern Snæfellsnes.*

28. *Collapsed lava tube in Hnappadalur.*

29. *Gold sand and sea-worn black lava rocks near Búdhir, Snæfellsnes.*

30. *Wave-worn rocks on the beach near Hellnar, western Snæfellsnes.*

31. Kelp on a black stone beach at Dritvík, western Snæfellsnes.

32. Abandoned farmstead constructed of turf, at Laufás, north of Akureyri, on the eastern shore of Eyjafjördhur.

33. Gate of the old farmstead at Laufás.

34. Junction of river canyons in Öxnadalsheidhi, west of Akureyri.

35. Hillside of moss and grass north of Dalvík, on the western shore of Eyjafjördhur.

36. Herdhubreidh, a table mountain surrounded by lava flows from the Askja volcano.

37. Hot spring east of Mývatn.

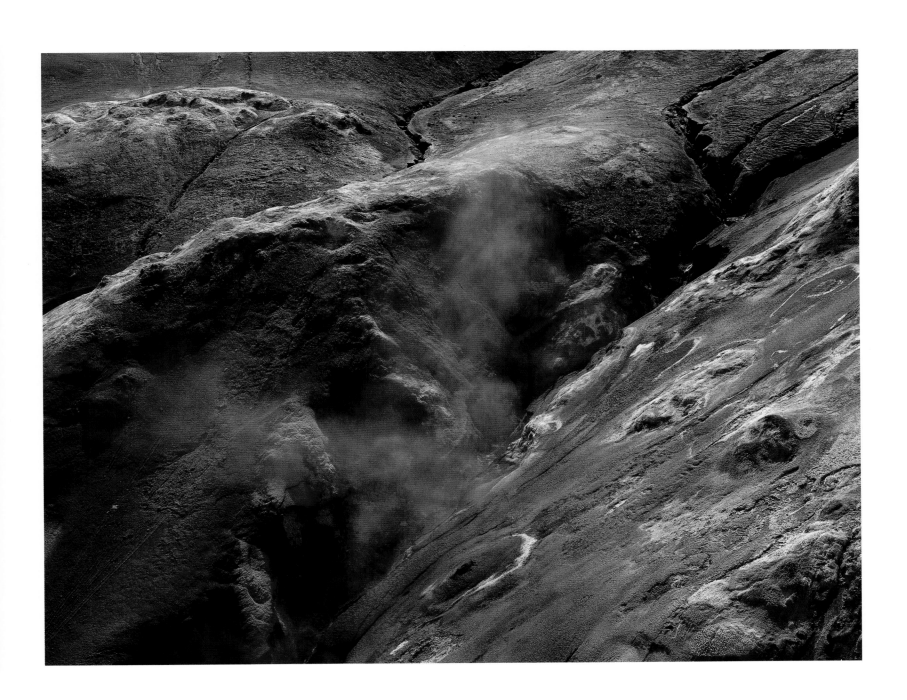

38. Mud pot at the hot springs east of Mývatn.

39. *Rare stand of birches at Vaglaskógur, east of Akureyri.*

40. The falls at Dettifoss.

41. Honeycomb weathering at Dimmuborgir, near Mývatn.

42. *Mountainside at the edge of Fagridalur, between Egilsstadhir and Búdhareyri, on the eastern coast.*

43. *Tarn with cotton grass at Fjardharheidhi, between Egilsstadhir and Seydhisfjördhur.*

44. *Lichens and black moss at Fjardharheidhi.*

45. *Sea cliff at Berufjördhur, on the eastern coast.*

46. *Kelp and sea lettuce on the beach at Berufjördhur.*

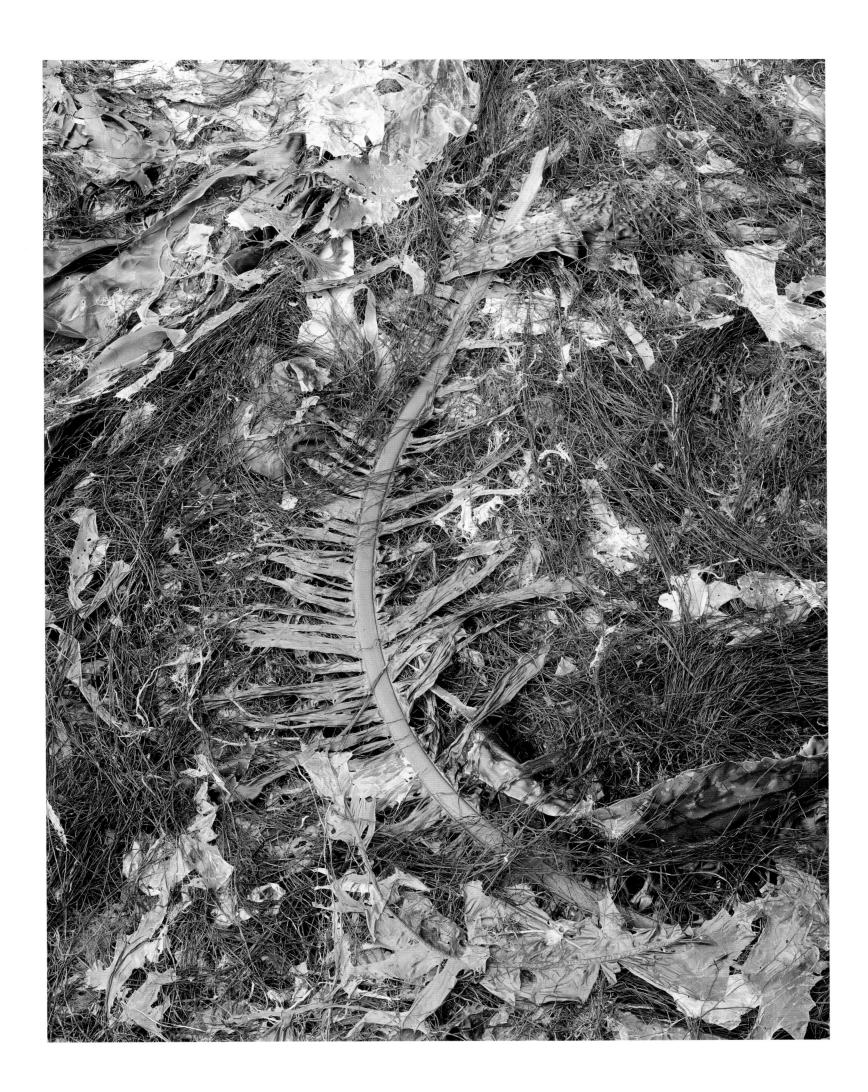

47. *The edge of Fláajökull, a finger glacier of Vatnajökull, near Höfn.*

48. *Flowering heath and round stones, near Fláajökull.*

49. *Glacial lake at the foot of Breidhamerkurjökull, a finger glacier of Vatnajökull.*

50. Lichens on round stones near Fláajökull.

51. Pond at the eastern edge of Öræfajökull, a finger glacier of Vatnajökull.

52. Farmhouse on a fjord on the eastern coast.

53. Talus on the southern coast, near Höfn.

54. Farmstead constructed of turf, at Glaumbær, north of Varmahlidh.

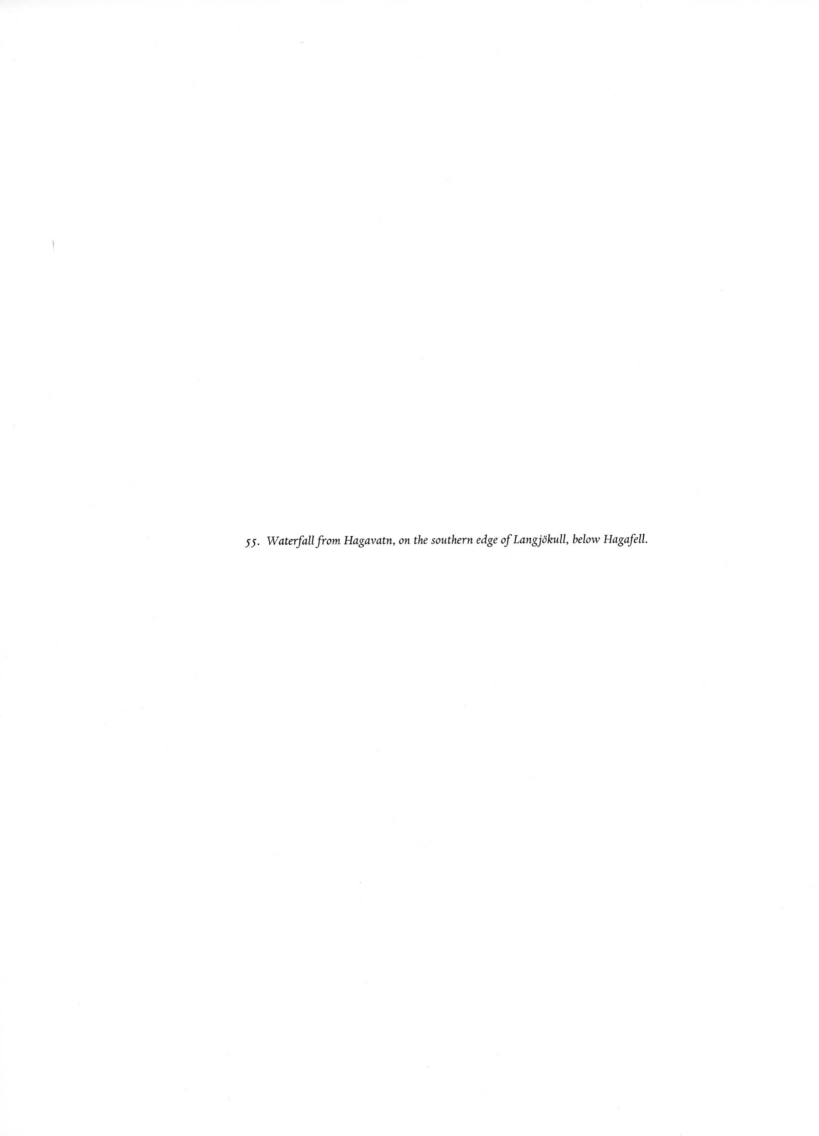

55. *Waterfall from Hagavatn, on the southern edge of Langjökull, below Hagafell.*

56. Thjórsá River, Thjórsádalur, with Mount Hekla on the horizon.

Edited by Terry Reece Hackford
Copyedited by Robin Jacobson
Production coordinated by Christina Holz Eckerson
Designed by Eleanor Morris Caponigro
Composition by Michael and Winifred Bixler
Separations, printing, and binding by
Dai Nippon Printing Co., Ltd.